My dearest Ca— 2005
I hope we —
every spot in this guide! we's start
checking them off — Love, Jim

WEST COAST
RV CAMPING

FOGHORN OUTDOORS®

WEST COAST RV CAMPING

The Complete Guide to More Than 1,800 RV Parks and Campgrounds in California, Oregon, and Washington

FIRST EDITION

Tom Stienstra

AVALON
TRAVEL

FOGHORN OUTDOORS
WEST COAST RV CAMPING
The Complete Guide to More Than
1,800 RV Parks and Campgrounds in
California, Oregon, and Washington

First Edition

Tom Stienstra

Text © 2004 by Tom Stienstra.
All rights reserved.
Maps © 2004 by Avalon Travel Publishing.
All rights reserved.

 Avalon Travel Publishing is an imprint of
Avalon Publishing Group, Inc.

AVALON
publishing group incorporated

Some photos and illustrations are used by permission
and are the property of the original copyright owners.

ISBN: 1-56691-671-2
ISSN: 1546-9786

Editor: Amy Scott
Series Manager: Marisa Solís
Copy Editor: Donna Leverenz
Research Editors: Pamela S. Padula, Washington and Oregon; Jeff Lupo, California
Proofreader: Erika Howsare
Graphics Coordinator: Susan Snyder
Production: Jacob Goolkasian and PDBD
Cover and Interior Designer Darren Alessi
Map Editor: Olivia Solís
Cartographers: Kat Kalamaras, Suzanne Service, Mike Morgenfeld
Indexers: Matt Kaye, Amy Scott

Front cover photo: © Robert Holmes

Printed in the United States of America by Worzalla Inc.

Please send all feedback about this book to:

FOGHORN OUTDOORS®
West Coast RV Camping
Avalon Travel Publishing
1400 65th Street, Suite 250
Emeryville, CA 94608, USA
atpfeedback@avalonpub.com
www.foghorn.com

Printing History
1st edition—April 2004
5 4 3 2

About the Author

GARY TODOROFF

Tom Stienstra has made it his life's work to explore the West—boating, fishing, camping, hiking, biking, and flying—searching for the best of the outdoors and then writing about it.

Tom is the nation's top-selling author of outdoors guidebooks. In 2003, he was inducted into the California Outdoor Hall of Fame and has twice been awarded National Outdoor Writer of the Year, newspaper division, by the Outdoor Writers Association of America. He has also been named California Outdoor Writer of the Year four times. Tom is the outdoors columnist for the San Francisco Chronicle, and his articles appear on www.SFGate.com and in newspapers around the country.

His wife, Stephani Stienstra, has co-authored two books with him. They live with their boys in Northern California.

You can contact Tom directly via the website www.TomStienstra .com. His other books are also available on his website, including:

Foghorn Outdoors California Camping
Foghorn Outdoors California Fishing
Foghorn Outdoors California Hiking (with Ann Marie Brown)
Foghorn Outdoors California Recreational Lakes & Rivers
Foghorn Outdoors California Wildlife (with illustrator Paul B. Johnson)
Foghorn Outdoors Northern California Cabins & Cottages
  (with Stephani Stienstra)
Foghorn Outdoors Oregon Camping
Foghorn Outdoors Pacific Northwest Camping
Foghorn Outdoors Tom Stienstra's Bay Area Recreation
Foghorn Outdoors Washington Camping (with Stephani Stienstra)

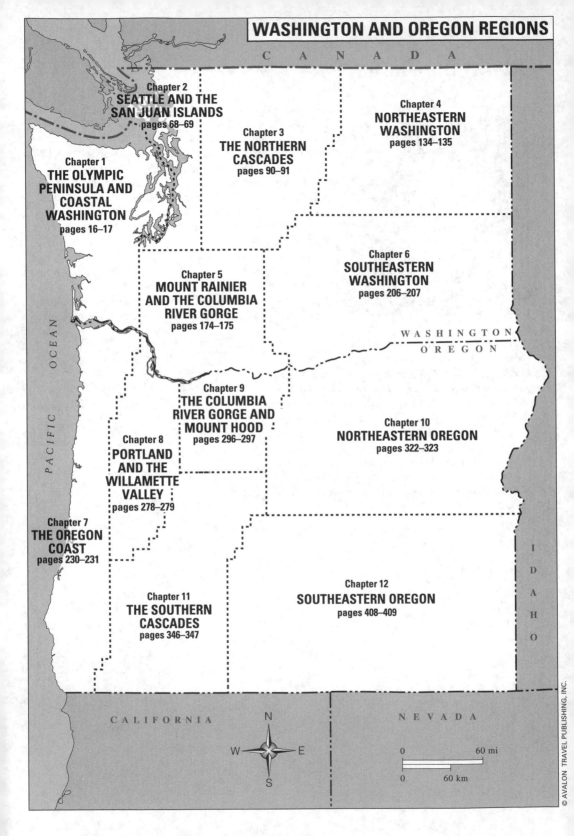

WASHINGTON AND OREGON REGIONS

CANADA

Chapter 2
SEATTLE AND THE
SAN JUAN ISLANDS
pages 68–69

Chapter 3
THE NORTHERN
CASCADES
pages 90–91

Chapter 4
NORTHEASTERN
WASHINGTON
pages 134–135

Chapter 1
THE OLYMPIC
PENINSULA AND
COASTAL
WASHINGTON
pages 16–17

Chapter 5
MOUNT RAINIER
AND THE COLUMBIA
RIVER GORGE
pages 174–175

Chapter 6
SOUTHEASTERN
WASHINGTON
pages 206–207

WASHINGTON
OREGON

PACIFIC OCEAN

Chapter 9
THE COLUMBIA
RIVER GORGE AND
MOUNT HOOD
pages 296–297

Chapter 10
NORTHEASTERN OREGON
pages 322–323

Chapter 8
PORTLAND
AND THE
WILLAMETTE
VALLEY
pages 278–279

Chapter 7
THE OREGON
COAST
pages 230–231

IDAHO

Chapter 11
THE SOUTHERN
CASCADES
pages 346–347

Chapter 12
SOUTHEASTERN OREGON
pages 408–409

CALIFORNIA

NEVADA

N
W E
S

0   60 mi
0   60 km

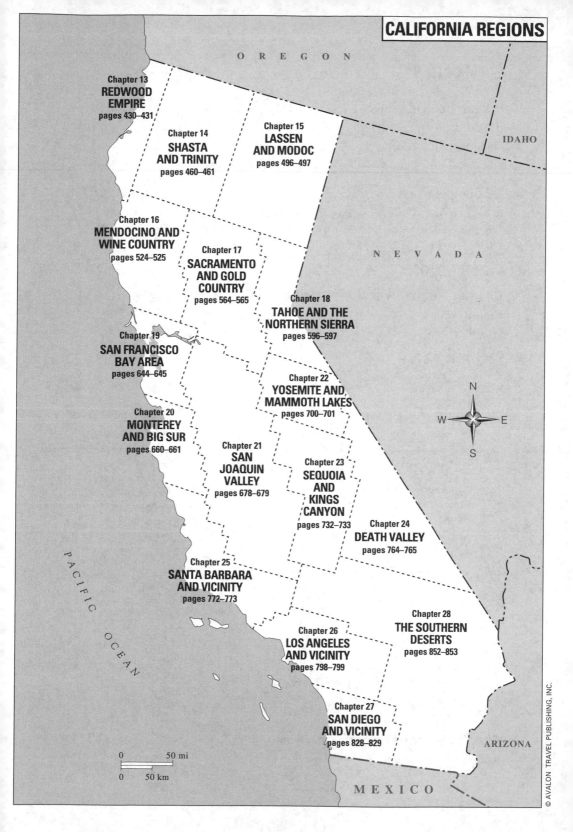

CALIFORNIA REGIONS

O R E G O N

IDAHO

Chapter 13
REDWOOD EMPIRE
pages 430–431

Chapter 14
SHASTA AND TRINITY
pages 460–461

Chapter 15
LASSEN AND MODOC
pages 496–497

Chapter 16
MENDOCINO AND WINE COUNTRY
pages 524–525

Chapter 17
SACRAMENTO AND GOLD COUNTRY
pages 564–565

N E V A D A

Chapter 18
TAHOE AND THE NORTHERN SIERRA
pages 596–597

Chapter 19
SAN FRANCISCO BAY AREA
pages 644–645

Chapter 22
YOSEMITE AND MAMMOTH LAKES
pages 700–701

Chapter 20
MONTEREY AND BIG SUR
pages 660–661

Chapter 21
SAN JOAQUIN VALLEY
pages 678–679

Chapter 23
SEQUOIA AND KINGS CANYON
pages 732–733

Chapter 24
DEATH VALLEY
pages 764–765

Chapter 25
SANTA BARBARA AND VICINITY
pages 772–773

Chapter 28
THE SOUTHERN DESERTS
pages 852–853

Chapter 26
LOS ANGELES AND VICINITY
pages 798–799

Chapter 27
SAN DIEGO AND VICINITY
pages 828–829

ARIZONA

P A C I F I C   O C E A N

N
W   E
S

0   50 mi
0   50 km

M E X I C O

© AVALON TRAVEL PUBLISHING, INC.

Contents

WASHINGTON

Chapter 28—The Southern Deserts 851

Including:
- Brite Lake
- Colorado River
- Joshua Tree National Park
- Lake Havasu
- Mojave National Preserve
- Mojave River

- Palm Springs
- Parker Valley
- Salton Sea
- Senator Wash Reservoir
- Taylor Lake
- Wiest Lake

Resources 877

Index 893

How to Use This Book

Foghorn Outdoors West Coast RV Camping is divided into 28 chapters based on major geographic regions in Washington, Oregon, and California. Each chapter begins with a map of the region. These maps show the location of all the RV parks and campgrounds in that chapter.

This guide can be navigated easily in two ways:

1. If you know the name of the specific RV park or campground you want to use, or the name of the surrounding geographical area or nearby feature (town, national or state park, forest, mountain, lake, river, etc.), look it up in the index and turn to the corresponding page.

2. If you know the general area you want to visit, turn to the map at the beginning of the chapter that covers the area. Each map shows by number all the RV parks and campgrounds in that chapter. You can then determine which RV parks or campgrounds are in or near your destination by their corresponding numbers. RV parks and campgrounds are listed sequentially in each chapter so you can turn to the page with the corresponding map number for the site you're interested in.

About the Site Profiles

Each RV park and campground in this book is listed in a consistent, easy-to-read format to help you choose the ideal camping spot. From a general overview of the setting to detailed driving directions, the profile will provide all the information you need. Here is an example:

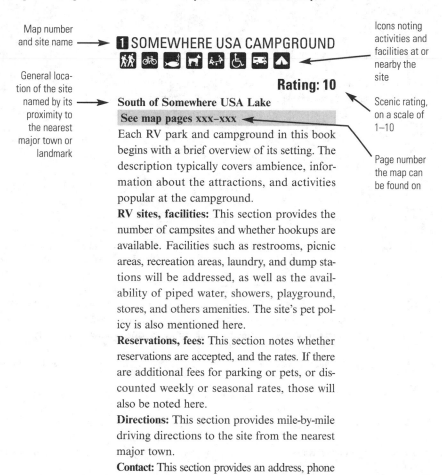

Map number and site name →

General location of the site named by its proximity to the nearest major town or landmark →

Icons noting activities and facilities at or nearby the site

Scenic rating, on a scale of 1–10

Page number the map can be found on

1 SOMEWHERE USA CAMPGROUND

Rating: 10

South of Somewhere USA Lake

See map pages xxx–xxx

Each RV park and campground in this book begins with a brief overview of its setting. The description typically covers ambience, information about the attractions, and activities popular at the campground.

RV sites, facilities: This section provides the number of campsites and whether hookups are available. Facilities such as restrooms, picnic areas, recreation areas, laundry, and dump stations will be addressed, as well as the availability of piped water, showers, playground, stores, and others amenities. The site's pet policy is also mentioned here.

Reservations, fees: This section notes whether reservations are accepted, and the rates. If there are additional fees for parking or pets, or discounted weekly or seasonal rates, those will also be noted here.

Directions: This section provides mile-by-mile driving directions to the site from the nearest major town.

Contact: This section provides an address, phone number, and email address and website, if available, for each RV park or campground.

About the Icons

The icons in this book are designed to provide at-a-glance information on activities, facilities, and services provided that are available on-site or within walking distance of each RV park and campground. The icons are not meant to represent every activity or service, but rather those that are most significant.

— Hiking trails are available.

— Biking trails or routes are available. This usually refers to mountain biking, although it may represent road cycling as well. Refer to the text for that site for details.

— Swimming opportunities are available.

— Fishing opportunities are available.

— Boating opportunities are available. Various types of vessels apply under this umbrella activity, including motorboats and personal watercrafts (Jet Skis). Refer to the text for that site for more details, including mph restrictions and boat ramp availability.

— Canoeing and/or kayaking opportunities are available. Typically, canoeing is available on inland lakes and rivers, whereas kayaking is available along the coast. Refer to the text for that site for more details.

— Winter sports are available. This general category may include activities such as downhill skiing, cross-country skiing, snowshoeing, snowmobiling, snowboarding, and ice skating. Refer to the text for that site for more details on which sports are available.

— Hot or cold springs are located nearby. Refer to the text for that site for more information.

— Pets are permitted. RV parks and campgrounds that allow pets may require an additional fee or that pets be leashed. RV sites and campgrounds may also restrict pet size or behavior. Refer to the text for that site for specific instructions or call in advance.

— A playground is available. An RV park or campground with a playground can be desirable for RVers traveling with children.

— Wheelchair access is provided, as advertised by site managers. However, concerned persons are advised to call the contact number of a site to be certain that their specific needs will be met.

— RV sites are provided.

— Tent sites are provided.

Our Commitment

We are committed to making *Foghorn Outdoors West Coast RV Camping* the most accurate, thorough, and enjoyable RV camping guide to Washington, Oregon, and California. Be aware that with the passing of time some of the fees listed herein may have changed, and campgrounds may have closed unexpectedly. If you have a specific need or concern, it's best to call the location ahead of time.

If you would like to comment on the book, whether it's to suggest an RV park or campground we overlooked or to let us know about any noteworthy experience—good or bad—that occurred while using *Foghorn Outdoors West Coast RV Camping* as your guide, we would appreciate hearing from you. Please address correspondence to:

Foghorn Outdoors West Coast RV Camping, First Edition
Avalon Travel Publishing
1400 65th Street, Suite 250
Emeryville, CA 94608
email: atpfeedback@avalonpub.com

If you send us an email, please put "Foghorn Outdoors West Coast RV Camping" in the subject line.

Introduction

Introduction

"Moving is the closest thing to being free," wrote Billy Joe Shaver, an old Texas cowboy songwriter.

He got it.

It's not just the getaway destinations, adventures, and array of sights that makes roaming the West the greatest RV adventure in America. It's the way it makes you feel inside when you're on the road, the anticipation of the trip ahead, all the hopes and dreams that inspire road trips across the West—it's the closest thing to being free.

I understand these feelings. I've traveled more than a million miles across Washington, Oregon, and California in the past 25 years. Although I love hiking, boating, and fishing, the real underlying force is staying on the move, roaming around, free, always curious to see what is around the next bend in the road.

All along the Pacific Coast, from Mission Bay near San Diego to Orcas Island near the Canadian border north of the Olympic Peninsula, you can discover a series of beautiful park campgrounds that seem perfectly spaced for the trip. One of the greatest road trips anywhere is Highway 1 on the coast, the best of it venturing north along the slow, curving two-laner from Morro Bay to Fort Bragg, California. In the fall, the road is largely free of traffic, the skies often clear of fog, and the bluff-top perches furnish a procession of stunning views of the rocky coast, with unpeopled foothills on one side and an ocean that stretches to forever on the other. Traveling slowly, you'll discover, can be ecstasy.

Another option is to cruise up and down Interstate 5, and then make side junctures into the Sierra Nevada in California, the Cascade Range in Oregon and Washington, or even a trip on a ferry boat out from Anacortes or Port Angeles in Washington to tour the San Juan Islands. Yosemite National Park is the No. 1 destination for most. Some of nature's most perfect artwork has been created in Yosemite and the adjoining eastern Sierra near Mammoth Lakes, as well as some of the most profound natural phenomena imaginable.

Cruising U.S. 395 along the Eastern Sierra is a preferred alternative for many, with the opportunity for easy side trips to many lakes. They include Bridgeport Reservoir, the June lakes, the Mammoth lakes, Convict Lake, and Crowley Lake. In addition, almost every lake's outlet stream provides prospects. This region has it all: beauty, variety, and a chance at the fish of a lifetime. There is also access to the Ansel Adams Wilderness, which features Banner and Ritter peaks, and lakes filled with fish.

Oregon and Washington feature similar stellar destinations, from pristine Crater Lake, a legend for its cobalt-blue waters, on north to Baker Lake in Mt. Baker–Snoqualmie National Forest in Washington. These are just a handful amid more than a thousand lakes that provide RV access in Washington, Oregon, and California.

There's one catch. To make a road trip work, you have to be able to find a spot to stop every night. That's why this book is a must-have for every RV owner. You'll never get stuck again. One of the worst feelings imaginable is cruising down the road in the early evening without a clue where you will park for the night, without any knowledge of the array of spots available. I call that being a prisoner of hope. My advice is to never hope your way through a vacation.

This book details more than 1,800 campgrounds and parks with RV sites. The listings, directions, facilities, and highlights are far more detailed than any RV guide ever published. To win your trust, we have done everything possible to make this book the most accurate guide in this field. After I completed the first draft, every entry was cross-checked with rangers and the owners of RV parks by three research editors, Stephani Cruickshank, Jeff Lupo, and Pamela Padula.

Regardless, things are always changing at RV parks and camps, and getting it right in a book requires year-round vigilance. Most commonly, prices go up. The prices in this book are the most up-to-date possible, but if price is the bottom-line concern, always verify prior to your visit.

Some of the highlights of this book include:

—More than 1,800 campgrounds and parks for RV camping. These include sites in privately owned RV parks; local, county, state, and national parks; national forests; and, in some rare cases, land managed by the Bureau of Land Management and Washington Department of Natural Resources.

—More than 30 detailed maps.

—Directions that are written as if a passenger is reading them aloud to the person driving, making them extremely driver-friendly.

—Detailed information about each camp's facilities, fees, reservation policies, setting, and nearby recreation options.

—Icons that quickly identify activities available at each site.

—Up-to-date, fact-checked information.

—Not included are sites that are extremely remote, very difficult to reach, or where the access road is extremely narrow or twisty.

Over the years, I have received many comments from campers, rangers, and park owners about what they are looking for in an RV guidebook. That is exactly what we are delivering in this book. After all, this is my full-time job. I understand how seriously people take their trips and what you need to know to make your trips work, every time.

You can roam for just a day or two. Or you can just keep on going. The road, as songwriter Robert Earl Keen says, goes on forever. More Americans than ever are fulfilling the dream of taking to the highway. While exotic air travel is in decline and distant adventure travel is flat, statistics show that since 2001, RV camping is up 20 percent, RV rentals are up 35 percent in California, and sales of all styles of RVs are up 8.5 percent across the country, according to the Recreational Vehicle Industry Association and other industry sources. The biggest increase in sales are to those aged 35 to 54—who own more RVs than any other age class. In addition, 1 in every 10 Americans over 55 now owns an RV.

Adventures are good for the soul. They can bond people for life. Adventures also make you feel good inside. Billy Joe Shaver was right. Moving really is the closest thing to being free.

—Tom Stienstra

Author's Picks

Prettiest Lakes

1. **Lake Tahoe,** California, pages 615, 618–619, 623–627
2. **Crater Lake,** Crater Lake National Park, Oregon, page 386
3. **Baker Lake,** Mt. Baker-Snoqualmie National Forest, Washington, pages 94–95
4. **Lower Sardine Lake,** Tahoe National Forest, California, page 604
5. **Crescent Lake,** Olympic National Park, Washington, page 374
6. **Tenaya Lake,** Yosemite National Park, California, page 713
7. **Lake Quinalt,** Olympic National Forest, Washington, pages 41–42
8. **Lake Sabrina,** Inyo National Forest, California, page 741
9. **Donner Lake,** Donner Memorial State Park, California, page 612
10. **Mountain Lake,** Moran State Park, Orcas Island, Washington, page 74

Prettiest Rivers

1. **Umpqua River,** Oregon, pages 257, 260, 376, 378, 381
2. **Smith River,** California, pages 434–436, 438–439
3. **Owyhee River,** Oregon, page 421
4. **Bogachiel River,** Washington, page 32
5. **McKenzie River,** Oregon, pages 354–356, 361
6. **Trinity River,** California, pages 475, 477–479, 483–484
7. **Rogue River,** Oregon, pages 269, 271–273, 388–389, 391–394
8. **Yuba River,** California, pages 575–576, 612
9. **Queets River,** Washington, page 33
10. **Deschutes River,** Oregon, pages 303, 358, 367, 370

Best Wildlife-Viewing

1. **Tule elk,** Point Reyes National Seashore, California, page 647
2. **Orcas,** Strait of Juan de Fuca, Washington, pages 21–23
3. **Roosevelt elk,** Prairie Creek Redwoods State Park, California, pages 442–443
4. **Gray whales,** Mendocino Coast, California, pages 528, 534–535, 551
5. **Bald eagles,** Tule Lake National Wildlife Refuge, California, page 499
6. **Black bears,** Sequoia National Park, California, pages 749, 752
7. **Roosevelt elk,** near Willapa Bay, Washington, page 58
8. **Black bears,** Yosemite National Park, California, pages 712–713, 715–717, 725
9. **Antelope,** Hart Mountain National Antelope Refuge, Oregon, page 425
10. **Deer and chukar,** Deschutes River, Oregon, pages 303, 358, 367, 370

Best Fishing

1. **San Diego deep sea and lakes for bass,** California, pages 841–842
2. **San Joaquin River Delta for largemouth bass,** California, pages 650–651, 681
3. **Umpqua River for smallmouth bass,** Oregon, pages 257, 260, 376, 378, 381
4. **Columbia River for sturgeon,** Washington/Oregon, pages 202–204, 299–301
5. **Omak Lake for cutthroat trout,** Washington, page 157
6. **Bogachiel River for steelhead,** Washington, page 32
7. **Rufus Woods Lake for rainbow trout,** Washington, page 162
8. **Lake San Antonio for bass,** California, page 775
9. **Fort Bragg for salmon,** California, pages 529–531
10. **Sacramento River,** Redding to Anderson, for rainbow trout, California, pages 490–491

RV Camping Tips

Many paths, one truth: There are nearly 40 styles of RVs in use, from the high-end 60-footers that resemble touring buses for rock stars, to the popular cab-over campers on pick-up trucks, to the pop-up trailers that can be towed by a small sedan. Regardless of what kind of rig you use, all share one similarity when you prepare for a trip: You must have good tires, brakes, and a cooling system for your engine.

During your trip, check fluid levels with every gas fill-up. These checks should include engine oil, brake fluid, engine coolant, transmission fluid, and power-steering fluid.

While these lists do not cover every imaginable item, they do serve as a checklist for primary items and a starting point to create your own list. My suggestion is to add items to these pages that are vital for your own vehicle.

Basic Maintenance

Here's a checklist for primary items; make sure that you have these and that they are in good working order before you go. Also be sure all mandatory routine maintenance is performed prior to your trip.

—Oil and filter
—Lube
—Transmission fluid
—Power-steering fluid
—Air filters
—Gas filter
—Batteries
—Tires (check air pressure, including spare tire)
—Wheel bearings
—Brakes and brake fluid
—Shocks
—Cooling system and coolant
—Electrical system, lights
—Heater and air conditioner
—Emergency flashers
—Tire-changing equipment
—Fire extinguisher
—Proof of insurance and registration
—All owner's manuals
—Road service card

Self-contained RVs
—Water system
—Propane gas
—Pilot light
—Electrical system
—Power converter
—Lights
—Stove
—Gray water tank and panel monitor
—Dump valve and sewer hose
—Toilet chemical and RV toilet paper

—Refrigerator
—Windows and shades
—Lube rollers or slider plates at the end of rams for slide-out rooms
—Fuses, including for slide-out motor
—Extra battery if camping without hookups
—Landing gear
—Stabilizer jacks
—Awning

Trailers and Fifth Wheels
—Safety chains
—Wheel bearings
—Perfect fit at tow junction
—Lube
—Lights
—Self-adjusting brakes

Food and Cooking
When it comes to food, you are only limited by your imagination. So there is no reason to ever settle for less than what is ideal for you. Add to this list as necessary.

—Primary foods for breakfasts, lunches, and dinners
—Bottled water and drinks
—Seasoned pepper and salt, spices
—Pots, pans, plates, glasses
—Cooking utensils
—Knives, forks, spoons
—Can opener
—Coffee maker and filters
—Matches or lighters
—Kitchen towels
—Napkins and paper towels
—Trash bags
—Wash rack and detergent
—Ice chest
—Charcoal

Sleeping Setup
Some things can't be compromised—ever. This is one of them. You must guarantee that you will get a good night's sleep. Your sleeping setup, whether in a bed or in a sleeping bag on a pad, must guarantee that you will be comfy, clean, dry, and warm, no matter what.

Start by making sure that the RV is level and solid, and then make sure that you have these essentials:
—Sleeping surface: bed mattress, air bed, or foam pad
—Bed: Sheets, blankets or sleeping bag
—Favorite pillows
—Blackout screens over windows
—Emergency ear plugs (snorers! hah!)
—Tent for children with pads, bags, and pillows

First Aid and Insect Protection

The most common injury on vacations is a sunburn. Close behind is the result of scratching a mosquito bite. Both are easily avoided. Although other mishaps are rare on vacations, campers should always be ready for them. In bright sun, always wear a hat that covers your ears, the tops of which can get singed quickly on a summer day. On trips to Central America, I learned that even on the hottest days, you can wear light long-sleeve shirts that provide sun protection yet are cool and ventilated.

A first-aid kit is a must. Here is a good starting list of basic sun and insect protection, plus basic first-aid supplies:
—Sun block
—Aloe sunburn cream
—Mosquito repellent
—AfterBite
—Chapstick
—Eye wash
—Band-Aids
—Adhesive towels and medical tape
—Antibiotic towels
—Burn ointment
—Ace bandage
—Moleskin or similar blister treatment
—Scissors
—Tweezers
—Sterile gloves
—Aspirin
—Excedrin, Tylenol, Ibuprofen, Advil, Aleve, or similar
—Tums or other antacid
—Prescription medications (such as an inhaler for asthmatics)
—Blood pressure monitoring equipment

Traveling with Pets

Many dogs and cats are considered members of the family. I recommend taking them along whenever possible. They always add to the trip. And after all, leaving them is a terrible moment, especially when they stare at you with those big, mournful eyes, and then you spend the next week thinking about them. My dog Rebel ended up traveling with me for 17 years. I believe one of the reasons he lived so long was because he was fit, happy, loved, had a job to do (camp security, or so he thought), and always had another adventure to look forward to. Of course, you just can't put your pet in the vehicle and figure everything will be fine. In addition, some pets are built for travel or camping, and some are not. Know the difference. A few precautions can prevent a lot of problems.

Start with your pet's comfort. Make certain your pet is cool, comfortable, and can sleep while you are driving. Once you arrive at your destination, create similar sleeping quarters at camp as at home. Be sure to make frequent stops for exercise, sniffing, and bathroom breaks.

To avoid frustration, always confirm that pets are permitted at planned destinations before you head out.
Plus keep these items in the RV:
—ID collar labeled with cell phone number
—Records of shots, licenses, and your vet's phone number
—Clean and filled water and food dishes

—Leash
—Poop scoop

Recreation

The most popular outdoor recreation activities in the West are hiking, biking, wildlife-watching, swimming, fishing, golfing, boating, kayaking and canoeing, and hunting. For this checklist, you may wish to cross off items for activities that you do not take part in and add items essential for your favorites.

—Maps
—Hiking boots
—Hiking socks
—Hat, sunglasses, sunscreen
—Day pack
—Camera
—Flashlight
—Identification guides
—Bike and tire repair kit
—Binoculars
—Swimming suit
—Life vests
—Sandals
—Beach chair
—Beach towels
—Fishing license with appropriate tags
—Fishing rod, reel with fresh line, tackle
—State fishing rulebook
—Golf clubs
—Boat with required safety equipment
—Hunting license with tags
—Rifle or shotgun and ammunition
—Hunting regulations

Protection Against Food Raiders

Bears, raccoons, and even blue jays specialize in the food-raiding business at camps. Bears, in particular, can be a real problem for people new to RV camping at parks with high bear populations. In rare cases, bears have even been known to break into unattended RVs in the pursuit of human goodies, especially Swiss Miss, Tang, butter, eggs, and ice cream. Raccoons can chew tiny holes in tents and destroy picnic baskets in their search. I've seen jays land on plastic bags hanging from tree limbs, rigged from rope as bear-proof food hangs, and then poke a hole in the plastic to get meat sticks. There are answers, of course. In the past few years, programs have been established at many state and national parks to reduce incidents with bears. The real problem, of course, is not bears, but the careless people who create incidents by not properly storing their food and disposing of garbage.

In areas with high bear density, owners of small truck campers or pop-up camper trailers can use a bear-proof food hang or bear-proof food canisters. When creating a bear-proof food hang, use the counter-balance method with either double plastic bags or canvas bags. If no tree limb is suitable for the counter-balance method for a bear-proof food hang, put all your food in a double bag, hoist it up to a limb, and then tie the end off on a different tree.

—Always use wildlife-proof metal food lockers available at major park campgrounds
—Do not leave food unattended on picnic tables or in camp
—Do not leave garbage unattended in camp
—Dispose of all garbage properly each day
—Do not leave food bags, cups, or anything that may appear as food within view of a bear who might peer into the window of an RV
—Do not put food inside a vehicle, under a vehicle, in a tent, or in a "hiding place"
—Report all aggressive bears to rangers

Getting Along

The most important element of any trip is the people you are with. That is why your choice of companions is so important. Your own behavior is equally consequential. Yet most people spend more time putting together their gear than considering why they enjoy or dislike the company of their chosen companions. Here are a few rules of behavior for a great trip:

— **No whining:** Nothing is more irritating than being around a whiner.
— **Activities must be agreed upon:** Always have a meeting of the minds with your companions over the general game plan.
— **Nobody's in charge:** It is impossible to be genuine friends if one person is always telling another what to do.
— **Equal chances at the fun stuff:** There must be an equal distribution of the fun stuff and the not-fun stuff.
— **No heroes:** Nobody cares about all your wonderful accomplishments. No gloating. The beauty of travel is simply how each person feels inside, the heart of the adventure.
— **Agree on a wake-up time:** You can then proceed on course together without the risk of whining.
— **Think of the other guy:** Count the number of times you say, "What do you think?"
— **Solo responsibilities:** When it is time for you to cook, make a campfire, or clean a fish, it means you can do so without worrying about somebody else getting their mitts in the way.
— **Don't let money get in the way:** Among friends, don't let somebody pay extra, because that person will likely try to control the trip, and yet at the same time, don't let somebody weasel out of paying a fair share.
— **Accordance on the food plan:** Always have complete agreement on what you plan to eat each day, and always check for food allergies such as nuts, onions, or cheese.

Outdoors with Kids

I've put this list together with the help of my own kids, Jeremy and Kris, and their mother, Stephani. Some of the lessons are obvious, some are not, but all are important:
—Take children to places where there is a guarantee of action, such as a park with wildlife-viewing.
—Be enthusiastic. Enthusiasm is contagious—if you aren't excited about an adventure, you can't expect a child to be.
—Always be seated when talking to someone small, so the adult and child are on the same level.
—Always show how to do something, never tell.
—Let kids be kids by letting the adventure happen, rather than trying to force it within some preconceived plan.
—Use short attention spans to your advantage by bringing along a surprise bag of candy and snacks.

—Make absolutely certain the child's sleeping bag is clean, dry, and warm, and that they feel safe, protected, and listened to.

—Introduce kids to outdoor ethics; they quickly relate to the concepts and long remember when they do something right that somebody else has done wrong.

—Take close-up photographs of them holding fish they have caught, blowing on the camp-fire, or completing other camp tasks.

—Keep track of how often you say, "What do you think?"

Predicting Weather

Weather lore can be valuable on trips. Small signs provided by nature and wildlife can be translated to provide a variety of weather information. By paying attention, I can often provide weather forecasts for specific areas that are more reliable than the broad-brush approach provided by weather services. Here is the list I have compiled over the years:

When the grass is dry at morning light,
Look for rain before the night.

No dew on the grass at 7?
Expect sign of rain by 11.

Short notice, soon to pass.
Long notice, long it will last.

When the wind is from the east,
'Tis fit for neither man nor beast.

When the wind is from the south,
The rain is in its mouth.

When the wind is from the west,
Then it is the very best.

Red sky at night, sailors' delight.
Red sky in the morning, sailors take warning.

When all the cows are pointed north,
Within a day rain will come forth.

Onion skins very thin, mild winter coming in.
Onion skins very tough, winter's going to be very rough.

When your boots make the squeak of snow,
Then very cold temperatures will surely show.

If a goose flies high, fair weather ahead.
If a goose flies low, foul weather will come instead.

Washington

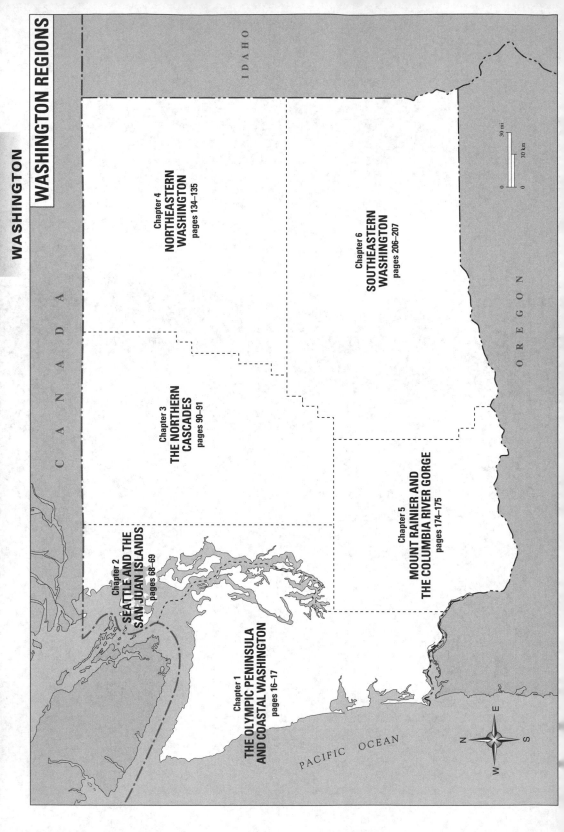

Chapter 4
NORTHEASTERN
WASHINGTON
pages 134–135

Chapter 6
SOUTHEASTERN
WASHINGTON
pages 206–207

Chapter 3
THE NORTHERN
CASCADES
pages 90–91

Chapter 5
MOUNT RAINIER AND
THE COLUMBIA RIVER GORGE
pages 174–175

Chapter 2
SEATTLE AND THE
SAN JUAN ISLANDS
pages 68–69

Chapter 1
THE OLYMPIC PENINSULA
AND COASTAL WASHINGTON
pages 16–17

IDAHO

CANADA

OREGON

PACIFIC OCEAN

30 mi
30 km
0
0

Washington

Chapter 1

The Olympic Peninsula and Coastal Washington

THE OLYMPIC PENINSULA AND COASTAL WASHINGTON

see Seattle and the
San Juan Islands
pages 68-69

TULALIP
INDIAN RES.

Puget

Sound

SEATTLE

Whidbey
Island

Skagit Bay

Vashon
Island

Port
Townsend

CANADA

UNITED STATES

Strait of Juan de Fuca

Neah
Bay

MAKAH INDIAN
RESERVATION

Ozette

Ozette
Lake

Clallam
Bay

Sappho

Lake
Crescent

Elwha

Olympic

National

Park

Mt. Deception
(7,788 ft.)

Mt. Olympus
(7,965 ft.)

River

Queets River

River

Hoh

Soleduck

River

River

Hood

Canal

Lake
Cushman

Olympic

National

Forest

Lake
Quinault

QUINAULT INDIAN
RESERVATION

Quinault

River

Taholah

N
E
S
W

1
2-4
5-6
7
8
9-10
11-12
13
14
15-16
17
18
19
20
21
22
23
24
25
26
27
28
29
30
31
32
33
34
35
36
37
38
39
40
41
42-43
44
45
46
47
48
49
50
51
52
53
54
55
56-58
59
60-62
63
64
65
66
67-68
71
72
106

5
5
3
16
3
101
101
101
112
112
113
110
109
29

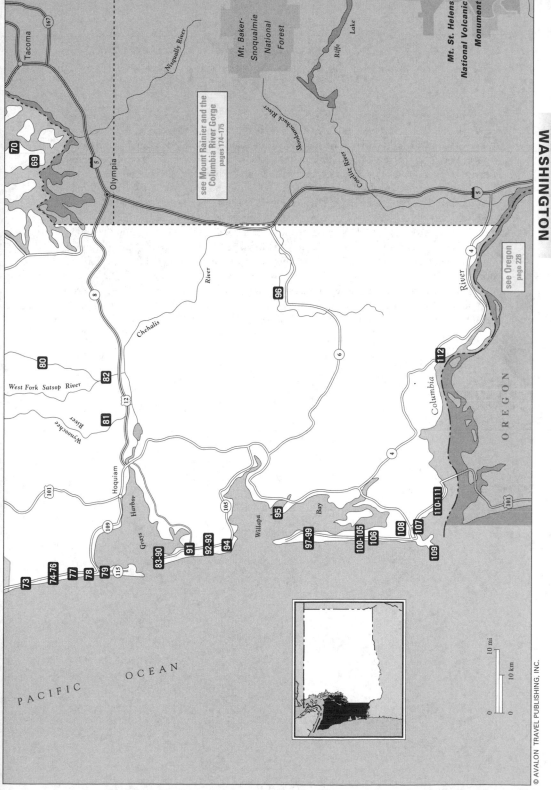

WASHINGTON

Tacoma

Olympia

see Mount Rainier and the
Columbia River Gorge
pages 174-175

Mt. Baker-
Snoqualmie
National
Forest

Riffe Lake

Mt. St. Helens
National Volcanic
Monument

Nisqually River

Skookumchuck River

Cowlitz River

70

69

80

82

81

West Fork Satsop River

Wynoochee River

Chehalis River

96

6

see Oregon
page 228

Columbia River

OREGON

112

Hoquiam

Grays Harbor

101

109

115

73

74-76

77

78

79

83-90

91

92-93

94

105

Willapa Bay

95

97-99

100-105

106

108

107

109

110-111

101

PACIFIC OCEAN

10 mi

10 km

© AVALON TRAVEL PUBLISHING, INC.

Chapter 1—The Olympic Peninsula and Coastal Washington   17

Chapter 1—The Olympic Peninsula and Coastal Washington

Vast, diverse, and beautiful, the Olympic Peninsula is like no other landscape in the world. Water borders the region on three sides: the Pacific Ocean to the west, the Strait of Juan de Fuca to the north, and the inlets of the Hood Canal to the east. At its center are Olympic National Park and Mount Olympus, with rainforests on its slopes feeding rivers and lakes that make up the most dynamic river complex in America.

Only heavy rainfall for months on end from fall through spring and coastal fog in the summer have saved this area from a massive residential boom. At the same time, those conditions make it outstanding for getaways and virtually all forms of recreation. A series of stellar campgrounds ring the perimeter foothills of Mount Olympus, both in Olympic National Park and at the state parks and areas managed by the Department of Natural Resources. Your campsite can be your launch pad for adventure—just be sure to bring your rain gear.

In winter, campers can explore the largest array of steelhead rivers anywhere—there is no better place in America to fish for steelhead. Almost every one of these rivers provides campsites, often within walking distance of prime fishing spots.

❶ OZETTE

Rating: 6

on Lake Ozette in Olympic National Park
See map pages 16–17

Many people visit this site located on the shore of Lake Ozette just a few miles from the Pacific Ocean. Set close to a trailhead road and ranger station, with multiple trailheads nearby, this camp is a favorite for both hikers and boaters and is one of the first to fill in the park.

RV sites, facilities: There are 15 sites for RVs up to 21 feet or tents. Drinking water, picnic tables, flush toilets, and fire grills are provided. A pay phone and limited cell phone reception are available. Leashed pets are permitted in the campground only.

Reservations, fees: Reservations are not accepted. The fee is $10 per night, plus a $10 national park entrance fee per vehicle. A senior discount is available. Open year-round.

Directions: From Port Angeles, drive west on U.S. 101 to the junction with Highway 112. Bear right on Highway 112 and drive to Hoko-Ozette Road. Turn left and drive 21 miles to the ranger station. The camp parking lot is across from the ranger station on the northwest corner of Lake Ozette.

Contact: Olympic National Park, 600 East Park Ave., Port Angeles, WA 98362, 360/565-3130, fax 360/565-3147; Ozette Ranger Station, 360/963-2729.

❷ VAN RIPER'S RESORT

Rating: 7

on Clallam Bay in Sekiu
See map pages 16–17

Part of this campground hugs the waterfront and the other part sits on a hill overlooking the Strait of Juan de Fuca. Most sites are graveled, many with views of the strait. Other sites are grassy, without views. Hiking, fishing, and boating are among the options here, with salmon fishing being the principal draw. The beaches in the area, a mixture of sand and gravel, provide diligent rock hounds with agates and fossils.

RV sites, facilities: There are 100 sites with par-

tial or full hookups (30 amps) for tents or RVs of any length; six are drive-through sites. Other accommodations include two cabins, mobile homes, a house, and 12 motel rooms. Electricity, drinking water, and picnic tables are provided. An RV dump station, pay phone, toilets, showers, firewood, and ice are available. A store, café, and laundry facilities are available within one mile. Boat docks, launching facilities, and rentals are available in spring and summer. Some facilities are wheelchair-accessible. Leashed pets are permitted. No pets are allowed in cabins or other buildings.

Reservations, fees: Reservations are not accepted for campsites. The fee is $11–18 per night. Open April to September. Major credit cards accepted.

Directions: From Aberdeen, drive north on U.S. 101 for 119 miles to Sappho and Highway 113. Turn north on Highway 113 and drive nine miles to Clallam Bay. Continue north on Highway 113/112 for two miles to Sekiu and Front Street. Turn right and drive .25 mile to the resort on the right.

Contact: Van Riper's Resort, P.O. Box 246, Sekiu, WA 98381, 360/963-2334, website: www .vanripersresort.com.

❸ OLSON'S RESORT

Rating: 5

in Sekiu
See map pages 16–17

This full-service camp is large and private. The nearby marina is salmon fishing headquarters. In fact, the resort caters to anglers, offering all-day salmon fishing trips and boat moorage. Chartered trips can be arranged by reservation. A tackle shop, cabins, houses, and a motel are also available. See the description of Van Riper's (prior listing) for details on the Sekiu area.

RV sites, facilities: There are 100 sites for RVs of any length or tents, 64 of which have full hookups. Seven cabins, 14 motel rooms, and four houses are also available. Picnic tables, drinking water, an RV dump station, flush toilets, showers, a laundry room, a store, and ice are available. Boat docks, launching facilities, boat rentals, bait, tackle, a fish-cleaning station, gear storage, gas, and diesel fuel are also available on-site. A restaurant is located one mile away. Call for pet policy.

Reservations, fees: Reservations are not accepted. The fee is $12–16 per night, plus $2 per person per night for more than two people. Cabins and other lodging are $45–110 per night. Major credit cards accepted. Open year-round.

Directions: From Aberdeen, head north on U.S. 101 and drive 119 miles to Sappho and Highway 113. Turn north on Highway 113 and drive nine miles to a fork with Highway 112. Continue straight on Highway 112 and continue to Sekiu and Front Street. Turn right and drive one block to the resort on the right.

Contact: Olson's Resort, P.O. Box 216, Sekiu, WA 98381, 360/963-2311, website: www.olsons resort.com.

4 COHO RESORT AND MARINA

Rating: 5

near Sekiu

See map pages 16–17

Set across the highway from water, this camp features campsites that are entirely concrete free, with gravel predominating and some grassy areas. Coho is one of several camps in the immediate area. A full-service marina nearby provides boating access. See the descriptions of Van Riper's Resort Hotel, Olson's Resort, and Surfside Resort in this chapter for information on the area.

RV sites, facilities: There are 108 sites for tents or RVs of any length and 100 sites for tents; 60 are full-hookup sites and the remainder are partial hookups (30 amps) with electricity and water. Cable TV is available at a few sites. An RV dump station, toilets, coin-operated showers, a café, a restaurant, pay phone, cell phone reception, laundry facilities, and ice are available. A full-service marina with docks, launching facilities, and gas is nearby. A store and an ATM are within one mile. Leashed pets are permitted.

Reservations, fees: Reservations are not accepted. The fee is $14–18 per night, plus $1 per person per night for more than two people. No credit cards are accepted. Open early May–late September.

Directions: From Aberdeen, drive north on U.S. 101 for 119 miles to Sappho and Highway 113.

Turn north on Highway 113 and drive nine miles to a junction with Highway 112. Continue straight on Highway 112 and continue toward Sekiu. The campground is located between Mileposts 15 and 16, about .75 mile before the town of Sekiu.

Contact: Coho Resort and Marina, 15572 Highway 112, Sekiu, WA 98381, 360/963-2333.

5 SURFSIDE RESORT

Rating: 7

in Sekiu

See map pages 16–17

This park is smaller, less crowded, and more secluded than many in the area. Campers can enjoy the park's private beach and panoramic views of the Strait of Juan de Fuca and Vancouver Island to the north. The spectacular sunsets here are a draw for many visitors. Nearby recreation options include marked hiking and bike trails within 30 miles, beachcombing, a full-service marina, and the finest fishing for miles.

RV sites, facilities: There are 10 drive-through sites for RVs of any length and 10 tent sites. Fire rings, picnic tables, electricity, and sewer hookups are provided. Drinking water, toilets and showers, an RV dump station, cell phone reception, and cable TV are available. Propane, a store, an ATM, a café, coin-operated laundry facilities, and ice are available within one mile. Boat docks, launching facilities, and rentals are located within one mile. Leashed pets are permitted.

Reservations, fees: Reservations are recommended. The fee is $12–20 per night. No credit cards are accepted. Open year-round.

Directions: From Aberdeen, drive north on U.S. 101 for 119 miles to Sappho and Highway 113. Turn north on Highway 113 and drive nine miles to a junction with Highway 112. Continue straight on Highway 112 and drive to Clallam Bay. Continue about one mile west; the campground is located on the left, halfway between the towns of Clallam Bay and Sekiu.

Contact: Surfside Resort, P.O. Box 39, Sekiu, WA 98381, 360/963-2723, website: www.ohwy.com /wa/s/surfsidr.htm.

6 SAM'S TRAILER AND RV PARK

Rating: 5

on Clallam Bay
See map pages 16–17
New owners promise improvements here. Sam's is an alternative to Van Riper's Resort, Olson's Resort, Surfside Resort, and Coho Resort and Marina on Clallam Bay. It's a family-oriented park with grassy sites and many recreation options nearby. Beaches and shopping are within walking distance. Those wanting to visit Cape Flattery, Hoh Rain Forest, or Port Angeles will find this a good central location.

RV sites, facilities: There are 25 sites with full hookups (20 amps) for RVs of any length; 10 are drive-through sites. Four tent sites are also available. Picnic tables are provided. Drinking water, fire rings, restrooms, showers, an RV dump station, cable TV, cell phone reception, and coin-operated laundry facilities are available. A store, an ATM, a café, and ice are available within one mile. Boat docks, launching facilities, and rentals are also available within one mile. Leashed pets are permitted.

Reservations, fees: Reservations are accepted. The fee is $9–16 per night. A senior discount is available. Major credit cards are accepted. Open year-round.

Directions: From Aberdeen, drive north on U.S. 101 for 119 miles to Sappho and Highway 113. Turn north on Highway 113 and drive nine miles to Clallam Bay and Highway 112. Continue straight on Highway 112 and drive into Clallam Bay. Just as you come into town, the campground is on the right at 17053 Highway 112.

Contact: Sam's Trailer and RV Park, P.O. Box 45, Clallam Bay, WA 98326, 360/963-2402.

7 LYRE RIVER PARK

Rating: 9

near the Lyre River
See map pages 16–17
With open space surrounding the park, this beautiful privately owned 23-acre camp is situated in a wooded area tucked between the Strait of Juan de Fuca and the Lyre River. Both freshwater and saltwater beaches lend the park a unique flavor. Kids can give their rods a try in the pond stocked with trout (a fee charged), while adult anglers can head for excellent fishing in the Lyre River (steelhead are tops during migrations) and along the nearby shoreline (for perch). Tubing down the river is popular here, and bike and hiking trails are available nearby.

RV sites, facilities: There are 97 sites for RVs of any length or tents; 55 have full hookups (20, 30, 50 amps) and 30 are drive-through sites. Picnic tables are provided and some sites have fire rings. Restrooms, propane, an RV dump station, a small seasonal store, a coin-operated laundry, pay phone, cell phone reception, and ice are available. Showers and firewood are available for a fee. Leashed pets are permitted.

Reservations, fees: Reservations are accepted. The fee is $18–28 per night, plus $2 per person per night for more than two people. Group reservations are welcome with an advance deposit. Major credit cards are accepted. Open year-round.

Directions: From Olympia on I-5, take U.S. 101 and drive north 127 miles (five miles past the town of Port Angeles) to a fork with Highway 112. Turn west on Highway 112 and drive 15 miles to West Lyre River Road. Turn right and drive .5 mile to the park on the right.

Contact: Lyre River Park, 596 West Lyre River Rd., Port Angeles, WA 98363, 360/928-3436, website: www.lyreriverpark.com.

8 WHISKEY CREEK BEACH

Rating: 7

on the Strait of Juan de Fuca
See map pages 16–17
Located on the beach along the Strait of Juan de Fuca, this campground covers 30 acres and sits next to vast timberland. It is popular with rock hounds. Surf fishing for perch and other species draws anglers, and this is an excellent launch point for sea kayaking. The setting is rustic, with 1.25 miles of beach access. Olympic National Park is located five miles away and offers numerous recreation opportunities, including miles of stellar hiking trails. This camp is a good option if the national park camps are full,

WASHINGTON

but note that almost one-third of the campground is permanently rented out.

RV sites, facilities: There are 30 sites for RVs or tents, including six with full hookups and five with partial hookups (20 amps), plus eight cabins on the beach. Picnic tables and fire rings are provided. Drinking water, vault toilets, cell phone reception, and a children's play area are available. Launching facilities for small boats are on-site. A store, a gas station, an ATM, and a coin-operated laundry are available within three miles. Leashed pets are permitted.

Reservations, fees: Reservations are accepted. The fees are $15 per night for tent sites, $18–25 per night for RV sites; pets are $1 per night. No credit cards are accepted. Open May to early October; cabins available year-round.

Directions: From Olympia on I-5, take U.S. 101 and drive north 127 miles (five miles past the town of Port Angeles) to a fork with Highway 112. Turn right (west) on Highway 112 and drive 13 miles (three miles past Joyce) to Whiskey Creek Beach Road. Turn right and continue 1.5 miles to the campground on the right (well marked).

Contact: Whiskey Creek Beach, P.O. Box 130, Joyce, WA 98343, 360/928-3489, fax 360/928-3218, website: www.whiskey-creek-beach.com.

9 CRESCENT BEACH RV

Rating: 7

on the Strait of Juan de Fuca
See map pages 16–17

Located on a half-mile stretch of sandy beach, this campground makes a perfect weekend spot. Popular activities include swimming, fishing, surfing, sea kayaking, and beachcombing. It borders Salt Creek Recreation Area, with direct access available. Numerous attractions and recreation options are available in Port Angeles.

RV sites, facilities: There are 41 sites for RVs or tents with partial or full hookups (30, 50 amps), with a separate area for tent camping. Picnic tables and fire rings are provided. Restrooms, showers, a coin-operated laundry, a pay phone, cell phone reception, a recreation field, and horseshoes are available. An RV dump station is nearby. An ATM is within three miles. Leashed pets are permitted.

Reservations, fees: Reservations are recommended. The fees are $25–30 per night, plus $5 per person per night for more than two people, $5 per additional vehicle per night unless towed, and $5 per pet per night. Weekly and monthly rates are available. Major credit cards are accepted. Open year-round.

Directions: From Olympia on I-5, take U.S. 101 and drive north 127 miles (five miles past the town of Port Angeles) to a fork with Highway 112. Turn right (west) on Highway 112 and drive 10 miles to Camp Hayden Road (between Mileposts 53 and 54). Turn right on Camp Hayden Road and drive four miles to the campground on the left, on the beach.

Contact: Crescent Beach RV, 2860 Crescent Beach Rd., Port Angeles, WA 98363, 360/928-3344, website: www.olypen.com/crescent.

10 SALT CREEK RECREATION AREA

Rating: 8

near the Strait of Juan de Fuca
See map pages 16–17

The former site of Camp Hayden, a World War II–era facility, Salt Creek Recreation Area is a great spot for gorgeous ocean views, fishing, and hiking near Striped Peak, which overlooks the campground. Only a small beach area is available because of the rugged coastline, but there is an exceptionally good spot for tidepool viewing on the park's north side. The park covers 198 acres and overlooks the Strait of Juan de Fuca. Recreation options include nearby hiking trails, swimming, fishing, horseshoes, and field sports. It's a good layover spot if you're planning to take the ferry out of Port Angeles to Victoria, British Columbia.

RV sites, facilities: There are 92 sites for RVs of any length or tents, some with partial hookups (20, 30 amps). Picnic tables are provided. Restrooms, flush toilets, coin-operated showers, pay phone, cell phone reception, an RV dump station, firewood, and a playground are available. Some facilities are wheelchair-accessible. Leashed pets are permitted. Park gates close at dusk.

Reservations, fees: Reservations are not accepted. The fee is $12–14 per night, plus $3 per additional vehicle per night; six campers maximum per site. Open year-round.

Directions: From Olympia on I-5, take U.S. 101 and drive north 127 miles (five miles past the town of Port Angeles) to a fork with Highway 112. Turn right (west) on Highway 112 and drive nine miles to Camp Hayden Road. Turn right (north) and drive three miles to the campground.

Contact: Salt Creek Recreation Area, Clallam County, 3506 Camp Hayden Rd., Port Angeles, WA 98363, 360/928-3441, website: www.clallam .net/countyparks.

11 PEABODY CREEK RV PARK

Rating: 5

in Port Angeles
See map pages 16–17

This three-acre RV park is right in the middle of town but offers a pleasant, streamside setting among many beautiful maple trees. Nearby recreation options include salmon fishing, an 18-hole golf course, marked biking trails, a full-service marina, and tennis courts. The park is within walking distance of shopping and ferry services.

RV sites, facilities: There are 36 sites with full hookups for RVs of any length (30, 50 amps), but note that 19 are permanent rentals. An RV dump station, restrooms with coin-operated showers, ice, cell phone reception, modem access, and coin-operated laundry facilities are available. A cable TV hookup is available for $3 per night. A store, café, and an ATM are within one block. Boat docks, launching facilities, and boat rentals are available within 1.5 miles. Leashed pets are permitted.

Reservations, fees: Reservations are accepted. The fee is $23 per night. Major credit cards are accepted. Open year-round.

Directions: From I-5 at Olympia, turn north on U.S. 101 and drive about 122 miles to Port Angeles and Lincoln Street. Bear left on Lincoln and drive .5 mile to Second Street and the park entrance on the right.

Contact: Peabody Creek RV Park, 127 South Lincoln, Port Angeles, WA 98362, 360/457-7092 (phone or fax) or 800/392-2361, website: www.members.tripod.peabodyrv.com.

12 AL'S RV PARK

Rating: 8

near Port Angeles
See map pages 16–17

This adult-oriented campground is set in the country at about 1,000 feet elevation yet is centrally located and not far from the Strait of Juan de Fuca. Nearby recreation options include an 18-hole golf course and a full-service marina. Olympic National Park and the Victoria ferry are a short drive away.

RV sites, facilities: There are 31 sites with full hookups (30, 50 amps), including some drive-through sites, for RVs up to 40 feet, and 20 sites for tents. Note that approximately one-third of the sites are taken by long-term renters. Picnic tables are provided. Restrooms, drinking water, flush toilets, showers, a pay phone, cell phone reception, cable TV, and laundry facilities are available. No fires are allowed. Telephone service is available for long-term renters. A store, a café, propane, and ice are located within one mile. Boat docks and launching facilities are available within two miles. Some facilities are wheelchair-accessible. Leashed pets are permitted.

Reservations, fees: Reservations are accepted at 360/457-9844 (preferred) or 800/357-1553. The fee is $15–25 per night, plus $2 per person per night for more than two people. Trailers are $25 per night. Weekly and monthly rates are available. Major credit cards are accepted. Open year-round.

Directions: From Port Angeles, take U.S. 101 west for two miles to North Brook Avenue. Turn right (north) on North Brook Avenue, then left (almost immediately) on Lees Creek Road, and drive .5 mile to the park on the right.

Contact: Al's RV Park, 521 North Lees Creek Rd., Port Angeles, WA 98362, 360/457-9844.

13 DUNGENESS RECREATION AREA

Rating: 5

near the Strait of Juan de Fuca
See map pages 16–17

This park overlooks the Strait of Juan de Fuca and is set near the Dungeness National Wildlife

Refuge. Quite popular, it fills up on summer weekends. A highlight, the refuge sits on a seven-mile spit with a historic lighthouse at its end. Bird-watchers often spot bald eagles in the wildlife refuge. Nearby recreation options include hiking on marked trails, fishing, and golfing. The toll ferry at Port Angeles can take you to Victoria, British Columbia.

RV sites, facilities: There are 65 sites, including five drive-through, for RVs of any length or tents. Picnic tables and fire grills are provided. Restrooms, drinking water, flush toilets, coin-operated showers, firewood, an RV dump station, cell phone reception, a pay phone, and a playground are available. An ATM is within three miles. Leashed pets are permitted. Entrance gates close at dusk year-round.

Reservations, fees: Reservations are not accepted. The fee is $12 per night, plus $3 per additional vehicle per night. Open February to October, with facilities limited to day use in the winter.

Directions: From Sequim, drive north on U.S. 101 for four miles to Kitchen-Dick Road. Turn right on Kitchen-Dick Road and drive four miles to the park on the left.

Contact: Dungeness Recreation Area, Clallam County, 554 Voice of America Rd., Sequim, WA 98382, 360/683-5847, website: www.clallam.net /countyparks.

14 SEQUIM WEST INN & RV PARK

Rating: 5

near the Dungeness River
See map pages 16–17
This two-acre camp is near the Dungeness River and within 10 miles of Dungeness Spit State Park. It's a pleasant spot with full facilities and an urban setting. An 18-hole golf course and a full-service marina at Sequim Bay are close by.

RV sites, facilities: There are 22 drive-through sites with full hookups (30, 50 amps) for RVs of any length or tents, 17 cabins, and 21 motel rooms. Picnic tables are provided. Restrooms, drinking water, flush toilets, showers, cable TV, a coin-operated laundry, a pay phone, cell phone reception, and ice are available. Propane, a store, an ATM, and a café are available within one mile. Leashed pets are permitted.

Reservations, fees: Reservations are accepted. The fee is $24–28, plus $1 per person per night for more than two people (under 18 free). Major credit cards are accepted. Open year-round.

Directions: From Sequim and U.S. 101, take the Washington Street exit and drive west on Washington Street for 2.7 miles to the park on the right.

Contact: Sequim West Inn & RV Park, 740 West Washington St., Sequim, WA 98382, 360/683-4144 or 800/528-4527, fax 360/683-6452, website: www.olypen.com/swi.

15 RAINBOW'S END RV PARK

Rating: 6

on Sequim Bay
See map pages 16–17
This park on Sequim Bay is pretty and clean and features a rainbow trout pond and a creek running through the campground. A weekly potluck dinner is offered in the summer, with free hamburgers and hot dogs. A special landscaped area and clubhouse are available for reunions, weddings, and other gatherings. Nearby recreation opportunities include an 18-hole golf course, marked bike trails, a full-service marina, and tennis courts.

RV sites, facilities: There are 39 sites with full hookups, including some drive-through sites, for RVs of any length plus several tent sites. Cable TV hookups are provided at RV sites. Picnic tables and fire grills are provided at tent sites. Restrooms, drinking water, flush toilets, showers, an RV dump station, propane, a coin-operated laundry, modem access, a pay phone, firewood, and a clubhouse are available. A store, a café, and ice are available within one mile. Leashed pets are permitted.

Reservations, fees: Reservations are recommended. The fee is $18.73 per night for tent sites and $22.50–30.31 for RV sites, plus $2 per person per night for more than two people. Weekly and monthly rates are available. Major credit cards are accepted. Open year-round.

Directions: From Sequim, drive west on U.S. 101 for one mile past the River Road exit to the park on the right (along the highway).

Contact: Rainbow's End RV Park, 261831 U.S.

101, Sequim, WA 98382, 360/683-3863, fax 360/683-2150, website: www.rainbowsendrvpark.com.

16 SEQUIM BAY RESORT

Rating: 5

on Sequim Bay
See map pages 16–17
This is Sequim Bay headquarters for salmon anglers. The camp is in a wooded, hilly area, close to many activity centers, and with an 18-hole golf course nearby.

RV sites, facilities: There are 43 sites with full hookups (20, 30 amps), including 34 drive-through, for RVs of any length, plus eight cabins. No tent camping is allowed. Restrooms, drinking water, flush toilets, showers, cable TV, a pay phone, cell phone reception, and a coin-operated laundry are available. Boat docks and launching facilities are located across the street from the resort. Leashed pets are permitted except in cabins.

Reservations, fees: Reservations are recommended. The fee is $21.50 per night, plus $3 per person per night for more than two people. Cabins are $35–65 per night, plus $5 per person for more than two people, and are rented by night with a two-night minimum May to September and by the month the rest of the year. Open year-round.

Directions: From Olympia on I-5, turn north on U.S. 101 and drive about 100 miles (near Sequim) to Whitefeather Way (located between Mileposts 267 and 268, 2.5 miles east of Sequim). Turn north on Whitefeather Way and drive .5 mile to West Sequim Bay Road. Turn left (west) and drive one block to the park on the left.

Contact: Sequim Bay Resort, 2634 West Sequim Bay Rd., Sequim, WA 98382, 360/681-3853, fax 360/681-3854.

17 SEQUIM BAY STATE PARK

Rating: 8

on Sequim Bay
See map pages 16–17
Sequim translates to "quiet waters," which is an appropriate description of this area. Set in the heart of Washington's rain shadow, a region with far less rainfall than the surrounding areas, Sequim averages only 17 inches of rainfall a year. The park features 4,909 feet of saltwater shoreline, and two natural overlapping sand bars protect the bay waters from the rough waves and currents of the Strait of Juan de Fuca. The park has only one mile of hiking trails. This 90-acre camp on Sequim Bay features an underwater park for scuba divers.

RV sites, facilities: There are 60 developed sites for RVs or tents, 16 sites with full hookups for RVs up to 30 feet (30 amps), and three primitive tent sites. Picnic tables and fire grills are provided. Restrooms, drinking water, flush toilets, showers, a sheltered picnic area, an amphitheater, athletic fields, a basketball court, a pay phone, cell phone reception, and a playground are available. Boat docks, launching facilities, and boat mooring are also available. An ATM is within three miles. Facilities are wheelchair-accessible. Leashed pets are permitted.

Reservations, fees: Reserve at 888/CAMP-OUT (888/226-7688) or online at www.parks.wa.gov /reservations ($7 reservation fee). The fee is $16–22 per night, plus $10 per additional vehicle per night. Boat mooring is $10–16 per night; $10 per night for bike-in sites. Major credit cards are accepted during peak season only. A senior discount is available. Open year-round.

Directions: From Olympia on I-5, turn north on U.S. 101 and drive 100 miles (near Sequim) to the park entrance on the right (along the highway). The park is located four miles southeast of the town of Sequim.

Contact: Sequim Bay State Park, 360/683-4235; state park information, 360/902-8844.

18 FORT WORDEN STATE PARK

Rating: 9

near Puget Sound
See map pages 16–17
This park is on the northeastern tip of the Olympic Peninsula, at the northern end of Port Townsend, on a high bluff overlooking Puget Sound. Highlights here include great lookouts and two miles of trails over the Strait of Juan de Fuca as it feeds into Puget Sound. The park covers 433 acres at historic Fort Worden (on which construction was begun in 1897 and decommissioned in 1953) and

includes buildings from the turn of the 20th century. It has 11,020 feet of saltwater shoreline. Recreation options include 12 miles of marked hiking and biking trails, with five miles of wheelchair-accessible trails. The Coast Artillery Museum, Rothschild House, and the Marine Science Center are open during the summer season. A ferry at Port Townsend will take you across the strait to Whidbey Island. Special note on reservations: This is an extremely popular park and campground, and reservations are required via the Internet up to five months in advance or over the counter up to four months in advance.

RV sites, facilities: There are 80 sites with partial or full hookups (20 amps), including some drive-through, for RVs up to 60 feet or tents, and five primitive, hike-in or bike-in tent sites. Picnic tables and fire grills are provided. Restrooms, drinking water, flush toilets, coin-operated showers, a laundry room, a pay phone, limited cell phone reception, a store, and firewood are available. A restaurant, conference facilities, a sheltered amphitheater, athletic fields, an ATM, and interpretive activities are available nearby. Boat docks, buoys, floats, and launching facilities are also nearby. Several golf courses are located in the area. Some facilities are wheelchair-accessible. Leashed pets are permitted.

Reservations, fees: Reservations are available at www.fortworden.org—click on Online Camping Reservations. The fee is $10–22 per night, plus $10 per additional vehicle per night; moorage is $10–16 per night. A senior discount is available. Major credit cards are accepted. Open year-round.

Directions: From Olympia, turn north on U.S. 101 and drive 86 miles to Highway 20 (Port Townsend turnoff). Turn north (right) on Highway 20 and drive 13 miles to Port Townsend. Continue through Port Townsend to Cherry Street. Turn left at Cherry Street and drive 1.75 miles to the park entrance at the end of the road.

Contact: Fort Worden State Park, 200 Battery Way, Port Townsend, WA 98638, 360/344-4400, fax 360/385-7240.

19 POINT HUDSON RESORT & MARINA

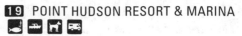

Rating: 6

in Port Townsend
See map pages 16–17

Point Hudson Resort is located on the site of an old Coast Guard station near the beach in Port Townsend. The park features ocean views and 2,000 feet of beach frontage. Known for its Victorian architecture, Port Townsend is called Washington's Victorian seaport. Fishing and boating are popular here, and nearby recreation opportunities include an 18-hole municipal golf course, a full-service marina, Old Fort Townsend State Park, Fort Flagler State Park, and Fort Worden State Park.

RV sites, facilities: There are 60 sites, most drive-through with full hookups (30, 50 amps), for RVs of any length. No tents are allowed. Restrooms, drinking water, flush toilets, showers, three restaurants, a pay phone, cell phone reception, and a coin-operated laundry are available. A 100-plus slip marina is on-site. An ATM is within two blocks. Leashed pets are permitted.

Reservations, fees: Reservations are encouraged. The fee is $19–25 per night. Major credit cards are accepted. Open year-round.

Directions: From Port Townsend on State Route 20, take the Water Street exit. Turn left (north) and continue (the road becomes Sims Way and then Water Street) to the end of Water Street at the marina. Turn left for registration.

Contact: Point Hudson Resort & Marina, 103 Hudson St., Port Townsend, WA 98368, 360/385-2828 or 800/228-2803, fax 360/385-7331, website: www.portofpt.com.

20 OLD FORT TOWNSEND STATE PARK

Rating: 10

near Quilcene
See map pages 16–17

This 367-acre park features a thickly wooded landscape, nearly 4,000 feet of saltwater shoreline on Port Townsend Bay, and 6.5 miles of hiking trails. Built in 1856, the historic fort is one of the oldest remaining in the state. The scenic campground has access to a good clamming beach, and visi-

WASHINGTON

tors can take a short self-guided walking tour of the fort. The park features several interpretive activities and a junior ranger program. Note that the nearest boat ramps are at Port Townsend, Fort Flagler, and Hadlock. Mooring buoys are located one mile south of Glenn Cove on the west side of Port Townsend Bay.

RV sites, facilities: There are 40 sites for RVs up to 40 feet or tents, three primitive tent sites, and one group site. Picnic tables and fire grills are provided. Restrooms, drinking water, flush toilets, coin-operated showers, a playground, boat buoys, firewood, cell phone reception, an amphitheater, an RV dump station, and a picnic area with a kitchen shelter are available. An ATM and a pay phone are within four miles. Leashed pets are permitted.

Reservations, fees: Reservations are not accepted for family sites. Group site reservations are required at 360/385-3595. The fee is $10–16 per night, plus $2 per person for more than four adults and $10 per additional vehicle per night. A senior discount is available. Major credit cards are accepted. Open mid-April to mid-September.

Directions: From Port Townsend and State Route 20, drive south on State Route 20 for two miles to Old Fort Townsend Road. Turn left and drive .5 mile to the park entrance road.

Contact: Old Fort Townsend State Park, 1370 Old Fort Townsend Rd., Port Townsend, WA 98368, 360/385-3595; state park information, 360/902-8844.

21 FORT FLAGLER STATE PARK

Rating: 10

near Port Townsend

See map pages 16–17

This beautiful park sits on a high bluff overlooking Puget Sound with views of the Olympic and Cascade Mountains. The park covers 784 acres and is surrounded on three sides by 19,100 feet of saltwater shoreline. Highlights include five miles of trails for hiking and biking, an interpretive trail, and a military museum featuring gun batteries that is open in the summer. Historic Fort Flagler is a pretty and unique state park, set on Marrowstone Island east of Port Townsend. The RV sites are situated right on the beach. Anglers like this spot for year-round rockfish and salmon fishing, and crabbing and clamming are good in season. The park offers an underwater park, which attracts scuba divers. Fort Flagler, under construction on some level from 1897 until its closure in 1953, offers tours. A youth hostel is also located in the park.

RV sites, facilities: There are 15 sites with partial hookups (30 amps) for RVs up to 50 feet, 101 tent sites, and two primitive tent sites. Picnic tables and fire grills are provided. Restrooms, drinking water, flush toilets, coin-operated showers, interpretive activities, an RV dump station, a store, a café, cell phone reception, boat buoys, floats, and a launch are available. A pay phone is available within 3.5 miles. Facilities are wheelchair-accessible. Leashed pets are permitted.

Reservations, fees: Reserve at 888/CAMP-OUT (888/226-7688), website: www.parks.wa.gov/reservations ($7 reservation fee). The fee is $10–22 per night. A senior discount is available. Major credit cards are accepted. Open March to October, weather permitting.

Directions: From Port Townsend at Highway 20, drive east on Highway 20 for three miles to Ness' Corner Road (at the traffic light). Continue straight onto Highway 19 and go eight miles to Oak Bay Road/State Route 116. Continue on State Route 116 and drive 10 miles to the park entrance.

Contact: Fort Flagler State Park, 360/385-1259, fax 360/379-1746; state park information, 360/902-8844.

22 BEAR CREEK MOTEL AND RV PARK

Rating: 7

on Bear Creek

See map pages 16–17

This quiet little spot is located where Bear Creek empties into the Sol Duc River. It's private and developed, with a choice of sunny or shaded sites in a wooded setting. There are many recreation options in the area, including fishing, hunting, and nature and hiking trails leading to the ocean. Sol Duc Hot Springs is 25 miles north and well worth the trip. A restaurant next to the camp serves family-style meals.

RV sites, facilities: There are 12 drive-through

sites for RVs of any length. Electricity (20 amps), drinking water, sewer hookups, and picnic tables are provided. Restrooms, showers, an RV dump station, a café, coin-operated laundry facilities, a pay phone, cell phone reception, and firewood are available. A motel is also located on the premises. Boat-launching facilities are available within a half mile. Leashed pets are permitted.

Reservations, fees: Reservations are not accepted. The fee is $15 per night. Major credit cards are accepted. Open year-round.

Directions: From Aberdeen, drive north on U.S. 101 to Forks. Continue past Forks for 15 miles to Milepost 205 (just past Sappho) to the campground on the right at 205860 Highway 101 West.

Contact: Bear Creek Motel and RV Park, P.O. Box 236, Beaver, WA 98305, 360/327-3660, website: www.hungrybearcafemotel.com.

23 KLAHOWYA

Rating: 9

on the Sol Duc River in Olympic National Forest

See map pages 16–17

Klahowya features great views of Lake Crescent and Mount Olympus. It makes a good choice if you don't want to venture far from U.S. 101 yet want to retain the feel of being in the Olympic National Forest. Set along the Sol Duc River, this 32-acre camp is pretty and wooded, with hiking trails nearby. A favorite, the Kloshe Nanitch Lookout Trail, is across the river and leads up to a lookout on Snider Ridge overlooking Sol Duc Valley. The Pioneer Path Interpretive Trail, an easy .3-mile loop that is wheelchair-accessible, starts in the camp. Fishing for salmon and steelhead, in season, can be good about a quarter mile downstream from camp; always check regulations. This camp gets medium use.

RV sites, facilities: There are 55 sites for RVs up to 30 feet and two walk-in sites requiring a 500-foot walk. Two sites have electrical hookups (30 amps). Picnic tables are provided. Drinking water, vault and flush toilets, limited cell phone reception, and wheelchair-accessible restrooms are available. An amphitheater with summer interpretive programs is also available. A boat ramp is nearby. Leashed pets are permitted.

Reservations, fees: Reservations are not accepted. The fee is $12 per night. The campground is open May to late September with full service. Limited service is available in the off-season. A senior discount is available.

Directions: From I-5 at Olympia, turn north on U.S. 101 and drive about 122 miles to Port Angeles. Continue on U.S. 101 past Port Angeles for about 36 miles (nine miles west of Lake Crescent) to the campground on the right side of the road, close to Milepost 212. (Coming from the other direction on U.S. 101, drive eight miles east of Sappho to the campground.)

Contact: Olympic National Forest, Pacific Ranger District, 437 Tillicum Ln., Forks, WA 98331, 360/374-6522, fax 360/374-1250.

24 FAIRHOLM

Rating: 9

on Lake Crescent in Olympic National Park Bay

See map pages 16–17

This camp is on the shore of Lake Crescent, a pretty lake situated within the boundary of Olympic National Park, at an elevation of 580 feet. The campsites lie along the western end of the lake, in a cove with a boat ramp. Located less than one mile off U.S. 101, Fairholm gets heavy use during tourist months; some highway noise is audible at some sites. A naturalist program is often available in the summer. Water-skiing is permitted at Lake Crescent, but personal watercraft are prohibited.

RV sites, facilities: There are 88 sites for RVs up to 21 feet or tents. Picnic tables and fire grills are provided. An RV dump station, restrooms, drinking water, and cell phone reception are available. A store, pay phone, and a café are located within one mile. Boat-launching facilities and rentals are nearby on Lake Crescent. Some facilities are wheelchair-accessible. Leashed pets are permitted.

Reservations, fees: Reservations are not accepted. The fee is $10 per night, plus a required $10 national park entrance fee. A senior discount is available. Open mid-April to mid-October, weather permitting.

Directions: From Port Angeles, drive west on

U.S. 101 for about 26 miles and continue along Lake Crescent to North Shore Road. Turn right and drive .5 mile to the camp on North Shore Road on the right.

Contact: Olympic National Park, 600 East Park Ave., Port Angeles, WA 98362, 360/565-3130, fax 360/565-3147.

25 SOL DUC

Rating: 10

on the Sol Duc River in Olympic National Park
See map pages 16–17

This site is a nice hideaway, with nearby Sol Duc Hot Springs a highlight. The problem is that this camp is very popular. It fills up quickly on weekends, and a fee is charged to use the hot springs, which have been fully developed since the early 1900s. The camp is set at 1,680 feet along the Sol Duc River. A naturalist program is available in the summer.

RV sites, facilities: There are 82 sites for RVs up to 21 feet or tents, including 10 drive-through sites for larger RVs, and one group site. Picnic tables and fire grills are provided. Restrooms, drinking water, and limited cell phone reception are available. An RV dump station is nearby, and a store, pay phone, and a café are within one mile. Some facilities are wheelchair-accessible. Leashed pets are permitted.

Reservations, fees: Reservations are taken for the group site only; phone 360/327-3534 from April 16 through October 31, phone 360/928-3380 from November 1 through April 15. The fees are $12 per night for individual sites and $20 per night and $1 per person for group sites, plus a $10 national park entrance fee per vehicle. A senior discount is available. Major credit cards are accepted. Open from May to late October, with limited winter facilities.

Directions: From I-5 at Olympia, turn north on U.S. 101 and drive about 122 miles to Port Angeles. Continue on U.S. 101 past Port Angeles for 27 miles, just past Lake Crescent. Turn left at the Sol Duc turnoff and drive 12 miles to the camp.

Contact: Olympic National Park, 600 East Park Ave., Port Angeles, WA 98362, 360/565-3130, fax 360/565-3147.

26 LOG CABIN RESORT

Rating: 10

on Lake Crescent in Olympic National Park Bay
See map pages 16–17

This pretty camp along the shore of Lake Crescent is a good spot for boaters as it features many sites near the water with excellent views. Fishing and swimming are two options at this family-oriented resort; the lake is home to a strain of Beardslee trout. Note that fishing became catch-and-release in 2000. Water-skiing is permitted, but no personal watercraft are allowed. A marked hiking trail traces the lake's 22-mile shoreline. This camp is extremely popular in the summer months, and you may need to make reservations 6 to 12 months in advance.

RV sites, facilities: There are 38 sites with full hookups (30 amps) for RVs up to 40 feet, plus 28 cabins. Picnic tables and fire barrels are provided. An RV dump station, restrooms, a store, a café, laundry facilities, ice, a pay phone, cell phone reception, and a recreation field are available. Showers and firewood are also available for a fee. Boat docks, launching facilities, and boat and hydrobike rentals are available. Some facilities are wheelchair-accessible. Leashed pets are permitted.

Reservations, fees: Reservations are recommended. The fees are $25–35 per night, plus $12 per person per night for more than two people (in cabins), and $12 per pet per night. Major credit cards are accepted. Open April to October.

Directions: From I-5 at Olympia, turn north on U.S. 101 and drive about 122 miles to Port Angeles. Continue on U.S. 101 past Port Angeles for about 18 miles to East Beach Road. Turn right and drive three miles (along Lake Crescent) to the camp on the left.

Contact: Log Cabin Resort, 3183 East Beach Rd., Port Angeles, WA 98363, 360/928-3325, fax 360/928-2088, website: www.logcabinresort.net.

WASHINGTON

27 ELWHA

Rating: 7

on the Elwha River in Olympic National Park Bay

See map pages 16–17

The Elwha River is the backdrop for this popular camp with excellent hiking trails close by in Olympic National Park. The elevation is 390 feet. Check at one of the visitors centers for maps and backcountry information; also see the description of neighboring Altaire (next listing) for more information.

RV sites, facilities: There are 40 sites for RVs up to 35 feet or tents. Picnic tables and fire grills are provided. Restrooms and drinking water are available, but no services are offered in the winter. Limited cell phone reception is available. Some facilities are wheelchair-accessible. Leashed pets are permitted.

Reservations, fees: Reservations are not accepted. The fee is $10 per night, plus a $10 national park entrance fee per vehicle. A senior discount is available. Major credit cards are accepted. Open year-round.

Directions: From Port Angeles, drive west on U.S. 101 for about nine miles (just past Lake Aldwell) to the signed entrance road on the left. Turn left at the entrance road and drive three miles south along the Elwha River to the campground on the left.

Contact: Olympic National Park, 600 East Park Ave., Port Angeles, WA 98362, 360/565-3130, fax 360/565-3147.

28 ALTAIRE

Rating: 8

on the Elwha River in Olympic National Park Bay

See map pages 16–17

A pretty and well-treed camp with easy highway access, this camp is set on the Elwha River about one mile from Lake Mills. Fishing is good in season; check regulations. The elevation is 450 feet. Altaire also makes for a nice layover spot before taking the ferry at Port Angeles to Victoria, British Columbia.

RV sites, facilities: There are 30 sites for RVs up to 21 feet or tents. Picnic tables and fire grills are provided. Restrooms, drinking water, and limited cell phone reception are available. A pay phone is available within a half mile. Some facilities are wheelchair-accessible. Leashed pets are permitted.

Reservations, fees: Reservations are not accepted. The fee is $10 per night, plus a $10 national park entrance fee per vehicle. A senior discount is available. Open June to September.

Directions: From I-5 at Olympia, turn north on U.S. 101 and drive about 122 miles to Port Angeles. Continue on U.S. 101 past Port Angeles for about nine miles (just past Lake Aldwell). Turn left at the signed entrance road and drive four miles south along the Elwha River.

Contact: Olympic National Park, 600 East Park Ave., Port Angeles, WA 98362, 360/565-3130, fax 360/565-3147.

29 KOA PORT ANGELES–SEQUIM

Rating: 5

near Port Angeles

See map pages 16–17

This is a private, developed camp covering 13 acres in a country setting. A pleasant park, it features the typical KOA offerings, including a pool, hot tub, recreation hall, and playground. Horseshoes and a sports field are also available. Hayrides are offered in the summer. Nearby recreation options include miniature golf, an 18-hole golf course, marked hiking trails, and tennis courts, and nearby side trips feature Victoria, Butchart Gardens, and whale-watching tours.

RV sites, facilities: There are 90 sites with full and partial hookups (20, 30, 50 amps), including 45 drive-through, for RVs of any length or tents, plus 12 cabins. Picnic tables and fire pits are provided. Restrooms, drinking water, flush toilets, showers, cable TV, cell phone reception, modem access, propane, firewood, an RV dump station, a store, a coin-operated laundry, ice, a playground, a recreation room, bike rentals, and a swimming pool are available. A café is located within two miles. Some facilities are wheelchair-accessible. Leashed pets are permitted.

Reservations, fees: Reservations are recommended

at 800/562-7558. The fee is $22–39 per night, plus $5 per person per night for more than two people, and $5 per additional vehicle per night. Cabins are $45–60 per night. There is no charge for children age five and under. Major credit cards are accepted. Open mid-March to mid-November.

Directions: From I-5 at Olympia, turn north on U.S. 101 and drive 116 miles to O'Brien Road, six miles southeast of Port Angeles. Turn left on O'Brien Road and drive half a block to the campground on the right.

Contact: KOA Port Angeles–Sequim, 80 O'Brien Rd., Port Angeles, WA 98362, 360/457-5916, fax 360/452-4248, website: www.koa.com.

30 HEART O' THE HILLS

Rating: 9

in Olympic National Park Bay
See map pages 16–17

Heart O' the Hills is nestled on the northern edge of Olympic National Park at an elevation of 1,807 feet. You can drive into the park on Hurricane Ridge Road and take one of numerous hiking trails. Little Lake Dawn is less than a half mile to the west, but note that most of the property around this lake is privately owned. Naturalist programs are available in summer months.

RV sites, facilities: There are 105 sites, five drive-through, for RVs up to 40 feet or tents. Picnic tables and fire grills are provided. Restrooms, drinking water, a pay phone, and limited cell phone reception are available. Some facilities are wheelchair-accessible. Leashed pets are permitted.

Reservations, fees: Reservations are not accepted. The fee is $10 per night, plus a $10 national park entrance fee per vehicle. A senior discount is available. Major credit cards are accepted. Open year-round, weather permitting.

Directions: From I-5 at Olympia, turn north on U.S. 101 and drive about 122 miles to Port Angeles to Hurricane Ridge Road. Turn left and drive five miles to the camp on the left. (Access roads can be impassable in severe weather.)

Contact: Olympic National Park, 600 East Park Ave., Port Angeles, WA 98362, 360/565-3130, fax 360/565-3147.

31 LONESOME CREEK RV RESORT

Rating: 8

on the Pacific Ocean
See map pages 16–17

This private, developed park is set along the Pacific Ocean and the coastal Dungeness National Wildlife Refuge. It has some of the few ocean sites available in the area and offers such recreation options as fishing, beachcombing, boating, whale-watching, and sunbathing.

RV sites, facilities: There are 42 sites with full hookups (50 amps) for RVs of any length, and six sites for tents. Picnic tables and fire rings are provided. Restrooms, coin-operated showers, a coin-operated laundry, a pay phone, limited cell phone reception, gasoline and propane, and a store with a deli and ice are available. Boat docks and launching facilities are located within one mile. Leashed pets are permitted.

Reservations, fees: Reservations are accepted for RV sites and are recommended for oceanfront sites. The fee is $15–18 per night for tent sites and $25–34 for RV sites. Major credit cards are accepted. Open year-round.

Directions: From Aberdeen, drive north on U.S. 101 for 108 miles to Forks. Continue past Forks for two miles to La Push Road/Highway 110. Turn left (west) and drive 14 miles to the campground on the left.

Contact: Lonesome Creek RV Resort, P.O. Box 250, La Push, WA 98350, 360/374-4338, fax 360/374-4153.

32 MORA

Rating: 8

near the Pacific Ocean in Olympic National Park
See map pages 16–17

At an elevation of 50 feet, this is a good out-of-the-way choice near the Pacific Ocean and the Olympic Coast Marine Sanctuary. The Quillayute River feeds into the ocean near the camp, and upstream lies the Bogachiel, a prime steelhead river in winter months. A naturalist program is available during the summer. This camp includes eight sites requiring short walks, several of which are stellar.

RV sites, facilities: There are 94 sites for RVs up to 21 feet or tents, including five drive-through sites for RVs of any length, and eight walk-in sites. Picnic tables and fire grills are provided. Restrooms, drinking water, limited cell phone reception, and an RV dump station are available. A pay phone is available nearby. A naturalist program is available in summer months. Some facilities are wheelchair-accessible. Leashed pets are permitted.

Reservations, fees: Reservations are not accepted. The fee is $10 per night, plus a $10 national park entrance fee per vehicle. A senior discount is available. Open year-round.

Directions: From Aberdeen, drive north on U.S. 101 for 108 miles to Forks. Continue past Forks for two miles to La Push Road (Highway 110). Turn left (west) and drive 12 miles to the campground on the left (well marked along the route).

Contact: Olympic National Park, 600 East Park Ave., Port Angeles, WA 98362, 360/565-3130, fax 360/565-3147.

33 THREE RIVERS RESORT

Rating: 8

on the Quillayute River
See map pages 16–17

This small, private camp is set at the junction of three rivers—the Quillayute, Sol Duck, and Bogachiel. Situated above this confluence, about six miles upstream from the ocean, this pretty spot features wooded, spacious sites. Hiking and fishing are popular here. Salmon and steelhead migrate upstream, best on the Sol Duc and Bogachiel Rivers; anglers should check regulations. The coastal Dungeness National Wildlife Refuge and Pacific Ocean, which often offer good whale-watching in the spring, are a short drive to the west. Hoh Rain Forest, a worthwhile side trip, is about 45 minutes away.

RV sites, facilities: There are 10 sites for RVs of any length or tents, and 14 sites with partial or full hookups for RVs only (20, 30, 50 amps), plus five rental cabins. Picnic tables, fire pits, and drinking water are provided. Restrooms, coin-operated showers, a store, a café, an ATM, a pay phone, limited cell phone reception, a coin-operated laundry, firewood, and ice are available. Leashed pets are permitted.

Reservations, fees: Reservations are accepted. The fee is $10–15 per night, plus $5 per pet per night. Major credit cards are accepted. Open year-round.

Directions: From Aberdeen, drive north on U.S. 101 for 108 miles to Forks. Continue past Forks for two miles to La Push Road/Highway 110. Turn left (west) and drive eight miles to the campground on the right.

Contact: Three Rivers Resort, 7764 La Push Rd., Forks, WA 98331, 360/374-5300, website: www .northolympic.com/threerivers.

34 BOGACHIEL STATE PARK

Rating: 6

on the Bogachiel River
See map pages 16–17

A good base camp for salmon or steelhead fishing trips, this 123-acre park is set on the Bogachiel River, with marked hiking trails in the area. It can be noisy at times because a logging mill is located directly across the river from the campground. Also note that highway noise is noticeable, and you can see the highway from some campsites. A one-mile hiking trail is nearby. Hunting is popular in the adjacent national forest. This region is heavily forested, with lush vegetation fed by 140 to 160 inches of rain on the average each year.

RV sites, facilities: There are six sites with water and electrical hookups (30 amps) for RVs up to 30 feet, 36 developed tent sites, and one primitive tent site. Picnic tables and fire grills are provided. Restrooms, drinking water, coin-operated showers, limited cell phone reception, an RV dump station, and a picnic area are available. A store, ice, and firewood are available within one mile. A primitive boat ramp is nearby. Leashed pets are permitted.

Reservations, fees: Reservations are not accepted. The fees are $16–22 per night, $10 per night for tent sites, plus $10 per additional vehicle per night. A senior discount is available. Open year-round.

Directions: From Olympia on I-5, take Exit 104 and drive north on U.S. 101 to the Aberdeen/Highway 8 exit. Turn west on Highway 8 and drive 36 miles to Aberdeen. Continue through Aberdeen four miles to U.S. 101. Turn north on U.S. 101 and drive 102 miles to the park (six miles south of Forks) on the left side of the road.

Contact: Bogachiel State Park, Northwest Region, 185983 U.S. 101, Forks, WA 98331, 360/374-6356; state park information, 360/902-8844.

35 HOH RIVER RESORT

Rating: 6

on the Hoh River
See map pages 16–17

This camp along U.S. 101 features a choice of grassy or graveled, shady sites and is most popular as a fishing camp. Although the Hoh River is nearby, you cannot see the river from the campsites. Marked hiking trails are nearby. This pleasant little park offers steelhead and salmon fishing as well as elk hunting in the fall. Horseshoes and a recreation field are provided for campers.

RV sites, facilities: There are 23 sites for RVs of any length or tents, some with full hookups, some with electrical hookups only (30 amps), and several cabins. Fire pits and picnic tables are provided. Restrooms, coin-operated showers, a coin-operated laundry, a store, a gas station, a pay phone, bait, firewood, and ice are available. A boat launch is located nearby. Leashed pets are permitted.

Reservations, fees: Reservations are accepted. The fee is $12–21 per night, plus $3 per additional vehicle per night. Major credit cards are accepted. Open year-round.

Directions: From Aberdeen, drive north on U.S. 101 for 90 miles to the resort (15 miles south of Forks) on the left.

Contact: Hoh River Resort, 175443 U.S. 101 S, Forks, WA 98331, 360/374-5566.

36 HOH

Rating: 10

in Olympic National Park
See map pages 16–17

This camp at a trailhead leading into the interior of Olympic National Park is located in the beautiful heart of a temperate, old-growth rainforest. Hoh Oxbow, Cottonwood, Willoughby Creek, and Minnie Peterson Campgrounds are nearby, set downstream on the Hoh River, outside national park boundaries. In the summer, naturalist programs are offered, and a visitors center is nearby. This is one of the most popular camps in the park. The elevation is 578 feet.

RV sites, facilities: There are 88 sites for RVs up to 21 feet or tents. Picnic tables and fire grills are provided. Restrooms, limited cell phone reception, and drinking water are available. An RV dump station and a pay phone are located nearby. Some facilities are wheelchair-accessible. Leashed pets are permitted.

Reservations, fees: Reservations are not accepted. The fee is $10 per night, plus a $10 national park entrance fee per vehicle. A senior discount is available. Major credit cards are accepted. Open year-round.

Directions: From Aberdeen, drive north on U.S. 101 for about 90 miles to Milepost 176. Turn east on Hoh River Road and drive 19 miles to the campground on the right (near the end of the road).

Contact: Olympic National Park, 600 East Park Ave., Port Angeles, WA 98362, 360/565-3130, fax 360/565-3147.

37 KALALOCH

Rating: 10

near the Pacific Ocean in Olympic National Park
See map pages 16–17

This camp, located on a bluff above the beach, offers some wonderful ocean-view sites—which explains its popularity. It can fill quickly. Like other camps on the coast of the Olympic Peninsula, heavy rain in winter and spring is common, and it's often foggy in the summer. A naturalist program is offered in the summer months. There are several good hiking trails in the area; check out the visitors center for maps and information. The pretty Queets River is located 5 miles south.

RV sites, facilities: There are 175 sites for RVs up to 21 feet or tents, including 10 drive-through sites for RVs up to 40 feet, plus one group site. Picnic tables and fire grills are provided. Restrooms, drinking water, a pay phone, limited cell phone reception, and an RV dump station are available. A store and a restaurant are located within one mile. Some facilities are wheelchair-accessible. Leashed pets are permitted in the campground.

Reservations, fees: Reservations are taken for the group site during summer only; call 800/365-CAMP (2267) or visit http://reservations.nps.gov. The fees are $12–16 per night for individual sites, $20 per night plus $2 per person for the group site, plus a $10 national park entrance fee per vehicle. A senior discount is available. Open year-round.

Directions: From Aberdeen, drive north on U.S. 101 for 83 miles to the campground on the left. It is located near the mouth of the Kalaloch River, five miles north of the U.S. 101 bridge over the Queets River.

Contact: Olympic National Park, 600 East Park Ave., Port Angeles, WA 98362, 360/565-3130, fax 360/565-3147.

38 CAPTAIN'S LANDING

Rating: 8

in Hansville

See map pages 16–17

This camp overlooks Puget Sound and sits right next to the water. Admiralty Inlet offers a rural escape, and the Point-No-Point is within walking distance and offers tours on weekends. Trout fishing at Buck Lake is three miles away. Grassy, open sites make this a good choice for campers wanting an in-town location. An 18-hole golf course and a full-service marina are close by. A wildlife sanctuary is five miles away. No open fires are permitted.

RV sites, facilities: There are 22 drive-through sites with full hookups (30 amps) for self-contained trailers or RVs of any length, plus four cabins. No restrooms are available. A store, ice, pay phone, and cell phone reception are available. Boat docks, launching facilities, and boat rentals are located within seven miles. An ATM and a casino are located nearby. Leashed pets are permitted.

Reservations, fees: Reservations are accepted. The fee is $28–35 per night. Open year-round.

Directions: From Bremerton, drive north on High-

way 16 for 10 miles (Highway 16 turns into Highway 3) and continue north on Highway 3 for 11 miles to Port Gamble. Bear southeast toward Kingston (still on Highway 3) to Hansville Road (at George's Corner). Turn left on Hansville Road and drive eight miles. The park is on the right side, at the bottom of the hill.

Contact: Captain's Landing, 39118 Hansville Rd. NE, Hansville, WA 98340, 360/638-2257, fax 360/638-2015.

39 KITSAP MEMORIAL STATE PARK

Rating: 10

on the Hood Canal

See map pages 16–17

Kitsap Memorial State Park is a beautiful spot for camping along the Hood Canal. The park covers only 58 acres but features sweeping views of the Hood Canal and 1,797 feet of shoreline. The park has 1.5 miles of hiking trails and two open grassy fields for family play. Note that the nearest boat launch is four miles away, north on State Route 3 at Salisbury County Park. An 18-hole golf course and swimming, fishing, and hiking at nearby Anderson Lake Recreation Area are among the activities available. A short drive north will take you to historic Old Fort Townsend, which is an excellent day trip.

RV sites, facilities: There are 25 sites for RVs up to 30 feet or tents, 18 sites with partial hookups (30 amps) for RVs, and three primitive tent sites. Picnic tables and fire grills are provided. Restrooms, drinking water, flush toilets, showers, an RV dump station, a sheltered picnic area, two pay phones, cell phone reception, and a playground are available. An ATM is within one mile. Two boat buoys are available. Leashed pets are permitted.

Reservations, fees: Reservations are accepted for the group camp only at 888/226-7688. The fee is $10–22 per night, plus $10 per each additional vehicle. A senior discount is available. Open year-round.

Directions: From Tacoma on I-5, turn north on Highway 16 and drive 44 miles (Highway 16 turns into Highway 3). Continue north on Highway 3 and drive six miles to Park Street. Turn left and drive 200 yards to the park entrance on the right (well marked). The park is located four miles south of the Hood Canal Bridge.

Contact: Kitsap Memorial State Park, 202 N.E. Park St., Poulsbo, WA 98370, 360/779-3205; state park information, 360/902-8844.

40 FALLS VIEW

Rating: 8

on the Big Quilcene River in Olympic National Forest

See map pages 16–17

A viewing area to a pretty waterfall on the Big Quilcene River, where you see a narrow, 100-foot cascade, is only a 150-foot walk from the campground. That explains why, despite the rustic setting, this spot on the edge of the Olympic National Forest has a host of facilities and is popular. Enjoy the setting of mixed conifers and rhododendrons along a one-mile scenic loop trail, which overlooks the river and provides views of the waterfall. A picnic area is also located near the waterfall.

RV sites, facilities: There are 30 sites for RVs up to 30 feet or tents. Picnic tables are provided. Restrooms, drinking water, and flush and vault toilets are available. An ATM and a pay phone are within seven miles. Some facilities are wheelchair-accessible. Leashed pets are permitted.

Reservations, fees: Reservations are not accepted. The fee is $10 per night. A senior discount is available. Open early May to September.

Directions: From Olympia on I-5, turn north on U.S. 101 and drive approximately 70 miles to the campground entrance on the left (located about four miles south of Quilcene).

Contact: Olympic National Forest, Quilcene Ranger District, P.O. Box 280, Quilcene, WA 98376, 360/765-2200, fax 360/765-2202.

41 RAINBOW GROUP CAMP

Rating: 7

near Quilcene in Olympic National Forest

See map pages 16–17

Rainbow Group Camp is in a rugged, primitive setting on the edge of Olympic National Forest. This area is heavily wooded with old-growth and new-growth forest, a variety of wildflowers, and spring-blooming rhododendrons. The Rainbow Canyon Trailhead, located at the far side of the campground, provides a short hike to the Big Quilcene River and a waterfall. It is fairly steep, but not a butt kicker. Forest roads provide considerable backcountry access (obtaining a U.S. Forest Service map is advisable). The nearest is Forest Road 2730, just .1 mile away, which leads to spectacular scenery at the Mt. Walker Observation Area. Olympic National Park is also just a short drive away.

RV sites, facilities: There are nine sites for small RVs and tents that are reserved for groups up to 50 people. Picnic tables and fire grills are provided. Drinking water and vault toilets are available. A store, a café, a coin-operated laundry, an ATM, a pay phone, and ice are within five miles. Leashed pets are permitted.

Reservations, fees: Reservations are required; phone 360/765-2200. The group site is $50 per night.

Directions: From I-5 at Olympia, go north on U.S. 101 and drive approximately 69 miles to the campground (about six miles past Dosewallips State Park) on the left (near Walker Pass).

Contact: Olympic National Forest, Quilcene Ranger District, P.O. Box 280, Quilcene, WA 98376, 360/765-2200, fax 360/765-2202.

42 COVE RV PARK

Rating: 5

near Dabob Bay

See map pages 16–17

This five-acre private camp enjoys a rural setting close to the shore of Dabob Bay, yet it is fully developed. Sites are grassy and graveled with a few trees. Scuba diving is popular in this area, and the park sells air for scuba tanks. Dosewallips State Park is a short drive away and a possible side trip.

RV sites, facilities: There are 32 sites with full hookups (30, 50 amps) for RVs up to 40 feet, six tent sites, one motel room, and one RV rental. Picnic tables and fire rings (in season) are provided. Restrooms, drinking water, flush toilets, coin-operated showers, Cable TV hookups, a pay phone, cell phone reception, propane, an RV dump station, a store, a coin-operated laundry, and ice are available. Boat docks and launching facilities are on the Hood Canal 2.2 miles from the park. An ATM is within 2.5 miles. Leashed pets are permitted.

Reservations, fees: Reservations are accepted. The fee is $14–20 per night, plus $3 per person per night for more than two people (over 12). Major credit cards are accepted. Open year-round.

Directions: From Olympia on I-5, drive north on U.S. 101 for 60 miles to Brinnon (located about one mile north of Dosewallips State Park). Continue three miles north on U.S. 101 to the park on the right (before Milepost 303).

Contact: Cove RV Park, 303075 U.S. 101, Brinnon, WA 98320, 360/796-4723 or 866/796-4723, fax 360/796-3452.

43 SEAL ROCK

Rating: 9

on Dabob Bay in Olympic National Forest

See map pages 16–17

Seal Rock is a 30-acre camp set along the shore near the mouth of Dabob Bay. This is one of the few national forest campgrounds anywhere located on saltwater. It brings with it the opportunity to harvest oysters and clams in season, and is an outstanding jumping-off point for scuba diving. Most campsites are located along the waterfront, spaced among trees. Carry-in boats, such as kayaks and canoes, can be launched from the north landing. The Native American Nature Trail and the Marine Biology Nature Trail begin at the day-use area. These are short walks, each less than a half mile. This camp is extremely popular in the summer, often filling up quickly.

RV sites, facilities: There are 40 sites for RVs up to 35 feet or tents. Picnic tables and fire rings are provided. Restrooms, drinking water, flush toilets, a picnic area, a pay telephone, and cell phone reception are available. Boat docks and launching facilities are nearby on the Hood Canal and in Dabob Bay. A camp host is on-site in summer. Some facilities, including viewing areas and trails, are wheelchair-accessible. Leashed pets are permitted.

Reservations, fees: Reservations are not accept-

ed. The fee is $12 per night. A senior discount is available. Open early May to late September.

Directions: From Olympia on I-5, drive north on U.S. 101 for 60 miles to Brinnon (located about one mile north of Dosewallips State Park). Continue two miles north on U.S. 101 to Seal Rock and the camp on the right.

Contact: Olympic National Forest, Quilcene Ranger District, P.O. Box 280, Quilcene, WA 98376, 360/765-2200, fax 360/765-2202.

44 COLLINS

Rating: 7

on the Duckabush River in Olympic National Forest

See map pages 16–17

Most vacationers cruising U.S. 101 don't have a clue about this quiet spot set on a great launch point for adventure, yet it's only five or six miles from the highway. This four-acre camp is located on the Duckabush River at 200 feet elevation. It has small, shaded sites, river access nearby, and plenty of fishing and hiking; check fishing regulations before you go. Just one mile from camp is the Duckabush Trail, which connects to trails in Olympic National Park. The Murhut Falls Trail starts about three miles from the campground, providing access to a .8-mile trail to the falls. It's an eight-mile drive to nearby Dosewallips State Park and a 30- to 35-minute drive to Olympic National Park.

RV sites, facilities: There are nine sites for RVs up to 21 feet and six tent sites. Picnic tables and fire rings are provided. No drinking water is available. Vault toilets are available. Some facilities are wheelchair-accessible. Leashed pets are permitted.

Reservations, fees: Reservations are not accepted. The fee is $10 per night. A senior discount is available. Open mid-May to September.

Directions: From Olympia on I-5, drive north on U.S. 101 for 59 miles to Forest Road 2510 (near Duckabush). Turn left on Forest Road 2510 and drive five miles west to the camp on the left.

Contact: Olympic National Forest, Hood Canal Ranger District, Hoodsport Office, P.O. Box 68, Hoodsport, WA 98548, 360/877-5254.

45 DOSEWALLIPS STATE PARK

Rating: 8

on Dosewallips Creek
See map pages 16–17

This state park features good shellfish harvesting in season, and to celebrate, it hosts an annual "Shellfish Shindig" every April. The 425-acre park is located on the shore of the Hood Canal at the mouth of Dosewallips River. It features 5,500 feet of saltwater shoreline on Hood Canal and 5,400 feet of shoreline on both sides of the Dosewallips River. All campsites are grassy and located in scenic, rustic settings. Mushrooming is available in season. Check regulations for fishing and clamming, which fluctuate according to time and season. This camp is popular because it's set right off a major highway; reservations or early arrival are advised. Access is not affected by the nearby slide area.

RV sites, facilities: There are 137 sites, including 40 with full hookups (30 amps), for RVs up to 60 feet or tents, three platform tent sites, and two reservable group sites. Picnic tables and fire rings are provided. Restrooms, drinking water, flush toilets, a pay phone, cell phone reception, coin-operated showers, a sheltered picnic area, interpretive activities, and a summer Junior Ranger Program are available. A wildlife-viewing platform, horseshoes, saltwater boat-launching facilities, a recreation hall, a store, a café, an ATM, and laundry facilities are available nearby. Some facilities are wheelchair-accessible. Leashed pets are permitted.

Reservations, fees: Reserve at 888/CAMP-OUT (888/226-7688) or online at www.parks.wa.gov /reservations ($7 reservation fee). The fees are $16–22 per night, plus $10 per additional vehicle per night; platform tent sites are $35 per night. A senior discount is available. Major credit cards are accepted. Open year-round.

Directions: From Olympia on I-5, drive north on U.S. 101 for 61 miles (one mile south of Brinnon) to the state park entrance on the right.

Contact: Dosewallips State Park, 360/796-4415; state park information, 360/902-8844.

46 SCENIC BEACH STATE PARK

Rating: 10

on the Hood Canal
See map pages 16–17

Scenic Beach is an exceptionally beautiful state park with beach access and superb views of the Olympic Mountains. It features 1,500 feet of saltwater beachfront on Hood Canal. The park is also known for its wild rhododendrons in spring. Wheelchair-accessible paths lead to a country garden, gazebo, rustic bridge, and large trees. Many species of birds and wildlife can often be seen here. This camp is also close to Green Mountain Forest, offering extensive hiking opportunities. A boat ramp is a half mile east of the park, with dock and moorage available at Seabeck, one mile east of the park. A nice touch here is that park staff will check out volleyballs and horseshoes during the summer.

RV sites, facilities: There are 52 sites, some drive-through, for RVs up to 60 feet or tents. Picnic tables and fire grills are provided. Restrooms, drinking water, flush toilets, coin-operated showers, a pay phone, cell phone reception, and an RV dump station are available. A sheltered picnic area, horseshoes, and volleyball fields (May–August) are available nearby. Some facilities are wheelchair-accessible. Leashed pets are permitted.

Reservations, fees: Reserve at 888/CAMP-OUT (888/226-7688) or online at www.parks.wa.gov /reservations ($7 reservation fee). The fee is $16 per night, plus $10 per additional vehicle per night. A senior discount is available. Open April to mid-November.

Directions: From Tacoma at I-5, turn north on Highway 16 and drive 30 miles to Bremerton and the junction with Highway 3. Turn north on Highway 3 and drive about nine miles and take the first Silverdale exit (Newberry Hill Road). Turn left and drive approximately three miles to the end of the road. Turn right on Seabeck Highway and drive six miles to Miami Beach Road. Turn right and drive 1.5 miles to the park.

Contact: Scenic Beach State Park, 360/830-5079; state park information, 360/902-8844.

WASHINGTON

47 FAY BAINBRIDGE STATE PARK

Rating: 10

on Bainbridge Island
See map pages 16–17

A beach park that offers beauty and great recreation, this camp is set on the edge of Puget Sound. The park covers just 17 acres but features 1,420 feet of saltwater shoreline on the northeast corner of the island. You can hike several miles along the beach at low tide; the water temperature is typically about 55°F in summer. The primitive walk-in sites are heavily wooded, and the developed sites have great views of the sound. On clear days, campers can enjoy views of Mount Rainier and Mount Baker to the east, and at night the park provides beautiful vistas of the lights of Seattle. Clamming (in season), diving, picnicking, beachcombing, and kite flying are popular here. In the winter months, there is excellent salmon fishing just offshore of the park.

RV sites, facilities: There are 26 sites for self-contained RVs up to 30 feet or tents plus 10 primitive tent sites. Picnic tables and fire grills are provided. Restrooms, drinking water, flush toilets, coin-operated showers, an RV dump station, a sheltered picnic area, horseshoes, and a playground are available. A store and a café are located within four miles. Boat docks, launching facilities, and mooring buoys are nearby. Some facilities are wheelchair-accessible. Leashed pets are permitted.

Reservations, fees: Reservations are not accepted. The fees are $10–16 per night, $22 for RVs with hookups, plus $10 per additional vehicle per night; mooring buoys are $10–16. A senior discount is available. Open mid-April to early October.

Directions: From Tacoma at I-5, turn north on Highway 16 and drive 30 miles to Bremerton to the junction with Highway 3. Turn north on Highway 3 and drive 18 miles to Highway 305. Turn south on Highway 305 and drive over the bridge to Bainbridge Island and continue three miles to Day Road. Turn left (northeast) and drive two miles to Sunrise Drive. Turn left (north) and drive two miles to the park entrance (well marked).

Note: From Seattle, this camp can be more easily accessed by taking the Bainbridge Island ferry and then Highway 305 north to the northeast end of the island.

Contact: Fay Bainbridge State Park, 206/842-3931; state park information, 360/902-8844.

48 ILLAHEE STATE PARK

Rating: 9

near Bremerton
See map pages 16–17

This 75-acre park, named for the Native American word for "earth" or "country," features the last stand of old-growth forest in Kitsap County, including one of the largest yew trees in America. The park also features 1,785 feet of saltwater frontage. The campsites are located in a pretty, forested area, and some are grassy. The shoreline is fairly rocky, set on the shore of Port Orchard Bay, although there is a small sandy area for sunbathers. Oyster gathering is popular here. A fishing pier is available for anglers. Note that large vessels can be difficult to launch at the ramp here.

RV sites, facilities: There are 25 sites for self-contained RVs up to 40 feet or tents (one with partial hookups), two primitive tent sites, and one group site for up to 40 people. Picnic tables and fire grills are provided. Restrooms, drinking water, flush toilets, showers, firewood, and a pier are available. Boat docks, launching facilities, five mooring buoys, and 356 feet of moorage float space are available. Two sheltered picnic areas, horseshoes, volleyball, a field, and a playground are nearby. A coin-operated laundry and ice are available within one mile. An ATM is within 1.5 miles. Some facilities are wheelchair-accessible. Leashed pets are permitted.

Reservations, fees: Reservations are not accepted for family sites. The fees are $10–15 per night, $21 for RVs with hookups, plus $10 per additional vehicle per night; mooring buoys and the float pier are $10–16 per night. The group site requires a $25 reservation fee plus $10 per person per night. A senior discount is available. Open year-round.

Directions: From Silverdale on Highway 3, drive to the Highway 303 exit. Turn left and drive about a quarter mile to the first stoplight (Wagga Way). Turn right and drive 7.5 miles to Sylvan Way.

Turn left and drive 1.5 miles to the park entrance on the left.

Contact: Illahee State Park, 360/478-6460; state park information, 360/902-8844.

49 MANCHESTER STATE PARK

Rating: 9

on Puget Sound

See map pages 16–17

Manchester State Park is on the edge of Middle Point, providing excellent lookouts across Puget Sound. The park covers 111 acres, with 3,400 feet of saltwater shoreline on Rich Passage in Puget Sound. The landscape is filled with fir and maple, which are very pretty in the fall. There are 1.9 miles of hiking trails, including an interpretive trail. The camp gets heavy use in the summer but relatively little use in the off-season, when you're almost always guaranteed a spot. Group and day-use reservations are available. Note that the beach is closed to shellfish harvesting. In the early 1900s, this park site was used as a U.S. Army coastal defense installation. A gun battery remains from the park's early days, along with a torpedo warehouse and a mining casemate that are on the register of National Historical Monuments.

RV sites, facilities: There are 50 sites, including 15 with partial hookups (30 amps), for RVs up to 60 feet or tents, three primitive tent sites, and one group site. Picnic tables and fire grills are provided. Restrooms, drinking water, flush toilets, showers, a pay phone, an RV dump station, and a sheltered picnic area are available. Some facilities are wheelchair-accessible. Leashed pets are permitted.

Reservations, fees: Reserve at 888/CAMP-OUT (888/226-7688) or online at www.parks.wa.gov/reservations ($7 reservation fee). The fee is $10–22 per night, plus $10 per additional vehicle per night. A senior discount is available. Major credit cards are accepted during peak season only. Open year-round, with limited winter facilities.

Directions: From Tacoma on I-5, turn north on Highway 16 and drive to the Sedgwick Road exit and Highway 160. Turn right (east) and drive on Highway 160 to Long Lake Road. Turn left and drive to Mile Hill Road. Turn right and drive one mile to Colchester Road. Turn left and drive

two miles to Main Street. Turn left onto Main Street then make an immediate right onto Beach Drive. Drive two miles on Beach Drive to Hilldale Road. Make a right on Hilldale Road and drive .25 mile to the park entrance.

Contact: Manchester State Park, P.O. Box 36, Manchester, WA 98353, 360/871-4065.

50 GRAVES CREEK

Rating: 6

near the Quinault River in Olympic National Park

See map pages 16–17

This camp, located at an elevation of 540 feet, sits a short distance from a trailhead leading into the backcountry of Olympic National Park. See an Olympic National Park and U.S. Forest Service map for details. The East Fork Quinault River is nearby, and there are lakes in the area.

RV sites, facilities: There are 30 sites for RVs up to 21 feet or tents. Picnic tables, fire grills, limited cell phone reception, and vault toilets are available. Drinking water is available except in winter. Some facilities are wheelchair-accessible. Leashed pets are permitted.

Reservations, fees: Reservations are not accepted. There is a $10-per-night fee, plus a $10 national park entrance fee per vehicle. A senior discount is available.

Directions: From Aberdeen, drive north on U.S. 101 for 38 miles to the Lake Quinault turnoff and South Shore Road. Turn east on South Shore Road and drive 18 miles (the road becomes unpaved) to the campground at the end of the road.

Contact: Olympic National Park, 600 East Park Ave., Port Angeles, WA 98362, 360/565-3130, fax 360/565-3147.

51 HAMMA HAMMA

Rating: 7

on the Hamma Hamma River in Olympic National Forest

See map pages 16–17

This camp is set on the Hamma Hamma River at an elevation of 600 feet. It's small and primitive, but it can be preferable to some of the developed

WASHINGTON

camps on the U.S. 101 circuit. The Civilian Conservation Corps is memorialized in a wheelchair-accessible interpretive trail that begins in the campground and leads .25 mile along the river. The sites are set among conifers and hardwoods.
RV sites, facilities: There are 12 sites for RVs up to 21 feet and three tent sites. Picnic tables and fire rings are provided. Hand-pumped water and vault toilets are available. Some facilities are wheelchair-accessible. Leashed pets are permitted.
Reservations, fees: Reservations are not accepted. The fee is $10 per night. A senior discount is available. Open May to September.
Directions: From Olympia on I-5, turn north on U.S. 101 and drive 37 miles to Hoodsport. Continue on U.S. 101 for 14 miles north to Forest Road 25. Turn left on Forest Road 25 and drive 6.5 miles to the camp on the left side of the road.
Contact: Olympic National Forest, Hood Canal Ranger District, Hoodsport Office, P.O. Box 68, Hoodsport, WA 98548, 360/877-5254, fax 360/352-2569.

52 LENA CREEK

Rating: 7

on the Hamma Hamma River in Olympic National Forest
See map pages 16–17
This seven-acre camp, set amid both conifers and hardwoods, is located where Lena Creek empties into the Hamma Hamma River. A popular trailhead camp, Lena Creek features a three-mile trail from camp to Lena Lake, with four additional miles to Upper Lena Lake. A map of Olympic National Forest details the trail and road system. The camp is rustic with some improvements.
RV sites, facilities: There are 14 sites for RVs up to 22 feet or tents. Picnic tables, drinking water, and fire rings are provided. Vault toilets are available. Some facilities are wheelchair-accessible. Leashed pets are permitted.
Reservations, fees: Reservations are not accepted. The fee is $10 per night. A senior discount is available. Open early May to September.
Directions: From Olympia on I-5, turn north on U.S. 101 and drive about 37 miles to Hoodsport. Continue north on U.S. 101 for 14 miles to For-

est Road 25. Turn west on Forest Road 25 and drive eight miles to the camp on the left.
Contact: Olympic National Forest, Hood Canal Ranger District, Hoodsport Office, P.O. Box 68, Hoodsport, WA 98548, 360/877-5254, fax 360/352-2569.

53 STAIRCASE

Rating: 9

on the North Fork of the Skokomish River in Olympic National Park
See map pages 16–17
This camp is located near the Staircase Rapids of the North Fork of the Skokomish River, about one mile from where it empties into Lake Cushman. The elevation is 765 feet. A major trailhead at the camp leads to the backcountry of Olympic National Park, and other trails are nearby. See an Olympic National Park and U.S. Forest Service map for details. Beautiful hiking is available along both sides of the river. Stock facilities are also available nearby.
RV sites, facilities: There are 56 sites for RVs up to 21 feet or tents. Picnic tables and fire grills are provided. Restrooms, drinking water, and limited cell phone reception are available. A pay phone is nearby. Some facilities are wheelchair-accessible. Leashed pets are permitted in camp.
Reservations, fees: Reservations are not accepted. There is a $10-per-night fee, plus a $10 national park entrance fee per vehicle. A senior discount is available. Open year-round, weather permitting.
Directions: From Olympia on I-5, take U.S. 101 and drive north about 37 miles to the town of Hoodsport and Lake Cushman Road (County Road 119). Turn left (west) and drive 17 miles to the camp at the end of the road (about one mile above the inlet of Lake Cushman). The last several miles of the road are unpaved.
Contact: Olympic National Park, 600 East Park Ave., Port Angeles, WA 98362, 360/565-3130, fax 360/565-3147.

54 BIG CREEK

Rating: 7

near Lake Cushman in Olympic National Forest

See map pages 16–17

Big Creek is an alternative to Staircase camp on the North Fork of Skokomish River and Camp Cushman on Lake Cushman, both of which get heavier use. The sites here are large and well spaced for privacy over 30 acres, primarily of second-growth forest. Big Creek runs adjacent to the campground. A four-mile loop trail extends from camp and connects to the Mt. Eleanor Trail.

RV sites, facilities: There are 23 sites for RVs up to 30 feet or tents, and two walk-in sites (requiring a .25-mile walk). Picnic tables and fire grills are provided. Drinking water, vault toilets, and sheltered picnic tables are available. A boat dock and ramp are located at nearby Lake Cushman. Leashed pets are permitted.

Reservations, fees: Reservations are not accepted. The fee is $10 per night. A senior discount is available. Open May to September.

Directions: From Olympia on I-5, take Exit 104 for U.S. 101/Highway 8. Drive north on U.S. 101 for 37 miles to Hoodsport and Lake Cushman Road (Highway 119). Turn left on Lake Cushman Road and drive nine miles (two miles north of Camp Cushman) to the T intersection. Turn left and the campground is on the right.

Contact: Olympic National Forest, Hood Canal Ranger District, Hoodsport Office, P.O. Box 68, Hoodsport, WA 94548, 360/877-5254, fax 360/352-2569.

55 CAMP CUSHMAN

Rating: 10

on Lake Cushman

See map pages 16–17

Set in the foothills of the Olympic Mountains on the shore of Lake Cushman, this park features a 10-mile-long blue-water mountain lake, eight miles of park shoreline, forested hillsides, and awesome views of snowcapped peaks. Beach access and good trout fishing are other highlights. The park has eight miles of hiking trails and five miles of bike trails. In fall, mushrooming is popular. Windsurfing, water-skiing, and swimming are all popular here. An 18-hole golf course is nearby.

RV sites, facilities: There are 50 sites, 30 with full hookups (30 amps) for RVs up to 60 feet, and two primitive sites. Picnic tables and fire grills are provided. Restrooms, drinking water, flush toilets, showers, a picnic area, an amphitheater, a store, a pay phone, ice, limited cell phone reception, horseshoes, volleyball, and firewood are available. Boat docks and launching facilities are located at nearby Lake Cushman. Leashed pets are permitted.

Reservations, fees: Reservations are accepted at 360/877-6770 or 866/259-2900. The fees are $16–22 per night, plus $6 per additional vehicle per night, and a $5 pet fee. Major credit cards are accepted. Open April to October.

Directions: From Olympia on I-5, take the U.S. 101 exit and drive north 37 miles to Hoodsport and Highway 119 (Lake Cushman Road). Turn left (west) on Lake Cushman Road and drive seven miles to the park on the left.

Contact: Camp Cushman, 866/259-2900, website: www.lakecushman.com.

56 WILLABY

Rating: 8

on Lake Quinault in Olympic National Forest

See map pages 16–17

This pretty, 14-acre wooded camp is on the shore of Lake Quinault at 200 feet elevation, adjacent to where Willaby Creek empties into the lake. Since it is part of the Quinault Indian Reservation, special fishing and boating regulations apply. Phone 360/276-8211 for more information. The campsites vary, with some open and featuring lake views, while others are more private, with no views. The tree cover consists of Douglas fir, western red cedar, western hemlock, and big leaf maple. The forest floor is covered with wall-to-wall greenery, with exceptional moss growth. The Quinault Rain Forest Nature Trail and the Quinault National Recreation Trail System are nearby. Lake Quinault covers about six square miles. This camp is concessionaire operated.

RV sites, facilities: There are 22 drive-in sites for RVs up to 32 feet or tents. Picnic tables and fire pits are provided. Drinking water, flush toilets, and electricity in the restrooms are available. Launching facilities and rentals are available. An ATM and a pay phone are within one mile. Some facilities are wheelchair-accessible. Leashed pets are permitted.

Reservations, fees: Reservations are not accepted. The fee is $15 per night. A senior discount is available. Open from Memorial Day weekend through September.

Directions: From Olympia on I-5, take Exit 104 and drive north on U.S. 101 to the Aberdeen/Highway 8 exit. Turn west on Highway 8 (becomes Highway 12) and drive 36 miles to Aberdeen. Continue through Aberdeen four miles to U.S. 101. Turn north on U.S. 101 and drive about 38 miles to the Lake Quinault turnoff and South Shore Road. Turn northeast on South Shore Road and drive 1.5 miles to the camp on the southern shore of the lake.

Contact: Olympic National Forest, Pacific Ranger District, Quinault Office, P.O. Box 9, Quinault, WA 98575, 360/288-2525, fax 360/352-2676.

57 FALLS CREEK

Rating: 8

on Lake Quinault in Olympic National Forest
See map pages 16–17

This scenic, wooded three-acre camp is set where Falls Creek empties into Quinault Lake. A canopy of lush big leaf maple hangs over the campground. The campsites feature both drive-in and walk-in sites, with the latter requiring about a 125-yard walk. The Quinault Rain Forest Nature Trail and Quinault National Recreation Trail System are nearby. The camp is located adjacent to the Quinault Ranger Station and historic Lake Quinault Lodge at an elevation of 200 feet. Special fishing and boating regulations apply; phone 360/276-8211 for more information.

RV sites, facilities: There are 20 sites for RVs up to 16 feet and 11 tent sites. Picnic tables and fire pits are provided. Drinking water, flush toilets, and electricity in the restrooms are available. Launching facilities are available. A camp host has firewood for sale. Four picnic sites are available nearby. An ATM and a pay phone are within a half mile. Some facilities are wheelchair-accessible. Leashed pets are permitted.

Reservations, fees: Reservations are not accepted. The fee is $14 per night. A senior discount is available. Open Memorial Day through Labor Day.

Directions: From Aberdeen, drive north on U.S. 101 for 38 miles to Quinault and South Shore Road. Turn right (northeast) and drive 2.5 miles to the camp on the southeast shore of Lake Quinault.

Contact: Olympic National Forest, Pacific Ranger District, Quinault Office, P.O. Box 9, Quinault, WA 98575, 360/288-2525, fax 360/352-2676.

58 GATTON CREEK

Rating: 9

on Lake Quinault in Olympic National Forest
See map pages 16–17

Although walk-in campsites are the focus here, RV sites are available in the parking area. This five-acre wooded camp is set on the shore of Lake Quinault (elevation 200 feet), where Gatton Creek empties into it. The walk-in sites feature great views across the lake to the forested slopes of Olympic National Park. The lake is part of the Quinault Indian Nation, which has jurisdiction here. Rules allow a 24 mph speed limit on the lake, but no towing and no personal watercraft. Special fishing and boating regulations apply; phone 360/276-8211 for more information. Lake Quinault covers about six square miles. The Quinault Rain Forest Nature Trail and the Quinault National Recreation Trail System are nearby. About nine miles of loop trails are accessible here. This camp, like the others on the lake, is concessionaire operated.

RV sites, facilities: There are eight overflow RV sites (in a parking area) and seven walk-in tent sites. Picnic tables and fire pits are provided. Pit toilets, firewood, and a picnic area are available. An ATM and a pay phone are within 1.5 miles. Some facilities are wheelchair-accessible. Leashed pets are permitted.

Reservations, fees: Reservations are not accepted. The fee is $12 per night. A senior discount is available. There is no charge for picnicking. Open May to September.

Directions: From Aberdeen, drive north on U.S. 101 for 38 miles to the Lake Quinault turnoff and South Shore Road. Turn right (northeast) and drive 3.5 miles to the camp on the southeast shore of Lake Quinault.

Contact: Olympic National Forest, Pacific Ranger District, Quinault Office, P.O. Box 9, Quinault, WA 98575, 360/288-2525, fax 360/352-2676.

59 COHO

Rating: 10

on Wynoochee Lake in Olympic National Forest

See map pages 16–17

This eight-acre camp is on the shore of Wynoochee Lake, which is 4.4 miles long and covers 1,140 acres. The camp is set at an elevation of 900 feet. The fishing season opens June 1 and closes October 31. Powerboats, water-skiing, and personal watercraft are permitted. Points of interest include the Working Forest Trail, Wynoochee Dam Viewpoint and exhibits, and the 16-mile Wynoochee Lake Shore Trail, which circles the lake. This is one of the most idyllic drive-to settings you could hope to find.

RV sites, facilities: There are 58 sites for RVs up to 36 feet or tents. Picnic tables are provided. Restrooms, flush toilets, and drinking water are available. An RV dump station and a pay phone are nearby. Boat docks and launching facilities are available at Wynoochee Lake. Some facilities are wheelchair-accessible. Leashed pets are permitted.

Reservations, fees: Reservations are not accepted. The fee is $12 per night for drive-in sites and $10 per night for walk-in sites. A senior discount is available. Open May to September.

Directions: From Olympia on I-5, take Exit 104 and drive north on U.S. 101 to the Aberdeen/Highway 8 exit. Turn west on Highway 8 and drive 36 miles (it becomes Highway 12 at Elma) to Montesano. Continue two miles on Highway 12 to Wynoochee Valley Road. Turn north on Wynoochee Valley Road and drive 12 miles to Forest Road 22. Continue north on Forest Road 22 (a gravel road) to Wynoochee Lake. Just south of the lake, bear left and drive on Forest Road 2294 (which runs along the lake's northwest shore)

for one mile to the camp on the west shore of Wynoochee Lake. Obtaining a U.S. Forest Service map is helpful.

Contact: Olympic National Forest, Hood Canal Ranger District, Hoodsport Office, P.O. Box 68, Hoodsport, WA 98548, 360/877-5254, fax 360/352-2569.

60 REST-A-WHILE RV PARK

Rating: 6

on the Hood Canal

See map pages 16–17

This seven-acre park, located at sea level on the Hood Canal, offers waterfront sites and a private beach for clamming and oyster gathering, not to mention plenty of opportunities to fish, boat, and scuba dive. It's an alternative to Potlatch State Park and Glen-Ayr RV Park.

RV sites, facilities: There are 80 sites with full hookups (30 amps), including some drive-through, for RVs of any length and two tent sites. Picnic tables are provided. Restrooms, portable fire rings, drinking water, flush toilets, showers, propane, firewood, a clubhouse, a store, a pay phone, cell phone reception, a seafood market, a drive-in restaurant, laundry facilities, and ice are available. A café is within walking distance. Boat docks, launching facilities, a scuba diving shop, seasonal boat and kayak rentals, and a private beach for clamming and oyster gathering (in season) are also available. An ATM is within two miles. Leashed pets are permitted.

Reservations, fees: Reservations are accepted. The fee is $20–30 per night, plus $2 per additional vehicle per night, and $4 per person per night for more than two people. Major credit cards are accepted. Open year-round.

Directions: From Olympia on I-5, take Exit 104 for U.S. 101/Highway 8. Drive north on U.S. 101 for 37 miles to Hoodsport. Continue 2.5 miles north on U.S. 101 to the park located at Milepost 329.

Contact: Rest-a-While RV Park, North 27001 U.S. 101, Hoodsport, WA 98548, 360/877-9474, website: www.restawhile.com.

61 GLEN-AYR RV PARK & MOTEL

Rating: 6

on the Hood Canal
See map pages 16–17
This adults-only, fully developed, nine-acre park is located at sea level on the Hood Canal, where there are opportunities to fish and scuba dive. Salmon fishing is especially excellent. Swimming and boating round out the options. The park has a spa, moorage, horseshoes, a recreation field, and a motel.

RV sites, facilities: There are 40 sites with full hookups (30 amps), including some drive-through, for RVs of any length, 14 motel rooms, and two suites with kitchens. Restrooms, drinking water, flush toilets, showers, picnic tables, propane, a spa, a recreation hall, horseshoes, a pay phone, cell phone reception, and a coin-operated laundry are available. A store, an ATM, a café, and ice are within one mile. A boat dock is located across the street from the park. Leashed pets are permitted.

Reservations, fees: Campers must be 18 years of age or older. Reservations are accepted. The fee is $27 per night, plus $4 per person per night for more than two people. Major credit cards are accepted. Open year-round.

Directions: From Olympia on I-5, take Exit 104 for U.S. 101/Highway 8. Drive north on U.S. 101 for 37 miles to Hoodsport. Continue one mile north on U.S. 101 to the park on the left.

Contact: Glen-Ayr RV Park & Motel, 25381 North U.S. 101, Hoodsport, WA 98548, 360/877-9522 or 800/367-9522, fax 360/877-5177, website: www.hoodsportwa.com.

62 MINERVA BEACH RESORT

Rating: 5

on the Hood Canal
See map pages 16–17
This resort is on Hood Canal, a layover spot if you're cruising up or down U.S. 101. For the highly sensitive, road noise is discernible. There are some permanent rentals here, but they are located in a separate area, apart from the campground. Recreational opportunities at this park include salmon fishing, crabbing, and digging for oysters and clams in season; check regulations. A winery is located three miles to the north. Nearby Potlatch State Park provides a good side trip.

RV sites, facilities: There are 23 sites with full hookups (30, 50 amps) for RVs up to 50 feet and 20 tent sites. Picnic tables and fire grills are provided. Restrooms, drinking water, flush toilets, coin-operated showers, cable TV, modem access, cell phone reception, a coin-operated laundry, limited groceries, ice, RV supplies, and propane are available. Horseshoes, an ATM, and a gift shop are nearby. Leashed pets are permitted.

Reservations, fees: Reservations are recommended. The fee is $16–22 per night, plus $2 per person per night for more than two people. Major credit cards are accepted. Open year-round.

Directions: From Tumwater/Olympia, take the U.S. 101 exit and drive north to Shelton. Continue north for 10 miles past Potlatch State Park to the resort entrance on the left.

Contact: Minerva Beach Resort, 21110 U.S. 101 N, Shelton, WA 98584, 360/877-5145 or 866/500-5145, website: http://home.att.net/~minervabeach/.

63 POTLATCH STATE PARK

Rating: 8

on the Hood Canal
See map pages 16–17
This state park is on the edge of the Northwest rain shadow, receiving less rainfall than most other areas of coastal Washington. The park has 9,570 feet of shoreline on the Hood Canal. There are 1.5 miles of trails for hiking and biking, but the shoreline and water bring people here for the good kayaking, windsurfing, scuba diving, clamming, and fishing. The park is named for the potlatch, which is a gift-giving ceremony of the Skokomish Indians. There are four major rivers, the Skokomish, Hamma Hamma, Duckabush, and Dosewallips, within a 30-mile radius of the park. The park receives an annual rainfall of 64 inches.

RV sites, facilities: There are 18 drive-through sites with full hookups (30, 50 amps) for RVs up to 35 feet, 17 developed tent sites, and two primitive tent sites. Picnic tables and fire grills are

WASHINGTON

provided. Restrooms, drinking water, flush toilets, showers, an RV dump station, firewood, an amphitheater, a pay phone, cell phone reception, a picnic area, and interpretive programs are available. Three mooring buoys are located at the park, and boat launching and docks are available nearby at the Hood Canal. An ATM is within three miles. Leashed pets are permitted.

Reservations, fees: Reservations are not accepted. The fees are $10–22 per night, plus $10 per additional vehicle per night, and $7–16 for mooring buoys. A senior discount is available. Open year-round.

Directions: From Olympia take the U.S. 101 and drive north to Shelton. Continue north for 9.7 miles to the Potlatch entrance.

Contact: Potlatch State Park, 360/877-5361; state park information, 360/902-8844.

64 ROBIN HOOD VILLAGE

Rating: 5

near the Hood Canal
See map pages 16–17

This wooded park is near a state park, Olympic National Forest, Mason Lake and Lake Cushman, and Hood Canal. Nearby recreation options include an 18-hole golf course.

RV sites, facilities: There are 16 sites with partial or full hookups (20, 30, 50 amps) for RVs of any length, four tent sites, and four cabins. Picnic tables are provided. Restrooms, drinking water, flush toilets, showers, a restaurant, an espresso stand, a liquor store, a pay phone, cell phone reception, a massage therapist, a beauty salon, a sauna, and a coin-operated laundry are available. Propane, an RV dump station, a store, and ice are available within one mile. Boat docks and launching facilities are located in the park. Leashed pets are permitted.

Reservations, fees: Reservations are accepted. The fee is $14–22 per night; cabins are $85–200 per night. Major credit cards are accepted. Open year-round.

Directions: From Tacoma, drive northeast on Highway 16 for about 30 miles to Bremerton and Highway 3. Turn south on Highway 3 and drive eight miles southwest to the town of Belfair and Highway 106. Bear right (southwest) on High-

way 106 and drive 13 miles to the campground along Hood Canal.

Contact: Robin Hood Village, East 6780 Hwy. 106, Union, WA 98592, 360/898-2163, fax 360/898-2164, website: www.robinhoodvillage.com.

65 TWANOH STATE PARK

Rating: 8

near Union
See map pages 16–17

This state park is set on the shore of Hood Canal at one of the warmest saltwater bodies in Puget Sound and likely the warmest saltwater beach in the state. Twanoh, from the Native American word meaning "gathering place," covers 182 acres, with 3,167 feet of saltwater shoreline. Swimming and oyster and crab harvesting (in season) are popular here. No clamming is allowed. Winter smelting is also popular; check regulations. In late fall, the chum salmon can be seen heading up the small creek; fishing for them is prohibited. Most of the park buildings are made of brick, stone, and round logs. They were built by the Civilian Conservation Corps in the 1930s. You'll also see extensive evidence of logging from the 1890s. Amenities include a tennis court, horseshoes, and a concession stand.

RV sites, facilities: There are nine sites for RVs up to 35 feet and 17 tent sites, 13 with full hookups and nine with partial hookups (20, 30 amps). Picnic tables and fire grills are provided. Flush toilets, a store, and a playground are available. Electricity, drinking water, sewer hookups, showers, a pay phone, cell phone reception, and firewood can be obtained for a fee. An ATM is within three miles. Some facilities are wheelchair-accessible. Leashed pets are permitted.

Reservations, fees: Reservations are not accepted. The fee is $10–22 per night. Open April to October.

Directions: From Bremerton, take Highway 3 southwest to Belfair and Highway 106. Turn west and drive eight miles to the park. If driving from U.S. 101, turn east on Highway 106 and drive 12 miles to the park.

Contact: Twanoh State Park, 360/275-2222; state park information, 360/902-8844.

66 BELFAIR STATE PARK

Rating: 8

on the Hood Canal
See map pages 16–17

Belfair State Park is situated along the southern edge of the Hood Canal, spanning 65 acres with 3,720 feet of saltwater shoreline. This park is known for its saltwater tidal flats, wetlands, and wind-blown beach grasses. Beach walking and swimming are good. The camp is set primarily amid conifer forest and marshlands on the Hood Canal with nearby streams, tideland, and wetlands. A gravel-rimmed pool that is separate from the Hood Canal creates a unique swimming area. A children's Easter egg hunt is held here each spring. Note that the DNR Tahuya Multiple-Use Area is nearby with trails for motorcycles, mountain biking, hiking, horseback riding, and off-road vehicles. Big Mission Creek and Little Mission Creek, both located in the park, are habitat for chum salmon during spawning season in fall.

RV sites, facilities: There are 47 sites with full hookups (30 amps) for RVs up to 65 feet and 137 sites for tents. Picnic tables and fire grills are provided. Restrooms, drinking water, flush toilets, coin-operated showers, a bathhouse, a pay phone, an RV dump station, a swimming lagoon, and a playground with horseshoes are available. A store and a restaurant are within one mile. An ATM is within three miles. Some facilities are wheelchair-accessible. Leashed pets are permitted.

Reservations, fees: Reserve at 888/CAMP-OUT (888/226-7688) or online at www.parks.wa.gov /reservations ($7 reservation fee). The fee is $16–22 per night, plus $10 per additional vehicle per night. A senior discount is available. Major credit cards are accepted. Open year-round.

Directions: From Tacoma on I-5, drive to the Highway 16 west exit. Take Highway 16 northwest and drive about 27 miles toward Bremerton and Belfair (after the Port Orchard exits, note that the highway merges into three lanes). Get in the left lane for the Belfair/State Route 3 south exit. Take that exit and turn left at the traffic signal. Take State Route 3 eight miles south to Belfair to State Route 300 (at the signal just after the Safeway). Turn right and drive three miles to the park entrance.

Contact: Belfair State Park, 360/275-0668; state park information, 360/902-8844.

67 JARRELL COVE STATE PARK

Rating: 8

on Harstine Island
See map pages 16–17

Most visitors to this park arrive by boat. Campsites are near the docks, set on a rolling, grassy area. The park covers just 43 acres but boasts 3,500 feet of saltwater shoreline on the northwest end of Harstine Island in South Puget Sound. The park's dense forest presses nearly to the water's edge at high tides—a beautiful setting. At low tides, tideland mud flats are unveiled. The beach is rocky and muddy, not exactly Hawaii. Hiking and biking is limited to just one mile of trail.

RV sites, facilities: There are 21 sites for RVs up to 30 feet or tents and a group camp for up to 64 people, which requires a short walk in. Picnic tables and fire grills are provided. Restrooms, drinking water, flush toilets, and coin-operated showers are available. Boat docks, a marine pumpout, and 14 mooring buoys are available. A picnic area and a horseshoe pit are nearby. Some facilities are wheelchair-accessible. Leashed pets are permitted.

Reservations, fees: Four family sites and the group site can be reserved at 888/CAMP-OUT (888/226-7688) or online at www.parks.wa.gov/reservations ($7 reservation fee). The fee is $10–15 per night, plus $10 per additional vehicle per night, and the mooring fee is $10–16; the group site requires a $25 reservation plus $2 per person with a 20-person minimum. A senior discount is available. Open year-round.

Directions: From Olympia on I-5, turn north on U.S. 101 and drive 22 miles to Shelton and Highway 3. Turn north on Highway 3 and drive about eight miles to Pickering Road. Turn right and drive to the Harstine Bridge. Turn left, cross the bridge to Harstine Island, and continue to a stop sign at North Island Drive. Turn left and drive four miles to Wingert Road. Turn left and drive .25 mile to the park on the left.

Contact: Jarrell Cove State Park, 360/426-9226; state park information, 360/902-8844.

68 JARRELL'S COVE MARINA

Rating: 6

near Shelton
See map pages 16–17
The marina and nearby Puget Sound are the big draws here. This small camp features 1,000 feet of shoreline and a half mile of public beach. Clamming is available in season.

RV sites, facilities: There are three sites with partial hookups (30 amps) for RVs up to 65 feet. Picnic tables and barbecues are provided. Restrooms, drinking water, flush toilets, showers, propane, an RV dump station, a store, limited cell phone reception, fishing licenses, bait and tackle, a laundry room, boat docks, boat rentals, gas, and diesel are available. A pay phone and ATM are nearby. Leashed pets are permitted.

Reservations, fees: Reservations are accepted. The fee is $30 per night. Major credit cards are accepted. Open year-round.

Directions: From Olympia on I-5, turn north on U.S. 101 and drive 22 miles to Shelton and Highway 3. Turn east on Highway 3 and drive about eight miles to Pickering Road. Turn right and drive to the Harstine Island Bridge. Turn left, cross the bridge to Harstine Island, and continue to a stop sign at North Island Drive. Turn left on North Island Drive and drive 2.8 miles to Haskell Hill Road. Turn left on Haskell Hill Road and drive one mile to the marina.

Contact: Jarrell's Cove Marina, 220 East Wilson Rd., Shelton, WA 98584, 360/426-8823.

69 JOEMMA BEACH STATE PARK

Rating: 8

on Puget Sound
See map pages 16–17
This beautiful camp set along the shore of the peninsula provides an alternative to nearby Penrose Point State Park. It covers 122 acres and features 3,000 feet of saltwater frontage on the Southeast Kitsap Peninsula. This area is often excellent for boating, fishing, and crabbing. It is a forested park with the bonus of a boat-in campsite. Hiking is limited to a trail that is less than a mile long.

RV sites, facilities: There are 19 sites for RVs up to 35 feet or tents and three primitive tent sites. Picnic tables, fire grills, and tent pads are provided. Vault toilets, drinking water, boat-launching facilities, cell phone reception, and a dock are available. Leashed pets are permitted.

Reservations, fees: Reservations are not accepted. The fee is $10–22, plus $10 per additional vehicle per night. A senior discount is available. Open year-round.

Directions: From Tacoma, drive north on Highway 16 for about 10 miles to Highway 302. Turn west and drive about five miles to Key Peninsula Highway. Turn south and drive about 15 miles to Whiteman Road. Turn right and drive four miles to Bay Road. Turn right and drive one mile to the park entrance (stay on the asphalt road when entering the park).

Contact: Joemma Beach State Park, 253/265-3606; state park information, 360/902-8844.

70 PENROSE POINT STATE PARK

Rating: 8

on Puget Sound
See map pages 16–17
This park on Carr Inlet in Puget Sound, overlooking Lake Bay, has a remote feel, but it's actually not far from Tacoma. The park covers 152 acres, with two miles of saltwater frontage on Mayo Cove and Carr Inlet. The camp has impressive stands of fir and cedars nearby, along with ferns and rhododendrons. The park has 2.5 miles of trails for biking and hiking. Bay Lake is a popular fishing lake for trout and is located one mile away; a boat launch is available there. Penrose is known for its excellent fishing, crabbing, clamming, and oysters. The nearest boat launch to Puget Sound is located three miles away in the town of Home.

RV sites, facilities: There are 82 developed sites for self-contained RVs up to 35 feet or tents and one hike-in/bike-in tent site. Picnic tables and fire grills are provided. Restrooms, drinking water, flush toilets, coin-operated showers, an RV dump station, horseshoes, a picnic area, a pay phone, cell phone reception, and a beach are available. Boat docks, a marine pump-out, and mooring buoys are nearby. Some facilities are wheelchair-accessible. Leashed pets are permitted.

Reservations, fees: Reserve at 888/CAMP-OUT (888/226-7688) or online at www.parks.wa.gov /reservations ($7 reservation fee). The fee is $10–16 per night, plus $10 per additional vehicle per night; buoys are $7 per night, and boat mooring is $10–16 per night. A senior discount is available. Major credit cards are accepted. Open March to September.

Directions: From Tacoma, drive north on Highway 16 for about 10 miles to Highway 302/Key Peninsula Highway. Turn west and drive about five miles to Key Peninsula Highway. Turn south and drive 9.2 miles through the towns of Key Center and Home to Cornwall Road KPS (second road after crossing the Home Bridge). Turn left and drive 1.25 miles to 158 Avenue KPS and the park entrance.

From State Highway 16 at Purdy, drive west on Highway 302 for five miles to the intersection with the Key Peninsula Highway. Turn south and drive nine miles to Cornwall Road KPS. Turn left on Cornwall Road KPS and drive 1.25 miles to 158th Avenue KPS. Turn left and drive to the park entrance.

Contact: Penrose Point State Park, 253/884-2514; state park information, 360/902-8844.

71 KOPACHUCK STATE PARK

Rating: 8

on Puget Sound
See map pages 16–17
This park is located on Henderson Bay on Puget Sound near Tacoma. Noteworthy are the scenic views and dramatic sunsets across the Puget Sound and Olympic Mountains. The park covers 109 acres, with 5,600 feet of saltwater shoreline. A unique element of this park is that it includes Cutts Island (also called Deadman's Island), located a half mile from shore, accessible only by boat (no camping on the island). The park has sandy beaches, located about 250 yards down the hill from the camp. Two miles of hiking trails are available. Fishing access is available

by boat only. A boat launch is located not far from camp.

RV sites, facilities: There are 41 developed sites for self-contained RVs up to 35 feet or tents, one primitive boat-in site for kayakers (no motorized boats permitted), and one group site for up to 40 people. Picnic tables and fire grills are provided. Restrooms, drinking water, flush toilets, coin-operated showers, an RV dump station, a pay phone, cell phone reception, a covered picnic area, a Junior Ranger program, interpretive activities, and boat buoys are available. Some facilities are wheelchair-accessible. Leashed pets are permitted.

Reservations, fees: Reservations are not accepted for family sites. The fee is $16 per night, plus $10 per person for the primitive boat-in site; the group site requires a $25 reservation fee, plus $2 per person with a 20-person minimum. A senior discount is available. Open April to September.

Directions: From Tacoma on I-5, turn north on Highway 16. Drive seven miles north to the second Gig Harbor exit. Take that exit and look for the sign for Kopachuck State Park. At the sign, turn west and drive five miles (the road changes names several times) to the camp (well marked).

Contact: Kopachuck State Park, 253/265-3606; state park information, 360/902-8844.

72 GIG HARBOR RV RESORT

Rating: 7

near Tacoma
See map pages 16–17
This is a popular layover spot for folks heading up to Bremerton. Just a short jaunt off the highway, it's pleasant, clean, and friendly. An 18-hole golf course, a full-service marina, and tennis courts are located nearby. Look for the great view of Mount Rainier from the end of the harbor.

RV sites, facilities: There are 93 sites, most with partial or full hookups (20, 30, 50 amps), including 28 drive-through sites and some long-term rentals, for RVs of any length or tents and one cabin. Restrooms, drinking water, flush toilets, showers, a pay phone, cell phone reception, modem access, propane, an RV dump station, a club room, a coin-operated laundry, ice, a playground with horseshoes, a sports field, and a heated swimming pool are available. An ATM is within 1.25 miles. Leashed pets are permitted. **Reservations, fees:** Reservations are recommended in the summer. The fee is $20–38 per night. A senior discount is available. Major credit cards are accepted. Open year-round.

Directions: From Tacoma, drive northwest on Highway 16 for 12 miles to Burnham Drive/North Rosedale exit. Take that exit and drive into the roundabout. Take an immediate right out of the roundabout onto Burnham Drive NW and drive one mile to the campground on the left.

Contact: Gig Harbor RV Resort, 9515 Burnham Dr. NW, Gig Harbor, WA 98332, 253/858-8138 or 800/526-8311, fax 253/858-8399.

73 PACIFIC BEACH STATE PARK

Rating: 10

on the Pacific Ocean
See map pages 16–17

This is the only state park campground in Washington where you can see the ocean from your campsite. Set on just nine acres, within the town of Pacific Beach, it boasts 2,300 feet of beachfront. This spot is great for long beach walks, although it can be windy, especially in the spring and early summer. Because of those winds, this is a great place for kite flying. Clamming (for razor clams) is permitted only in season. Note that rangers advise against swimming or body surfing because of strong riptides. Vehicle traffic is allowed seasonally on the uppermost portions of the beach, but ATVs are not allowed in the park, on the beach, or on sand dunes. This camp is popular and often fills up quickly.

RV sites, facilities: There are 32 sites with partial hookups (30 amps) for RVs up to 60 feet, 32 developed tent sites, and two primitive tent sites. Picnic tables are provided. Restrooms, drinking water, flush toilets, coin-operated showers, a pay phone, limited cell phone reception, an RV dump station, and a picnic area are available. An ATM is within a quarter mile. No fires are permitted. Some facilities are wheelchair-accessible. Leashed pets are permitted.

Reservations, fees: Reserve at 888/CAMP-OUT (888/226-7688) or online at www.parks.wa.gov /reservations ($7 reservation fee). The fee is $16–22 per night, and $10 per night for bike-in sites. A senior discount is available. Major credit cards are accepted. Open year-round.

Directions: From Hoquiam, drive north on State Route 109 for 37 miles to Pacific Beach and the park on the right.

Contact: Pacific Beach State Park, 148 Rte. 115, Hoquiam, WA 98550, 360/276-4297; state park information, 360/902-8844.

74 DRIFTWOOD ACRES OCEAN CAMPGROUND

Rating: 7

in Copalis Beach
See map pages 16–17

Driftwood Acres spreads over some 150 acres and features large RV sites and secluded tent sites. It is located along a tidal river basin, out of the wind. Most find the camp, with its beach access, evergreens, and marked hiking trails, to be family friendly. A bundle of firewood is provided for each night's stay. Clamming is often good in the area. Additional facilities within eight miles include an 18-hole golf course and a riding stable.

RV sites, facilities: There are 15 sites with partial hookups (20 amps) for RVs of any length and 29 tent sites. Picnic tables and fire pits are provided. Restrooms, drinking water, flush toilets, coin-operated showers, a free bundle of firewood, a recreation hall, limited cell phone reception, and an RV dump station are available. A clam-cleaning station is nearby. Propane, a tavern, an ATM, a pay phone, and ice are available within one mile. Leashed pets are permitted, but no Rottweilers, pit bulls, Dobermans, or aggressive dogs of any type.

Reservations, fees: Reservations are accepted. The fee is $25 per night in summer and $15–20 per night in winter, plus $5 per person ($2.50 for children) for more than two adults and two children and $5 per additional vehicle per night. Open year-round.

Directions: From Hoquiam, drive west on State Route 109 for 21 miles to Copalis Beach. Continue .5 mile north to the camp on the left, between Mileposts 21 and 22.

Contact: Driftwood Acres Ocean Campground,

P.O. Box 216, 3209 Rte. 109, Copalis Beach, WA 98535, 360/289-3484.

⁷⁵ SURF AND SAND RV PARK, COPALIS BEACH

Rating: 5

in Copalis Beach

See map pages 16–17

Although not particularly scenic, this five-acre park is a decent layover for an RV vacation and will do the job if you're tired and ready to get off U.S. 101. It does have beach access, possible with a 15-minute walk, but as of spring 2002, the creek had washed out the nearby road to the ocean, so check for status. The surrounding terrain is flat and grassy.

RV sites, facilities: There are 50 sites with partial or full hookups (30 amps), including 20 drive-through, for RVs of any length and 16 tent sites. Picnic tables and fire grills are provided. Restrooms, drinking water, flush toilets, showers, cable TV hookups, a coin-operated laundry, a café, a recreation room with kitchen facilities, limited cell phone reception, and ice are available. Propane is available within one mile. Leashed pets are permitted.

Reservations, fees: Reservations are accepted. The fee is $15–32, plus $4 per additional vehicle per night. Major credit cards are accepted. Open year-round.

Directions: From Hoquiam, drive west on State Route 109 for 21 miles to Copalis Beach and Heath Road. Turn left (west) on Heath Road and drive .2 mile to the campground entrance on the left.

Contact: Surf and Sand RV Park, Copalis Beach, P.O. Box 208, No. 8 McCullough, Copalis Beach, WA 98535, 360/289-2707.

⁷⁶ RIVERSIDE RV RESORT

Rating: 8

near Copalis Beach

See map pages 16–17

River access is a bonus at this nice and clean 10-acre park. Most sites have a river view. Salmon fishing can be good in the Copalis River, and a

boat ramp is available nearby for anglers. Other options include swimming (no lifeguards) and beachcombing.

RV sites, facilities: There are 53 sites with full hookups, including 20 drive-through, for RVs of any length and a large area for tents. Picnic tables and fire grills are provided. Restrooms, drinking water, flush toilets, showers, an RV dump station, a fish-cleaning station, cell phone reception, a hot tub, firewood, and a recreation hall are available. A café is within one mile. A boat dock and launching facilities are nearby. Leashed pets are permitted.

Reservations, fees: Reservations are accepted. The fee is $16 per night for tent sites and $21 per night for RV sites, plus $2 per person per night for more than two people. A senior discount is available. Major credit cards are accepted. Open year-round.

Directions: From Hoquiam, drive west on State Route 109 for 21 miles to Copalis Beach. The park is off the highway on the left.

Contact: Riverside RV Resort, P.O. Box 307, No. 6 Condra Rd., Copalis Beach, WA 98535, 360/289-2111, website: www.riversidervresort.net.

⁷⁷ TIDELANDS RESORT

Rating: 7

near Copalis Beach

See map pages 16–17

This flat, wooded campground covers 47 acres and provides beach access and a great ocean view. It's primarily an RV park, with pleasant, grassy sites. Ten sites are on sand dunes, while the remainder are in a wooded area. In the spring, azaleas and wildflowers abound. Horseshoes and a sports field offer recreation possibilities. Though more remote than at the other area sites, clamming is an option in season. Various festivals are held in the area from spring through fall.

RV sites, facilities: There are 100 sites, 55 with partial or full hookups (20, 30 amps), including some drive-through, for RVs of any length or tents, one three-bedroom trailer, and three two-bedroom cabins. Picnic tables and fire rings are provided. Restrooms, drinking water, flush toilets, coin-operated showers, an RV dump station, firewood, ice, cable TV, cell phone reception, and a playground are available. An ATM is within one mile. A casino, golf course, and horseback riding are available within five miles. Leashed pets are permitted.

Reservations, fees: Reservations are accepted. The fee is $15–21 per night; pets are $5 per night. A senior discount is available. Major credit cards are accepted. Open year-round.

Directions: From Hoquiam, drive west on State Route 109 for about 20 miles to the campground on the left. It is located between Mileposts 20 and 21, about one mile south of Copalis Beach.

Contact: Tidelands Resort, P.O. Box 36, Copalis Beach, WA 98535, 360/289-8963, website: www.tidelandsresort.com.

78 OCEAN MIST RESORT

Rating: 9

on Conners Creek

See map pages 16–17

Always call to determine whether space is available before planning a stay here. This is a membership resort RV campground, and members always come first. If space is available, they will rent sites to the public. Surf fishing is popular in the nearby Pacific Ocean, while the Copalis River offers salmon fishing. It's about a one-block walk to the beach, and a golf course is within five miles.

RV sites, facilities: There are 120 sites, most with full hookups (30, 50 amps), for RVs up to 45 feet, an area for dispersed camping for up to 20 tents, and three RV rentals. Picnic tables are provided. Restrooms, drinking water, flush toilets, showers, cable TV, cell phone reception, modem access, an RV dump station, two community fire pits, a hot tub, and a coin-operated laundry are available. A grocery store is within one mile in Ocean City. Leashed pets are permitted.

Reservations, fees: Reservations are required except in winter; phone 360/289-3656 or fax 360/289-2807. The fee is $20–30 per night; trailers are $60 per night. Major credit cards are accepted. Open year-round.

Directions: From Hoquiam, drive west on State Route 109 for 19 miles to the campground on the left (one mile north of Ocean City).

Contact: Ocean Mist Resort, 2781 Rte. 109, Ocean City, WA 98569, 360/289-3656, fax 360/289-2807, website: www.kmresorts.com.

79 OCEAN CITY STATE PARK

Rating: 9

near Hoquiam

See map pages 16–17

This 170-acre oceanfront camp, an excellent example of coastal wetlands and dune succession, features ocean beach, dunes, and dense thickets of pine surrounding freshwater marshes. The Ocean Shores Interpretive Center is located on the south end of Ocean Shores near the marina (open summer season only). This area is part of the Pacific Flyway, and the migratory route for gray whales and other marine mammals lies just offshore. Spring wildflowers are excellent and include lupine, buttercups, and wild strawberry. This is also a good area for surfing and kite flying, with springs typically windy. Beachcombing, clamming, and fishing are possibilities at this park. An 18-hole golf course is nearby.

RV sites, facilities: There are 149 standard sites for RVs or tents, 29 sites with full hookups (30 amps), including some drive-through, for RVs up to 55 feet, and three primitive tent sites. Picnic tables and fire rings are provided. Restrooms, drinking water, flush toilets, showers, a pay phone, cell phone reception, an RV dump station, a sheltered picnic area, and firewood are available. An ATM is within one mile. Some facilities are wheelchair-accessible. Leashed pets are permitted.

Reservations, fees: Reserve at 888/226-7688 (CAMP-OUT) or online at www.parks.wa.gov /reservations ($7 reservation fee). The fee is $6–22 per night. Major credit cards are accepted in summer only. A senior discount is available. Open year-round.

Directions: From Hoquiam, drive northwest on State Route 109 for 16 miles to State Route 115. Turn left and drive 1.2 miles south to the park on the right (1.5 miles north of Ocean Shores).

Contact: Ocean City State Park, 148 Rte. 115, Hoquiam, WA 98550, 360/289-3553; state park information, 360/902-8844.

WASHINGTON

80 SCHAFER STATE PARK

Rating: 8

on the Satsop River
See map pages 16–17

This unique destination boasts many interesting features, including buildings constructed from native stone. A heavily wooded, rural camp, Schafer State Park covers 119 acres along the East Fork of the Satsop River. The river is well known for fishing and rafting, with 4,200 feet of the river flowing through day-use and camping areas. Fish for sea-run cutthroat in summer, salmon in fall, and steelhead in late winter. There are good canoeing and kayaking spots, some with Class II and III rapids, along the Middle and West Forks of the Satsop. Two miles of hiking trails are also available. At one time, this park was the Schafer Logging Company Park and was used by employees and their families.

RV sites, facilities: There are six sites with partial hookups (30 amps) for RVs up to 40 feet, 42 developed tent sites, two primitive tent sites, and a group campsite. Picnic tables and fire grills are provided. Restrooms, drinking water, flush toilets, showers, two covered picnic shelters, interpretive activities, a pay phone, an RV dump station, a volleyball court, and horseshoes are available. Some facilities are wheelchair-accessible. Leashed pets are permitted.

Reservations, fees: Reservations are not accepted. The fee is $10–21 per night, plus $10 per additional vehicle per night. A senior discount is available. Open May to September.

Directions: From Olympia on I-5, take Exit 104 to U.S. 101. Drive west on U.S. 101 six miles to Highway 8. Turn west on Highway 8 to Elma (Highway 8 becomes Highway 12). Continue west on Highway 12 for seven miles to East Satsop Road (four miles east of Montesano). Turn right (north) and drive five miles to the park. The park is 12 miles north of Elma.

Contact: Schafer State Park, 360/482-3852; state park information, 360/902-8844.

81 LAKE SYLVIA STATE PARK

Rating: 8

on Lake Sylvia
See map pages 16–17

This 234-acre state park on the shore of Lake Sylvia features nearly three miles of freshwater shoreline. The park is located in a former logging camp in a wooded area midway between Olympia and the Pacific Ocean. Expect plenty of rustic charm, with displays of old logging gear, a giant ball carved out of wood from a single log, and some monstrous stumps. The lake is good for fishing and ideal for canoes, prams, or small boats with oars or electric motors; no gas motors are permitted. Five miles of hiking trails and a half-mile wheelchair-accessible trail meander through the park. Additional recreation options include trout fishing and swimming.

RV sites, facilities: There are 35 sites for self-contained RVs up to 30 feet or tents, six primitive tent sites, and one group site for up to 10 people. Picnic tables are provided. Drinking water and flush toilets are available. Fee showers, an RV dump station, cell phone reception, firewood, a picnic area, and a playground are available. Laundry facilities, a store, a pay phone, and ice are available within one mile. Some facilities are wheelchair-accessible. Leashed pets are permitted.

Reservations, fees: Reservations are not accepted for family sites. The fee is $10–16 per night, plus $10 per additional vehicle per night; the group site requires a $25 reservation fee plus $2 per person, with a 20-person minimum. A senior discount is available. Open late March to early October.

Directions: From Olympia on I-5, take Exit 104 to U.S. 101. Drive west on U.S. 101 six miles where it becomes Highway 8/12. Turn west on Highway 8/12 and drive 26 miles to Montesano and the first exit. Drive to Pioneer (the only stoplight in town). Turn left on Pioneer and drive three blocks to Third Street. Turn right and drive two miles to the park entrance (route is well signed).

Contact: Lake Sylvia State Park, Montesano, WA 98563, 360/249-3621; state park information, 360/902-8844.

82 TRAVEL INN RESORT

Rating: 7

on Lake Sylvia
See map pages 16–17

This is a membership campground, which means sites for RV travelers are available only if there is extra space. It can be difficult to get a spot from May to September, but the park opens up significantly in the off-season. There are five major rivers or lakes within 15 minutes of this camp (Satsop, Chehalis, Wynoochee, Black River, and Lake Sylvia). Nearby Lake Sylvia State Park provides multiple marked hiking trails. Additional recreation options include trout fishing, swimming, and golf (three miles away).

RV sites, facilities: There are 144 sites with partial or full hookups (30, 50 amps) for RVs of any length and 10 tent sites. Picnic tables are provided. Restrooms, drinking water, flush toilets, showers, a pay phone, cell phone reception, a coin-operated laundry, two community fire pits, a gazebo, a heated swimming pool (seasonal), a game room, cable TV, modem access, and a social hall are available. A grocery store, restaurant, and ATM are within one mile. Some facilities are wheelchair-accessible. Leashed pets are permitted.

Reservations, fees: Reservations are required May to September; call 866/460-3869 (Washington and Oregon residents only) or 360/482-3877. The fee is $30 per night (for nonmembers), plus $1 each for electricity or cable TV hookups. Open year-round.

Directions: From Olympia on I-5, take Exit 104 to U.S. 101. Drive west on U.S. 101 six miles to Highway 8. Turn west on Highway 8 and drive to Elma. Take the first Elma exit and at the stop sign at Highway 12, turn right. Drive about 200 yards to the end of the highway and a stop sign. Turn right and drive another 200 yards to the resort on the right.

Contact: Travel Inn Resort, 801 East Main St., Elma, WA 98541, 360/482-3877, website: www.kmresorts.com.

83 JOLLY ROGERS RV PARK

Rating: 7

near Westport Harbor
See map pages 16–17

A beachside RV park with gravel or grassy sites and nearby beach access, this camp covers one acre on Westport Harbor. It's a prime spot for watching ocean sunsets, and on a clear day, the snow-capped Cascades are visible. Westport Lighthouse and Westhaven State Parks are nearby and offer day-use facilities along the ocean.

RV sites, facilities: There are 25 sites with full hookups (20, 30 amps) for RVs of any length or tents. Restrooms, drinking water, flush toilets, showers, cable TV, cell phone reception, boat docks, and mooring are available. Propane, a store, a café, an ATM, a pay phone, and a laundry are available within one mile. Leashed pets are permitted.

Reservations, fees: Reservations are accepted. The fee is $18–20 per night. Open year-round.

Directions: From Aberdeen, drive south on State Route 105 for 22 miles southwest to Westport and Neddie Rose Drive. Turn right (north) and drive a short distance to the park on the right (Westport Docks).

Contact: Jolly Rogers RV Park, P.O. Box 342, Westport, WA 98595, tel./fax 360/268-0265.

84 GRIZZLY JOE'S RV PARK AND MARINA

Rating: 9

on Point Chehalis
See map pages 16–17

Grizzly Joe's is a landscaped, one-acre park with ocean views on three sides. Sites are graveled and level. Snow-capped Mount Rainier is visible, and the sunsets are spectacular. Westport Lighthouse and Westhaven State Parks are nearby with multiple recreational options.

RV sites, facilities: There are 35 sites with full hookups (30 amps) and drive-through for RVs of any length. Electricity, drinking water, sewer, and cable TV are provided. An RV dump station, flush toilets, showers, a patio/picnic area with fire pit, a fish-cleaning station, outdoor cooking facilities, a pay phone, cell phone reception, modem access, boat docks, and boat mooring are available. Propane, a store, a café, an ATM, laundry facilities, firewood, and ice are available within .25 mile. Leashed pets are permitted.

Reservations, fees: Reservations are recommended. The fee is $22 per night. Open year-round.

Directions: From Aberdeen, drive south on State Route 105 for 22 miles southwest to Westport and Neddie Rose Drive. Turn right and drive four blocks to the park at the end of the road.

Contact: Grizzly Joe's RV Park and Marina, P.O. Box 1755, 743 Neddie Rose Dr., Westport, WA 98595, 360/268-5555, fax 360/268-1212.

85 AMERICAN SUNSET RV RESORT

Rating: 8

near Westport Harbor
See map pages 16–17

If location is everything, then this RV camp, set on a peninsula near the ocean, is a big winner. It covers 32 acres and has its own hiking and biking trails. The park is divided into two areas: one for campers, another for long-term rentals. Nearby are Westhaven and Westport Lighthouse State Parks, popular with hikers, rock hounds, scuba divers, surfers, and surf anglers. Swimming (but not off the docks), fishing, and crabbing off the docks are also options. Monthly rentals are available.

RV sites, facilities: There are 120 sites with full hookups (20, 30, 50 amps), including some drive-through, for RVs up to 50 feet, 50 tent sites, and one trailer. Picnic tables and fire rings are provided. Restrooms, drinking water, flush toilets, showers, modem hookups (in office), a coin-operated laundry, a grocery store, propane, a seasonal heated pool, horseshoes, a playground, a fish-cleaning station, a pay phone, cell phone reception, and a 2,400-square-foot recreation hall are available. Hookups for phone and cable TV are available for extended stays only. A marina, an ATM, and a boat launch are within three blocks. Leashed pets are permitted.

Reservations, fees: Reservations are recommended during the summer; phone 800/JOY-CAMP (800/569-2267). The fee is $13–22.50 per night, plus $5 per additional vehicle per night and $2

per person for more than two people. A senior discount is available. Major credit cards are accepted. Open year-round.

Directions: From Aberdeen, drive south on State Route 105 for 22 miles southwest to Westport and Montesano Street (the first exit in Westport). Turn right (northeast) on Montesano and drive three miles to the resort on the left.

Contact: American Sunset RV Resort, 1209 N. Montesano St., Westport, WA 98595, 360/268-0207 or 800/569-2267, website: www.american sunsetrv.com.

86 COHO RV PARK, MOTEL & CHARTER

Rating: 4

near Westport Harbor
See map pages 16–17

Fishermen stake out this RV park as their base camp. Fishing is good nearby for salmon and rockfish. One of several parks in the immediate area, Coho covers two acres and has its own fishing and whale-watching charters. Nearby Westhaven and Westport Lighthouse State Parks are popular with rock hounds, scuba divers, and surf anglers. A full-service marina is within easy walking distance.

RV sites, facilities: There are 76 sites, including six drive-through, with full hookups (30, 50 amps) for RVs of any length. No tents are permitted. No open campfires are allowed. Restrooms, drinking water, flush toilets, coin-operated showers, cable TV, a pay phone, cell phone reception, a coin-operated laundry, a meeting hall, ice, and fishing charters are available. Boat docks, launching facilities, and an ATM are nearby. Propane, a store, and a café are within one mile. Leashed pets are permitted.

Reservations, fees: Reservations are accepted. The fee is $22–24 per night, plus $2 per person per night for more than two people. Major credit cards are accepted. Monthly rentals are available. Open year-round.

Directions: From Aberdeen, drive south on State Route 105 for 22 miles southwest to Westport and Montesano Street (the first exit in Westport). Turn right (northeast) and drive 3.5 miles to Nyhus Street. Turn left (northwest) and drive 2.5 blocks to the campground on the left.

Contact: Coho RV Park, Motel & Charter, 2501 North Nyhus St., Westport, WA 98595, 360/268-0111 or 800/572-0177, fax 360/268-9425, website: www.westportwa.com/coho.

87 TOTEM RV PARK

Rating: 8

in Westport
See map pages 16–17

This 3.2-acre park, remodeled in 2000, is 300 yards from the ocean and features an expanse of sand dunes between the park and the ocean. It has large, grassy sites close to Westhaven State Park, which offers day-use facilities. The owner is a fishing guide and can provide detailed fishing information. The salmon fishing within 10 miles of this park is often excellent in summer. Marked biking trails and a full-service marina are within five miles of the campground. A golf course may be opened just one block away in 2004 or 2005.

RV sites, facilities: There are 76 sites, most drive-through with partial or full hookups, for RVs of any length or tents. Picnic tables are provided. Restrooms, drinking water, flush toilets, coin-operated showers, an RV dump station, a pay phone, cell phone reception, modem access, an ATM, a coin-operated laundry, and ice are available. A pavilion, barbecue facilities with kitchen, and a fish-cleaning station are also available. Propane and a café are located next door. A store is within a half mile. Boat docks, launching facilities, and fishing charters are nearby. Leashed pets are permitted.

Reservations, fees: Reservations are accepted. The fee is $16.50–18.50 per night. Major credit cards are accepted. Open year-round.

Directions: From Aberdeen, drive southwest on State Route 105 for 20 miles to the turnoff for Westport. Turn right (north) on the State Route 105 spur and drive 4.2 miles to the docks and Nyhus Street. Turn left on Nyhus Street and drive two blocks to the park on the left.

Contact: Totem RV Park, P.O. Box 1166, 2421 North Nyhus St., Westport, WA 98595, 360/268-0025 or 888/TOTEM-RV (888/868-3678).

88 HOLAND CENTER

Rating: 6

in Westport
See map pages 16–17

This pleasant, 18-acre RV park is one of several in the immediate area. The sites are graveled or grassy with pine trees between and have ample space. There is no beach access from the park, but full recreational facilities are available nearby. About half of the sites are long-term rentals.

RV sites, facilities: There are 80 sites with full hookups (30 amps) for RVs up to 40 feet. No tents are allowed. Picnic tables are provided. Restrooms, drinking water, flush toilets, coin-operated showers, a coin-operated laundry, and storage sheds are available. Propane, a store, a café, a pay phone, an ATM, and ice are available within one mile. Boat docks and launching facilities are nearby. Leashed pets are permitted.

Reservations, fees: Reservations are accepted. The fee is $20 per night. Open year-round.

Directions: From Aberdeen, drive south on State Route 105 for 22 miles to Westport. Continue on State Route 105 to Wilson Street. The park is at the corner of State Route 105 and Wilson Street.

Contact: Holand Center, 201 Wilson St., Westport, WA 98595, 360/268-9582, fax 360/532-3818.

89 PACIFIC MOTEL AND RV PARK

Rating: 5

near Twin Harbors
See map pages 16–17

This five-acre park has grassy, shaded sites in a wooded setting. It's near Twin Harbors and Westport Lighthouse State Parks, both of which have beach access. A full-service marina is within two miles. About 25 percent of the sites are occupied with long-term rentals.

RV sites, facilities: There are 80 sites with full hookups (20, 30 amps), including some drive-through, for RVs of any length and 15 tent sites. Picnic tables and fire rings are provided. Restrooms, drinking water, flush toilets, coin-operated showers, an RV dump station, propane, a fish-cleaning station, a recreation hall with a kitchen, cable TV, cell phone reception, modem access, a pay phone and fax, coin-operated laundry facilities, and a heated swimming pool (seasonal) are available. A store, a café, and ice are available within one mile. Boat-launching facilities and boat docks are nearby in a full-service marina. Leashed pets are permitted.

Reservations, fees: Reservations are accepted. The fee is $15–20 per night, plus $2 per person per night for more than two people. Major credit cards are accepted. Open year-round.

Directions: From Aberdeen, drive south on State Route 105 for approximately 18 miles to the State Route 105 spur road to Westport. Turn right (north) and drive 1.7 miles to the park on the right.

Contact: Pacific Motel and RV Park, 330 South Forrest St., Westport, WA 98595, 360/268-9325, fax 360/268-6227, website: www.pacificmotel andrv.com.

90 ISLANDER RV PARK & MOTEL

Rating: 8

on Grays Harbor
See map pages 16–17

This .75-acre park is located on Grays Harbor, close to Westport Light and Westhaven State Parks, which offer oceanfront day-use facilities. On-site amenities include a hair salon, a gift shop, a restaurant, a motel, dancing, fishing charters, access to crabbing (in season), and whale-watching trips. This park is big with the surfing crowd, with good surf breaks located just across the street.

RV sites, facilities: There are 57 sites with full hookups, including 30 drive-through, for RVs up to 40 feet. No tent camping or open campfires are permitted. Restrooms, drinking water, flush toilets, showers, a coffee shop, a gift shop, an ATM, a pay phone, cell phone reception, fishing licenses, a restaurant, a coin-operated laundry, ice, a heated swimming pool (in season), boat docks, and fishing charters are available. Propane, an RV dump station, and a store are available within one mile. Leashed pets are permitted.

Reservations, fees: Reservations are accepted. The fee is $20–25 per night. Major credit cards are accepted. Open year-round.

Directions: From Aberdeen, drive south on State Route 105 for 22 miles to Westport and Montesano Street. Turn right and drive two miles (Montesano becomes Dock Street) to the docks and Westhaven Drive. Turn left and drive four blocks to Neddie Rose Avenue. Turn right and drive one block to the park on the right.

Contact: Islander RV Park & Motel, 421 East Neddie Rose, Westport, WA 98595, 360/268-9166 or 800/322-1740, fax 360/268-0902, website: www.westportislander.com.

91 TWIN HARBORS STATE PARK

Rating: 8

on the Pacific Ocean
See map pages 16–17

This park, the site of a military training ground in the 1930s, covers 172 acres and is located four miles south of Westhaven. The campsites are close together and often crammed to capacity in the summer. Highlights include beach access and marked hiking trails, including the Shifting Sands Nature Trail. The most popular recreation activities are surf fishing, surfing, beachcombing, and kite flying. Fishing boats can be chartered nearby in Westport.

RV sites, facilities: There are 307 sites, including 49 with full hookups, for RVs up to 35 feet or tents, five primitive tent sites, and one group site for up to 75 people. Picnic tables and fire grills are provided. Restrooms, drinking water, flush toilets, pay phones, cell phone reception, coin-operated showers, an RV dump station, interpretive activities, a picnic area with a kitchen shelter and electricity, and horseshoes are available. A store, an ATM, a café, and ice are available within one mile. Some facilities are wheelchair-accessible. Leashed pets are permitted.

Reservations, fees: Reserve at 888/CAMP-OUT (888/226-7688) or online at www.parks.wa.gov /reservations ($7 reservation fee). The fee is $10–22 per night, plus $10 per additional vehicle per night. A senior discount is available. The group site requires a $25 reservation fee and $2 per person with a 20-person minimum. Major credit cards are accepted in peak season only. Open year-round.

Directions: From Aberdeen, drive south on State

Route 105 for 17 miles to the park entrance on the left (three miles south of Westport).
Contact: Twin Harbors State Park, Twin Harbors State Park, Westport, WA 98595, 360/268-9717; state park information, 360/902-8844.

92 OCEAN GATE RESORT

Rating: 5

in Grayland
See map pages 16–17
This privately run, seven-acre park has beach access and offers an alternative to the publicly run Grayland Beach State Park. Fishing, beach biking, and beachcombing are highlights.
RV sites, facilities: There are 24 sites with full hookups (30 amps), including 12 drive-through, for RVs of any length, 20 tent sites, and six cabins. Picnic tables and fire rings are provided. Restrooms, drinking water, flush toilets, showers, cell phone reception, a covered picnic shelter with a barbecue, and a playground are available. Propane, a store, a café, an ATM, a pay phone, a laundry, and ice are available within one mile. Leashed pets are permitted.
Reservations, fees: Reservations are accepted. The fee is $15–22 per night, plus $5 per additional vehicle per night. There is an $8 per night pet fee for the cabins. Open year-round.
Directions: From Aberdeen, drive south on State Route 105 for 21 miles to a roundabout. Take State Route 105 left toward Grayland. The park is in Grayland on the right between Mileposts 26 and 27.
Contact: Ocean Gate Resort, P.O. Box 67, 1939 Rte. 105 S, Grayland, WA 98547, 360/267-1956 or 800/473-1956, website: www.oceangateresort.net.

93 WESTERN SHORES MOTEL AND RV PARK

Rating: 4

in Grayland
See map pages 16–17
This small, private park is designed for families. Beach access and golf are not far, and Twin Harbors and Grayland Beach State Parks are just a few minutes away. This is an excellent layover for tourists who want to get off U.S. 101. About one-third of the RV sites are filled with permanent rentals.
RV sites, facilities: There are 30 drive-through sites with full hookups (20, 30 amps) for RVs of any length. Picnic tables are provided. Restrooms, drinking water, flush toilets, showers, a community fire pit, cable TV, ice, propane, firewood, cell phone reception, snacks, and a playground are available. A store, ATM, restaurant, and a lounge are next door. A pay phone is nearby. Leashed pets are permitted.
Reservations, fees: Reservations are recommended. The fee is $15.50 per night. Major credit cards are accepted. Open year-round.
Directions: From Aberdeen, drive south on State Route 105 to Westport. Continue south on State Route 105 to Grayland. The RV park is located in town, right along State Route 105 on the right.
Contact: Western Shores Motel and RV Park, 2193 State Route 105, Grayland, WA 98547, 360/267-1611.

94 GRAYLAND BEACH STATE PARK

Rating: 8

on the Pacific Ocean
See map pages 16–17
This state park features 7,500 feet of beach frontage. All the campsites are within easy walking distance of the ocean, with the bonus of a quarter-mile self-guided interpretive trail that provides a route from the campground to the beach. The campsites are relatively spacious for a state park, but they are not especially private. This park is popular with out-of-towners, especially during summer. Recreation options include fishing, beachcombing, and kite flying. The best spot for surfing is five miles north at Westhaven State Park.
RV sites, facilities: There are 60 sites with full hookups for RVs (30 amps) up to 40 feet and three primitive tent sites. Picnic tables and fire grills are provided. Drinking water and vault toilets are available. Restrooms, drinking water, flush toilets, a pay phone, cell phone reception, and coin-operated showers are available. An ATM is within one mile. Some facilities are wheelchair-accessible. Leashed pets are permitted.

Reservations, fees: Reserve at 888/CAMP-OUT (888/226-7688) or online at www.parks.wa.gov /reservations ($7 reservation fee). The fee is $10–22 per night, plus $10 per additional vehicle per night. A senior discount is available. Major credit cards are accepted. Open year-round.

Directions: From Aberdeen, drive south on State Route 105 for 22 miles to the park entrance. The park is just south of the town of Grayland on the right (west).

Contact: Grayland Beach State Park, 360/268-9717; state park information, 360/902-8844.

95 BAY CENTER/WILLAPA BAY KOA

Rating: 7

on Willapa Bay
See map pages 16–17

This KOA is set on the shore of Willapa Bay, within walking distance of a beach that seems to stretch to infinity. A trail leads to the beach, and from here you can walk for miles in either direction. The beach sand is mixed with agates, driftwood, and seaweed. Dungeness crabs, clams, and oysters all live within the nearshore vicinity. Another bonus is that herds of Roosevelt elk roam the nearby woods. Believe it or not, there are also black bear, although they are seldom seen here. The park covers 11 acres, and the campsites are graveled and shaded.

RV sites, facilities: There are 11 sites with full hookups and 28 sites with partial hookups (20, 30, amps), including some drive-through, for RVs of any length, 25 tent sites, and two cabins. Picnic tables are provided. Restrooms, drinking water, flush toilets, showers, propane, an RV dump station, cable TV, modem hookups, cell phone reception, two courtesy phones, a recreation hall, a store, firewood, a coin-operated laundry, and ice are available. There is a café nearby. A marina is located a half mile away; boat docks and launching facilities are about three miles from camp on Willapa Bay. Leashed pets are permitted.

Reservations, fees: Reservations accepted at 800/562-7810. The fee is $21–32 per night, plus $4 per adult per night for more than two people. Major credit cards are accepted. Open mid-March to late October.

Directions: From Nemah on U.S. 101, drive north for five miles to Bay Center/Dike exit (located between Mileposts 42 and 43, 16 miles south of Raymond). Turn west and drive three miles to the campground.

Contact: Bay Center/Willapa Bay KOA, 457 Bay Center Rd., Bay Center, WA 98527, 360/875-6344, website: www.koa.com.

96 RAINBOW FALLS STATE PARK

Rating: 8

on the Chehalis River Bay
See map pages 16–17

This 139-acre park is set on the Chehalis River and boasts 3,400 feet of shoreline. The camp features stands of old-growth cedar and fir and is named after a few small cascades with drops of about 10 feet. The park has 10 miles of hiking trails, including an interpretive trail, seven miles of bike trails, and seven miles of horse trails. A pool at the base of Rainbow Falls is excellent for swimming. Another attraction, a small fuchsia garden, has more than 40 varieties. There are also several log structures built by the Civilian Conservation Corps in 1935.

RV sites, facilities: There are 47 sites for self-contained RVs up to 32 feet or tents, three primitive tent sites, three equestrian sites with hitching points and stock water, and one group site. Picnic tables and fire rings are provided. Restrooms, drinking water, flush toilets, coin-operated showers, an RV dump station, a picnic area, a pay phone, firewood, interpretive activities, a playground with horseshoes, and a softball field are available. Leashed pets are permitted.

Reservations, fees: Reservations are not accepted. The fee is $10–16 per night, plus $10 per additional vehicle per night. A senior discount is available. Open year-round.

Directions: From Chehalis on I-5, take Exit 77 to Highway 6. Turn west and drive 16 miles to the park entrance on the right.

Contact: Rainbow Falls State Park, 4008 Hwy. 6, Chehalis, WA 98532, 360/291-3767; state park information, 360/902-8844.

97 OCEAN PARK RESORT

Rating: 5

on Willapa Bay

See map pages 16–17

This wooded, 10-acre campground is located a half mile from Willapa Bay. With grassy, shaded sites, it caters primarily to RVs. Fishing, crabbing, and clamming are popular in season. Ocean Park has several festivals during the summer season. During these festivals, this resort fills up. To the north, Leadbetter Point State Park provides a side-trip option.

RV sites, facilities: There are 70 sites with full hookups (20, 30 amps), including some drive-through, for RVs of any length, seven tent sites, and two cottages (park model trailers). Picnic tables are provided. Fire pits are provided at tent sites. Restrooms, drinking water, flush toilets, coin-operated showers, propane, a recreation hall, a coin-operated laundry, a pay phone, cell phone reception, ice, a playground, firewood, a hot tub, and a heated swimming pool (in season) are available. A store, a café, and an ATM are within one mile. Boat docks and launching facilities are located nearby on Willapa Bay. Leashed pets are permitted, but no Rottweilers, pit bulls, or Doberman pinschers permitted.

Reservations, fees: Reservations are accepted. The fees are $23–25 per night, plus $3 per person per night for more than two people; cottages are $70–110 per night. Major credit cards are accepted. A senior discount is available. Open year-round.

Directions: From Kelso/Longview on I-5, turn west on Highway 4 and drive 63 miles to U.S. 101. Turn south on U.S. 101 and drive 13 miles to the junction with Highway 103. Turn right (north) on Highway 103 and drive 11 miles to the town of Ocean Park and 259th Street. Turn right (east) on 259th Street and drive two blocks to the resort at the end of the road.

Contact: Ocean Park Resort, P.O. Box 339, 25904 R St., Ocean Park, WA 98640, 360/665-4585 or 800/835-4634, website: www.opresort.com.

98 WESTGATE MOTEL AND TRAILER COURT

Rating: 9

near Long Beach

See map pages 16–17

Highlights at this pretty and clean four-acre camp include beach access, oceanfront sites, and all the amenities. There are 28 miles of beach that can be driven on. A nine-hole golf course is within 10 miles.

RV sites, facilities: There are 39 sites with full hookups (30 amps), including 15 drive-through, for RVs of any length and six cabins. Restrooms, drinking water, flush toilets, showers, cable TV, limited cell phone reception, a recreation hall, and ice are available. A store, a café, an ATM, a pay phone, and a coin-operated laundry are within four miles. Boat docks and launching facilities are located nearby on Willapa Bay. Leashed pets are permitted.

Reservations, fees: Reservations are accepted. The fees are $23–24 per night, plus $1 per person per night for more than two people; cabins are $55–65 per night. Major credit cards are accepted. Open year-round.

Directions: From Kelso/Longview on I-5, turn west on Highway 4 and drive 63 miles to U.S. 101. Turn south on U.S. 101 and drive 13 miles to the junction with Highway 103. Turn north on Highway 103 and drive 7.5 miles to the campground on the left (located at the south edge of the town of Ocean Park).

Contact: Westgate Motel and Trailer Court, 20803 Pacific Hwy., Ocean Park, WA 98640, 360/665-4211.

99 OCEAN AIRE RV PARK

Rating: 4

near Willapa Bay

See map pages 16–17

This camp is located in town, a half mile from the shore of Willapa Bay. Tennis courts are a quarter mile away, and a golf course is three miles away. Leadbetter Point State Park, about eight miles north, is open for day use and provides footpaths for walking through the state-designated natural area and wildlife refuge. Two-thirds of the sites are long-term rentals, making reservations essential for the remaining sites during the summer.

RV sites, facilities: There are 46 sites with full hookups (20 amps), including eight drive-through, for RVs of any length. No tents are allowed. Restrooms, drinking water, flush toilets, showers, picnic tables, cell phone reception, an RV dump station, and a coin-operated laundry are available. A store, ice, pay phone, and a café are available next door. Boat rentals are nearby on Willapa Bay. An ATM is within two blocks. Leashed pets are permitted.

Reservations, fees: Reservations are accepted. The fee is $16 per night, plus $3 per person per night for more than two people. Open year-round.

Directions: From Kelso/Longview on I-5, turn west on Highway 4 and drive 63 miles to U.S. 101. Turn south on U.S. 101 and drive 13 miles to the junction with Highway 103. Turn north on Highway 103 and drive 11 miles to the town of Ocean Park and 259th Street. Turn right on 259th Street and drive two blocks to the camp.

Contact: Ocean Aire RV Park, 25918 R St., Ocean Park, WA 98640, 360/665-4027, website: www.opchamber.com.

100 MA AND PA'S PACIFIC RV PARK

Rating: 7

near Long Beach
See map pages 16–17

I wanted to give them some kind of award for the name of this place, but I haven't figured out what to give them yet. This park covers six acres and features both beach access and spacious, grassy sites near the shore. Additional facilities within five miles of the campground include a nine-hole golf course, marked bike trails, and a riding stable.

RV sites, facilities: There are 53 sites with partial or full hookups (20, 30 amps) for RVs of any length and an area for dispersed tent camping. Restrooms, drinking water, flush toilets, coin-operated showers, picnic tables, a pay phone, cell phone reception, a coin-operated laundry, a recreation room, and ice are available. Propane, a store, and a café are within one mile, and an

ATM is within two miles. Leashed pets are permitted.

Reservations, fees: Reservations are recommended. The fee is $22–25 per night, plus $2 per person per night for more than two people, $5 per additional vehicle per night, and $2 per pet per night. Major credit cards are accepted. Open year-round.

Directions: From Kelso/Longview on I-5, turn west on Highway 4 and drive 63 miles to U.S. 101. Turn south on U.S. 101 and drive 13 miles to the junction with Highway 103. Turn north on Highway 103 and drive four miles to the park on the left.

Contact: Ma and Pa's Pacific RV Park, 10515 Pacific Hwy., Long Beach, WA 98631, 360/642-3253, fax 360/642-5039, website: www.maandpasrvpark.com.

101 ANDERSEN'S RV PARK ON THE OCEAN

Rating: 7

near Long Beach
See map pages 16–17

Timing is everything here. When the dates are announced for the local festivals, reservations start pouring in, and the sites at this park can be booked a year in advance. Fully remodeled in 2003, there have been extensive upgrades throughout this park. Located near Long Beach, this seven-acre camp features a path through the dunes that will get you to the beach in a flash. It is set in a flat, sandy area with gravel sites and grassy landscaping. Recreation options include beach bonfires, beachcombing, surf fishing, and clamming (seasonal). Additional facilities found within five miles of the campground include marked dune trails, a nine-hole golf course, a riding stable, and tennis courts.

RV sites, facilities: There are 60 sites with full hookups (20, 30, 50 amps) for RVs of any length. Picnic tables are provided. Restrooms, drinking water, flush toilets, showers, a meeting hall, cable TV, modem hookups, an RV dump station, a coin-operated laundry, ice, propane, a pay phone, cell phone reception, a fax machine, a children's playground, and a doggie playground are available. A store and a café are within two miles, and an ATM is within 3.5 miles. Leashed pets are permitted.

Reservations, fees: Reservations are accepted. The fee is $30–34 per night, plus $2 per person per night for more than two people. Major credit cards are accepted. Open year-round.

Directions: From Kelso/Longview on I-5, turn west on Highway 4 and drive 63 miles to U.S. 101. Turn south on U.S. 101 and drive 13 miles to the junction with Highway 103. Turn north on Highway 103 and drive five miles to the park on the left.

Contact: Andersen's RV Park on the Ocean, 1400 138th St., Long Beach, WA 98631, 360/642-2231 or 800/645-6795, website: www.andersensrv.com.

102 OCEANIC RV PARK

Rating: 3

in Long Beach
See map pages 16–17

This two-acre park is located in the heart of downtown, within walking distance of restaurants and stores. It is also within five miles of a nine-hole golf course, marked bike trails, and a full-service marina. An 18-hole golf course is within 10 miles.

RV sites, facilities: There are 20 drive-through sites with full hookups (20 amps) for RVs of any length. No tents are allowed. Restrooms, drinking water, flush toilets, cell phone reception, and showers are available. Propane, an RV dump station, a store, an ATM, a pay phone, a café, a coin-operated laundry, and ice are available within one mile. Boat docks, launching facilities, and boat rentals are nearby. Leashed pets are permitted.

Reservations, fees: Reservations are accepted. The fee is $14–21 per night, plus $2 per person per night for more than two people. Open year-round.

Directions: From Kelso/Longview on I-5, turn west on Highway 4 and drive 63 miles to U.S. 101. Turn south on U.S. 101 and drive 13 miles to the junction with Highway 103. Turn north on Highway 103 and drive two miles to Long Beach. Continue to the campground at the south junction of Pacific Highway (Highway 103) and Fifth Avenue on the right.

Contact: Oceanic RV Park, P.O. Box 242, 504

South Pacific Ave., Long Beach, WA 98631, 360/642-3836.

103 MERMAID INN AND SAND-LO RV PARK

Rating: 3

near Long Beach
See map pages 16–17

Situated along the highway, this tiny, three-acre park is within four blocks of the beach. It is also within five miles of an 18-hole golf course, a full-service marina, and a riding stable.

RV sites, facilities: There are 15 sites with full hookups (30 amps) for RVs of any length or tents. Restrooms, drinking water, flush toilets, showers, cable TV, modem access, limited cell phone reception, an RV dump station, and a coin-operated laundry are available. A restaurant and a pay phone are located next door. Propane, a store, an ATM, a café, and ice are available within one mile. Leashed pets are permitted in RV park only.

Reservations, fees: Reservations are accepted. The fee is $15–20, plus $1 per person per night for more than two people. Major credit cards are accepted. Open year-round.

Directions: From Kelso/Longview on I-5, turn west on Highway 4 and drive 63 miles to U.S. 101. Turn south on U.S. 101 and drive 13 miles to the junction with Highway 103. Turn north on Highway 103 and drive three miles to the park on the right.

Contact: Mermaid Inn and Sand-Lo RV Park, 1910 North Pacific Hwy., Long Beach, WA 98631, 360/642-2600, fax 360/642-3040.

104 DRIFTWOOD RV PARK

Rating: 5

near Long Beach
See map pages 16–17

New owners are hard at work improving everything imaginable here. This two-acre park features grassy, shaded sites and beach access. A fenced pet area is a bonus. Additional facilities within five miles of the campground include an 18-hole golf course and a full-service marina.

RV sites, facilities: There are 56 sites with full hookups (30 amps), including some drive-through, for RVs of any length. No tents are allowed. Heated restrooms, drinking water, flush toilets, showers, picnic tables, a coin-operated laundry, a meeting hall, cable TV, a courtesy phone, limited cell phone reception, modem access, and a fenced pet area are available. Propane, a store, an ATM, and a café are available within one block. A convenience store and restaurants are within five blocks. Leashed pets are permitted.

Reservations, fees: Reservations are recommended. The fee is $25 per night, plus $3 per person per night for more than two people. Major credit cards are accepted. Open year-round.

Directions: From Kelso/Longview on I-5, turn west on Highway 4 and drive 63 miles to U.S. 101. Turn south on U.S. 101 and drive 13 miles to the junction with Highway 103. Turn north on Highway 103 and drive 2.4 miles to the park on the right, at 14th North and Pacific.

Contact: Driftwood RV Park, P.O. Box 296, 1512 North Pacific Ave., Long Beach, WA 98631, 360/642-2711 or 888/567-1902, website: www .driftwood-rvpark.com.

105 SAND CASTLE RV PARK

Rating: 3

in Long Beach
See map pages 16–17

This park is across the highway from the ocean. Although not particularly scenic, it is clean and does provide nearby beach access. The park covers one acre and is one of several in the immediate area. Additional facilities found within five miles of the campground include a nine-hole golf course, marked bike trails, a full-service marina, and two riding stables. Note that 15 percent of the sites are permanent rentals.

RV sites, facilities: There are 38 sites with full hookups (30 amps), including some drive-through, for RVs of any length. Tents are permitted only with RVs. Restrooms, drinking water, flush toilets, coin-operated showers, cable TV hookups, modem access, cell phone reception, picnic tables, an RV dump station, a coin-operated laundry, and a pay phone are available. Propane, a store, an ATM, ice, and a café are available

within one mile. Boat docks, launching facilities, and rentals are within five miles. Leashed pets are permitted.

Reservations, fees: Reservations are accepted. The fee is $22–30, plus $1 per person per night for more than two people. A senior discount is available in the off-season. Major credit cards are accepted. Open year-round.

Directions: From Kelso/Longview on I-5, turn west on Highway 4 and drive 63 miles to U.S. 101. Turn south on U.S. 101 and drive 13 miles to the junction with Highway 103. Turn north on Highway 103 and drive two miles to the park on the right.

Contact: Sand Castle RV Park, 1100 North Pacific Hwy., Long Beach, WA 98631, 360/642-2174.

106 THE HISTORIC SOU'WESTER LODGE, CABINS, AND RV PARK

Rating: 7

in Seaview on the Long Beach Peninsula
See map pages 16–17

This one-of-a-kind place features a lodge that dates back to 1892, vintage trailers available for rent, and cottages. Various cultural events are held at the park throughout the year, including fireside evenings with theater and chamber music. The park covers three acres, provides beach access, and is one of the few sites in the immediate area that provides spots for tent camping. This park often attracts creative people such as musicians and artists, and some arrive for vacations in organized groups. It is definitely not for Howie and Ethel from Iowa. Fishing is a recreation option. The area features the Lewis and Clark Interpretive Center, a lighthouse, museums, fine dining, bicycle and boat rentals, bicycle and hiking trails, and bird sanctuaries. Additional facilities found within five miles of the campground include a nine-hole golf course, a full-service marina, and a riding stable. The lodge was originally built for U.S. Senator Henry Winslow Corbett.

RV sites, facilities: There are 60 sites with full hookups (20, 30 amps), some drive-through, for RVs of any length, 10 tent sites, a historic lodge, four cottages, and 12 1950s-style trailers in vintage condition. Restrooms, drinking water, flush toilets, showers, cable TV, modem access, a pay phone, cell phone reception, a coin-operated laundry, a classic-video library, a picnic area with pavilion, and community fire pits and grills are available. Propane, an RV dump station, a store, an ATM, a café, and ice are available within one mile. Boat-launching facilities are nearby. Leashed pets are permitted.

Reservations, fees: Reservations are accepted. The fee is $23–33, plus $2–3 per person per night for more than two people. Off-season discounts are available. Major credit cards are accepted. Open year-round.

Directions: From Kelso/Longview on I-5, turn west on Highway 4 and drive approximately 63 miles to U.S. 101. Turn south on U.S. 101 and drive 13 miles to the junction with Highway 103 (flashing light). Turn left to stay on U.S. 101 and drive one block to Seaview Beach Access Road (38th Place). Turn right and drive toward the ocean. Look for the campground on the left.

Contact: Sou'Wester Lodge, Cabins, and RV Park, P.O. Box 102, Seaview, WA 98644, 360/642-2542 (phone or fax), website: www.souwesterlodge.com.

107 FISHERMAN'S COVE RV PARK

Rating: 7

near Fort Canby State Park
See map pages 16–17

This five-acre park is located by the docks, near where the Pacific Ocean and the Columbia River meet. It has beach and fishing access nearby and caters to fishermen. Fish- and clam-cleaning facilities are available in the park. A maritime museum, hiking trails, a full-service marina, and a riding stable are within five miles of the park. About 15 percent of the sites are taken by full-time renters.

RV sites, facilities: There are 51 sites with full hookups (30, 50 amps), including some drive-through, for RVs of any length and some tent sites. Restrooms, drinking water, flush toilets, coin-operated showers, cable TV hookups, cell phone reception, an RV dump station, and a coin-operated laundry are available. Propane, a store, a pay phone, an ATM, and a café are available within one mile. Boat docks, launching facilities, and rentals are nearby. Leashed pets are permitted.

Reservations, fees: Reservations are accepted.

The fee is $10 for tents and $20 for RVs per night. Open year-round.

Directions: From Kelso/Longview on I-5, turn west on Highway 4 and drive 63 miles to U.S. 101. Turn south on U.S. 101 and drive 13 miles to the junction with Highway 103. Turn north on Highway 103 and drive two miles to Highway 100. Turn right (south) and drive to Ilwaco. At the junction of Spruce Street SW and First Street, turn right (west) on Spruce Street and drive one block to Second Avenue SW. Turn left (south) on Second Avenue SW and drive four blocks south to the campground on the right.

Contact: Fisherman's Cove RV Park, P.O. Box 921, 411 Second Ave. SW, Ilwaco, WA 98624, 360/642-3689 or 877/268-3789.

108 ILWACO KOA

Rating: 5

near Fort Canby State Park
See map pages 16–17

This 17-acre camp is about nine miles from the beach and includes a secluded area for tents. You'll find a boardwalk nearby, as well as the Lewis and Clark Museum, lighthouses, and an amusement park. Fishing is possible from a jetty or charter boats. Additional facilities found within five miles of the campground include a maritime museum, hiking trails, and a nine-hole golf course.

RV sites, facilities: There are 114 sites with full hookups (30 amps), including some drive-through, for RVs of any length, 26 tent sites, five secluded group sites, and five cabins. Restrooms, drinking water, flush toilets, showers, cable TV, propane, a pay phone, limited cell phone reception, an RV dump station, a recreation hall, a store, a laundry, ice, and a playground are available. Leashed pets are permitted.

Reservations, fees: Reservations are accepted; phone 800/562-3258. The fee is $25–35 per night, plus $5 per person per night for more than two people (children four and under free), and $6.50 for each additional vehicle. Cabins are $50 per night. Major credit cards are accepted. Open mid-May to mid-October.

Directions: From Astoria on the Astoria bridge, drive north on U.S. 101 for nine miles to the camp on the left.

Contact: Ilwaco KOA, P.O. Box 549, Ilwaco, WA 98624, tel./fax 360/642-3292, website: www.koa.com.

109 FORT CANBY STATE PARK

Rating: 10

on the Pacific Ocean

See map pages 16–17

This park covers 1,882 acres on the Long Beach Peninsula and is fronted by the Pacific Ocean. It offers access to two miles of ocean beach and two lighthouses. The park contains old-growth forest, lakes, both freshwater and saltwater marshes, streams, and tidelands. It is the choice spot in the area for tent campers. There are two places to camp: a general camping area and the Lake O'Neil area, which offers sites right on the water. Highlights at the park include hiking trails and opportunities for surf, jetty, and ocean fishing. An interpretive center highlights the Lewis and Clark expedition as well as maritime and military history. North Head Lighthouse is open for touring. Colbert House Museum is open during the summer.

RV sites, facilities: There are 250 sites, including 20 sites with partial hookups, and 60 sites with full hookups (30 amps) for RVs up to 45 feet or tents, three cabins, and 10 yurts. Picnic tables and fire grills are provided. Restrooms, drinking water, flush toilets, coin-operated showers, an RV dump station, a picnic area, interpretive activities, a horseshoe pit, athletic fields, a small store, a pay phone, limited cell phone reception, and firewood are available. An ATM is available within three blocks. Some facilities are wheelchair-accessible. Leashed pets are permitted.

Reservations, fees: Reserve at 888/CAMP-OUT (888/226-7688) or online at www.parks.wa.gov /reservations ($7 reservation fee). The fee is $16–22 per night; cabins and yurts $35 per night. A senior discount is available. Major credit cards are accepted. Open year-round.

Directions: From the junction of Highway 4 and Highway 101 (a flashing light, south of Nemah), turn west on Highway 101 (toward Ilwaco) and drive 10 miles to Ilwaco and Highway 100. Turn right and drive three miles to the park entrance on the right.

Contact: Fort Canby State Park, 360/642-3078; state park information, 360/902-8844.

110 RIVER'S END CAMPGROUND AND RV PARK

Rating: 6

near Fort Columbia State Park

See map pages 16–17

This wooded campground spreads over five acres and has riverside access. Salmon fishing is available here. Additional facilities found within five miles of the campground include marked bike trails and a full-service marina. Also nearby is Fort Columbia State Park.

RV sites, facilities: There are 54 sites with full hookups (20, 30 amps), including some drive-through, for RVs of any length and 10 tent sites. Picnic tables are provided at RV sites. Fire pits are provided at tent sites. Restrooms, drinking water, flush toilets, coin-operated showers, an RV dump station, a recreation hall, a coin-operated laundry, cell phone reception, firewood, a fish-cleaning station, ice, and a playground are available. A store, an ATM, and a café are within one mile. Boat docks, launching facilities, and rentals are nearby on the Columbia River. Leashed pets are permitted.

Reservations, fees: Reservations are accepted. The fee is $16–22 per night, plus $2 per person per night for more than two people. Open April to late October.

Directions: From Kelso/Longview on I-5, turn west on Highway 4 and drive 60 miles to Highway 401. Turn south on Highway 401 and drive 14 miles to the park entrance (just south of Chinook) on the left.

Contact: River's End Campground and RV Park, P.O. Box 280, 12 Bayview St., Chinook, WA 98614, 360/777-8317.

111 MAUCH'S SUNDOWN RV PARK

Rating: 5

near Fort Columbia State Park

See map pages 16–17

This is an adults-only park with about 35 percent of the sites rented long-term, usually throughout the summer. The park covers four acres, has riverside access, and is in a wooded, hilly setting with grassy sites. Nearby fishing from shore is available. It's near Fort Columbia State Park.

RV sites, facilities: There are 50 sites with full and partial hookups (30 amps) for RVs up to 40 feet. Restrooms, drinking water, flush toilets, coin-operated showers, picnic tables, an RV dump station, cable TV, a pay phone, limited cell phone reception, a coin-operated laundry, a store, propane, and ice are available. A café and an ATM are within three miles. Boat docks and launching facilities are nearby on the Columbia River. No tents, children, or large pets are permitted. Small pets are allowed.

Reservations, fees: Reservations are accepted. The fee is $10–20 per night, plus $1.50 per person per night for more than two people, and $1.50 per additional vehicle per night. A senior discount is available. Open year-round.

Directions: From Kelso/Longview on I-5, turn west on Highway 4 and drive 60 miles to Highway 401. Turn south on Highway 401 and drive to U.S. 101. Take U.S. 101 to the right and continue for .5 mile (do not go over the bridge) to the park on the right.

Contact: Mauch's Sundown RV Park, 158 Rte. 101, Chinook, WA 98614, 360/777-8713.

112 SKAMOKAWA VISTA PARK

Rating: 7

near the Columbia River
See map pages 16–17

Skamokawa, meaning "smoke on the water," is named for the effect produced by fog rolling up the Columbia River. This public camp covers 70 acres and features a half mile of sandy beach and a Lewis and Clark interpretive site installed in 2003. A short hiking trail is nearby. The camp also has nearby access to the Columbia River, where recreational options include fishing, swimming, and boating. Additional facilities found within five miles of the campground include a full-service marina and additional tennis courts. This park is in a growth mode, and there is a good chance that additional campsites and yurts will be added by 2004. In Skamokawa, a River Life Interpretive Center stays open year-round.

RV sites, facilities: There are 21 sites with partial hookups (30 amps) for RVs of any length, 16 sites with no hookups for tents or RVs, and four tent sites. Picnic tables and fire grills are provided. Restrooms, drinking water, flush toilets, coin-operated showers, a pay phone, cell phone reception, an RV dump station, boat-launching facilities, firewood, tennis courts, basketball courts, and a playground are available. A store, a café, and ice are available within one mile. Propane and an ATM are available within five miles. Boat docks and canoe and kayak rentals are nearby. Leashed pets are permitted.

Reservations, fees: Reservations are accepted. The fee is $15–25 per night. Open year-round.

Directions: From Kelso/Longview on I-5, turn west on Highway 4 and drive 35 miles to Skamokawa. Continue west on Highway 4 for .5 mile to the park on the left.

Contact: Skamokawa Vista Park, Port of Wahkiakum No. 2, P.O. Box 220, 13 Vista Park Rd., Skamokawa, WA 98647, 360/795-8605, fax 360/795-8611.

Washington

Chapter 2

Seattle and the
San Juan Islands

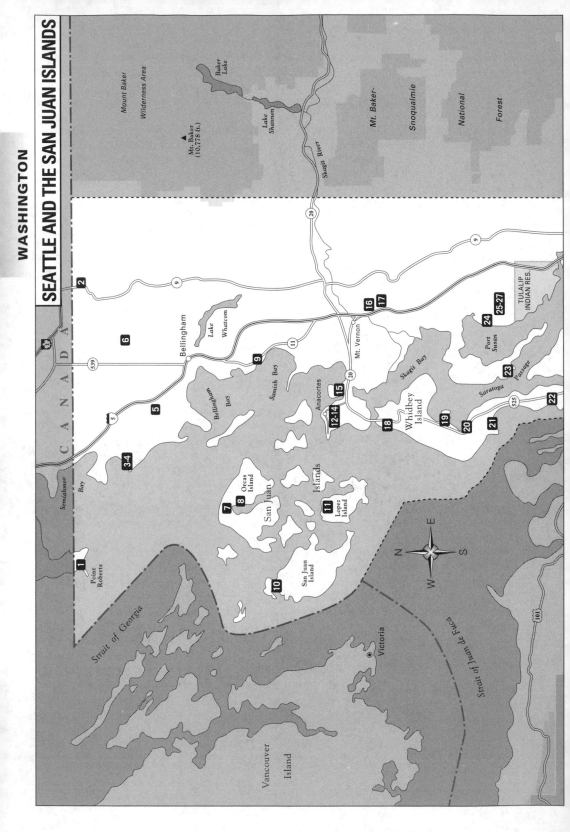

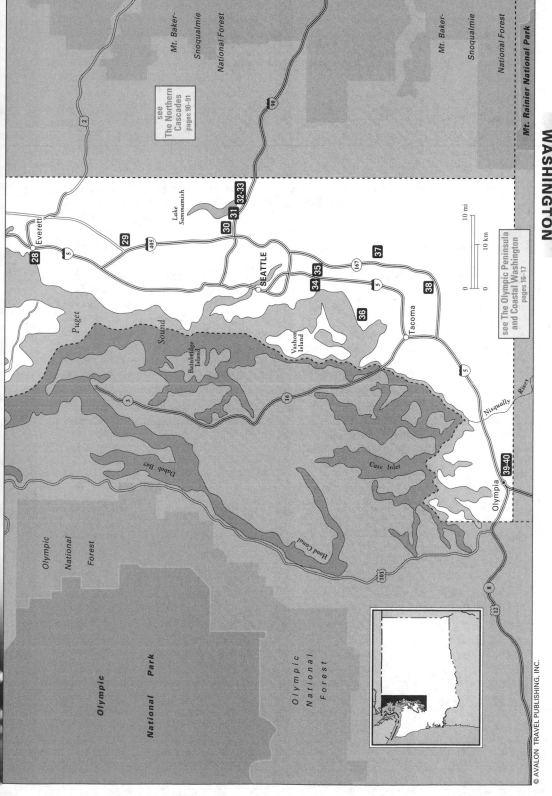

WASHINGTON

Mt. Rainier National Park

see
The Northern
Cascades
pages 90–91

Mt. Baker-
Snoqualmie
National Forest

Mt. Baker-
Snoqualmie
National Forest

2

90

32-33
31
30
29
28

405
5

Everett

Lake
Sammamish

SEATTLE

34
35
36
37
38

5

167

Tacoma

10 mi

10 km

see The Olympic Peninsula
and Coastal Washington
pages 1b–17

Puget

Sound

Bainbridge
Island

Vashon
Island

Case Inlet

39-40

Olympia

Nisqually River

5

3

16

Dabob Bay

Hood Canal

Olympic
National
Forest

Olympic
National
Forest

Olympic

National

Park

101

8

12

© AVALON TRAVEL PUBLISHING, INC.

Chapter 2—Seattle and the San Juan Islands

No metropolitan area in the world offers a wider array of recreation options than Seattle-Tacoma and its sphere of influence. At the center are water, woods, and islands. One of my favorite views anywhere is from the top of Mount Constitution on Orcas Island, where on a clear day you can look out over an infinity of sunswept charm. Take one look and you'll know this is why you came.

The scope of parks, campgrounds, and recreation on the islands in this region is preeminent. Even in an RV you'll have an array of excellent destinations, including many available by ferry transport. Many state parks offer gorgeous water-view campsites. Well-furnished RV parks along the I-5 corridor offer respite for vacationers in need of a layover, and hidden lakes, such as Cascade Lake on Orcas Island, will surprise you with their beauty.

But spend even a short time here and you will realize that you need some kind of boat to do it right. A powerboat, sailboat, or kayak offers instant access to adventure. With a powerboat, you get freedom from the traffic on the I-5 corridor, as well as near-unlimited access to destinations in Puget Sound and the linked inlets, bays, and canals. Fishing can be good, too. On calm days with light breezes, roaming the peaceful waters in a sailboat amid dozens of islands provides a segue to instant tranquillity. With near-perfect destinations like these, this area is quickly becoming the sea kayaking capital of the world.

People who live here year-round, fighting the rat maze of traffic on I-5, can easily fall into the trap of tunnel vision, never seeing beyond the line of cars ahead of them. Escape that tunnel. Scan the maps and pages in this region, and in the process, reward yourself with the best water-based adventure anywhere.

① WHALEN'S RV PARK

Rating: 6

on Point Roberts

See map pages 68–69

This RV park is located on Point Roberts, so remote you must drive through Canada and then return south into the United States to reach it. But don't hop on the bandwagon just yet. Take note that 80 percent of the campsites are booked for the entire summer. That makes reservations critical for anybody wishing to stay overnight. The park features a mix of woods and water, and has grassy sites and lots of trees. A recreation field is provided for campers. Nearby recreational options include an 18-hole golf course, a full-service marina, and tennis courts.

RV sites, facilities: There are 50 sites with partial hookups (30 amps) for RVs of any length and 100 sites for tents. Picnic tables and fire grills are provided. Restrooms, drinking water, flush toilets, coin-operated showers, an RV dump station, and firewood are available. A store, a café, a pay phone, cell phone reception, an ATM, a coin-operated laundry, and ice are available within one mile. Boat docks and launching facilities are nearby. Leashed pets are permitted.

Reservations, fees: Reservations are accepted. The fee is $15–20 per night. Major credit cards are accepted. Open May to late October.

Directions: From Bellingham, take I-5 north through Blaine and the border customs into Canada to Highway 99 North. Continue northwest on Highway BC 99N for 18 miles to BC 17. Turn and drive six miles to the town of Tsawwassen and 56th Street. Turn west and drive to Benson Road. Turn left on Benson Road and drive one mile to Boundary Bay Road. Turn left and drive one mile to Bay View Road. Turn left again and drive .5 mile to the park on the left.

Contact: Whalen's RV Park, Roosevelt and Derby, Point Roberts, WA 98281, 360/945-2874, fax 360/945-0934.

② SUMAS RV PARK

Rating: 5

in Sumas

See map pages 68–69

Located on the U.S.–Canadian border with 24-hour customs available nearby, this campground is a layover spot to spend American dollars before heading into British Columbia and making the conversion. The camp is set in the grassy flatlands; it has graveled sites with trees. Nearby recreation options include an 18-hole golf course and tennis courts.

RV sites, facilities: There are 50 sites with partial or full hookups (30, 50 amps), including 18 drive-through sites, for RVs of any length and 24 tent sites. Picnic tables, cable TV hookups, and fire rings are provided. Restrooms, drinking water, flush toilets, showers, an RV dump station, cell phone reception, a pay phone, coin-operated laundry, firewood, and a ballpark are available. A store, a café, an ATM, and ice are available within one mile. Leashed pets are permitted.

Reservations, fees: Reservations are accepted. The fee is $10–20 per night. Major credit cards are accepted. Open year-round.

Directions: From I-5 at Bellingham, take Exit 256 to Highway 539. Turn north on Highway 539 and drive 12 miles to Highway 536. Turn right (east) on Highway 536 (Badger Road) and drive 14 miles (the road becomes Highway 9) to Sumas and look for Cherry Street. Turn right (south) at Cherry Street (the road becomes Easterbrook Road) and drive two blocks to the park on the left.

Contact: Sumas RV Park, 9600 Easterbrook Rd., Sumas, WA 98295, 360/988-8875.

③ BIRCH BAY STATE PARK

Rating: 8

on Birch Bay

See map pages 68–69

Birch Bay State Park covers 194 acres and features nearly two miles of beach as well as great views of the Canadian Gulf Islands and the Cascade Mountains. For water lovers it has the best of both worlds, with 8,255 feet of saltwater

WASHINGTON

shoreline and 14,923 feet of freshwater shoreline on Terrell Creek. More than 100 different species of birds, many of which are migrating on the Pacific flyway, can be seen here. The Terrell Creek Marsh Interpretive Trail extends a half mile through both a forest of black birch trees and one of the few remaining saltwater/freshwater estuaries in northern Puget Sound. Bald eagles and great blue herons feed along the banks of Terrell Creek. Several 18-hole golf courses are located nearby. The campground is divided into two loops; hookups for RVs are in the North Loop.

RV sites, facilities: There are 20 sites with partial hookups for RVs up to 60 feet and 146 sites for tents or self-contained RVs. Picnic tables and fire grills are provided. Flush toilets, coin-operated showers, and an RV dump station are available. A boat ramp, launch facilities (for boats under 16 feet only), a picnic area with a sheltered kitchen with water and electricity, an amphitheater, a half-court basketball area, interpretive activities, and a camp host are available. A store, a restaurant, a pay phone, firewood, a coin-operated laundry, and ice are available within a half mile, and an ATM is within five miles. Some facilities are wheelchair-accessible. Leashed pets are permitted.

Reservations, fees: Reserve at 888/CAMP-OUT (888/226-7688) or online at www.parks.wa.gov /reservations ($7 reservation fee). The fee is $10–22 per night, plus $10 per additional vehicle per night. Major credit cards are accepted. A senior discount is available. Open year-round.

Directions: From Bellingham, drive north on I-5 to Exit 266. At Exit 266 take Grandview west and continue seven miles to Jackson Road. Turn right on Jackson Road and drive one mile to Helweg Road. Turn left and drive .25 mile to the reservation office.

Contact: Birch Bay State Park, 5105 Helweg Rd., Blaine, WA 98230, 360/371-2800, fax 360/371-0455; state park information, 360/902-8844, fax 360/856-2150.

4 BEACHSIDE RV PARK

Rating: 8

on Birch Bay
See map pages 68–69

This pretty park comes with the opportunity to occasionally view a pair of nesting eagles. Evergreens and bay views surround the park. Hiking, fishing, mountain biking, and nearby golf are also options.

RV sites, facilities: There are 26 sites with full hookups (30, 50 amps), including 24 drive-through sites, for RVs and 12 sites for tents. Picnic tables are provided. Restrooms, drinking water, flush toilets, showers, cell phone reception, a pay phone, modem access, a group fire pit, and a coin-operated laundry are available. An ATM and a restaurant are within a half mile, and a grocery store is within one mile. Leashed pets are permitted.

Reservations, fees: Reservations are recommended; call 360/371-5962. The fee is $14–22 per night. Major credit cards are accepted. A senior discount is available. Open year-round.

Directions: From Bellingham, drive north on I-5 to Exit 270. Turn west on Birch Bay–Lynden Road and drive five miles to Birch Bay Drive. Turn left and drive one mile to the park on the left.

Contact: Beachside RV Park, 7630 Birch Bay Dr., Birch Bay, WA 98230, tel./fax 360/371-5962.

5 THE CEDARS RV RESORT

Rating: 5

in Ferndale
See map pages 68–69

This campground provides more direct access from I-5 than Windmill Inn and KOA Lynden, and note that you can usually get a spot here. It's a nice, clean park covering 22 acres with spacious sites and trees. Horseshoes, a game room, and a recreation field provide possible activities for campers. Several golf courses are nearby.

RV sites, facilities: There are 127 sites with partial or full hookups (30, 50 amps), including drive-through sites, for RVs of any length or tents and a dispersed tent camping area on grass. Picnic tables and fire pits are provided. Restrooms, drinking water, flush toilets, showers, cell phone reception, a pay phone, modem hookups (at 50 sites), two RV dump stations, a coin-operated laundry, badminton, volleyball, a playground with horseshoes, a recreation room, an arcade, a pool (seasonal), a small store, and ice are available. An ATM is within one mile. Leashed pets are permitted.

WASHINGTON

Reservations, fees: Reservations are accepted. The fee is $20–29.50 per night. Major credit cards are accepted. Open year-round.

Directions: From Bellingham on I-5, drive north to Ferndale and Exit 263. Take Exit 263 and turn north on Portal Way. Drive less than one mile north to the campground on the left.

Contact: The Cedars RV Resort, 6335 Portal Way, Ferndale, WA 98248, 360/384-2622, fax 360/380-6365, website: www.holidaytrailsresorts.com.

6 KOA LYNDEN

Rating: 9

in Lynden

See map pages 68–69

Lynden is a quaint Dutch town. The park features green lawns, flowers, and trees surrounding a miniature golf course and ponds, where you can fish for trout. This KOA stars as a unique layover spot for vacationers heading north to Canada via Highway 539 and Highway 546. Nearby recreational options include an 18-hole golf course.

RV sites, facilities: There are 90 sites with partial or full hookups (30, 50 amps), including 25 drive-through, for RVs of any length, 40 tent sites, and 12 cabins. Picnic tables are provided. Restrooms, drinking water, flush toilets, showers, propane, an RV dump station, showers, firewood, a pay phone, cell phone reception, modem access, a recreation hall, a store, a café (summer season only), an espresso bar, an ice-cream parlor, laundry facilities, ice, a playground, miniature golf, and a swimming pool are available. Tackle and boat rentals are also available. An ATM is within 1.5 miles. Leashed pets are permitted.

Reservations, fees: Reservations are accepted at 800/562-4779. The fee is $29–35 per night for two campers, plus $4 for each additional person five years of age and up. Major credit cards are accepted. Call the park for group rates. Open year-round.

Directions: From I-5 at Bellingham, take Exit 256 to Highway 539. Turn north on Highway 539 and drive 12 miles to Highway 546. Turn east on Highway 546 (Badger Road) and drive three miles to Line Road. Turn right (south) on

Line Road and drive .5 mile to the campground on the right.

Contact: KOA Lynden, 8717 Line Rd., Lynden, WA 98264, 360/354-4772, fax 360/354-7050, website: www.koa.com.

7 WEST BEACH RESORT FERRY-IN

Rating: 9

on Orcas Island

See map pages 68–69

Right on the beach, this resort offers salmon fishing, boating, swimming, and an apple orchard. An excellent alternative to Moran State Park, which is often full, it offers the same recreation opportunities. The beaches at Orcas Island are prime spots for whale-watching and beautiful views, especially at sunrise and sunset.

RV sites, facilities: There are 62 sites with partial hookups (20, 30 amps) for RVs of any length or tents. There are also 18 cabins. Restrooms, coin-operated showers (from April to October only), a pay phone, a store, a playground, a coin-operated laundry, ice, cell phone reception, propane, modem access, and firewood are available. A hot tub is available for a fee. Also on-site are a boat ramp, a dock, gas, a marina, canoe and bike rentals, and kayak tours. Leashed pets are permitted.

Reservations, fees: Reservations are recommended. The fee is $25–35 per night for up to three people, plus $5 per additional vehicle per night, and $5 per pet per night. Major credit cards are accepted. Open May to October.

Directions: From Seattle on I-5, drive north to Burlington and Highway 20. Turn west on Highway 20 and drive 12 miles to the Highway 20 North spur, following signs to the San Juan Islands Ferry Terminal in Anacortes. Take the ferry to Orcas Island. From the ferry landing, turn left and drive 11 miles on Horseshoe Highway/Orcas Road to the entrance of Eastsound. A green sign directs you left toward Moran State Park. Turn left (continuing on Orcas Road) and drive .5 mile to Enchanted Forest Road. Turn left and drive to the end of Enchanted Forest Road and the resort.

Contact: West Beach Resort, 190 Waterfront

Way, Eastsound, WA 98245, 360/376-2240, fax 360/376-4746, website: www.westbeachresort.com.

8 MORAN STATE PARK FERRY-IN

Rating: 10

on Orcas Island
See map pages 68–69

This state park is drop-dead beautiful. It covers 5,252 acres, with surprise lakes (my favorite is Mountain Lake), hiking trails, and the best mountaintop views anywhere in the chain of islands. There are actually four separate campgrounds plus a primitive area. You can drive to the summit of Mount Constitution, which tops out at 2,409 feet, then climb up the steps to a stone observation tower (built in 1936 by the Civilian Conservation Corps) for sensational 360-degree views of Vancouver, Mount Baker, the San Juan Islands, the Cascade Mountains, and several cities on the distant shores of mainland America and Canada. No RVs are allowed on the winding road to the top. There are five freshwater lakes with fishing for rainbow trout, cutthroat trout, and kokanee salmon, 33 miles of hiking trails, 11 miles of biking trails, and six miles of horse trails. The landscape features old-growth forest, primarily lodgepole pine, and several small waterfalls. Nearby recreation options include a nine-hole golf course.

RV sites, facilities: There are 136 developed sites, including some drive-through sites, for RVs up to 45 feet long or tents, 15 primitive hike-in/bike-in tent sites, and one cabin for up to 10 people. Picnic tables and fire grills are provided. Restrooms, drinking water, flush toilets, coin-operated showers, an RV dump station, a picnic area with a log kitchen shelter, two courtesy phones, and firewood are available. Boat docks, limited fishing supplies, launching facilities, and boat rentals are located at the concession stand in the park. An ATM is within four miles. Some facilities are wheelchair-accessible. Leashed pets are permitted.

Reservations, fees: Reserve at 888/CAMP-OUT (888/226-7688) or online at www.parks.wa.gov /reservations ($7 reservation fee). The fees are $10–16 for tent and RV sites, and $10 for bike-in/hike-in sites, plus $10 per additional vehicle per night. Reserve a cabin at 800/360-4240. A senior discount is available. Major credit cards are accepted. Open year-round.

Directions: From Seattle on I-5, drive north to Burlington and Highway 20. Turn west on Highway 20 and drive 12 miles to the Highway 20 North spur, following signs to the San Juan Islands Ferry Terminal in Anacortes. Take the ferry to Orcas Island. From the ferry landing, turn left on Horseshoe Highway/Oras Road and drive 13 miles to Moran State Park (well marked). Stop at the campground registration booth for directions to your site.

Contact: Moran State Park Ferry-In, 3572 Olga Rd., Olga, WA 98279, 360/376-2326; state park information, 360/902-8844.

9 LARRABEE STATE PARK

Rating: 9

on Samish Bay
See map pages 68–69

This 2,683-acre state park sits on Samish Bay in Puget Sound and boasts 8,100 feet of saltwater shoreline. The park has two freshwater lakes, coves, and tidelands. Sunsets are often beautiful. The park has 13.7 miles of hiking trails and 11.7 miles of mountain-biking trails. The landscape is primarily forested with conifers, often with dense woodlands and vegetation, but also features marshlands, wetlands, streams, lakes, and Chuckanut Mountain. The area is known for Chuckanut sandstone. Fishing is available on Fragrance Lake and Lost Lake, which are hike-in lakes. Dating from 1915, this was the first state park established in Washington. The park lies on a beautiful stretch of coastline and offers prime spots for wildlife viewing. A relatively short drive south will take you to Anacortes, where you can catch a ferry to islands in the San Juan chain.

RV sites, facilities: There are 77 developed sites, including 22 with full hookups (30 amps), for RVs up to 60 feet or tents and 10 walk-in tent sites. Picnic tables and fire grills are provided. Restrooms, drinking water, flush toilets, coin-operated showers, an RV dump station, a pay phone, a picnic area with electricity and a covered shelter, and firewood are available. Boat-launching facilities are available nearby. An ATM is within five miles. Leashed pets are permitted.

Reservations, fees: Reserve at 888/CAMP-OUT (888/226-7688) or online at www.parks.wa.gov /reservations ($7 reservation fee). The fee is $10–22 per night, plus $10 per additional vehicle per night. A senior discount is available. Major credit cards are accepted in peak season only. Open year-round.

Directions: From Bellingham on I-5, take Exit 250 and turn on Fairhaven Parkway. Drive less than a mile to State Route 11/Chuckanut Drive (second stoplight). Turn left (stay left at the next stoplight) and drive six miles to the park entrance on the right.

Contact: Larrabee State Park, 245 Chuckanut, Bellingham, WA 98225, 360/676-2093; state park information, 360/902-8844, fax 360/676-2061.

10 LAKEDALE RESORT FERRY-IN

Rating: 7

on San Juan Island

See map pages 68–69

This is a nice spot for visitors who want the solitude of an island camp, yet all the amenities of a privately run campground. Fishing, swimming, and boating are available at the Lakedale Lakes. A sand volleyball court, a half-court basketball area, and a grassy sports field are also on-site. Roche Harbor and Wescott Bay are nearby to the north, and Friday Harbor and its restaurants are nearby to the south.

RV sites, facilities: There are 18 sites with partial hookups (30 amps) for tents or RVs up to 40 feet and 102 sites for tents. There are also six group sites, three tent cabins, six log cabins, and 10 luxury lodge rooms. Picnic tables and fire rings are provided. Restrooms, drinking water, flush toilets, showers, a pay phone, modem access, cell phone reception, firewood, a store, and ice are available. Boat docks, three swimming beaches, and boat, kayak, canoe, paddleboat, bike, camping gear, and fishing gear rentals are available on-site. An ATM is within six miles. Leashed pets are permitted.

Reservations, fees: Reservations are accepted. The fee is $21–31, plus $5–6 per person per night for more than two people, $11–13 per night per additional vehicle, and $1.50 per pet per night. Motorcycle and driver are $10–11 per night.

Major credit cards are accepted. A senior discount is available. Open mid-March to mid-October for camping. Cabin rentals are available year-round.

Directions: From Seattle on I-5, drive north to Burlington and Highway 20. Turn west on Highway 20 and drive 12 miles to the Highway 20 North spur, following signs to the San Juan Islands Ferry Terminal in Anacortes. Take the ferry to Friday Harbor on San Juan Island. From the ferry landing at Friday Harbor, drive two blocks on Spring Street to 2nd Street. Turn right (northwest) on 2nd Street and drive .5 mile to Tucker Avenue (it becomes Roche Harbor Road). Turn right (north) and continue four miles to the campground on the left.

Contact: Lakedale Resort, 4313 Roche Harbor Rd., Friday Harbor, WA 98250, 360/378-2350 or 800/617-CAMP (800/617-2267), fax 360/378-0944, website: www.lakedale.com.

11 SPENCER SPIT STATE PARK FERRY-IN

Rating: 9

on Lopez Island

See map pages 68–69

Spencer Spit State Park offers one of the few island campgrounds accessible to cars via ferry. It also features walk-in sites, which require anywhere from a 50-foot to a 200-yard walk to the tent sites. A sand spit extends far into the water and provides both a lagoon and good access to prime clamming areas (in season). The park covers 130 acres. Picnicking, beachcombing, and sunbathing are some pleasant activities for campers looking for relaxation.

RV sites, facilities: There are 30 sites for self-contained RVs up to 40 feet or tents, 14 walk-in sites, and two group sites. Picnic tables and fire grills are provided. Restrooms, drinking water, flush toilets, cell phone reception, a picnic area, and an RV dump station are available, and 16 mooring buoys are available on the Cascadia Marine Trail. Boat docks and a launch are within two miles. An ATM and a pay phone are within four miles. Some facilities are wheelchair-accessible. Leashed pets are permitted.

Reservations, fees: Reserve at 888/CAMP-OUT

(888/226-7688) or online at www.parks.wa.gov/reservations ($7 reservation fee). The fee is $10–16 per night, plus $10 per additional vehicle per night, and $7 for mooring buoys per night. Group sites are $40 for up to 20 people, plus $2 per person for up to 50 people. A senior discount is available. Major credit cards are accepted. Open March to October.

Directions: From Seattle on I-5, drive north to Burlington and Highway 20. Turn west on Highway 20 and drive 12 miles to the Highway 20 North spur, following signs to the San Juan Islands Ferry Terminal in Anacortes. Take the ferry to Lopez Island. The park is within four miles of the ferry terminal.

Contact: Spencer Spit State Park Ferry-In, 521A Bakerview Rd., Lopez, WA 98261, 360/468-2251; state park information, 360/902-8844, fax 360/856-2150.

12 PIONEER TRAILS RV RESORT & CAMPGROUND

Rating: 9

on Fidalgo Island in the San Juan Islands
See map pages 68–69
This site offers resort camping in the beautiful San Juan Islands. Tall trees, breathtaking views, and country hospitality can all be found here. Side trips include nearby Deception Pass State Park (eight minutes away) and ferries to Victoria, British Columbia, Friday Harbor, Orcas Island, and other nearby islands (it is imperative to arrive early at the ferry terminal). Nearby recreation activities include horseshoes, an 18-hole golf course, relaxing spas, and lake fishing.

RV sites, facilities: There are 111 sites with partial or full hookups (30, 50 amps), including some drive-through sites, for RVs up to 70 feet or tents, plus 24 covered wagons and five cabins. Picnic tables and fire rings are provided. Restrooms, drinking water, flush toilets, showers, an RV dump station, cable TV, a pay phone, cell phone reception, modem access, an ATM, and a coin-operated laundry are available. A recreation hall, a playground, and a sports field are nearby. If RV camping, leashed pets are permitted.

Reservations, fees: Reservations are recommended. A three-night minimum on holidays is required.

The fee is $18–25 per night, plus $5 per additional vehicle per night, $2–3 per person per night for more than two adults and two children, and $2 per pet per night. Major credit cards are accepted. Open year-round.

Directions: From Seattle on I-5, drive north to Burlington and take Exit 230 for Highway 20 West. Drive west on Highway 20 for 12 miles. At the traffic signal, turn left (still Highway 20, toward Oak Harbor/Deception Pass) and drive .5 mile to Miller Road. Turn right (west) on Miller Road, drive .25 mile, and look for the park on the right side of the road.

Contact: Pioneer Trails RV Resort & Campground, 7337 Miller Rd., Anacortes, WA 98221, 360/293-5355, 888/777-5355, or 360/299-2240, website: www.pioneertrails.com.

13 FIDALGO BAY RESORT

Rating: 5

on Fidalgo Bay
See map pages 68–69
This park is five minutes from Anacortes and right on Fidalgo Bay, providing easy access to boating, fishing, and swimming. A golf course is available two miles away. There are a few permanent rentals at this park.

RV sites, facilities: There are 187 sites with full hookups (30, 50 amps), including 60 drive-through sites and a few sites with phone hookups, for RVs up to 87 feet, and eight tent sites. Picnic tables are provided. Restrooms, drinking water, flush toilets, showers, modem access in the clubhouse, a large fire pit, a small boat launch, a grocery store, a dog run, a courtesy phone, cell phone reception, and a coin-operated laundry are available. Leashed pets are permitted, but they must be kept quiet.

Reservations, fees: Reservations are recommended; phone 800/727-5478. The fee is $25–40 per night, plus $2 per person per night for more than two people. Major credit cards are accepted. Open year-round.

Directions: From Seattle on I-5, drive north approximately 80 miles to Burlington and Highway 20 (exit 230). Turn west on Highway 20 and drive about 14 miles to Fidalgo Bay Road. Turn right on Fidalgo Bay Road and drive one mile to the resort on the right.

Contact: Fidalgo Bay Resort, 4701 Fidalgo Bay Rd., Anacortes, WA 98221, 360/293-5353 or 800/727-5478, fax 360/299-3010, website: www .fidalgobay.com.

14 WASHINGTON PARK

Rating: 6

in Washington Park
See map pages 68–69

This city park is set in the woods and features many hiking trails. A 2.3-mile paved loop route for vehicles, hikers, and bicyclists stretches around the perimeter of the park. The Washington State Ferry terminals are located 1.25 miles away, providing access to the San Juan Islands. This is a popular camp, and it's a good idea to arrive early to claim your spot.

RV sites, facilities: There are 73 sites, including 46 with partial hookups and six drive-through sites, for RVs up to 40 feet or tents and one group tent-only site for up to 30 people. Restrooms, drinking water, flush toilets, coin-operated showers, a pay phone, a playground, a recreation field, an RV dump station, and a coin-operated laundry are available. A day-use area is provided. A boat launch is also available. Leashed pets are permitted.

Reservations, fees: Reservations are accepted for residents of Anacortes only. The fee is $15–20 per night; the group site is $50 per night. Open year-round.

Directions: From Seattle on I-5, drive north to Burlington and Highway 20. Turn west on Highway 20 and drive to Anacortes and Commercial Avenue (Spur 20). Drive north on Commercial Avenue (Spur 20/Oak Avenue) to 12th Street. Turn left and drive towards the ferry terminals. At the intersection in front of the ferry terminals, proceed west on Sunset Avenue for one mile to the park entrance at the end of the road.

Contact: Washington Park, City of Anacortes, P.O. Box 547, Anacortes, WA 98221, 360/293-1927 or 360/293-1918, website: www.cityofanacortes.org.

15 BAY VIEW STATE PARK

Rating: 10

on Padilla Bay
See map pages 68–69

This campground on Padilla Bay has a large, grassy area for kids, making it a good choice for families. Bordering 11,000 acres of Padilla Bay and the National Estuarine Sanctuary, this 25-acre park boasts 1,285 feet of saltwater shoreline. From the park, you can enjoy views of the San Juan Islands fronting Padilla Bay. On a clear day, you can see the Olympic Mountains to the west and Mount Rainier to the south. Kayakers should note that Padilla Bay becomes a large mud flat during low tides. Windsurfing is becoming popular, but tracking tides and wind is required. Crabbing and clamming (in season) are best at other locations along Padilla Bay or Bellingham Bay. The Breazeale Padilla Bay Interpretive Center, featuring saltwater aquariums and displays highlighting area wildlife, is located a half mile north of the park. For a nice day trip, take the ferry at Anacortes to Lopez Island (there are several campgrounds there as well).

RV sites, facilities: There are 76 sites, some with partial hookups (30 amps), for self-contained RVs or tents, nine sites with full hookups for RVs up to 50 feet, three primitive sites, and one group tent site for up to 64 people. Picnic tables and fire rings are provided. Restrooms, drinking water, flush toilets, coin-operated showers, cell phone reception, an RV dump station, and a picnic area with a beach shelter are available. A beach play area with horseshoes, volleyball (no net supplied), interpretive activities, windsurfing, water-skiing, swimming, clamming, crabbing, oyster gathering (in season), boating, and 50 beach picnic sites are available. A pay phone, and an ATM are within four miles. A store and a coin-operated laundry are eight miles away in Burlington. Leashed pets are permitted. Note that some campsites are closed in winter months.

Reservations, fees: Reserve at 888/226-7688 (CAMP-OUT) or online at www.parks.wa.gov /reservations ($7 reservation fee). The fee is $10–22 per night, plus $10 per additional vehicle per night. Reservations are required for the group camp; there is a $7 reservation fee, plus

$2 per person per night. A senior discount is available. Major credit cards are accepted in summer. Open year-round.

Directions: From Seattle on I-5, drive north to Burlington and Exit 230 for Highway 20. Turn west on Highway 20 and drive seven miles west (toward Anacortes) to Bay View–Edison Road. Turn right (north) on Bay View–Edison Road and drive four miles to the park on the right.

Contact: Bay View State Park, 10901 Bay View–Edison Rd., Brighton, WA 98273, 360/757-0227; state park information, 360/902-8844, fax 360/676-2061.

16 BURLINGTON/ANACORTES KOA

Rating: 5

in Burlington

See map pages 68–69

This is a fine KOA campground, complete with all the amenities. The sites are spacious and comfortable. Possible side trips include tours of the Boeing plant, Victoria, Vancouver Island, and the San Juan Islands.

RV sites, facilities: There are 120 sites, most with partial or full hookups (30 amps), some drive-through, for RVs up to 70 feet or tents, and nine cabins. Restrooms, drinking water, flush toilets, showers, an RV dump station, cable TV, a pay phone, modem access, a coin-operated laundry, limited groceries, ice, propane, and a barbecue are available. An indoor heated pool, a spa with a sauna, a recreation hall, a game room, a playground, miniature golf, horseshoes, and a sports field are also available. An ATM is within 5.5 miles. Leashed pets are permitted.

Reservations, fees: Reservations are recommended in the summer; phone 800/562-9154. The fee is $24–33 per night, plus $2.50–4 per person per night for more than two people. Major credit cards are accepted. A senior discount is available. Open year-round.

Directions: From Seattle on I-5, drive north to Exit 232/Cook Road in Burlington. Take that exit to Cook Road. Turn right on Cook Road and drive 100 feet to Old Highway 99. Turn left and drive 3.5 miles to the campground on the right.

Contact: Burlington/Anacortes KOA, 6397 North Green Rd., Burlington, WA 98233, 360/724-5511, fax 360/724-4001, website: www.koa.com.

17 RIVERBEND RV PARK

Rating: 5

on the Skagit River

See map pages 68–69

Riverbend RV Park is a pleasant layover spot for I-5 travelers. While not particularly scenic, it is clean and spacious. Access to the Skagit River here is a high point, with fishing for salmon, trout, and Dolly Varden in season; check regulations. Nearby recreational options include a casino and an 18-hole golf course.

RV sites, facilities: There are 90 drive-through sites with full hookups (30, 50 amps) for RVs of any length and 25 tent sites. Picnic tables are provided at RV sites and barbecues are provided at tent sites. Restrooms, drinking water, flush toilets, coin-operated showers, an RV dump station, a pay phone, cell phone reception, modem access, a coin-operated laundry, and a playground with horseshoes are available. A store, a café, ice, and a swimming pool are available within a quarter mile. Leashed pets are permitted.

Reservations, fees: Reservations are accepted. The fee is $12–21.50 per night. Major credit cards are accepted. Open year-round.

Directions: From Seattle on I-5, drive north to Mt. Vernon and the College Way exit. Take the College Way exit and drive one block west to Freeway Drive. Turn right (north) and drive .25 mile to the end of the road and the park entrance on the left.

Contact: Riverbend RV Park, 305 West Stewart Rd., Mt. Vernon, WA 98273, 360/428-4044.

18 DECEPTION PASS STATE PARK

Rating: 10

on Whidbey Island

See map pages 68–69

Located at beautiful Deception Pass on the west side of Whidbey Island, this state park encompasses 4,134 acres with almost 15 miles of saltwater shoreline and six miles of freshwater shoreline on two lakes. The landscape ranges from old-growth forest to sand dunes. This diverse habitat has attracted 174 species of birds. An observation deck overlooks the Cranberry Lake wetlands. The park also features spectacular views of shoreline, mountains, and islands, often with dramatic sunsets. At one spot, rugged cliffs drop to the turbulent waters of Deception Pass. Recreation options include fishing at Pass Lake, a freshwater lake within the park. Fly-fishing for trout is a unique bonus for anglers. Note that each lake has different regulations for boating and fishing. Scuba diving is also popular, with an underwater park located nearby at Rosario Beach. The park provides 38 miles of hiking trails, 1.2 miles of wheelchair-accessible trails, and six miles of biking trails. There are several historic Civilian Conservation Corps buildings near the campground.

RV sites, facilities: There are 246 developed sites, 92 with partial hookups (30, 50 amps), including some drive-through, for RVs up to 50 feet or tents and five primitive tent sites. Picnic tables and fire rings are provided. Restrooms, drinking water, flush toilets, cell phone reception, coin-operated showers, and an RV dump station are available. A concession stand, an amphitheater, interpretive activities, a picnic area with electricity and a kitchen shelter, a boat launch, boat rentals, and mooring buoys are available nearby. An ATM and a pay phone are across the street. The facilities are wheelchair-accessible. Leashed pets are permitted.

Reservations, fees: Reserve at 888/CAMP-OUT (888/226-7688) or online at www.parks.wa.gov /reservations ($7 reservation fee). The fees are $10–22 per night, plus $10 per additional vehicle per night, and $10–16 for mooring buoys per night. A senior discount is available. Major credit cards are accepted. Open year-round, with limited winter services.

Directions: From Seattle on I-5, drive north to Burlington and Exit 230/Highway 20. Take that exit and drive west on Highway 20 for 12 miles to Highway 20 spur heading south. Turn south on Highway 20 and drive four miles (to the bridge at Deception Pass). Continue to the park (one mile south of the bridge) on the right.

Contact: Deception Pass State Park, 360/675-2417, fax 360/675-3288; state park information, 360/902-8844, fax 360/676-2061.

19 OAK HARBOR CITY BEACH PARK

Rating: 4

in Oak Harbor
See map pages 68–69
This popular park fills quickly on summer weekends. With graveled sites, it is geared toward RVers but is also suitable for tent campers. Fishing, swimming, boating, and sunbathing are all options at Oak Harbor City Beach Park. A full-service marina is next door. Within a few miles are an 18-hole golf course and tennis courts. Fort Ebey and Fort Casey State Parks are both a short drive away and make excellent side trips. There are more than three miles of hiking trails within the park.

RV sites, facilities: There are 56 sites with full hookups (40 amps) for RVs of any length. Restrooms, drinking water, flush toilets, a pay phone, an RV dump station, coin-operated showers, and a playground are available. Propane, a store, a café, a coin-operated laundry, an ATM, and ice are available within one mile. A swimming lagoon, wading pools, boat rentals, and a concession stand are available in summer. Boat-launching facilities are located at Oak Harbor Marina. Leashed pets are permitted.

Reservations, fees: Reservations are not accepted. The fee is $12–20 per night. Open year-round.

Directions: From Seattle on I-5, drive north to Burlington and Highway 20. Turn west on Highway 20 and drive 28 miles to the intersection of Highway 20 and Pioneer Way in the town of Oak Harbor on Whidbey Island. Continue straight through the intersection onto Beeksma Drive and drive about one block to the park on the left.

Contact: Oak Harbor City Beach Park, 865 SE Berrington Dr., Oak Harbor, WA 98277, 360/679-5551, website: www.oakharbor.org.

20 FORT EBEY STATE PARK

Rating: 9

on Whidbey Island
See map pages 68–69
This park is situated on the west side of Whidbey Island at Point Partridge. It covers 645 acres and has access to a rocky beach that is good for

WASHINGTON

exploring. There are also 28 miles of hiking and biking trails. Fort Ebey is the site of a historic World War II bunker, where concrete platforms mark the locations of the former gun batteries. Other options here include fishing and wildlife viewing. Limited fishing is available for small-mouth bass at Lake Pondilla, only about 100 yards away and a good place to see bald eagles. The saltwater shore access provides a good spot for surfing and paragliding.

RV sites, facilities: There are 50 developed camp-sites, including four sites with electricity (50 amps), for self-contained RVs up to 70 feet or tents and three primitive tent sites. Picnic tables and fire grills are provided. Restrooms, drinking water, flush toilets, cell phone reception, coin-operated showers, and a picnic area are available. An RV dump station is nearby. An ATM and a pay phone are within seven miles. Some facilities are wheelchair-accessible. Leashed pets are permitted.

Reservations, fees: Reserve at 888/CAMP-OUT (888/226-7688) or online at www.parks.wa.gov /reservations ($7 reservation fee). The fee is $10–22 per night, plus $10 per additional vehi-cle per night. Major credit cards are accepted. A senior discount is available. Open year-round.

Directions: From Seattle on I-5, drive north to Burlington and Exit 230/Highway 20. Turn west on Highway 20 and drive 23 miles (Whidbey Island) to Libbey Road (eight miles past Oak Harbor). Turn right and drive 1.5 miles to Hill Valley Drive. Turn left and enter the park.

Contact: Fort Ebey State Park, 400 Hill Valley Drive, Coupeville, WA 98239, 360/678-4636; state park information, 360/902-8844.

21 FORT CASEY STATE PARK

Rating: 10

on Whidbey Island
See map pages 68–69

Fort Casey State Park features a lighthouse and sweeping views of Admiralty Inlet and the Strait of Juan de Fuca. The park has 10,180 feet of salt-water shoreline on Puget Sound at Admiralty Inlet and includes Keystone Spit, a two-mile stretch of land separating Admiralty Inlet and Crocket Lake. The park covers 467 acres, with

just 1.8 miles of hiking trails, but as part of Ebey's Landing National Historic Reserve, it contains a coast artillery post featuring four historic guns on display. It is also a designated area for remote-control glider flying, with a parade field popu-lar for kite flying. The lighthouse and interpretive center are open seasonally. Fishing is often good in this area, in season. Another highlight that attracts divers is the underwater park, protected from waves and currents by an artificial rock jetty. You can also take a ferry from here to Port Townsend on the Olympic Peninsula.

RV sites, facilities: There are 35 developed camp-sites for self-contained RVs up to 40 feet or tents and three primitive tent sites. Picnic tables and fire grills are provided. Restrooms, drinking water, flush toilets, cell phone reception, coin-operated showers, firewood, an interpretive center, a pic-nic area, and an amphitheater are available. Boat-launching facilities are located in the park. Groceries and an ATM are available within five miles. Some facilities are wheelchair-accessible. Leashed pets are permitted.

Reservations, fees: Reservations are not accept-ed. The fee is $10–16 per night, plus $10 per addi-tional vehicle per night. A senior discount is available. Open year-round.

Directions: From Seattle on I-5, drive north to Burlington and Exit 230/Highway 20. Turn west on Highway 20 and drive 35 miles to Coupeville. In Coupeville, turn right on Main Street and drive for five miles (the road becomes Engle Road) to the campground entrance on the right.

Contact: Fort Casey State Park, 1280 Fort Casey, Coupeville, WA 98239, 360/678-4519; state park information, 360/902-8844.

22 SOUTH WHIDBEY STATE PARK

Rating: 10

on Whidbey Island
See map pages 68–69

This park is located on the southwest end of Whidbey Island, covers 347 acres, and provides opportunities for hiking, picnicking, and beach-combing along a sandy beach. There are spec-tacular views of Puget Sound and the Olympic Mountains. The park features old-growth forest, tidelands for clamming and crabbing (in season), and campsites set in the seclusion of a lush forest undergrowth. The park has 4,500 feet of saltwater shoreline on Admiralty Inlet and 3.5 miles of hiking trails.

RV sites, facilities: There are 50 sites, some with partial hookups (30 amps), for RVs up to 45 feet or tents, six primitive tent sites, and one group site. Picnic tables and fire grills are provided. Restrooms, drinking water, flush toilets, coin-operated showers, an RV dump station, a pay phone, cell phone reception, firewood, ice, a picnic area with a log kitchen shelter, an amphitheater, interpretive activities, and a Junior Ranger program are available. An ATM is within six miles. Some facilities are wheelchair-accessible. Leashed pets are permitted.

Reservations, fees: Reserve at 888/CAMP-OUT (888/226-7688) or online at www.parks.wa.gov /reservations ($7 reservation fee). The fee is $10–22 per night, plus $10 per night for each additional vehicle. A senior discount is available. Major credit cards are accepted. Open late February to October.

Directions: From Seattle on I-5, drive north to Burlington and the Highway 20 exit. Take Highway 20/525 west and drive 28 miles (past Coupeville on Whidbey Island) to where Highway 20 turns into Highway 525 west. Drive to Smugglers Cove Road (the park access road, well marked). The park can also be reached easily with a ferry ride from Mulkilteo (located southeast of Everett) to Clinton (this also makes a great bike trip to the state park).

Contact: South Whidbey State Park, 360/331-4559, fax 360/331-7669; state park information, 360/902-8844.

23 CAMANO ISLAND STATE PARK

Rating: 10

on Camano Island
See map pages 68–69

This park features panoramic views of Puget Sound, the Olympic Mountains, and Mount Rainier. Set on the southwest point of Camano Island, near Lowell Point and Elger Bay along the Saratoga Passage, this wooded camp offers quiet and private campsites. The park covers 134 acres and features 6,700 feet of rocky shoreline

and beach, three miles of hiking trails, and just one mile of bike trails. Flounder and salmon fishing are good in season. Clamming is excellent during low tides in June. A self-guided nature trail is also available.

RV sites, facilities: There are 87 developed campsites for self-contained RVs up to 45 feet or tents, one primitive tent site, and one group camp for up to 200 people. Picnic tables and fire grills are provided. Restrooms, drinking water, flush toilets, coin-operated showers, cell phone reception, firewood, an RV dump station, a playground, a picnic area with a kitchen shelter, summer interpretive programs, an amphitheater, and a large field for ballgames in the day-use area are available. Boat-launching facilities are located in the park. An 18-hole golf course is nearby. An ATM and a pay phone are within four miles. Leashed pets are permitted.

Reservations, fees: Reservations are not accepted for family camping. Reservations are required for the group camp; phone 360/387-3031. The fee is $10–15 per night, plus $10 per additional vehicle per night. The group reservation fee is $25, plus $2 per person per night. A senior discount is available. Open year-round.

Directions: From Seattle on I-5, drive north (17 miles north of Everett) to Exit 212. Take Exit 212 to Highway 532. Drive west on Highway 532 to Stanwood and continue three miles (to Camano Island) to a fork. Bear left at the fork and continue south on East Camano Drive (the road becomes Elger Bay Road) to Mountain View Road. Turn right and drive two miles (climbs a steep hill) and continue to Lowell Point Road. Turn left and continue to the park entrance at the end of the road. (The park is 14 miles southwest of Stanwood).

Contact: Camano Island State Park, 360/387-3031; state park information, 360/902-8844.

24 KAYAK POINT COUNTY PARK

Rating: 5

on Puget Sound
See map pages 68–69

This camp usually fills on summer weekends. Set on the shore of Puget Sound, this large, wooded county park covers 430 acres on Port Susan.

It provides good windsurfing and whale-watching and can be good for crabbing and fishing (in season). An 18-hole golf course is nearby.

RV sites, facilities: There are 34 sites with partial hookups (20, 30 amps), including some drive-through sites, for RVs up to 32 feet or tents, and 10 yurts with heat and electricity for up to six people. Picnic tables and fire rings are provided. Restrooms, drinking water, flush toilets, showers, firewood, a pay phone, cell phone reception, modem access, a picnic area with covered shelter, and a 300-foot fishing pier are available. Boat docks and launching facilities are located in the park. An ATM is within five miles. Some facilities are wheelchair-accessible. Leashed pets are permitted.

Reservations, fees: Reservations are accepted up to one year in advance for campsites and yurts. The fees are $12–20 per night for campsite and $40 per night for yurts. Major credit cards are accepted. Open year-round.

Directions: From Seattle on I-5, drive north past Everett to Exit 199 (Tulalip) at Marysville. Take Exit 199, bear left on Tulalip Road, and drive west for 13 miles (road name changes to Marine Drive) through the Tulalip Indian Reservation to the park entrance road on the left (marked for Kayak Point). Turn left and drive .5 mile to the park.

Contact: Kayak Point County Park, Snohomish County, 15610 Marine Dr., Stanwood, WA 98292, 425/388-6600 or 360/652-7992, fax 425/377-9509, website: www.co.snohomish.wa.us/parks.

25 WENBERG STATE PARK

Rating: 8

on Lake Goodwin

See map pages 68–69

This state park is set along the east shore of Lake Goodwin, where the trout fishing can be great. The park covers 46 acres with 1,140 feet of shoreline frontage on the lake. Powerboats are allowed, and a seasonal concession stand provides food and fishing supplies. This is a popular weekend spot for Seattle area residents.

RV sites, facilities: There are 30 sites with partial hookups (30 amps), including 10 drive-through, for RVs up to 50 feet and 46 developed tent sites.

Picnic tables and fire grills are provided. Restrooms, drinking water, flush toilets, coin-operated showers, an RV dump station, cell phone reception, a sheltered picnic area, a store (seasonal), and a playground are available. Boat-launching facilities are located on Lake Goodwin. A pay phone is within 1.5 miles and an ATM is within six miles. Leashed pets are permitted.

Reservations, fees: Reserve at 888/CAMP-OUT (888/226-7688) or online at www.parks.wa.gov/reservations ($7 reservation fee). The fee is $16–22 per night, plus $10 per additional vehicle per night. Boat launching is $5. A senior discount is available. Major credit cards are accepted. Open year-round.

Directions: From Seattle on I-5, drive north to Exit 206. Take exit 206/Smokey Point (Highway 531), turn west and continue 4.5 miles East Lake Goodwin Road. Turn left and drive one mile to the park entrance on the right.

Contact: Wenberg State Park, 360/652-7417; state park information, 360/902-8844.

26 CEDAR GROVE SHORES RV PARK

Rating: 5

on Lake Goodwin

See map pages 68–69

This wooded resort is on the shore of Lake Goodwin near Wenberg State Park. The camp is a busy place in summer, with highlights including trout fishing, water-skiing, and swimming. Tent campers should try Lake Goodwin Resort. An 18-hole golf course is nearby.

RV sites, facilities: There are 48 sites with full hookups (30, 50 amps), including some drive-through, for RVs up to 40 feet. No tents are permitted. Restrooms, drinking water, flush toilets, coin-operated showers, a coin-operated laundry, an RV dump station (fee), propane, ice, a clubhouse, a recreation room, horseshoes, volleyball, and firewood are available. A store, an ATM, a pay phone, and a café are within one mile. Boat docks and launching facilities are within 1,000 feet on Lake Goodwin. Some facilities are wheelchair-accessible. Leashed pets are permitted.

Reservations, fees: Reservations are accepted. The fee is $20–28 per night, plus $4 per person (under 16 free) per night for more than two people. Major credit cards are accepted. Open year-round.

Directions: From Seattle on I-5, drive north to Exit 206 (10 miles north of Everett). Take Exit 206/Smokey Point and drive west for 2.2 miles to Lakewood Road. Turn right and drive 3.2 miles to Westlake Goodwin Road. Turn left (the park is marked) and drive .75 mile to the park on the left.

Contact: Cedar Grove Shores RV Park, 16529 West Lake Goodwin Rd., Stanwood, WA 98292, 360/652-7083 or 866/342-4981.

27 LAKE GOODWIN RESORT

Rating: 5

on Lake Goodwin

See map pages 68–69

This private campground is set on Lake Goodwin, which is known for good trout fishing. Motorboats are permitted on the lake, and an 18-hole golf course is located nearby. Other activities include swimming in the lake, horseshoes, shuffleboard, and a recreation field.

RV sites, facilities: There are 85 sites with partial or full hookups (30, 50 amps), including eight drive-through sites for RVs of any length, 11 tent sites, and four cabins. Picnic tables and fire grills are provided. Restrooms, drinking water, flush toilets, coin-operated showers, propane, an RV dump station, a pay phone, cell phone reception, an ATM, recreation equipment, a store, a coin-operated laundry, ice, a playground, and firewood are available. Boat moorage and a fishing pier are located nearby on Lake Goodwin. Small leashed pets are permitted in RV sites only.

Reservations, fees: Reservations are accepted; phone 800/242-8169. The fee is $18–40 per night; cabins are $60–85 per night. Major credit cards are accepted. Open year-round.

Directions: From Seattle on I-5, drive north to Exit 206 (10 miles north of Everett). Take Exit 206/Smokey Point, turn west, and drive two miles to Highway 531. Bear right on Highway 531 and drive to a stop sign at Lakewood Road. Turn right at Lakewood Road and drive 3.5 miles to the park on the left.

Contact: Lake Goodwin Resort, 4726 Lakewood Rd., Stanwood, WA 98292, 360/652-8169, fax 360/652-4025.

28 LAKESIDE RV PARK

Rating: 6

in the town of Everett

See map pages 68–69

With 100 of the 150 RV spaces dedicated to permanent rentals, this camp can be a crapshoot for vacationers in summer; the remaining 50 spaces get filled nightly with travelers all summer. The park is landscaped with annuals, roses, other perennials, and shrubs, which provide privacy and gardens for each site. There's an artificially constructed lake stocked with trout year-round, providing fishing for a fee.

RV sites, facilities: There are 150 sites (50 non-permanent), including some drive-through, with full hookups (20, 30, 50 amps) for RVs up to 50 feet and nine tent sites. Restrooms, drinking water, flush toilets, showers, a coin-operated laundry, propane, a playground, a modem hookup, cell phone reception, and pay phones are available. An ATM is within a quarter mile. Some facilities are wheelchair-accessible. Leashed pets are permitted.

Reservations, fees: Reservations are recommended; phone 800/468-7275. The fee is $31.31–34.79 per night. A senior discount is available. Major credit cards are accepted. Open year-round.

Directions: From Seattle on I-5, drive north to Everett and Exit 186. Take Exit 186 and turn west on 128th Street. Drive about two miles to Old Highway 99. Turn left (south) on Old Highway 99 and drive .25 mile to the park on the left.

Contact: Lakeside RV Park, 12321 Hwy. 99 S, Everett, WA 98204, 425/347-2970 or 800/468-7275, fax 206/347-9052.

29 LAKE PLEASANT RV PARK

Rating: 6

on Lake Pleasant

See map pages 68–69

A large, developed camp geared primarily toward RVers, this park is located on Lake Pleasant. The setting is pretty, with lakeside sites and plenty of trees. Just off the highway, it's a popular camp, so expect lots of company, especially in summer. This is a good spot for a little trout fishing. Note that half of the 196 sites are permanent rentals. All sites are paved.

RV sites, facilities: There are 196 sites (half available for overnight use) with full hookups (30, 50 amps), including some drive-through sites, for RVs up to 45 feet. Picnic tables are provided. Restrooms, drinking water, flush toilets, showers, cable TV, cell phone reception, modem access, an RV dump station, two pay phones, a coin-operated laundry, a playground, and propane are available. An ATM is within a quarter mile. Some facilities are wheelchair-accessible. Leashed pets are permitted.

Reservations, fees: Reservations are recommended. The fee is $28 per night. Major credit cards are accepted. Open year-round.

Directions: From the junction of I-5 and I-405 (just south of Seattle), take I-405 and drive to Exit 26. Take that exit to the Bothell/Everett Highway over the freeway and drive south for about one mile; look for the park on the left side. It's marked by a large sign.

Contact: Lake Pleasant RV Park, 24025 Bothell/Everett Hwy. SE, Bothell, WA 98021, 425/487-1785 or 800/742-0386.

30 TRAILER INNS RV PARK AND RECREATION CENTER

Rating: 5

near Lake Sammamish State Park

See map pages 68–69

This park features all the amenities for RV travelers, and it's close to Lake Sammamish State Park, the closest park to downtown Seattle. Nearby recreation options include an 18-hole golf course, hiking trails, marked bike trails, and tennis courts.

RV sites, facilities: There are 103 sites, including half that are permanently rented and some drive-through sites, with partial or full hookups (30, 50 amps) for RVs up to 48 feet. Picnic tables are provided. Restrooms, drinking water, flush toilets, showers, propane, cell phone reception, a pay phone, modem access, a recreation hall, an indoor swimming pool, a hot tub and sauna, a

laundry room, ice, and a playground are available. An ATM, a store, and a café are within one mile. Leashed pets are permitted.

Reservations, fees: Reservations are accepted. The fee is $22–40 per night. Major credit cards are accepted. Open year-round.

Directions: At the junction of I-5 and I-90 south of Seattle, turn east on I-90 and drive 1.5 miles to Exit 11A. Take Exit 11A (a two-avenue exit) and stay in the right lane for 150th Avenue SE. After the lanes split, stay in the left lane and drive to the intersection of 150th Avenue SE and 37th. Continue straight through the light and look for the park entrance at the fifth driveway on the right (about one mile from I-90).

Contact: Trailer Inns RV Park and Recreation Center, 15531 Southeast 37th St., Bellevue, WA 98006, 425/747-9181, 509/248-1142, or 800/659-4684, fax 425/747-0858.

31 VASA PARK RESORT

Rating: 5

on Lake Sammamish

See map pages 68–69

I was giving a seminar in Bellevue one evening when a distraught-looking couple walked in and pleaded, "Where can we camp tonight?" I answered, "Just look in the book," and they ended up staying at this camp. It was the easiest sale ever made. This is the most rustic of the parks in the immediate Seattle area. The resort is on the western shore of Lake Sammamish, and the state park is at the south end of the lake. An 18-hole golf course, hiking trails, and marked bike trails are close by. The park is within easy driving distance of Seattle.

RV sites, facilities: There are 16 sites with partial hookups (30 amps) for RVs or tents and six sites with full hookups for RVs of any length. Picnic tables are provided. Restrooms, drinking water, flush toilets, coin-operated showers, a pay phone, cell phone reception, an RV dump station, a playground, and a boat-launching facility are available. Propane, firewood, a store, an ATM, and a café are available within one mile. Leashed pets are permitted within the campsites only.

Reservations, fees: Reservations are accepted. The fee is $20–25 per night, plus $3.25 per person per night for more than two people. Open mid-May to mid-October.

Directions: In Bellevue, drive east on I-90 to Exit 13. Take Exit 13 to West Lake Sammamish Parkway SE and drive north for one mile; the resort is on the right.

Contact: Vasa Park Resort, 3560 West Lake Sammamish Parkway SE, Bellevue, WA 98008, 425/746-3260, fax 425/746-0301.

32 ISSAQUAH VILLAGE RV PARK

Rating: 7

in Issaquah
See map pages 68–69

Although Issaquah Village RV Park doesn't allow tents, it's set in a beautiful environment ringed by the Cascade Mountains, making it a scenic alternative in the area. Lake Sammamish State Park is just a few miles north. Most of the sites are asphalt, and 20 percent are long-term rentals.

RV sites, facilities: There are 56 sites, including two drive-through sites, with full hookups for RVs of any length. No tents are allowed. Restrooms, drinking water, flush toilets, showers, cable TV, modem access, cell phone reception, an RV dump station, a pay phone, a coin-operated laundry, and propane are available. Picnic areas and a playground are also on-site. An ATM is within 1.5 miles. Some facilities are wheelchair-accessible. Leashed pets are permitted.

Reservations, fees: Reservations are recommended. The fee is $30–35 per night. Major credit cards are accepted. Open year-round.

Directions: From Seattle on I-405 (preferred) or I-5, drive to the junction of I-90. Take I-90 east and drive 17 miles to Issaquah and Exit 17. Take Exit 17 for Front Street and turn left; drive under the freeway and look for the first right. Take the first right for a very short distance and keep bearing right on the frontage road that parallels the freeway. Drive .25 mile to the park on the left.

Contact: Issaquah Village RV Park, 650 First Ave. NE, Issaquah, WA 98027, 425/392-9233 or 800/258-9233, website: http://home.earthlink.net/~issaquahrv.com.

33 BLUE SKY RV PARK

Rating: 5

near Lake Sammamish State Park
See map pages 68–69

Blue Sky RV Park is situated in an urban setting just outside of Seattle. It provides a good off-the-beaten-path alternative to the more crowded metro area yet is still only a short drive from the main attractions in the city. Nearby Lake Sammamish State Park provides more rustic recreation opportunities, including hiking and fishing. All sites are paved and level.

RV sites, facilities: There are 51 sites with full hookups (30, 50 amps), including some long-term rentals, for RVs. Restrooms, drinking water, flush toilets, showers, cable TV, modem access, cell phone reception, a coin-operated laundry, and a covered picnic pavilion with a barbecue are available. A pay phone and an ATM are within a half mile. Leashed pets are permitted.

Reservations, fees: Reservations are not accepted. The fee is $30 per night, plus $5 per person per night for more than two people. Open year-round.

Directions: From Seattle on I-5, drive to the junction with Highway 90. Turn east on Highway 90 and drive 22 miles to Exit 22 (Preston/Falls City exit). Take that exit to SE 82nd Street. Turn right on SE 82nd Street and drive a very short distance to 302nd Avenue SE. Turn left and drive .5 mile to the campground entrance at the end of the road.

Contact: Blue Sky RV Park, 9002 302nd Ave. SE, Issaquah, WA 98027, 425/222-7910.

34 SALTWATER STATE PARK

Rating: 7

near Seattle
See map pages 68–69

This state park is located halfway between Tacoma and Seattle. The cities jointly and literally buried a hatchet in the park to symbolize the end of their mutual competition. Campers still don't have it so peaceful, though. The camp is set on the flight path of Seattle-Tacoma International Airport, so it is often noisy from the jets. The park features tidepools and marine life, including salmon spawning in McSorley Creek in the fall. Scuba diving is good here with a nearby underwater reef. There are three trails for hiking and biking and four buildings from the 1930s built by the Civilian Conservation Corps. A Junior Ranger program is available. You'll find beautiful views of Maury and Vashon Islands and of the Olympic Mountains. Beaches offer clamming and picnic facilities.

RV sites, facilities: There are 52 sites for self-contained RVs up to 50 feet or tents and a group camp. Picnic tables and fire grills are provided. Restrooms, drinking water, flush toilets, showers, an RV dump station, a playground, a pay phone, cell phone reception, a picnic area, horseshoes, volleyball, interpretive activities, and firewood are available. A store, a restaurant, an ATM, and ice are available within one mile. Boat buoys are nearby on Puget Sound. Some facilities are wheelchair-accessible. Leashed pets are permitted.

Reservations, fees: Reservations are not accepted for individual sites. To reserve the group camp, phone 253/661-4956. The fee is $10–16 per night, plus $10 per additional vehicle per night. A senior discount is available. Open April to mid-September.

Directions: From the junction of I-5 and Highway 516 (located between Seattle and Tacoma three miles south of SeaTac International Airport), take Highway 516 and drive west for two miles to Highway 509. Turn left and drive one mile to the park access road on the right. Turn right (well marked) and drive .5 mile to the park on the shore of Puget Sound.

Contact: Saltwater State Park, 253/661-4956, fax 206/870-4294; state park information, 360/902-8844.

35 SEATTLE/TACOMA KOA

Rating: 5

in Kent
See map pages 68–69

This is a popular urban campground, not far from the highway yet in a pleasant setting. The sites are spacious and most are drive-through to accommodate large RVs. During the summer, take a tour of Seattle from the campground. The tour highlights include the Space Needle, Pikes Place Market, Safeco Field, and Puget Sound. A public golf course is located nearby.

RV sites, facilities: There are 140 sites, most with full hookups and the rest with partial hookups (30, 50 amps), for RVs of any length, and 18 tent sites. Restrooms, drinking water, flush toilets, showers, an RV dump station, a pay phone, cell phone reception, a coin-operated laundry, limited groceries, propane, ice, RV supplies, free movies, and a pancake breakfast are available. A large playground, a game room, a heated swimming pool, and a recreation hall are also on-site. An ATM is within two blocks. Some facilities are wheelchair-accessible. Leashed pets are permitted.

Reservations, fees: Reservations are recommended. The fee is $30–48 per night, plus $3.50 per person per night for more than two people. Major credit cards are accepted. Open year-round.

Directions: On I-5 in Seattle, take Exit 152 for 188th Street/Orillia. Drive east on Orillia for 2.5 miles (the road becomes 212th Street) to the campground on the right.

Contact: Seattle/Tacoma KOA, 5801 South 212th St., Kent, WA 98032, 253/872-8652 or 800/562-1892, fax 206/872-9221, website: www.koa.com.

36 DASH POINT STATE PARK

Rating: 8

near Tacoma
See map pages 68–69

This urban state park on Puget Sound features unobstructed water views. The park covers 398 acres, with 3,301 feet of saltwater shoreline and 11 miles of trails for hiking and biking. Fishing, windsurfing, swimming, and mountain biking are all popular. Tacoma offers a variety of activities and attractions, including the Tacoma Art Museum (with a children's gallery); the Washington State Historical Society Museum; the Seymour Botanical Conservatory at Wrights Park; Point Defiance Park, Zoo, and Aquarium; the Western Washington Forest Industries Museum; and the Fort Lewis Military Museum.

RV sites, facilities: There are 28 sites with partial hookups (30 amps) for RVs up to 35 feet,

WASHINGTON

110 tent sites, and two hike-in/bike-in sites. Picnic tables and fire grills are provided. Restrooms, drinking water, flush toilets, four pay phones, cell phone reception, showers, an RV dump station, a playground, an amphitheater, interpretive activities, two sheltered picnic areas, and firewood are available. An ATM is within 1.5 miles. Leashed pets are permitted.

Reservations, fees: Reserve at 888/CAMP-OUT (888/226-7688) or online at www.parks.wa.gov /reservations ($7 reservation fee). The fee is $10–22 per night, plus $10 per additional vehicle per night. A senior discount is available. Major credit cards are accepted in high season only. Open year-round.

Directions: On I-5, drive to Exit 143/320th Street. Take that exit and turn west on 320th Street and drive four miles to 47th Street (a T intersection). Turn right on 47th Street and drive to Highway 509 (another T intersection). Turn left on Highway 509/SW Dash Point Road and drive one mile to the park. Note: The camping area is on the west side of the road; the day-use area is on the east side of the road.

Contact: Dash Point State Park, 253/661-4955, fax 253/661-4995; state park information, 360/902-8844.

37 GAME FARM WILDERNESS PARK
🚶 ♿ 🎣 🐕 ♿ 🚐 ⛺

Rating: 6

on the Stuck River in Auburn

See map pages 68–69

The Game Farm Wilderness Park is just minutes from downtown Auburn and a short drive from Mount Rainier, the Seattle waterfront, and the Cascade Mountains. Located along the scenic Stuck River, it was demarcated with group outings in mind.

RV sites, facilities: There are six group campsites with partial hookups (20, 30 amps) for RVs or tents, with four sleeping units per site and a maximum of 16 people per site. Picnic tables and fire grills are provided. Restrooms, drinking water, flush toilets, a picnic shelter, cell phone reception, and an RV dump station are available. An ATM and pay phone are within two miles. Some facilities are wheelchair-accessible. Leashed pets are permitted.

Reservations, fees: Reservations are required in person at the Parks and Recreation Department. The fee for group sites is $25 per night for city residents and $35 for nonresidents, with a one-week maximum. Open April to October.

Directions: On I-5 (north of Tacoma), drive to Exit 142 and Highway 18. Turn east on Highway 18 and drive to the Auburn/Enumclaw exit. Take that exit and drive to the light at Auburn Way. Turn left on Auburn Way South and drive one mile to Howard Road. Exit to the right on Howard Road and drive .2 mile to the stop sign at R Street. Turn right on R Street and drive 1.5 miles to Stuck River Drive SE (just over the river). Turn left and drive .25 mile upriver to the park on the left at 2401 Stuck River Drive.

Contact: City of Auburn Parks and Recreation Department, 25 West Main St., Auburn, WA 98001, 253/931-3043, website: www.ci.auburn.wa.us.

38 MAJESTIC MOBILE MANOR RV PARK
🚶 🚲 🏊 ⛵ 🚣 🐕 🚐 ⛺

Rating: 7

on the Puyallup River

See map pages 68–69

This clean, pretty park along the Puyallup River with views of Mount Rainier caters to RVers. Recreation options within 10 miles include an 18-hole golf course, a full-service marina, and tennis courts. For information on the attractions in Tacoma, see the description of Dash Point State Park in this chapter.

RV sites, facilities: There are 118 sites with full hookups (30, 50 amps), including half reserved for long-term rentals, for RVs of any length and 12 tent sites available May to October only. Restrooms, drinking water, flush toilets, showers, propane, a pay phone, modem access, cell phone reception, an RV dump station, a recreation hall, a store, a coin-operated laundry, ice, and a swimming pool are available. Leashed pets are permitted.

Reservations, fees: Reservations are accepted. The fee is $16–24 per night, plus $2 per person per night for more than two people. Open year-round.

Directions: From near Tacoma on I-5, take Exit 135 to Highway 167. Drive east on Highway 167

(River Road) for four miles to the park on the right.

Contact: Majestic Mobile Manor RV Park, 7022 River Rd., Puyallup, WA 98371, 253/845-3144 or 800/348-3144, fax 253/841-2248, website: www.majesticrvpark.com.

39 OLYMPIA CAMPGROUND

Rating: 7

near Olympia
See map pages 68–69

This campground in a natural, wooded setting has all the comforts. Nearby recreation options include an 18-hole golf course, hiking trails, marked bike trails, and tennis courts.

RV sites, facilities: There are 95 sites with partial or full hookups (30 amps), including 40 drive-through, for RVs of any length or tents and two cabins. Picnic tables are provided. Fire rings are provided at some sites. Restrooms, drinking water, flush toilets, showers, propane, an RV dump station, a recreation hall, gas, cell phone reception, two pay phones, modem access, an ATM, a store, a coin-operated laundry, ice, a playground, a heated swimming pool in the summer, and firewood are available. A café is within two miles. Leashed pets are permitted with permission.

Reservations, fees: Reservations are accepted. The fee is $20–28 per night for two people, plus $4 per person per night for more than two people. Cabins are $42 per night for two people. Major credit cards are accepted. Open year-round.

Directions: From Olympia on I-5, take Exit 101 to Airdustrial Way. Bear east for .25 mile to Center Street. Turn right on Center Street and drive one mile to 83rd Avenue. Turn right on 83rd Avenue and drive .1 mile to the park on the left.

Contact: Olympia Campground, 1441 83rd Ave. SW, Olympia, WA 98512, 360/352-2551, website: www.olympiacampground.com.

40 NISQUALLY PLAZA RV PARK

Rating: 5

near McAlister Creek
See map pages 68–69

This campground is located on McAlister Creek, where salmon fishing and boating are popular. Nearby recreation opportunities include an 18-hole golf course and the Nisqually National Wildlife Refuge, which offers seven miles of foot trails for viewing a great variety of flora and fauna.

RV sites, facilities: There are 51 sites with full hookups, including six drive-through, for RVs up to 60 feet. Picnic tables are provided. Restrooms, drinking water, flush toilets, coin-operated showers, a pay phone, modem access, cell phone reception, an ATM, a restaurant and pub, a gift shop, marine supplies, boat-launching facilities, cable TV, a store, a café, a coin-operated laundry, electronic gate entry, ice, a playground, and a seasonal swimming pool are available. Some facilities are wheelchair-accessible. Leashed pets are permitted. Gates close at 11p.m.

Reservations, fees: Reservations are accepted. The fee is $25 per night, plus $2 per person per night for more than two people. Open year-round.

Directions: In Olympia on I-5, take Exit 114 and drive a short distance to Martin Way. Turn right and drive a short distance to the first road (located between two gas stations), a private access road for the park. Turn right and drive to the park.

Contact: Nisqually Plaza RV Park, 10220 Martin Way E, Olympia, WA 98516, 360/491-3831.

 **Washington**

Chapter 3
The Northern Cascades

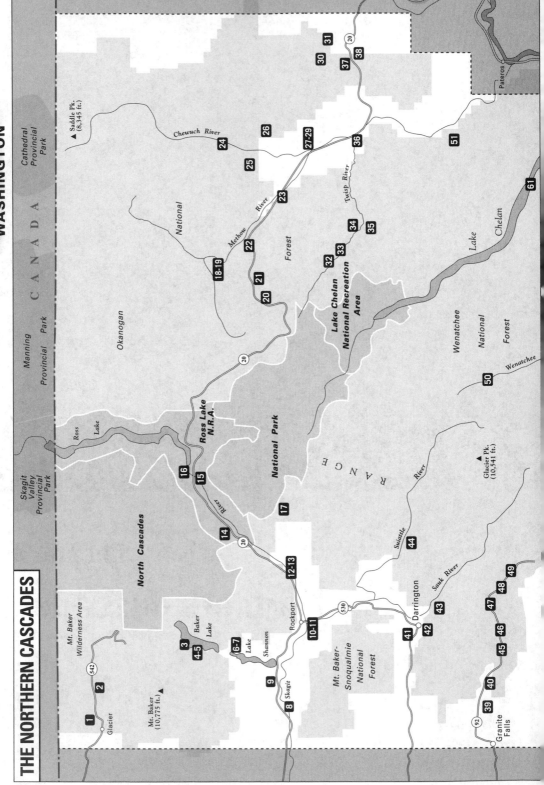

THE NORTHERN CASCADES

WASHINGTON

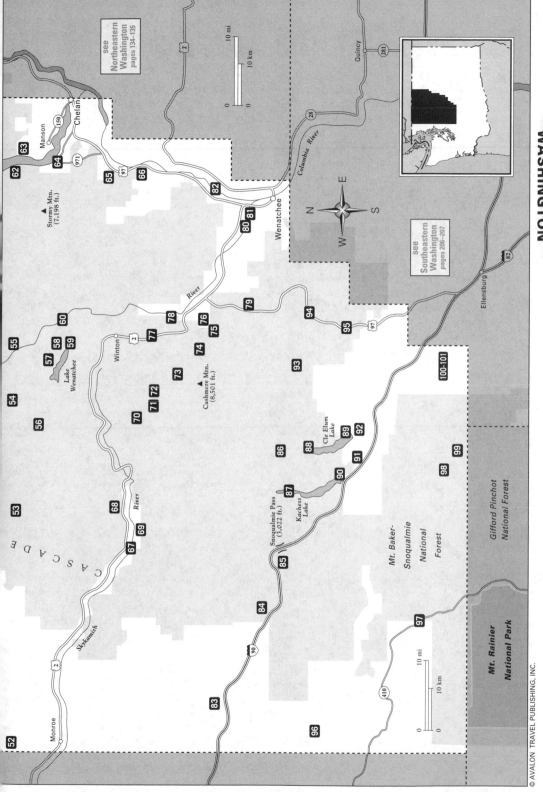

Chapter 3—The Northern Cascades

Mount Baker is the centerpiece in a forested landscape with hundreds of lakes, rivers, and hidden campgrounds. The only limit here is weather. The Northern Cascades are deluged with the nation's highest snowfall in winter; Mount Baker often receives a foot a day for weeks. Although that shortens the recreation season to just a few months in summer, it has another effect as well. With so many recreation destinations available for such a short time—literally hundreds over the course of three or four months—many remain largely undiscovered.

The vast number of forests, lakes, and streams can make choosing your destination the most difficult decision of all. With so many stellar spots to choose from, newcomers will be well served starting at the state parks, which offer beautiful settings that are easy to reach. Many camps set along roads provide choice layover spots for vacationing travelers.

After awhile, though, searching for the lesser-known camps in the national forests becomes more appealing. Many beautiful spots are set alongside lakes and streams, often with trailheads for hikes into nearby wilderness. These areas are among the wildest in America, featuring abundant wildlife, good fishing, and great hiking.

It's true that anybody can get an overview of the area by cruising the highways and camping at the roadside spots we list. But you can take this one the extra mile. Your dream spot may be waiting out there.

1 DOUGLAS FIR

Rating: 10

**on the Nooksack River in Mt. Baker–
Snoqualmie National Forest**

See map pages 90–91

Set along the Nooksack River, this camp features river views from some campsites. It is a beautiful camp, surrounded by old-growth Douglas fir, silver fir, and western hemlock. Trout fishing is available on the river, and there are hiking trails in the area, with a nearby trailhead.

RV sites, facilities: There are 28 sites for RVs up to 31 feet, trailers, or tents. Picnic tables and fire grills are provided. Drinking water, a picnic shelter, and vault toilets are available. A store, a café, a coin-operated laundry, a pay phone, and ice are available within five miles. Leashed pets are permitted.

Reservations, fees: Reservations are recommended. Reserve at 877/444-6777 or online at www.reserveusa.com ($9 reservation fee). The fee is $14 per night. Open May to September.

Directions: From Bellingham on I-5, take the Highway 542 exit and drive 31 miles to Glacier. Continue two miles northeast on Highway 542 to the campground on the left.

Contact: Mt. Baker–Snoqualmie National Forest, Mt. Baker Ranger District, Sedro-Woolley, WA 98284, 360/856-5700, fax 360/856-1934.

2 SILVER FIR

Rating: 9

on the North Fork of the Nooksack River in Mt. Baker–Snoqualmie National Forest

See map pages 90–91

This campground is set on the North Fork of the Nooksack River. It is within 30 minutes of the Heather Meadows area, which provides some of the best hiking trails in the entire region. In addition, a one-mile round-trip to Artist Ridge promises views of Mount Baker and Mount Shuksan. The first part of the trail to the first viewpoint is wheelchair-accessible. Fishing is available nearby, and in the winter the area offers cross-country skiing. You're strongly advised to obtain a U.S. Forest Service map in order to take maxi-

mum advantage of the recreational opportunities in the area.

RV sites, facilities: There are 20 sites for RVs up to 21 feet, trailers, or tents. Picnic tables and barbecue grills are provided. Drinking water, vault toilets, and a group picnic shelter are available. Leashed pets are permitted.

Reservations, fees: Reservations are accepted; reserve at 877/444-6777 or online at www.reserveusa.com ($9 reservation fee). The fee is $14 per night. A senior discount is available. Open May to September.

Directions: From I-5 at Bellingham, turn east on Highway 542 and drive 31 miles to Glacier. Continue east on Highway 542 for 12.5 miles to the campground on the right.

Contact: Mt. Baker–Snoqualmie National Forest, Mt. Baker Ranger District, 810 Rte. 20, Sedro-Woolley, WA 98284, 360/856-5700, fax 360/856-1934.

3 PARK CREEK

Rating: 6

near Baker Lake in Mt. Baker–Snoqualmie National Forest

See map pages 90–91

This pretty camp is set at an elevation of 800 feet on Park Creek amid a heavily wooded area comprised of old-growth Douglas fir and western hemlock. Park Creek is a feeder stream to nearby Baker Lake. The camp is primitive and small but gets its fair share of use.

RV sites, facilities: There are 11 sites for small RVs or tents. Picnic tables are provided. Vault toilets are available, but there is no drinking water. Boat docks, launching facilities, and rentals are nearby on Baker Lake. Leashed pets are permitted.

Reservations, fees: Reservations are recommended; reserve at 877/444-6777 or online at www.reserveusa.com ($9 reservation fee). The fee is $10 per night. A senior discount is available. Open mid-May to early September.

Directions: From I-5 at Burlington, turn east on State Route 20 and drive approximately 24 miles to Milepost 82 and Baker Lake Highway (Forest Road 11). Turn north on Baker Lake Highway and drive about 19.5 miles to Forest Road

1144. Turn left (northwest) and drive about 200 yards to the campground on the left. Obtaining a U.S. Forest Service map is helpful.

Contact: Mt. Baker–Snoqualmie National Forest, Mt. Baker Ranger District, 810 Rte. 20, Sedro-Woolley, WA 98284, 360/856-5700, fax 360/856-1934.

4 BOULDER CREEK

Rating: 8

near Baker Lake in Mt. Baker–Snoqualmie National Forest

See map pages 90–91

This camp provides an alternative to Horseshoe Cove. It is set on Boulder Creek about one mile from the shore of Baker Lake. Fishing is fair here for rainbow trout but is typically far better at Baker Lake. A boat launch is located at Panorama Point, about 15 minutes away. Wild berries can be found in the area in season. The campground offers prime views of Mount Baker.

RV sites, facilities: There are eight sites for RVs up to 30 feet or tents and a group site. Picnic tables and fire grills are provided. Pit toilets are available, but there is no drinking water. Boat docks and launching facilities are nearby on Baker Lake. Leashed pets are permitted.

Reservations, fees: Reservations are required for group sites and are available for some family sites; reserve at 877/444-6777 or online at www.reserveusa.com ($9 reservation fee). The fee is $10 per night for family sites and $40–55 per night for group sites. A senior discount is available. Open mid-May to early September.

Directions: From I-5 at Burlington, turn east on State Route 20 and drive approximately 24 miles to Milepost 82 and Baker Lake Highway (Forest Road 11). Turn north on Baker Lake Highway and drive 17.4 miles to the campground on the right.

Contact: Mt. Baker–Snoqualmie National Forest, Mt. Baker Ranger District, 810 Rte. 20, Sedro-Woolley, WA 98284, 360/856-5700, fax 360/856-1934.

5 PANORAMA POINT

Rating: 10

on Baker Lake in Mt. Baker–Snoqualmie National Forest

See map pages 90–91

With incredible scenic views of Mount Baker, Mount Shuk, Baker Lake, and Anderson Mountain, this camp is true to its name. Panorama Point is a well-maintained campground on the northwest shore of Baker Lake. The reservoir is one of the better fishing lakes in the area, often with good prospects for rainbow trout. Powerboating and water-skiing are permitted. Hiking trails are nearby.

RV sites, facilities: There are 15 sites for RVs up to 30 feet, trailers, or tents. Picnic tables are provided. Drinking water and vault toilets are available. A boat ramp is adjacent to the camp. Boat docks and rentals are nearby. Leashed pets are permitted.

Reservations, fees: Reservations are accepted for some sites; reserve at 877/444-6777 or online at www.reserveusa.com ($9 reservation fee). The fee is $14 per night. A senior discount is available. Open May to mid-September.

Directions: From I-5 at Burlington, turn east on State Route 20 and drive approximately 24 miles to Milepost 82 and Baker Lake Highway (Forest Road 11). Turn north on Baker Lake Highway and drive 18.7 miles to the campground entrance on the right on the shore of Baker.

Contact: Mt. Baker–Snoqualmie National Forest, Mt. Baker Ranger District, 810 Rte. 20, Sedro-Woolley, WA 98284, 360/856-5700, fax 360/856-1934.

6 HORSESHOE COVE

Rating: 9

on Baker Lake in Mt. Baker–Snoqualmie National Forest

See map pages 90–91

This camp is set along 5,000-acre Baker Lake. Anglers will often find good fishing for rainbow trout and kokanee salmon. Other highlights include swimming access from the campground and a boat ramp. Some hiking trails can be found nearby. The Baker Lake Basin has many trails, and the Mt. Baker National Recreation area is available within 30 minutes.

RV sites, facilities: There are 34 sites for RVs up to 30 feet, trailers, or tents and three group sites. Picnic tables and fire grills are provided. Drinking water and flush and vault toilets are available. A boat ramp and swimming beach are adjacent to camp. Leashed pets are permitted.

Reservations, fees: Reservations are accepted for some sites; reserve at 877/444-6777 or online at www.reserveusa.com ($9 reservation fee). The fee is $14 per night for family sites or $75 per night for group sites. Reservations are required for group sites. A senior discount is available. Open May to September.

Directions: From I-5 at Burlington, turn east on State Route 20 and drive approximately 24 miles to Milepost 82 and the Baker Lake Highway (Forest Road 11). Turn north on Baker Lake Highway and drive about 14.8 miles to Forest Road 1118. Turn east on Forest Road 1118 and drive two miles to the campground. A U.S. Forest Service map is recommended.

Contact: Mt. Baker–Snoqualmie National Forest, Mt. Baker Ranger District, 810 Rte. 20, Sedro-Woolley, WA 98284, 360/856-5700, fax 360/856-1934.

▨ BAY VIEW NORTH GROUP & SOUTH GROUP

Rating: 9

on Baker Lake in Mt. Baker–Snoqualmie National Forest
See map pages 90–91

These are both group camps set along Baker Lake. They are located in forest, though not dense forest, and there is an open feel to the area here. Many sites are close to the water. Baker Lake covers 5,000 acres and offers fishing for rainbow trout and kokanee salmon.

RV sites, facilities: There are two group sites at separate camps for 25 people with RVs, trailers, or tents. Picnic tables and fire grills are provided. Vault toilets are available. No drinking water is available. A boat ramp is located nearby near Horseshoe Cove Camp. Leashed pets are permitted.

Reservations, fees: Reserve at 877/444-6777 or online at www.reserveusa.com ($9 reservation fee). The fee is $75 per night. Major credit cards are accepted. Open mid-May to mid-September, weather permitting.

Directions: From I-5 at Burlington, turn east on State Route 20 and drive approximately 24 miles to Milepost 82 and the Baker Lake Highway (Forest Road 11). Turn north on Baker Lake Highway and drive about 14.8 miles to Forest Road 1118. Turn east on Forest Road 1118 and drive two miles to the campground (adjacent to Horseshoe Cove). A U.S. Forest Service map is recommended.

Contact: Mt. Baker–Snoqualmie National Forest, Mt. Baker Ranger District, 810 Rte. 20, Sedro-Woolley, WA 98284, 360/856-5700, fax 360/856-1934.

▨ RASAR STATE PARK

Rating: 8

on the Skagit River
See map pages 90–91

This park borders North Cascade National Park and is also near 10,778-foot Mount Baker and the Baker River watershed. Fishing and hiking are the attractions here. This park, the newest in the Washington State Parks system, was built with the goal to accommodate disabled campers in mind. Special sites, trails, and shower facilities are available. The elevation is 4,000 feet.

RV sites, facilities: There are 50 sites, including 20 with full hookups (30 amps) for RVs up to 40 feet, trailers, and tents, three primitive hike-in/bike-ins sites, 10 walk-in sites at which two four-person Adirondack shelters are available, and three group camps. Picnic tables and fire grills are provided. Restrooms, drinking water, flush toilets, coin-operated showers, cell phone reception, and a kitchen shelter are available. Firewood gathering is prohibited, but firewood is available for purchase. A pay phone is within two miles, and an ATM is within seven miles. Leashed pets are permitted.

Reservations, fees: Reservations are accepted. The fee is $10–22 per night, plus $10 per additional vehicle per night. Open year-round, weather permitting.

Directions: From Seattle, drive north on I-5 to

Burlington and the Highway 20 exit. Turn east on Highway 20/North Cascade Highway and drive 20 miles to Lusk Road. Turn right on Lusk Road and drive one mile to Cape Horn Road. Turn left on Cape Horn Road and drive one mile to the park entrance.

Contact: Rasar State Park, 38730 Cape Horn Rd., Concrete, WA 98237, 360/826-3942; state park information, 360/902-8844.

9 CREEKSIDE CAMPGROUND

Rating: 6

near the Skagit River
See map pages 90–91

This pretty, wooded campground is centrally located to nearby recreational opportunities at Baker Lake and the Skagit River. Trout fishing is good here, and tackle is available nearby.

RV sites, facilities: There are 29 sites with partial or full hookups (20, 30 amps) for RVs up to 40 feet, trailers, or tents plus several tent-only sites. Picnic tables are provided. Restrooms, drinking water, flush toilets, showers, an RV dump station, a store, a laundry room, horseshoes, a recreation hall, a pay phone, cell phone reception, and a playground are available. A café is within one mile. Leashed pets are permitted.

Reservations, fees: Reservations are recommended. The fees are $10 per night for tent sites and $22 per night for RV sites. Open year-round.

Directions: From Seattle, drive north on I-5 to Exit 232 (Cook Road). Take the exit up and over the highway to the flashing light and Cook Road. Turn left on Cook Road (Highway 20) and drive four miles to the light at Highway 20. Turn left at Highway 20 and drive 17 miles to Baker Lake Road (near Grasmere/Concrete). Turn left on Baker Lake Road and drive .25 mile to the camp.

Contact: Creekside Campground, 39602 Baker Lake Rd., Concrete, WA 98237, 360/826-3566.

10 ROCKPORT STATE PARK

Rating: 8

near the Skagit River
See map pages 90–91

This state park covers 670 acres and is set at the foot of Sauk Mountain (5,400 feet). This area was never logged, creating a natural forest with a canopy so dense that minimal sunlight penetrates to the ground. The park features more than 600 acres of old-growth Douglas firs. There are five miles of hiking trails amid this forest. In addition, a steep but climbable trail extends three miles (one-way) to the top of Sauk Mountain. The summit offers good views of the Skagat Valley and the Northern Cascades. A bonus at this camp: four Adirondack shelters, which have three sides and a roof. The Skagit River, a good steelhead stream, runs nearby. Rafting and kayaking are allowed on the Skagit, with the put-in not at the park, but on nearby State Route 20.

RV sites, facilities: There are 50 sites with full hookups (20 amps) for RVs up to 38 feet, three primitive tent sites, eight developed, walk-in tent sites, four Adirondack shelters, and one group tent site. Picnic tables and fire grills are provided. Restrooms, flush toilets, showers, cell phone reception, firewood, and an RV dump station are available. A store, gas, and ice are available within one mile. Some facilities are wheelchair-accessible. Leashed pets are permitted.

Reservations, fees: Reservations are required for the group site only; phone 360/853-8461. The fee is $10–22 per night, plus $10 per additional vehicle per night. Adirondack shelters are $21 per night. The group site is $40, plus $25 deposit, and $2 per person per night for over 20 people. Open April to late October.

Directions: From I-5 at Burlington, turn east on State Route 20 and drive 37 miles to Milepost 96. Look for the park entrance (one mile west of Rockport) on the right.

Contact: Rockport State Park, 51905 Rte. 20, Rockport, WA 98283, 360/853-8461; state park information, 360/902-8844.

11 HOWARD MILLER STEELHEAD PARK

Rating: 5

on the Skagit River
See map pages 90–91

This Skagit County Park provides grassy sites and access to the Skagit River, a designated Wild and Scenic River. The steelhead fishing is often good in season. Campsites at this spot are sunny and spacious. A bald eagle sanctuary is located at the east end of the park. November to January is the best time to see bald eagles here. This camp is most popular in July, August, and September, when the weather is best, but it also attracts visitors in early winter who arrive primarily for bald-eagle watching.

RV sites, facilities: There are 48 sites, including 18 with electrical and water hookups and 30 with electrical hookups (20, 30, 50 amps), for RVs of any length, trailers, or tents and 10 sites for tents. Picnic tables and fire pits are provided. Restrooms, drinking water, flush toilets, showers, an RV dump station, a clubhouse, a pay phone, a picnic shelter, Adirondacks (three-sided, roofed shelters), and a playground with horseshoes are available. A store and ice are available within one mile. Boat-launching facilities are located on the Skagit River. Some facilities and sites are wheelchair-accessible. Leashed pets are permitted.

Reservations, fees: Reservations are recommended ($2 reservation fee). The fee is $10–18 per night, plus $3 per additional vehicle per night. Major credit cards are accepted. Open year-round.

Directions: On I-5, drive to Exit 230/State Route 20 at Burlington. Turn east on State Route 20, and drive 44 miles to Rockport and Rockport-Darrington Road (Highway 530). Turn south and drive three blocks to the camp on the right.

Contact: Howard Miller Steelhead Park, P.O. Box 127, Rockport, WA 98283, 360/853-8808, fax 360/853-7315.

12 WILDERNESS VILLAGE AND RV PARK

Rating: 6

near the Skagit River
See map pages 90–91

This RV park is located near the Skagit River. Cool and wooded, it offers nice, grassy sites and nearby access to the river and fishing. Horseshoes and a sports field provide recreation alternatives. Rockport State Park and hiking trails are nearby. Bald eagles can often be viewed on the Skagit River in December and January. A one-mile trail (round-trip) can be accessed along the river.

RV sites, facilities: There are 32 drive-through sites with full hookups (30 amps) for RVs up to 45 feet and 20 tent sites. Picnic tables and fire rings are provided. Restrooms, flush toilets, coin-operated showers, cable TV, a pay phone, cell phone reception, a recreation hall, and a coin-operated laundry are available. A café and ice are available within two miles. An ATM is within 3.5 miles. Leashed pets are permitted.

Reservations, fees: Reservations are accepted. The fee is $12–19 per night. Open year-round.

Directions: From Burlington, drive east on State Route 20 for 44 miles to Rockport. Continue east on State Route 20 for four miles to the park. The park is between Mileposts 102 and 103 on the right.

Contact: Wilderness Village and RV Park, 57588 Rte. 20, Rockport, WA 98283, 360/873-2571.

13 SKAGIT RIVER RESORT

Rating: 9

on the Skagit River
See map pages 90–91

This beautiful camp is nestled in the trees close to the Skagit River. The resort covers 125 acres, including 1.5 miles of river frontage. One feature, a restaurant called "The Eatery," has received awards for its pecan pie and is also known for its home-style meals. Fishing, river walks, and nearby hiking trails among the glaciers and waterfalls can be accessed close to the campground. Three nearby hydroelectric plants also offer tours. This resort is popular from July to September, when reservations are often required to get a spot.

RV sites, facilities: There are 48 sites with full hookups (20, 30 amps), including some pull-through sites, for RVs, trailers, and tents plus 34 cabins and mobile homes. Restrooms, drinking water, flush toilets, coin-operated showers, an RV dump station, a pay phone, an ATM, modem access, a coin-operated laundry, horseshoes, a sports field for volleyball, croquet, and badminton, and a restaurant are available. Leashed pets are permitted.

Reservations, fees: Reservations are recommended. The fee is $10–20 per night. Major credit cards are accepted. There is an added charge for pets in the cabins. Open year-round.

Directions: From Burlington, drive east on State Route 20 for 44 miles to Rockport. Continue east on State Route 20 for six miles to the campground on the left (between Mileposts 103 and 104).

Contact: Skagit River Resort, 58468 Clark Cabin Rd., Rockport, WA 98283, 360/873-2250 or 800/273-2606, fax 360/873-4077, website: www.northcascades.com.

14 NEWHALEM CREEK & NEWHALEM CREEK GROUP

Rating: 7

near the Skagit River in Ross Lake National Recreation Area
See map pages 90–91

This spot is set along the Skagit River west of Newhalem at 500 feet elevation. Good hiking possibilities abound in the immediate area, and naturalist programs are available. Be sure to visit the North Cascades Visitor Center at the top of the hill from the campground. No firewood gathering is permitted here. If this camp is full, try Goodell Creek Campground, located just one mile west on State Route 20.

RV sites, facilities: There are 111 sites for RVs up to 32 feet or tents and two group sites for up to 24 people each. Picnic tables and fire grills are provided. Flush toilets, drinking water, cell phone reception, and an RV dump station are available. The group camp has a covered pavilion. A pay phone is within two miles. Some facilities are wheelchair-accessible. Leashed pets are permitted.

Reservations, fees: Reservations are not accepted for family sites but are required for group camps; phone 360/873-4590, ext. 17. The fee is $12 per night for family sites and $32 per night for group sites. A senior discount is available. Open mid-May to mid-October.

Directions: On I-5, drive to Exit 230/State Route 20 at Burlington. Turn east on State Route 20, and drive 46 miles to Marblemount. Continue 14 miles east on State Route 20 to the camp.

Contact: North Cascades National Park Headquarters, 810 Rte. 20, Sedro-Woolley, WA 98284, 360/856-5700, fax 360/856-1934.

15 GORGE LAKE

Rating: 9

on Gorge Lake on Skagit River in Ross Lake National Recreation Area
See map pages 90–91

This small camp is near the north shore of Gorge Lake, with lake views from many sites, and close to Colonial Creek and Goodell Creek. The elevation is 900 feet. Gorge Lake is very narrow and has trout fishing; check regulations. The camp is not well known and gets low use. One problem here is that the lake level can fluctuate (but not as much as Ross Lake), leaving the camps high and dry. No firewood gathering is permitted. Two other lakes are nearby on the Skagit River—Diablo Lake and Ross Lake.

RV sites, facilities: There are six sites for RVs up to 22 feet, trailers, or tents. Picnic tables and fire grills are provided. Vault toilets are available. No drinking water is available. Garbage must be packed out. A boat ramp is nearby. Leashed pets are permitted.

Reservations, fees: Reservations are not accepted. There is no fee for camping. Open late May to October.

Directions: From I-5 near Burlington, take exit 230 for State Route 20. Turn east on State Route 20 and drive 46 miles to Marblemount. Continue east on State Route 20 for another 20 miles to the junction with Diablo Road. Bear left and drive .6 mile to the campground on the right.

Contact: North Cascades National Park Headquarters, 810 Rte. 20, Sedro-Woolley, WA 98284, 360/856-5700, fax 360/856-1934.

16 COLONIAL CREEK

Rating: 7

on Diablo Lake in Ross Lake National Recreation Area
See map pages 90–91

Colonial Creek Campground (elevation 1,200 feet) sits along the shore of Diablo Lake in the Ross Lake National Recreation Area. The five-mile-long lake offers many hiking and fishing opportunities. A naturalist program and guided walks are available during the summer months. No firewood gathering is permitted at this campsite.

RV sites, facilities: There are 162 campsites for RVs, trailers, or tents, including a few walk-in tent sites; 18 lakefront sites remain open through the winter, but no services are available. Picnic tables and fire grills are provided. Flush toilets, drinking water, an RV dump station, three boat docks, and a boat ramp are available. Some facilities are wheelchair-accessible. Leashed pets are permitted.

Reservations, fees: Reservations are not accepted. The fee is $12 per night. A senior discount is available. Open mid-April to mid-October; 18 lakefront sites are open through the winter (no services provided).

Directions: From I-5 at Burlington, take Exit 230 and drive east to State Route 20. Turn east on State Route 20, drive 46 miles to Marblemount, and continue east on State Route 20 for 24 miles to the campground entrance.

Contact: North Cascades National Park Headquarters, 810 Rte. 20, Sedro-Woolley, WA 98284, 360/856-5700, fax 360/856-1934.

17 MARBLE CREEK

Rating: 7

on Marble Creek in Mt. Baker–Snoqualmie National Forest
See map pages 90–91

This primitive campground is set on Marble Creek amid old-growth Douglas fir and western hemlock. Fishing for rainbow trout is possible here. A trailhead to Hidden Lake just inside the boundary of North Cascades National Park can be found about five miles from camp at the end of Forest Road 1540. See a U.S. Forest Service map for details.

RV sites, facilities: There are 23 sites for RVs up to 25 feet, trailers, or tents. Picnic tables and fire grills are provided. Vault toilets are available, but there is no drinking water. Leashed pets are permitted.

Reservations, fees: Reserve at 877/444-6777 or online at www.reserveusa.com ($9 reservation fee). The fee is $10 per night. A senior discount is available. Open mid-May to mid-September.

Directions: From I-5, drive to Exit 230/State

Route 20 at Burlington. Turn east on State Route 20, and drive 46 miles to Marblemount and Forest Road 15 (Cascade River Road). Cross the bridge, turn east on Cascade River Road, and drive eight miles to Forest Road 1530. Turn south on Forest Road 1530 and drive one mile to the campground. Obtaining a U.S. Forest Service map is advised.

Contact: Mt. Baker–Snoqualmie National Forest, Mt. Baker Ranger District, 810 Rte. 20, Sedro-Woolley, WA 98284, 360/856-5700, fax 360/856-1934.

18 BALLARD

Rating: 6

near the Methow River in Okanogan and Wenatchee National Forests
See map pages 90–91

Ballard is set at an elevation of 2,521 feet, about a half mile from River Bend. Numerous hiking trails can be found in the area, as well as access to the West Fork Methow and Lost River Monument Creek trails. It is also possible to hike west and eventually hook up with the Pacific Crest Trail. See the description of Early Winters Campground in this chapter for area information. Livestock are not permitted in the campground, but a hitching rail and stock truck dock are available at the Robinson Creek Trailhead near the campground, where there are several primitive sites.

RV sites, facilities: There are six sites for RVs up to 20 feet, trailers, or tents. Picnic tables and fire grills are provided. Vault toilets are available, but there is no drinking water. Garbage must be packed out. Leashed pets are permitted. No livestock is permitted in camp.

Reservations, fees: Reservations are not accepted. The fee is $5 per night, plus $5 per additional vehicle per night. A senior discount is available. Open May to October, weather permitting.

Directions: From Burlington, drive east on State Route 20 for 120 miles to Mazama Road. Turn left on Mazama Road and drive .25 mile to County Road 9140. Turn left and drive northwest for seven miles to Lost River, where the pavement ends and the road soon becomes Forest Road 5400. Continue northwest on Forest Road 5400 for two miles to the campground on the left.

Contact: Okanogan and Wenatchee National Forests, Methow Valley Visitor Center, 24 West Chewuch Rd., Winthrop, WA 98862, 509/996-4000, fax 509/996-4051.

19 RIVER BEND

Rating: 6

on the Methow River in Okanogan and Wenatchee National Forests
See map pages 90–91

This campground is located along the Methow River at 2,600 feet elevation, about two miles from the boundary of the Pasayten Wilderness. Several trails near the camp provide access to the wilderness, and another trail follows the Methow River west for about eight miles before hooking up with the Pacific Crest Trail near Azurite Peak; a U.S. Forest Service map will show you the options. See the previous listing, Ballard Camp, for more information about the area.

RV sites, facilities: There are five sites for RVs up to 16 feet, trailers, or tents. Picnic tables and fire grills are provided. Vault toilets are available. No drinking water is available. Garbage must be packed out. A pay phone is within five miles. Leashed pets are permitted.

Reservations, fees: Reservations are not accepted. The fee is $5 per night, plus $5 per additional vehicle per night. A senior discount is available. Open June to late September.

Directions: From Burlington, drive east on State Route 20 for 120 miles to Mazama Road. Turn left on Mazama Road and drive .25 mile to County Road 9140. Turn left and drive northwest for seven miles to Lost River, where the pavement ends and the road soon becomes Forest Road 5400. Continue northwest on Forest Road 5400 for two miles to Forest Road 5400-600. Bear left (west) on Forest Road 5400-600 and drive .5 mile to the campground on the left.

Contact: Okanogan and Wenatchee National Forests, Methow Valley Visitor Center, 24 West Chewuch Rd., Winthrop, WA 98862, 509/996-4000, fax 509/996-3531.

20 LONE FIR

Rating: 9

on Early Winters Creek in Okanogan and Wenatchee National Forests
See map pages 90–91

Lone Fir is set at 3,640 feet elevation along the banks of Early Winters Creek. The area has had some timber operations in the past, but there are no nearby clear-cuts. To the west, Washington Pass Overlook offers a spectacular view. Anglers can fish in the creek, and many hiking and biking trails crisscross the area, including the trailhead for Cutthroat Lake. A U.S. Forest Service map will provide details. A loop trail through the campground woods is wheelchair-accessible for .4 mile. See the description of Early Winters Camp in this chapter for more information.

RV sites, facilities: There are 27 sites for RVs up to 36 feet, trailers, or tents. Picnic tables and fire grills are provided. Vault toilets are available. No drinking water is available. Garbage must be packed out. Leashed pets are permitted.

Reservations, fees: Reservations are not accepted. The fee is $8 per night, plus $8 per additional vehicle per night. A senior discount is available. Open June to late September.

Directions: From Burlington, drive east on State Route 20 for 107 miles to the campground (11 miles west of Mazama) on the right.

Contact: Okanogan and Wenatchee National Forests, Methow Valley Visitor Center, 24 West Chewuch Rd., Winthrop, WA 98862, 509/996-4000, fax 509/996-3531.

21 KLIPCHUCK

Rating: 7

on Early Winters Creek in Okanogan and Wenatchee National Forests
See map pages 90–91

This camp is located at an elevation of 3,000 feet along Early Winters Creek. The camp area is set amid majestic trees, primarily Douglas fir and subalpine firs. Klipchuck provides hiking aplenty, but note that rattlesnakes are occasionally seen in this area. A short loop trail from the camp leads about five miles up and over Delancy Ridge to Driveway Butte and down to the creek. Another trail starts nearby on Forest Road 200 (Sandy Butte-Cedar Creek Road) and goes two miles up Cedar Creek to lovely Cedar Creek Falls. Still another option from the campground is a two-mile trail along Early Winters Creek. This region is best visited in the spring and fall, with summer hot and dry. See the description of Early Winters Camp in this chapter for more information.

RV sites, facilities: There are 46 sites for RVs up to 34 feet, trailers, or tents. Sites can be combined to accommodate groups. Picnic tables and fire grills are provided. Drinking water and vault toilets are available. A pay phone is within five miles. Some facilities are wheelchair-accessible. Leashed pets are permitted.

Reservations, fees: Reservations are not accepted. The fee is $8 per night, plus $8 per additional vehicle per night. A senior discount is available. Open June to late September.

Directions: From Burlington, drive east on State Route 20 for 115 miles to Forest Road 300. (If you reach the Methow River Valley, you have gone four miles past the turnoff.) Turn left (marked) and drive northwest one mile to the camp at the end of the road.

Contact: Okanogan and Wenatchee National Forests, Methow Valley Visitor Center, 24 West Chewuch Rd., Winthrop, WA 98862, 509/996-4000, fax 509/996-3531.

22 EARLY WINTERS

Rating: 6

on Early Winters Creek in Okanogan and Wenatchee National Forests

See map pages 90–91

Located on each side of the highway, this campground has an unusual configuration. The confluence of Early Winters Creek and the Methow River mark the site. The elevation is 2,160 feet. You'll find great views of Goat Wall here. Campsites are flat, and the open landscape, set in a sparse lodgepole pine forest, lends an arid feel to the area. Several hiking trails can be found within five miles, including one that leads south to Cedar Creek Falls. Other possible side trips include Goat Wall to the north and the town of Winthrop

to the south, which boasts a historical museum, a state fish hatchery, and Pearrygin Lake State Park.

RV sites, facilities: There are 13 sites for RVs up to 24 feet, trailers, or tents. Picnic tables and fire grills are provided. Drinking water and vault toilets are available. There is a small store, pay phone, and snack bar in Mazama, about two miles away. Leashed pets are permitted.

Reservations, fees: Reservations are not accepted. The fee is $5 per night, plus $5 per additional vehicle per night. A senior discount is available. Open June to October, weather permitting.

Directions: From Burlington, drive east on State Route 20 for 116 miles to the campground (if you reach County Road 1163 near Mazama, you have gone two miles too far).

Contact: Okanogan and Wenatchee National Forests, Methow Valley Visitor Center, 24 West Chewuch Rd., Winthrop, WA 98862, 509/996-4000, fax 509/996-3531.

23 ROCKING HORSE RANCH

Rating: 7

in the Methow River Valley

See map pages 90–91

This ranch is good for campers with horses. Set in the lovely Methow River Valley, it's flanked on both sides by national forest. There are numerous trails nearby and a horse stable at the ranch. Owen Wister, who wrote the novel *The Virginian,* lived in the nearby town of Winthrop at the turn of the 20th century. Portions of the novel were based on his experiences in this area. Horse rentals and guided trips are available if you want to try to relive the stuff of legends.

RV sites, facilities: There are 10 drive-through sites with partial or full hookups (30 amps) for RVs of any length and 25 tent sites. Picnic tables are provided. Restrooms, flush toilets, showers, a horse stable, corrals, horseshoes, volleyball, and firewood are available. A pay phone is within five miles, and an ATM is within 10 miles. Some facilities are wheelchair-accessible. Leashed pets are permitted.

Reservations, fees: Reservations are accepted. The fee is $12–18 per night. Open late April to late October, weather permitting.

Directions: From Winthrop, drive west on State

Route 20 for nine miles to the campground on the right.

Contact: Rocking Horse Ranch, 18381 Hwy. 20, Winthrop, WA 98862, 509/996-2768, website: www.rockinghorsewinthrop.com.

24 CHEWUCH

Rating: 6

on the Chewuch River in Okanogan and Wenatchee National Forests

See map pages 90–91

Chewuch Camp is set along the Chewuch River at an elevation of 2,278 feet and is surrounded by ponderosa pines. There are also hiking and biking trails in the area. By traveling north, you can access trailheads that lead into the Pasayten Wilderness. See a U.S. Forest Service map for specific locations. This camp provides an alternative to the more developed nearby Falls Creek Campground.

RV sites, facilities: There are 16 sites for small self-contained RVs up to 35 feet, small trailers, and tents. Picnic tables and fire grills are provided. Vault toilets are available. No drinking water is available. Garbage must be packed out. Leashed pets are permitted.

Reservations, fees: Reservations are not accepted. The fee is $5 per vehicle. A senior discount is available. Open June to late September.

Directions: From Burlington, drive east on State Route 20 for 134 miles to Winthrop and County Road 1213/West Chewuch Road. Turn north on County Road 1213/West Chewuch Road and drive 6.5 miles (where it merges with Forest Road 51). Continue north on Forest Road 51 for seven miles to the campground on the right.

Contact: Okanogan and Wenatchee National Forests, Methow Valley Visitor Center, 24 West Chewuch Rd., Winthrop, WA 98862, 509/996-4000, fax 509/996-3531.

25 FLAT

Rating: 6

on Eightmile Creek in Okanogan and Wenatchee National Forests

See map pages 90–91

This campground is set along Eightmile Creek, two miles from where it empties into the Chewuch River. The elevation is 2,858 feet. Buck Lake is about three miles away. This is the closest of six camps to County Road 1213. Other options include Honeymoon, Nice, and Buck Lake.

RV sites, facilities: There are 12 sites for RVs up to 20 feet, trailers, or tents. Picnic tables and fire grills are provided, but there is no drinking water. Vault toilets are available. Garbage must be packed out. Leashed pets are permitted.

Reservations, fees: Reservations are not accepted. The fee is $5 per night, plus $5 per additional vehicle per night. A senior discount is available. Open June to late September.

Directions: From Burlington, drive east on State Route 20 for 134 miles to Winthrop and County Road 1213 (West Church Road). Drive three miles to Forest Road 5130 (Eightmile Creek Road). Turn left (northwest) and drive two miles to the campground on the left.

Contact: Okanogan and Wenatchee National Forests, Methow Valley Visitor Center, 24 West Chewuch Rd., Winthrop, WA 98862, 509/996-4000, fax 509/996-4051.

26 PEARRYGIN LAKE STATE PARK

Rating: 8

on Pearrygin Lake

See map pages 90–91

Pearrygin Lake is fed from underground springs and Pearrygin Creek, the lifeblood for this setting and the adjacent 578-acre state park. Located in the beautiful Methow Valley, it's ringed by the Northern Cascade Mountains. The park is known for its expansive green lawns, which lead to 8,200 feet of waterfront and sandy beaches. Old willows and ash provide shade. The camp is frequented by red-winged and yellow-headed blackbirds, as well as marmots. Wildflower and wildlife viewing are excellent in the spring. The campground has access to a sandy beach and facilities for swimming, boating, fishing, and hiking. The sites don't offer much privacy, but they are spacious, and a variety of recreation options make staying here worth it.

RV sites, facilities: There are 30 sites with full hookups (30 amps) for RVs up to 60 feet or tents, 53 tent sites, and two primitive hike-in/bike-in sites. Picnic tables and fire grills are provided. Restrooms, drinking water, flush toilets, coin-operated showers, a pay phone, cell phone reception, an RV dump station, and firewood are available. A store, a deli, and ice are located nearby. An ATM is within five miles. Boat-launching and dock facilities are available. Some facilities are wheelchair-accessible. Leashed pets are permitted.

Reservations, fees: Reserve at 888/CAMP-OUT (888/226-7688) or online at www.parks.wa.gov /reservations ($7 reservation fee); Reservations are accepted from April 15 to the last Sunday in October. The fee is $10–22 per night, plus $10 per additional vehicle per night. A senior discount is available. Major credit cards are accepted. Open April to October.

Directions: From Winthrop and State Route 20, drive north through town (road changes to East Chewuch Road). Continue 1.5 miles north from town to Bear Creek Road. Turn right and drive 1.5 miles to the end of the pavement and look for the cattle guard and the park entrance on the right. Turn right, drive over the cattle guard, and continue to the campground.

Contact: Pearrygin Lake State Park, 509/996-2370, fax 509/996-2630; state park information, 360/902-8844.

27 PINE-NEAR RV PARK

Rating: 7

on the Methow River
See map pages 90–91

This camp is an adequate layover spot for State Route 20 cruisers and a good alternative camp to the more crowded sites at Pearrygin Lake. The Shafer Historical Museum is located across the street. The Methow River is nearby; see the description of KOA Methow River in this chapter for information on the various activities available in the Winthrop area.

RV sites, facilities: There are 28 sites with full hookups (30, 50 amps), including 14 drive-through, for RVs of any length and 10 tent sites. Three mobile homes are for rent on a per-night basis. Picnic tables are provided. Restrooms, flush toilets, coin-operated showers, cell phone reception, an RV dump station, and a coin-operated laun-

dry are available. A store, an ATM, a pay phone, propane, and a café are available within one block. Leashed pets are permitted.

Reservations, fees: Reservations are accepted. The fee is $12–25 per night, plus $2 per person for more than two people and $2 per additional vehicle. Major credit cards are accepted. Open year-round.

Directions: From Winthrop, drive east on State Route 20 one block north of Riverside Drive to Castle Avenue. Turn right (east) and drive three blocks to the park on the left.

Contact: Pine-Near RV Park, Rte. 1, P.O. Box 400-32, Winthrop, WA 98862, 509/996-2391.

28 KOA METHOW RIVER-WINTHROP

Rating: 7

on the Methow River
See map pages 90–91

Here's another campground set along the Methow River, which offers opportunities for fishing, boating, swimming, and rafting. The park has a free shuttle into Winthrop, an interesting town with many restored, early-1900s buildings lining the main street. One such building, the Shafer Historical Museum, displays an array of period items. If you would like to observe wildlife, take a short, two-mile drive southeast out of Winthrop on County Road 9129 on the east side of the Methow River. Turn east on County Road 1631 into Davis Lake, and follow the signs to the Methow River Habitat Management Area Headquarters. Depending on the time of year, you may see mule deer, porcupine, bobcat, mountain lion, snowshoe hare, black bear, red squirrel, and many species of birds. If you're looking for something tamer, other nearby recreation options include an 18-hole golf course and tennis courts.

RV sites, facilities: There are 70 sites with partial or full hookups (20, 30, 50 amps), including some drive-through sites, for RVs of any length and 35 tent sites. There are also 17 one- and two-room cabins. Picnic tables and fire grills are provided. Restrooms, drinking water, flush toilets, showers, firewood, an RV dump station, a recreation hall, modem hookups, a pay phone, cell phone reception, bike and video rentals, a store, a laundry room, ice, a playground, and a swimming pool (seasonal) are available. Propane, an ATM, and a café are available within one mile. There is a courtesy shuttle to and from Winthrop. Leashed pets are permitted.

Reservations, fees: Reservations are accepted; phone 800/562-2158. The fee is $20–28 per night, plus $4 per person per night for more than two people, and $2 per child 5–17 per night. Major credit cards are accepted. Open mid-April to November.

Directions: From Winthrop, drive east on State Route 20 for one mile to the camp on the left. The camp is between Mileposts 194 and 195.

Contact: KOA Methow River-Winthrop, 1114 Rte. 20, Winthrop, WA 98862, 509/996-2258, website: www.koa.com.

29 BIG TWIN LAKE CAMPGROUND

Rating: 5

on Twin Lakes
See map pages 90–91

As you might figure from the name, this campground is set along the shore of Twin Lakes. With its sweeping lawn and shade trees, the camp features views of the lake from all campsites. No gas motors are permitted on the lake. Fly-fishing is good for rainbow trout, with special regulations in effect: one-fish limit, single barbless hook, artificials only. This is an ideal lake for a float tube, rowboat with a casting platform, or a pram. See the description of KOA Methow River in this chapter for information on the various activities available in the Winthrop area.

RV sites, facilities: There are 50 sites with partial or full hookups (30 amps), including 14 drivethrough sites for RVs up to 38 feet, and 35 tent sites. Picnic tables and fire grills are provided. Restrooms, drinking water, flush toilets, coin-operated showers, cell phone reception, an RV dump station, firewood, ice, and a playground are available. Boat docks, launching facilities, and rentals can be obtained on Big Twin Lake. An ATM and a pay phone are within two miles. Leashed pets are permitted.

Reservations, fees: Reservations are accepted. The fee is $13–19 per night (children free), plus $4 per additional vehicle per night. Open late April to late October.

Directions: From Winthrop, drive east on State Route 20 for three miles to Twin Lakes Road. Turn right (west) on Twin Lakes Road and drive two miles to the campground on the right.

Contact: Big Twin Lake Campground, 210 Twin Lakes Rd., Winthrop, WA 98862, 509/996-2650, website: www.methownet.com/bigtwin.

30 KERR

Rating: 6

on Salmon Creek in Okanogan National Forest
See map pages 90–91

This camp sits at an elevation of 3,100 feet along Salmon Creek, about four miles north of Conconully Reservoir, and is one of many campgrounds near the lake. Fishing prospects are marginal for trout here. There are numerous recreation options available at Conconully Reservoir, including far better fishing.

RV sites, facilities: There are 13 sites for RVs up to 21 feet, trailers, or tents. Picnic tables and fire grills are provided. Vault toilets are available, but there is no drinking water. Garbage must be packed out. Some facilities are wheelchair-accessible. Leashed pets are permitted.

Reservations, fees: Reservations are not accepted. The fee is $5 per night, plus $5 per additional vehicle per night. A senior discount is available. Open mid-May to mid-September.

Directions: From East Wenatchee, drive north on U.S. 97 for 88 miles to Okanogan and County Road 9229. Turn left (north) on County Road 9229 and drive 17.5 miles to Conconully and County Road 2361. Continue northwest on County Road 2361 and drive four miles (becomes Forest Road 38) to the campground on the left.

Contact: Okanogan and Wenatchee National Forests, Tonasket Ranger District, 1 West Winesap Ave., Tonasket, WA 98855, 509/486-2186, fax 509/486-5161.

31 ORIOLE

Rating: 6

on Salmon Creek in Okanogan National Forest
See map pages 90–91

This camp is located at 2,900 feet elevation along

Salmon Creek and offers a creek view from some of the campsites. This forest setting features well-spaced campsites among Western larch and lodgepole pine. This is a primitive camp, similar to Kerr and Salmon Meadows, also set on Salmon Creek.

RV sites, facilities: There are 10 sites for small RVs or tents. Picnic tables and fire grills are provided. Vault toilets are available, but there is no drinking water. Garbage must be packed out. Some facilities are wheelchair-accessible. Leashed pets are permitted.

Reservations, fees: Reservations are not accepted. The fee is $5 per night, plus $5 per additional vehicle per night. A senior discount is available. Open mid-May to mid-September.

Directions: From East Wenatchee, drive north on U.S. 97 for 88 miles to Okanogan and County Road 9229. Turn left (north) on County Road 9229 and drive 17.5 miles to Conconully and County Road 2361 (becomes Forest Road 38). Continue northwest on County Road 2361 and drive 2.5 miles to Forest Road 026. Turn left and drive one mile (crossing the creek) to the campground on the left.

Contact: Okanogan and Wenatchee National Forests, Tonasket Ranger District, 1 West Winesap Ave., Tonasket, WA 98855, 509/486-2186, fax 509/486-5161.

32 SOUTH CREEK

Rating: 6

on the Twisp River in Okanogan and
Wenatchee National Forests
See map pages 90–91

Although small, quiet, and little known, South Creek Campground packs a wallop with good recreation options. It's set at the confluence of the Twisp River and South Creek at a major trailhead that accesses the Lake Chelan–Sawtooth Wilderness. The South Creek Trailhead provides a hike to Louis Lake. The elevation at the camp is 3,100 feet. See a U.S. Forest Service map for details.

RV sites, facilities: There are four sites for small trailers or tents, plus a few sites with parking for RVs up to 30 feet. No drinking water is available. Picnic tables and fire grills are provided. A vault toilet is available. Garbage must be packed out. Leashed pets are permitted.

Reservations, fees: Reservations are not accepted. The fee is $5 per night, plus $5 per additional vehicle per night. A senior discount is available. Open late May to early September.

Directions: From Burlington, drive east on State Route 20 for 145 miles to Twisp and County Road 9114 (Twisp River Road). Turn west on County Road 9114 and drive 22 miles (becomes Forest Road 44). Continue west (becomes Forest Road 4440) to the campground on the left.

Contact: Okanogan and Wenatchee National Forests, Methow Valley Visitor Center, 24 West Chewuch Rd., Winthrop, WA 98862, 509/996-4000, fax 509/996-3531.

33 POPLAR FLAT

Rating: 7

on the Twisp River in Okanogan and
Wenatchee National Forests
See map pages 90–91

This campground is set at 2,900 feet elevation along the Twisp River. This area provides many wildlife-viewing opportunities for deer, black bear, and many species of birds. Several trails in the area, including the Twisp River Trail, follow streams and some provide access to the Lake Chelan–Sawtooth Wilderness. Twisp River Horse Camp, across the river from the campground, has facilities for horses.

RV sites, facilities: There are 16 sites for RVs up to 22 feet, trailers, or tents and one double site for up to 12 people. Picnic tables and fire grills are provided. Drinking water and vault toilets are available. A day-use picnic area with a shelter is nearby. Some facilities are wheelchair-accessible. Leashed pets are permitted.

Reservations, fees: Reservations are not accepted. The fee is $8 per night, plus $8 per additional vehicle per night. A senior discount is available. Open May to September.

Directions: From Burlington, drive east on State Route 20 for 145 miles to Twisp and County Road 9114 (Twisp River Road). Turn west on County Road 9114 and drive 11 miles (becomes Forest Road 44). Continue west for 9.5 miles to the campground on the left.

Contact: Okanogan and Wenatchee National Forests, Methow Valley Visitor Center, 24 West

Chewuch Rd., Winthrop, WA 98862, 509/996-4000, fax 509/996-3531.

34 WAR CREEK

Rating: 6

on the Twisp River in Okanogan and Wenatchee National Forests
See map pages 90–91

This trailhead camp is set at 2,400 feet elevation and provides several routes into the Lake Chelan–Sawtooth Wilderness. The War Creek Trail, Eagle Creek Trail, and Oval Creek Trail all offer wilderness access and trout fishing (check regulations). Backpackers can extend this trip into the Lake Chelan National Recreation Area, for a 15-mile trek that finishes off at the shore of Lake Chelan and the National Park Service outpost. Rattlesnakes are occasionally spotted in this region in the summer.

RV sites, facilities: There are 10 sites for RVs up to 22 feet, trailers, or tents. Drinking water, fire grills, and picnic tables are provided. Vault toilets and firewood are available. Leashed pets are permitted.

Reservations, fees: Reservations are not accepted. The fee is $5 per night, plus $5 per additional vehicle per night. A senior discount is available. Open May to September.

Directions: On I-5, drive to Exit 230/State Route 20 at Burlington. Turn east on State Route 20, and drive 145 miles to Twisp and County Road 9114 (Twisp River Road). Turn west on County Road 9114 and drive 11 miles (becomes Forest Road 44). Continue west on Forest Road 44 for 3.5 miles to the campground on the left.

Contact: Okanogan and Wenatchee National Forests, Methow Valley Visitor Center, 24 West Chewuch Rd., Winthrop, WA 98862, 509/996-4000, fax 509/996-3531.

35 TWISP RIVER HORSE CAMP

Rating: 7

on Twisp River in Okanogan and Wenatchee National Forests
See map pages 90–91

This camp is only for horses and their owners.

It is set on the Twisp River at an elevation of 3,000 feet. The camp features nearby access to trails, including the North Fork Twisp River Trail, which leads to Copper Pass, and the South Fork Twisp River Trail, which leads to Lake Chelan National Recreation Area and Twisp Pass. The South Creek Trail is also available and leads from the camp to Lake Chelan National Recreation Area.

RV sites, facilities: There are 12 sites for RVs up to 30 feet, trailers, or tents. Picnic tables and fire grills are provided. Vault toilets are available. No drinking water is available. Garbage must be packed out. For horses, a loading ramp, hitching rails, and feed stations are available. Leashed pets are permitted.

Reservations, fees: A Northwest Forest Pass ($5 daily fee or $30 annual fee per parked vehicle) is required. A senior discount is available. Open May to September.

Directions: On I-5, drive to Exit 230/State Route 20 at Burlington. Turn east on State Route 20, and drive 145 miles to Twisp and County Road 9114 (Twisp River Road). Turn west on County Road 9114 and drive 11 miles (becomes Forest Road 44). Continue west on Forest Road 44 for 3.5 miles to War Creek Campground on the left. Continue 250 yards to Forest Road 4430. Turn left (drive over the bridge) and drive approximately nine miles to the campground on the right.

Contact: Okanogan and Wenatchee National Forests, Methow Valley Visitor Center, 24 West Chewuch Rd., Winthrop, WA 98862, 509/996-4000, fax 509/996-3531.

36 RIVER BEND RV PARK

Rating: 6

near the Methow River
See map pages 90–91

The shore of the Methow River skirts this campground, and there is a nice separate area for tent campers set right along the river. Trout fishing, river rafting, and swimming are popular here. The description of KOA Methow River in this chapter details the recreation possibilities available within 10 miles.

RV sites, facilities: There are 69 sites with full hookups (30, 50 amps), including 30 drive-through sites and 31 riverfront sites, for RVs and trailers of any length, 12 tent sites, and rental trailers. Picnic tables and fire pits are provided. Restrooms, flush toilets, coin-operated showers, a pay phone, cell phone reception, an RV dump station, firewood, a store, a coin-operated laundry, ice, a playground with horseshoes, propane, modem access, and RV storage are available. An ATM is within two miles. Leashed pets are permitted.

Reservations, fees: Reservations are accepted. The fee is $16–23 per night, plus $2 per person per night for more than two people; $1 for children over 5. Major credit cards are accepted. Open year-round.

Directions: From Twisp, drive west on State Route 20 for two miles to the campground on the right.

Contact: River Bend RV Park, 19961 Rte. 20, Twisp, WA 98856, 509/997-3500 or 800/686-4498, website: www.riverbendrv.com.

37 LOUP LOUP

Rating: 6

near Loup Loup Ski Area in Okanogan National Forest

See map pages 90–91

This camp provides a good setup for large groups of up to 100 people. It is located next to the Loup Loup Ski Area at 4,200 feet elevation. The camp features a setting of Western larch trees, along with good access to biking and hiking trails as well as the ski area.

RV sites, facilities: There are 25 sites for RVs up to 24 feet, trailers, or tents. Picnic tables and fire rings are provided. Drinking water, vault toilets, and an RV dump station are available. Some facilities are wheelchair-accessible. Leashed pets are permitted.

Reservations, fees: Reservations are not accepted. The fee is $8 per night, plus $8 per additional vehicle per night. Open May to September, weather permitting.

Directions: From East Wenatchee, drive north on U.S. 97 for 88 miles to Okanogan and Highway 20. Turn west and drive 21 miles to Forest Road 42. Turn right (north) on Forest Road 42 and drive one mile to the campground on the left.

Contact: Okanogan and Wenatchee National Forests, Methow Valley Visitor Center, 24 West

Chewuch Rd., Winthrop, WA 98862, 509/996-4000, fax 509/996-3531.

38 SPORTSMAN'S CAMP

Rating: 6

on Sweat Creek, in Lower Loomis State Forest

See map pages 90–91

In season, this is a popular camp with hunters, who may bring horses; although there are no livestock facilities, horses are allowed in the camp. The landscape is shady and grassy with a small stream. Some roads in the area can be used by hikers and bikers. Highway 20 east of I-5 is a designated scenic route.

RV sites, facilities: There are six pull-through sites for RVs up to 30 feet, trailers, or tents and a small, dispersed area for tents. Picnic tables and fire pits are provided. Vault toilets are available, but there is no drinking water. A gazebo shelter with a fire pit is also available. Garbage must be packed out. Leashed pets are permitted.

Reservations, fees: Reservations are not accepted. There is no fee for camping. Open year-round, weather permitting.

Directions: From East Wenatchee, drive north on U.S. 97 for 88 miles to Okanogan and Highway 20. Turn west and drive 15 miles to Sweat Creek Road. Turn left on Sweat Creek Road and drive one mile to the campground on the right.

Contact: Department of Natural Resources, Northeast Region, P.O. Box 190, Colville, WA 99114-0190, 509/684-7474, fax 509/684-7484.

39 TURLO

Rating: 8

on the South Fork of the Stillaguamish River in Mt. Baker–Snoqualmie National Forest

See map pages 90–91

The westernmost camp on this stretch of Highway 92, Turlo is set at 900 feet elevation along the South Fork of the Stillaguamish River. A U.S. Forest Service Public Information Center is nearby. Riverside campsites are available, and the fishing can be good here. A few hiking trails can be found in the area; see a U.S.

Forest Service map or consult the nearby information center for trail locations.

RV sites, facilities: There are 19 sites for RVs up to 31 feet or tents. Picnic tables are provided. Vault toilets, drinking water, and firewood are available. A pay phone is across the street. A store, a café, and ice are available one mile away. Leashed pets are permitted.

Reservations, fees: Reserve at 877/444-6777 or online at www.reserveusa.com ($9 reservation fee). The fee is $14 per night, plus $7 per additional vehicle per night. Open mid-May to late September.

Directions: From Seattle, drive north on I-5 to Everett and U.S. 2. Turn east on U.S. 2 and drive five miles to Highway 9. Turn north and drive four miles to Highway 92. Turn east on Highway 92 and drive approximately 15 miles to the town of Granite Falls. Continue another 11 miles east on Highway 92 to the campground entrance on the right.

Contact: Mt. Baker–Snoqualmie National Forest, Darrington Ranger District, 1405 Emmens St., Darrington, WA 98241, 360/436-1155, fax 360/436-1309.

40 VERLOT

Rating: 9

on the South Fork of the Stillaguamish River in Mt. Baker–Snoqualmie National Forest

See map pages 90–91

This pretty campground is set along the South Fork of the Stillaguamish River. Some campsites provide river views. The camp is a short distance from the Lake Twenty-Two Research Natural Area and the Maid of the Woods Trail. A U.S. Forest Service map details back roads and hiking trails. Fishing is another recreation option.

RV sites, facilities: There are 26 sites for RVs up to 31 feet, trailers, or tents. Picnic tables and fire rings are provided. Restrooms, drinking water, and flush toilets are available. A store, a café, and ice are available within one mile. A pay phone is across the street. Leashed pets are permitted.

Reservations, fees: Reservations are accepted. Reserve at 877/444-6777 or online at www .reserveusa.com ($9 reservation fee). The fee is $14 per night, plus $7 per additional vehicle per night. Open mid-May to late September.

Directions: From Seattle, drive north on I-5 to Everett and U.S. 2. Turn east on U.S. 2 and drive five miles to Highway 9. Turn north and drive four miles to Highway 92. Turn east on Highway 92 and drive approximately 15 miles to the town of Granite Falls, and continue another 11.6 miles east on Highway 92 to the campground entrance on the right.

Contact: Mt. Baker–Snoqualmie National Forest, Darrington Ranger District, 1405 Emmens St., Darrington, WA 98241, 360/436-1155, fax 360/1309.

41 SQUIRE CREEK COUNTY PARK

Rating: 7

on Squire Creek

See map pages 90–91

This pretty RV park is set amid old-growth forest, primarily Douglas fir and cedar, along Squire Creek. A family-oriented park, it often fills on summer weekends. The park covers 12.2 acres and features several nearby trailheads. A trail from the park provides a 4.5-mile loop that heads toward White Horse Mountain. Other trailheads are available within five miles in nearby Mt. Baker–Snoqualmie National Forest, about three miles from the boundaries of the Boulder River Wilderness. No alcohol is permitted in this park.

RV sites, facilities: There are 34 drive-through sites for RVs up to 25 feet, trailers, or tents and two sites for trailers up to 70 feet long. Picnic tables and fire rings are provided. Restrooms, drinking water, flush toilets, modem access, cell phone reception, and firewood are available. A store is located three miles east in Darrington. A pay phone and an ATM are within 1.5 miles. Some facilities are wheelchair-accessible. Leashed pets are permitted.

Reservations, fees: Reservations are not accepted. The fee is $14 per night. A senior discount is available. Open year-round.

Directions: From Seattle, drive north on I-5 to Exit 208 and the junction with Highway 530. Turn east on Highway 530 and drive 26 miles to the park on the left. The park is at Milepost 45.2.

Contact: Squire Creek County Park, 360/436-1283; Snohomish County Parks, 425/388-6600.

42 CASCADE KAMLOOPS TROUT FARM AND RV PARK

Rating: 5

in Darrington

See map pages 90–91

Campers will find a little bit of both worlds at this campground—a rustic quietness with all facilities available. A bonus is the trout pond, which is stocked year-round. No boats are allowed. Nearby recreation options include marked hiking trails, snowmobiling, cross-country skiing, river rafting, and tennis.

RV sites, facilities: There are 32 sites with full hookups (20, 30 amps) for RVs of any length and four tent sites. Picnic tables and fire rings are provided. Restrooms, drinking water, flush toilets, showers, an RV dump station, modem access, cell phone reception, firewood, a coin-operated laundry, a trout pond, and a recreation hall are available. Propane, a store, an ATM, a pay phone, a café, and ice are available within one mile. Leashed pets are permitted.

Reservations, fees: Reservations are accepted. The fee is $14–18 per night, plus $2 per person per night for more than two people over 12. Open year-round.

Directions: From Seattle, drive north on I-5 to Exit 208 and the junction with Highway 530. Turn east on Highway 530 and drive 32 miles to Darrington and Madison Street. Turn right on Madison Street and drive about four blocks to Darrington Street. Turn right and drive two blocks to the park on the right.

Contact: Cascade Kamloops Trout Farm and RV Park, 1240 Darrington St., Darrington, WA 98241, 360/436-1003, website: www.glacierview.net/kamloops.

43 CLEAR CREEK

Rating: 8

on Clear Creek and the Sauk River in Mt. Baker–Snoqualmie National Forest

See map pages 90–91

This nice, secluded spot is set in old-growth fir on the water but doesn't get heavy use. It's located at the confluence of Clear Creek and the Sauk River, a designated Wild and Scenic River. Fishing is available for rainbow trout, Dolly Varden trout, whitefish, and steelhead in season. A trail from camp leads about one mile up to Frog Pond.

RV sites, facilities: There are 13 sites for RVs up to 21 feet, trailers, or tents. Picnic tables and fire grills are provided. Cell phone reception, vault toilets, and firewood are available. There is no drinking water. A store, an ATM, a pay phone, a café, a coin-operated laundry, and ice are available within four miles. Some facilities are wheelchair-accessible. Leashed pets are permitted.

Reservations, fees: Reserve at 877/444-6777 or online at www.reserveusa.com ($9 reservation fee). The fee is $10 per night, plus $5 per additional vehicle. A senior discount is available. Open late May to mid-October.

Directions: From Seattle, drive north on I-5 to Exit 208 and the junction with Highway 530. Turn east on Highway 530 and drive 32 miles to Darrington and Forest Road 20 (Mountain Loop Highway). Turn south on Forest Road 20 and drive 3.3 miles to the campground entrance on the left.

Contact: Mt. Baker–Snoqualmie National Forest, Darrington Ranger District, 1405 Emmens St., Darrington, WA 98241, 360/436-1155, fax 360/436-1309.

44 BUCK CREEK

Rating: 9

near the Suiattle River in Mt. Baker–Snoqualmie National Forest

See map pages 90–91

Quiet and remote, this primitive campground is set along Buck Creek near its confluence with the Suiattle River in the Glacier Peak Wilderness. An interpretive trail runs along Buck Creek and provides access to fishing on the stream for rainbow trout, Dolly Varden, whitefish, and steelhead in season. There's a large (18 feet by 18 feet) Adirondack shelter by the creek and stands of old-growth timber. A zigzagging trail routed into the Glacier Peak Wilderness is accessible about one mile west of camp. See a U.S. Forest Service map for specifics.

RV sites, facilities: There are 26 sites for RVs up to 30 feet, trailers, or tents. Picnic tables and fire grills are provided. Vault toilets, cell phone reception, and firewood are available. No drinking water is available. Leashed pets are permitted.

Reservations, fees: Reserve at 877/444-6777 or online at www.reserveusa.com ($9 reservation fee). The fee is $10 per night, plus $5 per additional vehicle. A senior discount is available. Open late May to late September.

Directions: From Seattle, drive north on I-5 to Exit 208 and the junction with Highway 530. Turn east on Highway 530 and drive 32 miles to Darrington. Continue 7.5 miles on Highway 530 to Forest Road 26 (Suiattle River Road). Turn right (southeast) on Forest Road 26 and drive 14 miles to the campground on the left. Obtaining a U.S. Forest Service map is essential.

Contact: Mt. Baker–Snoqualmie National Forest, Darrington Ranger District, 1405 Emmens St., Darrington, WA 98241, 360/436-1155, fax 360/436-1309.

45 GOLD BASIN

Rating: 9

**on the South Fork of the Stillaguamish River
in Mt. Baker–Snoqualmie National Forest
See map pages 90–91**

This is the largest campground in Mt. Baker–Snoqualmie National Forest, and since it's loaded with facilities, it's a favorite with RVers. Set at 1,100 feet along the South Fork of the Stillaguamish River, the campground features riverside sites, easy access, and a wheelchair-accessible interpretive trail. This area once provided good fishing, but a slide upstream put clay silt into the water, and it has hurt the fishing. Rafting and hiking are options.

RV sites, facilities: There are 83 sites for RVs up to 60 feet, trailers, or, tents, 10 tent sites, and two group sites for up to 50 people. Picnic tables and fire rings are provided. Drinking water, restrooms, vault toilets, showers, and firewood are available. A store, a café, a pay phone, and ice are available within 2.5 miles. Some facilities are wheelchair-accessible. Leashed pets are permitted.

Reservations, fees: Some sites can be reserved; reserve at 877/444-6777 or online at www.reserveusa.com ($9 reservation fee). The fee is

$16 per night, plus $7 per additional vehicle; group sites are $75–100 per night. Open mid-May to early October.

Directions: From Seattle, drive north on I-5 to Everett and Highway 92. Turn east on Highway 92 and drive about 15 miles to the town of Granite Falls and Mountain Loop Highway. Continue east on Mountain Loop Highway for 13.5 miles to the campground entrance on the left.

Contact: Mt. Baker–Snoqualmie National Forest, Darrington Ranger District, 1405 Emmens St., Darrington, WA 98241, 360/436-1155, fax 360/436-1309.

46 ESSWINE GROUP CAMP

Rating: 6

**in Mt. Baker–Snoqualmie National Forest
See map pages 90–91**

This small, quiet camp is a great place for a restful group getaway. The only drawback? No drinking water. Fishing access is available nearby. The Boulder River Wilderness is located to the north; see a U.S. Forest Service map for trailhead locations.

RV sites, facilities: This is a specially designated group campground for small RVs or tents for up to 25 people. Picnic tables are provided. Vault toilets and firewood are available, but there is no drinking water. A store, a café, an ATM, a pay phone, and ice are available within five miles. Leashed pets are permitted.

Reservations, fees: Reservations are required; phone 877/444-6777 or reserve online at www.reserveusa.com ($9 reservation fee). The fee is $60 per night. Open mid-May to September.

Directions: From Seattle, drive north on I-5 to Everett and Highway 92. Turn east on Highway 92 and drive about 15 miles to the town of Granite Falls and Mountain Loop Highway (Forest Road 7). Continue northeast on Mountain Loop Highway for 16 miles to the campground entrance on the left.

Contact: Mt. Baker–Snoqualmie National Forest, Darrington Ranger District, 1405 Emmens St., Darrington, WA 98241, 360/436-1155, fax 360/436-1309.

47 BOARDMAN CREEK

Rating: 7

on the South Fork of the Stillaguamish River in Mt. Baker–Snoqualmie National Forest

See map pages 90–91

Roomy sites and river access are highlights at this pretty riverside camp. The fishing near here can be excellent for rainbow trout, Dolly Varden, whitefish, and steelhead in season. Forest roads in the area will take you to several backcountry lakes, including Boardman Lake, Lake Evan, and Ashland Lakes. Get a U.S. Forest Service map, set up your camp, and go for it.

RV sites, facilities: There are eight sites for RVs of any length, trailers, or tents. Picnic tables and fire grills are provided. Vault toilets and cell phone reception are available. No drinking water is available. An ATM and pay phone are within six miles. Leashed pets are permitted.

Reservations, fees: Reservations are not accepted. The fee is $8 per night, plus $4 per additional vehicle. A senior discount is available. Open late May to early September.

Directions: From Seattle, drive north on I-5 to Everett and Highway 92. Turn east on Highway 92 and drive about 15 miles to the town of Granite Falls and Mountain Loop Highway. Continue northeast on Mountain Loop Highway for 16.5 miles to the campground entrance on the left.

Contact: Mt. Baker–Snoqualmie National Forest, Darrington Ranger District, 1405 Emmens St., Darrington, WA 98241, 360/436-1155, fax 360/436-1309.

48 RED BRIDGE

Rating: 9

on the South Fork of Stillaguamish River in Mt. Baker–Snoqualmie National Forest

See map pages 90–91

Red Bridge is another classic spot, one of several in the vicinity, and a good base camp for a backpacking expedition. The campground is set at 1,300 feet elevation on the South Fork of the Stillaguamish River near Mallardy Creek. It has pretty, riverside sites with old-growth fir. A trail-

head two miles east of camp leads to Granite Pass in the Boulder River Wilderness.

RV sites, facilities: There are 16 sites for RVs up to 31 feet, trailers, or tents. Picnic tables are provided. Vault toilets are available, but there is no drinking water. Some facilities are wheelchair-accessible. Leashed pets are permitted.

Reservations, fees: Reserve at 877/444-6777 or online at www.reserveusa.com ($9 reservation fee). The fee is $10 per night. Open late May to mid-September.

Directions: From Seattle, drive north on I-5 to Everett and Highway 92. Turn east on Highway 92 and drive about 15 miles to the town of Granite Falls and Mountain Loop Highway. Continue northeast on Mountain Loop Highway for 18 miles to the campground entrance on the right.

Contact: Mt. Baker–Snoqualmie National Forest, Darrington Ranger District, 1405 Emmens St., Darrington, WA 98241, 360/436-1155, fax 360/436-1309.

49 COAL CREEK GROUP CAMP

Rating: 8

on the South Fork of the Stillaguamish River in Mt. Baker–Snoqualmie National Forest

See map pages 90–91

A U.S. Forest Service map will unlock the beautiful country around this campground set along the South Fork of the Stillaguamish River. Fishing access is available for rainbow trout, Dolly Varden, whitefish, and steelhead in season. Nearby forest roads lead to Coal Lake and a trailhead that takes you to other backcountry lakes.

RV sites, facilities: There is one group site for small RVs or tents for up to 25 people. Picnic tables and fire grills are provided. Vault toilets and firewood are available. There is no drinking water. Leashed pets are permitted.

Reservations, fees: Reserve at 877/444-6777 or online at www.reserveusa.com ($9 reservation fee). The fee is $60 per night for the entire camp. Open mid-May to late September.

Directions: From Seattle, drive north on I-5 to Everett and Highway 92. Turn east on Highway 92 and drive about 15 miles to the town of Granite Falls and Mountain Loop Highway (Forest Road 7). Continue northeast on Mountain Loop

WASHINGTON

Highway for 23.5 miles to the campground entrance on the left.

Contact: Mt. Baker–Snoqualmie National Forest, Darrington Ranger District, 1405 Emmens St., Darrington, WA 98241, 360/436-1155, fax 360/436-1309.

50 PHELPS CREEK

Rating: 7

on the Chiwawa River in Wenatchee National Forest
See map pages 90–91

This campground is set at an elevation of 2,800 feet at the confluence of Phelps Creek and the Chiwawa River. There's a key trailhead for backpackers and horseback riders nearby that provides access to the Glacier Peak Wilderness and Spider Meadows. The Phelps Creek Trail is routed out to Spider Meadows, a five-mile hike one-way, and the Buck Creek Trail extends into the Glacier Peak Wilderness. The Chiwawa River is closed to fishing downstream of Buck Creek to protect endangered species. A U.S. Forest Service map is advisable.

RV sites, facilities: There are seven sites for RVs, tents, or trailers up to 30 feet long. Picnic tables and fire grills are provided. Pit toilets are available, but there is no drinking water. Garbage must be packed out. Horse facilities including loading ramps and high lines are nearby. Leashed pets are permitted.

Reservations, fees: A Northwest Forest Pass ($5 daily fee or $30 annual fee per parked vehicle) is required. A senior discount is available. Open mid-June to mid-October.

Directions: From Seattle, drive north on I-5 to Everett and U.S. 2. Turn east on U.S. 2 and drive 87 miles to State Route 207. Turn north on State Route 207 and drive five miles to Chiwawa Loop Road. Turn right (east) on Chiwawa Loop Road and drive 1.4 miles to Chiwawa Valley Road (Forest Road 6200). Bear left (north) and continue for 23.6 miles to the campground.

Contact: Okanogan and Wenatchee National Forests, Lake Wenatchee and Leavenworth Ranger District, Lake Wenatchee Office, 22976 Hwy. 207, Leavenworth, WA 98826, 509/763-3103, fax 509/763-3211.

51 FOGGY DEW

Rating: 6

on Foggy Dew Creek in Okanogan and Wenatchee National Forests
See map pages 90–91

This private, remote campground is set at the confluence of Foggy Dew Creek and the North Fork of Old Creek. The elevation is 2,400 feet. Several trails for hiking and horseback riding nearby provide access to various backcountry lakes and streams. To get to the trailheads, follow the forest roads near camp. Bicycles are allowed on Trails 417, 429, and 431. There is also access to a motorcycle-use area. See a U.S. Forest Service map for options.

RV sites, facilities: There are 13 sites for RVs up to 22 feet, trailers, or tents. Picnic tables and fire grills are provided. Vault toilets are available. No drinking water is available. Garbage must be packed out. Leashed pets are permitted.

Reservations, fees: Reservations are not accepted. The fee is $5 per night, plus $5 per additional vehicle per night. A senior discount is available. Open late May to early September.

Directions: From Burlington, drive east on State Route 20 for 145 miles to Twisp. Continue east on State Route 20 for three miles to Highway 153. Turn south on Highway 153 and drive 12 miles to County Road 1029 (Gold Creek Road). Turn right (south) and drive one mile to Forest Road 4340. Turn right (west) and drive four miles to the campground on the left.

Contact: Okanogan and Wenatchee National Forests, Methow Valley Visitor Center, 24 West Chewuch Rd., Winthrop, WA 98862, 509/996-4000, fax 509/996-3531.

52 FLOWING LAKE COUNTY PARK

Rating: 6

near Snohomish
See map pages 90–91

This campground has a little something for everyone, including swimming, powerboating, waterskiing, and good fishing on Flowing Lake. The campsites are in a wooded setting (that is, no lake view), and it is a one-eighth-mile walk to the

WASHINGTON

beach. A one-mile nature trail is nearby. Note the private homes on the lake; all visitors are asked to respect the privacy of the owners.

RV sites, facilities: There are 40 sites, 15 drive-through, most with partial hookups (30 amps) for RVs up to 40 feet, trailers, or tents, four cabins, and one group site. Picnic tables and fire grills are provided. Restrooms, drinking water, flush toilets, coin-operated showers, cell phone reception, a pay phone, an RV dump station, and firewood are available. Picnic areas with covered shelters, a fishing dock, and launching facilities are available nearby. An ATM is within three miles. Some facilities are wheelchair-accessible. Leashed pets are permitted.

Reservations, fees: Reservations are not accepted for family sites. The fee is $14–20 per night, plus $5 for a second tent. Cabins are $40–45. Reservations are required at the group site, which is $20 per night plus $2 per person. Major credit cards are accepted. Open year-round with limited winter facilities.

Directions: From Seattle, drive north on I-5 to Everett and U.S. 2. Turn east on U.S. 2, drive to Milepost 10, and look for 100 Street SE (Westwick Road). Turn left and drive two miles to a 90-degree corner onto 171st Avenue Southeast. Drive two miles to 48th Street Southeast. Turn right and drive about .5 mile into the park at the end of the road.

Contact: Flowing Lake County Park, Snohomish County, 360/568-2274 or 425/388-6600, website: www.co.snohomish.wa.us/parks.

53 TROUBLESOME CREEK

Rating: 9

on the North Fork of the Skykomish River in Mt. Baker–Snoqualmie National Forest

See map pages 90–91

This campground is set along the North Fork of the Skykomish River among old-growth pine and fir. Highlights include a half-mile nature trail adjacent to the camp as well as rafting and good fishing in the river. A must-do trip here is the hike out to Blanca Lake. The trailhead is a short drive; then hike 3.5 miles to the lake, which is drop-dead beautiful with blue-green water fed by glacier-melt.

RV sites, facilities: There are 24 sites for RVs up to 21 feet, trailers, or tents and six walk-in tent sites requiring about a 100-foot walk. Picnic tables and fire rings are provided. Drinking water and vault toilets are available. Some facilities are wheelchair-accessible. Leashed pets are permitted.

Reservations, fees: Some sites, including three that are wheelchair-accessible, may be reserved at 877/444-6777 or online at www.reserveusa.com ($9 reservation fee). The fee is $14 per night, plus $7 per additional vehicle per night. A senior discount is available. Open Memorial Day through Labor Day, weather permitting.

Directions: From Seattle, drive north on I-5 to Everett and U.S. 2. Turn east on U.S. 2 and drive 36 miles to the town of Index and Forest Road 63 (Index-Galena Road). Turn left (northeast) on Forest Road 63 and drive 11 miles to the campground on the right.

Contact: Mt. Baker–Snoqualmie National Forest, Skykomish Ranger District, P.O. Box 305, Skykomish, WA 98288, 360/677-2414, fax 425/744-3265.

54 NAPEEQUA CROSSING

Rating: 8

on the White and Napeequa Rivers in Wenatchee National Forest

See map pages 90–91

A trail across the road from this camp on the White River heads east for about 3.5 miles to Twin Lakes in the Glacier Peak Wilderness. It's definitely worth the hike, with scenic views and wildlife observation as your reward. But note that Twin Lakes is closed to fishing. Sightings of osprey, bald eagles, and golden eagles can brighten the trip. This is also an excellent spot for fall colors.

RV sites, facilities: There are five sites for RVs up to 30 feet, trailers, or tents. Picnic tables and fire grills are provided. Vault toilets are available, but there is no drinking water. Garbage must be packed out. Leashed pets are permitted.

Reservations, fees: Reservations are not accepted. There is no fee for camping. Open year-round, weather and snow level permitting.

Directions: From Leavenworth, drive west on U.S. 2 for 14 miles to Coles Corner and State

Route 207. Turn north and drive 10 miles to Forest Road 6400 (White River Road). Turn right and drive 5.9 miles to the campground on the left.
Contact: Okanogan and Wenatchee National Forests, Lake Wenatchee and Leavenworth Ranger District, Lake Wenatchee Office, 22976 Rte. 207, Leavenworth, WA 98826, 509/763-3103, fax 509/763-3211.

55 SILVER FALLS

Rating: 10

on the Entiat River in Wenatchee National Forest
See map pages 90–91

This campground is set in an enchanted spot at the confluence of Silver Creek and the Entiat River. A trail from camp leads a half mile to the base of beautiful Silver Falls. This trail continues in a loop for another half mile past the falls, and then back to camp. There is also a 1.5-mile interpretive trail along the river. Fishing is available above Entiat Falls, located two to three miles upriver from Silver Falls. The elevation at the camp is 2,400 feet.

RV sites, facilities: There are 30 sites for RVs up to 35 feet, trailers, or tents plus one group site for 30 to 50 people. Picnic tables and fire grills are provided. Drinking water and vault toilets are available. A camp host is available on summer weekends. Some facilities are wheelchair-accessible. Leashed pets are permitted.

Reservations, fees: Reservations are required for groups only; reserve at 877/444-6777 or online at www.reserveusa.com ($9 reservation fee). The fees are $9 per vehicle per night in family sites and $60 a night for the group site. A senior discount is available. Open mid-May to mid-October.

Directions: From Seattle, drive north on I-5 to Everett and U.S. 2. Turn east on U.S. 2 and drive 120 miles to U.S. 97-A. Turn north on U.S. 97-A and drive 18.5 miles to Entiat River Road. Turn left (northwest) and drive 30 miles to the campground on the left.

Contact: Okanogan and Wenatchee National Forests, Entiat Ranger District, P.O. Box 476, Entiat, WA 98822, 509/784-1511, fax 509/784-1150.

56 LAKE CREEK/WENATCHEE

Rating: 6

on the Little Wenatchee River in Wenatchee National Forest
See map pages 90–91

Fishing for rainbow trout can be good at this camp, which is in a remote and primitive spot along the Little Wenatchee River. Berry picking is a bonus in late summer. The elevation is 2,300 feet. Note that there is another Lake Creek Camp in the Entiat Ranger District.

RV sites, facilities: There are eight sites for RVs of any length, trailers, or tents. Picnic tables and fire grills are provided, but there is no drinking water. Vault toilets are available. An ATM and pay phone are within 3.5 miles. Garbage must be packed out. Leashed pets are permitted.

Reservations, fees: Reservations are not accepted. There is no fee for camping. Open May to late October, weather permitting.

Directions: From Seattle, drive north on I-5 to Everett and U.S. 2. Turn east on U.S. 2 and drive 87 miles to State Route 207. Turn north on State Route 207 and drive 11 miles to Forest Road 6500. Turn left (west) on Forest Road 6500 and drive 9.5 miles to the campground on the left.

Contact: Okanogan and Wenatchee National Forests, Lake Wenatchee and Leavenworth Ranger District, Lake Wenatchee Office, 22976 Rte. 207, Leavenworth, WA 98826, 509/763-3103, fax 509/763-3211.

57 LAKE WENATCHEE STATE PARK

Rating: 8

on Lake Wenatchee
See map pages 90–91

Lake Wenatchee is the centerpiece of a 489-acre park with two miles of waterfront. Glaciers and the Wenatchee River feed Lake Wenatchee, and the river, which bisects the park, helps make it a natural wildlife area. Visitors should be aware of bears; all food must be stored in bear-proof facilities. Lake Wenatchee is set in a transition zone between the wet, western Washington woodlands and the sparse pine and fir of the eastern Cascades. Thanks to a nice location and drive-in sites that are spaced just right, you can expect plenty of company at this campground. The secluded campsites are at the southeast end of Lake Wenatchee, which offers plenty of recreation opportunities, with a boat launch nearby. There are eight miles of hiking trails, seven miles of bike trails, five miles of horse trails in and around the park, plus a 1.1-mile interpretive snowshoe trail in winter. Note that no horse facilities are available right in the park. In winter, there are 15 miles of multiuse trails for snowshoeing, cross-country skiing, and other nonmotorized sports.

RV sites, facilities: There are 197 sites for RVs up to 50 feet or tents with 42 scheduled to have hookups (50 amps) by 2004. Picnic tables and fire grills are provided. Restrooms, drinking water, flush toilets, showers, an RV dump station, a store, ice, firewood, a pay phone, cell phone reception, a playground, and horse rentals are available. A boat dock, launching facilities, rentals, and golf are nearby. An ATM is within a half mile. Leashed pets are permitted.

Reservations, fees: Reserve at 888/CAMP-OUT (888/226-7688) or online at www.parks.wa.gov /reservations ($7 reservation fee). The fee is $10–22 per night, plus $10 per additional vehicle per night. A senior discount is available. Major credit cards are accepted. Open year-round, with limited winter facilities.

Directions: From Leavenworth, drive west on U.S. 2 for 15 miles to State Route 207 at Coles Corner. Turn right (north) and drive three miles to the park entrance on the left.

Contact: Lake Wenatchee State Park, 21588 Hwy. 207, Leavenworth, WA 98826, 509/763-3101, fax 509/763-1029; state park information, 360/902-8844.

58 MIDWAY VILLAGE AND GROCERY

Rating: 5

near the Wenatchee River
See map pages 90–91

This private campground is located about a quarter mile from the Wenatchee River, and one mile from Lake Wenatchee State Park and Fish Lake, which is noted for good fishing year-round. There is good hiking and mountain biking out of the camp. Nearby recreation options include boat-

ing, fishing, water-skiing, swimming, windsurfing, hiking, and bike riding. The average annual snowfall is 12 feet. There is a snowmobile trail across the road from Midway Village. Snowmobile races are held in winter months within a quarter mile of the campground. Winter options include cross-country and downhill skiing, dogsledding (20 miles east of Stevens Pass Ski Area), snowshoeing, and ice fishing.

RV sites, facilities: There are 18 sites with full hookups (20, 30 amps) for RVs up to 40 feet and two RV rentals. Picnic tables and barbecues are provided. Restrooms, flush toilets, showers, firewood, a café, a coin-operated laundry, a pay phone, cell phone reception, ice, propane, and a children's playground with horseshoes and volleyball are available. A convenience store and gas are on-site. Boat docks, launching facilities, and rentals are nearby. An ATM is within five miles. Leashed pets are permitted.

Reservations, fees: Reservations are accepted. The fee is $16.50–22 per night. Major credit cards are accepted. Open year-round.

Directions: From Seattle, drive north on I-5 to Everett and U.S. 2. Turn east on U.S. 2 and drive 88 miles over Steven's Pass to Coles Corner at State Route 207. Turn left (north) on State Route 207 and drive four miles, crossing the bridge over the Wenatchee River to a Y intersection. Turn right at the Y and drive .25 mile to the park on the right.

Contact: Midway Village and Grocery, 14193 Chiwawa Loop Rd., Leavenworth, WA 98826, 509/763-3344, fax 509/763-3519.

59 NASON CREEK

Rating: 7

near Lake Wenatchee in Wenatchee National Forest
See map pages 90–91

This campground is located on Nason Creek near Lake Wenatchee, bordering Lake Wenatchee State Park. Recreation activities include swimming, fishing, and water-skiing. Horseback riding and golf are available nearby.

RV sites, facilities: There are 73 sites, including some drive-through, for RVs of any length, trailers, or tents. Picnic tables and fire grills are provided. Restrooms, drinking water, flush toilets, and electricity are available. Boat-launching facilities are nearby. A pay phone and an ATM are within 3.5 miles. Some facilities are wheelchair-accessible.

Reservations, fees: Reservations are not accepted. The fee is $12 per night, plus $9 per additional vehicle. A senior discount is available. Open May to mid-October.

Directions: From Seattle, drive north on I-5 to Everett and U.S. 2. Turn east on U.S. 2 and drive 87 miles to State Route 207. Turn north on State Route 207 and drive 3.5 miles to Cedar Brae Road. Turn west and drive 100 yards to the campground.

Contact: Okanogan and Wenatchee National Forests, Lake Wenatchee and Leavenworth Ranger District, Lake Wenatchee Office, 22976 Rte. 207, Leavenworth, WA 98826, 509/763-3103, fax 509/763-3211.

60 GOOSE CREEK

Rating: 7

on Goose Creek in Wenatchee National Forest
See map pages 90–91

With trails for dirt bikes available directly from the camp, Goose Creek is used primarily by motorcycle riders. A main trail links to the Entiat off-road-vehicle trail system, so this camp gets high use during the summer. The camp is set near a small creek.

RV sites, facilities: There are 29 sites for RVs of any length, trailers, or tents. Picnic tables and fire rings are provided. Drinking water and vault toilets are available. An ATM and a pay phone are within 10 miles. Leashed pets are permitted.

Reservations, fees: Reservations are not accepted. The fee is $7 per vehicle per night. A senior discount is available. Open May to mid-October.

Directions: From Seattle, drive north on I-5 to Everett and U.S. 2. Turn east on U.S. 2 and drive 87 miles to State Route 207. Turn north on State Route 207 and drive 4.5 miles to Chiwawa Loop Road. Turn right and drive two miles to Chiwawa Valley Road/Forest Road 6200. Turn left and drive three miles to Forest Road 6100. Turn right and drive .25 mile to the camp on the right.

Contact: Okanogan and Wenatchee National

Forests, Lake Wenatchee and Leavenworth Ranger District, Lake Wenatchee Office, 22976 Rte. 207, Leavenworth, WA 98826, 509/763-3103, fax 509/763-3211.

61 SNOWBERRY BOWL

Rating: 7

near Lake Chelan in Wenatchee National Forest
See map pages 90–91

Snowberry Bowl is less than four miles from Twenty-Five Mile Creek State Park and Lake Chelan. Nestled amid a forest of Douglas fir and Ponderosa pine, which provide privacy screening, it sits at an elevation of 2,000 feet. The camp is most often used as an overflow camp when the state park fills up. It opened in 2001 and is not well known.

RV sites, facilities: There are seven sites for RVs up to 40 feet, trailers, or tents and two double sites for up to 15 people each. Picnic tables, fire grills, and tent pads on sand are provided. Drinking water and vault toilets are available. A pay phone is within four miles. Some facilities are wheelchair-accessible. Leashed pets are permitted.

Reservations, fees: Reservations are not accepted. The fees are $9 per night and $18 for double sites. A senior discount is available. Open year-round, with limited winter facilities.

Directions: From Chelan, drive south on Highway 97A for three miles to South Lakeshore Road. Turn right and drive 13.5 miles (passing the state park) to Shady Pass Road. Turn left and drive 2.5 miles to a Y intersection with Slide Ridge Road. Bear left and drive .5 mile to the campground on the right.

Contact: Okanogan and Wenatchee National Forests, Chelan Ranger District, 428 West Woodin Ave., Chelan, WA 98816, 509/682-2576, fax 509/682-9004.

62 TWENTY-FIVE MILE CREEK STATE PARK

Rating: 8

near Lake Chelan
See map pages 90–91

This campground is located on Twenty-Five Mile Creek near where it empties into Lake Chelan. A 235-acre marine camping park, it sits on the forested south shore of Lake Chelan. The park separates the mountain from the lake and is surrounded by spectacular scenery, featuring a rocky terrain with forested areas. It's known for its boat access. You can use this park as your launching point for exploring the up-lake wilderness portions of Lake Chelan. Fishing access for trout and salmon is close by. Fishing supplies, a dock, a modern marina, and boat moorage are available. There is also a small wading area for kids. Forest Road 5900, which heads west from the park, accesses several trailheads leading into the U.S. Forest Service lands of the Chelan Mountains. Obtain a U.S. Forest Service map of Wenatchee National Forest for details. Note that a ferry can take visitors to a roadless community at the head of the lake.

RV sites, facilities: There are 21 sites with partial or full hookups (20 amps) for RVs up to 30 feet and 53 sites for tents. Picnic tables and fire grills are provided. Drinking water and flush toilets are available. An RV dump station, firewood, a pay phone, a boat dock, a fishing pier, a marina, a boat ramp, boat moorage, a picnic area, gasoline, and a grocery store are available nearby.

Reservations, fees: Reserve at 888/CAMP-OUT (888/226-7688)or online at www.parks.wa.gov /reservations ($7 reservation fee). The fee is $16–22 per night, plus $2 per person for more than four people and $10 per additional vehicle. Marina slips are $10 per night. A senior discount is available. Major credit cards are accepted. Open April to October.

Directions: From Chelan, drive south on Highway 97A for three miles to South Lakeshore Road. Turn right and drive 15 miles to the park on the right.

Contact: Twenty-Five Mile Creek State Park, South Lakeshore Rd., Chelan, WA 98816, 509/687-3710; state park information, 360/902-8844; Lake Chelan Boat Company, 509/682-4584, website: www.ladyofthelake.com.

63 KAMEI CAMPGROUND & RV PARK

Rating: 6

on Lake Wapato
See map pages 90–91

This resort is on Lake Wapato, about two miles from Lake Chelan, and close to a casino. Note that this is a seasonal lake that closes midsummer. If you have an extra day, take the ferryboat ride on Lake Chelan.

RV sites, facilities: There are 50 sites, some with partial hookups (20, 50 amps), for RVs of any length, trailers, or tents. Picnic tables are provided. Restrooms, drinking water, flush toilets, showers, cell phone reception, and ice are available. Boat docks, launching facilities, and boat rentals are nearby. A pay phone and an ATM are within four miles. Leashed pets are permitted.

Reservations, fees: Reservations are accepted beginning in January. The fee is $16–17 per night, plus $4 per person for more than four people. Open late April to early September.

Directions: From Chelan, drive west on Highway 150 for seven miles to Wapato Lake Road. Turn north on Wapato Lake Road and drive three miles to the resort on Wapato Lake Road.

Contact: Kamei Campground & RV Park, Wapato Lake Rd. Rte. 1, Manson, WA 98831, 509/687-3690.

64 LAKE CHELAN STATE PARK

Rating: 10

on Lake Chelan
See map pages 90–91

This park is the recreation headquarters for Lake Chelan. It provides boat docks and concession stands on the shore of the 55-mile lake. The park covers 127 acres, featuring 6,000 feet of shoreline on the forested south shore. Summers tend to be hot and dry, but expansive lawns provide a fresh feel, especially in the early evenings, looking out on the lake. A daily ferry service provides access to the roadless community at the head of the lake. The word "chelan" is Native American and translates to both "lake" and "blue water." Water sports include fishing, swimming, scuba diving, and water-skiing.

RV sites, facilities: There are 35 sites with partial or full hookups (20 amps) for RVs up to 30 feet, 109 developed tent sites, and two primitive tent sites. Picnic tables and fire grills are provided. Restrooms, drinking water, flush toilets, showers, firewood, a picnic area with a kitchen shelter, an RV dump station, a store, a pay phone, ice, a playground, a beach area, a boat dock, and launching facilities and moorage are available. A restaurant is across the street, and an ATM and groceries are within 10 miles. Some facilities are wheelchair-accessible.

Reservations, fees: Reserve at 888/CAMP-OUT (888/226-7688) or online at www.parks.wa.gov /reservations ($7 reservation fee). The fee is $10–22 per night, plus $10 per additional vehicle per night. Major credit cards are accepted. A senior discount is available. Open mid-March to October.

Directions: From Wenatchee, drive north on U.S. 97-A for 27 miles to State Route 971 (Navarre Coulee Road). Turn left (north) and drive seven miles to the end of the highway at South Lakeshore Road. Turn right, then immediately look for the park entrance to the left.

Contact: Lake Chelan State Park, 509/687-3710; state park information, 360/902-8844.

65 DAROGA STATE PARK

Rating: 6

on the Columbia River
See map pages 90–91

This 90-acre state park is set along 1.5 miles of shoreline on the Columbia River. It sits on the elevated edge of the desert "scab-lands." This camp fills up quickly on summer weekends. The Desert Canyon Golf Course is two miles away. Fishing, along with walking and biking trails, are available out of the camp.

RV sites, facilities: There are 28 sites with partial hookups (30 amps), including eight drive-through sites, for RVs up to 40 feet, trailers, and tents, 17 walk-in or boat-in sites (requiring a quarter-mile trip), and two group sites for 20 to 100

people. Picnic tables and fire pits are provided. Restrooms, drinking water, flush toilets (near RV sites) and vault toilets (near walk-in sites), showers, an RV dump station, ice, firewood, cell phone reception, a pay phone, a swimming beach, boat-launching facilities and docks, a picnic area with a kitchen shelter, and a playground with a baseball field, basketball courts, softball, and soccer fields are available. An ATM is within five miles. Leashed pets are permitted.

Reservations, fees: Reservations are accepted for group sites only; reserve at 888/CAMP-OUT (888/226-7688) or online at www.parks.wa.gov /reservations ($7 reservation fee). The fees are $10–22, plus $10 per additional vehicle per night; group sites are $25 plus $2 per person per night, with a minimum of 20 people. A senior discount is available. Open mid-March to mid-October, weather permitting.

Directions: From East Wenatchee, drive north on Highway 97 (east side of Columbia River) for 18 miles to the camp. For boat-in camps, launch boats from the ramp at the park and drive .25 mile.

Contact: Daroga State Park, 509/664-6380; state park information, 360/902-8844.

66 ENTIAT CITY PARK

Rating: 8

on the Columbia River
See map pages 90–91

If you're hurting for a spot for the night, you can usually find a campsite here. Lake Entiat is actually a dammed portion of the Columbia River. Access to nearby launching facilities makes this a good camping spot for boaters.

RV sites, facilities: There are 31 sites with partial hookups (30 amps) for RVs of any length and 25 tent sites. Picnic tables are provided. Restrooms, drinking water, flush toilets, coin-operated showers, an RV dump station, cell phone reception, a pay phone, a playground, propane, a store, a café, a laundry room, and ice are available. Boat docks and launching facilities are nearby. An ATM is within one mile. No open fires, dogs, or alcohol are permitted.

Reservations, fees: Reservation are available at 800/736-8428. The fee is $20–25 per night, plus $2 per extra person above four people per night. Open mid-April to mid-September.

Directions: From Wenatchee, drive north on U.S. 97-A for 16 miles to Entiat; the park entrance is on the right (Shearson Street is adjacent on the left). Turn right and drive to the park along the shore of Lake Entiat.

Contact: Entiat City Park, P.O. Box 228, Entiat, WA 98822, 800/736-8428; city offices, 509/784-1500.

67 MONEY CREEK CAMPGROUND

Rating: 5

on the Skykomish River in Mt. Baker–Snoqualmie National Forest
See map pages 90–91

You have a little surprise waiting for you here. Trains go by regularly day and night, and the first time it happens while you're in deep sleep, you might just launch a hole right through the top of your tent. The Burlington Northern/Santa Fe Railroad runs along the western boundary of the campground. By now you've got the picture: This can be a noisy camp. Money Creek Campground is on the Skykomish River, with hiking trails a few miles away. The best of these is the Dorothy Lake Trail. This camp was renovated in 2002.

RV sites, facilities: There are 25 sites for RVs up to 40 feet, trailers, or tents. Picnic tables are provided. Vault toilets, cell phone reception, and drinking water are available. A store, a café, a pay phone, an ATM, and ice are within 3.5 miles. Some facilities are wheelchair-accessible. Leashed pets are permitted.

Reservations, fees: Some sites can be reserved at 877/444-6777 or online at www.reserveusa.com ($9 reservation fee). The fee is $14 per night, plus $7 per additional vehicle per night. A senior discount is available. Open Memorial Day Weekend through Labor Day Weekend.

Directions: From Seattle, drive north on I-5 to Everett and U.S. 2. Turn east on U.S. 2 and drive 46 miles to Old Cascade Highway, 11 miles east of Index. Turn south on Old Cascade Highway and drive across the bridge to the campground.

Contact: Mt. Baker–Snoqualmie National Forest, Skykomish Ranger District, P.O. Box 305, Skykomish, WA 98288, 360/677-2414, fax 425/744-3265.

68 BECKLER RIVER

Rating: 7

on the Beckler River in Mt. Baker–Snoqualmie National Forest
See map pages 90–91

Located on the Beckler River at an elevation of 900 feet, this camp has scenic riverside sites in second-growth timber, primarily Douglas fir, cedar, and big leaf maple. Fishing at the campground is poor; it's better well up the river. The Skykomish Ranger Station is just a couple of miles away; maps are available for sale.

RV sites, facilities: There are 27 sites for RVs up to 40 feet, trailers, or tents. Picnic tables and fire grills are provided. Vault toilets, drinking water, and cell phone reception are available. A store, a café, an ATM, a pay phone, and ice are available within two miles. Some sites and facilities are wheelchair-accessible. Leashed pets are permitted.

Reservations, fees: Some sites can be reserved at 877/444-6777 or online at www.reserveusa.com ($9 reservation fee). The fee is $14 per night, plus $7 per additional vehicle per night. A senior discount is available. Open Memorial Day through Labor Day.

Directions: From Seattle, drive north on I-5 to Everett and U.S. 2. Turn east on U.S. 2 and drive 49 miles to Skykomish. Continue east on U.S. 2 for .5 mile to Forest Road 65. Turn left (north) on Forest Road 65 and drive 1.6 miles to the camp on the left.

Contact: Mt. Baker–Snoqualmie National Forest, Skykomish Ranger District, P.O. Box 305, Skykomish, WA 98288, 360/677-2414, fax 425/744-3265.

69 MILLER RIVER GROUP

Rating: 8

near the Alpine Lakes Wilderness in Mt. Baker–Snoqualmie National Forest
See map pages 90–91

This campground is located along the Miller River, a short distance from the boundary of the Alpine Lakes Wilderness. If you continue another seven miles on Forest Road 6410, you'll get to a trailhead leading to Dorothy Lake, a 1.5-mile hike. This pretty lake is two miles long. The trail continues past the lake to many other backcountry lakes. The group limit in wilderness is 12 people. A U.S. Forest Service map is essential.

RV sites, facilities: This is a group camp with 18 sites for up to 100 people with RVs up to 40 feet, trailers, or tents. Picnic tables and fire grills are provided. Vault toilets, drinking water, a group barbecue, and a 24-foot group table are available. A store, a café, a pay phone, an ATM, and ice are within six miles. Some facilities are wheelchair-accessible. Leashed pets are permitted.

Reservations, fees: Reservations are required; reserve at 877/444-6777 or online at www .reserveusa.com ($9 reservation fee). The fees are $75 for the first 50 people, $125 for 51–75, and $150 for 76–100 campers. Open mid-May to late September.

Directions: From Seattle, drive north on I-5 to Everett and U.S. 2. Turn east on U.S. 2 and drive 46 miles to Old Cascade Highway, 11 miles east of Index. Turn south on Old Cascade Highway (across the bridge) and drive one mile to Forest Road 6410. Turn right (south) and drive two miles to the campground on the left.

Contact: Mt. Baker–Snoqualmie National Forest, Skykomish Ranger District, P.O. Box 305, Skykomish, WA 98288, 360/677-2414, fax 425/744-3265.

70 BLACKPINE CREEK HORSE CAMP

Rating: 8

near the Alpine Lakes Wilderness in Wenatchee National Forest
See map pages 90–91

A base camp for horse pack trips, Blackpine Creek Horse Camp is for horse campers only. It is set on Black Pine Creek near Icicle Creek, at a major trailhead leading into the Alpine Lakes Wilderness. It's one of seven rustic camps on the creek, with the distinction of being the only one with facilities for horses. The elevation is 3,000 feet.

RV sites, facilities: There are 10 drive-through sites for RVs up to 21 feet, trailers, or tents. Picnic tables and fire grills are provided. Drinking water and vault toilets are available. Horse facilities,

including a loading ramp, are also available. Leashed pets are permitted.

Reservations, fees: Reservations are not accepted. The fee is $10 per vehicle per night. A senior discount is available. Open mid-May to late October.

Directions: From Seattle, drive north on I-5 to Everett and U.S. 2. Turn east on U.S. 2 and drive 103 miles to Leavenworth and County Road 76 (Icicle River Road). Turn south and drive 19.2 miles to the campground on the left.

Contact: Okanogan and Wenatchee National Forests, Leavenworth Ranger District, 600 Sherbourne, Leavenworth, WA 98826, 509/548-6977, fax 509/548-5817.

71 ROCK ISLAND

Rating: 8

near the Alpine Lakes Wilderness in Wenatchee National Forest
See map pages 90–91

Rock Island is one of several campgrounds in the immediate area along Icicle Creek and is located about one mile from the trailhead that takes hikers into the Alpine Lakes Wilderness. This is a pretty spot with good fishing access. The elevation is 2,900 feet.

RV sites, facilities: There are 22 sites for RVs up to 21 feet, trailers, or tents. Picnic tables and fire grills are provided. Drinking water and vault toilets are available. Some facilities are wheelchair-accessible. Leashed pets are permitted.

Reservations, fees: Reservations are not accepted. The fee is $10 per vehicle per night, plus $9 per additional vehicle. A senior discount is available. Open May to late October.

Directions: From Seattle, drive north on I-5 to Everett and U.S. 2. Turn east on U.S. 2 and drive 103 miles to Leavenworth and County Road 76 (Icicle River Road). Turn south and drive 17.7 miles to the campground.

Contact: Okanogan and Wenatchee National Forests, Leavenworth Ranger District, 600 Sherbourne, Leavenworth, WA 98826, 509/548-6977, fax 509/548-5817.

72 CHATTER CREEK

Rating: 8

near the Alpine Lakes Wilderness in Wenatchee National Forest
See map pages 90–91

Icicle and Chatter Creeks are the backdrop for this creekside campground. The elevation is 2,800 feet. Trails lead out in several directions from the camp into the Alpine Lakes Wilderness.

RV sites, facilities: There are 12 sites for RVs up to 21 feet, trailers, or tents and one group site for up to 45 people. Picnic tables and fire grills are provided. Drinking water and vault toilets are available. Leashed pets are permitted.

Reservations, fees: Reservations are required only for group sites; reserve at 877/444-6777 or online at www.reserveusa.com ($9 reservation fee). The fees are $10 per night for single sites, plus $9 per additional vehicle, and $70 per night for the group site. A senior discount is available. Open May to late October.

Directions: From Seattle, drive north on I-5 to Everett and U.S. 2. Turn east on U.S. 2 and drive 103 miles to Leavenworth and County Road 76 (Icicle River Road). Turn south and drive 16.1 miles to the campground on the right.

Contact: Okanogan and Wenatchee National Forests, Leavenworth Ranger District, 600 Sherbourne, Leavenworth, WA 98826, 509/548-6977, fax 509/548-5817.

73 IDA CREEK

Rating: 8

on Icicle Creek in Wenatchee National Forest
See map pages 90–91

This campground is one of several small, quiet camps along Icicle and Ida Creeks, with recreation options similar to Chatter Creek and Rock Island Campgrounds (see previous listings).

RV sites, facilities: There are five sites for RVs up to 21 feet, trailers, or tents and five tent sites. Picnic tables and fire grills are provided. Drinking water and vault toilets are available. Some facilities are wheelchair-accessible. Leashed pets are permitted.

Reservations, fees: Reservations are not accepted.

The fee is $10 per night, plus $9 per additional vehicle. A senior discount is available. Open May to late October.

Directions: From Seattle, drive north on I-5 to Everett and U.S. 2. Turn east on U.S. 2 and drive 103 miles to Leavenworth and County Road 76 (Icicle River Road). Turn south and drive 14.2 miles to the campground on the left.

Contact: Okanogan and Wenatchee National Forests, Leavenworth Ranger District, 600 Sherbourne, Leavenworth, WA 98826, 509/548-6977, fax 509/548-5817.

74 JOHNNY CREEK

Rating: 8

on Icicle Creek in Wenatchee National Forest
See map pages 90–91

This campground is split into two parts and sits on both sides of the road, along Icicle and Johnny Creeks. It is fairly popular. Upper Johnny has a forest setting, whereas Lower Johnny is set alongside the creek, with adjacent forest. The elevation is 2,300 feet.

RV sites, facilities: There are 65 sites for RVs up to 50 feet, trailers, or tents. Picnic tables and fire grills are provided. Drinking water and vault toilets are available. Some facilities are wheelchair-accessible. Leashed pets are permitted.

Reservations, fees: Reservations are not accepted. The fee is $10–11 per night, plus $9–10 per additional vehicle. A senior discount is available. Open May to late October.

Directions: From Seattle, drive north on I-5 to Everett and U.S. 2. Turn east on U.S. 2 and drive 103 miles to Leavenworth and County Road 76 (Icicle River Road). Turn south and drive 12.4 miles to the campground (with camps on each side of the road).

Contact: Okanogan and Wenatchee National Forests, Leavenworth Ranger District, 600 Sherbourne, Leavenworth, WA 98826, 509/548-6977, fax 509/548-5817.

WASHINGTON

75 EIGHTMILE

Rating: 8

near the Alpine Lakes Wilderness in Wenatchee National Forest

See map pages 90–91

This camp is set in the vicinity of trout fishing and hiking. Trailheads are available within two miles of the campground along Icicle and Eightmile Creeks, providing access to fishing, as well as a backpacking route into the Alpine Lakes Wilderness. The elevation is 1,800 feet. Horseback-riding opportunities are within four miles and golf is within five miles.

RV sites, facilities: There are 45 sites for RVs up to 50 feet, trailers, or tents and one group site for up to 70 people. Picnic tables and fire grills are provided. Drinking water, vault toilets, and cell phone reception are available. An ATM and pay phone are within eight miles. Some facilities are wheelchair-accessible. Leashed pets are permitted.

Reservations, fees: Reservations are required only for the group site; phone 800/274-6104 (reservation fee). The fees are $11 per night, plus $10 per additional vehicle, and $70 per night for the group site. A senior discount is available. Open mid-April to late October.

Directions: From Seattle, drive north on I-5 to Everett and U.S. 2. Turn east on U.S. 2 and drive 103 miles to Leavenworth and County Road 76 (Icicle River Road). Turn south and drive eight miles to the campground on the left.

Contact: Okanogan and Wenatchee National Forests, Leavenworth Ranger District, 600 Sherbourne, Leavenworth, WA 98826, 509/548-6977, fax 509/548-5817.

76 ICICLE RIVER RV RESORT

Rating: 9

on Icicle River

See map pages 90–91

Icicle River RV Resort is one of two campgrounds in the immediate area. The other is Pine Village KOA/Leavenworth. Note that no tent camping is permitted here, but six cabins are available for rent. This pretty, wooded spot is set along the Icicle River, where fishing and swimming are available. The park is clean and scenic and even has its own putting green. An 18-hole golf course and hiking trails are nearby.

RV sites, facilities: There are 114 sites with partial or full hookups (30, 50 amps) for RVs of any length and six rustic cabins. Picnic tables and fire pits (at some sites) are provided. Restrooms, drinking water, flush toilets, showers, modem access, two pay phones, cell phone reception, a hot tub, firewood, and propane are available. A putting green, horseshoes, and two pavilions are on-site. An ATM and groceries are available within five miles. Leashed pets are permitted.

Reservations, fees: Reservations are accepted. The fee is $26.50–32.50 per night, plus $4 per additional vehicle per night and $3–4 per person per night for more than two people. Major credit cards are accepted. Open April to October, weather permitting.

Directions: From Seattle, drive north on I-5 to Everett and U.S. 2. Turn east on U.S. 2 and drive 103 miles to Leavenworth and County Road 76 (Icicle River Road). Turn south (right) and drive three miles to the park on the left.

Contact: Icicle River RV Resort, 7305 Icicle Rd., Leavenworth, WA 98826, 509/548-5420, fax 509/548-6207, website: www.icicleriverrv.com.

77 TUMWATER

Rating: 7

near the Alpine Lakes Wilderness in Wenatchee National Forest

See map pages 90–91

This large, popular camp provides a little bit of both worlds. It provides a good layover spot for campers cruising U.S. 2. But it also features two nearby forest roads, each less than a mile long, which end at trailheads that provide access to the Alpine Lakes Wilderness. If you don't like to hike, no problem. The camp is on the Wenatchee River in Tumwater Canyon. This section of river is closed to fishing. The elevation is 2,050 feet.

RV sites, facilities: There are 84 sites for RVs up to 50 feet, trailers, or tents and one group site for up to 75 people. Drinking water, fire grills, and picnic tables are provided. Flush toilets are

available. Some facilities are wheelchair-accessible. Leashed pets are permitted.

Reservations, fees: Reservations are required only for the group site; phone 877/444-6777 or reserve online at www.reserveusa.com ($9 reservation fee). The fees are $12 per night, plus $11 per additional vehicle, and $80 for group sites. A senior discount is available. Open May to mid-October.

Directions: From Seattle, drive north on I-5 to Everett and U.S. 2. Turn east on U.S. 2 and drive 93 miles to the campground (10 miles west of Leavenworth).

Contact: Okanogan and Wenatchee National Forests, Leavenworth Ranger District, 509/548-6977, fax 509/548-5817.

78 PINE VILLAGE KOA/LEAVENWORTH

Rating: 8

near the Wenatchee River
See map pages 90–91

This lovely resort is located near the "Bavarian village" of Leavenworth, to which the park provides a free shuttle in the summer. The spectacularly scenic area is surrounded by the Cascade Mountains and set among Ponderosa pines. The camp has access to the Wenatchee River, not to mention many luxurious extras, including a hot tub and a heated pool. The park allows campfires and has firewood available. Nearby recreation options include an 18-hole golf course and hiking trails. Make a point to spend a day in Leavenworth if possible; it offers authentic German food and architecture, along with music and art shows in the summer.

RV sites, facilities: There are 135 sites, including 22 drive-through, for RVs up to 45 feet, 40 tent sites, 20 cabins, nine lodges, and two cottages. Picnic tables and fire grills are provided. Restrooms, drinking water, flush toilets, showers, an RV dump station, firewood, a recreation hall, cable TV, a store, a laundry room, two pay phones, cell phone reception, modem access, ice, a playground with horseshoes and volleyball, a spa, a heated swimming pool, and a beach area are available. Propane, an ATM, and a café are available within one mile. Some facilities are wheelchair-accessible. Leashed pets are permitted.

Reservations, fees: Reservations are accepted at 800/562-5709. The fee is $21–38 per night, plus $5 per additional vehicle per night and $4.50 per person per night for more than two people. Cabins are $50–65, cottages $109–139, and lodges $115–145. Major credit cards are accepted. Open April to November.

Directions: From Spokane on Highway 2, drive west 192 miles to Leavenworth and Riverbend Drive. Turn right (north), and drive .5 mile to the campground entrance on the right.

Contact: Pine Village KOA/Leavenworth, 11401 River Bend Dr., Leavenworth, WA 98826, 509/548-7709 (phone or fax), website: www.koa.com.

79 BLU SHASTIN RV PARK

Rating: 6

near Peshastin Creek
See map pages 90–91

This park is set in a mountainous area near Peshastin Creek. Gold panning in the river is a popular activity here, and during the gold rush, the Peshastin was the best-producing river in the state. The camp has sites on the riverbank and plenty of shade trees. A heated pool, a recreation field, and horseshoes provide possible activities in the park. Hiking trails and marked bike trails are nearby.

RV sites, facilities: There are 86 sites with full hookups (30 amps), including four drive-through sites, for RVs of any length, trailers, or tents. Picnic tables and fire rings are provided. Restrooms, drinking water, flush toilets, showers, pay phone, cell phone reception, a recreation hall, firewood, a coin-operated laundry, ice, a playground, horseshoes, a game room with Ping Pong and video games, badminton, volleyball, and a heated swimming pool are available. Propane, a store, and a café are available within seven miles. An ATM is within a quarter mile. Leashed pets are permitted.

Reservations, fees: Reservations are recommended. The fee is $20–25 per night. Major credit cards are accepted. Open year-round.

Directions: From Leavenworth, drive south on U.S. 2 for four miles to U.S. 97. Turn south (right) on U.S. 97 and drive seven miles to the park on the right.

Contact: Blu Shastin RV Park, 3300 Hwy. 97,

Peshastin, WA 98847, 509/548-4184 or 888/548-4184, website: www.blushastin.com.

80 WENATCHEE RIVER COUNTY PARK

⬛⬛⬛⬛⬛

Rating: 5

on the Wenatchee River
See map pages 90–91

This camp is set along the Wenatchee River, situated between the highway and the river. Renovated in 2003, many sites were moved to alleviate highway noise. Other improvements have made this a great place for RV cruisers. You can usually get a tree-covered site in the campground, despite it being a small park. The adjacent river is fast moving and provides white-water rafting, with a put-in spot at the park. Fishing has been poor in the past but is improving due to upstream work and hatchery output.

RV sites, facilities: There are 50 sites, including 43 with full hookups (20, 30, 50 amps), for RVs up to 50 feet (three drive-through), seven tent sites, and one cabin. Picnic tables and fire grills are provided. Restrooms, drinking water, flush toilets, a pay phone, cell phone reception, and showers are available. A store and a restaurant are within one mile. An ATM is within five miles. Leashed pets are permitted.

Reservations, fees: Reservations are available at 509/667-7503. The fee is $15–22 per night, plus $5 per person for more than four people and $5 per additional vehicle per night. Major credit cards are accepted. Open April to September.

Directions: From Wenatchee and U.S. 2, drive west on U.S. 2 for 4.7 miles to the campground on the left.

Contact: Chelan County Commissioner, 350 Orondo Ave., Wenatchee, WA 98801, 509/667-7503 or 509/667-6215, fax 509/667-5914, website: www.co.chelan.wa.us.

81 WENATCHEE CONFLUENCE STATE PARK

⬛⬛⬛⬛⬛⬛⬛⬛⬛⬛

Rating: 10

on the Columbia River
See map pages 90–91

This 197-acre state park is set at the confluence of the Wenatchee and Columbia Rivers. The park features expansive lawns shaded by deciduous trees and fronted by the two rivers. Wenatchee Confluence has something of a dual personality: The north portion of the park is urban and recreational, while the southern section is a designated natural wetland area. There are 10.5 miles of paved trail for hiking, biking, and in-line skating. Pedestrian bridges cross both the Wenatchee and Columbia Rivers. An interpretive hiking trail is available in the Horan Natural Area. Other recreation possibilities include fishing, swimming, boating, and water-skiing. Sports enthusiasts will find playing fields as well as tennis and basketball courts. Daroga State Park and Lake Chelan to the north offer side trip possibilities.

RV sites, facilities: There are 59 sites with full hookups (30 amps) for RVs up to 65 feet, six developed tent sites, and a group site for tents for up to 300 people. Picnic tables and fire grills are provided. Restrooms, drinking water, flush toilets, coin-operated showers, a pay phone, cell phone reception, a boat launch, an RV dump station, a swimming beach, a playground, and athletic fields are available. An ATM and groceries are available within one block. Some facilities are wheelchair-accessible. Leashed pets are permitted.

Reservations, fees: Reserve at 888/CAMP-OUT (888/226-7688) or online at www.parks.wa.gov/reservations ($7 reservation fee). The fee is $16–22 per night, plus $6 per additional vehicle per night. Major credit cards are accepted in summer. A senior discount is available. Open year-round.

Directions: From Wenatchee and U.S. 2, take the Easy Street exit and drive south to Penny Road. Turn left and drive a short distance to Chester Kimm Street. Turn right and drive to a T intersection and Old Station Road. Turn left on Old Station Road and drive past the railroad tracks to the park on the right. The park is 1.3 miles from U.S. 2.

Contact: Wenatchee Confluence State Park, 333 Olds Station Rd., Wenatchee, WA 98801, 509/664-6373, fax 509/662-0459; state park information, 360/902-8844.

WASHINGTON

82 LINCOLN ROCK STATE PARK

Rating: 5

on Lake Entiat
See map pages 90–91

Lincoln Rock State Park is an 80-acre park set along the shore of Lake Entiat. The lake was created by the Rocky Reach Dam on the Columbia River. The park is named for a basalt outcropping that is said to resemble the profile of Abraham Lincoln. The park features lawns and shade trees amid an arid landscape. There are two miles of hiking and bike trails, paved and flat. Water sports include swimming, boating, and water-skiing. Beavers are occasionally visible in the Columbia River.

RV sites, facilities: There are 94 sites, some with partial or full hookups (30 amps), for RVs up to 65 feet. Picnic tables and fire grills are provided. Restrooms, drinking water, flush toilets, coin-operated showers, a pay phone, cell phone reception, an RV dump station, a playground, an athletic fields, horseshoes, a swimming beach, an amphitheater, and three picnic shelters with electricity are available. Boat docks, moorage, and launching facilities are located on Lake Entiat. An ATM and firewood are available within a quarter mile. Some facilities are wheelchair-accessible. Leashed pets are permitted.

Reservations, fees: Reserve at 888/CAMP-OUT (888/226-7688) or online at www.parks.wa.gov /reservations ($7 reservation fee). The fee is $16–22 per night, plus $10 per additional vehicle per night. A senior discount is available. Major credit cards are accepted. Open March to mid-October.

Directions: From East Wenatchee, drive northeast on U.S. 2 for seven miles to the park on the left.

Contact: Lincoln Rock State Park, 509/884-8702, fax 509/886-1704; state park information, 360/902-8844.

83 SNOQUALMIE RIVER CAMPGROUND & RV PARK

Rating: 7

on the Snoqualmie River
See map pages 90–91

If you're in the Seattle area and stuck for a place for the night, this pretty 10-acre park set along the Snoqualmie River may be a welcome option. Activities include fishing, swimming, road biking, and rafting. Nearby recreation options include several nine-hole golf courses. A worthwhile side trip is beautiful Snoqualmie Falls, 3.5 miles away in the famed Twin Peaks country.

RV sites, facilities: There are 112 sites, 92 with partial or full hookups (30 amps), including 12 long-term rentals, for RVs of any length, and 50 tent sites. Picnic tables are provided. Restrooms, drinking water, flush toilets, showers, cell phone reception, modem access, a pay phone, firewood, and a playground are available. Propane, a store, a café, an ATM, and ice are available within two miles. Boat-launching facilities are available within a half mile. Leashed pets are permitted.

Reservations, fees: Reservations are accepted. The fee is $21–25 per night, plus $3.50 per person per night for more than two people and $2.50 per pet per night. Major credit cards are accepted. Open April to October.

Directions: From the junction of I-5 and I-90 south of Seattle, turn east on I-90. Drive east for 26 miles to Exit 22 (Preston–Fall City). Take that exit and turn north on Preston–Fall City Road and drive 4.5 miles to SE 44th Place. Turn east and drive one mile to the campground at the end of the road.

Contact: Snoqualmie River Campground & RV Park, 425/222-5545.

84 TINKHAM

Rating: 9

on the Snoqualmie River in Mt. Baker–Snoqualmie National Forest
See map pages 90–91

About half the campsites here face the Snoqualmie River, making this a pretty spot. Fishing can be good; check regulations. The camp is set at an elevation of 1,600 feet. The creek provides hiking options. This camp is often used as an overflow for Denny Creek Camp. Wilderness trails for the Alpines Lakes Wilderness are located 5 to 10 miles away from the camp.

RV sites, facilities: There are 47 sites for RVs up to 35 feet, trailers, or tents. Picnic tables and fire pits are provided. Drinking water and vault toilets are available. Some facilities are wheelchair-accessible. Leashed pets are permitted.

Reservations, fees: Some sites can be reserved at 877/444-6777 or online at www.reserveusa.com ($9 reservation fee). The fee is $14 per night, plus $7 per additional vehicle per night. Open late May to early September.

Directions: In Seattle on I-5, turn east on I-90. Drive east on I-90 to Exit 42. Take that exit and turn right on Tinkham Road (Forest Road 55), and drive southeast 1.5 miles to the campground on the left. Obtaining a U.S. Forest Service map is advisable.

Contact: Mt. Baker–Snoqualmie National Forest, Snoqualmie Ranger District, North Bend Office, 42404 SE North Bend Way, North Bend, WA 98045, 425/888-1421, fax 425/888-1910.

85 DENNY CREEK

Rating: 9

on Denny Creek
See map pages 90–91

This camp is set at 1,900 feet elevation along Denny Creek, which is pretty and offers nearby recreation access. The campground is secluded in an area of Douglas fir, hemlock, and cedar, with hiking trails available in addition to swimming. The Denny Creek Trail starts from the campground and provides a 3.5-mile round-trip hike that features Keckwulee Falls and Denny Creek Waterslide. You can also climb to Hemlock Pass and Melakwa Lake. There is access for backpackers into the Alpine Lakes Wilderness.

RV sites, facilities: There are 33 sites, some with partial hookups (30 amps), for trailers or tents up to 35 feet and one group site for up to 35 people. Picnic tables and fire grills are provided. Drinking water, flush toilets, and firewood are available. Some facilities are wheelchair-accessible. Leashed pets are permitted.

Reservations, fees: Reserve at 877/444-6777 or online at www.reserveusa.com ($9 reservation fee). The fee is $14–18 per night, plus $7 per additional vehicle per night. The group site is $75 per night. A senior discount is available. Open late May to early October, weather permitting.

Directions: In Seattle on I-5, turn east on I-90. Drive east on I-90 to Exit 47. Take that exit, cross the freeway, and at the T intersection turn right and drive .25 mile to Denny Creek Road (Forest Road 58). Turn left on Denny Creek Road and drive two miles to the campground on the left.

Contact: Mt. Baker–Snoqualmie National Forest, Snoqualmie Ranger District, North Bend Office, 42404 SE North Bend Way, North Bend, WA 98045, 425/888-1421, fax 425/888-1910.

86 SALMON LA SAC

Rating: 6

on the Cle Elum River in Wenatchee National Forest
See map pages 90–91

This is a base camp for backpackers and day hikers and is also popular with kayakers. It's located along the Cle Elum River at 2,400 feet elevation, about a quarter mile from a major trailhead, the Salmon La Sac Trailhead. Hikers can follow creeks heading off in several directions, including into the Alpine Lakes Wilderness. A campground host is available for information.

RV sites, facilities: There are 99 sites, including 12 double sites, for RVs up to 21 feet, trailers, or tents. Picnic tables and fire grills are provided. Drinking water and flush toilets are available. Leashed pets are permitted.

Reservations, fees: Some sites can be reserved at 877/444-6777 or online at www.reserveusa.com ($9 reservation fee). The fee is $14–28 per night, plus $11 per additional vehicle per night. A senior discount is available. Open late May to early September.

Directions: In Seattle on I-5, turn east on I-90. Drive east on I-90 for 78 miles to Exit 80 (two miles before Cle Elum). Take that exit, turn north on Bullfrog Road, and drive three miles to Highway 903. Continue north on Highway 903 for 21 miles to the campground on the left.

Contact: Okanogan and Wenatchee National Forests, Cle Elum Ranger District, West Second St., Cle Elum, WA 98922, 509/674-4411, fax 509/674-1530.

87 KACHESS & KACHESS GROUP

Rating: 8

on Kachess Lake in Wenatchee National Forest
See map pages 90-91
This is the only campground on the shore of Kachess Lake, but note that the water level often drops significantly in summer due to irrigation needs. It is the most popular campground in the local area, often filling in July and August, especially on weekends. Recreation opportunities include water-skiing, fishing, hiking, and bicycling. A trail from camp heads north into the Alpine Lakes Wilderness; see a U.S. Forest Service map for details. The elevation is 2,300 feet.
RV sites, facilities: There are 120 sites, including 30 double sites, for RVs up to 32 feet, trailers, or tents. A group site is also available. Picnic tables and fire grills are provided. Drinking water, cell phone reception, and vault toilets are available. Restrooms and dump stations are located at Kachess Lake. Some facilities are wheelchair-accessible. Leashed pets are permitted but aren't allowed in swimming areas.
Reservations, fees: Some sites can be reserved at 877/444-6777 or online at www.reserveusa.com ($9 reservation fee). The fee is $14–28 per night, plus $11 per additional vehicle per night. The group fee is $80 per night. A senior discount is available. Open late May to mid-September.
Directions: In Seattle on I-5, turn east on I-90. Drive east on I-90 for 59 miles to Exit 62. Take that exit to Forest Road 49 and turn northeast; drive 5.5 miles to the campground on the right at the end of the paved road.
Contact: Okanogan and Wenatchee National Forests, Cle Elum Ranger District, West Second St., Cle Elum, WA 98922, 509/674-4411, fax 509/674-1530.

88 CLE ELUM RIVER & CLE ELUM GROUP

Rating: 6

on the Cle Elum River in Wenatchee National Forest
See map pages 90-91
The gravel roads in the campground make this setting a bit more rustic than nearby Salmon La Sac. It serves as a valuable overflow campground for Salmon La Sac and is similar in setting and opportunities. The group site fills on most summer weekends. A nearby trailhead provides access into the Alpine Lakes Wilderness.
RV sites, facilities: There are 23 sites, including some pull-through, for RVs up to 21 feet, trailers, or tents and a group site for up to 100 people. Picnic tables and fire grills are provided. Drinking water and vault toilets are available. A pay phone is within five miles. Leashed pets are permitted.
Reservations, fees: Reservations are not accepted for family sites. Reservations are required for the group site; reserve at 877/444-6777 or online at www.reserveusa.com ($9 reservation fee). The fee is $11–22 per night, plus $9 per additional vehicle per night. The group site is $100 per night. A senior discount is available. Open late May to mid-September.
Directions: In Seattle on I-5, turn east on I-90. Drive east on I-90 for 78 miles to Exit 80 (two miles before Cle Elum). Take that exit, turn north on Bullfrog Road, and drive three miles to Highway 903. Continue north on Highway 903 for 14 miles to the campground on the left.
Contact: Okanogan and Wenatchee National Forests, Cle Elum Ranger District, West Second St., Cle Elum, WA 98922, 509/674-4411, fax 509/674-1530.

89 WISH POOSH

Rating: 7

on Cle Elum Lake in Wenatchee National Forest
See map pages 90-91
This popular camp is set on the shore of Cle Elum Lake. It fills up on summer weekends and holidays. It is great during midweek, when many sites are usually available. Although the lake is near the camp, note that in summer the lake level often lowers significantly due to irrigation needs. Water-skiing, sailing, fishing, and swimming are among the recreation possibilities. The camp sits at an elevation of 2,400 feet.
RV sites, facilities: There are 34 sites, including five double sites, for RVs up to 21 feet, trailers,

WASHINGTON

or tents. Picnic tables and fire grills are provided. Restrooms, drinking water, flush toilets, cell phone reception, and firewood are available. Boat-launching facilities are located on Cle Elum Lake. A restaurant, ATM, pay phone, and ice are available nearby. Leashed pets are permitted.

Reservations, fees: Reservations are not accepted. The fee is $14–28 per night, plus $10 per additional vehicle per night. A senior discount is available. Open mid-May to mid-September.

Directions: In Seattle on I-5, turn east on I-90. Drive east on I-90 for 78 miles to Exit 80 (two miles before Cle Elum). Take that exit, turn north on Bullfrog Road, and drive three miles to Highway 903. Continue north on Highway 903 for nine miles to the campground on the left.

Contact: Okanogan and Wenatchee National Forests, Cle Elum Ranger District, West Second St., Cle Elum, WA 98922, 509/674-4411, fax 509/674-1530.

90 CRYSTAL SPRINGS

Rating: 5

on Yakima River in Wenatchee National Forest
See map pages 90–91

This campground is just off I-90, and if you think that means lots of highway noise, well, you are correct. This camp is worth knowing as an overflow campground from the more desirable Kachess Campground. It is set at 2,400 feet elevation and features the Yakima River and some old-growth trees. It's a short drive to Kachess and Keechelus Lakes. Both lakes have boat ramps. The Summit at Snoqualmie Ski Area is at the north end of Keechelus Lake.

RV sites, facilities: There are 22 sites, including some drive-through sites, and two double sites for RVs up to 21 feet, trailers, or tents. Picnic tables and fire grills are provided. Drinking water, vault toilets, cell phone reception, and firewood are available. An ATM and pay phone are within 10 miles. Leashed pets are permitted.

Reservations, fees: Reservations are not accepted. The fee is $12–24 per night, plus $9 per additional vehicle per night. A senior discount is available. Open mid-May to mid-September.

Directions: In Seattle on I-5, turn east on I-90. Drive east on I-90 for 60 miles to Exit 62. Take

that exit and turn right (south) on Forest Road 54, and drive .5 mile to the campground on the right.

Contact: Okanogan and Wenatchee National Forests, Cle Elum Ranger District, West Second St., Cle Elum, WA 98922, 509/674-4411, fax 509/674-1530.

91 LAKE EASTON STATE PARK

Rating: 8

on Lake Easton
See map pages 90–91

This campground offers many recreational opportunities. For starters, it's set along the shore of Lake Easton on the Yakima River in the Cascade foothills. The landscape features old-growth forest, dense vegetation, and freshwater marshes, and the park covers 256 acres of the best of it. Two miles of trails for hiking and biking are available. The park provides opportunities for both summer and winter recreation, including swimming, fishing, boating, cross-country skiing, and snowmobiling. Note that high-speed boating is not allowed because Lake Easton is a shallow reservoir with stumps often hidden just below the water surface. There is a 10 mph speed limit for boats. Nearby recreation options include an 18-hole golf course and hiking trails. Kachess Lake and Keechelus Lake are just a short drive away.

RV sites, facilities: There are 45 sites with full hookups (20, 30 amps) for RVs up to 60 feet, 92 developed tent sites, two primitive tent sites, and one group site. Picnic tables and fire grills are provided. Restrooms, drinking water, flush toilets, showers, cell phone reception, a pay phone, an RV dump station, an amphitheater, a playground with basketball and horseshoes, and firewood are available. A café, an ATM, and ice are available within one mile. Boat-launching facilities and floats are located on Lake Easton. Some facilities are wheelchair-accessible. Leashed pets are permitted.

Reservations, fees: Reserve at 888/CAMP-OUT (888/226-7688) or online at www.parks.wa.gov /reservations ($7 reservation fee). The fee is $10–22 per night, plus $10 per additional vehicle per night. The group site is $2 per person with a minimum of 20 people. A senior discount is available. Major credit cards are accepted. Open May to mid-October, with limited winter facilities.

Directions: From Seattle, drive east on I-90 for 68 miles to Exit 70; the park entrance is on the right (it is located one mile west of the town of Easton).

Contact: Lake Easton State Park, P.O. Box 26, Easton, WA 98925, 509/656-2586, fax 509/656-2294; state park information, 360/902-8844.

92 CAYUSE HORSE CAMP

Rating: 6

on the Cle Elum River in Wenatchee National Forest

See map pages 90–91

This camp is for horse campers only. It's located along the Cle Elum River at major trailheads for horses and hikers and marked trails for bikers. The elevation is 2,400 feet. See Salmon La Sac Campground in this chapter for further information.

RV sites, facilities: There are 13 sites, including three double sites, for RVs, trailers, or tents with some sites 25 feet and some up to 40 feet long. Picnic tables and fire pits are provided. Drinking water and vault toilets are available. Stock facilities include corrals, troughs, and hitching posts are on-site. Bring your own stock feed. Leashed pets are permitted.

Reservations, fees: Some sites are available by reservation. Reserve at 877/444-6777 or online at www.reserveusa.com ($9 reservation fee). The fee is $14 per night, plus $11 per night for each additional vehicle. A senior discount is available. Open mid-May to mid-September, depending on weather.

Directions: In Seattle on I-5, turn east on I-90. Drive east on I-90 for 78 miles to Exit 80 (two miles before Cle Elum). Take that exit and turn north on Bullfrog Road; drive three miles to Highway 903. Continue north on Highway 903 for 18 miles to the campground on the right.

Contact: Okanogan and Wenatchee National Forests, Cle Elum Ranger District, West Second St., Cle Elum, WA 98922, 509/674-4411, fax 509/674-1530.

93 BEVERLY

Rating: 8

on the North Fork of the Teanaway River in Wenatchee National Forest

See map pages 90–91

This primitive campground is set on the North Fork of the Teanaway River, a scenic area of the river. It is primarily a hiker's camp, with several trails leading up nearby creeks and into the Alpine Lakes Wilderness. Self-issued permits are required for wilderness hiking. Fishing is poor. The elevation is 3,100 feet.

RV sites, facilities: There are 14 sites for RVs up to 21 feet, trailers, or tents. Picnic tables and fire grills are provided. Vault toilets are available, but there is no drinking water. Garbage must be packed out. Leashed pets are permitted.

Reservations, fees: Reservations are not accepted. The fee is $5 per night per vehicle. Open June to mid-November.

Directions: In Seattle on I-5, turn east on I-90. Drive east on I-90 for 80 miles to Cle Elum and Exit 85. Take Exit 85 to Highway 970. Turn east on Highway 970 and drive 6.5 miles to Teanaway Road (County Road 970). Turn left (north) on Teanaway Road and drive 13 miles to the end of the paved road. Bear right (north) on Forest Road 9737 and drive four miles to the campground on the left.

Contact: Okanogan and Wenatchee National Forests, Cle Elum Ranger District, West Second St., Cle Elum, WA 98922, 509/674-4411, fax 509/674-1530.

94 SWAUK

Rating: 6

on Swauk Creek in Wenatchee National Forest

See map pages 90–91

Some decent hiking trails can be found at this campground along Swauk Creek. A short loop trail, about a one-mile round-trip, is the most popular. Fishing is marginal, and there is some highway noise from U.S. 97. The elevation is 3,200 feet. Three miles east of the camp on Forest Road 9716 is the Swauk Forest Discovery Trail. This three-mile interpretive trail explains some of the effects of logging and U.S. Forest Service management of the forest habitat.

RV sites, facilities: There are 22 sites, including two double sites, for RVs up to 21 feet, trailers, or tents. Fire grills and picnic tables are provided. Drinking water, vault toilets, and firewood are available. Leashed pets are permitted.

Reservations, fees: Reservations are not accepted. The fee is $11–22 per night, plus $9 per additional vehicle per night. A senior discount is available. Open mid-May to late September.

Directions: In Seattle on I-5, turn east on I-90. Drive east on I-90 for 80 miles to Cle Elum and Exit 85. Take Exit 85 to County Road 970. Turn northeast on County Road 970 and drive 12 miles to where the road becomes U.S. 97. Turn north on U.S. 97 and drive 10 miles to the campground on the right (near Swauk Pass).

Contact: Okanogan and Wenatchee National Forests, Cle Elum Ranger District, West Second St., Cle Elum, WA 98922, 509/674-4411, fax 509/674-1530.

95 MINERAL SPRINGS
🏕️ 🚣 🐕 🚐 ⛺

Rating: 6

on Swauk Creek in Wenatchee National Forest
See map pages 90–91

This campground at the confluence of Medicine and Swauk Creeks is one of two campgrounds along U.S. 97. Note that this camp is set along a highway, so there is some highway noise. Fishing, berry picking, and hunting are good in season in this area. It is at an elevation of 2,700 feet. Most use the camp as a one-night layover spot.

RV sites, facilities: There are 12 sites for RVs up to 21 feet, trailers, or tents. Picnic tables and fire rings are provided. Drinking water, vault toilets, and cell phone reception are available. A restaurant, ATM, and pay phone are nearby. Leashed pets are permitted.

Reservations, fees: Reservations are not accepted. The fee is $11 per night, plus $9 per additional vehicle per night. A senior discount is available. Open mid-May to late September.

Directions: From Seattle, drive northeast on I-90 for 80 miles to Cle Elum and Exit 85 and Highway 970. Turn northeast on Highway 970 and drive 12 miles to U.S. 97. Continue north-

east (the road becomes U.S. 97) and drive about seven miles to the campground on the left.

Contact: Okanogan and Wenatchee National Forests, Cle Elum Ranger District, 830 West Second St., Cle Elum, WA 98922, 509/674-4411, fax 509/674-1530.

96 KANASKAT-PALMER STATE PARK
🏕️ 🚣 🚐 🗡️ 🐕 ♿ 🚐 ⛺

Rating: 8

on the Green River
See map pages 90–91

This wooded campground offers private campsites near the Green River. The park covers 320 acres with two miles of river frontage. It is set on a small, low, forested plateau. In winter and spring, the river is ideal for expert-level rafting and kayaking, and the park is used as a put-in spot for the rafting run down the Green River Gorge. This area has much mining history, though all mines have recently been closed and are being filled. Nearby Flaming Geyser gets its name from a coal seam. In winter, the river attracts a run of steelhead. The park has three miles of hiking trails.

RV sites, facilities: There are 31 sites for RVs or tents and 19 sites (10 drive-through) with partial hookups (30 amps) for RVs up to 50 feet long. Picnic tables are provided. Restrooms, drinking water, flush toilets, showers, two pay phones, a sheltered picnic area, horseshoes, and an RV dump station are available. Some facilities are wheelchair-accessible. Leashed pets are permitted.

Reservations, fees: Reserve at 888/CAMP-OUT (888/226-7688) or online at www.parks.wa.gov/reservations ($7 reservation fee). The fee is $16–22 per night, plus $10 per additional vehicle per night. A senior discount is available. Major credit cards are accepted in high season only. Open year-round, with limited facilities in the winter.

Directions: From Puyallup at the junction of Highway 167 and Highway 410, turn southeast on Highway 410 and drive 25 miles to Enumclaw and Farman Road. Turn northeast (left) on Farman Road and drive 10 miles to the park on the left.

Contact: Kanaskat-Palmer State Park, 360/886-0148; state park information, 360/902-8844.

97 DALLES

Rating: 10

in Mt. Baker–Snoqualmie National Forest
See map pages 90–91

This campground is set at the confluence of Minnehaha Creek and the White River. Aptly, its name means "rapids." A nature trail is nearby, and the White River entrance to Mount Rainier National Park is about 14 miles south on Highway 410. The camp sits amid a grove of old-growth trees; a particular point of interest is a huge old Douglas fir that is 9.5 feet in diameter and more than 235 feet tall. This is one of the prettiest camps in the area. It gets moderate use in summer.

RV sites, facilities: There are 44 sites for RVs up to 21 feet, trailers, or tents. Picnic tables and fire grills are provided. Vault toilets, drinking water, and firewood are available. There is a large shaded picnic area for day use. An ATM and a pay phone are within six miles. Leashed pets are permitted.

Reservations, fees: Reservations are accepted for some sites; reserve at 877/444-6777 or online at www.reserveusa.com ($9 reservation fee). The fee is $14 per night, plus $7 per additional vehicle per night. A senior discount is available. Open May to late September.

Directions: From Enumclaw, drive east on Highway 410 for 25.5 miles to the campground (three miles inside the forest boundary) on the right.

Contact: Mt. Baker–Snoqualmie National Forest, White River Ranger District, 450 Roosevelt Ave. E, Enumclaw, WA 98022, 360/825-6585, fax 360/825-0660.

98 CROW CREEK

Rating: 5

on the Little Naches River in Wenatchee National Forest
See map pages 90–91

This campground on the Little Naches River is popular with off-road bikers and four-wheel-drive cowboys and is similar to the following camp,

Kaner Flat, except that there is no drinking water. It is set at 2,900 feet elevation. A trail heading out from the camp leads into the backcountry and then forks in several directions. One route leads to the American River, another follows West Quartz Creek, and another goes along Fife's Ridge into the Norse Peak Wilderness (where no motorized vehicles are permitted). See a U.S. Forest Service map for details. There is good seasonal hunting and fishing in this area.

RV sites, facilities: There are 15 sites for RVs up to 30 feet, trailers, or tents. Picnic tables and fire grills are provided. Vault toilets are available, but there is no drinking water. Downed firewood may be gathered. Leashed pets are permitted.

Reservations, fees: Reservations are not accepted. The fee is $7 per night, plus $5 per additional vehicle per night. A senior discount is available. Open early May to late November.

Directions: From Yakima, drive northwest on U.S. 12 for 18 miles to Highway 410. Bear northwest on Highway 410 and drive 24.5 miles to Forest Road 1900. Turn northwest and drive 2.5 miles to Forest Road 1902. Turn west and drive .5 mile to the campground on the right.

Contact: Okanogan and Wenatchee National Forests, Naches Ranger District, 10237 U.S. 12, Naches, WA 98937, 509/653-2205, fax 509/653-2638.

99 KANER FLAT

Rating: 7

near the Little Naches River in Wenatchee National Forest
See map pages 90–91

This campground is set near the Little Naches River, at an elevation of 2,678 feet. It is located at the site of a wagon-train camp on the Old Naches Trail, a route used in the 1800s by wagon trains, Native Americans, and the U.S. Cavalry on their way to west side markets. The Naches Trail is now used by motorcyclists and narrow-clearance four-wheel-drive enthusiasts. This camp is popular among them, similar to Crow Creek campground. Kaner Flat is larger, though, so it handles more multiple user groups.

RV sites, facilities: There are 41 sites for RVs up to 30 feet, trailers, or tents, including two wheelchair-accessible sites. Picnic tables and fire grills are provided. Drinking water and vault toilets are available. Some facilities are wheelchair-accessible. Leashed pets are permitted.

Reservations, fees: Reservations are not accepted. The fee is $10 per night, plus $5 for each additional vehicle. A senior discount is available. Open late May to late November.

Directions: From Yakima, drive northwest on U.S. 12 for 18 miles to Highway 410. Bear northwest on Highway 410 and drive 25 miles to Forest Road 1900. Turn northwest and drive 2.5 miles to the campground on the right.

Contact: Okanogan and Wenatchee National Forests, Naches Ranger District, 10061 U.S. 12, Naches, WA 98937, 509/653-2205, fax 509/653-2638.

100 TANEUM

Rating: 7

on Taneum Creek in Wenatchee National Forest

See map pages 90–91

This rustic spot is set along Taneum Creek, with an elevation of 2,400 feet. It is located several miles away from the camps popular with the off-road-vehicle crowd. This is more of a quiet getaway, not a base camp. Ponderosa pines add to the setting. Trout fishing is popular here in the summer. The camp receives moderate use.

RV sites, facilities: There are 13 sites for RVs up to 21 feet and one double site. Picnic tables and fire rings are provided. Drinking water and firewood are available. Some facilities are wheelchair-accessible. Leashed pets are permitted.

Reservations, fees: Reservations are not accepted. The fee is $11–22 per night for single sites, plus $9 for each additional vehicle. A senior discount is available. Open June to late September.

Directions: From Ellensburg, drive west on U.S. 90 for about six miles to the Thorpe exit (#101). Turn south on the Thorpe Highway and drive .75 mile to Thorpe Cemetery Road. Turn right

and drive west for 11 miles (it becomes Taneum Road, then Forest Road 33), to the campground entrance on the left.

Contact: Okanogan and Wenatchee National Forests, Cle Elum Ranger District, 830 West Second St., Cle Elum, CA 98922, 509/674-4411, fax 509/674-1530.

101 ICEWATER CREEK

Rating: 7

on Taneum Creek in Wenatchee National Forest

See map pages 90–91

Icewater Creek Camp is similar to Taneum Camp, except that the trees are smaller and the sites are a bit more open. It is most popular with off-road motorcyclists because there are two ORV trails leading from the camp, both of which network with an extensive system of off-road riding trails. The best route extends along the South Fork Taneium River area. Fishing is fair, primarily for six- to eight-inch cutthroat trout.

RV sites, facilities: There are 14 sites for RVs up to 26 feet or tents. Picnic tables and fire rings are provided. Drinking water and firewood are available. Some facilities are wheelchair-accessible. Leashed pets are permitted.

Reservations, fees: Reservations are not accepted. The fees are $11 for single sites and $22 for the double site, plus $9 for each additional vehicle. A senior discount is available. Open May to late September.

Directions: From Ellensburg, drive west on U.S. 90 for about six miles to the Thorpe exit (#101). Turn south on the Thorpe Highway and drive .75 mile to Thorpe Cemetery Road. Turn right and drive 13.5 miles (it becomes Taneum Road, then Forest Road 33), to the campground entrance.

Contact: Okanogan and Wenatchee National Forests, Cle Elum Ranger District, 830 West Second St., Cle Elum, CA 98922, 509/674-4411, fax 509/674-1530.

 **Washington**

Chapter 4

Northeastern Washington

WASHINGTON

see
The Northern Cascades
pages 90–91

Okanogan

National

Forest

Okanogan
National
Forest

Tonasket

Moses Mtn.
(6,774 ft.)
▲

C O L V I L L E

I N D I A N

R E S E R V A T I O N

River

Methow

River

Lake
Chelan

Wenatchee

National

Forest

Pateros

Columbia

River

Banks

Lake

Coulee
City

Lake
Lenore

Wenatchee

N
W — E
S

see
Southeastern
Washington
pages 206–207

1
2
3-5
6
7-8 **9**
10
12-14
21-23
24-27
28
29
30
49
50
61
62
63
64
65
66-67
68
69
76-78
79-80
81

Sanpoil

97

20

20

97

17

174

155

174

17

2

97

28

21

3

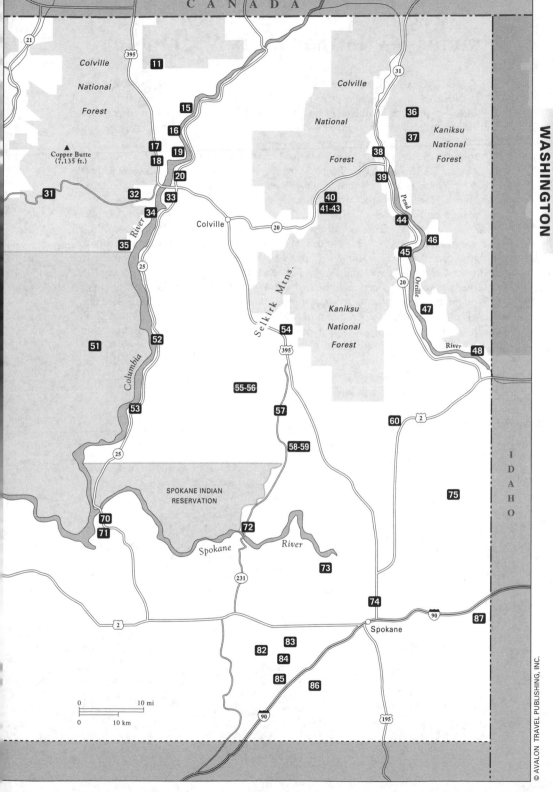

Chapter 4—Northeastern Washington

A lot of people call this area "God's country." You know why? Because nobody else could have thought of it. The vast number of lakes, streams, and national forests provides an unlimited land of adventure. You could spend a lifetime here—your days hiking, fishing, and exploring, your nights camping out and staring up at the stars.

And that's exactly what some people do, like Rich Landers, the outdoors writer for the *Spokane Spokesman-Review*. People know they have it good here, living on the threshold of a fantastic land of adventure, but with a population base in Spokane that creates a financial center with career opportunities.

The landscape features a variety of settings. The national forests (Colville, Kaniksu, Wenatchee), in the northern tier of the state, are ideal for a mountain hideaway. You'll find remote ridges and valleys with conifers, along with many small streams and lakes. In the valleys, the region is carved by the Pacific Northwest's largest river system, featuring the Columbia River, Franklin D. Roosevelt Lake, and the Spokane River. These waterways are best for campers interested in water views, boating, and full facilities.

While many well-known destinations are stellar, our favorites are the lesser-known sites. There are dozens of such camps in this area, often along the shore of a small lake, that provide good fishing and hiking. You could search across the land and not find a better region for outdoor adventure. This is a wilderness to enjoy.

1 OSOYOOS LAKE VETERAN'S MEMORIAL STATE PARK

Rating: 9

on Osoyoos Lake
See map pages 134–135

The park is set along the shore of Osoyoos Lake, a 14-mile-long lake created from the Okanogan River, located south of the Canadian Rockies. The park covers 47 acres and provides a base of operations for a fishing vacation. The lake has rainbow trout, kokanee salmon, smallmouth bass, crappie, and perch. Water sports are also popular in the summer, and in winter it is an ideal location for ice skating, ice fishing, and snow play. Fishing gear and concessions are available at the park. Expansive lawns lead down to the sandy shore of the lake. Osoyoos Lake is a winter nesting area for geese. The park also features a war veteran's memorial. A nine-hole golf course is located nearby. A history note: Many years ago, the area was the site of the annual okanogan (rendezvous) of the Washington and British Columbia Indians. They would gather and share supplies of fish and game for the year.

RV sites, facilities: There are 80 sites for self-contained RVs up to 45 feet or tents and six primitive tent sites. Picnic tables and fire grills are provided. Restrooms, flush toilets, showers, an RV dump station, cell phone reception, two pay phones, a store, a café, firewood, and a playground with horseshoes and volleyball are available. A coin-operated laundry facility and ice are available within one mile. An ATM is within 1.5 miles. Boat-launching and dock facilities are available. Leashed pets are permitted.

Reservations, fees: Reserve at 888/CAMP-OUT (888/226-7688) or online at www.parks.wa.gov/reservations ($7 reservation fee). The fee is $10–22 per night, plus $10 per additional vehicle per night. Major credit cards are accepted. Open year-round, with limited facilities in winter.

Directions: From Oroville, on U.S. 97 just south of the Canadian border, drive north on U.S. 97 for one mile to the park entrance on the right.

Contact: Osoyoos Lake Veteran's Memorial State Park, tel./fax 509/476-3321; state park information, 360/902-8844.

2 SUN COVE RESORT

Rating: 9

on Wannacut Lake
See map pages 134–135

This beautiful resort is surrounded by trees and hills and set along the shore of Wannacut Lake, a spring-fed lake that doesn't get much traffic. The lake is approximately three miles long and three-quarters of a mile wide. An 8 mph speed limit is enforced for boats. Fishing, swimming, boating, and hiking are all summertime options. The park provides full facilities, including a heated pool, a playground, and a recreation hall. For the horsy set, a guided trail and overnight rides are available one mile from the resort.

RV sites, facilities: There are 28 drive-through sites with full hookups (30 amps) for RVs of any length, 22 tent sites, two cottages, and 10 motel units with kitchens. Picnic tables are provided. Restrooms, flush toilets, coin-operated showers, an RV dump station, a recreation hall, a store, a café, a laundry room, ice, a playground, and a swimming pool are available. Boat docks, launching facilities, and rentals are also available. Some facilities are wheelchair-accessible. Leashed pets are permitted except in buildings.

Reservations, fees: Reservations are accepted. The fee is $20 per night, plus $2 per person for more than four people. Major credit cards are accepted. Open late April to October.

Directions: From Oroville (on U.S. 97 just south of the Canadian border), drive south on Highway 97 for 10 miles to Ellisford. Turn right (west) and drive one mile to Old Highway 97. Turn left (south) and drive for one mile to the Loomis Highway. Turn right (west) and drive six miles to Wannacut Lake Road. Turn right and drive five miles to the campground entrance on the right.

Contact: Sun Cove Resort, 93 East Wannacut Ln., Oroville, WA 98844, tel./fax 509/476-2223.

3 SPECTACLE LAKE RESORT

Rating: 7

on Spectacle Lake
See map pages 134–135

This pleasant resort on the shore of long, narrow

Spectacle Lake has grassy, shaded sites. Space is usually available here, although reservations are accepted. Recreation options include boating, fishing, swimming, water-skiing, and hunting (in season).

RV sites, facilities: There are 36 sites with full hookups (20, 30 amps) for RVs of any length or tents and 16 motel rooms with kitchenettes. Picnic tables are provided. Restrooms, flush toilets, showers, propane, an RV dump station, a store, a coin-operated laundry, ice, a playground, a recreation hall, a pay phone, cell phone reception, modem access, an exercise room, and a heated swimming pool are available. Boat docks, launching facilities, and rentals are also available. Leashed pets are permitted.

Reservations, fees: Reservations are accepted. The fee is $17 per night, plus $1.50 per person per night for more than two people. Major credit cards are accepted. Open mid-April to late October.

Directions: In Tonasket on U.S. 97, turn west (left if arriving from south), cross the bridge, and continue to Highway 7. Turn right on Highway 7 and drive about 12 miles to Holmes Road. Turn left (south) on Holmes Road and drive .75 mile to McCammon Road. Turn right (west) and drive one block to the park at the end of the road.

Contact: Spectacle Lake Resort, 10 McCammon Rd., Tonasket, WA 98855, tel./fax 509/223-3433, website: www.spectaclelakeresort.com.

4 RAINBOW RESORT

Rating: 7

on Spectacle Lake
See map pages 134–135

This resort on Spectacle Lake is an alternative to Spectacle Lake Resort. Major renovations were completed in late 2000. The camp features pretty lake views and full facilities. Nearby activities include swimming, fishing, hunting, tennis, and horseback riding, including overnight trail rides.

RV sites, facilities: There are 54 sites with full hookups (30, 50 amps) for RVs of any length, including 34 drive-through sites, and 14 tent sites with electricity and water. Picnic tables and fire pits are provided. Restrooms, flush toilets, show-

ers, ice, a recreation room, cell phone reception, horseshoes, volleyball, boat docks, boat rentals, and launching facilities are available. Leashed pets are permitted.

Reservations, fees: Reservations are accepted. The fee is $23 per night, plus $3 per person for more than four people. Major credit cards are accepted. Open April to October.

Directions: From Ellisford, turn west on Loomis Highway and drive 9.5 miles to the resort on the left.

Contact: Rainbow Resort, 761 Loomis Hwy., Tonasket, WA 98855, 509/223-3700 or 800/347-4375.

5 SPECTACLE FALLS RESORT

Rating: 8

on Spectacle Lake
See map pages 134–135

Spectacle Falls Resort is set on the shore of Spectacle Lake. It is open only as long as fishing is available, which means an early closing in July. Be sure to phone ahead of time to verify that the resort is open. Nearby recreation options include hiking, swimming, fishing, tennis, and horseback riding, including guided trails and overnight rides. Rainbow Resort provides an alternative.

RV sites, facilities: There are 20 drive-through sites with full hookups (30 amps) for RVs of any length, 10 tent sites, and four mobile homes available for rent. Picnic tables are provided. Restrooms, flush toilets, showers, an RV dump station, ice, cell phone reception, boat docks, launching facilities, and boat rentals are available. A pay phone is within 2.5 miles. Leashed pets are permitted.

Reservations, fees: Reservations are accepted. The fee is $16.50 per night, plus $2 per person per night for more than two people and $2 per additional vehicle per night. Open mid-April to late July.

Directions: From Tonasket on U.S. 97, turn northwest on Loomis Highway and drive 15 miles to the resort on the left.

Contact: Spectacle Falls Resort, 879 Loomis Hwy., Tonasket, WA 98855, 509/223-4141.

6 LOST LAKE

Rating: 7

on Lost Lake in Okanogan National Forest

See map pages 134–135

This camp is set on the shore of Lost Lake at an elevation of 3,800 feet. It keeps visitors happy as a launch point for fishing, swimming, hiking, hunting, and horseback riding. Only electric motors are permitted on the lake (that is, no gas motors). The lake is similar to Beth and Beaver Lakes (see Beth Lake and Beaver Lake camp listings in this chapter), but it is rounder. The Big Tree Botanical Area is about one mile away. Note that the group site is often booked one year in advance.

RV sites, facilities: There are 12 single and six double sites for RVs up to 31 feet or tents. There is also one group unit available by reservation only. Picnic tables and fire rings are provided. Drinking water and vault toilets are available. Boat docks and launching facilities are nearby. Leashed pets are permitted.

Reservations, fees: Reservations are required for the group site; phone 509/486-2186. The fees are $8 per vehicle per night at single and multiple sites, group fees are $40 for up to 25 people, $60 for 26–50 people, and $80 for 51–100 people. A senior discount is available. Open late May to mid-September, weather permitting.

Directions: From East Wenatchee, drive north on U.S. 97 for 20 miles to Tonasket and Highway 20. Turn east on Highway 20 and drive 20 miles to Bonaparte Lake Road (County Road 4953). Turn left (north) and drive six miles to Forest Road 32. Turn right (north) and drive three miles to Forest Road 33. Bear left (northwest) and drive three miles to a four-way intersection. Turn left on Forest Road 33-050 and drive .3 mile to the campground on the right.

Contact: Okanogan and Wenatchee National Forests, Tonasket Ranger District, 1 West Winesap Ave., Tonasket, WA 98855, 509/486-2186, fax 509/486-5161.

7 BONAPARTE LAKE

Rating: 7

on Bonaparte Lake in Okanogan National Forest

See map pages 134–135

This campground is located on the southern shore of Bonaparte Lake at an elevation of 3,600 feet. The lake is stocked with rainbow trout, brook trout, and mackinaw trout. See the description of Bonaparte Lake Resort (see next listing) for lake recreation information. Several trails nearby provide access to Mt. Bonaparte Lookout. Consult a U.S. Forest Service map for details.

RV sites, facilities: There are 15 single and 10 multiple sites for RVs up to 31 feet or tents, three bike-in/hike-in sites (require a walk of less than 100 feet), and one group site that can accommodate up to 30 people. Picnic tables and fire grills are provided. Drinking water and vault toilets are available. An RV dump station, a store, a pay phone, a café, and ice are available within one mile. Boat docks and launching facilities are also available. Some facilities are wheelchair-accessible, including a fishing dock. Leashed pets are permitted.

Reservations, fees: Reservations are not accepted. The fee is $8 per night, plus $8 per additional vehicle. A senior discount is available. Open mid-May to mid-September, weather permitting.

Directions: From East Wenatchee, drive north on U.S. 97 for 20 miles to Tonasket and Highway 20. Turn east on Highway 20 and drive 20 miles to Bonaparte Lake Road (County Road 4953). Turn left (north) and drive six miles to Bonaparte Lake and Forest Road 32 and the campground on the left.

Contact: Okanogan and Wenatchee National Forests, Tonasket Ranger District, 1 West Winesap Ave., Tonasket, WA 98855, 509/486-2186, fax 509/486-5161.

8 BONAPARTE LAKE RESORT

Rating: 6

on Bonaparte Lake

See map pages 134–135

Fishing is popular at this resort, which is set on

WASHINGTON

the southeast shore of Bonaparte Lake. A 10 mph speed limit keeps the lake quiet, ideal for fishing. Other recreational activities include hiking and hunting in the nearby U.S. Forest Service lands and snowmobiling and cross-country skiing in the winter.

RV sites, facilities: There are 35 sites, including many with full hookups (20 amps) and some drive-through sites, for RVs of any length, 10 tent sites, and 10 cabins. Picnic tables are provided. Restrooms, flush toilets, showers, propane, an RV dump station, firewood, a recreation hall, a store, a restaurant, a laundry room, ice, a pay phone, a playground, boat docks, launching facilities, and boat rentals (licensed drivers only) are available. Leashed pets are permitted.

Reservations, fees: Reservations are accepted. The fee is $10–18 per night. Open April to late October.

Directions: From East Wenatchee, drive north on U.S. 97 for 20 miles to Tonasket and Highway 20. Turn east on Highway 20 and drive 20 miles to Bonaparte Lake Road (County Road 4953). Turn left (north) and drive six miles to Bonaparte Lake and the resort on the left.

Contact: Bonaparte Lake Resort, 615 Bonaparte Rd., Tonasket, WA 98855, 509/486-2828.

9 BETH LAKE

Rating: 7

on Beth Lake in Okanogan National Forest
See map pages 134–135

This campground is set between Beth Lake and Beaver Lake, both small, narrow lakes stocked with rainbow trout and brook trout. The elevation is 2,800 feet. A 1.9-mile-long hiking trail (one-way) connects the two lakes. Other side trips in the area include Lost Lake, Bonaparte Lake, and several hiking trails, one of which leads up to the Mt. Bonaparte Lookout.

RV sites, facilities: There are 14 sites for RVs up to 31 feet or tents plus one multiple site. Picnic tables and fire rings are provided. Drinking water and vault toilets are available. Boat-launching facilities are available nearby. Some facilities are wheelchair-accessible. Leashed pets are permitted.

Reservations, fees: Reservations are not accepted. The fee is $6 per vehicle per night. A sen-

ior discount is available. Open mid-May to mid-September.

Directions: From East Wenatchee, drive north on U.S. 97 for 20 miles to Tonasket and Highway 20. Turn east on Highway 20 and drive 20 miles to Bonaparte Lake Road (County Road 4953). Turn left (north) and drive six miles to Bonaparte Lake and Forest Road 32. Bear right (north) and drive six miles to County Road 9480. Turn left (northwest) and drive one mile to the campground on the left.

Contact: Okanogan and Wenatchee National Forests, Tonasket Ranger District, 1 West Winesap Ave., Tonasket, WA 98855, 509/486-2186, fax 509/486-5161.

10 BEAVER LAKE

Rating: 7

on Beaver Lake in Okanogan National Forest
See map pages 134–135

This camp calls the southeastern shore of long, narrow Beaver Lake home. Situated at 2,700 feet elevation, it is one of several lakes in this area. Beth Lake, the previous listing, is nearby and accessible with an hour-long hike. The lake is stocked with trout. Fishing, swimming, hunting, and hiking are all possibilities here. See the descriptions for Beth Lake, Lost Lake, and Bonaparte Lake earlier in this chapter for information on the other lakes in the area.

RV sites, facilities: There are nine single and two multiple sites for RVs up to 21 feet or tents. Picnic tables are provided. Vault toilets and drinking water are available. Boat-launching facilities are available within 100 yards of the campground. No boats with gas engines are permitted. Leashed pets are permitted.

Reservations, fees: Reservations are not accepted. The fee is $6 per vehicle per night. A senior discount is available. Open mid-May to mid-September.

Directions: From East Wenatchee, drive north on U.S. 97 for 20 miles to Tonasket and Highway 20. Turn east on Highway 20 and drive 20 miles to Bonaparte Lake Road (County Road 4953). Turn left (north) and drive six miles to Bonaparte Lake and Forest Road 32. Bear right (north) and drive six miles to the campground on the left.

Contact: Okanogan and Wenatchee National Forests, Tonasket Ranger District, 1 West Winesap Ave., Tonasket, WA 98855, 509/486-2186, fax 509/486-5161.

11 PIERRE LAKE

Rating: 8

on Pierre Lake in Colville National Forest
See map pages 134–135

Pierre Lake, just 105 acres, is a quiet jewel of a camp near the Canadian border. The camp is set on the west shore of the lake. This popular camp is only a short drive from U.S. 395, and usually fills on summer weekends. The lake has fishing for rainbow trout, cutthroat trout, brook trout, crappie, bass, and catfish. There is no speed limit, but the lake is too small for big, fast boats.

RV sites, facilities: There are 15 sites for RVs up to 24 feet or tents. Picnic tables and fire grills are provided. Vault toilets are available. No drinking water is available. Garbage must be packed out. Boat docks and launching facilities are available on-site. A convenience store, a pay phone, and ice are available within seven miles. Some facilities are wheelchair-accessible. Leashed pets are permitted.

Reservations, fees: Reservations are not accepted. The fee is $6 per night, free in winter. A senior discount is available. Open year-round, no facilities in winter.

Directions: From Spokane, drive north on U.S. 395 for 74 miles to Colville. Continue north on U.S. 395 for about 25 miles to Barstow and Pierre Lake Round (County Road 4013). Turn right (north) on Pierre Lake Road and drive nine miles to the campground on the west side of Pierre Lake.

Contact: Colville National Forest, Three Rivers Ranger District, 255 West 11th St., Kettle Falls, WA 99141, 509/738-6111, fax 509/738-7701.

12 CURLEW LAKE STATE PARK

Rating: 8

on Curlew Lake
See map pages 134–135

Boredom is banned at this park, which is on the

eastern shore of Curlew Lake. The park covers 123 acres, and the lake is 5.5 miles long. Fishing is often good for trout and largemouth bass at the lake, and there are additional fishable lakes and streams in the immediate region. There is also beach access, swimming, water-skiing, and hiking, with two miles of hiking and biking trails in the park. The park is also used as a base for bicycle tour groups, with mountain biking available on a fairly steep trail that provides a view of the valley. An active osprey nest can be viewed from the park. Nearby recreation options include an 18-hole golf course. The park borders an air field and is located in the heart of a historic gold-mining district.

RV sites, facilities: There are 20 sites with partial or full hookups (30 amps) for RVs up to 40 feet, 57 developed tent sites, and five primitive fly-in tent sites. Picnic tables are provided. Restrooms, flush toilets, showers, an RV dump station, electricity, drinking water, cell phone reception, a pay phone, and boat-launching and dock facilities are available. Boat fuel is available at the marina. An ATM and groceries are available within seven miles. An amphitheater with interpretive activities is available nearby. Leashed pets are permitted.

Reservations, fees: Reservations are not accepted. The fee is $10–22 per night, plus $10 per additional vehicle per night. A senior discount is available. Open April to October.

Directions: From Spokane on I-90, turn north on U.S. 395 and drive 87 miles to Kettle Falls and Highway 20. Turn west on Highway 20 and continue 39 miles to Highway 21 (two miles east of Republic). Turn north and drive six miles to the park entrance on the left, immediately following the airport.

Contact: Curlew Lake State Park, 509/775-3592; state park information, 360/902-8844, fax 509/775-0822.

13 TIFFANYS RESORT

Rating: 7

on Curlew Lake
See map pages 134–135

Tiffanys Resort is located in a pretty, wooded setting along the western shore of Curlew Lake.

This 6.5-mile-long lake is good for water-skiing. Fishing can be good for rainbow trout and large-mouth bass. Most of the sites are fairly spacious. This is a smaller, more private alternative to Black Beach Resort.

RV sites, facilities: There are 15 sites with full hookups (20, 30 amps) for RVs of any length and four tent sites. Picnic tables and fire pits are provided. Restrooms, flush toilets, showers, firewood, a pay phone, a store, a coin-operated laundry, ice, a playground, and a swimming beach are available. Boat docks, launching facilities, and rentals are available. An ATM is within 10 miles. Leashed pets are permitted.

Reservations, fees: Reservations are accepted. The fee is $20–22 per night, plus $4 per person for more than four people. Major credit cards are accepted. Open April to late October.

Directions: From Colville, drive west on Highway 20 for 36 miles into the town of Republic and Klondike Road. Turn right on Klondike Road and drive 10.2 miles (Klondike Road will turn into West Curlew Lake Road) to Tiffany Road. Turn right and drive .5 mile to the resort at the end of the road.

Contact: Tiffanys Resort, 58 Tiffany Rd., Republic, WA 99166, 509/775-3152, website: www.tiffanysresort.com.

14 BLACK BEACH RESORT

Rating: 7

on Curlew Lake

See map pages 134–135

Here's another resort along Curlew Lake. This one is much larger, with beautiful waterfront sites and full facilities. Water-skiing, swimming, and fishing are all options.

RV sites, facilities: There are 120 sites with full hookups (20, 30 amps), including 60 drive-through sites, for RVs of any length, nine tent sites, and 13 lodging units. Picnic tables and fire pits are provided. Restrooms, flush toilets, coin-operated showers, a pay phone, an RV dump station, a store, a coin-operated laundry, ice, and a playground are available. Boat docks, launching facilities, and rentals are also located at the resort. An ATM is within 7.5 miles. Leashed pets are permitted.

Reservations, fees: Reservations are accepted.

The fee is $18–21 per night, plus $3 per person for more than four people. Major credit cards are accepted. A senior discount is available. Open April to October; two campsites and five rental units are available in winter.

Directions: From Colville, drive west on Highway 20 for 48 miles to the town of Republic and the T intersection at Klondike Road. Turn right and drive 7.5 miles to the resort sign at Black Beach Road. Turn right and drive .75 mile to the resort entrance.

Contact: Black Beach Resort, 80 Black Beach Rd., Republic, WA 99166, tel./fax 509/775-3989, website: www.blackbeachresort.com.

15 NORTH GORGE

Rating: 7

on Franklin Roosevelt Lake in Lake Roosevelt National Recreation Area

See map pages 134–135

This is the first and northernmost of many campgrounds I discovered along the shore of 130-mile-long Franklin Roosevelt Lake, which was formed by damming the Columbia River at Coulee. This camp is set on the west shore of Lake Roosevelt National Recreation Area. Recreation options include water-skiing and swimming, plus fishing for walleye, trout, bass, and sunfish. During the winter, the lake level lowers; for a unique trip, walk along the lake's barren edge. Note that this campground provides full facilities from May 1 through September 30, then limited facilities in the off-season. See the description of Spring Canyon in this chapter for more recreation information.

RV sites, facilities: There are 10 sites for RVs up to 26 feet or tents. Picnic tables and fire grills are provided. Drinking water, vault toilets, cell phone reception, boat docks, and launching facilities are available. (Note that if the lake level drops below an elevation of 1,272 feet, there is no drinking water.) Some facilities are wheelchair-accessible. Leashed pets are permitted.

Reservations, fees: Reservations are not accepted. The fee is $10 per night ($5 per night in off-season), and a $6 boat-launch fee. A senior discount is available. Open year-round.

Directions: From Spokane on I-90, drive north

on U.S. 395 for 84 miles to the town of Kettle Falls and Highway 25. Turn right (north) on Highway 25 and drive 20 miles to the campground entrance.

Contact: Lake Roosevelt National Recreation Area, 1008 Crest Dr., Coulee Dam, WA 99116-1259, 509/633-9441, fax 509/633-9332.

16 SNAG COVE

Rating: 8

on Franklin Roosevelt Lake in Lake Roosevelt National Recreation Area
See map pages 134–135

Snag Cove has a setting similar to North Gorge campground (see previous listing). It is set amid Ponderosa pines along the west shore of Franklin Roosevelt Lake, within Lake Roosevelt National Recreation Area. This small camp has just nine sites, but the nearby boat launch makes it a find.

RV sites, facilities: There are nine sites for RVs up to 26 feet or tents. Picnic tables and fire grills are provided. Vault toilets and cell phone reception are available. When the lake level drops, there is no drinking water. Boat-launching facilities and docks are nearby. Some facilities are wheelchair-accessible. Leashed pets are permitted.

Reservations, fees: Reservations are not accepted. The fee is $5–10 per night; there is a $6 boat-launch fee. A senior discount is available. Open year-round, weather permitting.

Directions: From Spokane, turn north on U.S. 395 and drive 84 miles to the town of Kettle Falls. Continue north on U.S. 395 (crossing the Columbia River) for seven miles to the Hedlund Bridge turnoff. Turn right, cross Hedlund Bridge, and drive 7.5 miles to the campground on the right.

Contact: Lake Roosevelt National Recreation Area, 1008 Crest Dr., Coulee Dam, WA 99116-1259, 509/633-9441, fax 509/633-9332.

17 WHISPERING PINES RV RESORT AND CAMPGROUND

Rating: 7

on Franklin Roosevelt Lake
See map pages 134–135

This campground is set along the long, narrow Kettle River Arm of Franklin Roosevelt Lake and near the border crossing into Canada. A country resort, it is usually quiet and peaceful. A highlight is easy access to the lake. A one-mile loop nature trail is available along the lake shore, where wild turkeys and deer are often spotted. The campground is excellent for bird-watching and fishing. It's close to marked bike trails, a full-service marina, and tennis courts. Riding stables are available 20 miles away, and three golf courses are within 15 miles. A good side trip is to Colville National Forest East Portal Interpretive Area, 10 miles away. (Drive south to the junction of Highway 20 and continue southwest for about six miles.) Highlights include a nature trail and the Bangs Mountain auto tour, a five-mile drive that takes you through old-growth forest to Bangs Mountain Vista overlooking the Roosevelt Lake–Kettle Falls area.

RV sites, facilities: There are 42 sites with full hookups (30, 50 amps), including 40 drive-through sites, for RVs of any length or tents, 15 tent sites, two cabins, three rental trailers, and two motel rooms with kitchens. An overflow camping area is also available. Picnic tables and fire grills are provided. Restrooms, drinking water, flush toilets, coin-operated showers, a pay phone, cell phone reception, an RV dump station, a coin-operated laundry, a playground with horseshoes and volleyball, modem hookups, a store, and firewood are available. Lake swimming and fishing are available on-site. A restaurant is within five miles, and an ATM and groceries are within six miles. Leashed pets are permitted.

Reservations, fees: Reservations are accepted. The fee is $12–22 per night, plus $1 per person per night for more than four people. Weekly and monthly rates are available. Open year-round.

Directions: From Spokane, turn north on U.S. 395 and drive 84 miles to the town of Kettle Falls. Continue north on U.S. 395 for 6.5 miles (toward Canada) to the campground entrance road on the right (Roosevelt Road). Turn east at the sign for the campground and drive 300 yards to the camp on the right.

Contact: Whispering Pines RV Resort and Campground, Roosevelt Rd., Kettle Falls, WA 99141, tel./fax 509/738-2593 or 800/597-4423, website: www.whisperingpinesresort.net.

18 KETTLE RIVER

Rating: 7

on Franklin Roosevelt Lake in Lake Roosevelt National Recreation Area

See map pages 134–135

This campground is set along the long, narrow Kettle River Arm of Franklin Roosevelt Lake, and features campsites amid Ponderosa pines. If the lake level drops below an elevation of 1,272 feet, there is no drinking water. The nearest boat launch is located at Napoleon Bridge.

RV sites, facilities: There are 13 sites for RVs up to 16 feet or tents. Picnic tables and fire grills are provided. Vault toilets and cell phone reception are available. When the lake level drops, there is no drinking water. A pay phone and groceries are available within eight miles, and an ATM is within 10 miles. Boat docks are nearby. Some facilities are wheelchair-accessible. Leashed pets are permitted.

Reservations, fees: Reservations are not accepted. The fee is $5–10 per night. A senior discount is available. Open year-round, weather permitting.

Directions: From Spokane, turn north on U.S. 395 and drive 84 miles to the town of Kettle Falls. Continue north on U.S. 395 (crossing the Columbia River) for seven miles to the campground on the right.

Contact: Lake Roosevelt National Recreation Area, 1008 Crest Dr., Coulee Dam, WA 99116-1259, 509/633-9441, fax 509/633-9332.

19 EVANS

Rating: 9

on Franklin Roosevelt Lake in Lake Roosevelt National Recreation Area

See map pages 134–135

This campground is another in a series along the shore of Franklin Roosevelt Lake. This one sits along the eastern shoreline, just south of the town of Evans. Fishing, swimming, and water-skiing are among the activities here. See the description of Spring Canyon in this chapter for more information.

RV sites, facilities: There are 46 sites for RVs up to 26 feet or tents and one group site for up to

44 people. Picnic tables and fire grills are provided. Drinking water, flush toilets, and cell phone reception are available. A boat dock, launch facilities, an RV dump station, and a picnic area are available nearby. Groceries and a pay phone are available within three miles. An ATM is within eight miles. Some facilities are wheelchair-accessible. Leashed pets are permitted.

Reservations, fees: Reservations are not accepted for family sites; reservations for the group site are required at 509/633-3860. The fee is $5–10 per night; there is a $6 launch fee. Open year-round, with limited facilities in the winter.

Directions: From Spokane on I-90, drive north on U.S. 395 for 84 miles to the town of Kettle Falls and Highway 25. Turn right (north) on Highway 25 and drive eight miles to the campground entrance on the left.

Contact: Lake Roosevelt National Recreation Area, 1008 Crest Dr., Coulee Dam, WA 99116-1259, 509/633-9441, fax 509/633-9332.

20 MARCUS ISLAND

Rating: 8

on Franklin Roosevelt Lake in Lake Roosevelt National Recreation Area

See map pages 134–135

This campground, located south of Evans camp on the eastern shore of Franklin Roosevelt Lake, is quite similar to that camp. Water-skiing, fishing, and swimming are the primary recreation options. See the description of Spring Canyon in this chapter for information about the park and side-trip options in the area.

RV sites, facilities: There are 25 sites for RVs up to 20 feet or tents. Picnic tables and fire grills are provided. Drinking water, vault toilets, cell phone reception, and a picnic area are available. (Note that if the lake level drops below an elevation of 1,272 feet, there is no drinking water.) A boat launch and dock are available nearby. A store and a pay phone are within one mile, and an ATM is within six miles. Some facilities are wheelchair-accessible. Leashed pets are permitted.

Reservations, fees: Reservations are not accepted. The fee is $5–10 per night; boat launching is $6 per boat. A senior discount is available. Open year-round, weather permitting.

Directions: From Spokane on I-90, drive north on U.S. 395 for 84 miles to the town of Kettle Falls and Highway 25. Turn right (north) on Highway 25 and drive four miles to the campground entrance on the left.

Contact: Lake Roosevelt National Recreation Area, 1008 Crest Dr., Coulee Dam, WA 99116-1259, 509/633-9441, fax 509/633-9332.

21 JACK'S RV PARK AND MOTEL

Rating: 5

near Conconully Reservoir

See map pages 134–135

This park is in the town of Conconully, set between Conconully Reservoir and Conconully Lake. Horseshoes can be found in the park, and nearby recreation options include hiking trails, fishing, hunting (in season), and water sports (summer and winter) at the lake.

RV sites, facilities: There are 57 sites with full hookups (30 amps), including 27 drive-through sites, for RVs of any length. Picnic tables are provided. Restrooms, flush toilets, showers, propane, a covered barbecue building, modem access, a five-hole putting green, shuffleboard, darts, basketball, and a coin-operated laundry are available. A store, a café, an ATM, a pay phone, and ice are available within two blocks. Boat docks, launching facilities, and rentals are nearby. Leashed pets are permitted.

Reservations, fees: Reservations are accepted. The fee is $21 per night, plus $2 per person per night for more than four people and $6 per additional vehicle (more than two) per night. Major credit cards are accepted. Open mid-April to October, weather permitting.

Directions: From U.S. 97 in Okanogan, turn north (left if arriving from the south) on Pine Street/Conconully Highway and drive 17.5 miles northwest to Conconully and Broadway Street. Turn right (east) and drive one block to A Avenue. Turn left (north) on A Avenue and drive less than one block to the park on the right.

Contact: Jack's RV Park and Motel, P.O. Box 98, Conconully, WA 98819, 509/826-0132 or 800/893-5668, website: www.jacksrv.com.

22 KOZY KABINS AND RV PARK

Rating: 7

near Conconully Reservoir

See map pages 134–135

This quiet and private park in Conconully has a small creek running through it and plenty of greenery. A full-service marina is located close by. If you continue northeast of town on County Road 4015, the road will get a bit narrow for awhile, but will widen again when you enter the Sinlahekin Habitat Management Area, which is managed by the Department of Fish and Game. There are some primitive campsites in this valley, especially along the shores of the lakes in the area.

RV sites, facilities: There are 15 sites with full hookups (30 amps) for RVs up to 40 feet, six tent sites, and eight cabins. Picnic tables are provided. Restrooms, flush toilets, a community fire pit, coin-operated showers, and firewood are available. Propane, an RV dump station, a store, a café, a coin-operated laundry, a pay phone, an ATM, and ice are available within one block. Boat docks, launching facilities, and boat rentals are nearby. Leashed pets are permitted.

Reservations, fees: Reservations are accepted. The fee is $8–16 per night, plus $2.75 per additional vehicle. Cabins are $37–45 per night. Major credit cards are accepted. Open year-round.

Directions: From U.S. 97 in Okanogan, turn north (left if arriving from the south) on Pine Street/Conconully Highway and drive 17.5 miles northwest to Conconully and Broadway Street. Turn right (east) and drive one block to A Avenue. The park is at the junction of A Avenue and Broadway.

Contact: Kozy Kabins and RV Park, P.O. Box 82, 111 East Broadway, Conconully, WA 98819, 509/826-6780 or 888/502-2246, website: www .conconully.com.

23 MAPLE FLATS RV PARK AND RESORT

Rating: 9

near Conconully Reservoir

See map pages 134–135

This campground near Conconully Reservoir is

in a beautiful setting, situated in a valley between two lakes. Nearby recreation options include hiking and biking on the many nature trails in the area, an 18-hole golf course (15 miles away), and trout fishing in the well-stocked Upper Conconully Lake and Lower Conconully Reservoir.

RV sites, facilities: There are 25 drive-through sites with full hookups (30 amps) for RVs of any length, a dispersed camping area with room for six tents, and one apartment with a kitchen for rent. Picnic tables are provided. Restrooms, flush toilets, showers, a coin-operated laundry, modem access, seasonal fire pits, and a covered gazebo with electricity are available. Groceries, dining, dancing, a pay phone, an ATM, and propane, as well as boat, snowmobile, and personal watercraft rentals are available within two blocks. Boat docks and launching facilities are also nearby. Leashed pets are permitted.

Reservations, fees: Reservations are accepted. The fee is $15–20 per night, plus $2 per person for more than two people. Open April to October.

Directions: From U.S. 97 in Okanogan, turn north (left if arriving from the south) on Pine Street/Conconully Highway and drive 17.5 miles northwest to Conconully and Silver Street. Turn right (east) and drive one block to A Avenue. Turn left (north) on A Avenue and drive to the park on the right.

Contact: Maple Flats RV Park and Resort, P.O. Box 126, 310 A Ave., Conconully, WA 98819, tel./fax 509/826-4231 or 800/683-1180, website: www.conconully.com.

24 CONCONULLY STATE PARK

Rating: 9

on Conconully Reservoir
See map pages 134–135

This park, dating to 1910, is considered a fisherman's paradise, with trout, bass, and kokanee salmon. The park is set along Conconully Reservoir and covers 81 acres, with 5,400 feet of shoreline. A boat launch, beach access, swimming, and fishing provide all sorts of water sports possibilities. A half-mile nature trail is available. A side-trip option is to Sinlahekin Habitat Management Area, which is accessible via County

Road 4015. This route heads northeast along the shore of Conconully Reservoir on the other side of U.S. 97. The road is narrow at first, but then becomes wider as it enters the Habitat Management Area.

RV sites, facilities: There are 84 sites for self-contained RVs up to 60 feet or tents. Picnic tables and fire grills are provided. Restrooms, flush toilets, showers, an RV dump station, firewood, boat-launching and dock facilities, cell phone reception, a pay phone, and a playground are available. A store, an ATM, a café, a coin-operated laundry, and ice are available within a quarter mile. A picnic area with covered shelter and electricity, horseshoes, a baseball field, and interpretive activities are available nearby. Leashed pets are permitted.

Reservations, fees: Reservations are not accepted. The fee is $15 per night, plus $10 per additional vehicle per night. A senior discount is available. Open year-round, with no services in winter.

Directions: On U.S. 97 at Omak, take the North Omak exit. At the base of the hill, turn right and drive two miles until you reach Conconully Road. Turn right and drive 19 miles north to the park entrance.

Contact: Conconully State Park, P.O. Box 95, Conconully, WA 98819, tel./fax 509/826-7408; state park information, 360/902-8844.

25 CONCONULLY RESERVOIR RESORT

Rating: 6

on Upper Conconully Reservoir
See map pages 134–135

This resort is one of several set along the shore of Conconully Reservoir. Tents are permitted, but this is a prime vacation destination for RVers. Trout fishing, swimming, and boating are all options here.

RV sites, facilities: There are 11 sites with full hookups (30 amps) for RVs of any length, four cabins, and one apartment. Picnic tables and fire rings are provided. Restrooms, flush toilets, coin-operated showers, and ice are available. Propane, an RV dump station, a store with tackle, an ATM, a pay phone, a café, and a coin-operated laundry are available within one mile. Boat docks, launching facilities, and a variety of boat rentals are available. Leashed pets are permitted.

Reservations, fees: Reservations are accepted. The fee is $23 per night, plus $2 per person per night for more than two people. Major credit cards are accepted. Open late April to late October.

Directions: From U.S. 97 in Okanogan, turn north (left if arriving from the south) on Pine Street/Conconully Highway and drive 17.5 miles northwest to Conconully and Lake Street. Turn right on Lake Street and drive one mile to the park on the right.

Contact: Conconully Reservoir Resort, P.O. Box 131, 102 Sinlahekin Rd., Conconully, WA 98819, 509/826-0813 or 800/850-0813, fax 509/826-1292.

26 LIAR'S COVE RESORT

Rating: 6

on Conconully Reservoir
See map pages 134–135

Roomy sites for RVs can be found at this camp on the shore of Conconully Reservoir. Tents are allowed, too. Fishing, swimming, boating, and hiking opportunities are available on-site.

RV sites, facilities: There are 30 sites with full hookups (20, 30 amps), including 20 drive-through sites, for RVs up to 50 feet or tents, two cabins, one mobile home, and three motel rooms. Picnic tables and fire pits are provided. Restrooms, flush toilets, coin-operated showers, modem access, a pay phone, a horseshoe pit, cable TV, and ice are available. Propane, an RV dump station, a store, and a café are available within one mile. Boat docks, launching facilities, and boat rentals are available. Some facilities are wheelchair-accessible. Leashed pets are permitted.

Reservations, fees: Reservations are accepted. The fee is $22–23 per night, plus $2 per person per night for more than two people. Open April to October.

Directions: From U.S. 97 in Okanogan, turn north (left if arriving from the south) on Pine Street/Conconully Highway and drive 16.5 miles northwest to Conconully and look for the park on the left. It's located a quarter mile south of Conconully.

Contact: Liar's Cove Resort, P.O. Box 72, Conconully, WA 98819, 509/826-1288 or 800/830-1288, website: www.omakchronicle.com/liarscove.

27 SHADY PINES RESORT

Rating: 6

on Conconully Reservoir
See map pages 134–135

This camp is on the western shore of Conconully Reservoir, with great access to trout fishing (in season), swimming, and water-skiing. It is near Conconully State Park and provides a possible option if the state park campground is full—a common occurrence in summer. But note that on summer weekends, this camp often fills as well. See the descriptions of Kozy Kabins and RV Park and Conconully State Park in this chapter for area information.

RV sites, facilities: There are 23 sites for RVs up to 45 feet, including 21 sites with full hookups (30, 50 amps), 14 drive-through sites, two tent sites, and six cabins. Picnic tables and fire rings are provided. Restrooms, flush toilets, cell phone reception, modem access, massage therapy, coin-operated showers, ice, and firewood are available. Propane, an RV dump station, a store, a café, an ATM, a pay phone, and a coin-operated laundry are available within one mile. Boat-launching facilities and boat rentals are available. Leashed pets are permitted.

Reservations, fees: Reservations are accepted. The fee is $19–21 per night, plus $5 per person per night for more than four people. Cabins are $69–79 per night. Major credit cards are accepted. Open mid-April to late October.

Directions: From U.S. 97 in Okanogan, turn north (left if arriving from the south) on Pine Street/Conconully Highway and drive 16.5 miles northwest to Conconully and Broadway Street. Turn left (west) and drive one mile. The park is on the west shore of the lake.

Contact: Shady Pines Resort, P.O. Box 44, 125 West Fork Rd., Conconully, WA 98819, 509/826-2287 or 800/552-2287, website: www.shadypinesresort.com.

28 SWAN LAKE

Rating: 8

on Swan Lake in Colville National Forest
See map pages 134–135

Scenic views greet visitors on the drive to Swan Lake and at the campground as well. The camp is on the shore of Swan Lake, at an elevation of 3,700 feet. The Swan Lake Trail, a beautiful hiking trail, circles the lake. Fishing for rainbow trout is an option. Swimming, boating (gas motors prohibited), mountain biking, and hiking are some of the possibilities here. This is a good out-of-the-way spot for RV cruisers seeking a rustic setting. It commonly fills on summer weekends.

RV sites, facilities: There are 25 sites for RVs up to 31 feet or tents. Picnic tables and fire grills are provided. Drinking water, vault toilets, and cell phone reception are available. A picnic shelter with a barbecue, firewood, a boat dock, and launching facilities are available nearby. Gas motors are prohibited on the lake. Leashed pets are permitted.

Reservations, fees: Reservations are not accepted. The fee is $12 per night, plus $2 per additional vehicle per night. A senior discount is available. Open mid-May to September.

Directions: From Spokane on I-90, turn north on U.S. 395 and drive 87 miles to Highway 20. Turn west on Highway 20 and drive 36 miles to the town of Republic and Highway 21. Turn south on Highway 21 and drive seven miles to Forest Road 53 (Scatter Creek Road). Turn right (southwest) on Forest Road 53 and drive eight miles to the campground at the end of the road.

Contact: Colville National Forest, Republic Ranger District, Republic, WA 99166, 509/775-3305, fax 509/775-7401.

29 LONG LAKE

Rating: 9

on Long Lake in Colville National Forest
See map pages 134–135

Long Lake is the third and smallest of the three lakes in this area (the others are Swan Lake and Ferry Lake). Expert fly fishermen can get a quality experience here angling for cutthroat trout.

No gas motors are allowed on the lake, and fishing is restricted (fly-fishing only), but it's ideal for a float tube or a pram. The lake is adjacent to little Fish Lake, and a half-mile trail runs between the two. The drive on Highway 21 south of Republic is particularly beautiful, with views of the Sanpoil River.

RV sites, facilities: There are 12 sites for RVs up to 21 feet or tents. Picnic tables and fire grills are provided. Drinking water, vault toilets, and cell phone reception are available. Garbage must be packed out. Primitive launching facilities are nearby. Leashed pets are permitted.

Reservations, fees: Reservations are not accepted. The fee is $10 per night, plus $2 per additional vehicle per night. Open May to September, weather permitting.

Directions: From Spokane on I-90, turn north on U.S. 395 and drive 87 miles to Highway 20. Turn west on Highway 20 and drive 36 miles to the town of Republic and Highway 21. Turn south on Highway 21 and drive seven miles to Forest Road 53 (Scatter Creek Road). Turn right (southwest) on Forest Road 53 and drive seven miles to Forest Road 400. Turn south and drive 1.5 miles to the camp on the right.

Contact: Colville National Forest, Republic Ranger District, 180 North Jefferson, Republic, WA 99166, 509/775-3305, fax 509/775-7401.

30 TEN MILE

Rating: 7

on the Sanpoil River in Colville National Forest
See map pages 134–135

This spot is secluded and primitive. Located about nine miles from Swan Lake, Ferry Lake, and Long Lake, this campground along the Sanpoil River is a good choice for a multiday trip visiting each of the lakes. The Sanpoil River provides fishing for rainbow trout, and a hiking trail leads west from camp for about 2.5 miles.

RV sites, facilities: There are nine sites for RVs up to 21 feet or tents. Picnic tables and fire rings are provided. Vault toilets and cell phone reception are available. No drinking water is available. Garbage must be packed out. Leashed pets are permitted.

Reservations, fees: Reservations are not accepted. The fee is $8 per night, plus $2 per additional

WASHINGTON

vehicle per night. A senior discount is available. Open mid-May to mid-October, weather permitting.

Directions: From Spokane on I-90, turn north on U.S. 395 and drive 87 miles to Highway 20. Turn west on Highway 20 and drive 40 miles to Republic and Highway 21. Turn south on Highway 21 and drive 10 miles to the campground entrance on the left.

Contact: Colville National Forest, Republic Ranger District, 180 North Jefferson, Republic, WA 99166, 509/775-3305, fax 509/775-7401.

31 SHERMAN PASS OVERLOOK

Rating: 6

at Sherman Pass in Colville National Forest
See map pages 134–135

Sherman Pass Scenic Byway (Highway 20) runs through here, so the camp does have some road noise. This roadside campground is located near Sherman Pass (5,575 feet elevation), one of the few high-elevation mountain passes maintained and open year-round in Washington. Several nearby trails provide access to various peaks and vistas in the area. One of the best is the Kettle Crest National Recreation Trail, with the trailhead located one mile from camp. This trail extends for 45 miles, generally running north to south, and provides spectacular views of the Cascades on clear days. No other campgrounds are in the immediate vicinity.

RV sites, facilities: There are nine sites for RVs up to 24 feet or tents. Picnic tables and fire grills are provided. Vault toilets are available. No drinking water is available. Garbage must be packed out. Some facilities are wheelchair-accessible. Leashed pets are permitted.

Reservations, fees: Reservations are not accepted. The fee is $6 per night. A senior discount is available. Open mid-May to mid-October.

Directions: From Spokane on I-90, turn north on U.S. 395 and drive 87 miles to Highway 20. Turn west on Highway 20 and drive 19.5 miles to the campground on the right.

Contact: Colville National Forest, Three Rivers Ranger District, 255 West 11th St., Kettle Falls, WA 99141, 509/738-6111, fax 509/738-7701.

32 CANYON CREEK

Rating: 7

near the Long Flume Heritage Site in Colville National Forest
See map pages 134–135

The campground is located .4 mile from the highway, just far enough to keep it from road noise. It's a popular spot among campers looking for a layover spot, with the bonus of trout fishing in the nearby creek. Canyon Creek is within hiking distance of the Long Flume Heritage Site. The camp is set in a pretty area not far from the Columbia River, which offers a myriad of recreation options. A side trip option is the Bangs Mountain Auto Tour, featuring a scenic route with mountain vistas.

RV sites, facilities: There are 12 sites for RVs up to 30 feet or tents. Picnic tables and fire grills are provided. Vault toilets and cell phone reception are available. No drinking water is available. An ATM is within nine miles and a pay phone within six miles. Garbage must be packed out. Some facilities are wheelchair-accessible. Leashed pets are permitted.

Reservations, fees: Reservations are not accepted. The fee is $6 per night. Open year-round, with limited facilities in winter.

Directions: From Spokane, drive north on U.S. 395 for 87 miles, crossing the Columbia River. Turn left on Highway 20 and drive south for six miles to Forest Road 2000-136. Turn left and drive .25 mile to the campground entrance on the left.

Contact: Colville National Forest, Three Rivers, Ranger District, 255 West 11th St., Kettle Falls, WA 99141, 509/738-6111, fax 509/738-7701.

33 KETTLE FALLS

Rating: 8

on Franklin Roosevelt Lake in Lake Roosevelt National Recreation Area
See map pages 134–135

This campground only fills occasionally. It's located along the eastern shore of Roosevelt Lake, about two miles south of the highway bridge near West Kettle Falls. In the summer, the rangers offer campfire programs in the evenings. Water-skiing, swimming, and fishing are all options. Local side trips include St. Paul's Mission in Kettle Falls, which was built in 1846 and is one of the oldest churches in Washington.

RV sites, facilities: There are 76 sites for RVs up to 26 feet or tents and two group sites for up to 50 people. Picnic tables and fire grills are provided. Restrooms, drinking water, flush toilets, cell phone reception, an RV dump station, firewood, a small marina with a store, and a playground are available. A larger store is available within one mile, and an ATM and a pay phone are within 2.5 miles. Boat docks, fuel, and launching facilities are available. Some facilities are wheelchair-accessible. Leashed pets are permitted.

Reservations, fees: Reservations are not accepted for family sites but are required for group sites; phone 509/633-3860. The fee is $5–10 per night; there is a $6 boat-launch fee. A senior discount is available. Major credit cards are accepted. Open year-round, with limited facilities in winter.

Directions: From Spokane, drive north on U.S. 395 for 84 miles to the town of Kettle Falls. Continue on U.S. 395 for three miles to Kettle Park Road on the left. Turn left and drive two miles to the campground on the right.

Contact: Lake Roosevelt National Recreation Area, 1008 Crest Dr., Coulee Dam, WA 99116-1259, 509/633-9441, fax 509/633-9332.

34 HAAG COVE

Rating: 8

on Franklin Roosevelt Lake in Lake Roosevelt National Recreation Area
See map pages 134–135

This campground is tucked away in a cove along the western shore of Franklin Roosevelt Lake (Columbia River), about two miles south of Highway 20. A good side trip is to the Sherman Creek Habitat Management Area, located just north of camp. It's rugged and steep, but a good place to see and photograph wildlife, including bald eagles, golden eagles, and 200 other species of birds, along with the occasional black bear, cougar, and moose. Note that no boat launch is available at

this camp, but boat ramps are available at Kettle Falls and French Rock. Also note that no drinking water is available if the lake level drops below an elevation of 1,275 feet.

RV sites, facilities: There are 16 sites for RVs up to 26 feet or tents. Picnic tables and fire grills are provided. Drinking water, vault toilets, and cell phone reception are available. An ATM and pay phone are within 10 miles. Boat docks are available nearby. Leashed pets are permitted.

Reservations, fees: Reservations are not accepted. The fee is $5–10 per night. A senior discount is available. Open year-round, weather permitting.

Directions: From Spokane, drive north on U.S. 395 for 84 miles to the town of Kettle Falls and Highway 20. Continue on Highway 20 and drive 7.5 miles to Kettle Falls Road. Turn left (south) and drive two miles to the campground on the right.

Contact: Lake Roosevelt National Recreation Area, 1008 Crest Dr., Coulee Dam, WA 99116-1259, 509/633-9441, fax 509/633-9332.

35 LAKE ELLEN AND LAKE ELLEN WEST

Rating: 7

on Lake Ellen in Colville National Forest
See map pages 134–135

This 82-acre lake is a favorite for powerboating (with no speed limit) and fishing for rainbow trout, which are a good size and plentiful early in the season. Many people use this lake for trolling; exercise caution when water-skiing in a fishing area. There are two small camps available here. The boat launch is located at the west end of the lake. The camp is located about three miles west of the Columbia River and the Lake Roosevelt National Recreation Area. See a U.S. Forest Service map for details.

RV sites, facilities: There are 11 sites at Lake Ellen and five sites at Lake Ellen West for RVs up to 22 feet or tents. Picnic tables are provided, but there is no drinking water. Vault toilets and a boat dock are available. Garbage must be packed out. Some facilities are wheelchair-accessible. Leashed pets are permitted.

Reservations, fees: Reservations are not accepted. The fee is $6 per night. A senior discount is available. Open year-round with limited facilities in winter.

Directions: From Spokane, drive north on U.S. 395 for 87 miles, crossing the Columbia River. Turn left on Country Road 3 and drive south for 4.5 miles to County Road 412. Turn right on County Road 412 (well-maintained gravel) and drive five miles to the Lake Ellen Campground or continue another .7 mile to Lake Ellen West Campground.

Contact: Colville National Forest, Three Rivers Ranger District, 255 West 11th St., Kettle Falls, WA 99141, 509/738-6111, fax 509/738-7701.

36 EAST SULLIVAN CAMPGROUND

Rating: 7

on Sullivan Lake in Colville National Forest
See map pages 134–135

This campground is the largest one on Sullivan Lake and by far the most popular. It fills up in summer. The camp is located on the lake's north shore. Some come here to try to catch the giant brown trout or the smaller, more plentiful rainbow trout. The boating and hiking are also good. The beautiful Salmo-Priest Wilderness is located just three miles to the east. It gets light use, which means quiet, private trails. This is a prime place to view wildlife, so carry binoculars while hiking for a chance to spot the rare Woodland caribou and Rocky Mountain bighorn sheep. A nearby grass airstrip provides an opportunity for fly-in camping, but pilots should note that there are chuck holes present and holes from lots of ground squirrels. Only planes suited for primitive landing conditions should be flown in; check FAA guide to airports.

RV sites, facilities: There are 38 sites, including some drive-through sites, for RVs up to 45 feet or tents and one group area for up to 30 people. Picnic tables and fire grills are provided. Drinking water and vault toilets are available. A boat dock, launching facilities, a picnic area, a swimming area and platform, a pay phone, a camp host, and an RV dump station are nearby. An ATM is within 10 miles. Some facilities are wheelchair-accessible. Leashed pets are permitted.

Reservations, fees: Reserve at 877/444-6777 or online at www.reserveusa.com ($9 reservation

fee). The fee is $10 per night, plus $5 per night per additional vehicle; the group site is $50 per night. A senior discount is available. Open late May to September.

Directions: From Spokane, drive north on U.S. 395 for six miles to U.S. 2. Turn northeast on U.S. 2 and drive 30 miles to the Metaline turnoff and Highway 211 West. Turn northwest on Highway 211 West and drive 15 miles to Usk and Highway 20. Turn left (northwest) and drive 34 miles to Tiger and Highway 31. Continue on Highway 31 and drive 15 miles to the town of Metaline Falls (Highway 31 is also known as Lehigh Avenue in town); continue 2.5 miles to Sullivan Lake Road (County Road 9345). Turn right (east) on Sullivan Lake Road and drive eight miles to Sullivan Creek Road. Turn left (east) and drive .25 mile to the campground on the right.

Contact: Colville National Forest, Sullivan Lake Ranger District, 12641 Sullivan Lake Rd., Metaline Falls, WA 99153-9701, 509/446-7500, fax 509/446-7580.

37 NOISY CREEK AND NOISY CREEK GROUP

Rating: 7

on Sullivan Lake in Colville National Forest
See map pages 134–135

This campground is situated on the southeast end of Sullivan Lake, adjacent to where Noisy Creek pours into Sullivan Lake. It's a beautiful spot, but campsites do not have views of the lake. Note that the lake level can be drawn down for irrigation, leaving this camp well above the lake in winter months. The Noisy Creek Trail near camp heads east along Noisy Creek and then north up to Hall Mountain (elevation 6,323 feet), a distance of 5.3 miles; this is bighorn sheep country. The Lakeshore Trailhead is located at the nearby day-use area, directly on the water. Waterskiing is allowed on the 3.5-mile-long lake, and the boat ramp near the camp provides a good launch point.

RV sites, facilities: There are 19 sites for RVs up to 45 feet and one group camp for up to 40 people. If the group camp is not reserved, it is available as an overflow area. Picnic tables and fire grills are provided. Drinking water and vault toilets are available. Boat-launching facilities and a picnic area are nearby. A pay phone is within four miles. Leashed pets are permitted.

Reservations, fees: Reserve at 877/444-6777 or online at www.reserveusa.com ($9 reservation fee). The fee is $10 per night, plus $5 per additional vehicle. The group site is $50 per night. A senior discount is available. Open year-round, with no services in winter.

Directions: From Spokane, drive north on U.S. 395 for six miles to U.S. 2. Turn northeast on U.S. 2 and drive 30 miles to the Metaline turnoff and Highway 211 West. Turn northwest on Highway 211 West and drive 15 miles to Usk and Highway 20. Turn left (northwest) and drive 34 miles to Tiger and Highway 31. Continue on Highway 31 and drive 15 miles to the town of Metaline Falls (Highway 31 is known as Lehigh Avenue in town); continue 2.5 miles to Sullivan Lake Road (County Road 9345). Turn right (east) on Sullivan Lake Road and drive eight miles to the campground on the right (on the south end of Sullivan Lake).

Contact: Colville National Forest, Sullivan Lake Ranger District, 12641 Sullivan Lake Rd., Metaline Falls, WA 99153, 509/446-7500, fax 509/446-7580.

38 EDGEWATER

Rating: 6

on the Pend Oreille River in Colville National Forest
See map pages 134–135

Edgewater Camp is set on the shore of the Pend Oreille River about two miles upstream from the Box Canyon Dam. Although not far out of Ione, the camp has a primitive feel to it. Fishing for largemouth bass, rainbow trout, and brown trout is popular here.

RV sites, facilities: There are 20 sites for RVs up to 40 feet or tents. Picnic tables and fire grills are provided. Drinking water, vault toilets, and cell phone reception are available. A boat launch and six picnic sites for day use are available nearby. An ATM and pay phone are within three miles. Leashed pets are permitted.

Reservations, fees: Reservations are not accepted. The fee is $10 per night, plus $5 per addi-

tional vehicle per night. A senior discount is available. Open late May to early September.

Directions: From Spokane, drive north on U.S. 395 for six miles to U.S. 2. Turn northeast on U.S. 2 and drive 30 miles to the Metaline turnoff and Highway 211 West. Turn northwest on Highway 211 West and drive four miles to just south of Ione. Turn right on Country Road 9345, cross the orange bridge, and take a sharp left onto Country Road 3669. Turn left (north) on County Road 3669 and drive two miles to the campground entrance road on the left. Turn left and drive .25 mile to the campground.

Contact: Colville National Forest, Sullivan Lake Ranger District, 12641 Sullivan Lake Rd., Metaline Falls, WA 99153-9701, 509/446-7500, fax 509/446-7580.

39 IONE RV PARK AND MOTEL

Rating: 8

on the Pend Oreille River
See map pages 134–135

This camp is a good layover spot for campers with RVs or trailers who want to stay in town. The park sits on the shore of the Pend Oreille River, which offers fishing, swimming, several bike trails, and boating. In the winter, bighorn sheep may be spotted north of town.

RV sites, facilities: There are 19 sites with full hookups (20, 30, 50 amps) for RVs of any length, seven tent sites, and 11 motel rooms. Picnic tables are provided. Restrooms, drinking water, flush toilets, showers, an RV dump station, cell phone reception, a pay phone, and a coin-operated laundry are available. A store, ATM, a café, and ice are available within one mile. Boat docks, launching facilities, and a playground are nearby. Leashed pets are permitted.

Reservations, fees: Reservations are accepted. The fee is $5–18 per night. Major credit cards are accepted. Open year-round.

Directions: From Spokane, drive north on U.S. 2 for 48 miles to the junction with Highway 211 at the Washington/Idaho border. Turn west on Highway 211 and drive 48 miles northwest to Tiger and Highway 31. Turn north on Highway 31 and drive four miles to Ione. Cross a spillway (it looks like a bridge) on Highway 31 and continue to the campground on the right.

Contact: Ione RV Park and Motel, P.O. Box 730, Ione, WA 99139, 509/442-3213.

40 LAKE THOMAS

Rating: 6

on Lake Thomas in Colville National Forest
See map pages 134–135

This camp on the shore of Lake Thomas offers a less crowded alternative to the campgrounds at Lake Gillette. The lake provides fishing for cutthroat trout. Other nearby options include Lake Gillette and Gillette Campgrounds and Beaver Lodge Resort; see these listings for recreation information.

RV sites, facilities: There are 15 sites for small RVs up to 16 feet or tents. Picnic tables, fire grills, and tent pads are provided. Drinking water, vault toilets, and firewood are available. An RV dump station is within one mile. A pay phone is within 1.5 miles. Boat docks, launching facilities, and rentals are nearby. Leashed pets are permitted.

Reservations, fees: Reservations are not accepted. The fee is $10 per night. A senior discount is available. Open mid-May to late September.

Directions: From Spokane, drive north on U.S. 395 for 74 miles to Colville and Highway 20. Turn east on Highway 20 and drive 23 miles to County Road 4987 (Lake Gillette Road). Turn right (east) on Lake Gillette Road and drive one mile to the campground on the left.

Contact: Colville National Forest, Three Rivers Ranger District, Colville Office, 755 South Main St., Colville, WA 99114, 509/684-7000, fax 509/684-7285.

41 LAKE GILLETTE

Rating: 8

on Lake Gillette in Colville National Forest
See map pages 134–135

This pretty and popular camp is situated right on the shore of Lake Gillette. Like neighboring East Gillette Campground, it fills up quickly in the summer with off-road motorcyclists. The camp is popular with off-road vehicle (ORV)

users. An ORV system can't be accessed directly from the campground but is close by. Fishing at Lake Gillette is best for cutthroat trout.

RV sites, facilities: There are 14 sites for RVs up to 31 feet or tents. Drinking water, fire grills, and picnic tables are provided. Vault toilets, an RV dump station, and an amphitheater are available. A store and ice are available within one mile. Boat docks, launching facilities, and rentals are nearby. A pay phone is within one mile. Some facilities are wheelchair-accessible. Leashed pets are permitted.

Reservations, fees: Reservations are not accepted. The fee is $10–20 per night. A senior discount is available. Open mid-May to late September.

Directions: From Spokane, drive north on U.S. 395 for 74 miles to Colville and Highway 20. Turn east on Highway 20 and drive 23 miles to County Road 4987 (Lake Gillette Road). Turn right (east) on Lake Gillette Road and drive .5 mile to the campground on the left.

Contact: Colville National Forest, Three Rivers Ranger District, Colville Office, 755 South Main St., Colville, WA 99114, 509/684-7000, fax 509/684-7280.

42 GILLETTE

Rating: 7

near Lake Gillette in Colville National Forest
See map pages 134–135

This beautiful and extremely popular campground, just south of Beaver Lodge Resort and Lake Thomas, is near Lake Gillette, one in a chain of four lakes. There are a few multiuse trails in the area. See the description of Beaver Lodge Resort (the next listing) for other recreation information. Be sure to make reservations early.

RV sites, facilities: There are 30 sites for RVs up to 31 feet or tents. Picnic tables and fire grills are provided. Drinking water, vault toilets, and an RV dump station are available. A store, a pay phone, and ice are available within one mile. Boat docks, launching facilities, and rentals are nearby. Some facilities are wheelchair-accessible. Leashed pets are permitted.

Reservations, fees: Reservations are not accepted.

The fee is $8 per night. A senior discount is available. Open mid-May to late September.

Directions: From Spokane, drive north on U.S. 395 for 74 miles to Colville and Highway 20. Turn east on Highway 20 and drive 23 miles to County Road 4987 (Lake Gillette Road). Turn right (east) on Lake Gillette Road and drive .5 mile to the campground on the right.

Contact: Colville National Forest, Three Rivers Ranger District, Colville Office, 755 South Main St., Colville, WA 99114, 509/684-7000 or 509/684-7010, fax 509/684-7280.

43 BEAVER LODGE RESORT

Rating: 9

on Lake Thomas
See map pages 134–135

This developed camp is set along the shore of Lake Gillette, one in a chain of four lakes. A highlight in this area is the numerous opportunities for off-road vehicles (ORVs), with a network of ORV trails. In addition, hiking trails and marked bike trails are close to the camp. In winter cross-country skiing is available, and downhill skiing is available 30 miles away.

RV sites, facilities: There are 45 sites for RVs up to 40 feet or tents, six with full hookups (30 amps), 10 with partial hookups, a separate tent camping area, and seven cabins. Picnic tables and fire grills are provided. Restrooms, drinking water, flush toilets, showers, gasoline, propane, firewood, a pay phone, a store, a café, ice, boat rentals, and a playground are available. An RV dump station is within one mile. Boat docks and launching facilities are nearby. Leashed pets are permitted.

Reservations, fees: Reservations are accepted. The fee is $10–16 per night; cabins are $45–65 per night. Major credit cards are accepted. Open year-round.

Directions: From Spokane, drive north on U.S. 395 for 74 miles to Colville and Highway 20. Turn east on Highway 20 and drive 25 miles to the lodge on the right.

Contact: Beaver Lodge Resort, 2430 Hwy. 20 E, Colville, WA 99114, 509/684-5657, fax 509/685-9426, website: www.beaverlodgeresort.com.

44 BLUESLIDE RESORT

Rating: 7

on the Pend Oreille River
See map pages 134–135

This resort, situated along the western shore of the Pend Oreille River, offers a headquarters for fishermen and vacationers. Four to five bass tournaments are held each spring during May and June, and the river is stocked with both rainbow trout and bass. The resort offers full facilities for anglers, including tackle, boat rentals, and a marina with the only boat gas for 53 miles. The park is lovely, with grassy, shaded sites, and is located along the waterfowl migratory path. Lots of groups camp here in the summer. Recreation options include bicycling nearby. The only other campground in the vicinity is the Outpost Resort (see next listing).

RV sites, facilities: There are 44 sites with partial or full hookups (20, 30, 50 amps) including four drive-through sites, for RVs of any length or tents, seven tent sites, four motel units, and five cabins. Picnic tables and fire pits are provided. Restrooms, drinking water, flush toilets, showers, an RV dump station, a meeting hall, several sports fields, a pay phone, modem access, cell phone reception, a store, propane, a laundry room, ice, firewood, a playground with basketball, tetherball, volleyball, and horseshoes, a heated swimming pool, boat docks, launching facilities, and boat fuel are available. Leashed pets are permitted.

Reservations, fees: Reservations are recommended. The fee is $15–20 per night, plus $2 per person per night for more than two people. Cabins are $50–70 per night and motel rooms are $40–43 per night. Major credit cards are accepted. Open year-round, but only cabins are available in the winter.

Directions: From Spokane on Highway 2, drive north 25 miles to Highway 211. Turn left on Highway 211 and drive 18 miles to Highway 20 Turn left on Highway 20 and drive 22 miles to the park entrance on the right.

Contact: Blueslide Resort, 400041 Rte. 20, Cusick, WA 99119, 509/445-1327.

WASHINGTON

45 CHERIE'S OUTPOST RESORT

Rating: 8

on the Pend Oreille River

See map pages 134–135

This comfortable campground in a pretty setting along the west shore of the Pend Oreille River has fairly spacious sites and views of snow-capped mountains. Many species of birds and mammals live in this area. Fishing, hunting, and snowmobiling are popular activities (check regulations). The park is under new ownership as of 2002, bringing extensive renovations throughout the resort. If you're cruising Highway 20, Blueslide Resort is located about five miles north, the nearest alternative if this camp is full.

RV sites, facilities: There are 12 sites with full hookups (30 amps) for RVs of any length (four drive-through), 12 tent sites, and five cabins. Picnic tables and fire pits are provided. Flush toilets, an RV dump station, a store, propane, cell phone reception, emergency supplies, a café, ice, electricity, drinking water, sports fields, volleyball, horseshoes, a 1952 fire engine for climbing, a community fire pit, sewer hookups, showers, a swimming area, boat rentals, boat docks, and launching facilities are available. A pay phone is within five miles. Leashed pets are permitted.

Reservations, fees: Reservations are accepted. The fee is $10–15 per night, plus a $5 fee for boat launch for day use (free for campers). Major credit cards are accepted. Open year-round, with limited winter facilities.

Directions: From Spokane on Highway 2, drive north for 25 miles to Highway 211. Turn left onto Highway 211 and drive 18 miles to Highway 20. Turn left on Highway 20. Turn left on Highway 20 and drive 17.5 miles to the resort on the right.

Contact: Cherie's Outpost Resort, 405351 Hwy. 20, Cusick, WA 99119, 509/445-1317 or 888/888-9064, fax 509/445-2278, website: www.povn.com /outpostresort.

46 PANHANDLE

Rating: 9

on the Pend Oreille River in Colville National Forest

See map pages 134–135

In the tall trees and with views of the river, here's a scenic spot to set up camp along the eastern shore of the Pend Oreille River. This camp makes a good base for a fishing or water-skiing trip and is popular with bicyclists and mountain bikers. Fishing for largemouth and smallmouth bass is the most popular activity, with an annual bass tournament held every summer in the area. The campground is located in an area of mature trees directly across the river from Cherie's Outpost Resort. A network of hiking trails can be accessed by taking Forest Roads to the east. See a U.S. Forest Service map for details.

RV sites, facilities: There are 13 sites for RVs up to 35 feet or tents. Picnic tables and fire grills are provided. Drinking water, vault toilets, and cell phone reception are available. A small boat launch is nearby. Some facilities are wheelchair-accessible. Leashed pets are permitted.

Reservations, fees: Reserve at 877/444-6777 or online at www.reserveusa.com ($9 reservation fee). The fee is $10 per night, plus $5 per additional vehicle per night. A senior discount is available. Open late May to mid-September.

Directions: From Spokane, drive north on U.S. 395 for six miles to U.S. 2. Turn north on U.S. 2 and drive 30 miles to the Metaline turnoff and Highway 211 West. Take Highway 211 West and drive for 15 miles to the junction of Highway 20. Cross Highway 20, driving through the town of Usk. Continue across the Pend Oreille River to Le Clerc Road (County Road 9325). Turn left and drive 15 miles north on Le Clerc Road to the campground on the left.

Contact: Colville National Forest, Newport Ranger District, 315 North Warren Ave., Newport, WA 99156, 509/447-7300, fax 509/447-7301.

WASHINGTON

47 SOUTH SKOOKUM LAKE

Rating: 7

on South Skookum Lake in Colville National Forest

See map pages 134–135

This camp is situated on the western shore of South Skookum Lake, at the foot of Kings Mountain (elevation 4,383 feet). This is a good fishing lake, stocked with cutthroat trout, and is popular with families. The lake's small size (10 acres) makes large boats unadvisable. A 1.3-mile-long hiking trail circles the water, and a spur trail leads to a lake overview.

RV sites, facilities: There are 25 sites for RVs up to 30 feet or tents. Picnic tables and fire rings are provided. Drinking water, vault toilets, and cell phone reception are available. A boat ramp for small boats, two docks, and a wheelchair-accessible fishing dock are available nearby. An ATM and a pay phone are within eight miles. Leashed pets are permitted.

Reservations, fees: Reservations are not accepted. The fee is $10 per night, plus $5 per additional vehicle per night. A senior discount is available. Open late May to late September.

Directions: From Spokane, drive north on U.S. 395 for six miles to U.S. 2. Turn north on U.S. 2 and drive 30 miles to the Metaline turnoff and Highway 211 West. Turn northwest on Highway 211 West and drive 15 miles to Usk and Highway 20. Drive north on Highway 20 a short distance to Kings Lake/Boswell Road (County Road 3389). Turn right (east) on Kings Lake/Boswell Road (County Road 3389) and drive eight miles (over the Pend Oreille River) to the campground entrance road. Turn right and drive .25 mile to the campground.

Contact: Colville National Forest, Newport Ranger District, 315 North Warren Ave., Newport, WA 99156, 509/447-7300, fax 509/447-7301.

48 PIONEER PARK

Rating: 8

on the Pend Oreille River in Colville National Forest

See map pages 134–135

Pioneer Park Campground is set along the Pend Oreille River near Newport. The launch and adjoining parking area are suitable for larger boats. Water-skiing and water sports are popular here. There is an interpretive trail with a boardwalk and beautiful views of the river. Signs along the way explain the history of the Kalispell tribe.

RV sites, facilities: There are 17 sites for RVs up to 35 feet or tents. Picnic tables and fire rings are provided. Drinking water, vault toilets, and a picnic area are available. Boat docks, launching facilities, and rentals are nearby. An ATM and a pay phone are within eight miles. Some facilities are wheelchair-accessible. Leashed pets are permitted.

Reservations, fees: Reserve at 877/444-6777 or online at www.reserveusa.com ($9 reservation fee). The fee is $10 per night, plus $5 per additional vehicle per night. A senior discount is available. Open May to late September, weather permitting.

Directions: From Spokane, drive north on U.S. 395 for six miles to U.S. 2. Turn north on U.S. 2 and drive 41 miles to Newport. Continue across the Pend Oreille River to Le Clerc Road (County Road 9325). Turn left on Le Clerc Road and drive two miles to the campground on the left.

Contact: Colville National Forest, Newport Ranger District, 315 North Warren Ave., Newport, WA 99156, 509/447-7300, fax 509/447-7301.

49 EASTSIDE PARK AND CARL PRECHT MEMORIAL RV PARK

Rating: 6

on the Okanogan River

See map pages 134–135

This city park is in the town of Omak, along the shore of the Okanogan River. The RV park covers about 10 acres of the 76-acre park and features campsites positioned on concrete pads surrounded by grass. Trout fishing is often good at nearby Omak Lake, and there is a boat ramp near the campground. Recreation options include a pool and sports fields.

RV sites, facilities: There are 68 drive-through sites with full hookups (20, 30 amps) for RVs of any length and 25 tent sites. Picnic tables are provided. Restrooms, flush toilets, coin-operated showers, an RV dump station, a swimming pool, a playground with horseshoes, a skateboarding park, basketball and tennis courts, and a fitness trail are available. A store, a café, a coin-operated laundry, an ATM, a pay phone, and ice are available within one mile. Boat-launching facilities are nearby. An 18-hole golf course is within five miles. Some facilities are wheelchair-accessible. Leashed pets are permitted.

Reservations, fees: Reservations are not accepted. The fee is $14 per night. Open April to October, weather permitting.

Directions: From U.S. 97 in Omak, turn east (right, if coming from the south) on Highway 155 and drive .3 mile to the campground on the left.

Contact: City of Omak, P.O. Box 72, Omak, WA 98841, 509/826-1170, fax 509/826-6531.

50 AMERICAN LEGION PARK

Rating: 6

on the Okanogan River
See map pages 134–135

This city park is located along the shore of the Okanogan River in an urban setting. The sites are graveled and sunny. Anglers may want to try their hand at the excellent bass fishing here. There is a historical museum at the park.

RV sites, facilities: There are 35 sites for RVs of any length or tents. Picnic tables are provided. Restrooms, drinking water, flush toilets, and coin-operated showers are available. A store, a café, a coin-operated laundry, an ATM, and ice are available within one mile. Leashed pets are permitted.

Reservations, fees: Reservations are not accepted. The fee is $3–5 per vehicle per night. Open May to October, weather permitting.

Directions: From East Wenatchee, drive north on U.S. 97 for 88 miles to Okanogan and Highway 215. Turn left (north) on Highway 215 and

drive about three miles to the campground on the right.

Contact: Okanogan City Hall, P.O. Box 752, Okanogan, WA 98840, 509/422-3600, fax 509/422-0747, website: www.okanoganwash.com.

51 RAINBOW BEACH RESORT

Rating: 8

on Twin Lakes Reservoir
See map pages 134–135

This quality resort is located along the shore of Twin Lakes in the Colville Indian Reservation. Busy in summer, the camp fills up virtually every day in July and August. Nearby recreation options include hiking trails, marked bike trails, a full-service marina, and tennis courts.

RV sites, facilities: There are 14 sites with full hookups, including five drive-through sites, for RVs of any length, seven tent sites, and 26 cabins. Picnic tables are provided. Restrooms, drinking water, flush toilets, coin-operated showers, propane, an RV dump station, firewood, a recreation hall, a store, a laundry room, ice, boat rentals, docks and launching facilities, and a playground with volleyball and horseshoes are available. Leashed pets are permitted.

Reservations, fees: Reservations are recommended. The fee is $11–21 per night, with an extra charge for RV campers with tents. Pets are $10 per entire stay. Major credit cards are accepted. Campsites are available April to October; cabins are available year-round.

Directions: From Spokane, drive north on U.S. 395 for 84 miles to the town of Kettle Falls and Highway 20. Turn east on Highway 20 and drive five miles to the turnoff for Inchelium Highway. Turn left (south) and drive about 20 miles to Inchelium and Bridge Creek–Twin Lakes County Road. Turn right (west) and drive two miles to Stranger Creek Road. Turn left and drive .25 mile to the resort on the right.

Contact: Rainbow Beach Resort, 18 North Twin Lakes Rd., Inchelium, WA 99138, 509/722-5901, fax 509/722-7080.

52 GIFFORD

Rating: 7

on Franklin Roosevelt Lake in Lake Roosevelt National Recreation Area
See map pages 134–135

Fishing and water-skiing are two of the draws at this camp on the eastern shore of Franklin Roosevelt Lake (Columbia River). The nearby boat ramp is a big plus.

RV sites, facilities: There are 42 sites for RVs up to 20 feet or tents and one group site for up to 43 people. Picnic tables and fire grills are provided. Drinking water, vault toilets, and cell phone reception are available. Boat docks and launching facilities, an RV dump station, and a picnic area are nearby. Some facilities are wheelchair-accessible. Leashed pets are permitted.

Reservations, fees: Reservations are not accepted for family sites but are required for the group site; phone 509/633-3860. The fee is $5–10 per night; there is a $6 boat-launch fee. A senior discount is available. Open year-round, with limited winter facilities.

Directions: From Spokane on I-90, drive west for four miles to U.S. 2. Turn west on U.S. 2 and drive 34 miles to Davenport and Highway 25. Turn right (north) on Highway 25 and drive 60 miles to the campground (located about three miles south of Gifford) on the left.

Contact: Lake Roosevelt National Recreation Area, 1008 Crest Dr., Coulee Dam, WA 99116-1259, 509/633-9441, fax 509/633-9332.

53 HUNTERS PARK

Rating: 8

on Franklin Roosevelt Lake in Lake Roosevelt National Recreation Area
See map pages 134–135

This campground, on a shoreline point along Franklin Roosevelt Lake (Columbia River), offers good swimming, fishing, and water-skiing. It is located on the east shore of the lake, adjacent to the mouth of Hunters Creek and near the town of Hunters. Note: No drinking water is available if the lake level drops below an elevation of 1,245 feet.

RV sites, facilities: There are 37 sites for RVs up to 26 feet or tents and three group sites for up to 25 people each. Picnic tables and fire grills are provided. Drinking water and vault toilets are available. Restrooms, drinking water, flush toilets, cell phone reception, an RV dump station, and a picnic area are available. A store and ice are available within one mile. Boat docks and launching facilities are nearby. Some facilities are wheelchair-accessible. Leashed pets are permitted.

Reservations, fees: Reservations are not accepted for family sites but are required for group sites; phone 509/633-3860. The fee is $5–10 per night; there is a $6 boat-launch fee. A senior discount is available. Open year-round, with limited winter facilities.

Directions: From Spokane on I-90, drive west for four miles to U.S. 2. Turn west on U.S. 2 and drive 34 miles to Davenport and Highway 25. Turn north on Highway 25 and drive 47 miles to Hunters and the campground access road on the left side (west side) of the road (well marked). Turn left at the access road and drive two miles to the campground at the end of the road.

Contact: Lake Roosevelt National Recreation Area, 1008 Crest Dr., Coulee Dam, WA 99116-1259, 509/633-9441, fax 509/633-9332.

54 THE 49ER MOTEL AND RV PARK

Rating: 6

near Chewelah
See map pages 134–135

This region is the heart of mining country. The park is located in a mountainous setting next to a motel and has grassy sites. Nearby recreation options include a 27-hole golf course, hiking trails, and marked bike trails. This park is a good deal for RV cruisers—a rustic setting right in town. Numerous lakes are available within the area, providing good trout and bass fishing. In winter, note that the 49 Degrees Ski & Snowboard Park is located 12 miles to the east.

RV sites, facilities: There are 27 sites with full hookups (20, 30 amps), including mostly drive-through sites, for RVs up to 30 feet or tents and 13 motel rooms. Picnic tables are provided. Restrooms, drinking water, flush toilets, showers, an RV dump station, cable TV, a spa, cell phone reception, a recreation hall, and an indoor heated swimming pool are available. Propane, a store, a café, ice, and a coin-operated laundry are available within one mile. An ATM and pay phones are within a quarter mile. Leashed pets are permitted.

Reservations, fees: Reservations are accepted. The fee is $15–20 per night, with weekly and monthly rates available, plus $5 per person for more than four people and $4 per pet per night. Major credit cards are accepted. Open year-round.

Directions: From Spokane, drive north on U.S. 395 and go 48 miles to Chewelah; the park is on the right (on U.S. 395 at the south edge of town, well marked).

Contact: The 49er Motel and RV Park, South 311 Park St., Chewelah, WA 99109, 509/935-8613 or 888/412-1994, fax 509/935-8705, website: www .theofficenet.com/~49er.

55 WINONA BEACH RESORT AND RV PARK

Rating: 9

on Waitts Lake
See map pages 134–135

This beautiful and comfortable resort on the shore of Waitts Lake has spacious sites and friendly folks. The park fills up in July and August, and note that cabins here are available during this time by the week, not the night. In the spring, fishing for brown trout and rainbow trout can be quite good. The trout head to deeper water in the summer, and bluegill and perch are easier to catch then. Water-skiing and windsurfing are also popular. A casino and golf course are located nearby, and in winter, skiing and snowboarding are available nearby.

RV sites, facilities: There are 54 sites with full hookups (30, 50 amps), including 20 lakeside sites and two drive-through sites, for RVs up to 40 feet or tents, seven tent sites, and seven cabins. Picnic tables and fire rings are provided. Restrooms, drinking water, flush toilets, cell phone reception, coin-operated showers, an RV dump station, firewood, a snack bar, a general store, a swimming beach, an antique store, ice,

and a playground with volleyball, horseshoes, and basketball are available. Boat docks, launching facilities, and rentals are on-site. A pay phone is within three miles. Leashed pets are permitted.

Reservations, fees: Reservations are accepted. The fee is $15–22 per night, plus $2 per additional vehicle per night and $3 per pet per night. Major credit cards are accepted. Open April to September.

Directions: From Spokane, drive north on U.S. 395 for 42 miles to the Valley-Waitts Lake exit. Turn left (west) at that exit and drive one mile to Highway 231. Turn right (north) on Highway 231 and drive 1.5 miles to the town of Valley and Valley–Waitts Lake Road. Turn left and drive three miles to Winona Beach Road. Turn left and drive .25 mile to the resort at the end of the road.

Contact: Winona Beach Resort and RV Park, 33022 Winona Beach Rd., Valley, WA 99181, 509/937-2231, fax 509/937-2215, website: www .gocampingamerica.com/winona.

56 SILVER BEACH RESORT

Rating: 6

on Waitts Lake
See map pages 134–135

Silver Beach Resort offers grassy sites on the shore of Waitts Lake, where fishing and water-skiing are popular. See the previous description of Winona Beach Resort and RV Park for information about the lake and area activities.

RV sites, facilities: There are 53 sites with full hookups (20, 30 amps), including four drive-through sites, for RVs up to 38 feet and seven cabins. Picnic tables and fire pits are provided. Restrooms, drinking water, flush toilets, coin-operated showers, propane, an RV dump station, a store, a restaurant, a coin-operated laundry, ice, a playground, boat docks, launching facilities, and boat rentals are available. Leashed pets are permitted.

Reservations, fees: Reservations are accepted. The fee is $21 per night, plus $2 per person per night for more than two people and $2 per pet per night. Major credit cards are accepted. Open mid-April to mid-October, weather permitting.

Directions: From Spokane, drive north on U.S.

395 for 42 miles to the Valley–Waitts Lake exit. Turn left (west) at that exit and drive six miles to Waitts Lake and the resort on the left-hand side near the shore of the lake.

Contact: Silver Beach Resort, 3323 Waitts Lake Rd., Valley, WA 99181, 509/937-2811, fax 509/937-2812.

57 JUMP OFF JOE LAKE RESORT

Rating: 7

on Jump Off Joe Lake
See map pages 134–135

Located on the edge of Jump Off Joe Lake, this wooded campground offers lake views and easy boating access. Recreational activities include boating, fishing, and swimming. Spokane and Grand Coulee Dam are both within a short drive and provide excellent side-trip options. Within 10 miles to the north are an 18-hole golf course and casino.

RV sites, facilities: There are 20 sites with full hookups (20, 30 amps), including one drive-through site, for RVs or tents, 20 sites for tents, and five cabins. Picnic tables and fire rings are provided. Restrooms, drinking water, flush toilets, showers, a coin-operated laundry, horseshoes, a recreation field, a store, a swimming beach, and a barbecue are available. The camp also rents boats and has a boat ramp and 350-foot dock. An ATM and pay phone are within five miles. Some facilities are wheelchair-accessible. Leashed pets are permitted.

Reservations, fees: Reservations are recommended. The fee is $16.50–19.50 per night, plus $2 per person per night for over four people and $2.50 per pet per night. Major credit cards are accepted. Open April to October.

Directions: From Spokane, drive north on U.S. 395 for about 40 miles (three miles south of the town of Valley) to the Jump Off Joe Road exit (Milepost 198). Take that exit, turn west, and drive 1.2 miles to the campground on the right.

Contact: Jump Off Joe Lake Resort, 3290 East Jump Off Joe Rd., Valley, WA 99181, 509/937-2133.

58 SHORE ACRES

Rating: 8

on Loon Lake
See map pages 134–135

Located along the shore of Loon Lake at 2,400 feet elevation, this family-oriented campground has a long expanse of beach and offers an alternative to Granite Point Park across the lake. Water-skiing and fishing are popular pastimes here. New owners are busy making extensive renovations to the park. See the description of Granite Point Park (next listing) for details about the fishing opportunities.

RV sites, facilities: There are 30 sites with full hookups (50 amps) for RVs up to 40 feet or tents and 10 cabins. Picnic tables are provided. Restrooms, drinking water, flush toilets, fire pits, cell phone reception, modem access, a snack bar, a party boat, showers, an RV dump station, cable TV, a general store with fishing tackle and supplies, firewood, propane, ice, a playground, a swimming area, boat docks, boat rentals, and launching facilities are available. An ATM is within 3.5 miles. Leashed pets are permitted in RV sites only.

Reservations, fees: Reservations are recommended. The fee is $26 per night. Cabins are $480–615 per week in July and August, $80–100 per night the rest of the year. Major credit cards are accepted. Open mid-April to September.

Directions: From Spokane, drive north on U.S. 395 for 30 miles to Highway 292. Turn west on Highway 292 and drive two miles to Shore Acres Road. Turn left and drive another two miles to the park.

Contact: Shore Acres, 41987 Shore Acres Rd., Loon Lake, WA 99148, 509/233-2474 or 800/900-2474, fax 509/233-8052, website: www.shoreacresresort.com.

59 GRANITE POINT PARK

Rating: 8

on Loon Lake
See map pages 134–135

This resort is located on the shore of Loon Lake, a clear, clean, spring-fed lake that covers 1,200 acres and features a sandy beach and swimming area. The campground features grass sites, no concrete. In the spring, the mackinaw trout range from 4 to 30 pounds and can be taken by deep-water trolling (downriggers suggested). Easier to catch are the kokanee salmon and rainbow trout in the 12- to 14-inch class. A sprinkling of perch, sunfish, and bass come out of their hiding places when the weather heats up. Water-skiing and windsurfing are popular in summer months. Two golf courses are available within 10 miles.

RV sites, facilities: There are 80 sites with full hookups (30 amps) for RVs up to 40 feet and 25 cottages with kitchens (no tents allowed). Picnic tables and barbecues are provided. Restrooms, drinking water, flush toilets, showers, a recreation hall, a store, a snack bar, a pay phone, cell phone reception, a coin-operated laundry, ice, a playground with basketball, volleyball, and horseshoes, three swimming areas with a .75-mile beach, two swimming docks, boat docks, boat rentals, and launching facilities are available. Propane is available within one mile. An ATM is within 1.5 miles. Pets are not permitted.

Reservations, fees: Reservations are accepted. The fee is $25 per night, plus $2 per person per night for more than two people. Open early May to late September.

Directions: From Spokane, drive north on U.S. 395 for 26 miles (eight miles past the town of Deer Park) to the campground on the left.

Contact: Granite Point Park, 41000 Granite Point Rd., Loon Lake, WA 99148, 509/233-2100, website: www.granitepointpark.com.

60 PEND OREILLE COUNTY PARK

Rating: 6

near Newport

See map pages 134–135

This 440-acre park is wooded and features hiking trails throughout. There is some road noise from U.S. 2, but it's not intolerable. This park is not a bad choice if you're looking for a layover spot, and it's a good alternative to the often-crowded Mount Spokane State Park. Nearby activities include fishing and hunting.

RV sites, facilities: There are two sites for RVs up to 30 feet and 34 sites for tents. Picnic tables

and barbecues are provided. Restrooms, drinking water, flush toilets, cell phone reception, and showers are available. A pay phone is within five miles. Leashed pets are permitted.

Reservations, fees: Reservations are accepted; phone 509/447-4821. The fee is $10–13 per night. Open late May to late September, with some sites available in the off-season by special arrangement.

Directions: From Spokane, drive north on Highway 2 for 35 miles to the county park entrance on the left.

From Newport, drive east on Highway 2 for 13 miles to the park entrance on the right.

Contact: Pend Oreille County Department of Parks and Recreation, P.O. Box 5066, Newport, WA 99156, 509/447-4821, website: www.co.pend-oreille.wa.us.

61 ALTA LAKE STATE PARK

Rating: 8

on Alta Lake

See map pages 134–135

This state park is nestled among the pines along the shore of Alta Lake. The park covers 181 acres, and the lake is two miles long and a half mile wide. Alta Lake brightens a region where the mountains and pines meet the desert and features good trout fishing in summer, along with a boat launch and a half-mile-long swimming beach. Windsurfing is often excellent on windy afternoons. Because of its small size and many hidden rocks just under the lake surface, it can be dangerous for water-skiing. An 18-hole golf course and a riding stable are close by, and a nice one-mile hiking trail leads up to a scenic lookout. Lake Chelan is about 30 minutes away.

RV sites, facilities: There are 32 sites with partial hookups (30 amps) for RVs up to 40 feet, 157 developed tent sites, and a group site for 20 to 88 people. Picnic tables and fire grills are provided. Restrooms, flush toilets, showers, electricity, a pay phone, cell phone reception, firewood, and an RV dump station are available. A picnic area with a shelter and boat-launching facilities are available. A store, a café, and ice can be found within one mile. Some facilities are wheelchair-accessible. Leashed pets are permitted.

Reservations, fees: Reservations are not accepted

for family sites. The fee is $15–21 per night, plus $10 per person for more than two people and $6 per additional vehicle per night. Group reservations are required at 509/923-2473; the group fee is $25, plus $2 per person per night. A senior discount is available. Open April to October.

Directions: From East Wenatchee, drive north on U.S. 97 for 64 miles to Highway 153 (just south of Pateros). Turn left (northwest) on Highway 153 and drive two miles to Alta Lake Road. Turn left (southwest) and drive two miles to the park at the end of the road.

Contact: Alta Lake State Park, 509/923-2473, fax 509/923-2980; state park information, 360/902-8844.

62 BRIDGEPORT STATE PARK

Rating: 8

on Rufus Woods Lake
See map pages 134–135

Bridgeport State Park is located along the shore of Rufus Woods Lake, a reservoir on the Columbia River above Chief Joseph Dam. It's a big place, covering 748 acres, including 7,500 feet of shoreline and 18 acres of lawn, with some shade amid the desert landscape. Highlights include beach access and a boat launch. A unique feature, the "haystacks," which are unusual volcanic formations that resemble their name, stand out as the park's most striking characteristic. Fishing is good within the park; fishing outside of park boundaries requires a Colville Tribe Fishing License (for sale at the Bridgeport Hardware Store), in addition to a state fishing license. The lake has plenty of rainbow trout and walleye. A half-mile walking trail is available out of camp. Windsurfing in the afternoon wind and water-skiing are popular at the lake. Recreation options include an 18-hole golf course.

RV sites, facilities: There are 14 sites for self-contained RVs or tents, 20 sites with water and electrical hookups (30 amps) for RVs up to 45 feet, and one group site. Picnic tables and fire grills are provided. Restrooms, flush toilets, cell phone reception, a pay phone, coin-operated showers, firewood, a picnic area, and an RV dump station are available. A store, a café, ATM, and ice are available within two miles. Boat docks and launch-

ing facilities are nearby on both the upper and lower portions of the reservoir. Interpretive programs are available in summer. Leashed pets are permitted.

Reservations, fees: Reservations are not accepted for family sites but are required for groups. The fee is $16–22 per night. A senior discount is available. Open April to October.

Directions: From East Wenatchee, drive north on U.S. 97 for 71 miles to Highway 17. Turn south on Highway 17 and drive eight miles southeast to the park entrance on the left.

Contact: Bridgeport State Park, P.O. Box 846, Bridgeport, WA 98813, tel./fax 509/686-7231; state park information, 360/902-8844.

63 LAKESHORE RV PARK AND MARINA

Rating: 7

on Lake Chelan
See map pages 134–135

This municipal park and marina on Lake Chelan is a popular family camp, with fishing, swimming, boating, and hiking among the available activities. The camp fills up in the summer, including on weekdays in July and August. This RV park covers 22 acres, featuring a large marina and a 15-acre day-use area. There is an 18-hole putting course, bumper boats, go-carts, and a bungee trampoline within the park. An 18-hole championship golf course and putting green, lighted tennis courts, and a visitors center are nearby. A trip worth taking, the ferry ride goes to several landings on the lake; the ferry terminal is a half mile from the park.

RV sites, facilities: There are 163 sites with full hookups (20, 30, 50 amps) for RVs of any length or tents. Picnic tables are provided. Restrooms, flush toilets, coin-operated showers, a pay phone, cell phone reception, a snack bar, a children's playground, tennis courts, basketball, volleyball, a swimming beach, a skate park, an RV dump station, and a covered picnic area with a shelter are available. A store, an ATM, a café, a coin-operated laundry, ice, a playground, and propane are available within one mile. Boat docks and launching facilities are on-site.

Reservations, fees: Reservations are accepted. The fee is $13–35 per night, plus $5 per person for more than four people and $6 per additional vehicle per night. Major credit cards are accepted. Open year-round.

Directions: From East Wenatchee, drive north on Highway 97-A for 40 miles to Chelan (after crossing the Dan Gordon Bridge, the road name changes to Saunders Street). Continue for .1 mile to Johnson Street. Turn left and drive .2 mile (becomes Highway 150/Manson Highway) to the campground on the left.

Contact: City of Chelan, P.O. Box 1669, Chelan, WA 98816, 509/682-8024, fax 509/682-8248, website: www.chelancityparks.com.

64 STEAMBOAT ROCK STATE PARK

Rating: 10

on Banks Lake

See map pages 134–135

Steamboat Rock State Park is an oasis in desert surroundings. The park covers 3,522 acres and features nine miles of shoreline along Banks Lake, a reservoir created by the Grand Coulee Dam. Dominating the landscape is the columnar basaltic rock, with a surface area of 600 acres, that rises 800 feet above the lake. Two campground areas and a large day-use area are set on green lawns sheltered by tall poplars. The park has 13 miles of hiking and biking trails, as well as 10 miles of horse trails. There is also a swimming beach. Fishing and water-skiing are popular; so is rock-climbing. A hiking trail leads to Northrup Lake. Horse trails are available in nearby Northrup Canyon. Note that the one downer is mosquitoes, which are very prevalent in early summer. During the winter, the park is used by snowmobilers, cross-country skiers, and ice anglers.

RV sites, facilities: There are 100 sites with full hookups (30 amps) for RVs up to 50 feet long, 26 sites for tents or self-contained RVs, and 92 primitive campsites. Picnic tables and fire grills are provided. Restrooms, flush toilets, showers, an RV dump station, cell phone reception, a pay phone, a café, and a playground with volleyball are available. Boat-launching facilities, docks, and a marine dump station are nearby. An ATM is within 10 miles. Some facilities are wheelchair-accessible. Leashed pets are permitted.

Reservations, fees: Reserve at 888/CAMP-OUT

(888/226-7688) or online at www.parks.wa.gov/reservations ($7 reservation fee). The fee is $10–22 per night, plus $10 per additional vehicle per night. A senior discount is available. Major credit cards are accepted. Open year-round, with limited winter facilities.

Directions: From East Wenatchee, drive north U.S. 2 for 70 miles to Highway 155 (five miles east of Coulee City). Turn north and drive 18 miles to the park on the left.

Contact: Steamboat Rock State Park, P.O. Box 370, Electric City, WA 99123, 509/633-1304; state park information, 360/902-8844.

65 COULEE PLAYLAND RESORT

Rating: 7

near the Grand Coulee Dam

See map pages 134–135

This park on North Banks Lake, south of the Grand Coulee Dam, is pretty and well treed, with spacious sites for both RVs and tents. The Grand Coulee Laser Light Show is just two miles away and is well worth a visit. Boating, fishing for many species, and water-skiing are all popular. In addition, hiking trails, marked bike trails, a full-service marina, and tennis courts are close by.

RV sites, facilities: There are 65 sites with full hookups (20, 30 amps) for RVs of any length or tents, and one yurt, which sleeps five. Picnic tables and fire grills are provided. Restrooms, flush toilets, coin-operated showers, an RV dump station, a store, a coin-operated laundry, a pay phone, an ATM, modem access, cell phone reception, firewood, ice, a playground, boat docks, launching facilities, boat rentals, gas, and a bait and tackle shop are available. Propane and a café are available within one mile. Pets are permitted.

Reservations, fees: Reservations are accepted. The fee is $19–22 per night, plus $10 per additional vehicle per night. Major credit cards are accepted. Open year-round, with limited winter facilities.

Directions: From the junction of Highway 17 and U.S. 2 (north of Ephrata), drive east on U.S. 2 for five miles to Highway 155. Turn left (north) and drive 26 miles to Grand Coulee and Electric City. The campground is just off the highway on the left.

Contact: Coulee Playland Resort, P.O. Box 457, 401 Coulee Blvd., Electric City, WA 99123, 509/633-2671, website: www.couleeplayland.com.

66 SPRING CANYON

Rating: 6

on Franklin Roosevelt Lake in Lake Roosevelt National Recreation Area
See map pages 134–135

This large, developed campground is a popular vacation destination. Fishing for bass, walleye, trout, and sunfish is popular at Franklin Roosevelt Lake, as is water-skiing. The campground is not far from Grand Coulee Dam. Lake Roosevelt National Recreation Area offers numerous recreation options, such as free programs conducted by rangers that include guided canoe trips, campfire talks, and guided hikes. This lake is known as a prime location to view bald eagles, especially in winter. Side-trip options include visiting the Colville Tribal Museum in the town of Coulee Dam and touring the Grand Coulee Dam Visitor Center. Almost one mile long and twice as high as Niagara Falls, the dam is one of the largest concrete structures ever built. It is open for self-guided tours.

RV sites, facilities: There are 87 sites for self-contained RVs up to 26 feet or tents and one group site for up to 25 people. Picnic tables and fire grills are provided. Restrooms, flush toilets, an RV dump station, a snack bar, a picnic area, cell phone reception, and a playground are available. An ATM and a pay phone are within four miles. Boat docks, launching facilities, marine fuel, and a marine dump station are available nearby. Some facilities are wheelchair-accessible. Leashed pets are permitted.

Reservations, fees: Reservations are not accepted for family sites. The fee is $5–10 per night with a $6 boat launch fee. Reservations are required for the group site at 509/633-3830. A senior discount is available. Open year-round, weather permitting.

Directions: From the junction of I-90 and Highway 17 (just south of Moses Lake), drive north on Highway 17 for 45 miles to U.S. 2. Turn east on U.S. 2 and drive five miles to Highway 155. Turn left (north) and drive 26 miles to Grand Coulee and Highway 174. Turn right (east) on Highway 174 and drive three miles to the campground entrance on the left.

Contact: Lake Roosevelt National Recreation Area, 1008 Crest Dr., Coulee Dam, WA 99116-1259, 509/633-9441, fax 509/633-5125.

67 LAKEVIEW TERRACE MOBILE AND RV PARK

Rating: 6

near Franklin Roosevelt Lake
See map pages 134–135

This pleasant resort is situated near Franklin Roosevelt Lake, which was created by Grand Coulee Dam. It provides a slightly less crowded alternative to the national park camps in the vicinity. See the description of Spring Canyon above for water recreation options. A full-service marina and tennis courts are nearby.

RV sites, facilities: There are 20 drive-through sites with full hookups (20, 30, 50 amps) for RVs of any length, 20 tent sites, and a group camp for up to 100 tents. Picnic tables and fire pits are provided. Restrooms, flush toilets, a coin-operated laundry, cell phone reception, and a playground are available. Boat docks, launching facilities, and rentals are nearby. An ATM and pay phone are within three miles. Leashed pets are permitted.

Reservations, fees: Reservations are accepted. The fee is $15–20 per night, plus $1 per person for more than four people. The group site is $15 per tent. A senior discount is available. Major credit cards are accepted. Open year-round.

Directions: From Grand Coulee, drive east on Highway 174 for 3.5 miles east to the park entrance on the left.

Contact: Lakeview Terrace Mobile and RV Park, 44900 Rte. 174 N, Grand Coulee, WA 99133, 509/633-2169, website: www.lakeviewterracepark.com.

68 KELLER FERRY

Rating: 7

on Franklin Roosevelt Lake in Lake Roosevelt National Recreation Area
See map pages 134–135

This camp is set along the shore of Franklin Roosevelt Lake, a large reservoir created by Grand Coulee Dam, which sits about 15 miles west of camp. Franklin Roosevelt Lake is known for its walleye fishing; although more than 30 species live in this lake, 90 percent of those caught are walleye. They average one to four pounds and always travel in schools. Trout and salmon often swim below the bluffs near Keller Ferry. Waterskiing, fishing, and swimming are all recreation options here.

RV sites, facilities: There are 55 sites for RVs up to 16 feet or tents and two group sites for up to 25 people each. Picnic tables and fire grills are provided. Drinking water, vault toilets, and cell phone reception are available. An RV dump station, ice, a picnic area, a public telephone, and a playground are available nearby. Boat docks, launching facilities, fuel, and a marine dump station are also available. Some facilities are wheelchair-accessible. Leashed pets are permitted.

Reservations, fees: Reservations are not accepted for family sites. The fee is $5–10 per night, with a $6 boat launch fee. Reservations are required for group sites; phone 509/633-3830. A senior discount is available. Open year-round, weather permitting.

Directions: From Spokane on U.S. 90, turn west on U.S. 2 and drive 71 miles to Wilbur and Highway 21. Turn north and drive 14 miles to the campground on the left.

Contact: Lake Roosevelt National Recreation Area, 1008 Crest Dr., Coulee Dam, WA 99116-1259, 509/633-9441, fax 509/633-9332.

69 RIVER RUE RV PARK

Rating: 7

near the Columbia River
See map pages 134–135

This camp is located in high desert terrain yet is surrounded by lots of trees. You can fish, swim,

water-ski, or rent a houseboat at Lake Roosevelt, which is one mile away. Another nearby side trip is to the Grand Coulee Dam. A nine-hole golf course is available in Wilbur.

RV sites, facilities: There are 73 sites for RVs of any length or tents, including some with full hookups (20, 30, 50 amps), some with partial hookups, and some drive-through sites. Picnic tables and fire rings are provided. Restrooms, showers, an RV dump station, an ATM, cell phone reception, modem access, a courtesy phone, limited groceries, ice, a snack bar, RV supplies, fishing tackle, and propane are available. Recreational facilities include a playground, volleyball, and horseshoes. Some facilities are wheelchair-accessible. Leashed pets are permitted.

Reservations, fees: Reservations are recommended. The fee is $15–23 per night, plus $2 per person per night for more than two people. Major credit cards are accepted. A senior discount is available. Open April to October.

Directions: On U.S. 2 at Wilbur, drive west on U.S. 2 for one mile to Highway 174. Turn north on Highway 174 and drive .25 mile to Highway 21. Turn right (north) on Highway 21 and drive 13 miles to the park on the right.

Contact: River Rue RV Park, 44892 State Rte. 21 N, Wilbur, WA 99185, 509/647-2647, website: www.riverrue.com.

70 SEVEN BAYS RESORT AND MARINA

Rating: 6

on Franklin Roosevelt Lake
See map pages 134–135

Friendly folks run this resort on the shore of Roosevelt Lake, where the highlights include manicured, grassy, lakeside sites among deciduous trees. This camp is an alternative to Fort Spokane and Hawk Creek. A full-service marina sets this spot apart from the others.

RV sites, facilities: There are 32 sites with full hookups (20 amps), including two drive-through sites, for RVs up to 50 feet and 24 tent sites. Picnic tables are provided. Restrooms, drinking water, flush toilets, coin-operated showers, propane, cell phone reception, a pay phone, an RV dump station, a store, a café, a coin-operated laundry, and ice are available. Boat rentals, docks, and launching facilities are located at the resort. An ATM is within four miles. Leashed pets are permitted.

Reservations, fees: Reservations are accepted. The fee is $12–18 per night; extra tents are $5 per night. Major credit cards are accepted. Open year-round.

Directions: From Spokane on I-90, drive west for four miles to U.S. 2. Turn west on U.S. 2 and drive 34 miles to Highway 25. Turn north on Highway 25 and drive 23 miles to Miles-Creston Road. Turn left and drive five miles to the resort on the right.

Contact: Seven Bays Resort, Rte. 1, 1250 Marina Dr., Seven Bays, WA 99122, 509/725-1676.

71 FORT SPOKANE

Rating: 8

on Franklin Roosevelt Lake in Lake Roosevelt National Recreation Area

See map pages 134–135

Rangers offer evening campfire programs and guided daytime activities at this modern campground on the shore of Roosevelt Lake. This park also hosts living-history demonstrations. Fort Spokane is one of 28 campgrounds on the 130-mile-long lake. A 190-mile scenic vehicle route encircles most of the lake.

RV sites, facilities: There are 67 sites for RVs up to 26 feet or tents and two group sites for up to 30 people each. Picnic tables and fire grills are provided. Restrooms, drinking water, flush toilets, an RV dump station, and a playground are available. A picnic area is nearby. A store and ice are available within one mile. Boat docks, launching facilities, and a marine dump station are nearby. Some facilities are wheelchair-accessible. Leashed pets are permitted.

Reservations, fees: Reservations are not accepted for family sites but are required for group sites; phone 509/633-3830. The fee is $5–10 per night, with a $6 boat launch fee. A senior discount is available. Open year-round, with limited winter facilities.

Directions: From Spokane on I-90, drive west for four miles to U.S. 2. Turn west on U.S. 2 and drive 34 miles to Davenport and Highway 25.

Turn right (north) on Highway 25 and drive 22 miles to the campground entrance on the right. **Contact:** Lake Roosevelt National Recreation Area, 1008 Crest Dr., Coulee Dam, WA 99116-1259, 509/633-9441, fax 509/633-9332.

72 LONG LAKE CAMP AND PICNIC AREA

Rating: 8

on the Spokane River

See map pages 134–135

This campground is located about 45 minutes from Spokane and is set on a terrace above Long Lake (Spokane River), where fishing can be good for rainbow trout and occasional brown trout. This area is also popular for powerboating, waterskiing, and personal watercraft use. Crowded in summer, it gets a lot of use from residents of the Spokane area.

RV sites, facilities: There are 12 sites for small RVs up to 30 feet or tents. Picnic tables, fire grills, and tent pads are provided. Drinking water and vault toilets are available. A boat launch, a dock, a swimming beach, and a day-use area are nearby. Most of the facilities are wheelchair-accessible.

Reservations, fees: Reservations are not accepted. There is no fee for camping. Open April to September.

Directions: From Spokane on I-90, drive west for four miles to U.S. 2. Turn west on U.S. 2 and drive 21 miles to Reardan and Highway 231. Turn north on Highway 231 and drive 14.2 miles to Long Lake Dam Road (Highway 291). Turn right and drive 4.7 miles to the campground entrance on the right.

Contact: Department of Natural Resources, Northeast Region, P.O. Box 190, Colville, WA 99114-0190, 509/684-7474, fax 509/684-7484.

73 RIVERSIDE STATE PARK

Rating: 8

near Spokane

See map pages 134–135

This 10,000-acre park is set along the Spokane and Little Spokane Rivers and features freshwater river shores and a beautiful mountainous countryside. There are many recreation options, including canoeing, kayaking, and whitewater rafting, and fishing for bass, crappie, and perch. There are 55 miles of hiking and biking trails, featuring the 37-mile Centennial Trail, and 25 miles of trails for horseback riding, as well as riding stables. The park also has a 600-acre riding area for dirt bikes and off-road vehicles and snowmobiles in winter. An 18-hole golf course is located nearby. A local point of interest is the unique Bowl and Pitcher Lava Formation in the river. The park offers the Spokane House Interpretive Center, and a Junior Ranger program.

RV sites, facilities: There are 17 sites with partial hookups (30 amps) for RVs up to 45 feet or tents, 22 tent sites, three primitive tent sites, and two large group sites. Picnic tables and fire grills are provided. Restrooms, drinking water, flush toilets, showers, a picnic area with a kitchen shelter and electricity, an RV dump station, interpretive programs, and firewood are available. A store, a restaurant, an ATM, and ice are available within three miles. Boat-launching facilities and a dock are located on-site. Leashed pets are permitted.

Reservations, fees: Reservations are not accepted for family sites. The fee is $10–22 per night, plus $10 per additional vehicle per night. Group site reservations are required at least two weeks in advance; phone 509/465-5064. A senior discount is available. Open year-round.

Directions: In Spokane on I-90, take Exit 280/Maple Street North (cross the Maple Street Bridge), and drive north 1.1 miles to Maxwell Street (becomes Pettit Street). Turn left (west) and drive 1.9 miles, bearing left along the Spokane River to the park entrance. From the park entrance, continue for 1.5 miles on Aubrey L. White Parkway to the campground.

Contact: Riverside State Park, 9711 West Charles Rd., Nine Mile Falls, WA 99026, 509/465-5064, fax 509/465-5571, website: www.riversidestatepark .org; state park information, 360/902-8844.

74 TRAILER INNS RV PARK

Rating: 5

in Spokane
See map pages 134–135

This large RV park makes a perfect layover spot

on the way to Idaho. It's as close to a hotel as an RV park can get. Nearby recreation options include an 18-hole golf course, a racquet club, and tennis courts.

RV sites, facilities: There are 97 sites with full hookups, including 30 drive-through sites, for RVs of any length or tents. Picnic tables are provided. Restrooms, drinking water, flush toilets, showers, propane, cable TV, a TV room, a coin-operated laundry, ice, and a playground are available. An RV dump station, a store, and a café are within one mile. Leashed pets are permitted.

Reservations, fees: Reservations are accepted. The fee is $15–23 per night for two vehicles per site. Major credit cards are accepted. Open year-round.

Directions: Note that your route will depend on your direction: In Spokane eastbound on I-90, take Exit 285 (Sprague Avenue/Thierman Road) to Thierman Road. Drive .1 mile on Thierman Road to Fourth Avenue. Turn right (west) on Fourth Avenue and drive two blocks to the campground. In Spokane westbound on I-90, take Exit 284 (Havana Street). Drive one block south on Havana Street to Fourth Avenue. Turn left (east) on Fourth Avenue and drive one mile to the park.

Contact: Trailer Inns RV Park, 6021 East Fourth Ave., Spokane, WA 99212, 509/535-1811 or 800/659-4864, website: www.trailerinnsrv.com.

75 MOUNT SPOKANE STATE PARK

Rating: 8

on Mount Spokane
See map pages 134–135

This state park provides one of the better short trips available out of Spokane. It is set on the slopes of Mount Spokane (5,883 feet), and little brother, Mount Kit Carson (5,180 feet), sits alongside it. The park covers 13,643 acres in the Selkirk Mountains and features a stunning view from the top of Mount Spokane. The old lookout area takes in Washington, Idaho, Montana, and Canada. The park has 86 miles of hiking trails, occasionally routed into old-growth forest and amid granite outcroppings. The park is popular with bicyclists and mountain bikers. The Mt. Spokane Ski Resort operates here in winter. The park receives an average of 220 inches of snow annually.

RV sites, facilities: There are 12 sites for self-contained RVs up to 30 feet or tents. Picnic tables and fire grills are provided. Restrooms, drinking water, and flush toilets are available. A picnic area with a kitchen shelter, interpretive activities, and a café are available nearby. A restaurant, groceries, and a pay phone are available within seven miles. Leashed pets are permitted.

Reservations, fees: Reservations are not accepted. The fee is $15 per night, plus $10 per additional vehicle per night. Open June to September, weather permitting.

Directions: From Spokane, drive north on U.S. 395 for six miles to U.S. 2. Turn north on U.S. 2 and drive six miles to Highway 206. Turn northeast on Highway 206 and drive 15 miles north to the park.

Contact: Mount Spokane State Park, 509/238-4258, fax 509/238-4078; state park information, 360/902-8844.

76 BLUE LAKE RESORT

Rating: 6

on Blue Lake
See map pages 134–135

Blue Lake Resort is set in a desertlike area along the shore of Blue Lake between Sun Lakes State Park and Lake Lenore Caves State Park. Both parks make excellent side trips. Activities at Blue Lake include trout fishing, swimming, and boating. Tackle and boat rentals are available at the resort.

RV sites, facilities: There are 56 sites with partial or full hookups (20 amps), including six drive-through sites, for RVs of any length, 30 tent sites, and 10 cabins. Picnic tables and fire pits are provided. Restrooms, flush toilets, showers, a pay phone, an RV dump station, firewood, a store, ice, a roped swimming area, volleyball, a playground, boat docks, launching facilities, and boat rentals are available. An ATM is within 10 miles. Leashed pets are permitted.

Reservations, fees: Reservations are accepted. The fee is $15.50 per night, plus $5 per person for more than four people and $5 for each additional vehicle; pets are $2–5 per night. Cabins are $36–74 per night. Major credit cards are accepted. Open mid-April to late September.

Directions: From the junction of I-90 and Highway 17 (just south of Moses Lake), drive north on Highway 17 for 36 miles to the park on the right.

Contact: Blue Lake Resort, 31199 Hwy. 17 N, Coulee City, WA 99115, 509/632-5364 or 509/632-5388.

77 SUN VILLAGE RESORT

Rating: 6

on Blue Lake and Park Lake
See map pages 134–135

Like Blue Lake Resort, this campground is situated along the shore of Blue Lake. The hot desert setting is perfect for swimming and fishing. Late July and early August are the busiest times of the year here. See the description of Sun Lakes State Park in this chapter for information on the nearby state parks and other recreation options.

RV sites, facilities: There are 86 sites, including 40 drive-through and most with full hookups (20, 30 amps), for RVs of any length, four tent sites, and 19 cabins. Picnic tables are provided. Restrooms, flush toilets, coin-operated showers, group fire pits, propane, an RV dump station, a coin-operated laundry, a store, bait and tackle, firewood, ice, a playground, boat docks, launching facilities, and boat rentals are available. Leashed pets are permitted.

Reservations, fees: Reservations are accepted. The fee is $18.50 per night, plus $3–5 per person over the maximum number allowed per site or cabin, $4 per additional vehicle per night, and $3 per pet per night. Cabins are $49–106 per night. Major credit cards are accepted. Open late April to late September.

Directions: From the junction of I-90 and Highway 17 (just south of Moses Lake), drive north on Highway 17 for 36 miles to Blue Lake and Park Lake Road. Turn right (east) on Park Lake Road (the south entrance) and drive .5 mile to the resort on the right.

Contact: Sun Village Resort, 33575 Park Lake Rd. NE, Coulee City, WA 99115, 509/632-5664 or 888/632-5664, fax 509/632-5360.

78 COULEE LODGE RESORT

Rating: 8

on Blue Lake
See map pages 134–135

This camp is set at Blue Lake, which often provides outstanding fishing for trout in early spring. It is one of five camps in the general area and one of three in the immediate vicinity. Blue Lake offers plenty of summertime recreation options, including a swimming beach. See the following description of Sun Lakes State Park for details.

RV sites, facilities: There are 22 sites with full hookups (30 amps), including seven drive-through sites, for RVs up to 35 feet and 14 tent sites. Picnic tables and fire pits are provided. Restrooms, flush toilets, coin-operated showers, propane, an RV dump station, a store, firewood, a coin-operated laundry, boat docks, a boat and personal watercraft rentals, launching facilities, and ice are available. A pay phone is within two miles. A café is within five miles, and an ATM is within seven miles. Some facilities are wheelchair-accessible. Leashed pets are permitted.

Reservations, fees: Reservations are accepted. The fee is $16–25 per night, plus $3 per person for more than two people, $3 per additional vehicle per night, and $2 per pet per night. Major credit cards are accepted. Open early April to mid-September.

Directions: From the junction of I-90 and Highway 17 (just south of Moses Lake), drive north on Highway 17 for 39 miles to the north end of Blue Lake.

Contact: Coulee Lodge Resort, 33017 Park Lake Rd. NE, Coulee City, WA, 509/632-5565, fax 509/632-8607, website: www.couleelodgeresort.com.

79 SUN LAKES STATE PARK

Rating: 10

on Park Lake
See map pages 134–135

Sun Lakes State Park is situated on the shore of Park Lake, which is used primarily by anglers, boaters, and water-skiers. This 4,027-acre park near the foot of Dry Falls features 12 miles of shoreline. Dry Falls, a former waterfall, is now

a stark 400-foot-high climb, 3.5 miles wide. During the Ice Age floods, this waterfall was 10 times the size of Niagara Falls. An interpretive center at Dry Falls is open May to September. Now, back to the present: There are nine lakes in the park. A trail at the north end of Lake Lenore leads to the Lake Lenore Caves. Nearby recreation possibilities include a nine-hole golf course and miniature golf.

RV sites, facilities: There are 162 sites for self-contained RVs or tents, 18 sites with full hookups (30 amps) for RVs up to 50 feet, and one group campsite for up to 40 people. Picnic tables and fire pits are provided. Restrooms, flush toilets, coin-operated showers, an RV dump station, electricity, drinking water, and sewer hookups are available. A store, a snack bar, ice, firewood, and a coin-operated laundry are available within one mile. Boat docks, launching facilities, and rentals are nearby. An ATM is within 3.5 miles. Some facilities are wheelchair-accessible. Leashed pets are permitted.

Reservations, fees: Reserve at 888/CAMP-OUT (888/226-7688) or online at www.parks.wa.gov /reservations ($7 reservation fee). The fee is $16–22 per night, plus $10 per night per additional vehicle. The group site is $25 plus $2 per person per night. A senior discount is available. Major credit cards are accepted. Open year-round.

Directions: From Ephrata, drive northeast on Highway 28 to Soap Lake and Highway 17. Turn north on Highway 17 and drive 17 miles to the park on the right.

Contact: Sun Lakes State Park, 509/632-5583, fax 509/632-5971; state park information, 360/902-8844.

80 SUN LAKES PARK RESORT

Rating: 8

Sun Lakes State Park
See map pages 134–135

Run by the concessionaire that operates within Sun Lakes State Park, this camp offers full facilities and is a slightly more developed alternative to the state campground. It is right on the water and very scenic. See the description of Sun Lakes State Park above for activities information.

RV sites, facilities: There are 108 sites with full

hookups (30, 50 amps), including 64 drive-through, for RVs of any length or tents, 50 cabins, and 10 mobile home rentals. Picnic tables and fire grills are provided. Restrooms, flush toilets, coin-operated showers, propane, an RV dump station, a store, firewood, a gift shop, mini golf, a nine-hole golf course, a pay phone, a snack bar, a coin-operated laundry, ice, a playground, boat rentals, and a heated swimming pool are available. Boat docks, boat rentals, and launching facilities are nearby. An ATM is within five miles. Some facilities are wheelchair-accessible. Leashed pets are permitted. **Reservations, fees:** Reservations are accepted. The fee is $25–27 per night, plus $5 per additional vehicle per night and $7 per person per night over four people; children 16 and under free. Cabins are $60–82, and mobile home rentals are $114. Open mid-April to mid-October, weather permitting. **Directions:** From Ephrata, drive northeast on Highway 28 to Soap Lake and Highway 17. Turn north on Highway 17 and drive 17 miles to the Sun Lakes Park on the right. Enter the park and drive to the resort (well marked). **Contact:** Sun Lakes Park Resort, 34228 Park Lake Rd. NE, Coulee City, WA 99115, 509/632-5291, fax 509/754-6240, website: www.sunlakes parkresort.com.

81 COULEE CITY PARK

Rating: 6

on Banks Lake
See map pages 134–135

Coulee City Park is a well-maintained park located in shade trees on the southern shore of 30-mile-long Banks Lake. You can see the highway from the park, and there is some highway noise. Campsites are usually available. The busiest time of the year is Memorial Day weekend because of the local rodeo. Boating, fishing, and water-skiing are popular. An 18-hole golf course is close by. **RV sites, facilities:** There are 55 sites for RVs up to 35 feet and 100 tent sites, including 32 drive-through sites with full hookups (30, 50 amps). Picnic tables and fire rings are provided. Restrooms, flush toilets, showers, group fire pits, an RV dump station, and a playground are available. Boat docks and launching facilities are on-site. Propane, firewood, a store, a restaurant, a

café, a coin-operated laundry, and ice are available within one mile. Some facilities are wheelchair-accessible. **Reservations, fees:** Reservations are not accepted. The fee is $12–17 per night, plus $2 per additional vehicle. Open mid-April to late October, weather permitting. **Directions:** From Coulee City, drive east on U.S. 2 for .5 mile to the park on the left. **Contact:** Coulee City Park, P.O. Box 398, Coulee City, WA 99115, 509/632-5331, website: www .couleecity.com.

82 WEST MEDICAL LAKE RESORT

Rating: 7

on West Medical Lake
See map pages 134–135

This resort functions primarily as a fish camp for anglers. There are actually two lakes: West Medical is the larger of the two and has better fishing, with boat rentals available; Medical Lake is just one-quarter-mile wide and one-half-mile long, and boating is restricted to rowboats, canoes, kayaks, and sailboats. The lakes got their names from the wondrous medical powers once attributed to their waters. This is a popular spot for Spokane locals and the only campground on West Medical Lake. **RV sites, facilities:** There are 12 sites with full hookups and six with partial hookups (20, 30 amps) for RVs up to 40 feet and 20 tent sites. At tent sites, fire pits are provided. Picnic tables, restrooms, drinking water, flush toilets, showers, a café, bait, tackle, and ice are available. Boat and fishing docks, launching facilities, a fish-cleaning station, and boat and barge rentals are nearby. An ATM, pay phone, and groceries are available within one mile. Leashed pets are permitted. **Reservations, fees:** Reservations are recommended. The fee is $15 per night. Open late April to September. **Directions:** In Seattle on I-90, drive west to Exit 264 and Cheney/Salnave Road. Take that exit and turn north on Salnave Road; drive six miles to Fancher Road. Turn right (west) and drive 200 yards. Bear left on Fancher Road and drive 200 yards to the campground. **Contact:** West Medical Lake Resort, 1432 West

Fancher Rd., Medical Lake, WA 99022, 509/299-3921, website: http://goodwin.org/resort/.

83 PICNIC PINES ON SILVER LAKE

Rating: 8

on Silver Lake
See map pages 134–135

This shorefront resort on Silver Lake caters primarily to RVers, although tent campers are welcome. Fishing can be excellent here. Nearby recreation options include marked bike trails, a full-service marina, and tennis courts. New owners took over this operation in April 2002. See the description of West Medical Lake Resort above for further details.

RV sites, facilities: There are 18 sites, six with full hookups and 12 with electricity, for RVs up to 35 feet and 10 tent sites. Hookups are available only from mid-March to mid-October. Picnic tables and fire pits are provided. Restrooms, drinking water, flush toilets, showers, a store, a restaurant, a lounge, courtesy phones, cell phone reception, a bait shop, boat docks, boat rentals, launching facilities, ice, and a swimming beach are available. Propane, an ATM, and a coin-operated laundry are available within two miles. Leashed pets are permitted.

Reservations, fees: Reservations are accepted. The fee is $15–19 per night. Major credit cards are accepted. Open year-round.

Directions: In Spokane on I-90, drive west to Exit 270 and Medical Lake Road. Take that exit and turn west on Medical Lake Road; drive three miles to Silver Lake Road. Turn left and drive .5 mile to the park on the left.

Contact: Picnic Pines on Silver Lake, South 9212 Silver Lake Rd., Medical Lake, WA 99022, 509/299-6902.

84 MALLARD BAY RESORT

Rating: 8

on Clear Lake
See map pages 134–135

This resort is on the shore of Clear Lake, which is two miles long, a half-mile wide, and used for fishing, water-skiing, windsurfing, and sailing.

Most of the campsites are lakeshore sites on a 20-acre peninsula. Marked bike trails and tennis courts are nearby.

RV sites, facilities: There are 50 sites with partial hookups (20, 30, 50 amps) for RVs of any length or tents, plus two camping cabins. Picnic tables and fire pits are provided. Restrooms, drinking water, flush toilets, showers, propane, an RV dump station, a store, a tackle shop, ice, swimming facilities with a diving board, a playground, a basketball court, boat docks, launching facilities, a fishing pier, fish-cleaning stations, and boat rentals are available. Leashed pets are permitted.

Reservations, fees: Reservations are accepted. The fee is $16 per night, plus $3 per person for more than four people and $3 per additional vehicle per night. Cabins are $39 per night. Open mid-April to Labor Day Weekend.

Directions: In Spokane on I-90, drive west to Exit 264 and Salnave Road. Take that exit and turn north on Salnave Road; drive 1.5 miles to a junction signed by Mallard Bay Resort. Turn right at that sign and drive .5 mile on a dirt road to the resort at the end of the road.

Contact: Mallard Bay Resort, 14601 Salnave Rd., Cheney, WA 99004, 509/299-3830.

85 RAINBOW COVE RV AND FISHING RESORT

Rating: 7

on Clear Lake
See map pages 134–135

This resort at Clear Lake features a 300-foot dock with benches that can be used for fishing. If you figured that most people here are anglers, well, that is correct. Fishing can be good for rainbow trout, brown trout, largemouth bass, crappie, bullhead, and catfish. Most of the campsites are at least partially shaded. Summer weekends are often busy.

RV sites, facilities: There are 16 sites with partial hookups (30 amps) for RVs up to 40 feet, four tent sites, and two rustic floating/sleeping cabins. Picnic tables and fire pits are provided. Restrooms, drinking water, flush toilets, showers, a café, ice, bait and tackle, boat docks, boat rentals, and launching facilities and moorage are available. Leashed pets are permitted.

Reservations, fees: Reservations are accepted. The fee is $17–20 per night, plus $3 per person per night for more than two people. Open mid-April to mid-September.

Directions: In Spokane on I-90, drive west to Exit 264 and Salnave Road. Take that exit and turn right (north) on Salnave Road; then make another immediate right onto Clear Lake Road. Turn right (north) on Clear Lake Road and drive three miles to the resort on the left (well signed).

Contact: Rainbow Cove RV and Fishing Resort, 12514 South Clear Lake Rd., Medical Lake, WA 99022, 509/299-3717.

86 YOGI BEAR'S CAMP RESORT

Rating: 6

west of Spokane

See map pages 134–135

This resort is located 15 minutes from downtown Spokane yet provides a wooded, rural setting. It features towering Ponderosa pines. Highlights include an 18-hole golf course next door and several other courses within 20 minutes of the resort.

RV sites, facilities: There are 168 sites with full hookups, including 63 drive-through sites, for RVs up to 70 feet or tents, five cabins, and six bungalows. Restrooms, drinking water, flush toilets, showers, a pay phone, cell phone reception, cable TV, modem-friendly phone service, an RV dump station, propane, a coin-operated laundry, an RV wash station, and three playgrounds are available. Other facilities include a camp store, an activity center with an indoor pool, a spa, an exercise room, a game room, a snack shack, a dog walk, and various sports facilities (volleyball, basketball, badminton, miniature golf, and organized recreational activities in summer). Some facilities are wheelchair-accessible. Leashed pets are permitted.

Reservations, fees: Reservations are accepted. The fees are $20–25 per night for tent sites and $27–40 per night for RV sites, plus $5 per person for more than four people. Major credit cards are accepted. Open year-round.

Directions: In Spokane on I-90, drive to Exit 272 and Westbow Road. Take that exit, turn east on Westbow Road, and drive to Thomas Mallen Road. Turn right (south) on Thomas Mallen Road and drive .5 mile to the campground on the right.

Contact: Yogi Bear's Camp Resort, 7520 South Thomas Mallen Rd., Cheney, WA 99004, 509/747-9415 or 800/494-7275, fax 509/459-0148, website: www.jellystonewa.com.

87 KOA SPOKANE

Rating: 5

on the Spokane River

See map pages 134–135

This KOA campground is located close to the shore of the Spokane River. Also nearby you'll find the Centennial Trail, as well as an 18-hole golf course and tennis courts.

RV sites, facilities: There are 150 sites with full hookups (30, 50 amps), including 109 drive-through sites, for RVs of any length, 50 tent sites, and three cabins. Picnic tables are provided. Restrooms, drinking water, flush toilets, showers, cable TV, an RV dump station, a recreation hall, a playground, a store, pay phones, cell phone reception, basketball, volleyball, a laundry room, ice, modem access, summer ice-cream socials, and a swimming pool are available. An ATM is within a quarter mile. A café and groceries are available within two miles. Some facilities are wheelchair-accessible. Leashed pets are permitted.

Reservations, fees: Reservations are accepted at 800/562-3309. The fee is $28–32 per night. Major credit cards are accepted. Open year-round.

Directions: From Spokane, drive east on I-90 for 13 miles to Exit 293. Take that exit to Barker Road. Turn north on Barker Road and drive 1.5 miles to the campground on the left.

Contact: KOA Spokane, 3025 North Barker, Otis Orchards, WA 99027, 509/924-4722 or 800/562-3309, website: www.koa.com.

 **Washington**

Mount Rainier and the Columbia River Gorge

MOUNT RAINIER AND THE COLUMBIA RIVER GORGE

see
The Northern
Cascades
pages 90–91

see
Southeastern
Washington
pages 206–207

see
Seattle and the
San Juan Islands
pages 68–69

see The Olympic Peninsula
and Coastal Washington
pages 16–17

Wenatchee
National Forest

Mt. Rainier
National Park

Mt. Rainier
(14,411 ft.)

Mt. Adams
(12,276 ft.)

Gifford
Pinchot
National
Forest

Mt. Baker-
Snoqualmie
National Forest

Mt. St. Helens
National Volcanic
Monument

Nisqually River

Chehalis

River

Riffe
Lake

Mayfield
Lake

Silver Lake

Naches

River

Rimrock
Lake

AHTANUM RIDGE

YAKAMA   INDIAN

RESERVATION

Lincoln   Plateau

C A S C A D E

R A N G E

Olympia

Centralia

Chehalis

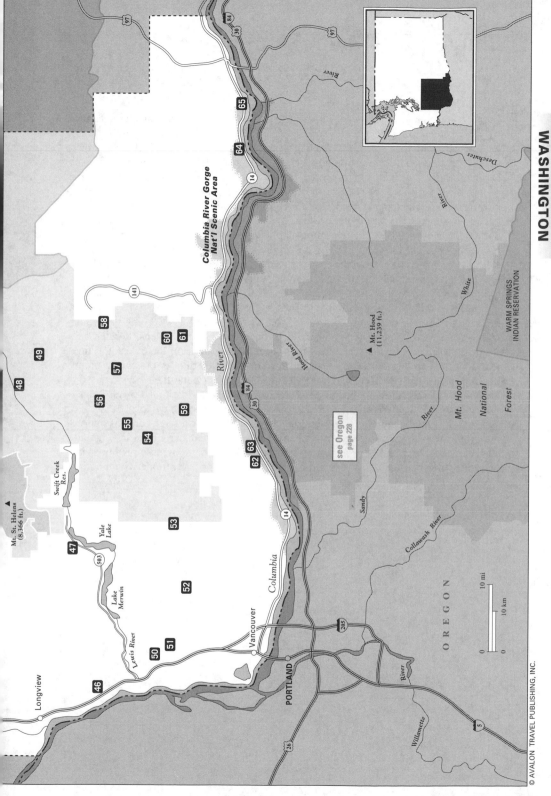

Columbia River Gorge
Nat'l Scenic Area

Mt. Hood
(11,239 ft.) ▲

see Oregon
page 228

WARM SPRINGS
INDIAN RESERVATION

Deschutes

White

River

Hood River

River

Mt. Hood   National   Forest

Sandy

River

Collawash River

O R E G O N

Willamette

River

PORTLAND

Vancouver

Columbia

Mt. St. Helens
(8,366 ft.) ▲

Swift Creek
Res.

Yale
Lake

Lake
Merwin

Lewis River

Longview

River

48
49
58
60
61
57
56
59
55
54
63
62
53
52
51
50
47
46

97
84
30
65
64
14
141
30
14
503
205
5
26

10 mi
10 km
0
0

© AVALON TRAVEL PUBLISHING, INC.

Chapter 5—Mount Rainier and the Columbia River Gorge

As you stand at the rim of Mount St. Helens, the greatest natural spectacle anywhere on the planet is at your boot tips. The top 1,300 feet of the old volcano, along with the entire north flank, has been blown clean off. The half-moon crater walls drop almost 2,100 feet straight down to a lava plug dome, a mile across and still building, where a wisp of smoke emerges from its center. At its edges, the rising plumes of dust from continuous rock falls can be deceptive—you may think a small eruption is in progress. It's like looking inside the bowels of the earth.

The plug dome gives way to the blast zone, where the mountain has completely blown out its side and spreads out across 230 square miles of devastation. From here, it's largely a moonscape but for Spirit Lake on the northeast flank, where thousands of trees are still floating, log-jammed from the eruption in May 1980. Beyond this scene rises 14,411-foot Mount Rainier to the north, 12,276-foot Mount Adams to the northeast, and 11,235-foot Mount Hood to the south, all pristine jewels in contrast to the nearby remains.

I've hiked most of the Pacific Crest Trail and climbed most of the West's highest mountains, but no view compares to this. You could explore this sweeping panorama of a land for years. The most famous spots in this region are St. Helens, Rainier, and Adams; the latter are two of the three most beautiful mountains in the Cascade Range (Mount Shasta in Northern California is the third). All of them offer outstanding touring and hiking, with excellent camps of all kinds available around their perimeters. St. Helens provides the most eye-popping views and most developed visitors centers, Rainier the most pristine wilderness, and Adams some of the best lakeside camps.

That's just the beginning. The Western Cascades span down river canyons and up mountain subridges, both filled with streams and lakes. There are camps throughout. At the same time, the I-5 corridor and its network of linked highways also provide many privately developed RV parks fully furnished with everything a vacationer could desire.

1 COLUMBUS PARK

Rating: 7

on Black Lake

See map pages 174–175

This spot along the shore of Black Lake is pretty enough for special events, such as weddings and reunions. The campsites are wooded, and a stream (no fishing) runs through the campground. Black Lake is good for fishing. An 18-hole golf course is nearby.

RV sites, facilities: There are 29 sites with partial hookups (30 amps) for RVs up to 40 feet and three tent sites. Picnic tables and fire rings are provided. Restrooms, drinking water, flush toilets, showers, an RV dump station, a coin-operated laundry, firewood, a playground with volleyball and horseshoes, boat docks, and launching facilities are available. A picnic area for special events is nearby. Propane, ice, an ATM, a pay phone, and a store are available within one mile; there is a restaurant within three miles. Some facilities are wheelchair-accessible. Leashed pets are permitted.

Reservations, fees: Reservations are recommended during summer. The fee is $13–16.26 per night. Open year-round.

Directions: From I-5 in Olympia, take the U.S. 101 exit (exit 104) and drive 1.7 miles northwest to Black Lake Boulevard. Turn left (south) on Black Lake Boulevard and drive 3.5 miles to the park on the left.

Contact: Columbus Park, 5700 Black Lake Blvd. SW, Olympia, WA 98512, 360/786-9460 or 800/848-9460, website: www.columbuspark.net.

2 AMERICAN HERITAGE CAMPGROUND

Rating: 7

near Olympia

See map pages 174–175

This spacious, wooded campground situated just a half mile off the highway is close to many activities, including an 18-hole golf course, hiking trails, marked bike trails, and tennis courts. The park features novelty cycle rentals, free wagon rides, and free nightly movies. It's exceptionally clean and pretty, making for a pleasant layover

on your way up or down I-5. The park has a 5,000-square-foot pavilion for special events or groups.

RV sites, facilities: There are 72 sites with partial or full hookups (30 amps) for RVs of any length or tents, 23 tent sites, and one cabin. Picnic tables and fire rings are provided. Restrooms, drinking water, flush toilets, showers, propane, cell phone reception, pay phones, an RV dump station, a recreation hall, a group pavilion, recreation programs, a store, a coin-operated laundry, ice, a playground, a heated swimming pool, and firewood are available. An ATM is within 1.5 miles. Leashed pets are permitted.

Reservations, fees: Reservations are accepted. The fee is $20–28 per night for two people, plus $4 per person per night for more than two adults and two children. Major credit cards are accepted. Open Memorial Day through Labor Day weekend.

Directions: From Olympia, drive five miles south on I-5 to Exit 99. Take that exit and drive .25 mile east to Kimmie Street. Turn right (south) on Kimmie Street and drive .25 mile to the end of the road to the campground on the left.

Contact: American Heritage Campground, 9610 Kimmie St. SW, Olympia, WA 98512, 360/943-8778, website: www.americanheritagecampground .com.

3 MILLERSYLVANIA STATE PARK

Rating: 8

on Deep Lake

See map pages 174–175

This state park is set on the shore of Deep Lake and features 3,300 feet of waterfront. The park has 8.6 miles of hiking and biking trails amid an abundance of old-growth cedar and fir trees. Boating at Deep Lake is restricted to hand-launched boats, with a 5 mph speed limit. A fishing dock is available at the boat-launch area. Another highlight is a one-mile fitness trail with workout stations. Remnants of a narrow-gauge railroad and several skid trails used in the 1800s by the logging industry are still present on park roads.

RV sites, facilities: There are 48 sites with full hookups (30 amps) for RVs up to 45 feet, 120 developed tent sites, and four primitive tent sites.

Picnic tables and fire grills are provided. Restrooms, drinking water, flush toilets, coin-operated showers, an RV dump station, a playground, boat docks and launching facilities, and firewood are available. A picnic area, summer interpretive activities, and horseshoes are also nearby. A store, a restaurant, and ice are available within two miles. Some facilities are wheelchair-accessible. Leashed pets are permitted.

Reservations, fees: Reserve at 888/CAMP-OUT (888/226-7688) or online at www.parks.wa.gov /reservations ($7 reservation fee). The fee is $10–22 per night, plus $10 per additional vehicle per night. The group site is $7 plus $2 per person with a minumum of 20 people and a maximum of 40. A senior discount is available. Major credit cards are accepted in summer. Open year-round.

Directions: From Olympia, drive south on I-5 for 10 miles to Exit 95 and Highway 121. Turn east on Maytown Road (Highway 121) and drive 2.7 miles to Tilley Road. Turn left (north) and drive 1.3 miles to the park.

Contact: Millersylvania State Park, 360/753-1519; state park information, 360/902-8844.

⁴ OFFUT LAKE RESORT

Rating: 8

on Offut Lake

See map pages 174–175

This wooded campground is on Offut Lake, just enough off the beaten track to provide a bit of seclusion. Fishing, swimming, and boating are favorite activities here. Anglers will find everything they need, including tackle and boat rentals, at the resort. Boating is restricted to a 5 mph speed limit, and no gas motors are permitted at the resort. Several fishing derbies are held here every year.

RV sites, facilities: There are 51 sites with partial or full hookups (20, 30, 50 amps) for RVs up to 40 feet, 25 tent sites, and nine cabins. Picnic tables and fire rings are provided. Restrooms, drinking water, flush toilets, coin-operated showers, an ATM, a pay phone, cell phone reception, modem access, a picnic shelter, an RV dump station, firewood, a store with bait and tackle, fishing licenses, groceries, propane, a laundry room, ice, and a playground with basketball and horseshoes are available. Boat rentals and docks are available;

no gas motors permitted. Some facilities are wheelchair-accessible. Leashed pets are permitted.

Reservations, fees: Reservations are accepted. The fee is $17–24 per night, plus $5 per person per night for more than two adults and two children, $2 per additional vehicle per night, and $1–2 per pet. Major credit cards are accepted. Open year-round.

Directions: From Olympia, drive south on I-5 for seven miles to Exit 99. Take that exit and turn east on 93rd Avenue; drive four miles to Old Highway 99. Turn south and drive four miles to Offut Lake Road. Turn left (east) and drive 1.5 miles to the resort.

Contact: Offut Lake Resort, 4005 120th Ave. SE, Tenino, WA 98589, 360/264-2438, website: www.offutlakeresort.com.

⁵ RAINBOW RESORT

Rating: 8

on Tanwax Lake

See map pages 174–175

This wooded park along the shore of Tanwax Lake has spacious sites with views of the mountains and the lake. Highlights include good fishing in a seasonal fish pond and a stable. Powerboating and water-skiing are popular on hot summer weekends.

RV sites, facilities: There are about 50 sites with full hookups (30 amps) for RVs up to 40 feet or tents. Picnic tables are provided. Restrooms, drinking water, flush toilets, coin-operated showers, propane, a recreation hall, a store, a coin-operated laundry, a café, ice, cell phone reception, cable TV, boat docks, boat rentals, and launching facilities are available. Leashed pets are permitted.

Reservations, fees: Reservations are accepted. The fee is $21 per night, plus $3 per person per night for more than two people and $3 per pet. A senior discount is available. Major credit cards are accepted. Open year-round.

Directions: From Tacoma, drive south on I-5 to Exit 127 and Highway 512. Turn east on Highway 512 and drive to Highway 161. Turn south on Highway 161 and drive to Tanwax Drive. Turn left (east) on Tanwax Drive and drive 200 yards to the resort.

Contact: Rainbow Resort, 34217 Tanwax Court

E, Eatonville, WA 98328, 360/879-5115, fax 360/879-5116, website: www.rainbowrvresort.com.

6 HENLEY'S SILVER LAKE RESORT

Rating: 7

on Silver Lake
See map pages 174–175

Silver Lake is a 150-acre spring-fed lake that can provide good trout fishing. This full-facility resort is set up as family vacation destination. A rarity, this private campground caters both to tent campers and RVers. Silver Lake is beautiful and stocked with trout. Highlights include a 250-foot fishing dock and 50 rental rowboats.

RV sites, facilities: There are 36 sites with partial or full hookups (30 amps), including two drive-through, for RVs up to 30 feet, a very large area for dispersed tent camping, and six cabins. Restrooms, drinking water, flush toilets, a pay phone, cell phone reception, snacks, boat rentals, a boat ramp, and a dock are available. An ATM is within four miles. Leashed pets are permitted except in the cabins.

Reservations, fees: Reservations are accepted. The fee is $10–15 per night. Open the first day of fishing season in April to late October, weather permitting.

Directions: From Tacoma, drive south on I-5 for five miles to Exit 127 and Highway 512. Turn east of Highway 512 and drive two miles to Highway 7. Turn south on Highway 7 and drive 19 miles (two miles straight beyond the blinking light) to Silver Lake Road on the right (well marked). Turn right and drive .25 mile to the resort entrance on the left.

Contact: Henley's Silver Lake Resort, 40718 South Silver Lake Rd. E, Eatonville, WA 98328, 360/832-3580, website: www.washingtonlakes.com.

7 WHITE RIVER

Rating: 7

on the White River in Mount Rainier National Park
See map pages 174–175

This campground is set on the White River at 4,400 feet elevation. The Glacier Basin Trail, a seven-mile round-trip, starts at the campground and leads along the Emmons Moraine to a view of the Emmons Glacier, the largest glacier in the continental United States. It is sometimes possible to spot mountain goats, as well as mountain climbers, on the surrounding mountain slopes. Note that another trail near camp leads a short distance (but vertically, for a rise of 2,200 feet) to the Sunrise Visitor Center. Local rangers recommend that trailers be left at the White River Campground and that the 11-mile road trip to Sunrise be made by car. From there, you can take several trails that lead to backcountry lakes and glaciers. Climbers planning to summit Mount Rainier often use White River as their base camp. Also note that this campground is located in what is considered to be a geohazard zone, where there is risk of a mudflow. It's never happened, but minor incidents have occurred up-slope from the camp.

RV sites, facilities: There are 112 sites for RVs up to 20 feet or tents. Picnic tables and fire grills are provided. Flush toilets, drinking water, a pay phone, and cell phone reception are available. A small amphitheater is nearby. Some facilities are wheelchair-accessible. Leashed pets are permitted in camp, but not on trails or in the wilderness.

Reservations, fees: Reservations are not accepted. The fee is $12 per night. Major credit cards are accepted. Open mid-June to mid-September.

Directions: From Enumclaw, drive southeast on Highway 410 to the entrance of Mount Rainier National Park and White River Road. Turn right and drive seven miles to the campground on the left.

Contact: Mount Rainier National Park, Tahoma Woods, Star Rte., Ashford, WA 98304, 360/569-2211, fax 360/569-2187.

8 SILVER SPRINGS

Rating: 9

in Mt. Baker–Snoqualmie National Forest
See map pages 174–175

This campground along the White River on the northeastern border of Mount Rainier National Park offers a good alternative to the more crowded camps in the park. It's located in a beautiful section of old-growth forest, primarily with

Douglas fir, cedar, and hemlock, and is very scenic. Recreational options are limited to hiking. A U.S. Forest Service information center is located one mile away from the campground entrance on Highway 410.

RV sites, facilities: There are 55 sites for RVs up to 21 feet or tents and one group site for up to 50 people. Picnic tables and fire grills are provided. Flush toilets, drinking water, and a pay phone are available. Downed firewood can be gathered. The group site has a picnic shelter. Some facilities are wheelchair-accessible. Leashed pets are permitted.

Reservations, fees: Reservations are accepted for some sites; phone 877/444-6777 or reserve online at www.reserveusa.com ($9 reservation fee). The fee is $14 per night, plus $6 per additional vehicle. The group site is $75 per night. A senior discount is available. Open mid-May to late September.

Directions: From Enumclaw, drive east on Highway 410 for 31 miles (one mile south of the turnoff for Corral Pass) to the campground entrance on the right.

Contact: Mt. Baker–Snoqualmie National Forest, White River Ranger District, 450 Roosevelt Ave. E, Enumclaw, WA 98022, 360/825-6585, fax 360/825-0660.

9 LODGEPOLE

Rating: 6

on the American River in Wenatchee National Forest

See map pages 174–175

This campground is set at an elevation of 3,500 feet along the American River, just eight miles east of the boundary of Mount Rainier National Park. See the description of Gateway Inn and RV Park in this chapter for information on Mount Rainier. Fishing access is available nearby. The campground was remodeled in 2001.

RV sites, facilities: There are 33 sites for RVs up to 20 feet or tents. Picnic tables and fire grills are provided. Drinking water, vault toilets, and garbage service are available. Leashed pets are permitted.

Reservations, fees: Reservations are not accepted. The fee is $13–15 per night, plus $5 for each

additional vehicle and a $2 surcharge on holidays and summer weekends. A senior discount is available. Open late May to mid-October, weather permitting.

Directions: From Yakima, drive northwest on U.S. 12 for 18 miles to Highway 410. Bear northwest on Highway 410 and drive 40.5 miles (eight miles east of the national park boundary) to the campground on the right.

Contact: Okanogan and Wenatchee National Forests, Naches Ranger District, 10237 U.S. 12, Naches, WA 98937, 509/653-2205, fax 509/653-2638.

10 PLEASANT VALLEY

Rating: 7

on the American River in Wenatchee National Forest

See map pages 174–175

This campground, set at an elevation of 3,300 feet, provides a good base camp for a hiking or fishing trip. A trail from the camp follows Kettle Creek up to the American Ridge and Kettle Lake in the William O. Douglas Wilderness. It joins another trail that follows the ridge and then drops down to Bumping Lake. A U.S. Forest Service map is essential. You can fish here for whitefish, steelhead, trout, and salmon in season; check regulations. In the winter, the area is popular with cross-country skiers. The campground was remodeled in 2001.

RV sites, facilities: There are 16 sites for RVs up to 32 feet or tents. Picnic tables and fire grills are provided. Drinking water, garbage service, vault toilets, and a picnic shelter are available. Downed firewood may be gathered. Some facilities are wheelchair-accessible. Leashed pets are permitted.

Reservations, fees: Reservations are not accepted. The fees are $13–15 per night for single sites and $26 per night for double sites, plus $5 for each additional vehicle and a $2 surcharge on holidays and summer weekends. A senior discount is available. Open mid-May to mid-November.

Directions: From Yakima, drive northwest on U.S. 12 for 18 miles to Highway 410. Bear northwest on Highway 410 and drive 37 miles to the campground on the left.

Contact: Okanogan and Wenatchee National Forests, Naches Ranger District, 10237 U.S. 12, Naches, WA 98937, 509/653-2205, fax 509/653-2638.

11 CEDAR SPRINGS

Rating: 6

on the Bumping River in Wenatchee National Forest

See map pages 174–175

The Bumping River runs alongside this camp, set at an elevation of 2,800 feet. Fishing here follows the seasons for trout, steelhead, and whitefish; check regulations. If you continue driving southwest for 11 miles on Forest Road 1800/Bumping River Road, you'll reach Bumping Lake, where recreation options abound.

RV sites, facilities: There are 15 sites for RVs up to 22 feet or tents, including two multifamily sites. Picnic tables and fire grills are provided. Drinking water and vault toilets are available. Leashed pets are permitted.

Reservations, fees: Reservations are not accepted. The fees are $13–15 per night for single sites and $26 per night for double sites, plus $5 for each additional vehicle and a $2 surcharge on holidays and summer weekends. A senior discount is available. Open late May to October.

Directions: From Yakima, drive northwest on U.S. 12 for 18 miles to Highway 410. Bear northwest on Highway 410 and drive 28.5 miles to the campground access road (Forest Road 1800/Bumping River Road). Turn southwest and drive .5 mile to the campground on the left.

Contact: Okanogan and Wenatchee National Forests, Naches Ranger District, 10237 U.S. 12, Naches, WA 98937, 509/653-2205, fax 509/653-2638.

12 SAWMILL FLAT

Rating: 6

on the Naches River in Wenatchee National Forest

See map pages 174–175

This campground on the Naches River near Halfway Flat is used more by off-road motorcyclists than others. It offers fishing access and a hiking trail that leads west from Halfway Flat Campground for several miles into the backcountry; note that you must wade across the river to reach Halfway Flat from Sawmill Flat. Fishing is primarily for trout in summer, whitefish in winter; check regulations. Another trailhead is located at Boulder Cave to the south. See a U.S. Forest Service map for details.

RV sites, facilities: There are 24 sites for RVs up to 24 feet or tents. Picnic tables and fire grills are provided. Drinking water, vault toilets, an RV dump station, and an Adirondack group shelter are available. Downed firewood may be gathered. A camp host is available in summer. Some facilities are wheelchair-accessible, including one campsite. Leashed pets are permitted.

Reservations, fees: Reservations are not accepted. The fee is $13–15 per night, plus $5 for each additional vehicle and a $2 surcharge on holidays and summer weekends. A senior discount is available. Open May to October, weather permitting.

Directions: From Yakima, drive northwest on U.S. 12 for 18 miles to Highway 410. Bear northwest on Highway 410 and drive 23.5 miles to the campground on the left.

Contact: Okanogan and Wenatchee National Forests, Naches Ranger District, 10237 U.S. 12, Naches, WA 98937, 509/653-2205, fax 509/653-2638.

13 SODA SPRINGS

Rating: 6

on the Bumping River in Wenatchee National Forest

See map pages 174–175

Highlights at this camp along Bumping Creek include natural mineral springs and a nature trail. The mineral spring is located next to a trail across the river from the campground, where the water bubbles up out of the ground. This cold-water spring is popular with some campers for soaking and drinking. Many campers use this camp for access to nearby Bumping Lake. Fishing access is available.

RV sites, facilities: There are 26 sites for RVs up to 30 feet or tents. Picnic tables and fire grills are provided. Drinking water, vault toilets, an RV dump station, several picnic shelters with fireplaces, and garbage service are available. Some facilities are wheelchair-accessible. Leashed pets are permitted.

Reservations, fees: Reservations are not accepted. The fee is $13–15 per night, plus $5 for each additional vehicle and a $2 surcharge on holidays and summer weekends. A senior discount is available. Open May to late November, weather permitting.

Directions: From Yakima, drive northwest on U.S. 12 for 18 miles to Highway 410. Turn left (northwest) on Highway 410 and drive 28.5 miles to Forest Road 1800. Turn left (southwest) and drive five miles (along the Bumping River) to the campground on the left.

Contact: Okanogan and Wenatchee National Forests, Naches Ranger District, 10237 U.S. 12, Naches, WA 98937, 509/653-2205, fax 509/653-2638.

14 LOWER BUMPING LAKE

Rating: 7

on Bumping Lake in Wenatchee National Forest
See map pages 174–175
This camp is set at an elevation of 3,200 feet near Bumping Lake amid a forest of primarily lodgepole pine. This popular campground features a variety of water activities at Bumping Lake, including water-skiing, fishing (salmon and trout), and swimming. A boat ramp is available near the camp. There are also several hiking trails that go into the William O. Douglas Wilderness surrounding the lake.

RV sites, facilities: There are 23 sites for RVs up to 50 feet or tents. Picnic tables and fire grills are provided. Drinking water, vault toilets, and an RV dump station are available. Boat-launching facilities are located nearby at Upper Bumping Lake Campground. Some facilities are wheelchair-accessible. Leashed pets are permitted.

Reservations, fees: Reservations are not accepted. The fees are $13–15 per night and $26 for a double site, plus $5 for each additional vehicle and a $2 surcharge on holidays and summer weekends. A senior discount is available. Open mid-May to late November, weather permitting.

Directions: From Yakima, drive northwest on U.S. 12 for 18 miles to Highway 410. Turn left (northwest) on Highway 410 and drive 28.5 miles to Forest Road 1800. Turn left (southwest) and drive 11 miles (along the Bumping River); look for the campground entrance road on the right (now paved all the way).

Contact: Okanogan and Wenatchee National Forests, Naches Ranger District, 10237 U.S. 12, Naches, WA 98937, 509/653-2205, fax 509/653-2638.

15 UPPER BUMPING LAKE

Rating: 7

on Bumping Lake in Wenatchee National Forest
See map pages 174–175
Woods and water—this spot has them both. The cold lake is stocked with trout, and the nearby boat launch makes it a winner for campers with boats. This popular camp fills up quickly on summer weekends. A variety of water activities is allowed at Bumping Lake, including water-skiing, fishing (salmon and trout), and swimming. Six picnic sites are situated adjacent to the boat facilities. In addition, several hiking trails lead into the William O. Douglas Wilderness surrounding the lake. One of the more developed camps in the area, this camp was remodeled in 2001.

RV sites, facilities: There are 45 sites for RVs up to 30 feet or tents. Picnic tables and fire grills are provided. Drinking water, vault toilets, and firewood are available. Boat docks, launching facilities, rentals, and an RV dump station are nearby. Leashed pets are permitted.

Reservations, fees: Reservations are not accepted. The fee is $13–15 per night, plus $5 for each additional vehicle and a $2 surcharge on holidays and summer weekends. A senior discount is available. Open mid-May to late November, weather permitting.

Directions: From Yakima, drive northwest on U.S. 12 for 18 miles to Highway 410. Turn left (northwest) on Highway 410 and drive 28.5 miles to Forest Road 1800. Turn left (southwest) and drive 11 miles (along the Bumping River) to the end of the pavement; look for the campground entrance road on the right.

Contact: Okanogan and Wenatchee National Forests, Naches Ranger District, 10237 U.S. 12, Naches, WA 98937, 509/653-2205, fax 509/653-2638.

16 ALDER LAKE RECREATION AREA

Rating: 6

on Alder Lake

See map pages 174–175

This recreation area at Alder Lake features three camping areas: Rocky Point, Alder Lake Park, and Boathouse. Alder Lake is a 3,065-acre lake (7.5 miles long) often with good fishing for kokanee salmon, rainbow trout, and cutthroat trout. Rocky Point is near the mouth of feeder streams, often the best fishing spots on the lake. At the east end of the lake, anglers can catch catfish, perch, and crappie. The campsites are set near the water with lots of trees and shrubbery. On clear, warm summer weekends these camps can get crowded. The camps are always booked full for summer holiday weekends as soon as reservations are available in January. Another potential downer, the water level fluctuates here. Powerboating, water-skiing, and personal watercraft are allowed at this lake. Mount Rainier Scenic Railroad leaves from Elbe regularly and makes its way through the forests to Mineral Lake. It features open deck cars, live music, and restored passenger cars.

RV sites, facilities: There are four camping areas with approximately 196 sites with partial or full hookups (30, 50 amps) for RVs of any length, 68 tent sites, and one group site with full hookups (50 amps) for up to 20 RVs. Alder Lake Camp is the largest and most developed; Rocky Point is a nearby overflow camp for RVs, with no tent sites available; and Boathouse Camp is smaller (24 sites), with partial electricity hookups for self-contained RVs. Picnic tables and fire grills are provided. Drinking water, flush toilets, and coin-operated showers are available. Boat docks and launching facilities are available nearby. A swimming beach, a day-use picnic area, a fishing dock, a small convenience store, an ATM, and an RV dump station are also available nearby. Some facilities are wheelchair-accessible. Leashed pets are permitted.

Reservations, fees: Reservations are recommended and are available in person or by mail; applications can be downloaded from the website. The fee is $16–23 per night, plus $6 per additional vehicle per night. The group camp is $23 per night per site. A senior discount is available. Day-use fees apply on weekends and holidays. Major credit cards are accepted. Open year-round, excluding December 20 through January 2.

Directions: From Chehalis, drive south on I-5 for 10 miles to U.S. 12. Turn east and drive 31 miles to Morton and Highway 7. Turn north on Highway 7 and drive 17 miles to Elbe. Bear left on Highway 7 and drive to the park entrance road on the left (on the east shore of Alder Lake). Turn left and drive .2 mile to the park entrance gate.

Contact: Alder Lake Recreation Area, Tacoma Power at 50324 School Rd., Eatonville, WA 98328, 360/569-2778, fax 253/502-8631, website: www.tacomapower.com.

17 GATEWAY INN AND RV PARK

Rating: 7

near Mount Rainier National Park

See map pages 174–175

This park is located fewer than 100 feet from the southwestern entrance to Mount Rainier National Park. In turn, it can provide a launching point for your vacation. One option: Enter the park at the Nisqually (southwestern) entrance to Mount Rainier National Park, then drive on Nisqually Paradise Road for about five miles to Longmire Museum; general park information and exhibits about the plants and geology of the area are available. If you then continue into the park for 10 more miles, you'll arrive at the Jackson Visitor Center in Paradise, which has more exhibits and an observation deck. This road is the only one into the park that's open year-round. Winter activities in the park include cross-country skiing, snowshoeing, and inner-tube sledding down slopes.

RV sites, facilities: There are 16 sites with full hookups (30, 50 amps) for RVs of any length, a dispersed area for up to seven tents, and nine cabins. Picnic tables are provided. Drinking water, portable toilets, a pay phone, and cell phone reception are available. A restaurant, a gift shop, and a mini-mart are on-site. Leashed pets are permitted.

Reservations, fees: Reservations are accepted. The fee is $12–22 per night. Cabins are $69–99 per night, plus $10 per person per night for more than two people. A senior discount is available. Major credit cards are accepted. Open April to September.

Directions: From Chehalis, drive south on I-5 for 10 miles to U.S. 12. Turn east and drive 31 miles to Morton and Highway 7. Turn north on Highway 7 and drive 17 miles to Elbe and Highway 706. Turn east on Highway 706 and drive 13 miles to the campground on the right.

Contact: Gateway Inn and RV Park, 38820 Hwy. 706 E, Ashford, WA 98304, 360/569-2506, website: www.gatewaytomtrainier.com.

18 MOUNTHAVEN RESORT

Rating: 7

near Mount Rainier National Park
See map pages 174–175

This campground is located within a half mile of the Nisqually entrance to Mount Rainier National Park, the only entrance open year-round. See the previous description of Gateway Inn and RV Park for information about the national park. A creek runs through this wooded camp.

RV sites, facilities: There are 17 sites with full hookups (20, 30 amps) for RVs of any length, one tent site, and 11 furnished cabins. Picnic tables and fire pits are provided. Restrooms, drinking water, flush toilets, one shower, a pay phone, a coin-operated laundry, firewood, and a playground are available. A restaurant, an ATM, and groceries are nearby. Leashed pets are permitted.

Reservations, fees: Reserve at 800/456-9380. The fee is $15–25 per night. Cabins are $74–219 per night. Major credit cards are accepted. Open year-round.

Directions: From Chehalis, drive south on I-5 for 10 miles to U.S. 12. Turn east and drive 31 miles to Morton and Highway 7. Turn north on Highway 7 and drive 17 miles to Elbe and Highway 706. Turn east on Highway 706 and drive to Ashford; continue for six miles to the campground on the right.

Contact: Mounthaven Resort, 38210 Hwy. 706

E, Ashford, WA 98304, 360/569-2594, fax 360/569-2949, website: www.mounthaven.com.

19 SUNSHINE POINT

Rating: 7

in Mount Rainier National Park
See map pages 174–175

This campground is one of several in Mount Rainier National Park located near the Nisqually entrance. The others include Ipsut Creek, Cougar Rock, White River, Mounthaven, Gateway, and Ohanapecosh. The elevation is 2,000 feet. See the description of Gateway Inn and RV Park earlier in this chapter for information about nearby sights and facilities.

RV sites, facilities: There are 18 sites for RVs up to 25 feet or tents. Picnic tables and fire rings are provided. Drinking water, a pay phone, and vault toilets are available. An ATM is within six miles. Some facilities are wheelchair-accessible. Leashed pets are permitted in the camp but not on trails or in the wilderness.

Reservations, fees: Reservations are not accepted. The fee is $12 per night, plus $5 per additional vehicle per night and a $10 park entrance fee. A senior discount is available. Major credit cards are accepted. Open year-round.

Directions: From Chehalis, drive south on I-5 for 10 miles to U.S. 12. Turn east and drive 31 miles to Morton and Highway 7. Turn north on Highway 7 and drive 17 miles to Elbe and Highway 706. Turn east on Highway 706 and drive 12 miles to the park entrance. The campground is just inside the park entrance on the right.

Contact: Mount Rainier National Park, Tahoma Woods, Star Rte., Ashford, WA 98304, 360/569-2211, fax 360/569-2187.

20 BIG CREEK

Rating: 8

on Big Creek in Gifford Pinchot National Forest
See map pages 174–175

This camp is useful as an overflow spot for Mount Rainier and Puget Sound area campers. It is along a stream next to a rural residential area in

WASHINGTON

a forest setting made up of Douglas fir, western hemlock, western red cedar, and big leaf and vine maple. RV drivers should note that the required turning radius is fairly tight.

RV sites, facilities: There are 28 sites for RVs up to 25 feet or tents. Picnic tables and fire rings are provided. Drinking water, vault toilets, and cell phone reception are available. An ATM, a pay phone, and groceries are available within eight miles. Leashed pets are permitted.

Reservations, fees: Reservations are recommended; phone 877/444-6777 or reserve online at www.reserveusa.com ($9 reservation fee). The fees are $13 for a single and $26 for a double site per night, plus $5 for each additional vehicle. A senior discount is available. Open late May to mid-September.

Directions: On I-5, drive to Exit 68 (south of Chehalis) and U.S. 12. Turn east on U.S. 12 and drive 62 miles to Packwood and Forest Road 52/Skate Creek Road. Turn left (northwest) and drive 23 miles to the campground on the left.

Contact: Gifford Pinchot National Forest, Cowlitz Valley Ranger District, P.O. Box 670, Randle, WA 98377-0670, 360/497-1100, fax 360/497-1102.

21 COUGAR ROCK

Rating: 9

in Mount Rainier National Park

See map pages 174–175

Cougar Rock is a national park campground set at 3,180 feet elevation at the foot of awesome Mount Rainier. To the east lies Paradise, connected by the Wonderland Trail. It begins at the visitors center and provides stellar views of Mount Rainier and the Nisqually Glacier. Fishing tends to be marginal. As in all national parks, no trout are stocked, and lakes without natural fisheries provide zilch. See the earlier listing for Gateway Inn and RV Park for information on the nearby park sights and visitors centers.

RV sites, facilities: There are 173 sites for RVs up to 35 feet or tents and five group sites for 24 to 40 people each. Picnic tables and fire rings are provided. Restrooms, drinking water, flush toilets, an RV dump station, a pay phone, and an amphitheater are available. A camp store is

located two miles away. Some facilities are wheelchair-accessible. Leashed pets are permitted.

Reservations, fees: Reserve at 800/365-CAMP (800/365-2267) or http://reservations.nps.gov. The fee is $15 per night, plus a $10 park entrance fee and $6 per additional vehicle per night; group sites are $40–64 per night. A senior discount is available. Major credit cards are accepted. Open mid-May to mid-October.

Directions: From Tacoma, drive south on I-5 for five miles to Highway 512. Turn east of Highway 512 and drive two miles to Highway 7. Turn south on Highway 7 and drive to Elbe and Highway 706. Continue east on Highway 706 and drive 12 miles to the park entrance. Continue eight miles to the campground entrance on the left (about two miles past the Longmire developed area).

Contact: Mount Rainier National Park, Tahoma Woods, Star Rte., Ashford, WA 98304, 360/569-2211, fax 360/569-2187.

22 OHANAPECOSH

Rating: 8

on the Ohanapecosh River in Mount Rainier National Park

See map pages 174–175

This camp is at an elevation of 1,914 feet at the foot of North America's most beautiful volcano, 14,410-foot Mount Rainier. It is also set along the Ohanapecosh River, near the Ohanapecosh Visitor Center, which features exhibits on the history of the forest, plus visitor information. A half-mile loop trail leads from the campground, behind the visitors center, to Ohanapecosh Hot Springs. The Silver Falls Trail, a three-mile loop trail, follows the Ohanapecosh River to 75-foot Silver Falls. Warning: Do not climb on the rocks near the waterfall; they are wet and slippery. Note that Stevens Canyon Road heading west and Highway 123 heading north are closed by snowfall in winter.

RV sites, facilities: There are 188 sites for RVs up to 32 feet or tents and one group site for up to 25 people. Picnic tables are provided. Flush toilets, drinking water, a pay phone, and an RV dump station are available. An amphitheater is nearby. Some facilities are wheelchair-accessible.

WASHINGTON

Leashed pets are permitted in camp but not on trails.

Reservations, fees: Reserve at 800/365-CAMP (800/365-2267) or online at http://reservations.nps.gov. The fee is $15 per night, plus a $10 per vehicle park entrance fee. The group site is $40 per night. A senior discount is available. Major credit cards are accepted. Open mid-May to September.

Directions: On I-5, drive to Exit 68 (south of Chehalis) and U.S. 12. Turn east on U.S. 12 and drive 72 miles (seven miles past Packwood) to Highway 123. Turn north and drive five miles to the Ohanapecosh entrance to the park. As you enter the park, the camp is on the left, next to the visitors center.

Contact: Mount Rainier National Park, Tahoma Woods, Ashford, WA 98304, 360/569-2211, fax 360/569-2187.

23 PACKWOOD TRAILER AND RV PARK

Rating: 6

in Packwood

See map pages 174–175

This is a pleasant campground, especially in the fall when the maples turn color. Groups are welcome. Mount Rainier National Park is located just 25 miles north, and this camp provides a good alternative if the park is full. Nearby recreation options include a riding stable, hiking, fishing, and tennis courts.

RV sites, facilities: There are 88 sites, most with full hookups (30 amps), for RVs of any length and 15 tent sites. Picnic tables are provided. Restrooms, drinking water, flush toilets, showers, some fire rings, an RV dump station, a store, cable TV, a pay phone, cell phone reception, and a coin-operated laundry are available. A café and propane are available within walking distance. Leashed pets are permitted.

Reservations, fees: Reservations are accepted. The fee is $11–22 per night, plus $3 per person for more than two people and $3 per additional vehicle per night. Major credit cards are accepted. Open early March to mid-November.

Directions: On I-5, drive to Exit 68 (south of Chehalis) and U.S. 12. Turn east on U.S. 12 and drive 65 miles to Packwood. The park is on the

north side of the highway in town at 19285 U.S. Highway 12.

Contact: Packwood Trailer and RV Park, P.O. Box 309, Packwood, WA 98361, 360/494-5145, fax 360/494-2255.

24 LA WIS WIS

Rating: 9

on the Cowlitz River in Gifford Pinchot National Forest

See map pages 174–175

This camp is ideally located for day trips to Mount Rainier and Mount St. Helens. It's set at an elevation of 1,400 feet along the Clear Fork of the Cowlitz River, near the confluence with the Ohanapecosh River. Trout fishing is an option. The landscape features an old-growth forest, a mix of Douglas fir, western hemlock, western red cedar, and Pacific yew, with an undergrowth of big leaf maple. A 200-yard trail provides access to the Blue Hole on the Ohanapecosh River, a deep pool designated by an observation point and interpretive signs. Another trail leads less than a quarter mile to Purcell Falls. The entrance to Mount Rainier National Park is about seven miles south of the camp.

RV sites, facilities: There are 115 sites for RVs up to 24 feet or tents. Picnic tables and fire rings are provided. Flush and vault toilets, drinking water, and firewood are available. An ATM, pay phone, and groceries are available within six miles. Some facilities are wheelchair-accessible. Leashed pets are permitted.

Reservations, fees: Reserve at 877/444-6777 ($9 reservation fee) or online at www.reserveusa.com. The fee is $16–28 per night, plus $5 per additional vehicle per night. A senior discount is available. The maximum stay is 14 days. Open mid-May to late September.

Directions: On I-5, drive to Exit 68 (south of Chehalis) and U.S. 12. Turn east on U.S. 12 and drive 69 miles (about six miles past Packwood) to Forest Road 1272. Turn left and drive .5 mile to the campground on the left.

Contact: Gifford Pinchot National Forest, Cowlitz Valley Ranger District, P.O. Box 670, Randle, WA 98377-0670, 360/497-1100, fax 360/497-1102.

25 WHITE PASS

Rating: 7

on Leech Lake in Wenatchee National Forest
See map pages 174–175
This campground on the shore of Leech Lake sits at an elevation of 4,500 feet and boasts nearby trails leading into the Goat Rocks Wilderness to the south and the William O. Douglas Wilderness to the north. A trailhead for the Pacific Crest Trail is also nearby. Beautiful Leech Lake is popular for fly-fishing for rainbow trout. Note that this is the only type of fishing allowed here; check regulations. No gas motors are permitted on Leech Lake. White Pass Ski Area is located across the highway, less than a quarter mile away.
RV sites, facilities: There are 16 sites for RVs up to 20 feet or tents. Picnic tables and fire grills are provided. Vault toilets are available, but there is no drinking water. A store, a café, a coin-operated laundry, a pay phone, and ice are available within one mile. Boat-launching facilities are nearby. No gas motors on boats are allowed; electric motors are permitted. Leashed pets are permitted.
Reservations, fees: Reservations are not accepted. The fee is $5 per night. A senior discount is available. Open late May to late October.
Directions: On I-5, drive to Exit 68 (south of Chehalis) and U.S. 12. Turn east on U.S. 12 and drive 84 miles (three miles past the White Pass Ski Area) to the campground entrance road on the left side. Turn north and drive 200 yards to Leech Lake and the campground.
Contact: Okanogan and Wenatchee National Forests, Naches Ranger District, 10237 U.S. 12, Naches, WA 98937, 509/653-2205, fax 509/653-2638.

26 CLEAR LAKE SOUTH

Rating: 7

in Wenatchee National Forest
See map pages 174–175
This campground (elevation 3,100 feet) is located near the east shore of Clear Lake, which is the forebay for Rimrock Lake. Fishing and swimming are recreation options. For winter travelers, several Sno-Parks in the area offer snowmobiling

and cross-country skiing. White Pass Ski Area is close by. Many hiking trails lie to the north; see a U.S. Forest Service map for details.
RV sites, facilities: There are 22 sites for RVs up to 22 feet or tents. Picnic tables and fire grills are provided. Drinking water and vault toilets are available. Downed firewood may be gathered. Boat-launching facilities are nearby. An ATM and pay phone are within seven miles. Leashed pets are permitted.
Reservations, fees: Reservations are not accepted. The fee is $10 per night, plus $5 per additional vehicle per night. Open mid-April to late November, weather permitting.
Directions: From Yakima, drive northwest on I-82 for 17 miles to the junction with Highway 410. Turn west on U.S. 12 and drive 31 miles to Forest Road 1200. Turn left (south) and drive one mile to Forest Road 1200-740. Continue south and drive .25 mile to the campground.
Contact: Okanogan and Wenatchee National Forests, Naches Ranger District, 10237 U.S. 12, Naches, WA 98937, 509/653-2205, fax 509/653-2638.

27 SILVER BEACH RESORT

Rating: 8

on Rimrock Lake
See map pages 174–175
This resort along the shore of Rimrock Lake is one of several camps in the immediate area. It's very scenic, with beautiful lakefront sites. Hiking trails, marked bike trails, a full-service marina, and a riding stable are close by.
RV sites, facilities: There are 97 sites, most with full hookups (30 amps), for RVs up to 40 feet or tents, three cabins with kitchens, and 16 motel rooms. Picnic tables and fire pits are provided. A restroom, coin-operated showers, a café, a store, a pay phone, cell phone reception, an RV dump station, bait and tackle, propane, ice, a playground, a hot tub, boat docks, launching facilities, and boat and personal watercraft rentals are available. An ATM is within nine miles. Leashed pets are permitted.
Reservations, fees: Reservations are accepted. The fee is $15–20 per night, plus $5 per additional vehicle per night; cabins are $75 per night.

Major credit cards are accepted. Open year-round, with limited winter facilities.

Directions: From Yakima, drive northwest on U.S. 12 for 40 miles to the resort on the left.

Contact: Silver Beach Resort, 40350 Hwy. 12, Rimrock, WA 98937, 509/672-2500.

28 INDIAN CREEK

Rating: 7

on Rimrock Lake in Wenatchee National Forest

See map pages 174–175

Fishing, swimming, and water-skiing are among the activities at this shorefront campground on Rimrock Lake (elevation 3,000 feet). The camp is adjacent to Silver Beach Resort. This is a developed lake and an extremely popular campground, often filling on summer weekends. Fishing is often good for rainbow trout. Many excellent hiking trails to the north, about 5 to 10 miles from the campground, lead into the William O. Douglas Wilderness, including the treasured Indian Creek Trail.

RV sites, facilities: There are 39 sites for RVs up to 32 feet or tents. Picnic tables and fire grills are provided. Drinking water and vault toilets are available. Downed firewood may be gathered. A café, a store, ice, boat docks, launching facilities, and rentals are nearby. Leashed pets are permitted.

Reservations, fees: Reservations are not accepted. The fee is $13–15 per night, plus $5 per additional vehicle per night and a $2 surcharge on holidays and summer weekends. Open late May to mid-September.

Directions: From Yakima, drive northwest on I-82 for 17 miles to the junction with U.S. 12. Turn west on U.S. 12 and drive 20 miles to Rimrock Lake and the campground entrance at the lake.

Contact: Okanogan and Wenatchee National Forests, Naches Ranger District, 10237 U.S. 12, Naches, WA 98937, 509/653-2205, fax 509/653-2638.

29 SOUTH FORK

Rating: 8

on the South Fork of the Tieton River in Wenatchee National Forest

See map pages 174–175

This campground (at 3,000 feet elevation) is set along the South Fork of the Tieton River, less than one mile from where it empties into Rimrock Lake. Note that fishing is prohibited to protect the bull trout. By traveling a bit farther south on Tieton River Road, you can see the huge Blue Slide, an enormous prehistoric rock and earth slide that has a curious blue tinge to it.

RV sites, facilities: There are nine sites for RVs up to 20 feet or tents. Picnic tables and fire grills are provided. Vault toilets and garbage service are available, but there is no drinking water. Leashed pets are permitted.

Reservations, fees: Reservations are not accepted. The fee is $7 per night, plus $5 per additional vehicle per night. Open late May to mid-October.

Directions: From Yakima, drive northwest on I-82 for 17 miles to the junction with U.S. 12. Turn west on U.S. 12 and drive 22 miles to Forest Road 1200. Turn left (south) and drive four miles to Forest Road 1203. Bear left and drive .75 mile to Forest Road 1203-517. Turn right and drive 200 feet to the campground.

Contact: Okanogan and Wenatchee National Forests, Naches Ranger District, 10237 U.S. 12, Naches, WA 98937, 509/653-2205, fax 509/653-2638.

30 STAN HEDWALL PARK

Rating: 5

on the Newaukum River

See map pages 174–175

This park is set along the Newaukum River, and its proximity to I-5 makes it a good layover spot for vacation travelers. Recreational opportunities include fishing, hiking, and golf (an 18-hole course and hiking trails are nearby).

RV sites, facilities: There are 29 sites with partial hookups (20, 30, 50 amps) for RVs up to 61 feet. Picnic tables are provided. Restrooms, drinking water, some fire pits, cell phone reception, a pay phone, flush toilets, coin-operated showers, an RV dump station, cable TV, and a playground are available. Propane, a store, a café, and a coin-operated laundry are available within 1.5 miles. Leashed pets are permitted.

Reservations, fees: Reservations are accepted two weeks or more in advance, when paid in full, with a seven-night-maximum stay. The fee is $15 per night. Open March to November, weather permitting.

Directions: Near Chehalis on I-5, take Exit 76 to Rice Road. Turn south and drive one-eighth mile to the park.

Contact: Stan Hedwall Park, City of Chehalis, P.O. Box 871, Chehalis, WA 98532, 360/748-0271, fax 360/748-6993.

31 LEWIS AND CLARK STATE PARK

Rating: 8

near Chehalis

See map pages 174–175

The highlight of this state park is an immense old-growth forest that contains some good hiking trails and a half-mile nature trail. This famous grove lost half of its old-growth trees along the highway when they were blown down in the legendary 1962 Columbus Day storm. This was a cataclysmic event for what is one of the last major stands of old-growth forest in the state. The park covers 621 acres and features primarily Douglas fir and red cedar, wetlands, and dense vegetation. There are eight miles of hiking trails and five miles of horse trails. June is Youth Fishing Month, when youngsters age 14 and under can fish the creek. Jackson Tours, on which visitors can see a pioneer home built in 1845 north of the Columbia River, are available year-round by appointment.

RV sites, facilities: There are 25 sites for self-contained RVs up to 30 feet or tents, 10 with partial hookups (30 amps), five horse camp sites, two primitive sites, two group camps for up to 50 people each, and an environmental learning center for up to 50 people. Picnic tables and fire grills are provided. Restrooms, drinking water, flush toilets, coin-operated showers, firewood, cell phone reception, a pay phone, a picnic area, an amphitheater, horseshoes, volleyball, and badminton are available. Leashed pets are permitted.

Reservations, fees: Reservations are not accepted for family sites. The fee is $10–21 per night, plus $10 per additional vehicle per night. Group sites require a $25 reservation, plus $2 per person with a 20-person minimum and 50-person maximum. For reservations for the Environmental Learning Center, phone 800/360-4240. A senior discount is available. Open year-round with limited facilities in winter.

Directions: From Chehalis, drive south on I-5 to Exit 68 and U.S. 12. Drive east on U.S. 12 for three miles to Jackson Highway. Turn right and drive three miles to the park entrance on the right.

Contact: Lewis and Clark State Park, 4583 Jackson Hwy., Winlock, WA 98596, 360/864-2643, fax 360/864-2515; state park information, 360/902-8844.

32 IKE KINSWA STATE PARK

Rating: 8

at Mayfield Lake

See map pages 174–175

This state park, named after a prominent Cowlitz Indian, Ike Kinswa, is set alongside the north shore of Mayfield Lake. The lake features 8.5 miles of shoreline, forested campsites, and 2.5 miles of hiking and biking trails. Mayfield Lake is a treasure trove of recreational possibilities. Fishing is a year-round affair here, with trout and tiger muskie often good. Boating, kayaking, canoeing, personal watercraft use, water-skiing, and swimming are all popular. Two fish hatcheries are located nearby. A spectacular view of Mount St. Helens can be found at a vista point 11 miles east. This popular campground often fills on summer weekends. Be sure to reserve well in advance.

RV sites, facilities: There are 41 sites with full hookups (30 amps) and 31 with partial hookups for RVs up to 60 feet, 30 developed tent sites, and two primitive tent sites. Picnic tables and fire grills are provided. Restrooms, drinking water, flush toilets, showers, a pay phone, cell phone reception, a snack bar, paddleboat rentals, an RV dump station, a store, a playground, a picnic area, horseshoes, and firewood are available.

Boat docks and launching facilities are also available. An ATM, coin-operated laundry, and groceries are available within 3.5 miles. Some facilities are wheelchair-accessible. Leashed pets are permitted.

Reservations, fees: Reserve at 888/CAMP-OUT (888/226-7688) or online at www.parks.wa.gov /reservations ($7 reservation fee). The fee is $10–22 per night, plus $10 per additional vehicle per night. A senior discount is available. Major credit cards are accepted in summer. Open year-round.

Directions: From Longview, drive north on I-5 to Exit 68 and U.S. 12. Turn east on U.S. 12 and drive 14 miles to Silver Creek Road (State Route 122). Turn north and drive 1.9 miles to a Y intersection. Bear right on State Route 122/Harmony Road and drive 1.6 miles to the park entrance.

Contact: Ike Kinswa State Park, State Rte. 122, Silver Creek, WA 98585, 360/983-3402, fax 360/983-3332; state park information, 360/902-8844.

33 MAYFIELD LAKE PARK

Rating: 7

on Mayfield Lake
See map pages 174–175

Mayfield Lake is the centerpiece of this 50-acre park. The camp has a relaxing atmosphere and comfortable, wooded sites. Insider's tip: Campsites 42 through 54 are set along the lake's shoreline. Fishing is primarily for trout, bass, and silver salmon. Other recreational activities include water-skiing, swimming, and boating. For a great side trip, tour nearby Mount St. Helens. Note that this camp was managed for years as a county park. Tacoma Power first established new management in spring 2002.

RV sites, facilities: There are 54 sites for self-contained RVs up to 70 feet or tents. Picnic tables and fire grills are provided. Restrooms, drinking water, flush toilets, coin-operated showers, a pay phone, and a barbecue are available. An RV dump station is within a half mile. Some facilities are wheelchair-accessible. Leashed pets are permitted.

Reservations, fees: Reservations are recommended. The fee is $16–20 per night, plus $4 per person for more than four people and $6 per addition-

al vehicle per night. Day-use fees apply on weekends and holidays. Major credit cards are accepted. A senior discount is available. Open mid-April to mid-October.

Directions: From Longview, drive north on I-5 to Exit 68 and U.S. 12. Turn east on U.S. 12 and drive 11 miles. Look for the campground entrance signs on the left.

Contact: Mayfield Lake Park, 360/985-2364, fax 360/985-7825, website: www.tacomapower.com.

34 HARMONY LAKESIDE RV PARK

Rating: 7

near Mayfield Lake
See map pages 174–175

This beautifully landscaped park fills up on weekends in July and August. It is set on Mayfield Lake, a 10-mile-long lake with numerous recreational activities, including fishing, boating, and water-skiing. Some sites feature lake views. The park is within an hour's drive of Mount Saint Helens and Mount Rainier. Ike Kinswa State Park is a nearby side-trip option.

RV sites, facilities: There are 80 sites with partial or full hookups (20, 30, 50 amps) for RVs of any length or tents. Picnic tables and fire grills are provided. Restrooms, drinking water, flush toilets, coin-operated showers, an RV dump station, cell phone reception, modem access, boat rentals, ice, firewood, a pay phone, boat docks, and launching facilities are available. Group facilities, including a banquet and meeting room, are also available. An ATM, groceries, bait and tackle, and fishing licenses are available within 2.5 miles. Leashed pets are permitted.

Reservations, fees: Reservations are recommended. The fee is $25–30 per night, plus $3 per person for more than four people and $2 per pet per night. Monthly rates are available. Major credit cards are accepted. Open year-round.

Directions: From Longview, drive north on I-5 to Exit 68 and U.S. 12. Turn east on U.S. 12 and drive 21 miles to Mossyrock (Highway 122). Turn left (north) and drive 2.3 miles to the park on the left.

Contact: Harmony Lakeside RV Park, 563 State Rte. 122, Silver Creek, WA 98585, 360/983-3804, fax 360/983-8345, website: www.mayfieldlake.com.

35 MOSSYROCK PARK

Rating: 8

at Riffe Lake

See map pages 174–175

This park is located along the southwest shore of Riffe Lake. It is an extremely popular campground for several reasons. For anglers, it provides the best of both worlds: a boat launch on Riffe Lake, which offers coho salmon, rainbow trout, and bass, and nearby Swofford Pond, a 240-acre pond stocked with rainbow trout, brown trout, bass, catfish, and bluegill. Swofford Pond is located south of Mossyrock on Swofford Road; no gas motors are permitted. This campground provides access to a half-mile loop nature trail. Bald eagles and osprey nest on the north side of the lake in the 14,000-acre Cowlitz Wildlife Area.

RV sites, facilities: There are 141 sites, including 77 with full hookups (30 amps), for RVs or tents, 12 walk-in sites, one group camp with 60 sites, and a primitive group camp with 10 sites. Picnic tables and fire rings are provided. Restrooms, drinking water, flush toilets, showers, a courtesy phone, cell phone reception, an RV dump station, a fishing bridge, fish-cleaning stations, a boat launch, a playground, a swimming area, a horseshoe pit, a volleyball net, and interpretive displays are available. In summer, a camp host is available. Boat rentals are nearby. Groceries, an ATM, and a pay phone are available within three miles. Some facilities are wheelchair-accessible. Leashed pets are permitted.

Reservations, fees: Reservations are recommended; phone 360/983-3900. The fee is $10–19 per night, plus $6 per additional vehicle per night. There is a $5 day-use fee on weekends and holidays. Call for group site prices. A senior discount is available. Major credit cards are accepted in summer. Open year-round, excluding December 20 through January 20.

Directions: On I-5, drive to Exit 68 and Highway 12 East. Take Highway 12 East and drive 21 miles to Williams Street (flashing yellow light). Turn right and drive several blocks in the town of Mossyrock to a T intersection with State Street. Turn left and drive 3.5 miles (becomes Mossyrock Road East, then Ajlune Road) to the park. Ajlune Roads lead right into the park.

Contact: Mossyrock Park, Tacoma Power, 50324 School Rd., Eatonville, WA 98328, 360/983-3900, fax 360/983-3906, website: www.tacomapower.com.

36 TAIDNAPAM PARK

Rating: 8

at Riffe Lake

See map pages 174–175

This 50-acre park is located at the east end of Riffe Lake. Nestled in the cover of Douglas fir and maple, it is surrounded by thousands of acres of undeveloped greenbelt. Fishing is open year-round at the lake, with coho salmon, rainbow trout, and bass available. This camp was named after the Upper Cowlitz Indians, also known as "Taidnapam." Since it often fills in summer, the walk-in sites are an outstanding option.

RV sites, facilities: There are 52 sites with partial or full hookups (30 amps) for RVs up to 70 feet or tents, 16 walk-in sites, and one group camp with 22 sites and a kitchen shelter. Picnic tables and fire rings are provided. Restrooms, drinking water, flush toilets, cell phone reception, showers, an RV dump station, a fishing bridge, fish-cleaning stations, a boat launch, a playground, a swimming area, a horseshoe pit, a volleyball net, and interpretive displays are available. An ATM, pay phone, and groceries are within 10 miles. Some facilities are wheelchair-accessible. Leashed pets are permitted.

Reservations, fees: Reservations are accepted after January 2 of each year for summer months by mail at P.O Box 277, Glenoma, WA, 98336. The fee is $11–22 per night, plus $6 per additional vehicle per night. Call for group site prices. A senior discount is available. Major credit cards are accepted in summer season. Open year-round, excluding December 20 through January 2.

Directions: On I-5, drive to Exit 68 and Highway 12 East. Take Highway 12 East and drive 37 miles (five miles past Morton) to Kosmos Road. Turn right and drive 200 yards to 100 Champion Haul Road (a gravel road). Turn left and drive four miles to the park.

Contact: Taidnapam Park, Tacoma Power, 50324 School Rd., Eatonville, WA 98328, 360/497-7707, website: www.tacomapower.com.

WASHINGTON

37 IRON CREEK

Rating: 7

**on the Cispus River in Gifford Pinchot
National Forest**

See map pages 174–175

This popular U.S. Forest Service campground is set along the Cispus River near its confluence with Iron Creek. Trout fishing is available. The landscape features primarily Douglas fir, western red cedar, and old-growth forest on fairly flat terrain. The camp is also located along the access route that leads to the best viewing areas of Mount St. Helens on the eastern flank. Take a 25-mile drive to Windy Ridge Vista Point for a breathtaking view of Spirit Lake and the blast zone of the volcano.

RV sites, facilities: There are 98 sites for RVs up to 45 feet or tents. Picnic tables and fire rings are provided. Drinking water, vault toilets, and firewood are available. Some facilities are wheelchair-accessible. Leashed pets are permitted.

Reservations, fees: Reserve at 877/444-6777 or online at www.reserveusa.com ($9 reservation fee). The fees are $14–16 per night or $28 per night for a double site, plus $5 per additional vehicle per night. A senior discount is available. Open mid-May to late September.

Directions: From Olympia, drive south on I-5 to Exit 68 and U.S. 12. Turn east on U.S. 12 and drive 48 miles to Randle and Highway 131. Turn south on Highway 131 and drive one mile (becomes Forest Road 25). Continue south on Forest Road 25 and drive nine miles to a fork. Bear left at the fork, continue across the bridge, turn left, and drive two miles to the campground entrance on the left (along the south shore of the Cispus River).

Contact: Gifford Pinchot National Forest, Cowlitz Valley Ranger District, P.O. Box 670, Randle, WA 98377-0670, 360/497-1100, fax 360/497-1102.

38 NORTH FORK AND NORTH FORK GROUP

Rating: 6

**on the Cispus River in Gifford Pinchot
National Forest**

See map pages 174–175

This campground along the North Cispus River offers single sites, double sites, and a group camp, along with a river flowing between the sites for individual and group use. The elevation is 1,500 feet. The campsites are set back from the river in a well-forested area. A national forest map details the backcountry access to the Valley Trail, which is routed up the Cispus River Valley for about 15 miles. This trailhead provides access for hikers, bikers, all-terrain vehicles, and horses. Note that if you explore Road 2300-083 for 15 miles west you will find Layser Cave, a Native American archeological site that is open to the public.

RV sites, facilities: There are 33 sites for RVs up to 31 feet or tents and an adjacent group camp with three sites. Picnic tables and fire grills are provided. Drinking water, vault toilets, and firewood are available. Leashed pets are permitted.

Reservations, fees: Reserve at 877/444-6777 or online at www.reserveusa.com ($9 reservation fee). The fees are $14–16 per night, plus $5 per additional vehicle per night, and $71–89 for group sites. A senior discount is available. Open mid-May to late September.

Directions: From Olympia, drive south on I-5 to Exit 68 and U.S. 12. Turn east on U.S. 12 and drive 48 miles to Randle and Highway 131. Turn south on Highway 131 and drive one mile to Forest Road 23. Bear left and drive 13 miles to the campground on the left.

Contact: Gifford Pinchot National Forest, Cowlitz Ranger District, P.O. Box 670, Randle, WA 98377, 360/497-1100, fax 360/497-1102.

39 BLUE LAKE CREEK

Rating: 7

**near Blue Lake in Gifford Pinchot National
Forest**

See map pages 174–175

This camp is set at an elevation of 1,900 feet

along Blue Lake Creek. With access to a network of all-terrain-vehicle (ATV) trails, it is a significant camp for ATV owners. There is nearby access to the Valley Trail, which features 25 to 30 miles of trail. This camp is also near the launch point for the 3.5-mile hike to Blue Lake; the trailhead lies about a half mile from camp.

RV sites, facilities: There are 11 sites for RVs up to 31 feet or tents. Picnic tables and fire rings are provided. Drinking water and vault toilets are available. Firewood can be gathered outside of the campground area. Leashed pets are permitted.

Reservations, fees: Reserve at 877/444-6777 or online at www.reserveusa.com ($9 reservation fee). The fee is $12 per night, plsu $5 per additional vehicle per night. A senior discount is available. Open mid-May to late September.

Directions: From Olympia, drive south on I-5 to Exit 68 and U.S. 12. Turn east on U.S. 12 and drive 48 miles to Randle and Highway 131. Turn south on Highway 131 and drive one mile to Forest Road 23. Turn south and drive about 18 miles to the campground on the left.

Contact: Gifford Pinchot National Forest, Cowlitz Ranger District, P.O. Box 670, Randle, WA 98377, 360/497-1100, fax 360/497-1102.

40 ADAMS FORK

Rating: 7

on the Cispus River in Gifford Pinchot National Forest

See map pages 174–175

This campground is set at 2,600 feet elevation along the Upper Cispus River near Adams Creek and is popular with off-road-vehicle (ORV) enthusiasts. Many miles of trails in this area are designed for use by ORVs. A trail that is just a half mile away leads north to Blue Lake, which is about a five-mile hike (one-way) from the camp. Most of the campsites are small, but a few are large enough for comfortable RV use. The area has many towering trees. The Cispus River provides trout fishing.

RV sites, facilities: There are 24 sites for RVs up to 21 feet or tents and two group sites. Picnic tables and fire grills are provided. Drinking water and vault toilets are available. Firewood may be gathered outside the campground area. Some

facilities are wheelchair-accessible. Leashed pets are permitted.

Reservations, fees: Reservations are accepted; phone 877/444-6777 or reserve online at www.reserveusa.com ($9 reservation fee). The fees are $14 per night for single sites, $28 per night for double sites, and $22–35 per night for group sites; plus $5 per additional vehicle per night. A senior discount is available. Open May to late October.

Directions: On I-5, drive to Exit 68 (south of Chehalis) and U.S. 12. Turn east on U.S. 12 and drive 48 miles to Randle and U.S. 131. Turn right (south) and drive one mile to Forest Road 23. Turn left (southeast) and drive 18 miles to Forest Road 21. Turn left (southeast) on Forest Road 21 and drive five miles to Forest Road 56. Turn right on Forest Road 56 and drive 200 yards to the campground on the left.

Contact: Gifford Pinchot National Forest, Cowlitz Valley Ranger District, P.O. Box 670, Randle, WA 98377, 360/497-1100, fax 360/497-1102.

41 RIVER OAKS RV PARK & CAMPGROUND

Rating: 8

on the Cowlitz River

See map pages 174–175

This camp is right on the Cowlitz River, with opportunities for boating and fishing—and nearby access to Mount St. Helens. In most years in the spring, the river is the site of a big smelt run, and they come thick. Using a dip net, you can sometimes fill a five-gallon bucket with just a couple of dips. Two horse ranches are located nearby.

RV sites, facilities: There are 24 sites with full hookups (30, 50 amps), including 12 long-term rentals and 15 drive-through, for RVs up to 40 feet and 50 tent sites. Restrooms, drinking water, flush toilets, showers, picnic tables, fire rings, firewood, cell phone reception, and a laundry room are available. Propane, a store, bait and tackle, an ATM, a pay phone, and a café are available within a quarter mile. Boat-launching facilities, mooring buoys, and a fishing shelter are nearby. Leashed pets are permitted.

Reservations, fees: Reservations are accepted. The fee is $15–22 per night, plus $3 per person for more than four people. A senior discount is available. Open year-round.

Directions: From Castle Rock on I-5, take Exit 59 for Highway 506. Turn west on Highway 506 and drive .3 mile to the park on the left.

Contact: River Oaks RV Park & Campground, 491 Hwy. 506, Toledo, WA 98591, 360/864-2895.

42 MOUNT ST. HELENS RV PARK

Rating: 6

near Silver Lake
See map pages 174–175

This RV park is located just outside Castle Rock, only three miles from the Mount St. Helens Visitor Center. It is close to the highway. Good fishing and boating are available nearby on Silver Lake.

RV sites, facilities: There are 90 sites with partial or full hookups (30 amps) for RVs up to 40 feet or tents. Restrooms, drinking water, flush toilets, coin-operated showers, cable TV, cell phone reception, a coin-operated laundry, an RV dump station, and ice are available. Horseshoes, a recreation hall, and a playground are also provided. A pay phone is one block away. An ATM and groceries are within two miles. Some facilities are wheelchair-accessible. Leashed pets are permitted.

Reservations, fees: Reservations are recommended in the summer; phone 360/274-8522. The fee is $22–24 per night, plus $1 per person per night for more than two people. Major credit cards are accepted. Open year-round.

Directions: From Longview, drive 10 miles north on I-5 to Castle Rock and Exit 49 and Highway 504. Take Exit 49 and drive east on Highway 504 for two miles to Schaffran Road. Turn left (well signed) and drive to the park at the top of the hill.

Contact: Mount St. Helens RV Park, 167 Schaffran Rd., Castle Rock, WA 98611, 360/274-8522, fax 360/274-4529, website: www.mtsthelens rvpark.com.

43 PARADISE COVE RESORT & RV PARK

Rating: 7

near the Toutle River
See map pages 174–175

This wooded park is situated about 400 yards from the Toutle River and a half mile from the Cowlitz River. Take your pick: Seaquest State Park and Silver Lake to the east provide two excellent, activity-filled side-trip options. This is a major stopover for visits to Mount St. Helens. New owners took over in 2002 and are making extensive renovations throughout the park.

RV sites, facilities: There are 52 sites with full hookups (30, 50 amps), including many drive-through, for RVs of any length, and a large dispersed tent camping area. Picnic tables are provided. Restrooms, drinking water, flush toilets, showers, a pay phone, cell phone reception, a coin-operated laundry, a store, and ice are available. Boat-launching facilities are nearby. An ATM is within two miles. Leashed pets are permitted.

Reservations, fees: Reservations are accepted. The fee is $16–22 per night. A senior discount is available. Major credit cards are accepted. Open year-round.

Directions: From Longview, drive 15 miles north on I-5 to Castle Rock and Exit 52. Take Exit 52 and look for the park on Frontage Road, just off the freeway (within view of the freeway).

Contact: Paradise Cove Resort & RV Park, 112 Burma Rd., Castle Rock, WA 98611, 360/274-6785.

44 SEAQUEST STATE PARK

Rating: 6

near Silver Lake
See map pages 174–175

This camp fills nightly because it is set along the paved road to the awesome Johnston Ridge Observatory, the premier lookout of Mount St. Helens. This state park is located adjacent to Silver Lake, one of western Washington's finest fishing lakes for bass and trout. But that's not all. The Mount St. Helens Visitor Center, which reopened in 2002, is located across the road from the park entrance. This 425-acre park features a one-mile wetlands interpretive trail and a heavily forested park with six miles of trails for hiking and biking. The irony of the place is that some out-of-towners on vacation think that this park is located on the ocean because of its name, Seaquest. The park has nothing to do with the ocean, of course. It is named after Alfred L. Seaquest, who donated the property to the state for parkland. One interesting fact: He stipulated in his will that if liquor were ever sold on the property that the land would be transferred to Willamette University. The park is popular for day use as well as camping.

RV sites, facilities: There are 92 sites, including 16 with full hookups (30 amps) and 18 with partial hookups, for RVs up to 45 feet or tents, four primitive tent sites, and one group camp. Picnic tables and fire grills are provided. Restrooms, drinking water, flush toilets, showers, a picnic area, a playground, six horseshoes, a ball field, an RV dump station, a pay phone, cell phone reception, and firewood are available. A store, ATM, and a boat launch are within two miles. Some facilities are wheelchair-accessible. Leashed pets are permitted.

Reservations, fees: Reserve at 888/CAMP-OUT (888/226-7688) or online at www.parks.wa.gov /reservations ($7 reservation fee). The fee is $10–22 per night, plus $10 per additional vehicle per night. The group camp has a $7 reservation fee, plus $2 per person per night with a minimum of 20 people and a maximum of 55. A senior discount is available. Major credit cards are accepted. Open year-round.

Directions: From Longview, drive 10 miles north on I-5 to Castle Rock and Exit 49 and Highway 504. Take Exit 49 and drive east on Highway 504 for six miles to the park.

Contact: Seaquest State Park, 360/274-8633, fax 360/274-9285; state park information, 360/902-8844.

45 SILVER LAKE MOTEL AND RESORT

Rating: 8

on Silver Lake
See map pages 174–175

This park is near the shore of Silver Lake and features a view of Mount St. Helens. One of Washington's better lakes for largemouth bass and trout, it also has perch, crappie, and bluegill. Powerboating and water-skiing are popular. This spot is considered a great fisherman's camp. The grassy sites are set along a horseshoe-shaped driveway. Access is quick to Mount St. Helens, which is located to the nearby east.

RV sites, facilities: There are 22 sites with partial hookups (30, 50 amps) for RVs of any length, 11 tent sites, five cabins, and six motel rooms. Picnic tables and fire grills are provided. Restrooms, drinking water, flush toilets, coin-operated showers, a store, a pay phone, ice, boat docks, boat rentals, launching facilities, and a playground are available. An RV dump station is within one mile, and a café, groceries, and an ATM are available within four miles. Leashed pets are permitted.

Reservations, fees: Reservations are accepted. The fee is $16–24 per night, plus $2 per person for more than four people and $5 per additional vehicle per night. There is a $5 pet fee per night for motel rooms. Major credit cards are accepted. Open year-round.

Directions: From Longview, drive 10 miles north on I-5 to Castle Rock and Exit 49 and Highway 504. Take Exit 49 and drive east on Highway 504 for 6.5 miles to the park on the right.

Contact: Silver Lake Motel and Resort, 3201 Spirit Lake Hwy., Silver Lake, WA 98645, 360/274-6141, fax 360/274-2183, website: www.silverlake -resort.com.

46 CAMP KALAMA RV AND CAMPGROUND

Rating: 6

on the Kalama River
See map pages 174–175

This camp is covered in oak trees and has a rustic setting, with open and wooded areas and some accommodations for tent campers. It's set along the Kalama River, where salmon and steelhead fishing is popular. A full-service marina is nearby. The Columbia River is a half mile away.

RV sites, facilities: There are 118 sites with partial or full hookups (20, 30, 50 amps), including drive-through, for RVs of any length and 50 tent sites. Picnic tables are provided. Restrooms, drinking water, flush toilets, coin-operated showers, fire pits, cable TV, propane, an RV dump station, a store, pay phones, cell phone reception, a café, a beauty shop, a banquet room, firewood, a coin-operated laundry, ice, boat-launching facilities, beach area, and a playground are available. An ATM is within two miles. Some facilities are wheelchair-accessible. Leashed pets are permitted.

Reservations, fees: Reservations are accepted. The fee is $17–28 per night, plus $1.50 per person per night for more than two adults, $1.50 per additional vehicle over two vehicles per night, and $1 per pet. A senior discount is available. Major credit cards are accepted. Open year-round.

Directions: From near Kalama (between Kelso and Woodland) on I-5, take Exit 32 and drive south on the frontage road for one block to the campground.

Contact: Camp Kalama RV and Campground, 5055 Meeker Dr., Kalama, WA 98625, 360/673-2456 or 800/750-2456, fax 360/673-2324, website: www.campkalama.com.

47 LONE FIR RESORT

🚶 🏊 🎣 🚐 🐴 🚌 ⛺

Rating: 4

near Yale Lake
See map pages 174–175

This private campground is located near Yale Lake (the smallest of four lakes in the area) and, with grassy sites and plenty of shade trees, is designed primarily for RV use. New owners took over in 2002, making extensive renovations throughout the park. Mount St. Helens provides a side-trip option. The trailhead for the summit climb is located nearby at Climber's Bivouac on the south flank of the volcano; a primitive campground with dispersed sites for hikers only is available here. Note: This trailhead is the only one available for the summit climb.

RV sites, facilities: There are 32 sites with full hookups (30 amps), including two drive-through, for RVs of any length, eight tent sites, and 18 motel units. Picnic tables are provided. Fire pits are provided at tent sites. Restrooms, drinking water, flush toilets, a laundry room, coin-operated showers, ice, a snack bar, an ATM, a gift shop, horseshoes, a children's playground, a covered community fire pit, a pay phone, barbecues, and a swimming pool in summer are available. Propane, a store, and a restaurant are within one mile. Boat docks and launching facilities are nearby. Pets and motorbikes are permitted.

Reservations, fees: Reservations are accepted. The fee is $15–25 per night, plus $2 per person per night for more than two people. A senior discount is available if paying cash. Major credit cards are accepted. Open year-round.

Directions: In Woodland on I-5, take Exit 21 for Highway 503. Drive east on Highway 503 for 29 miles to Cougar and the resort turnoff (marked, in town, with the park visible from the road) on the left.

Contact: Lone Fir Resort, 16806 Lewis River Rd., Cougar, WA 98616, 360/238-5210, fax 360/238-5122, website: www.lonefirresort.com.

48 LOWER FALLS

🚶 🚴 🎣 🐴 🦽 🚌 ⛺

Rating: 10

on the Lewis River in Gifford Pinchot National Forest
See map pages 174–175

This camp is set at 1,400 feet elevation in the primary viewing area for six major waterfalls on the Lewis River. The spectacular Lewis River Trail is available for hiking or horseback riding, and it features a wheelchair-accessible loop. Several other hiking trails in the area branch off along backcountry streams. The sites are paved and set among large fir trees on gently sloping ground; access roads were designed for easy RV parking. Note that above the falls, the calm water in the river looks safe, but it is not! Stay out. In addition, the trail goes along cliffs, providing beautiful views but potentially dangerous hiking.

RV sites, facilities: There are 42 sites for RVs up to 35 feet or tents and two group sites for up to 20 people each. Picnic tables and fire grills are provided. Drinking water and composting toilets are available. Leashed pets are permitted.

Reservations, fees: Reservations are not accepted. The fees are $14 per night for single sites and $28 per night for double sites, plus $5 per additional vehicle per night. Group sites are $33 per night. A senior discount is available. Open May to September.

Directions: From Woodland on I-5, take Exit 21 for Highway 503. Drive east on Highway 503 for 23 miles to Highway 503 spur. Drive northeast on Highway 503 spur for seven miles (becomes Forest Road 90). Continue east on Forest Road 90 for 30 miles to the campground (along the Lewis River) on the right.

Contact: Gifford Pinchot National Forest, Mount St. Helens National Volcanic Monument, 42218 N.E. Yale Bridge Rd., Amboy, WA 98601-0369, 360/247-3900, fax 360/247-3901.

49 TILLICUM AND SADDLE

Rating: 8

near Meadow Lake in Gifford Pinchot National Forest
See map pages 174–175

These two pretty camps are primitive but well forested and within walking distance of several recreation options. A 4.5-mile trail from the Tillicum camp leads southwest past little Meadow Lake to Squaw Butte, then over to Big Creek. It's a nice hike, as well as an excellent ride for mountain bikers. This area is premium for picking huckleberries in August and early September. The Lone Butte area about five miles to the south provides a side trip. There are two lakes nearby, Big and Little Mosquito Lakes, which are fed by Mosquito Creek. And, while we're on the subject, mosquito attacks in late spring and early summer can be like squadrons of World War II bombers moving in. The Pacific Crest Trail passes right by Saddle camp.

RV sites, facilities: There are 37 sites for RVs up to 18 feet or tents and eight sites for tents only. Picnic tables and fire grills are provided. Pit toilets and firewood are available, but there is no drinking water. Garbage must be packed out. Leashed pets are permitted.

Reservations, fees: There are no reservation and no fee at Saddle Campground. A Northwest Forest Pass ($5 daily fee or $30 annual fee per parked vehicle) is required at Tillicum Campground. Open mid-June to late September.

Directions: From Vancouver (Washington) on I-205, take Highway 14 and drive east for 66 miles to Highway 141. Turn north on Highway 141 and drive 23 miles to Trout Lake and County Road 141 (Forest Road 24). Turn right (north) on Forest Road 88. Drive 12 miles to Big Tire Junction. Turn left on Forest Road 8851 and drive four miles to Forest Road 24. Turn left and drive one mile to the campground entrance on the right.

Contact: Gifford Pinchot National Forest, Mount St. Helens National Volcanic Monument, 42218 N.E. Yale Bridge Rd., Amboy, WA 98601, 360/247-3900, fax 360/247-3901.

50 PARADISE POINT STATE PARK

Rating: 8

on the East Fork of the Lewis River
See map pages 174–175

This park is named for the serenity that once blessed this area. Alas, it has lost much of that peacefulness since the freeway went in next to the park. To reduce traffic noise, stay at one of the wooded sites in the small apple orchard. The sites in the grassy areas have little noise buffer. This park covers 88 acres and features 1,680 feet of river frontage. The two-mile hiking trail is good for families and children. Note that the dirt boat ramp is primitive and nonfunctional when the water level drops and is recommended for car-top boats only. Fishing on the East Fork of the Lewis River is a bonus.

RV sites, facilities: There are 70 sites for self-contained RVs up to 40 feet or tents and nine primitive tent sites. Picnic tables and fire grills are provided. Restrooms, drinking water, flush toilets, showers, cell phone reception, a pay phone, an RV dump station, firewood, an amphitheater, and summer interpretive programs are available. A primitive, dirt boat-launching area is located nearby on the East Fork of the Lewis River. An ATM, coin-operated laundry, and groceries are available within five miles. Leashed pets are permitted.

Reservations, fees: Reserve at 888/CAMP-OUT (888/226-7688) or online at www.parks.wa.gov/reservations ($7 reservation fee). The fee is $10–16, plus $10 per additional vehicle per night. Major credit cards are accepted. Open April to late September, weekends only in winter.

Directions: From Vancouver (Washington), drive north on I-5 for 15 miles to Exit 16 (La Center/Paradise Point State Park exit). Take that exit and turn right, then almost immediately at Paradise Park Road, turn left and drive one mile to the park.

Contact: Paradise Point State Park, 360/263-2350; state park information, 360/902-8844.

WASHINGTON

51 BIG FIR CAMPGROUND AND RV PARK

🏃 🛶 ⚓ 🐕 🚐 ⛺

Rating: 6

near Paradise Point State Park
See map pages 174–175

This campground is set in a heavily wooded, rural area not far from Paradise Point State Park. It's nestled among hills and features shaded gravel sites and wild berries. The East Fork of the Lewis River is nearby, offering great trout and steelhead fishing in season. See the previous description of Paradise Point State Park for details on the area.

RV sites, facilities: There are 37 sites with full hookups (30, 50 amps), including three drive-through, for RVs of any length and 33 tent sites. Picnic tables and barbecues are provided (no wood fires allowed). Restrooms, drinking water, flush toilets, coin-operated showers, volleyball, croquet, a horseshoe pit, board games, a store, a pay phone, cell phone reception, and ice are available. Boat-launching facilities and an ATM are within 1.5 miles. Leashed pets are permitted.

Reservations, fees: Reservations are accepted. The fee is $16–22 per night, plus $2 per person for more than two adults and three children. Major credit cards are accepted. Open year-round.

Directions: From Vancouver (Washington), drive north on I-5 to Exit 14 (Ridgefield exit). Take that exit to 269th Street. Drive east on 269th Street (the road changes names several times) for two miles to 10th Avenue. Turn right and drive to the first intersection at 259th Street. Turn left and drive two miles to the park on the right (route is well marked).

Contact: Big Fir Campground and RV Park, 5515 NE 259th St., Ridgefield, WA 98642, 360/887-8970 or 800/532-4397.

52 BATTLE GROUND LAKE STATE PARK

🏃 🚲 ⚓ 🛶 🚣 🐕 🛶 ♿ 🚐 ⛺

Rating: 8

on Battle Ground Lake
See map pages 174–175

The centerpiece of this state park is Battle Ground Lake, a spring-fed lake that is stocked with trout but is popular for bass and catfish fishing as well.

The lake is of volcanic origin, fed by water from underground lava tubes, and is considered a smaller version of Crater Lake in Oregon. The park covers 280 acres, primarily forested with conifers, in the foothills of the Cascade Mountains. There are 10 miles of trails for hiking and biking, including a trail around the lake, and five miles of trails for horses; a primitive equestrian camp is also available. The lake is good for swimming and fishing, and it has a nice beach area; no gas-powered boats are allowed. If you're traveling on I-5 and looking for a layover, this camp, just 15 minutes from the highway, is ideal. In July and August, the area hosts several fairs and celebrations. Like many of the easy-access state parks on I-5, this one fills up quickly on weekends. The average annual rainfall is 35 inches.

RV sites, facilities: There are 33 sites for self-contained RVs up to 50 feet or tents and 15 primitive tent sites. Two cabins that sleep four are available year-round. Picnic tables and fire grills are provided. Restrooms, drinking water, flush toilets, showers, an RV dump station, a store, firewood, pay phones, cell phone reception, a snack bar, a restaurant, a sheltered picnic area, summer interpretive programs, a playground with horseshoes, and an athletic field are available. An ATM and groceries are available within four miles. Boat-launching facilities and rentals are nearby. Some facilities are wheelchair-accessible. Leashed pets are permitted.

Reservations, fees: Reserve at 888/CAMP-OUT (888/226-7688) or online at www.parks.wa.gov /reservations ($7 reservation fee). The fee is $10–22 per night; cabins are $39 per night. Major credit cards are accepted. A senior discount is available. Open year-round.

Directions: From I-5 southbound, take Exit 14 and drive to the city of Battle Ground (well marked); continue to the east end of town to Grace Avenue. Turn left and drive three miles (a marked route) to the park.

From I-5 northbound, take Exit 9 and drive to the city of Battle Ground (well marked); continue to the east end of town to Grace Avenue. Turn left and drive three miles (a marked route) to the park.

Contact: Battle Ground Lake State Park, tel./fax 360/687-4621; state park information, 360/902-8844.

53 SUNSET

Rating: 9

on the East Fork of the Lewis River in Gifford Pinchot National Forest

See map pages 174–175

This campground is located at an elevation of 1,000 feet along the East Fork of the Lewis River. Fishing, hiking, and huckleberry and mushroom picking are some of the favored pursuits of visitors. Scenic Sunset Falls is located just upstream of the campground. A barrier-free viewing trail leads to an overlook.

RV sites, facilities: There are 10 sites for RVs up to 22 feet or tents and six walk-in sites. Picnic tables and fire grills are provided. Drinking water (well water) and vault toilets are available. Leashed pets are permitted.

Reservations, fees: Reservations are not accepted. The fee is $14 per night, plus $5 per additional vehicle per night. Open year-round.

Directions: From Vancouver (Washington), drive north on I-5 about seven miles to County Road 502. Turn east on Highway 502 and drive six miles to Highway 503. Turn left and drive north for five miles to Lucia Falls Road. Turn right and drive eight miles to Moulton Falls and Old County Road 12. Turn right on Old County Road 12 and drive seven miles to the Forest Boundary and the campground entrance on the right.

Contact: Gifford Pinchot National Forest, Mount St. Helens National Volcanic Monument, 42218 N.E. Yale Bridge Rd., Amboy, WA 98601, 360/247-3900, fax 360/449-7801.

54 BEAVER

Rating: 7

on the Wind River in Gifford Pinchot National Forest

See map pages 174–175

This campground is the closest one north of Stevenson in the Columbia Gorge. Set along the Wind River at an elevation of 1,053 feet, it features pretty, shaded sites. No fishing is permitted. The campsites are paved, and a large grassy day-use area is nearby. Hiking highlights include two nearby trailheads. Two miles north lies the

trailhead for the Trapper Creek Wilderness, with 30 miles of trails, including a loop possibility. Three miles north is the Falls Creek Trail.

RV sites, facilities: There are 24 sites for RVs up to 25 feet or tents and one group site for up to 40 campers. Picnic tables and fire grills are provided. Drinking water, vault toilets, and cell phone reception are available. Some facilities are wheelchair-accessible. Leashed pets are permitted.

Reservations, fees: Reservations are accepted for family sites and required for the group site. Reserve at 877/444-6777 or online at www.reserveusa.com ($9 reservation fee). The fee is $13–26 per night, plus $5 per additional vehicle per night. The group site is $91 per night. A senior discount is available. Open mid-April to late September.

Directions: From Vancouver (Washington), take Highway 14 east and drive 50 miles to Carson and the Wind River Highway (County Road 80). Turn left (north) and drive 12 miles to the campground entrance (three miles past Stabler) on the left.

Contact: Gifford Pinchot National Forest, Mount Adams Ranger District, 2455 Hwy. 141, Trout Lake, WA 98650, 509/395-3400, fax 509/395-9384.

55 PARADISE CREEK

Rating: 9

on Paradise Creek and the Wind River in Gifford Pinchot National Forest

See map pages 174–175

This camp is located deep in Gifford Pinchot National Forest among old-growth woods, primarily Douglas fir, cedar, and western hemlock, at the confluence of Paradise Creek and the Wind River. It gets light use despite easy access and easy RV parking. The campsites are well shaded. Lava Butte, located a short distance from the camp, is accessible by trail; the 1.2-mile round-trip hike from the campground provides a good view of the valley. Fishing is closed here. The elevation is 1,500 feet.

RV sites, facilities: There are 42 sites for RVs up to 25 feet or tents. Picnic tables and fire grills are provided. Drinking water and vault toilets are available. Some facilities are wheelchair-accessible. Leashed pets are permitted.

Reservations, fees: Reserve at 877/444-6777 or online at www.reserveusa.com ($9 reservation fee). The fee is $13–15 per night, plus $5 per additional vehicle per night. Open mid-May to mid-November.

Directions: From Vancouver (Washington), take Highway 14 east and drive 50 miles to Carson and the Wind River Highway (County Road 30). Turn north on the Wind River Highway and drive 20 miles to the camp on the right.

Contact: Gifford Pinchot National Forest, Mount Adams Ranger District, 2455 Hwy. 141, Trout Lake, WA, 98650, 509/395-3400, fax 509/395-9384.

WASHINGTON

56 CULTUS CREEK

Rating: 7

near the Indian Heaven Wilderness in Gifford Pinchot National Forest

See map pages 174–175

This camp is set at an elevation of 4,000 feet along Cultus Creek on the edge of the Indian Heaven Wilderness. It offers nearby access to trails that will take you into the backcountry, which has numerous small meadows and lakes among old-growth stands of fir and pine. Horse trails are available as well. Access to the Pacific Crest Trail requires a two-mile climb. This camp is popular during the fall huckleberry season, when picking is good here, but gets light use the rest of the year. Situated amid gentle terrain, the sites are graveled and level.

RV sites, facilities: There are 43 sites for RVs up to 32 feet or tents. Picnic tables and fire grills are provided. Drinking water, vault toilets, and firewood are available. Garbage must be packed out. Some facilities are wheelchair-accessible. Leashed pets are permitted.

Reservations, fees: Reservations are not accepted. A Northwest Forest Pass ($5 daily fee or $30 annual fee per parked vehicle) is required. Open June to September.

Directions: From Vancouver (Washington) on I-205, take Highway 14 east and drive 66 miles to State Route 141. Turn north on State Route 141 and drive 28 miles (becomes Forest Road 24); continue two miles to a junction. Turn right (staying on Forest Road 24) and drive 13.5 miles to the campground.

Contact: Gifford Pinchot National Forest, Mount

Adams Ranger District, 2455 Hwy. 141, Trout Lake, WA 98650, 509/395-3400, fax 509/395-9384.

57 PETERSON PRAIRIE AND PETERSON PRAIRIE GROUP

Rating: 8

near the town of Trout Lake in Gifford Pinchot National Forest

See map pages 174–175

Here's a good base camp if you want to have a short ride to town as well as access to the nearby wilderness areas. Peterson Prairie is a prime spot for huckleberry picking in the fall. A trail from the camp leads about one mile to nearby ice caves; a stairway into the caves provides access to a variety of ice formations. The camp is closed in winter, but an area Sno-Park with snowmobiling and cross-country skiing trails is open for winter recreation. The elevation is 2,800 feet.

RV sites, facilities: There are 23 sites for RVs up to 32 feet or tents, one group site for up to 50 people, and one historic cabin. Picnic tables and fire grills are provided. Drinking water, vault toilets, cell phone reception, and firewood are available. A camp host is available in summer. Some facilities are wheelchair-accessible. Leashed pets are permitted.

Reservations, fees: Reservations are required for the group site only; phone 877/444-6777 or reserve online at www.reserveusa.com ($9 reservation fee). The fees are $13–26 per night for individual and double sites, plus $5 per additional vehicle per night, and $32–67 per night for the group site. A senior discount is available. Open May to late September.

Directions: From Hood River, Oregon, drive north on Highway 35 (over the Columbia River) to Highway 14. Turn left and drive two miles to Highway 141. Turn right (north) on Highway 141 and drive 23 miles to Forest Road 24 (five miles beyond and southwest of the town of Trout Lake). Bear right (west) and drive 2.5 miles to the campground on the left.

Contact: Gifford Pinchot National Forest, Mount Adams Ranger District, 2455 Hwy. 141, Trout Lake, WA 98650, 509/395-3400, fax 509/395-9384.

58 TROUT LAKE CREEK

Rating: 7

on Trout Lake Creek in Gifford Pinchot National Forest

See map pages 174–175

This spot makes a popular base camp for folks fishing at Trout Lake (five miles away). During the day, many anglers will fish at the lake, where fishing is good for stocked rainbow trout, then return to this camp for the night. Some bonus brook trout are occasionally caught at Trout Lake. The camp is set along a creek in a forest of Douglas fir. In season, berry picking can be good here.

RV sites, facilities: There are 17 sites for RVs up to 32 feet or tents. Picnic tables and fire rings are provided. Pits toilets are available. Garbage must be packed out. Leashed pets are permitted.

Reservations, fees: A Northwest Forest Pass ($5 daily fee or $30 annual fee per parked vehicle) is required. A senior discount is available. Open May to September.

Directions: From Hood River, Oregon, drive north on Highway 35 (over the Columbia River) to Highway 14. Turn left and drive two miles to Highway 141. Turn right (north) on Highway 141 and drive 25 miles north to Forest Road 88. Turn right and drive four miles to Forest Road 8810. Turn right and drive 1.5 miles to Forest Road 8810-010. Turn right and drive .25 mile to the campground on the right.

Contact: Gifford Pinchot National Forest, Mount Adams Ranger District, 2455 Hwy. 141, Trout Lake, WA 98650, 509/395-3400, fax 509/395-9384.

59 PANTHER CREEK AND PANTHER CREEK HORSE CAMP

Rating: 8

on Panther Creek in Gifford Pinchot National Forest

See map pages 174–175

This campground is set along Panther Creek in a second-growth forest of Douglas fir and western hemlock, adjacent to an old-growth forest. The sites are well defined, and despite a paved road to the campground and easy parking and access, it gets light use. The camp lies 3.5 miles from the Wind River, an option for those who enjoy fishing, hiking, and horseback riding. The Pacific Crest Trail is accessible from the adjacent Panther Creek Horse Camp. The elevation is 912 feet.

RV sites, facilities: There are 33 sites for RVs up to 25 feet or tents, and the adjacent horse camp has one equestrian site, with a stock loading ramp. Picnic tables and fire rings are provided. Drinking water and pits toilets are available. Garbage must be packed out. Leashed pets are permitted.

Reservations, fees: Reserve at 877/444-6777 or online at www.reserveusa.com ($9 reservation fee). The fee is $13–26 per night, plus $5 per additional vehicle per night. A senior discount is available. Open mid-May to mid-September.

Directions: From Vancouver, Washington, take Highway 14 east and drive 50 miles to Carson and the Wind River Highway (County Road 30). Turn north and drive 5.5 miles to Forest Road 65, and drive 2.5 miles to the camp on the right.

Contact: Gifford Pinchot National Forest, Wind River Work Center, 1262 Hemlock Rd., Carson, WA 98610, 509/427-3200, fax 509/427-4633.

60 OKLAHOMA

Rating: 7

on the Little White Salmon River in Gifford Pinchot National Forest

See map pages 174–175

This pretty campground is set along Little White Salmon River at an elevation of 1,700 feet. Fishing can be excellent in this area. The river is stocked in the spring with rainbow trout. The camp, which gets light use, has some open meadow but is generally flat. Close to the Columbia River Gorge, it features paved road all the way into the campground and easy RV parking. As to why they named the camp "Oklahoma," who knows? If you do, drop me a line.

RV sites, facilities: There are 23 sites for RVs up to 22 feet or tents. Drinking water, fire rings, and picnic tables are provided. Vault toilets are available. A pay phone is within 10 miles. Some facilities are wheelchair-accessible. Leashed pets are permitted.

Reservations, fees: Reservations are accepted; phone 877/444-6777 or reserve online at www.reserveusa.com ($9 reservation fee). The fee is $13 per night, plus $5 for each additional vehicle. A senior discount is available. Open mid-May to mid-September.

Directions: From Hood River, Oregon, drive north on Highway 35 for one mile over the Columbia River to Highway 14. Turn left on Highway 14 and drive about five miles to Cook and County Road 1800. Turn right (north) and drive 14 miles (becomes Cook-Underwood Road, then turn right on Willard Road, then Oklahoma Road) to the campground entrance at the end of the paved road.

Contact: Gifford Pinchot National Forest, Mt. Adams Ranger District, 2455 Hwy. 141, Trout Lake, WA 98650, 509/395-3400, fax 509/395-9384.

61 MOSS CREEK

Rating: 7

on the Little White Salmon River in Gifford Pinchot National Forest
See map pages 174–175

This campground is set at 1,400 feet elevation, about one mile from the Little White Salmon River. Although a short distance from Willard and Big Cedars County Park, the camp gets light use. The river provides good fishing prospects for trout in the spring, usually with few other people around. The sites are generally small but are shaded and still functional for most RVs. The road is paved all the way to the campground.

RV sites, facilities: There are 17 sites for RVs up to 32 feet or tents. Picnic tables and fire grills are provided. Drinking water and vault toilets are available. A pay phone is two miles away, and groceries are available within 10 miles. A camp host is available in the summer. Some facilities are wheelchair-accessible. Leashed pets are permitted.

Reservations, fees: Reservations are accepted; phone 877/444-6777 or reserve online at www.reserveusa.com ($9 reservation fee). The fee is $13 per night; plus $5 for each additional vehicle. A senior discount is available. Open mid-May to mid-September.

Directions: From Hood River, Oregon, drive north on Highway 35 for one mile over the Columbia River to Highway 14. Turn left on Highway

14 and drive about five miles to Cook and County Road 1800. Turn right (north) and drive 10 miles (becomes Cook-Underwood Road, then turn right on Willard Road, then Oklahoma Road) to the campground entrance on the right.

Contact: Gifford Pinchot National Forest, Mt. Adams Ranger District, 2455 Hwy. 141, Trout Lake, CA 98650, 509/395-3400, fax 509/395-9384.

62 BEACON ROCK RESORT

Rating: 7

on the Columbia River
See map pages 174–175

This trailer park is set along the Columbia River, a short distance from Beacon Rock State Park. See the following description of the state park for details. Nearby recreation options include a nine-hole golf course four miles away and two 18-hole golf courses, eight and 12 miles away, respectively.

RV sites, facilities: There are 20 sites with full hookups (20, 30, 50 amps), including three drive-through, for RVs up to 45 feet and a grassy area for tents. Picnic tables and fire rings are provided. Restrooms, drinking water, flush toilets, coin-operated showers, propane, a store, a recreation hall, a coin-operated laundry, and ice are available. A pay phone is within one mile, and an ATM is within three miles. Boat-launching facilities are available within a quarter mile on the Columbia River. Leashed pets are permitted.

Reservations, fees: Reservations are accepted with a deposit. The fee is $13–18 per night, plus $2 per person per night for more than two people and $5 per additional vehicle per night. Open year-round.

Directions: From Vancouver, Washington, on I-205, take Highway 14 and drive east for 27 miles to Skamania. Look for the park along Highway 14 on the right at the corner of Moorage Road.

Contact: Beacon Rock Resort, 62 Moorage Rd., Skamania, WA 98648, 509/427-8473.

63 BEACON ROCK STATE PARK

Rating: 8

on the Columbia River

See map pages 174–175

This state park features Beacon Rock, the second largest monolith in the world, which overlooks the Columbia River Gorge. The park is located in the heart of the Columbia River Gorge National Scenic Area. The Beacon Rock Summit Trail, a 1.8-mile round-trip hike, provides panoramic views of the gorge. The rock is also excellent for rock-climbing, with the climbing season running from mid-July to January for the Southeast and South faces. The Northwest Corner is open year-round. Lewis and Clark gave Beacon Rock its name on their expedition to the Pacific Ocean in 1805. The park covers nearly 5,000 acres and includes 9,500 feet of shoreline along the Columbia River and more then 20 miles of nearby roads open for hiking, mountain biking, and horseback riding. An eight-mile loop trail to Hamilton Mountain (2,300 feet elevation) is one of the best hikes, featuring even better views than from Beacon Rock. Fishing for sturgeon, salmon, steelhead, smallmouth bass (often excellent), and walleye is available on the Lower Columbia River below Bonneville Dam, in season; check regulations.

RV sites, facilities: There are 29 developed sites for self-contained RVs up to 40 feet or tents, one hike-in/bike-in site, and one group site for up to 200 people. Picnic tables and fire grills are provided. Restrooms, drinking water, flush toilets, coin-operated showers, a picnic area, two sheltered kitchen areas with electricity, and a playground are available. An ATM and pay phone are within two miles. Boat docks and launching facilities are within 2.5 miles. Some facilities are wheelchair-accessible. Leashed pets are permitted.

Reservations, fees: Reservations are not accepted for family sites but are required for group camp. Reserve at 888/CAMP-OUT (888/226-7688) or online at www.parks.wa.gov/reservations ($7 reservation fee). The fee is $10–16 per night, plus $10 per additional vehicle; there is a $5 launch fee and a $10–16 fee for boat mooring. The group site requires a $7 reservation fee

plus $2 per person with a 20-person minimum and 200-person maximum. A senior discount is available. Open April to October.

Directions: From Vancouver, Washington, on I-205, take Highway 14 and drive east for 35 miles. The park straddles the highway; follow the signs to the campground.

Contact: Beacon Rock State Park, 34841 Rte. 14, Skamania, WA 98648, 509/427-8265, fax 509/427-4471; state park information, 360/902-8844.

64 HORSETHIEF LAKE STATE PARK

Rating: 10

near Dalles Dam

See map pages 174–175

This 338-acre park boasts 7,500 feet of Columbia River shoreline. It also adjoins the 3,000-acre Dalles Mountain Ranch State Park. Horsethief Butte, adjacent to the lake, dominates the skyline. Horsethief Lake, created by The Dalles Dam, covers approximately 90 acres and is part of the Columbia River. Lupine and balsam root bloom in mid-April and create spectacular fields of purple and gold. Rock-climbing in the park is popular, but the river canyon is often windy, especially in late spring and early summer. Most people find the place as a spot camp while driving along the Columbia River Highway. There are hiking trails and access to both the lake and the Columbia River. Non-powered boats are allowed, and anglers can try for trout and bass. Guided tours on weekends feature pictographs and petroglyphs; reservations are required at 509/767-1159. See the following description of Maryhill State Park for information on other recreation options in the region.

RV sites, facilities: There are 16 sites, eight with partial hookups (30 amps), for self-contained RVs up to 30 feet or tents and two primitive tent sites. Picnic tables and fire grills are provided. Drinking water, flush toilets, firewood, cell phone reception, an RV dump station, a horseshoe pit, and a picnic area are available. A store and a café are within two miles. Boat-launching facilities are located on both the lake and the river. An ATM and groceries are available within three miles. Leashed pets are permitted.

Reservations, fees: Reservations are not accepted. The fee is $10–22 per night, plus $10 per additional vehicle per night. A senior discount is available. Open early April to late October.

Directions: From The Dalles in Oregon, turn north on Highway 197, cross over the Columbia River, and drive four miles to Highway 14. Turn right (east) and drive two miles to Milepost 85 and the park entrance on the right.

Contact: Horsethief Lake State Park, 509/767-1159, fax 509/767-4304; state park information, 360/902-8844.

65 MARYHILL STATE PARK

Rating: 8

on the Columbia River

See map pages 174–175

This 99-acre park has 4,700 feet of frontage along the Columbia River. Fishing, water-skiing, and windsurfing are among the recreation possibilities. The climate here is pleasant from March to mid-November. Two interesting places can be found near Maryhill: One is a full-scale replica of Stonehenge, located on a bluff overlooking the Columbia River, about one mile from the park. The other is the historic Mary Hill Home Museum of Art, which is open to the public; Mary Hill's husband, Sam Hill, constructed the Stonehenge replica.

RV sites, facilities: There are 50 sites with full hookups (50 amps) for RVs up to 50 feet and 20 tent sites, including three primitive sites. Picnic tables and fire pits are provided. Restrooms, flush toilets, cell phone reception, a pay phone, showers, an RV dump station, boat docks, launching facilities, and a picnic area with covered shelters are available. A café, ATM, and groceries are within one mile. Some facilities are wheelchair-accessible. Leashed pets are permitted.

Reservations, fees: Reservations are accepted for the group site only; Reserve at 888/CAMP-OUT (226-7688) or online at www.parks.wa.gov/reservations ($7 reservation fee). The fee is $10–22 per night, plus $10 per additional vehicle per night. The group site is $25, plus $2 per person per night with a minimum of 20 people. Call 360/902-8844 for group camping information. A senior discount is available. Major credit cards are accepted. Open year-round.

Directions: From Goldendale and U.S. 97, drive 12 miles south to the park on the left.

Contact: Maryhill State Park, 509/773-5007, fax 509/773-6337; state park information, 360/902-8844.

Washington

Chapter 6

Southeastern
Washington

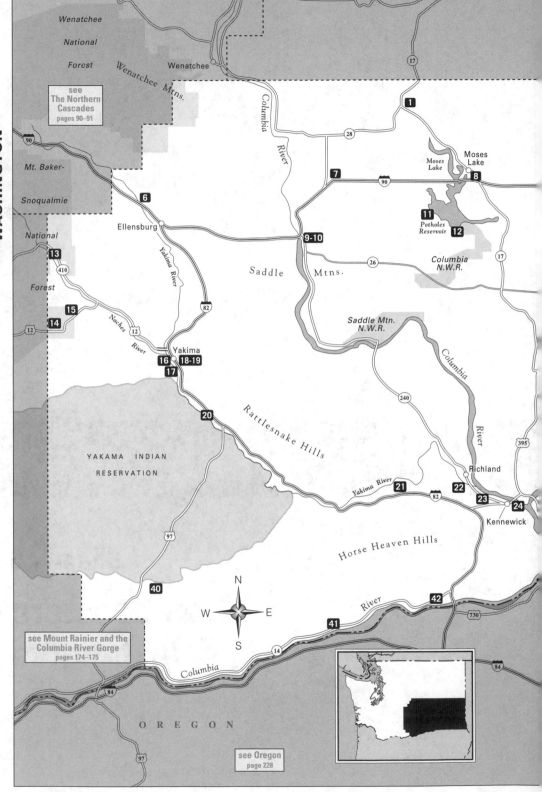

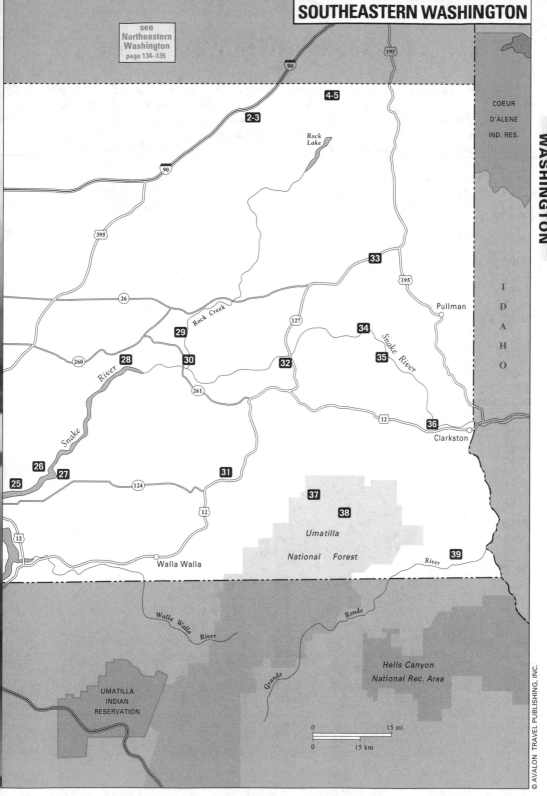

see
Northeastern
Washington
page 134–135

COEUR
D'ALENE
IND. RES.

WASHINGTON

4-5

2-3

Rock
Lake

90

90

195

395

33

195

Pullman

I
D
A
H
O

26

Rock Creek

127

34

29

35

Snake River

260

28

30

261

32

Snake River

12

36

Clarkston

26

27

124

31

12

37

38

Umatilla

National   Forest

River

39

12

Walla Walla

Walla Walla River

Ronde

Grande

UMATILLA
INDIAN
RESERVATION

Hells Canyon
National Rec. Area

0   15 mi
0   15 km

© AVALON TRAVEL PUBLISHING, INC.

Chapter 6—Southeastern Washington

The expansive domain of southeastern Washington is a surprise for many newcomers. Instead of the high mountains of the Cascades, there are rolling hills. Instead of forests, there are miles of wheat fields (Washington's second-largest export crop behind lumber). Instead of a multitude of streams, there are giant rivers—the Columbia and Snake. Just one pocket of mountains and a somewhat sparse forest sit in the southeast corner of the state, in a remote sector of Umatilla National Forest.

The Lewis and Clark expedition was routed through this area some two hundred years ago, and today, several major highways, including I-82 and U.S. 395, bring out-of-town visitors through the region en route to other destinations. A network of camps is set along these highways, including RV parks created to serve the needs of travelers. Of the 16 area parks, the 13 state parks offer the best campgrounds. The prettiest picture you will find is of Palouse Falls, where a gorgeous fountain of water pours through a desert gorge.

1 OASIS RV PARK AND GOLF

Rating: 5

near Soap Lake

See map pages 206–207

This area can be extremely warm and arid during the summer months, but, fortunately, Oasis RV Park offers shaded sites. There are two fishing ponds at the resort: One has crappie, while the other is for kids and has trout and bass. There is also a par-three nine-hole golf course at the park. Mineral baths are located just a few miles north.

RV sites, facilities: There are 68 sites with full hookups (20, 30 amps) for RVs of any length, 10 are drive-through, and 38 tent sites. Picnic tables are provided. A restroom with flush toilets and coin-operated showers is available. A par-three nine-hole golf course, an RV dump station, a store, propane, a coin-operated laundry, ice, a swimming pool, a pay phone, cell phone reception, and a fishing pond for children are available. A café is within one mile. Leashed pets are permitted.

Reservations, fees: Reservations are recommended. The fee is $15–20 per night, plus $2 per person for more than four people and $2 per additional vehicle. Major credit cards are accepted. A senior discount is available. Open year-round, with limited winter facilities.

Directions: From Spokane, drive west on I-90 to the Moses Lake exit and Highway 17. Turn northeast and drive 17 miles to the Y junction with Highway 282. Take Highway 282 and drive four miles to Highway 281/283 (a stoplight). Turn left and drive 1.25 miles to the park on the right (just before reaching the town of Ephrata).

Contact: Oasis RV Park and Golf, 2541 Basin St. SW, Ephrata, WA 98823, 509/754-5102 or 877/754-5102.

2 FOUR SEASONS CAMPGROUND AND RESORT

Rating: 7

on Sprague Lake

See map pages 206–207

This campground along the shore of Sprague Lake, one of the top fishing waters in the state, has spacious sites with plenty of vegetation. The fishing for rainbow trout is best in May and June, with some bass in spring and fall. Because there is an abundance of natural feed in the lake, the fish reach larger sizes here than in neighboring lakes. Walleye up to 11 pounds are taken here. Perch, crappie, blue gill, and catfish are also abundant. From late July to August, a fair algae bloom is a turnoff for swimmers and water-skiers.

RV sites, facilities: There are 38 sites with partial or full hookups (20, 30, 50 amps), including some drive-through sites, for RVs of any length, 25 tent sites, and four furnished cabins for up to six people. Picnic tables and fire grills are provided. Restrooms, drinking water, flush toilets, coin-operated showers, cell phone reception, an RV dump station, firewood, ice, a store with fishing tackle, a fish-cleaning station, a small basketball court, and a swimming pool are available. Boat and fishing docks, launching facilities, and rentals are nearby. An ATM is within six miles. Leashed pets are permitted.

Reservations, fees: Reservations are accepted. The fee is $16–23 per night, plus $2 per person for more than four people and $1 per pet per night. Cabins are $70–85 per night. Open March to October, weather permitting.

Directions: From Spokane, drive west on I-90 for about 40 miles to Exit 245. Take Exit 245 and drive south to Fourth Street. Turn right and drive one block to B Street. Turn left and drive two blocks to First Street. Turn right and drive .5 mile to a Y intersection. Bear right to Doerschlag Road and drive one mile to Lake Road. Turn left and drive four miles to Bob Lee Road. Turn left and drive one mile to the campground at the end of the road.

Contact: Four Seasons Campground and Resort, 2384 North Bob Lee Rd., Sprague, WA 99032, tel./fax 509/257-2332, website: www.fourseasons campground.com.

3 SPRAGUE LAKE RESORT

Rating: 5

on Sprague Lake

See map pages 206–207

This developed campground is located on the

shore of Sprague Lake, about 35 miles from Spokane. It offers a pleasant, grassy setting with many cottonwood and native trees on the property. See the prior listing for Four Seasons Campground and Resort for more information about Sprague Lake.

RV sites, facilities: There are 30 drive-through sites with partial or full hookups (30 amps) for RVs of any length and 50 tent sites. Picnic tables and fire grills are provided. Restrooms, drinking water, flush toilets, coin-operated showers, an RV dump station, a coin-operated laundry, ice, firewood, a playground, boat docks, bait and tackle, cell phone reception, launching facilities, and rentals are available. An ATM and pay phone are within two miles. Leashed pets are permitted.

Reservations, fees: Reservations are accepted. The fee is $16–21 per night, plus $1 per person per night for more than two people. Open April to October.

Directions: In Spokane, drive west on I-90 to the Sprague Business Center exit. Take that exit to Sprague Lake Road and drive two miles to the resort on the left (well signed).

Contact: Sprague Lake Resort, 1999 Sprague Lake Resort Rd., Sprague, WA 99032, tel./fax 509/257-2864, website: www.spraguelakeresort .com.

4 KLINK'S WILLIAMS LAKE RESORT

Rating: 6

on Williams Lake

See map pages 206–207

This family-oriented resort is on the shore of Williams Lake, which is less than 3.5 miles long and is popular for swimming and water-skiing. The newly renovated resort has a swimming area with a floating dock. This lake is also one of the top fishing lakes in the region for rainbow trout and cutthroat trout. Rocky cliffs border the lake in some areas. Turnbull National Wildlife Refuge is within seven miles. Note that about 100 permanent residents live at the resort.

RV sites, facilities: There are 60 sites with partial or full hookups (20, 30, 50 amps), including one drive-through site, for RVs of any length, 15 tent sites, and three log cabins. Picnic tables are provided. Restrooms, drinking water, flush toi-

lets, coin-operated showers, propane, an RV dump station, firewood, a store, a café, some portable fire rings, a pay phone, a restaurant, ice, a playground, boat docks, launching facilities, fishing, and boat, kayak, and paddleboat rentals are available. Leashed pets are permitted.

Reservations, fees: Reservations are accepted. The fee is $17–20 per night, plus $2 per person for more than two adults and two children and $1.50 per pet per night. Major credit cards are accepted. Open early April to mid-October.

Directions: From Spokane, drive west on I-90 for 10 miles to Exit 270 and Highway 904. Turn south on Highway 904 and drive four miles to Cheney and Cheney Plaza Road. Turn left (south) on Cheney Plaza Road and drive 11.2 miles to Williams Lake Road. Turn right (west) and drive 2.2 miles to the campground on the left.

Contact: Klink's Williams Lake Resort, 18617 West Williams Lake Rd., Cheney, WA 99004, 509/235-2391 or 800/274-1540, fax 509/235-2817, website: www.klinksresort.com.

5 BUNKER'S RESORT

Rating: 8

on Williams Lake

See map pages 206–207

This campground is on the shore of Williams Lake. See the previous description of Klink's Williams Lake Resort for information on the lake.

RV sites, facilities: There are 10 drive-through sites with partial or full hookups (20 amps) for RVs of any length, 10 sites for tents, and four furnished cabins. Fire pits are provided at tent sites. Picnic tables, restrooms, drinking water, flush toilets, showers, propane, an RV dump station, cell phone reception, a pay phone, a restaurant, a store, ice, boat and fishing docks, launching facilities, and rentals are available. Leashed pets are permitted.

Reservations, fees: Reservations are accepted. The fee is $15–24.50 per night, plus $5 per person for over four people. Cabins are $65–80 per night. Major credit cards are accepted. Open mid-April to September.

Directions: From Spokane, drive west on I-90 for 10 miles to Exit 270 and Highway 904. Turn south on Highway 904 and drive six miles to

Cheney and Mullinex Road. Turn left (south) on Mullinex Road and drive 12 miles to the resort. **Contact:** Bunker's Resort, 36402 South Bunker Landing Rd., Cheney, WA 99004, 509/235-5212 or 509/235-8707.

6 ELLENSBURG KOA

Rating: 8

on the Yakima River
See map pages 206–207

This KOA is one of the few campgrounds in a 25-mile radius. Exceptionally clean and scenic, it offers well-maintained, shaded campsites along the Yakima River. Rafting and fly-fishing on the nearby Yakima River are popular activities. Other nearby recreation options include an 18-hole golf course. The Kittitas County Historical Museum is in town at Third and Pine Streets, and the Clymer Art Museum is nearby. The Ginkgo Petrified Forest is within 20 miles.

RV sites, facilities: There are 104 sites for RVs of any length, including 48 drive-through sites, some with full hookups (20, 30, 50 amps) and the rest with water and electricity, and 40 tent sites. Picnic tables and fire rings are provided. Restrooms, flush toilets, showers, an RV dump station, a video arcade, a store, a coin-operated laundry, ice, a playground, video rentals, a snack bar, propane, peddlebike and raft rentals, a pay phone, cell phone reception, a horseshoe pit, volleyball, a seasonal wading pool, and a heated swimming pool are available. An ATM and a café are within a quarter mile. Groceries are available within 10 miles. Extra parking is available for horse trailers, vans, and boats. Leashed pets are permitted.

Reservations, fees: Reserve at 800/562-7616. The fee is $25–35 per night, plus $2–4 per person per night for more than two people (children five and under are free) and $3 per additional vehicle per night. Major credit cards are accepted. Open year-round.

Directions: From Seattle, drive east on I-90 for 106 miles to Exit 106 (near Ellensburg). Take that exit and continue .25 mile to Thorp Highway. Turn right at Thorp Highway and drive a short distance to the KOA entrance (well marked). **Contact:** Ellensburg KOA, 32 Thorp Hwy. S,
Ellensburg, WA 98926, 509/925-9319, fax 509/925-3607, website: www.koa.com.

7 SHADY TREE RV PARK

Rating: 8

near George
See map pages 206–207

With shade trees and grassy sites, this camp is an oasis in a desertlike area. A natural outdoor amphitheater just eight miles away seats 20,000 and is the scene of major concerts from June to September. The camp is one mile from Moses Lake State Park and about 30 miles from Martha Lake, a small and public lake which provides another recreation option.

RV sites, facilities: There are 41 sites with full hookups (30, 50 amps) for RVs of any length, including four drive-through, and 30 tent sites. Picnic tables are provided. A restroom with flush toilets, showers, cell phone reception, an RV dump station, a horseshoe pit, and a coin-operated laundry are available. An ATM and pay phone are across the street. Leashed pets are permitted.

Reservations, fees: Reservations are not accepted. The fee is $22–30 per night, plus $5 per person per night for more than two people over age seven for RV sites and $10 per person per night for tent sites. Open year-round.

Directions: From Spokane, drive west on I-90 to Exit 151 (two miles east of George). Take that exit and bear right to the campground right at the corner (just off the highway at the intersection of Highways 281 and 283).

Contact: Shady Tree RV Park, 1099 Hwy. 283 N, Quincy, WA 98848, tel./fax 509/785-2851.

8 BIG SUN RESORT

Rating: 5

near Moses Lake State Park
See map pages 206–207

This park sits a short distance from Moses Lake State Park, which is open for day-use only. The primary appeal is Moses Lake, where you will find shady picnic spots with tables and fire grills, beach access, and moorage floats. Water-skiing

WASHINGTON

is allowed on the lake. New owners are anticipated for this resort in 2004.

RV sites, facilities: There are 42 sites with full hookups (30 amps) for RVs of any length, including 13 drive-through, and 10 tent sites. Picnic tables are provided. A restroom with flush toilets and pay showers is available. A coin-operated laundry, ice, cable TV, some fire pits, cell phone reception, pay phones, rowboat rentals and launch facilities, and a playground are available. An ATM is within a quarter mile. A restaurant is within one mile, and groceries are available within three miles. Boat docks, launching facilities, and rentals are nearby. Leashed pets are permitted.

Reservations, fees: Reservations are accepted. The fee is $13.50–22 per night, plus $2 per person ($1 per child) per night for more than two people. Major credit cards are accepted. Open March to October.

Directions: From Spokane, drive west on I-90 to Moses Lake and Exit 176. Exit right onto Broadway and drive .5 mile to Burress Avenue. Turn west on Burress Avenue and drive one block to the park.

Contact: Big Sun Resort, 2300 West Marina, Moses Lake, WA 98837, 509/765-8294.

9 GINKGO-WANAPUM STATE PARK

Rating: 7

on the Columbia River and Wanapum Lake
See map pages 206–207

Ginkgo Petrified Forest State Park is one of the most unusual fossil forests in the world, and it is registered as a national natural landmark. Although a completely separate park, it is linked to Wanapum State Recreation Area. Camping is permitted only at Wanapum, which is seven miles south of the main entrance at Ginkgo. The site of an ancient petrified forest, the park features an interpretive center and trail. The petrified forest is open weekends and holidays from November to March. Ginkgo is set along Wanapum Lake in the course of the Columbia River. This is a huge recreation area, covering 7,740 acres and surrounding the 27,000 acres of Wanapum Lake. Recreation options include hiking (three miles of trails), swimming, boating, water-skiing,

and fishing. There are also several historical Civilian Conservation Corps structures from the 1930s. The campground at Wanapum is set up primarily for RVs, with full hookups, restrooms, and showers. Note that the park always fills up during the Gorge concert season.

RV sites, facilities: There are 50 sites with full hookups (30 amps) for RVs up to 60 feet long. Picnic tables, fire grills, a pay phone, coin-operated showers, cell phone reception, and flush toilets are provided. Showers and firewood are available for an extra fee. Boat docks, launching facilities, and a picnic area are nearby. Groceries and an ATM are available within six miles. Leashed pets are permitted.

Reservations, fees: Reserve at 888/CAMP-OUT (888/226-7688) or online at website: www.parks .wa.gov/reservations ($7 reservation fee). The fee is $22 per night, plus $10 per additional vehicle per night. A senior discount is available. Open April to October.

Directions: From Spokane, drive west on I-90 to the Vantage Highway/Huntzinger Road (Exit 136). Take that exit, turn south on Vantage Highway/Huntzinger Road, and drive three miles south to the park on the left.

Contact: Ginkgo-Wanapum State Park, Vantage, WA 98950, 509/856-2700; state park information, 360/902-8844.

10 VANTAGE RIVERSTONE RESORT

Rating: 6

on the Columbia River
See map pages 206–207

This campground offers pleasant, grassy sites overlooking the Columbia River, which lies a short distance from the state park (see Ginkgo-Wanapum State Park above). This campground is the only one in the immediate area that provides space for tent camping. The next closest camp is 12 miles away at Shady Tree RV Park in George.

RV sites, facilities: There are 50 sites with full hookups (30, 50 amps) for RVs of any length and 200-plus tent sites. Picnic tables, a restroom with flush toilets, showers, an RV dump station, a recreation hall, a coin-operated laundry, a pay phone, cell phone reception, ice, a playground, and a heated indoor swimming pool are available. A store, two cafés, and an ATM are located next to the resort. Boat docks and launching facilities are nearby. Leashed pets are permitted.

Reservations, fees: Reservations are accepted. The fee is $20–23 per night, plus $10 per person for more than two people. Major credit cards are accepted. Open year-round.

Directions: From Spokane, drive west on I-90 to Vantage and the Vantage Highway (Exit 136). Take that exit, turn north, and drive north for three blocks to the resort on the left.

Contact: Vantage Riverstone Resort, P.O. Box 1101, Vantage, WA 98950, 509/856-2230 or 509/856-2800, website: www.vantagewa.com.

11 POTHOLES STATE PARK

Rating: 8

on Potholes Reservoir
See map pages 206–207

This park is set on Potholes Reservoir, also known as O'Sullivan Reservoir (because of the O'Sullivan Dam), where fishing is the highlight. Trout, walleye, crappie, and perch are among the species taken here. Water-skiing and hiking (three miles of hiking trails) are two other recreation options. A sand beach is near the campground. The surrounding terrain is desertlike with freshwater marshes. A side trip to the Columbia Wildlife Refuge, located two miles east of the park, is recommended. Note that Potholes Reservoir is often confused with the Potholes Lakes, which are 3 to 10 miles away.

RV sites, facilities: There are 125 sites for RVs up to 50 feet or tents, 60 with full hookups (20 amps). Picnic tables and fire grills are provided. Flush toilets, coin-operated showers, two pay phones, cell phone reception, firewood, an RV dump station, a store, a playground, and a picnic area with a shelter are available. Boat-launching facilities, rentals, and an ATM are nearby. Leashed pets are permitted.

Reservations, fees: Reserve at 888/CAMP-OUT (888/226-7688) or online at www.parks.wa.gov /reservations ($7 reservation fee). The fee is $10–22 per night, plus $10 per additional vehicle per night. A senior discount is available. Open year-round.

Directions: From I-90 at Moses Lake, take Exit 179 and Highway 17. Turn south and drive nine miles to Highway 262/O'Sullivan Dam Road. Turn right (west) and drive 11 miles to the resort on the southern shore of Potholes Reservoir (well signed).

Contact: Potholes State Park, 6762 Hwy. 262 E, Othello, WA 99344, 509/346-2759, fax 509/346-1732; state park information, 360/902-8844.

12 MAR DON RESORT

Rating: 7

near Potholes Reservoir
See map pages 206–207

This resort is located on Potholes Reservoir and provides opportunities for fishing, swimming, and boating. A marina, tackle, and boat rentals are all available. Hiking trails and marked bike trails are close by. There are also a 25-unit motel and two rental homes at the resort. Many visitors find the café and cocktail lounge a nice bonus. The Columbia National Wildlife Refuge is located to the nearby south and provides exceptional bird-watching, with pelicans and kingfishers common and bald eagles and migratory sandhill cranes often seen.

RV sites, facilities: There are 275 sites for RVs of any length or tents, including 90 with partial or full hookups (30 amps) and seven with drive-through sites, and 97 tent sites. Electricity, drinking water, and picnic tables are provided. A restroom with flush toilets, coin-operated showers, propane, two pay phones, cell phone reception, modem access, an RV dump station, a store, a coin-operated laundry, ice, a playground, boat moorage, boat rentals, and launching facilities are available. An ATM is within one mile. Some facilities are wheelchair-accessible. Leashed pets are permitted.

Reservations, fees: Reserve at 800/416-2736. The fee is $20–26 per night, plus $3 per person for more than four people, $5 per additional vehicle per night, and $3 per pet per night. A senior discount is available. Major credit cards are accepted. Open year-round.

Directions: From Spokane, drive west on I-90 to Moses Lake and Exit 179 and Highway 17. Turn south and drive nine miles to Highway 262. Turn west and drive 10 miles to the resort on the southern shore of Potholes Reservoir.

Contact: Mar Don Resort, 8198 Hwy. 262 SE, Othello, WA 99344, 509/346-2651, fax 509/346-9493, website: www.mardonresort.com.

13 SQUAW ROCK RESORT

Rating: 8

on the Naches River
See map pages 206–207

This park, situated in a stand of old-growth fir and pine on the Naches River, is close to a host of activities, including trout fishing, hiking trails, and marked bike trails. The park has a pool and hot tub. The nearby town of Naches, located southeast of the campground on State Route 410, offers all services.

RV sites, facilities: There are 65 sites, most with full hookups (20, 30, 50 amps), for RVs of any length, 25 tent sites, five cabins, and five motel rooms. Picnic tables are provided. Restrooms, flush toilets, showers, propane, an RV dump station, cable TV, a pay phone, a store, a café, ice, a playground, a hot tub, and a swimming pool are available. Leashed pets are permitted.

Reservations, fees: Reservations are accepted. The fee is $15–24 per night, plus $2 per person per night for more than two people. Major credit cards are accepted. A senior discount is available. Open year-round.

Directions: From Yakima, drive northwest on U.S. 12 for 18 miles to State Route 410. Continue straight on State Route 410 and drive 15 miles to the campground on the left (Mile Marker 102).

Contact: Squaw Rock Resort, 15070 State Rte. 410, Naches, WA 98937, 509/658-2926, fax 509/658-2927, website: www.squawrockresort.com.

14 HAUSE CREEK

Rating: 7

on the Tieton River in Wenatchee National Forest
See map pages 206–207

Several creeks converge at this campground along the Tieton River (elevation 2,500 feet). The Tieton Dam, which creates Rimrock Lake, is located just upstream. Hause Creek is one of the larger, more developed camps in the area.

RV sites, facilities: There are 42 sites for RVs up to 30 feet or tents. Picnic tables and fire grills are provided. Drinking water and flush toilets are available. Boat docks, launching facilities, and rentals are located on Rimrock Lake. A pay phone is within 4.5 miles. Some facilities are wheelchair-accessible. Leashed pets are permitted.

Reservations, fees: Reservations are accepted; phone 877/444-6777 or reserve online at www.reserveusa.com ($9 reservation fee). The fees are $13–15 per night and $26 for double sites, plus $5 per additional vehicle per night. A senior discount is available. Open late May to late October, weather permitting.

Directions: From Yakima on U.S. 12, drive west for 20 miles to the junction with Highway 410. Bear left and stay on Highway 12; drive 15 miles to the camp entrance on the left.

Contact: Okanogan and Wenatchee National Forests, Naches Ranger District, 10061 U.S. 12, Naches, WA 98937, 509/653-2205, fax 509/653-2638.

15 WINDY POINT

Rating: 5

on the Tieton River in Wenatchee National Forest
See map pages 206–207

This campground, located along the Tieton River at an elevation of 2,000 feet, is more isolated than the camps set westward toward Rimrock Lake. Drinking water is a bonus. Fishing access is available.

RV sites, facilities: There are 15 sites for RVs up to 22 feet or tents. Picnic tables and fire grills are provided. Drinking water, vault toilets, and cell phone reception are available. Garbage service and firewood are available nearby. Leashed pets are permitted.

Reservations, fees: Reservations are not accepted. The fee is $13–15 per night, plus $5 per additional vehicle per night. A senior discount is available. Open April to late October, weather permitting.

Directions: From Yakima on U.S. 12, drive west for 20 miles to the junction with Highway 410.

Bear left and stay on Highway 12; drive nine miles to the camp entrance on the left.

Contact: Okanogan and Wenatchee National Forests, Naches Ranger District, 10061 U.S. 12, Naches, WA 98937, 509/653-2205, fax 509/653-2638.

16 CIRCLE H RV RANCH

Rating: 8

in Yakima
See map pages 206–207

This pleasant, centrally located, and clean park with a Western flavor has comfortable, spacious sites among ornamental trees and roses. Nearby recreation options include several 18-hole golf courses, hiking trails, and marked bike trails. See the KOA Yakima listing in this chapter for information on points of interest in Yakima.

RV sites, facilities: There are 64 sites with full hookups (20, 30, 50 amps) for RVs of any length, including 16 drive-through sites, and 12 tent sites. Picnic tables are provided. Restrooms, flush toilets, showers, two recreation halls, a coin-operated laundry, a hot tub, two pay phones, cell phone reception, modem access, two playgrounds with horseshoes, a tennis court, volleyball and basketball, a video arcade, a mini-golf course, and a swimming pool are available. Propane, a store, a café, and ice are available within one mile. Mini-storage units are available for a fee. An ATM is within a quarter mile. Leashed pets are permitted.

Reservations, fees: Reservations are accepted. The fee is $16–21 per night, plus $3 per person per night for more than two people. Major credit cards are accepted. Open year-round.

Directions: In Yakima on I-82, take Exit 34 and drive one block to South 18th Street. Turn right (north) and drive .25 mile to the campground on the right.

Contact: Circle H RV Ranch, 1107 South 18th St., Yakima, WA 98901, 509/457-3683, website: www.circlehrvranch.com.

17 TRAILER INN RV PARK

Rating: 7

in Yakima
See map pages 206–207

Like the Trailer Inn RV Park in Spokane, this spot has many of the luxuries you'd find in a hotel, including a pool, a hot tub, on-site security, and a large-screen TV. An 18-hole golf course, hiking trails, marked bike trails, and tennis courts are close by. It's especially pretty in the fall when the sycamores turn color. See the description of KOA Yakima in this chapter for information on some of the points of interest in Yakima.

RV sites, facilities: There are 154 sites with full hookups (30, 50 amps) for RVs of any length or tents; 30 are drive-through sites. Picnic tables are provided. Restrooms, flush toilets, showers, propane, a recreation hall, a coin-operated laundry, ice, an indoor heated swimming pool, a whirlpool, a TV room with a 52-inch-screen TV, a dog walk, an enclosed barbecue (no open fires permitted), and a playground are available. A store and a café are within one block. Leashed pets are permitted.

Reservations, fees: Reservations are accepted. The fee is $17–25 per night, plus $5 per person per night for more than two people and $5 per additional vehicle per night. Major credit cards are accepted. Open year-round.

Directions: In Yakima on I-82, take Exit 31-A and drive south for one block on North First Street to the park on the right (west side of the road).

Contact: Trailer Inn RV Park, 1610 North First St., Yakima, WA 98901, tel./fax 509/452-9561 or 800/659-4784, website: www.trailerinnsrv.com.

18 YAKIMA SPORTSMAN STATE PARK

Rating: 8

on the Yakima River
See map pages 206–207

This park is located on the floodplain of the Yakima River and is an irrigated area in an otherwise desert landscape. Several deciduous trees shade the camping and picnic areas. More than 140 bird species have been identified in the park.

It is a popular layover spot for visitors attending events in the Yakima area. There is a fishing pond for children (no anglers over age 15 are allowed). Hiking is permitted along two miles of unpaved roadway on the river dike. Kayaking and rafting are possible at this park on the Yakima River. No swimming is allowed. Nearby recreation options include an 18-hole golf course and hiking trails. See the following description of KOA Yakima for information on other points of interest in Yakima.

RV sites, facilities: There are 28 sites for self-contained RVs or tents, 37 drive-through sites with full hookups (30 amps) for RVs up to 60 feet, and two primitive tent sites. Picnic tables and fire grills are provided. Flush toilets, an RV dump station, a pay phone, cell phone reception, and a playground are available. Showers and firewood are available for an extra fee. A store, an ATM, and ice are within one mile. Some facilities are wheelchair-accessible. Leashed pets are permitted.

Reservations, fees: Reservations are accepted. The fee is $6–22 per night, plus $6 per additional vehicle per night. Major credit cards are accepted. A senior discount is available. Open year-round.

Directions: In Yakima, drive on I-82 to Milepost 34 and the Highway 24 exit. Turn east on Highway 24 and drive one mile to Keys Road. Turn left and drive one mile to the park entrance on the left.

Contact: Yakima Sportsman State Park, 509/575-2774, fax 509/454-4114; state park information, 360/902-8844.

19 KOA YAKIMA

Rating: 6

on the Yakima River
See map pages 206–207
This campground along the Yakima River offers well-maintained, shaded sites and fishing access. Some points of interest in Yakima are the Yakima Valley Museum and the Yakima Trolley Lines, which offer rides on restored trolley cars originally built in 1906. Indian Rock Paintings State Park is located five miles west of Yakima on U.S. 12. Nearby recreation options include an 18-hole golf course, hiking trails, marked bike trails, and tennis courts. A casino is located two miles to the west.

RV sites, facilities: There are 120 sites, some with full hookups (30, 50 amps), the rest with water and electricity, for RVs of any length, 40 tent sites, and 10 cabins. Picnic tables are provided. Restrooms, flush toilets, showers, propane, a pay phone, cell phone reception, an RV dump station, a recreation hall, a store, a coin-operated laundry, ice, a pool, a playground with horseshoes, a basketball court, fishing ponds, firewood, bike rentals, and boat rentals including paddleboats are available. A café, ATM, and groceries are available within one mile. Leashed pets are permitted.

Reservations, fees: Reserve at 800/562-5773. The fee is $22–29 per night, plus $3 per person per night for more than two people. Cabins are $42–49 per night. Major credit cards are accepted. Open year-round.

Directions: In Yakima, drive on I-82 to Milepost 34 and the Highway 24 exit. Turn east on Highway 24 and drive one mile to Keys Road. Turn north on Keys Road and drive 300 yards to the campground on the left.

Contact: KOA Yakima, 1500 Keys Rd., Yakima, WA 98901, 509/248-5882, fax 509/469-3986, website: www.koa.com.

20 YAKAMA NATION RV RESORT

Rating: 3

near the Yakima River
See map pages 206–207
The park is within the Yakama Indian Reservation (the tribe spells its name differently from the river and town), close to a casino and movie theater. The Toppenish National Wildlife Refuge, the best side trip, is almost always a good spot to see a large variety of birds. For information, phone 509/545-8588. Nearby Toppenish, a historic Old West town with a museum, is also worth a side trip.

RV sites, facilities: There are 125 sites with full hookups (20, 30, 50 amps) for RVs of any length, 10 tent sites, and 14 tepees for up to 10 people each. Picnic tables and fire pits are provided. Restrooms, flush toilets, showers, modem hookups, a pay phone, cell phone reception, an RV dump station, garbage service, a playground, a recreation room, an exercise room, a jogging track, ball courts, bicycle rentals, a heated pool, and a coin-operated laundry are available. A picnic shelter with drinking water, propane, and a sink is available in the tent area. A restaurant, ATM, and grocery store are within 1.5 miles. Leashed pets are permitted.

Reservations, fees: Reservations are recommended; phone 800/874-3087. The fee is $20–26 per night, plus $2 per person per night for more than two people. Tepees are $50 per night for five campers, plus $5 for each additional person. Major credit cards are accepted. Open year-round.

Directions: From Yakima, drive south on U.S. 97 for 16 miles to the resort on the right.

Contact: Yakama Nation RV Resort, 280 Buster Rd., Toppenish, WA 98948, 509/865-2000 or 800/874-3087, website: www.yakamanation.com.

21 BEACH RV PARK AND CAMPGROUND

Rating: 8

on the Yakima River
See map pages 206–207

If it's getting late, you'd best stop here because it's the only option for a long stretch. This park along the shore of the Yakima River is a pleasant spot with spacious RV sites, a large grassy area, and poplar trees and shrubs that provide privacy between sites. Nearby recreation options include an 18-hole golf course, a full-service marina, and tennis courts. The park was sold in 2000, and the new owner installed a deck overlooking the river.

RV sites, facilities: There are 35 sites with full hookups (30, 50 amps) for RVs of any length; five are drive-through sites. Electricity, drinking water, sewer hookups, and cable TV are provided. Flush toilets, showers, a pay phone, cell phone reception, modem access, and a coin-operated laundry are available. Boat-launching facilities are nearby. Propane, an RV dump station, a store, and a café are available within one mile. An ATM is within two miles. Leashed pets are permitted.

Reservations, fees: Reservations are accepted. The fee is $24 per night. Open year-round.

Directions: From Pasco, drive west on U.S. 12 past Richland and continue eight miles to Exit 96 and the Benton City/West Richland exit. Take that exit and drive one block north to Abby Avenue. Turn left (west) and drive 1.5 blocks to the park on the left.

Contact: Beach RV Park, 113 Abby Ave., Benton City, WA 99320, tel./fax 509/588-5959, website: www.angelfire.com/wa2/beachrvpark.

22 DESERT GOLD RV PARK AND MOTEL

Rating: 6

near the Columbia River
See map pages 206–207

Desert Gold is a nice RV park located about one mile from the Columbia River. Nearby recreation options include an 18-hole golf course, hiking trails, a full-service marina, and tennis courts. You can also visit the Department of Energy public information center at the Hanford Science Center. The RV park has a pool and spa if you just want to relax without going anywhere.

RV sites, facilities: There are 90 sites with full hookups (30 amps) for RVs of any length, including 15 drive-through sites, and 29 motel rooms, including 19 with kitchenettes. Picnic tables and cable TV are provided. Flush toilets, showers, propane, an RV dump station, a store, a pay phone, cell phone reception, modem access, a coin-operated laundry, ice, a game/meeting room, video rentals, and a seasonal hot tub and swimming pool are available. Boat docks and launching facilities are nearby on the Columbia River. A café is within one mile. An ATM is within two blocks. Leashed pets are permitted.

Reservations, fees: Reservations are accepted. The fee is $24 per night, plus $1.50 per person per night for more than two people. Major credit cards are accepted. Open year-round.

Directions: In Richland on I-182, take Exit 3 (Queensgate). Turn right and drive to Columbia Park Trail (the first left). Turn left and drive about two miles to the park.

Contact: Desert Gold RV Park and Motel, 611 Columbia Park Trail, Richland, WA 99352, 509/627-1000 or 800/788-GOLD (800/788-4653), fax 509/627-3467.

23 COLUMBIA PARK CAMPGROUND

Rating: 7

on the Columbia River
See map pages 206–207

This campground is set in a grassy suburban area on the Columbia River, adjacent to 605-acre Columbia Park. Nearby activities include water-skiing on the Columbia River, an 18-hole golf course, hiking trails, marked bike trails, tennis courts, and Frisbee golf. The sun can feel like a branding iron during the summer here.

RV sites, facilities: There are 58 sites, including 30 with partial hookups (30, 50 amps), for RVs of any length or tents; 14 are drive-through. Picnic tables and fire grills are provided. Drinking water, restrooms, flush toilets, showers, an RV dump station, a pay phone, cell phone reception, firewood, ice, a small store, and a playground with horseshoes are available. Group picnic shelters and a snack bar are available nearby. A store and a café are within one mile. Boat docks and launching facilities are nearby. Some facilities are wheelchair-accessible. Leashed pets are permitted.

Reservations, fees: Reservations are accepted at 509/585-4529. The fee is $9–16 per night. Major credit cards are accepted. Open early April to early October.

Directions: In Kennewick on U.S. 395/Highway 240, drive west toward the Columbia River to the first exit, signed Columbia Park. Take that exit and continue to the campground along the highway. The campground is located adjacent to Columbia Park.

Contact: Columbia Park Campground, 6515 Columbia Park Trail, Kennewick, WA 99336, 509/585-4529, fax 509/586-9022.

24 ARROWHEAD RV PARK

Rating: 5

near the Columbia River
See map pages 206–207

Arrowhead provides a decent layover spot in Pasco. Nearby recreation options include an 18-hole golf course, a full-service marina, and tennis courts.

RV sites, facilities: There are 80 sites with full hookups (30 amps) for RVs of any length, including 33 drive-through sites, and 35 tent sites. Drinking water, sewer hookups, cell phone reception, and picnic tables are provided. Flush toilets, showers, a pay phone, and a coin-operated laundry are available. A store, an ATM, and a café are within walking distance. Small pets are permitted (no pit bulls, Rottweilers, or Doberman pinschers).

Reservations, fees: Reservations are accepted. The fee is $20–30 per night for two people, plus $5 per person and $3 per child per night for more than two people and $1 per pet per night. Open year-round.

Directions: In Pasco on U.S. 395 North, take the Hillsboro Street exit, turn east, and drive a short distance to Commercial Avenue. Turn right (south) and drive .25 mile to the park entrance on the right.

Contact: Arrowhead RV Park, 3120 Commercial Ave., Pasco, WA 99301, 509/545-8206.

25 HOOD PARK

Rating: 6

on Lake Wallula
See map pages 206–207

This 99-acre park is set on Lake Wallula. All the campsites at the main campground are paved; an overflow camping area and boat camping are also available. This park is a more developed, nearby alternative to Columbia Park Campground and provides access for swimming and boating. There are hiking trails throughout the park, along with two fishing ponds. Other recreation options include basketball and horseshoes. McNary Wildlife Refuge is right next door, and Sacajawea State Park is within four miles.

RV sites, facilities: There are 69 sites for RVs up to 60 feet or tents, including 25 pull-through sites with full hookups, and an overflow camping area with 90 sites. Picnic tables and fire grills are provided. Drinking water, restrooms, flush toilets, showers, an RV dump station, a playground, horseshoes, a basketball court, a swimming beach, a covered picnic area, two pay phones, cell phone reception, and an amphitheater are available. Summer programs are offered. A restaurant and convenience store are within two miles. Boat docks

WASHINGTON

and launching facilities are nearby. An ATM is within four miles. Some facilities are wheelchair-accessible. Leashed pets are permitted.

Reservations, fees: Reservations are accepted; phone 877/444-6777 or reserve online at www.reserveusa.com ($9 reservation fee). The fees are $16–18 per night and $8 per night in the overflow area and for boat camping. A senior discount is available. Open early April to September. Park gates are locked from 10 P.M.–6 A.M.

Directions: In Pasco, drive southeast on U.S. 12 for three miles to the junction with Highway 124. Turn left (east) on Highway 124 and drive an extremely short distance to the park entrance on the left.

Contact: U.S. Army Corps of Engineers, 2763 Monument Dr., Burbank, WA 99323, 509/547-7781, fax 509/543-3201.

26 CHARBONNEAU PARK

Rating: 6

on the Snake River
See map pages 206–207
This shorefront camp is the centerpiece of a 244-acre park that is set along the Snake River just above Ice Harbor Dam. It is a good spot for fishing, boating, swimming, and water-skiing. An overflow camping area provides an insurance policy if the numbered sites are full.

RV sites, facilities: There are 54 sites for RVs up to 60 feet or tents, including 18 pull-through sites with full hookups (30 amps), and an overflow camping area. Picnic tables and fire grills are provided. Flush toilets, showers, tent pads, an RV dump station, a pay phone, and a playground with a volleyball net are available. A marina with boat docks, launching facilities, a marine dump station, a swimming beach, a store, ice, and group shelters with electricity are nearby. An ATM and groceries are available within 10 miles. Some facilities are wheelchair-accessible. Leashed pets are permitted.

Reservations, fees: Reservations are accepted; phone 877/444-6777 or reserve online at www.reserveusa.com ($9 reservation fee). The fee is $16–20 per night. Overflow camping is $8 per night. A senior discount is available. Open April to October with full facilities; there are lim-

ited facilities and no fee the rest of the year. Park gates are locked from 10 P.M.–6 A.M.

Directions: In Pasco, drive southeast on U.S. 12 for five miles to Highway 124. Turn east and drive eight miles to Sun Harbor Road. Turn north and drive two miles to the park.

Contact: U.S. Army Corps of Engineers, 2763 Monument Dr., Burbank, WA 99323, 509/547-7781, fax 509/543-3201.

27 FISHHOOK PARK

Rating: 6

on the Snake River
See map pages 206–207
If you're driving along Highway 124 and you need a spot for the night, make the turn on Fishhook Park Road and check out this wooded camp along the Snake River. It is a nice spot within a 46-acre park set on Lake Sacajawea. The park provides some lawn area, along with places to swim, fish, and water-ski. A one-mile walk along railroad tracks will take you to a fishing pond. This park is popular on summer weekends.

RV sites, facilities: There are 41 sites with partial hookups (30 amps) for RVs up to 45 feet or tents, including eight drive-through sites, and 20 tent sites. Picnic tables and fire grills are provided. Drinking water, flush toilets, showers, an RV dump station, cell phone reception, and a playground are available. Boat docks, launching facilities, a swimming beach, and group shelters with electricity are nearby. An ATM, pay phone, and groceries are available within two miles. Some facilities are wheelchair-accessible. Leashed pets are permitted. Park gates are locked from 10 P.M. to 6 A.M.

Reservations, fees: Reservations are accepted; phone 877/444-6777 or reserve online at www.reserveusa.com ($9 reservation fee). The fee is $12–20 per night. A senior discount is available. Open April to September.

Directions: In Pasco, drive southeast on U.S. 12 for five miles to Highway 124. Turn east and drive 18 miles to Fishhook Park Road. Turn left on Fishhook Park Road and drive four miles to the park.

Contact: U.S. Army Corps of Engineers, 2763 Monument Dr., Burbank, WA 99323, 509/547-7781, fax 509/543-3201.

28 WINDUST

Rating: 6

on Lake Sacajawea
See map pages 206–207

With no other campgrounds within a 20-mile radius, Windust is the only game in town. The camp is located along the shore of Lake Sacajawea near the Lower Monumental Dam on the Snake River. The park covers 54 acres. Swimming and fishing are popular.

RV sites, facilities: Open camping areas at both ends of the park provide space for 24 RVs or tents. Picnic tables and fire grills are provided. Vault toilets and garbage bins are available year-round. Flush toilets are available from April to September. Drinking water, a playground and horseshoe pit, a swimming beach, and covered sun shelters are available nearby. Boat docks and launching facilities are nearby. Some facilities are wheelchair-accessible. Leashed pets are permitted.

Reservations, fees: Reservations are accepted; phone 877/444-6777 or reserve online at www.reserveusa.com ($9 reservation fee). The fee is $10 per night. A senior discount is available. Open year-round, with limited facilities and no fee from October to March.

Directions: From Pasco, drive east on U.S. 12 for four miles to Pasco/Kahlotus Highway. Turn east and drive 28 miles to Burr Canyon Road. Turn right on Burr Canyon Road and drive 5.2 miles to the park (from the north, Burr Canyon Road becomes Highway 263).

Contact: U.S. Army Corps of Engineers, 2763 Monument Dr., Burbank, WA 99323, 509/547-7781, fax 509/543-3201.

29 PALOUSE FALLS STATE PARK

Rating: 10

on the Snake and Palouse Rivers
See map pages 206–207

This remote state park is well worth the trip. Spectacular 198-foot Palouse Falls is a sight not to miss. A quarter-mile wheelchair-accessible trail leads to a waterfall overlook. The park is set upstream of the confluence of the Snake and Palouse Rivers, and it does not receive heavy use, even in summer. The park covers 1,282 acres and features a waterfall observation shelter, shaded picnic facilities, historical displays, and an abundance of wildlife.

RV sites, facilities: There are 10 primitive campsites for self-contained RVs up to 40 feet or tents. Picnic tables and fire grills are provided. Vault toilets, and a picnic area are available. Some facilities are wheelchair-accessible. Leashed pets are permitted.

Reservations, fees: Reservations are not accepted. The fee is $8 per night, plus $10 per additional vehicle per night. A senior discount is available. Open April to late September, weather permitting.

Directions: From Starbuck, drive northwest on Highway 261 for 16.4 miles (crossing the river) to the park entrance and Palouse Falls Road. Turn right and drive two miles to the park.

Contact: Palouse Falls State Park, 509/646-3252, fax 509/646-3297; state park information, 360/902-8844.

30 LYON'S FERRY PARK

Rating: 8

on the Snake River
See map pages 206–207

This park, covering 1,282 acres, is located at the confluence of the Snake and Palouse Rivers. Although not a high-destination park, it is loaded with activities. A three-quarter-mile trail leads to a lookout point with interpretive plaques. In addition, another short hike from camp can take you to the Marmes Rock Shelter, where the Marmes Man—the oldest human remains ever found in the Western Hemisphere—was unearthed in 1968. Many other recreation options include boating, fishing, swimming, and water-skiing. Note that high winds can occur suddenly and surprise many boaters. Another feature is the nearby terrain. The park is part of hundreds of square miles of "peeled ground," which span west from Spokane to the Cascades and south to the Snake River and which some geologists call "the strangest landscape this side of Mars." A good side trip is a visit to beautiful 198-foot Palouse Falls, located 10 miles north. In 2003 the park reopened under Northwest Land Management.

RV sites, facilities: There are 49 sites, including 12 pull-through sites for RVs up to 45 feet or tents. Picnic tables and fire grills are provided. Restrooms, flush toilets, cell phone reception, coin-operated showers, and an RV dump station are available. A bathhouse, a sheltered picnic area, a snack bar, a boat dock, and a boat launch and moorage are available nearby. An ATM and pay phone are within seven miles. Some facilities are wheelchair-accessible. Leashed pets are permitted.

Reservations, fees: Reservations are not accepted. The fee is $14 per night, plus $5 per additional vehicle per night. The boat launch fee is $5, and there is a $5 day-use fee. A senior discount is available. Open April to September, weather permitting.

Directions: From Starbuck, drive northwest on Highway 261 for 14.2 miles (crossing the river) to the park entrance (just north of the river on the right). Turn right and drive to the park.

Contact: Lyon's Ferry Park, 509/646-3252, fax 509/646-3297.

31 LEWIS AND CLARK TRAIL STATE PARK

Rating: 8

on the Lewis and Clark Trail

See map pages 206–207

Fishing for rainbow trout and brown trout can be excellent here. The park is set on 37 acres with frontage along the Touchet River. The landscape is an unusual mixture of old-growth forest and riparian habitat, featuring long-leafed Ponderosa pine and cottonwood amid the surrounding arid prairie grasslands. An interpretive display explains much of it, as well as the history of the area. A Saturday evening living-history program depicts the story of Lewis and Clark and the site's history here on the original Lewis and Clark Trail. In winter, cross-country skiing and snowshoeing are good here. Note: If it's getting late and you need to stop, consider this camp because it's the only one within 36 miles.

RV sites, facilities: There are 24 sites for self-contained RVs up to 28 feet or tents, four primitive tent sites, and two large group camps. Picnic tables and fire grills are provided. Restrooms,

flush toilets, cell phone reception, showers, firewood, and an RV dump station are available. Two fire circles, an amphitheater, a picnic area, badminton, a baseball field, and a volleyball court are available nearby. A store, an ATM, a café, and ice are available within five miles. Leashed pets are permitted.

Reservations, fees: Reservations are not accepted for individual sites. For group camp reservations, phone 509/337-6457. The fee is $8–15 per night, plus $10 per additional vehicle per night. Open year-round, with limited winter facilities.

Directions: From Walla Walla, drive east on U.S. 12 for 22 miles to Waitsburg. Bear right on U.S. 12 and drive east for 4.5 miles to the park entrance on the left.

Contact: Lewis and Clark Trail State Park, 36149 Highway 12, Dayton, WA 99328, tel./fax 509/337-6457; state park information, 360/902-8844.

32 CENTRAL FERRY PARK

Rating: 8

on the Snake River

See map pages 206–207

This campground is the only one within a 20-mile radius, yet it's a great spot to hunker down and enjoy the world. This 185-acre park is set on 10,000-acre Lake Bryan, a reservoir situated on the Snake River and created by Little Goose Dam. With summer daytime temperatures in the 90s and even 100s occasionally, boating is popular at the desert lake. Despite the lake, the surrounding terrain is dry, courtesy of just eight inches of average rainfall per year, as well as basaltic lava flows, according to geologic evidence. The park is named after a ferry that once operated in this area. A beach, boating, waterskiing, swimming, and fishing for bass and catfish are all options here. Navigational locks are on the lake. In 2003 the park reopened under Northwest Land Management.

RV sites, facilities: There are 60 sites with full hookups (30 amps) for RVs up to 45 feet, eight primitive tent sites, and one group camp accommodating up to 100 people. Picnic tables and fire grills are provided. Restrooms, flush toilets, coin-operated showers, cell phone reception, an RV dump station, a group fire ring, a day-use picnic area with a covered kitchen shelter, a swimming beach and bathhouse, beachside shade structures, volleyball courts, and three horseshoe pit areas are available. A pay phone is nearby. Boat docks, launching facilities, and a fishing pier are within the park. A store and a restaurant are within five miles. Some facilities are wheelchair-accessible. Leashed pets are permitted.

Reservations, fees: Reservations not accepted. The fee is $14–21 per night, plus $5 per additional vehicle per night. Major credit cards are accepted. Open mid-March to mid-November.

Directions: From Spokane, drive south on U.S. 195 for 59 miles to Highway 26. Turn west on Highway 26 and drive 17 miles southwest to the town of Dusty and Highway 127. Turn south on Highway 127 and drive 17 miles to the park entrance on the right (set on the north shore of the Snake River).

Contact: Central Ferry Park, 10152 Rte. 127, Pomeroy, WA 99347, 509/549-3551 or 509/549-3645.

33 PALOUSE EMPIRE FAIRGROUNDS AND HORSE CAMP

🏃 🚵 🏠 ♿ 🚐 ⛰️

Rating: 6

west of Colfax, Whitman County
See map pages 206–207
This camp consists primarily of a large lawn area with shade trees and is set just off the road. The highway noise, surprisingly, is relatively limited. All sites are on grass. The park covers 47 acres, with paved trails available around the adjacent fairgrounds. This area is agricultural, with rolling hills, and it is considered the "Lentil Capital of the World." With wash racks, corrals, arenas, and water troughs, the camp encourages horse campers to stay here. It fills up for the Palouse Empire Fair in mid-September. They turn back the clock every Labor Day weekend with the annual "Threshing Bee," featuring demonstrations of historical farming practices dating back to the early 1900s, including the use of draft horses.

RV sites, facilities: There are 60 sites with partial hookups (30 amps) for RVs of any length or tents. Large groups can be accommodated. Picnic tables are provided. Restrooms, drinking water, flush toilets, showers, and an RV dump

station are available. Restaurants, gas, an ATM, a pay phone, and supplies are available 4.5 miles away in Colfax. Some facilities are wheelchair-accessible. Leashed pets are permitted.

Reservations, fees: Reservations are accepted; phone 509/397-6263. The fee is $15 per night; horse stalls are $10 per night. Open year-round with limited winter facilities.

Directions: From Colfax and Highway 26, drive west on Highway 26 for 4.5 miles to the fairgrounds on the right.

Contact: Palouse Empire Fairgrounds and Horse Camp, Whitman County, North 310 Main, Colfax, WA 99111, 509/397-6238 or 509/397-3753, website: www.palouseempirefair.org.

34 BOYER PARK AND MARINA

🏃 🚵 🏊 🎣 ⛵ 🐕 ♿ 🚐 ⛰️

Rating: 7

on Lake Bryan on the Snake River
See map pages 206–207
This 99-acre park on the north shore of Lake Bryan is located two miles from the Lower Granite Dam. It features 3.5 miles of trails for hiking and biking, and the lake is popular for water-skiing and fishing for sturgeon, steelhead, and salmon. The camp features shade trees; all campsites are paved and bordered by a grassy day-use area. The landscape is flat and open, and it gets hot here in summer. The camp is well above the water level, typically about 100 feet above the lakeshore. The camp commonly fills on summer weekends.

RV sites, facilities: There are 28 sites, including 12 with full hookups (30, 50 amps) and 16 with partial hookups (no sewer), for RVs up to 40 feet or tents, four motel rooms, and one three-bedroom apartment. Picnic tables and fire grills are provided. Restrooms, drinking water, flush toilets, showers, and an RV dump station are available. A coin-operated laundry, covered shelters, a swimming area, a snack bar, a store, ice, gas, modem access, and pay phones are available. A restaurant, a marina, boat docks, a boat launch, and a marine dump station are also available. Some facilities are wheelchair-accessible. Leashed pets are permitted.

Reservations, fees: Reserve at 509/397-3208. The fee is $10–22 per night, plus $2 per person for more than four people, $6 per vehicle for more than two vehicles, and $5 per tent for more than two tents. A senior discount is available. Major credit cards are accepted. Open year-round, with limited winter facilities.

Directions: From U.S. 195 at Colfax, turn southwest on Almota Road and drive 17 miles to the park and campground.

Contact: Port of Whitman County, Boyer Park and Marina, Almota Inn, 1753 Granite Rd., Colfax, WA 99111, 509/397-3208, fax 509/397-3181.

35 WAWAWAI COUNTY PARK

Rating: 7

on Lower Granite Lake, Whitman County
See map pages 206–207

This park covers just 49 acres but is set near the inlet to Lower Granite Lake, about a quarter mile from the lake. The camp itself is situated on a hillside, and all sites are paved. Some sites have views of a bay, but not the entire lake. Tree cover is a plus. So is a half-mile loop trail that leads to a bird-viewing platform. A diverse mix of wildlife and geology makes interpretive hikes with naturalists often popular. One strange note: An underground house built in 1980 has been converted to a ranger's residence. This camp often fills on summer weekends. Note: No campfires are allowed June to October.

RV sites, facilities: There are nine sites for self-contained RVs up to 24 feet or tents. Picnic tables and fire grills are provided. Drinking water and vault toilets are available. A playground with a volleyball net and a group covered shelter is nearby. Some facilities are wheelchair-accessible. Leashed pets are permitted.

Reservations, fees: Reservations are not accepted. The fee is $15 per night, plus $5 per additional vehicle. Open year-round.

Directions: From Colfax, drive south on U.S. 195 for 16 miles to Wawawai-Pullman Road (located just west of Pullman). Turn right (west) and drive about 10 miles to Wawawai Road. Turn right on Wawawai Road (signed) and drive to the park on Lower Granite Lake.

Contact: Wawawai County Park, Whitman County, North 310 Main, Colfax, WA 99111, 509/397-6238, website: www.whitmancounty.org.

36 CHIEF TIMOTHY PARK

Rating: 8

on the Snake River
See map pages 206–207

This unusual state park is set on a bridged island in the Snake River and is accessible by car. The park covers 282 acres with two miles of shoreline. It features a desert landscape, and the park is on an island composed of glacial tills. Recreation options include 2.5 miles of hiking trails, a beach area, and water sports, including fishing, swimming, boating, water-skiing, and sailing, plus docks for boating campers. Call the Clarkston Chamber of Commerce at 509/758-7712 for details. This park reopened in 2003 under Northwest Land Management.

RV sites, facilities: There are 66 sites, including 25 with full hookups (20, 30 amps) and eight with partial hookups (water and electricity), for RVs up to 60 feet or tents, 17 self-contained RV sites, and 16 tent sites. Picnic tables and fire grills are provided. Restrooms, flush toilets, showers, cell phone reception, firewood, an RV dump station, a picnic area, and a playground with volleyball courts and horseshoes are available. Boat docks and launching facilities are nearby. Groceries, an ATM, and a pay phone are available within seven miles. Some facilities are wheelchair-accessible. Leashed pets are permitted.

Reservations, fees: Reservations are not accepted. The fee is $19–21 per night, plus $5 per additional vehicle per night and a $5 day-use fee. A senior discount is available. Major credit cards are accepted. Open early May to late November.

Directions: From Clarkston on the Washington/Idaho border, drive west on U.S. 12 for seven miles to the signed park entrance road on the right. Turn north and drive one mile to the park, which is on a bridged island in the Snake River.

Contact: Chief Timothy Park, 13766 Hwy. 12, Clarkston, WA 99403, 509/758-9580.

WASHINGTON

37 TUCANNON

Rating: 8

in Umatilla National Forest
See map pages 206–207
For people willing to rough it, this backcountry camp in Umatilla National Forest is the place, with plenty of hiking, fishing, and hunting, all in a rugged setting. The camp is set along the Tucannon River, which offers a myriad of recreation options for vacationers. It is popular from early spring (best time for fishing) through fall (when it makes a good hunting camp). In summer, several nearby ponds are stocked with trout, making it a good family destination. There is some tree cover. The elevation is 2,600 feet.

RV sites, facilities: There are 13 sites for RVs up to 21 feet or tents. Picnic tables and fire grills are provided. Vault toilets are available, but there is no drinking water. Garbage must be packed out. Two covered shelters are available nearby. A pay phone is within 8.5 miles. Leashed pets are permitted.

Reservations, fees: Reservations are not accepted. The fee is $5 per night. Open year-round, weather permitting.

Directions: From Clarkston, drive west on U.S. 12 for 37 miles to Pomeroy. Continue west for five miles to Tatman Mountain Road (signed for Camp Wooten). Turn left (south) and drive 19 miles (becomes Forest Road 47). Once inside the national forest boundary, continue southwest on Forest Road 47 for four miles to the campground on the left.

Contact: Umatilla National Forest, Pomeroy Ranger District, 71 West Main St., Pomeroy, WA 99347, 509/843-1891, fax 509/843-4621.

38 TEAL SPRING

Rating: 8

in Umatilla National Forest
See map pages 206–207
The views of the Tucannon drainage and the Wenaha-Tucannon Wilderness are astonishing from the nearby lookout. Teal Spring Camp is set at 5,600 feet elevation and is one of several small, primitive camps in the area. Trails in the immediate area provide a variety of good day-hiking options. A U.S. Forest Service map details the backcountry roads, trails, and streams. Hunting is popular in the fall.

RV sites, facilities: There are five sites for RVs up to 26 feet or tents. Vault toilets and cell phone reception are available, but there is no drinking water. Picnic tables and fire grills are provided. Garbage must be packed out. Some facilities are wheelchair-accessible. Leashed pets are permitted.

Reservations, fees: Reservations are not accepted. There is no fee for camping. Open June to mid-November, weather permitting.

Directions: From Clarkston, drive west on U.S. 12 for 37 miles to Pomeroy and Highway 128. Turn south and drive 25 miles to Forest Road 42 (to the Clearwater Lookout Tower). Turn left and continue on Forest Road 42; drive one mile to the campground entrance road. Turn right and drive 200 yards to the campground.

Contact: Umatilla National Forest, Pomeroy Ranger District, 71 West Main St., Pomeroy, WA 99347, 509/843-1891, fax 509/843-4621.

39 FIELDS SPRING STATE PARK

Rating: 8

near Puffer Butte
See map pages 206–207
This 792-acre state park is located in the Blue Mountains and is set in a forested landscape atop Puffer Butte, offering a spectacular view of three states and the Grande Ronde River. A hiking trail leads up to Puffer Butte at 4,500 feet elevation, providing a panoramic view of the Snake River Canyon, the Wallowa Mountains, and Idaho, Oregon, and Washington. This park is noted for its variety of bird life and wildflowers. There are seven miles of mountain-biking trails, along with three miles of hiking trails. In winter, recreation opportunities include cross-country skiing, snowmobiling, snowshoeing, and general snow play. Basalt dominates the landscape. Not many people know about this spot, yet it's a good one, tucked away in the southeast corner of the state. It also has a designated environmental learning center. Two day-use areas with boat launches, managed by the Department of Fish and Game,

are within about 25 miles of the park. One is the Snake River Access, 22.5 miles south of Asotin on Snake River Road; the other is the Grande Ronde River Access, 24 miles south of Asotin on the same road.

RV sites, facilities: There are 20 sites for self-contained RVs up to 30 feet or tents, two primitive tent sites, and two tepees. Picnic tables and fire grills are provided. Restrooms, drinking water, cell phone reception, flush toilets, an RV dump station, two picnic shelters with electricity, two sheltered fire circles, a playground with horseshoes, a softball field, and volleyball courts are available. Showers and firewood are available for a fee. A store, a pay phone, a restaurant, and ice are available within four miles. Some facilities are wheelchair-accessible. Leashed pets are permitted.

Reservations, fees: Reservations are not accepted. The fee is $10–16 per night, plus $10 per additional vehicle per night. A senior discount is available. Open year-round, with limited winter facilities.

Directions: From Clarkston, turn south on Highway 129 and drive 28.5 miles (just south of Rattlesnake Pass) to the park entrance on the left (east) side of the road.

Contact: Fields Spring State Park, P.O. Box 86, Anatone, WA 99401, tel./fax 509/256-3332; state park information, 360/902-8844.

40 BROOKS MEMORIAL STATE PARK

Rating: 7

near the Goldendale Observatory
See map pages 206–207

This 700-acre park is near the barren hills of the South Yakima Valley and in the lodgepole pine forests of the Simcoe Mountains. It is set at an elevation of nearly 3,000 feet. Highlights include nine miles of hiking trails, a 1.5-mile-long nature trail that runs along the Little Klickitat River, and occasionally excellent fishing for trout. You can extend your trip into the mountains, where you'll find open meadows with a panoramic view of Mount Hood. The environmental learning center provides nature talks, and a lodge and cabins are available for groups. Other activities near the park include stargazing at the Goldendale Observatory, visiting the Maryhill Museum, viewing the replica of Stonehenge on State Route 14, and driving the historic Columbia Highway in nearby Oregon. The Yakama Indian Nation is located two miles north of the park.

RV sites, facilities: There are 22 developed sites for small self-contained RVs or tents, 23 sites with partial hookups (20 amps) for RVs up to 50 feet, and a group camp for up to 50 people. There is also an environmental learning center with seven cabins and one lodge available for groups. Picnic tables and fire grills are provided. Restrooms, flush toilets, coin-operated showers, an RV dump station, and a playground are available. A picnic area with covered shelters and electricity and a ball field are nearby. A store is also nearby. Leashed pets are permitted.

Reservations, fees: Reservations are accepted for group sites only; call 800/360-4240. The fee is $15–21 per night, plus $10 per additional vehicle per night. Group sites are $2 per person per night with a minimum of 20 people and a maximum of 50. A senior discount is available. Open year-round, with limited winter facilities.

Directions: From Toppenish, drive south on U.S. 97 for 40 miles to the park on the right (well signed).

Contact: Brooks Memorial State Park, 509/773-4611, fax 509/773-6428; state park information, 360/902-8844.

41 CROW BUTTE PARK

Rating: 8

on the Columbia River
See map pages 206–207

How would you like to be stranded on a romantic island? Well, this park offers that possibility. This park is set on an island in the Columbia River and is the only campground in a 25-mile radius. Sometimes referred to as "The Maui of the Columbia," the park covers 1,312 acres and has several miles of shoreline. It is set on the Lewis and Clark Trail, with the camp situated in a partially protected bay. The highlight of 3.5 miles of hiking trails is a mile-long path that leads to the top of a butte, where you can see Mount Hood, Mount Adams, and the Columbia River Valley. Water-skiing, sailboarding, fishing, swimming, and hiking are among the possibilities here. One downer: Keep an eye out for rattlesnakes, which are occasionally spotted. The Umatilla National Wildlife Refuge is adjacent to the park and allows fishing and hunting in specified areas. This is no longer a state park; it has been taken over by a nonprofit community organization.

RV sites, facilities: There are 50 sites with full hookups (30 amps) for RVs up to 60 feet or tents, including 24 pull-through sites, one primitive tent sites, and one group camp. Fire grills and picnic tables are provided. Restrooms, flush toilets, coin-operated showers, a pay phone, cell phone reception, a sheltered picnic area, a swimming beach, a snack bar, and an RV dump station are available. A store is open on summer weekends. Boat-launching and moorage facilities are nearby. Some facilities are wheelchair-accessible. Leashed pets are permitted.

Reservations, fees: Reserve at 509/875-2644. The fees are $15–20 per night for RV or tent sites, plus $5 per additional vehicle per night. The group site is $50 per night. Moorage fees are $5 per night. Open year-round, with limited winter facilities.

Directions: From the junction of I-82/U.S. 395 and Highway 20 at Plymouth, just north of the Columbia River, turn west on Highway 14. Drive to Paterson and continue west for 13 miles to the park entrance road at Milepost 155 on the right. Turn right and drive one mile (across the bridge) to the park on the island.

Contact: Crow Butte Assocciation, 509/875-2644, website: www.crowbutte.com.

42 PLYMOUTH PARK

Rating: 7

on Lake Umatilla, Benton County
See map pages 206–207

Plymouth Park is a family and RV-style campground set on Lake Umatilla on the Columbia River. The 112-acre park is not located on the shore of the lake, rather about a quarter-mile drive from the water. The camp has tree cover, which is a nice plus, and it fills up on most summer weekends. Each campsite has a tent pad.

RV sites, facilities: There are 32 sites, including 29 pull-through sites and 16 with partial hookups (30, 50 amps), for RVs up to 40 feet or tents. Picnic tables and fire grills are provided. Restrooms, drinking water, flush toilets, showers, an RV dump station, cell phone reception, and a coin-operated laundry are available. A boat dock, boat launch, swimming areas, and covered shelters are also available. A tavern is within two miles. An ATM, a pay phone, and groceries are available within five miles. Some facilities are wheelchair-accessible. Leashed pets are permitted.

Reservations, fees: Reserve at 877/444-6777 or online at www.reserveusa.com ($9 reservation fee). The fee is $16–18 per night. A senior discount is available. Major credit cards are accepted. Open early April to October.

Directions: From Richland and I-82, drive south on I-82 for about 30 miles to Highway 14. Turn west on Highway 14 and drive two miles to the Plymouth exit. Take that exit and drive to Christy Road; continue for 200 yards to the park entrance on the left.

Contact: U.S. Army Corps of Engineers, Portland District, 509/783-1270 (campground) or 541/506-7819.

WASHINGTON

Oregon

OREGON REGIONS

WASHINGTON

IDAHO

NEVADA

CALIFORNIA

PACIFIC OCEAN

N E / W S (compass)

30 mi
30 km
0

Chapter 7
THE OREGON COAST
pages 230–231

Chapter 8
PORTLAND AND THE WILLAMETTE VALLEY
pages 278–279

Chapter 9
THE COLUMBIA RIVER GORGE AND MOUNT HOOD
pages 296–297

Chapter 10
NORTHEASTERN OREGON
pages 322–323

Chapter 11
THE SOUTHERN CASCADES
pages 346–347

Chapter 12
SOUTHEASTERN OREGON
pages 408–409

Oregon

Chapter 7
The Oregon Coast

THE OREGON COAST

Mt. St. Helena National Volcanic Monument

Gifford Pinchot National Forest

see Washington page 14

WASHINGTON

OREGON

Columbia River

Clatsop State Forest

Nehalem River

Tillamook State Forest

PORTLAND

Mt. Hood National Forest

see The Columbia River Gorge and Mount Hood pages 296–297

see Portland and the Willamette Valley pages 278–279

Salem

Willamette River

Willamette National Forest

Green Peter Res.

Fern Ridge Res.

Siuslaw N.F.

Siuslaw National Forest

Astoria

Tillamook

Tillamook Bay

Cape Falcon

Newport

Yaquina Bay

Alsea Bay

1-3 4 5-6 7 8 9 10 11 12 13 14 15 16 17 18 19 20 21-22 23 24-25 26 27-29 30 31 32-35 36-38 39 40 41 42-43 44

N E S W

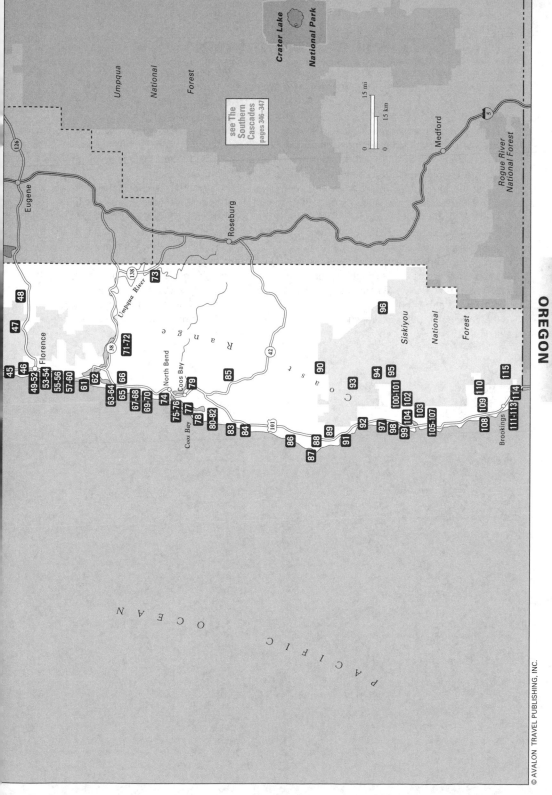

OREGON

see The
Southern
Cascades
pages 346-347

Crater Lake
National Park

Umpqua *National* *Forest*

Eugene

Roseburg

Medford

Rogue River
National Forest

Siskiyou *National* *Forest*

Florence

Umpqua River

North Bend

Coos Bay

Coos Bay

C o a s t *R a n g e*

Brookings

P A C I F I C   O C E A N

© AVALON TRAVEL PUBLISHING, INC.

Chapter 7—The Oregon Coast

If you want to treat yourself to vacation memories you'll treasure forever, take a drive (and then stop overnight) along U.S. 101 on the Oregon Coast. Here you'll see some of the most dramatic coastal frontage in North America: tidewater rock gardens, cliff-top views that seem to stretch to forever, vast sand dunes, protected bays, beautiful streams with giant salmon and steelhead (in fall and winter), and three major national forests. I prefer cruising north to south, in the right lane close to the coastline and with the wind behind me; it often seems I'm on the edge of never-never land.

On the way, you'll cross the Columbia River on the border of Oregon and Washington. The river is so wide here that it looks like an inland sea. I find that the best way to appreciate this massive waterway is to get off the main highway and explore the many coastal streams by two-lane road. There are numerous routes, from tiny Highway 15 on the Little Nestucca River to well-known Highway 38 along the beautiful Umpqua.

The most spectacular region on the coast may be the Oregon Dunes National Recreation Area, which spans roughly from Coos Bay north past Florence to near the mouth of the Siuslaw River. Whenever I visit, I feel like I'm instantly transported to another universe. I have a photo from the dunes in my office. While I'm writing, I often look at the image of a lone raptor soaring past a pyramid of sand—it's my window to this wonderful otherworld.

1 FORT STEVENS STATE PARK

Rating: 8

at the mouth of the Columbia River
See map pages 230–231

This classic spot is at the northern tip of Oregon, right where the Columbia River enters the Pacific Ocean. A historic military area and shipwreck site, freshwater lake, swimming, beachcombing, trails, and wildlife viewing make Fort Stevens a uniquely diversified park. Covering 3,700 acres, the park has nine miles of bike trails and six miles of hiking trails, providing exploration through spruce and hemlock forests, wetlands, dunes, and shore pines. The trailhead for the Oregon Coast Trail is here as well. History buffs will find a museum, tours of the fort and artillery batteries, and the remains of the *Peter Iredale* shipwreck.

RV sites, facilities: There are 170 sites with full hookups (20, 30, 50 amps) and 303 sites with partial hookups for RVs up to 50 feet, 42 tent sites, and a special camping area for hikers and bicyclists; 15 yurts and four group tent areas are also available. Picnic tables and fire grills are provided. Drinking water, flush toilets, a pay phone, cell phone reception, an RV dump station, a transfer and recycling station, showers, firewood, and a playground are available. An ATM, coin-operated laundry, and groceries are available within three miles. Boat docks and launching facilities are nearby. Some facilities are wheelchair-accessible. Leashed pets are permitted.

Reservations, fees: Reserve at 800/452-5687 or online at www.OregonStateParks.org ($7 reservation fee). The fees are $17–21 per night and $4 for hikers/bikers, plus $7 per night per additional vehicle. Group sites are $65 per night; yurts are $29 per night. Major credit cards are accepted. Open year-round.

Directions: From Portland, turn west on U.S. 26 and drive 73 miles to the junction with U.S. 101. Turn right (north) on U.S. 101 and drive about 15 miles (about .25 mile past the Camp Rilea Army Base). Turn west on Highway 104 at the sign for Fort Stevens State Park and drive about one mile to Ocean View Cemetery Road. Turn left and drive about 2.5 miles (Ocean View Cemetery Road becomes Ridge Road) to the park entrance on the left.

Contact: Fort Stevens State Park, 100 Peter Iredale Rd., Hammond, OR 97121, 503/861-1671 or 800/551-6949, fax 503/861-1672.

2 ASTORIA/WARRENTON SEASIDE KOA

Rating: 3

near Fort Stevens State Park
See map pages 230–231

This campground is nestled in a wooded area adjacent to Fort Stevens State Park, and tours of that historical military site can be arranged. This camp provides an excellent alternative if the state park campground is full. A host of activities are available in the immediate area, including bicycling, hiking, deep-sea fishing, and beachcombing. Horse stables are within 10 miles. See the description of Fort Stevens State Park above for further details about the area.

RV sites, facilities: There are 311 sites, 103 with full hookups (30, 50 amps) and 82 with partial hookups for RVs up to 80 feet or tents, 14 tent sites, and 54 one- and two-bedroom cabins. Cable TV, restrooms, showers, security, a pay phone, a laundry room, limited groceries, ice, an ATM, modem access, cell phone reception, snacks, RV supplies, propane, and a barbecue are available. Recreational facilities include a playground, a game room, a recreation field, horseshoes, a spa, and a heated swimming pool. Some facilities are wheelchair-accessible. Leashed pets are permitted.

Reservations, fees: Reserve at 800/562-8506. The fee is $23–66 per night, plus $3.50–4.50 per person for more than two people. Cabins are $40–66 per night for two people. Major credit cards are accepted. Open year-round.

Directions: From Portland, turn west on U.S. 26 and drive 73 miles to the junction with U.S. 101. Turn right (north) on U.S. 101 and drive about 15 miles (about .25 mile past the Camp Rilea Army Base). Turn west on Perkins Road/Highway 104 at the sign for Fort Stevens State Park and drive about one mile to Ocean View Cemetery Road. Turn left and drive about 2.5 miles (Ocean View Cemetery Road becomes Ridge Road) to the campground directly across from the state park.

OREGON

Contact: Astoria/Warrenton Seaside KOA, 1100 NW Ridge Rd., Hammond, OR 97121, 503/861-2606, fax 503/861-3209, website: www.koa.com.

3 KAMPERS WEST CAMPGROUND

Rating: 7

near Fort Stevens State Park
See map pages 230–231
Just four miles from Fort Stevens State Park, this privately run camp offers full RV services. Nearby recreation possibilities include an 18-hole golf course, hiking trails, marked bike trails, and a riding stable.

RV sites, facilities: There are 180 sites for RVs of any length, most with full hookups (30, 50 amps) and some with partial hookups (30 amps), a small area for tents only, and three park-model cabins. Picnic tables are provided. Flush toilets, propane, drinking water, pay phones, cell phone reception, modem access, an RV dump station, showers, some fire rings, laundry facilities, and ice are available. A store, an ATM, groceries, and a café are within 2.5 miles. Leashed pets are permitted.

Reservations, fees: Reservations are accepted. The fee is $20–27.50 per night. Major credit cards are accepted. Open year-round.

Directions: From Portland, turn west on U.S. 30 and drive 105 miles north and west to Astoria and the junction of U.S. 101. Turn south and drive 6.5 miles to the Warrenton/Hammond Junction. Turn west on Warrenton and drive 1.5 miles to the campground on the right.

Contact: Kampers West Campground, 1140 N.W. Warrenton Dr., Warrenton, OR 97146, 503/861-1814, fax 503/861-3620, website: www .kamperswest.com.

4 VENICE RV PARK

Rating: 3

on the Neawanna River
See map pages 230–231
This park along the Necanium and Neawanna Rivers is less than a mile from the beach. A great bonus: Crab pot rentals are available. The seaside offers beautiful ocean beaches for fishing

and surfing, plus moped and bike rentals, shops, and a theater. The city provides swings and volleyball nets on the beach. Several 18-hole golf courses are nearby.

RV sites, facilities: There are 31 sites, including 13 drive-through with full hookups (30 amps), for RVs of any length and four tent sites. Drinking water, cable TV, barbecue grills, and picnic tables are provided. Flush toilets, showers, a laundry room, a riverside fire pit, cell phone reception, a pay phone, modem access, and ice are available. A store and a café are within one mile. Leashed pets are permitted.

Reservations, fees: Reservations are preferred. The fees are $25 per night for RV sites and $12 per night for tent sites, plus $2 per person for more than two people, $2 per additional vehicle, and one-time $2 pet charge. Major credit cards are accepted. Open year-round.

Directions: From Portland on I-5, turn west on U.S. 26 and drive 73 miles to the junction with U.S. 101. Turn north on U.S. 101 and drive four miles to Seaside. Continue to the north end of town and turn left (west) on 24th Avenue. The campground is on the corner at 1032 24th Avenue.

Contact: Venice RV Park, 1032 24th Ave., Seaside, OR 97138, 503/738-8851.

5 SEA RANCH RV PARK

Rating: 9

near the Pacific Ocean
See map pages 230–231
This resort is in a wooded area with nearby access to the beach. Activities at the camp include stream fishing, horseback riding, and swimming at the seashore. A golf course is six miles away, and the historic Lewis and Clark Trail is nearby. Elk hunters camp here in season. The beach and the town of Cannon Beach are within walking distance of the resort.

RV sites, facilities: There are 80 sites, many with full hookups (20, 30 amps), for RVs up to 40 feet or tents and three cabins with fireplace and porch that sleep four each. Restrooms, drinking water, showers, an RV dump station, cell phone reception, and a pay phone are available. An ATM and groceries are available within a half mile. Leashed pets are permitted.

OREGON

Reservations, fees: Reservations are recommended. The fee is $20–25 per night, plus $2 per person for more than two people, $3 per additional vehicle, and $2 per pet per night. Cabins are $55–65 per night. Major credit cards are accepted. Open year-round.

Directions: From Portland on I-5, turn west on U.S. 26 and drive 73 miles to the junction with U.S. 101. Turn south on U.S. 101 and drive three miles to the Cannon Beach exit. The park is south .3 mile on the left.

Contact: Sea Ranch RV Park, P.O. Box 214, 415 Fir St., Cannon Beach, OR 97110, 503/436-2815, website: www.cannon-beach.net/searanch.

6 RV RESORT AT CANNON BEACH

Rating: 9

near Ecola State Park
See map pages 230–231
This private resort is located about seven blocks from one of the nicest beaches in the region and about two miles from Ecola State Park. From the town of Cannon Beach, you can walk for miles in either direction. Nearby recreational facilities include marked bike trails, a riding stable, and tennis courts. The city shuttle service stops here.

RV sites, facilities: There are 100 sites, many with full hookups (30, 50 amps), for RVs of any length; 11 are drive-through sites. Drinking water, fire pits, and picnic tables are provided. Flush toilets, propane, showers, firewood, a recreation hall, a store, a spa, a pay phone, cell phone reception, modem access, a laundry room, ice, a playground, and a swimming pool are available. An ATM is within a half mile. Leashed pets are permitted.

Reservations, fees: Reserve at 800/847-2231. The fee is $26–38 per night. Major credit cards are accepted. Open year-round.

Directions: From Portland on I-5, turn west on U.S. 26 and drive 73 miles to the junction with U.S. 101. Turn south on U.S. 101 and drive four miles to the Cannon Beach exit at Milepost 29.5. Turn left (east) and drive 200 feet to the campground.

Contact: RV Resort at Cannon Beach, P.O. Box 1037, 345 Elk Creek Rd., Cannon Beach, OR

97110, 503/436-2231, fax 503/436-1527, website: www.cbrvresort.com.

7 NEHALEM BAY STATE PARK

Rating: 7

on the Pacific Ocean
See map pages 230–231
This state park on a sandy point separating the Pacific Ocean from Nehalem Bay features six miles of beach frontage. Crabbing and fishing on the bay are popular. The neighboring towns of Manzanita and Nehalem offer fine dining and shopping. The Oregon Coast Trail passes through the park. A horse camp with corrals and a 7.5-mile equestrian trail are available. There is also a 1.75-mile bike trail. An airport is in the park, and there are airstrip fly-in campsites.

RV sites, facilities: There are 274 sites with partial hookups (30 amps) for RVs up to 60 feet, a special camping area for hikers and bicyclists, and six primitive fly-in sites next to the airport. There are also 18 yurts and 17 sites with stock corrals. Drinking water, picnic tables, and fire grills are provided. Flush toilets, an RV dump station, a pay phone, cell phone reception, showers, and firewood are available. Boat-launching facilities are nearby on Nehalem Bay, and an airstrip is in the park. An ATM is within one mile, and a coin-operated laundry is within 10 miles. Some facilities are wheelchair-accessible. Leashed pets are permitted.

Reservations, fees: Reserve at 800/452-5687 or online at www.OregonStateParks.org ($6 reservation fee). The fee is $20 per night, plus $7 per additional vehicle; hikers/bikers are $4 per person per night. Yurts are $27 per night; horse sites are $10 per night. Major credit cards are accepted. Open year-round.

Directions: From Portland, drive west on U.S. 26 for 73 miles to the junction with U.S. 101. Turn south on U.S. 101 and drive 19 miles to Manzanita. Turn right (west) on the park entrance road and drive 1.5 miles to the campground.

Contact: Nehalem Bay State Park, 9500 Sandpiper Ln., Nehalem, OR 97131, 503/368-5154 or 800/551-6949, fax 503/368-5090.

OREGON

8 NEHALEM FALLS

Rating: 10

in Tillamook State Forest
See map pages 230–231
This beautiful campground, amid old-growth hemlock and spruce, is available within a two-minute walk of lovely Nehalem Falls. A half-mile loop trail follows the adjacent Nehalem River, where fishing and swimming are options.

RV sites, facilities: There are 14 sites for RVs up to 40 feet or tents, four walk-in tent sites, and one group site. Drinking water, picnic tables, garbage bins, fire grills, and vault toilets are available. A pay phone is within eight miles. Some facilities are wheelchair-accessible. Leashed pets are permitted.

Reservations, fees: Reservations are not accepted. The fee is $10 per night, plus $2 per additional vehicle. Walk-in sites are $5 per night. Reservations are required for the group site, which is $25 per night; phone 503/842-2545. Open Memorial Day weekend through October.

Directions: From Tillamook on U.S. 101 northbound, drive 22 miles to Highway 53. Turn right (east) and drive 1.3 miles to Miami Foley Road. Turn right (south) and drive one mile to Foss Road (narrow and rough). Turn left and drive seven miles to the campground on the left (the last one-eighth mile is dirt).

Contact: Tillamook State Forest, Tillamook District, 5005 E. 3rd St., Tillamook, OR 97141, 503/842-2545, fax 503/842-3143, website: www.odf .state.or.us.

9 JONES CREEK

Rating: 7

on the Wilson River in Tillamook State Forest
See map pages 230–231
Set in a forest of fir, hemlock, spruce, and alder, campsites here are spacious and private. The adjacent Wilson River provides opportunities for steelhead and salmon fishing (artificial lures only). A scenic 3.5-mile trail runs along the riverfront. The camp fills up on holidays and weekends.

RV sites, facilities: There are 28 sites for RVs or tents (27 are 50 feet long and one is 72 feet long and pull-through), nine walk-in tent sites, and

one group site. A camp host is on-site, and drinking water, picnic tables, fire grills, vault toilets, garbage bins, and a horseshoe pit are available. Some facilities are wheelchair-accessible. Leashed pets are permitted.

Reservations, fees: Reservations are not accepted. The fee is $10 per night, plus $2 per additional vehicle. Walk-in sites are $5 per night. Reservations are required for the group site, which is $25 per night; phone 503/842-2545. Open Memorial Day weekend through October.

Directions: From Portland, turn west on U.S. 26 and drive 24 miles to Highway 6. Turn west on Highway 6 and drive 28 miles to Milepost 22.7 and North Fork Road. Turn right and drive .25 mile to the campground on the left.

Contact: Tillamook State Forest, Tillamook District, 5005 E. 3rd St., Tillamook, OR 97141, 503/842-2545, fax 503/842-3143, website: www.odf .state.or.us.

10 GALES CREEK

Rating: 7

on Gales Creek in Tillamook State Forest
See map pages 230–231
Gales Creek runs through this heavily forested camp. The Gales Creek Trailhead is accessible from camp, providing hiking and mountain biking opportunities. A day-use picnic area is also available.

RV sites, facilities: There are 19 sites for RVs up to 35 feet or tents and four walk-in tent sites. Drinking water, picnic tables, fire grills, garbage bins, and vault toilets are available. A pay phone is within four miles. Some facilities are wheelchair-accessible. Leashed pets are permitted.

Reservations, fees: Reservations are not accepted. The fees are $10 per night for family sites or $5 per night for walk-in sites, plus $2 per night per additional vehicle. Open Memorial Day weekend through October.

Directions: From Portland, turn west on U.S. 26 and drive 24 miles to Highway 6. Turn west on Highway 6 and drive 17 miles to the campground entrance road (Rogers Road) on the right at Milepost 35. Turn right on Rogers Road and drive one mile to the campground.

Contact: Tillamook State Forest, Forest Grove

OREGON

District, 801 Gales Creek Rd., Forest Grove, OR 97116, 503/357-2191, website: www.odf.state.or.us.

11 BROWNS CAMP

Rating: 6

in Tillamook State Forest

See map pages 230–231

This camp is located next to the Devil's Lake Fork of the Wilson River and has sites with and without tree cover. Surrounded by miles of off-highway-vehicle (OHV) trails, it caters to OHV campers. Don't expect peace and quiet. No fishing is allowed here.

RV sites, facilities: There are 29 sites for RVs up to 45 feet or tents. Drinking water, picnic tables, fire grills, garbage bins, and vault toilets are available. Some facilities are wheelchair-accessible. Leashed pets are permitted.

Reservations, fees: Reservations are not accepted. The fee is $10 per night, plus $2 per additional vehicle. Open March to November.

Directions: From Portland, turn west on U.S. 26 and drive 24 miles to Highway 6. Turn west on Highway 6 and drive 19 miles to Beaver Dam Road. Turn left (south) and drive 2.5 miles to Scoggins Road. Turn left (southeast) and drive .5 mile to the campground.

Contact: Tillamook State Forest, Forest Grove District, 801 Gales Creek Rd., Forest Grove, OR 97116, 503/357-2191, website: www.odf.state.or.us.

12 BARVIEW JETTY COUNTY PARK

Rating: 7

near Garibaldi

See map pages 230–231

This Tillamook County park covers 160 acres and is near the beach, in a wooded area adjacent to Tillamook Bay. The sites are set on grassy hills. Nearby recreation options include an 18-hole golf course, hiking trails, bike trails, surf and scuba fishing, and a full-service marina.

RV sites, facilities: There are 249 sites, including 60 with full hookups (30, 50 amps), for RVs of any length or tents and five group sites. Picnic tables and fire rings are provided. Drinking water,

flush toilets, an RV dump station, showers, a pay phone, cell phone reception, and a playground are available. Propane, a store, a café, and ice are within 1.5 miles. Leashed pets are permitted.

Reservations, fees: Reservations are accepted for some sites. The fees are $15–20 per night, plus $5 for each additional vehicle or tent, a $2 for dump station fee, a $2 shower fee for nonregistered guests (free for registered campers), and $5 for firewood; group sites are $25–30. Major credit cards are accepted. Open year-round.

Directions: From Portland on I-5, turn west on U.S. 26 and drive 24 miles to Highway 6. Turn left on Highway 6 and drive 44 miles to Tillamook. Turn north on U.S. 101 and drive 12 miles to the park on the left (two miles north of the town of Garibaldi).

Contact: Barview Jetty County Park, P.O. Box 633, Garibaldi, OR 97118, 503/322-3522.

13 BIAK-BY-THE-SEA RV PARK

Rating: 7

on Tillamook Bay

See map pages 230–231

This park along the shore of Tillamook Bay is a prime retreat for deep-sea fishing, crabbing, clamming, surf fishing, scuba diving, and beachcombing. The nearby town of Tillamook is home to a cheese factory and a historical museum. A good side trip is to Cape Meares State Park, where you can hike through the national wildlife preserve and see seabirds nesting along the cliffs. A golf course is nearby. Note that about 30 of the sites are monthly rentals.

RV sites, facilities: There are 45 drive-through sites with full hookups (30 amps) for RVs of any length. Cable TV is provided. Flush toilets, coin-operated showers, picnic tables, a pay phone, cell phone reception, and coin-operated laundry facilities are available. Propane, a store, a café, an ATM, and ice are within two blocks. Boat docks, launching facilities, and rentals are nearby. Leashed pets are permitted.

Reservations, fees: Reservations are recommended. The fee is $20 per night, plus $1 per pet per night. Major credit cards are accepted. Open year-round.

Directions: From Portland, turn west on U.S. 26 and drive 24 miles to Highway 6. Turn west on

Highway 6 and drive 44 miles to Tillamook and U.S. 101. Turn north and drive 10 miles to 7th Street. Turn left on 7th Street and drive to the park on the left (just over the tracks).

Contact: Biak-by-the-Sea RV Park, P.O. Box 396, Garibaldi, OR 97118, 503/322-2111.

14 PACIFIC CAMPGROUND

Rating: 6

on Tillamook Bay
See map pages 230–231

This campground is located at the southern end of Tillamook Bay, not far from the Wilson River. The Tillamook Cheese Factory—which offers tours—is just south of the park. An 18-hole golf course is also nearby. See the previous description of Biak-by-the-Sea RV Park for more information about the area.

RV sites, facilities: There are 31 drive-through sites with full hookups (20, 30, 50 amps) for RVs of any length and 20 tent sites. Picnic tables and fire rings are provided. Drinking water, flush toilets, cable TV, cell phone reception, showers, firewood, and ice are available. A store, ATM, pay phone, coin-operated laundry, and a café are within one mile. Leashed pets (except in the tent area) and motorbikes are permitted.

Reservations, fees: Reservations are accepted. The fee is $13–23 per night for two people, plus $1 per person for more than two people and $1 per additional vehicle. Open year-round.

Directions: From Portland, turn west on U.S. 26 and drive 24 miles to Highway 6. Turn west on Highway 6 and drive 44 miles to Tillamook. Turn north on U.S. 101 and drive 1.5 miles to the campground entrance across from the Tillamook Cheese Factory.

Contact: Pacific Campground, 1950 Suppress Rd. N, Tillamook, OR 97141, 503/842-5201, fax 503/842-0588.

15 PLEASANT VALLEY RV PARK

Rating: 8

on the Tillamook River
See map pages 230–231

This campground along the Tillamook River is very clean and features many recreation options in the immediate area.

RV sites, facilities: There are 30 sites with full hookups (50 amps) and 46 with partial hookups for RVs of any length, 10 tent sites, and two cabins. Picnic tables and fire rings are provided. Drinking water, flush toilets, propane, an RV dump station, modem access, a pay phone, showers, firewood, a recreation hall, cable TV, a store, a coin-operated laundry, ice, and a playground are available. Boat-launching facilities are nearby. An ATM is within seven miles. Leashed pets are permitted.

Reservations, fees: Reservations are accepted. The fee is $16–21.50 per night, plus $2 per person for more than two people; cabins are $27 per night. A senior discount is available. Major credit cards are accepted. Open year-round.

Directions: From Portland, turn west on U.S. 26 and drive 24 miles to Highway 6. Turn west on Highway 6 and drive 44 miles to Tillamook and U.S. 101. Turn south on U.S. 101 and drive 6.5 miles to the campground entrance on the right.

Contact: Pleasant Valley RV Park, 11880 U.S. 101 S, Tillamook, OR 97141, 503/842-4779, fax 503/842-2293, website: www.pvrvpark.com.

16 NETARTS BAY RV PARK AND MARINA

Rating: 8

on Netarts Bay
See map pages 230–231

This camp is one of two on the east shore of Netarts Bay. A golf course is eight miles away. Sunsets and wildlife viewing are notable here. Some sites are filled with rentals for the summer season. No tent campers are permitted. This RV park was formerly known as Bay Shore RV Park.

RV sites, facilities: There are 83 sites for RVs of any length; 11 are drive-through sites with full hookups (20, 30, 50 amps). Picnic tables are provided. Drinking water, flush toilets, propane, cell phone reception, a pay phone, modem access, coin-operated showers, a meeting room, a coin-operated laundry, crab-cooking facilities, crab bait, and ice are available. Boat docks, launching facilities, and rentals are available on-site. A store, an ATM, and a café are within one mile. Leashed pets are permitted.

Reservations, fees: Reservations are recommended. The fee is $19–27 per night. Major credit cards are accepted. Monthly rentals are available. Open year-round.

Directions: From Portland, turn west on U.S. 26 and drive 24 miles to Highway 6. Turn west on Highway 6 and drive 44 miles to Tillamook and Netarts Highway. Turn west on Netarts Highway and drive six miles to the campground entrance.

Contact: Netarts Bay RV Park and Marina, 2260 Bilyeu, P.O. Box 218, Netarts, OR 97413, 503/842-7774, website: www.netartsbay.com.

17 CAPE LOOKOUT STATE PARK

Rating: 8

near Netarts Bay
See map pages 230–231

Cape Lookout is on a sand spit between Netarts Bay and the ocean and has more than eight miles of hiking and walking trails that wind through old-growth forest. The Cape Lookout Trail follows the headland for more than two miles. Another walk will take you out through a variety of estuarine habitats along the five-mile sand spit that extends between the ocean and Netarts Bay. With many species to view, this area is a paradise for bird-watchers. You might also catch a glimpse of the local hang gliders and para gliders that frequent the park. Fishing is another option here.

RV sites, facilities: There are 39 sites with partial or full hookups (20, 30, 50 amps) for RVs up to 60 feet, 173 tent sites, a special tent camping area for hikers and bicyclists, four group sites for up to 25 people each, three cabins, and 10 yurts. Picnic tables and fire grills are provided. Flush toilets, an RV dump station, a pay phone, cell phone reception, showers, garbage bins, and firewood are available. A restaurant is within one mile. An ATM and groceries are available within six miles. Some facilities are wheelchair-accessible. Leashed pets are permitted.

Reservations, fees: Reserve at 800/452-5687 or online at www.OregonStateParks.org ($6 reservation fee). The fees are $16–20 per night plus $7 per additional vehicle, $4 per person per night

for hikers/bikers, $40–60 for group sites, $45–65 for cabins, and $27 per night for yurts. Major credit cards are accepted. Open year-round.

Directions: From Portland, turn west on U.S. 26 and drive 24 miles to Highway 6. Turn west on Highway 6 and drive 44 miles to Tillamook. Turn southwest on Netarts Road and drive 11 miles to the park entrance on the right.

Contact: Cape Lookout State Park, 13000 Whiskey Creek Rd. W, Tillamook, OR 97141, 503/842-4981.

18 CAMPER COVE RV PARK AND CAMPGROUND

Rating: 6

on Beaver Creek
See map pages 230–231

This small, wooded campground along Beaver Creek is set just far enough off the highway to provide quiet. The park can be used as a base camp for anglers, with seasonal steelhead and salmon fishing in the nearby Nestucca River. It gets crowded here, especially in the summer, so be sure to make a reservation whenever possible. Ocean beaches are four miles away.

RV sites, facilities: There are 17 sites with full hookups (20, 30, 50 amps) for RVs up to 40 feet, five tent sites, and three cabins. Picnic tables and fire rings are provided. Drinking water, flush toilets, an RV dump station, coin-operated showers, a store, cell phone reception, firewood, a recreation hall, laundry facilities, and ice are available. A pay phone is within 2.5 miles, and an ATM is within 10 miles. Leashed pets are permitted.

Reservations, fees: Reservations are accepted. The fees are $20 per night for RV sites and $15 per night for tent sites, plus $3 per person for more than two people and $3 per night per additional vehicle; cabin rentals are $30–40 per night. A senior discount is available. Open year-round.

Directions: From Portland, turn west on U.S. 26 and drive 24 miles to Highway 6. Turn west on Highway 6 and drive 44 miles to Tillamook and U.S. 101. Turn south on U.S. 101 and drive 12 miles to the park entrance on the right (2.5 miles north of Beaver).

Contact: Camper Cove RV Park and Campground, P.O. Box 42, Beaver, OR 97108, 503/398-5334, website: www.amadevice.com/campercove.

19 DOVRE, FAN CREEK, ALDER GLEN

Rating: 5

on the Nestucca River
See map pages 230–231

This is a series of three BLM campgrounds set along the Nestucca River. The camps, separated by alder trees and shrubs, are near the river, and some have river views. Tourists don't know about these spots. The Nestucca is a gentle river, with the water not deep enough for swimming.

RV sites, facilities: Dovre has 10 sites (for RVs up to 16 feet), Fan Creek has 11 sites, and Alder Glen has 11 sites for RVs up to 28 feet or tents. Picnic tables and fire grills are provided. Drinking water and vault toilets are available. Garbage must be packed out. Some facilities, including a fishing pier at Alder Glen, are wheelchair-accessible. Leashed pets are permitted.

Reservations, fees: Reservations are not accepted. The fee is $6 per night, plus $4 per additional vehicle with a limit of two vehicles per site. A senior discount is available. Open late April to late October, weather permitting.

Directions: On U.S. 101 southwest of Portland, drive to the tiny town of Beaver and Blaine Road. Turn east on Blaine Road (keep right; Blaine Road turns into Nestucca River Access Road) and drive 17.5 miles to Alder Glen. Continue east for seven more miles to reach Fan Creek and nine more miles to reach Dovre (the last two miles are steep, winding, and narrow).

Contact: Bureau of Land Management, Salem District, 1717 Fabry Rd. SE, Salem, OR 97306, 503/375-5646, fax 503/375-5622.

20 HEBO LAKE

Rating: 7

on Hebo Lake in Siuslaw National Forest
See map pages 230–231

This U.S. Forest Service campground along the shore of Hebo Lake is a secluded spot with sites nestled under trees. The trailhead for the eight-mile-long Pioneer-Indian Trail is located in the campground. The trail around the lake is wheelchair-accessible.

RV sites, facilities: There are 15 sites for RVs up to 18 feet or tents. Picnic tables and fire pits are provided. Drinking water, garbage bins, and vault toilets are available. Boats with electric motors are allowed on the lake. A pay phone and groceries are available within five miles, and an ATM is within six miles. Some facilities are wheelchair-accessible. Leashed pets are permitted.

Reservations, fees: Reservations are not accepted. The fee is $10 per night, plus $5 per additional vehicle. A senior discount is available. Open May to mid-October, weather permitting.

Directions: On U.S. 101 southwest of Portland, drive to the town of Hebo and Highway 22. Turn east on Highway 22 and drive .25 mile to Forest Road 14. Turn left (east) and drive five miles to the campground (the last five miles are steep, winding, and narrow).

Contact: Siuslaw National Forest, Hebo Ranger District, 31525 Hwy. 22, Hebo, OR 97122, 503/392-3161, fax 503/392-4203.

21 CAPE KIWANDA RV PARK

Rating: 8

on the Pacific Ocean
See map pages 230–231

This park is a short distance from Cape Kiwanda State Park, which is open for day use only. Highlights at the park include a boat launch and hiking trails that lead out to the cape. Four miles south at Nestucca Spit, there is another day-use park, providing additional recreational options. The point extends about three miles and is a good spot for bird-watching. The campsites do not have ocean views.

RV sites, facilities: There are 147 sites with full hookups (30, 50 amps) for RVs of any length, 25 tent sites, and 11 camping cabins. Picnic tables and fire rings are provided. Drinking water, flush toilets, an RV dump station, showers, firewood, a recreation hall, laundry facilities, propane, a seafood market, a gift shop, an ATM, a pay phone, modem access, cell phone reception, and a playground are available. Propane, a store, a café, and ice are within one mile. Boat docks, launching facilities, and rentals are nearby. Leashed pets are permitted.

Reservations, fees: Reservations are accepted. The fee is $17–27 per night, plus $2 per person

OREGON

for more than two people and $2 per additional vehicle. Cabins are $50–60 per night. Major credit cards are accepted. Open year-round.

Directions: From Portland, turn west on U.S. 26 and drive 24 miles to Highway 6. Turn west on Highway 6 and drive 44 miles to Tillamook and U.S. 101. Turn south on U.S. 101 and drive 25 miles to the Pacific City exit and Brooten Road. Turn right and drive three miles toward Pacific City and Three Capes Drive. Turn left, cross the bridge, and bear right on Three Capes Drive. Continue one mile north to the park on the right.

Contact: Cape Kiwanda RV Park, P.O. Box 129, 33315, Cape Kiwanda Dr., Pacific City, OR 97135, 503/965-6230, fax 503/965-6235, website: www .capekiwandarvpark.com.

22 WEBB PARK

Rating: 7

near the Pacific Ocean
See map pages 230–231

This public campground provides an excellent alternative to the more crowded commercial RV parks off U.S. 101. Although not as developed, it offers a quiet, private setting and access to the ocean. Fishing and swimming are among your options here. The camp is just behind the new inn at Cape Kiwanda (Kiwanda Inn) and across the street from the Pelican Brew Pub and dinner house.

RV sites, facilities: There are 37 sites for RVs or tents, seven with partial hookups (30 amps). Picnic tables and fire rings are provided. Drinking water, showers, flush toilets, cell phone reception, an RV dump station, and beach launching are available. A pay phone, coin-operated laundry, and deli are next door. An ATM is within two blocks, and groceries are available within 1.5 miles. Leashed pets are permitted.

Reservations, fees: Reserve at 503/965-5001 ($5 reservation fee). The fee is $14–16 per night. Open year-round.

Directions: From Portland, turn west on U.S. 26 and drive 24 miles to Highway 6. Turn west on Highway 6 and drive 44 miles to Tillamook and U.S. 101. Turn south on U.S. 101 and drive about 25 miles to the Pacific City exit and Highway 30. From Pacific City, turn right (north) and drive to the four-way stop at McPhillips Drive. Turn

left and drive .5 mile to Cape Kiwanda and the park on the right.

Contact: Webb Park, Tillamook County Parks, P.O. Box 572, Pacific City, OR 97135, 503/965-5001, fax 503/842-2721, website: www.co.tillamook .or.us.

23 WANDERING SPIRIT RV PARK

Rating: 6

on Rock Creek
See map pages 230–231

The major draw here is the nearby casino, but there is the added benefit of shaded sites next to Rock Creek and the confluence of the Yamhill River, which provides fishing and swimming options. Fishing is good for steelhead and salmon in season. Golf courses and wineries are available within 10 miles. There is a combination of both monthly rentals and overnighters at this park.

RV sites, facilities: There are 105 sites with full hookups (30, 50 amps) for RVs up to 45 feet and 20 tent sites. Picnic tables are provided. Drinking water, electricity, sewer hookups, restrooms, showers, an RV dump station, coin-operated laundry facilities, RV supplies, and a small store are available. Propane, a clubhouse, a basketball hoop, cable TV, a pay phone, modem access, cell phone reception, an exercise room, and a game room are also available on-site. A 24-hour free bus shuttles campers to and from the Spirit Mountain Casino, restaurants, and shops less than two miles away. An ATM is available within one block. Some facilities are wheelchair-accessible. Leashed pets are permitted.

Reservations, fees: Reserve at 800/390-6980. The fees are $12 for tents per night and $22 for RVs per night, plus $2 per person for more than two people. Monthly rates are available. Major credit cards are accepted. Open year-round.

Directions: From Salem, drive west on Highway 22 about 25 miles to Highway 18. Turn west on Highway 18 and drive about nine miles to the park on the left.

Contact: Wandering Spirit RV Park, 28800 Salmon River Hwy., Grand Ronde, OR 97347, 503/879-5700, fax 503/879-5171, website: www .onlinemac.com/business/wander.

24 DEVIL'S LAKE STATE PARK

Rating: 7

on Devil's Lake
See map pages 230–231

Oregon's only coastal camp in the midst of a city, Devil's Lake is the center of summertime activity. A take-your-pick deal: You can boat, canoe, kayak, fish, or water-ski. For something different, head west and explore the seven miles of beaches. Lincoln City also has several arts and crafts galleries. East Devil's Lake is two miles east and offers a boat ramp and picnic facilities.

RV sites, facilities: There are 31 sites with full hookups (50 amps) for RVs up to 60 feet and 54 tent sites. There are also 10 yurts and a separate area for hikers and bikers. Picnic tables and fire grills are provided. Drinking water, garbage bins, flush toilets, showers, a pay phone, cell phone reception, and firewood are available. An ATM and groceries are available within a half mile. Boat docks and launching facilities are nearby. Some facilities are wheelchair-accessible. Leashed pets are permitted.

Reservations, fees: Reserve at 800/452-5687 or online at www.OregonStateParks.org ($6 reservation fee). The fees are $17–22 per night plus $7 per additional vehicle, $4 per person per night for hikers/bikers, and $29 per night for yurts. Boat mooring is $7 per night. Major credit cards are accepted. Open year-round.

Directions: From Portland, drive south on Highway 99 to Highway 18. Turn west on Highway 18 and drive 47 miles to U.S. 101. Turn south on U.S. 101 and drive five miles to Lincoln City. Follow the signs to the park.

Contact: Devil's Lake State Park, 1452 N.E. 6th St., Lincoln City, OR 97367, 541/994-2002.

25 KOA LINCOLN CITY

Rating: 7

near the Pacific Ocean
See map pages 230–231

This area offers opportunities for beachcombing, tidepool viewing, and fishing along a seven-mile stretch of beach. Nearby recreation options

include an 18-hole golf course, tennis courts, and horseback riding facilities.

RV sites, facilities: There are 23 sites with full hookups for RVs up to 60 feet, 29 sites with partial hookups (20, 30, 50 amps), 15 sites for tents, and 14 camping cabins. Picnic tables are provided. Drinking water, cable TV, modem access, flush toilets, an RV dump station, pay phones, showers, a store, a café, fire rings, a gift shop, propane, ice, RV supplies, video rentals, an ATM, cell phone reception, a game room, coin-operated laundry facilities, firewood, and a playground are available. Leashed pets are permitted.

Reservations, fees: Reserve at 800/562-2791. The fee is $26–55 per night, plus $3 per person for more than two people and $5 per additional vehicle. Major credit cards are accepted. Open year-round.

Directions: From Portland, drive south on Highway 99 West to Highway 18. Turn west on Highway 18 and drive 47 miles to U.S. 101. Turn south on U.S. 101 and drive 1.5 miles to East Devil's Lake Road. Turn east (left) on East Devil's Lake Road and drive one mile to the park.

Contact: KOA Lincoln City, 5298 N.E. Park Ln., Otis, OR 97368, 541/994-2961, fax 541/994-9454, website: www.koa.com.

26 BEVERLY BEACH STATE PARK

Rating: 7

on the Pacific Ocean
See map pages 230–231

This beautiful campground is set in a wooded, grassy area on the east side of U.S. 101. Giant, wind-sculpted trees surround the campsites along Spencer Creek. Like magic, you walk through a tunnel under the roadway and emerge on a beach that extends from Yaquina Head to the headlands of Otter Rock and from which a lighthouse is visible. A one-mile hiking trail is available. Just a mile to the north lies a small day-use state park called Devil's Punchbowl, named for an unusual bowl-shaped rock formation with caverns under it where the waves rumble about. For some great ocean views, head north one more mile to the Otter Crest Wayside. The Oregon Coast Aquarium is within a few minutes' drive.

RV sites, facilities: There are 129 sites with partial

OREGON

or full hookups (20, 30 amps) for RVs of any length, 129 tent sites, a special camping area for hikers and bicyclists, and a reserved group area. There is also a village of 21 yurts. Picnic tables and fire grills are provided. Drinking water, flush toilets, showers, a coin-operated laundry, cell phone reception, pay phones, and an RV dump station are available. An ATM and groceries are available within seven miles. Some facilities are wheelchair-accessible. Leashed pets are permitted.

Reservations, fees: Reserve at 800/452-5687 or online at www.OregonStateParks.org ($6 reservation fee). The fees are $14–22 per night plus $7 per additional vehicle, $4 per person per night for hikers/bikers, $29 per night for yurts, and $43–60 for group sites. Major credit cards are accepted. Open year-round.

Directions: From I-5 at Albany, turn west on U.S. 20 and drive 66 miles to Newport and U.S. 101. Turn north on U.S. 101 and drive seven miles to the park entrance.

Contact: Beverly Beach State Park, 198 N.E. 123rd St., Newport, OR 97365, 541/265-9278 or 800/551-6949.

27 AGATE BEACH RV PARK

Rating: 6

near the Pacific Ocean
See map pages 230–231
This park is located a short distance from Agate Beach Wayside, a small state park with beach access. Agate hunting can be good. Sometimes a layer of sand covers the agates, and you have to dig a bit. But other times wave action will clear the sand, unveiling the agates at low tides. Beverly Beach State Park is 4.5 miles north. About half of the sites are filled with monthly rentals.

RV sites, facilities: There are 32 sites, 25 with full hookups (30 amps) and five with partial hookups, for RVs up to 40 feet. Drinking water, cable TV, and picnic tables are provided. Flush toilets, an RV dump station, cell phone reception, showers, a dog run, and a laundry room are available. A pay phone is across the street. A store, ATM, and ice are within one mile. Leashed pets are permitted, with some species restricted.

Reservations, fees: Reservations are accepted. The fee is $21.50–23.50 per night, plus $1 per person for more than two people and $1 per additional vehicle. Major credit cards are accepted. Open year-round.

Directions: From Albany, drive west on U.S. 20 for 66 miles to Newport and U.S. 101. Turn north on U.S. 101 and drive three miles to the park on the north end of town.

Contact: Agate Beach RV Park, 6138 N. Coast Hwy., Newport, OR 97365, 541/265-7670.

28 HARBOR VILLAGE RV PARK

Rating: 6

on Yaquina Bay
See map pages 230–231
This wooded and landscaped park is set near the shore of Yaquina Bay. See the description of Port of Newport Marina and RV Park for information on attractions in Newport. Nearby recreation options include clamming, crabbing, deep-sea fishing, an 18-hole golf course, hiking trails, and a full-service marina. No tent campers are permitted.

RV sites, facilities: There are 40 sites with full hookups (30 amps) for RVs up to 40 feet. Picnic tables are provided. Drinking water, flush toilets, showers, a pay phone, cell phone reception, modem access, and a laundry room are available. Propane, a store, an ATM, and a café are within one mile. Boat docks, launching facilities, and rentals are nearby. One leashed pet per site is permitted.

Reservations, fees: Reservations are accepted. The fee is $20 per night, plus $3 per person for more than two people. Major credit cards are accepted. Open year-round.

Directions: From Albany, drive west on U.S. 20 for 65.5 miles into Newport and John Moore Road (lighted intersection). Turn left (south) on John Moore Road and drive .5 mile to the bay and Bay Boulevard. Bear left and drive a short distance to the park entrance on the left.

Contact: Harbor Village RV Park, 923 S.E. Bay Blvd., Newport, OR 97365, 541/265-5088, fax 541/265-5895, website: www.harborvillagerv park.com.

OREGON

29 PORT OF NEWPORT MARINA AND RV PARK

Rating: 7

on Yaquina Bay
See map pages 230–231

This public park is set along the shore of Yaquina Bay near Newport, a resort town that offers a variety of attractions. Among them are ocean fishing, a museum and aquarium at the nearby Hatfield Marine Science Center, the Undersea Garden, the Waxworks, Ripley's Believe It or Not, and the Lincoln County Historical Society Museum. Nearby recreation options include an 18-hole golf course, hiking trails, and a full-service marina.

RV sites, facilities: There are 115 sites with full hookups (30, 50 amps) for RVs of any length. Drinking water, flush toilets, coin-operated showers, cable TV, a store, an ATM, a pay phone, modem access, cell phone reception, a coin-operated laundry, and ice are available. A marina with boat docks and launching facilities is onsite. Leashed pets are permitted.

Reservations, fees: Reserve at 541/867-3321. The fee is $24 per night, plus $1 per person for more than two people. Major credit cards are accepted. Open year-round.

Directions: From Albany, drive west on U.S. 20 for 66 miles to Newport and U.S. 101. Turn south on U.S. 101 and drive .5 mile (over the bridge) to Marine Science Drive. Take the first right after the bridge, and drive .5 mile to the park entrance on the left.

Contact: Port of Newport Marina and RV Park, 600 S.E. Bay Blvd., Newport, OR 97365 (physical address: 2301 S.E. O.S.U. Dr., Newport, OR 97365), 541/867-3321, fax 541/867-3352, website: www.portofnewport.com.

30 SOUTH BEACH STATE PARK

Rating: 7

on the Pacific Ocean
See map pages 230–231

This park along the beach offers opportunities for beachcombing, fishing, crabbing, windsurfing, boating, and hiking. In fact, the Oregon

Coast Trail passes right through the park. A primitive hike-in campground is also available. The park is within walking distance of Oregon Aquarium. A nice plus: An on-duty naturalist provides campground talks (seasonal). For information on attractions in Newport, see the description of Port of Newport Marina and RV Park above.

RV sites, facilities: There are 227 sites with partial hookups (30 amps) for RVs of any length and an area of six primitive tent sites for hikers and bicyclists. There are also three group sites and 27 yurts. Picnic tables and fire grills are provided. Drinking water, restrooms with flush toilets and showers, garbage bins, a pay phone, cell phone reception, recycling, an RV dump station, and firewood are available. An ATM is within two miles. Some facilities are wheelchair-accessible. Leashed pets are permitted.

Reservations, fees: Reserve at 800/452-5687 or online at www.OregonStateParks.org ($6 reservation fee). The fees are $9–22 per night plus $7 per additional vehicle, $4 per person per night for hikers/bicyclists, and $64 for group sites. Yurts are $29. Major credit cards are accepted. Open year-round.

Directions: From Albany, drive west on U.S. 20 for 66 miles to Newport and U.S. 101. Turn south and drive three miles to the park entrance on the right.

Contact: South Beach State Park, 5580 S. Coast Hwy., South Beach, OR 97366, 541/867-4715.

31 SEAL ROCKS RV COVE

Rating: 8

near Seal Rock State Park
See map pages 230–231

This RV park is situated on the rugged coastline near Seal Rock State Park (open for day use only), where you may find seals, sea lions, and a variety of birds. The ocean views are stunning, and a fascinating tidepool full of aquatic life is located directly across the street.

RV sites, facilities: There are 26 sites with full hookups (30, 50 amps) for RVs of any length—two are drive-through sites—and 16 tent sites. Picnic tables and fire rings are provided. Drinking water, flush toilets, cable TV, showers, and firewood are available. A store, an ATM, a pay phone, a coin-operated laundry, a café, and ice are within a half mile. Leashed pets are permitted.

Reservations, fees: Reservations are accepted. The fee is $15–31 per night, plus $1–3 per person for more than two people and $3 per additional vehicle unless towed. Open year-round.

Directions: From Albany, drive west on U.S. 20 for 66 miles to Newport and U.S. 101. Turn south and drive 10 miles to the town of Seal Rock. Continue south on U.S. 101 for .25 mile to the park entrance on the left.

Contact: Seal Rocks RV Cove, 1276 N.W. Cross St., P.O. Box 71, Seal Rock, OR 97376, 541/563-3955, website: www.sealrocksrv.com.

32 DRIFT CREEK LANDING

Rating: 6

on the Alsea River

See map pages 230–231

This campground is set along the shore of the Alsea River in a heavily treed and mountainous area. The Oregon Coast Aquarium is 15 miles away, and an 18-hole golf course is nearby. There are 10 mobile homes on this property with long-term renters. For more information on the area, see the description of Waldport/Newport KOA in this chapter.

RV sites, facilities: There are 50 sites with full hookups (30 amps) for RVs of any length and an area for tent camping. Drinking water, flush toilets, private telephone service, cable TV, propane, coin-operated showers, a recreation hall, a store, a café, a coin-operated laundry, cell phone reception, modem access, an ATM, boat docks, boat rentals, and launching facilities are available. A pay phone is within a half mile. Leashed pets are permitted.

Reservations, fees: Reservations are accepted. The fee is $22 per night, plus $2 per person for more than two people and $5 per additional vehicle. A senior discount is available. Major credit cards are accepted. Open year-round.

Directions: From Albany, drive west on U.S. 20 for 66 miles to Newport and U.S. 101. Turn south and drive 14 miles to Waldport and Highway 34. Turn east on Highway 34 and drive 3.7 miles to the campground on the left.

Contact: Drift Creek Landing, 3851 Hwy. 34,

Waldport, OR 97394, 541/563-3610, fax 541/563-5234, website: www.driftcreeklanding.com.

33 FISHIN' HOLE RV PARK & MARINA

Rating: 6

on the Alsea River

See map pages 230–231

This campground is one of several along the shore of the Alsea River. About half of the sites here are filled with monthly rentals. For information on the area, see the description of Waldport/Newport KOA in this chapter.

RV sites, facilities: There are 20 sites for RVs of any length—10 with full hookups (30 amps)—16 tent sites, and one cabin. Drinking water, picnic tables, flush toilets, showers, a coin-operated laundry, boat docks, boat rentals, and launching facilities are available. An ATM and groceries are available within four miles. Leashed pets are permitted.

Reservations, fees: Reserve at 877/770-6137. The fees are $15–18 for RV sites and $10 per night for tent sites, plus $2 per person for more than two people and $1 per night for cable TV. Cabins are $35–42 for up to four people. Open year-round.

Directions: From Albany, drive west on U.S. 20 for 66 miles to Newport and U.S. 101. Turn south and drive 14 miles to Waldport and Highway 34. Turn east on Highway 34 and drive four miles to the entrance on the left.

Contact: Fishin' Hole RV Park & Marina, 3911 Hwy. 34, Waldport, OR 97394, 541/563-3401.

34 CHINOOK RV PARK

Rating: 7

on the Alsea River

See map pages 230–231

This trailer park is set along the shore of the Alsea River, about 3.5 miles from the ocean. The park is filled primarily with monthly rentals. Campsites are rented on a space-available basis. As a result, RV sites with hookups are almost never available; sites without hookups can almost always be found here as an emergency backup spot. For more information on the area, see the description of Waldport/Newport KOA in this chapter.

RV sites, facilities: There are 22 sites with full hookups (50 amps) and 12 sites with partial hookups (30 amps) for RVs of any length plus six sites for tents. Drinking water, cable TV, flush toilets, showers, and a laundry room are available. A café is next door. A store, pay phone, and ice are available within one mile. Propane and an ATM are available 3.5 miles away. Boat docks are nearby. Leashed pets are permitted.

Reservations, fees: Reservations are accepted. The fee is $10–16 per night, plus $2 per person for more than two people. Open year-round.

Directions: From Albany, drive west on U.S. 20 for 66 miles to Newport and U.S. 101. Turn south and drive 14 miles to Waldport and Highway 34. Turn east on Highway 34 and drive 3.5 miles to the park entrance on the left.

Contact: Chinook RV Park, 3299 Highway 34, Waldport, OR 97394, 541/563-3485.

35 TAYLOR'S LANDING

Rating: 9

on the Alsea River

See map pages 230–231

This campground is set along the Alsea River. Fall, when the salmon fishing is best, is the prime time here and the park often fills. For more information on the area, see the following description of Waldport/Newport KOA.

RV sites, facilities: There are 38 sites with full hookups (30 amps) for RVs and six tent sites. Picnic tables are provided. Drinking water, flush toilets, propane, showers, a café, and a laundry room are available. Boat docks, launching facilities, and rentals are nearby. An ATM and a pay phone are within three miles. Leashed pets are permitted.

Reservations, fees: Reservations are accepted. The fee is $19–25 per night, plus $1 per person for more than two people. Monthly rates available. Open year-round.

Directions: From Albany, drive west on U.S. 20 for 66 miles to Newport and U.S. 101. Turn south and drive 14 miles to Waldport and Highway 34. Turn east on Highway 34 and drive seven miles to the entrance on the right.

Contact: Taylor's Landing, 7164 Alsea Hwy. 34, Waldport, OR 97394, tel./fax 541/528-3388.

36 WALDPORT/NEWPORT KOA

Rating: 8

on Alsea Bay

See map pages 230–231

This pretty park, set amid some of the oldest pine trees in Oregon, is within walking distance of the beach, the bay, and downtown Waldport—and to top it off, the campsites have beautiful ocean views. Alsea Bay's sandy and rocky shoreline makes this area a favorite with anglers. The crabbing and clamming can also be quite good. South Beach State Park, about five miles north on U.S. 101, offers more fishing and a boat ramp along Beaver Creek. It's open for day use only. Other nearby recreation options include hiking trails, marked bike trails, the Oregon Coast Aquarium, and a marina.

RV sites, facilities: There are 75 sites with full hookups (30, 50 amps) for RVs up to 40 feet, 12 tent sites, and 15 cabins. Picnic tables and fire rings are provided. Drinking water, flush toilets, showers, a courtesy phone, cell phone reception, and a recreation hall are available. Propane, an RV dump station, a store, an ATM, a café, a coin-operated laundry, and ice are within one mile. Boat docks, launching facilities, and boat rentals are also available. Leashed pets are permitted.

Reservations, fees: Reserve at 800/562-3443. The fee is $18–47 per night, plus $2–5 per person for more than two people. Major credit cards are accepted. Open year-round.

Directions: From Albany, drive west on U.S. 20 for 66 miles to Newport and U.S. 101. Turn south and drive to Milepost 155 at the north end of the Alsea Bay Bridge. The park is on the west side of the bridge.

Contact: Waldport/Newport KOA, 1330 N.W. Pacific Coast Hwy., P.O. Box 397, Waldport, OR 97394, 541/563-2250, fax 541/563-4098, website: www.koa.com.

37 BEACHSIDE STATE PARK

Rating: 7

near Alsea Bay
See map pages 230–231

This state park offers about nine miles of beach and is not far from Alsea Bay and the Alsea River. Every site is seconds from the beach. Within 30 miles in either direction, you'll find visitors centers, tidepools, hiking and driving tours, three lighthouses, crabbing, clamming, fishing, an aquarium, and science centers. See the description of Waldport/Newport KOA in this chapter for more information on the fishing opportunities in the area.

RV sites, facilities: There are 33 sites with partial hookups (30 amps) for RVs up to 40 feet, 28 sites for tents, two yurts, and a special camping area for hikers and bicyclists. Picnic tables and fire grills are provided. Drinking water, garbage bins, flush toilets, showers, recycling, and firewood are available. An ATM, groceries, and a coin-operated laundry are available within four miles. Some facilities are wheelchair-accessible. Leashed pets are permitted.

Reservations, fees: Reserve at 800/452-5687 or online at www.OregonStateParks.org ($7 reservation fee). The fees are $13–21 per night plus $7 per additional vehicle, and $4 per person per night for hikers/bicyclists; yurts are $29 per night. Major credit cards are accepted. Open mid-March to October, weather permitting.

Directions: From Albany, drive west on U.S. 20 for 66 miles to Newport and U.S. 101. Turn south on U.S. 101 and drive 16 miles to Waldport. Continue south on U.S. 101 for four miles to the park entrance on the right.

Contact: Beachside State Park, P.O. Box 693, Waldport, OR 97394, 541/563-3220, fax 541/563-3657.

38 TILLICUM BEACH

Rating: 8

on the Pacific Ocean in Siuslaw National Forest
See map pages 230–231

Ocean-view campsites are a big draw at this campground just south of Beachside State Park. Nearby forest roads provide access to streams in the mountains east of the beach area. A U.S. Forest Service map details the possibilities. Since it's just off the highway and along the water, this camp fills up very quickly in the summer, so expect crowds.

RV sites, facilities: There are 61 sites for RVs up to 40 feet or tents. Picnic tables and fire grills are provided. Flush toilets, garbage bins, drinking water, a pay phone, and cell phone reception are available. An ATM and groceries are available within a half mile. Leashed pets are permitted.

Reservations, fees: Reservations are accepted at 877/444-6777 or online at www.reserveusa.com ($9 reservation fee). The fee is $15 per night, plus $5 per additional vehicle. A senior discount is available. Open year-round.

Directions: From Albany, drive west on U.S. 20 for 66 miles to Newport and U.S. 101. Turn south on U.S. 101 and drive 14 miles to Waldport. Continue south on U.S. 101 for 4.5 miles to the campground entrance on the right.

Contact: Siuslaw National Forest, Waldport Ranger District, P.O. Box 400, 1049 S.W. Pacific Coast Hwy., Waldport, OR 97394, 541/563-3211, fax 541/563-3124; concessionaire, 541/547-3679.

39 BLACKBERRY

Rating: 7

on the Alsea River in Siuslaw National Forest
See map pages 230–231

Blackberry makes a good base camp for a fishing trip on the Alsea River. The U.S. Forest Service provides boat launches and picnic areas at several spots along this stretch of river. Often there is a camp host, who can give you inside information on nearby recreational opportunities. Large fir trees and lawn separate the sites.

RV sites, facilities: There are 32 sites for RVs or tents. Picnic tables and fire grills are provided. Drinking water, garbage bins, cell phone reception, and flush toilets are available. A boat ramp is on-site. Leashed pets are permitted.

Reservations, fees: Reservations are not accepted. The fee is $10 per night, plus $5 per additional vehicle. A senior discount is available. Open year-round.

Directions: From Albany, drive west on U.S. 20

for 15 miles to Philomath and Highway 34. Turn south on Highway 34 and drive 41 miles to the campground entrance.

Contact: Siuslaw National Forest, Waldport Ranger District, 1049 S.W. Pacific Coast Hwy., P.O. Box 400, Waldport, OR 97394, 541/563-3211, fax 541/563-3124.

40 ALSEA FALLS

Rating: 8

adjacent to the South Fork of the Alsea River
See map pages 230–231

Enjoy the beautiful surroundings of Alsea Falls by exploring the trails that wander through this park and lead to a picnic area by the falls. Trails to McBee Park and Green Peak Falls are accessible from the campground along the South Fork of the river. The campsites are situated in a 40-year-old forest of Douglas fir and vine maple. On a warm day, Alsea Falls offers cool relief along the river. The area was named after its original inhabitants, the Alsi Indians.

RV sites, facilities: There are 22 sites for RVs up to 26 feet or tents. Fire pits are provided. Drinking water, vault toilets, garbage bins, and fireplaces for wood and charcoal are available. A pay phone and an ATM are within 9.5 miles. Leashed pets are permitted.

Reservations, fees: Reservations are not accepted. The fee is $10 per night, plus $5 per additional vehicle. A senior discount is available. Open mid-May to late September.

Directions: From Albany, drive west on U.S. 20 for nine miles to Corvallis. Turn left (south) onto Highway 99 and drive 15 miles to County Road 45120. Turn right (west) and drive five miles to Alpine Junction. Continue along the South Fork Alsea Access Road for nine miles to the campground on the right.

Contact: Bureau of Land Management, Salem District Office, 1717 Fabry Rd. SE, Salem, OR 97306, 503/375-5646, fax 503/375-5622.

41 CAPE PERPETUA

Rating: 8

on Cape Creek in Siuslaw National Forest
See map pages 230–231

This U.S. Forest Service campground is set along Cape Creek in the Cape Perpetua Scenic Area. The visitor information center provides hiking and driving maps to guide you through this spectacular region, and also shows a movie about the area. Maps highlight the tidepool and picnic spots. The coastal cliffs are perfect for whale-watching from December to March. Neptune State Park is just south and offers additional rugged coastline vistas.

RV sites, facilities: There are 37 sites for RVs up to 22 feet or tents plus one group site that can accommodate 100 people. Picnic tables and fire grills are provided. Flush toilets, drinking water, and garbage bins are available. A pay phone and an ATM are within three miles. Leashed pets are permitted.

Reservations, fees: Reservations are accepted at 877/444-6777 or online at www.reserveusa.com ($9 reservation fee). The fee is $15 per night, plus $5 per additional vehicle. The group site is $125 per night. A senior discount is available. Open year-round.

Directions: From Albany, drive west on U.S. 20 for 66 miles to Newport and U.S. 101. Turn south and drive 23 miles to Yachats. Continue three miles south on U.S. 101 to the entrance on the left.

Contact: Siuslaw National Forest, Waldport Ranger District, 1049 S.W. Pacific Coast Hwy., P.O. Box 400, Waldport, OR 97394, 541/563-3211, fax 541/563-3124; concessionaire, 541/822-3799.

42 SEA PERCH

Rating: 8

near Cape Perpetua
See map pages 230–231

Sea Perch sits right in the middle of one of the most scenic areas on the Oregon coast. This private camp just south of Cape Perpetua has sites on the beach and in lawn areas, plus its own shell museum and gift shop. Big rigs are welcome here.

No tent camping is permitted. For more information on the area, see the previous description of Cape Perpetua.

RV sites, facilities: There are 18 back-up sites with full hookups (30, 50 amps) and 17 pull-through sites with partial hookups (30 amps) for RVs of any length. Picnic tables are provided. Flush toilets, an RV dump station, showers, a pay phone, a recreation hall, a laundry room, ice, a store, modem hookups, and a beach are available. Campfires are permitted on the beach. Leashed pets are permitted.

Reservations, fees: Reservations are accepted. The fee is $28–32 per night June to October, $28 in the off-season, plus $2 per person for more than two people. Major credit cards are accepted. Open year-round.

Directions: From Albany, drive west on U.S. 20 for 66 miles to Newport and U.S. 101. Turn south and drive 23 miles to Yachats. Continue south on U.S. 101 for 6.5 miles to the campground at Milepost 171 on the right.

Contact: Sea Perch Campground, 95480 U.S. 101, Yachats, OR 97498, 541/547-3505.

43 ROCK CREEK

Rating: 7

on Rock Creek in Siuslaw National Forest
See map pages 230–231

This little campground is set along Rock Creek just a quarter mile from the ocean. It's a premium spot for coastal-highway travelers, although it can get packed very quickly. An excellent side trip is to Cape Perpetua, a designated scenic area a few miles up the coast. The cape offers beautiful ocean views and a visitors center that will supply you with information on nature trails, picnic spots, tidepools, and where to find the best viewpoints in the area.

RV sites, facilities: There are 16 sites for RVs up to 22 feet or tents. Fire grills and picnic tables are provided. Flush toilets, garbage bins, and drinking water are available. A pay phone, an ATM, and groceries are available within 10 miles. Leashed pets are permitted.

Reservations, fees: Reservations are not accepted. The fee is $15 per night, plus $5 per additional vehicle. A senior discount is available. Open year-round.

Directions: From Albany, drive west on U.S. 20 for 66 miles to Newport and U.S. 101. Turn south and drive 23 miles to Yachats. Continue south on U.S. 101 for 10 miles to the campground entrance on the left.

Contact: Siuslaw National Forest, Waldport Ranger District, 1049 S.W. Pacific Coast Hwy., P.O. Box 400, Waldport, OR 97394, 541/563-3211, fax 541/563-3124; concessionaire, 541/547-3679.

44 CARL G. WASHBURNE STATE PARK

Rating: 7

on the Pacific Ocean
See map pages 230–231

These spacious campsites feature a buffer of native plants between you and the highway. At night you can hear the pounding surf. A creek runs through the campground, and elk have been known to wander through. Short hikes lead from the campground to a two-mile-long beach, extensive tidepools along the base of the cliffs, and a three-mile trail to Heceta Head Lighthouse. Just three miles south of the park are the Sea Lion Caves, where an elevator takes visitors down into a cavern for an insider's view of the life of a sea lion. The park also offers Junior Ranger programs.

RV sites, facilities: There are 58 sites with full hookups (20 amps) for RVs up to 45 feet, seven primitive walk-in sites, and two yurts. A special area is available for hikers and bicyclists. Picnic tables and fire rings are provided. Drinking water, flush toilets, showers, an RV dump station, a pay phone, badmitton and volleyball courts, a sandbox, and firewood are available. An ATM is within 10 miles. Leashed pets are permitted.

Reservations, fees: Reservations are not accepted. The fees are $17–21 per night plus $7 per additional vehicle, $4 per person per night for hikers/bicyclists, and $29 per night for yurts. Major credit cards are accepted. Open year-round.

Directions: From Eugene, drive west on Highway 126 for 61 miles to Florence and U.S. 101. Turn north on U.S. 101 and drive 12.5 miles to the park entrance road (well signed, 10 miles

OREGON

south of the town of Yachats). Turn right (east) and drive a short distance to the park.

Contact: Carl G. Washburne State Park, 93111 U.S. 101 N, Florence, OR 97439, 541/547-3416 or 800/551-6949.

45 ALDER DUNE

Rating: 7

near Alder Lake in Siuslaw National Forest
See map pages 230–231

This wooded campground is situated near four lakes—Alder Lake, Sutton Lake, Dune Lake, and Mercer Lake (the largest). A boat launch is available at Sutton Lake. A recreation option is to explore the expansive sand dunes in the area by foot. There is no off-road-vehicle access here. See the description of Harbor Vista County Park in this chapter for other information on the area.

RV sites, facilities: There are 39 sites for RVs up to 30 feet or tents. Picnic tables and fire grills are provided. Flush toilets, garbage bins, drinking water, and cell phone reception are available. Leashed pets are permitted.

Reservations, fees: Reservations are not accepted. The fee is $15 per night, plus $7 per additional vehicle. An ATM, a pay phone, a coin-operated laundry, and coin-operated showers are within 4.5 miles. A senior discount is available. Open mid-May to mid-September.

Directions: From Eugene, drive west on Highway 126 for 61 miles to Florence and U.S. 101. Turn north on U.S. 101 and drive eight miles to the campground on the left.

Contact: Siuslaw National Forest, Mapleton Ranger District, 4480 U.S. 101, Building G, Florence, OR 97439, 541/902-8526, fax 541/902-6946.

46 SUTTON

Rating: 7

near Sutton Lake in Siuslaw National Forest
See map pages 230–231

This campground is located adjacent to Sutton Creek, not far from Sutton Lake. Vegetation provides some privacy between sites. Holman Vista on Sutton Beach Road provides a beautiful view of the dunes and ocean. Wading and fishing are both popular. A hiking trail system leads from the camp out to the dunes. There is no off-road-vehicle access here. An alternative camp is Alder Dune to the north.

RV sites, facilities: There are 80 sites, 20 with partial hookups (20 amps), for RVs up to 30 feet or tents and two group sites. Picnic tables and fire grills are provided. Flush toilets, garbage bins, drinking water, and cell phone reception are available. A boat ramp is nearby. An ATM, a pay phone, a coin-operated laundry, and coin-operated showers are within four miles. Leashed pets are permitted.

Reservations, fees: Reserve at 877/444-6777 or online at www.reserveusa.com ($9 reservation fee). The fees are $15–17 per night, plus $7 per additional vehicle, and $75–120 for group sites. A senior discount is available. Open year-round.

Directions: From Eugene, drive west on Highway 126 for 61 miles to Florence and U.S. 101. Turn north on U.S. 101 and drive six miles to Sutton Beach Road (Forest Road 794). Turn northwest and drive 1.5 miles to the campground entrance.

Contact: Siuslaw National Forest, Mapleton Ranger District, 4480 U.S. 101, Building G, Florence, OR 97439, 541/902-8526, fax 541/902-6946.

47 MAPLE LANE TRAILER PARK-MARINA

Rating: 5

on the Siuslaw River
See map pages 230–231

This park along the shore of the Siuslaw River in Mapleton is close to hiking trails. The general area is surrounded by Siuslaw National Forest land. A U.S. Forest Service map details nearby backcountry side-trip options. Fall is the most popular time of the year here, as it's prime time for salmon fishing on Siuslaw.

RV sites, facilities: There are 46 sites with full hookups (20, 30 amps) for RVs up to 35 feet and two tent sites. Drinking water, flush toilets, propane, an RV dump station, picnic tables, fire rings, cell phone reception, and showers are available. A store, an ATM, a pay phone, a café, and ice are behind the park. A bait and tackle shop is open during the fishing season. Boat docks and launching facilities are on-site. Small pets (under 15 pounds) are permitted.

Reservations, fees: Reservations are accepted. The fee is $7–14 per night, plus $1.50 per person for more than two people and $2 per additional vehicle. Open year-round.

Directions: From Eugene, drive west on Highway 126 for 47 miles to Mapleton. Continue on Highway 126 for .25 mile past the business district to the park entrance on the left.

Contact: Maple Lane Trailer Park-Marina, 10730 Hwy.126, Mapleton, OR 97453, 541/268-4822.

48 ARCHIE KNOWLES

Rating: 6

on Knowles Creek in Siuslaw National Forest
See map pages 230–231

This little campground along Knowles Creek about three miles east of Mapleton is rustic with a mix of forested and lawn areas, yet it offers easy proximity to the highway.

RV sites, facilities: There are nine sites for RVs up to 16 feet or tents. Picnic tables and fire grills are provided. Chemical toilets, garbage bins, and drinking water are available. An ATM, a pay phone, and a coin-operated laundry are within three miles. Leashed pets are permitted.

Reservations, fees: Reservations are not accepted. The fee is $10 per night, plus $7 per additional vehicle. A senior discount is available. Open May to late September.

Directions: From Eugene, drive west on Highway 126 for 44 miles to the campground entrance (three miles east of Mapleton).

Contact: Siuslaw National Forest, Mapleton Ranger District, 4480 U.S. 101, Building G, Florence, OR 97439, 541/902-8526, fax 541/902-6946.

49 HARBOR VISTA COUNTY PARK

Rating: 6

near Florence
See map pages 230–231

This county park out among the dunes near the entrance to the harbor offers a great lookout point from its observation deck. A number of side trips are available, including to the Sea Lion

Caves, Darlington State Park, Jessie M. Honeyman Memorial State Park (see the description in this chapter), and the Indian Forest, just four miles north. Florence also has displays of Native American dwellings and crafts.

RV sites, facilities: There are 38 sites with partial hookups (30, 50 amps) for RVs up to 60 feet or tents. Picnic tables and garbage bins are provided. Flush toilets, cell phone reception, an RV dump station, coin-operated showers, drinking water, a pay phone, and a playground are available. An ATM and groceries are available within four miles. Leashed pets are permitted.

Reservations, fees: Reserve at 541/997-5987 (at least 14 days in advance, $14 reservation fee). The fee is $20 per night, plus $6.50 per night for a third vehicle. Open year-round.

Directions: From Eugene, drive west on Highway 126 for 61 miles to Florence and U.S. 101. Turn right (north) and drive four miles to 35th Street. Turn left and drive to where it dead-ends into Rhododendron Drive. Turn right and drive 1.4 miles to North Jetty Road. Turn left and drive half a block to Harbor Vista Road. Turn left and continue to the campground at 87658 Harbor Vista Road.

Note: Follow these exact directions. Visitors to this park taking a different route will discover that part of Harbor Vista Road is now gated.

Contact: Harbor Vista County Park, 87658 Harbor Vista Rd., Florence, OR 97439, 541/997-5987, website: www.co.lane.or.us/park.

50 B AND E WAYSIDE MOBILE HOME AND RV PARK

Rating: 5

near Florence
See map pages 230–231

This landscaped park is beautifully maintained, clean, and quiet. The property features a 28-unit mobile home park that is adjacent to this RV park. Some sites at the RV park are taken by monthly rentals. No tent camping is allowed. See the descriptions of Harbor Vista County Park and Port of Siuslaw RV Park and Marina for side-trip ideas. Nearby recreation options include two golf courses and a riding stable (two miles away).

RV sites, facilities: There are 24 sites with full

hookups (30 amps) for RVs of any length. Picnic tables and fire rings are provided. Drinking water, flush toilets, an RV dump station, a recreation hall, pool tables, a library, a mail room, showers, and a laundry room are available. Propane, a store, ice, a café, an ATM, and a restaurant are within two miles. A pay phone is across the street. Boat-launching facilities are nearby. Small leashed pets are permitted.

Reservations, fees: Reservations are accepted. The fee is $22 per night, plus $2 per person for more than two people. Open year-round.

Directions: From Eugene, drive west on Highway 126 for 61 miles to Florence and U.S. 101. Turn north on U.S. 101 and drive 1.8 miles to the park on the right.

Contact: B and E Wayside Mobile Home and RV Park, 3760 U.S. 101 N, Florence, OR 97439, 541/997-6451.

51 PORT OF SIUSLAW RV PARK AND MARINA

🚶🚴🛶🎣🛥️🐕♿🚐⛺

Rating: 8

on the Siuslaw River

See map pages 230–231

This public resort can be found along the Siuslaw River in a grassy, urban setting. Anglers with boats will find that the U.S. 101 bridge support pilings make good spots for crabbing as well as fishing for perch and flounder. A new set of docks with drinking water, electricity, gasoline, security, and a fish-cleaning station are available. The sea lion caves and estuary are a bonus for wildlife lovers, and nearby lakes make swimming and water-skiing a possibility. Golf is within driving distance, and horses can be rented about nine miles away.

RV sites, facilities: There are 84 sites with full hookups (20, 30 amps) for RVs of any length or tents. Picnic tables and drinking water are provided. Flush toilets, an RV dump station, cable TV, showers, a laundry room, and boat docks are available. A café and ice are within one mile. Leashed pets are permitted.

Reservations, fees: Reserve at 541/997-3040. The fee is $20–22 per night. Major credit cards are accepted. Open year-round.

Directions: From Eugene, drive west on Highway

126 for 61 miles to Florence and U.S. 101. Turn south on U.S. 101 and drive to Harbor Street. Turn left (east) on Harbor Street and drive about three blocks to the park and marina.

Contact: Port of Siuslaw RV Park and Marina, 080 Harbor St., P.O. Box 1638, Florence, OR 97439, 541/997-3040, fax 541/997-9407.

52 JESSIE M. HONEYMAN MEMORIAL STATE PARK

🚶🚴🛶🎣🛥️🐕♿🚐⛺

Rating: 7

near Cleowax Lake

See map pages 230–231

This popular state park is within walking distance of the shore of Cleowax Lake and adjacent to the dunes of the Oregon Dunes National Recreation Area. Dunes stretch for two miles between the park and the ocean. The dunes here are quite impressive, with some reaching to 500 feet. In the winter, the area is open to OHV use. For thrill seekers, sand boards (for sand-boarding on the dunes) are available to rent in nearby Florence. The two lakes in the park offer facilities for boating, fishing, and swimming. A one-mile hiking trail with access to the dunes is available in the park, and off-road-vehicle trails are nearby in the sand dunes.

RV sites, facilities: There are 141 sites with partial or full hookups (20, 30, 50 amps) for RVs up to 60 feet, 237 sites for tents, a special camping area for hikers and bicyclists, six group tent areas, and 10 yurts. Picnic tables, garbage bins, and fire grills are provided. Drinking water, flush toilets, an RV dump station, showers, evening interpretive programs and events, and firewood are available. An ATM is within three miles. Boat docks and launching facilities are nearby. Some facilities are wheelchair-accessible. Leashed pets are permitted.

Reservations, fees: Reserve at 800/452-5687 or online at www.OregonStateParks.org ($6 reservation fee). The fees are $13–21 per night plus $7 per additional vehicle, $4 per person per night for hikers/bicyclists, $29 per night for yurts, and $64 per night for group sites. Open year-round.

Directions: From Eugene, drive west on Highway 126 for 61 miles to Florence and U.S. 101.

OREGON

Turn south on U.S. 101 and drive three miles to the park entrance on the right.

Contact: Jessie M. Honeyman Memorial State Park, 84505 U.S. 101, Florence, OR 97439, 541/997-3641 or 800/551-6949, fax 541/997-3252.

53 LAKESHORE RV PARK

Rating: 5

on Woahink Lake
See map pages 230–231

Here's a prime area for vacationers. This park is set along the shore of Woahink Lake, a popular spot to fish for trout, perch, catfish, crappie, bluegill, and bass. It's adjacent to Jessie M. Honeyman Memorial State Park and the Oregon Dunes National Recreation Area. Off-road-vehicle access to the dunes is four miles northeast of the park. Hiking trails through the dunes can be found at Honeyman Memorial State Park. If you set out across the dunes off the trail, note your path. People hiking off trail commonly get lost here.

RV sites, facilities: There are 20 sites with full hookups (30 amps) for RVs of any length; six are drive-through sites. No tent camping is allowed. Picnic tables are provided. Drinking water, flush toilets, cable TV hookups, modem access, cell phone reception, showers, and a laundry room are available. An ATM, pay phone, and groceries are available within two miles. A café is within three miles. Boat docks are nearby. Leashed pets are permitted.

Reservations, fees: Reservations are accepted. The fee is $20 per night, plus $2 per person for more than two people. Monthly rentals are available. Open year-round.

Directions: From Eugene, drive west on Highway 126 for 61 miles to Florence and U.S. 101. Turn south on U.S. 101 and drive four miles to Milepost 195 and the park on the left.

Contact: Lakeshore RV Park, 83763 U.S. 101, Florence, OR 97439, tel./fax 541/997-2741, website: www.lakeshorerv.com.

54 WOAHINK LAKE RV RESORT

Rating: 7

on Woahink Lake
See map pages 230–231

One of several RV parks in the Florence area, this quiet, clean camp is across from Woahink Lake, where trout fishing is an option. Nearby Oregon Dunes National Recreation Area makes a good side trip.

RV sites, facilities: There are 76 sites with full hookups (20, 30, 50 amps) for RVs of any length and one cabin. No tent camping is allowed. Picnic tables are provided. Drinking water, restrooms, showers, cable TV, a pay phone, modem access, cell phone reception, and a laundry room are available. Recreational facilities include horseshoes, a recreation hall, a game room, and a boat dock. An ATM is within 4.5 miles. One large or two small leashed pets per site are permitted.

Reservations, fees: Reservations are recommended. The fee is $25 per night, plus $2 per person for more than two people and $6 per additional vehicle. Major credit cards are accepted. Open year-round.

Directions: From Eugene, drive west on Highway 126 for 61 miles to Florence and U.S. 101. Turn south on U.S. 101 and drive 5.1 miles to the camp on the right.

Contact: Woahink Lake RV Resort, 83570 U.S. 101 S, Florence, OR 97439, 541/997-6454, reservations 800/659-6454, fax 541/902-0481, website: www.ohwy.com/or/w/woahlkrv.htm.

55 MERCER LAKE RESORT

Rating: 7

on Mercer Lake
See map pages 230–231

This resort is along the shore of Mercer Lake, one of a number of lakes that have formed among the ancient dunes in this area.

RV sites, facilities: There are 11 sites, four drive-through with full hookups (20, 30 amps) and seven with partial hookups, for RVs of any length, and 10 cabins. No open fires and no tent camping are allowed. Picnic tables are provided. Drinking water, flush toilets, an RV dump station,

OREGON

showers, a small store, a laundry room, a pay phone, modem access, and ice are available. Boat docks, launching facilities, and fishing boat rentals are on-site. Leashed pets are permitted.

Reservations, fees: Reserve at 800/355-3633. The fee is $17–21 per night, plus $2 per person for more than four people and $2 per additional vehicle. Cabins are $45–100, depending on season. Major credit cards are accepted. Open year-round.

Directions: From Eugene, drive west on Highway 126 for 61 miles to Florence and U.S. 101. Turn north on U.S. 101 and drive five miles to Mercer Lake Road. Turn east and drive just under one mile to Bay Berry Lane. Turn left and drive to the resort.

Contact: Mercer Lake Resort, 88875 Bay Berry Ln., Florence, OR 97439, 541/997-3633, fax 541/997-5096, website: www.mlroregon.com.

56 CARTER LAKE

Rating: 9

on Carter Lake in Oregon Dunes National Recreation Area

See map pages 230–231

This campground sits on the north shore of Carter Lake, and you can fish almost right from your campsite. Boating, swimming, and fishing are permitted on this long, narrow lake, which is set among dunes overgrown with vegetation. The nearby Taylor Dunes Trail is an easy half-mile wheelchair-accessible trail to the dunes past Taylor Lake. Hiking is allowed in the dunes, but there is no off-road-vehicle access here. If you want off-road access, head north one mile to Siltcoos Road, turn west, and drive 1.3 miles to Driftwood II.

RV sites, facilities: There are 23 sites for RVs up to 35 feet or tents. Picnic tables, garbage service, and fire grills are provided. Drinking water and flush toilets are available. A pay phone is within 1.5 miles, and an ATM, groceries, a coin-operated laundry, and coin-operated showers are available within nine miles. Leashed pets are permitted.

Reservations, fees: Reserve at 877/444-6777 or online at www.reserveusa.com ($9 reservation fee). The fee is $15 per night, plus $7 per additional vehicle. A senior discount is available. Open early May to late September.

Directions: From Eugene, drive west on Highway 126 for 61 miles to Florence and U.S. 101. Turn south on U.S. 101 and drive 8.5 miles to Forest Road 1084. Turn right on Forest Road 1084 and drive west 200 yards to the camp.

Contact: Oregon Dunes National Recreation Area, Visitor Center, 855 U.S. 101, Reedsport, OR 97467, 541/271-3611, fax 541/750-7244.

57 DRIFTWOOD II

Rating: 7

near Siltcoos Lake in Oregon Dunes National Recreation Area

See map pages 230–231

Primarily a campground for off-road vehicles, Driftwood II is near the ocean, but without an ocean view, in the Oregon Dunes National Recreation Area. It has off-road-vehicle access. Several small lakes, the Siltcoos River, and Siltcoos Lake are nearby. Note that ATV use is prohibited between 10 P.M. and 6 A.M.

RV sites, facilities: There are 68 sites for RVs up to 50 feet or tents. Picnic tables, garbage service, and fire grills are provided. Drinking water, flush and vault toilets, a pay phone, and cell phone reception are available. An RV dump station is within five miles. An ATM, groceries, a coin-operated laundry, and coin-operated showers are available within 8.5 miles. Boat docks, launching facilities, and rentals can be found about four miles away on Siltcoos Lake. Some facilities are wheelchair-accessible. Leashed pets are permitted.

Reservations, fees: Reserve at 877/444-6777 or online at www.reserveusa.com ($9 reservation fee). The fee is $15 per night, plus $7 per night for each additional vehicle. A senior discount is available. Open year-round.

Directions: From Eugene, drive west on Highway 126 for 61 miles to Florence and U.S. 101. Turn south on U.S. 101 and drive seven miles to Siltcoos Beach Road. Turn right and drive 1.5 miles west to the campground.

Contact: Oregon Dunes National Recreation Area, Visitor Center, 855 U.S. 101, Reedsport, OR 97467, 541/271-3611, fax 541/750-7244.

OREGON

58 LAGOON

Rating: 9

near Siltcoos Lake in Oregon Dunes National Recreation Area

See map pages 230–231

One of several campgrounds in the area, this camp is located along the lagoon, about one mile from Siltcoos Lake, and a half mile inland. The Lagoon Trail offers prime wildlife viewing for marine birds and other aquatic species.

RV sites, facilities: There are 39 sites for RVs up to 35 feet or tents. Picnic tables, garbage service, and fire grills are provided. Drinking water, flush and vault toilets, a pay phone, and cell phone reception are available. An RV dump station is within five miles. Boat docks, launching facilities, and rentals are nearby on Siltcoos Lake. An ATM, groceries, a coin-operated laundry, and coin-operated showers are available within 8.5 miles. Leashed pets are permitted.

Reservations, fees: Reservations are not accepted. The fee is $15 per night, plus $7 per additional vehicle. A senior discount is available. Open year-round.

Directions: From Eugene, drive west on Highway 126 for 61 miles to Florence and U.S. 101. Turn south on U.S. 101 and drive seven miles to Siltcoos Beach Road. Turn right on Siltcoos Beach Road and drive west for 1.2 miles to the campground.

Contact: Oregon Dunes National Recreation Area, Visitor Center, 855 U.S. 101, Reedsport, OR 97467, 541/271-3611, fax 541/750-7244.

59 DARLINGS RESORT

Rating: 7

on Siltcoos Lake

See map pages 230–231

This park, in a rural area along the north shore of Siltcoos Lake, is adjacent to the extensive Oregon Dunes National Recreation Area. Sites are right on the lake; fish from your picnic table. An access point to the dunes for hikers and off-road vehicles is just across the highway. The lake has a full-service marina. About half the sites are taken by monthly rentals.

RV sites, facilities: There are 42 sites, 18 with full hookups (20, 30 amps), for RVs of any length. No tent camping is allowed. Picnic tables and fire rings are provided. Drinking water, flush toilets, showers, firewood, cable TV hookups, a store, a tavern, a deli, boat docks, boat rentals, launching facilities, and a laundry room are available. An ATM and pay phone are within five miles. Leashed pets are permitted.

Reservations, fees: Reservations are accepted. The fee is $22.50 per night, plus $5 per additional vehicle. Major credit cards are accepted. Open year-round.

Directions: From Eugene, drive west on Highway 126 for 61 miles to Florence and U.S. 101. Turn south on U.S. 101 and drive five miles to North Beach Road. Turn east and drive .5 mile to the resort.

Contact: Darlings Resort, 4879 Darling Loop, Florence, OR 97439, 541/997-2841, website: www.darlingsresort.com.

60 WAXMYRTLE

Rating: 7

near Siltcoos Lake in Oregon Dunes National Recreation Area

See map pages 230–231

One of three camps in the immediate vicinity, Waxmyrtle is adjacent to Lagoon and less than a mile from Driftwood II. The camp is near the Siltcoos River and a couple of miles from Siltcoos Lake, a good-sized lake with boating facilities where you can water-ski, fish, and swim. A pleasant hiking trail here meanders through the dunes and along the estuary.

RV sites, facilities: There are 55 sites for RVs up to 35 feet or tents. Picnic tables, garbage service, and fire grills are provided. Drinking water and flush toilets are available. Boat docks, launching facilities, and rentals are nearby on Siltcoos Lake. Leashed pets are permitted.

Reservations, fees: Reservations are not accepted. The fee is $15 per night, plus $7 per additional vehicle. A senior discount is available. Open late May to early October.

Directions: From Eugene, drive west on Highway 126 for 61 miles to Florence and U.S. 101. Turn south on U.S. 101 and drive seven miles to

OREGON

Siltcoos Beach Road. Turn right and drive 1.3 miles west to the campground.

Contact: Oregon Dunes National Recreation Area, Visitor Center, 855 U.S. 101, Reedsport, OR 97467, 541/271-3611, fax 541/750-7244.

61 TAHKENITCH LANDING

Rating: 6

near Tahkenitch Lake in Oregon Dunes National Recreation Area

See map pages 230–231

This camp overlooking Tahkenitch Lake has easy access for fishing and swimming. Fishing is excellent on Tahkenitch, which means "a lake with many fingers." There is no drinking water here, but water, a boat ramp, and a dock are available nearby at the lake.

RV sites, facilities: There are 27 sites for RVs up to 30 feet or tents. Picnic tables and garbage service are provided. Vault toilets, boat-launching facilities, cell phone reception, and a floating dock are available, but there is no drinking water. An ATM, a pay phone, and a store are within seven miles. Leashed pets are permitted.

Reservations, fees: Reservations are not accepted. The fee is $15 per night, plus $7 per additional vehicle. A senior discount is available. Open year-round.

Directions: From Eugene, drive west on Highway 126 for 61 miles to Florence and U.S. 101. Turn south on U.S. 101 and drive 14 miles to the campground on the east side of the road.

Contact: Oregon Dunes National Recreation Area, Visitor Center, 855 U.S. 101, Reedsport, OR 97467, 541/271-3611, fax 541/750-7244.

62 TAHKENITCH

Rating: 7

near Tahkenitch Lake in Oregon Dunes National Recreation Area

See map pages 230–231

This very pretty campground is in a wooded area across the highway from Tahkenitch Lake, which has numerous coves and backwater areas for fishing and swimming. A hiking trail close to the camp goes through the dunes out to the beach, as well as to Threemile Lake. If this camp is full, Tahkenitch Landing provides space nearby.

RV sites, facilities: There are 34 sites for RVs up to 30 feet or tents. Picnic tables, garbage service, and fire grills are provided. Drinking water, flush and vault toilets, and cell phone reception are available. Boat docks and launching facilities are on the lake across the highway. An ATM and pay phone are within seven miles. Leashed pets are permitted.

Reservations, fees: Reservations are accepted at 877/444-6777 or online at www.reserveusa.com ($9 reservation fee). The fee is $15 per night, plus $7 per additional vehicle. A senior discount is available. Open mid-May to late September.

Directions: From Eugene, drive west on Highway 126 for 61 miles to Florence and U.S. 101. Turn south on U.S. 101 and drive 14 miles. The campground entrance is on the right.

Contact: Oregon Dunes National Recreation Area, Visitor Center, 855 U.S. 101, Reedsport, OR 97467, 541/271-3611, fax 541/750-7244.

63 DISCOVERY POINT RESORT & RV PARK

Rating: 7

on Winchester Bay

See map pages 230–231

This resort sits on the shore of Winchester Bay in a fishing village near the mouth of the Umpqua River, adjacent to sandy dunes. The park was designed around motor sports, and ATVs are available for rent. It is somewhat noisy, but that's what most people come here for.

RV sites, facilities: There are 60 sites with full hookups (30 amps), 20 drive-through, for RVs of any length, 12 tent sites, and eight cabins. Picnic tables and fire rings are provided. Drinking water, flush toilets, showers, a pay phone, a store, a laundry room, cable TV hookups, and ice are available. An RV dump station, ATM, and propane are within 1.5 miles. Boat docks and launching facilities are nearby. Leashed pets are permitted.

Reservations, fees: Reservations are accepted. The fees are $15 for tent sites, $24–27 for RV sites. Major credit cards are accepted. Open year-round.

Directions: From Eugene, drive south on I-5 for about 35 miles to Exit 162 and Highway 38. Turn west on Highway 38 and drive 64 miles to Reedsport and U.S. 101. Turn south on U.S. 101 and drive three miles to the Windy Cove exit near Winchester Bay. Take that exit and drive west 1.5 miles to the resort.

Contact: Discovery Point Resort & RV Park, 242 Discovery Point Ln., Winchester Bay, OR 97467, 541/271-3443, fax 541/271-9285, website: www .discoverypointresort.com.

64 WINDY COVE COUNTY PARK

Rating: 7

on the Pacific Ocean

See map pages 230–231

This Douglas County park actually comprises two parks, Windy Cove A and B. Set near ocean beaches and sand dunes, both offer a variety of additional recreational opportunities, including an 18-hole golf course, hiking trails, and a lighthouse.

RV sites, facilities: There are 63 sites with full hookups (30, 50 amps) for RVs up to 60 feet, four sites with partial hookups, and 29 tent sites. Picnic tables and fire rings are provided. Drinking water, flush toilets, showers, and cable TV are available. Propane, an RV dump station, a store, a café, a coin-operated laundry, an ATM, a pay phone, and ice are within one mile. Boat docks, launching facilities, boat charters, and rentals are nearby. Leashed pets are permitted.

Reservations, fees: Reserve at 541/440-4500. The fee is $12–17 per night, plus $3 per additional vehicle. Major credit cards are accepted. A senior discount is available for residents of Douglas County. Open year-round.

Directions: From Eugene, drive south on I-5 to Exit 162 and Highway 38. Turn west on Highway 38 and drive 64 miles to Reedsport and U.S. 101. Turn south on U.S. 101 and drive three miles to the Windy Cove exit near Winchester Bay. Take that exit and drive west to the park on the left.

Contact: Windy Cove County Park, 684 Salmon Harbor Dr., Reedsport, OR 97467, 541/271-5634 or 541/271-4138, website: www.co.douglas.or.us /parks.

65 UMPQUA LIGHTHOUSE STATE PARK

Rating: 7

on the Umpqua River

See map pages 230–231

This park is located near Lake Marie and less than a mile from Salmon Harbor on Winchester Bay. Near the mouth of the Umpqua River, this unusual area features dunes as high as 500 feet. Hiking trails lead out of the park and into the Oregon Dunes National Recreation Area. The park offers more than two miles of beach access on the ocean and a half mile along the Umpqua River. The adjacent lighthouse is still in operation, and tours are available during the summer season.

RV sites, facilities: There are 20 sites with full hookups (20, 30 amps) for RVs up to 45 feet, 24 tent sites, two cabins, two standard yurts, and six deluxe yurts. Garbage bins, picnic tables, and fire rings are provided. Flush toilets, showers, a pay phone, cell phone reception, and firewood are available. Boat docks and launching facilities are on the Umpqua River. A coin-operated laundry is within one mile, and an ATM is within five miles. Leashed pets are permitted.

Reservations, fees: Reserve at 800/452-5687 or online at www.OregonStateParks.org ($6 reservation fee). The fees are $12–20 per night plus $7 per night for an additional vehicle, $4 per person per night for hikers/bikers, $35 for cabins, and $27–65 for yurts. Major credit cards are accepted. Open year-round.

Directions: From Eugene, drive south on I-5 to Exit 162 and Highway 38. Turn west on Highway 38 and drive 64 miles to Reedsport and U.S. 101. Turn south on U.S. 101 and drive six miles to Umpqua Lighthouse Road. Turn right and drive one mile to the park.

Contact: Umpqua Lighthouse State Park, 460 Lighthouse Rd., Reedsport, OR 97467, 541/271-4118 or 800/551-6949.

66 WILLIAM M. TUGMAN STATE PARK

Rating: 7

on Eel Lake

See map pages 230–231

This campground is set along the shore of Eel

OREGON

Lake, which offers almost five miles of shoreline for swimming, fishing, boating, and sailing. It's perfect for bass fishing. A boat ramp is available, but there is a 10 mph speed limit for boats. Oregon Dunes National Recreation Area is across the highway. Hiking is available just a few miles north at Umpqua Lighthouse State Park. A trail along the south end of the lake allows hikers to get away from the developed areas of the park and explore the lake's many outlets. This camp has gone from three to 13 yurts, and they are almost always booked.

RV sites, facilities: There are 99 sites with water and electrical hookups for RVs up to 50 feet, a special camping area for hikers, and 13 yurts. Picnic tables and fire rings are provided. Drinking water, flush toilets, an RV dump station, a pay phone, showers, firewood, and a picnic shelter are available. Boat docks and launching facilities are nearby. An ATM is within two miles. Some facilities are wheelchair-accessible. Leashed pets are permitted.

Reservations, fees: Reserve at 800/452-5687 or online at www.OregonStateParks.org ($6 reservation fee). The fees are $15 per night plus $7 per additional vehicle, $4 per person per night for hikers/bicyclists, and $27 per night for yurts. Major credit cards are accepted. Open year-round.

Directions: From Eugene, drive south on I-5 to Exit 162 and Highway 38. Turn west on Highway 38 and drive 64 miles to Reedsport and U.S. 101. Turn south on U.S. 101 and drive eight miles to the park entrance on the left.

Contact: William M. Tugman State Park, 72549 Highway 101, Lakeside, OR 97449, 541/759-3604 or 800/551-6949.

67 NORTH LAKE RESORT AND MARINA

Rating: 9

on Tenmile Lake
See map pages 230–231

This 55-acre resort along the shore of Tenmile Lake is wooded and secluded, with a private beach, and makes the perfect layover spot for U.S. 101 travelers. The lake has a full-service marina, and bass fishing can be good here. The park recently underwent extensive renovations

throughout. About 10 percent of the sites are taken by summer season rentals.

RV sites, facilities: There are 25 sites with full hookups (50 amps) and 30 with partial hookups, both for RVs up to 65 feet, and 35 tent sites. Picnic tables are provided. Drinking water, flush toilets, an RV dump station, a fish-cleaning station, showers, firewood, a store, ice, modem access, cable TV hookups, cell phone reception, drinking water, fire rings, boat rentals, a boat launch, a pay phone, coin-operated laundry facilities, horseshoes, and a volleyball court are available. A café and boat docks are also available. An ATM is within .75 mile. Leashed pets are permitted.

Reservations, fees: Reservations are accepted. The fees are $25 per night for RV sites, $20 per night for tent sites. Major credit cards are accepted. Open April to October.

Directions: From Eugene, drive south on I-5 to Exit 162 and Highway 38. Turn west on Highway 38 and drive 64 miles to Reedsport and U.S. 101. Turn south on U.S. 101 and drive 11 miles to the Lakeside exit. Take that exit and drive east on North Lake Avenue for .75 mile, then continue on North Lake Road for .75 mile to the resort on the left.

Contact: North Lake Resort and Marina, 2090 North Lake Rd., Lakeside, OR 97449, 541/759-3515, fax 541/759-3326.

68 OSPREY POINT RV RESORT

Rating: 7

on Tenmile Lake
See map pages 230–231

Tenmile is one of Oregon's premier bass fishing lakes and yet is located only three miles from the ocean. The resort is situated in a large, open area adjacent to Tenmile Lake and a half mile from North Lake. A navigable canal connects the lakes. The Oregon Dunes National Recreation Area provides nearby hiking trails, and Elliot State Forest offers wooded trails. With occasional live entertainment, Osprey Point is more a destination resort than an overnight stop.

RV sites, facilities: There are 132 sites with full hookups (20, 30, 50 amps), some pull-through, for RVs of any size or tents, 20 tent sites, and four park-model rentals. Picnic tables and fire rings are provided. Drinking water, restrooms with flush toilets and showers, garbage bins, modem access, cable TV hookups, telephone hookups, an RV dump station, coin-operated laundry facilities, a restaurant, a cocktail lounge, a grocery store, a full service marina with boat docks, a pay phone, cell phone reception, a launch, a fishing pier, a fish-cleaning station, horseshoes, volleyball, tether ball, a recreation hall, a video arcade, beauty and barber shops, and a pizza parlor are available. An ATM is within a half mile. Leashed pets are permitted.

Reservations, fees: Reservations are accepted. The fees are $24–34 per night for RV sites and $18 per night for tent sites, plus $3.50 per person for more than two people and $2.50 per additional vehicle. Major credit cards are accepted. Open year-round.

Directions: From Coos Bay, drive north on U.S. 101 for 13 miles to the Lakeside exit. Take that exit east into town (across the railroad tracks) to North Lake Road. Turn left (north) on North Lake Road and drive .5 mile to the resort on the right.

Contact: Osprey Point RV Resort, 1505 North Lake Rd., Lakeside, OR 97449, 541/759-2801, fax 541/759-3198, website: www.ospreypoint.net.

69 EEL CREEK

Rating: 8

near Eel Lake in Oregon Dunes National Recreation Area
See map pages 230–231

This campground along Eel Creek is located near both Eel and Tenmile Lakes. Whereas Tenmile Lake allows water-skiing, Eel Lake does not. Nearby trails offer access to the Umpqua Dunes Scenic Area, where you'll find spectacular scenery in an area closed to off-road vehicles. Off-road access is available at Spinreel.

RV sites, facilities: There are 52 sites for RVs up to 35 feet or tents. Picnic tables, garbage service, fire grills, and cell phone reception are provided. Drinking water and flush and vault toilets are available. An ATM and a pay phone are within one mile. Boat docks, launching facilities, and rentals are nearby. Leashed pets are permitted.

Reservations, fees: Reserve at 877/444-6777 or online at www.reserveusa.com ($9 reservation fee). The fees are $15 per night for single sites and $24 for double sites, plus $7 per additional vehicle. A senior discount is available. Open year-round.

Directions: From Eugene, drive south on I-5 to Exit 162 and Highway 38. Turn west on Highway 38 and drive 64 miles to Reedsport and U.S. 101. Turn south on U.S. 101 and drive 10.5 miles to the park entrance.

Contact: Oregon Dunes National Recreation Area, Visitor Center, 855 U.S. 101, Reedsport, OR 97467, 541/271-3611, fax 541/750-7244.

70 SPINREEL

Rating: 6

on Tenmile Creek in Oregon Dunes National Recreation Area
See map pages 230–231

This campground, primarily for off-road-vehicle enthusiasts, is several miles inland at the outlet of Tenmile Lake in the Oregon Dunes National Recreation Area. A boat launch is near the camp. Other recreational opportunities include hiking trails and off-road-vehicle access to the dunes. Off-road-vehicle rentals are available adjacent to the camp.

RV sites, facilities: There are 36 sites for RVs up to 40 feet or tents. Drinking water, garbage service, and flush toilets are available. Picnic tables and fire grills are provided. Firewood, a store, and a coin-operated laundry are nearby. Boat docks, launching facilities, and rentals are available on Tenmile Lake. An ATM, a pay phone, and a store are within four miles. Leashed pets are permitted.

Reservations, fees: Reserve at 877/444-6777 or online at www.reserveusa.com ($9 reservation fee). The fee is $15 per night, plus $7 per additional vehicle. A senior discount is available. Open year-round.

Directions: From Coos Bay, drive north on U.S. 101 for 10 miles to the campground entrance road (well signed). Turn northwest and drive one mile to the campground.

Contact: Oregon Dunes National Recreation Area, Visitor Center, 855 U.S. 101, Reedsport, OR 97467, 541/271-3611, fax 541/750-7244.

OREGON

71 LOON LAKE RECREATION AREA

Rating: 8

on Loon Lake

See map pages 230–231

Loon Lake was created 1,400 years ago when a nearby mountain crumbled and slid downhill, damming the creek with house-sized boulders. Today the lake is a half mile wide and nearly two miles long, covers 260 acres, and is more than 100 feet deep in places. Its ideal location provides a warm, wind-sheltered summer climate for various water activities. A nature trail leads to a waterfall about a quarter mile away. Evening interpretive programs are held during summer weekends.

RV sites, facilities: There are 60 sites for RVs of any length or tents. There are also six group sites for up to 15 people per site. Picnic tables and fire pits are provided. Drinking water, restrooms with flush toilets and showers, garbage bins, an RV dump station, two pay phones, a sand beach, a boat ramp, and moorings are available. Gasoline is available within one mile. Leashed pets are permitted.

Reservations, fees: Reservations are accepted; phone Coos Bay Bureau of Land Management office at 541/756-0100 for information. The fee is $15 per night, plus $7 per additional vehicle. Group sites are $45 per night. Major credit cards are accepted. A senior discount is available. Open late May to mid-September, weather permitting.

Directions: From Eugene, drive south on I-5 to Exit 162 and Highway 38. Turn west on Highway 38 and drive 43 miles to Milepost 13.5 and the County Road 3 exit. Turn south and drive 7.5 miles to the campground.

Contact: Bureau of Land Management, Coos Bay District Office, 1300 Airport Ln., North Bend, OR 97459, 541/756-0100, fax 541/751-4303.

72 LOON LAKE LODGE RESORT

Rating: 8

on Loon Lake

See map pages 230–231

This resort, nestled among the tall trees on pretty Loon Lake, boasts one mile of lake frontage.

It's not a long drive from either U.S. 101 or I-5, making it an ideal layover spot for travelers eager to get off the highway. The lake offers good bass fishing, swimming, boating, and water-skiing.

RV sites, facilities: There are 100 sites, 50 with partial hookups (20, 30 amps), for RVs up to 40 feet or tents, group sites, cabins, and a motel. Picnic tables and fire rings are provided. Drinking water, a pay phone, security, a game room, a restaurant, a bar, a grocery store, ice, gas, and a beach are available. A boat ramp, dock, marina, and rentals are also available. No pets are permitted.

Reservations, fees: Reservations are recommended. The fee is $16–19 per night, plus $4 per person for more than two people and $4 per additional vehicle. Major credit cards are accepted. Open year-round.

Directions: From Eugene, drive south on I-5 to Exit 162 and Highway 38. Turn west on Highway 38 and drive 43 miles to Milepost 13.5 and the County Road 3 exit. Turn south and drive 8.2 miles to the resort on the right.

Contact: Loon Lake Lodge Resort, 9011 Loon Lake Rd., Reedsport, OR 97467, 541/599-2244, fax 541/599-2274.

73 TYEE

Rating: 7

on the Umpqua River

See map pages 230–231

Here's a classic spot set at 240 feet elevation along the Umpqua River, which has great steelhead, salmon, and small mouth bass fishing in season. Boat launches are available a few miles upstream and downstream of the campground. The camp isn't far from I-5, and it's the only campground in the immediate vicinity. Another plus: This campground was renovated in 2001. Because Tyee has become popular, another camp will be constructed one mile down the road, likely available in 2004.

RV sites, facilities: There are 15 sites for RVs up to 25 feet or tents. Drinking water, garbage service, fire grills, and picnic tables are provided. Vault toilets, a day-use area with horseshoes, and a pavilion with a barbecue, water, electricity, and 10 tables are available. A camp host is on-site. A

OREGON

store is within one mile. Some facilities are wheelchair-accessible. Leashed pets are permitted.

Reservations, fees: Reservations are not accepted. The fee is $8 per night, plus $3 for each additional vehicle. A senior discount is available. Open year-round.

Directions: From Roseburg, drive north on I-5 to Exit 136 and Highway 138. Take that exit and drive west on Highway 138 for 12 miles. Cross Bullock Bridge and continue to County Road 57. Turn right and drive .5 mile to the campground entrance.

Contact: Bureau of Land Management, Roseburg District, 777 N.W. Garden Valley Blvd., Roseburg, OR 97470, 541/440-4930, fax 541/440-4948.

74 OREGON DUNES KOA

Rating: 5

six miles north of North Bend, next to the Oregon Dunes National Recreation Area

See map pages 230–231

This ATV-friendly park has direct access to Oregon Dunes National Recreation Area, which offers miles of ATV trails. This fairly open campground features a landscape of grass, young trees, and a small lake. The ocean is a 15-minute drive away. Mill Casino is about six miles south on U.S. 101. Freshwater and ocean fishing are nearby. A golf course is about five miles away.

RV sites, facilities: There are 50 sites with full hookups (30, 50 amps) for RVs of any size or tents, 10 tent sites, and three cabins. Picnic tables and fire rings are provided. Drinking water, restrooms with flush toilets and showers, garbage bins, modem access, satellite TV hookups, wheelchair facilities, a coin-operated laundry, a small store, a pay phone, cell phone reception, horseshoes, volleyball, and a picnic shelter with electricity, a sink, and electric cooktops are available. ORV rentals are nearby. An ATM is within 3.5 miles. Leashed pets are permitted, except in cabins.

Reservations, fees: Reservations are recommended; phone 800/562-4236. The fee is $20–42 per night, plus $2.50–3.50 per person for more than two people and $4.50 per additional vehicle. Major credit cards are accepted. Open year-round.

Directions: From Coos Bay, drive north on U.S.

101 past North Bend for six miles to Milepost 229 and the campground entrance road on the left.

Contact: Oregon Dunes KOA, 68632 U.S. 101, North Bend, OR 97459, 541/756-4851, fax 541/756-8838, website: www.koa.com.

75 WILD MARE HORSE CAMP

Rating: 7

in Oregon Dunes National Recreation Area

See map pages 230–231

This horse camp has paved parking, with single and double corrals. No off-road vehicles are allowed within the campground. Horses can be ridden straight out into the dunes—they cannot be ridden on the developed trails. The heavily treed shoreline gives rise to treed sites with some bushes.

RV sites, facilities: There are 12 horse campsites for RVs up to 50 feet or tents with a maximum of two vehicles per site. Picnic tables and fire pits are provided. Drinking water, vault toilets, cell phone reception, and garbage bins are available. A pay phone, ATM, and casino are within 3.5 miles. Leashed pets are permitted.

Reservations, fees: Reserve at 877/444-6777 or online at www.reserveusa.com ($9 reservation fee). The fee is $15 per night, plus $7 per additional vehicle. Major credit cards are accepted. A senior discount is available. Open year-round.

Directions: From Coos Bay, drive north on U.S. 101 for 1.5 miles to Horsfall Dunes and Beach Access Road. Turn left and drive west for one mile to the campground access road. Turn right and drive .75 mile to the campground on the left.

Contact: Oregon Dunes National Recreation Area, Visitor Center, 855 U.S. 101, Reedsport, OR 97467, 541/271-3611, fax 541/750-7244.

76 BLUEBILL

Rating: 6

on Bluebill Lake in Oregon Dunes National Recreation Area

See map pages 230–231

This campground gets very little camping pressure although there are some good hiking trails available. It's located next to little Bluebill Lake, which sometimes dries up during the summer.

A one-mile trail goes around the lake bed. The camp is a short distance from Horsfall Lake, which is surrounded by private property. If you continue west on the forest road, you'll come to a picnicking and parking area near the beach. This spot provides off-road-vehicle access to the dunes at the Horsfall day-use area and Horsfall Beach.

RV sites, facilities: There are 18 sites for RVs up to 30 feet or tents. Picnic tables, garbage service, and fire grills are provided. Vault toilets and drinking water are available. Leashed pets are permitted.

Reservations, fees: Reservations are not accepted. The fee is $15 per night, plus $7 per night for each additional vehicle. A senior discount is available. Open May to November.

Directions: From Coos Bay, drive north on U.S. 101 for 1.5 miles north to Horsfall Dunes and Beach Access Road. Turn west and drive one mile to Horsfall Road. Turn northwest and drive two miles to the campground entrance.

Contact: Oregon Dunes National Recreation Area, Visitor Center, 855 U.S. 101, Reedsport, OR 97467, 541/271-3611, fax 541/750-7244.

77 HORSFALL

Rating: 4

in Oregon Dunes National Recreation Area
See map pages 230–231

This campground is actually a nice, large paved area for parking RVs. It's the staging area for off-road-vehicle access into the southern section of Oregon Dunes National Recreation Area. If Horsfall is full, try nearby Horsfall Beach, an overflow area with 41 tent and RV sites.

RV sites, facilities: There are 70 sites for RVs up to 50 feet. Drinking water, garbage service, coin-operated showers, a pay phone, cell phone reception, and flush toilets are available. An ATM and groceries are available within three miles. Leashed pets are permitted.

Reservations, fees: Reserve at 877/444-6777 or online at www.reserveusa.com ($9 reservation fee). The fee is $15 per night, plus $7 per additional vehicle. A senior discount is available. Open year-round.

Directions: From Coos Bay, drive north on U.S.

101 for 1.5 miles to Horsfall Road. Turn west on Horsfall Road and drive about one mile to the campground access road. Turn on the campground access road (well signed) and drive .5 mile to the campground.

Contact: Oregon Dunes National Recreation Area, Visitor Center, 855 U.S. 101, Reedsport, OR 97467, 541/271-3611, fax 541/750-7244.

78 SUNSET BAY STATE PARK

Rating: 8

near Sunset Bay
See map pages 230–231

Situated in one of the most scenic areas on the Oregon Coast, this park features beautiful, sandy beaches protected by towering sea cliffs. A network of hiking trails connects Sunset Bay with nearby Shore Acres and Cape Arago Parks. Swimming, boating, fishing, clamming, and golfing are some of the recreation options here.

RV sites, facilities: There are 66 sites for self-contained RVs or tents, 29 sites with full hookups (20, 30 amps) for RVs up to 47 feet, a separate area for hikers and bicyclists, eight yurts, and two group camps for more than 25 people. Picnic tables and fire rings are provided. Drinking water, flush toilets, showers, a meeting hall, a boat ramp, garbage bins, a pay phone, and firewood are available. A restaurant is within three miles. An ATM is within eight miles. Some facilities are wheelchair-accessible. Leashed pets are permitted.

Reservations, fees: Reserve at 800/452-5687 or online at www.OregonStateParks.org ($6 reservation fee). The fees are $13–20 per night plus $7 per additional vehicle, $4 per person per night for hikers/bicyclists, $27 for yurts, and $60 for group camps. Major credit cards are accepted. Open year-round.

Directions: In Coos Bay, take the Charleston/State Parks exit to Newmark Avenue and drive west for three miles to Cape Arago Highway. Turn left and drive about five miles south to Charleston and cross the South Slough Bridge. Continue on Cape Arago Highway about three miles to the park entrance on the left.

Contact: Sunset Bay State Park, 89814 Cape Arago Hwy., Coos Bay, OR 97420, 541/888-4902.

79 KELLEY'S RV PARK

Rating: 5

near Coos Bay
See map pages 230–231
This clean, well-maintained RV park is situated in the town of Coos Bay, well known for its rock-fish and salmon fishing and for its past lumber industry. A shaded picnic area here overlooks the bay. A full-service marina nearby is a giant plus. Note that more than half of the sites are filled with monthly rentals.

RV sites, facilities: There are 38 sites with full hookups (30 amps) for RVs of any length or tents; three are drive-through sites. Picnic tables are provided. Drinking water, flush toilets, modem access, coin-operated showers, a pay phone, cell phone reception, and a laundry room are available. Boat docks and launching facilities are nearby. Propane, a store, an ATM, and a café are available within a mile. Leashed pets are permitted.

Reservations, fees: Reservations are accepted. The fee is $15–16 per night, plus $2 per person for more than two people. Major credit cards are accepted. Monthly rentals are available. Open year-round.

Directions: In Coos Bay on U.S. 101, drive to the Charleston exit. Take that exit (the road changes names several times) to South Empire Boulevard and drive 4.5 miles to the park at 555 South Empire Boulevard.

Contact: Kelley's RV Park, 555 S. Empire Blvd., Coos Bay, OR 97420, 541/888-6531, website: www .rverschoice.com.

80 BASTENDORFF BEACH PARK

Rating: 8

near Cape Arago State Park
See map pages 230–231
This campground provides access to the ocean. Nearby activities include sand-dune buggy riding, golfing, clamming, crabbing, fishing, swimming, whale-watching, and boating. Horses may be rented near Bandon. A nice side trip is to Shore Acres State Park and Botanical Gardens, about 2.5 miles away.

RV sites, facilities: There are 74 sites with partial hookups (30, 50 amps) for RVs up to 40 feet, 25 tent sites, and two cabins. Picnic tables and fire rings are provided. Drinking water, restrooms, showers, an RV dump station, a pay phone, cell phone reception, a fish-cleaning station, horse-shoes, a playground, basketball courts, and a pic-nic area with a shelter and barbecue are available. An ATM is within two miles. Some facilities are wheelchair-accessible. Leashed pets are permitted.

Reservations, fees: Reservations are not accept-ed. The fees are $15–18 per night and $10–14 in the off-season, plus $5 per additional vehicle. Cabins are $30 per night. A senior discount is available. Major credit cards are accepted. Phone 541/396-3121, ext. 354, for reservations for the shelter and cabins. Open year-round.

Directions: In Coos Bay, take the Charleston/State Parks exit to Newmark Avenue and drive west for three miles to Cape Arago Highway. Turn left and drive about five miles south to Charleston and cross the South Slough Bridge. Continue on Cape Arago Highway about two miles to the park entrance.

Contact: Coos County Parks, Coos County Court-house, 250 N. Baxter St., Coquille, OR 97423, website: www.cooscountyparks.com; Bastendorff Beach Park, 4250 Bastendorff Beach Road, Coos Bay, OR 97420, 541/888-5353.

81 CHARLESTON MARINA RV PARK

Rating: 7

on Coos Bay
See map pages 230–231
This large, developed public park and marina is located in Charleston on the Pacific Ocean. Recre-ational activities in and near the campground include hiking, swimming, clamming, crabbing, boating, huckleberry and blackberry picking, and fishing for tuna, salmon, and halibut.

RV sites, facilities: There are 98 sites with full hookups (30, 50 amps), 10 drive-through, for RVs up to 50 feet or tents and two yurts. Drinking water, satellite TV, restrooms, showers, an RV dump station, a pay phone, a laundry room, RV supplies, a playground, cell phone reception, and propane are available. A marina with a board-ing dock and launch ramp are nearby. An ATM

OREGON

and groceries are available within three blocks. Some facilities are wheelchair-accessible. Leashed pets are permitted.

Reservations, fees: Reservations are advised. The fees are $10–21 per night and $30 per night for yurts, plus $1 per additional vehicle. Major credit cards are accepted. Open year-round.

Directions: In Coos Bay, take the Charleston/State Parks exit to Newmark Avenue and drive west for three miles to Cape Arago Highway. Turn left and drive about five miles south to Charleston and cross the South Slough Bridge; continue to Boat Basin Drive. Turn right and drive .25 mile to Kingfisher Drive. Turn right and drive 200 feet to the campground on the left.

Contact: Charleston Marina RV Park, P.O. Box 5433, Charleston, OR 97420-0607, 541/888-9512 or 541/888-2548, fax 541/888-6111, website: www.charlestonmarina.com.

82 OCEANSIDE RV PARK

Rating: 7

near the Pacific Ocean
See map pages 230–231

One of several private, developed parks in the Charleston area, this park is within walking distance of the Pacific Ocean, with opportunities for swimming, fishing, clamming, crabbing, and boating. A marina is 1.5 miles away.

RV sites, facilities: There are 70 full-hookup sites (30, 50 amps) for RVs of any length and 10 tent sites. Drinking water, restrooms, showers, a pay phone, modem access, cell phone reception, a fish-cleaning station, and propane are available. Equipment for crabbing and clamming is also available. An ATM and groceries are available within two miles. Some facilities are wheelchair-accessible. Leashed pets are permitted.

Reservations, fees: Reserve at 800/570-2598. The fees are $24 per night for RV sites and $15 per night for tent sites, plus $5 per additional vehicle. A senior discount is available. Major credit cards are accepted. Open year-round.

Directions: In Coos Bay, take the Charleston Ocean Beaches exit to Newmark Avenue and drive west for three miles to Cape Arago Highway. Turn left and drive about five miles south to Charleston and cross the South Slough Bridge.

Continue on Cape Arago Highway for 1.8 miles to the park entrance on the right.

Contact: Oceanside RV Park, 90281 Cape Arago Hwy., Charleston, OR 97420, 541/888-2598 or 800/570-2598, website: www.harborside.com /~oceanside.

83 BULLARDS BEACH STATE PARK

Rating: 7

on the Coquille River
See map pages 230–231

The Coquille River, which has good fishing in season for both boaters and crabbers, is the centerpiece of this park with four miles of shore access. If fishing is not your thing, the park also has several hiking trails. The Coquille River Lighthouse is at the end of the road that wanders through the park. During the summer there are tours to the tower. Equestrians can explore the seven-mile horse trail.

RV sites, facilities: There are 185 sites with partial or full hookups (20, 30 amps) for RVs up to 64 feet; 13 yurts are also available, including three that are wheelchair-accessible. Each yurt can sleep five people. A special area for horses and an area reserved for hikers and bicyclists are also available. Picnic tables and fire rings are provided. Drinking water, flush toilets, garbage bins, an RV dump station, showers, firewood, a pay phone, cell phone reception, and a yurt meeting hall are available. Boat docks and launching facilities are in the park on the Coquille River. An ATM is within three miles. Some facilities are wheelchair-accessible. Leashed pets are permitted.

Reservations, fees: Reserve at 800/452-5687 or online at www.OregonStateParks.org ($6 reservation fee). The fees are $16–20 per night plus $7 per additional vehicle, $4 per person per night for hikers/bicyclists, and $27 per night for yurts. Horse camping is $12–16 per night. Major credit cards are accepted. Open year-round.

Directions: In Coos Bay, drive south on U.S. 101 for about 22 miles to the park on the right (two miles north of Bandon).

Contact: Bullards Beach State Park, P.O. Box 569, Bandon, OR 97411, 541/347-2209, fax 541/347-4656.

OREGON

84 BANDON RV PARK

Rating: 6

near Bullards Beach State Park
See map pages 230–231

This in-town RV park is a good base for many adventures. Some sites are filled with rentals, primarily fishermen, for the summer season. Rock hounds will enjoy combing for agates and other semiprecious stones hidden along the beaches, while kids can explore the West Coast Game Park Walk-Through Safari petting zoo seven miles south of town. Bandon State Park, four miles south of town, has a nice wading spot in the creek at the north end of the park. Nearby recreation opportunities include two 18-hole golf courses, a riding stable, and tennis courts. Bullards Beach is about 2.5 miles north. Nice folks run this place.

RV sites, facilities: There are 44 sites with full hookups (30 amps) for RVs of any length; some are drive-through sites. Picnic tables are provided. Drinking water, flush toilets, cable TV, showers, a courtesy phone, modem access, cell phone reception, and a laundry room are available. Propane and a store are within two blocks. Boat docks and launching facilities are nearby. An ATM and a pay phone are within two miles. Leashed pets are permitted.

Reservations, fees: Reserve at 800/393-4122. The fee is $20–22 per night, plus $2 per person for more than two people. Major credit cards are accepted. Open year-round.

Directions: From Coos Bay, drive south on U.S. 101 for 26 miles to Bandon and the Highway 42S junction. Continue south on U.S. 101 for one block to the park.

Contact: Bandon RV Park, 935 2nd St. SE, Bandon, OR 97411, 541/347-4122, website: www .bandon.com.

85 LAVERNE COUNTY PARK

Rating: 9

in Fairview on the North Fork of the Coquille River
See map pages 230–231

This beautiful park sits on a river with a small waterfall and many trees, including a myrtle grove and old-growth Douglas fir. Mountain bikers can take an old wagon road, and golfers can enjoy any of several courses in the area. There are a few hiking trails and a very popular swimming hole. Fishing includes salmon, steelhead, and trout, and the wildlife includes deer, elk, bear, raccoons, and cougar. You can take a side trip to the museums at Myrtle Point and Coos Bay, which display local Indian items, or visit an old stagecoach house in Dora.

RV sites, facilities: There are 76 sites for RVs of any length or tents, half of which have partial hookups (20, 30 amps). There is also a large group site at West Laverne B with 22 RV hookups (20, 30 amps). One cabin is also available. Picnic tables and fire pits are provided. Drinking water, restrooms with flush toilets and showers (two barrier-free), garbage bins, an RV dump station, a playground, four cooking shelters with barbecues, a swimming hole (unsupervised), horseshoes, and volleyball and baseball areas are available. An ATM, store, and restaurant are within 1.5 miles. Propane, a store, and gasoline are within five miles. Leashed pets are permitted, and there is a pet area.

Reservations, fees: Reservations are not accepted for family sites. The fee is $10–15 per night, plus $5 per additional vehicle. Reservations for the group site and cabin ($5 reservation fee) are available at 541/396-3121, ext. 354; the group site is $130 per night for the first six camping units, then $15 per unit. The cabin is $30 per night. A senior discount is available for Coos County residents. Major credit cards are accepted. Open year-round.

Directions: From Coos Bay, drive south on U.S. 101 for six miles to the junction with Highway 42. Turn east and drive 11 miles to Coquille and West Central. Turn left and drive .5 mile to Fairview McKinley Road. Turn right and drive eight miles to the Fairview Store. Continue east another five miles (past the store) to the park on the right.

Contact: Laverne County Park, Coos County, 61217 Fairview McKinley Rd., Coquille, OR 97423, 541/396-2344, website: www.co.coos.or.us.

OREGON

86 KOA BANDON–PORT ORFORD

Rating: 7

near the Elk River
See map pages 230–231

This spot is considered to be just a layover camp, but it offers large, secluded sites nestled among big trees and coastal ferns. A new pool and spa are now open. The Elk and Sixes Rivers, where the fishing can be good, are minutes away, and Cape Blanco State Park is just a few miles down the road.

RV sites, facilities: There are 26 drive-through sites for RVs of any length and 46 tent sites. Six cabins are also available. Picnic tables and fire pits are provided. Drinking water, flush toilets, propane, an RV dump station, showers, firewood, a recreation hall, a store, a laundry room, ice, a playground, a pay phone, modem access, and cell phone reception are available. An ATM is within nine miles. Leashed pets are permitted.

Reservations, fees: Reserve at 800/562-3298. The fee is $24–30 per night, plus $3 per person for more than two people and $5 per additional vehicle. Major credit cards are accepted. Open year-round.

Directions: From Coos Bay, drive south on U.S. 101 for 50 miles to the campground at Milepost 286 near Langlois, on the west side of the highway.

Contact: KOA Bandon–Port Orford, 46612 U.S. 101, Langlois, OR 97450, 541/348-2358, website: www.koa.com.

87 CAPE BLANCO STATE PARK

Rating: 8

between the Sixes and Elk Rivers
See map pages 230–231

This large park is named for the white (blanco) chalk appearance of the sea cliffs here, which rise 200 feet above the ocean. Sea lions inhabit the offshore rocks, and trails and a road lead to the sandy beach below the cliffs. Another highlight is the good access to the Sixes River, which runs for more than two miles through the meadows and forests of the park. Trails for horseback riding are also available; beach rides are also pop-

ular. More than eight miles of trails lead through woodland and wetland settings and feature spectacular ocean vistas. Lighthouse and historic Hughes House tours (seasonal) are on-site.

RV sites, facilities: There are 54 sites with water and electrical hookups for RVs up to 65 feet or tents. Other options are a special camp for horses, a camping area reserved for hikers and bicyclists, four cabins, and one primitive group site that can accommodate up to 100 people. Picnic tables and fire grills are provided. Drinking water, garbage bins, firewood, a pay phone, cell phone reception, flush toilets, showers, and an RV dump station are available. A store is within five miles, and an ATM and coin-operated laundry are within nine miles. Some facilities are wheelchair-accessible. Leashed pets are permitted.

Reservations, fees: No reservations are available for single sites. The fees are $16 per night plus $7 per additional vehicles, and $4 per person per night for hikers/bikers. Reserve the cabins, the group site, and the horse camp at 800/452-5687 or online at www.OregonStateParks.org ($6 reservation fee). The group site is $60 for the first 25 people, then $2.40 per person. Major credit cards are accepted. Open year-round.

Directions: From Coos Bay, turn south on U.S. 101 and drive approximately 46 miles (south of Sixes, five miles north of Port Orford) to Cape Blanco Road. Turn right (northwest) and drive five miles to the campground on the left.

Contact: Humbug Mountain State Park, P.O. Box 1345, Port Orford, OR 97465, 541/332-6774. (This park is under the same management as Humbug Mountain State Park.)

88 SIXES RIVER

Rating: 6

on the Sixes River
See map pages 230–231

Set along the banks of the Sixes River at an elevation of 4,303 feet, this camp is a favorite of miners, fishermen, and nature lovers. This is a recreational gold panning area. Anybody using a powered dredge must be registered and have a permit through the Department of Environmental Quality (dredging is permitted from July 15 through September). No permit is required when panning by hand. The camp roads are paved.

RV sites, facilities: There are 19 sites for RVs up to 26 feet or tents. Picnic tables, garbage service, and fire grills are provided. Drinking water and vault toilets are available. Leashed pets are permitted.

Reservations, fees: Reservations are not accepted. The fee is $5 per night, plus $3 for each additional vehicle, with a 14-day stay limit. A senior discount is available. Open year-round.

Directions: From Coos Bay, drive south on U.S. 101 for 40 miles to Sixes and Sixes River Road. Turn left (east) on Sixes River Road and drive 11 miles to the campground. The last .5 mile is an unpaved road.

Contact: Bureau of Land Management, Coos Bay District, 1300 Airport Ln., North Bend, OR 97459, 541/756-0100, fax 541/751-4303.

89 ELK RIVER CAMPGROUND

Rating: 7

near the Elk River
See map pages 230–231

This quiet and restful camp makes an excellent base for fall and winter fishing on the Elk River, which is known for its premier salmon fishing. A one-mile private access road goes to the river, so guests get their personal fishing holes. About half of the sites are taken by monthly rentals.

RV sites, facilities: There are 50 sites for RVs up to 40 feet or tents, all with full hookups (30 amps). Picnic tables are provided. Drinking water, restrooms, showers, an RV dump station, a pay phone, modem access, cable TV, cell phone reception, and a laundry room are available. Recreational facilities include a sports field, horseshoes, a recreation hall, and a boat ramp. An ATM and a store are within three miles. Some facilities are wheelchair-accessible. Leashed pets are permitted.

Reservations, fees: Reservations are recommended. The fee is $11–17 per night, plus $1 per person for more than two people. Weekly and monthly rates are available. Open year-round.

Directions: From Port Orford, drive north on U.S. 101 for 1.5 miles to Elk River Road (Milepost

297). Turn right (east) on Elk River Road and drive 1.8 miles to the campground on the left.

Contact: Elk River Campground, 93363 Elk River Rd., Port Orford, OR 97465, 541/332-2255.

90 POWERS COUNTY PARK

Rating: 9

near the South Fork of the Coquille River
See map pages 230–231

This private and secluded public park in a wooded, mountainous area is a great stop for travelers going between I-5 and the coast. A small lake at the park provides a spot for visitors to boat, swim, and fish for trout. Only nonmotorized boats allowed. On display at the park are an old steam donkey and a hand-carved totem pole. This park is reputed to have the biggest cedar tree in Oregon.

RV sites, facilities: There are 70 sites with partial hookups (20, 30 amps) for RVs up to 40 feet or tents. One cabin is also available. Drinking water, restrooms, showers, an RV dump station, and a pay phone are available. Other facilities include a boat ramp, horseshoes, a playground, three large picnic shelters, tennis courts, and a recreation field. Supplies are available within one mile. Some facilities are wheelchair-accessible. Leashed pets are permitted.

Reservations, fees: Reserve at 541/396-3121, ext. 354. The fees are $10–15 per night and $30 per night for cabins. A senior discount is available. Major credit cards are accepted. Open year-round. U.S. 101 for six miles to the junction with Highway 42. Turn east and drive 20 miles to Myrtle Point. Continue on Highway 42 to the Powers Highway (Highway 242) exit. Turn right (southwest) and drive 19 miles to the park on the right.

Contact: Powers County Park, P.O. Box 12, Powers, OR 97466-0012, 541/396-3121, or 541/439-2791, website: www.co.coos.or.us.

91 PORT ORFORD RV VILLAGE

Rating: 5

near the Elk and Sixes Rivers
See map pages 230–231

The hosts make you feel at home at this friendly mom-and-pop campground in Port Orford. An informal group campfire and happy/social hour are scheduled each evening. Other nice touches include a small heated gazebo where you can get coffee each morning and a patio where you can sit. Fishing is good during the fall and winter on the nearby Elk and Sixes Rivers, and the campground has a smokehouse, a freezer, and a cleaning table. Some sites here are taken by summer season rentals, and some are taken by permanent residents.

RV sites, facilities: There are 49 sites with full hookups (30 amps) for RVs of any length and seven tent sites. Picnic tables are provided. Drinking water, flush toilets, propane, an RV dump station, a craft room, showers, a recreation hall, and a laundry room are available. Boat docks and launching facilities are nearby. Lake, river, and ocean are all within 1.5 miles. Leashed pets are permitted.

Reservations, fees: Reservations are accepted. The fee is $20 per night, plus $1 per person for more than two people. A senior discount is available. Open year-round.

Directions: In Port Orford on U.S. 101, drive to Madrona Avenue. Turn east and drive two blocks (road becomes Port Orford Loop) to the park on the left.

Contact: Port Orford RV Village, 2855 Port Orford Loop Rd., P.O. Box 697, Port Orford, OR 97465, 541/332-1041.

92 HUMBUG MOUNTAIN STATE PARK

Rating: 7

near the Pacific Ocean
See map pages 230–231

This park and campground are dominated by Humbug Mountain (1,756 feet elevation) and surrounded by forested hills. The campground enjoys some of the warmest weather on the Oregon coast. Windsurfing and scuba diving are popular, as is hiking the three-mile trail to Humbug Peak. Both ocean and freshwater fishing are accessible nearby.

RV sites, facilities: There are 35 sites with partial hookups for RVs up to 55 feet and 63 tent sites. A special camping area is provided for hikers and bicyclists. Picnic tables and fire rings are

provided. Drinking water, flush toilets, a pay phone, garbage bins, showers, and firewood are available. An ATM, a store, and a coin-operated laundry are within six miles. Leashed pets are permitted.

Reservations, fees: Reservations are not accepted for family sites. The fees are $14–16 per night plus $7 per additional vehicles, and $4 per person per night for hikers/bicyclists. Group sites can be reserved at 541/332-6774. Group sites are $60 for the first 25 people, then $2.40 per person after that. Major credit cards are accepted. Open year-round.

Directions: From Port Orford, drive south on U.S. 101 for six miles to the park entrance on the left.

Contact: Humbug Mountain State Park, P.O. Box 1345, Port Orford, OR 97465, 541/332-6774 or 800/551-6949.

93 DAPHNE GROVE

Rating: 7

on the South Fork of the Coquille River in Siskiyou National Forest
See map pages 230–231

This prime spot (at 1,000 feet elevation) along the South Fork of the Coquille River, surrounded by old-growth Douglas fir, cedar, and maple, is far enough out of the way to attract little attention. No fishing is allowed. The road is paved all the way to, and in, the campground, a plus for RVs and "city cars."

RV sites, facilities: There are 15 sites for RVs up to 30 feet or tents. Picnic tables, garbage bins, and fire grills are provided. Vault toilets and drinking water are available. Some facilities are wheelchair-accessible. Leashed pets are permitted.

Reservations, fees: Reservations are not accepted. The fee is $8 per night from late May to late September, plus $3 per additional vehicle, and free the rest of the year. A senior discount is available. Open year-round, with limited winter facilities.

Directions: From Coos Bay, drive south on U.S. 101 for six miles to the junction with Highway 42. Turn east and drive 20 miles to Myrtle Point. Continue on Highway 42 to Powers Highway (Highway 242). Turn right (southwest) and drive 18 miles to Powers and County Road 90.

Turn south and drive 4.3 miles to Forest Road 33. Turn south and drive 10.5 miles to the campground entrance.

Contact: Siskiyou National Forest, Powers Ranger District, 42861 Hwy. 242, Powers, OR 97466, 541/439-6200, fax 541/439-6217.

94 SQUAW LAKE

Rating: 8

on Squaw Lake in Siskiyou National Forest
See map pages 230–231

This campground (at 2,200 feet elevation) along the shore of one-acre Squaw Lake is set in rich, old-growth forest. Squaw is more of a pond than a lake, but it is stocked with trout in the spring. Get there early; the fish are generally gone by midsummer. The trailheads for the Panther Ridge Trail and Coquille River Falls Trail are a 10-minute drive from the campground. It's strongly advised that you obtain a U.S. Forest Service map detailing the backcountry roads and trails.

RV sites, facilities: There are seven partially developed sites for RVs up to 21 feet or tents. Picnic tables and fire rings are provided. Pit toilets are available. There is no drinking water, and all garbage must be packed out. Leashed pets are permitted.

Reservations, fees: Reservations are not accepted. There is no fee for camping. Open year-round.

Directions: From Coos Bay, drive south on U.S. 101 for six miles to the junction with Highway 42. Turn east and drive 20 miles to Myrtle Point. Continue on Highway 42 to Powers Highway (Highway 242). Turn right (southwest) and drive 18 miles to Powers and County Road 90. Turn south and drive 4.3 miles to Forest Road 33. Turn south and drive 12.5 miles to Forest Road 3348. Turn southeast and drive 4.5 miles to the campground entrance road. Turn east and drive one mile to the campground. The road is paved for all but the last .5 mile.

Contact: Siskiyou National Forest, Powers Ranger District, 42861 Hwy. 242, Powers, OR 97466, 541/439-6200, fax 541/439-6217.

95 ILLAHE

Rating: 7

on the Rogue River in Siskiyou National Forest
See map pages 230–231

This quiet and isolated camping area has great hiking opportunities, beginning at the nearby Upper Rogue River Trail. Boating and fishing are just a mile away at Foster Bar Campground. This pretty spot offers privacy between sites and is hidden from the majority of tourists. Deer are in abundance here.

RV sites, facilities: There are 14 sites for RVs up to 16 feet or tents. Picnic tables and fire rings are provided. Drinking water and flush toilets are available. A store is within five miles. Boat docks and a pay phone are within one mile. Leashed pets are permitted.

Reservations, fees: Reservations are not accepted. The fee is $5 per night, plus $3 for each additional vehicle. A senior discount is available. Open year-round.

Directions: From Gold Beach on U.S. 101, turn east on County Road 595. Drive east for 35 miles (it becomes Forest Road 33) to a junction for Illahe, Illahe Campground, and Foster Bar. Turn right on County Road 375 and drive five miles to the campground.

Contact: Siskiyou National Forest, Gold Beach Ranger District, 29279 Ellensburg Ave., Gold Beach, OR 97444, 541/247-3600, fax 541/247-3617.

96 SAM BROWN AND SAM BROWN HORSE CAMP

Rating: 4

near Grants Pass in Siskiyou National Forest
See map pages 230–231

This campground is located in an isolated area near Grants Pass along Briggs Creek in a valley of pine and Douglas fir. It is set at an elevation of 2,500 feet. Many sites lie in the shade of trees, and a creek runs along one side of the campground. Taylor Creek Trail, Briggs Creek Trail, and Dutchy Creek Trail are nearby and are popular for hiking and horseback riding. An amphitheater is available for small group presentations.

OREGON

Although the campground was spared, the Biscuit Fire of 2002 did burn nearby areas.

RV sites, facilities: There are 33 sites for RVs of any length or tents at Sam Brown and seven equestrian tent sites with small corrals across the road at Sam Brown Horse Camp. At Sam Brown, picnic tables and fire rings or grills are provided. Drinking water, vault toilets, and cell phone reception are available. A picnic shelter, solar shower (bag not provided), and an amphitheater are available. Some facilities are wheelchair-accessible.

Reservations, fees: Reservations are not accepted. The fee is $5 per night, plus $2 for an additional vehicle. A senior discount is available. Open late May to mid-October.

Directions: From Grants Pass, drive north on I-5 for 3.5 miles to Exit 61 (Merlin-Galice Road). Take that exit and drive northwest for 12.5 miles to Forest Road 25. Turn left on Forest Road 25 and head southwest for 13.5 miles to the campground.

Contact: Siskiyou National Forest, Galice Ranger District, 200 N.E. Greenfield Road, Grants Pass, OR 97526, 541/471-6500, fax 541/471-6514.

97 ARIZONA BEACH CAMPGROUND

Rating: 7

near Gold Beach
See map pages 230–231

This pleasant campground offers grassy, tree-lined sites along a half mile of ocean beach frontage. Many of the RV sites are located along the beach. A creek runs through the campground, and you can swim at the mouth of it in the summer. Elk and deer roam nearby. A small lake is available for fishing.

RV sites, facilities: There are 78 sites for RVs of any length with full hookups (30, 50 amps), including seven drive-through sites, and 48 sites for self-contained RVs or tents. Picnic tables and fire grills are provided. Drinking water, flush toilets, propane, an RV dump station, showers, firewood, a store, a laundry room, a recreation room, a pay phone, modem access, gold panning, and a playground are available. Leashed pets are permitted.

Reservations, fees: Reservations are accepted. The fees are $25–28 per night for RV sites and $16 per night for tent sites, plus $3 per person for more than four people and $5 for an addi-

tional vehicle. A senior discount is available. Major credit cards are accepted. Monthly rates are available. Open year-round.

Directions: From Gold Beach, drive north on U.S. 101 for 14 miles to the campground on the right.

Contact: Arizona Beach Campground, 36939 Arizona Ranch Rd., Port Orford, OR 97465, 541/332-6491, fax, 541/332-5504, website: www.arizonabeachrv.com.

98 HONEYBEAR CAMPGROUND

Rating: 10

near Gold Beach
See map pages 230–231

This campground offers wooded sites with ocean views. The owners have built a huge, authentic chalet, which contains a German deli, a recreation area, and a big dance floor. On summer nights, they hold dances with live music. A restaurant is available on-site with authentic German food.

RV sites, facilities: There are 65 sites for RVs of any length, including 30 drive-through sites with full hookups (30 amps) and 15 with patios, and 20 tent sites. Picnic tables and fire rings are provided. Drinking water, flush toilets, cable TV, an RV dump station, showers, firewood, a recreation hall, a restaurant, a store, a laundry room, ice, and a playground are available. An ATM is within eight miles. Leashed pets are permitted.

Reservations, fees: Reserve at 800/822-4444. The fee is $14.95–25 per night, plus $2 per person for more than two people and $1 per additional vehicle. Open year-round, weather permitting.

Directions: From Gold Beach, drive north on U.S. 101 for nine miles to Ophir Road near Milepost 321. Turn north and drive two miles to the campground on the right side of the road.

Contact: Honeybear Campground, 34161 Ophir Rd., P.O. Box 97, Ophir, OR 97464, 541/247-2765, website: www.honeybearrv.com.

99 NESIKA BEACH RV PARK

Rating: 7

near Gold Beach
See map pages 230–231

This campground next to Nesika Beach is a good

layover spot for U.S. 101 cruisers. An 18-hole golf course is close by. There are many long-term rentals here.

RV sites, facilities: There are 32 sites for RVs of any length, including 18 with full hookups (30 amps) and 14 with partial hookups, and six tent sites. Picnic tables are provided. Drinking water, flush toilets, an RV dump station, showers, cable TV, a pay phone, cell phone reception, a store, a laundry room, and ice are available. An ATM is within six miles. Leashed pets are permitted.

Reservations, fees: Reservations are accepted. The fee is $12–19 per night, plus $1 per person for more than two people. A senior discount is available. Monthly rates are available. Open year-round.

Directions: From Gold Beach, drive north on U.S. 101 for six miles to Nesika Road. Turn left and drive .75 mile west to the campground on the right.

Contact: Nesika Beach RV Park, 32887 Nesika Rd., Gold Beach, OR 97444, tel./fax 541/247-6077.

100 QUOSATANA

Rating: 6

on the Rogue River in Siskiyou National Forest
See map pages 230–231

This campground is set along the banks of the Rogue River, upstream from the much smaller Lobster Creek Campground. The campground features a large, grassy area and a barrier-free trail with interpretive signs. Ocean access is just a short drive away, and the quaint town of Gold Beach offers a decent side trip. Nearby Otter Point State Park (day use only) has further recreation options. The Shrader Old-Growth Trail and Myrtle Tree Trail provide nearby hiking opportunities. Quosatana makes a good base camp for a hiking or fishing trip.

RV sites, facilities: There are 42 sites for RVs up to 32 feet or tents. Drinking water, fire grills, garbage bins, and picnic tables are provided. Flush toilets, an RV dump station, a fish-cleaning station, and a boat ramp are available. Some facilities are wheelchair-accessible. Leashed pets are permitted.

Reservations, fees: Reservations are not accepted. The fee is $8–10 per night, plus $3 for each

additional vehicle. A senior discount is available. Open year-round.

Directions: From Gold Beach on U.S. 101, turn east on County Road 595 and drive 13 miles (it becomes Forest Road 33) to the campground on the left.

Contact: Siskiyou National Forest, Gold Beach Ranger District, 29279 Ellensburg Ave., Gold Beach, OR 97444, 541/247-3600, fax 541/247-3617.

101 LOBSTER CREEK

Rating: 6

on the Rogue River in Siskiyou National Forest
See map pages 230–231

This small campground on a river bar along the Rogue River is about a 15-minute drive from Gold Beach, and it makes a good base for a fishing trip. The area is heavily forested with myrtle and Douglas fir, and the Shrader Old-Growth Trail and Myrtle Tree Trail are nearby.

RV sites, facilities: There are six sites for RVs up to 21 feet or tents. Fire rings and picnic tables are provided. Flush toilets are available, but there is no drinking water and all garbage must be packed out. A boat launch is also available. An ATM and a pay phone are within 10 miles. Leashed pets are permitted.

Reservations, fees: Reservations are not accepted. The fee is $5 per night, plus $3 for each additional vehicle. Camping is also permitted on a gravel bar area for $3 per night. A senior discount is available. Open mid-May to mid-October.

Directions: From Gold Beach on U.S. 101, turn east on County Road 595 and drive 10 miles (it becomes Forest Road 33) to the campground on the left.

Contact: Siskiyou National Forest, Gold Beach Ranger District, 29279 Ellensburg Ave. (Highway 101), Gold Beach, OR 97444, 541/247-3600, fax 541/247-3617.

102 KIMBALL CREEK BEND RV RESORT

Rating: 6

on the Rogue River
See map pages 230–231

This campground on the scenic Rogue River is

just far enough from the coast to provide quiet and its own distinct character. Nearby recreation options include a nine-hole golf course, hiking trails, and boating facilities.

RV sites, facilities: There are 56 sites with full hookups (30 amps), 18 drive-through, for RVs of any length, 13 tent sites, group sites, two park-model cabins, and three motel rooms. Picnic tables are provided. Fire rings, drinking water, flush toilets, propane, an RV dump station, showers, a recreation hall, a store, a laundry room, a pay phone, modem access, cell phone reception, ice, and a playground are available. Boat docks and launching facilities are also available. An ATM is within eight miles. Leashed pets are permitted.

Reservations, fees: Reserve at 888/814-0633. The fees are $23–34.50 per night for RVs and $20 per night for tents, plus $1–3 per person for more than two people. Major credit cards are accepted. Open year-round.

Directions: From Gold Beach, drive north on U.S. 101 for one mile (on the north side of the Rogue River) to Rogue River Road. Turn east and drive about eight miles to the campground.

Contact: Kimball Creek Bend RV Resort, 97136 North Bank Rogue, Gold Beach, OR 97444, 541/247-7580, website: www.kimballcreek.com.

103 LUCKY LODGE RV PARK

Rating: 6

on the Rogue River
See map pages 230–231

Lucky Lodge is a good layover spot for U.S. 101 travelers who want to get off the highway circuit. Set on the shore of the Rogue River, it offers opportunities for fishing, boating, and swimming. Most sites have a view of the river. Nearby recreation options include hiking trails. This park has a few long-term rentals.

RV sites, facilities: There are 32 sites with full hookups (30, 50 amps), most drive-through, for RVs of any length, four tent sites, and two cabins. Picnic tables are provided. Drinking water, flush toilets, propane, an RV dump station, showers, firewood, a recreation hall, and a laundry room are available. Boat docks, rentals, and an ATM are within eight miles. Leashed pets are permitted.

Reservations, fees: Reservations are accepted. The fees are $21–24 per night for RVs and $15 per night for tents, plus $3 per person for more than two people. Open year-round.

Directions: From Gold Beach, drive north on U.S. 101 for four miles (on the north side of the Rogue River) to Rogue River Road. Turn east and drive .25 mile to the campground.

Contact: Lucky Lodge RV Park, 32040 Watson Ln., Gold Beach, OR 97444, 541/247-7618.

104 INDIAN CREEK RV PARK

Rating: 7

on the Rogue River
See map pages 230–231

This campground is set along the Rogue River on the outskirts of the town of Gold Beach. Nearby recreation options include a riding stable, riding trails, and boat trips on the Rogue.

RV sites, facilities: There are 100 sites with full hookups (30 amps) for RVs of any length and 25 tent sites. Picnic tables are provided. Drinking water, flush toilets, showers, firewood, a recreation hall, a store, a sauna, a café, a laundry room, ice, cable TV, a pay phone, cell phone reception, and a playground are available. Propane is within two miles. Boat docks, launching facilities, and rentals are nearby. Leashed pets are permitted.

Reservations, fees: Reservations are accepted. The fee is $15–25 per night, plus $1 per person for more than two people. Major credit cards are accepted. A senior discount is available. Open early May to early October.

Directions: On U.S. 101, drive to the northern end of Gold Beach to Jerry's Flat Road (just south of the Patterson Bridge). Turn east on Jerry's Flat Road and drive .5 mile to the campground.

Contact: Indian Creek RV Park, 94680 Jerry's Flat Rd., Gold Beach, OR 97444, 541/247-7704, website: www.harborside.com/~indiancreek/.

105 IRELAND'S OCEAN VIEW RV PARK

Rating: 8

on the Pacific Ocean
See map pages 230–231

One of the newest RV parks in the area, this spot

is situated on the beach in the quaint little town of Gold Beach, only one mile from the famous Rogue River. This park is very clean and features blacktop roads and grass beside each site. Recreation options include beachcombing, fishing, and boating. Great ocean views are possible from the observatory/lighthouse.

RV sites, facilities: There are 33 sites with full hookups (20, 30, 50 amps) for RVs up to 40 feet. Tent camping is permitted only in combination with an RV. Picnic tables are provided. Drinking water, cable TV, phones, showers, restrooms, a laundry room, modem access, cell phone reception, a recreation room, horseshoes, and picnic areas are available. An ATM is within three blocks. Leashed pets are permitted.

Reservations, fees: Reservations are recommended. The fee is $15–25 per night, plus $1 per person for more than two people and $2 per additional vehicle. Monthly rates are available. Open year-round.

Directions: On U.S. 101, drive to the southern end of Gold Beach (U.S. 101 becomes Ellensburg Avenue) and look for the camp at 29272 Ellensburg Avenue (across from the U.S. Forest Service office).

Contact: Ireland's Ocean View RV Park, 29272 Ellensburg Ave., P.O. Box 727, Gold Beach, OR 97444, 541/247-0148, website: www.irelandsrvpark.com.

106 OCEANSIDE RV PARK

Rating: 5

on the Pacific Ocean
See map pages 230–231

Set 100 yards from the ocean, this park is close to beachcombing terrain, marked bike trails, and boating facilities. The park is also adjacent to the mouth of the Rogue River, in the Port of Gold Beach.

RV sites, facilities: There are 80 sites—20 drive-through, 30 with full hookups (30 amps), and 50 with partial hookups—for RVs of any length and two yurts. No tent camping is allowed. Picnic tables are provided. Drinking water, flush toilets, showers, a coin-operated laundry, cable TV, a pay phone, cell phone reception, modem access, a small store, and ice are available. Propane, an

RV dump station, a store, and a café are within two miles. Boat docks, launching facilities, and rentals are nearby. Leashed pets are permitted.

Reservations, fees: Reservations are recommended. The fee is $13–22, plus $1 per person for more than two people, and $30 per night for yurts. Major credit cards are accepted. Open year-round.

Directions: On U.S. 101, drive to central Gold Beach and the intersection with Moore Street. Turn west and drive two blocks to Airport Way. Turn right and drive three blocks to South Jetty Road. Turn left and look for the park on the left.

Contact: Oceanside RV Park, P.O. Box 1107, Gold Beach, OR 97444, 541/247-2301.

107 AGNESS RV PARK

Rating: 6

on the Rogue River
See map pages 230–231

Agness RV Park is a destination campground on the scenic Rogue River in the middle of the Siskiyou National Forest. Fishing is the main focus here. Boating is sharply limited because the nearest pullout is 12 miles downstream. It's advisable to obtain a U.S. Forest Service map detailing the backcountry. Note that more than half of the sites are taken by summer season rentals. There are also some year-round rentals. Tent camping is permitted at RV sites.

RV sites, facilities: There are 84 sites, 52 with full hookups (30 amps), for RVs of any length or tents. Picnic tables are provided. Drinking water, flush toilets, an RV dump station, a pay phone, showers, a covered pavilion with barbecues, and a laundry room are available. A store, a café, propane, and ice are within 100 yards. Boat-launching facilities are nearby. Pets are permitted.

Reservations, fees: Reservations are accepted. The fee os $19 per night, plus $2 per person for more than two people. Major credit cards are accepted. Monthly rates are available. Open year-round.

Directions: In Gold Beach, drive on U.S. 101 to the southern end of the Rogue River Bridge and Jerry's Flat Road. Turn east on Jerry's Flat Road and you'll see the entrance to the campground on the left.

Contact: Agness RV Park, 4215 Agness Rd.,

OREGON

Agness, OR 97406, tel./fax 541/247-2813, website: www.agnessrv.com.

108 WHALESHEAD BEACH RESORT

Rating: 7

near the Pacific Ocean
See map pages 230–231

This resort, about a quarter mile from the beach, is set in a forested area with a small stream nearby. Activities at and around the camp include ocean and river fishing, jet boat trips, whale-watching excursions, and a golf course (13 miles away). Each campsite has a deck, and all cabins have either an ocean view or a creekside setting. One unique feature is a tunnel that connects the campground to a trail to the beach.

RV sites, facilities: There are 115 sites for RVs of any length, 58 with full hookups (20, 30, 50 amps) and seven with partial hookups, five tent sites, and 18 cabins. Cable TV, restrooms, showers, drinking water, a pay phone, a laundry room, picnic tables, fire rings, a courtesy phone, modem access, cell phone reception, limited groceries, ice, snacks, RV supplies, propane, horseshoes, and a restaurant are available. An RV dump station, ATM, and pay phone are six miles away. Some facilities are wheelchair-accessible. Leashed pets are permitted.

Reservations, fees: Reservations are recommended. The fees are $22–25 per night for RV sites and $18 per night for tent sites, plus $2 per person for more than two people, $2 per additional vehicle, $10 per pet. Major credit cards are accepted. Open year-round.

Directions: From Brookings, drive 6.5 miles north on U.S. 101 to Milepost 349.5 and look for the park on the right.

Contact: Whaleshead Beach Resort, 19921 Whaleshead Rd., Brookings, OR 97415, 541/469-7446, fax 541/469-7447, website: www.whalesheadresort.com.

109 LOEB STATE PARK

Rating: 8

near the Chetco River
See map pages 230–231

This park is set in a canyon formed by the Chetco River. The campsites are nestled in a beautiful old myrtle grove. A three-quarter-mile self-guided River View Trail adjacent to the Chetco River leads to the northernmost redwood grove in the United States. Nature programs and interpretive tours are available.

RV sites, facilities: There are 50 sites with partial hookups (30 amps) for RVs up to 50 feet or tents and three log cabins. Picnic tables and fire grills are provided. Drinking water, garbage bins, flush toilets, a pay phone, cell phone reception, and firewood are available. An ATM is within 10 miles. Leashed pets are permitted.

Reservations, fees: Reservations not accepted for family sites. Cabin reservations can be made at 800/452-5687 or online at www.OregonStateParks .org ($7 reservation fee). The fees are $12–16 per night, plus $7 for additional vehicles, and $35 per night for cabins. Major credit cards are accepted. Open year-round.

Directions: Take U.S. 101 to south Brookings and County Road 784 (North Bank Chetco River Road). Turn northeast and drive 10 miles northeast on North Bank Road to the park entrance on the right.

Contact: Harris Beach State Park, 1655 U.S. 101, Brookings, OR 97415, 541/469-2021 or 800/551-6949.

110 LITTLE REDWOOD

Rating: 7

on the Chetco River in Siskiyou National Forest
See map pages 230–231

This campground is set among old-growth fir trees near the banks of the Chetco River. An official put-in spot for rafting and river boats, the camp is also on the main western access route to the Kalmiopsis Wilderness, which is about 20 miles away. Campsites are fairly private, though close together.

RV sites, facilities: There are 11 sites for RVs up to 16 feet or tents. Picnic tables, garbage containers, and fire grills are provided. Drinking water and vault toilets are available. Leashed pets are permitted.

Reservations, fees: Reservations are not accepted. The fee is $10 per night, plus $3 for an additional vehicle; towed vehicles are free. A senior discount is available. Open late May to mid-September.

OREGON

Directions: Take U.S. 101 to south Brookings and County Road 784 (North Bank Chetco River Road). Turn northeast on North Bank Chetco River Road and drive 13.5 miles (the road becomes Forest Road 1376) to the campground.

Contact: Siskiyou National Forest, Chetco Ranger District, 539 Chetco Ave., P.O. Box 4580, Brookings, OR 97415, 541/412-6000, fax 541/412-6025.

111 HARRIS BEACH STATE PARK

Rating: 8

on the Pacific Ocean
See map pages 230–231

This park, featuring sandy beaches interspersed with eroded sea stacks, boasts the largest island off the Oregon coast. Bird Island (also called Goat Island) is a breeding site for such rare birds as the tufted puffin. The park's beauty changes with the seasons. Wildlife viewing opportunities are abundant (gray whales, harbor seals, and sea lions). In the fall and winter, the nearby Chetco River attracts good runs of salmon and steelhead, respectively.

RV sites, facilities: There are 63 sites for self-contained RVs or tents and 86 sites with partial or full hookups for RVs up to 50 feet long. There are six yurts, each accommodating five people, and a special camping area for hikers and bicyclists. Picnic tables, garbage bins, and fire grills are provided. Electricity, drinking water, sewer and cable TV hookups, flush toilets, an RV dump station, showers, a laundry room, and firewood are available. Some facilities are wheelchair-accessible. Leashed pets are permitted.

Reservations, fees: Reserve at 800/452-5687 or online at www.OregonStateParks.org ($7 reservation fee). The fees are $13–22 per night plus $7 per night for an additional vehicle, $4 per night per person for hikers/bikers, and $29 per night for yurts. Major credit cards are accepted. Open year-round.

Directions: From Brookings, drive north on U.S. 101 for two miles to the park entrance on the left.

Contact: Harris Beach State Park, 1655 U.S. 101, Brookings, OR 97415, 541/469-2021.

112 PORT OF BROOKINGS HARBOR BEACHFRONT RV PARK

Rating: 8

on the Pacific Ocean
See map pages 230–231

This park, located just past the Oregon/California border on the Pacific Ocean, makes a great layover spot. Oceanfront sites are available, and recreational activities include boating, fishing, and swimming. Nearby Harris Beach State Park, with its beach access and hiking trails, makes a good side trip.

RV sites, facilities: There are 138 sites for RVs of any length, including 129 with full hookups (30, 50 amps) and nine with partial hookups, and 25 tent sites. Drinking water, restrooms, showers, cable TV, an RV dump station, a pay phone, a laundry room, ice, a café, cell phone reception, and modem access are available. A marina with a boat ramp, a boat dock, and snacks is available nearby. An ATM is within a half mile. Some facilities are wheelchair-accessible. Leashed pets are permitted.

Reservations, fees: Reservations are recommended. The fee is $14–28 per night, plus $2 per person for more than two people. Major credit cards are accepted. Open year-round.

Directions: From Brookings, drive south on U.S. 101 for 2.5 miles to Benham Lane. Turn west on Benham Lane and drive .5 mile (it becomes Lower Harbor Road) to Boat Basin Road. Turn left and drive two blocks to the park on the right.

Contact: Port of Brookings Harbor Beachfront RV Park, 16035 Boat Basin Rd., Brookings, OR 97415, 541/469-5867 or 800/441-0856 in Oregon, website: www.port-brookings-harbor.org.

113 AT RIVERS EDGE RV RESORT

Rating: 7

on the Chetco River
See map pages 230–231

This campground lies along the banks of the Chetco River, just upstream from Brookings Harbor. A favorite spot for fishermen, it features salmon and steelhead fishing on the Chetco in the fall and winter. Deep-sea trips for salmon

OREGON

or rockfish are available nearby in the summer. This resort looks like the Rhine Valley in Germany, a pretty canyon between the trees and the river. A golf course is nearby.

RV sites, facilities: There are 110 sites with full hookups (30, 50 amps), including 15 drive-through, for RVs of any length and five cabins. Drinking water, flush toilets, propane, fire rings, modem access, cell phone reception, an RV dump station, showers, a recreation hall with exercise equipment, a laundry room, a recycling station, a small boat launch, and cable TV are available. An ATM and pay phone are within two miles. Leashed pets are permitted.

Reservations, fees: Reservations are recommended at 888/295-1441. The fees are $22–30 per night for RV sites and $16 per night for tent sites, plus $3 per person for more than two people. Open year-round.

Directions: On U.S. 101, drive to the southern end of Brookings (harbor side) and to South Bank Chetco River Road (a cloverleaf exit). Turn east on South Bank Chetco River Road and drive 1.5 miles to the park entrance on the left (a slanted left turn, through the pillars, well signed).

Contact: At Rivers Edge RV Resort, 98203 South Bank Chetco Rd., Brookings, OR 97415, 541/469-3356, website: www.atriversedge.com.

114 SEA BIRD RV PARK

Rating: 5

on the Pacific Ocean
See map pages 230–231

This is one of several campgrounds in the area. Nearby recreation options include marked bike trails, a full-service marina, and tennis courts. A nice, neat park, it features paved roads and granite sites. There is also a beach for surfing near the park. In summer, most of the sites are reserved for the season.

RV sites, facilities: There are 60 sites with full hookups (30 amps) for RVs up to 40 feet; nine are drive-through sites. No tent camping is allowed. Picnic tables are provided. Drinking water, flush

toilets, an RV dump station, a pay phone, modem access, cell phone reception, showers, a recreation hall, and a laundry room are available. Boat docks, launching facilities, and rentals are nearby. An ATM is within six blocks. Leashed pets are permitted.

Reservations, fees: Reservations are accepted. The fee is $16 per night, plus $1 per person for more than two people. A senior discount is available. Open year-round.

Directions: In Brookings, drive south on U.S. 101 to the Chetco River Bridge. Continue .25 mile south on U.S. 101 to the park entrance on the left.

Contact: Sea Bird RV Park, 16429 U.S. 101 S, P.O. Box 1026, Brookings, OR 97415, 541/469-3512.

115 WINCHUCK

Rating: 6

on the Winchuck River in Siskiyou National Forest
See map pages 230–231

This forested campground hugs the banks of the Winchuck River, an out-of-the-way stream that out-of-towners don't know exists. It's quiet, remote, and not that far from the coast, although it feels like an inland spot.

RV sites, facilities: There are 15 sites for RVs up to 30 feet or tents. Picnic tables, garbage bins, and fire grills are provided. Vault toilets and drinking water are available. Some facilities are wheelchair-accessible. Leashed pets are permitted.

Reservations, fees: Reservations are not accepted. The fee is $10 per night, plus $3 for each additional nontowed vehicle. A senior discount is available. Open late May to mid-September.

Directions: From Brookings, drive south on U.S. 101 for 5.5 miles to County Road 896 (the road turns into Forest Road 1107). Turn east and drive six miles to Forest Road 1107. Turn east and drive one mile to the campground.

Contact: Siskiyou National Forest, Chetco Ranger District, 539 Chetco Ave., P.O. Box 4580, Brookings, OR 97415, 541/412-6000, fax 541/412-6025.

OREGON

Oregon

Chapter 8

Portland and the Willamette Valley

PORTLAND AND THE WILLAMETTE VALLEY

WASHINGTON

Gifford Pinchot

National Forest

see Washington
page 14

Columbia River
Gorge Nat'l Scenic
Area

Longview

Columbia River

see The Columbia River
Gorge and Mount Hood
pages 296–297

Mt. Hood

National

Forest

River

Cascade Range

Clackamas

Vancouver
Lake

PORTLAND

5

2

1

River

30

3

26

River

99E

7

8

5

9

211

212

4-5

205

12

13

14

Salem

10-11

Willamette

99W

6

18

22

Columbia

Astoria

Clatsop
State Forest

River

Nehalem

Tillamook
State Forest

Trask Mtn.▲
(3,423 ft.)

Siuslaw
National
Forest

101

Tillamook Bay

PACIFIC

OCEAN

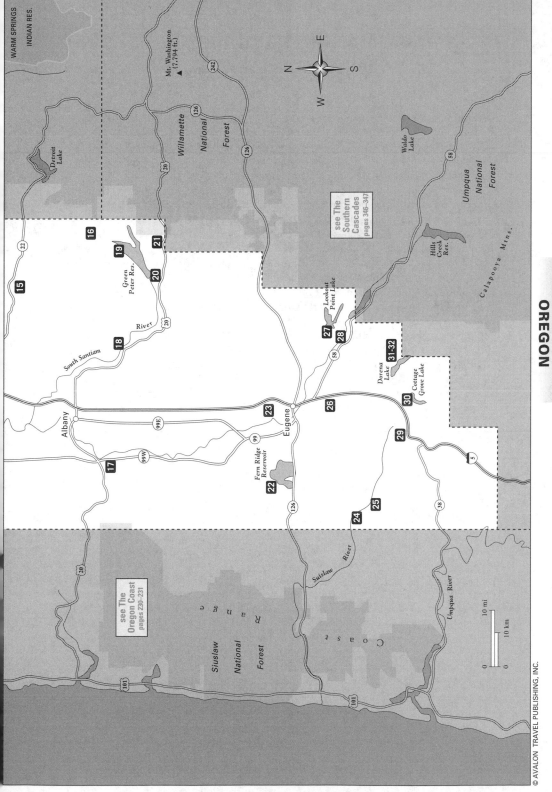

OREGON

© AVALON TRAVEL PUBLISHING, INC.

Chapter 8—Portland and the Willamette Valley

For most tourists, Oregon is little more than a stretch of I-5 from Portland to Cottage Grove. Although there are some interesting things about this area—it's Oregon's business center—the glimpse provided from I-5 doesn't capture the beauty of much of the state. Residents, however, know the secret: Not only can you earn a good living here, but it's also a great jump-off point to adventure.

To discover what the locals know, venture east to west on the slow two-lane highways bordering the streams. Among the most notable are Highway 26 along the Nacanticum River, little Highway 6 along the Wilson, Highway 22 along Three Rivers, tiny Highway 15 on the Little Nestucca, Highway 18 on the Salmon River, Highway 34 on the Alsea, Highway 126 on the Siuslaw, and Highway 38 on the Umpqua (my favorite). These roads provide routes to reach the coast and can be used to create beautiful loop trips, with many hidden campgrounds to choose from while en route.

There are also parks and a number of lakes in the foothills set along dammed rivers. The highlight is Silver Falls State Park, Oregon's largest state park, with a seven-mile hike that is routed past 10 awesome waterfalls, some falling more than 100 feet from their brinks. Lakes are plentiful, too, including Green Peter Reservoir on the Santiam River, Cottage Grove Reservoir, Dorena Lake, and Fall Creek Reservoir.

Portland is a great hub for finding recreation in the region. To the east is the Columbia River corridor and Mount Hood and its surrounding wilderness and national forest. To the south is Eugene, which leads to the McKenzie and Willamette Rivers and offers a good launch station to the Three Sisters in the east.

1 SCAPPOOSE RV PARK

Rating: 6

in Scappoose

See map pages 278–279

This county-operated RV park is next to the rural Scappoose airport, making it a convenient spot for private pilots. The sites are partially shaded with spruce, oak, and maple trees. Set on the edge of a dike, it is less than a mile from the Columbia River and about a 30-minute drive from Portland.

RV sites, facilities: There are seven sites for RVs up to 40 feet, six with full hookups (30 amps), and several tent sites in dispersed areas. Picnic tables and fire grills are provided. Drinking water, a restroom with flush toilets and showers, an RV dump station, cell phone reception, firewood, and a playground with equipment and horseshoes are available. A pay phone is within a quarter mile, and an ATM and coin-operated laundry are within two miles. Leashed pets are permitted.

Reservations, fees: Reserve at 503/397-2353. The fee is $14–18 per night, plus $7 for each additional vehicle. A senior discount is available. Open year-round.

Directions: From Portland, turn west on U.S. 30 and drive to Scappoose. Continue one mile north on U.S. 30 to West Lane Road. Turn right (east) and drive .75 mile to Honeyman Road. Turn left and drive one block to the park on the right.

Contact: Columbia County Forest, Parks and Recreation, 503/397-2353; Scappoose RV Park, 34038 N. Honeyman Rd., Scappoose, OR 97056, 503/543-3225, website: www.columbia-center.org /co/parks.

2 JANTZEN BEACH RV PARK

Rating: 6

near the Columbia River

See map pages 278–279

This RV campground is near the banks of the Columbia River on the outskirts of Portland. Recreation options include seasonal swimming. An 18-hole golf course and tennis courts are close by. Many recreation opportunities are available in the Portland area. Numerous marinas on the Willamette and Columbia Rivers offer boat trips and rentals, and the city parks and nearby state parks have hiking, bicycling, and horseback riding possibilities. The Columbia River Highway (U.S. 30) is a scenic drive. If golf is your game, Portland has 18 public golf courses. The winter ski areas at Mount Hood are within an hour's drive.

RV sites, facilities: There are 169 sites with full hookups (20, 30, 50 amps) for RVs of any length. No tents are allowed. Picnic tables are provided. Drinking water, flush toilets, showers, a recreation hall, a laundry room, cable TV, cell phone reception, a pay phone, modem access, a playground, and a swimming pool (seasonal) are available. Propane, a store, ice, an ATM, and a café are within one mile. Boat docks, launching facilities, and rentals are nearby. Leashed pets are permitted.

Reservations, fees: Reserve at 800/443-7248. The fee is $26 per night, plus $1 per person for more than two people. Major credit cards are accepted. Weekly and monthly rates are available. Open year-round.

Directions: From Portland on I-5, drive four miles north to the Jantzen Beach exit (Exit 308) and take Hayden Island Drive. Turn west on Hayden Island Drive and drive .5 mile to the park on the right.

Contact: Jantzen Beach RV Park, 1503 N. Hayden Island Dr., Portland, OR 97217, 503/289-7626.

3 RV PARK OF PORTLAND

Rating: 6

in Tualatin

See map pages 278–279

This park, just south of Portland in a wooded setting, has spacious sites, all with access to lawn areas. More than half of the sites are taken by monthly and long-term rentals.

RV sites, facilities: There are 100 sites with full hookups (20, 30, 50 amps), most of them drive-through sites for RVs of any length. No tents are allowed. Picnic tables are provided. Drinking water, flush toilets, showers, a laundry room, a pay phone, cell phone reception, modem access, and cable TV are available. Propane, a store, a café, an ATM, a children's playground, and ice are within a half mile. Leashed pets are permitted.

Reservations, fees: Reserve at 800/856-2066. The fee is $21.50–25.05 per night, plus $2 per person for more than two people. Major credit cards are accepted. Open year-round.

Directions: From Portland, drive south on I-5 to Tualatin and Exit 289. Take Exit 289, turn east on Nyberg Road, and drive .5 mile to the campground on the left.

Contact: RV Park of Portland, 6645 SW Nyberg Rd., Tualatin, OR 97062, 503/692-0225, website: www.rvparkofportland.com.

4 BARTON PARK

Rating: 6

near the Clackamas River
See map pages 278–279

Getting here may seem a bit of a maze, but the trip is well worth it. This camp is set on the Clackamas River and is surrounded by woods and tall trees. The nearby Clackamas River can provide good salmon fishing.

RV sites, facilities: There are 98 sites for RVs of any length or tents, 87 with partial hookups (20, 30, 50 amps), and 11 tent sites. Drinking water, restrooms, showers, an RV dump station, a pay phone, cell phone reception, and a barbecue are available. Recreational facilities include horseshoes, a playground, volleyball, baseball, and a boat ramp. An ATM is within a quarter mile. Supplies are available within one mile. Leashed pets are permitted.

Reservations, fees: Reservations are recommended at 503/353-4414. The fee is $12–16 per night. Major credit cards are accepted for reservations. Open May to October.

Directions: From Portland, drive south on I-5 to I-205. Turn east and drive about 20 miles to the Clackamas/Estacada exit (Highway 212). Turn east on Highway 212 and drive about 3.2 miles to the Carver exit (Highway 224). Turn right on Highway 224 and drive about 6.5 miles to the town of Barton and Baker's Ferry Road. Turn right and drive .25 mile to Barton Park Road. Turn left and drive to the park on the left.

Contact: Clackamas County Parks Department, 9101 SE Sunnybrook Blvd., Clackamas, OR 97015, 503/353-4414, fax 503/353-4420, website: www.co.clackamas.or.us/dtd/parks.

5 METZLER PARK

Rating: 8

on Clear Creek
See map pages 278–279

This county campground on a small stream not far from the Clackamas River is a hot spot for fishing, swimming, and picnicking. Be sure to make your reservation early at this very popular park.

RV sites, facilities: There are 60 sites with partial hookups (30, 50 amps) for RVs up to 40 feet or tents and 10 tent sites. Picnic tables and fire rings are provided. Drinking water, restrooms, showers, an RV dump station, a pay phone, a playground, and a recreation field with basketball, volleyball, and baseball are available. Propane, ice, an ATM, and laundry facilities are available within five miles. Leashed pets are permitted.

Reservations, fees: Reservations are recommended at 503/353-4414. The fee is $12–16 per night. Major credit cards are accepted with reservations. Open May to September.

Directions: From Portland, drive east on U.S. 26 from Gresham 11 miles to Sandy and Highway 211. Turn right (south) and drive six miles to a junction. Turn south (still Highway 211) and drive over the bridge to South Springwater Road. Turn right on South Springwater Road and drive about .25 mile to Metzler Park Road. Turn left on Metzler Park Road and drive .75 mile to the park.

Contact: Clackamas County Parks Department, 9101 SE Sunnybrook Blvd., Clackamas, OR 97015, 503/353-4414, fax 503/353-4420, website: www.co.clackamas.or.us.

6 MULKEY RV PARK

Rating: 7

near the South Yamhill River
See map pages 278–279

If you're in the area and looking for a camping spot, you'd best stop here—there are no other campgrounds within 30 miles. This wooded park is set near the South Yamhill River. Nearby recreation options include an 18-hole golf course, tennis courts, and the Western Deer Park and Arboretum, which has a playground.

RV sites, facilities: There are 70 sites with full hookups (30, 50 amps) for RVs of any length or tents. Drinking water, flush toilets, showers, a store, propane, and laundry facilities are available. An ATM is within 3.5 miles. Leashed pets are permitted.

Reservations, fees: Reserve at 877/472-2475. The fee is $15–20 per night, plus $3 per person for more than two people. Monthly rates are available. Major credit cards are accepted. Open year-round.

Directions: From Portland, turn south on Highway 99 and drive about 31 miles to McMinnville and Highway 18. Turn southwest on Highway 18 and drive 3.5 miles to the park entrance on the left.

Contact: Mulkey RV Park, 14325 SW Hwy. 18, McMinnville, OR 97128, 503/472-2475, fax 503/472-0718.

7 CHAMPOEG STATE HERITAGE AREA

Rating: 7

on the Willamette River
See map pages 278–279

Situated on the south bank of the Willamette River, this state park features an interpretive center, a botanical garden with native plants, and hiking and bike trails. In July, a pageant reenacting the early history of the area is staged Thursday through Sunday evenings. Also worth a tour: a log cabin museum, the historic Newell House, and a visitors center.

RV sites, facilities: There are 84 sites for RVs up to 50 feet, eight with full hookups (30 amps) and the rest with partial hookups, and six tent sites. Three group areas can also accommodate a maximum of 25 people each, plus offer six walk-in sites, six cabins, six yurts, a hiker/biker camp, an RV group area with 10 sites with electric hookups only. Picnic tables and fire grills are provided. Drinking water, garbage bins, flush toilets, a pay phone, cell phone reception, an RV dump station, showers, a group recreation hall for up to 55 people, and firewood are available. An ATM is within four miles. Boat docking facilities are

nearby. Some facilities are wheelchair-accessible. Leashed pets are permitted.

Reservations, fees: Reserve at 800/452-5687 ($6 reservation fee) or online at www.oregonstateparks .org. The fees are $16–20 per night and $4 per person per night for hiker/biker sites. The group camp area is $80 for up to 10 camping units, then $8 per additional unit. Yurts are $29 per night and cabins are $37 per night. There is a $7 fee per night for an additional vehicle. Major credit cards are accepted. Open year-round, with limited winter facilities in day-use areas.

Directions: From Portland, drive south on I-5 to Exit 278, the Donald/Aurora exit. Take that exit and turn right (west) on Ehlen Road and drive three miles to Case Road. Turn north and drive 5.5 miles (the road becomes Champoeg Road) to the park on the right.

Contact: Champoeg State Heritage Area, 8239 Champoeg Rd. NE, Saint Paul, OR 97137, 503/678-1251.

OREGON

8 ISBERG RV PARK

Rating: 7

near Aurora
See map pages 278–279

This RV campground is located in a rural area just off the main highway. The setting is very pretty, thanks to lots of evergreen trees that shelter the camp from the highway. Portland and Salem are just 20 minutes away.

RV sites, facilities: There are 148 sites with full hookups (30, 50 amps) for RVs of any length. Drinking water, flush toilets, propane, showers, a recreation hall, cable TV, a pay phone, an ATM, cell phone reception, a store, a swimming pool, a laundry room, and ice are available. Leashed pets are permitted.

Reservations, fees: Reservations are accepted. The fee is $25 per night. Major credit cards are accepted. Weekly and monthly rates are available. Open year-round.

Directions: From Portland, drive south on I-5 to Exit 278, the Donald/Aurora exit. Take that exit and turn left (east) on Ehlen Road and drive to Dolores Way. Turn right on Dolores Way and drive .25 mile to the park on the right.

Contact: Isberg RV Park, 21599 Dolores Way

NE, Aurora, OR 97002, 503/678-2646, fax 503/678-2724.

9 FEYRER MEMORIAL PARK

Rating: 5

on the Molalla River
See map pages 278–279

On the scenic Molalla River, this county park offers swimming and excellent salmon fishing. A superb option for weary I-5 cruisers, the park is only 30 minutes off the highway and provides a peaceful, serene environment.

RV sites, facilities: There are 20 sites with full hookups (30, 50 amps) for RVs up to 40 feet or tents. Drinking water, restrooms, showers, an RV dump station, cell phone reception, and a pay phone are available. A playground and recreation field are also on-site. Supplies, an ATM, and a coin-operated laundry are available within three miles. Some facilities are wheelchair-accessible. Leashed pets are permitted.

Reservations, fees: Reservations are recommended at 503/353-4414. The fee is $12–16 per night. Major credit cards are accepted with reservations. Open May to September.

Directions: From Portland, drive south on I-5 to Woodburn and Exit 271. Take that exit and drive east on Highway 214; continue (the road changes to Highway 211 at the crossing with Highway 99E) to Molalla and go straight through the four-way stop to Mathias Road (becomes Feyrer Park Road). Drive 1.9 miles to the park on the left.

Contact: Clackamas County Parks Department, 9101 SE Sunnybrook Blvd., Clackamas, OR 97015, 503/353-4414, fax 503/353-4420, website: www.co.clackamas.or.us.

10 FOREST GLEN RV RESORT

Rating: 6

south of Salem
See map pages 278–279

This RV resort is directly behind ThrillVille USA, an amusement park with rides, miniature golf, go-carts, waterslides, and a snack bar. ThrillVille is open during the summer. Another bonus: The campground has a fishing pond with bass and trout, and in 2003 a new pool and spa were installed. A winery tour at Willamette Vineyards is available just one mile south via I-5, and a golf course is located one mile to the north. Campsites here are often more private and shaded than in many RV parks. The park also hosts weekly activities, including bingo and meals served on weekends. A big plus for overnighters: There are no monthly rentals.

RV sites, facilities: There are 70 sites with full hookups (30 amps) for RVs of any length. Picnic tables and fire pits are provided. Drinking water, flush toilets, showers, a pay phone, modem access, cell phone reception, a seasonal ATM, a pool, a spa, and a laundry room are available. A playground is available nearby. A store, a café, and ice are within two miles. Some facilities are wheelchair-accessible. Leashed pets are permitted.

Reservations, fees: Reservations are not accepted. The fee is $30.50 per night. Major credit cards are accepted. Open year-round.

Directions: From Salem, drive south on I-5 for one mile to Exit 248. Take that exit and turn left on Delaney Road and drive 100 yards to Enchanted Way. Turn right and drive .25 mile to the park on the left.

Contact: Forest Glen RV Resort, 8372 Enchanted Way, Turner, OR 97392, tel./fax 503/363-7616, website: www.forestglenresort/homestead.com.

11 SALEM CAMPGROUND AND RVS

Rating: 5

in Salem
See map pages 278–279

This park with shaded sites is located just off I-5 in Salem. A picnic area and a lake for swimming are within walking distance, and a nine-hole golf course, hiking trails, a riding stable, and tennis courts are nearby.

RV sites, facilities: There are 190 sites with full hookups (30, 50 amps) for RVs of any length, most of which are drive-through sites, and 30 tent sites. Picnic tables are provided. Drinking water, flush toilets, propane, an RV dump station, showers, a recreation hall with a game room, a store, a laundry room, ice, a playground, a pay phone, cell phone reception, and modem access are available. An ATM is within a quarter mile.

OREGON

A café is within one mile. Leashed pets are permitted with the exception of pit bulls and rottweilers.

Reservations, fees: Reserve at 800/826-9605. The fee is $16–25 per night, plus $2 per person for more than two people. Major credit cards are accepted. Open year-round.

Directions: From Salem on I-5, take Exit 253 to Highway 22. Turn east and drive .25 mile to Lancaster Drive. Turn right on Lancaster Drive and drive to Hagers Grove Road. Turn right on Hagers Grove Road and drive to the park.

Contact: Salem Campground and RVs, 3700 Hagers Grove Rd. SE, Salem, OR 97301, 503/581-6736, fax 503/581-9945, website: www.salemrv.com.

12 SILVER FALLS STATE PARK

Rating: 8

near Salem

See map pages 278–279

Oregon's largest state park, Silver Falls covers more than 8,700 acres. Numerous trails crisscross the area. One of which, a seven-mile jaunt, meanders past 10 majestic waterfalls (some more than 100 feet high) in the rain forest of Silver Creek Canyon. Four of these falls have an amphitheater-like surrounding where you can walk behind the falls and feel the misty spray. A horse camp and a 14-mile, multiuse equestrian trail are available in the park. A rustic nature lodge and group lodging facilities are also on-site.

RV sites, facilities: There are 54 sites with partial hookups (30 amps) for RVs up to 60 feet, 51 tent sites, three group sites, a six-site horse camp, and 14 cabins. Picnic tables and fire rings are provided. Drinking water, garbage bins, flush toilets, showers, an RV dump station, firewood, and a playground are available. Some facilities are wheelchair-accessible. Leashed pets are permitted.

Reservations, fees: Reserve at 800/452-5687 or online at www.oregonstateparks.org ($6 reservation fee). The fees are $12–20 per night; the tent group site is $60 per night, the RV group site is $80 per night for the first 10 units and then $8 per additional unit. Horse campsites are $16 per night; the group horse camp is $48 per night for a maximum of 12 horses. There is a $7 per night charge for an additional vehicle. Major credit cards are accepted. Open year-round.

Directions: From Salem on I-5, take Exit 253 to Highway 22. Turn east and drive five miles to Highway 214. Turn left (east) and drive 15 miles to the park.

Contact: Silver Falls State Park, 20024 Silver Falls Hwy. SE, Sublimity, OR 97385, 503/873-8681 or 800/551-6949, fax 503/873-8925.

13 FISHERMEN'S BEND

Rating: 7

on the North Santiam River

See map pages 278–279

Fishermen's Bend is a popular site for anglers of all ages, and the sites are spacious. A barrier-free fishing and river viewing area and a network of trails provide access to more than a mile of river. There's a one-mile, self-guided nature trail, and the nature center has a variety of displays. The amphitheater has films and activities on weekends.

RV sites, facilities: There are 39 sites for RVs or tents; 20 are pull-through with water hookups and 20 are tent/camper sites with water spigots nearby. There are also three group sites available for up to 60 people each and two cabins. Drinking water, picnic tables, and fire pits are provided. Restrooms with flush toilets, sinks, and hot showers; a pay phone; cell phone reception; firewood; an RV dump station; and garbage containers are available. A boat ramp, three group picnic areas, a picnic shelter, and a day-use area with playgrounds, horseshoes, and baseball, volleyball, and basketball courts and fields are also available. The front gate closes at 10 P.M. Some facilities are wheelchair-accessible. Leashed pets are permitted.

Reservations, fees: Reserve at 888/242-4256 ($7 reservation fee). The fees are $12–18 per night, $60–80 per night for group sites, and $35 per night for cabins. A senior discount is available. Open mid-May to mid-October.

Directions: From Salem on I-5, take Exit 253 to Highway 22. Turn east and drive 28 miles to the campground on the right.

Contact: Bureau of Land Management, Salem District Office, 1717 Fabry Rd. SE, Salem, OR

97306, 503/375-5646; reservations 888/242-4256, fax 503/375-5622, website: www.or.blm.gov/salem.

14 ELKHORN VALLEY

Rating: 7

on the Little North Santiam River
See map pages 278–279

This pretty campground along the Little North Santiam River, not far from the North Fork of the Santiam River, has easy access, an on-site host, and is only a short drive away from a major metropolitan area. The front gate is locked from 10 P.M.–7 a.m. daily.

RV sites, facilities: There are 24 sites for RVs up to 24 feet or tents. Picnic tables, garbage bins, fire grills, drinking water, vault toilets, and firewood are available. A pay phone is within three miles. Leashed pets are permitted.

Reservations, fees: Reservations are not accepted. The fee is $10 per night, plus $5 per night for an additional vehicle after two. There is a 14-day stay limit. A senior discount is available. Open mid-May to late September.

Directions: From Salem on I-5, take Exit 253 to Highway 22. Turn east and drive 25 miles to Elkhorn Road (North Fork Road). Turn left (northeast) and drive nine miles to the campground on the left.

Contact: Bureau of Land Management, Salem District Office, 1717 Fabry Rd. SE, Salem, OR 97306, 503/375-5646, fax 503/375-5622, website: www.or.blm.gov/salem.

15 JOHN NEAL MEMORIAL PARK

Rating: 6

on the North Santiam River
See map pages 278–279

This camp is on the banks of the North Santiam River, offering good boating and trout fishing possibilities. Other recreation options include exploring lakes and trails in the adjacent national forest land or visiting Silver Falls State Park.

RV sites, facilities: There are 40 sites for self-contained RVs or tents and 14 sites which can be reserved as a group area. Picnic tables and fire rings are provided. Restrooms, garbage bins, cell phone reception, and drinking water are available. Recreational facilities include a boat ramp, a playground, horseshoes, a barbecue, and a recreation field. Ice and a grocery store are within one mile. An ATM and a pay phone are within three miles. Leashed pets are permitted.

Reservations, fees: Reservations are not accepted for family sites. The fee is $11 per night. Reservations are available for the group site ($50 reservation fee) which is $100 per night. A senior discount is available. Major credit cards are accepted for reservations. Open May to October, weather permitting.

Directions: From Salem, drive east on Highway 22 for about 20 miles to Highway 226. Turn right and drive south for two miles to Lyons and John Neal Park Road. Turn east and drive a short distance to the campground on the left.

Contact: Linn County Parks Department, 3010 Ferry St. SW, Albany, OR 97322, 541/967-3917, fax 541/924-6915, website: www.co.linn.or.us.

16 YELLOWBOTTOM

Rating: 7

on Quartzville Creek
See map pages 278–279

Out-of-town visitors always miss this campground across the road from Quartzville Creek. It's nestled under a canopy of old-growth forest. The Rhododendron Trail, which is just under a mile, provides a challenging hike through forest and patches of rhododendrons. Some folks pan for gold here. Though primitive, the camp is ideal for a quiet getaway weekend.

RV sites, facilities: There are 20 sites for RVs up to 28 feet or tents; 10 are drive-through. Picnic tables, garbage bins, and fire grills are provided. Drinking water, vault toilets, and firewood are available. There is a camp host. Some facilities are wheelchair-accessible. Leashed pets are permitted.

Reservations, fees: Reservations are not accepted. The fee is $8 per night, with a 14-day stay limit, plus $5 per night for an additional vehicle after two. A senior discount is available. Open mid-May to late September.

Directions: From Albany, drive east on U.S. 20 for about 35 miles (through Sweet Home) to Quartzville Road. Turn left (northeast) on

Quartzville Road and drive 24 miles to the campground on the left.

Contact: Bureau of Land Management, Salem District, 1717 Fabry Rd. SE, Salem, OR 97306, 503/375-5646, fax 503/375-5622.

17 WILLAMETTE CITY PARK

Rating: 8

on the Willamette River
See map pages 278–279

This 287-acre city park sits on the banks of the Willamette River, just outside Corvallis. The camping area is actually a large clearing near the entrance to the park, which has been left in its natural state. There are trails leading down to the river, and the bird-watching is good here.

RV sites, facilities: There are 13 sites for RVs of any length or tents. Flush toilets, drinking water, a covered outdoor kitchen area, picnic tables, and a children's playground are available. Propane, a store, a café, a coin-operated laundry, and ice are within one mile. Boat docks and launching facilities are also within one mile. An RV dump station is in town, three miles away. Leashed pets are permitted.

Reservations, fees: Reservations are not accepted. The fee is $12 per night, plus $5 per additional vehicle. Open April to mid-November.

Directions: On I-5, take Exit 228 (five miles south of Albany) to Highway 34. Turn west and drive nine miles to Corvallis and Highway 99 W. Turn left (south) and drive 1.3 mile to Southeast Goodnight Road. Turn left (east) and drive one mile to the park.

Contact: Corvallis Department of Parks and Recreation, 1310 SW Avery Park Dr., Corvallis, OR 97333, 541/766-6918, fax 541/754-1701, website: www.ci.corvallis.or.us/pr/prhome.html.

18 WATERLOO COUNTY CAMPGROUND

Rating: 8

on the South Santiam River
See map pages 278–279

This campground features more than a mile of South Santiam River frontage. Swimming, fishing, picnicking, and field sports are options here.

Small boats with trolling motors are the only boats usable here.

RV sites, facilities: There are 122 sites for RVs or tents; 102 have partial hookups (30 amps). Picnic tables and fire pits are provided. Drinking water, a pay phone, cell phone reception, and restrooms with showers are available. Boat ramps and a playground are in the surrounding day-use area. A small grocery store is within one mile. Leashed pets are permitted.

Reservations, fees: Reservations are accepted at 541/967-3917 ($11 reservation fee). The fee is $13–16 per night, plus $5 fee for one additional vehicle. Senior discounts are available. Major credit cards are accepted for reservations. Open year-round.

Directions: From Albany, drive east on U.S. 20 for about 20 miles through Lebanon to the Waterloo exit. Turn north at the Waterloo exit and drive approximately two miles to the camp on the right. The camp is on the south side of the South Santiam River.

Contact: Linn County Parks Department, 3010 Ferry St. SW, Albany, OR 97322, 541/967-3917, fax 541/924-6915, website: www.co.linn.or.us.

19 WHITCOMB CREEK COUNTY PARK

Rating: 8

on Green Peter Reservoir
See map pages 278–279

This camp is on the north shore of Green Peter Reservoir in a wooded area with lots of ferns, which gives it a rain-forest feel. Recreation options include swimming, sailing, hiking, and picnicking. Two boat ramps are on the reservoir about a mile from camp.

RV sites, facilities: There are 39 sites for RVs or tents and one group area for up to 100 people. Picnic tables and fire rings are provided. Drinking water is available to haul from several different locations; vault toilets, cell phone reception, and garbage bins are available. Facilities are within 15 miles. Leashed pets are permitted.

Reservations, fees: Reservations are not accepted for family sites but are required for the group site at 541/967-3917 ($50 reservation fee). The fees are $11 per night and $100 per night for the group site. A senior discount is available. Major credit cards are accepted for reservations. Open April to October.

Directions: From Albany, drive east on U.S. 20 for about 35 miles (through Lebanon and Sweet Home) to the Quartzville Road exit (near Foster Reservoir). Turn north on Quartzville Road and drive 10 miles to the campground.

Contact: Linn County Parks Department, 3010 Ferry St. SW, Albany, OR 97322, 541/967-3917, fax 541/924-6915, website: www.co.linn.or.us.

20 SUNNYSIDE COUNTY PARK

Rating: 8

on Foster Reservoir
See map pages 278–279

This is Linn County's most popular park. Recreation options include boating, fishing, water-skiing, and swimming. A golf course is within 15 miles.

RV sites, facilities: There are 165 sites, most with partial hookups (30, 50 amps), for RVs up to 60 feet or tents. Twenty-seven sites are reserved for groups, who must take a minimum of eight sites, with a maximum of eight people per site. Drinking water, flush toilets, showers, an RV dump station, a pay phone, cell phone reception, firewood, picnic areas, volleyball courts, a boat ramp, and moorage are available. Additional facilities are within two miles. An ATM is within six miles. Leashed pets are permitted.

Reservations, fees: Reservations are accepted ($11 reservation fee, $50 reservation fee for group site). The fee is $13–16 per night, plus $5 for one additional vehicle. Senior discounts are available. Open year-round.

Directions: From Albany, drive east on U.S. 20 for about 35 miles (through Lebanon and Sweet Home) to the Quartzville Road exit (near Foster Reservoir). Turn north on Quartzville Road and drive one mile to the campground on the right. The camp is on the south side of Foster Reservoir.

Contact: Linn County Parks Department, 3010 Ferry St. SW, Albany, OR 97322, 541/967-3917, fax 541/924-0202, website: www.co.linn.or.us.

21 CASCADIA STATE PARK

Rating: 7

on the Santiam River
See map pages 278–279

The highlight of this 258-acre park is Soda Creek Falls, with a fun three-quarter-mile hike to reach it. The park is set along the banks of the Santiam River. A newer trail ushers you through Douglas fir trees along the river, a good place to fish and swim. It's a great spot for a more intimate getaway for hikers, and also for reunions and meetings for families, Boy Scouts, and other groups.

RV sites, facilities: There are 25 primitive sites for self-contained RVs up to 30 feet or tents and two group areas for tents. Picnic tables, garbage bins, and fire grills are provided. Drinking water, flush toilets, firewood, and cell phone reception are available. Some facilities are wheelchair-accessible. Leashed pets are permitted.

Reservations, fees: Reservations are accepted for group areas only at 503/854-3406. The fee is $9–14 per night, plus $4 per night for an additional vehicle. Group sites are $60 for up to 25 people and $2.40 for each additional person. Major credit cards are accepted. Open March to October, weather permitting.

Directions: From Albany, drive east on U.S. 20 for 40 miles to the park on the left (14 miles east of the town of Sweet Home).

Contact: Cascadia State Park, P.O. Box 736, Cascadia, OR 97329, 541/367-6021 or 800/551-6949.

22 RICHARDSON PARK

Rating: 7

on Fern Ridge Reservoir
See map pages 278–279

This pretty Lane County park is a favorite for sailing and sailboards, as the wind is consistent. Boating and water-skiing are also popular. A walking trail around the reservoir doubles as a bike trail. Additional activities include swimming, fishing, and wildlife viewing. The Corps of Engineers has wildlife areas nearby.

RV sites, facilities: There are 88 sites with partial hookups (20, 30, 50 amps) for RVs of any

OREGON

length or tents and four double sites. Picnic tables and fire pits are provided. Drinking water, an RV dump station, garbage bins, and restrooms with flush toilets, sinks, and hot showers are available. A part-time attended marina with minimal supplies—including ice, a boat launch, and transient boat docks—unsupervised swimming, and a playground are available in the park. An ATM is within three miles. There is a small town within five miles. Some facilities are wheelchair-accessible. Leashed pets are permitted.

Reservations, fees: Reservations are accepted at 541/935-2005 ($14 reservation fee). The fee is $20 per night, plus $6.50 per additional vehicle. The maximum stay is 14 days in a 30-day period. Open mid-April to mid-October.

Directions: In Eugene on I-5, drive to Exit 195B and Belt Line Road. Turn west on Belt Line Road and drive 6.5 miles to Junction City Airport exit and Highway 99. Turn left on Highway 99 and drive north for .5 mile to Clear Lake Road. Turn left and drive 8.2 miles to the campground on the left.

Contact: Richardson Park, 25950 Richardson Park Rd., Junction City, OR 97448, 541/935-2005, website: www.lakecounty.org/parks.

23 EUGENE KAMPING WORLD

Rating: 5

near the Willamette River
See map pages 278–279

Eugene is one of Oregon's major cities, but it offers many riverside parks and hiking opportunities. Both the Willamette and McKenzie Rivers run right through town. The McKenzie, in particular, can provide good trout fishing. A golf course is nearby.

RV sites, facilities: There are 110 sites (77 drive-through) for RVs of any length and 30 tent sites. There are 89 sites with full hookups (30, 50 amps) and 21 sites with partial hookups. Picnic tables are provided. Drinking water, flush toilets, propane, an RV dump station, showers, a recreation hall, cable TV, a pay phone, cell phone reception, modem access, a miniature golf course, a store, a laundry room, a meeting room, ice, and a playground are available. An ATM is within two

blocks. A café is within one mile. Small, leashed pets are permitted.

Reservations, fees: Reserve at 800/343-3008. The fee is $16–22 per night, plus $1.50 per person for more than two people and $1 for an additional vehicle. Major credit cards are accepted. Open year-round.

Directions: From Eugene, drive north on I-5 for seven miles to Coburg and Exit 199. Take that exit and drive west for .25 mile to South Stewart Way (the campground access road). Turn left and drive up the driveway.

Contact: Eugene Kamping World, 90932 S. Stewart Way, Coburg, OR 97408, 541/343-4832, fax 541/343-3313.

24 WHITTAKER CREEK

Rating: 7

near the Siuslaw River
See map pages 278–279

This campground is home to one of the area's premier salmon spawning grounds, where annual runs of chinook, coho salmon, and steelhead can be viewed. The Old Growth Ridge Trail is accessible from the campground. This moderately difficult trail ascends 1,000 feet above the Siuslaw River through a stand of old-growth Douglas fir. Fishing is for trout and crayfish.

RV sites, facilities: There are 31 sites for RVs up to 35 feet or tents. Picnic tables and fire pits are provided. A camp host is on-site, and drinking water, vault toilets, garbage bins, boat ramp (no motors allowed), a swimming beach, a playground, and a picnic shelter are available. A pay phone is within nine miles. Some facilities are wheelchair-accessible. Leashed pets are permitted.

Reservations, fees: Reservations are not accepted. The fee is $8 per night, plus $5 for each additional vehicle. A senior discount is available. Open mid-May to mid-October, weather permitting.

Directions: From Eugene, drive west on Highway 126 for 33 miles to Siuslaw River Road. Turn left (south) and drive two miles to the campground on the right.

Contact: Bureau of Land Management, Eugene District Office, 2890 Chad Dr., P.O. Box 10226, Eugene, OR 97440-2226, 541/683-6600, fax 541/683-6981.

OREGON

25 CLAY CREEK

Rating: 7

near the Siuslaw River
See map pages 278–279
Clay Creek Trail, a two-mile loop, takes you to a ridge overlooking the river valley and is well worth the walk. Fishing for trout and crayfish is popular. Sites are situated in a forest of cedars, Douglas fir, and maple trees. The campground gets a medium amount of use.

RV sites, facilities: There are 21 sites for RVs up to 35 feet or tents. Picnic tables and fire pits are provided. Drinking water, vault toilets, garbage bins, a swimming beach, a softball field, horseshoes, a playground, and two group picnic shelters with fireplaces are available. A camp host is on-site. Some facilities are wheelchair-accessible. Leashed pets are permitted.

Reservations, fees: Reservations are not accepted. The fee is $8 per night, plus $5 for each additional vehicle. A senior discount is available. Open mid-May to mid-October, weather permitting.

Directions: From Eugene, drive west on Highway 126 for 33 miles to Siuslaw River Road. Turn left (south) and drive 9.7 miles to Siuslaw River Access Road. Bear left and continue six miles to the campground on the right.

Contact: Bureau of Land Management, Eugene District Office, 2890 Chad Dr., P.O. Box 10226, Eugene, OR 97440-2226, 541/683-6600, fax 541/683-6981.

26 KOA SHERWOOD FOREST

Rating: 5

near Eugene
See map pages 278–279
Seven miles south of Eugene, this KOA provides an easy-to-reach layover for RV travelers heading up and down on I-5. Nearby recreational facilities include a golf course.

RV sites, facilities: There are 100 sites with full hookups (30, 50 amps) for RVs of any length, 20 tent sites, and three cabins. Picnic tables are provided. Drinking water, flush toilets, a pay phone, modem access, cell phone reception, showers, an RV dump station, a recreation hall, a store, a laundry room, ice, a playground, and a swimming pool are available. Propane and an ATM are available within one block. A café is within one mile. Leashed pets are permitted.

Reservations, fees: Reserve at 800/541-4110. The fee is $21–26 per night, plus $2 per person for more than two people. Cabins are $37. Major credit cards are accepted. Open year-round.

Directions: From Eugene, drive south on I-5 for seven miles to the Creswell exit. Take that exit and turn west on Oregon Avenue and drive one-half block to the campground at 298 East Oregon Avenue.

Contact: KOA Sherwood Forest, 298 E. Oregon Ave., Creswell, OR 97426, 541/895-4110, fax 541/895-5037, website: www.koa.com.

27 CASCARA CAMPGROUND

Rating: 7

in Fall Creek Reservoir State Recreation Area
See map pages 278–279
Campsites are near the water with great views. Most of these spacious sites have Douglas fir and white fir tree cover. Water recreation is the primary activity here. Personal watercraft and water-skiing are allowed. The lake level drops in August, and water temperatures are ideal for summer swimming.

RV sites, facilities: There are 42 sites for RVs or tents and five walk-in sites for tents. Picnic tables, garbage service, and fire grills are provided. Drinking water, vault toilets, cell phone reception, and firewood are available. A boat launch, dock, and swimming area are also available. A pay phone is within 5.5 miles. An ATM and a store are within 10 miles. A camp host is on-site. Leashed pets are permitted.

Reservations, fees: Reservations are not accepted. The fee is $15 per night, plus $5 for each additional vehicle. Major credit cards are accepted. Open May to September.

Directions: From south Eugene on I-5, take Exit 188 to Highway 58. Drive 11 miles south to Lowell and Pioneer Street (at the covered bridge). Turn left and drive less than .25 mile to West Boundary Road. Turn left and drive one block to Lowell Jasper Road. Turn right and drive 1.5

miles to Unity and Place Road. Turn right and drive about one mile to a fork with North Shore Road (Big Fall Creek Road). Bear left onto Big Fall Creek Road and drive about eight miles to the head of Fall Creek Reservoir and Peninsula Road (Forest Road 6250). Turn right and drive .5 mile to the campground.

Contact: Oregon State Parks, Southern Willamette Management Unit, 541/937-1173 or 800/551-6949, website: www.oregonstateparks.org.

28 DEXTER SHORES RV PARK

Rating: 7

near Dexter Point Reservoir
See map pages 278–279

If you're driving on I-5, this RV park is well worth the 15-minute drive out of Springfield. It's across the street from Dexter Point Reservoir, where fishing and boating are permitted. Nearby Dexter and Fall Creek Lakes offer swimming, sailing, windsurfing, and water-skiing. There are three authentic Sioux tepees on the property in the summer and three cabins.

RV sites, facilities: There are 56 sites with full hookups (30, 50 amps) for RVs up to 40 feet, five tent sites, three tepees, and three one-bedroom cabins. Picnic tables and fire pits are provided. Drinking water, flush toilets, showers, an RV dump station, a pay phone, cell phone reception, modem access, cable TV, firewood, a laundry room, and a playground are available. Propane, a café, a restaurant, an ATM, and ice are within one mile. Boat docks and launching facilities are nearby. Leashed pets permitted, but no pets or smoking is allowed in the vacation rentals.

Reservations, fees: Reserve at 866/558-9777. The fees are $16–26 per night and $25–35 per night for tepees, plus $3–7 per person for more than two people and $1 per pet per night. Major credit cards are accepted. No pets are allowed in tepees or cabins. Open year-round.

Directions: From south Eugene on I-5, drive to Exit 188A and Highway 58. Take Highway 58 east and drive 11.5 miles to Lost Creek Road. Turn right (south) and drive to Dexter Road. Turn left (in front of the café) and drive east for one-half block to the park on the right.

Contact: Dexter Shores RV Park, P.O. Box 70, Dexter, OR 97431, 541/937-3711, fax 541/937-1724, website: www.dextershoresrvpark.com.

29 PASS CREEK COUNTY PARK

Rating: 7

near Cottage Grove
See map pages 278–279

This decent layover spot for travelers on I-5 is situated in a wooded, hilly area and features many shaded sites. Mountain views give the park scenic value. There is a covered pavilion and gazebo with barbecue grills for get-togethers. You can find fishing and other water activities 11 miles away; history buffs can look for a covered bridge eight miles away. There are no other campgrounds in the immediate area, so if it's late and you need a place to stay, grab this one.

RV sites, facilities: There are 30 sites with full hookups (20, 30, 50 amps) for RVs up to 30 feet and 30 tent sites. Picnic tables and fire rings are provided. Drinking water, flush toilets, showers, cell phone reception, and a playground are available. A store, a café, a pay phone, and ice are within one mile. Leashed pets are permitted.

Reservations, fees: Reservations are not accepted. The fee is $11–14 per night, plus $3 for additional vehicles unless towed. A senior discount is available for Douglas County residents. Major credit cards are accepted. Open year-round.

Directions: On I-5, drive to Exit 163 (between Roseburg and Eugene). Take Exit 163 and turn west on Curtain Park Road. Drive west (under the freeway) for a very short distance to the park entrance.

Contact: Pass Creek County Park, 201 Curtain Park Rd., P.O. Box 81, Curtin, OR 97428, 541/942-3281, website: www.co.douglas.or.us/parks.

30 COTTAGE GROVE LAKE/PINE MEADOWS

Rating: 6

on Cottage Grove Reservoir
See map pages 278–279

This campground is surrounded by a varied landscape—marshland, grassland, and forest—near the banks of Cottage Grove Reservoir. Boating,

OREGON

fishing, water-skiing, and swimming are among the recreation options. It's an easy hop from I-5.

RV sites, facilities: There are 92 sites for RVs up to 40 feet or tents, with some drive-through sites. Drinking water, picnic tables, garbage bins, and fire rings are provided. Flush toilets, showers, an RV dump station, a children's play area, an amphitheater, interpretive displays, and a swimming area are available. A boat dock, launching facilities, and a small store are nearby. Leashed pets are permitted.

Reservations, fees: Reserve at 877/444-6777 or online at www.reserveusa.com ($9 reservation fee). The fee is $14 per night for up to eight people, plus $4 per night for an additional vehicle. A senior discount is available. Open mid-May to mid-September.

Directions: From Eugene, drive south on I-5 past Cottage Grove to Exit 172. Take that exit to London Road and drive south for 4.5 miles to Reservoir Road. Turn left and drive three miles to the camp entrance on the right.

Contact: U.S. Army Corps of Engineers, Recreation Information, Cottage Grove, OR 97424, 541/942-8657 or 541/942-5631, fax 541/942-1305, website: www.nwp.usace.army.mil.

31 BAKER BAY COUNTY PARK

Rating: 6

on Dorena Lake

See map pages 278–279

This campground is set along the shore of Dorena Lake, where fishing, sailing, water-skiing, canoeing, swimming, and boating are among the recreation options. Row River Trail follows part of the lake for a hike or bike ride, and there are covered bridges in the area. For golf, head to Cottage Grove.

RV sites, facilities: There are 49 sites for self-contained RVs up to 35 feet or tents, plus two group sites for up to 25 people per group. Picnic tables and fire grills are provided. Drinking water, flush toilets, coin-operated showers, a pay phone, cell phone reception, firewood, garbage bins, and an RV dump station are available. A concession stand with ice is in the park. A store and ATM are within 2.5 miles. Boat docks and launching facilities are nearby, with seasonal on-shore facil-

ities for catamarans. Some facilities are wheelchair-accessible. Leashed pets are permitted.

Reservations, fees: Reservations are not accepted for family sites. The fee is $16 per night for a single site, plus $5 for an additional vehicle. Reservations are required for group sites ($40 deposit) at 541/942-7669; the fee is $40 per night. Open mid-April to mid-October.

Directions: From Eugene, drive south on I-5 for 22 miles to Cottage Grove and Exit 174 (Dorena Lake exit). Take that exit to Row Road and drive east for 4.4 miles (the road becomes Shore View Drive). Bear right and drive 2.8 miles to the campground entrance on the left.

Contact: Baker Bay County Park, 35635 Shore View Dr., Dorena, OR 97434, 541/942-7669, website: www.co.lane.or.us/parks.

32 SCHWARZ PARK

Rating: 7

on Dorena Lake

See map pages 278–279

This large campground is set before Dorena Lake on the Row River, where fishing, swimming, boating, and water-skiing are among the recreation options. Note that chances of rain are high May to mid-June and that there is a posted warning for consumption of fish from Dorena Lake. The Row River Trail parallels Dorena Lake's north shoreline. The paved trail is approximately 13.5 miles long and is excellent for walking, bike riding, and shoreline access.

RV sites, facilities: There are 72 sites for RVs of any length and six group sites. Picnic tables and fire rings are provided. Drinking water, flush toilets, showers, garbage bins, a pay phone, cell phone reception, and an RV dump station are available. Boat-launching facilities are on the lake about two miles upstream. A coin-operated laundry is within five miles, and an ATM is within nine miles. Three sites are wheelchair-accessible. Leashed pets are permitted.

Reservations, fees: Reserve at 877/444-6777 or online at www.reserveusa.com. The fees are $12 per night for individual sites and $90 per night for group sites, plus $4 per night for an additional vehicle. A senior discount is available. Open late April to late September.

Directions: From Eugene, drive south on I-5 for 22 miles to Cottage Grove and Exit 174. Take that exit to Shoreview Drive and continue (past Row Road) six miles east to the campground entrance.

Contact: U.S. Army Corps of Engineers, Recreation Information, Cottage Grove, OR 97424, 541/942-1418 or 541/942-5631, fax 541/942-1305.

OREGON

Oregon

Chapter 9

The Columbia River Gorge and Mount Hood

THE COLUMBIA RIVER GORGE AND MOUNT HOOD

see Washington
page 14

WASHINGTON

Columbia River Gorge
National Scenic Area

Gifford Pinchot

National Forest

Columbia River

The Dalles

Hood River

Hood River

Mt. Hood
(11,235 ft.)

Wapinitia Pass
(3,952 ft.)

White River

Deschutes River

Range

Mt. Hood

Sandy River

Clackamas River

10 mi

10 km

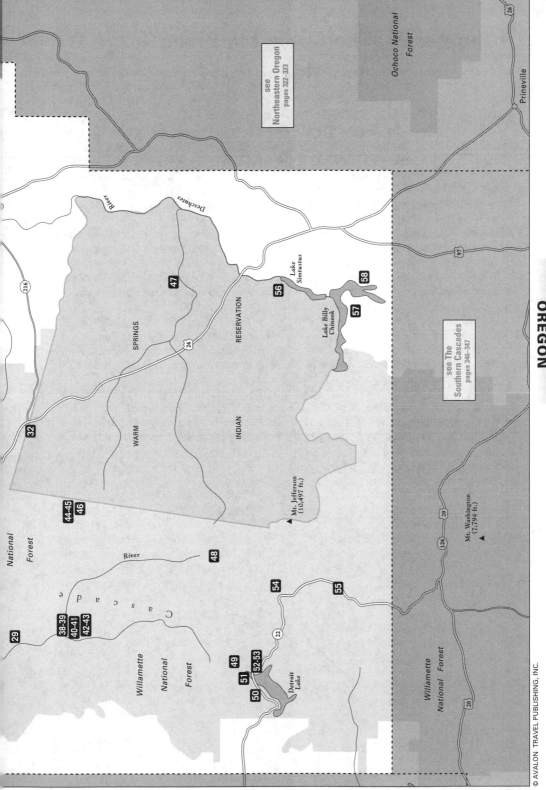

OREGON

see
Northeastern Oregon
pages 322-323

see The
Southern Cascades
pages 346-347

Ochoco National
Forest

Prineville

Deschutes River

Deschutes

River

Lake
Simtustus

Lake Billy
Chinook

WARM   SPRINGS

INDIAN   RESERVATION

Mt. Jefferson
(10,497 ft.)

Mt. Washington
(7,794 ft.)

National
Forest

River

Cascade

Willamette
National
Forest

Willamette   National   Forest

Detroit
Lake

© AVALON TRAVEL PUBLISHING, INC.

Chapter 9—The Columbia River Gorge and Mount Hood

OREGON

The Columbia River area is at once a living history lesson, a geological wonder, and a recreation paradise. The waterway is probably best known as the route the Lewis and Clark expedition followed two centuries ago. It's also famous for carving out a deep gorge through the Cascade Range that divides Oregon. And nearby Mount Hood and its surrounding national forest and many lakes provide almost unlimited opportunities for camping, hiking, and fishing.

The Columbia spans hundreds of square miles and is linked to a watershed that in turn is connected to the Snake River, which covers thousands of square miles. I-84 provides a major route along the southern shore of the Columbia, but the river view is not what you will remember. After you depart the traffic of the Portland area, driving west to east, you will pass along the wooded foothills of the Cascade Range to the south. When you pass Hood River, the world suddenly changes. The trees disappear. In their place are rolling grasslands that seem to extend for as far as you can see. It is often hot and dry here, with strong winds blowing straight down the river.

However, the entire time you are within the realm of Mount Hood. At 11,239 feet, Hood is a beautiful mountain, shaped like a diamond, its flanks supporting many stellar destinations, including with campsites and small lakes set in forest. Snowmelt feeds many major rivers as well as numerous smaller streams, which roll down Mount Hood in every direction.

The transformation of the Gorge-area landscape from forest to grasslands to high desert is quick and striking. Particularly remarkable is how the Deschutes River has cut a path through the desert bluffs. And while the Deschutes is one of Oregon's better steelhead streams, unless you're fishing, you are more likely to encounter a desert chukar on a rock perch than anything water-bound.

1 CROWN POINT RV PARK

Rating: 6

near the Columbia River
See map pages 296–297

This little park is located near the Columbia River along scenic U.S. 30. Nearby Crown Point State Park is open during the day and offers views of the Columbia River Gorge and the historic Vista House, a memorial built in 1918 to honor Oregon's pioneers. Multnomah Falls offers another possible side trip.

RV sites, facilities: There are 21 sites, including two drive-through sites, with full hookups (30 amps) for RVs of any length and five tent sites. Picnic tables are provided. Drinking water, flush toilets, an RV dump station, coin-operated showers, a pay phone, cell phone reception, modem access, a beauty shop, and a laundry room are available. A store, an ATM, and ice are within walking distance. Leashed pets are permitted.

Reservations, fees: Reservations are accepted. The fee is $15–24 per night. A senior discount is available. Open year-round.

Directions: From Portland on I-84 eastbound, drive 16 miles to Exit 22 and Corbett. Take that exit and turn right on Corbett Hill Road. Drive 1.5 miles to a Y intersection with East Historic Columbia River Highway. Bear left and drive .25 mile to the park on the right.

Note: The recommended route has a 10 percent grade for 1.5 miles. An alternate route: from Portland on I-84 eastbound, drive to Exit 18/Lewis and Clark State Park. Take that exit to East Historic Columbia River Highway and drive seven miles to the park on the right.

Contact: Crown Point RV Park, 37000 E. Historic Columbia River Hwy., Corbett, OR 97019, 503/695-5207, fax 503/695-3217.

2 OXBOW REGIONAL PARK

Rating: 7

on the Sandy River
See map pages 296–297

This 1,200-acre park along the Sandy River, a short distance from the Columbia River Gorge, is a designated natural preservation area. Fish-ing, swimming, and nonmotorized boating are permitted here.

RV sites, facilities: There are 67 sites for RVs up to 35 feet or tents. Picnic tables and fire pits are provided. Drinking water, flush and vault toilets, coin-operated showers, a pay phone, firewood, barbecues, and two playgrounds are available. Boat-launching facilities are nearby. An ATM, a coin-operated laundry, and groceries are within 10 miles. Gates lock at sunset and open at 6:30 A.M. No alcohol is allowed. No pets are permitted.

Reservations, fees: Reservations are not accepted. The fee is $13 per night for up to six people, plus $4 per additional vehicle and a park entrance fee of $3 per vehicle. Open year-round but subject to periodic closure; call for current status.

Directions: From Portland on I-84, drive to Exit 17. Turn south on Highway 257 and drive 3.5 miles to Division Street. Turn left and drive eight miles to the park on the left.

Contact: Oxbow Regional Park, 3010 SE Oxbow Pkwy., Gresham, OR 97080, 503/663-4708. The park is managed by Metro-Region Parks and Green Spaces.

3 AINSWORTH STATE PARK

Rating: 8

along the Columbia River Gorge
See map pages 296–297

This state park is set along the scenic Columbia River Gorge, home to the world's greatest concentration of high waterfalls, including famous Multnomah Falls. From the Nesmith Point Trailhead, located three miles away, hike to a great view of St. Peter's Dome. Anglers should check out the Bonneville Fish Hatchery.

RV sites, facilities: There are 45 sites with full hookups (30 amps) for RVs up to 60 feet and six walk-in sites. Picnic tables and fire grills are provided. Drinking water, flush toilets, cell phone reception, showers, garbage bins, an RV dump station, and firewood are available. An ATM, a coin-operated laundry, and a store are within nine miles. Leashed pets are permitted.

Reservations, fees: Reservations are not accepted. The fee is $13–18 per night, plus $7 per additional

OREGON

vehicle. Major credit cards are accepted. Open March to October, weather permitting.

Directions: From Portland on I-84 eastbound, drive 37 miles to Exit 35. Turn southwest on the Columbia River Scenic Highway and continue a short distance to the park. An alternate route is to take the historic Columbia River Highway, a designated scenic highway, all the way from Portland (37 miles).

Contact: Columbia River Gorge District, Oregon State Parks, P.O. Box 100, Corbett, OR 97019, 503/695-2301 or 800/551-6949.

4 EAGLE CREEK

Rating: 8

near the Columbia Wilderness in Mount Hood National Forest
See map pages 296–297

Eagle Creek is the oldest Forest Service Camp in America. Set at 400 feet elevation among old-growth Douglas fir and hemlock, it makes a good base camp for a hiking trip. The Eagle Creek Trail leaves the campground and goes 13 miles to Wahtum Lake, where it intersects with the Pacific Crest Trail. A primitive campground sits at the 7.5-mile point. The upper seven miles of the trail pass through the Hatfield Wilderness.

RV sites, facilities: There are 20 sites for RVs up to 22 feet or tents and one group site. Picnic tables and fire grills are provided. Drinking water, garbage bins, flush toilets, and cell phone reception are available. Boat docks and launching facilities are nearby on the Columbia River. A pay phone is across the street, and an ATM is within 7.5 miles. Leashed pets are permitted.

Reservations, fees: Reservations are not accepted. The fee is $10 per night, plus $5 per additional vehicle. A senior discount is available. Reservations are required for groups. Open mid-May to October.

Directions: From Portland, drive east on I-84 for 40 miles to Bonneville. Continue east for two miles to the campground.

Contact: Columbia River Gorge National Scenic Area, 902 Wasco Ave., Suite 200, Hood River, OR 97031, 541/386-2333, fax 541/386-1916.

5 CASCADE LOCKS MARINE PARK

Rating: 8

in Cascade Locks
See map pages 296–297

This public riverfront park covers 200 acres and offers a museum and boat rides. The salmon fishing is excellent here. Stern-wheeler brunch and dinner cruises are available, as well as day-long excursions.

RV sites, facilities: There are 30 sites for RVs of any length or tents. Picnic tables are provided. Drinking water, flush toilets, an RV dump station, showers, a pay phone, cell phone reception, boat docks, launching facilities, and a playground are available. Propane, a store, a café, an ATM, a coin-operated laundry, and ice are within one mile. Leashed pets are permitted.

Reservations, fees: Reservations are not accepted. The fee is $15 per night. Open year-round, with limited winter facilities.

Directions: From Portland, drive east on I-84 for 44 miles to Cascade Locks. Take Exit 44 to Wanapa Street and drive .5 mile to the sign for the park on the left. Turn left and drive to the park (well signed).

Contact: Cascade Locks Marine Park, P.O. Box 307, 355 Wanapa St., Cascade Locks, OR 97014, 541/374-8619, fax 541/374-8428, website: www.sternwheeler.com. Campground managed by Port of Cascade Locks.

6 KOA CASCADE LOCKS

Rating: 5

near the Columbia River
See map pages 296–297

This KOA is a good layover spot for RVers touring the Columbia River corridor. The campground offers level, shaded RV sites and grassy tent sites. Nearby recreation options include bike trails, hiking trails, and tennis courts. The 200-acre Cascade Locks Marine Park is close by and offers everything from museums to boat trips.

RV sites, facilities: There are 78 sites with full hookups (30, 50 amps) for RVs of any length or tents, nine cabins, and two cottages. Picnic tables are provided. Drinking water, flush toilets, propane, an RV dump station, showers, firewood, a hot tub, cable TV hookups, a pay phone, cell phone reception, modem access, a recreation hall, a store, a laundry room, ice, a playground, and a heated swimming pool are available. A café and ATM are within 1.5 miles. Leashed pets are permitted.

Reservations, fees: Reserve at 800/562-8698. The fee is $20–28 per night, plus $3–4 per person for more than two people. Cabins are $30–50 per night, cottages are $49–114 per night. Major credit cards are accepted. Open February to November.

Directions: From Portland, drive east on I-84 for 44 miles to Cascade Locks and Exit 44. Turn east on Forest Lane and drive one mile to the campground.

Contact: KOA Cascade Locks, 841 NW Forest Ln., Cascade Locks, OR 97014, 541/374-8668, website: www.koa.com.

7 HERMAN CREEK HORSE CAMP

Rating: 5

near the Pacific Crest Trail in Mount Hood National Forest

See map pages 296–297

This rustic campground with spacious sites sits at 1,000 feet elevation and is about a half mile from Herman Creek, not far from the Pacific Crest Trail. This area, separated from Washington by the Columbia River, is particularly beautiful. There are many recreation options here, including biking, hiking, fishing, and boat trips.

RV sites, facilities: There are seven sites for RVs up to 24 feet or tents. Drinking water, garbage bins, fire grills, and picnic tables are provided. Stock handling facilities and cell phone reception are available. An RV dump station, showers, a store, an ATM, a pay phone, a café, a coin-operated laundry, and ice are nearby. Leashed pets are permitted.

Reservations, fees: Reservations are not accepted. The fee is $8 per night, plus $5 per additional vehicle. A senior discount is available. Open mid-May to October.

Directions: From Portland, drive east on I-84 for 44 miles to Cascade Locks and Exit 44. Take that exit and drive straight ahead to the frontage road (Wanapa Street). Continue 1.5 miles (the road becomes Herman Creek Road) to the campground on the right.

Contact: Columbia River Gorge National Scenic Area, 902 Wasco Ave., Suite 200, Hood River, OR 97031, 541/386-2333, fax 541/386-1916.

8 WYETH

Rating: 5

on Gordon Creek in Mount Hood National Forest

See map pages 296–297

Wyeth makes a good layover spot for Columbia River corridor cruisers. The camp is set at 400 feet elevation along Gordon Creek, near the Columbia River. See the previous description of Herman Creek Horse Camp for recreation details.

RV sites, facilities: There are 16 sites for RVs up to 32 feet or tents and three group sites. Fire grills, cell phone reception, and picnic tables are provided. Drinking water and flush toilets are available. An ATM and pay phone are within eight miles. Leashed pets are permitted.

Reservations, fees: Reservations are not accepted. The fee is $10 per night, plus $5 per additional vehicle. A senior discount is available. Open mid-May to October.

Directions: From Portland, drive east on I-84 for 44 miles to Cascade Locks. Continue east on I-84 for seven miles to Wyeth and Exit 51. Turn right and drive .25 mile to the campground entrance.

Contact: Columbia River Gorge National Scenic Area, 902 Wasco Ave., Suite 200, Hood River, OR 97031, 541/386-2333, fax 541/386-1916.

9 VIENTO STATE PARK

Rating: 8

along the Columbia River Gorge

See map pages 296–297

This park along the Columbia River Gorge offers scenic hiking trails and some of the best windsurfing in the Gorge. Sites are often available because of low use. Just eight miles to the east, old U.S. 30 skirts the Columbia River, offering a picturesque drive. Viento has a day-use picnic area right next to a babbling creek. Look for weekend interpretive programs during the summer. There are several other day-use state parks along I-84 just west of Viento, including Wygant, Vinzenz Lausmann, and Seneca Fouts. All offer quality hiking trails and scenic views. Note: there is some noise due to the campground's location next to railroad tracks.

RV sites, facilities: There are 56 sites with partial hookups (20, 30 amps) for RVs up to 30 feet, with some sites accessible for RVs up to 40 feet, and 17 tent sites. Picnic tables and fire grills are provided. Drinking water, garbage bins, a pay phone, cell phone reception, flush toilets, showers, firewood, and a playground are available. An ATM, a coin-operated laundry, and a store are within eight miles. Leashed pets are permitted.

Reservations, fees: Reservations are not accepted. The fee is $13–16 per night, plus $7 per additional vehicle. Major credit cards are accepted. Open March to October, weather permitting.

Directions: From Portland, drive east on I-84 for 56 miles to Exit 56 (eight miles west of Hood River). Take Exit 56 and drive to the park entrance. The park is set on both sides of I-84.

Contact: Columbia River Gorge District, Oregon State Parks, P.O. Box 126, Hood River, OR 97031, 541/374-8811 or 800/551-6949.

10 TUCKER COUNTY PARK

Rating: 6

on the Hood River
See map pages 296–297

This county park along the banks of the Hood River is just far enough out of the way to be missed by most of the tourist traffic. Many people who choose this county park come for the windsurfing. Other recreation opportunities include trout fishing, rafting, and kayaking.

RV sites, facilities: There are 13 sites with partial hookups (20, 30 amps) for RVs up to 30 feet or tents and 80 tent sites. Picnic tables and fire rings are provided. Drinking water, flush toilets, showers, cell phone reception, firewood, and a playground are available. A store, a café, a pay phone, an ATM, and ice are within two miles. A coin-operated laundry is within four miles. Most facilities are wheelchair-accessible. Leashed pets are permitted.

Reservations, fees: Reservations are not accepted. The fee is $13–14 per night, plus $6 per extra tent and $2 per additional vehicle. Open April to October.

Directions: From Portland, turn east on I-84 and drive about 65 miles to the town of Hood River and Exit 62. Take the exit and drive east on Cascade Street and continue to 13th Street (first light). Turn right (south) and drive through and out of town; 13th Street becomes Tucker Road and then Dee Highway (Highway 281). Follow the signs to Parkdale. The park is four miles out of town on the right.

Contact: Hood River County Parks, 918 18th St., Hood River, OR 97031, 541/387-6889, fax 541/386-6325, website: www.co.hood-river.or.us.

11 MEMALOOSE STATE PARK

Rating: 7

in the Columbia River Gorge
See map pages 296–297

This park borrows its name from nearby Memaloose Island, which ancient Native Americans used as a sacred burial ground. Set along the hottest part of the scenic Columbia River Gorge, it makes a prime layover spot for campers cruising the Oregon-Washington border. Nature programs and interpretive events are also held here. This popular camp receives a good deal of traffic, so plan on arriving early to claim a spot even if you have a reservation.

RV sites, facilities: There are 43 sites with full hookups (30 amps) for RVs up to 60 feet and 67 tent sites. Picnic tables and fire grills are provided. Drinking water, garbage bins, flush toilets, a pay phone, cell phone reception, an RV dump station, solar showers, and firewood are available. Leashed pets are permitted.

Reservations, fees: Reserve at 800/452-5687 or online at www.OregonStateParks.org ($7 reservation fee). The fee is $12–20 per night, plus $7 per additional vehicle. Major credit cards are accepted. Open mid-March to late October.

Directions: This park is accessible only to westbound traffic on I-84. From The Dalles, drive west on I-84 for 11 miles to the signed turnoff. (The park is about 75 miles east of Portland.)

Contact: Columbia River Gorge District, Oregon

State Parks, P.O. Box 100, Corbett, OR 97019, 541/478-3008 or 800/551-6949.

12 LONE PINE RV PARK

Rating: 7

near the Columbia River
See map pages 296–297
This private park isn't far from the Columbia River, where fishing and boating are options. The area gets hot weather and occasional winds shooting through the river canyon during summer. Nearby recreation possibilities include an 18-hole golf course and tennis courts.

RV sites, facilities: There are 25 sites with full hookups (30 amps), including 17 drive-through, for RVs of any length. Drinking water, flush toilets, showers, picnic tables, cell phone reception, a café, a laundry room, ice, and a playground are available. An ATM and a pay phone are within one block. Boat docks and launching facilities are nearby. Leashed pets are permitted.

Reservations, fees: Reservations are accepted. The fee is $22–25 per night. Open year-round.

Directions: From Portland, turn east on I-84 and drive about 90 miles to The Dalles and Exit 87. Take Exit 87 to U.S. 197 and drive less than .25 mile to the park.

Contact: Lone Pine RV Park, 335 U.S. 197, The Dalles, OR 97058, 541/506-3755.

13 DESCHUTES RIVER STATE RECREATION AREA

Rating: 7

on the Deschutes River
See map pages 296–297
This tree-shaded park along the Deschutes River in the Deschutes Canyon offers bicycling and hiking trails and good steelhead fishing in season. The Atiyeh Deschutes River Trail at river level is a favorite jaunt for hikers; be sure to look for the basketlike hanging nests of the orioles. A small day-use state park called Heritage Landing, which has a boat ramp and restroom facilities, is located across the river. The U.S. Army Corps of Engineers offers a free train ride and tour of the dam at The Dalles during the sum-

mer. Good rafting is a bonus here. For 25 miles upstream, the river is mostly inaccessible by car. Many fishermen launch boats here and then go upstream to steelhead fishing grounds. Note that boat fishing is not allowed here; you must wade into the river or fish from shore.

RV sites, facilities: There are 35 primitive sites for self-contained RVs up to 30 feet or tents and 34 sites with partial hookups (30, 50 amps). There is also a group area for RVs and tents. Picnic tables and fire grills are provided. Drinking water, garbage bins, a pay phone, cell phone reception, and flush toilets are available. An ATM is within five miles. Coin-operated showers are within seven miles. Leashed pets are permitted.

Reservations, fees: Reserve at 800/452-5687 or online at www.OregonStateParks.org ($6 reservation fee). The fee is $8–16 per night, plus $5 per additional vehicle. Major credit cards are accepted. Open year-round, with limited services November to March.

Directions: From Portland, turn east on I-84 and drive about 90 miles to The Dalles. Continue east on I-84 for 12 miles to Exit 97, turn right, and drive 50 feet to Biggs-Rufus Highway. Turn left and drive about one mile, cross the Deschutes River, and turn right to the campground entrance.

Contact: Deschutes River State Recreation Area, 89600 Biggs-Rufus Hwy., Wasco, OR 97065, 541/739-2322 or 800/452-5687.

14 LE PAGE PARK

Rating: 6

on the John Day River
See map pages 296–297
One half of the campsites are adjacent to the John Day River and the other half are on the other side of the road at this partially shaded campground. The John Day River feeds into the Columbia just one-eighth mile north of the campground. Anglers come for the smallmouth bass, catfish, and bluegill during the summer. The day-use area has a swimming beach, a lawn, a boat launch, and boat docks. Wildlife viewing can be exceptional here, as well as salmon and steelhead fishing. There are several other campgrounds nearby.

RV sites, facilities: There are 22 partial hookup (50 amps) sites for RVs up to 40 feet or tents and five tent sites. Picnic tables and fire pits are provided. Drinking water, a pay phone, and restrooms with flush toilets, sinks, and hot showers are available. A boat ramp, docks, a dump station, and garbage containers are also available. Food, a laundry facility, and an ATM are available five miles away in the town of Rufus. Leashed pets are permitted.

Reservations, fees: Reservations are not accepted. The fee is $10–16 per night, plus $3 per additional vehicle and a $1 day-use fee. Major credit cards are accepted. A senior discount is available. Open April to October.

Directions: From Portland on I-84, drive east 120 miles (30 miles past The Dalles) to Exit 114, the John Day River Recreation Area. The campground is just off I-84.

Contact: Army Corps of Engineers, Portland District, P.O. Box 2946, Portland, OR 97208-2946, 503/808-5150, fax 503/808-4515.

OREGON

15 LOST LAKE

Rating: 9

on Lost Lake in Mount Hood National Forest
See map pages 296–297

Only nonmotorized boats are allowed on this clear, 240-acre lake set against the Cascade Range. The campground is nestled in an old-growth forest of cedar, Douglas fir, and hemlock trees at 3,200 feet elevation. Some sites have a lake view, and the campground affords a great view of Mount Hood. Significant improvements to this campground were completed in late 1999.

RV sites, facilities: There are 125 sites for RVs up to 32 feet or tents, and there is one large, separate group site. A horse camp with a corral is also available. Picnic tables and fire rings with grills are provided. Drinking water, vault toilets, cell phone reception, garbage containers, a dump station, and a covered picnic shelter are available. Cabins, a grocery store, showers, beach picnic areas, a boat launch, and boat rentals are nearby. Many sites are wheelchair-accessible, and there is barrier-free boating and fishing, as well as 3.5 miles of barrier-free trails. Leashed pets are permitted.

Reservations, fees: Reservations are not accepted. The fee is $15–20 per night, plus $5 per addi-

tional vehicle. Major credit cards are accepted. Reservations are required for the group site at 541/386-6366; the group site $40 per night. A senior discount is available. Open mid-May to mid-October, weather permitting.

Directions: From Portland, drive 62 miles east on I-84 to the city of Hood River. Take Exit 62/Westcliff exit to Cascade Road and drive east on Cascade Road to 13th Street. Turn right on 13th Street and drive through Hood River Heights. The road turns into Dee Highway. Continue seven miles, then turn right onto Lost Lake Road (Forest Road 13). Continue seven miles to the campground.

Contact: Mount Hood National Forest, Hood River Ranger District, 6780 Hwy. 35, Mount Hood, OR 97041, 541/352-6002, or 541/386-6366, fax 541/352-7365.

16 EIGHTMILE CROSSING

Rating: 7

on Eightmile Creek in Mount Hood National Forest
See map pages 296–297

This campground is set at an elevation of 4,200 feet along Eightmile Creek. Although pretty and shaded, with sites scattered along the banks of the creek, it gets relatively little camping pressure. From the day-use area you have access to a nice hiking trail that runs along Eightmile Creek. In addition, a three-quarter-mile wheelchair-accessible trail links Eightmile Campground to Lower Crossing Campground. The fishing can be good here, so bring your gear.

RV sites, facilities: There are 21 sites for RVs up to 30 feet or tents. No drinking water is available, and all garbage must be packed out. Picnic tables and fire grills are provided. Vault toilets are available. Leashed pets are permitted.

Reservations, fees: Reservations are not accepted. A Northwest Forest Pass ($5 daily fee or $30 annual fee per parked vehicle) is required. Open year-round.

Directions: From Portland, turn east on I-84 and drive about 90 miles to Exit 87. Take Exit 87 and turn south on U.S. 197; drive 13 miles to Dufur and Dufur Valley Road. Turn right on Dufur Valley Road and drive west for 12 miles to Forest Road 44. Continue west on Forest Road 44 for four miles to Forest Road 4430. Turn right and drive a short distance to the campground.

Contact: Mount Hood National Forest, Barlow Ranger District, 780 NE Court St., Dufur, OR 97021, 541/467-2291, fax 541/467-2271.

17 MCNEIL

Rating: 5

on the Clear Fork of the Sandy River in Mount Hood National Forest

See map pages 296–297

This campground is set at an elevation of 2,040 feet in Old Maid Flat, a special geological area along the Clear Fork of the Sandy River. There's a good view of Mount Hood from the campground entrance. Several trails nearby provide access to the wilderness backcountry. See a U.S. Forest Service map for details.

RV sites, facilities: There are 34 sites for RVs up to 22 feet or tents. Picnic tables and vault toilets are provided. There is no drinking water at the camp, but drinking water can be obtained across the street at Riley Horse Camp. A pay phone is within five miles, and an ATM is within seven miles. Leashed pets are permitted.

Reservations, fees: Reservations are not accepted. The fee is $10 per night, plus $5 per additional vehicle. A senior discount is available. Open May to late September.

Directions: From Portland, drive 40 miles east on U.S. 26 to Zigzag. Turn left on County Road 18/East Lolo Pass Road and drive 4.5 miles to Forest Road 1825. Turn right on Forest Road 1825, drive less than one mile, bear right onto a bridge to stay on Forest Road 1825, and drive .25 mile to the campground on the left.

Contact: Mount Hood National Forest, Zigzag Ranger District, Mount Hood Information Center, 65000 E. Hwy. 26, Welches, OR 97067, 503/622-7674, fax 503/622-7625.

18 LOST CREEK

Rating: 8

on Lost Creek in Mount Hood National Forest

See map pages 296–297

This campground near McNeil and Riley has some of the same opportunities. Set in a cool, lush area on a creek at 2,600 feet elevation, it's barrier-free and offers an interpretive nature trail about one mile long as well as a wheelchair-accessible fishing pier.

RV sites, facilities: There are nine sites for RVs up to 22 feet and five walk-in sites for tents. Drinking water, garbage service, fire grills, vault toilets, and picnic tables are provided. A pay phone is within eight miles, and an ATM is within 10 miles. Some facilities are wheelchair-accessible. Leashed pets are permitted.

Reservations, fees: Reserve at 877/444-6777 or online at www.reserveusa.com ($9 reservation fee). The fees are $14 for a single site and $28 for a double site, plus $7 per additional vehicle. A senior discount is available. Open May to late September.

Directions: From Portland, drive 40 miles east on U.S. 26 to Zigzag. Turn north on County Road 18/East Lolo Pass Road and drive 4.5 miles to Forest Road 1825. Turn right and drive two miles to a fork. Bear right and drive .25 mile to the campground on the right.

Contact: Mount Hood National Forest, Zigzag Ranger District, Mount Hood Information Center, 65000 E. Hwy. 26, Welches, OR 97067, 503/622-7674, fax 503/622-7625.

19 TOLL GATE

Rating: 8

on the Zigzag River in Mount Hood National Forest

See map pages 296–297

This shady campground along the banks of the Zigzag River near Rhododendron is extremely popular, and finding a site on a summer weekend can be next to impossible. Luckily you can get a reservation. There are numerous hiking trails in the area. The nearest one leads east for several miles along the river. The campground features a historic Civilian Conservation Corps shelter from the 1930s, which can be used by campers.

RV sites, facilities: There are nine sites for RVs up to 16 feet and 14 tent sites. Picnic tables and fire grills are provided. Drinking water, garbage service, pit toilets, and cell phone reception are available. A pay phone is within a half mile, and an ATM is within three miles. Leashed pets are permitted.

Reservations, fees: Reserve at 877/444-6777 or online at www.reserveusa.com ($9 reservation fee). The fees are $14–16 per night for single sites and $28 per night for double sites, plus $7 per additional vehicle. A senior discount is available. Open late May to late September.

Directions: From Portland, drive east on U.S. 26 for 40 miles to Zigzag. Continue 2.5 miles southeast on U.S. 26 to the campground entrance.

Contact: Mount Hood National Forest, Zigzag Ranger District, Mount Hood Information Center, 65000 E. Hwy. 26, Welches, OR 97067, 503/622-7674, fax 503/622-7625.

20 GREEN CANYON

Rating: 8

on the Salmon River in Mount Hood National Forest

See map pages 296–297

Few out-of-towners know about this winner. But the locals do, and they keep the place hopping in the summer. The camp sits at 1,600 feet elevation along the banks of the Salmon River. A long trail cuts through the area and parallels the river, passing through a magnificent old-growth forest. See a U.S. Forest Service map for details.

RV sites, facilities: There are 15 sites for RVs up to 22 feet or tents. Picnic tables, garbage service, and fire grills are provided. Pit toilets are available. Drinking water is intermittently available. A store, a café, a pay phone, an ATM, and ice are within five miles. Some facilities are wheelchair-accessible. Leashed pets are permitted.

Reservations, fees: Reservations are not accepted. The fee is $14–16 per night, plus $7 per additional vehicle. A senior discount is available. Open May to late September.

Directions: From Portland, drive east on U.S. 26 for 39 miles to Forest Road 2618 (Salmon River Road) near Zigzag. Turn right and drive 4.5 miles to the campground on the right.

Contact: Mount Hood National Forest, Zigzag Ranger District, Mount Hood Information Center, 65000 E. Hwy. 26, Welches, OR 97067, 503/622-7674, fax 503/622-7625.

21 CAMP CREEK

Rating: 8

near the Zigzag River in Mount Hood National Forest

See map pages 296–297

This campground is set at 2,200 feet elevation along Camp Creek, not far from the Zigzag River. It looks similar to Toll Gate but is larger and farther from the road. A hiking trail runs through camp and along the river; another one leads south to Still Creek. This campground, along with Toll Gate to the west, is very popular and you'll probably need a reservation.

RV sites, facilities: There are 24 sites for RVs up to 22 feet or tents. Drinking water, garbage bins, fire grills, cell phone reception, and picnic tables are provided. Vault toilets are available. A pay phone is within two miles, and an ATM is within five miles. Leashed pets are permitted.

Reservations, fees: Reserve at 877/444-6777 or online at www.reserveusa.com ($9 reservation fee). The fees are $14–16 per night and $12 for a double site, plus $7 per additional vehicle. A senior discount is available. Open late May to late September.

Directions: From Portland, drive east on U.S. 26 for 40 miles to Zigzag. Continue southeast on U.S. 26 for about four miles to the camp on the right.

Contact: Mount Hood National Forest, Zigzag Ranger District, Mount Hood Information Center, 65000 E. Hwy. 26, Welches, OR 97067, 503/622-7674, fax 503/622-7625.

22 STILL CREEK

Rating: 6

on Still Creek in Mount Hood National Forest

See map pages 296–297

This primitive camp, shaded primarily by fir and hemlock, sits along Still Creek where the creek pours off Mount Hood's south slope. Adjacent to Summit Meadows and site of a pioneer gravesite from the Oregon Trail days, it's a great place for mountain views, sunsets, and wildlife. Anglers should bring along their rods; the fishing in Still

Creek can be excellent. The camp sits at 3,600 feet elevation.

RV sites, facilities: There are 27 sites for self-contained RVs up to 16 feet or tents. Picnic tables, garbage service, and fire grills are provided. Pit toilets, drinking water, and cell phone reception are available. A pay phone is within 1.5 miles. Leashed pets are permitted.

Reservations, fees: Reserve at 877/444-6777 or online at www.reserveusa.com ($9 reservation fee). The fee is $14 per night, plus $7 per additional vehicle. A senior discount is available. Open mid-June to late September.

Directions: From Portland, drive 55 miles east on U.S. 26 to Government Camp. Continue east on U.S. 26 for one mile to Forest Road 2650. Turn right and drive south for 500 yards to the campground.

Contact: Mount Hood National Forest, Zigzag Ranger District, Mount Hood Information Center, 65000 E. Hwy. 26, Welches, OR 97067, 503/622-7674, fax 503/622-7625.

23 MILO McIVER STATE PARK

Rating: 7

on the Clackamas River

See map pages 296–297

Though only 45 minutes from Portland, this park is far enough off the beaten track to provide a feeling of separation from the metropolitan area. It's set along the banks of the Clackamas River and has a boat ramp. Hiking trails are available, and a 4.5-mile equestrian trail is also accessible. A fish hatchery is a nearby point of interest. Every April, 300 actors participate in a Civil War re-enactment here.

RV sites, facilities: There are 44 sites with partial hookups (30 amps) for RVs up to 85 feet, nine primitive tent sites, one hiker/biker site, and three group tent areas for a maximum of 50 people. Picnic tables and fire grills are provided. Drinking water, garbage bins, flush toilets, a pay phone, cell phone reception, an RV dump station, showers, picnic shelters, and firewood are available. Boat-launching facilities and Frisbee golf are nearby. An ATM and a coin-operated laundry are within four miles. Most facilities are wheelchair-accessible. Leashed pets are permitted.

Reservations, fees: Reserve at 800/452-5687 or online at www.oregonstateparks.org ($6 reservation fee). The fee is $6–17 per night, plus $7 per additional vehicle, and group sites are $64 per night for up to 25 people, with a $2.40 charge for each additional person. Major credit cards are accepted. Open mid-March to October.

Directions: From Portland, drive east on U.S. 26 from Gresham 11 miles to Sandy and Highway 211. Turn right (south) and drive six miles to a junction. Turn south (still Highway 211) and drive five miles to the park entrance road on the right.

Contact: Milo McIver State Park, 24101 South Entrance Rd., Estacada, OR 97023, 503/630-7150 or 800/551-6949.

24 PROMONTORY

Rating: 7

on North Fork Reservoir

See map pages 296–297

This Portland General Electric camp on North Fork Reservoir is part of a large recreation area and park. The water is calm and ideal for boating, and the trout fishing is excellent. This reservoir is actually a dammed-up section of the Clackamas River. A trail travels along about one mile of the lake shoreline.

RV sites, facilities: There are 47 sites for RVs up to 35 feet or tents, one group site for up to 35 people, and five yurts. There are no RV hookups. Restrooms, garbage bins, showers, a pay phone, limited groceries, ice, a playground, horseshoes, covered picnic shelters with sinks and electric stoves, and snacks are available. A fish-cleaning station, a fishing pier, a children's fishing pond, a boat ramp, a dock, and boat rentals are also on-site. An ATM, a coin-operated laundry, and a store are within seven miles. Some facilities, including restrooms, some sites, the boat ramp, and the fishing pier, are wheelchair-accessible. Leashed pets are permitted.

Reservations, fees: Reserve at 503/630-7229. The fees are $15 per night; $25 per night for a yurt. Major credit cards are accepted. Open mid-May to September.

Directions: From Portland, drive east on U.S. 26 from Gresham 11 miles to Sandy and Highway 211. Turn right (south) and drive six miles to a

OREGON

junction. Turn south (still Highway 211) and drive six miles to Estacada. Continue south on Highway 224 and drive seven miles to the campground on the right. The route is well signed.

Contact: Portland General Electric, 121 SW Salmon St., Portland, OR 97204, 503/464-8515, fax 503/464-2944, website: www.portlandgeneral.com/parks.

25 LAZY BEND

Rating: 8

on the Clackamas River in Mount Hood National Forest

See map pages 296–297

This campground is set at 800 feet elevation along the banks of the Clackamas River near the large North Fork Reservoir. It's far enough off the highway to provide a secluded, primitive feeling, though it fills quickly on weekends and holidays. Only catch-and-release fishing is allowed in the Clackamas.

RV sites, facilities: There are 21 sites for RVs up to 16 feet or tents. Picnic tables, garbage service, and fireplaces are provided. Drinking water and flush toilets are available. An ATM and pay phone are within 10 miles. Leashed pets are permitted.

Reservations, fees: Reserve at 877/444-6777 or online at www.reserveusa.com ($9 reservation fee). The fee is $14 per night, plus $7 per additional vehicle. A senior discount is available. Open late April through Labor Day.

Directions: From Portland, drive east on U.S. 26 from Gresham 11 miles to Sandy and Highway 211. Turn right (south) and drive six miles to a junction. Turn south (still Highway 211) and drive six miles to Estacada. Continue south on Highway 224 and drive 10.5 miles to the campground on the right.

Contact: Mount Hood National Forest, Clackamas River Ranger District, 595 NW Industrial Way, Estacada, OR 97023, 503/630-6861, fax 503/630-2299.

26 ARMSTRONG

Rating: 5

on the Clackamas River in Mount Hood National Forest

See map pages 296–297

This campground is set at an elevation of 900 feet along the banks of the Clackamas River and offers good fishing access. Fishing is catch-and-release only.

RV sites, facilities: There are 12 sites for RVs up to 16 feet or tents. Picnic tables and fire rings are provided. Vault toilets and drinking water are available. Garbage service is available in the summer only. An ATM and pay phone are within six miles. Some facilities are wheelchair-accessible. Leashed pets are permitted.

Reservations, fees: Reserve at 877/444-6777 or online at www.reserveusa.com ($9 reservation fee). The fee is $14 per night, plus $7 per additional vehicle. A senior discount is available. Open year-round, with limited winter services.

Directions: From Portland, drive east on U.S. 26 from Gresham 11 miles to Sandy and Highway 211. Turn right (south) and drive six miles to a junction. Turn south (still Highway 211) and drive six miles to Estacada. Continue south on Highway 224 and drive 15 miles to the campground on the right.

Contact: Mount Hood National Forest, Clackamas River Ranger District, 595 NW Industrial Way, Estacada, OR 97023, 503/630-6861, fax 503/630-2299.

27 CARTER BRIDGE

Rating: 5

on the Clackamas River in Mount Hood National Forest

See map pages 296–297

This small, flat campground is popular with anglers. The Clackamas River flows along one end, and the other end borders the highway, with the attendant traffic noise.

RV sites, facilities: There are 15 sites for RVs up to 28 feet or tents. Picnic tables and fire pits are provided. Drinking water, vault toilets, and garbage

OREGON

bins are available. Some facilities are wheelchair-accessible. Leashed pets are permitted.

Reservations, fees: Reserve at 877/444-6777 or online at www.reserveusa.com ($9 reservation fee). The fee is $12 per night, plus $6 per additional vehicle. A senior discount is available. Open late May to early September, weather permitting.

Directions: From Portland, drive east on U.S. 26 from Gresham 11 miles to Sandy and Highway 211. Turn right (south) and drive six miles to a junction. Turn south (still Highway 211) and drive six miles to Estacada. Continue south on Highway 224 and drive 15.2 miles to the campground on the left.

Contact: Mount Hood National Forest, Clackamas River Ranger District, 595 NW Industrial Way, Estacada, OR 97023, 503/630-6861, fax 503/630-2299.

28 LOCKABY

Rating: 6

on the Clackamas River in Mount Hood National Forest

See map pages 296–297

This campground is set at an elevation of 900 feet along the banks of the Clackamas River, next to Armstrong. Fishing in the Clackamas River is catch-and-release only.

RV sites, facilities: There are 30 sites for RVs up to 16 feet or tents. Picnic tables, fireplaces, drinking water, garbage service, and vault toilets are available. Leashed pets are permitted.

Reservations, fees: Reserve at 877/444-6777 or online at www.reserveusa.com ($9 reservation fee). The fee is $14 per night, plus $7 per additional vehicle. A senior discount is available. Open late May to early September.

Directions: From Portland, drive east on U.S. 26 from Gresham 11 miles to Sandy and Highway 211. Turn right (south) and drive six miles to a junction. Turn south (still Highway 211) and drive six miles to Estacada. Continue south on Highway 224 and drive 15.3 miles to the campground on the left.

Contact: Mount Hood National Forest, Clackamas River Ranger District, Estacada Ranger Station, 595 NW Industrial Way, Estacada, OR 97023, 503/630-6861, fax 503/630-2299.

29 ROARING RIVER

Rating: 8

on the Roaring River in Mount Hood National Forest

See map pages 296–297

This campground, set among old-growth cedars at the confluence of the Roaring and Clackamas Rivers at an elevation of 1,000 feet, has access to the Dry Ridge Trail. The trail starts in camp, and it's a butt-kicker of an uphill climb. Several other trails into the adjacent roadless area are accessible from camp. See a U.S. Forest Service map for details.

RV sites, facilities: There are 19 sites for RVs up to 16 feet or tents. Picnic tables, garbage service, fireplaces, drinking water, and vault toilets are available. Leashed pets are permitted.

Reservations, fees: Reserve at 877/444-6777 or online at www.reserveusa.com ($9 reservation fee). The fee is $14 per night, plus $7 per additional vehicle. A senior discount is available. Open mid-May to mid-September.

Directions: From Portland, drive east on U.S. 26 from Gresham 11 miles to Sandy and Highway 211. Turn right (south) and drive six miles to a junction. Turn south (still Highway 211) and drive six miles to Estacada and Highway 224. Bear south on Highway 224 and drive 18 miles to the campground on the left.

Contact: Mount Hood National Forest, Clackamas River Ranger District, 595 NW Industrial Way, Estacada, OR 97023, 503/630-6861, fax 503/630-2299.

30 TRILLIUM LAKE

Rating: 9

on Trillium Lake in Mount Hood National Forest

See map pages 296–297

This campground is set at 3,600 feet elevation along the shores of Trillium Lake, which is about a half mile long and a quarter mile wide. Fishing is good in the evening here, and the nearby boat ramp makes this an ideal camp for anglers. The lake is also great for canoes, rafts, and small rowboats. Trillium Lake is an extremely popular vacation destination, so expect plenty of company. Reservations are highly recommended.

RV sites, facilities: There are 55 sites for RVs up to 40 feet or tents. Picnic tables and fire grills are provided. Pit toilets, drinking water, and cell phone reception are available. Boat docks and launching facilities are available on the lake, but no motors are allowed. An ATM and pay phone are within 2.5 miles. Some sites are wheelchair-accessible. Leashed pets are permitted.

Reservations, fees: Reserve at 877/444-6777 or online at www.reserveusa.com ($9 reservation fee). The fees are $14–16 per night for single sites and $28 per night for double sites, plus $7 per additional vehicle. A senior discount is available. Open late May to late September.

Directions: From Portland, drive east on U.S. 26 for 55 miles to the small town of Government Camp. Continue east on U.S. 26 for 1.5 miles to Forest Road 2656. Turn right and drive 1.3 miles to the campground on the right.

Contact: Mount Hood National Forest, Zigzag Ranger District, Mount Hood Information Center, 65000 E. Hwy. 26, Welches, OR 97067, 503/622-7674, fax 503/622-7625.

31 FROG LAKE

Rating: 6

near the Pacific Crest Trail in Mount Hood National Forest
See map pages 296–297

This classic spot in the Cascade Range is situated on the shore of little Frog Lake (more of a pond than a lake), at an elevation of 3,800 feet and a short distance from the Pacific Crest Trail. Several other trails lead to nearby lakes. Clear Lake, to the south, provides a possible day trip and offers more recreation options.

RV sites, facilities: There are 33 sites for RVs up to 22 feet or tents. Drinking water, garbage bins, and picnic tables are provided. Vault toilets and firewood are available. Boat-launching facilities are nearby. No motorized boats are allowed. Some facilities are wheelchair-accessible. Leashed pets are permitted.

Reservations, fees: Reserve at 877/444-6777 or online at www.reserveusa.com ($9 reservation fee). The fee is $12 per night, plus $6 per additional vehicle. A senior discount is available. Open mid-June to mid-September, weather permitting.

Directions: From Portland, drive east on U.S. 26 for 57 miles to the junction with Highway 35 (two miles past Government Camp). Turn right (southeast) on U.S. 26 and drive seven miles to Forest Road 2610. Turn southeast and drive .5 mile to the campground.

Contact: Mount Hood National Forest, Hood River Ranger District, 6780 Hwy. 35, Mount Hood, OR 97041, 541/352-6002, fax 541/352-7365.

32 CLEAR CREEK CROSSING

Rating: 7

on Clear Creek in Mount Hood National Forest
See map pages 296–297

This secluded, little-known spot is set along the banks of Clear Creek at an elevation of 3,600 feet. Clear Creek Trail, a very pretty walk, begins at the campground. Fishing and hiking are two recreation options here.

RV sites, facilities: There are seven sites for RVs up to 16 feet or tents. Picnic tables and fire grills are provided. Vault toilets are available. There is no drinking water, and all garbage must be packed out. A pay phone is within six miles. Leashed pets are permitted.

Reservations, fees: Reservations are not accepted. A Northwest Forest Pass ($5 daily fee or $30 annual fee per parked vehicle) is required. Open year-round, weather permitting.

Directions: From Portland, drive east on U.S. 26 for 55 miles to Government Camp. Continue three miles to a junction, turn right on U.S. 26, and drive south for 12 miles to Highway 216. Turn left (east) on Highway 216 and drive three miles to Forest Road 2130. Turn left (north) on Forest Road 2130 and drive three miles to the campground.

Contact: Mount Hood National Forest, Barlow Ranger District, 780 NE Court St., Dufur, OR 97021, 541/467-2291, fax 541/467-2271.

OREGON

33 WHITE RIVER STATION

Rating: 9

on the White River in Mount Hood National Forest

See map pages 296–297

This tiny campground is set along the White River at an elevation of 3,000 feet. It is on Old Barlow Road, an original wagon trail used by early settlers. One of several small, secluded camps in the area, White River Station is quiet and private, but with poor fishing prospects.

RV sites, facilities: There are five sites for RVs up to 32 feet or tents. Picnic tables and fire grills are provided. Vault toilets are available, but there is no drinking water and no garbage service; pack out all garbage. Leashed pets are permitted.

Reservations, fees: Reservations are not accepted. A Northwest Forest Pass ($5 daily fee or $30 annual fee per parked vehicle) is required. Open year-round, weather permitting.

Directions: From Portland, drive east on U.S. 26 for 57 miles to the junction with Highway 35 (two miles past Government Camp). Turn left on Highway 35 and drive two miles east to Forest Road 48. Turn right (south) and drive nine miles southeast to Forest Road 43. Turn right and drive .25 mile to Forest Road 3530. Turn left and drive 1.5 miles to the campground on the left.

Contact: Mount Hood National Forest, Barlow Ranger District, 780 NE Court St., Dufur, OR 97021, 541/467-2291, fax 541/467-2271.

34 FOREST CREEK

Rating: 6

on Forest Creek in Mount Hood National Forest

See map pages 296–297

The elevation here is 3,000 feet. This very old camp is set along Forest Creek on the original Barlow Road, which was once used by early settlers. Shaded by old-growth Douglas fir and ponderosa pine forest, you'll find solitude here. See a U.S. Forest Service map for specific roads and trails.

RV sites, facilities: There are eight sites for RVs up to 16 feet or tents. No drinking water is available. Picnic tables and fire grills are provided.

Vault toilets are available. All garbage must be packed out. Leashed pets are permitted.

Reservations, fees: Reservations are not accepted. A Northwest Forest Pass ($5 daily fee or $30 annual fee per parked vehicle) is required. Open year-round, weather permitting.

Directions: From Portland, turn east on I-84 and drive 91 miles to The Dalles, Exit 87, and Highway 197. Turn south and drive 31 miles to Tygh Valley and Wamic Market Road. Turn right and drive west for six miles to Forest Road 48. Continue west and drive 12.5 miles southwest to Forest Road 4885. Turn left and drive one mile to Forest Road 3530. Turn left to the campground.

Contact: Mount Hood National Forest, Barlow Ranger District, 780 NE Court St., Dufur, OR 97021, 541/467-2291, fax 541/467-2271.

35 ROCK CREEK RESERVOIR

Rating: 7

on Rock Creek Reservoir in Mount Hood National Forest

See map pages 296–297

Fishing is excellent, and the environment is perfect for canoes or rafts at this campground along the shore of Rock Creek Reservoir. Enjoy views of Mount Hood from the day-use area. No hiking trails are in the immediate vicinity, but there are many old forest roads that are ideal for walking or mountain biking. The camp sits at 2,200 feet elevation.

RV sites, facilities: There are 33 sites for RVs up to 18 feet or tents. Picnic tables, garbage service, and fire grills are provided. Vault toilets, drinking water, and firewood are available. There are boat docks nearby, but no motorboats are allowed on the reservoir. A pay phone is within seven miles. Some facilities are wheelchair-accessible. Leashed pets are permitted.

Reservations, fees: Reserve at 877/444-6777 or online at www.reserveusa.com ($9 reservation fee). The fee is $14–16 per night. A senior discount is available. Open mid-April to early October.

Directions: From Portland, turn east on I-84 and drive 91 miles to The Dalles, Exit 87, and Highway 197. Turn south and drive 31 miles to Tygh Valley and Wamic Market Road. Turn right and drive west for six miles to Forest Road 48. Turn west and drive one mile to Forest Road 4820. Turn west and drive a short distance to the campground.

Contact: Mount Hood National Forest, Barlow Ranger District, 780 NE Court St., Dufur, OR 97021, 541/467-2291, fax 541/467-2271.

36 PINE HOLLOW LAKESIDE RESORT

Rating: 8

on Pine Hollow Reservoir
See map pages 296–297

This resort on the shore of Pine Hollow Reservoir is the best game in town for RV campers, with some shaded lakefront sites and scenic views. Year-round fishing, boating, swimming, and water-skiing are some recreation options here.

RV sites, facilities: There are 75 sites with partial hookups (20, 30 amps) for RVs, 35 tent sites, and 10 cabins. Picnic tables are provided. Drinking water, flush toilets, propane, an RV dump station, showers, firewood, a store, a laundry room, and ice are available. A restaurant and lounge are next door. Boat docks, launching facilities, and boat and personal watercraft rentals are nearby. Leashed pets are permitted.

Reservations, fees: Reservations are accepted. The fee is $17–24 per night, plus $2 per person for more than two people, $2 per additional vehicle, and $2 per pet per night. Major credit cards are accepted. Open mid-March to October.

Directions: From Portland, turn east on I-84 and drive 91 miles to The Dalles, Exit 87, and Highway 197. Turn south and drive 31 miles to Tygh Valley and Wamic Market Road. Turn west and drive 4.5 miles to Ross Road. Turn north and drive 3.5 miles to the campground.

Contact: Pine Hollow Lakeside Resort, 34 N. Mariposa Dr., Wamic, OR 97063, 541/544-2271, website: www.pinehollowlakeside.com.

37 WASCO COUNTY FAIRGROUNDS

Rating: 6

near Badger Creek
See map pages 296–297

This county campground is set near the confluence of Badger and Tygh Creeks. Hiking trails, marked bike trails, and tennis courts are nearby. This is a popular area for hunting and fishing. The Deschutes River is within eight miles and is a great choice for rafting and kayaking. Tennis courts are available within 10 miles.

RV sites, facilities: There are 120 sites with full hookups (20, 30, 50 amps), 95 drive-through, for RVs of any length and 50 tent sites. Picnic tables are provided. Drinking water, flush toilets, an RV dump station, a pay phone, garbage bins, and coin-operated showers are available. Two community kitchens are available for a fee. A store, a café, and ice are within one mile. Horse facilities, including stalls and an arena, are available. An ATM and a coin-operated laundry are within 10 miles. Some facilities are wheelchair-accessible. Leashed pets are permitted.

Reservations, fees: Reservations are not accepted for family sites. The fee is $12–15 per night, plus $3 per additional vehicle. Group reservations are available. Open May to October.

Directions: From Portland, turn east on I-84 and drive 91 miles to The Dalles, Exit 87, and Highway 197. Turn south and drive 31 miles to Tygh Valley and Main Street. Turn right at Main Street and drive two blocks to Fairgrounds Road. Turn right and drive one mile to the fairgrounds on the right.

Contact: Wasco County, 81849 Fairgrounds Rd., Tygh Valley, OR 97063, 541/483-2288 or 541/483-2288.

38 SUNSTRIP

Rating: 3

on the Clackamas River in Mount Hood National Forest
See map pages 296–297

This campground on the banks of the Clackamas River offers fishing and rafting access. One of several camps along the Highway 224 corridor, Sunstrip is a favorite with rafting enthusiasts and can fill up quickly on weekends. Note: This campground, squeezed between the river and the highway and traversed by power lines, may be a turn-off for those wanting another kind of experience.

RV sites, facilities: There are nine sites for RVs up to 18 feet or tents. Picnic tables, garbage service, fireplaces, drinking water, and vault toilets are available. Leashed pets are permitted.

Reservations, fees: Reserve at 877/444-6777 or online at www.reserveusa.com ($9 reservation fee). The fee is $14 per night, plus $7 per additional vehicle. A senior discount is available. Open year-round, with limited winter services.

Directions: From Portland, drive east on U.S. 26 from Gresham 11 miles to Sandy and Highway 211. Turn right (south) and drive six miles to a junction. Turn south (still Highway 211) and drive six miles to Estacada and Highway 224. Bear south on Highway 224 and drive 19 miles to the campground.

Contact: Mount Hood National Forest, Clackamas River Ranger District, 595 NW Industrial Way, Estacada, OR 97023, 503/630-6861, fax 503/630-2299.

39 RAINBOW

Rating: 6

on the Oak Grove Fork of the Clackamas River in Mount Hood National Forest
See map pages 296–297

This campground is set at an elevation of 1,400 feet along the banks of the Oak Grove Fork of the Clackamas River, not far from where it empties into the Clackamas River. The camp is less than a quarter mile from Ripplebrook Campground.

RV sites, facilities: There are 17 sites for RVs up to 16 feet or tents. There is no drinking water. Garbage service is provided during the summer. Fire grills and picnic tables are provided. Vault toilets are available. Leashed pets are permitted.

Reservations, fees: Reserve at 877/444-6777 or online at www.reserveusa.com ($9 reservation fee). The fee is $14 per night, plus $7 per additional vehicle. A senior discount is available. Open year-round, with limited winter services.

Directions: From Portland, drive east on U.S. 26 from Gresham 11 miles to Sandy and Highway 211. Turn right (south) and drive six miles to a junction. Turn south (still Highway 211) and drive six miles to Estacada and Highway 224. Bear south on Highway 224 and drive 27 miles in national forest (the road becomes Forest Road

46). Continue south and drive about 100 yards to the campground on the right.

Contact: Mount Hood National Forest, Clackamas River Ranger District, 595 NW Industrial Way, Estacada, OR 97023, 503/630-6861, fax 503/630-2299.

40 INDIAN HENRY

Rating: 8

on the Clackamas River in Mount Hood National Forest
See map pages 296–297

One of the most popular campgrounds in the Clackamas River Ranger District, Indian Henry sits along the banks of the Clackamas River at an elevation of 1,250 feet and has a wheelchair-accessible trail. Group campsites and an amphitheater are available. The nearby Clackamas River Trail has fishing access.

RV sites, facilities: There are 86 sites for RVs up to 22 feet or tents and eight group tent sites. Picnic tables, garbage service, and fire grills are provided. Flush toilets, a sanitary dump station, a pay phone, and drinking water are available. Some facilities are wheelchair-accessible. Leashed pets are permitted.

Reservations, fees: Reserve at 877/444-6777 or online at www.reserveusa.com ($9 reservation fee). The fee is $14 per night, plus $7 per additional vehicle; group sites are $35 per night. A senior discount is available. Open late May to early September.

Directions: From Portland, drive east on U.S. 26 from Gresham 11 miles to Sandy and Highway 211. Turn right (south) and drive six miles to a junction. Turn south (still Highway 211) and drive six miles to Estacada and Highway 224. Bear south on Highway 224 and drive 23 miles to Forest Road 4620. Turn right and drive .5 mile southeast to the campground on the left.

Contact: Mount Hood National Forest, Clackamas River Ranger District, 595 NW Industrial Way, Estacada, OR 97023, 503/630-6861, fax 503/630-2299.

OREGON

41 RIPPLEBROOK

Rating: 7

on the Oak Grove Fork of the Clackamas River in Mount Hood National Forest

See map pages 296-297

Shaded sites with river views are a highlight at this campground along the banks of the Oak Grove Fork of the Clackamas River, where anglers are limited to artificial lures and catch-and-release only. Note that the road to this camp was closed for two years in the late 1990s, and only recently have campers begun to return.

RV sites, facilities: There are 13 sites for RVs up to 16 feet. Picnic tables, garbage service, and fire grills are provided. Vault toilets are available, but there is no drinking water. A pay phone is within one mile. Leashed pets are permitted; horses are not allowed in the campground.

Reservations, fees: Reserve at 877/444-6777 or online at www.reserveusa.com ($9 reservation fee). The fee is $14 per night, plus $6 per additional vehicle. A senior discount is available. Open late April to late September.

Directions: From Portland, drive east on U.S. 26 from Gresham 11 miles to Sandy and Highway 211. Turn right (south) and drive six miles to a junction. Turn south (still Highway 211) and drive six miles to Estacada and Highway 224. Bear south on Highway 224 and drive 26.5 miles to the campground entrance on the left.

Contact: Mount Hood National Forest, Clackamas River Ranger District, 595 NW Industrial Way, Estacada, OR 97023, 503/630-6861, fax 503/630-2299.

42 RIVERSIDE

Rating: 8

on the Clackamas River in Mount Hood National Forest

See map pages 296-297

The banks of the Clackamas River are home to this campground (elevation 1,400 feet). A trail worth hiking leaves the camp and follows the river for four miles north. Fishing is another option here, and several old forest roads in the vicinity make excellent mountain biking trails.

RV sites, facilities: There are 16 sites for RVs up to 22 feet or tents. Picnic tables, garbage service, and fire grills are provided. Vault toilets and drinking water are available. Leashed pets are permitted; no horses are allowed in the campground.

Reservations, fees: Reserve at 877/444-6777 or online at www.reserveusa.com ($9 reservation fee). The fee is $14 per night, plus $7 per additional vehicle. A senior discount is available. Open mid-May to late September.

Directions: From Portland, drive east on U.S. 26 from Gresham 11 miles to Sandy and Highway 211. Turn right (south) and drive six miles to a junction. Turn south (still Highway 211) and drive six miles to Estacada and Highway 224. Bear south on Highway 224 and drive 27 miles and into national forest (Highway 224 becomes Forest Road 46). Continue 2.5 miles south on Forest Road 46 to the campground on the right.

Contact: Mount Hood National Forest, Clackamas River Ranger District, 595 NW Industrial Way, Estacada, OR 97023, 503/630-6861, fax 503/630-2299.

43 KINGFISHER

Rating: 7

on the Hot Springs Fork of the Collawash River in Mount Hood National Forest

See map pages 296-297

This pretty campground, set at an elevation of 1,250 feet among old-growth forest, is situated along the banks of the Hot Springs Fork of the Collawash River. It's about three miles from Bagby Hot Springs, a U.S. Forest Service day-use area. The hot springs are an easy 1.5-mile hike from the day-use area. The camp provides fishing access.

RV sites, facilities: There are 23 sites for RVs up to 16 feet or tents. Picnic tables and fireplaces are provided. Garbage service is provided during the summer. Vault toilets and drinking water are available. A pay phone is within 10 miles. Leashed pets are permitted.

Reservations, fees: Reserve at 877/444-6777 or online at www.reserveusa.com ($9 reservation fee). The fee is $14 per night, plus $7 per additional

OREGON

vehicle. A senior discount is available. Open year-round, with limited winter facilities.

Directions: From Portland, drive east on U.S. 26 from Gresham 11 miles to Sandy and Highway 211. Turn right (south) and drive six miles to a junction. Turn south (still Highway 211) and drive six miles to Estacada and Highway 224. Bear south on Highway 224 and drive 27 miles in national forest (the road becomes Forest Road 46). Continue south on Forest Road 46 for 3.5 miles to Forest Road 63. Turn right and drive three miles to Forest Road 70. Turn right again and drive 1.8 miles to the campground on the left.

Contact: Mount Hood National Forest, Clackamas River Ranger District, 595 NW Industrial Way, Estacada, OR 97023, 503/630-6861, fax 503/630-2299.

44 HOODVIEW

Rating: 9

on Timothy Lake in Mount Hood National Forest

See map pages 296–297

This camp is set at 3,200 feet elevation along the south shore of Timothy Lake. A trail out of camp branches south for a few miles and, if followed to the east, eventually leads to the Pacific Crest Trail.

RV sites, facilities: There are 43 sites for RVs up to 31 feet or tents. Picnic tables, garbage service, and fire grills are provided. Drinking water, firewood, cell phone reception, and vault toilets are available. A boat ramp is nearby; motorized boats are allowed but are limited to a speed of 10 mph. Leashed pets are permitted.

Reservations, fees: Reserve at 877/444-6777 or online at www.reserveusa.com ($9 reservation fee). The fee is $14–16 per night, plus $7 per additional vehicle. A senior discount is available. Open late May to mid-September, weather permitting.

Directions: From Portland, turn east on U.S. 26 and drive 57 miles (just past the town of Government Camp) to the junction with Highway 35. Turn southeast on U.S. 26 and drive 15 miles to Forest Road 42 (Skyline Road). Turn right and drive eight miles to Forest Road 57. Turn

right and drive three miles to the campground on the right.

Contact: Mount Hood National Forest, Zigzag Ranger District, Mount Hood Information Center, 65000 E. Hwy. 26, Welches, OR 97067, 503/622-7674, fax 503/622-7625.

45 LITTLE CRATER

Rating: 5

on Little Crater Lake in Mount Hood National Forest

See map pages 296–297

Little Crater campground is set at 3,200 feet elevation next to Crater Creek and scenic Little Crater Lake. This camp is popular with hunters in the fall. Both the drinking water and the lake water flow from an artesian well, and the water is numbingly cold. The Pacific Crest Trail is located near camp, providing hiking trail access. Fishing is poor at Little Crater Lake; no motorized boats are allowed. Bring your mosquito repellent; you'll need it.

RV sites, facilities: There are 16 sites for RVs up to 22 feet or tents. Picnic tables, garbage bins, and fire grills are provided. Vault toilets, firewood, and drinking water are available. Leashed pets are permitted.

Reservations, fees: Reserve at 877/444-6777 or online at www.reserveusa.com ($9 reservation fee). The fee is $12 per night, plus $7 per additional vehicle. A senior discount is available. Open June to mid-September.

Directions: From Portland, drive east on U.S. 26 for 57 miles to the junction with Highway 35 (two miles past Government Camp). Turn right (southeast) on U.S. 26 and drive 15 miles to Forest Road 42 (Skyline Road). Turn right and drive about six miles to Forest Road 58. Turn right and drive about 2.5 miles to the campground on the left.

Contact: Mount Hood National Forest, Zigzag Ranger District, Mount Hood Information Center, 65000 E. Hwy. 26, Welches, OR 97067, 503/622-7674, fax 503/622-7625.

OREGON

46 CLACKAMAS LAKE

Rating: 7

near the Clackamas River in Mount Hood National Forest

See map pages 296–297

This camp, set at 3,400 feet elevation, is a good place to go to escape the hordes of people at the lakeside sites in neighboring camps. The Pacific Crest Trail passes nearby, and Timothy Lake requires little more than a one-mile hike from camp. This is a popular spot for campers with horses.

RV sites, facilities: There are 46 sites for RVs up to 16 feet, trailers, horse trailers, or tents. Horses are permitted at the first 19 sites. Drinking water, garbage service, fire grills, and picnic tables are provided. Vault toilets and firewood are available. Boat docks and launching facilities are nearby at Timothy Lake, but only nonmotorized boats are allowed on Clackamas Lake. Leashed pets are permitted.

Reservations, fees: Reservations are accepted for some sites ($8.65 reservation fee). The fee is $14 per night, plus $7 per additional vehicle. A senior discount is available. Open June to mid-September.

Directions: From Portland, turn east on U.S. 26 and drive 57 miles (just past the town of Government Camp) to the junction with Highway 35. Turn southeast on U.S. 26 and drive 15 miles to Forest Road 42 (Skyline Road). Turn right and drive eight miles to Forest Road 57. Continue 500 feet (on Forest Road 42) past the Clackamas Lake Historic Ranger Station to Forest Road 4270. Turn left and drive .5 mile to the campground on the left.

Contact: Mount Hood National Forest, Zigzag Ranger District, Mount Hood Information Center, 65000 E. Hwy. 26, Welches, OR 97067, 503/622-7674, fax 503/622-7625.

47 KAH-NEE-TA RESORT

Rating: 7

on the Warm Springs Indian Reservation

See map pages 296–297

This resort features a stellar-rated, full-concept spa, with the bonus of a nearby casino. It is also the only public camp on the east side of the Warm Springs Indian Reservation; there are no other camps within 30 miles. The Warm Springs River runs nearby. Recreation options in the area include an 18-hole golf course, miniature golf, biking and hiking trails, a riding stable, and tennis courts.

RV sites, facilities: There are 50 drive-through sites with full hookups (50 amps) for RVs of any length. Picnic tables are provided. Drinking water, flush toilets, propane, cable TV, an RV dump station, a pay phone, an ATM, cell phone reception, modem access, showers, a concession stand, laundry facilities, ice, a playground, a spa with a therapist, mineral baths, and an Olympic-sized, spring-fed swimming pool with a 140-foot water slide are available. Some facilities are wheelchair-accessible. Leashed pets are permitted, but some areas are restricted.

Reservations, fees: Reserve at 800/554-4786. The fee is $38 per night for three people with a two-night minimum on weekends, three-night minimum on holiday weekends. Major credit cards are accepted. Open year-round.

Directions: From Portland, turn east on U.S. 26 and drive about 105 miles to Warm Springs and Agency Hot Springs Road on the left. Turn left and drive 11 miles northeast to Kah-Nee-Ta and the resort on the right.

Contact: Kah-Nee-Ta Resort, P.O. Box 1240, Warm Springs, OR 97761, 541/553-1112, fax 541/553-1071, website: www.kah-nee-taresort.com.

48 BREITENBUSH

Rating: 8

on the Breitenbush River in Willamette National Forest

See map pages 296–297

There is fishing access at this campground along the Breitenbush River. Nearby recreation options include the South Breitenbush Gorge National Recreation Trail, three miles away, and Breitenbush Hot Springs, just over a mile away.

RV sites, facilities: There are 29 sites for RVs up to 70 feet or tents. Picnic tables, garbage service (summer only), and fire grills are provided. Drinking water, vault toilets, and cell phone reception are available. Leashed pets are permitted.

OREGON

Reservations, fees: Reservations are not accepted. The fees are $10 per night for a single site and $20 per night for a double site, plus $5 per additional vehicle. A senior discount is available. Open year-round, weather permitting, with limited winter facilities.

Directions: From Salem on I-5, take Exit 253, turn east on Highway 22, and drive 50 miles to Detroit. Turn left (north) on Forest Road 46/Breitenbush Road and drive 10 miles to the campground on the right.

Contact: Willamette National Forest, Detroit Ranger District, HC 73, P.O. Box 320, Mill City, OR 97360, 503/854-3366, fax 503/854-4239.

49 HUMBUG

Rating: 9

on the Breitenbush River in Willamette National Forest
See map pages 296–297

Fishing and hiking are popular at this campground along the banks of the Breitenbush River, about four miles from where it empties into Detroit Lake. The lake offers many other recreation opportunities. The Humbug Flat Trailhead is behind Sites 9 and 10, and a scenic stroll through an old-growth forest follows the Breitenbush River. The rhododendrons put on a spectacular show from May to July.

RV sites, facilities: There are 21 sites for RVs up to 70 feet or tents. Picnic tables, garbage service (summer only), fire grills, drinking water, cell phone reception, and vault toilets are available. An ATM and pay phone are within five miles. Leashed pets are permitted.

Reservations, fees: Reservations are not accepted. The fee is $10 per night, plus $5 per additional vehicle. A senior discount is available. Open year-round, weather permitting, with limited winter facilities.

Directions: From Salem on I-5, take Exit 253, turn east on Highway 22, and drive 52 miles to Detroit. Turn left on Forest Road 46/Breitenbush Road and drive five miles northeast to the campground on the right.

Contact: Willamette National Forest, Detroit Ranger District, HC 73, P.O. Box 320, Mill City, OR 97360, 503/854-3366, fax 503/854-4239.

50 DETROIT LAKE STATE PARK

Rating: 7

on Detroit Lake
See map pages 296–297

This campground is set at 1,600 feet elevation along the shore of Detroit Lake, which is 400 feet deep, nine miles long, and has more than 32 miles of shoreline. The park offers a fishing dock and a moorage area, and a boat ramp and bathhouse are available nearby at the Mongold Day Use Area. There is great trout fishing here, year-round.

RV sites, facilities: There are 72 sites with full hookups (30 amps), 106 sites with partial hookups for RVs up to 60 feet, 132 tent sites, and 82 boat slips. Drinking water, garbage bins, fire grills, and picnic tables are provided. Flush toilets, showers, two pay phones, two playgrounds, swimming areas, a store, a visitors center, and firewood are available. Two boat docks and launching facilities are nearby. An ATM is within two miles. Leashed pets are permitted.

Reservations, fees: Reserve at 800/452-5687 or online at www.OregonStateParks.org ($6 reservation fee). The fee is $16–20 per night, plus $7 per additional vehicle. Boating moorage is $7 per night. Major credit cards are accepted. Open March to November, weather permitting.

Directions: From Salem, drive east on Highway 22 for 50 miles to the park entrance on the right (located two miles west of Detroit).

Contact: Detroit Lake State Park, P.O. Box 549, Detroit, OR 97342, 503/854-3346, or 503/854-3406.

51 SOUTHSHORE

Rating: 9

on Detroit Lake in Willamette National Forest
See map pages 296–297

This popular camp is set along the south shore of Detroit Lake, where fishing, swimming, and water-skiing are some of the recreation options. The Stahlman Point Trailhead is about a half mile from camp. There's a day-use area for picnicking and swimming. The views of the lake and surrounding mountains are outstanding.

OREGON

RV sites, facilities: There are 27 sites for RVs up to 70 feet or tents and eight walk-in tent sites. Picnic tables and fire rings are provided. Vault toilets, garbage service, cell phone reception, and drinking water are available. Boat-launching facilities are nearby at a day-use area. A pay phone is within four miles and an ATM within 6.5 miles. Leashed pets are permitted.

Reservations, fees: Reservations are not accepted. The fees are $12 for single site and $24 for double site, plus $5 per additional vehicle. Open mid-April to late September, with a gate preventing access during the off-season.

Directions: From Salem, drive east on Highway 22 for 52 miles to Detroit. Continue southeast on Highway 22 for 2.5 miles to Forest Road 10 (Blowout Road). Turn right and drive four miles to the campground on the right.

Contact: Willamette National Forest, Detroit Ranger District, HC 73, Box 320, Mill City, OR 97360, 503/854-3366, fax 503/854-4239.

52 COVE CREEK

Rating: 10

on Detroit Lake in Willamette National Forest
See map pages 296–297

See the description of Southshore and Hoover in this chapter for recreation options.

RV sites, facilities: There are 63 sites for RVs up to 80 feet or tents and one group site for up to 70 people. Picnic tables, garbage service, and fire rings are provided. Drinking water, restrooms with flush toilets and coin-operated showers, garbage bins, cell phone reception, and a boat ramp are available. A pay phone is within three miles and an ATM within 5.5 miles. Some facilities are wheelchair-accessible. Leashed pets are permitted.

Reservations, fees: Reservations are not accepted for family sites. The fees are $16 per night for single sites and $32 for double sites, plus $5 per additional vehicle. Reservations are available for the group site at 877/444-6777 or online at www.reserveusa.com ($9 reservation fee); the fee is $150 per night. A senior discount is available. Open late May to late September.

Directions: From Salem, drive east on Highway 22 for 52 miles to Detroit. Continue southeast on Highway 22 for 2.5 miles to Forest Road 10

(Blowout Road). Turn right and drive three miles to the campground on the right.

Contact: Willamette National Forest, Detroit Ranger District, HC 73, Box 320, Mill City, OR 97360, 503/854-3366, fax 503/854-4239.

53 HOOVER

Rating: 9

on Detroit Lake in Willamette National Forest
See map pages 296–297

This campground is along the eastern arm of Detroit Lake, near the mouth of the Santiam River. It features a wheelchair-accessible fishing area and nature trail. You're likely to see osprey fishing during the day, a truly special sight. See the description of Southshore in this chapter for other recreation options.

RV sites, facilities: There are 37 sites for RVs up to 110 feet or tents. Picnic tables, garbage service, cell phone reception, and fire grills are provided. Flush toilets and drinking water are available. Boat docks and launching facilities are nearby. A pay phone is within one mile, and an ATM is within 3.5 miles. Some facilities are wheelchair-accessible. Leashed pets are permitted.

Reservations, fees: Reservations are not accepted. The fees are $12 for a single site per night and $24 for a double site, plus $5 per additional vehicle. A senior discount is available. Open mid-April to late September; a gate prevents access in the off-season.

Directions: From Salem, drive east on Highway 22 for 52 miles to Detroit. Continue southeast on Highway 22 for 2.5 miles to Forest Road 10 (Blowout Road). Turn right and drive one mile to the campground on the right.

Contact: Willamette National Forest, Detroit Ranger District, HC 73, Box 320, Mill City, OR 97360, 503/854-3366, fax 503/854-4239.

54 WHISPERING FALLS

Rating: 10

on the North Santiam River near Detroit Lake in Willamette National Forest
See map pages 296–297

This popular campground sits on the banks of

OREGON

the North Santiam River, where you can fish. If the campsites at Detroit Lake are crowded, this camp provides a more secluded option, and it's only about a 10-minute drive from the lake. Ospreys sometimes nest near the campground.

RV sites, facilities: There are 16 sites for RVs up to 80 feet or tents. Picnic tables, garbage service, and fire grills are provided. Drinking water and flush toilets are available. Leashed pets are permitted.

Reservations, fees: Reservations are not accepted. The fee is $10 per night, plus $5 per additional vehicle. A senior discount is available. Open mid-April to late September; a gate prevents access in the off-season.

Directions: From Salem, drive east on Highway 22 for 50 miles to Detroit. Continue east on Highway 22 for eight miles to the campground on the right.

Contact: Willamette National Forest, Detroit Ranger District, HC 73, Box 320, Mill City, OR 97360, 503/854-3366, fax 503/854-4239.

55 MARION FORKS

Rating: 8

on the Santiam River in Willamette National Forest

See map pages 296–297

This campground is situated along Marion Creek, adjacent to the Marion Forks Fish Hatchery. A U.S. Forest Service guard station and a restaurant are across Highway 22. The area boasts some quality hiking trails; the nearest is Independence Rock Trail, a quarter mile north of the campground.

RV sites, facilities: There are 15 sites for RVs up to 50 feet or tents. Picnic tables, fire grills, and garbage containers are provided. Pit toilets and drinking water are available. Leashed pets are permitted.

Reservations, fees: Reservations are not accepted. The fee is $10 per night, plus $5 per additional vehicle. A senior discount is available. Open year-round, weather permitting, with no winter services.

Directions: From Salem, drive east on Highway 22 for 50 miles to Detroit. Continue southeast

on Highway 22 for 16 miles to the campground on the left.

Contact: Willamette National Forest, Detroit Ranger District, HC 73, Box 320, Mill City, OR 97360, 503/854-3366, fax 503/854-4239.

56 PELTON

Rating: 8

on Lake Simtustus in Deschutes National Forest

See map pages 296–297

This campground claims a half mile of shoreline along the north side of Lake Simtustus. Campsites here are shaded with juniper in an area of rolling hills and sagebrush. One section of the lake is accessible for water-skiing and personal watercraft. Simtustus is a trophy fishing lake for kokanee and rainbow, brown, and bull trout. Cove Palisades State Park, about 15 miles south, provides additional recreational opportunities. Watch for osprey and bald and golden eagles.

RV sites, facilities: There are 71 sites, 30 with partial hookups (30 amps), for RVs up to 40 feet or tents, one group site for up to 50 people, and five yurts. Drinking water, picnic tables, garbage service, and fire grills are provided. Restrooms, a restaurant, a pay phone, a small store, gasoline, and a picnic shelter with sinks and electric stoves are available. Also, a full-service marina with boat rentals, a boat launch, boat dock, fishing pier, swimming beach, volleyball courts, horseshoes, and a playground is available. An ATM, groceries, and a pay phone are available within five miles. Leashed pets are permitted.

Reservations, fees: Reserve at 541/475-0517. The fees are $15–21 per night for individual sites, $65 per night for the group site, and $25 per night for yurts. Major credit cards are accepted. Open mid-April to October.

Directions: From Portland, drive south on U.S. 26 for 108 miles to the town of Warm Springs. Continue south two miles to Pelton Dam Road. Turn right and drive three miles to the campground on the right.

Contact: Portland General Electric, 121 SW Salmon St., Portland, OR 97204, 503/464-8515, fax 503/464-2944, website: www.portlandgeneral.com/parks.

57 COVE PALISADES STATE PARK

Rating: 7

on Lake Billy Chinook
See map pages 296–297

This park is a half mile away from the shore of Lake Billy Chinook, where some lakeshore cabins are available. There are two separate campgrounds within the park, Crooked River Campground and the Deschutes River Campground. Here in Oregon's high desert region, the weather is sunny and warm in the summer and chilly but generally mild in the winter. Towering cliffs surround the lake, and about 10 miles of hiking trails crisscross the area. Two popular special events are held here annually: Lake Billy Chinook Day in September and the Eagle Watch in February.

RV sites, facilities: There are 178 sites with partial or full hookups (20, 30 amps) for RVs up to 60 feet, 94 tent sites, three cabins, and a group area. Picnic tables and fire grills are provided. Drinking water, garbage bins, flush toilets, an RV dump station, showers, a coin-operated laundry, firewood, a pay phone, a store, a restaurant, and ice are available. Boat docks, launching facilities, a marina, and boat rentals are nearby. An ATM is within three-quarters of a mile of Crooked River and five miles from Deschutes River. Some facilities are wheelchair-accessible. Leashed pets are permitted.

Reservations, fees: Reserve at 800/452-5687 or online at www.OregonStateParks.org ($6 reservation fee). The fees are $17–21 per night for individual sites, $70 per night for cabins, and $64 per night for the group area, plus $7 per additional vehicle. Major credit cards are accepted. Open year-round.

Directions: From Bend, drive north on U.S. 97 for 13 miles to Redmond and continue north for 15 miles to the Culver Highway. Take the Culver Highway north to Culver and continue two miles to Gem Lane. Turn left and drive two miles to Frazier Drive. Turn left and drive a short distance to Peck Road. Turn right and drive to the park entrance.

Contact: Cove Palisades State Park, 7300 Jordan Rd., Culver, OR 97734, 541/546-3412 or 800/551-6949.

58 KOA MADRAS/CULVER

Rating: 6

near Lake Billy Chinook
See map pages 296–297

This campground has a relaxing atmosphere, with some mountain views. It is about three miles from Lake Billy Chinook, a steep-sided reservoir formed where the Crooked River, Metolius River, Deschutes River, and Squaw Creek all merge. Like much of the country east of the Cascades, this is a high desert area.

RV sites, facilities: There are 68 drive-through sites with full hookups (20, 30, 50 amps) for RVs of any length and 31 tent sites. Picnic tables and fire rings are provided. Drinking water, flush toilets, a pay phone, modem access, cell phone reception, propane, an RV dump station, showers, firewood, a recreation hall, a store, a laundry room, ice, a playground, and a swimming pool are available. Boat docks and launching facilities are nearby. An ATM is within three miles. Leashed pets are permitted.

Reservations, fees: Reserve at 800/562-1992. The fee is $19–30 per night, plus $2–4 per person for more than two people. Major credit cards are accepted. Open year-round.

Directions: From Madras, drive south on U.S. 97 for nine miles to Jericho Lane. Turn east and drive .5 mile to the campground.

Contact: KOA Madras/Culver, S.W. Jericho Ln., Culver, OR 97734, 541/546-3046, fax 541/546-7972, website: www.koa.com.

Oregon

Chapter 10
Northeastern Oregon

WASHINGTON

Lake
Wallula

Columbia   River

Boardman

Pendleton

Biggs

see The Columbia
River Gorge
and Mount Hood
pages 296–297

John Day River

Deschutes R.

Butter Creek

Umatilla   National   Forest

John Day

Mt.
Vernon

River

Ochoco National Forest

Aldrich   Mtns.

Prineville

Malheur
National
Forest

Crooked   River

Paulina

Prineville
Reservoir

Silvies

0   10 mi

0   10 km

1
2
3
8
9
10
11
12
28
29
30
32
31
33
34
35
36
37
38
39
40
48

84
30
730
395
82
12
74
207
19
97
126
26
380
395

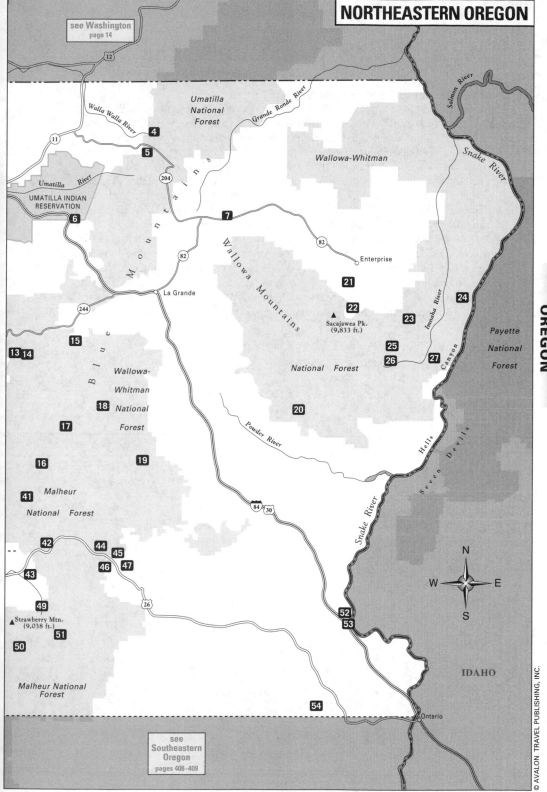

see Washington
page 14

12

11

4

5

204

Walla Walla River

Umatilla River

Umatilla
National
Forest

Grande Ronde River

Wallowa-Whitman

Salmon River

Snake River

UMATILLA INDIAN
RESERVATION

6

7

82

Enterprise

82

21

Wallowa Mountains

22

Sacajawea Pk.
(9,833 ft.)

23

Immaha River

24

25

26

27

Hells Canyon

Payette
National
Forest

La Grande

244

Blue

15

13 14

Wallowa-

Whitman

National

Forest

18

17

16

19

National Forest

20

Powder River

Seven Devils

Snake River

Malheur

41

National Forest

84 30

42

44

45

43

46 47

49

26

Strawberry Mtn.
(9,038 ft.)

51

50

Malheur National
Forest

52

53

IDAHO

54

Ontario

N
W   E
S

see
Southeastern
Oregon
pages 408–409

OREGON

© AVALON TRAVEL PUBLISHING, INC.

Chapter 10—Northeastern Oregon

It might be difficult to believe that there are many places left in America that are little known and little traveled. Yet that is how it is in northeastern Oregon. Even long-time residents often overlook this area of Oregon (the same is true with the southeastern portion of the state, detailed in Chapter 12). With its high desert abutting craggy Blue Mountains, it just doesn't look like the archetypal Oregon.

In this corner of the state you'll find Wallowa-Whitman National Forest and little-known sections of Umatilla, Malheur, and Ochoco National Forests. Idaho, the Snake River, and the Hells Canyon National Recreation Area border this region to the east. My favorite destinations are the Wallowa Mountains and the Eagle Cap Wilderness, a wildlife paradise with deer, elk, bears, mountain lions, and bighorn sheep.

This region covers a huge swatch of land, most of it explored by few. But those few have learned to love it for its unique qualities. Among the highlights are the John Day River and its headwaters, the Strawberry Mountain Wilderness in Malheur National Forest, and various sections of the linked John Day Fossil Beds National Monument. One of the prettiest spots in northeastern Oregon is Wallowa Lake State Park, where 9,000-foot snowcapped mountains surround a pristine lake on three sides.

OREGON

1 BOARDMAN MARINA PARK

Rating: 7

on the Columbia River

See map pages 322–323

This campground is set near the Columbia River among maple, sycamore, and linden trees. In addition to fishing for bass, walleye, and crappie, nearby recreation options include a golf course, a marina, and tennis courts.

RV sites, facilities: There are 63 sites with full hookups (20, 30, 50 amps) for RVs of any length or tents. Picnic tables are provided. Drinking water, flush toilets, showers, fire grills, an RV dump station, garbage bins, coin-operated laundry facilities, a day-use area with picnic shelters, a pay phone, firewood, and a boat dock are available. A boat marina, gasoline, propane, ice, and a grocery store are within one mile. Leashed pets are permitted.

Reservations, fees: Reserve at 888/481-7217 or online at www.visitboardman.com. The fees are $20–22 per night for RV sites and $10 per night for tent sites, plus $2 per night for a third vehicle. Open year-round.

Directions: From Portland on I-84 eastbound, drive 164 miles to Boardman and Exit 164. Take that exit and turn left (north) on Main Street. Drive .5 mile to the park on the left.

Contact: Boardman Marina Park, 1 West Marine Dr., P.O. Box 8, Boardman, OR 97818, 541/481-7217, fax 541/481-2828.

2 HAT ROCK CAMPGROUND

Rating: 7

near the Columbia River

See map pages 322–323

This campground is not far from Hat Rock State Park, a day-use area with a boat launch along the banks of the Columbia River. The campground itself is very pretty, with lots of trees, and offers close access to the river and fishing.

RV sites, facilities: There are 60 sites for RVs of any length, 30 with full hookups (20, 30, 50 amps) and 30 with partial hookups, and eight tent sites. Picnic tables are provided. Drinking water, flush toilets, an RV dump station, showers, a store, fire pits, a pay phone, a café, a laundry room, a

swimming pool, and ice are available. Boat docks and launching facilities are nearby. An ATM is within 5.5 miles. Leashed pets are permitted.

Reservations, fees: Reserve at 541/567-4188 or 541/567-0917. The fee is $16 per night, $8 per night on Tuesdays and Wednesdays, plus $2 per person for more than two people. Open year-round.

Directions: From Portland, drive east on U.S. 84 for roughly 170 miles past Boardman to the junction of U.S. 84 and U.S. 730. Turn northeast on U.S. 730 and drive 18 miles to the junction with I-82. Continue east on U.S. 730 for one mile to the state park access road. Turn left (north) and drive .5 mile to the park on the left.

Contact: Hat Rock Campground, 82280 Hat Rock Rd., Hermiston, OR 97838, 541/567-4188; Hat Rock Store, 541/567-0917.

3 FORT HENRIETTA RV PARK

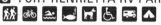

Rating: 7

on the Umatilla River

See map pages 322–323

This park, located in the historic community of Echo, sits along the Umatilla River, which provides some good trout fishing. The park offers a quiet, pleasant layover spot for travelers cruising I-84.

RV sites, facilities: There are seven sites with full hookups (30, 50 amps), two with partial hookups, for RVs up to 80 feet and an area for dispersed tent camping. Drinking water, cable TV, a pay phone, restrooms, showers, and an RV dump station are available. The camp is within walking distance of two restaurants. An ATM is within three miles. Some facilities are wheelchair-accessible. Licensed, leashed pets are permitted.

Reservations, fees: Reservations are not accepted. The fee is $16–18 per night, plus $2 per person for more than two people. Open year-round.

Directions: From Pendleton, drive west on I-84 to Exit 188 and the Echo Highway. Take the exit, turn southeast, and drive one mile; cross the railroad tracks and drive to Dupont Street. Turn south and drive .3 mile to Main Street. Turn west and drive one block to the park on the left.

Contact: Echo City Hall, P.O. Box 9, Echo, OR 97826, 541/376-8411, fax 541/376-8218, website: www.echo-oregon.com.

OREGON

4 WOODWARD

Rating: 7

near Langdon Lake in Umatilla National Forest
See map pages 322–323
Nestled among the trees at an elevation of 4,950 feet, with some privacy screening between campsites, this popular campground has a view of Langdon Lake (though campers do not have access to the private lake). A flat trail circles the camp.

RV sites, facilities: There are 18 sites for RVs up to 30 feet or tents. Drinking water, picnic tables, garbage bins, fire grills, and wheelchair-accessible vault toilets are provided. A picnic shelter is available. A pay phone is within one mile. Leashed pets are permitted.

Reservations, fees: Reservations are not accepted. The fee is $10 per night, plus $5 per night for an additional vehicle. Open mid-June to mid-October, weather permitting.

Directions: From Pendleton on I-84, turn north on Highway 11 and drive approximately 27 miles to Weston and Highway 204. Turn east on Highway 204 and drive 17 miles to the campground along the highway (near Langdon Lake).

Contact: Umatilla National Forest, Walla Walla Ranger District, 1415 W. Rose St., Walla Walla, WA 99362, 509/525-6290, fax 509/522-6000; Bluewood Recreation Management, 509/382-4725.

5 TARGET MEADOWS

Rating: 6

near the South Fork of the Walla Walla River in Umatilla National Forest
See map pages 322–323
This quiet campground with shady sites and a sunny meadow is set at 4,800 feet elevation and is adjacent to the Burnt Cabin Trailhead, which leads to the South Fork of the Walla Walla River. An old military site can be viewed here.

RV sites, facilities: There are 20 sites for RVs up to 30 feet or tents. Drinking water, picnic tables, and fire grills are provided. Garbage bins and vault toilets are available. A pay phone is within four miles. Leashed pets are permitted.

Reservations, fees: Reservations are not accepted. The fee is $10 per night, plus $5 per night for an additional vehicle. A senior discount is available. Open mid-June to mid-November, weather permitting.

Directions: From Pendleton, drive north on Highway 11 for 16 miles to Highway 204 near Weston. Turn east on Highway 204 and drive 17.5 miles to Forest Road 64. Turn left and drive .5 mile to Forest Road 6401. Turn left (north) and drive two miles to Road 6401-050. Turn right (north) and drive .5 mile to the camp.

Contact: Umatilla National Forest, Walla Walla Ranger District, 1415 W. Rose St., Walla Walla, WA 99362, 509/522-6290, fax 509/522-6000; Bluewood Recreation Management, 509/382-4725.

6 EMIGRANT SPRINGS STATE HERITAGE AREA

Rating: 7

near the Umatilla Indian Reservation
See map pages 322–323
Perched near the summit of the Blue Mountains, Emigrant Springs provides an opportunity to explore a popular pioneer stopover along the Oregon Trail. The park is nestled in an old-growth forest, lush with flora and teeming with native wildlife. You can explore nearby attractions, such as the Blue Mountain Crossing Oregon Trail interpretive park or the Pendleton Woolen Mills and underground tours.

RV sites, facilities: There are 18 sites with full hookups (20, 50 amps) for RVs up to 60 feet, 33 tent sites, a designated horse camp, and eight cabins. Picnic tables and fire grills are provided. Drinking water, garbage bins, flush toilets, a pay phone, cell phone reception, showers, firewood, some horse facilities, a community building with a kitchen, a basketball court, an amphitheater, and a baseball field are available. Leashed pets are permitted.

Reservations, fees: Reserve at 800/452-5687 or online at www.oregonstateparks.org ($6 reservation fee). The fees are $14–16 per night for campsites, $20–35 per night for cabins, and $14 per night for horse campsites, plus $7 per night per additional vehicle. Major credit cards are accepted. Cabins and four tent sites are open year-round. Full operations are open mid-April to October, weather permitting.

Directions: From Pendleton, drive southeast on I-84 for 26 miles to Exit 234. Take that exit to Old Oregon Trail Road (frontage road) and drive .5 mile to the park on the right.

Contact: Emigrant Springs State Heritage Area, P.O. Box 85, Meacham, OR 97859, 541/983-2277, fax 541/983-2279.

7 MINAM STATE PARK

Rating: 7

near the Grande Ronde River
See map pages 322–323

In a remote, steep valley, this park has a landscape dominated by large pine trees. The Wallowa River flows through the park and is noted for its fishing and rafting, especially for spring and fall steelhead fishing. Wildlife is abundant, including deer, elk, bear, cougar, and occasionally mountain sheep downriver. The park is small and pretty, well worth the detour off I-84 necessary to get here.

RV sites, facilities: There are 12 primitive sites for self-contained RVs up to 71 feet or tents. Picnic tables and fire grills are provided. Drinking water is available May 1 to October 15. Garbage bins, vault toilets, and cell phone reception are available. Raft rentals are available nearby. Leashed pets are permitted.

Reservations, fees: Reservations are not accepted. The fee is $7–10 per night, plus $7 per night for an additional vehicle. Major credit cards are accepted. Open year-round, with no winter facilities.

Directions: From LaGrande, drive northeast on Highway 82 for 18 miles to Elgin, then continue 14 miles to the park entrance road. Turn left (north) and drive two miles to the park.

Contact: Minam State Park, 541/432-8855.

8 CUTSFORTH FOREST PARK

Rating: 8

on Willow Creek
See map pages 322–323

This secluded, private county park is set beside a small, wheelchair-accessible pond in a quiet, wooded area. Trout fishing is available in the stocked ponds. Three of the campsites have corrals available. See the following description of Anson Wright Memorial Park for details on the area.

RV sites, facilities: There are 35 sites for RVs up to 35 feet or tents, 20 with full hookups (30 amps) and seven with partial hookups. Drinking water, restrooms, showers, cell phone reception, horseshoes, firewood, ice, and a playground are available. A large building with kitchen facilities is available for rent by groups. Supplies are available in Heppner (22 miles away). Some facilities are wheelchair-accessible. Leashed pets are permitted.

Reservations, fees: Reserve at 541/989-9500. The fee is $9–14 per night, plus $2 per additional vehicle and $5 for a horse corral. Major credit cards are accepted. Open early May to late November, weather permitting.

Directions: From Pendleton on I-84, drive west for 27 miles to Exit 182 and Highway 207 (Heppner Highway). Turn south and drive 32 miles to Lexington and Highway 74. Turn left (southeast) on Highway 74 and drive 10 miles to Heppner. Continue south on Highway 207 for .5 mile to Willow Creek Road. Turn left on Willow Creek Road and drive 23 miles to the park.

Contact: Morrow County Public Works, P.O. Box 428, Lexington, OR 97839, 541/989-9500, fax 541/989-8352, website: www.heppner.net /parks/index.html.

9 ANSON WRIGHT MEMORIAL PARK

Rating: 7

on Rock Creek
See map pages 322–323

Set among wooded hills along a small stream, this county park offers visitors prime trout fishing in several stocked ponds as well as hiking opportunities. One of the fishing ponds is wheelchair-accessible. Attractions in the area include the Pendleton Mills, Emigrant Springs State Park, Hardman Ghost Town (10 miles away), and the Columbia River.

RV sites, facilities: There are 24 sites for RVs up to 35 feet, including 20 sites with full hookups (30 amps) and three sites with partial hookups, and 25 sites for tents. Drinking water, restrooms, showers, a pay phone, cell phone reception, a barbecue, firewood, ice, and a playground are

OREGON

available. Some facilities are wheelchair-accessible. Leashed pets are permitted.

Reservations, fees: Reserve at 541/989-9500. The fee is $9–14 per night, plus $2 for additional vehicle. Open late spring to early fall.

Directions: From Pendleton, drive west on I-84 for 27 miles to Exit 182 and Highway 207 (Heppner Highway). Turn south and drive 32 miles to Lexington and Highway 74. Turn left (south) and drive 10 miles to Heppner. Continue south on Highway 207 for 11 miles to Ruggs and a fork. Bear left at the fork (still Highway 207) and drive 12 miles to the park on the right.

Contact: Morrow County Public Works, P.O. Box 428, Lexington, OR 97839, 541/989-9500, fax 541/989-8352, website: www.heppner.net /parks/index.html.

10 BULL PRAIRIE

Rating: 8

on Bull Prairie Lake in Umatilla National Forest

See map pages 322–323

This campground is set along the shore of Bull Prairie Lake, a 24-acre lake at 4,000 feet elevation. Boating (no motors permitted), swimming, fishing, and hunting are some of the options here. A hiking trail circles the lake. This spot attracts little attention from out-of-towners, yet it offers plenty of recreation opportunities, making it an ideal vacation destination for many.

RV sites, facilities: There are 28 sites for RVs up to 31 feet or tents. Picnic tables and fire grills are provided. Drinking water, an RV dump station, garbage bins (summer only), firewood, and vault toilets are available. Boat docks, launching facilities, and a wheelchair-accessible boat ramp are on-site. Leashed pets are permitted.

Reservations, fees: Reservations are not accepted. The fee is $12 per night, plus $5 per night per additional vehicle. A senior discount is available. Open May to October.

Directions: From Heppner, drive south on Highway 207 for roughly 35 miles to the national forest boundary and continue four miles to Forest Road 2039 (paved). Turn left and drive three miles northeast to the campground on the right.

Contact: Umatilla National Forest, Heppner

Ranger District, P.O. Box 7, Heppner, OR 97836, 541/676-9187, fax 541/676-2105; Bluewood Recreation Management, 509/382-4725.

11 UKIAH-DALE FOREST STATE SCENIC CORRIDOR

Rating: 7

near the North Fork of the John Day River

See map pages 322–323

Fishing is a prime activity at this Camas Creek campground, set at an elevation of 3,140 feet near the banks of the North Fork of the John Day River. It's a good layover for visitors cruising U.S. 395 looking for a spot for the night. Emigrant Springs State Park near Pendleton is a possible side trip.

RV sites, facilities: There are 28 primitive sites for self-contained RVs up to 50 feet or tents. Picnic tables and fire pits are provided. Drinking water, firewood, and flush toilets are available. A pay phone is within three miles. Leashed pets are permitted.

Reservations, fees: Reservations are not accepted. The fee is $9 per night, plus $7 per additional vehicle. Open mid-April to late October, weather permitting.

Directions: From Pendleton, drive south on U.S. 395 for 50 miles to Highway 244 (near Ukiah). Continue south on U.S. 395 for three miles to the park.

Contact: Emigrant Springs State Heritage Area, P.O. Box 85, Meacham, OR 97859, 800/551-6949; Emigrant Springs State Park, 541/983-2277.

12 TOLLBRIDGE

Rating: 4

on the North Fork of the John Day River in Umatilla National Forest

See map pages 322–323

This small, secluded campground (elevation 3,800 feet) lies at the confluence of Desolation Creek and the North Fork of the John Day River and is adjacent to the Bridge Creek Wildlife Area. It can be beautiful or ugly, depending upon which direction you look. It's dusty in the summer, and tree cover is sparse. Hunting and fishing are two options here. Look for the geological interpretive sign in the camp.

RV sites, facilities: There are seven sites for RVs up to 31 feet or tents. Picnic tables and fire grills are provided. A vault toilet is available, but there is no drinking water, and all garbage must be packed out. Leashed pets are permitted.

Reservations, fees: Reservations are not accepted. The fee is $5 per night, with a 14-day stay limit. A senior discount is available. Open May to November.

Directions: From Pendleton, drive south on U.S. 395 for 50 miles to the intersection with Highway 244. Continue south on U.S. 395 for 18 miles to Forest Road 55 (one mile north of Dale). Turn left and drive .5 mile southeast to Forest Road 10 and the campground access road. Drive a short distance to the campground.

Contact: Umatilla National Forest, North Fork John Day Ranger District, P.O. Box 158, Ukiah, OR 97880, 541/427-3231, fax 541/276-5026.

13 LANE CREEK

Rating: 4

on Camas Creek in Umatilla National Forest
See map pages 322–323

This campground is set at 3,850 feet elevation along Camas Creek and Lane Creek, just inside the forest boundary, and provides easy access to all the amenities of town. It's a popular stop for overnighters passing through. Some of the sites close to the highway get traffic noise. Highlights include hot springs (privately owned) and good hunting and fishing. A U.S. Forest Service map details the back roads.

RV sites, facilities: There are eight sites for RVs up to 45 feet or tents and one group site. Picnic tables, garbage bins, and fire grills are provided. Vault toilets are available. No drinking water is provided. A pay phone is within 10 miles. Leashed pets are permitted.

Reservations, fees: Reservations are not accepted. The fees are $5 per night and $10 for the group site. A senior discount is available. Open May to November.

Directions: From Pendleton, drive south on U.S. 395 for 50 miles to Ukiah and Highway 244.

Turn east on Highway 244 and drive nine miles to the campground.

Contact: Umatilla National Forest, North Fork John Day Ranger District, P.O. Box 158, Ukiah, OR 97880, 541/427-3231, fax 541/276-5026.

14 BEAR WALLOW CREEK

Rating: 5

on Bear Wallow Creek in Umatilla
National Forest
See map pages 322–323

Set near the confluence of Bear Wallow and Camus Creeks at an elevation of 3,900 feet, this camp is one of three off Highway 244. The others are Lane Creek and Frazier. Quiet and primitive, the camp is used primarily in the summer. A three-quarter-mile interpretive trail highlighting the steelhead habitat meanders next to Bear Wallow Creek. The trail is wheelchair-accessible.

RV sites, facilities: There are eight sites for RVs up to 30 feet or tents and one group site. No drinking water is available, and garbage bins are provided in the summer only. Picnic tables and fire grills are provided. Vault toilets are available. A pay phone is within 10 miles. Some facilities are wheelchair-accessible. Leashed pets are permitted.

Reservations, fees: Reservations are not accepted. The fee is $5 per night, with a 14-day stay limit; the group site is $10 per night. A senior discount is available. Open March to November.

Directions: From Pendleton, drive south on U.S. 395 for 50 miles to Ukiah and Highway 244. Turn east on Highway 244 and drive 10 miles to the camp.

Contact: Umatilla National Forest, North Fork John Day Ranger District, P.O. Box 158, Ukiah, OR 97880, 541/427-3231, fax 541/276-5026.

15 SPOOL CART

Rating: 6

on the Grande Ronde River in Wallowa-
Whitman National Forest
See map pages 322–323

This campground, set at 3,500 feet elevation on the banks of the Grande Ronde River, gets its

OREGON

name from the large cable spools that were left on a cart here for some years. Hilgard Junction State Park to the north provides numerous recreation options, and the Oregon Trail Interpretive Park is nearby. This camp is popular with hunters in the fall. It's advisable to obtain a map of Wallowa-Whitman National Forest, which details the back roads and other side trips.

RV sites, facilities: There are 16 sites for RVs up to 22 feet or tents. Picnic tables and fire grills are provided. Firewood, vault toilets, and cell phone reception are available. There is no drinking water, and all garbage must be packed out. The sites are fully wheelchair-accessible. Leashed pets are permitted.

Reservations, fees: Reservations are not accepted. The fee is $5 per night. A senior discount is available. Open late May to late November.

Directions: From Pendleton, drive southeast on U.S. 84 for 42 miles to Highway 244. Turn southwest and drive 13 miles to Forest Road 51. Turn south and drive seven miles to the campground on the right.

Contact: Wallowa-Whitman National Forest, LaGrande Ranger District, 3502 Hwy. 30, LaGrande, OR 97850, 541/963-7186, fax 541/962-8580.

16 OLIVE LAKE

Rating: 9

on Olive Lake in Umatilla National Forest
See map pages 322–323

This campground is set at 6,100 feet along the shore of Olive Lake, between two sections of the North Fork John Day Wilderness. Dammed to hold an increased volume of water, the glacial lake is a beautiful tint of blue. Motorized boats are allowed, but water-skiing is prohibited. Fishing is fair for kokanee salmon and cutthroat, rainbow, and brook trout. Sections of the old wooden pipeline for the historic Fremont Powerhouse can still be seen. Nearby trails provide access to the wilderness; motorbikes and mountain bikes are not permitted there. The old mining town of Granite is 12 miles east of camp.

RV sites, facilities: There are 28 sites for RVs up to 31 feet or tents (four sites available for RVs up to 45 feet) and two group sites. Vault toilets

are available, but there is no drinking water, and garbage must be packed out. Picnic tables and fire grills are provided. Boat docks, launching facilities, and two picnic areas are available. Leashed pets are permitted.

Reservations, fees: Reservations are not accepted. The fee is $5 per night, with a 14-day stay limit; $10 for a group camp. A senior discount is available. Open June to mid-October, weather permitting.

Directions: From Pendleton, drive south on U.S. 395 for 62 miles to Forest Road 55 (one mile north of Dale). Turn right and drive .5 mile to Forest Road 10. Turn right on Forest Road 10 and drive 26 miles to the campground on the right.

Contact: Umatilla National Forest, North Fork John Day Ranger District, P.O. Box 158, Ukiah, OR 97880, 541/427-3231, fax 541/276-5026.

17 NORTH FORK JOHN DAY

Rating: 6

on the North Fork of the John Day River in Umatilla National Forest
See map pages 322–323

This campground is set in a conifer stand along the banks of the North Fork of the John Day River and makes an ideal base camp for a wilderness backpacking trip. In the fall, it has a great view of salmon spawning in the river. A horse-handling area is also available for wilderness users. Trails from camp lead into the North Fork John Day Wilderness. The camp is set at an elevation of 5,200 feet at the intersection of Elkhorn and Blue Mountain National Forest Scenic Byways. No motorbikes are permitted in the wilderness.

RV sites, facilities: There are 18 sites for RVs up to 22 feet or tents and one group camp. Picnic tables and fire rings are provided. Vault toilets are available. There is no drinking water. All garbage must be packed out. Leashed pets are permitted.

Reservations, fees: Reservations are not accepted. The fee is $5 per night, with a 14-day stay limit; $10 for a group camp. A senior discount is available. Open June to November. For trailhead use only, a Northwest Forest Pass ($5 daily

OREGON

fee or $30 annual fee per parked vehicle) is required.

Directions: From Pendleton, drive south on U.S. 395 for 50 miles to Highway 244. Turn east on Highway 244 and drive one mile to Ukiah and Forest Road 52. Turn south on Forest Road 52 and drive 36 miles to the campground.

Contact: Umatilla National Forest, North Fork John Day Ranger District, P.O. Box 158, Ukiah, OR 97880, 541/427-3231, fax 541/276-5026.

18 ANTHONY LAKES

Rating: 10

on Anthony Lake in Wallowa-Whitman National Forest

See map pages 322–323

This campground is set at 7,100 feet elevation, adjacent to Anthony Lake, where boating without motors is permitted. Sites are wooded, providing good screening between them. Alas, mosquitoes are often in particular abundance. Several smaller lakes within two miles by car or trail are ideal for trout fishing from a raft, float tube, or canoe. Sometimes mountain goats can be seen from the Elkhorn Crest Trail, which begins near here. Weekends and holidays are full.

RV sites, facilities: There are 37 sites for RVs up to 22 feet or tents and one group site. Drinking water, fire grills, garbage bins (summer only), and picnic tables are provided. Vault toilets are available. Some facilities are wheelchair-accessible. Leashed pets are permitted.

Reservations, fees: Reservations are not accepted for family sites. The fee is $11 per night, plus $5 per additional vehicle. Group reservations are required at 541/894-2505; the group site is $30–75 per night. A senior discount is available. Open July to late September.

Directions: From Baker City on I-84, turn north on U.S. 30. Drive north for 10 miles to Haines and County Road 1146 (signed for Anthony Lakes Ski Resort). Turn left on County Road 1146 and drive 20 miles (the road becomes Forest Road 73) to the campground on the left.

Contact: Wallowa-Whitman National Forest, Baker Ranger District, 3165 10th St., Baker City, OR 97814, 541/523-4476 or 541/894-2505, fax 541/523-1965.

19 UNION CREEK

Rating: 8

on Phillips Lake in Wallowa-Whitman National Forest

See map pages 322–323

This campground along the north shore of Phillips Lake is easy to reach yet missed by most I-84 travelers. It's the largest of three camps on the lake and the only one with drinking water. An old narrow-gauge railroad has been restored and runs up the valley from McEwen Depot (six miles from the campground) to Sumpter (10 miles away). Visit Sumpter to see an old dredge.

RV sites, facilities: There are 58 sites with full hookups (20 amps) for RVs up to 32 feet or tents. Picnic tables and fire rings are provided. Drinking water, garbage bins, cell phone reception, flush toilets, an RV dump station, firewood, and ice are available. Boat docks and launching facilities, a pay phone, a store, and an ATM are adjacent to the campground. Some facilities are wheelchair-accessible. Leashed pets are permitted.

Reservations, fees: Reservations are not accepted for family sites. The fee is $11–20 per night, plus $5 per additional vehicle. A senior discount is available. Open from mid-April to mid-September.

Directions: From Baker City, drive southwest on Highway 7 for 20 miles to the campground.

Contact: Wallowa-Whitman National Forest, Baker Ranger District, 3165 10th St., Baker City, OR 97814, 541/523-4476, fax 541/523-1965; concessionaire, Recreation Resource Management, 541/894-2505.

20 TWO COLOR

Rating: 6

on Eagle Creek in Wallowa-Whitman National Forest

See map pages 322–323

This campground is set at 4,800 feet elevation along the banks of Eagle Creek, about a mile north of Tamarack. Another option for campers is nearby Boulder Park campground, three miles northeast on Forest Road 7755.

RV sites, facilities: There are six sites for RVs up to 22 feet and 14 sites for tents. Picnic tables and fire grills are provided. Drinking water, vault toilets, and cell phone reception are available, but garbage must be packed out. Leashed pets are permitted.

Reservations, fees: Reservations are not accepted. The fee is $5 per night. A senior discount is available. Open mid-June to late October.

Directions: From Baker City, drive north on I-84 for six miles to Highway 203. Turn east on Highway 203 and drive 17 miles to Medical Springs and Big Springs Road (Forest Road 67). Turn left on Forest Road 67 and drive 15.5 miles (staying on Forest Road 67 at all Y junctions) to Forest Road 77. Turn left and drive .25 mile to the camp.

Contact: Wallowa-Whitman National Forest, LaGrande Ranger District, 3502 Hwy. 30, LaGrande, OR 97850, 541/963-7186, fax 541/962-8580.

21 MOUNTAIN VIEW MOTEL AND RV PARK

Rating: 3

near Wallowa Lake
See map pages 322–323

This park is centrally located for exploring the greater Wallowa Lake area. Enjoy views of the Seven Devils Mountains and the Eagle Cap Wilderness from here. Nearby recreational facilities include a golf course, hiking trails, bike paths, and a riding stable. Fishing and jet boating are also nearby options. This park is under new ownership and considerable improvements are constantly underway.

RV sites, facilities: There are 30 sites with full hookups (20, 30, 50 amps), including some drive-through, for RVs of any length, a few tent sites, and nine rooms/cabins. Drinking water, flush toilets, a pay phone, modem access, cell phone reception, and showers are available. Propane, a store, a café, and a coin-operated laundry are within two miles. Leashed pets are permitted.

Reservations, fees: Reservations are accepted. The fees are $20 per night for RV sites and $16 per night for tent sites, plus $3–5 per person for more than two people. A senior discount is available. Major credit cards are accepted. Open year-round.

Directions: From LaGrande, turn north on Highway 82 and drive 62 miles to Enterprise and the junction with Highway 3. Continue south on Highway 82 for five miles to the campground (1.5 miles north of Joseph).

Contact: Mountain View Motel and RV Park, 83450 Joseph Hwy., Joseph, OR 97846, 541/432-2982 or tel./fax 866/262-9891.

22 WALLOWA LAKE STATE PARK

Rating: 8

on Wallowa Lake
See map pages 322–323

Surrounded on three sides by 9,000-foot snow-capped mountains and large, clear Wallowa Lake, this area is popular for fishing and boating recreation, including water-skiing and parasailing. You can also enjoy hiking, horseback riding, bumper boats, canoeing, miniature golf, or a tram ride up 4,000 feet to a mountaintop. A nearby artist community makes world-class bronze castings and tours are available. This is also the gateway to Hells Canyon, the deepest gorge in North America. Other highlights include a pretty one-mile nature trail and trailheads that provide access into the Eagle Cap Wilderness. A marina is nearby for boaters and anglers. Picnicking, swimming, and wildlife viewing are a few of the other activities available to visitors.

RV sites, facilities: There are 121 full-hookup sites for RVs up to 90 feet, 89 tent sites, some hiker/biker sites, three group tent areas, two yurts, and one deluxe cabin. Picnic tables and fire pits are provided. Drinking water, garbage bins, flush toilets, an RV dump station, showers, and firewood are available. A store, an ATM, a café, and ice are within one mile. Boat docks, launching facilities, and rentals are nearby. Some facilities are wheelchair-accessible. Leashed pets are permitted.

Reservations, fees: Reserve at 800/452-5687 or online at www.OregonStateParks.org ($6 reservation fee). The fees are $11–21 per night, $4 per night for hiker/biker sites, $65 per night for group areas, $29 per night for yurts, and $58–79 per night for the deluxe cabin, plus $7 per night per additional vehicle. Major credit cards are accepted. Open year-round.

Directions: From LaGrande, turn east on High-

OREGON

way 82 and drive 62 miles to Enterprise and the junction with Highway 3. Continue south on Highway 82 to Joseph. Continue for six miles to the south shore of the lake and the campground.
Contact: Wallowa Lake State Park, 72214 Marina Ln., Joseph, OR 97846, 541/432-4185.

23 BLACKHORSE

Rating: 7

on the Imnaha River in Wallowa-Whitman National Forest
See map pages 322–323
This campground along the banks of the Imnaha River in Hells Canyon National Recreation Area is located in a secluded section of Wallowa-Whitman National Forest at an elevation of 4,000 feet.
RV sites, facilities: There are 16 sites for RVs up to 30 feet or tents. Picnic tables and fire grills are provided. Drinking water and vault toilets are available, but all garbage must be packed out. Leashed pets are permitted.
Reservations, fees: Reservations are not accepted. The fee is $5 per night. A senior discount is available. Open June to late October.
Directions: From I-84 at LaGrande, turn north on Highway 82 and drive 62 miles to Enterprise. Continue six miles south to Joseph and then drive eight miles east on Highway 350. Turn south on Forest Road 39 and drive 29 miles to the campground.
Contact: Hells Canyon National Recreation Area, Wallowa Mountains Visitor Center, 88401 Hwy. 82, Enterprise, OR 97828, 541/426-5546.

24 LAKE FORK

Rating: 6

on Lake Fork Creek in Wallowa-Whitman National Forest
See map pages 322–323
This little campground (at 3,200 feet elevation) along the banks of Lake Fork Creek is tucked away off the main road and makes an ideal jumping-off point for a backpacking trip. A trail from camp follows the creek west for about 10 miles to Fish Lake, then continues to several smaller lakes.
RV sites, facilities: There are 10 sites for RVs up to 22 feet or tents. Picnic tables and fire grills

are provided. Drinking water and vault toilets are available, but all garbage must be packed out. Leashed pets are permitted.
Reservations, fees: Reservations are not accepted. The fee is $5 per night. A senior discount is available. Open June to late October, weather permitting.
Directions: From Baker City, drive east on Highway 86 for 82 miles to Forest Road 39. Turn north and drive 7.5 miles to the campground entrance road on the left.
Contact: Hells Canyon National Recreation Area, Wallowa Mountains Visitor Center, 88401 Hwy. 82, Enterprise, OR 97828, 541/426-5546, fax 541/426-5522.

25 LICK CREEK

Rating: 7

on Lick Creek in Wallowa-Whitman National Forest
See map pages 322–323
This campground is set at an elevation of 5,400 feet in parklike surroundings along the banks of Lick Creek in Hells Canyon National Recreation Area. It is secluded and pretty. Tall Douglas fir, white fir, tamarack, and lodgepole pine are interspersed throughout the campground, providing habitat for some of the birds and small mammals you might see.
RV sites, facilities: There are five sites for RVs up to 30 feet and seven tent sites. Picnic tables and fire grills are provided. Vault toilets are available, but there is no drinking water, and garbage must be packed out. Leashed pets are permitted.
Reservations, fees: Reservations are not accepted. The fee is $5 per night. A senior discount is available. Open mid-June to late October, weather permitting.
Directions: From LaGrande, turn north on Highway 82 and drive 62 miles to Enterprise and the junction with Highway 3. Continue south on Highway 82 to Joseph and Highway 350. Turn east and drive 7.5 miles to Forest Road 39. Turn south and drive 15 miles to the campground.
Contact: Hells Canyon National Recreation Area, Wallowa Mountains Visitor Center, 88401 Hwy. 82, Enterprise, OR 97828, 541/426-5546, fax 541/426-5522.

26 OLLOKOT

Rating: 5

on the Imnaha River in Wallowa-Whitman National Forest
See map pages 322–323

This campground sits on the banks of the Imnaha River in Hells Canyon National Recreation Area at an elevation of 4,000 feet. It's named for Chief Joseph's brother, a member of the Nez Perce tribe. For those seeking a little more solitude, this could be the spot.

RV sites, facilities: There are 12 sites for RVs up to 30 feet or tents. Picnic tables and fire grills are provided. Drinking water and vault toilets are available, but all garbage must be packed out. Leashed pets are permitted.

Reservations, fees: Reservations are not accepted. The fee is $5 per night. A senior discount is available. Open June to late October, weather permitting.

Directions: From I-84 at LaGrande, turn north on Highway 82 and drive 62 miles to Enterprise. Continue six miles south to Joseph, and then drive 7.5 miles east on Highway 350. Turn south on Forest Road 39 and drive 30 miles to the campground.

Contact: Hells Canyon National Recreation Area, Wallowa Mountains Visitor Center, 88401 Hwy. 82, Enterprise, OR 97828, 541/426-5546, fax 541/426-5522.

27 INDIAN CROSSING

Rating: 6

on the Imnaha River in Wallowa-Whitman National Forest
See map pages 322–323

This campground is set at an elevation of 4,500 feet and is more developed than nearby Evergreen and Hidden Campgrounds, which accept RVs but are better designed for tent camping. A trailhead for the Eagle Cap Wilderness is near this camp. Obtain a U.S. Forest Service map for side-trip possibilities.

RV sites, facilities: There are 14 sites for RVs up to 30 feet or tents. Drinking water, picnic tables, and fire grills are provided, but all garbage must

be packed out. Vault toilets and horse facilities are available. Leashed pets are permitted.

Reservations, fees: Reservations are not accepted. The fee is $5 per night. A senior discount is available. Open June to late October, weather permitting.

Directions: From LaGrande, turn north on Highway 82 and drive 62 miles to Enterprise and the junction with Highway 3. Continue on Highway 82 for six miles to Joseph and Highway 350. Turn east on Highway 350 and drive 7.5 miles to Forest Road 39. Turn south and drive about 30 miles to Forest Road 3960. Turn right and drive 10 miles to the campground at the end of the road.

Contact: Hells Canyon National Recreation Area, Wallowa Mountains Visitor Center, 88401 Hwy. 82, Enterprise, OR 97828, 541/426-5546, fax 541/426-5522.

28 OCHOCO DIVIDE

Rating: 5

in Ochoco National Forest
See map pages 322–323

This camp is set at an elevation of 4,700 feet amid an old-growth stand of ponderosa pine just off scenic U.S. 26. An unused forest road on the far side of the campground provides an easy stretch walk after a long day of driving. Most visitors arrive late in the day and leave early in the morning, so the area is normally quiet during the day. Marks Creek is nearby, and the Bandit Springs Rest Stop, one mile west, is the jumping-off point for a network of trails.

RV sites, facilities: There are 28 sites for RVs up to 30 feet or tents and a separate area with walk-in and bike-in sites. Picnic tables and fire pits are provided. Drinking water, garbage bins, and vault toilets are available. Some facilities are wheelchair-accessible. Leashed pets are permitted.

Reservations, fees: Reservations are not accepted. The fee is $10 per night, plus $5 per night for an additional vehicle. A senior discount is available. Open late May to mid-November, weather permitting.

Directions: From Prineville, drive east on U.S. 26 for 30 miles to the campground at the summit of Ochoco Pass.

Contact: Ochoco National Forest, Lookout Mountain Ranger District, P.O. Box 490, Prineville, OR 97754, 541/416-6500, fax 541/416-6695.

29 OCHOCO FOREST CAMP

Rating: 4

in Ochoco National Forest
See map pages 322–323
Campsites here are set at an elevation of 4,000 feet along Ochoco Creek in a lush setting of ponderosa pine and aspen. Fishing for rainbow trout is fair. A large group picnic area with a beautiful log shelter, perfect for weddings, family reunions, and other group events, is available by reservation. The nearby Lookout Mountain Trail provides access to the Lookout Mountain Recreation Area, 15,000 acres without roads. Don't expect privacy and solitude at this campground.
RV sites, facilities: There are six sites for RVs up to 24 feet or tents. Picnic tables and fire rings are provided. Drinking water, garbage bins, and vault toilets are available. Boat-launching facilities are nearby at Walton Lake (only electric motors are allowed). Some facilities are wheelchair-accessible. Leashed pets are permitted.
Reservations, fees: Reservations are not accepted. The fee is $10 per night, plus $5 per night for an additional vehicle. A senior discount is available. Open mid-May to November, weather permitting.
Directions: From Prineville, drive east on U.S. 26 for 16.5 miles to County Road 23. Turn right on County Road 23 and drive nine miles (County Road 23 becomes Forest Road 42) to the campground, across from the Ochoco Ranger Station.
Contact: Ochoco National Forest, Lookout Mountain Ranger District, P.O. Box 490, Prineville, OR 97754, 541/416-6500, fax 541/416-6695.

30 WALTON LAKE

Rating: 7

on Walton Lake in Ochoco National Forest
See map pages 322–323
This campground sits among old-growth ponderosa pine and mountain meadows along the shore of small Walton Lake, where fishing and swimming are popular; only nonmotorized boats or those with electric motors are allowed. Hik-

ers can explore a nearby trail that leads south to Round Mountain. The lake is stocked with rainbow trout, and the fishing can range from middle-of-the-road fair right up to downright excellent.
RV sites, facilities: There are 30 sites for RVs up to 31 feet or tents and one group site. Picnic tables, garbage bins, and fire grills are provided. Drinking water and vault toilets are available. Boat-launching facilities are nearby (only electric motors are allowed). Some facilities are wheelchair-accessible. Leashed pets are permitted.
Reservations, fees: Reservations are not accepted for family sites. The fee is $10–12 per night, plus $7 per night for an additional vehicle. Reservations for the group site are required; reserve at 877/444-6777 or online at www.reserveusa.com ($9 reservation fee). The group site is $25 per night. A senior discount is available. Open June to late September.
Directions: From Prineville, drive east on U.S. 26 for 16.5 miles to County Road 23. Turn right (northeast) and drive nine miles (County Road 23 becomes Forest Road 42) to the Ochoco Ranger Station and Forest Road 22. Drive north on Forest Road 22 for seven miles to the campground.
Contact: Ochoco National Forest, Big Summit/Lookout Mountain Ranger District, Ochoco Ranger District, Prineville, OR 97754-9612, 541/416-6645.

31 CROOK COUNTY RV PARK

Rating: 6

near the Crooked River
See map pages 322–323
This campground is in a landscaped and grassy area near the Crooked River, where fly-fishing is popular. The camp is set right next to the Crook County Fairgrounds, which, in season, offers horse races, rodeos, rock festivals, llama shows, and expositions.
RV sites, facilities: There are 81 sites with full hookups (30, 50 amps) for RVs up to 70 feet or tents and two sleeping cabins. Picnic tables are provided. Drinking water, flush toilets, an RV dump station, cable TV, a pay phone, cell phone reception, modem access, ice, vending machines, and showers are available. A small store, an ATM,

a restaurant, laundry facilities, and propane are available within one mile. Some facilities are wheelchair-accessible. Leashed pets are permitted.

Reservations, fees: Reserve at 800/609-2599. The fees are $9 per night for tent sites and $20–22 for RVs, plus $1 per additional vehicle. Weekly and monthly rates are available. Cabins are $25 per night. Major credit cards are accepted. Open year-round.

Directions: From Redmond, drive east on Highway 126 for 18 miles to Prineville (Highway 126 becomes 3rd Street). Turn east on 3rd Street and drive to Main Street. Turn right on Main Street and drive about .5 mile south to the campground on the left, next to the fairgrounds.

Contact: Crook County RV Park, 1040 S. Main St., Prineville, OR 97754, 541/447-2599, fax 541/416-9022, website: www.rvcampground.com/or/crookcounty.

32 OCHOCO LAKE

Rating: 6

on Ochoco Lake
See map pages 322–323
This is one of the nicer camps along U.S. 26 in eastern Oregon. The state park is located on the shore adjacent to Ochoco Lake, where boating and fishing are popular pastimes. Some quality hiking trails can be found in the area.

RV sites, facilities: There are 22 primitive sites for self-contained RVs up to 30 feet or tents and a special area for hikers and bicyclists. Picnic tables, garbage bins, and fire grills are provided. Drinking water, firewood, hot showers, cell phone reception, and flush toilets are available. Boat-launching facilities and a pay phone are nearby. An ATM, store, and coin-operated laundry are within seven miles. Leashed pets are permitted.

Reservations, fees: Reservations are not accepted. The fees are $14 per night for family sites and $4 per person hike-in/bike-in sites, plus $7 per additional vehicle. Open April to October, weather permitting.

Directions: From Prineville, drive east on U.S. 26 for seven miles to the park entrance on the right.

Contact: Crook County Parks and Recreation, 398 NE Fairview St., Prineville, OR 97754, 541/447-1209, fax 541/447-9894.

33 CHIMNEY ROCK

Rating: 6

on the Crooked River
See map pages 322–323
This well-spaced campground is a favorite for picnicking and wildlife viewing. The Chimney Rock Trailhead, just across the highway, is the jump-off point for the 1.7-mile, moderately difficult hike to Chimney Rock. There are numerous scenic overlooks along the trail, and wildlife sightings are common. The elevation here is 3,000 feet. Chimney Rock Campground is one of nine BLM camps along a six-mile stretch of Highway 27.

RV sites, facilities: There are 20 sites for RVs of any length or tents. Drinking water and picnic tables are provided. Vault toilets and garbage bins are available. Wheelchair-accessible toilets, tables, and a fishing dock are also available. Leashed pets are permitted.

Reservations, fees: Reservations are not accepted. The fee is $8 per night, plus $2 per night for an additional vehicle. A senior discount is available. Open year-round.

Directions: In Prineville, drive south on Highway 27 for 16.4 miles to the campground (the road is twisty and winding).

Contact: Bureau of Land Management, Prineville District, 3050 NE 3rd St., Prineville, OR 97754, 541/416-6700, fax 541/416-6798.

34 PRINEVILLE RESERVOIR STATE PARK

Rating: 7

on Prineville Reservoir
See map pages 322–323
This state park is set along the shore of Prineville Reservoir, which formed with the damming of the Crooked River. Swimming, boating, fishing, and water-skiing are among the activities here. The nearby boat docks and ramp are a bonus. The reservoir supports rainbow and cutthroat trout, small and largemouth bass, catfish, and crappie. You can even ice fish in the winter. This is one of two campgrounds on the lake; the other is Prineville Reservoir Resort (RVs only).

RV sites, facilities: There are 22 sites with full

OREGON

hookups (30, 50 amps), 23 with partial hookups, for RVs up to 40 feet, 23 tent sites, two rustic cabins, and three deluxe cabins. Picnic tables and fire rings are provided. Drinking water, flush toilets, garbage bins, boat moorage, showers, and firewood are available. Boat docks and launching facilities are nearby. Leashed pets are permitted.

Reservations, fees: Reserve at 800/452-5687 or online at www.OregonStateParks.org ($6 reservation fee). The fees are $16–20 per night and $35–65 per night for cabins. Boat moorage is $7 per night. Major credit cards are accepted. Open year-round.

Directions: From Prineville, drive east on U.S. 26 for one mile to Combs Flat Road. Turn right (south) and drive one mile to Juniper Canyon Road. Turn right (south) and drive 15 miles to the campground.

Contact: Prineville Reservoir State Park, 19020 SE Parkland Dr., Prineville, OR 97754, 541/447-4363 or 800/551-6949.

35 PRINEVILLE RESERVOIR RESORT

Rating: 6

on Prineville Reservoir

See map pages 322–323

This resort sits on the shore of Prineville Reservoir in the high desert, a good spot for water sports and fishing. The mostly shaded sites are a combination of dirt and gravel. The camp features easy access to the reservoir and some colorful rock formations to check out.

RV sites, facilities: There are 71 sites with partial hookups (20 amps), including two drive-through, for RVs of any length, seven motel rooms, and one primitive cabin. Picnic tables and fire pits are provided. Drinking water, flush toilets, propane, a pay phone, cell phone reception, an RV dump station, showers, firewood, a store, a café, and ice are available. A full-service marina, a boat ramp, and boat rentals are on-site. Leashed pets are permitted.

Reservations, fees: Reserve at 541/447-7468. The fee is $14–21 per night. Major credit cards are accepted. A senior discount is available. Open early May to mid-September, weather permitting.

Directions: From Prineville, drive east on U.S. 26 for one mile to Combs Flat Road. Turn right

(south) and drive one mile to Juniper Canyon Road. Turn right (south) and drive 18 miles to the campground.

Contact: Prineville Reservoir Resort, 19600 SE Juniper Canyon Rd., Prineville, OR 97754, 541/447-7468.

36 DEEP CREEK

Rating: 5

on the North Fork of the Crooked River in Ochoco National Forest

See map pages 322–323

This small camp on the edge of high desert gets little use, but it's in a nice spot—the confluence of Deep Creek and the North Fork of the Crooked River. Highlights include pretty, shady sites and river access. Fishing is possible here.

RV sites, facilities: There are six sites for RVs up to 22 feet or tents. Picnic tables and fire grills are provided. Drinking water and vault toilets are available. Garbage must be packed out. Leashed pets are permitted.

Reservations, fees: Reservations are not accepted. The fee is $8 per night, plus $3 per additional vehicle. A senior discount is available. Open June to mid-October.

Directions: From Prineville, drive east on U.S. 26 for 16.5 miles to County Route 23. Turn right (northeast) and drive 8.5 miles (it becomes Forest Road 42). Continue east on Forest Road 42 for 23.5 miles to the campground.

Contact: Ochoco National Forest, Lookout Mountain Ranger District, P.O. Box 490, Prineville, OR 97754, 541/416-6500, fax 541/416-6695.

37 WOLF CREEK

Rating: 5

on Wolf Creek in Ochoco National Forest

See map pages 322–323

This campground is set along the banks of Wolf Creek, a nice trout stream that runs through Ochoco National Forest. A quality spot, it features some excellent hiking trails to the northeast in the Black Canyon Wilderness.

RV sites, facilities: There are 12 sites for RVs up to 22 feet or tents. Picnic tables and fire grills are provided, but there is no drinking water, and all garbage must be packed out. Vault toilets are available. Leashed pets are permitted.

Reservations, fees: Reservations are not accepted. The fee is $6 per night, with a 14-day stay limit, plus $3 per night for an additional vehicle. A senior discount is available. Open May to early November.

Directions: From Prineville, drive southeast on Combs Flat Road (Paulina Highway) for 55 miles to Paulina. Continue east for 3.5 miles to County Road 112. Turn left (north) and drive 6.5 miles to Forest Road 42. Turn north and drive 1.5 miles to the campground.

Contact: Ochoco National Forest, Paulina Ranger District, 7803 Beaver Creek Rd., Paulina, OR 97751, 541/477-6900, fax 541/477-6949.

OREGON

38 SUGAR CREEK

Rating: 6

on Sugar Creek in Ochoco National Forest
See map pages 322–323

This small, quiet, and remote campground sits on the banks of Sugar Creek. It is set at an elevation of 4,000 feet. A three-quarter-mile trail loops along the creek. The camp also offers a covered group shelter in the day-use area and a wheelchair-accessible trail. Because of the presence of bald eagles, there may be seasonal closures on land access in the area. Be sure to check posted notices.

RV sites, facilities: There are 17 sites for RVs up to 21 feet or tents. Picnic tables, garbage bins, and fire grills are provided. Drinking water, a picnic shelter, and vault toilets are available. Some facilities are wheelchair-accessible. Leashed pets are permitted.

Reservations, fees: Reservations are not accepted. The fee is $8 per night, with a 14-day stay limit, plus $3 per night for an additional vehicle. A senior discount is available. Open June to early November.

Directions: From Prineville, drive southeast on Combs Flat Road (Paulina Highway) for 55 miles to Paulina. Continue east and drive 3.5 miles to a fork with County Road 112. Bear left at the fork onto County Road 112 and drive 7.5 miles to Forest Road 58. Continue on Forest Road 58 for 2.25 miles to the campground on the right.

Contact: Ochoco National Forest, Paulina Ranger District, 7803 Beaver Creek Rd., Paulina, OR 97751, 541/477-6900, fax 541/477-6949.

39 CLYDE HOLLIDAY STATE RECREATION SITE

Rating: 7

near the John Day River
See map pages 322–323

Think of this campground as an oasis. Its tall, willowy cottonwood trees provide shade and serenity, giving you that private, secluded feeling. It borders the John Day River, and you're as likely to have wildlife neighbors as human ones; Rocky Mountain elk and mule deer are frequent visitors. You might also see steelhead rushing upriver to spawn.

RV sites, facilities: There are 31 sites with partial hookups (20, 30, 50 amps) for RVs up to 60 feet, a hiker/biker tent area, and two tepees. Picnic tables and fire grills are provided. Drinking water, firewood, an RV dump station, showers, a pay phone, cell phone reception, and flush toilets are available. An ATM and a coin-operated laundry are within one mile, and a store is within six miles. Leashed pets are permitted.

Reservations, fees: Reservations are not accepted. The fees are $17 per night, $4 per person per night for hike-in/bike-in sites, and $28 per night for tepees, plus $7 per night for an additional vehicle. Major credit cards are accepted. The campground is open March to November, weather permitting.

Directions: From John Day, drive west on U.S. 26 for six miles to the park on the left.

Contact: Clyde Holliday State Recreation Site, P.O. Box 10, Mt. Vernon, OR 97865, 541/932-4453 or 800/551-6949.

40 MAGONE LAKE

Rating: 8

on Magone Lake in Malheur National Forest
See map pages 322–323

This campground is set along the shore of little Magone Lake at an elevation of 5,100 feet. A 1.8-mile trail rings the lake, and the section extending from the beach area to the campground (about a quarter mile) is barrier-free. A half-mile trail leads to Magone Slide, an unusual geological formation. Swimming, fishing, sailing, and canoeing are some of the popular activities at this lake. Easy-access bike trails can be found within a quarter mile of the campground.

RV sites, facilities: There are 18 sites for RVs up to 40 feet, four of which are drive-through sites, and three sites for tents. There is a separate group camping site designed for 10 families, and a picnic shelter that can accommodate 50 to 100 people. Picnic tables and fire grills are provided. Drinking water, composting toilets, a boat ramp, and a beach area are available. Boat docks and launching facilities are nearby. Some facilities are wheelchair-accessible. Leashed pets are permitted.

Reservations, fees: Reservations are not accepted for family sites. The fee is $10 per night, plus $2.50 per additional vehicle. Reservations are required for the group site and group picnic shelter; phone 541/820-3863. Group sites are $60 per night. A senior discount is available. Open May to November, weather permitting.

Directions: From John Day, drive east on U.S. 26 for eight miles to County Road 18. Turn north and drive 10 miles to Forest Road 3620. Turn left (west) on Forest Road 3620 and drive 1.5 miles to Forest Road 3618. Turn right (northwest) and drive 1.5 miles to the campground.

Contact: Malheur National Forest, Blue Mountain Ranger District, P.O. Box 909, John Day, OR 97845, 541/575-3000, fax 541/575-3001.

41 MIDDLE FORK

Rating: 6

on the Middle Fork of the John Day River in Malheur National Forest

See map pages 322–323

Scattered along the banks of the Middle Fork of the John Day River at 4,100 feet elevation, these rustic campsites are easy to reach off a paved road. Besides wildlife-watching and berry picking, the main activity at this camp is fishing, so bring along your fly rod, and pinch down your barbs for catch-and-release. The John Day is a state scenic waterway.

RV sites, facilities: There are 10 sites for RVs up

to 30 feet or tents. Picnic tables and fire grills are provided. Vault toilets are available. There is no drinking water, and all garbage must be packed out. Some facilities are wheelchair-accessible. Leashed pets are permitted.

Reservations, fees: Reservations are not accepted. The fee is $5 per night, plus $2.50 per night for an additional vehicle. A senior discount is available. Open May to November, weather permitting.

Directions: From John Day, drive northeast on U.S. 26 for 28 miles to Highway 7. Turn left (north) and drive one mile to County Road 20. Turn left and drive five miles to the campground on the left.

Contact: Malheur National Forest, Blue Mountain Ranger District, P.O. Box 909, John Day, OR 97845, 541/575-3000, fax 541/575-3001.

42 DIXIE

Rating: 5

near Dixie Summit in Malheur National Forest

See map pages 322–323

This campground is at Dixie Summit (elevation 5,300 feet) near Bridge Creek, where you can toss in a fishing line. The camp is just off U.S. 26, close enough to provide easy access. It draws overnighters, but otherwise gets light use. The Sumpter Valley Railroad interpretive site is one mile west on U.S. 26.

RV sites, facilities: There are 11 sites for RVs up to 30 feet or tents. Picnic tables, vault toilets, and fire grills are provided. Drinking water and cell phone reception are available, but all garbage must be packed out. A store, a café, gas, a pay phone, and ice are available within six miles. Some facilities are wheelchair-accessible. Leashed pets are permitted.

Reservations, fees: Reservations are not accepted. The fee is $5 per night, plus $2.50 per night for an additional vehicle. A senior discount is available. Open May to November, weather permitting.

Directions: From John Day, drive northeast on U.S. 26 for 24 miles to Forest Road 365. Turn left and drive .25 mile to the campground.

Contact: Malheur National Forest, Blue Mountain Ranger District, P.O. Box 909, John Day, OR 97845, 541/575-3000, fax 541/575-3001.

43 DEPOT PARK

Rating: 6

on the John Day River
See map pages 322–323

This urban park on grassy flatlands provides access to the John Day River, a good trout fishing spot. The camp is a more developed alternative to the many U.S. Forest Service campgrounds in the area. Depot Park features a historic rail depot on the premises as well as a related museum. Nearby attractions include the Strawberry Mountain Wilderness (prime hiking trails) and Clyde Holliday State Recreation Site.

RV sites, facilities: There are 20 sites with full hookups (30, 50 amps) for RVs up to 35 feet or tents. Picnic tables and fire rings are provided. Restrooms, showers, an RV dump station, a gazebo, a picnic area, and a pay phone are provided. An ATM, groceries, and a coin-operated laundry are available within three blocks. Leashed pets are permitted.

Reservations, fees: Reservations are not accepted. The fee is $11–16 per night. Open May to November, weather permitting.

Directions: From John Day, drive east on U.S. 26 for 13 miles to Prairie City and the junction of U.S. 26 and Main Street. Turn right (south) on Main Street and drive three blocks to the park (well signed).

Contact: Prairie City Hall, P.O. Box 370, Prairie City, OR 97869, 541/820-3605.

44 WETMORE

Rating: 7

on the Middle Fork of the Burnt River in Wallowa-Whitman National Forest
See map pages 322–323

This campground, set at an elevation of 4,320 feet near the Middle Fork of the Burnt River, makes a nice base camp for a fishing or hiking trip. The stream can provide good trout fishing. Trails are detailed on a map of Wallowa-Whitman National Forest. In addition, an excellent half-mile, wheelchair-accessible trail passes through old-growth forest. Watch for bald eagles.

RV sites, facilities: There are 16 sites for RVs up to 28 feet or tents. Picnic tables and fire grills are provided. Drinking water, firewood, and vault toilets are available, but all garbage must be packed out. Some facilities are wheelchair-accessible. Leashed pets are permitted.

Reservations, fees: Reservations are not accepted. The fee is $5 per night. A senior discount is available. Open late May to mid-September.

Directions: From John Day, drive east on U.S. 26 for 29 miles to Austin Junction. Continue east on U.S. 26 for 11.5 miles to the campground.

Contact: Wallowa-Whitman National Forest, Unity Ranger District, 214 Main St., P.O. Box 39, Unity, OR 97884, 541/446-3351, fax 541/523-1479.

45 OREGON

Rating: 6

near Austin Junction in Wallowa-Whitman National Forest
See map pages 322–323

This campground at 4,880 feet elevation is just off U.S. 26 and is the staging area for ATV enthusiasts; several ATV trails crisscross the area. The camp is surrounded by hillside, Douglas fir, white fir, and tamarack. Bald eagles nest in the area.

RV sites, facilities: There are 11 sites for RVs up to 28 feet or tents. Picnic tables and fire grills are provided. Drinking water and vault toilets are available, but garbage must be packed out. Leashed pets are permitted.

Reservations, fees: Reservations are not accepted. The fee is $5 per night. A senior discount is available. Open May to mid-September.

Directions: From John Day, drive east on U.S. 26 for 29 miles to Austin Junction. Continue east for 20 miles to the campground.

Contact: Wallowa-Whitman National Forest, Unity Ranger District, 214 Main St., P.O. Box 39, Unity, OR 97884, 541/446-3351, fax 541/523-1479.

46 YELLOW PINE

Rating: 7

near the Middle Fork of the Burnt River
See map pages 322–323

Highlights of this camp include easy access and good recreation potential. The camp offers a

OREGON

number of hiking trails; one half-mile-long, wheel-chair-accessible trail connects to the Wetmore Campground. Yellow Pine is similar to Oregon campground, but larger. Keep an eye out for bald eagles in this area.

RV sites, facilities: There are 21 sites for RVs up to 28 feet or tents. Picnic tables and fire grills are provided. Drinking water, an RV dump station, and vault toilets are available, but all garbage must be packed out. Leashed pets are permitted.

Reservations, fees: Reservations are not accepted. The fee is $5 per night. A senior discount is available. Open late May to mid-September.

Directions: From John Day, drive east on U.S. 26 for 29 miles to Austin Junction. Continue east for 11 miles to the campground.

Contact: Wallowa-Whitman National Forest, Unity Ranger District, 214 Main St., P.O. Box 39, Unity, OR 97884, 541/446-3351, fax 541/523-1479.

47 UNITY LAKE STATE RECREATION SITE

Rating: 7

on Unity Reservoir
See map pages 322–323

This camp, set along the east shore of Unity Reservoir, is a popular spot in good weather. Campers can choose from hiking, swimming, boating, fishing, picnicking, or enjoying the scenic views. Set in the high desert, this grassy park provides a contrast to the sagebrush and cheat grass of the bordering land.

RV sites, facilities: There are 35 sites with partial hookups (20, 30 amps) for RVs of any length or tents, a separate area for hikers and bicyclists, and two tepees. Picnic tables and fire grills are provided. Drinking water, flush toilets, garbage bins, a pay phone, cell phone reception, showers, an RV dump station, and firewood are available. Boat docks and launching facilities are nearby. A store and coin-operated laundry are available within five miles. Some facilities are wheelchair-accessible. Leashed pets are permitted.

Reservations, fees: Reservations are not accepted. The fees are $10–17 per night, $4 per person for hike-in/bike-in sites, and $28 per night for tepees, plus $7 per night for an additional vehicle. Major credit cards are accepted. Open

mid-April to late October.

Directions: From John Day, drive east on U.S. 26 for 50 miles to Highway 245. Turn left (north) on Highway 245 and drive three miles to the park on the left.

Contact: Clyde Holliday State Recreation Site, P.O. Box 10, Mt. Vernon, OR 97820, 541/932-4453 or 800/551-6949.

48 STARR

Rating: 4

on Starr Ridge in Malheur National Forest
See map pages 322–323

A good layover spot for travelers on U.S. 395, Starr happens to be adjacent to Starr Ski Bowl, which is popular in winter for skiing and sledding. The camp itself doesn't offer much in the way of recreation, but to the northeast is the Strawberry Mountain Wilderness, which has a number of trails, lakes, and streams. The camp sits at an elevation of 5,100 feet.

RV sites, facilities: There are eight sites for RVs up to 25 feet or tents. Picnic tables and fire grills are provided. Vault toilets are available. There is no drinking water, and all garbage must be packed out. A pay phone is within eight miles. Some facilities are wheelchair-accessible. Leashed pets are permitted.

Reservations, fees: Reservations are not accepted. The fee is $4 per night, plus $2 per night for an additional vehicle. A senior discount is available. Open early May to November.

Directions: From John Day, drive south on U.S. 395 for 15 miles to the campground.

Contact: Malheur National Forest, Blue Mountain Ranger District, P.O. Box 909, John Day, OR 97845, 541/575-3000, fax 541/575-3001.

49 TROUT FARM

Rating: 6

near Prairie City in Malheur National Forest
See map pages 322–323

This campground (4,900 feet elevation) is situated on the Upper John Day River, which provides good trout fishing with easy access for people who don't wish to travel off paved roads.

A picnic shelter is available for family picnics, and a small pond at the campground has a wheelchair-accessible trail.

RV sites, facilities: There are six sites for RVs up to 21 feet or tents. Picnic tables and fire grills are provided. Drinking water and wheelchair-accessible vault toilets are available, but all garbage must be packed out. Leashed pets are permitted.

Reservations, fees: Reservations are not accepted. The fee is $6 per night, plus $3 per additional vehicle. A senior discount is available. Open June to mid-October.

Directions: From John Day, drive east on U.S. 26 for 13 miles to Prairie City and County Road 62. Turn right and drive 15 miles to the campground entrance on the right.

Contact: Malheur National Forest, Prairie City Ranger District, P.O. Box 337, Prairie City, OR 97869, 541/820-3311, fax 541/820-3838.

50 PARISH CABIN

Rating: 6

on Little Bear Creek in Malheur National Forest

See map pages 322–323

This campground along the banks of Little Bear Creek (elevation 4,900 feet) is in a pretty spot that's not heavily used. The creek offers limited fishing. The road is paved all the way to the campground. This campground is popular with groups of families and hunters in season.

RV sites, facilities: There are 16 sites for RVs up to 32 feet or tents. Picnic tables and fire grills are provided. Drinking water, vault toilets, and horse facilities are available. Leashed pets are permitted. All garbage must be packed out. Some facilities are wheelchair-accessible. Leashed pets are permitted.

Reservations, fees: Reservations are not accepted. The fee is $6 per night, plus $3 per additional vehicle. A senior discount is available. Open mid-May to late November.

Directions: From John Day, drive south on U.S. 395 for 10 miles to Forest Road 15. Turn left and drive 16 miles southeast to Forest Road 16. Turn right onto Forest Road 16 and drive a short distance to the campground on the right.

Contact: Malheur National Forest, Blue Moun-

tain Ranger District, P.O. Box 909, John Day, OR 97845, 541/575-3000, fax 541/575-3001.

51 BIG CREEK

Rating: 6

near the Strawberry Mountain Wilderness in Malheur National Forest

See map pages 322–323

This campground is set at an elevation of 5,100 feet along the banks of Big Creek. Nearby forest roads provide access to the Strawberry Mountain Wilderness. Other recreation options include fishing and mountain biking. Note that fishing is restricted to the use of artificial lures with a single, barbless hook. In the appropriate seasons, elk, bear, coyote, and deer are hunted here.

RV sites, facilities: There are 15 sites for RVs up to 16 feet or tents. Picnic tables and fire grills are provided. Drinking water, cell phone reception, and wheelchair-accessible vault toilets are available. All garbage must be packed out. Leashed pets are permitted.

Reservations, fees: Reservations are not accepted. The fee is $5 per night, plus $2.50 per night for an additional vehicle. A senior discount is available. Open mid-May to mid-November.

Directions: From John Day, drive east on U.S. 26 for 13 miles to Prairie City and County Road 62. Turn right and drive 24 miles to Forest Road 16. Turn right and drive six miles to Forest Road 815. Turn right and drive .5 mile to the campground on the right.

Contact: Malheur National Forest, Prairie City Ranger District, P.O. Box 337, Prairie City, OR 97869, 541/820-3311, fax 541/820-3838.

52 SPRING RECREATION SITE

Rating: 5

on the Snake River

See map pages 322–323

One of two camps in or near Huntington, this campground sits along the banks of the Snake River Reservoir. A more developed alternative, Farewell Bend State Recreation Area offers showers and all the other luxuries a camper could want. Fishing is popular at this reservoir.

RV sites, facilities: There are 35 sites for RVs of any length or tents. Picnic tables, garbage service, and fire grills are provided. Drinking water (summer only), vault toilets, and cell phone reception are available. Boat-launching facilities and a fish-cleaning station are on-site. A pay phone and an ATM are within three miles. Leashed pets are permitted.

Reservations, fees: Reservations are not accepted. The fee is $5 per night per vehicle, with a 14-day stay limit. A senior discount is available. Open year-round, with fees charged May 1 to October 31.

Directions: From Ontario (near the Oregon/Idaho border), drive northwest on I-84 for 28 miles to Huntington and Snake River Road. Turn northeast on Snake River Road and drive three miles to the campground.

Contact: Bureau of Land Management, Baker City Office, 3165 10th St., Baker City, OR 97814, 541/523-1256, fax 541/523-1965.

53 FAREWELL BEND STATE RECREATION AREA

Rating: 7

on the Snake River
See map pages 322–323

This campground offers a desert experience on the banks of the Snake River's Brownlee Reservoir. Situated along the Oregon Trail, it offers historic interpretive displays and an evening interpretive program at the amphitheater (seasonal). Among the amenities are horseshoes, basketball hoops, and a sand volleyball court.

RV sites, facilities: There are 101 sites with partial hookups (20, 30 amps) for RVs up to 56 feet and 30 tent sites. There are also four tepees, two cabins, two covered camper wagons, and a group tent area. Picnic tables and barbecues are provided. Drinking water, garbage bins, flush toilets, an RV dump station, a pay phone, cell phone reception, showers, and firewood are available. Boat-launching facilities are nearby. An ATM is within one mile, and a coin-operated laundry is within four miles. Leashed pets are permitted.

Reservations, fees: Reserve at 800/452-5687 or online at ww.oregonstateparks.org. The fees are $12–18 per night, tepees or covered wagons $29

a night, and cabins $35 per night, plus $7 per night for an additional vehicle. Major credit cards are accepted. Open year-round, with limited winter facilities.

Directions: From Ontario (near the Oregon/Idaho border), drive northwest on I-84 for 21 miles to Exit 353 and the park entrance on the right side of the road.

Contact: Farewell Bend State Recreation Area, 23751 Old Hwy. 30, Huntington, OR 97907, 541/869-2365 or 800/551-6949.

54 BULLY CREEK PARK

Rating: 7

on Bully Creek Reservoir
See map pages 322–323

The reservoir is set in a kind of high desert area with sagebrush and poplar trees for shade. People come here to swim, boat, water-ski, and fish (mostly for warm-water fish, such as crappie and large and smallmouth bass). You can bicycle on the gravel roads. It's beautiful if you like the desert, and the sunsets are worth the trip. The primitive setting is home to deer, antelope, jackrabbits, squirrels, and many birds. The elevation is 2,300 feet. No monthly rentals are permitted here, a big plus for overnighters.

RV sites, facilities: There are 40 sites with partial hookups (20, 30, 50 amps) for RVs up to 45 feet or tents and four group sites. Picnic tables and fire pits are provided. Drinking water, flush toilets, showers, ice, garbage bins, firewood, a dump station, and a boat ramp and launch dock are available. A restaurant, a café, groceries, a small store, a pay phone, an ATM, gasoline, propane, charcoal, and a coin-operated laundry are within 10 miles. Leashed pets are permitted.

Reservations, fees: Reservations are accepted ($10 deposit). The fee is $10 per sleeping unit per night. Open April to mid-November, weather permitting.

Directions: From Ontario (near the Oregon/Idaho border), drive west on U.S. 20/26 for 12 miles to Vale and Graham Boulevard. Turn northwest on Graham Boulevard and drive five miles to Bully Creek Road. Turn left (west) and drive three miles to Bully Creek Park.

Contact: Bully Creek Park, 2475 Bully Creek Rd., Vale, OR 97918, 541/473-2969, fax 541/473-9462.

Oregon

Chapter 11
The Southern Cascades

THE SOUTHERN CASCADES

Lake Billy Chinook

see The Columbia River Gorge and Mount Hood
pages 296–297

[12] [23]

Deschutes River

97

[26] [27] [28] [29]

Bend

[25]

[24]

20

[13]

[8-11]

[7]

[6]

[4]

[5]

Mt. Hood National Forest

Deschutes National Forest

[38]

[41]

[39-40]

[42]

[50]

[52]

[51] [60] [61]

[47-49]

Crane Prairie Res.

[53-56] [57]

[58]

[59]

Wickiup Reservoir

Newberry Nat'l Volcanic Monument

Deschutes National Forest

31

[67-72]

Waldo Lake

[44]

[45] [46]

58

[66]

[65]

North Umpqua River

[85-87]

[14]

[15]

[22]

[21] [20]

[19]

[18]

[17]

[16]

Willamette National Forest

126

[1] [2] [3]

see Portland and the Willamette Valley
pages 278–279

[37]

[36]

[34]

[35]

[43]

[33]

[32]

[31]

[30]

[62]

[63]

[64]

Hills Creek Reservoir

C a s c a d e   R a n g e

5

Willamette River

Eugene

Fern Ridge Reservoir

20

5

126

Umpqua

[73]

[74]

[75]

138

[77] [78]

[79] [80] [81]

River

N E S W

5

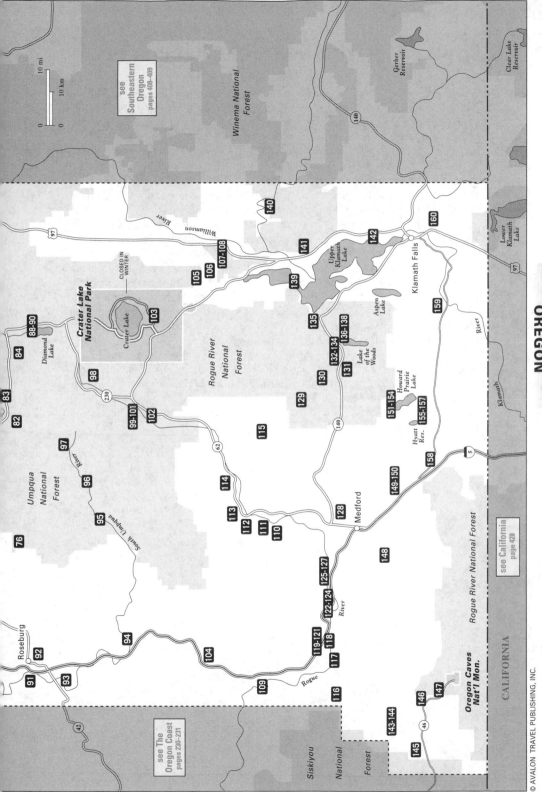

OREGON

© AVALON TRAVEL PUBLISHING, INC.

Chapter 11—The Southern Cascades

This region of Oregon is famous for one of its lakes, but it holds many fantastic recreation secrets. The crown jewel is Crater Lake, of course, and visitors come from all over the world to see its vast cobalt-blue waters within the clifflike walls. The lake's Rim Drive is one of those trips that everybody should have on their life's to-do list.

Beyond the lake, though, you'll find stellar camping, hiking, and fishing spots. The best among them are neighboring Mount Washington Wilderness and Three Sisters Wilderness in Willamette National Forest, accessible via a beautiful drive on the McKenzie River Highway (Highway 126) east from Eugene and Springfield.

But wait, there's more. Wickiup Reservoir, Crane Prairie, and Waldo Lake provide camping, boating, and good fishing. Wickiup, in turn, feeds into the headwaters of the Deschutes River, a prime steelhead locale. The Umpqua and Rogue National Forests offer some great water-sport destinations, including the headwaters of the North Umpqua, one of the prettiest rivers in North America; Diamond Lake; and the headwaters of the Rogue River. Upper Klamath Lake and the Klamath Basin are the No. 1 wintering areas in America for bald eagles. Klamath Lake also provides a chance to catch huge but elusive trout, as does the nearby Williamson River out of Chiloquin. All of this is but a small sampling of one of Oregon's best regions for adventure.

This region is all the more special for me because it evokes powerful personal memories. One of these is of a time at Hills Creek Reservoir southeast of Eugene. My canoe flipped on a cold winter day, and I almost drowned after 20 minutes in the icy water. After I'd gone down for the count twice, my brother Bob jumped in, swam out, grabbed the front of the flipped canoe, and towed me to shore. Then, once ashore, he kept me awake, preventing me from lapsing into a coma from hypothermia.

Thanks, Bob.

1 TROUT CREEK

Rating: 8

on the South Santiam River in Willamette National Forest

See map pages 346–347

This campground is set along the banks of the South Santiam River, about seven miles east of Cascadia. Fishing and swimming are two of the recreation possibilities here. There is a historic shelter and the remains of stonework from the era of the Civilian Conservation Corps. The Trout Creek Trail, just across the highway, leads into the Menagerie Wilderness. The Long Ranch Elk Viewing Area is immediately west of the campground, and at the Trout Creek Trailhead you'll also find a short trail leading to an elk-viewing platform. Nearby is the Old Santiam Wagon Road.

RV sites, facilities: There are 24 sites for RVs of any length or tents. Picnic tables, garbage bins, and fire grills are provided. Drinking water and vault toilets are available. A pay phone is within six miles. Some facilities are wheelchair-accessible. Leashed pets are permitted.

Reservations, fees: Reservations are not accepted. The fee is $10 per night, plus $5 per additional vehicle. A senior discount is available. Open May to October.

Directions: From Albany, drive east on U.S. 20 for 45 miles (19 miles past Sweet Home) to the campground entrance on the right.

Contact: Willamette National Forest, Sweet Home Ranger District, 3225 Hwy. 20, Sweet Home, OR 97386, 541/367-5168, fax 541/367-9221.

2 YUKWAH

Rating: 7

on the Santiam River in Willamette National Forest

See map pages 346–347

Yukwah campground is in a second-growth Douglas fir forest on the banks of the Santiam River. The camp is a quarter mile east of Trout Creek campground and offers the same recreation possibilities. The camp features a half-mile, compacted-surface interpretive trail that's barrier-free.

RV sites, facilities: There are 19 sites for RVs of any length or tents, including a deluxe group site for four or five families and three large RVs. Picnic tables, garbage bins, and fire grills are provided. Drinking water, vault toilets, a large picnic area, and a fishing platform are available. A pay phone is within 6.5 miles. Some facilities, including a fishing platform, are wheelchair-accessible. Leashed pets are permitted.

Reservations, fees: Reservations are not accepted. The fee is $10 per night, plus $5 per additional vehicle. The deluxe site is $20 per night. A senior discount is available. Open May to October.

Directions: From Albany, drive east on U.S. 20 for 45 miles (19 miles past Sweet Home) to the campground.

Contact: Willamette National Forest, Sweet Home Ranger District, 3225 Hwy. 20, Sweet Home, OR 97386, 541/367-5168, fax 541/367-9221.

3 FERNVIEW

Rating: 7

on the Santiam River in Willamette National Forest

See map pages 346–347

This campground is set high above the confluence of Boulder Creek and the Santiam River, just south of the Menagerie Wilderness. A stepped walkway leads down to the river. Just across U.S. 20 lies the Rooster Rock Trail, which leads to—where else?—Rooster Rock, the site of an old lookout tower. The Old Santiam Wagon Road runs through the back of the campground. The camp is best suited for tent and small RV camping; the sites are small.

RV sites, facilities: There are 11 sites for RVs up to 22 feet or tents. Picnic tables, garbage bins, and fire grills are provided. Drinking water and vault toilets are available. Some facilities are wheelchair-accessible. Leashed pets are permitted.

Reservations, fees: Reservations are not accepted. The fee is $10 per night, plus $5 per additional vehicle. A senior discount is available. Open May to October.

Directions: From Albany drive east on U.S. 20 for 49 miles (23 miles past Sweet Home) to the campground entrance on the right.

Contact: Willamette National Forest, Sweet Home

OREGON

Ranger District, 3225 Hwy. 20, Sweet Home, OR 97386, 541/367-5168, fax 541/367-9221.

◢ COLDWATER COVE

Rating: 10

on Clear Lake in Willamette National Forest
See map pages 346–347

This campground sits at 3,000 feet elevation on the south shore of Clear Lake, a spring-fed lake formed by a natural lava dam and the source of the McKenzie River. No motors are permitted on the lake, making it ideal for anglers in rowboats or canoes. The northern section of the McKenzie River National Recreation Trail passes by the camp.

RV sites, facilities: There are 35 sites for RVs up to 30 feet or tents. Picnic tables, garbage service, and fire grills are provided. Drinking water and vault toilets are available. Boat docks, launching facilities, rowboats, a pay phone, a store, a café, and cabin rentals are available nearby at Clear Lake Resort. Some facilities are wheelchair-accessible. Leashed pets are permitted.

Reservations, fees: Reserve at 877/444-6777 or online at www.reserveusa.com ($9 reservation fee). The fee is $14 per night, plus $7 per additional vehicle. A senior discount is available. Open late May to early October.

Directions: From Eugene, drive east on Highway 126 for 47 miles to the town of McKenzie Bridge. Continue on Highway 126 for 14 miles to Forest Road 770. Turn right (east) and drive to the campground.

Contact: Willamette National Forest, McKenzie Ranger District, 57600 McKenzie Hwy., McKenzie Bridge, OR 97413, 541/822-3381, fax 541/822-7254.

◢ ICE CAP

Rating: 9

on Carmen Reservoir in Willamette National Forest
See map pages 346–347

This campground (3,000 feet elevation) is on a hill above Carmen Reservoir, which was created by a dam on the McKenzie River. The McKen-

zie River National Recreation Trail passes by the camp, and Koosah Falls and Sahalie Falls are nearby. Clear Lake, a popular local vacation destination, is two miles away.

RV sites, facilities: There are 11 sites for RVs up to 16 feet or tents and 11 tent sites. Picnic tables, cell phone reception, garbage service, and fire grills are provided. Drinking water, flush toilets, boat-launching facilities, a pay phone, and boat rentals are about two miles away at Clear Lake Resort. Only nonmotorized boats are allowed on Carmen Reservoir. Leashed pets are permitted.

Reservations, fees: Reservations are not accepted. The fee is $14 per night, plus $6 per additional vehicle. A senior discount is available. Open mid-May to mid-September.

Directions: From Eugene, drive east on Highway 126 for 47 miles to the town of McKenzie Bridge. Continue on Highway 126 for 19 miles to the campground entrance road on the left. Turn left and drive 200 yards to the campground.

Contact: Willamette National Forest, McKenzie Ranger District, 57600 McKenzie Hwy., McKenzie Bridge, OR 97413, 541/822-3381, fax 541/822-7254.

◢ BIG LAKE

Rating: 9

on Big Lake in Willamette National Forest
See map pages 346–347

This jewel of a spot on the north shore of Big Lake at 4,650 feet elevation offers a host of activities, including fishing, swimming, water-skiing, and hiking. Big Lake has heavy motorized boat use. One of the better hikes is the five-mile wilderness loop trail (Patjens Lakes Trail) that heads out from the south shore of the lake and cuts past a few small lakes before returning. There's a great view of Mount Washington from the lake. The Pacific Crest Trail is only a half mile away.

RV sites, facilities: There are 49 sites for RVs up to 16 feet or tents. Picnic tables, garbage service, and fire grills are provided. Drinking water, vault and flush toilets, and cell phone reception are available. Boat ramps and launching facilities are nearby. A pay phone is within two miles. Leashed pets are permitted.

Reservations, fees: Reserve at 877/444-6777 or

OREGON

online at www.reserveusa.com ($9 reservation fee). The fee is $14 per night, plus $7 per additional vehicle. A senior discount is available. Open mid-June to early October.

Directions: From Eugene, drive east on Highway 126 for 47 miles to the town of McKenzie Bridge. Continue northeast on Highway 126 for 40 miles to Big Lake Road (Forest Road 2690). Turn right and drive three miles to the campground on the left.

Contact: Willamette National Forest, McKenzie Ranger District, 57600 McKenzie Hwy., McKenzie Bridge, OR 97413, 541/822-3381, fax 541/822-7254.

7 LINK CREEK

Rating: 6

on Suttle Lake in Deschutes National Forest
See map pages 346–347

This campground (elevation 3,450 feet) is at the west end of Suttle Lake. The high-speed boating area is on this end of the lake, making it a popular spot with water-skiers.

RV sites, facilities: There are 33 sites for RVs up to 40 feet or tents. Picnic tables, garbage service, and fire grills are provided. Drinking water and vault toilets are available. Boat docks, launching facilities, and rentals are nearby. A pay phone is within one mile. Leashed pets are permitted.

Reservations, fees: Reserve at 877/444-6777 or online at www.reserveusa.com ($9 reservation fee). The fee is $14 per night, plus $6 per additional vehicle. A senior discount is available. Open mid-April to mid-October.

Directions: From Albany, drive east on U.S. 20 for 74 miles to the junction of U.S. 20 and Highway 126. Continue east on Highway 126 for 12 miles to Forest Road 2070 (Suttle Lake). Turn right and drive a short distance to the campground.

Contact: Deschutes National Forest, Sisters Ranger District, P.O. Box 249, Sisters, OR 97759, 541/549-7700, fax 541/549-7746.

8 BLACK BUTTE RESORT MOTEL AND RV PARK

Rating: 6

near the Metolius River
See map pages 346–347

This RV park offers a choice of graveled or grassy sites in a clean, scenic environment. Rafting, kayaking, and fly-fishing (catch-and-release only) are popular activities at this campground. Other campgrounds, such as Camp Sherman, are set up for tent campers with space for RVs.

RV sites, facilities: There are 30 sites with full hookups (30, 50 amps) and 11 sites with partial hookups for RVs of any length. Picnic tables and barbecues are provided. Drinking water, flush toilets, modem access, showers, firewood, and a laundry room are available. Propane, an RV dump station, a pay phone, horseshoes, a volleyball area, a store, a café, and ice are within one block. Leashed pets are permitted.

Reservations, fees: Reservations are encouraged. The fee is $19–23 per night, plus $3 per person for more than two people. A senior discount is available. Major credit cards are accepted. Open year-round.

Directions: From Albany, drive east on U.S. 20 for 87 miles (near Black Butte) to the sign for Camp Sherman. Turn north on Forest Road 1419 and drive 4.5 miles to a stop sign and the camp access road. Turn right and drive .5 mile to the campground on the right.

Contact: Black Butte Resort Motel and RV Park, 25635 SW Forest Service Rd. 1419, Camp Sherman, OR 97730, 541/595-6514 or 877/595-6514, fax 541/595-5971, website: www.blackbutte-resort.com.

9 SMILING RIVER

Rating: 5

on the Metolius River in Deschutes National Forest
See map pages 346–347

Here's another camp along the banks of the Metolius River. It's set at an elevation of 2,900 feet. Other campgrounds, such as Camp Sherman, are set up for tent campers with space for RVs.

RV sites, facilities: There are 37 sites for RVs up

to 30 feet or tents. A few sites can accommodate RVs up to 40 feet. Picnic tables, garbage service, and fire grills are provided. Vault toilets and drinking water are available. Leashed pets are permitted.

Reservations, fees: Reservations are not accepted. The fee is $14 per night, plus $7 per additional vehicle. A senior discount is available. Open May to mid-October.

Directions: From Albany, drive east on U.S. 20 for 87 miles (near Black Butte) to the sign for Camp Sherman and Forest Road 14. Turn left on Forest Road 14 and drive five miles to Camp Sherman, the store, and Forest Road 900. Turn left on Forest Road 900 and drive one mile to the campground on the left.

Contact: Deschutes National Forest, Sisters Ranger District, P.O. Box 249, Sisters, OR 97759, 541/549-7700, fax 541/549-7746; Hoodoo Recreation Services, 541/822-3799, website: www.hoodoo.com.

10 PIONEER FORD

Rating: 7

on the Metolius River in Deschutes National Forest

See map pages 346–347

This quiet and serene wooded campground is set along the banks of the Metolius River and features grassy sites.

RV sites, facilities: There are 18 sites for RVs up to 40 feet or tents and two tent sites. Drinking water, garbage service, and fire grills are provided. Vault toilets and a barrier-free picnic shelter are available. A pay phone is within two miles. Leashed pets are permitted.

Reservations, fees: Reservations are not accepted. The fee is $14 per night, plus $7 per additional vehicle. A senior discount is available. Open April to September.

Directions: From Albany, drive east on U.S. 20 for 87 miles (near Black Butte) to the sign for Camp Sherman and Forest Road 14. Turn left on Forest Road 14 and drive 11 miles to the campground on the left.

Contact: Deschutes National Forest, Sisters Ranger District, P.O. Box 249, Sisters, OR 97759, 541/549-7700, fax 541/549-7746; Hoodoo Recreation Services, 541/822-3799, website: www.hoodoo.com.

11 COLD SPRINGS RESORT AND RV PARK

Rating: 7

on the Metolius River

See map pages 346–347

This pretty, wooded RV park on the Metolius River is world-famous for its fly-fishing and features an acre of riverfront lawn. Nearby recreation options include a golf course, swimming, boating, water-skiing, windsurfing, hiking and biking trails, a riding stable, and tennis courts. Winter activities vary from alpine and Nordic skiing to sledding, snowmobiling, and winter camping. A private bridge leads from the resort to Camp Sherman; the towns of Sisters and Bend are nearby (15 miles and 35 miles, respectively).

RV sites, facilities: There are 40 sites with full hookups (20, 30 amps) for RVs of any length, plus five cabins on the river. Fire pits, picnic tables, and patios are provided. Drinking water, restrooms, showers, laundry facilities, firewood, and a riverfront picnic facility are available. Propane, a store with groceries, fishing and sport supplies, a café, a post office, and ice are within a quarter mile. Leashed pets are permitted.

Reservations, fees: Reservations are accepted. The fee is $22–24 per night, plus $2 per person for more than two people and $1 per pet per night. Major credit cards are accepted. Open year-round.

Directions: From Albany, drive east on U.S. 20 for 87 miles (near Black Butte) to the sign for Camp Sherman. Turn north and drive about five miles to the stop sign. Turn right at the stop sign and drive about 300 feet to Cold Springs Resort Lane. Turn right and drive through the forest and the meadow, crossing Cold Springs Creek, to the resort.

Contact: Cold Springs Resort and RV Park, 25615 Cold Springs Resort Ln., Camp Sherman, OR 97730, 541/595-6271, fax 541/595-1400, website: www.coldsprings-resort.com.

12 HAYSTACK RESERVOIR

Rating: 5

**on Haystack Reservoir in Crooked River
National Grassland**

See map pages 346–347

This campground can be found in the high desert along the shore of Haystack Reservoir, a bright spot in an expansive desert landscape. The camps feature a moderate amount of privacy, as well as views of nearby Mount Jefferson. Haystack Lake receives a moderate number of people who boat, water-ski, swim, or fish. The camping and fishing crowds are also rated as moderate. A camp host is on-site.

RV sites, facilities: There are 24 sites for RVs up to 22 feet or tents. Picnic tables and fire grills are provided. Vault toilets and drinking water are available. A store, a café, a pay phone, and ice are within five miles. Boat docks and launching facilities are nearby. Leashed pets are permitted.

Reservations, fees: Reservations are not accepted. The fee is $8 per night, plus $3 per additional vehicle and a $3 day-use fee. Open mid-May to September.

Directions: From Madras, drive south on U.S. 97 for 10 miles to County Road 100. Turn southeast and drive three miles to Forest Road 96. Turn north and drive .5 mile to the campground.

Contact: Crooked River National Grassland, 813 SW Hwy. 97, Madras, OR 97741, 541/475-9272 or 541/416-6640, fax 541/416-6694.

13 KOA SISTERS/BEND

Rating: 7

on Branchwater Lake

See map pages 346–347

This park is located amid wooded mountains outside of Sisters at an elevation of 3,200 feet. Branchwater Lake offers swimming and good trout fishing. See the description of Belknap Springs Lodge for information about the surrounding area.

RV sites, facilities: There are 64 sites with full hookups (30 amps) for RVs up to 90 feet or tents and three cabins. Drinking water, cable TV, rest-

rooms, showers, an RV dump station, security, a pay phone, a laundry room, modem access, cell phone reception, limited groceries, ice, snacks, RV supplies, propane, and a barbecue are available. Recreational facilities include a sports field, a playground, a game room, horseshoes, a spa, and a heated swimming pool. An ATM is within three miles. Some facilities are wheelchair-accessible. Leashed pets are permitted.

Reservations, fees: Reserve at 800/562-0363. The fee is $20–40 per night, plus $2–4 per person for more than two people. Major credit cards are accepted. Open late March to November, weather permitting.

Directions: From Eugene, drive east on Highway 126 to its junction with U.S. 20. Turn east and drive 26 miles to Sisters. Continue southeast on U.S. 20 for three miles to the park on the right side of the highway.

Contact: KOA Sisters/Bend, 67667 Hwy. 20 W, Bend, OR 97701, 541/549-3021, fax 541/549-8144, website: www.koa.com.

14 TRAILBRIDGE

Rating: 6

**on Trailbridge Reservoir in Willamette National
Forest**

See map pages 346–347

This campground is set along the shore of Trailbridge Reservoir, where recreation options include boating, fishing, and hiking. Highway 126 east of McKenzie Bridge is a designated scenic route, providing a pleasant trip to the camp and making Trailbridge an exceptional spot for car campers. For a good side trip, take the beautiful 40-minute drive east to the little town of Sisters. From this camp there is access to the McKenzie River National Recreation Trail.

RV sites, facilities: There are 100-plus sites for RVs of any length and 28 sites for tents, with unlimited RV space at Trailbridge Flats. Picnic tables, garbage service, and fire grills are provided. Drinking water and vault and flush toilets are available. Boat ramps are nearby. Leashed pets are permitted.

Reservations, fees: Reservations are not accepted. The fee is $6 per night, plus $3 per additional

OREGON

vehicle. A senior discount is available. Open late April to late September.

Directions: From Eugene, drive east on Highway 126 for 47 miles to the town of McKenzie Bridge. Continue on Highway 126 for 13 miles to the signed turnoff for Trailbridge Reservoir. Turn left on Forest Road 1477 and drive a short distance; then bear left and continue .25 mile to the campground.

Contact: Willamette National Forest, McKenzie Ranger District, 57600 McKenzie Hwy., McKenzie Bridge, OR 97413, 541/822-3381, fax 541/822-7254.

15 OLALLIE

Rating: 7

on the McKenzie River in Willamette National Forest

See map pages 346–347

This campground (2,000 feet elevation) along the banks of the McKenzie River offers opportunities for boating, fishing, and hiking. Fishing for rainbow trout usually is good. Another bonus is easy access from Highway 126. The campground is two miles southwest of Trailbridge Reservoir off Highway 126.

RV sites, facilities: There are 17 sites for RVs up to 30 feet or tents. Picnic tables, garbage service, and fire grills are provided. Vault toilets and drinking water are available. A boat launch is nearby (nonmotorized boats only). Leashed pets are permitted.

Reservations, fees: Reserve at 877/444-6777 or online at www.reserveusa.com ($9 reservation fee). The fee is $12 per night, plus $6 per additional vehicle. Open mid-April to September, weather permitting.

Directions: From Eugene, drive east on Highway 126 for 47 miles to the town of McKenzie Bridge. Continue on Highway 126 for 11 miles to the campground on the left.

Contact: Willamette National Forest, McKenzie Ranger District, 57600 McKenzie Hwy., McKenzie Bridge, OR 97413, 541/822-3381, fax 541/822-7254.

16 MONA

Rating: 8

near Blue River Reservoir in Willamette National Forest

See map pages 346–347

This forested campground is set along the shore of Blue River Reservoir, close to where the Blue River joins it. A boat ramp is located across the river from the campground. After launching a boat, campers can ground it near the campsite. This camp is extremely popular when the reservoir is full.

RV sites, facilities: There are 23 sites for RVs up to 21 feet or tents. Picnic tables, garbage bins, and fire grills are provided. Drinking water, flush toilets, and cell phone reception are available. An ATM and a pay phone are within six miles. Some facilities are wheelchair-accessible. Leashed pets are permitted.

Reservations, fees: Reservations are not accepted. The fees are $12 per night and $20 per night for double sites, plus $6 per additional vehicle. A senior discount is available. Open mid-April to late September.

Directions: From Eugene, drive east on Highway 126 for 41 miles to Blue River. Continue east on Highway 126 for three miles to Forest Road 15. Turn north and drive three miles to the campground.

Contact: Willamette National Forest, McKenzie River Ranger District, Blue River Forest Service Center, P.O. Box 199, Blue River, OR 97413, 541/822-3317, fax 541/822-1255.

17 PATIO RV PARK

Rating: 7

near the South Fork of the McKenzie River

See map pages 346–347

This RV park is situated near the banks of the South Fork of the McKenzie River, not far from Cougar Lake, which offers opportunities for fishing, swimming, and water-skiing. Nearby recreation options include a golf course, hiking trails, and bike paths.

RV sites, facilities: There are 60 sites with full hookups (30, 50 amps) for RVs of any length.

OREGON

Picnic tables are provided. Drinking water, flush toilets, showers, firewood, cell phone reception, modem access, a recreation hall, video rentals, full group kitchen facilities, cable TV, and a laundry room are available. A store, an ATM, a pay phone, and a café are within two miles. Leashed pets are permitted.

Reservations, fees: Reserve at 800/650-0290. The fee is $23–25 per night, plus $2 per person for more than two people. Group rates are available. A senior discount is available. Major credit cards are accepted. Open year-round, weather permitting.

Directions: From Eugene, drive east on Highway 126 for 37 miles to the town of Blue River. Continue east on Highway 126 for six miles to McKenzie River Drive. Turn east and drive two miles to the park on the right.

Contact: Patio RV Park, 55636 McKenzie River Dr., Blue River, OR 97413, 541/822-3596, fax 541/822-8392, website: http://hometown.aol.com/thepatio.

18 DELTA

Rating: 8

on the McKenzie River in Willamette National Forest

See map pages 346–347

This popular campground sits along the banks of the McKenzie River. This spot is heavily forested, primarily with old-growth Douglas fir. The Delta Old Growth Nature Trail, a half-mile wheelchair-accessible interpretive trail, is adjacent to the campground. The camp also features an amphitheater. Nearby are Blue River and Cougar Reservoirs (seven and five miles away, respectively), both of which offer trout fishing, waterskiing, and swimming.

RV sites, facilities: There are 38 sites for RVs up to 36 feet or tents. Picnic tables, garbage bins, and fire grills are provided. Drinking water, vault toilets, and cell phone reception are available. An ATM and a pay phone are within three miles. Some facilities are wheelchair-accessible. Leashed pets are permitted.

Reservations, fees: Reservations are not accepted. The fees are $12 per night and $20 per night for a double site, plus $6 per additional vehicle.

A senior discount is available. Open mid-May to mid-October, weather permitting.

Directions: From Eugene, drive east on Highway 126 for 37 miles to the town of Blue River. Continue east on Highway 126 for five miles to Forest Road 19 (Aufderheide Scenic Byway). Turn right (south) and drive .1 mile to Forest Road 400. Turn right and drive one mile to the campground.

Contact: Willamette National Forest, McKenzie River Ranger District, Blue River Forest Service Center, P.O. Box 199, Blue River, OR 97413, 541/822-3317, fax 541/822-1255.

19 MCKENZIE BRIDGE

Rating: 8

on the McKenzie River in Willamette National Forest

See map pages 346–347

This campground (1,400 feet elevation) is set along the banks of the McKenzie River, one mile from the town of McKenzie Bridge. This stretch of river provides good evening fly-fishing for trout during the summer.

RV sites, facilities: There are 20 sites for RVs up to 35 feet or tents. Picnic tables, garbage service, and fire rings are provided. Vault toilets and drinking water are available. A grocery store, gasoline, restaurants, and a pay phone are available within one mile. Only nonmotorized boats are permitted. An ATM is within three miles. Leashed pets are permitted.

Reservations, fees: Reserve at 877/444-6777 or online at www.reserveusa.com ($9 reservation fee). The fee is $12 per night, plus $6 per additional vehicle. A senior discount is available. Open late April to early September.

Directions: From Eugene, drive east on Highway 126 for 46 miles to the campground entrance on the right (one mile west of the town of McKenzie Bridge).

Contact: Willamette National Forest, McKenzie Ranger District, 57600 McKenzie Hwy., McKenzie Bridge, OR 97413, 541/822-3381, fax 541/822-7254.

20 HORSE CREEK GROUP CAMP

Rating: 9

on Horse Creek in Willamette National Forest
See map pages 346–347

This campground reserved for groups is set on the banks of Horse Creek near the town of McKenzie Bridge. In spite of the name, no horse camping is permitted. Fishing is catch-and-release only. The camp sits at 1,400 feet elevation.

RV sites, facilities: This is a group site with 21 sites for RVs up to 35 feet or tents. Picnic tables, garbage service, and fire grills are provided. Drinking water, vault toilets, and cell phone reception are available. A pay phone is within two miles, and an ATM is within five miles. Leashed pets are permitted.

Reservations, fees: Reserve at 877/444-6777 or online at www.reserveusa.com ($9 reservation fee). The fees are $40 per night for up to 49 people and $60 per night for 50–100 people. Open May to October, weather permitting.

Directions: From Eugene, drive east on Highway 126 for 47 miles to the town of McKenzie Bridge and Horse Creek Road. Turn right (south) on Horse Creek Road and drive three miles to the campground on the left.

Contact: Willamette National Forest, McKenzie Ranger District, 57600 McKenzie Hwy., McKenzie Bridge, OR 97413, 541/822-3381, fax 541/822-7254.

21 PARADISE

Rating: 9

on the McKenzie River in Willamette National Forest
See map pages 346–347

This campground (1,600 feet elevation) along the banks of the McKenzie River may be right off the highway, but it offers a rustic, streamside setting with access to the McKenzie River National Recreation Trail. Trout fishing can be good here.

RV sites, facilities: There are 64 sites for RVs up to 40 feet or tents. Picnic tables, garbage service, and fire rings are provided. Flush, vault, and pit toilets, drinking water, a boat ramp, and firewood are available. A pay phone is within one

mile, and an ATM is within six miles. Leashed pets are permitted.

Reservations, fees: Reserve at 877/444-6777 or online at www.reserveusa.com ($9 reservation fee). The fees are $14 per night and $25 per night for double sites, plus $7 per additional vehicle. A senior discount is available. Open late April to mid-October.

Directions: From Eugene, drive east on Highway 126 for 47 miles to the town of McKenzie Bridge. Continue east on Highway 126 for 3.5 miles to the campground on the left.

Contact: Willamette National Forest, McKenzie Ranger District, 57600 McKenzie Hwy., McKenzie Bridge, OR 97413, 541/822-3381, fax 541/822-7254.

22 BELKNAP HOT SPRINGS RESORT

Rating: 9

on the McKenzie River
See map pages 346–347

This beautiful park has been featured on at least one magazine cover. It's in a wooded, mountainous area on the McKenzie River. Trout fishing can be excellent here. If you're looking for hiking opportunities, check out the Three Sisters and Mount Washington Wilderness Areas, both accessible by driving west of Sisters on Highway 242. Exceptionally scenic and pristine expanses of forest, they are well worth exploring. The Pacific Crest Trail runs north and south through both wilderness areas.

RV sites, facilities: There are 14 sites with full hookups (30, 50 amps) and 28 with partial hookups for RVs of any length, 15 sites for tents, a lodge with 18 rooms, and six cabins. Drinking water, restrooms, showers, an RV dump station, a store, and a pay phone are available. Recreational facilities include a hot-spring fed swimming pool, a recreation field, and a recreation hall. A coin-operated laundry is within 1.5 miles, and an ATM is within nine miles. Some facilities are wheelchair-accessible. Leashed pets are permitted at the campground and in three of the cabins. Pets are not permitted in the other cabins and lodge rooms.

Reservations, fees: Reserve at 541/822-3512. The

OREGON

fee is $19–20 per night, plus $7 per person for more than two people. Open year-round.

Directions: From Eugene, drive east on Highway 126 for 56 miles to Belknap Spring Road. Turn left and drive .5 mile. The road dead-ends at the lodge.

Contact: Belknap Hot Springs Resort, P.O. Box 2001, 59296 Belknap Springs Rd., McKenzie Bridge, OR 97413, 541/822-3512, fax 541/822-3327.

23 CROOKED RIVER RANCH RV PARK

Rating: 6

near Smith Rock State Park
See map pages 346–347

Spectacular wildlife abounds in this area. This campground is a short distance from Smith Rock State Park, which contains unusual, colorful volcanic formations overlooking the Crooked River Canyon. Lake Billy Chinook to the north is a good spot for water-skiing and fishing for bass and panfish. The park has a basketball court and a softball field; nearby recreation options include fishing, golf, and tennis. One of Oregon's nicest golf courses is next door.

RV sites, facilities: There are 87 sites for RVs of any length, including 35 with full hookups (20, 30, 50 amps), 45 with partial hookups, and 15 drive-through sites, plus 20 tent sites. Drinking water, flush toilets, an RV dump station, cable TV, a pay phone, cell phone reception, showers, a store, a café, laundry facilities, ice, a playground, a kiddie pool, and an Olympic-size swimming pool are available. An ATM is within a quarter mile. Leashed pets are permitted.

Reservations, fees: Reserve at 800/841-0563. The fee is $14–24 per night. Major credit cards are accepted. Open mid-March to late October.

Directions: From Redmond, drive north on U.S. 97 for six miles to Lower Bridge Way. Turn west on Lower Bridge Way at Terrebonne and drive to 43rd Street. Turn right and drive seven miles (the road names changes to Chinook, then to Clubhouse Road) to Hays Lane. Turn right on Hays Lane and drive .25 mile to the park.

Contact: Crooked River Ranch RV Park, P.O. Box 1448, Crooked River Ranch, OR 97760, 541/923-1441 or 800/841-0563, website: www.crookedriverranch.com.

24 INDIAN FORD

Rating: 4

on Indian Ford Creek in Deschutes National Forest
See map pages 346–347

This campground is on the banks of Indian Ford Creek at an elevation of 3,250 feet. There's a lot of traffic noise from U.S. 20. The camp is used primarily by overnighters on their way to the town of Sisters. The campground is sprinkled with aspen trees, and great bird-watching opportunities are available.

RV sites, facilities: There are 25 sites for RVs up to 40 feet or tents. Picnic tables, garbage service, and fire grills are provided. Vault toilets are available. There is no drinking water. A pay phone, an ATM, a coin-operated laundry, and groceries are available within six miles. Leashed pets are permitted.

Reservations, fees: Reservations are not accepted. The fee is $10 per night, plus $5 per additional vehicle. A senior discount is available. Open May to mid-October.

Directions: From Albany, drive east on U.S. 20 to the junction with Highway 126. Continue east on Highway 126 and drive 21 miles to the campground on the left.

Contact: Deschutes National Forest, Sisters Ranger District, P.O. Box 249, Sisters, OR 97759, 541/549-7700, fax 541/549-7746.

25 COLD SPRINGS

Rating: 7

in Deschutes National Forest
See map pages 346–347

This wooded campground is set at 3,400 feet elevation at the source of a small creek. It's just far enough off the main drag to be missed by many campers. Spring and early summer are the times for great bird-watching in the area's abundant aspen.

RV sites, facilities: There are 23 sites for RVs up to 40 feet or tents. Picnic tables, fire grills, and garbage service are provided. Vault toilets and drinking water are available. A pay phone, an ATM, a coin-operated laundry, and groceries are available within six miles. Leashed pets are permitted.

Reservations, fees: Reservations are not accepted. The fee is $14 per night, plus $7 per additional vehicle. A senior discount is available. Open May to September.

Directions: From Albany, drive east on U.S. 20 to the junction with Highway 126. Continue east on Highway 126 and drive 26 miles to Sisters and Highway 242. Turn right and drive 4.2 miles to the campground on the right.

Contact: Deschutes National Forest, Sisters Ranger District, P.O. Box 249, Sisters, OR 97759, 541/549-7700, fax 541/549-7746.

26 TUMALO STATE PARK

Rating: 7

on the Deschutes River
See map pages 346–347

Trout fishing can be good at this camp along the banks of the Deschutes River, just five miles from Bend. Mount Bachelor is just up the road and provides plenty of winter recreation opportunities. The swimming area is generally safe and a good spot for children. Rafting is also an option here.

RV sites, facilities: There are 21 sites with full hookups (20, 30 amps) for RVs up to 44 feet, 61 sites for tents, a special camping area for hikers and bicyclists, seven yurts, and a group area for tent camping. Picnic tables and fire grills are provided. Drinking water, flush toilets, showers, firewood, ice, a pay phone, and a playground are available. A store, a café, and ice are within one mile. An ATM is within five miles, and a coin-operated laundry is within 10 miles. Leashed pets are permitted.

Reservations, fees: Reserve at 800/452-5687 or online at www.oregonstateparks.org ($6 reservation fee). The fees are $17–21 per night, $4 per night for hikers/bikers, $29 per night for yurts, and $64 per night for the group area, plus $7 per additional vehicle. Major credit cards are accepted. Open year-round.

Directions: From Bend, drive north on U.S. 97 for two miles to U.S. 20 West. Turn northwest and drive five miles to Tumalo Junction. Turn

left at Tumalo Junction onto Cook Avenue, and drive one mile to the campground.

Contact: High Desert Management Unit, 62976 O. B. Riley Rd., Bend, OR 97701, 541/388-6055 or 800/551-6949.

27 BEND KAMPGROUND

Rating: 6

near Bend
See map pages 346–347

Recreation options near this camp include a golf course, hiking trails, bike paths, and tennis courts.

RV sites, facilities: There are 34 sites with full hookups (30, 50 amps) and 35 with partial hookups for RVs of any length, 40 of which are drive-through sites, plus 20 tent sites. Drinking water and picnic tables are provided. Flush toilets, showers, a laundry room, a pay phone, cell phone reception, an ATM, modem access, a store, a deli, ice, firewood, a playground, a swimming pool, a recreation room, propane, gasoline, and an RV dump station are available. Leashed pets are permitted.

Reservations, fees: Reserve at 800/713-5333. The fee is $18–28 per night, plus $2–3 per person for more than two people and $4 per additional vehicle. Major credit cards are accepted. Open year-round.

Directions: In Bend, drive north on U.S. 97 for two miles to the park entrance road.

Contact: Bend Kampground, 63615 N. U.S. 97, Bend, OR 97701, 541/382-7738, fax 541/382-3149.

28 SCANDIA RV AND MOBILE PARK

Rating: 5

near the Deschutes River
See map pages 346–347

This park near the Deschutes River is close to a golf course, a stable, bike paths, and tennis courts and is in the middle of a beautiful pine forest.

RV sites, facilities: There are 60 sites with full hookups (20, 30, 50 amps) for RVs of any length or tents; 10 are drive-through sites. Drinking water, picnic tables, cable TV, a pay phone, modem access, cell phone reception, and sewer hookups are provided. Flush toilets, showers, and a laundry room are available. Propane, an RV dump station, a store, an ATM, a café, and ice are within one mile. Leashed pets are permitted.

Reservations, fees: Reserve at 541/382-6206. The fee is $22 per night, plus $2 per person for more than two people. Major credit cards are accepted. Open year-round.

Directions: In Bend, drive south on U.S. 97 for .5 mile to the park entrance.

Contact: Scandia RV and Mobile Park, 61415 S. U.S. 97, Bend, OR 97702, 541/382-6206, fax 541/382-4087.

29 CROWN VILLA RV RESORT

Rating: 6

near Bend

See map pages 346–347

This RV park offers large and landscaped grassy sites. Nearby recreation options include horseback riding and golf.

RV sites, facilities: There are 116 sites for RVs of any length; 106 have full hookups (50 amps) and 10 have partial hookups. Picnic tables are provided. Drinking water, flush toilets, showers, cable TV, a laundry room, propane, ice, a courtyard with fire pits, spa, big screen TV, a lounge with a full kitchen, tennis courts, a volleyball area, a putting green, shuffleboard, an RV dump station, cell phone reception, a pay phone, modem access, and a playground are available. A store, an ATM, and a café are within one mile. Leashed pets are permitted.

Reservations, fees: Reservations are accepted. The fee is $30–45 per night, plus $2.50 per person for more than two people. A senior discount is available. Major credit cards are accepted. Open year-round.

Directions: From Bend, drive south on Business 97 for three miles to Murphy Road. Turn left and drive to Brosterhous Road. Turn right and drive to the park.

Contact: Crown Villa RV Resort, 60801 Brosterhous Rd., Bend, OR 97702, 541/388-1131.

30 BLACK CANYON

Rating: 7

on the Middle Fork of the Willamette River in Willamette National Forest

See map pages 346–347

This campground is set along the banks of the Middle Fork of the Willamette River, not far above Lookout Point Reservoir, where fishing and boating are available. The camp is pretty and wooded and has comfortable sites. Within the camp is a one-mile-long nature trail with interpretive signs. Weekend programs are staged in the amphitheater in July and August. You will hear train noise from the other side of the river.

RV sites, facilities: There are 72 sites for RVs up to 44 feet or tents. Picnic tables, garbage service, and fire grills are provided. Drinking water, vault toilets, cell phone reception, and firewood are available. An RV dump station, a café, a pay phone, an ATM, and a coin-operated laundry are within six miles. Launching facilities are nearby at the south end of Lookout Point Reservoir. Some facilities are wheelchair-accessible. Leashed pets are permitted.

Reservations, fees: Reservations are not accepted. The fee is $14–20 per night, plus $7 per additional vehicle. Open late April to late September.

Directions: From south Eugene on I-5, take Exit 188 to Highway 58. Drive southeast on Highway 58 for 27 miles to the camp on the left (six miles west of Oakridge).

Contact: Willamette National Forest, Middle Fork Ranger District, Lowell Service Center, 60 Pioneer St., Lowell, OR 97452, 541/937-2129, fax 541/937-2032.

31 WINBERRY

Rating: 6

on Winberry Creek in Willamette National Forest

See map pages 346–347

This campground is on Winberry Creek in a tree-shaded area. The closest hiking option is Station Butte Trail, just downstream from the campground on Forest Road 1802-150. Be cautious—poison oak grows at the top of the butte.

OREGON

RV sites, facilities: There are two sites for RVs up to 16 feet and five sites for tents. Picnic tables, garbage service, and fire grills are provided. Drinking water, vault toilets, cell phone reception, and two A-frame shelters are available. Leashed pets are permitted.

Reservations, fees: Reservations are not accepted. The fee is $12–25 per night, plus $6 per additional vehicle. A senior discount is available. Open late May to early October, weather permitting.

Directions: From south Eugene on I-5, take Exit 188 to Highway 58. Drive 11 miles south to Lowell and Pioneer Street (at the covered bridge). Turn left and drive less than .25 mile to West Boundary Road. Turn left and drive one block to Lowell Jasper Road. Turn right and drive 1.5 miles to Unity and Place Road. Turn right and drive about one mile to a fork with Winberry Road. Bear right and drive six miles (the road becomes Forest Road 1802). Continue 3.5 miles to the campground.

Contact: Willamette National Forest, Middle Fork Ranger District, Lowell Service Center, 60 Pioneer St., Lowell, OR 97452, 541/937-2129, fax 541/937-2032.

32 BEDROCK

Rating: 6

on Fall Creek in Willamette National Forest
See map pages 346–347

This campground along the banks of Fall Creek is one of the access points for the scenic Fall Creek National Recreation Trail, which in turn offers access to Jones Trail, a six-mile uphill climb.

RV sites, facilities: There are 19 sites for RVs up to 22 feet or tents. Picnic tables, garbage service, and fire grills are provided. Vault toilets, drinking water, and cell phone reception are available. Leashed pets are permitted.

Reservations, fees: Reservations are not accepted. The fee is $12 per night, plus $6 per additional vehicle. A senior discount is available. Open May to October.

Directions: From south Eugene on I-5, take Exit 188 to Highway 58. Drive 25 miles south to Lowell and Pioneer Street (at the covered bridge). Turn left and drive less than .25 mile to West

Boundary Road. Turn left and drive one block to Lowell Jasper Road. Turn right and drive 1.5 miles to Unity and Place Road. Turn right and drive about one mile to a fork with North Shore Road. Bear left onto North Shore Road (Big Fall Creek Road) and drive about 14 miles (the road becomes Forest Road 18) to the campground on the left.

Contact: Willamette National Forest, Middle Fork Ranger District, Lowell Service Center, 60 Pioneer St., Lowell, OR 97452, 541/937-2129, fax 541/937-2032.

33 PUMA CREEK

Rating: 6

on Fall Creek in Willamette National Forest
See map pages 346–347

This campground is set along the banks of Fall Creek, across from the Fall Creek National Recreation Trail. It's one of four camps in the immediate area.

RV sites, facilities: There are 11 sites for RVs up to 20 feet or tents. Picnic tables, garbage containers, and fire grills are provided. Vault toilets and drinking water are available. Leashed pets are permitted.

Reservations, fees: Reservations are not accepted. The fee is $12 per night, plus $6 per additional vehicle. A senior discount is available. Open May to early October.

Directions: From I-5 south of Eugene, take Exit 188 to Highway 58. Drive about 25 miles to Lowell. Turn left at Pioneer Street (at the covered bridge), drive .2 mile and turn left on West Boundary Road. Drive one block and turn right at Lowell Jasper Road. Drive 1.5 miles to Place Road and turn right. Drive about one mile to a fork and bear left onto North Shore Road (Big Fall Creek Road). Drive about 16 miles (the road becomes Forest Road 18) to the campground on the left.

Contact: Willamette National Forest, Middle Fork Ranger District, Lowell Service Center, 60 Pioneer St., Lowell, OR 97452, 541/937-2129, fax 541/937-2032.

OREGON

34 FRENCH PETE

Rating: 8

on the South Fork of the McKenzie River in Willamette National Forest

See map pages 346–347

This quiet, wooded campground is set on the banks of the South Fork of the McKenzie River and French Pete Creek. Fishing is catch-and-release only. A trail across the road from the campground provides access to the Three Sisters Wilderness. French Pete is only two miles from Cougar Reservoir, and the camp attracts campers wanting to use Cougar Reservoir facilities. Two more primitive camps (Homestead and Frissell Crossing) are located a few miles southeast on the same road.

RV sites, facilities: There are 17 sites for RVs up to 30 feet or tents. Picnic tables, garbage containers, and fire grills are provided. Drinking water and vault toilets are available. Some facilities are wheelchair-accessible. Leashed pets are permitted.

Reservations, fees: Reservations are not accepted. The fees are $12 per night and $25 for a double site, plus $6 for additional vehicle. A senior discount is available. Open mid-May to mid-September.

Directions: From Eugene, drive east on Highway 126 for 41 miles to the town of Blue River. Continue east on Highway 126 for five miles to Forest Road 19 (Aufderheide Scenic Byway). Turn right (south) and drive 11 miles to the campground.

Contact: Willamette National Forest, McKenzie River Ranger District, Blue River Forest Service Center, P.O. Box 199, Blue River, OR 97413, 541/822-3317, fax 541/822-1255.

35 KIAHANIE

Rating: 5

on the West Fork of the Willamette River in Willamette National Forest

See map pages 346–347

This is one heck of a spot for fly-fishing (the only kind allowed). This remote campground is set at 2,200 feet elevation along the North Fork of the Willamette River, a designated Wild and Scenic River. If you want beauty and quiet among enormous Douglas fir trees, you came to the right place. An even more remote campground, Box Canyon Horse Camp, is farther north on Forest Road 19.

RV sites, facilities: There are 19 sites for RVs up to 24 feet or tents. Picnic tables, garbage bins, a recycling center, and fire rings are provided. Drinking water and vault toilets are available. Leashed pets are permitted.

Reservations, fees: Reservations are not accepted. The fee is $12 per night, plus $6 per additional vehicle. Open late May to September.

Directions: From south Eugene on I-5, take Exit 188 to Highway 58. Drive 31 miles southeast on Highway 58 to Westfir. Take the Westfir exit and drive two miles to Westfir and the junction with Aufderheide Scenic Byway (Forest Road 19). Bear left (northeast) and drive 19 miles to the campground.

Contact: Willamette National Forest, Middle Fork Ranger District, 46375 Hwy. 58, Westfir, OR 97492, 541/782-2283, fax 541/782-5306.

36 HOMESTEAD

Rating: 8

on the South Fork of the McKenzie River in Willamette National Forest

See map pages 346–347

This quiet little campground is set among the trees along the banks of the South Fork of the McKenzie River. It's primitive, little known, and free. Nearby Frissell Crossing has water available from a hand pump.

RV sites, facilities: There are seven sites for RVs up to 32 feet or tents. Picnic tables and fire grills are provided. Vault toilets are available, but there is no drinking water. All garbage must be packed out. Leashed pets are permitted.

Reservations, fees: Reservations are not accepted. There is no fee for camping. Open year-round.

Directions: From Eugene, drive east on Highway 126 for 41 miles to Blue River. Continue east on Highway 126 for five miles to Forest Road 19 (Aufderheide Scenic Byway). Turn south on Forest Road 19 and drive 17 miles to the camp.

Contact: Willamette National Forest, McKenzie

River Ranger District, 57600 McKenzie Highway, Mckenzie Bridge, OR, 97413, 541/822-3381, fax 541/922-7254.

37 FRISSELL CROSSING

🚶 🚲 🐕 🚐 ⛺

Rating: 8

near the Three Sisters Wilderness in Willamette National Forest

See map pages 346–347

This campground (elevation 2,800 feet) sits on the banks of the South Fork of the McKenzie River, adjacent to a trailhead that provides access to the backcountry of the Three Sisters Wilderness. Frissell Crossing is the only camp in the immediate area that has drinking water. If you're looking for solitude, this place should be heaven to you. Homestead provides a free, primitive alternative.

RV sites, facilities: There are 12 sites for RVs up to 36 feet or tents. Picnic tables, garbage bins, and fire grills are provided. Drinking water and vault toilets are available. Leashed pets are permitted.

Reservations, fees: Reservations are not accepted. The fee is $12 per night, plus $6 per additional vehicle. A senior discount is available. Open mid-May to mid-September.

Directions: From Eugene, drive east on Highway 126 for 37 miles to Blue River. Continue east on Highway 126 for five miles to Forest Road 19 (Aufderheide Scenic Byway). Turn south and drive 23 miles to the camp.

Contact: Willamette National Forest, McKenzie River Ranger District, 57600 McKenzie Highway, Mckenzie Bridge, OR, 97413, 541/822-3381, fax 541/922-7254.

38 SODA CREEK

🚶 🎣 🚤 🍴 🐕 ♿ 🚐 ⛺

Rating: 5

near Sparks Lake in Deschutes National Forest

See map pages 346–347

This campground, nestled between two meadows in a pastoral setting, is on the road to Sparks Lake. Boating—particularly canoeing—is ideal at Sparks Lake, about a two-mile drive away. Also at Sparks Lake, a loop trail hugs the shore; about

a half mile of it is paved and barrier-free. Only fly-fishing is permitted. The camp sits at 5,450 feet elevation.

RV sites, facilities: There are 10 sites for RVs up to 22 feet or tents. Picnic tables and fire grills are provided. Vault toilets and cell phone reception are available. There is no drinking water, and all garbage must be packed out. Leashed pets are permitted.

Reservations, fees: Reservations are not accepted. A Northwest Forest Pass ($5 daily fee or $30 annual fee per parked vehicle) is required. A senior discount is available. Open July to October, weather permitting.

Directions: From Bend, drive southwest on Cascades Lakes Highway (also called Century Drive Highway and County Road 46) for 26.2 miles to Forest Road 400 (at sign for Sparks Lake). Turn left (east) and drive 100 yards to the campground.

Contact: Deschutes National Forest, Bend–Fort Rock Ranger District, 1230 NE 3rd St., Suite A-262, Bend, OR 97701, 541/383-4000, fax 541/383-4700.

39 POINT

🚶 🎣 🚣 🚤 🍴 🐕 ♿ 🚐 ⛺

Rating: 8

on Elk Lake in Deschutes National Forest

See map pages 346–347

This campground is situated along the shore of Elk Lake at an elevation of 4,900 feet. Fishing for kokanee salmon, rainbow trout, and brown trout can be good; hiking is another option. Swimming and water sports are popular during warm weather.

RV sites, facilities: There are 10 sites for RVs up to 22 feet or tents. Picnic tables, garbage service, and fire grills are provided. Vault toilets and drinking water are available. Boat docks and launching facilities are on-site. Boat rentals, a store, a restaurant, gas, and propane are at Elk Lake Resort, one mile away. Leashed pets are permitted.

Reservations, fees: Reservations are not accepted. The fee is $10 per night, plus $5 per additional vehicle and $10 for an additional RV. A senior discount is available. Open late May to late September, weather permitting.

Directions: From Bend, drive southwest on Cascades Lakes Highway (Century Drive Highway, which becomes County Road 46) for 34 miles to the campground on the left.

Contact: Deschutes National Forest, Bend–Fort Rock Ranger District, 1230 NE 3rd St., Suite A-262, Bend, OR 97701, 541/383-4000, fax 541/383-4700.

40 ELK LAKE

Rating: 8

on Elk Lake in Deschutes National Forest
See map pages 346–347

This campground hugs the shore of Elk Lake at 4,900 feet elevation. It is adjacent to Elk Lake Resort, which has boat rentals, a store, a restaurant, gas, and propane. Elk Lake is popular for windsurfing and sailing. See the previous description of Point for recreation options.

RV sites, facilities: There are 23 sites for RVs up to 22 feet or tents. Picnic tables, garbage service, and fire grills are provided. Vault toilets, drinking water, and cell phone reception are available. Boat-launching facilities are on-site. Boat rentals can be obtained nearby. Leashed pets are permitted.

Reservations, fees: Reservations are not accepted. The fee is $10 per night, plus $5 per additional vehicle and $10 per extra RV. A senior discount is available. Open June to September, weather permitting.

Directions: From Bend, drive southwest on Cascades Lakes Highway (Century Drive Highway, which becomes County Road 46) and drive 33.1 miles to the campground at the north end of Elk Lake.

Contact: Deschutes National Forest, Bend–Fort Rock Ranger District, 1230 NE 3rd St., Suite A-262, Bend, OR 97701, 541/383-4000, fax 541/383-4700.

41 SOUTH

Rating: 8

on Hosmer Lake in Deschutes National Forest
See map pages 346–347

This campground is located along the shore of Hosmer Lake, adjacent to Mallard Marsh.

RV sites, facilities: There are 23 sites for RVs up to 22 feet or tents. Picnic tables, garbage service, and fire grills are provided. Vault toilets, cell phone reception, and boat launch facilities are available. No drinking water is provided. Leashed pets are permitted.

Reservations, fees: Reservations are not accepted. The fee is $5 per night per vehicle. A senior discount is available. Open late May to late September, weather permitting.

Directions: From Bend, drive southwest on Cascades Lakes Highway (Century Drive Highway, which becomes County Road 46) and drive 35.5 miles to Forest Road 4625. Turn left (east) and drive 1.2 miles to the campground on the right.

Contact: Deschutes National Forest, Bend–Fort Rock Ranger District, 1230 NE 3rd St., Suite A-262, Bend, OR 97701, 541/383-4000, fax 541/383-4700.

42 LAVA LAKE

Rating: 10

on Lava Lake in Deschutes National Forest
See map pages 346–347

This well-designed campground sits on the shore of pretty Lava Lake at 4,750 feet elevation. Mount Bachelor and the Three Sisters are in the background, making a classic picture. Boating and fishing are popular here. A bonus is nearby Lava Lake Resort, which has showers, laundry facilities, an RV dump station, a store, gasoline, and propane.

RV sites, facilities: There are 43 sites for RVs up to 30 feet or tents. Picnic tables, garbage service, and fire grills are provided. Vault toilets, drinking water, cell phone reception, and a fish-cleaning station are available. Boat docks and launching facilities are on-site. Boat rentals are nearby. Some facilities are wheelchair-accessible. Leashed pets are permitted.

Reservations, fees: Reservations are not accepted. The fee is $10 per night, plus $5 per additional vehicle and $10 per extra RV. A senior discount is available. Open mid-April to October, weather permitting.

Directions: From Bend, drive southwest on Cascades Lakes Highway (Century Drive Highway, which becomes County Road 46) and drive 38.4

miles to Forest Road 4600-500. Turn left (east) and drive one mile to the campground.

Contact: Deschutes National Forest, Bend–Fort Rock Ranger District, 1230 NE 3rd St., Suite A-262, Bend, OR 97701, 541/383-4000, fax 541/383-4700.

43 SALMON CREEK FALLS

Rating: 8

on Salmon Creek in Willamette National Forest
See map pages 346–347

This pretty campground sits in a lush, old-growth forest, right along Salmon Creek. The rocky gorge area creates two small but beautiful waterfalls and several deep pools in the clear, blue-green waters. Springtime brings a full range of wildflowers and wild thimbleberries; hazelnuts abound in the summer. This area is a popular recreation spot.

RV sites, facilities: There are 14 sites for RVs up to 24 feet or tents. Picnic tables, garbage bins, and fire grills are provided. Drinking water, vault toilets, and cell phone reception are available. A store, a café, a coin-operated laundry, a pay phone, an ATM, and ice are available within five miles. Leashed pets are permitted.

Reservations, fees: Reservations are not accepted. The fee is $12 per night, plus $6 per additional vehicle. A senior discount is available. Open late April to September.

Directions: From south Eugene on I-5, take Exit 188 to Highway 58. Drive southeast on Highway 58 for 35 miles to Oakridge and the signal light for downtown. Turn left on Crestview Street and drive .25 mile to 1st Street. Turn right and drive six miles (the road becomes Forest Road 24, then Salmon Creek Road) to the campground entrance on the right.

Contact: Willamette National Forest, Middle Fork Ranger District, 46375 Hwy. 58, Westfir, OR 97492, 541/782-2283, fax 541/782-5306.

44 NORTH WALDO

Rating: 10

on Waldo Lake in Willamette National Forest
See map pages 346–347

This camp, at an elevation of 5,400 feet, is the most popular of the Waldo Lake campgrounds. The drier environment supports fewer mosquitoes, but they can still be plentiful in season. The boat launch is deeper than the others on the lake, making it more accommodating for large sailboats. North Waldo is also a popular starting point to many wilderness trails and lakes, most notably the Rigdon, Wahanna, and Torrey Lakes trails. Waldo Lake has the special distinction of being one of the three purest lakes in the world. Of those three lakes, two are in Oregon (the other is Crater Lake), and the third is in Siberia. Amphitheater programs are presented here on weekends from late July to Labor Day.

RV sites, facilities: There are 58 sites for RVs up to 30 feet or tents. Picnic tables, garbage bins, and fire rings are provided. Drinking water, vault and flush toilets, cell phone reception, a swimming area, a recycle center, and an amphitheater are available. A pay phone is within eight miles. Boat-launching facilities are available. Leashed pets are permitted.

Reservations, fees: Reservations are not accepted. The fee is $12–14 per night, plus $7 per additional vehicle. A senior discount is available. A Northwest Forest Pass ($5 daily fee or $30 annual fee per parked vehicle) is required at the nearby boat launch and trailheads. Open July to September, weather permitting.

Directions: From Eugene, drive south on I-5 for four miles to Exit 188 and Highway 58. Turn southeast and drive about 60 miles southeast to Waldo Lake Road (Forest Road 5897). Turn left and drive north on Waldo Lake Road for 14 miles to Forest Road 5898. Turn left and drive about two miles to the campground at the northeast end of Waldo Lake.

Contact: Willamette National Forest, Middle Fork Ranger District, 46375 Hwy. 58, Westfir, OR 97492, 541/782-2283, fax 541/782-5306.

45 ISLET

Rating: 10

on Waldo Lake in Willamette National Forest
See map pages 346–347

You'll find sandy beaches and an interpretive sign at this campground at the north end of Waldo Lake. The winds blow consistently every after-

OREGON

noon. A picnic table placed strategically on the rock jetty provides a great spot to enjoy a sunset. A one-mile shoreline trail stretches between Islet and North Waldo Campground. Bring your mosquito repellent June to August; you'll need it. For more information, see the previous description of North Waldo.

RV sites, facilities: There are 55 sites for RVs up to 30 feet or tents. Picnic tables, garbage bins, and fire rings are provided. Drinking water, vault toilets, a recycling center, and cell phone reception are available. Boat-launching facilities are available. A pay phone is within 7.5 miles. Leashed pets are permitted.

Reservations, fees: Reservations are not accepted. The fees are $12 per night and $20 per night for double sites, plus $6 per additional vehicle. A senior discount is available. A Northwest Forest Pass ($5 daily fee or $30 annual fee per parked vehicle) is required at the nearby boat launch and trailheads. Open July to September, weather permitting.

Directions: From Eugene, drive south on I-5 for four miles to Exit 188 and Highway 58. Turn southeast and drive about 60 miles southeast to Waldo Lake Road (Forest Road 5897). Turn left and drive north on Waldo Lake Road for 14 miles to Forest Road 5898. Turn left and continue 1.5 miles to the campground at the northeast end of Waldo Lake.

Contact: Willamette National Forest, Middle Fork Ranger District, 46375 Hwy. 58, Westfir, OR 97492, 541/782-2283, fax 541/782-5306.

46 SHADOW BAY

Rating: 10

on Waldo Lake in Willamette National Forest
See map pages 346–347

This campground is situated on a large bay at the south end of Waldo Lake. It has a considerably wetter environment than either North Waldo or Islet, supporting a more diverse and prolific ground cover as well as more mosquitoes. The camp receives considerably lighter use than North Waldo. You have access to the Shore Line Trail and then the Waldo Lake Trail from here. The boating speed limit is 10 mph for all of Waldo Lake.

RV sites, facilities: There are 92 sites for RVs up to 24 feet or tents. Picnic tables, garbage bins, a recycle center, and fire grills are provided. Drink-

ing water, vault and flush toilets, and cell phone reception are available. Boat-launching facilities are nearby. Leashed pets are permitted.

Reservations, fees: Reservations are not accepted. The fee is $14 per night, plus $7 per additional vehicle. A senior discount is available. A Northwest Forest Pass ($5 daily fee or $30 annual fee per parked vehicle) is required at the nearby boat launch and trailheads. Open July to September, weather permitting.

Directions: From Eugene, drive south on I-5 for four miles to Exit 188 and Highway 58. Turn southeast and drive about 60 miles southeast to Waldo Lake Road (Forest Road 5897). Turn left on Waldo Lake Road and drive north for 6.5 miles to the Shadow Bay turnoff. Turn left and drive on Forest Road 5896 to the campground at the south end of Waldo Lake.

Contact: Willamette National Forest, Middle Fork Ranger District, 46375 Hwy. 58, Westfir, OR 97492, 541/782-2283, fax 541/782-5306.

47 CRANE PRAIRIE

Rating: 6

on Crane Prairie Reservoir in Deschutes National Forest
See map pages 346–347

This campground along the north shore of Crane Prairie Reservoir is a good spot for fishing and boating. World-renowned for rainbow trout fishing, this reservoir is also popular for bass fishing.

RV sites, facilities: There are 130 sites for RVs up to 30 feet and six sites for tents. Picnic tables, garbage service, and fire grills are provided. Drinking water, vault toilets, and cell phone reception are available. Boat docks, launching facilities, and a fish-cleaning station are available on-site. Boat rentals, showers, and gas are nearby. Some facilities are wheelchair-accessible. Leashed pets are permitted.

Reservations, fees: Reservations are not accepted. The fee is $10–12 per night, plus $5 per additional vehicle and $10 per extra RV. A senior discount is available. Open April 20 to October, weather permitting.

Directions: From Bend, drive south on U.S. 97 for 26.8 miles to Wickiup Junction and County Road 43. Turn right (west) on County Road 43 and drive 11 miles to Forest Road 42. Continue west on Forest Road 42 for 5.4 miles to Forest Road 4270. Turn right (north) and drive 4.2 miles to the campground on the left.

Contact: Deschutes National Forest, Bend–Fort Rock Ranger District, 1230 NE 3rd St., Suite A-262, Bend, OR 97701, 541/383-4000, fax 541/383-4700.

48 QUINN RIVER

Rating: 5

on Crane Prairie Reservoir in Deschutes National Forest
See map pages 346–347

This campground is set along the western shore of Crane Prairie Reservoir, a popular spot for anglers and a great spot for bird-watching. A separate, large parking lot is available for boats and trailers. Boat speed is limited to 10 mph here. The elevation is 4,450 feet.

RV sites, facilities: There are 41 sites for RVs up to 30 feet or tents. Picnic tables, garbage service, and fire grills are provided. Drinking water, vault toilets, and cell phone reception are available. Boat launch facilities are available. Some facilities are wheelchair-accessible. Leashed pets are permitted.

Reservations, fees: Reservations are not accepted. The fee is $10 per night, plus $5 per additional vehicle and $10 per extra RV. A senior discount is available. Open late April to mid-October.

Directions: From Bend, drive southwest on Cascade Lakes Highway (Century Drive Highway, which becomes County Road 46) and drive 48 miles to the campground.

Contact: Deschutes National Forest, Bend–Fort Rock Ranger District, 1230 NE 3rd St., Suite A-262, Bend, OR 97701, 541/383-4000, fax 541/383-4700.

49 ROCK CREEK

Rating: 5

on Crane Prairie Reservoir in Deschutes National Forest
See map pages 346–347

This campground is set along the west shore of Crane Prairie Reservoir. There are other campgrounds at Crane Prairie for self-contained RVs, but no hookups or RV services. See the previous description of Quinn River for more information. The elevation is 4,450 feet.

RV sites, facilities: There are 31 sites for RVs up to 30 feet or tents. Picnic tables, garbage service, and fire grills are provided. Drinking water, a fish-cleaning station, cell phone reception, and vault toilets are available. Boat docks and launching facilities are on-site. Some facilities are wheelchair-accessible. Leashed pets are permitted.

Reservations, fees: Reservations are not accepted. The fee is $10 per night, plus $5 per additional vehicle and $10 per extra RV. A senior discount is available. Open mid-April to October, weather permitting.

Directions: From Bend, drive southwest on Cascade Lakes Highway (Century Drive Highway, which becomes County Road 46) for 48.8 miles to the campground.

Contact: Deschutes National Forest, Bend–Fort Rock Ranger District, 1230 NE 3rd St., Suite A-262, Bend, OR 97701, 541/383-4000, fax 541/383-4700.

50 FALL RIVER

Rating: 5

on the Fall River in Deschutes National Forest
See map pages 346–347

This campground is on the Fall River, where fishing is restricted to fly-fishing only. Check the regulations for other restrictions. Fall River is beautiful, crystal clear, and cold. Fall River Trail meanders along the river for 3.5 miles and is open for bicycling. The elevation is 4,300 feet.

RV sites, facilities: There are 10 sites for RVs up to 22 feet or tents. Picnic tables, garbage service, and fire grills are provided. Vault toilets and cell phone reception are available. There is no drinking water. Leashed pets are permitted.

Reservations, fees: Reservations are not accepted. The fee is $5 per night per vehicle. A senior discount is available. Open mid-April to October, weather permitting.

Directions: From Bend, drive south on U.S. 97 for 17.3 miles to Forest Road 42. Turn right (southwest) and drive 12.2 miles to the campground.

OREGON

Contact: Deschutes National Forest, Bend–Fort Rock Ranger District, 1230 NE 3rd St., Suite A-262, Bend, OR 97701, 541/383-4000, fax 541/383-4700.

51 BIG RIVER

Rating: 4

on the Deschutes River in Deschutes National Forest

See map pages 346–347

This is a good spot. Located between the banks of the Deschutes River and the road, it has easy access and is popular as an overnight camp. Rafting, fishing, and motorized boating are permitted.

RV sites, facilities: There are nine sites for RVs up to 22 feet or tents and two tent sites. There is also one group site that can accommodate up to 60 people. Picnic tables, garbage service, and fire grills are provided. Vault toilets and cell phone reception are available. There is no drinking water. Boat-launching facilities are on-site. Some facilities are wheelchair-accessible. Leashed pets are permitted.

Reservations, fees: Reservations are not accepted. The fee is $5 per night. A senior discount is available. Open April to September.

Directions: From Bend, drive south on U.S. 97 for 17.3 miles to Forest Road 42. Turn right (west) and drive 7.9 miles to the campground.

Contact: Deschutes National Forest, Bend–Fort Rock Ranger District, 1230 NE 3rd St., Suite A-262, Bend, OR 97701, 541/383-4000, fax 541/383-4700.

52 PRAIRIE

Rating: 4

on Paulina Creek in Deschutes National Forest

See map pages 346–347

Here's another good overnight campground that is quiet and private. This camp along the banks of Paulina Creek is about a half mile from the trailhead for the Peter Skene Ogden National Recreation Trail. The elevation is 4,300 feet.

RV sites, facilities: There are 16 sites for RVs up to 30 feet or tents. Picnic tables, garbage service, and fire grills are provided. Drinking water, firewood, and vault toilets are available. Leashed pets are permitted.

Reservations, fees: Reservations are not accepted. The fee is $10 per night, plus $5 per additional vehicle and $10 per extra RV. A senior discount is available. Open mid-May to October, weather permitting.

Directions: From Bend, drive south on U.S. 97 for 23.5 miles to County Road 21 (Paulina/East Lake Road). Turn left (east) and drive 3.1 miles to the campground.

Contact: Deschutes National Forest, Bend–Fort Rock Ranger District, 1230 NE 3rd St., Suite A-262, Bend, OR 97701, 541/383-4000, fax 541/383-4700.

53 NORTH TWIN LAKE

Rating: 6

on North Twin Lake in Deschutes National Forest

See map pages 346–347

This campground on the shore of North Twin Lake is a popular weekend spot for families. Although small and fairly primitive, it has lake access and a pretty setting. Only nonmotorized boats are permitted. The elevation is 4,350 feet.

RV sites, facilities: There are 19 sites for RVs up to 22 feet or tents. Picnic tables and fire grills are provided. Vault toilets and cell phone reception are available. There is no drinking water. Boat-launching facilities are on-site. Leashed pets are permitted.

Reservations, fees: Reservations are not accepted. The fee is $5 per night. A senior discount is available. Open June to late September, weather permitting.

Directions: From Bend, drive south on Highway 97 for 26.8 miles to Road 43 (Wickiup Junction). Turn right (west) and drive 11 miles to Road 42. Turn left (west) and drive 4.6 miles to Road 4260. Turn left (south) and drive .2 mile to the campground entrance on the left.

Contact: Deschutes National Forest, Bend–Fort Rock Ranger District, 1230 NE 3rd St., Suite A-262, Bend, OR 97701, 541/383-4000, fax 541/383-4700.

OREGON

54 TWIN LAKES RESORT

Rating: 8

on Twin Lakes

See map pages 346–347

This resort is a popular family vacation destination with a full-service marina and all the amenities, including beach areas. Recreational activities vary from hiking to fishing, swimming, and boating on Wickiup Reservoir. Nearby South Twin Lake is popular with paddleboaters and kayakers (no motors allowed). It's stocked with rainbow trout. See the following descriptions of West South Twin and South Twin Lake for more information.

RV sites, facilities: There are 22 full-hookup sites (30 amps) for RVs of any length and 14 cabins. Restrooms, showers, an RV dump station, a laundry room, cell phone reception, a store, a full-service restaurant, ice, snacks, some RV supplies, propane, gasoline, and a barbecue are available. A boat ramp, rentals, and a dock are provided; no motors are permitted on South Twin Lake. Leashed pets are permitted.

Reservations, fees: Reservations are recommended. The fees are $28 per night, $15 for overflow sites, and $60–145 per night for cabins, plus $8 per person for more than two people and $5 per pet per night in cabins. Major credit cards are accepted. Open late April to mid-October.

Directions: From Bend, drive south on Highway 97 for 26.8 miles to Road 43 (Wickiup Junction). Turn right (west) and drive 11 miles to Road 42. Turn left (west) and drive 4.6 miles to Road 4260. Turn left (south) and drive two miles to the campground entrance on the left.

Contact: Twin Lakes Resort, 11200 S. Century Drive, P.O. Box 3550, Sunriver, OR 97707, 541/593-6526, fax 541/410-4688, website: www.twinlakesresortoregon.com.

55 SOUTH TWIN LAKE

Rating: 6

on South Twin Lake in Deschutes National Forest

See map pages 346–347

This campground is on the shore of South Twin Lake, a popular spot for swimming, fishing, and boating (nonmotorized only). The elevation is 4,350 feet. See the following description of West South Twin for more information.

RV sites, facilities: There are 24 sites for RVs up to 26 feet or tents. Picnic tables, garbage service, and fire grills are provided. Drinking water and vault and flush toilets are available. Boat-launching facilities (small boats only), boat rentals, a restaurant, a store, propane, gasoline, showers, and laundry facilities are nearby. Some facilities are wheelchair-accessible. Leashed pets are permitted.

Reservations, fees: Reservations are not accepted. The fee is $14 per night, plus $7 per additional vehicle and $14 per extra RV. A senior discount is available. Open mid-April to October, weather permitting.

Directions: From Bend, drive south on Highway 97 for 26.8 miles to Road 43 (Wickiup Junction). Turn right (west) and drive 11 miles to Road 42. Turn left (west) and drive 4.6 miles to Road 4260. Turn left (south) and drive .2 mile to the campground entrance on the left.

Contact: Deschutes National Forest, Bend–Fort Rock Ranger District, 1230 NE 3rd St., Suite A-262, Bend, OR 97701, 541/383-4000, fax 541/383-4700.

56 WEST SOUTH TWIN

Rating: 4

on South Twin Lake in Deschutes National Forest

See map pages 346–347

A major access point to the Wickiup Reservoir, this camp is set on South Twin Lake adjacent to the reservoir. It's a popular angling spot with very good kokanee salmon fishing. Twin Lakes Resort is adjacent to West South Twin. The elevation is 4,350 feet.

RV sites, facilities: There are 24 sites for RVs up to 30 feet. Picnic tables, garbage service, and fire grills are provided. Drinking water, flush toilets, and cell phone reception are available. Boat-launching facilities are on-site, and boat rentals, a restaurant, showers, a coin-operated laundry, gas, propane, cabins, and a store are nearby. Leashed pets are permitted.

Reservations, fees: Reservations are not accepted. The fee is $10 per night, plus $5 per addi-

OREGON

tional vehicle and $10 per extra RV. A senior discount is available. Open mid-May to mid-October, weather permitting.

Directions: From Bend, drive south on Highway 97 for 26.8 miles to Road 43 (Wickiup Junction). Turn right (west) and drive 11 miles to Road 42. Turn left (west) and drive 4.6 miles to Road 4260. Turn left (south) and drive two miles to the campground entrance on the right.

Contact: Deschutes National Forest, Bend–Fort Rock Ranger District, 1230 NE 3rd St., Suite A-262, Bend, OR 97701, 541/383-4000, fax 541/383-4700.

57 GULL POINT

Rating: 5

on Wickiup Reservoir in Deschutes National Forest

See map pages 346–347

This campground sits in an open ponderosa stand on the north shore of Wickiup Reservoir. You'll find good fishing for kokanee salmon here. About two miles from West South Twin campground, Gull Point is the most popular campground on Wickiup Reservoir.

RV sites, facilities: There are 79 sites for RVs up to 30 feet or tents. There are also two group sites for up to 25 people. Picnic tables, garbage service, and fire grills are provided. Drinking water, an RV dump station, cell phone reception, and flush and vault toilets are available. Boat-launching facilities and fish-cleaning stations are on-site. Some facilities are wheelchair-accessible. Leashed pets are permitted.

Reservations, fees: Reservations are not accepted for family sites. The fee is $12 per night, plus $6 per additional vehicle and $12 per extra RV. Reservations are required for the group site at 541/382-9443. The group site is $60 per night. A senior discount is available. Open mid-April to October, weather permitting.

Directions: From Bend, drive south on Highway 97 for 26.8 miles to Road 43 (Wickiup Junction). Turn right (west) and drive 11 miles to Road 42. Turn left (west) and drive 4.6 miles to Road 4260. Turn left (south) and drive three miles to the campground entrance on the right.

Contact: Deschutes National Forest, Bend–Fort

Rock Ranger District, 1230 NE 3rd St., Suite A-262, Bend, OR 97701, 541/383-4000, fax 541/383-4700.

58 NORTH DAVIS CREEK

Rating: 4

on North Davis Creek in Deschutes National Forest

See map pages 346–347

This remote, secluded campground is set along a western channel that feeds into Wickiup Reservoir. It receives little use. In late summer, the reservoir level tends to drop. Fishing for brown and rainbow trout as well as kokanee salmon is good here. The elevation is 4,350 feet.

RV sites, facilities: There are 15 sites for RVs up to 22 feet or tents. Picnic tables, garbage service, and fire grills are provided. Drinking water, vault toilets, and cell phone reception are available. Boat-launching facilities are on-site. Leashed pets are permitted.

Reservations, fees: Reservations are not accepted. The fee is $8 per night, plus $5 for each additional vehicle and $8 per extra RV. A senior discount is available. Open May to late October.

Directions: From Bend, drive southwest on Cascade Lake Highway (Highway 46/Forest Road 46) for 56.2 miles to the campground on the left.

Contact: Deschutes National Forest, Bend–Fort Rock Ranger District, 1230 NE 3rd St., Suite A-262, Bend, OR 97701, 541/383-4000, fax 541/383-4700.

59 GOLD LAKE

Rating: 8

on Gold Lake in Willamette National Forest

See map pages 346–347

This campground wins the popularity contest for high use. Although motors are not allowed on this small lake (100 acres, 25 feet deep), rafts and rowboats provide excellent fishing access. A primitive log shelter built in the early 1940s provides a dry picnic area. In the spring and summer, this area abounds with wildflowers and huckleberries. The Gold Lake Bog is another special attraction where one can often see deer, elk, and smaller wildlife.

RV sites, facilities: There are 25 sites for RVs up to 22 feet or tents. Picnic tables, garbage bins, and fire grills are provided. Drinking water and vault toilets are available. A pay phone is within 3.5 miles. Boat docks and launching facilities are nearby. Leashed pets are permitted.

Reservations, fees: Reservations are not accepted. The fee is $14 per night, plus $7 per additional vehicle. A senior discount is available. Open June to September, weather permitting.

Directions: From Eugene, drive south on I-5 for five miles to Exit 188 and Highway 58. Turn east and drive 35 miles to the town of Oakridge. From Oakridge, continue east on Highway 58 for 28 miles to Gold Lake Road (Forest Road 500). Turn left (north) and drive two miles to the campground on the right.

Contact: Willamette National Forest, Middle Fork Ranger District, 46375 Hwy. 58, Westfir, OR 97492, 541/782-2283, fax 541/782-5306.

60 LAPINE STATE PARK

Rating: 7

on the Deschutes River
See map pages 346–347

This clean, quiet campground sits next to a twisting, cold river brimming with trout, a nearby legendary fly-fishing spot, and a giant tree. Be sure to visit Oregon's "Big Tree," the largest ponderosa pine in the state. The camp is set in a subalpine pine forest, and you just might see an eagle an osprey grabbing breakfast right in front of you. Many high mountain lakes are in proximity, as is snow-skiing in the winter.

RV sites, facilities: There are 134 sites, including 84 with full hookups (20 amps) and 39 with partial hookups, for self-contained RVs up to 85 feet or tents. There are also five cabins and three yurts. Picnic tables and fire grills are provided. Drinking water, restrooms with flush toilets and showers, garbage bins, a pay phone, cell phone reception, an RV dump station, and firewood are available. An ATM and a coin-operated laundry are within nine miles. Leashed pets are permitted.

Reservations, fees: Reserve at 800/452-5687 or online at www.oregonstateparks.org ($6 reservation fee). The fee is $17 per night, plus $7 per additional vehicle. Yurts are $29 per night, and cabins are $37 per night. Major credit cards are accepted. Open year-round.

Directions: From Bend, turn south on U.S. 97 and drive 23 miles to State Recreation Road. Turn right and drive four miles to the park.

Contact: LaPine State Park, Oregon State Parks, 15800 State Recreation Rd., LaPine, OR 97739, 541/536-2071 or 800/551-6949.

61 HIDDEN PINES RV PARK

Rating: 7

near the Little Deschutes River
See map pages 346–347

So you think you've come far enough, eh? If you want a spot in a privately run RV park two miles from the bank of the Little Deschutes River, you've found it. Within a 30-minute drive are two reservoirs, four lakes, and a golf course. The nearby town of LaPine is the gateway to the Newberry National Volcanic Monument.

RV sites, facilities: There are 25 sites for RVs up to 40 feet, of which 16 are pull-through sites, and six tent sites. Picnic tables are provided. Drinking water, flush toilets, an RV dump station, showers, a pay phone, cell phone reception, modem access, a laundry room, RV supplies, propane, a community fire ring with firewood, and ice are available. An ATM is within 2.5 miles. The full-service community of LaPine is about five miles away. Leashed pets are allowed with restrictions; call first.

Reservations, fees: Reservations are accepted. The fee is $17.50–23 per night, plus $2 per person for more than two people. Major credit cards are accepted. Open year-round.

Directions: From Bend, drive south on U.S. 97 for 24 miles to Wickiup Junction and Milepost 165 and County Road 43/Burgess Road (lighted). Turn right (west) on County Road 43 (Burgess Road) and drive 2.4 miles to Pine Forest Road. Turn left and drive .7 mile to Wright Avenue. Turn left onto Elderberry Lane, and drive one block to the campground.

Contact: Hidden Pines RV Park, 52158 Elderberry Ln., LaPine, OR 97739, tel./fax 541/536-2265.

OREGON

62 SHARPS CREEK

Rating: 5

on Sharps Creek
See map pages 346–347

Like nearby Rujada, this camp on the banks of Sharps Creek is just far enough off the beaten path to be missed by most campers. It's quiet, primitive, and remote, and fishing, swimming, and gold panning are popular activities in the day-use area.

RV sites, facilities: There are 10 sites for RVs up to 35 feet or tents. Picnic tables and fire pits are provided. Drinking water, vault toilets, and firewood are available. A camp host is here in summer. Some facilities are wheelchair-accessible. Leashed pets are permitted.

Reservations, fees: Reservations are not accepted. The fee is $5 per night, with a 14-day stay limit, plus $3 per additional vehicle. A senior discount is available. Open mid-May to mid-October, weather permitting.

Directions: From Eugene, drive south on I-5 to Cottage Grove and Exit 174. Take that exit and drive east on Row River Road for 18 miles to Sharps Creek Road. Turn south and drive four miles to the campground.

Contact: Bureau of Land Management, 2890 Chad Dr., Eugene District, P.O. Box 10226, Eugene, OR 97408, 541/683-6600, fax 541/683-6981.

63 RUJADA

Rating: 7

on Layng Creek in Umpqua National Forest
See map pages 346–347

This campground is situated on a river terrace on the banks of Layng Creek, right at the national forest border. The Swordfern Trail follows Layng Creek through a beautiful forest within a lush fern grotto. There is a fair swimming hole near the campground. Those with patience and persistence can fish in the creek. By continuing east on Forest Road 17, you reach a trailhead that leads a half mile to beautiful Spirit Falls, a spectacular 60-foot waterfall. A bit farther east is another easy trail, which leads to Moon Falls, even more awe inspiring at 125 feet.

RV sites, facilities: There are 11 sites for RVs up to 22 feet or tents. Picnic tables, garbage bins, and fire pits are provided. Flush toilets, drinking water, and a softball field are available. Some facilities are wheelchair-accessible. Leashed pets are permitted.

Reservations, fees: Reservations are not accepted for camping but are accepted for large groups for day use. The fee is $7 per night, plus $3 per additional vehicle. A senior discount is available. Open late May to late September.

Directions: From Eugene, drive south on I-5 to Cottage Grove and Exit 174. Take that exit and drive east on Row River Road for 19 miles to Layng Creek Road (Forest Road 17). Turn left and drive two miles to the campground on the right.

Contact: Umpqua National Forest, Cottage Grove Ranger District, 78405 Cedar Park Rd., Cottage Grove, OR 97424, 541/767-5000, fax 541/767-5075.

64 PACKARD CREEK

Rating: 6

on Hills Creek Reservoir in Willamette National Forest
See map pages 346–347

Situated on a large flat beside Hills Creek Reservoir, this campground is extremely popular with families and fills up on weekends and holidays. The mix of vegetation in the campground includes an abundance of poison oak. The speed limit around the swimming area and boat ramp is 5 mph.

RV sites, facilities: There are 33 sites for RVs up to 28 feet or tents. Picnic tables, garbage bins, and fire rings are provided. Drinking water, vault toilets, cell phone reception, and firewood are available. Fishing and boat docks, boat-launching facilities, a roped swimming area, a picnic shelter, and an amphitheater are available. An ATM, a pay phone, and a store are within 8.5 miles. Some sites have their own docks. Some facilities are wheelchair-accessible. Leashed pets are permitted.

Reservations, fees: Reservations are not accepted. The fees are $12 per night and $20 per night for a double site, plus $6 per additional vehicle.

A senior discount is available. Open mid-April to mid-September.

Directions: From Eugene, drive south on I-5 for four miles to Exit 188 and Highway 58. Turn southeast and drive 35 miles to Oakridge. Continue east on Highway 58 for two miles to Kitson Springs Road. Turn right and drive .5 mile to Forest Road 21. Turn right and continue six miles to the campground.

Contact: Willamette National Forest, Middle Fork Ranger District, 46375 Hwy. 58, Westfir, OR 97492, 541/782-2283, fax 541/782-5306.

65 SAND PRAIRIE

Rating: 6

on the Willamette River in Willamette National Forest
See map pages 346–347

Situated at 1,600 feet elevation in a mixed stand of Douglas fir, western hemlock, cedar, dogwood, and hazelnut, this campground provides easy access to the Middle Fork of the Willamette River. An access road leads to the south (upstream) end of the Hills Creek Reservoir. The 27-mile Middle Fork Trail begins at the south end of the campground. Fishing is good here; you can expect to catch large-scale suckers, rainbows, and cutthroat trout in the Middle Fork.

RV sites, facilities: There are 21 sites for RVs up to 22 feet or tents. Picnic tables, garbage bins, and fire rings are provided. Vault and flush toilets, a group picnic area, and drinking water are available. A boat launch is nearby on Hills Creek Reservoir. Some facilities are wheelchair-accessible. Leashed pets are permitted.

Reservations, fees: Reservations are not accepted. The fee is $12 per night, plus $6 per additional vehicle. A senior discount is available. Open May to September.

Directions: From Eugene, drive south on I-5 for four miles to Exit 188 and Highway 58. Turn southeast and drive 35 miles to Oakridge. Continue east on Highway 58 for two miles to Kitson Springs Road. Turn right and drive .5 mile to Forest Road 21. Turn right and continue 11 miles to the campground.

Contact: Willamette National Forest, Middle

Fork Ranger District, 46375 Hwy. 58, Westfir, OR 97492, 541/782-2283, fax 541/782-5306.

66 BLUE POOL

Rating: 4

on Salt Creek in Willamette National Forest
See map pages 346–347

This campground is situated in an old-growth forest alongside Salt Creek at 1,900 feet elevation. The camp features a large picnic area along the creek with picnic tables, a large grassy area, and fire stoves built in the 1930s by the Civilian Conservation Corps. A half mile east of the campground on Highway 58 is McCredie Hot Springs. This spot is undeveloped, without any facilities. Exercise caution when using the hot springs; they can be very hot.

RV sites, facilities: There are 24 sites for RVs up to 20 feet or tents. Picnic tables, garbage bins, a recycling center, and fire rings are provided. Drinking water and pit and flush toilets are available. A pay phone, an ATM, and a store are within nine miles. Leashed pets are permitted.

Reservations, fees: Reservations are not accepted. The fee is $12 per night, plus $6 per additional vehicle. A senior discount is available. Open mid-May to mid-September.

Directions: From Eugene, drive south on I-5 for four miles to Exit 188 and Highway 58. Turn southeast and drive 35 miles to Oakridge. Continue east on Highway 58 for nine miles to the campground.

Contact: Willamette National Forest, Middle Fork Ranger District, 46375 Hwy. 58, Westfir, OR 97492, 541/782-2283, fax 541/782-5306.

67 TRAPPER CREEK

Rating: 8

on Odell Lake in Deschutes National Forest
See map pages 346–347

The west end of Odell Lake is the setting for this camp. Boat docks and rentals are nearby at the Shelter Cove Resort. One of Oregon's prime fisheries for kokanee salmon and mackinaw (lake trout), this lake also has some huge brown trout.

RV sites, facilities: There are 32 sites for RVs up

to 35 feet or tents. Picnic tables, garbage service, and fire grills are provided. Drinking water, vault toilets, cell phone reception, and a boat launch are available. Firewood may be gathered from the surrounding area. A store, a coin-operated laundry, a pay phone, an ATM, and ice are within one mile. Leashed pets are permitted.

Reservations, fees: Reservations are not accepted. The fee is $5 per night, plus $5 per additional vehicle. A senior discount is available. Open June to September, weather permitting.

Directions: From Eugene, drive south on I-5 for five miles to Exit 188 and Highway 58. Turn east and drive 61 miles to the turnoff for Odell Lake and Forest Road 5810. Turn right on Forest Road 5810 and drive 1.9 miles to the campground on the left.

Contact: Deschutes National Forest, Crescent Ranger District, P.O. Box 208, Crescent, OR 97733, 541/433-3200, fax 541/433-3224.

68 SHELTER COVE RESORT

Rating: 9

on Odell Lake
See map pages 346–347
This private resort along the north shore of Odell Lake is at the base of the Diamond Peak Wilderness and offers opportunities for hiking, fishing, and swimming. The cabins sit right on the lakefront. A general store and tackle shop are available.

RV sites, facilities: There are 65 drive-through sites with partial hookups (30 amps) for RVs up to 40 feet, three tent sites, and 12 cabins. Picnic tables and fire pits are provided. Drinking water, flush toilets, showers, a store, a pay phone, cell phone reception, an ATM, horseshoes, laundry facilities, and ice are available. Boat docks, launching facilities, and boat rentals are on-site. Leashed pets are permitted.

Reservations, fees: Reserve at 800/647-2729. The fee is $12–21 per night. Major credit cards are accepted. Open year-round.

Directions: From Eugene, drive south on I-5 for five miles to Exit 188 and Highway 58. Turn east and drive 61 miles to the turnoff for Odell Lake and West Odell Lake Road. Take that road and drive south for 1.8 miles to the camp.

Contact: Shelter Cove Resort, West Odell Lake Rd., Hwy. 58, P.O. Box 52, Crescent Lake, OR 97425, 541/433-2548, website: www.sheltercoveresort.com.

69 ODELL CREEK

Rating: 9

on Odell Lake in Deschutes National Forest
See map pages 346–347
You can fish, swim, and hike at this campground (4,800 feet elevation) along the east shore of Odell Lake. A trail from the nearby Crater Buttes trailhead leads southwest into the Diamond Peak Wilderness and provides access to several small lakes in the backcountry. Another trail follows the north shore of the lake. Boat docks, launching facilities, and rentals are nearby at the Odell Lake Lodge and Resort, adjacent to the campground. Windy afternoons are common here.

RV sites, facilities: There are 21 sites for RVs up to 35 feet or tents. Picnic tables, garbage service, and fire grills are provided. Drinking water, vault toilets, and cell phone reception are available. Firewood may be gathered from the surrounding area. Leashed pets are permitted.

Reservations, fees: Reservations are not accepted. The fee is $11 per night, plus $5 per additional vehicle. A senior discount is available. Open mid-May to late September, weather permitting.

Directions: From Eugene, drive south on I-5 for five miles to Exit 188 and Highway 58. Turn east and drive 68 miles to Odell Lake and Forest Road 680 (at the east end of the lake). Turn right on Forest Road 680 and drive 400 yards to the campground on the right.

Contact: Deschutes National Forest, Crescent Ranger District, P.O. Box 208, Crescent, OR 97733, 541/433-3200, fax 541/433-3224.

70 SUNSET COVE

Rating: 8

on Odell Lake in Deschutes National Forest
See map pages 346–347
This campground is on the northeast shore of Odell Lake. Boat docks and rentals are available nearby at Odell Lake Lodge and Resort. Campsites are surrounded by large Douglas fir and

some white pine. The camp backs up to the highway; expect to hear the noise.

RV sites, facilities: There are 20 sites for RVs up to 35 feet or tents. Picnic tables and fire grills are provided. Drinking water, vault toilets, a barrier-free boat launch and day-use area, cell phone reception, and fish-cleaning facilities are available. Firewood may be gathered from the surrounding area. Leashed pets are permitted.

Reservations, fees: Reservations are not accepted. The fee is $11 per night, plus $5 per additional vehicle. A senior discount is available. Open mid-May to mid-October, weather permitting.

Directions: From Eugene, drive south on I-5 for five miles to Exit 188 and Highway 58. Turn east and drive 67 miles to the campground on the right.

Contact: Deschutes National Forest, Crescent Ranger District, P.O. Box 208, Crescent, OR 97733, 541/433-3200, fax 541/433-3224.

71 PRINCESS CREEK

Rating: 9

on Odell Lake in Deschutes National Forest
See map pages 346–347

This wooded campground is on the northeast shore of Odell Lake, but it backs up to the highway; expect traffic noise. See the description of Odell Creek in this chapter for recreation details. Boat docks and rentals are available nearby at the Shelter Cove Resort.

RV sites, facilities: There are 46 sites for RVs up to 35 feet or tents. Picnic tables and fire grills are provided. Vault toilets, and boat-launching facilities are available, but there is no drinking water. Firewood may be gathered from the surrounding area. Showers, a store, coin-operated laundry facilities, and ice are within five miles. Leashed pets are permitted.

Reservations, fees: Reservations are not accepted. The fee is $11–13 per night, plus $5 per additional vehicle. A senior discount is available. Open mid-May to September, weather permitting.

Directions: From Eugene, drive south on I-5 for five miles to Exit 188 and Highway 58. Turn east and drive 64 miles to the campground on the right.

Contact: Deschutes National Forest, Crescent Ranger District, P.O. Box 208, Crescent, OR 97733, 541/433-3200, fax 541/433-3224.

72 SPRING

Rating: 8

on Crescent Lake in Deschutes National Forest
See map pages 346–347

This campground is set in a lodgepole pine forest on the southern shore of Crescent Lake. Sites are open and some are on the lake with Diamond Peak views. The camp is at an elevation of 4,850 feet.

RV sites, facilities: There are 68 sites for RVs up to 35 feet or tents. Picnic tables, garbage service, and fire grills are provided. Drinking water, vault toilets, and boat-launching facilities are available. Firewood may be gathered from the surrounding area. Leashed pets are permitted.

Reservations, fees: Reservations are not accepted. The fee is $11–13 per night, plus $5 per additional vehicle. A senior discount is available. Open June to September, weather permitting.

Directions: From Eugene, drive south on I-5 for five miles to Exit 188 and Highway 58. Turn east and drive 70 miles to Crescent Lake Highway (Forest Road 60). Turn right and drive eight miles west to the campground entrance road on the left. Turn left and drive one mile to the campground.

Contact: Deschutes National Forest, Crescent Ranger District, P.O. Box 208, Crescent, OR 97733, 541/433-3200, fax 541/433-3224.

73 WHISTLER'S BEND

Rating: 7

on the North Umpqua River
See map pages 346–347

This Douglas County park along the banks of the North Umpqua River is an idyllic spot because it gets little pressure from outsiders, yet it is just a 20-minute drive from I-5. Two boat ramps accommodate boaters, and fishing is a plus. A wildlife reserve provides habitat for deer.

RV sites, facilities: There are 23 sites for RVs up to 35 feet or tents and two yurts. Group camping is available. Picnic tables and fire grills are

OREGON

provided. Drinking water, flush toilets, cell phone reception, showers, a playground, and launching facilities are available. An ATM, a pay phone, a coin-operated laundry, and a store are within four miles. Leashed pets are permitted.

Reservations, fees: Reservations are not accepted for tent or RV sites. The fee is $10 per night, plus $3 per additional vehicle. Reserve yurts or group camps at 541/440-4500. Yurts are $28 per night, and the group camp is $40 for up to 25 people, $70 for 26–50 people, and $100 for 51 or more people. A senior discount is available for Douglas County residents. Major credit cards are accepted. Open year-round.

Directions: From Roseburg, drive east on Highway 138 for 13 miles to Whistler's Bend Park Road (well signed). Turn left and drive two miles to the end of the road and the park entrance.

Contact: Whistler's Bend, 2828 Whistlers Park Rd., Roseburg, OR 97470, 541/673-4863, website: www.co.douglas.or.us/parks.

74 MILLPOND

Rating: 8

on Rock Creek
See map pages 346–347

Rock Creek flows past Millpond and empties into the North Umpqua River five miles downstream. Just below this confluence is the Rock Creek Fish Hatchery, which is open year-round to visitors, with free access. This campground along the banks of Rock Creek is the first camp you'll see along Rock Creek Road, which accounts for its relative popularity in this area. No fishing is allowed in Rock Creek. Note that a new campground called Lone Pine is scheduled to open just down the road in spring 2004.

RV sites, facilities: There are 12 sites for RVs up to 40 feet or tents. Picnic tables, garbage service, and fire grills are provided. A camp host is on-site, and flush and vault toilets, drinking water, cell phone reception, firewood, a ball field, a playground, and a pavilion (with 24 picnic tables, sinks, electricity, and fireplaces) are available. An ATM and pay phone are within 10 miles. Some facilities are wheelchair-accessible. Leashed pets are permitted.

Reservations, fees: Reservations are not accept-ed. The fee is $8 per night, with a 14-day stay limit, plus $3 per additional vehicle. A senior discount is available. Open mid-May to mid-November.

Directions: From Roseburg, drive east on Highway 138 for 22 miles to Rock Creek Road. Turn left (north) and drive five miles to the campground on the right.

Contact: Bureau of Land Management, Roseburg District, 777 NW Garden Valley Blvd., Roseburg, OR 97470, 541/440-4930, fax 541/440-4948, website: www.or.blm.gov/roseburg.

75 SUSAN CREEK

Rating: 9

on the North Umpqua River
See map pages 346–347

This popular campground is set along the banks of the North Umpqua Wild and Scenic River. This pretty setting features plenty of trees and river access. Highlights include two barrier-free trails, one traveling a half mile to the day-use area. From there, a hike of about three-quarters of a mile leads to the 50-foot Susan Creek Falls. Beyond this point, the trail is no longer barrier-free and becomes moderately difficult. Another four-tenths of a mile up the trail are the Susan Creek Indian Mounds. These moss-covered rocks are believed to be a spiritual site and are visited by Native Americans in search of guardian spirit visions. This area also boasts an excellent osprey interpretive site with a viewing platform along the river.

RV sites, facilities: There are 31 sites for RVs up to 35 feet long. Picnic tables, garbage service, and fire grills are provided. Flush toilets, drinking water, showers, cell phone reception, firewood, and a camp host are available. A pay phone and an ATM are within 10 miles. Some facilities and trails are wheelchair-accessible. Leashed pets are permitted.

Reservations, fees: Reservations are not accepted. The fee is $11 per night, with a 14-day stay limit, plus $3 per additional vehicle. A senior discount is available. Open late April to mid-November.

Directions: From Roseburg, drive east on Highway 138 for 29.5 miles to the campground (turnoff well signed).

OREGON

Contact: Bureau of Land Management, Roseburg District, NW 777 Garden Valley Blvd., Roseburg, OR 97470, 541/440-4930, fax 541/440-4948, website: www.or.blm.gov/roseburg.

76 WOLF CREEK

Rating: 6

on the Little River in Umpqua National Forest

See map pages 346–347

This pretty Little River camp is located at the entrance to the national forest, near the Wolf Creek Civilian Conservation Center. It is set at an elevation of 1,100 feet, with easy access to civilization. This camp has abundant wildflowers in the spring. If you want to get deeper into the Cascades, Hemlock Lake and Lake of the Woods are about 21 and 15 miles east, respectively.

RV sites, facilities: There are eight sites for RVs up to 30 feet or tents and one group site for up to 130 people. A covered pavilion for groups, 14 tables, and stone fireplaces are available. Picnic tables, fire grills, garbage bins, horseshoes, a softball field, and a volleyball court are provided. Flush toilets and drinking water are available. A pay phone is within five miles. Some facilities are wheelchair-accessible. Leashed pets are permitted.

Reservations, fees: Reservations are not accepted for family sites. The fee is $8 per night, plus $3 per additional vehicle. Reservations are required for the group site at 541/496-3532. The fee is $80 per night. There is a 14-day stay limit. A senior discount is available. Open mid-May to September.

Directions: From Roseburg on I-5, take Exit 120. Drive east on Highway 138 for 18 miles to Glide and County Road 17. Turn southeast and drive 12 miles (the road becomes Little River Road) to the campground.

Contact: Umpqua National Forest, North Umpqua Ranger District, 18782 North Umpqua Hwy., Glide, OR 97443, 541/496-3532, fax 541/496-3534.

77 ISLAND

Rating: 8

on the Umpqua River in Umpqua National Forest

See map pages 346–347

The North Umpqua is one of Oregon's most beautiful rivers, and this scenic campground is set along its banks at a spot popular for both rafting and steelhead fishing. Note: fly-fishing only is allowed and with a 20-inch minimum size limit; check regulations. A hiking trail that leads east and west along the river is accessible a short drive to the west. See a U.S. Forest Service map for details.

RV sites, facilities: There are seven sites for RVs up to 24 feet or tents. Picnic tables, garbage bins, and fire grills are provided. There is no drinking water. A pay phone is within 1.5 miles. Some facilities are wheelchair-accessible. Leashed pets are permitted.

Reservations, fees: Reservations are not accepted. The fee is $7 per night, plus $3 per additional vehicle. A senior discount is available. Open year-round.

Directions: From Roseburg, drive east on Highway 138 for 40 miles (just past Steamboat). The campground is along the highway.

Contact: Umpqua National Forest, North Umpqua Ranger District, 18782 North Umpqua Hwy., Glide, OR 97443, 541/496-3532, fax 541/496-3534.

78 CANTON CREEK

Rating: 8

near the North Umpqua River in Umpqua National Forest

See map pages 346–347

This campground (1,195 feet elevation) is set at the confluence of Canton and Steamboat Creeks, less than a mile from the North Umpqua River, and gets moderate overnight use—but lots of day swimmers come here in July and August. No fishing is permitted on Steamboat or Canton Creeks because they are spawning areas for steelhead and salmon. Steamboat Falls is six miles north on Forest Road 38. See the following description of Steamboat Falls for other area details.

RV sites, facilities: There are five sites for RVs up to 22 feet or tents. Picnic tables, garbage bins, and fire grills are provided. Drinking water, a covered picnic gazebo, and flush toilets are available. Leashed pets are permitted.

Reservations, fees: Reservations are not accepted. The fee is $7 per night, plus $3 per additional vehicle. A senior discount is available. Open mid-May to mid-October.

Directions: From Roseburg, drive east on Highway 138 for 39 miles to Steamboat and Forest Road 38 (Steamboat Creek Road). Turn left and drive .25 mile to the campground.

Contact: Umpqua National Forest, North Umpqua Ranger District, 18782 North Umpqua Hwy., Glide, OR 97443, 541/496-3532, fax 541/496-3534.

79 STEAMBOAT FALLS

Rating: 8

on Steamboat Creek in Umpqua National Forest

See map pages 346–347

This Steamboat Creek campground boasts some excellent scenery at beautiful Steamboat Falls, which features a fish ladder that provides passage for steelhead and salmon on their upstream migration. No fishing is permitted in Steamboat Creek. Other nearby camping options are Island and Canton Creek.

RV sites, facilities: There are 10 sites for RVs up to 24 feet or tents. Picnic tables, garbage bins, vault toilets, and fire grills are provided. There is no drinking water. A pay phone is within seven miles. Leashed pets are permitted.

Reservations, fees: Reservations are not accepted. The fee is $6 per night, plus $3 per additional vehicle. There is a 14-day stay limit. A senior discount is available. Open year-round, with no fee November to late May.

Directions: From Roseburg on I-5, take Exit 120 to Highway 138. Drive east on Highway 138 to Steamboat and Forest Road 38. Turn left on Forest Road 38 (Steamboat Creek Road) and drive six miles to a fork with Forest Road 3810. Bear right and drive one mile to the campground.

80 EAGLE ROCK

Rating: 9

on the North Umpqua River in Umpqua National Forest

See map pages 346–347

This camp is set next to the North Umpqua River and adjacent to the Boulder Creek Wilderness. It is named after Eagle Rock, which, along with Rattlesnake Rock, towers above the campground. The camp offers outstanding views of these unusual rock formations. It gets moderate use, even heavy on weekends. The camp sits at 1,676 feet elevation near Boulder Flat, a major launch point for rafting. Fishing here is restricted to the use of artificial lures with a single barbless hook; check regulations.

RV sites, facilities: There are 25 sites for RVs up to 30 feet or tents. Picnic tables and fire grills are provided. Vault toilets and garbage bins are available. There is no drinking water. A store, a pay phone, propane, and ice are within five miles. Some facilities are wheelchair-accessible. Leashed pets are permitted.

Reservations, fees: Reservations are not accepted. The fee is $8 per night, plus $3 per additional vehicle. A senior discount is available. Open mid-May to late September.

Directions: From Roseburg, drive east on Highway 138 for 53 miles to the campground on the left.

Contact: Umpqua National Forest, North Umpqua Ranger District, 18782 North Umpqua Hwy., Glide, OR 97443, 541/496-3532, fax 541/496-3534.

81 BOULDER FLAT

Rating: 8

on the North Umpqua River in Umpqua National Forest

See map pages 346–347

This campground is set along the banks of the

North Umpqua River at the confluence with Boulder Creek. There's good trout fishing here (fly-fishing only) and outstanding scenery. The camp sits at a major launching point for white-water rafting. Across the river from the campground, a trail follows Boulder Creek north for 10.5 miles through the Boulder Creek Wilderness, a climb in elevation from 2,000 to 5,400 feet. It's a good thumper for backpackers. Access to the trail is at Soda Springs Dam, two miles east of the camp. A little over a mile to the east you can see some huge, dramatic pillars of volcanic rock, colored with lichen.

RV sites, facilities: There are 11 sites for RVs up to 24 feet or tents. Picnic tables, garbage bins, and fire grills are provided. Vault toilets and cell phone reception are available. There is no drinking water. A store, propane, and ice are within five miles. A raft launch is on-site. Leashed pets are permitted.

Reservations, fees: Reservations are not accepted. The fee is $7 per night, plus $3 per additional vehicle. A senior discount is available. Open year-round.

Directions: From Roseburg, drive east on Highway 138 for 54 miles to the campground on the left.

Contact: Umpqua National Forest, North Umpqua Ranger District, 18782 North Umpqua Hwy., Glide, OR 97443, 541/496-3532, fax 541/496-3534.

82 HORSESHOE BEND

Rating: 8

on the Umpqua River in Umpqua National Forest
See map pages 346–347

This campground, at an elevation of 1,300 feet, is in the middle of a big bend in the North Umpqua River. This spot is a major launching point for white-water rafting. Fly-fishing is also popular here.

RV sites, facilities: There are 24 sites for RVs up to 35 feet or tents and one group site for up to 70 people. Picnic tables, fire grills, garbage bins, drinking water, and flush toilets are provided. A coin-operated laundry, a store, gas, a pay phone, and propane are available two miles east. Raft-launch-

ing facilities are nearby. Some facilities are wheelchair-accessible. Leashed pets are permitted.

Reservations, fees: Reservations are not accepted for family sites. The fee is $11 per night, plus $3 per additional vehicle. A senior discount is available. Reservations are required for the group site at 541/496-3532. The fee is $70 per night. Open mid-May to late September.

Directions: From Roseburg on I-5, take Exit 120. Drive east on Highway 138 for 47 miles to Forest Road 4750. Turn right and drive south a short distance to the campground.

Contact: Umpqua National Forest, North Umpqua Ranger District, 18782 North Umpqua Hwy., Glide, OR 97443, 541/496-3532, fax 541/496-3534.

83 TOKETEE LAKE

Rating: 7

on Toketee Lake in Umpqua National Forest
See map pages 346–347

This campground is located just north of Toketee Lake and is set at an elevation of 2,200 feet. The North Umpqua River Trail passes near camp and continues east along the river for many miles. Die-hard hikers can also take the trail west, where it meanders for a while before heading north near the Boulder Creek Wilderness. Toketee Lake, an 80-acre reservoir with a 10 mph speed limit, offers a good population of brown and rainbow trout and many recreation options. A worthwhile point of interest is Toketee Falls, just west of the lake turnoff. Another is Umpqua Hot Springs, a few miles northeast of the camp. The area sustains a wide variety of wildlife; you might see otter, beaver, great blue heron, kingfishers, a variety of ducks and geese, and bald eagles in fall and winter.

RV sites, facilities: There are 32 sites for RVs up to 22 feet or tents and one group site for up to 30 people. Picnic tables, garbage bins, and fire grills are provided. Vault toilets are available, but there is no drinking water. Boat docks and launching facilities are nearby. Leashed pets are permitted.

Reservations, fees: Reservations are not accepted for family sites. The fee is $7 per night, plus $3 per additional vehicle. Reservations are required for the group site at 541/498-2531. The fee is $15 per night. Open year-round.

Directions: From Roseburg, drive east on Highway 138 for 59 miles to Forest Road 34. Turn left and drive .25 mile. Turn left again and drive to the campground entrance on the right.

Contact: Umpqua National Forest, Diamond Lake Ranger District, 2020 Toketee Ranger Station Rd., Idleyld Park, OR 97447, 541/498-2531, fax 541/498-2515.

84 CLEARWATER FALLS

Rating: 8

on the Clearwater River in Umpqua National Forest

See map pages 346–347

The main attraction at this campground along the banks of the Clearwater River is the cascading section of stream called Clearwater Falls. The camp sits at an elevation of 4,100 feet. Two miles from the main campground is another camping area with eight more sites that include picnic tables and fire rings.

RV sites, facilities: There are nine sites for self-contained RVs up to 30 feet or tents. Picnic tables and fire grills are provided. Vault toilets are available, but there is no drinking water. An ATM and pay phone are within 10 miles. Leashed pets are permitted.

Reservations, fees: Reservations are not accepted. The fee is $6 per night, plus $2 per additional vehicle. A senior discount is available. Open mid-May to late October.

Directions: From Roseburg on I-5, take Exit 124 for Highway 138. Drive east on Highway 138 for 70 miles to a signed turn for Clearwater Falls. Turn right and drive one-eighth mile to the campground.

Contact: Umpqua National Forest, Diamond Lake Ranger District, 2020 Toketee Ranger Station Rd., Idleyld Park, OR 97447, 541/498-2531, fax 541/498-2515.

85 EAST LEMOLO

Rating: 8

on Lemolo Lake in Umpqua National Forest

See map pages 346–347

This campground is on the southeastern shore of Lemolo Lake, where boating and fishing are some of the recreation possibilities. Boats with motors are allowed. Large German brown trout, a wild, native fish, can be taken on troll and fly. Lemolo Lake also provides fishing for kokanee, brook trout, and a sprinkling of rainbow trout. The North Umpqua River and its adjacent trail lie just beyond the north shore of the lake. If you hike for two miles northwest of the lake, you can reach spectacular Lemolo Falls.

RV sites, facilities: There are 15 sites for small RVs up to 22 feet or tents. No drinking water is available. Picnic tables, garbage bins, and fire rings are provided. Vault toilets and cell phone reception are available. Boat docks, launching facilities, and rentals are nearby. An ATM and a pay phone are within 10 miles. Leashed pets are permitted.

Reservations, fees: Reservations are not accepted. The fee is $6 per night, plus $2 per additional vehicle. A senior discount is available. Open mid-May to late October.

Directions: From Roseburg, drive east on Highway 138 for 74 miles to Forest Road 2610 (three miles east of Clearwater Falls). Turn north and drive three miles to Forest Road 2614. Turn right and drive two miles to Forest Road 2614-430. Turn left and drive a short distance to the campground at the end of the road.

Contact: Umpqua National Forest, Diamond Lake Ranger District, 2020 Toketee Ranger Station Rd., Idleyld Park, OR 97447, 541/498-2531, fax 541/498-2515.

86 POOLE CREEK

Rating: 8

on Lemolo Lake in Umpqua National Forest

See map pages 346–347

This campground on the western shore of Lemolo Lake isn't far from Lemolo Lake Resort, which is open for recreation year-round. The camp is just south of the mouth of Poole Creek in a lodgepole pine, mountain hemlock, and Shasta red fir forest. This is by far the most popular U.S. Forest Service camp at the lake, especially with water-skiers, who are allowed to ski in designated areas of the lake. See the previous description of East Lemolo for more information.

RV sites, facilities: There are 59 sites for RVs up

OREGON

to 30 feet or tents and a group site for up to 60 people. Picnic tables and fire grills are provided. Drinking water, vault toilets, and cell phone reception are available. A grocery store, a restaurant, a lounge, boat docks, launching facilities, and rentals are nearby. An ATM and a pay phone are within 10 miles. Leashed pets are permitted.

Reservations, fees: Reservations are not accepted for individual sites. The fee is $9–12 per night, plus $3 per additional vehicle. Group reservations can be made at 877/444-6777 or online at www.reserveusa.com ($9 reservation fee). A senior discount is available. Open late April to late October.

Directions: From Roseburg, drive east on Highway 138 for 73 miles to Forest Road 2610 (Bird's Point Road). Turn north and drive four miles to the signed turnoff for the campground entrance on the right.

Contact: Umpqua National Forest, Diamond Lake Ranger District, 2020 Toketee Ranger Station Rd., Idleyld Park, OR 97447, 541/498-2531, fax 541/498-2515.

87 INLET

Rating: 5

on Lemolo Lake in Umpqua National Forest
See map pages 346–347

This campground sits on the eastern inlet of Lemolo Lake, hidden in the deep, green, and quiet forest where the North Umpqua River rushes into Lemolo Reservoir. The lake exceeds 100 feet in depth in some spots. The camp is just across the road from the North Umpqua River Trail, which is routed east into the Oregon Cascades Recreation Area and the Mt. Thielsen Wilderness. See the description of East Lemolo in this chapter for more recreation details.

RV sites, facilities: There are 14 sites for RVs up to 22 feet or tents. Vault toilets, cell phone reception, and garbage bins are available, but there is no drinking water. Picnic tables and fire grills are provided. Boat docks, launching facilities, rentals, a restaurant, a lounge, groceries, and a gas station are nearby. An ATM and a pay phone are within 10 miles. Leashed pets are permitted.

Reservations, fees: Reservations are not accept-

ed. The fee is $6 per night, plus $2 per additional vehicle. A senior discount is available. Open mid-May to late October.

Directions: From Roseburg, drive east on Highway 138 for 74 miles to Forest Road 2614. Turn north and drive three miles to Forest Road 2614-400. Turn east and drive three miles to the campground.

Contact: Umpqua National Forest, Diamond Lake Ranger District, 2020 Toketee Ranger Station Rd., Idleyld Park, OR 97447, 541/498-2531, fax 541/498-2515.

88 BROKEN ARROW

Rating: 6

on Diamond Lake in Umpqua National Forest
See map pages 346–347

This campground sits at 5,190 feet elevation near the south shore of Diamond Lake, the largest natural lake in Umpqua National Forest. Set back from the lake, it is surrounded by lodgepole pine and features views of Mount Bailey and Mount Thielsen. Boating, fishing, swimming, hiking, and bicycling keep visitors busy here. Concerns over the size of the trout have initiated a trout-planting program of one- and two-pound rainbow trout. Diamond Lake is quite popular with anglers because of its good trout trolling, particularly in early summer. Diamond Lake is adjacent to the Mount Thielsen Wilderness, Crater Lake National Park, and Mount Bailey, all of which offer a variety of recreation opportunities year-round.

RV sites, facilities: There are 117 sites for RVs up to 35 feet or tents and group sites for 40 to 104 people. Picnic tables, fire grills, and garbage bins are provided. Drinking water, flush toilets, showers, an RV dump station, and cell phone reception are available. A pay phone and an ATM are within three miles. Boat docks, launching facilities, and rentals are nearby. Some facilities are wheelchair-accessible. Leashed pets are permitted.

Reservations, fees: Reservations are not accepted for family sites. The fee is $9–12 per night, plus $3 per additional vehicle. Reservations are required for the group site; phone 877/444-6777 or reserve online at www.reserveusa.com ($9 reservation fee). The fee is $45–110 per night. A

OREGON

senior discount is available. Open late May to mid-September.

Directions: From Roseburg on I-5, take Exit 124. Drive east on Highway 138 for 78 miles to Diamond Lake exit. Turn right and drive three miles to the junction with the loop road. Turn right (south) and drive one mile to the campground entrance on the left.

Contact: Umpqua National Forest, Diamond Lake Ranger District, 2020 Toketee Ranger Station Rd., Idleyld Park, OR 97447, 541/498-2531, fax 541/498-2515.

89 THIELSEN VIEW

Rating: 7

on Diamond Lake in Umpqua National Forest
See map pages 346–347

This campground sits along the west shore of Diamond Lake in the shadow of majestic Mount Bailey. There is a beautiful view of Mount Thielsen from here. See the previous description of Broken Arrow for information on recreation opportunities.

RV sites, facilities: There are 59 sites for RVs up to 30 feet or tents. Picnic tables, fire grills, and garbage bins are provided. Drinking water, vault toilets, and cell phone reception are available. An ATM and a pay phone are within four miles. Boat docks, launching facilities, and rentals are nearby. Some facilities are wheelchair-accessible. Leashed pets are permitted.

Reservations, fees: Reservations are not accepted. The fee is $9–12 per night, plus $3 per additional vehicle. A senior discount is available. Open late May to late September.

Directions: From Roseburg on I-5, take Exit 124. Drive east on Highway 138 for 78 miles to Diamond Lake exit. Turn right and drive three-eighths of a mile. Turn right again and drive four miles to the campground entrance on the left.

Contact: Umpqua National Forest, Diamond Lake Ranger District, 2020 Toketee Ranger Station Rd., Idleyld Park, OR 97447, 541/498-2531, fax 541/498-2515.

90 DIAMOND LAKE

Rating: 9

on Diamond Lake in Umpqua National Forest
See map pages 346–347

This extremely popular camp along the east shore of Diamond Lake has all the luxuries: flush toilets, showers, and drinking water. There are campfire programs every Friday and Saturday night in the summer. See the description of Broken Arrow in this chapter for recreation information.

RV sites, facilities: There are 238 sites for RVs up to 45 feet or tents. Picnic tables, garbage bins, and fire grills are provided. Flush toilets, showers, drinking water, an RV dump station, firewood, cell phone reception, and an amphitheater are available. Boat docks, launching facilities, boat rentals, and a fish-cleaning station are nearby. A pay phone and an ATM are within two miles. Leashed pets are permitted.

Reservations, fees: Reserve at 877/444-6777 or online at www.reserveusa.com ($9 reservation fee). The fee is $10–20 per night, plus $5 per additional vehicle. A senior discount is available. Open late April to late October.

Directions: From Roseburg on I-5, take Exit 124. Drive east on Highway 138 for 80 miles to Diamond Lake exit. Turn right and drive three-eighths of a mile. Turn right again and drive two miles to the campground entrance on the right.

Contact: Umpqua National Forest, Diamond Lake Ranger District, 2020 Toketee Ranger Station Rd., Idleyld Park, OR 97447, 541/498-2531, fax 541/498-2515.

91 TWIN RIVERS VACATION PARK

Rating: 6

near the Umpqua River
See map pages 346–347

This wooded campground near the Umpqua River features large, shaded pull-through sites and more than 100 kinds of trees on the property. Nearby recreation options include a golf course, a county park, and bike paths. Rafting, kayaking, drift boating, and fishing are popular at the park.

RV sites, facilities: There are 72 sites for RVs of any length; 35 are drive-through with full hookups

(30, 50 amps). Picnic tables and fire rings are provided. Drinking water, cable TV, flush toilets, propane, showers, firewood, a store, a laundry room, cell phone reception, modem access, ice, and a playground are available. Boat-launching facilities are nearby. A pay phone is within a quarter mile, and an ATM is within six miles. Leashed pets are permitted.

Reservations, fees: Reservations are accepted. The fee is $18–28 per night, plus $2 per person for more than two people. Major credit cards are accepted. Open year-round.

Directions: In Roseburg on I-5, take Exit 125 to Garden Valley Road. Drive west for five miles (over the river) to Old Garden Valley Road. Turn left and drive 1.5 miles to River Forks Park Road. Turn left and drive to the entrance to the park.

Contact: Twin Rivers Vacation Park, 433 River Forks Park Rd., Roseburg, OR 97470, 541/673-3811.

92 DOUGLAS COUNTY FAIRGROUNDS RV PARK

Rating: 8

on the South Umpqua River
See map pages 346–347

This 74-acre county park is very easily accessible off the highway. Nearby Umpqua River, one of Oregon's prettiest rivers, often has good fishing in season. A golf course, bike paths, and tennis courts are nearby. Horse stalls and a boat ramp are available at the nearby fairgrounds. The campground fills up the third weekend in March during the annual fiddlers' convention.

RV sites, facilities: There are 50 sites with partial hookups (30 amps) for RVs of any length or tents. Tent camping is limited to two nights. Picnic tables are provided. Drinking water, flush toilets, an RV dump station, cell phone reception, a pay phone, a boat ramp, and showers are available. A store, an ATM, a café, a coin-operated laundry, and ice are within one mile. Some facilities are wheelchair-accessible. Leashed pets are permitted.

Reservations, fees: Reservations are not accepted. The fee is $20 per night, with a 14-day stay limit. Open year-round, except one week in August

during the county fair. Phone ahead to confirm current status.

Directions: From I-5 in Roseburg, take Exit 123 and drive south under the freeway to Frear Street. Turn right and enter the park.

Contact: Douglas County Fairgrounds & Speedway, 2110 SW Frear St., Roseburg, OR 97470, 541/957-7010, fax 541/440-6023.

93 WILDLIFE SAFARI RV PARK

Rating: 6

near Roseburg
See map pages 346–347

This park is part of the Wildlife Safari Park in Winston (near Roseburg), which offers a walk-through petting zoo. Nearby recreation options include an 18-hole golf course, hiking trails, and marked bike trails.

RV sites, facilities: There are 15 drive-through sites for self-contained RVs, and nine sites with partial hookups (20, 30 amps). Drinking water, picnic tables, garbage bins, cell phone reception, a pay phone, a gift shop, an ATM, and an RV dump station are available. Leashed pets are permitted.

Reservations, fees: Reservations are not accepted. The fee is $8–10 per night. The campground is closed in the winter.

Directions: From Roseburg, drive south on I-5 for five miles to Exit 119 and Highway 42. Take Highway 42 southwest for three miles to Looking Glass Road (just before reaching Winston). Turn right and drive one block to Safari Road. Turn right and enter the park.

Contact: Wildlife Safari RV Park, 1291 Safari Rd., P.O. Box 1600, Winston, OR 97496, 541/679-6761, fax 541/679-9210, website: www.maserith.com/safari.

94 CHARLES V. STANTON PARK

Rating: 7

on the South Umpqua River
See map pages 346–347

This campground, set along the banks of the South Umpqua River, is an all-season spot with a nice beach for swimming in the summer, good steelhead fishing in the winter, and wild grape picking in the fall.

RV sites, facilities: There are 20 sites with full hookups (30 amps) for RVs up to 30 feet, 20 tent sites, and one group area for tents or RVs. Picnic tables and fire rings or barbecues are provided. Drinking water, flush toilets, showers, an RV dump station, a pay phone, cell phone reception, a pavilion, and a playground are available. Propane, a store, an ATM, a café, a coin-operated laundry, and ice are within one mile. Leashed pets are permitted.

Reservations, fees: Reservations are not accepted for family sites. The fee is $11–14 per night. Group reservations are required ($10 reservation fee); phone 541/440-4500. The fee is $160 per night. A senior discount is available for county residents. Major credit cards are accepted. Open year-round.

Directions: Depending on your direction on I-5, there are two routes to reach this campground. In Canyonville northbound on I-5, take Exit 99 and drive one mile north on the frontage road to the campground on the right. Otherwise, in Canyonville southbound on I-5, take Exit 101 and drive one mile south on the frontage road to the campground on the left.

Contact: Charles V. Stanton Park, Douglas County Parks, 1540 Stanton Park Rd., Canyonville, OR 97417, 541/839-4483, fax 541/440-4500, website: www.co.douglas.or.us/parks.

95 BOULDER CREEK

Rating: 4

on the South Umpqua River in Umpqua National Forest

See map pages 346–347

This campground, set at 1,400 feet elevation, is on the banks of the South Umpqua River near Boulder Creek. No fishing is allowed here.

RV sites, facilities: There are 12 sites for RVs up to 25 feet or tents. Picnic tables, fire grills, and garbage bins are provided. Vault toilets are available, but there is no drinking water. Leashed pets are permitted.

Reservations, fees: Reservations are not accepted. The fee is $5 per night. Open late May to late October.

Directions: At Canyonville on I-5, take Exit 99 to County Road 1. Drive east on County Road

1 for 25 miles to Tiller and County Road 46. Turn left and drive six miles northeast (County Road 46 turns into South Umpqua Road/Forest Road 28). Continue northeast and drive seven miles to the camp.

Contact: Umpqua National Forest, Tiller Ranger District, 27812 Tiller Trail Hwy., Tiller, OR 97484, 541/825-3201, fax 541/825-3259.

96 COVER

Rating: 4

on Jackson Creek in Umpqua National Forest

See map pages 346–347

If you want quiet, this camp set at 1,700 feet elevation along the banks of Jackson Creek is the right place, since hardly anyone knows about it. Cover gets light use during the summer. During the fall hunting season, however, it is known to fill. If you head east to Forest Road 68 and follow the road south, you'll have access to a major trail into the Rogue-Umpqua Divide Wilderness. Be sure not to miss the world's largest sugar pine tree, a few miles west of camp. No fishing is allowed here.

RV sites, facilities: There are seven sites for RVs up to 40 feet or tents. Picnic tables, fire grills, and garbage bins are provided. Vault toilets are available, but there is no drinking water. Leashed pets are permitted.

Reservations, fees: Reservations are not accepted. The fee is $5 per night. Open year-round.

Directions: At Canyonville on I-5, take Exit 99 to County Road 1. Drive east on County Road 1 for 25 miles to Tiller and County Road 46. Turn left and drive five miles to Forest Road 29 (Jackson Creek Road). Turn right and drive east for 12 miles to the campground on the right.

Contact: Umpqua National Forest, Tiller Ranger District, 27812 Tiller Trail Hwy., Tiller, OR 97484, 541/825-3201, fax 541/825-3259.

97 CAMP COMFORT

Rating: 6

on the South Umpqua River in Umpqua National Forest

See map pages 346–347

This campground is set near the upper South

OREGON

Umpqua River, deep in the Umpqua National Forest, at an elevation of 2,000 feet. Large old-growth cedars shade the campsites. No fishing is permitted. A good side trip is visiting South Umpqua Falls (you will pass the access point while driving to this camp). Nearby trailheads (see a map of Umpqua National Forest) provide access to Rogue-Umpqua Divide Wilderness. By the way, those familiar with this camp might remember a rain shelter. It's gone now, having burned down.

RV sites, facilities: There are five sites for RVs up to 22 feet or tents. Picnic tables, fire grills, and garbage bins are provided. A wheelchair-accessible vault toilet is available. There is no drinking water. Leashed pets are permitted.

Reservations, fees: Reservations are not accepted. The fee is $5 per night. Open year-round.

Directions: At Canyonville on I-5, take Exit 99 to County Road 1. Drive east on County Road 1 for 25 miles to Tiller and County Road 46. Turn left and drive six miles northeast (County Road 46 turns into South Umpqua Road/Forest Road 28). Continue northeast and drive 18 miles to the camp on the right.

Contact: Umpqua National Forest, Tiller Ranger District, 27812 Tiller Trail Hwy., Tiller, OR 97484, 541/825-3201, fax 541/825-3259.

98 HAMAKER

Rating: 8

near the Upper Rogue River in Rogue River National Forest
See map pages 346–347

Set at 4,000 feet elevation near the Upper Rogue River, Hamaker is a beautiful little spot high in a mountain meadow. Wildflowers and wildlife abound in the spring and early summer. One of the least-used camps in the area, it's a prime camp for Crater Lake visitors.

RV sites, facilities: There are 10 sites for RVs up to 30 feet or tents. Picnic tables, fire grills, garbage service, and stoves are provided. Drinking water, vault toilets, and firewood are available. Leashed pets are permitted.

Reservations, fees: Reservations are not accepted. The fee is $10 per night, plus $5 per addi-

tional vehicle per night. A senior discount is available. Open late May to late October.

Directions: From Medford, drive northeast on Highway 62 for 57 miles (just past Union Creek) to Highway 230. Turn left (north) and drive 11 miles to a junction with Forest Road 6530. Continue on Forest Road 6530 for .5 mile to Forest Road 6530-900. Turn right and drive .5 mile to the campground on the right.

Contact: Rogue River National Forest, Prospect Ranger District, 47201 Hwy. 62, Prospect, OR 97536, 541/560-3400, fax 541/560-3444.

99 FAREWELL BEND

Rating: 7

on the Upper Rogue River in Rogue River National Forest
See map pages 346–347

This extremely popular campground is set at an elevation of 3,400 feet along the banks of the Upper Rogue River near the Rogue River Gorge. A quarter-mile barrier-free trail leads from camp to the Rogue Gorge Viewpoint and is definitely worth the trip. The Upper Rogue River Trail passes near camp. This spot attracts a lot of the campers visiting Crater Lake. See the following description of Union Creek for more information.

RV sites, facilities: There are 61 sites for RVs up to 40 feet or tents. Picnic tables, fire grills, and fire rings are provided. Drinking water, flush toilets, and firewood are available. Some facilities are wheelchair-accessible. Leashed pets are permitted.

Reservations, fees: Reservations are not accepted. The fee is $14 per night, plus $7 per additional vehicle a night. A senior discount is available. Open late May to late October.

Directions: From Medford, drive northeast on Highway 62 for 59 miles (near Union Creek) to the campground on the left.

Contact: Rogue River National Forest, Prospect Ranger District, 47201 Hwy. 62, Prospect, OR 97536, 541/560-3400, fax 541/560-3444.

100 UNION CREEK

Rating: 8

near the Upper Rogue River in Rogue River National Forest

See map pages 346–347

One of the most popular camps in the district, this spot is more developed than the nearby camps of Mill Creek (tents only), River Bridge (tents only), and Natural Bridge. It's set at 3,200 feet elevation along the banks of Union Creek, where the creek joins the Upper Rogue River. The Upper Rogue River Trail passes near camp. Interpretive programs are offered in the summer, and a convenience store and a restaurant are within walking distance. A private riding stable is less than one mile away.

RV sites, facilities: There are 74 sites for RVs up to 35 feet or tents. Picnic tables, garbage service, and fire grills are provided. Drinking water, vault toilets, and firewood are available. A store, a pay phone, and a restaurant are within walking distance. At least one toilet and one site are wheelchair-accessible. Leashed pets are permitted.

Reservations, fees: Reservations are not accepted. The fee is $10 per night, plus $5 per second vehicle per night. A senior discount is available. Open mid-May to mid-October.

Directions: From Medford, drive northeast on Highway 62 for 56 miles (near Union Creek) to the campground on the left.

Contact: Rogue River National Forest, Prospect Ranger District, 47201 Hwy. 62, Prospect, OR 97536, 541/560-3400, fax 541/560-3444.

101 NATURAL BRIDGE

Rating: 8

on the Upper Rogue River Trail in Rogue River National Forest

See map pages 346–347

Expect lots of company in midsummer at this popular camp, which sits at an elevation of 3,200 feet, where the Upper Rogue River runs underground. The Upper Rogue River Trail passes by the camp and follows the river for many miles to the Pacific Crest Trail in Crater Lake National Park. An interpretive area and a spectacular geo-

logical viewpoint are adjacent to the camp. A quarter-mile, barrier-free trail is also available.

RV sites, facilities: There are 17 sites for RVs up to 35 feet or tents. Picnic tables, garbage service, and fire grills are provided. Vault toilets are available, but there is no drinking water. A pay phone is within two miles. One toilet and one site are wheelchair-accessible. Leashed pets are permitted.

Reservations, fees: Reservations are not accepted. The fee is $6 per night, plus $3 per additional vehicle. A senior discount is available. Open early May to early November.

Directions: From Medford, drive northeast on Highway 62 for 54 miles (near Union Creek) to Forest Road 300. Turn left and drive one mile west to the campground on the right.

Contact: Rogue River National Forest, Prospect Ranger District, 47201 Hwy. 62, Prospect, OR 97536, 541/560-3400, fax 541/560-3444.

102 ABBOTT CREEK

Rating: 8

on Abbott and Woodruff Creeks in Rogue River National Forest

See map pages 346–347

Set at an elevation of 3,100 feet, at the confluence of Abbott and Woodruff Creeks about two miles from the Upper Rogue River, this camp is a better choice for visitors with children than some of the others along the Rogue River. Abbott Creek is small and tame compared to the roaring Rogue. The kids probably still won't be tempted to dip their toes, however, because the water usually runs at a body-numbing 42 degrees, even in the summer.

RV sites, facilities: There are 25 sites for RVs up to 45 feet or tents. Picnic tables, garbage service, and fire grills are provided. Drinking water, vault toilets, and firewood are available. Leashed pets are permitted.

Reservations, fees: Reservations are not accepted. The fee is $10 per night, plus $5 per additional vehicle per night. A senior discount is available. Open late May to late October.

Directions: From Medford, drive northeast on Highway 62 for 47 miles (near Union Creek) to

Forest Road 68. Turn left and drive 3.5 miles west to the campground on the left.

Contact: Rogue River National Forest, Prospect Ranger District, 47201 Hwy. 62, Prospect, OR 97536, 541/560-3400, fax 541/560-3444.

103 MAZAMA
🚶🚴 🐕 ♿ 🚐 ⛺

Rating: 6

near the Pacific Crest Trail in Crater Lake National Park

See map pages 346–347

This camp sits at 6,000 feet elevation and is known for cold nights, even in late June and early September. I once got caught in a snowstorm here at the opening in June. A nearby store is a great convenience. The Pacific Crest Trail passes near the camp, but the only trail access down to Crater Lake is at Cleetwood Cove.

RV sites, facilities: There are 212 sites for RVs up to 32 feet or tents. Picnic tables, fire grills, and garbage bins are provided. Drinking water, flush toilets, an RV dump station, a pay phone, coin-operated showers, a laundry room, gas pumps, a mini-mart, firewood, and ice are available. An ATM is within three miles. Some facilities are wheelchair-accessible. Leashed pets are permitted on paved roads only.

Reservations, fees: Reservations are not accepted. The fee is $15–19 per night, plus a $10 park entrance fee per vehicle and $3.50 per person for more than four people. A senior discount is available. Open late June to early October.

Directions: From I-5 at Medford, turn east on Highway 62 and drive 72 miles into Crater Lake National Park and to Annie Springs junction. Turn left and drive to the national park entrance kiosk. Just beyond the kiosk, turn right to the campground and Mazama store entrance.

Contact: Crater Lake National Park, P.O. Box 7, Crater lake, OR 97604, 541/594-3000.

104 MEADOW WOOD RV PARK
🚶🚴 🏊 🐕 ♿ 🚐 ⛺

Rating: 6

in Glendale

See map pages 346–347

Meadow Wood is a good option for RVers look-ing for a camping spot along I-5. It features 80 wooded acres and all the amenities. Nearby attractions include a ghost town, gold panning, and Wolf Creek Tavern.

RV sites, facilities: There are 64 sites (32 drive-through) for RVs of any length, of which 23 sites have full hookups (20, 30, 50 amps), and 25 tent sites. Picnic tables and fire pits are provided. Drinking water, flush toilets, propane, an RV dump station, showers, firewood, a store, a laundry room, ice, a playground, and a heated swimming pool are available. An ATM is within five miles. Leashed pets are permitted.

Reservations, fees: Reserve at 800/606-1274. The fee is $13–22 per night, plus $2 per person for more than two people. A senior discount is available. Major credit cards are accepted. Monthly rentals are available. Open year-round.

Directions: Depending on your direction on I-5, there are two routes to reach this campground. From Roseburg, drive south on I-5 to Exit 86 (near Glendale). Take that exit and drive south on the frontage road for three miles to Barton Road. Turn east and drive .25 mile to Autumn Lane. Turn south on Autumn Lane and drive .75 mile to the park. Otherwise, from Grants Pass, drive north on I-5 to Exit 83 (near Glendale) and drive east for .25 mile to Autumn Lane. Turn south on Autumn Lane and drive one mile to the park.

Contact: Meadow Wood RV Park, 869 Autumn Ln., Glendale, OR 97442, 541/832-3114 or 800/606-1274, fax 541/832-2454, website: www.meadow-woodrvpark.com.

105 JACKSON F. KIMBALL STATE PARK
🚶 🐟 🐕 🚐 ⛺

Rating: 7

on the Wood River

See map pages 346–347

This primitive state campground at the headwaters of the Wood River is another nice spot just far enough off the main drag to remain a secret. Wood River offers fine fishing that's accessible from the park by canoe. A walking trail leads from the campground to a clear spring bubbling from a rocky hillside.

RV sites, facilities: There are 10 primitive sites for self-contained RVs up to 45 feet or tents. Pic-

OREGON

nic tables, fire grills, and garbage bins are provided. Vault toilets and cell phone reception are available. There is no drinking water. A pay phone and a store are within three miles. Leashed pets are permitted.

Reservations, fees: Reservations are not accepted. The fee is $9 per night, plus $7 per additional vehicle. Open mid-April to late October.

Directions: From Klamath Falls, drive north on U.S. 97 for 21 miles to Highway 62. Turn northwest on Highway 62 and drive 10 miles to Highway 232 (near Fort Klamath). Turn north and drive three miles to the campground.

Contact: Jackson F. Kimball State Park, c/o Collier Memorial State Park, 46000 Hwy. 97 N, Chiloquin, OR 97624, 541/783-2471 or 800/551-6949.

106 CRATER LAKE RESORT

Rating: 6

on Fort Creek, close to the Wood River
See map pages 346–347

This campground, set among huge pine trees, is on the banks of the beautiful, crystal-clear Fort Creek, just outside Fort Klamath, the site of numerous military campaigns against the Modoc Indians in the late 1800s.

RV sites, facilities: There are 23 sites, 11 with full hookups (30, 50 amps) and 12 with partial hookups, for RVs of any length, some tent sites, nine cabins, and one log cabin. Picnic tables and fire pits are provided. Drinking water, flush toilets, showers, a recreation hall, and a laundry room are available. Propane, a store, a café, and ice are within one mile. Leashed pets are permitted.

Reservations, fees: Reservations are accepted. The fees are $5 per person per night for tent sites and $20–22 per night for RV sites, plus $2 per person for more than two people and $2 per pet per night. Cabins are $50–90 per night. Open mid-April to mid-October.

Directions: From Klamath Falls, drive north on U.S. 97 for 21 miles to Highway 62. Bear left on Highway 62 and drive 12.5 miles north to the campground (just before reaching Fort Klamath).

Contact: Crater Lake Resort, P.O. Box 457, Fort Klamath, OR 97626, 541/381-2349, website: www.craterlakeresort.com.

107 COLLIER MEMORIAL STATE PARK

Rating: 7

on the Williamson River
See map pages 346–347

This campground is set at the confluence of Spring Creek and the Williamson River, both of which are superior trout streams. A nature trail is also available. The park features a pioneer village and one of the state's finer logging museums. Movies about old-time logging and other activities are shown on weekend nights during the summer.

RV sites, facilities: There are 18 sites for self-contained RVs or tents and 50 sites with full hookups (30 amps) for RVs up to 100 feet long. Picnic tables and fire grills are provided. Drinking water, flush toilets, garbage bins, an RV dump station, a pay phone, showers, firewood, a laundry room, a playground, and a day-use hitching area are available. Some facilities are wheelchair-accessible. Leashed pets are permitted.

Reservations, fees: Reservations are not accepted. The fee is $16–21 per night, plus $7 per additional vehicle. Major credit cards are accepted. Open April to late October, weather permitting.

Directions: From Klamath Falls, drive north on U.S. 97 for 28 miles to the park on the left (well signed).

Contact: Collier Memorial State Park, 46000 Hwy. 97 N, Chiloquin, OR 97624, 541/783-2471 or 800/551-6949.

108 WILLIAMSON RIVER

Rating: 6

near Collier Memorial State Park in Winema National Forest
See map pages 346–347

Another great little spot is discovered, this one at 4,200 feet elevation, with excellent trout fishing along the banks of the Williamson River. Although accessible to a world-famous fly-fishing river, the camp does not get high use. Mosquitoes are numerous in spring and early summer, which can drive people away. A map of Winema National Forest details the back roads and trails. Collier Memorial State Park provides a nearby side-trip option.

OREGON

RV sites, facilities: There are seven sites for RVs up to 30 feet and three tent sites. Picnic tables, garbage bins, and fire grills are provided. Drinking water, vault toilets, and cell phone reception are available. Two restaurants, a pay phone, an ATM, and a casino are within five miles. Some facilities are wheelchair-accessible. Leashed pets are permitted.

Reservations, fees: Reservations are not accepted. The fee is $6 per night, plus $2 per additional vehicle. A senior discount is available. Open mid-May to late November 25, weather permitting.

Directions: From Klamath Falls, drive north on U.S. 97 for 30 miles to Chiloquin. Continue north on U.S. 97 for 5.5 miles to Forest Road 9730 on the right. Turn northeast and drive one mile to the campground.

Contact: Winema National Forest, Klamath Ranger District, 1936 California Ave., Klamath Falls, OR 97601, 541/885-3400, fax 541/885-3452.

109 INDIAN MARY PARK

Rating: 9

on the Rogue River
See map pages 346–347

This park is the crown jewel of the Josephine County parks. Set right on the Rogue River at an elevation of 900 to 1,000 feet, the park sports hiking trails, a picnic shelter for 150 people, swimming (unsupervised), fishing, Frisbee golf, and a historic mining town nearby. The Rogue River is famous for its rafting, which can be done commercially or on your own.

RV sites, facilities: There are 68 sites for RVs of up to 40 feet, 44 with full hookups (50 amps) and 14 with partial hookups, 34 sites for tents, and two yurts. Picnic tables and fire pits are provided. Drinking water, restrooms with flush toilets and coin-operated showers, a pay phone, cell phone reception, a barrier-free campsite and restroom, garbage bins, an RV dump station, a boat ramp, a playground, ice, and firewood are available. A store and café are four miles away, and laundry facilities are 16 miles away. An ATM is within seven miles. Leashed pets are permitted.

Reservations, fees: Reserve at 541/474-5285. The fees are $15–20 per night, plus $5 for a third vehicle, and $28 for a yurt per night with a $28 refund-able cleaning deposit. Major credit cards are accepted. Open year-round.

Directions: From Grants Pass, drive north on I-5 for 3.5 miles to Exit 61 (Merlin-Galice Road). Take that exit and drive northwest for 10 miles to Indian Mary Park on the right.

Contact: Josephine County Parks, 125 Ringuette St., Grants Pass, OR 97527, 541/474-5285, fax 541/474-5288, website: www.co.josephine.or.us/parks/index.htm.

110 SHADY TRAILS RV PARK AND CAMP

Rating: 7

on the Rogue River
See map pages 346–347

This grassy park with many shaded sites is set along the banks of the Rogue River in a wooded, mountainous area. Recreation options include fishing on the Rogue River and exploring Casey State Park.

RV sites, facilities: There are 61 sites with full hookups (30, 50 amps) for RVs of any length and 10 tent sites. Picnic tables are provided. Drinking water, flush toilets, cable TV, propane, an RV dump station, showers, a coin-operated laundry, cell phone reception, a store, ice, and a playground are available. A café is within one mile. An ATM and pay phone are within 1.5 miles. Boat-launching facilities are nearby. Leashed pets are permitted.

Reservations, fees: Reservations are accepted. The fees are $25–30 per night for RV sites and $20 per night for tent sites, plus $2 per night for each additional person. Open year-round.

Directions: From I-5 at Medford, drive northeast on Highway 62 for 23 miles to the campground.

Contact: Shady Trails RV Park and Camp, 1 Meadow Ln., Shady Cove, OR 97539, 541/878-2206.

111 FLY CASTERS RV PARK

Rating: 6

on the Rogue River
See map pages 346–347

This spot along the banks of the Rogue River is a good base camp for RVers who want to fish or hike. The county park, located across the river in Shady Cove, offers picnic facilities and a boat ramp. Lost Creek Lake is about a 15-minute drive northeast. No tent camping is permitted at this park. Note that about half of the sites are taken by long-term rentals.

RV sites, facilities: There are 47 sites with full hookups (30, 50 amps) for RVs of any length; two are drive-through sites. Picnic tables are provided. Drinking water, flush toilets, propane, showers, cable TV, modem access, cell phone reception, a clubhouse, and a laundry room are available. A store, a café, a pay phone, an ATM, and ice are within one mile. Boat-launching facilities are nearby. Leashed pets are permitted.

Reservations, fees: Reservations are accepted. The fee is $25–36 per night, plus $1 per person for more than two people. Major credit cards are accepted. Monthly rates are available. Open year-round.

Directions: From Medford, drive northeast on Highway 62 for 23 miles to the campground on the right (it is 2.7 miles south of the junction of Highways 62 and 227).

Contact: Fly Casters RV Park, 21655 Crater Lake Hwy., P.O. Box 699, Shady Cove, OR 97539, 541/878-2749, fax 541/878-2742.

112 BEAR MOUNTAIN RV PARK

Rating: 7

on the Rogue River

See map pages 346–347

This campground is set in an open, grassy area across the highway from the Rogue River about three miles from Lost Creek Lake, where boat ramps and picnic areas are available for day use. The Rogue is famous for its steelhead and salmon fishing, and rafting, kayaking, and driftboating are popular. The campsites here are spacious and shaded.

RV sites, facilities: There are 37 drive-through sites with full hookups (20, 30, 50 amps) for RVs of any length and seven tent sites. Picnic tables are provided. Drinking water, flush toilets, propane, an RV dump station, showers, a laundry room, propane, a courtesy phone, cell phone reception, ice, and a playground are available. A store and a café are within one mile. A pay phone is with-

in two miles, and an ATM is within five miles. Boat docks and launching facilities are nearby. Leashed pets are permitted.

Reservations, fees: Reserve at 541/878-2400 (from Oregon) or 800/586-2327 (from outside Oregon). The fee is $14–18 per night, plus $2 per person for more than two people and $2 per additional vehicle. Major credit cards are accepted. Open year-round.

Directions: From Medford, drive northeast on Highway 62 to the junction with Highway 227. Continue east on Highway 62 for 2.5 more miles to the campground.

Contact: Bear Mountain RV Park, 27301 Hwy. 62, Trail, OR 97541, 541/878-2400.

113 ROGUE ELK CAMPGROUND

Rating: 8

on the Rogue River east of the city of Trail

See map pages 346–347

Set right on the Rogue River at an elevation of 1,476 feet, the park has hiking trails, creek swimming (unsupervised), fishing, rafting, a Douglas fir forest, and wildlife. The forest is very beautiful here. Lost Creek Lake on Highway 62 makes a good side trip.

RV sites, facilities: There are 37 sites for RVs of up to 25 feet or tents; 15 with partial hookups (20 amps). Picnic tables and fire pits are provided. Drinking water, restrooms with flush toilets and coin-operated showers, garbage bins, an RV dump station, a pay phone, cell phone reception, a soft drink machine, a boat ramp, and a playground are available. A café, a mini-mart, an ATM, ice, laundry facilities, and firewood are available within three miles. Some facilities are wheelchair-accessible. Leashed pets are permitted.

Reservations, fees: Reservations are not accepted. The fee is $16–18 per night, plus $6 for a third vehicle and $1 per pet per night. A senior discount is available. Open mid-April to mid-October.

Directions: From Medford, take Exit 30 for the Crater Lake Highway (Highway 62) and drive northeast on Highway 62 for 29 miles to the park entrance (well signed).

Contact: Jackson County Parks, 400 Antelope Rd., White City, OR 97503, 541/774-8183, fax

OREGON

541/774-6320, website: www.jacksoncountyparks .com.

114 JOSEPH H. STEWART STATE PARK

🚶 🚵 🏊 ⛵ 🎣 🚤 🐕 👨‍👩‍👧 🚐 ⛺

Rating: 7

on Lost Creek Reservoir
See map pages 346–347

This state park is on the shore of Lost Creek Reservoir, a lake with a marina, a beach, and boat rentals. Home to eight miles of hiking and biking trails, the park is about 40 miles from Crater Lake National Park and makes an excellent jumping-off point for an exploration of southern Oregon.

RV sites, facilities: There are 151 sites with partial hookups (20, 30 amps) for self-contained RVs or tents, including some sites for RVs up to 80 feet long, 50 sites for self-contained RVs or tents, and two group tent areas. Picnic tables and fire grills are provided. Flush toilets, garbage bins, drinking water, an RV dump station, showers, firewood, and a playground are available. Boat rentals and launching facilities are nearby. An ATM is within two miles. Leashed pets are permitted.

Reservations, fees: Reservations are not accepted for the family sites. The fee is $14–16 per night, plus $7 per additional vehicle. Reservations for the group site are available; reserve at 800/452-5687 or online at www.oregonstateparks.org ($6 reservation fee). The fee is $60 per night. Major credit cards are accepted. Open mid-April to late October.

Directions: From Medford, drive northeast on Highway 62 for 34 miles to the Lost Creek Reservoir and the campground on the left.

Contact: Joseph H. Stewart State Park, 35251 Hwy. 62, Trail, OR 97541, 541/560-3334 or 800/551-6949.

115 WHISKEY SPRINGS

🚶 🎣 🏊 🐕 ♿ 🚐 ⛺

Rating: 9

near Butte Falls in Rogue River
National Forest
See map pages 346–347

This campground at Whiskey Springs is one of the larger, more developed backwoods U.S. For-est Service camps in the area. A one-mile, wheelchair-accessible nature trail passes nearby. You can see beaver dams and woodpeckers here. The camp is set at 3,200 feet elevation.

RV sites, facilities: There are 36 sites for RVs up to 30 feet or tents. Picnic tables, garbage service, and fire grills are provided. Drinking water, vault toilets, and firewood are available. Boat docks, launching facilities, and rentals are within 1.5 miles. Some facilities are wheelchair-accessible. Leashed pets are permitted.

Reservations, fees: Reservations are not accepted. The fee is $10 per night, plus $5 per additional vehicle a night. A senior discount is available. Open late May to September.

Directions: From Medford, drive northeast on Highway 62 for 16 miles to the Butte Falls Highway. Turn right and drive east for 16 miles to the town of Butte Falls. Continue southeast on Butte Falls Highway for nine miles to Forest Road 3065. Turn left on Forest Road 3065 and drive 300 yards to the campground on the left.

Contact: Rogue River National Forest, Butte Falls Ranger District, 800 Laurel St., P.O. Box 227, Butte Falls, OR 97522, 541/865-2700, fax 541/865-2795.

116 GRANTS PASS/REDWOOD HIGHWAY KOA

🚶 🚵 🐕 👨‍👩‍👧 🚐 ⛺

Rating: 8

near Grants Pass
See map pages 346–347

This KOA campground along two creeks in the hills outside of Grants Pass attracts bird-watchers. It also makes a perfect layover spot for travelers who want to get away from the highway for a while. For an interesting side trip, drive south down scenic U.S. 199 to Cave Junction or Illinois River State Park.

RV sites, facilities: There are 40 sites, eight with full hookups (20, 30, 50 amps) and 22 with partial hookups, for RVs up to 56 feet or tents, one cabin, and one RV rental. Drinking water, restrooms, a playground, modem access, showers, drinking water, an RV dump station, security, a pay phone, a laundry room, limited groceries, ice, RV supplies, propane, a recreation hall, a playground, and a recreation field, and a barbecue are available. Leashed pets are permitted.

Reservations, fees: Reserve at 800/562-7556. The fee is $21–30 per night, plus $2–3 per person for more than two people. Major credit cards are accepted. Open year-round.

Directions: In Grants Pass on I-5, take the U.S. 199 exit. Turn southwest on U.S. 199 and drive 14.5 miles to the campground on the right (at Milepost 14.5).

Contact: Grants Pass/Redwood Highway KOA, 13370 Redwood Hwy., Wilderville, OR 97543, 541/476-6508, fax 541/474-3987, website: www .koa.com.

117 SCHROEDER

Rating: 9

on the Rogue River
See map pages 346–347

Trout fishing, swimming, and boating are among the possibilities at this camp along the Rogue River. Just a short jog off the highway, it makes an excellent layover for I-5 travelers. It's not a highly publicized camp, so many tourists pass by it in favor of the more commercial camps in the area. The park is close to Hellgate Excursions, which provides jet-boat trips on the Rogue River. Tennis courts are close by.

RV sites, facilities: There are 28 sites, three with partial hookups (50 amps), for RVs up to 40 feet, 22 tent sites, and two yurts. Drinking water, restrooms, coin-operated showers, cell phone reception, and a pay phone are available. Recreational facilities include horseshoes, tennis, volleyball, a recreation field, a barbecue, a playground, and a boat ramp. An ATM is within four miles. Some facilities are wheelchair-accessible. Leashed pets are permitted.

Reservations, fees: Reserve at 541/474-5285. The fee is $15–20 per night, plus $5 for a third vehicle. Major credit cards are accepted. Open year-round.

Directions: In Grants Pass on I-5, take Exit 58 to U.S. 199. Drive west on U.S. 199 for four miles to the campground.

Contact: Josephine County Parks, 125 Ringuette St., Grants Pass, OR 97527, 541/474-5285, fax

541/474-5288, website: www.co.josephine.or .us/parks/index.htm.

118 ROGUE VALLEY OVERNITERS

Rating: 5

near the Rogue River
See map pages 346–347

This park is just off the freeway in Grants Pass, the jumping-off point for trips down the Rogue River. The summer heat in this part of Oregon can surprise visitors in late June and early July. This is a nice, comfortable park with shade trees.

RV sites, facilities: There are 110 sites with full hookups (50 amps) for RVs up to 70 feet or tents; 26 are drive-through sites. Drinking water, flush toilets, an RV dump station, modem access, cell phone reception, cable TV, showers, and a laundry room are available. An ATM and pay phone are across the street. Propane, a store, a café, and ice are available within one mile. Leashed pets are permitted.

Reservations, fees: Reservations are accepted. The fee is $23 per night, plus $2 per person for more than two people. A senior discount is available. Open year-round.

Directions: In Grants Pass on I-5, take Exit 58 to 6th Street. Drive south on 6th Street for .25 mile to the park on the right.

Contact: Rogue Valley Overniters, 1806 NW 6th St., Grants Pass, OR 97526, 541/479-2208.

119 WHITE HORSE

Rating: 9

on the Rogue River
See map pages 346–347

This pleasant county park on the banks of the Rogue River is one of several parks in the Grants Pass area that provides opportunities for trout fishing, hiking, bird-watching, and boating. Wildlife Images, a wildlife rehabilitation center, is nearby. Possible side trips include Oregon Caves, Kerby Museum, and Crater Lake National Park (two hours away).

RV sites, facilities: There are 42 sites for RVs up to 40 feet or tents, including eight with full hookups (30 amps), one group site for 12 to 18 people,

OREGON

and one yurt. Picnic tables and fire rings are provided. Drinking water, restrooms, coin-operated showers, fire grills, horseshoes, a picnic shelter, and a playground are available. A pay phone is next door, and an ATM is within eight miles. Leashed pets are permitted.

Reservations, fees: Reserve at 541/474-5285. The fees are $15–20 per night, plus $5 for a third vehicle, and $28 for a yurt per night with a $28 refundable cleaning deposit. Major credit cards are accepted. Open year-round, but only to self-contained RVs in the winter.

Directions: In Grants Pass on I-5, take Exit 58 to 6th Street. Drive south on 6th Street to G Street. Turn west and drive seven miles (the road becomes Upper River Road, then Lower River Road). The park is on the left at 7600 Lower River Road.

Contact: Josephine County Parks, 125 Ringuette St., Grants Pass, OR 97527, 541/474-5285, fax 541/474-5288, website: www.co.josephine.or.us/parks/index.htm.

120 GRANTS PASS OVERNITERS

Rating: 6

near Grants Pass

See map pages 346–347

This wooded park, set in a rural area just outside Grants Pass, is mostly shaded. Several other campgrounds are in the area. Don't let the name mislead you; whereas several spaces are reserved for overnighters, there are many monthly rentals at the park.

RV sites, facilities: There are 26 drive-through sites with full hookups (20, 30, 50 amps) for RVs of any length. Picnic tables are provided. Drinking water, flush toilets, showers, a laundry room, and a swimming pool are available. A store, a pay phone, and an ATM are within one mile. Leashed pets are permitted.

Reservations, fees: Reservations are accepted. The fee is $18 per night, plus $1 per person for more than two people. Open year-round.

Directions: From Grants Pass, drive north on I-5 for three miles to Exit 61 and bear right to a stop sign and Highland Avenue. Turn left and drive a very short distance to the campground on the right.

Contact: Grants Pass Overniters, 5941 Highland Ave., Grants Pass, OR 97526, 541/479-7289.

121 RIVER PARK RV RESORT

Rating: 6

on the Rogue River

See map pages 346–347

This park has a quiet, serene riverfront setting, yet it is close to all the conveniences of a small city. The highlight here is 700 feet of Rogue River frontage for trout fishing and swimming. It's one of several parks in the immediate area.

RV sites, facilities: There are 47 sites with full hookups (30 amps) for RVs of any length and three tent sites. Drinking water, cable TV, restrooms, modem access, cell phone reception, showers, an RV dump station, a pay phone, laundry facilities, and ice are available. Leashed pets are permitted.

Reservations, fees: Reserve at 800/677-8857. The fee is $25 per night, plus $3 per person for more than two people. Major credit cards are accepted. Open year-round.

Directions: In Grants Pass on I-5, take Exit 55 west to Highway 199. Drive west two miles to Parkdale. Turn left on Parkdale and drive one block to Highway 99. Turn left on Highway 99 and drive two miles to the park on the left.

Contact: River Park RV Resort, 2956 Rogue River Hwy., Grants Pass, OR 97527, 541/479-0046 or 800/677-8857, fax 541/471-1448, website: www.riverparkrvresort.com.

122 CIRCLE W RV PARK

Rating: 6

on the Rogue River

See map pages 346–347

This campground along the Rogue River is close to chartered boat trips down the Rogue and a golf course. Fishing and swimming access are available from the campground. No tents are permitted here.

RV sites, facilities: There are 25 sites, 18 with full hookups (30, 50 amps) and seven with partial hookups, for RVs of any length; four are drive-through sites. Picnic tables are provided. Drink-

OREGON

ing water, flush toilets, an RV dump station, a pay phone, cell phone reception, showers, a laundry room, RV supplies, and ice are available. A boat dock is nearby. An ATM is within two miles. Leashed pets are permitted.

Reservations, fees: Reservations are accepted. The fee is $22 per night, plus $1.50 per person for more than two people. Open year-round.

Directions: From Grants Pass, drive south on I-5 for 10 miles to Exit 48 at Rogue River. Take that exit west (over the bridge) to Highway 99. Turn right and drive west one mile to the camp.

Contact: Circle W RV Park, 8110 Rogue River Hwy., Grants Pass, OR 97527, 541/582-1686.

123 HAVE A NICE DAY CAMPGROUND

Rating: 6

on the Rogue River
See map pages 346–347

This campground with grassy, shaded sites is set along the Rogue River, where fishing, swimming, and boating are options. It has nice river views. The park is currently undergoing extensive site renovations.

RV sites, facilities: There are 10 sites with full hookups (30, 50 amps) for RVs of any length or tents, 18 sites for RVs only, and five sites for tents. Picnic tables and fire rings are provided. Drinking water, flush toilets, an RV dump station, a pay phone, cell phone reception, cable TV, showers, a laundry room, jet-boat excursion bookings, and a playground are available. A store, an ATM, and a café are within two miles. Boat docks and launching facilities are nearby. Leashed pets are permitted.

Reservations, fees: Reservations are accepted. The fee is $17–22 per night, plus $2 per person for more than four people. Monthly rentals are available. Open year-round, weather permitting, with limited winter facilities.

Directions: From Grants Pass, drive south on I-5 for seven miles to Exit 48 at Rogue River. Take that exit and drive west over the bridge to Highway 99. Turn right (downriver) and drive west for 1.5 miles to the campground (on both sides of the road).

Contact: Have a Nice Day Campground, 7275 Rogue River Hwy., Grants Pass, OR 97527, 541/582-1421.

124 RIVERFRONT RV PARK

Rating: 6

on the Rogue River
See map pages 346–347

This spot is convenient to good fishing, swimming, and boating on the Rogue River. Many of these large sites face the river. This park features a round driveway, so there is no backing up. There are only two tent sites, and some sites are rented for the entire summer season.

RV sites, facilities: There are 22 sites, 20 with full hookups (20, 30, amps) and two with partial hookups, for RVs of any length, and two tent sites. Picnic tables are provided. Drinking water, flush toilets, cable TV, an RV dump station, showers, a pay phone, cell phone reception, a laundry room, and ice are available. Propane, a store, and a café are within two miles. An ATM is within three miles. Fishing docks, boat docks, and launching facilities are nearby. Small leashed pets are permitted.

Reservations, fees: Reservations are accepted. The fee is $20 per night, plus $2.50 per person for more than two people. Monthly rates are available. Open year-round.

Directions: From Grants Pass, drive south on I-5 for seven miles to Exit 48 and Highway 99. Take that exit, bear west on Highway 99, and drive two miles to the park on the right.

Contact: Riverfront RV Park, 7060 Rogue River Hwy., Grants Pass, OR 97527, 541/582-0985.

125 LAZY ACRES RV & MOTEL

Rating: 6

on the Rogue River
See map pages 346–347

This wooded campground on the Rogue River may be a bit less scenic than KOA Gold n' Rogue (see listing in this chapter), but its evergreen, maple, and birch trees still make this a beautiful spot. The camp also offers the same recreation options. No tent camping is permitted.

RV sites, facilities: There are 68 sites with full

OREGON

hookups (30, 50 amps) for RVs of any length and a four-unit motel. Picnic tables are provided. Drinking water, flush toilets, propane, cable TV, coin-operated showers, cell phone reception, an RV dump station, a playground, and a laundry room are available. Boat docks are nearby. A pay phone and an ATM are within four blocks. Leashed pets are permitted.

Reservations, fees: Reservations are accepted. The fee is $22 per night, plus $2 per person for more than two people. Major credit cards are accepted. Monthly rates are available. Open year-round.

Directions: From Medford, drive north on I-5 for 18 miles to the South Gold Hill exit. Take that exit and drive .25 mile north to 2nd Avenue. Turn west and drive 1.2 miles to the campground on the left.

Contact: Lazy Acres RV & Motel, 1550 2nd Ave., Gold Hill, OR 97525, 541/855-7000.

126 VALLEY OF THE ROGUE STATE PARK

Rating: 7

on the Rogue River
See map pages 346–347

With easy highway access, this popular spot along the banks of the Rogue River often fills to near capacity during the summer. Recreation options include fishing and boating. This spot makes a good base camp for taking in the Rogue Valley and surrounding attractions: Crater Lake National Park, Oregon Caves National Monument, historic Jacksonville, Ashland's Shakespeare Festival, or the Britt Music Festival.

RV sites, facilities: There are 21 sites for self-contained RVs or tents, 98 sites with full hookups (30, 50 amps), and 48 sites with partial hookups for RVs up to 75 feet. Three group tent areas for up to 25 people each and six yurts are also available. Picnic tables and fire grills are provided. Flush toilets, drinking water, garbage bins, cell phone reception, pay phones, an RV dump station, showers, firewood, two laundry rooms, a meeting hall, and playgrounds are available. A restaurant is nearby. An ATM is within three miles. Boat-launching facilities are nearby. Some facilities are wheelchair-accessible. Leashed pets are permitted.

Reservations, fees: Reserve at 800/452-5687 or online at www.oregonstateparks.org ($6 reservation fee). The fees are $16–20 per night, group areas are $60, and yurts are $27 per night, plus $7 per additional vehicle per night. Open year-round. Major credit cards are accepted.

Directions: From Grants Pass, drive south on I-5 for 12 miles to Exit 45B. Take that exit, turn right, and drive 200 feet to the park on the right.

Contact: Valley of the Rogue State Park, 3792 N. River Rd., Gold Hill, OR 97525, 541/582-1118.

127 KOA GOLD N' ROGUE

Rating: 6

on the Rogue River
See map pages 346–347

This campground is a half mile from the Rogue River, with a golf course, bike paths, and the Oregon Vortex in the vicinity. It's one of the many camps between Gold Hill and Grants Pass.

RV sites, facilities: There are 97 sites (49 drive-through), 64 with full hookups (30, 50 amps) and nine with partial hookups, for RVs of any length, nine tent sites, and four cabins. Picnic tables are provided. Drinking water, flush toilets, propane, an RV dump station, a pay phone, modem access, cell phone reception, barbecues, showers, firewood, a store, a laundry room, ice, a playground, and a swimming pool are available. A café and an ATM are within one mile, and boat-launching facilities are within five miles. Leashed pets are permitted.

Reservations, fees: Reserve at 800/562-7608. The fee is $24–32 per night, plus $2 per person for more than two people. Major credit cards are accepted. Open year-round.

Directions: From Medford, drive north on I-5 for 10 miles to South Gold Hill and Exit 40. Take that exit, turn right, and drive .25 mile to Blackwell Road. Turn right (on a paved road) and drive .25 mile to the park.

Contact: KOA Gold n' Rogue, 12297 Blackwell Rd., Central Point, OR 97525, 541/855-7710, website: www.koa.com.

OREGON

128 MEDFORD OAKS RV PARK

Rating: 6

near Eagle Point
See map pages 346–347
This park is in a quiet, rural setting among the trees. Just a short hop off I-5, it's an excellent choice for travelers heading south to California. The campground is located along the shore of a pond that provides good fishing.

RV sites, facilities: There are 66 sites, 18 with full hookups (30, 50 amps) and 32 with partial hookups, for RVs of any length or tents, 18 tent-only sites, and three cabins. Drinking water, restrooms, showers, an RV dump station, a courtesy phone, modem access, a laundry room, limited groceries, ice, RV supplies, and propane are available. Recreational facilities include a seasonal, heated swimming pool with a slide, movies, video games, pool tables, horseshoes, table tennis, a recreation field for baseball and volleyball, and a playground. A pay phone and an ATM are within seven miles. Call for pet policy.

Reservations, fees: Reservations are recommended. The fee is $17–30 per night. Group rates are available. Major credit cards are accepted. Open year-round.

Directions: From Medford, drive northeast on Highway 62 for five miles to Highway 140. Turn east on Highway 140 and drive 6.8 miles to the campground on the left.

Contact: Medford Oaks RV Park, 7049 Hwy. 140, Eagle Point, OR 97524, 541/826-5103, fax 541/826-5984, website: www.medfordoaks.com.

129 WILLOW LAKE RESORT

Rating: 9

on Willow Lake
See map pages 346–347
This campground is on the shore of Willow Lake. A hiking trail starts near camp.

RV sites, facilities: There are 20 drive-through sites with full hookups (30 amps) for RVs, 17 sites with partial hookups for RVs of any length, and 29 tent sites. There are also four cabins for up to six people each. Picnic tables and fire rings are provided. Flush toilets, an RV dump station,

coin-operated showers, a pay phone, and firewood are available. An ATM and a coin-operated laundry are within eight miles. Leashed pets are permitted.

Reservations, fees: The fee is $16–20 per night, plus $1 per pet per night. Reservations are accepted for cabins only at 541/560-3900. Major credit cards are accepted. A senior discount is available. Open mid-March to October.

Directions: From Medford, drive northeast on Highway 62 for 15 miles to Butte Falls Highway. Turn east and drive 25 miles to Willow Lake Road. Turn south and drive two miles to the campground.

Contact: Jackson County Parks, 400 Antelope Rd., White City, OR 97503, 541/774-8183, fax 541/774-6320, website: www.jacksoncountyparks.com.

130 WILLOW PRAIRIE & EQUESTRIAN CAMP

Rating: 7

near Fish Lake in Rogue River National Forest
See map pages 346–347
There are two campgrounds here, including one for equestrian campers. This spot is located near the origin of the west branch of Willow Creek and next to a beaver swamp and several large ponds that attract sandhill cranes, ducks, geese, elk, and deer. A number of riding trails pass nearby. A map of Rogue River National Forest details the back roads and can help you get here. Fish Lake is four miles south.

RV sites, facilities: There are 10 sites for RVs up to 16 feet or tents, one primitive cabin with cots, and an equestrian campground. Picnic tables and fire grills are provided. Drinking water, vault toilets, cell phone reception, and garbage service are provided. The equestrian camp has 10 sites for small RVs or tents, two stock water troughs, and horse corrals. A store, a café, a pay phone, and ice are within five miles. Boat docks, launching facilities, and rentals are nearby. A camp host is on-site. Leashed pets are permitted.

Reservations, fees: Reservations are not accepted for tent and RV sites. The fee is $6 per night, plus $3 per additional vehicle. Reservations are required for the equestrian camp and cabin at

OREGON

541/865-2700. A senior discount is available. Open late May to late October.

Directions: From Medford, drive northeast on Highway 62 for five miles to Exit 30 and Highway 140. Turn east on Highway 140 and drive 31.5 miles to Forest Road 37. Turn left and drive north 1.5 miles to Forest Road 3738. Turn left and drive one mile west to Forest Road 3735. Turn left and drive 100 yards to the campground. For the equestrian camp, continue for .25 mile to the campground entrance.

Contact: Rogue River National Forest, Butte Falls Ranger District, 800 Laurel St., Butte Falls, OR 97522, 541/865-2700, fax 541/865-2795.

131 NORTH FORK

Rating: 7

near Fish Lake in Rogue River National Forest
See map pages 346–347

Here is a small, pretty campground with easy access from the highway and proximity to Fish Lake. Situated on the North Fork of Little Butte Creek at an elevation of 4,500 feet, it's fairly popular, so get your spot early. Excellent fly-fishing can be found along the Fish Lake Trail, which leads directly out of camp.

RV sites, facilities: There are three sites for RVs up to 24 feet and six tent sites. Picnic tables and fire grills are provided. All garbage must be packed out. Vault toilets and drinking water are available. Boat docks, launching facilities, and rentals are nearby. Some facilities are wheelchair-accessible, including a barrier-free vault toilet. Leashed pets are permitted.

Reservations, fees: Reservations are not accepted. The fee is $8 per night, plus $4 per additional vehicle. A senior discount is available. Open early May to October.

Directions: From Medford, drive northeast on Highway 62 for five miles to Exit 30 and Highway 140. Turn east on Highway 140 and drive 31.5 miles to Forest Road 37. Turn south and drive .5 mile to the campground.

Contact: Rogue River National Forest, Ashland Ranger District, 645 Washington St., Ashland, OR 97520, 541/482-3333, fax 541/858-2402.

132 FISH LAKE

Rating: 8

on Fish Lake in Rogue River National Forest
See map pages 346–347

Bikes and boats can be rented here by the hour or by the day, a nice bonus. Add it up: Boating, fishing, hiking, and bicycling are among the recreation options at this campground on the north shore of Fish Lake. An easy one-mile access trail to the Pacific Crest Trail is also available. If this campground is full, Doe Point and Fish Lake Resort are nearby.

RV sites, facilities: There are 17 sites for RVs up to 32 feet or tents and two walk-in sites for tents. One site is wheelchair-accessible. Picnic tables, fire grills, and garbage bins are provided. Drinking water, flush toilets, a pay phone, cell phone reception, an RV dump station, a wheelchair-accessible picnic shelter, a store, a café, firewood, and ice are available. Boat docks, launching facilities, and rentals are nearby. Leashed pets are permitted.

Reservations, fees: Reservations are not accepted for family sites. The fee is $14 per night, plus $7 per additional vehicle per night. Reservations for the group site are required at 541/560-3900. A senior discount is available. Open mid-May to mid-October, weather permitting.

Directions: From Medford, drive northeast on Highway 62 for five miles to Highway 140. Turn east on Highway 140 and drive 30 miles to the campground on the right.

Contact: Rogue River National Forest, Ashland Ranger District, 645 Washington St., Ashland, OR 97520, 541/482-3333, fax 541/858-2402.

133 DOE POINT

Rating: 8

on Fish Lake in Rogue River National Forest
See map pages 346–347

This campground (at 4,600 feet elevation) sits along the north shore of Fish Lake, nearly adjacent to Fish Lake Campground. Doe Point is slightly preferable because of its dense vegetation, offering shaded, quiet, well-screened sites. Privacy, rare at many campgrounds, can be found here. Recreation options include boating, fish-

OREGON

ing, hiking, and biking, plus an easy one-mile access trail to the Pacific Crest Trail.

RV sites, facilities: There are 25 sites for RVs up to 32 feet or tents and five walk-in tent sites. Picnic tables and fire grills are provided. Drinking water, garbage service, flush toilets, a store, a pay phone, cell phone reception, a café, firewood, and ice are available. Boat docks, launching facilities, boat rentals, showers, and an RV dump station are nearby. Leashed pets are permitted.

Reservations, fees: Reservations are not accepted. The fee is $12 per night, plus $6 per additional vehicle. A senior discount is available. Open mid-May to late September.

Directions: From Medford, drive northeast on Highway 62 for five miles to Exit 30 and Highway 140. Turn east on Highway 140 and drive 30 miles to the campground on the right.

Contact: Rogue River National Forest, Ashland Ranger District, 645 Washington St., Ashland, OR 97520, 541/482-3333, fax 541/858-2402.

134 FISH LAKE RESORT

Rating: 7

on Fish Lake

See map pages 346–347

This resort along Fish Lake is privately operated under permit by the U.S. Forest Service and offers a resort-type feel, catering primarily to families. Hiking, bicycling, fishing, and boating are some of the activities here. This is the largest and most developed of the three camps at Fish Lake. Cozy cabins are available for rent. Boat speed on the lake is limited to 10 mph.

RV sites, facilities: There are 45 sites with full hookups (30 amps) for RVs up to 40 feet, 12 tent sites, and 11 cabins. Picnic tables and fire rings are provided. Drinking water, flush toilets, garbage bins, propane, an RV dump station, showers, a pay phone, cell phone reception, a recreation hall, a store, a café, a laundry room, ice, boat docks, boat rentals, and launching facilities are available. Leashed pets are permitted.

Reservations, fees: Reserve at 541/949-8500. The fee is $16–30 per night. Major credit cards are accepted. Open May to October, weather permitting, with some winter recreation.

Directions: From Medford, drive northeast on

Highway 62 for five miles to Highway 140. Turn east on Highway 140 and drive 30 miles to Fish Lake Road. Turn right (south) and drive .5 mile to the campground on the left.

Contact: Fish Lake Resort, P.O. Box 990, Eagle Point, OR 97524, 541/949-8500, website: www.fishlakeresort.net.

135 ROCKY POINT RESORT

Rating: 7

on Upper Klamath Lake

See map pages 346–347

Rocky Point Resort, at the Upper Klamath Wildlife Refuge, boasts 10 miles of canoe routes, with opportunities for fishing, boating, and canoeing.

RV sites, facilities: There are 28 sites, (some drive-through), 17 with full hookups (50 amps) and 11 with partial hookups, for RVs up to 40 feet, five tent sites, four cabins, and five motel rooms. Picnic tables and fire rings are provided. Restrooms, drinking water, flush toilets, a pay phone, cell phone reception, showers, firewood, a store, a laundry room, ice, a marina with boat gas, and boat and canoe rentals are available. There is a free boat launch and game area. A restaurant and lounge overlook the lake. Leashed pets are permitted.

Reservations, fees: Reservations are accepted. The fee is $16–21 per night, plus $2 per person for more than two people and $1 per pet per night. Cabins are $80–109 per night, and motel rooms are $65 per night plus $5 per person over two people. Major credit cards are accepted. Open April to November.

Directions: From Klamath Falls, drive northeast on Highway 140 for about 25 miles to Rocky Point Road. Turn north and drive three miles to the campground.

Contact: Rocky Point Resort, 28121 Rocky Point Rd., Klamath Falls, OR 97601, 541/356-2287, fax 541/356-2222, website: www.rockypointoregon.com.

136 LAKE OF THE WOODS RESORT

Rating: 9

on Lake of the Woods

See map pages 346–347

On beautiful Lake of the Woods, this resort offers

OREGON

fishing (three kinds of trout, catfish, and bass) and boating in a secluded forest setting. It's on one of the most beautiful lakes in the Cascade Mountains, surrounded by tall pine trees. A family-oriented campground, it has all the amenities. In the winter, snowmobiling and cross-country skiing are popular (you can rent equipment at the resort). Attractions in the area include the Mountain Lakes Wilderness and the Pacific Crest Trail.

RV sites, facilities: There are 27 sites with full hookups (30 amps) for RVs up to 35 feet or tents, plus 15 cabins that can accommodate one to six people. Picnic tables and fire rings are provided. Drinking water, restrooms, showers, an RV dump station, a pay phone, cell phone reception, modem access, a laundry room, ice, snacks, two restaurants, a lounge, and propane are available. There are also a boat ramp, a dock, a marina, boat and mountain bike rentals, and a barbecue. Leashed pets are permitted.

Reservations, fees: Reservations are not accepted for family sites. The fees are $17–25 per night and $32 per night for double sites, plus $4 per additional vehicle and $5 per pet. Cabins are $69–269 per night. Major credit cards are accepted. Open year-round, weather permitting.

Directions: In Medford on I-5, take Exit 14 to Highway 66. Drive east for less than a mile to Dead Indian Memorial Road. Turn left (east) and drive 40 miles to Lake of the Woods Road. Turn north and drive less than .5 mile to the resort.

Contact: Lake of the Woods Resort, 950 Harriman Rte., Klamath Falls, OR 97601, 541/949-8300, fax 541/949-8229, website: www.lakeofthewoodsresort.com.

137 ASPEN POINT

Rating: 8

on Lake of the Woods in Winema National Forest

See map pages 346–347

This campground (at 5,000 feet elevation) is near the north shore of Lake of the Woods, adjacent to Lake of the Woods Resort. It's heavily timbered with old-growth fir and has a great view of Mount McLoughlin (9,495 feet). A hiking trail just north of camp leads north for several miles, wandering around Fourmile Lake and extending into the Sky Lakes Wilderness. Other trails nearby head into the Mountain Lakes Wilderness. Fishing, swimming, boating, and water-skiing are among the activities here. Note that of the 60 campsites, 20 are available by reservation and the rest are first-come, first-served.

RV sites, facilities: There are 60 sites for RVs up to 40 feet or tents. Picnic tables, garbage bins, and fire grills are provided. Drinking water, an RV dump station, cell phone reception, and flush toilets are available. Boat docks, launching facilities, rentals, and a pay phone are nearby. Leashed pets are permitted.

Reservations, fees: Reserve at 877/444-6777 or online at www.reserveusa.com ($9 reservation fee). The fee is $13 per night, plus $6 per additional vehicle. A senior discount is available. Open late May to early September.

Directions: In Medford on I-5, take Exit 14 to Highway 66. Drive east for less than a mile to Dead Indian Memorial Road. Turn left (east) and drive 40 miles to Lake of the Woods. Turn left onto Forest Service Road 3704 (on the east side of the lake). Drive .5 mile to the campground entrance on the left.

Contact: Winema National Forest, Klamath Ranger District, 1936 California Ave., Klamath Falls, OR 97601, 541/885-3400, fax 541/885-3452.

138 SUNSET

Rating: 8

near Lake of the Woods in Winema National Forest

See map pages 346–347

This campground (at 5,000 feet elevation) near the eastern shore of Lake of the Woods is fully developed and offers a myriad of recreation options. It's popular for both fishing and boating. Of the 67 sites, 20 are available by reservation.

RV sites, facilities: There are 67 sites for RVs up to 40 feet or tents. Picnic tables, garbage bins, and fire grills are provided. Drinking water, flush toilets, and cell phone reception are available. Boat docks, launching facilities, and rentals are nearby. Some facilities are wheelchair-accessible. Leashed pets are permitted.

Reservations, fees: Reserve at 877/444-6777 or online at www.reserveusa.com ($9 reservation fee). The fee is $13 per night, plus $6 per additional vehicle. A senior discount is available. Open June to mid-September.

Directions: In Medford on I-5, take Exit 14 to Highway 66. Drive east for less than a mile to Dead Indian Memorial Road. Turn left (east) and drive 40 miles to Lake of the Woods. Stay on Dead Indian Road on the east side of the lake, and continue for 1.5 miles to the campground entrance on the left.

Contact: Winema National Forest, Klamath Ranger District, 1936 California Ave., Klamath Falls, OR 97601, 541/885-3400, fax 541/885-3452.

139 AGENCY LAKE RESORT

Rating: 5

on Agency Lake

See map pages 346–347

This campground is on Agency Lake in an open, grassy area with some shaded sites. It has more than 750 feet of lakefront property, offering world-class trout fishing. Look across the lake and watch the sun set on the Cascades. There are many beautiful weeping willows. See the description of Rocky Point Resort earlier in this chapter for more information.

RV sites, facilities: There are 18 sites for RVs of any length, 10 with full hookups (30, 50 amps) and eight with partial hookups, 15 tent sites, three cabins, and one rental trailer. Picnic tables are provided. Drinking water, flush toilets, showers, a general store, ice, cell phone reception, boat docks, launching facilities, and marine gas are available. Leashed pets are permitted.

Reservations, fees: Reservations are accepted. The fee is $12–20 per night. Major credit cards are accepted. Open year-round, weather permitting.

Directions: From Klamath Falls, drive north on U.S. 97 for 17 miles to Modoc Point Road. Turn left (north) and drive about 10 miles to the campground on the left.

Contact: Agency Lake Resort, 37000 Modoc Point Rd., Chiloquin, OR 97624, 541/783-2489, website: www.kfalls.net/~agncylke.

140 POTTER'S PARK

Rating: 6

on the Sprague River

See map pages 346–347

This park on a bluff overlooking the river is in a wooded setting and bordered by the Sprague River and the Winema National Forest. For the most part, the area east of Klamath Lake doesn't get much attention.

RV sites, facilities: There are 22 sites with full hookups (20, 50 amps) for RVs of any length. Picnic tables are provided. Drinking water, flush toilets, showers, firewood, a convenience store, a telephone, and ice are available. Leashed pets are permitted.

Reservations, fees: Reservations are accepted. The fee is $13.50–15 per night, plus $2.50–5 per person for more than two people. Monthly rates are available. Open year-round, with limited winter facilities.

Directions: From Klamath Falls, drive north on U.S. 97 for 27 miles to Chiloquin and Sprague River Highway. Turn east on Sprague River Highway and drive 12 miles to the resort.

Contact: Potter's Park, 11700 Sprague River Rd., Chiloquin, OR 97624, 541/783-2253.

141 WATERWHEEL CAMPGROUND

Rating: 6

on the Williamson River

See map pages 346–347

This rural campground right on the Williamson River is close to hiking trails. Fishing can be excellent here, with a boat ramp and fishing tackle right at the camp.

RV sites, facilities: There are 28 sites for RVs of any length, 10 with full hookups (30 amps) and 18 with partial hookups; 22 are drive-through sites, plus six tent sites. Picnic tables and fire rings or barbecues are provided. Drinking water, flush toilets, propane, an RV dump station, showers, firewood, a store, a laundry room, a pay phone, cell phone reception, modem access, ice, and a playground are available. A café and an ATM are within one mile. Boat docks and launching facilities are nearby. Leashed pets are permitted.

Reservations, fees: Reservations are accepted. The fee is $16–23 per night, plus $1.50 per person for more than two people. Major credit cards are accepted. Open year-round, weather permitting.
Directions: From Klamath Falls, drive north on U.S. 97 for 20 miles to the campground (.25 mile south of the junction of U.S. 97 and Highway 62).
Contact: Waterwheel Campground, 200 Williamson River Dr., Chiloquin, OR 97624, 541/783-2738.

142 OREGON 8 MOTEL AND RV PARK

Rating: 6

on Upper Klamath Lake
See map pages 346–347
This campground, surrounded by mountains, big rocks, and trees, is near Hanks Marsh on the southeast shore of Upper Klamath Lake, within 50 miles of Crater Lake. Nearby recreation options include a golf course, bike paths, and a marina.
RV sites, facilities: There are 30 sites with full hookups (30 amps) for RVs of any length. Picnic tables and barbecues are provided. Drinking water, flush toilets, showers, cable TV, a recreation hall, a laundry room, ice, and a swimming pool are available. Propane, a store, and a café are within one mile. An ATM and a pay phone are within two miles. Leashed pets are permitted.
Reservations, fees: Reservations are accepted. The fee is $24–27 per night, plus $2 per person for more than two people and $1 per pet per night. Major credit cards are accepted. A senior discount is available. Open year-round, with limited winter facilities.
Directions: From Klamath Falls, drive north on U.S. 97 for 3.5 miles to the campground on the right (Milepost 270-271).
Contact: Oregon 8 Motel and RV Park, 5225 Hwy. 97 N, Klamath Falls, OR 97601, 541/883-3431.

143 LAKE SELMAC

Rating: 9

on Lake Selmac
See map pages 346–347
Nestled in a wooded, mountainous area, this 300-acre park offers swimming, hiking, boating, sail-ing, and good trout fishing on beautiful Lake Selmac. Seasonal hosts and an assistant park ranger are on-site.
RV sites, facilities: There are 81 sites, 38 with full hookups (30 amps) for RVs up to 40 feet or tents, and two yurts. Picnic tables and fire rings are provided. Facilities include drinking water, rest-rooms, coin-operated showers, an RV dump sta-tion, a pay phone, snacks, a barbecue, horseshoes, a playground, a recreation field, two boat ramps, and a dock. Some facilities are wheelchair-acces-sible. Leashed pets are permitted.
Reservations, fees: Reserve at 541/474-5285. The fees are $15–20 per night, plus $5 for a third vehi-cle, and $28 per night for a yurt plus a $28 refund-able deposit. Major credit cards are accepted. Open year-round, with limited winter service.
Directions: In Grants Pass on I-5, take the U.S. 199 exit. Turn southwest on U.S. 199 and drive for 23 miles to Selma and the Lake Selmac exit (Lakeshore Drive). Turn left (east) and drive two miles to the lake and the campground entrance.
Contact: Josephine County Parks, 125 Ringuette St., Grants Pass, OR 97527, 541/474-5285, fax 541/474-5288, website: www.co.josephine.or .us/parks/index.htm.

144 LAKE SELMAC RESORT

Rating: 7

on Lake Selmac
See map pages 346–347
This resort is set along the shore of Lake Selmac. Fishing is great for largemouth bass (the state record has been set here three times). Trout, crap-pie, bluegill, and catfish are also catchable here. There is a 10 mph speed limit on the lake. A trail circles the lake, and hikers, bikers, and horses are welcome. A golf course is about six miles away. Oregon Caves National Monument, about 30 miles away, makes a good side trip.
RV sites, facilities: There are 29 sites for RVs of any length or tents. Picnic tables and fire rings are provided. Drinking water, flush toilets, show-ers, firewood, a pay phone, fishing supplies, bait, an 18-hole miniature golf course, a store, a café, a laundry room, ice, and a playground are avail-able. Boat docks and launching facilities are near-by, and rentals are on-site. Horseback riding trails

OREGON

are available in the summer. Corrals are available for horse campers. An ATM is within three miles. Leashed pets are permitted.

Reservations, fees: Reservations are accepted. The fee is $17–19 per night for up to four people. Major credit cards are accepted. Open year-round, with limited winter facilities.

Directions: In Grants Pass on I-5, take the U.S. 199 exit. Turn southwest on U.S. 199 and drive 23 miles to Selma and the Lake Selmac exit (Lakeshore Drive). Turn left (east) and drive 2.5 miles to the lake and the resort on the left.

Contact: Lake Selmac Resort, 2700 Lakeshore Dr., Selma, OR 97538, 541/597-2277, website: www.lakeselmacresort.com.

145 TOWN AND COUNTRY RV PARK

Rating: 7

on the Illinois River
See map pages 346–347

This park on the Illinois River provides good opportunities for swimming and boating (no motors are permitted). Nearby side trips include Oregon Caves National Monument (21 miles) and Grants Pass (31 miles). Crescent City is 50 miles away. Note that a majority of the campground is taken by monthly rentals, with the remainder available for overnighters.

RV sites, facilities: There are 51 sites with full hookups (30, 50 amps) for RVs of any length or tents. Drinking water, cable TV, showers, restrooms, cell phone reception, a laundry room, and ice are available. Horseshoes, a clubhouse, and a playground are also available. An ATM and a pay phone are within two miles. Leashed pets are permitted.

Reservations, fees: Reservations are recommended. The fee is $18.50 for two people per night, plus $2 per additional person per night. Monthly rates are available. A senior discount is available. Open year-round.

Directions: In Grants Pass on I-5, take Exit 55 for U.S. 199. Bear southwest on U.S. 199 for 32 miles to Cave Junction and the campground.

Contact: Town and Country RV Park, 28288 Redwood Hwy., Cave Junction, OR 97523, tel./fax 541/592-2656.

146 COUNTRY HILLS RESORT

Rating: 7

near Oregon Caves National Monument
See map pages 346–347

Lots of sites at this wooded camp border Sucker Creek, a popular spot for swimming. Lake Selmac and Oregon Caves National Monument provide nearby side-trip options.

RV sites, facilities: There are 16 sites with partial hookups (20, 30 amps) for RVs of any length, two are drive-through, plus 12 tent sites. There are also six cabins and a five-unit motel. Picnic tables and fire pits are provided. Drinking water, flush toilets, showers, drinking water, electricity, firewood, a small store, a laundry room, a pay phone, volleyball, basketball, horseshoes, a motel, an ice-cream parlor, an outdoor café, and ice are available. An ATM is within eight miles. Leashed pets are permitted.

Reservations, fees: Reservations are accepted. The fees are $19 per night for RV sites, $15 per night for tent sites. Major credit cards are accepted. Open year-round.

Directions: In Grants Pass on I-5, take Exit 55 for U.S. 199. Bear southwest on U.S. 199 for 30 miles to Cave Junction and Highway 46. Turn east on Highway 46 and drive eight miles to the campground on the right.

Contact: Country Hills Resort, 7901 Caves Hwy., Cave Junction, OR 97523, 541/592-3406, fax 541/592-3406.

147 GRAYBACK

Rating: 7

near Oregon Caves National Monument in Siskiyou National Forest
See map pages 346–347

This wooded campground at an elevation of 2,000 feet along the banks of Sucker Creek has sites with ample shade and is a good choice if you're planning to visit Oregon Caves National Monument, about 10 miles away. The camp, set in a grove of old-growth firs, is a prime place for bird-watching. A half-mile barrier-free trail cuts through the camp.

RV sites, facilities: There are 37 sites for RVs up to 30 feet or tents; one site has a full hookup (20 amps). Picnic tables, garbage bins, and fire grills are provided. Flush toilets, drinking water, and cell phone reception are available. Some facilities are wheelchair-accessible. Leashed pets are permitted.

Reservations, fees: Reservations are not accepted. The fee is $15 per night, plus $5 per additional vehicle. A senior discount is available. Open May to October.

Directions: In Grants Pass on I-5, take Exit 55 for U.S. 199. Bear southwest on U.S. 199 for 30 miles to Cave Junction and Highway 46. Turn east on Highway 46 and drive 12 miles to the campground.

Contact: Siskiyou National Forest, Illinois Valley Ranger District, 26568 Redwood Hwy., Cave Junction, OR 97523, 541/592-4000, fax 541/592-4010.

148 CANTRALL-BUCKLEY PARK AND GROUP CAMP

Rating: 8

on the Applegate River

See map pages 346–347

This county park outside of Medford offers pleasant, shady sites in a wooded setting. The Applegate River, which has good trout fishing, runs nearby.

RV sites, facilities: There are 25 sites for self-contained RVs up to 25 feet or tents and one group area for 60 to 100 people. Picnic tables and fire pits are provided. Drinking water, restrooms, coin-operated showers, cell phone reception, and a pay phone are available. Recreational facilities include horseshoes, a playground, and a recreation field. An ATM is within one mile. Leashed pets are permitted.

Reservations, fees: Reservations are not accepted. The fee is $10 per night, plus $1 per pet per night. A senior discount is available. Reservations for the group site are required at 541/774-8183. Major credit cards are accepted with reservations only. Open year-round.

Directions: In Medford on I-5, take the Jacksonville exit to the Jacksonville Highway. Drive west on the Jacksonville Highway (Highway 238) for seven miles to Jacksonsville. Bear left on Highway 238 and drive to Hamilton Road. Turn south on Hamilton Road and drive to Cantrall Road. Turn right on Cantrall and drive to the campground.

Contact: Jackson County Parks, 400 Antelope Rd., White City, OR 97503, 541/774-8183, fax 541/774-6320, website: www.jacksoncountyparks.com.

149 THE WELLSPRINGS

Rating: 5

near Ashland

See map pages 346–347

This wooded campground has mineral hot springs that empty into a swimming pool, not a hot pool (80 degrees). Hot mineral baths are available in private rooms. Swimming and saunas are available for a fee, and there is also a hot pool (100–102 degrees). This is an old Indian birthing ground. Nearby recreation options include a golf course, hiking trails, a bike path, and tennis courts. Boating, fishing, and water-skiing are within 10 miles. Some may remember this campground under its former name, Jackson Hot Springs.

RV sites, facilities: There are 20 drive-through sites with full hookups (30 amps) for RVs of any length, 30 tent sites, and three tepees. Picnic tables are provided. Drinking water, flush toilets, showers, a laundry room, a pay phone, cell phone reception, ice, and a swimming pool are available. A store and an ATM are within one block. Propane is within one mile. Pets are permitted with a deposit.

Reservations, fees: Reservations are not accepted. The fees are $14–20 per night for one person, plus $8 per person for more than one person, and $25 per tepee per night for up to three people. Major credit cards are accepted. Open year-round.

Directions: From Ashland, drive north on I-5 to Exit 19. Take that exit and drive west for .25 mile to the stoplight at Highway 99. Turn right and drive 500 feet to the campground.

Contact: The WellSprings, 2253 Hwy. 99 N, Ashland, OR 97520, tel./fax 541/482-3776.

150 GLENYAN CAMPGROUND OF ASHLAND

Rating: 7

near Emigrant Lake

See map pages 346–347

This campground within seven miles of Ashland

offers shady sites near Emigrant Lake. Recreation options in the area include a golf course, hiking trails, a bike path, and tennis courts. It's an easy jump from I-5 at Ashland.

RV sites, facilities: There are 23 sites for RVs up to 40 feet or tents; 12 have full hookups (30 amps) and 38 have partial hookups. Picnic tables, fire rings, and barbecues are provided. Drinking water, flush toilets, propane, an RV dump station, showers, a pay phone, modem access, wireless Internet, cell phone reception, firewood, a recreation hall, a store, a laundry room, ice, a playground, and a swimming pool are available. An ATM is within 3.5 miles. Leashed pets are permitted.

Reservations, fees: Reserve at 877/453-6926. The fee is $18.50–24 per night, plus $2 per person for more than two people. Major credit cards are accepted. A senior discount is available. Open year-round.

Directions: From Ashland, drive east on Highway 66 for 3.5 miles to the campground on the right.

Contact: Glenyan Campground of Ashland, 5310 Hwy. 66, Ashland, OR 97520, 541/488-1785, website: www.glenyancampground.com.

151 HOWARD PRAIRIE LAKE RESORT

Rating: 7

on Howard Prairie Lake
See map pages 346–347

This wooded campground is located along the shore of Howard Prairie Lake, where hiking, swimming, fishing, and boating are among the recreation options. This is one of the largest campgrounds in more than 100 miles.

RV sites, facilities: There are 300 sites, about half with partial or full hookups (20, 30 amps), for RVs of any length or tents and 20 furnished RV rentals. Picnic tables and fire pits are provided. Drinking water, flush toilets, propane, a pay phone, modem access, cell phone reception, an RV dump station, showers, firewood, a store, a café, a laundry room, boat docks, boat rentals, moorage, and launching facilities are available. Leashed pets are permitted.

Reservations, fees: Reservations are not accepted. The fee is $17–21 per night, plus $5 per person for more than two people. Major credit cards are accepted. Open mid-April to October.

Directions: In Ashland on I-5, take Exit 14 to Highway 66. Drive east for less than a mile to Dead Indian Memorial Road. Turn left (east) and drive 17 miles to Howard Prairie Road. Turn right (south) and drive two miles to the reservoir.

Contact: Howard Prairie Lake Resort, 3249 Hyatt Prairie Rd., Ashland, OR 97520, 541/482-1979, fax 541/488-7485, website: www.howardprairieresort.com.

152 LILY GLEN CAMPGROUND

Rating: 6

near Howard Prairie Lake
See map pages 346–347

Set along the shore of Howard Prairie Lake, this horse camp is a secluded, primitive getaway. Trout fishing is available. Tubb Springs Wayside State Park and the nearby Rogue River National Forest are possible side trips. There is also nearby access to the Pacific Crest Trail.

RV sites, facilities: There are 26 sites for self-contained RVs or tents and two group sites for 60 to 100 people. Picnic tables, drinking water, vault toilets, cell phone reception, individual corrals, and a large barn are available. A pay phone and an ATM are within two miles. Some facilities are wheelchair-accessible. Leashed pets are permitted.

Reservations, fees: Reservations are not accepted for family sites. The fee is $14–16 per night, plus $1 per pet per night. Make group reservations at 541/774-8183; the fee is $75–125 per night. Major credit cards are accepted for reservations. A senior discount is available. Open year-round, with limited winter services.

Directions: In Ashland on I-5, take Exit 14 to Highway 66. Drive east for less than a mile to Dead Indian Memorial Road. Turn left (east) and drive 17 miles to the campground.

Contact: Jackson County Parks, 400 Antelope Rd., White City, OR 97503, 541/774-8183, fax 541/774-6320, website: www.jacksoncountyparks.com.

153 WILLOW POINT

Rating: 7

near Howard Prairie Lake
See map pages 346–347

Willow Point is the most popular of the three

county campgrounds on Howard Prairie Lake. It offers flat sites in an area well covered by trees. Another county park campground, Grizzly, is available at the lake as well for self-contained RVs and tent campers; there are no hookups.

RV sites, facilities: There are 40 sites for self-contained RVs up to 30 feet or tents. Picnic tables and fire rings are provided. Drinking water, vault toilets, cell phone reception, and garbage bins are available. A boat ramp is nearby. A store, a café, an ATM, a pay phone, laundry facilities, and boat rentals are within four miles. Some facilities are wheelchair-accessible. Leashed pets are permitted.

Reservations, fees: Reservations are not accepted for family sites. The fee is $14 per night, plus $1 per pet per night. Major credit cards are accepted for reservations. A senior discount is available. Open mid-April to October.

Directions: In Ashland on I-5, take Exit 14 to Highway 66. Drive east for less than a mile to Dead Indian Memorial Road. Turn left (east) and drive 17 miles to Howard Prairie Road. Turn right (south) and drive three miles to the reservoir.

Contact: Jackson County Parks, 400 Antelope Rd., White City, OR 97503, 541/774-8183, fax 541/774-6320, website: www.jacksoncountyparks.com.

154 KLUM LANDING

Rating: 7

near Howard Prairie Lake
See map pages 346–347

Klum Landing is one of three county campgrounds on Howard Prairie Lake. The others are Grizzly and Willow Point. A bonus at this one is that coin-operated showers are available.

RV sites, facilities: There are 30 sites for self-contained RVs up to 30 feet or tents. Picnic tables and fire rings are provided. Drinking water, garbage bins, cell phone reception, and restrooms with flush toilets and showers are available. A boat ramp is nearby. A store, a pay phone, an ATM, a café, laundry facilities, and boat rentals are available at Howard Prairie Lake Resort. Some facilities are wheelchair-accessible. Leashed pets are permitted.

Reservations, fees: Reservations are not accepted. The fee is $16 per night, plus $1 per pet per

night. A senior discount is available. Open mid-April to October.

Directions: In Ashland on I-5, take Exit 14 to Highway 66. Drive east for less than a mile to Dead Indian Memorial Road. Turn left (east) and drive 17 miles to Howard Prairie Road. Turn right (south) and drive eight miles to Howard Prairie Dam Road. Turn left (east) and drive one mile to the campground.

Contact: Jackson County Parks, 400 Antelope Rd., White City, OR 97503, 541/774-8183, fax 541/774-6320, website: www.jacksoncountyparks.com.

155 HYATT LAKE

Rating: 8

on Hyatt Lake
See map pages 346–347

This campground is situated on the south end of Hyatt Lake, which has six miles of shoreline. Fishing is good for brook and rainbow trout and smallmouth bass. Another campground option is Wildcat, about two miles north, with 12 semi-primitive sites. The boat speed limit here is 10 mph.

RV sites, facilities: There are 47 sites for RVs up to 40 feet or tents, one horse campsite, two group sites, and a few walk-in tent sites. Picnic tables and fire grills are provided. Drinking water, flush toilets, showers, garbage service, a pay phone, cell phone reception, an RV dump station, a group kitchen, a fish-cleaning station, a day-use area, athletic fields, a playground, horseshoes, and two boat ramps are available. Some facilities are wheelchair-accessible. Leashed pets are permitted.

Reservations, fees: Reservations are not accepted for individual sites. The fee is $12–15 per night, plus $3 per additional vehicle, with a 14-day stay limit. Campsites with horse facilities are $10 per night. Reserve group sites at 541/618-2306. The group site fee is $45–100 per night. Sites at nearby primitive Wildcat Campground are $7 per night. A senior discount is available. Open late April to October, weather permitting.

Directions: From Ashland, drive east on Highway 66 for 17 miles to East Hyatt Lake Road. Turn north and drive three miles to the campground entrance on the right.

Contact: Bureau of Land Management, Medford

District, 3040 Biddle Rd., Medford, OR 97504, 541/618-2200, fax 541/618-2400.

156 HYATT LAKE RESORT

Rating: 7

on Hyatt Lake
See map pages 346–347

This campground is set along the shore of Hyatt Lake, just west of the dam, where hiking and fishing are some of the recreation options. This is a scaled-down alternative to the resort at adjacent Howard Prairie Lake. The Pacific Crest Trail is just half a mile away.

RV sites, facilities: There are 22 sites with full hookups (30, 50 amps) for RVs of any length, including four drive-through sites, and 13 tent sites. There are also four cabins with no kitchen facilities; each sleeps four. Picnic tables and fire pits are provided. Drinking water, flush toilets, a pay phone, cell phone reception, an RV dump station, showers, a store, a laundry room, ice, and boat rentals are available. Boat docks and launching facilities are on the resort property. Leashed pets are permitted.

Reservations, fees: Reservations are accepted. The fee is $15–20 per night, plus $5 per extra tent or vehicle. Major credit cards are accepted. Open April to October.

Directions: From Ashland, drive east on Highway 66 for 17 miles to East Hyatt Lake Road. Turn north and drive three miles to Hyatt Prairie Road. Turn left and drive one mile to the resort.

Contact: Hyatt Lake Resort, 7979 Hyatt Prairie Rd., Ashland, OR 97520, 541/482-3331, website: www.hyattlake.com.

157 CAMPER'S COVE

Rating: 7

on Hyatt Lake
See map pages 346–347

This campground is set about 400 feet from the shore of Hyatt Lake, with the Pacific Crest Trail passing about a mile away. It is in a cove east of the dam. No tents are permitted here.

RV sites, facilities: There are 23 sites with full hookups (30 amps), seven drive-through, for RVs

up to 30 feet. Picnic tables are provided. Drinking water, flush toilets, showers, firewood, a restaurant, a pay phone, cell phone reception, a store, a café, a bar, a lounge, and ice are available. Boat docks are nearby. Leashed pets are permitted.

Reservations, fees: Reservations are accepted. The fee is $18 per night, plus $1 per person for more than two people. Major credit cards are accepted. Open year-round.

Directions: From Ashland drive east on Highway 66 for 17 miles to Hyatt Lake Access Road. Turn north and drive three miles to Hyatt Prairie Road. Turn left and drive 2.5 miles (over the dam) to the resort.

Contact: Camper's Cove, 7900 Hyatt Prairie Rd., Ashland, OR 97520, 541/482-1201, website: www.camperscove.com.

158 EMIGRANT CAMPGROUND

Rating: 8

on Emigrant Lake
See map pages 346–347

This camp is nestled among the trees above Emigrant Lake, a well-known recreational area. Activities at this park include swimming, hiking, boating, water-skiing, and fishing. There are also two super water slides. The park has its own swimming cove (unsupervised). Side-trip possibilities include exploring nearby Mount Ashland, where a ski area operates in the winter, and visiting the world-renowned Shakespeare Festival in Ashland as well as historic Jacksonville and the Britt Music Festival.

RV sites, facilities: There are 42 sites for self-contained RVs up to 30 feet or tents, 32 sites with full hookups (50 amps) for RVs, an overflow area, and one group camp area for up to 75 people. Restrooms, coin-operated showers, an RV dump station, a pay phone, cell phone reception, snacks in summer, and a barbecue are available. A group picnic and barbecue area is also available. Recreational facilities include horseshoes, volleyball, and a recreation field. Two boat ramps are provided. An ATM, coin-operated laundry, and food facilities are within six miles. Some facilities are wheelchair-accessible. Pets are permitted in designated areas only.

Reservations, fees: Reserve RV sites and the group site at 541/774-8183. The fee is $16–20 per night

OREGON

for RV and family sites; the group site is $100 per night. Major credit cards are accepted for reservations. A senior discount is available. Open mid-April to October.

Directions: From Ashland, drive east on Highway 66 for five miles to the campground.

Contact: Jackson County Parks, 400 Antelope Rd., White City, OR 97503, 541/774-8183, fax 541/774-6320, website: www.jacksoncountyparks.com.

159 TOPSY

Rating: 7

on the Upper Klamath River
See map pages 346–347

This campground is on Boyle Reservoir near the Upper Klamath River, a good spot for trout fishing and a top river for rafters (experts only, or nonexperts with professional licensed guides). There are Class IV and V rapids about four miles southwest at Caldera, Satan's Gate, and Hells Corner. I flipped at Caldera and ended up swimming for it, finally getting out at an eddy. Luckily, I was wearing a dry suit and the best lifejacket available, perfect fitting, which saved my butt. The area is good for mountain biking, too.

RV sites, facilities: There are 13 sites for RVs up to 40 feet. Picnic tables and fire grills are provided. Drinking water, vault toilets, garbage service, cell phone reception, and an RV dump station are available. Boat-launching facilities are nearby. An ATM and a pay phone are within six miles. A camp host is on-site. Some facilities are wheelchair-accessible. Leashed pets are permitted.

Reservations, fees: Reservations are not accepted. The fee is $7 per night, plus $4 per additional vehicle, with a 14-day stay limit. A senior discount is available. Open early May to late September.

Directions: From Klamath Falls, drive west on Highway 66 for 18 miles to Topsy Road. Turn south on Topsy Road and drive one mile to the campground on the right.

Contact: Bureau of Land Management, Klamath Falls Resource Area, 2795 Anderson Ave., Building 25, Klamath Falls, OR 97603, 541/883-6916, fax 541/884-2097.

160 TINGLEY LAKE ESTATES

Rating: 7

on Tingley Lake
See map pages 346–347

This privately operated RV park provides a layover for travelers crossing the Oregon border on U.S. 97. You can see California's Mount Shasta from this park right on the lake. All sites have a view of Tingley Lake, which has opportunities for bass fishing, boating, and swimming. Note that about half of the 16 sites at this park are booked for the entire summer season. A nice bonus: Free use of rowboats and canoes is included with the price.

RV sites, facilities: There are 10 sites for RVs of any length; three have full hookups (30 amps) and seven have partial hookups, and six tent sites. Picnic tables and barbecues are provided. Drinking water, telephone and cable TV hookups, cell phone reception, flush toilets, showers, boat docks, and a playground are available. A store, a café, and ice are within two miles. A pay phone and an ATM are within four miles. Leashed pets are permitted.

Reservations, fees: Reservations are accepted. The fee is $15–18 per night, plus $2 per person for more than two people. Monthly rates are available. Open year-round, weather permitting, with limited winter services.

Directions: From Klamath Falls, drive southwest on U.S. 97 for seven miles to Old Midland Road. Turn east and drive two miles to Tingley Lane. Turn right (south) and drive .5 mile to the park.

Contact: Tingley Lake Estates, 11800 Tingley Ln., Klamath Falls, OR 97603, tel./fax 541/882-8386.

OREGON

Oregon

Chapter 12
Southeastern Oregon

OREGON

see The
Southern
Cascades
pages 346–347

Deschutes

National

Forest

Bend

20

Ochoco National Forest

7

Ochoco
National Forest

Newberry Nat'l
Volcanic Mon.

Wickiup
Reservoir

1-3   4-6
East
Lake

Paulina
Lake

Deschutes
National
Forest

16

Moon
Res.

395

Silver Lake

97

Winema

National

Forest

Fremont

National

Forest

31

Silver
Lake

18
19

Summer
Lake

N
W   E
S

Great Sandy Desert

Warner Lakes

Fremont   20   21

23
24   25

22

31

Lake
Abert

National

Forest

Mountains

140

Gerber
Res.

32

33

34

Fremont

Drews
Res.

36   37

38

39

395

35

Lakeview

Goose

39

Lake

Hart Mountain

National Antelope

Refuge

Hart
Lake

Crump
Lake

40

140

Fremont

National

Forest

Charles

Antelope

Lower
Klamath Lake

Tule
Lake

Clear Lake
Res.

CALIFORNIA

Lava Beds
Nati'l Mon.

Modoc National

Forest

see
California
page 428

39

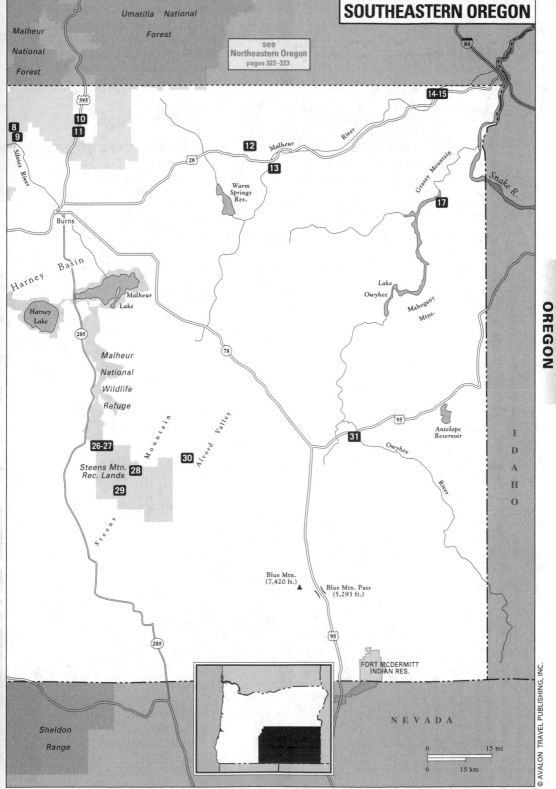

see
Northeastern Oregon
pages 322–323

Umatilla   National

Malheur   Forest

National

Forest

Malheur   River

Silvies River

Grassy Mountain

Snake R.

8
9

10
11

14-15

12

20

13

17

Warm
Springs
Res.

Burns

Lake
Owyhee

Harney   Basin

Malheur
Lake

Mahogany
Mtns.

Harney
Lake

205

Malheur

National

Wildlife

Refuge

78

95

Antelope
Reservoir

31

Owyhee

26-27

Mountain

Alvord Valley

30

River

Steens Mtn.
Rec. Lands

28

29

Steens

I
D
A
H
O

OREGON

Blue Mtn.
(7,420 ft.)

Blue Mtn. Pass
(5,293 ft.)

205

95

FORT MCDERMITT
INDIAN RES.

Sheldon

Range

NEVADA

0   15 mi

0   15 km

Chapter 12—Southeastern Oregon

Some people think that southeastern Oregon is one big chunk of nothing. They are only half right. True, this high-desert region is dry and foreboding, with many miles between camps in several areas. However, because this part of Oregon is so under-visited, often you'll have vast areas of great land all to yourself.

Among the southeast's highlights are the Newberry Volcanic Monument, with East and Paulina Lakes set within its craters; Paulina is one of the best lakes for a chance to catch big brown trout in the Western United States. Here as well is the launch point for one of the best canoe trips, the Owyhee River. This watershed is like nothing most have ever seen. It looks like a miniature Grand Canyon, with steep, orange walls and the river cutting a circuitous route through the desert. I have paddled a canoe through most of it, from remote stretches below the Jarbridge Mountains in Nevada through Idaho and then into Oregon.

Be aware, though, if you tour this area of Oregon, to keep an eye on your gas tank and be alert about how far you are from the coming night's campground. You can cover a hellacious number of miles between a chance for gas and a camp.

1 PAULINA LAKE

Rating: 8

on Paulina Lake in Deschutes National Forest
See map pages 408–409

This campground (6,350 feet elevation) is set along the south shore of Paulina Lake and within the Newberry National Volcanic Monument. The lake itself sits in a volcanic crater. Nearby trails provide access to the remains of volcanic activity, including craters and obsidian flows. My longtime friend Guy Carl caught the state's record brown trout here, right after I'd written a story about his unique method of using giant Rapala and Rebel bass lures for giant browns. However, according to Todd Brown at Paulina Lake Resort, that record has since been beaten by Ron Lane of Olancha, CA, who on October 4, 2002, caught a brown weighing in at 28 pounds, five ounces. Whooowheee! The boat speed limit here is 10 mph. The camp is adjacent to Paulina Lake Resort. The recreation options here include boating, sailing, fishing, and hiking. Note that food-raiding bears are common at all the campgrounds in the Newberry Caldera area, and that all food must be kept out of reach. Do not store food in vehicles.

RV sites, facilities: There are 69 sites for RVs up to 30 feet. Picnic tables, garbage service, and fire grills are provided. Drinking water and flush and vault toilets are available. Boat docks, launching facilities, boat rentals, a small store, a coin-operated laundry, coin-operated showers, a restaurant, cabins, gas, and propane are within five miles. The Newberry RV dump station is nearby. Some facilities are wheelchair-accessible. Leashed pets are permitted.

Reservations, fees: Reservations are not accepted. The fee is $10–12 per vehicle per night for the first two RVs, plus $5 for each additional vehicle. A senior discount is available. Open late May to late October.

Directions: From Bend, drive south on U.S. 97 for 23.5 miles to County Road 21 (Paulina/East Lake Road). Turn left (east) and drive 12.9 miles to the campground.

Contact: Deschutes National Forest, Bend–Fort Rock Ranger District, 1230 NE 3rd St., Suite A-262, Bend, OR 97701, 541/383-4000, fax 541/383-4700.

2 CHIEF PAULINA HORSE CAMP

Rating: 4

on Paulina Lake in Deschutes National Forest
See map pages 408–409

This campground is set at an elevation of 6,400 feet, about a quarter mile from the south shore of Paulina Lake. Horse trails and a vista point are close by. See the previous description of Paulina Lake for additional recreation information.

RV sites, facilities: There are 14 sites for RVs up to 30 feet or tents. Picnic tables, garbage service, horse corrals, and fire grills are provided. Vault toilets are available, but there is no drinking water. Boat docks and rentals are nearby. A pay phone is within two miles. Leashed pets are permitted.

Reservations, fees: Reservations are not accepted. The fee is $12 per night, plus $5 per additional vehicle. A senior discount is available. Open late May to late October, weather permitting.

Directions: From Bend, drive south on U.S. 97 for 23.5 miles to County Road 21 (Paulina/East Lake Road). Turn left (east) and drive 14 miles to the campground.

Contact: Deschutes National Forest, Bend–Fort Rock Ranger District, 1230 NE 3rd St., Suite A-262, Bend, OR 97701, 541/383-4000, fax 541/383-4700.

3 LITTLE CRATER

Rating: 8

near Paulina Lake in Deschutes National Forest
See map pages 408–409

This campground is set at 6,350 feet elevation near the east shore of Paulina Lake in Newberry National Volcanic Monument, a caldera. This camp is very popular. See the earlier description of Paulina Lake for more information.

RV sites, facilities: There are 50 sites for RVs up to 30 feet or tents. Picnic tables, garbage service, and fire grills are provided. Drinking water and vault toilets are available. Boat docks and launching facilities are on-site, and boat rentals are nearby. A pay phone is within four miles. Some facilities are wheelchair-accessible. Leashed pets are permitted.

Reservations, fees: Reservations are not accepted. The fee is $14 per vehicle per night for the first two vehicles, plus $5 per additional vehicle. A senior discount is available. Parking at the trailhead at the campground requires a Northwest Forest Pass ($5 daily fee or $30 annual fee per parked vehicle). Open late May to late October.

Directions: From Bend, drive south on U.S. 97 for 23.5 miles to County Road 21 (Paulina/East Lake Road). Turn left (east) and drive 14.5 miles to Forest Road 2110. Turn left (north) and drive .5 mile to the campground.

Contact: Deschutes National Forest, Bend–Fort Rock Ranger District, 1230 NE 3rd St., Suite A-262, Bend, OR 97701, 541/383-4000, fax 541/383-4700.

4 CINDER HILL

Rating: 7

on East Lake in Deschutes National Forest
See map pages 408–409
The campground is situated along the northeast shore of East Lake at an elevation of 6,400 feet. Located within the Newberry National Volcanic Monument, Cinder Hill makes a good base camp for area activities. Boating, fishing, and hiking are among the recreation options here. Boat speed is limited to 10 mph.

RV sites, facilities: There are 110 sites for RVs up to 30 feet or tents. Picnic tables, garbage service, and fire grills are provided. Drinking water and flush and vault toilets are available. Boat docks and launching facilities are on-site, and boat rentals, a store, a restaurant, showers, a pay phone, a coin-operated laundry, and cabins are nearby at East Lake Resort. Some facilities are wheelchair-accessible. Leashed pets are permitted.

Reservations, fees: Reservations are not accepted. The fee is $10–12 per vehicle per night for the first two vehicles, plus $5 per additional vehicle. Parking at the trailhead at the campground requires a Northwest Forest Pass ($5 daily fee or $30 annual fee per parked vehicle). A senior discount is available. Open late May to late October.

Directions: From Bend, drive south on U.S. 97 for 23.5 miles to County Road 21 (Paulina/East Lake Road). Turn left (east) and drive 17.6 miles

to Forest Road 2110-700. Turn left (north) and drive .5 mile to the campground.

Contact: Deschutes National Forest, Bend–Fort Rock Ranger District, 1230 NE 3rd St., Suite A-262, Bend, OR 97701, 541/383-4000, fax 541/383-4700.

5 EAST LAKE

Rating: 8

on East Lake in Deschutes National Forest
See map pages 408–409
This campground is set along the south shore of East Lake at an elevation of 6,400 feet. Boating and fishing are popular here, and hiking trails provide access to signs of former volcanic activity in the area. East Lake Campground is similar to Cinder Hill (see previous listing), but smaller. Boat speed is limited to 10 mph.

RV sites, facilities: There are 29 sites for RVs up to 30 feet or tents. Picnic tables, garbage service, and fire grills are provided. Drinking water and flush and vault toilets are available. Boat docks, launching facilities, rentals, and a pay phone are nearby. Some facilities are wheelchair-accessible. Leashed pets are permitted.

Reservations, fees: Reservations are not accepted. The fee is $10–12 per vehicle per night for the first two vehicles, plus $5 per additional vehicle. A senior discount is available. Open late May to late October.

Directions: From Bend, drive south on U.S. 97 for 23.5 miles to County Road 21 (Paulina/East Lake Road). Turn left (east) and drive 16.6 miles to the campground.

Contact: Deschutes National Forest, Bend–Fort Rock Ranger District, 1230 NE 3rd St., Suite A-262, Bend, OR 97701, 541/383-4000, fax 541/383-4700.

6 EAST LAKE RESORT AND RV PARK

Rating: 7

on East Lake
See map pages 408–409
This resort offers shaded sites in a wooded, mountainous setting on the east shore of East Lake.

Opportunities for fishing, boating, and swimming abound.

RV sites, facilities: There are 38 sites with partial hookups (30, 50 amps) for RVs up to 40 feet or tents and 16 cabins. Picnic tables, barbecues, and fire pits are provided. Drinking water, flush toilets, propane, showers, barbecues, cabins, firewood, a store, a pay phone, a café, a laundry room, ice, boat-launching facilities, boat rentals, moorage, and a playground are available. A dump station is on-site. Leashed pets are permitted.

Reservations, fees: Reservations are accepted. The fee is $15 per night. Cabins are $50–145. Major credit cards are accepted. Open mid-May to mid-October, weather permitting.

Directions: From Bend, drive south on U.S. 97 for 23.5 miles to County Road 21 (Paulina/East Lake Road). Turn left (east) and drive 18 miles to the campground at the end of the road.

Contact: East Lake Resort and RV Park, P.O. Box 95, La Pine, OR 97739, 541/536-2230, website: www.eastlakeresort.com.

⑦ DELINTMENT LAKE

Rating: 7

on Delintment Lake in Malheur National Forest
See map pages 408–409

This very pretty, forested camp is set along the shore of Delintment Lake. Originally a beaver pond, the lake was gradually developed to its current size of 57 acres. It is now pretty and blue and is stocked with trout, providing good bank and boat fishing. Here's an insider's note: Rainbow trout here average 12 to 18 inches.

RV sites, facilities: There are 29 sites for RVs up to 30 feet or tents. Picnic tables and fire grills are provided. Drinking water, a group picnic area on the lake with tables and grills, and vault toilets are available. Boat-launching facilities are in the campground. Some facilities are wheelchair-accessible. Leashed pets are permitted.

Reservations, fees: Reservations are not accepted. The fee is $7 per night, plus $3 per night for an additional vehicle. A senior discount is available. Open May to October.

Directions: From Burns, drive southwest on U.S. 20 for three miles to County Road 127. Turn right (northwest) and drive about 18 miles to Forest

Road 41. Turn left on Forest Road 41 and drive about 35 miles (staying on Forest Road 41 at all junctions, paved all the way) to the campground at the lake.

Contact: Malheur National Forest, Emigrant Creek Ranger District, 265 Hwy. 20 S, Hines, OR 97738, 541/573-4300, fax 541/573-4398.

⑧ YELLOWJACKET

Rating: 8

on Yellowjacket Lake in Malheur National Forest
See map pages 408–409

This campground (elevation 4,800 feet) in the ponderosa pines is set along the shore of Yellowjacket Lake, where fishing for rainbow trout can be very good in the summer. The camp is quiet and uncrowded.

RV sites, facilities: There are 20 sites for RVs up to 22 feet or tents. Picnic tables, drinking water, and vault toilets are available, but all garbage must be packed out. A boat launch is nearby. Leashed pets are permitted.

Reservations, fees: Reservations are not accepted. The fee is $7 per night, plus $3 per night for an additional vehicle, except for towed vehicles. A senior discount is available. Open late May to October, weather permitting.

Directions: From Burns, drive southwest on U.S. 20 for three miles to County Road 127. Turn right (northwest) and drive 32 miles to Forest Road 37. Turn right and drive three miles to Forest Road 3745. Turn right and drive one mile to the campground on the right.

Contact: Malheur National Forest, Emigrant Creek Ranger District, 265 Hwy. 20 S, Hines, OR 97738, 541/573-4300, fax 541/573-4398.

⑨ FALLS

Rating: 5

near Emigrant Creek in Malheur National Forest
See map pages 408–409

Falls camp is set in a beautiful meadow next to Emigrant Creek and is surrounded by ponderosa pine forests. This campground is a great place

OREGON

to see wildflowers in the early summer. A short trail leads to a small waterfall on the creek, from which the camp gets its name. Fly-fishing and mountain biking are good here, as well as at nearby Emigrant (see listing in Chapter 11), set two miles down the road. The elevation is 5,200 feet.

RV sites, facilities: There are seven sites for RVs up to 30 feet or tents. Picnic tables and fire grills are provided. Drinking water and vault toilets are available. Garbage must be packed out. Some facilities are wheelchair-accessible. Leashed pets are permitted.

Reservations, fees: Reservations are not accepted. The fee is $7 per night, plus $3 per night for an additional vehicle, except for towed vehicles. A senior discount is available. Open May to October.

Directions: From Burns, drive southwest on U.S. 20 for three miles to County Road 127. Turn right (northwest) and drive 25 miles (passing Forest Road 41 on the left) to Forest Road 43 and the junction for Allison Guard Station, Delintment Lake, and Paulina. Turn left on Forest Road 43 and drive eight miles to the campground on the left.

Contact: Malheur National Forest, Emigrant Creek Ranger District, 265 Hwy. 20 S, Hines, OR 97738, 541/573-4300, fax 541/573-4398.

10 JOAQUIN MILLER HORSE CAMP

Rating: 5

in Malheur National Forest
See map pages 408–409

Campsites are spread out and there's a fair amount of privacy at this camp set among mature ponderosa pines and adjacent to a meadow. Expect some highway noise. Lots of old logging roads are available for walking, biking, and horseback riding. The camp gets low use, and while it caters to horse campers, all are welcome. Campers with horses are strongly advised to arrive early before holiday weekends to claim the campsites nearest to the corrals.

RV sites, facilities: There are 18 sites for RVs up to 28 feet or tents. Picnic tables and fire rings are provided. Drinking water and vault toilets are available. All garbage must be packed out.

Stock facilities include four corrals and hitching rails. Leashed pets are permitted.

Reservations, fees: Reservations are not accepted. There is no fee for camping. Open mid-May to November, weather permitting.

Directions: From Burns, drive north on U.S. 395 for 19 miles to the campground on the left (this turnoff is easy to miss; watch for a very small green sign on the right that says, "Joaquin Miller Horse Camp").

Contact: Malheur National Forest, Emigrant Creek Ranger District, 265 Hwy. 20 S, Hines, OR 97738, 541/573-4300, fax 541/573-4398.

11 IDLEWILD

Rating: 8

in Devine Canyon in Malheur National Forest
See map pages 408–409

This campground is set at an elevation of 5,300 feet in Devine Canyon, a designated Sno-Park in the winter that's popular with locals for snowmobiling and cross-country skiing. Several hiking and biking trailheads start here, including the Divine Summit Interpretive Loop Trail and the Idlewild Loop Trail. Since it provides easy access and a pretty setting, it's also a popular spot for visitors traveling up U.S. 395 and in need of a stopover. Bird-watching for white-headed woodpeckers and goshawks is popular. Expect to hear some highway noise. But the ponderosa pine forest and area trails are so beautiful that this area can feel divine, even if Devine Canyon and neighboring Devine Ridge are spelled after the guy who named the place in the good old days when nobody worried about spelling.

RV sites, facilities: There are five sites for RVs up to 30 feet and 26 sites for tents. Picnic tables, fire grills, and picnic areas are provided. Drinking water, a group picnic shelter, cell phone reception, and vault toilets are available. Some facilities are wheelchair-accessible. Leashed pets are permitted.

Reservations, fees: Reservations are not accepted. The fee is $7 per night, plus $3 per night for an additional vehicle, except for towed vehicles. A senior discount is available. Open late May to mid-October.

Directions: From Burns, drive north on U.S. 395 for 17 miles to the campground on the right.

Contact: Malheur National Forest, Emigrant Creek Ranger District, 265 Hwy. 20 S, Hines, OR 97738, 541/573-4300, fax 541/573-4398.

12 CHUKAR PARK

Rating: 7

near the North Fork of the Malheur River

See map pages 408–409

This campground is set along the banks of the North Fork of the Malheur River. The general area provides habitat for chukar, an upland game bird species. Hunting can be good in season during the fall but requires much hiking in rugged terrain. Trout fishing is also popular here. The BLM asks that visitors please respect the surrounding private property.

RV sites, facilities: There are 18 sites for RVs up to 28 feet or tents. Picnic tables, fire grills, and garbage services are provided. Drinking water (May to October only) and vault toilets are available. A pay phone and a store are within six miles. Leashed pets are permitted.

Reservations, fees: Reservations are not accepted. The fee is $5 per night per vehicle, with a 14-day stay limit. A senior discount is available. Open year-round, with limited winter facilities.

Directions: From Burns, drive north on U.S. 395 for three miles to U.S. 20. Turn east and drive 55 miles to Juntura and Beulah Reservoir Road. Turn northwest and drive six miles to the campground.

Contact: Bureau of Land Management, Vale District, 100 Oregon St., Vale, OR 97918-9630, 541/473-3144, fax 541/473-6213.

13 OASIS MOTEL & RV PARK

Rating: 6

in Juntura

See map pages 408–409

One of the only camps in the area, this well-maintained RV park is close to Chukar Park. New owners here have been busy making extensive improvements throughout. See the prior description of Chukar Park for more details.

RV sites, facilities: There are 22 sites with full hookups (20, 30, 50 amps), including eight drive-through, for RVs of any length, and nine motel rooms. Drinking water, flush toilets, showers, cell phone reception, a pay phone, a community fire pit with a 16-person table, a café, and ice are available. Leashed pets are permitted.

Reservations, fees: Reservations are recommended. The fee is $16 per night, plus $5 per pet per night in motel rooms. Open year-round.

Directions: From Burns, drive north on U.S. 395 for three miles to U.S. 20. Turn east and drive 55 miles to Juntura. The park is in Juntura (a very small town) along U.S. 20.

Contact: Oasis Motel & RV Park, P.O. Box 277, Juntura, OR 97911, 541/277-3605, fax 541/277-3312.

14 PROSPECTOR RV PARK

Rating: 5

in Vale

See map pages 408–409

Prospector is one of two RV parks (Golden Wheel Motel and Westerner RV Park is the other) for travelers in the Vale area. For tents, this one is more comfortable, featuring a specifically designated wooded and grassy area. It claims to be a fishing and hunting paradise, and it even has a game bird cleaning room. It is set on the historic Oregon Trail.

RV sites, facilities: There are 36 drive-through sites, 32 with full hookups (20, 30, 50 amps) and four with partial hookups, for RVs of any length, 10 tent sites, plus a separate area for tents. Picnic tables are provided. Drinking water, flush toilets, propane, cell phone reception, modem access, an RV dump station, showers, a laundry room, and ice are available. A store and an ATM are within two blocks. A café is within one mile. Leashed pets are permitted.

Reservations, fees: Reservations are accepted. The fees are $20 per RV and tents are $8 per person per night, plus $2–5 per person for more than two people. Major credit cards are accepted. Open year-round.

Directions: From Ontario (near the Oregon/Idaho border), drive west on U.S. 20/26 for 12 miles to Vale and U.S. 26. Turn north on U.S. 26 and

OREGON

drive .5 mile to Hope Street. Turn east and drive one block east to the park on the left.

Contact: Prospector RV Park, 511 N. 11th St. E, Vale, OR 97918, 541/473-3879.

15 GOLDEN WHEEL MOTEL AND WESTERNER RV PARK

Rating: 5

on the Malheur River
See map pages 408–409

This campground on the banks of the Malheur River and right on the Oregon Trail provides a good layover spot for travelers heading to or from Idaho on U.S. 20/26. See the previous description of Prospector RV Park for more information.

RV sites, facilities: There are 10 sites with full hookups (20, 30, 50 amps) for RVs of any length or tents and 14 motel rooms. Picnic tables are provided. Drinking water, flush toilets, cable TV, a pay phone, cell phone reception, showers, a laundry room, and ice are available. Propane, a store, a café, an ATM, and a swimming pool are within two blocks. Leashed pets are permitted.

Reservations, fees: Reservations are accepted. The fee is $10 per night, plus $1 per person for more than two people. Major credit cards are accepted. Open year-round.

Directions: From Ontario (near the Oregon/Idaho border), drive west on U.S. 20/26 for 12 miles to Vale and to the junction of U.S. 26. The campground is on the left at the junction of U.S. 20 and U.S. 26.

Contact: Golden Wheel Motel and Westerner RV Park, 317 A St. E, Vale, OR 97918, 541/473-3947.

16 CHICKAHOMINY RESERVOIR

Rating: 4

on Chickahominy Reservoir
See map pages 408–409

While a good spot for group camping, this camp is set in the high desert with no shade. Weather conditions can be extreme, so come prepared. The camp is used primarily as an overnight stop for travelers driving through the area. Boats with motors are allowed on the reservoir. There is a

new access road on the northwest side of the reservoir for day use. The nearest services are eight miles east (via U.S. 20) in Riley.

RV sites, facilities: There are 28 sites for RVs up to 35 feet or tents. Picnic tables, garbage bins, and fire grills are provided. Drinking water and vault toilets are available. A fish-cleaning station is nearby. A pay phone and a store are within eight miles. Some facilities are wheelchair-accessible. Leashed pets are permitted.

Reservations, fees: Reservations are not accepted. The fee is $8 per night per vehicle, with a stay limit of 14 days. Open April to October, weather permitting.

Directions: From Burns, drive west on U.S. 20 for 30 miles to the campground on the right.

Contact: Bureau of Land Management, Burns District, 28910 Hwy. 20 W, Hines, OR 97738, 541/573-4400, fax 541/573-4411, website: www.or.blm.gov/burns.

17 LAKE OWYHEE STATE PARK

Rating: 7

on Owyhee Lake
See map pages 408–409

This state park is set along the shore of 53-mile-long Owyhee Lake, a good lake for water-skiing in the day and fishing for warm-water species in the morning and evening. Owyhee is famous for its superb bass fishing. The place even has floating restrooms. Other highlights include views of unusual geological formations and huge rock pinnacles from the park. Bighorn sheep, pronghorn antelope, golden eagles, coyotes, mule deer, wild horses, and mountain lions live around here.

RV sites, facilities: There are 33 sites with partial hookups (50 amps) for RVs up to 45 feet and seven sites for tents. There are also two tepees and 35 primitive sites. Picnic tables and fire grills are provided. Drinking water, garbage bins, flush toilets, an RV dump station, a pay phone, a store, and showers are available. Boat docks and launching facilities are nearby. Leashed pets are permitted.

Reservations, fees: Reservations are accepted for tepees only ($6 reservation fee) at 800/452-5687 or online at www.oregonstateparks.org. The fees are $14–16 per night, tepees are $27 per night, and primitive sites are $8, plus $5–7 per night for an additional vehicle. Major credit cards are accepted. Open early April to October.

Directions: From Ontario (near the Oregon/Idaho border), drive south on U.S. 20/26 for six miles to the Nyssa exit. Turn south and drive eight miles to Nyssa and Highway 201. Turn southeast on Highway 201 and drive eight miles to Owyhee. Turn right (east) and drive about 22 miles to road's end and the entrance to the park.

Contact: Lake Owyhee State Park, 3012 Island Ave., 541/339-2331 or 800/551-6949, website: www.owyheeresort.com.

18 THOMPSON RESERVOIR

Rating: 3

on Thompson Reservoir in Fremont National Forest

See map pages 408–409

Located on the north shore of Thompson Reservoir among black-bark ponderosa pines the height of telephone poles, this simple and pretty camp features shaded sites close to the water. This area is popular for fishing and boating. See the following description of East Bay for more information. Water in the reservoir fluctuates and sometimes dries up too much to launch a boat in late summer.

RV sites, facilities: There are 20 sites for RVs up to 22 feet or tents, plus a separate group camping area. Picnic tables and fire grills are provided. Drinking water, vault toilets, and cell phone reception are available, but all garbage must be packed out. Boat-launching facilities are nearby. Leashed pets are permitted.

Reservations, fees: Reservations are not accepted. There is no fee for camping. Open May to mid-November.

Directions: From Bend, drive south on U.S. 97 for 32 miles to Highway 31. Turn southeast on Highway 31 and drive 48 miles to County Road 4-11 (one mile west of the town of Silver Lake). Turn right and drive six miles (the road becomes Forest Road 27) and continue south for nine miles to the campground entrance road. Turn left and drive one mile to the camp.

Contact: Fremont National Forest, Silver Lake

Ranger District, P.O. Box 129, Hwy. 31, Silver Lake, OR 97638, 541/576-2107, fax 541/576-7587.

19 EAST BAY

Rating: 3

on Thompson Reservoir in Fremont National Forest

See map pages 408–409

This campground on the east shore of Thompson Reservoir has paved roads, but it's still a long way from home, so be sure to bring all of your supplies with you. A day-use area is adjacent to the camp.

RV sites, facilities: There are 17 sites, including two drive-through, for RVs of any length or tents. Picnic tables, garbage bins, and fire grills are provided. Drinking water, vault toilets, and a fishing pier are available. Boat-launching facilities are nearby. Some facilities are wheelchair-accessible. Leashed pets are permitted.

Reservations, fees: Reservations are not accepted. The fee is $8 per night, plus $5 per additional vehicle. A senior discount is available. Open May to mid-November.

Directions: From Bend, drive south on U.S. 97 for 32 miles to Highway 31. Turn southeast on Highway 31 and drive 49 miles to Silver Lake. Turn right (south) on Country Road 4-12 and drive six miles (turns into Country Road 28). Continue six miles to East Bay Campground Road. Turn right (west) and continue one mile to the campground.

Contact: Fremont National Forest, Silver Lake Ranger District, P.O. Box 129, Hwy. 31, Silver Lake, OR 97638, 541/576-2107, fax 541/576-7587.

20 DEAD HORSE LAKE

Rating: 9

on Dead Horse Lake in Fremont National Forest

See map pages 408–409

The shore of Dead Horse Lake is home to this camp (at 7,372 feet elevation). It generally fills on most weekends and holidays. A hiking trail winds around the perimeter of the lake, hooking up with other trails along the way. One original

OREGON

Civilian Conservation Corps canoe, a relic of the 1930s, remains in the lake. Good side trips are nearby in Fremont National Forest. See the following description of Campbell Lake for more information.

RV sites, facilities: There are nine sites for self-contained RVs up to 30 feet or tents and a separate area with seven sites for group camping. Picnic tables and fire grills are provided. Drinking water and vault toilets are available, but all garbage must be packed out. A boat launch is nearby. Boats with electric motors are permitted, but gas motors are prohibited. Leashed pets are permitted.

Reservations, fees: Reservations are not accepted. There is no fee for camping. Open July to October.

Directions: From Lakeview, drive north on U.S. 395 for 23 miles to Highway 31. Turn northwest and drive 22 miles to Paisley. Continue on Highway 31 for .5 mile to Mill Street. Turn west on Mill Street and drive 20 miles (the road becomes Forest Road 033); continue to the T intersection with Forest Road 28. Turn right and drive 11 miles (watch for the turn to Campbell–Dead Horse Lakes) to Forest Road 033. Turn left and drive three miles (gravel road) to the campground.

Contact: Fremont National Forest, Paisley Ranger District, P.O. Box 67, Paisley, OR 97636, 541/943-3114, fax 541/943-4479.

21 CAMPBELL LAKE

Rating: 9

on Campbell Lake in Fremont National Forest

See map pages 408–409

This campground on the pebbled shore of Campbell Lake is near Dead Horse Lake campground. These high-elevation, crystal-clear lakes were formed during the glacier period. Evidence of the past glacial nature of this area can be found on the nearby Lakes Trail system. Both camps are very busy, filling most weekends in July and August. No boats with gas motors are permitted on Campbell Lake. Good side trips are available in Fremont National Forest. A U.S. Forest Service map details the back roads.

RV sites, facilities: There are 21 sites for RVs up to 32 feet or tents. Picnic tables and fire grills

are provided. Drinking water and vault toilets are available. A boat launch is adjacent to the camp. Boats with electric motors are permitted, but gas motors are prohibited. All garbage must be packed out. Leashed pets are permitted.

Reservations, fees: Reservations are not accepted. There is no fee for camping. Open July to late October.

Directions: From Lakeview, drive north on U.S. 395 for 23 miles to Highway 31. Turn northwest and drive 22 miles to Paisley. Continue on Highway 31 for .5 mile to Mill Street. Turn west on Mill Street and drive 20 miles (the road becomes Forest Road 33) and continue to the T intersection with Forest Road 28. Turn right and drive eight miles to Forest Road 033 (gravel road). Turn left and drive two miles to the campground.

Contact: Fremont National Forest, Paisley Ranger District, P.O. Box 67, Paisley, OR 97636, 541/943-3114, fax 541/943-4479.

22 CORRAL CREEK

Rating: 4

near the Gearhart Mountain Wilderness in Fremont National Forest

See map pages 408–409

Set along Corral Creek, this camp is adjacent to a trailhead that provides access into the Gearhart Mountain Wilderness, making it a prime base camp for a backpacking trip. Access is also available from camp to the Palisade Rocks, a worthwhile side trip. Another option is Quartz Mountain Snowpark, which is 14 miles east of the campground. The elevation is 6,000 feet.

RV sites, facilities: There are six sites for RVs up to 16 feet or tents. Picnic tables and fire grills are provided. Vault toilets are available. There is no drinking water, and all garbage must be packed out. Stock facilities include hitching posts, stalls, and corrals are on-site. Leashed pets are permitted.

Reservations, fees: Reservations are not accepted. There is no fee for camping. Open mid-May to late October.

Directions: From Klamath Falls, drive east on Highway 140 for 53 miles to the town of Bly. Continue east on Highway 140 for another 13 miles to Forest Road 3660. Turn left and drive

13 miles to Forest Road 34. Turn right and drive about one-eighth mile to Forest Road 012 and continue to the campground.

Contact: Fremont National Forest, Bly Ranger District, P.O. Box 25, Bly, OR 97622, 541/353-2427, fax 541/353-2750.

23 DAIRY POINT

Rating: 6

on Dairy Creek in Fremont National Forest
See map pages 408–409

This campground, elevation 5,200 feet, is situated next to the Dairy Creek Bridge in a stand of ponderosa pine and white fir at the edge of a large and open meadow. The setting is beautiful and peaceful, with a towering backdrop of mountains. In the spring, wildflowers are a sight to behold; bird-watching can also be excellent this time of year. Fishing and inner tubing are popular activities at Dairy Creek. Warning: This campground is suitable for large groups and is often full on holidays and most weekends.

RV sites, facilities: There are four sites for self-contained RVs up to 30 feet or tents. Picnic tables, fire grills, a vault toilet, and drinking water are provided. All garbage must be packed out. Leashed pets are permitted.

Reservations, fees: Reservations are not accepted. There is no fee for camping. Open mid-May to October.

Directions: From Lakeview, drive north on U.S. 395 for 23 miles to Highway 31. Turn northwest and drive 22 miles to Paisley. Continue on Highway 31 for .5 mile to Mill Street. Turn west on Mill Street and drive 20 miles (the road becomes Forest Road 33); continue to the T intersection with Forest Road 28. Turn left and drive two miles (crossing the Dairy Creek Bridge) to Forest Road 3428. Turn left and drive to the campground (just past the intersection on the left).

Contact: Fremont National Forest, Paisley Ranger District, P.O. Box 67, Paisley, OR 97636, 541/943-3114, fax 541/943-4479.

24 HAPPY CAMP

Rating: 6

on Dairy Creek in Fremont National Forest
See map pages 408–409

Here's a pleasant spot with open sites along Dairy Creek, though only one site is close to the water. The camp features three old Depression-era Civilian Conservation Corps picnic shelters, preserved in their original state. Horseshoes are provided. Fishing is available here for rainbow trout, though the creek is no longer stocked. The camp sits at 5,289 feet elevation.

RV sites, facilities: There are nine sites for RVs up to 16 feet or tents. Picnic tables and fire grills are provided. Vault toilets are available, but there is no drinking water. All garbage must be packed out. Leashed pets are permitted.

Reservations, fees: Reservations are not accepted. There is no fee for camping. Open mid-May to late October.

Directions: From Lakeview, drive north on U.S. 395 for 23 miles to Highway 31. Turn northwest and drive 22 miles to Paisley. Continue on Highway 31 for .5 mile to Mill Street. Turn west on Mill Street and drive 20 miles (the road becomes Forest Road 33); continue to the T intersection with Forest Road 28. Turn left and drive two miles (just before Dairy Creek) to Forest Road 047. Turn right and drive two miles (gravel) to the campground on the left.

Contact: Fremont National Forest, Paisley Ranger District, P.O. Box 67, Paisley, OR 97636, 541/943-3114, fax 541/943-4479.

25 MARSTER SPRING

Rating: 6

on the Chewaucan River in Fremont National Forest
See map pages 408–409

This pretty campground is set at an elevation of 4,845 feet on the banks of the Chewaucan River, a good fishing area. The largest of several popular camps in this river corridor, Marster Spring sits right on the river among ponderosa pine trees yet is close to the town of Paisley. The Fremont National Recreation Trail is accessible at the

Chewaucan Crossing Trailhead, a quarter mile to the south.

RV sites, facilities: There are 11 sites for RVs up to 22 feet or tents. Picnic tables and fire grills are provided. Drinking water and vault toilets are available. A pay phone and an ATM are within seven miles. Leashed pets are permitted.

Reservations, fees: Reservations are not accepted. There is no fee for camping. Open May to October.

Directions: From Lakeview, drive north on U.S. 395 for 23 miles to Highway 31. Turn northwest and drive 22 miles to Paisley. Continue on Highway 31 for .5 mile to Mill Street. Turn west on Mill Street and drive seven miles (the road becomes Forest Road 33) to the campground on the left.

Contact: Fremont National Forest, Paisley Ranger District, P.O. Box 67, Paisley, OR 97636, 541/943-3114, fax 541/943-4479.

26 STEENS MOUNTAIN RESORT

Rating: 9

on the Blitzen River
See map pages 408–409

The self-proclaimed "gateway to the Steens Mountains," this resort is bordered by the Malheur National Wildlife Refuge on three sides, and it has great views. The mile-high mountain and surrounding gorges make an excellent photo opportunity. Hiking and hunting are other possibilities in the area. Fishing is available on the Blitzen River, with easy access from the camp.

RV sites, facilities: There are 20 sites with full hookups (30, 50 amps), 30 sites with partial hookups for RVs of any length, 28 sites for tents, plus nine cabins and one rental home. Drinking water, restrooms, showers, a store, a pay phone, modem access, an RV dump station, laundry facilities, ice, and fishing and hunting licenses are available. Leashed pets are permitted.

Reservations, fees: Reserve at 800/542-3765. The fee is $12–20 per night, plus $5 per person for more than two people. Cabins are $50–75 per night, plus $10 per pet per night in cabins. Major credit cards are accepted. Open year-round.

Directions: From Burns, drive east on Highway 78 for two miles to Highway 205. Turn south on Highway 205 and drive 59 miles to Frenchglen

and Steens Mountain Road. Turn east and drive three miles to the resort on the right.

Contact: Steens Mountain Resort, 35678 Resort Ln., Frenchglen, OR 97736, 541/493-2415, website: www.steensmountainresort.com.

27 PAGE SPRINGS

Rating: 7

near Malheur National Wildlife Refuge
See map pages 408–409

This campground is adjacent to the Malheur National Wildlife Refuge. The Frenchglen Hotel (three miles away) is administered by the state parks department and offers overnight accommodations and meals. Activities include hiking on the area trails, plus bird-watching, fishing, hunting, and sightseeing.

RV sites, facilities: There are 36 sites for RVs up to 35 feet or tents. Picnic tables, garbage service, and fire grills are provided. Drinking water, vault toilets, and cell phone reception are available. A day-use area with a shelter is nearby. A pay phone is within three miles. Some facilities are wheelchair-accessible. Leashed pets are permitted.

Reservations, fees: Reservations are not accepted. The fee is $8 per vehicle per night, with a 14-day stay limit. A senior discount is available. Open year-round.

Directions: From Burns, drive east on Highway 78 for two miles to Highway 205. Turn south on Highway 205 and drive 60 miles to Frenchglen and Steens Mountain Loop Road. Turn east and drive three miles to the campground.

Contact: Bureau of Land Management, Burns District, 28910 Hwy. 20 W, Hines, OR 97738, 541/573-4400, fax 541/573-4411.

28 FISH LAKE

Rating: 8

on Fish Lake
See map pages 408–409

The shore of Fish Lake is the setting for this primitive but pretty camp. Set among the aspens at 7,400 feet elevation, it can make an excellent weekend getaway spot for sightseeing. Trout fish-

OREGON

ing is an option, made easier by the boat ramp near camp.

RV sites, facilities: There are 23 sites for RVs up to 35 feet or tents. Picnic tables, garbage bins, and fire grills are provided. Drinking water, vault toilets, and cell phone reception are available. Boat-launching facilities are nearby (nonmotorized boats only). Some facilities are wheelchair-accessible. Leashed pets are permitted.

Reservations, fees: Reservations are not accepted. The fee is $8 per vehicle per night, with a 14-day stay limit. A senior discount is available. Open from June to October, weather permitting.

Directions: From Burns, drive east on Highway 78 for two miles to Highway 205. Turn south on Highway 205 and drive 60 miles to Frenchglen and Steens Mountain Loop Road. Turn east and drive 20 miles to the campground.

Contact: Bureau of Land Management, Burns District, 28910 Hwy. 20 W, Hines, OR 97738, 541/573-4400, fax 541/573-4411.

29 SOUTH STEENS

Rating: 6

in the Steens Mountain Wilderness
See map pages 408–409

This campground is on the edge of the Steens Mountain Wilderness. The area features deep, glacier-carved gorges, volcanic uplifts, stunning scenery, and a rare chance to see elk and bighorn sheep. Redband trout fishing is a mile away at Donner und Blitzen River and its tributaries, a new reserve. This campground is also good for horse campers, providing them with a separate area from the other campers. Trails are accessible from the campground. Note: The road beyond the campground is not recommended for RV travel.

RV sites, facilities: There are 36 sites for RVs of up to 35 feet or tents; 15 of the sites are designated for horse campers. Picnic tables, hitching posts, and fire grills are provided. Drinking water, vault toilets, and cell phone reception are available. Some facilities are wheelchair-accessible. Leashed pets are permitted.

Reservations, fees: Reservations are not accepted. The fee is $6 per vehicle per night. There is a 14-day stay limit. A senior discount is available. Open May to October, weather permitting.

Directions: From Burns, drive east on Highway 78 for two miles to Highway 205. Turn south on Highway 205 and drive 60 miles to Frenchglen. Continue south on Highway 205 for 10 miles to Steens South Loop Road. Turn left (east) and drive 18 miles to the campground on the right.

Contact: Bureau of Land Management, Burns District, 28910 Hwy. 20 W, Hines, OR 97738, 541/573-4400, fax 541/573-4411.

30 MANN LAKE

Rating: 8

on Mann Lake
See map pages 408–409

Mann Lake has two small boat ramps and a policy of electric motors only. Fishing, including wintertime ice fishing, and wildlife viewing are popular here. Weather can be extreme. The campground sits at the base of Steens Mountain and is open, with sagebrush and no trees. The scenic, high desert camp is mainly used as a fishing camp; please respect private property on land parcels next to the lake. Fishing can be very good for cutthroat trout. Nearby Alvord Desert is also an attraction.

RV sites, facilities: There are dispersed sites for RVs of up to 35 feet or tents; there are open areas on each side of the lake. No drinking water is available. Cell phone reception is available. Garbage must be packed out. Some facilities are wheelchair-accessible. Leashed pets are permitted.

Reservations, fees: Reservations are not accepted. There is no fee for camping. Open year-round.

Directions: From Burns, drive southeast on Highway 78 for 65 miles to Fields/Denio Road (Folly Farm Road). Turn right (south) and drive 22 miles to the campground at Mann Lake.

Contact: Bureau of Land Management, Burns District, 28910 Hwy. 20 W, Hines, OR 97738, 541/573-4400, fax 541/573-4411.

31 ROME LAUNCH

Rating: 6

on the Owyhee River
See map pages 408–409

This campground is used mainly by people rafting

the Owyhee River and overnighters passing through. A few cottonwood trees and sagebrush live in this campground. There are some farms and ranches in the area. Campsites are adjacent to the Owyhee River. I have canoed most of the Owyhee from the headwaters in Nevada below the Jarbidge Mountains all the way through Idaho and into Oregon, and I would rate this river as one of the top canoeing destinations in North America. The Owyhee Canyon is quite dramatic, like a miniature Grand Canyon. Rome Launch is also a good wildlife-viewing area; mountain lions and bobcats have been spotted. Note: No motorized boats are allowed on the river.

RV sites, facilities: There are five sites for RVs up to 32 feet or tents. Picnic tables and fire rings are provided. Drinking water, vault toilets, and a boat launch are available. No firewood is available, and all garbage must be packed out. Leashed pets are permitted.

Reservations, fees: Reservations are not accepted. There is no fee for camping. Open March to November, weather permitting.

Directions: From Burns Junction, drive east on U.S. 95 for 15 miles to Jordan Valley and the signed turnoff for the Owyhee River and BLM-Rome boat launch. Turn south and drive .25 mile to the campground.

Contact: Bureau of Land Management, Vale District, 100 Oregon St., Vale, OR 97918-9630, 541/473-3144, fax 541/473-6213.

32 GERBER RESERVOIR

Rating: 6

on Gerber Reservoir
See map pages 408–409

This camp can be found at an elevation of 4,800 feet alongside the west shore of Gerber Reservoir (10 mph boat speed limit). Off the beaten path, Gerber attracts mainly locals. Recreation options include swimming, fishing, boating, and hiking.

RV sites, facilities: There are 50 sites for RVs up to 30 feet or tents. Picnic tables and fire grills are provided. Drinking water, firewood, an RV dump station, vault toilets, cell phone reception, a boat ramp, a boat dock, launching facilities, and a fish-cleaning station are available. Some

facilities are wheelchair-accessible. Leashed pets are permitted.

Reservations, fees: Reservations are not accepted. The fee is $7 per night, plus $4 per night per additional vehicle. A senior discount is available. Open year-round, with drinking water and services available May to mid-September.

Directions: From Klamath Falls, drive east on Highway 140 for 16 miles to Dairy and Highway 70. Turn south on Highway 70 and drive seven miles to Bonanza and East Langell Valley Road. Turn east on East Langell Valley Road and drive 11 miles to Gerber Road. Turn left on Gerber Road and drive eight miles to the campground on the right.

Contact: Bureau of Land Management, Klamath Falls Resource Area, 2795 Anderson Ave., Building 25, Klamath Falls, OR 97603, 541/883-6916, fax 541/884-2097, website: www.or.blm.gov /lakeview.

33 LOFTON RESERVOIR

Rating: 6

on Lofton Reservoir in Fremont National Forest
See map pages 408–409

This remote campground sits on the shore of Lofton Reservoir, a small lake that can provide the best trout fishing in this region. Other nearby lakes are accessible by forest roads. This area marks the beginning of the Great Basin, a high-desert area that extends to Idaho. A large fire burned much of the surrounding forest about 20 years ago, making this campground an oasis of sorts.

RV sites, facilities: There are 26 sites for RVs up to 22 feet or tents. Picnic tables and fire grills are provided. Vault toilets are available. No drinking water is available. Garbage must be packed out. Fully accessible boat docks and launching facilities are nearby. Leashed pets are permitted.

Reservations, fees: Reservations are not accepted. There is no fee for camping. Open mid-May to late October.

Directions: From Klamath Falls, drive east on Highway 140 for 54 miles to Bly. Continue east on Highway 140 for 13 miles to Forest Road 3715. Turn right and drive seven miles to Forest Road

013. Turn left on Forest Road 013 and drive one mile to the campground.

Contact: Fremont National Forest, Bly Ranger District, P.O. Box 25, Bly, OR 97622, 541/353-2427, fax 541/353-2750.

34 COTTONWOOD RECREATION AREA

Rating: 6

on Cottonwood Meadow Lake in Fremont National Forest

See map pages 408–409

This campground along the shore of little Cottonwood Meadow Lake is one of the better spots in the vicinity for fishing and hiking. Boats with electric motors are allowed on the lake, but gas motors are prohibited. Three hiking trails wind around the lake, and facilities for horses include hitching posts, feeders, water, and corrals. The camp is set at an elevation of 6,130 feet in a forested setting with aspen and many huge ponderosa pines.

RV sites, facilities: There are 21 sites for RVs up to 28 feet or tents. Picnic tables and fire grills are provided. Drinking water, vault toilets, and cell phone reception are available, but all garbage must be packed out. Boat docks are nearby. Electric motors are allowed, but gas motors are prohibited on the lake. The boating speed limit is 5 mph. Leashed pets are permitted.

Reservations, fees: Reservations are not accepted. There is no fee for camping. Open early June to mid-October, weather permitting.

Directions: From Lakeview, drive west on Highway 140 for 24 miles to Forest Road 3870. Turn right and drive about 10 miles to the campground.

Contact: Fremont National Forest, Lakeview Ranger District, 18049 Hwy. 395, Lakeview, OR 97630, 541/947-3334, fax 541/947-6375.

35 MUD CREEK

Rating: 4

on Mud Creek in Fremont National Forest

See map pages 408–409

This remote and quiet camp (at 6,600 feet elevation) is set in an isolated stand of lodgepole pines along the banks of Mud Creek. Drake Peak (8,405 feet elevation) is nearby. There are no other camps in the immediate vicinity. Fishing in Mud Creek is surprisingly good.

RV sites, facilities: There are seven sites for RVs up to 16 feet or tents. Drinking water, picnic tables, fire grills, and vault toilets are available. Leashed pets are permitted.

Reservations, fees: Reservations are not accepted. There is no fee for camping. Open June to mid-October, weather permitting.

Directions: From Lakeview, drive five miles north on U.S. 395 to Highway 140. Turn right on Highway 140 and drive eight miles to Forest Road 3615. Turn left and drive seven miles to the campground.

Contact: Fremont National Forest, Lakeview Ranger District, 18049 Hwy. 395, Lakeview, OR 97630, 541/947-3334, fax 541/947-6375.

36 JUNIPERS RESERVOIR RV RESORT

Rating: 6

on Junipers Reservoir

See map pages 408–409

This resort on an 8,000-acre cattle ranch is situated in a designated Oregon Wildlife Viewing Area, and campers may catch glimpses of seldom-seen species. Many nature-walking trails meander through the park, and guests can also take driving tours. Fishing for catfish and trout can be good, and, because it is a private lake, no fishing license is required. The area is popular for mountain biking. The summer climate is mild and pleasant. Antelope, deer, and elk can be spotted in this area.

RV sites, facilities: There are 23 sites with full hookups (20, 30, 50 amps), 17 with partial hookups, for RVs of any length and 15 tent sites. Drinking water, restrooms, showers, an RV dump station, a courtesy phone, cell phone reception, modem access, a laundry room, and ice are available. Recreational facilities include a recreation hall, a volleyball court, and horseshoes. A pay phone is within five miles, and an ATM is within 10 miles. Some facilities are wheelchair-accessible. Leashed pets are permitted.

Reservations, fees: Reservations are recommended. The fee is $22.50–25 per night. A senior discount is available. Open May to mid-October.

Directions: From Lakeview, drive west on High-way 140 for 10 miles to the resort (at Milepost 86.5) on the right.

Contact: Junipers Reservoir RV Resort, 91029 Hwy. 140 W, Lakeview, OR 97630, 541/947-2050, website: www.junipersrv.com.

37 DREWS CREEK

Rating: 9

near Lakeview in Fremont National Forest
See map pages 408–409

This is an exceptionally beautiful campground, set along Drews Creek at 4,900 feet elevation. Gorgeous wild roses grow near the creek, and several unmarked trails lead to nearby hills where campers can enjoy scenic views. A great spot for a family trip, Drews Creek features horseshoes, an area for baseball, and a large group barbecue, making it equally popular with group campers. Fishing is available in nearby Dog Lake, which also provides facilities for boating. Water-skiing is another option at Drews Reservoir, two miles to the west.

RV sites, facilities: There are five sites for RVs up to 30 feet or tents. Picnic tables, fire grills, vault toilets, cell phone reception, and drinking water are provided. All garbage must be packed out. Leashed pets are permitted.

Reservations, fees: Reservations are not accepted. There is no fee for camping. Open early June to mid-October, weather permitting.

Directions: From Lakeview, drive west on High-way 140 for 10 miles to County Road 1-13. Turn left and drive four miles to County Road 1-11D. Turn right and drive six miles (the road will become Forest Road 4017) to the bridge that provides access to the campground.

Contact: Fremont National Forest, Lakeview Ranger District, 18049 Hwy. 395, Lakeview, OR 97630, 541/947-3334, fax 541/947-6375.

38 DOG LAKE

Rating: 5

on Dog Lake in Fremont National Forest
See map pages 408–409

This campground is located on the west shore of Dog Lake at an elevation of 5,100 feet. Fishing and boats with motors are permitted, though speeds are limited to 5 mph. Dog Lake provides a popular fishery for bass, perch, and crappie. Native Americans named the lake for its resemblance in shape to the hind leg of a dog. Prospects for seeing waterfowl and eagles are good.

RV sites, facilities: There are eight sites for RVs up to 16 feet or tents. Drinking water, picnic tables, and fire grills are provided. Vault toilets and cell phone reception are available. Garbage must be packed out. A boat launch is nearby. Leashed pets are permitted.

Reservations, fees: Reservations are not accepted. There is no fee for camping. Open mid-April to mid-October, weather permitting.

Directions: From Lakeview, drive west on High-way 140 for seven miles to County Road 1-13. Turn left on County Road 1-13 and drive four miles to County Road 1-11D (Dog Lake Road). Turn right and drive four miles (the road becomes Forest Road 4017) into national forest. Continue on Forest Road 4017 for 12 miles (two miles past Drew Reservoir) to Dog Lake and the campground entrance on the left.

Contact: Fremont National Forest, Lakeview Ranger District, 18049 Hwy. 395, Lakeview, OR 97630, 541/947-3334, fax 541/947-6375.

39 GOOSE LAKE STATE PARK

Rating: 7

on Goose Lake
See map pages 408–409

This park is situated on the east shore of unusual Goose Lake, which lies half in Oregon and half in California. Waterfowl from the Pacific flyway frequent this out-of-the-way spot. It is home to many species of birds and other wildlife, including a large herd of mule deer that spends much of the time in the campground. When the lake is full, canoes and personal watercraft are popular here.

RV sites, facilities: There are 48 sites with partial hookups (20 amps) for RVs up to 50 feet or tents. Picnic tables, fire grills, garbage bins, and drinking water are provided. Flush toilets, showers, an RV dump station, cell phone reception,

OREGON

and firewood are available. Boat-launching facilities are nearby. Leashed pets are permitted.

Reservations, fees: Reservations are not accepted. The fee is $16 per night, plus $5 per night per additional vehicle. Open from mid-April to late October.

Directions: From Lakeview, drive south on U.S. 395 for 14 miles to the California border and Stateline Road. Turn right (west) and drive one mile to the campground.

Contact: Goose Lake State Park, P.O. Box 207, New Pine Creek, OR 97635, 541/947-3111 or 800/551-6949.

40 ADEL STORE AND RV PARK

Rating: 5

in Adel
See map pages 408–409

This remote park is the only game in town, so you'd better grab it while you can. New owners took over in March 2003, and they are working to make extensive renovations throughout. Recreation options in the area include hang gliding, rockhounding, or visiting Hart Mountain National Antelope Refuge, 40 miles north of Adel. Deep Creek and Twenty-mile Creek are nearby.

RV sites, facilities: There are eight sites with full hookups (30 amps) for RVs of any length. A store, a small café, a tavern, gasoline, diesel, cell phone reception, and ice are available. A pay phone is across the street. Leashed pets are permitted.

Reservations, fees: Reservations are accepted. The fee is $15 per night, plus $10 per additional vehicle. Major credit cards are accepted. Open year-round.

Directions: From Lakeview, drive five miles north on U.S. 395 to Highway 140. Turn right (east) on Highway 140 and drive 28 miles to Adel (a very small town). The RV park is in town along Highway 140 on the right.

Contact: Adel Store and RV Park, P.O. Box 58, Adel, OR 97620, 541/947-3850.

OREGON

© SUSAN SNYDER

California

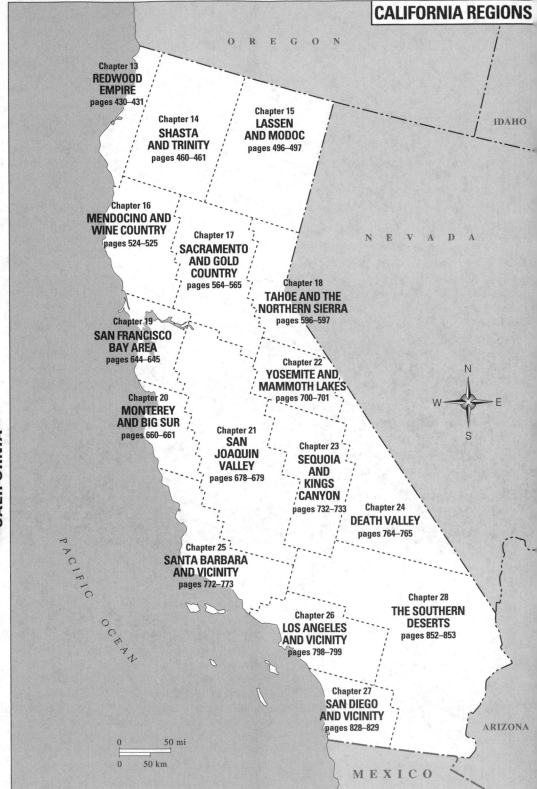

O R E G O N

IDAHO

Chapter 13
REDWOOD EMPIRE
pages 430–431

Chapter 14
SHASTA AND TRINITY
pages 460–461

Chapter 15
LASSEN AND MODOC
pages 496–497

N E V A D A

Chapter 16
MENDOCINO AND WINE COUNTRY
pages 524–525

Chapter 17
SACRAMENTO AND GOLD COUNTRY
pages 564–565

Chapter 18
TAHOE AND THE NORTHERN SIERRA
pages 596–597

Chapter 19
SAN FRANCISCO BAY AREA
pages 644–645

Chapter 22
YOSEMITE AND MAMMOTH LAKES
pages 700–701

Chapter 20
MONTEREY AND BIG SUR
pages 660–661

Chapter 21
SAN JOAQUIN VALLEY
pages 678–679

Chapter 23
SEQUOIA AND KINGS CANYON
pages 732–733

Chapter 24
DEATH VALLEY
pages 764–765

Chapter 25
SANTA BARBARA AND VICINITY
pages 772–773

Chapter 28
THE SOUTHERN DESERTS
pages 852–853

Chapter 26
LOS ANGELES AND VICINITY
pages 798–799

Chapter 27
SAN DIEGO AND VICINITY
pages 828–829

ARIZONA

N
W E
S

P A C I F I C   O C E A N

CALIFORNIA

0   50 mi
0   50 km

M E X I C O

California

Chapter 13
Redwood Empire

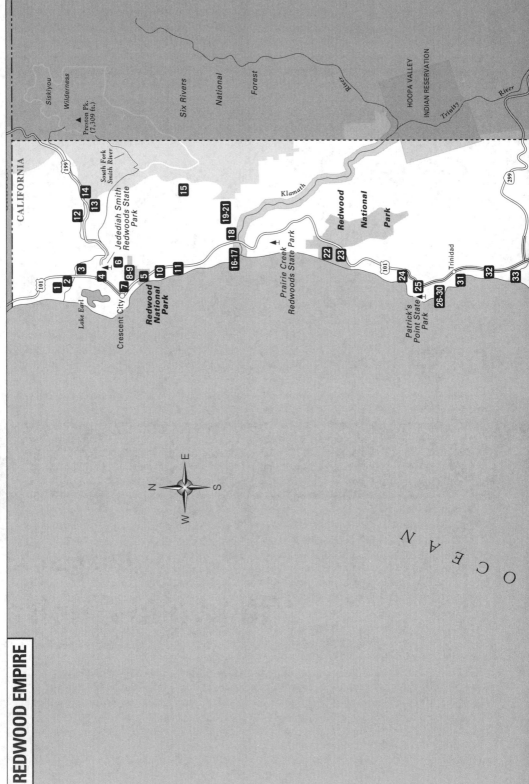

REDWOOD EMPIRE

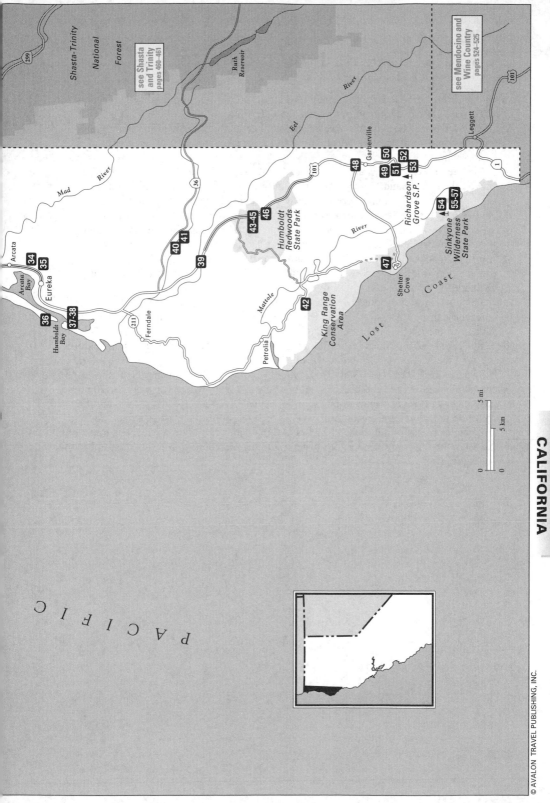

CALIFORNIA

Chapter 13—Redwood Empire

Visitors come from around the world to the Redwood Empire for one reason: to see the groves of giant redwoods, the tallest trees in the world. On a perfect day in the redwoods here, refracted sunlight beams through the forest canopy, creating a solemn, cathedral-like effect. It feels as if you are standing in the center of the earth's pure magic.

But the redwood forests are only one of the attractions in this area. The Smith River canyon, Del Norte and Humboldt Coasts, and the remote edge of the Siskiyou Wilderness in Six Rivers National Forest all make this region like none other in the world.

On sunny days in late summer, some visitors are incredulous that so few people live in the Redwood Empire. The reason is the same one that explains why the trees grow so tall: rain in the winter—often for weeks at a time—and fog in the summer. If the sun does manage to appear, it's an event almost worthy of calling the police to say you've spotted a large, yellow Unidentified Flying Object. So most folks are content to just visit.

Three stellar areas should be on your must-see list for outstanding days of adventure here: the redwood parks from Trinidad to Klamath River, the Smith River Recreation Area, and the Lost Coast.

I've hiked every trailhead from Trinidad to Crescent City and the hikes here feature some of the best adventuring day trips in Northern California. A good place to start is Prairie Creek Redwoods State Park, where you can see fantastic herds of Roosevelt elk. Then head over to the beach by hiking Fern Canyon, where you walk for 20 minutes at the bottom of a canyon adjacent to vertical walls covered with ferns, and then continue north on the Coastal Trail, where you'll pass through pristine woodlands and fantastic expanses of untouched beaches. All the trails through the redwoods north of the Klamath River are winners; it's just a matter of matching your level of ambition to the right hike.

The Smith River Recreation Area is equally gorgeous. The Smith is one of the last major free-flowing rivers in America. Wild, pristine, and beautiful, it's set in a series of gorges and bordered by national forest. The centerpiece is Jedediah Smith State Park and its grove of monster-sized redwoods. South Fork Road provides an extended tour into Six Rivers National Forest along the South Fork Smith River, with the option of visiting many of the largest trees in Jedediah Smith State Park. The turnoff is on U.S. 199 just northeast of the town of Hiouchi. Turn right, cross two bridges, and you will arrive at a fork in the road. Turning left at the fork will take you along the South Fork Smith River and deep into Six Rivers National Forest. Turning right at the fork will take you to a series of trailheads for hikes into redwoods. Of these, the best is the Boy Scout Tree Trail.

The Lost Coast is often overlooked by visitors because of the difficulty in reaching it; your only access is via a slow, curvy road through the Mattole River Valley, past Petrolia, and out to a piece of coast. The experience is like being in suspended animation—your surroundings peaceful and pristine, with a striking lack of people. One of the best ways to capture the sensation is to drive out near the mouth of the Mattole, then hike south on the Coast Trail long enough to get a feel for the area.

Compared to other regions in California, this corner of the state is somewhat one-dimensional. The emphasis here is primarily on exploring the redwoods and the coast, and to some extent, the Smith River. Most of the campgrounds here are designed with that in mind.

Many private campgrounds are set on U.S. 101 as well as near the mouths of the Smith and Klamath Rivers. These make fine base camps for fishing trips when the salmon are running. The state and national park campgrounds in the redwoods are in high demand, and reservations are often necessary in the peak vacation season. On the opposite end of the spectrum are primitive and remote settings in Six Rivers National Forest, the Lost Coast, and even a few surprise nuggets in Redwood National Park.

CALIFORNIA

1 SALMON HARBOR RESORT

Rating: 6

on the Smith River
See map pages 430–431
If location is everything, this privately operated campground rates high for salmon fishermen in the fall. It is set near the mouth of the Smith River, where salmon enter and school in the deep river holes in October. The fish are big, often in the 20-pound range, occasionally surpassing even 40 pounds. Year-round this is a good layover for RV cruisers looking for a spot near the Oregon border. It is actually an RV parking area with hookups, set within a mobile home park. Salmon Harbor Resort overlooks the ocean, with good beachcombing and driftwood and agate hunting nearby.

RV sites, facilities: There are 93 sites for RVs or tents, 88 with full hookups (30, 50 amps) for RVs up to 40 feet. Picnic tables and fire grills are provided. Drinking water, flush toilets, showers, cell phone reception, telephones, coin-operated laundry, storage sheds, modem hookups, cable TV, and a recreation room are available. A grocery store, ice, gas, a restaurant, and a bar are available within three miles. An ATM is nearby. Leashed pets are permitted.

Reservations, fees: Reservations are accepted at 800/332-6139. The fee is $25 per night, plus $1.50 per person for more than two people. A senior discount is available. Open year-round.

Directions: From Crescent City, drive north on U.S. 101 for 13 miles to the town of Smith River. Continue three miles north on U.S. 101 to the Salmon Harbor Road exit. Turn left on Salmon Harbor Road, drive a short distance, and look for Salmon Harbor Resort at the end of the road.

Contact: Salmon Harbor Resort, 707/487-3341.

2 BEST WESTERN & SHIP ASHORE RESORT RV PARK

Rating: 7

on the Smith River
See map pages 430–431
This is a famous spot for Smith River fishermen in late fall and all through winter, when the tales get taller as the evening gets late. In the summer, the resort has become quite popular with people cruising the coast on U.S. 101. The park is set on five acres of land adjacent to the lower Smith River. The salmon and steelhead seem to come in one size here—big—but they can be as elusive as Bigfoot. If you want to hear how big these fish can be, just check into the Captain's Galley restaurant any fall or winter evening. Salmon average 15 to 25 pounds, occasionally bigger, with 50-pounders caught each year, and steelhead average 10 to 14 pounds, with bigger fish occasionally hooked as well.

RV sites, facilities: There are 200 RV sites, including 80 permanent sites for mobile homes, some pull-through sites, most with full hookups, and a separate area for 10 to 15 tents. Motel rooms are also available. Picnic tables are provided. Flush toilets, showers, a coin-operated laundry, propane, a restaurant, a boat dock, a boat ramp, and some patios are available. A grocery store is two miles away. Leashed pets are permitted.

Reservations, fees: Reservations are accepted. The fee is $10 for two people for the first night and $15 per night thereafter. Major credit cards are accepted. Open year-round.

Directions: From Crescent City, drive north on U.S. 101 for 16 miles, three miles past the town of Smith River, to the Ship Ashore sign at Chinook Street. At Chinook Street, turn left and drive a short distance (less than half a block) to the motel lobby to register.

Contact: Best Western & Ship Ashore Resort RV Park, 707/487-3141, fax 707/487-7070.

3 RAMBLIN' ROSE RESORT

Rating: 8

near the Smith River
See map pages 430–431
Ramblin' Rose is an RV park set amid redwood trees, some of them giant, with Tyrone Creek running just behind the campground. The big trees are the highlight of the area, of course, with Redwood National Park and Jedediah Smith Redwoods State Park just to the east on U.S. 199. Nearby attractions include the beach to the immediate west and the Smith River to the north.

RV sites, facilities: There are 93 RV sites with

full hookups (30 amps), including some drive-through sites, seven tent sites, and two cabins. Picnic tables are provided. There is also a separate mobile park with full-time residents. Restrooms, drinking water, showers, telephone hookups, limited cell phone reception, a fitness and health club, volleyball, horseshoes, croquet, and badminton are available. A mini–convenience store, ice, and a coin-operated laundry are also available. Leashed pets are permitted.

Reservations, fees: Reservations are accepted. The fees are $22.50 per night for RV sites and $18 per night for tent sites, plus $2 per person for more than two people. For reservations, phone 877/387-4831. Open year-round.

Directions: From Crescent City, take U.S. 101 north for four miles to the junction of U.S. 199. Continue north on U.S. 101 for another four miles to the campground at 6701 U.S. 101 N in Crescent City.

Contact: Ramblin' Rose Resort, 707/487-4831, website: www.ramblinroserv.com.

▲ CRESCENT CITY REDWOODS KOA

Rating: 6

five miles north of Crescent City
See map pages 430–431

This KOA camp is on the edge of a recreation wonderland, a perfect jump-off spot for a vacation. The camp itself includes those little KOA Kamping Kabins, which are cute log cabins with electricity and heat, as well as the larger Kamping Kottages; just make sure you bring your sleeping bag and pillows. The park covers 20 acres, featuring both open and wooded areas. In addition, there are two nine-hole golf courses nearby. The camp is only a 10-minute drive to Redwood National Park, Jedediah Smith Redwoods State Park, and the Smith River National Recreation Area. It is also only a 10-minute drive to the beach and Tolowa Dunes Wildlife Area to the east and to Crescent City Harbor to the south.

RV sites, facilities: There are 50 sites with full hookups (30, 50 amps) for RVs up to 40 feet and 37 tent sites; 17 cabins and one cottage are also available. Picnic tables and fire grills are provided. An RV dump station, flush toilets, showers, a coin-operated laundry, modem access,

limited cell phone reception, a playground, propane, groceries, ice, and wood are available. A recreation room, pool table, Ping Pong, horseshoes, go-carts, pedal carts, bike rentals, basketball, and volleyball are on the property. An ATM is within four miles. Leashed pets are permitted.

Reservations, fees: Reservations are accepted at 800/562-5754. The fees are $24–32 per night and $39–59 for two-room cabins, plus $3.50 per person for more than two people and $2.50 per night for children 8–17 years; children seven and under are free. A senior discount is available. Major credit cards are accepted. Open year-round.

Directions: From Crescent City, take U.S. 101 north for five miles to the junction of U.S. 101 and U.S. 199. Continue north on U.S. 101 for one mile and look for the campground entrance on the right (east) side of the road.

Contact: Crescent City Redwoods KOA, 707/464-5744, website: www.koa.com.

▲ JEDEDIAH SMITH REDWOODS STATE PARK

Rating: 10

on the Smith River
See map pages 430–431

This is a beautiful park set along the Smith River, where the campsites are sprinkled amid a grove of old-growth redwoods. Reservations are usually a necessity during the summer. This park covers 10,000 acres on both sides of the Smith River, a jewel, the last major free-flowing river in California. There are 20 miles of hiking and nature trails, river access, a visitors center with exhibits, and a nature store. The park has hiking trails that lead right out of the campground; one is routed along the beautiful Smith River, and another heads through forest, across U.S. 199, and hooks up with the Simpson-Reed Interpretive Trail. In the summer, interpretive programs are available. There is also a good put-in spot at the park for river access in a drift boat, canoe, or raft. The fishing is best for steelhead from mid-January through March. The best hikes are on the south side of the Smith River, accessible via Howland Hill Road, including the Boy Scout Tree Trail and Stout Grove (for access, see the following listing for Hiouchi Hamlet RV Resort).

CALIFORNIA

Note that in winter, 100 inches of cumulative rainfall is common.

RV sites, facilities: There are 106 sites for RVs up to 36 feet or tents and trailers up to 31 feet and five hike-in/bike-in sites. Picnic tables, fire grills, and food lockers are provided. Drinking water, flush toilets, coin-operated showers, a pay phone, and an RV dump station are available. Propane, groceries, and a coin-operated laundry are available within one mile. Some facilities are wheelchair-accessible. Leashed pets are permitted only in the campground and on roads.

Reservations, fees: Reservations are accepted with a $7.50 reservation fee at 800/444-PARK (800/444-7275) or www.reserveamerica.com. The fees are $12–15 per night, and $2 per person per night for hike-in, bike-in sites. A senior discount is available. Open year-round.

Directions: From Crescent City, drive north on U.S. 101 for four miles to the junction with U.S. 199. Turn east at U.S. 199 and drive five miles. Turn right at the well-signed entrance station.

Contact: Redwood National and State Parks, 1111 2nd St., Crescent City, CA 95531, 707/464-6101, fax 707/464-1812.

6 HIOUCHI HAMLET RV RESORT

Rating: 7

near the Smith River
See map pages 430–431

This park is out of the wind and fog you get on the coast and set instead in the heart of the forest country. It makes a good base camp for a steelhead trip in winter. Insiders know that right next door, the fried chicken at the Hamlet's market is always good for a quick hit. An excellent side trip is to drive just east of Hiouchi on U.S. 199, turn right, and cross over two bridges, where you will reach a fork in the road. Turn left for a great scenic drive along the South Fork Smith River or turn right to get backdoor access to Jedediah Smith Redwoods State Park and three great trailheads for hiking in the redwoods. My favorite of the latter is the Boy Scout Tree Trail.

RV sites, facilities: There are 125 sites for RVs of any length, most with full hookups (30, 50 amps) and cable TV, and six tent sites. The RV sites

include some drive-through sites and 40 full-time residents. Park-model RVs and furnished apartments with kitchenettes are also available. Flush toilets, showers, an RV dump station, a coin-operated laundry, modem hookups, an ATM, horseshoes, groceries, propane, and a deli are available. A motel and café are nearby. A golf course is within three miles. Some facilities are wheelchair-accessible. Leashed pets are permitted.

Reservations, fees: Reservations are accepted. The fee is $22–26.70 per night. A senior discount is available. Major credit cards are accepted. Open year-round.

Directions: From Crescent City, drive five miles north on U.S. 101 to U.S. 199. Turn east (right) on U.S. 199 and drive about five miles (just past the entrance to Jedediah Smith State Park) to the town of Hiouchi. In Hiouchi, turn left at the well-signed campground entrance.

Contact: Hiouchi Hamlet RV Resort, 707/458-3321 or 800/722-9468, fax 707/458-4223.

7 BAYSIDE RV PARK

Rating: 6

in Crescent City
See map pages 430–431

If you are towing a boat, you just found your personal heaven: this RV park is directly adjacent to the boat docking area in Crescent City Harbor. There are several walks in the immediate area, including exploring the harbor and ocean frontage. For a quick change of scenery, it is only a 15-minute drive to Redwood National Park and Jedediah Smith Redwoods State Park along U.S. 199 to the north.

RV sites, facilities: There are 110 sites for RVs up to 34 feet, including some drive-through sites with full hookups (30 amps), including cable TV. Picnic tables are provided. Flush toilets, showers, limited cell phone reception, and a coin-operated laundry are available. A modem hookup is available at the park office. An ATM is within a quarter mile. Leashed pets are permitted.

Reservations, fees: Reservations are accepted at 800/446-9482. The fee is $18 per night, plus $2 per person for more than two people. Open year-round.

Directions: From U.S. 101 at the southern end of Crescent City, turn west at Citizen Dock Road and drive a very short distance to the campground.

Contact: Bayside RV Park, 707/464-9482.

8 VILLAGE CAMPER INN RV PARK

Rating: 7

in Crescent City
See map pages 430–431

Woods and water, that's what attracts visitors to California's north coast. Village Camper Inn provides nearby access to big woods and big water. This RV park is on 20 acres of wooded land, with the giant redwoods along U.S. 199 about a 10-minute drive away. In addition, you'll find some premium beachcombing for driftwood and agates a mile away on the spectacular rocky beaches just west of town.

RV sites, facilities: There are 135 RV sites, including some drive-through sites, most with full hookups (30, 50 amps), and a separate area for tents. Picnic tables are provided. Drinking water, an RV dump station, flush toilets, showers, a coin-operated laundry, limited cell phone reception, and cable TV hookups are available. An ATM is within one mile. Leashed pets are permitted.

Reservations, fees: Reservations are accepted. The fee is $16–20 per night, plus $2 per person for more than two people and $1 for children. Major credit cards are accepted. Open year-round.

Directions: From North U.S. 101 in Crescent City: Take the Parkway Drive exit and drive .5 mile to the campground on the right.

From South U.S. 101 in Crescent City: Take the Washington Boulevard exit. Turn left on Washington Boulevard and drive one block to Parkway Drive. Turn left on Parkway and drive one block to the campground on the right.

Contact: Village Camper Inn RV Park, 707/464-3544, website: www.villagecamperinn.com.

9 SUNSET HARBOR RV PARK

Rating: 4

in Crescent City
See map pages 430–431

People camp here with their RVs to be close to the action in Crescent City and to the nearby harbor and beach frontage. For starters, drive a few minutes to the northwest side of town, where the sea is sprinkled with gigantic rocks and boulders, for dramatic ocean views and spectacular sunsets. For finishers, go down to the west side of town for great walks along the ocean parkway or south to the harbor and adjacent beach, which is long and expansive.

RV sites, facilities: There are 69 sites with full hookups (30, 50 amps), including cable TV, for RVs up to 60 feet. Picnic tables are provided. Flush toilets, showers, cell phone reception, and a coin-operated laundry are available. A modem hookup is available in the park office. A grocery store, an ATM, and a recreation room are nearby. Restrooms and showers are wheelchair-accessible. Leashed pets are permitted.

Reservations, fees: Reservations are accepted. The fee is $22 per night, plus $2 per person for more than two people; monthly rates are available. Major credit cards are accepted. Open year-round.

Directions: In Crescent City on U.S. 101, drive to King Street. At King Street, turn east and drive one block to the park entrance at the end of the road.

Contact: Sunset Harbor RV Park, 707/464-3423.

10 DEL NORTE COAST REDWOODS STATE PARK

Rating: 8

near Crescent City
See map pages 430–431

The campsites are set in a series of loops in the forest, so while there are a lot of sites, you still feel a sense of privacy here. In addition to redwoods, there are also good stands of alders, along with a rambling stream fed by several creeks. It makes for a very pretty setting, with a good loop hike available right out of the camp. This park covers 6,400 acres, featuring 50 percent old-growth coastal redwoods and eight miles of wild coastline. Topography is fairly steep, with elevations ranging from sea level to 1,277 feet. This range is oriented in a north-to-south direction, with steep cliffs adjacent to the ocean. That makes most of the rocky seacoast generally inaccessible except by the Damnation Trail and Footsteps Rock Trail. The best coastal access is at Wilson

Beach or False Klamath Cove, where there is a half mile of sandy beach bordered by excellent tidepools. The forest interior is dense, with redwoods as well as tanoaks, madrones, red alder, big leaf maple, and California bay. One reason for the lush growth is what rangers call the "nurturing" coastal climate. Nurturing, in this case, means rain like you wouldn't believe in the winter, often more than 100 inches in a season, and lots of fog in the summer. Interpretive programs are conducted here. Insider's note: hike-in and bike-in campers beware. There is a 900-foot elevation change over the course of two miles between the U.S. 101 access road and the campground.

RV sites, facilities: There are 107 sites for tents or RVs up to 31 feet and trailers up to 27 feet and 38 tent sites. Hike-in/bike-in sites are also available. Picnic tables, fire grills, and food lockers are provided. Drinking water, RV dump station, flush toilets, and coin-operated showers are available. Some facilities are wheelchair-accessible. Leashed pets are permitted only in the campground.

Reservations, fees: Reservations are accepted with a $7.50 reservation fee at 800/444-PARK (800/444-7275) or www.reserveamerica.com. The fees are $12–15 per night and $2 per person per night for hike-in/bike-in sites. Open May through September.

Directions: From Crescent City, drive seven miles south on U.S. 101 to a signed access road for Del Norte Coast Redwoods State Park. Turn left at the park entrance.

Contact: Redwood National and State Parks, 1111 2nd St., Crescent City, CA 95531, 707/464-6101, fax 707/464-1812.

11 MYSTIC FOREST RV PARK

Rating: 6

near the Klamath River

See map pages 430–431

Yes, Paul Bunyan exists. After all, how do you think the Mojave got turned into a desert? Babe, the giant blue ox, is still around too, as you will discover at the Trees of Mystery north of Klamath, where a dinosaur-sized Paul Bunyan guards the parking lot. Less than a mile away is the Mystic Forest RV Park. Though Mystic Forest and the Trees of Mystery are not associated commercially, the link is obvious as soon as you arrive. The park features gravel roads, redwood trees, and grassy sites amid a 50-acre park designed primarily for RVs with a separate area for tents.

RV sites, facilities: There are 30 RV sites with full hookups (30 amps), including 15 drive-through, and a separate area for tents with 14 sites. Picnic tables and fire rings are provided. Drinking water, flush toilets, showers, a playground, a coin-operated laundry, an 18-hole mini-golf course, a game room, limited cell phone reception, modem access, a small store and gift shop, and wood are available. A clubhouse with a kitchen is available for groups. An ATM is nearby. Some facilities are wheelchair-accessible. Leashed pets are permitted.

Reservations, fees: Reservations are accepted. The fee is $14–20 per night, plus $2 per person for more than two people. Major credit cards are accepted. Open year-round.

Directions: From Eureka, drive north on U.S. 101 to Klamath and continue north for four miles. Look for the entrance sign on the left side of the road. If you reach the Trees of Mystery, you have gone a mile too far north.

Contact: Mystic Forest RV Park, 707/482-4901, fax 707/482-0704, website: www.mysticforestrv.com.

12 PANTHER FLAT

Rating: 8

on the Smith River in Six Rivers National Forest

See map pages 430–431

This is an ideal alternative to the often-crowded Jedediah Smith Redwoods State Park. The park provides easy road access since it is set right along U.S. 199, the two-laner that runs beside the Smith River. This is the largest and one of the feature campgrounds in the Smith River National Recreation Area, with excellent prospects for salmon and steelhead fishing in the fall and winter respectively, and outstanding hiking and backpacking in the summer. A great nearby hike is the Stony Creek Trail, an easy walk along the North Fork Smith River; the trailhead is in nearby Gasquet on Stoney Creek Road. Redwood National Park is a short drive to the west. The Siskiyou Wilderness is a short drive to the southeast via forest roads detailed on Forest Service maps. The wild and scenic Smith River system provides swimming, sunbathing, kayaking for experts, and beautiful scenery.

RV sites, facilities: There are 39 sites for RVs up to 35 feet, trailers up to 40 feet, and tents. Picnic tables and fire grills are provided. Drinking water, flush toilets, limited cell phone reception, and hot showers are available. A camp host is on-site. Propane, groceries, and a coin-operated laundry are nearby. Several campsites are wheelchair-accessible. Leashed pets are permitted.

Reservations, fees: Reservations are recommended and may be made with a $9 reservation fee at 877/444-6777 or www.reserveusa.com. The fee is $15 per night, plus $5 for additional vehicles. A senior discount is available. Open year-round.

Directions: From Crescent City, drive north on U.S. 101 for four miles to the junction with U.S. 199. At U.S. 199, turn east and drive 15 miles to Gasquet. From Gasquet, continue for 2.3 miles east on U.S. 199 and look for the entrance to the campground on the left side of the highway.

Contact: Smith River National Recreation Area, Six Rivers National Forest, P.O. Box 228, Gasquet, CA 95543, 707/457-3131, fax 707/457-3794.

13 GRASSY FLAT

Rating: 4

on the Smith River in Six Rivers National Forest
See map pages 430–431

This is one in a series of three easy-to-reach Forest Service camps set near U.S. 199 along the beautiful Smith River. It's a classic wild river, popular in the summer with kayakers, and the steelhead come huge in the winter for the crafty few. The camp itself is directly across from a Cal-Trans waste area, and if you hit it when the crews are working, it can be noisy here. Most of the time, however, it is peaceful and quiet. In the winter when the camp is closed, fishermen will often park at the piped gate, and then walk past the camp to a good steelhead spot.

RV sites, facilities: There are 15 sites for RVs up to 30 feet or tents and four walk-in tent sites. Picnic tables and fire grills are provided. Drinking water and vault toilets are available. Propane and

groceries are available nearby. Some facilities are wheelchair-accessible. Leashed pets are permitted.

Reservations, fees: Reservations are accepted with a $9 reservation fee at 877/444-6777 or www.reserveusa.com. The fee is $10 per night, plus $5 for each additional vehicle. A senior discount is available. Open late May through mid-September.

Directions: From Crescent City, drive north on U.S. 101 for four miles to the junction with U.S. 199, turn east on U.S. 199, and drive 15 miles to Gasquet. From Gasquet, continue east on U.S. 199 for 4.4 miles and look for the campground entrance on the right side of the road.

Contact: Smith River National Recreation Area, Six Rivers National Forest, P.O. Box 228, Gasquet, CA 95543, 707/457-3131, fax 707/457-3794.

14 PATRICK CREEK

Rating: 8

in Six Rivers National Forest
See map pages 430–431

This is one of the prettiest spots along U.S. 199, where Patrick Creek enters the upper Smith River. This section of the Smith looks something like a large trout stream, rolling green past a boulder-lined shore, complete with forest canopy. There are no trout of course, but rather salmon and steelhead in the fall and winter, and only their little smolts pooling up in the summer. A big plus for this camp is its nearby access to excellent hiking in the Siskiyou Wilderness, especially the great day hike to Buck Lake. It is essential to have a map of Six Rivers National Forest, both for driving directions to the trailhead and for the hiking route. You can buy maps at the information center for the Smith River National Recreation Area on the north side of U.S. 199 in Gasquet. An option at this camp is Patrick Creek Lodge, on the opposite side of the highway from the campground, which has a fine restaurant and bar. A paved trail connects the campground to Patrick Creek Lodge.

RV sites, facilities: There are 13 sites for RVs up to 35 feet or tents. Picnic tables and fire grills are provided. Drinking water, flush toilets, and restrooms are available. Some facilities are wheelchair-accessible. Leashed pets are permitted.

CALIFORNIA

Reservations, fees: Reservations are accepted with a $9 reservation fee at 877/444-6777 or www.reserveusa.com. The fee is $13 per night, plus $5 for each additional vehicle. A senior discount is available. Open late May through mid-September.

Directions: From Crescent City, drive north on U.S. 101 for three miles to the junction with U.S. 199, turn east on U.S. 199, and drive 15 miles to Gasquet. From Gasquet, continue east on U.S. 199 for 7.5 miles and look for the campground entrance on the right side of the road.

Contact: Smith River National Recreation Area, Six Rivers National Forest, P.O. Box 228, Gasquet, CA 95543, 707/457-3131, fax 707/457-3794.

15 BIG FLAT

Rating: 7

on Hurdygurdy Creek in Six Rivers National Forest
See map pages 430–431

This camp provides an ideal setting for those who know of it, which is why it gets quite a bit of use for a relatively remote camp. Set along Hurdygurdy Creek, near where the creek enters the South Fork of the Smith River, it provides nearby access to the South Kelsey Trail, an outstanding hiking route whether you are walking for a few hours or backpacking for days. In the summer, it is a good layover for rafters or kayakers paddling the South Fork of the Smith River.

RV sites, facilities: There are 28 sites for RVs up to 22 feet or tents. Picnic tables and fire grills are provided. Vault toilets are available. There is no drinking water, and you must pack out your garbage. Leashed pets are permitted.

Reservations, fees: Reservations are not accepted. The fee is $8 per night, plus $5 per night for each additional vehicle. A senior discount is available. Open May through mid-September.

Directions: From Crescent City, drive north on U.S. 101 for four miles to the junction with U.S. 199, turn east on U.S. 199, and drive five miles to Hiouchi. Continue just past Hiouchi, turn right at South Fork Road, and cross two bridges. At the Y, turn left on South Fork Road and drive about 14 miles to Big Flat Road/County Road 405. At Big Flat Road, turn left and drive .25

mile to the campground entrance road (Forest Road 15N59) on the left. Turn left and drive a short distance to the camp on the left.

Contact: Smith River National Recreation Area, Six Rivers National Forest, P.O. Box 228, Gasquet, CA 95543, 707/457-3131, fax 707/457-3794.

16 RIVERSIDE RV PARK

Rating: 7

on the Klamath River
See map pages 430–431

This RV park features lots of trees and grassy areas along the Klamath River. This is one in a series of RV parks near the town of Klamath along the lower Klamath River. It provides an option for RV cruisers looking for a layover spot on a U.S. 101 tour or a base of operations for a Klamath River fishing trip. There's good salmon fishing starting in late summer, peaking at Labor Day, and continuing into fall on the Klamath River.

RV sites, facilities: There are 93 sites, including 30 drive-through, with full hookups (20, 30, 50 amps) for RVs or tents. Drinking water, flush toilets, showers, modem access, and cable TV are available. Boat rentals and a dock are also available. A restaurant is within one mile. An ATM is within three miles. Leashed pets are permitted.

Reservations, fees: Reservations are accepted. The fee is $9–20 per night. Monthly rates are available. Open year-round.

Directions: From Eureka, drive north on U.S. 101 to Klamath. Continue north for two miles to the campground on the west (on the left if driving north).

Contact: Riverside RV Park, 707/482-2523.

17 CHINOOK RV RESORT

Rating: 7

on the Klamath River
See map pages 430–431

The camping area at this park consists of grassy RV sites that overlook the Klamath River. Chinook RV Resort is another of the more well-known parks on the lower Klamath. A boat ramp, fishing supplies, and all the advice you can ask for are available.

RV sites, facilities: There are 70 RV sites with full hookups (30 amps), including some drive-through sites, a suite for rent, and a grassy tent area. Picnic tables and fire grills are provided. Drinking water, flush toilets, showers, cable TV, modem access, limited cell phone reception, a playground, a coin-operated laundry, a recreation room, propane, groceries, RV supplies, a boat ramp, boat rentals, and a tackle shop are available. An ATM is within three miles. Leashed pets are permitted.

Reservations, fees: Reservations are accepted. The fee is $22 per night, plus $2 per person per night for more than two people and $2 per each additional vehicle. Major credit cards are accepted. A senior discount is available. Open year-round.

Directions: From Eureka, drive north on U.S. 101 to Klamath. After crossing the bridge at the Klamath River, continue north on U.S. 101 for a mile to the campground on the left.

Contact: Chinook RV Resort, 707/482-3511, fax 707/482-3030.

18 CAMP MARIGOLD

Rating: 7

near the Klamath River
See map pages 430–431

Camp Marigold is surrounded by wonder: Redwood National Park, towering redwoods, Pacific Ocean beaches, driftwood, agates, fossilized rocks, blackberries, Fern Canyon, Lagoon Creek Park, and the Trees of Mystery. Fishing is available nearby, in season, for several species, including king salmon, steelhead, red tail perch, and candlefish. The camp has 3.5 acres of landscaped gardens with hiking trails . . . get the idea? Well, there's more: it is only two miles to the Klamath River, in case you can't find enough to do already.

RV sites, facilities: There are 40 sites with full hookups (30 amps) for RVs up to 35 feet or tents. Park-model RVs are also available. Picnic tables and barbecues are provided. Drinking water, restrooms, hot showers, limited cell phone reception, cable TV, and a coin-operated laundry are available. Cabins (with fully equipped kitchenettes

and bedding, for two to six people) and a group lodge (with a kitchen, for up to 15 people) are also available. An ATM is nearby. Small leashed pets are permitted.

Reservations, fees: Reservations are recommended. The fee is $10–15 per night, plus $5 for each additional person (maximum 15). Monthly rates are available. Major credit cards are accepted. Open year-round.

Directions: From Eureka, drive 60 miles north on U.S. 101 to the campground at 16101 U.S. 101, four miles north of the Klamath River Bridge, on the right side of the road. The camp is a mile south of the Trees of Mystery.

Contact: Camp Marigold, 707/482-3585 or 800/621-8513, website: www.northcoast.com /~campmar.

19 CAMPER CORRAL

Rating: 6

on the Klamath River
See map pages 430–431

This resort offers 3,000 feet of Klamath River frontage, grassy tent sites, berry picking, access to the ocean, and hiking trails nearby. And, of course, in the fall it has salmon, the main attraction on the lower Klamath. Organized recreation is available in summer. This campground is right across the street from a gigantic drive-through redwood tree and the center for jet boat tours on the Klamath River.

RV sites, facilities: There are 140 sites, including 100 drive-through sites, many with full hookups (30 amps), for RVs or tents. Picnic tables and fire grills are provided. Drinking water, flush toilets, showers, a heated swimming pool, a recreation hall, a playground, an RV dump station, a coin-operated laundry, cell phone reception, modem access, cable TV, ice, and a bait and tackle shop are available. Basketball, volleyball, badminton, shuffleboard, horseshoes, and tetherball are also available. An ATM is nearby. Leashed pets are permitted.

Reservations, fees: Reservations are accepted. The fee is $16–25 per night, plus $2 per night for each additional vehicle and $2 per person per night for more than two people. Monthly rates

CALIFORNIA

are available. Major credit cards are accepted. Open April through October.

Directions: From Eureka, drive north on U.S. 101 to Klamath. Just after crossing the Klamath River Bridge, take the Terwer Valley Road exit. At the stop sign, turn left and drive a short distance west to the campground.

Contact: Camper Corral, 707/482-5741, website: www.campercorral.net.

20 STEELHEAD LODGE

Rating: 6

on the Klamath River

See map pages 430–431

Many anglers use this park as headquarters when the salmon and steelhead get going in August. The park has grassy sites near the Klamath River.

RV sites, facilities: There are 36 sites, including 10 drive-through, with full hookups (30 amps) for RVs or tents. Picnic tables are provided. Drinking water, flush toilets, cell phone reception, showers, and ice are available. A bar, restaurant, and motel are also available. An ATM is nearby. The bar and restaurant are wheelchair-accessible. Leashed pets are permitted.

Reservations, fees: Reservations are accepted. The fee is $15 per night. Major credit cards are accepted. Open year-round.

Directions: From Eureka, drive north on U.S. 101 to Klamath and the junction with Highway 169. Turn east on Highway 169 and drive 3.2 miles to Terwer Riffle Road. Turn right (south) on Terwer Riffle Road and drive one block to Steelhead Lodge on the right.

Contact: Steelhead Lodge, 707/482-8145. For a fishing report, call 707/482-7775.

21 TERWER PARK

Rating: 7

on the Klamath River

See map pages 430–431

This RV park is situated near the Terwer Riffle, one of the better shore-fishing spots for steelhead and salmon on the lower Klamath River. You get grassy sites, river access, and some fair trails along the Klamath. When the salmon arrive in late August and September, Terwer Riffle can be loaded with fish, as well as boaters and shore anglers—a wild scene. Note that at this park, tent campers are separated from the RV park, with tent camping at a grassy area near the river.

RV sites, facilities: There are 87 RV sites, including 12 drive-through sites, with full hookups plus a few long-term residents. A separate tent area is available. Picnic tables are provided. Flush toilets, hot showers, and a coin-operated laundry are available. A pulley boat launch is nearby. Leashed pets are permitted.

Reservations, fees: Reservations are accepted. The fee is $10–13.50 per night, plus $5 for a second vehicle. Monthly rates are available. Open year-round.

Directions: From Eureka, drive north on U.S. 101 to Klamath and the junction with Highway 169. Turn east on Highway 169 and drive 3.5 miles to Terwer Riffle Road. Turn right on Terwer Riffle Road and drive seven blocks (about .5 mile) to the park at the end of the road (641 Terwer Riffle Rd).

Contact: Terwer Park, 707/482-3855, website: www.terwerpark.com.

22 GOLD BLUFF BEACH

Rating: 8

in Prairie Creek Redwoods State Park

See map pages 430–431

The campsites here are set in a sandy, exposed area with man-made windbreaks with a huge, expansive beach on one side and a backdrop of 100- to 200-foot cliffs on the other side. You can walk for miles at this beach, often without seeing another soul, and there is a great trail routed north through forest, with many hidden little waterfalls. In addition, the Fern Canyon Trail, one of the best 30-minute hikes in California, is at the end of Davison Road. Hikers walk along a stream in a narrow canyon, its vertical walls covered with magnificent ferns. There are some herds of elk in the area, often right along the access road. These camps are rarely used in the winter because of the region's heavy rain and winds. The expanse of beach here is awesome, covering 10 miles of huge, pristine ocean frontage. Campfire programs are offered in summer.

CALIFORNIA

RV sites, facilities: There are 25 sites for RVs up to 24 feet (no trailers or vehicles wider than eight feet) or tents. Fire grills, food lockers, and tables are provided. Drinking water, limited cell phone reception, flush toilets, and solar showers are available. Leashed pets are permitted.

Reservations, fees: Reservations are not accepted. The fee is $12–15 per night. A senior discount is available. Open year-round.

Directions: From Eureka, drive north on U.S. 101 for 45 miles to Orick. At Orick, continue north on U.S. 101 for three miles to Davison Road. Turn left (west) on Davison Road and drive six miles to the campground on the left. Note: no vehicles more than 24 feet long or more than eight feet wide are permitted on Davison Road, which is narrow and very bumpy.

Contact: Prairie Creek Redwoods State Park, 707/464-6101, ext. 5301 or 5300 (Visitor Center).

23 ELK PRAIRIE

Rating: 9

in Prairie Creek Redwoods State Park
See map pages 430–431

Herds of Roosevelt elk wander free in this remarkable 14,000-acre park. Great opportunities for photographs abound, with the elk often found right along the highway and access roads. Where there are meadows, there are elk; it's about that simple. An elky here, an elky there, making this one of the best places to see wildlife in California. Remember that these are wild animals, they are huge, and they can be unpredictable; in other words, enjoy them, but don't harass them or get too close. This park consists of old-growth coastal redwoods, prairie lands, and 10 miles of scenic, open beach (Gold Bluff Beach). The interior of the park can be reached by 75 miles of hiking, biking, and nature trails, including a trailhead for a great bike ride at the campground. There are many additional trailheads and a beautiful tour of giant redwoods along the Drury Scenic Parkway. A visitors center and summer interpretive programs with guided walks and junior ranger programs are available. Because of the prevalent coastal fog, the understory of the forest is very dense. Western azalea and rhododendron bloom in May and June, and the Rhododendron Trail is a favorite for seeing this display. From November through May, always bring your rain gear. Summer temperatures range from 40 to 75°F; winter temperatures range from 35 to 55°F.

RV sites, facilities: There are 75 sites for RVs up to 27 feet, or trailers up to 24 feet, or tents. Picnic tables, fire grills, and bear-proof food lockers are provided. Drinking water, flush toilets, an RV dump station, and coin-operated showers are available. Some facilities are wheelchair-accessible. Leashed pets are permitted.

Reservations, fees: Reservations are accepted with a $7.50 reservation fee at 800/444-PARK (800/444-7275) or www.reserveamerica.com. The fee is $12–15 per night. A senior discount is available. Open year-round.

Directions: From Eureka, drive 45 miles north on U.S. 101 to Orick. At Orick, continue north on U.S. 101 for five miles to the Newton B. Drury Scenic Parkway. Take the exit for the Newton B. Drury Scenic Parkway and drive north for a mile to the park. Turn left at the park entrance.

Contact: Prairie Creek Redwoods State Park, 707/464-6101, ext. 5301 or 5300 (Visitor Center).

24 BIG LAGOON COUNTY PARK

Rating: 7

overlooking the Pacific Ocean
See map pages 430–431

This is a remarkable, huge lagoon that borders the Pacific Ocean. It provides good boating, excellent exploring, fair fishing, and good duck hunting in the winter. It's a good spot to paddle a canoe around on a calm day. A lot of out-of-towners cruise by, note the lagoon's proximity to the ocean, and figure it must be salt water. Wrong! Not only is it freshwater, but it provides a long shot for anglers trying for rainbow trout. One reason not many RV drivers stop here is that most of them are drawn farther north (another eight miles) to Freshwater Lagoon.

RV sites, facilities: There are 26 sites for RVs or tents, including one with partial hookups (30 amps). Picnic tables and fire grills are provided. Drinking water, flush toilets, a pay phone, and limited cell phone reception are available. A boat

CALIFORNIA

ramp is also available. Some facilities are wheelchair-accessible. Leashed pets are permitted.

Reservations, fees: Reservations are not accepted. The fee is $12 per night per vehicle, plus a $3 day-use fee and $1 per pet per night. Open year-round.

Directions: From Eureka, drive 22 miles north on U.S. 101 to Trinidad. At Trinidad, continue north on U.S. 101 for eight miles to Big Lagoon Park Road. Turn left (west) at Big Lagoon Park Road and drive two miles to the park.

Contact: Humboldt County Parks, 707/445-7652.

25 PATRICK'S POINT STATE PARK

Rating: 9

near Trinidad
See map pages 430–431

This pretty park covers 640 acres of coastal headlands and is filled with Sitka spruce, dramatic ocean lookouts, and several beautiful beaches, including one with agates, one with tidepools, and another with an expansive stretch of beachfront leading to a lagoon. You can best see it on the Rim Trail, which has many little cutoff routes to the lookouts and down to the beaches. The campground is sheltered in the forest, and while it is often foggy and damp in the summer, it is always beautiful. A Native American village, constructed by the Yurok tribe, is also here. At the north end of the park, a short hike to see the bizarre "Octopus Trees" is a good side trip, with trees that are growing atop downed logs, their root systems exposed like octopus tentacles; the trail here loops through a grove of old-growth Sitka spruce. In addition, there are several miles of pristine beach to the north that extends to the lagoons. Interpretive programs are available. The forest here is dense, with spruce, hemlock, pine, fir, and red alder covering an ocean headland. Night and morning fog are common almost year-round, and there are periods where it doesn't lift for days. This area gets 60 inches of rain per year on the average. For camping, plan on making reservations.

RV sites, facilities: There are 124 sites for RVs or tents, including 39 sites for RVs only up to 31 feet long. Fire grills, food lockers, and picnic tables are provided. Drinking water, flush toilets, limited cell phone reception, and coin-operated showers are available. An ATM is within five miles. Some facilities are wheelchair-accessible. Leashed pets are permitted at campsites but not on trails or beaches.

Reservations, fees: Reservations are accepted with a $7.50 reservation fee at 800/444-PARK (800/444-7275) or www.reserveamerica.com. The fee is $15 per night. A senior discount is available. Open year-round.

Directions: From Eureka, drive north on U.S. 101 for 22 miles to Trinidad. At Trinidad, continue north on U.S. 101 for 5.5 miles to Patrick's Point Drive. Take that exit and at the stop sign, turn left and drive .5 mile to the park entrance.

Contact: Patrick's Point State Park, 707/677-3570.

26 SOUNDS OF THE SEA RV PARK

Rating: 6

in Trinidad
See map pages 430–431

The Trinidad area, about 20 miles north of Eureka, is one of the great places on this planet. Nearby Patrick's Point State Park is one of the highlights, with a Sitka spruce forest, beautiful coastal lookouts, a great easy hike on the Rim Trail, and access to several secluded beaches. To the nearby south at Trinidad Head is a small harbor and dock, with deep-sea and salmon fishing trips available. A breezy beach is to the immediate north of the Seascape Restaurant. A bonus at this privately operated RV park is good berry picking.

RV sites, facilities: There are 52 RV sites, including some drive-through, with full hookups (30, 50 amps). Picnic tables and fire rings are provided. Restrooms, showers, an RV dump station, cell phone reception, modem access, a coin-operated laundry, a grocery store, gift shop, cable TV, and ice are available. An ATM is nearby. Leashed pets are permitted.

Reservations, fees: Reservations are accepted. The fee is $28 per night. Major credit cards are accepted. Open year-round.

Directions: From Eureka, drive north on U.S. 101 for 28 miles to Trinidad. In Trinidad, continue north on U.S. 101 for five miles to the

CALIFORNIA

Patrick's Point exit. Take the Patrick's Point exit, turn left, and drive .5 mile to the campground. **Contact:** Sounds of the Sea RV Park, 707/677-3271, website: www.northcoast.com/~gupie.

27 SYLVAN HARBOR RV PARK AND CABINS

Rating: 8

in Trinidad
See map pages 430–431
This park is designed as an RV park and fish camp, with cleaning tables and canning facilities available on site. It is a short distance from the boat hoist at Trinidad Pier. Beauty surrounds Sylvan Harbor on all sides for miles. Visitors come to enjoy the various beaches, go agate hunting, or look for driftwood on the beach. Nearby Patrick's Point State Park is an excellent getaway side trip. This is one of several privately operated parks in the Trinidad area, offering a choice of shaded or open sites near the ocean. (For more information about recreation options nearby, see the previous listing for Sounds of the Sea.)

RV sites, facilities: There are 70 sites with full hookups (20, 30, 50 amps) for RVs up to 35 feet. Three cabins are available. Drinking water, restrooms, showers, an RV dump station, limited cell phone reception, modem access, a coin-operated laundry, and propane are available. An ATM is within one mile. Leashed pets are permitted.

Reservations, fees: Reservations are accepted for cabins only. The fee is $20 per night for RV sites, plus $2 per person for more than two people; call for cabin fees. Open year-round.

Directions: From Eureka, drive north on U.S. 101 for 28 miles to Trinidad. Take the Trinidad exit to the stop sign at Seawood Drive. Turn left and drive a short distance under the freeway to Patrick's Point Drive. Turn right and drive one mile to the campground on the right.

Contact: Sylvan Harbor RV Park and Cabins, tel./fax 707/677-9988, website: www.sylvanharbor.com.

28 VIEW CREST LODGE AND CAMPGROUND

Rating: 8

in Trinidad
See map pages 430–431
View Crest Campground is one of the premium spots in Trinidad, with pretty cottages available as well as campsites for RVs and tents. A bonus here is the remarkable flights of swallows, many of which have nests at the cottages. Recreation options include deep-sea and salmon fishing at Trinidad Harbor to the nearby south, and outstanding easy hiking at Patrick's Point State Park to the nearby north.

RV sites, facilities: There are 25 RV sites with full hookups (20, 30 amps), including nine drive-through sites, and a separate area for tents; 12 cottages are available. Picnic tables and fire rings are provided. Drinking water, restrooms, showers, limited cell phone reception, an RV dump station, cable TV hookups, RV storage, a coin-operated laundry, and wood are available. Leashed pets are permitted only in the campground.

Reservations, fees: Reservations are accepted. The fee is $16–22 per night, plus $1 per person per night for more than two people. Major credit cards are accepted. Open year-round.

Directions: From Eureka, drive north on U.S. 101 for 28 miles to Trinidad. Take the Trinidad exit to the stop sign at Seawood Drive. Turn left and drive a short distance under the freeway to Patrick's Point Drive. Turn right and drive two miles to the campground on the right.

Contact: View Crest Lodge and Campground, 707/677-3393, fax 707/677-9363, website: www.viewcrestlodge.com.

29 MIDWAY RV PARK

Rating: 6

in Trinidad
See map pages 430–431
This is one of several privately developed campgrounds in Trinidad. In the summer, salmon fishing can be excellent just off Trinidad Head. In the fall, rock fishing is the way to go, and in winter,

CALIFORNIA

crabbing is tops. Patrick's Point State Park provides a nearby side-trip option to the north.

RV sites, facilities: There are 65 RV sites with full hookups (20, 30 amps) and four tent sites. Picnic tables are provided. Drinking water, restrooms, showers, cable TV, a pay phone, modem access, cell phone reception, a club room, a playground, propane, a coin-operated laundry, a fish-cleaning station, and RV storage are available. An ATM is nearby. Some facilities are wheelchair-accessible. Leashed pets are permitted.

Reservations, fees: Reservations are recommended in the summer. The fee is $18–24 per night, plus $3 per person per night for more than two people. A senior discount is available. Major credit cards are accepted. Open year-round.

Directions: From Eureka, drive north on U.S. 101 for 20 miles to Trinidad. Take the first Trinidad exit to the stop sign at Seawood Drive. Turn left and drive a short distance under the freeway to Patrick's Point Drive. Turn right on Patrick's Point Drive and drive .5 mile to the campground on the right.

Contact: Midway RV Park, tel./fax 707/677-3934.

30 EMERALD FOREST

Rating: 5

in Trinidad
See map pages 430–431

This campground is set on 12 acres of redwoods, often dark and wet, with the ocean at Trinidad Head only about a five-minute drive away. This is a nice spot with nice folks.

RV sites, facilities: There are 55 sites for RVs, including 14 drive-through sites, with partial or full hookups (30 amps), and 30 tent sites. There are also 15 cabins with kitchens. Picnic tables, fire rings, and barbecues are provided. Restrooms, showers, free cable TV in RV sites, limited cell phone reception, and a playground are available. A mini-mart, ice, wood, a coin-operated laundry, a meeting hall with a kitchen and fireplace (seats about 40), and propane are also available. Modem hookups, volleyball, horseshoes, badminton, and a video arcade are on-site. An ATM is nearby. Leashed pets are permitted, except in the tent sites.

Reservations, fees: Reservations are recommended

in the summer. The fee is $19–25 per night, plus $2.50 per person per night for more than two people. Call for cabin prices and pet fees. Major credit cards are accepted. Open year-round.

Directions: From Eureka, drive north on U.S. 101 for 28 miles to Trinidad. Take the Trinidad exit. Turn right on Patrick's Point Drive and drive about .7 mile north to the campground on the right side of the road.

Contact: Emerald Forest, 707/677-3554, fax 707/677-0963, website: www.cabinsintheredwoods.com.

31 HIDDEN CREEK RV PARK

Rating: 5

in Trinidad
See map pages 430–431

To tell you the truth, there really isn't much hidden about this RV park, but you might be hard-pressed to find year-round Parker Creek. Regardless, it is still in a pretty location in Trinidad, with the Trinidad pier, adjacent harbor, restaurants, and beach all within a drive of just a minute or two. Some of California's best deep-sea fishing for salmon, lingcod, and rockfish is available on boats out of Trinidad Harbor, and there are annual derbies for salmon, lingcod, and halibut. Crab and albacore tuna are also caught here, and there's beachcombing for agates and driftwood on the beach to the immediate north.

RV sites, facilities: There are 56 RV sites (some with permanent residents) with partial or full hookups, including cable TV, six drive-through sites, four sites for tents, and one mobile home. Several group sites are also available. Picnic tables are provided. Patios, restrooms, showers, propane, a fish-cleaning station, ice, and an RV dump station are available. Leashed pets are permitted.

Reservations, fees: Reservations are recommended in the summer. The fee is $14–21 per night, plus $2 per person per night for more than two people. Long-term rates are available. A senior discount is available. Open year-round.

Directions: From Eureka, drive north on U.S. 101 for 28 miles to Trinidad. Take the Trinidad exit to the stop sign. Turn right at Westhaven Drive and drive a short distance to the RV park on the left at 199 N. Westhaven.

Contact: Hidden Creek RV Park, 707/677-3775, fax 707/677-3886.

32 CLAM BEACH COUNTY PARK

Rating: 7

near McKinleyville
See map pages 430–431

Here awaits a beach that seems to stretch on forever, one of the great places to bring a lover, dog, children, or, hey, all three. The campsites are a bit exposed, making winds out of the north a problem in the spring, but the direct beach access largely makes up for it. The park gets its name from the good clamming that is available, but you must come equipped with a clam gun or special clam shovel, and then be out when minus low tides arrive at daybreak. Most people just enjoy playing tag with the waves, taking long romantic walks, or throwing sticks for the dog.

RV sites, facilities: RV parking is allowed on the paved lot, and there are 12 sites for tents. Picnic tables and fire rings are provided. Drinking water and vault toilets are available. Propane, a grocery store, and a coin-operated laundry are available in McKinleyville. Leashed pets are permitted.

Reservations, fees: Reservations are not accepted. The fee is $8 per night per vehicle, plus $1 per pet per night. Open year-round.

Directions: From Eureka, drive north on U.S. 101 to McKinleyville. Just past McKinleyville, turn west at the sign for Clam Beach and drive two blocks to the campground, which is adjacent to Little River State Beach.

Contact: Humboldt County Parks, 707/445-7652.

33 MAD RIVER RAPIDS RV PARK

Rating: 7

in Arcata
See map pages 430–431

This camp is near the farmlands on the outskirts of town, in a pastoral, quiet setting. There is a great bike ride nearby on a trail routed along the Mad River, and it is also excellent for taking a dog for a walk. Nearby Arcata is a unique town, a bit of the old and a bit of the new, and the

Arcata Marsh at the north end of Humboldt Bay provides a scenic and easy bicycle trip, as well as an excellent destination for hiking, sightseeing, and bird-watching.

RV sites, facilities: There are 92 RV sites with full hookups (30, 50 amps), including 50 long-term rentals and 40 drive-through sites. Picnic tables are provided. Fire grills are provided at two sites. Drinking water, patios, restrooms, showers, an RV dump station, cell phone reception, an ATM, modem access, a recreation room, tennis courts, a fitness room, a playground, basketball courts, horseshoes, a swimming pool, a spa, cable TV, VCR rentals, a restaurant, a grocery store, and a coin-operated laundry are available. Some facilities are wheelchair-accessible. Leashed pets are permitted.

Reservations, fees: Reservations are accepted. The fee is $26–33 per night. Major credit cards are accepted. A senior discount is available. Open year-round.

Directions: From the junction of U.S. 101 and Highway 299 in Arcata, drive .25 mile north on U.S. 101 to the Guintoli Lane exit. At the exit, turn left (west) on Janes Road and drive two blocks west to the park on the left.

Contact: Mad River Rapids RV Park, 707/822-7275 or 800/822-7776, fax 707/822-7286, website: www.madriverrv.com.

34 WIDOW WHITE CREEK RV PARK

Rating: 5

in McKinleyville
See map pages 430–431

This privately operated park provides extremely easy access from the highway. Nearby recreation options include the Mad River, where there is a nice picnic site near the hatchery, productive steelhead fishing in the winter, and good perch fishing in the surf where the Mad River enters the ocean. Ocean fishing for salmon is possible in the summer. Get this—nearby are the "world's largest totem poles." They'll tell you all about it.

RV sites, facilities: There are 40 RV sites, including 30 long-term rentals and some drive-through sites, with full hookups (30, 50 amps) and a separate area for tents. Picnic tables are provided.

Drinking water, restrooms, showers, a playground, modem access, limited cell phone reception, an RV dump station, and a coin-operated laundry are available. An ATM is within one mile. Some facilities are wheelchair-accessible. Leashed pets are permitted.

Reservations, fees: Reservations are accepted. The fee is $18–22 per night. Monthly rates are available. Open year-round.

Directions: From Eureka, drive north on U.S. 101 and continue for 4.5 miles past the junction with Highway 299 to the Murray Road exit. Take the exit, turn right (east) on Murray Road, and drive a half block to the park on the left.

Contact: Widow White Creek RV Park, 707/839-1137.

35 EUREKA KOA

Rating: 2

in Eureka

See map pages 430–431

This is a year-round KOA camp for U.S. 101 cruisers looking for a layover spot in Eureka. A bonus here is a few of those little KOA Kamping Kabins, the log-style jobs that win on cuteness alone. The closest significant recreation option is the Arcata Marsh on Humboldt Bay, a richly diverse spot with good trails for biking and hiking or just parking and looking at the water. Another option is excellent salmon fishing in June, July, and August.

RV sites, facilities: There are 140 RV sites—42 are drive-through with full hookups (30, 50 amps) and some have partial hookups. There are also 26 tent sites and eight bike-in/hike-in sites. Group sites, 10 camping cabins, and two cottages are available. Picnic tables and fire pits are provided. Drinking water, flush toilets, showers, a playground, a recreation room, a heated swimming pool, two hot tubs, a grocery store, a coin-operated laundry, an RV dump station, limited cell phone reception, propane, ice, wood, a fax machine, and modem access are available. Some facilities are wheelchair-accessible. Leashed pets are permitted.

Reservations, fees: Reservations are accepted at 800/562-3136. The fee is $20–30 per night, plus $3 per person for more than two people. Cabins are $50 per night for four people; cottages are $120 per night for four people. A senior discount is available. Major credit cards are accepted. Open year-round.

Directions: From Eureka, drive north on U.S. 101 for four miles to KOA Drive (well signed on east side of highway). Turn right on KOA Drive and drive to 4050 N. U.S. 101.

Contact: Eureka KOA, 707/822-4243, fax 707/822-0126, website: www.koa.com.

36 SAMOA BOAT LAUNCH COUNTY PARK

Rating: 7

on Humboldt Bay

See map pages 430–431

The nearby vicinity of the boat ramp, with access to Humboldt Bay and the Pacific Ocean, makes this a star attraction for campers towing their fishing boats. At the park you get good beach-combing and clamming at low tides and a chance to see a huge variety of seabirds, highlighted by egrets and herons. There's a reason: directly across the bay is the Humboldt Bay National Wildlife Refuge. This park is near the famed all-you-can-eat, logger-style Samoa Cookhouse.

RV sites, facilities: There are 24 sites for RVs or tents. Picnic tables and fire grills are provided. Drinking water and flush toilets are available. A boat ramp, cell phone reception, a grocery store, propane, an ATM, and a coin-operated laundry are available in Eureka (about five miles away). Leashed pets are permitted.

Reservations, fees: Reservations are not accepted. The fee is $12 per night per vehicle, plus $1 per pet per night. There is a three-day minimum stay. Open year-round.

Directions: From U.S. 101 in Eureka, turn west on Highway 255 and drive two miles until it dead-ends at New Navy Base Road. At New Navy Base Road, turn left and drive five miles to the end of the Samoa Peninsula and the campground entrance.

Contact: Humboldt County Parks, 707/445-7652, website: www.humboldtnation.com.

CALIFORNIA

37 E-Z LANDING RV PARK AND MARINA

Rating: 7

on Humboldt Bay
See map pages 430–431

This is a good base camp for salmon trips in July and August when big schools of king salmon often teem just west of the entrance of Humboldt Bay. A nearby boat ramp with access to Humboldt Bay has been in disrepair and was scheduled for repair and a return to operation by 2003; call first if you plan on launching a boat here. It's not the prettiest camp in the world, with quite a bit of asphalt, but most people use this camp as a simple parking spot for sleeping and getting down to the business of the day: fishing. This spot is ideal for ocean fishing, clamming, beachcombing, and boating.

RV sites, facilities: There are 45 RV sites with full hookups (30 amps), including about half long-term and 20 drive-through sites. Patios, flush toilets, showers, modem hookups, cell phone reception, marine gas, ice, a coin-operated laundry, a party boat for fishing, bait, and tackle are available. An ATM is within 3.5 miles. Some facilities are wheelchair-accessible. Leashed pets are permitted.

Reservations, fees: Reservations are accepted. The fee is $19 per night. Major credit cards are accepted. Open year-round.

Directions: From Eureka, drive 3.5 miles south on U.S. 101 to King Salmon Avenue. Turn west (right) on King Salmon Avenue (it becomes Buhne Drive) and drive for a half mile to where the road turns. Turn left (south) on Buhne Drive and go .5 mile to the park on the left (1875 Buhne Drive).

Contact: E-Z Landing RV Park and Marina, 707/442-1118, fax 707/442-1999.

38 JOHNNY'S MARINA AND RV PARK

Rating: 5

on Humboldt Bay
See map pages 430–431

This is a good base camp for salmon fishing during the peak season—always call, since the season changes each year as set by the Department of Fish and Game. Mooring for private boats is available, a nice plus for campers trailering boats. Other recreation activities include beachcombing, clamming, and perch fishing from shore. The owners have run this place for more than 50 years.

RV sites, facilities: There are 53 sites with full hookups (20, 30 amps), including several long-term rentals and three drive-through sites for RVs up to 40 feet. Patios, restrooms, showers, gasoline, and an RV dump station are provided. A coin-operated laundry and a boat dock are available. Leashed pets are permitted.

Reservations, fees: Reservations are accepted. The fee is $20 per night. Open year-round.

Directions: From Eureka, drive 3.5 miles south on U.S. 101 to King Salmon Avenue. Turn west (right) on King Salmon Avenue (it becomes Buhne Drive). Continue about .5 mile to the park on the left (1821 Buhne Drive).

Contact: Johnny's Marina and RV Park, 707/442-2284, fax 707/443-4608.

39 STAFFORD RV PARK

Rating: 6

near Scotia
See map pages 430–431

This is a privately operated park for RVs that provides several side-trip options: a tour of the giant sawmill in Scotia, a tour of giant redwoods on the Avenue of the Giants, access to the nearby Eel River, and, best of all, the nearby Redwood National Park. One of the better park information centers in California is here, with maps and information about hikes, bike rides, and driving tours.

RV sites, facilities: There are 50 RV sites, including many drive-through sites, with partial or full hookups (30, 50 amps), 30 tent sites, group sites, and four sleeping cabins. Picnic tables and fire grills are provided. Drinking water, flush toilets, showers, limited cell phone reception, and a coin-operated laundry are available. Some facilities are wheelchair-accessible. Leashed pets are permitted.

Reservations, fees: Reservations are accepted. The fee is $18–25 per night. A senior discount is available. Major credit cards are accepted in summer only. Monthly rates are available. Open

CALIFORNIA

year-round, with a reduced number of sites in the winter.

Directions: From Eureka, drive south on U.S. 101 to Scotia. At Scotia, continue south for three miles to Stafford Road. Turn right (west) on Stafford Road and at the first stop sign, turn left under the overpass, and drive a short distance to North Road. At North Road, turn right and drive .25 mile to the park on the right (385 North Road).

Contact: Stafford RV Park, 707/764-3416, website: www.staffordrvpark.com.

40 VAN DUZEN COUNTY PARK

Rating: 6

on the Van Duzen River

See map pages 430–431

This campground is set at the headwaters of the Van Duzen River, one of the Eel River's major tributaries. The river is subject to tremendous fluctuations in flows and height, so low in the fall that it is often temporarily closed to fishing by the Department of Fish and Game, and so high in the winter that only fools would stick their toes in. For a short period in late spring, it provides a benign run for rafting and canoeing, putting in at Grizzly Creek and taking out at Van Duzen. In October, you'll find an excellent salmon fishing spot where the Van Duzen enters the Eel.

RV sites, facilities: There are 30 sites for RVs or tents, including five with partial hookups (30 amps). Picnic tables and fire grills are provided. Drinking water, flush toilets, and coin-operated showers are available. A grocery store and a coin-operated laundry are nearby. Some facilities are wheelchair-accessible. Leashed pets are permitted.

Reservations, fees: Reservations are not accepted. The fee is $12 per night per vehicle, plus $1 per pet per night. There is a 10-day maximum stay. Open year-round.

Directions: From Eureka, drive south on U.S. 101 to the junction of Highway 36 at Alton. Turn east on Highway 36 and drive 12 miles to the campground.

Contact: Humboldt County Parks, 707/445-7652, website: www.humboldtnation.com.

41 GRIZZLY CREEK REDWOODS STATE PARK

Rating: 7

near Bridgeville

See map pages 430–431

Most summer vacationers hit the campgrounds on the Redwood Highway, that is, U.S. 101. However, this camp is just far enough off the beaten path to provide some semblance of seclusion. It is set in redwoods, quite beautiful, with fair hiking and good access to the adjacent Van Duzen River. The park encompasses only a few acres, yet it is very quiet and private. There are 4.5 miles of hiking trails, a visitors center with exhibits, and a bookstore. The Cheatham Grove in this park is an exceptional stand of coast redwoods. In the winter one of the better holes for steelhead fishing is accessible here. Nearby attractions include the Victorian village of Ferndale and Fort Humboldt to the north, Humoldt Redwoods State Park to the south, and Ruth Lake to the more distant east.

RV sites, facilities: There are 12 sites for RVs up to 30 feet or trailers up to 18 feet and 18 tent sites. Picnic tables and fire grills are provided. Drinking water, flush toilets, and showers are available. A grocery store is within 3.5 miles. Some facilities are wheelchair-accessible. Leashed pets are permitted in the campground but not on trails or at the day-use beach area.

Reservations, fees: Reservations are accepted with a $7.50 reservation fee at 800/444-PARK (800/444-7275) or www.reserveamerica.com. The fee is $15 per night, plus a $4 day-use fee. A senior discount is available. Open year-round.

Directions: From Eureka, drive south on U.S. 101 to the junction of Highway 36 at Alton. Turn east on Highway 36 and drive about 17 miles to the campground on the right.

Contact: Grizzly Creek Redwoods State Park, 707/777-3683, fax 707/777-3159.

42 A. W. WAY COUNTY PARK

Rating: 8

on the Mattole River

See map pages 430–431

This secluded camp provides a home for visitors

to the "Lost Coast," the beautiful coastal stretch of California far from any semblance of urban life. The highlight here is the Mattole River, a great steelhead stream when flows are suitable between January and mid-March. Nearby is excellent hiking in the King Range National Conservation Area. For the great hike out to the abandoned Punta Gorda Lighthouse, drive to the trailhead on the left side of Lighthouse Road. This area is typically bombarded with monsoon-level rains in winter.

RV sites, facilities: There are 30 sites for RVs or tents. Picnic tables and fire grills are provided. Drinking water, flush toilets, and outdoor showers are available. A grocery store, a coin-operated laundry, and propane are available nearby. Leashed pets are permitted.

Reservations, fees: Reservations are not accepted. The fee is $12 per night per vehicle, plus $1 per pet. Open year-round.

Directions: From Garberville, drive north on U.S. 101 to the South Fork–Honeydew exit. Turn west on South Fork–Honeydew Road and drive 31 miles (the road alternates between pavement, gravel, dirt, then pavement again, steep and curvy) to the park entrance on the left side of the road. The park is 7.5 miles south of the town of Petrolia.

Contact: Humboldt County Parks, 707/445-7652.

43 ALBEE CREEK

Rating: 8

in Humboldt Redwoods State Park
See map pages 430–431

Humboldt Redwoods State Park is a massive sprawl of forest that is known for some unusual giant trees in the Federation Grove and Big Tree Area. The park covers 52,000 acres, including more than 7,000 acres of old-growth coast redwoods. It has 100 miles of hiking trails, many excellent, both short and long. The camp is in a redwood grove, and the smell of these trees has a special magic. Nearby Albee Creek, a benign trickle most of the year, can flood in the winter after heavy rains. A visitors center with exhibits and seasonal interpretive programs, campfire talks, nature walks, and junior ranger programs are available.

RV sites, facilities: There are 33 sites for RVs

up to 31 feet and trailers up to 21 feet and 39 sites for tents. Picnic tables, fire grills, and food lockers are provided. Drinking water, flush toilets, and showers are available. Leashed pets are permitted.

Reservations, fees: Reservations are accepted with a $7.50 reservation fee at 800/444-PARK (800/444-7275) or www.reserveamerica.com. The fee is $12–15 per night. A senior discount is available. Open May through September.

Directions: From Eureka, drive south on U.S. 101 about 11 miles to the Honeydew exit (if you reach Weott, you have gone two miles too far). At Mattole Road, turn west and drive five miles to the campground on the right.

Contact: Humboldt Redwoods State Park, 707/946-2409, fax 707/946-2326.

44 BURLINGTON

Rating: 7

in Humboldt Redwoods State Park
See map pages 430–431

This camp is one of the centerpieces of Humboldt Redwoods State Park, California's largest redwood state park. It includes the Rockefeller Forest, the largest remaining contiguous old-growth coast redwood forest in the world. The trees here are thousands of years old and have never been logged; they are as pristine now as 200 years ago. This camp is often at capacity during the tourist months. You get shady campsites with big redwood stumps that kids can play on. Good hiking is available on trails routed through the redwoods, and in winter, steelhead fishing is often good on the nearby Eel River. The park has 100 miles of trails, but it is the little half-mile Founders Grove Nature Trail that has the quickest payoff and requires the least effort. The average rainfall here is 65 inches per year, with most occurring between October and May. Morning and evening fog in the summer keeps the temperature cool in the river basin.

RV sites, facilities: There are 57 sites for RVs up to 30 feet, trailers up to 24 feet, or tents. Picnic tables, fire grills, and food lockers are provided. Drinking water, flush toilets, and showers are available. Some facilities are wheelchair-accessible. Leashed pets are permitted.

CALIFORNIA

Reservations, fees: Reservations are accepted with a $7.50 reservation fee at 800/444-PARK (800/444-7275) or www.reserveamerica.com. The fee is $12–15 per night. A senior discount is available. Open year-round.

Directions: From Eureka, drive south on U.S. 101 for 45 miles to the Weott/Newton Road exit. Turn right on Newton Road and continue to the T junction where Newton Road meets the Avenue of the Giants. Turn left on the Avenue of the Giants and drive two miles to the campground entrance on the left.

Contact: Humboldt Redwoods State Park, 707/946-2409, fax 707/946-2326.

45 HIDDEN SPRINGS

Rating: 7

in Humboldt Redwoods State Park
See map pages 430–431

This camp gets heavy use from May through September, but the campsites have been situated in a way that offers relative seclusion. Side trips include good hiking on trails routed through redwoods and a touring drive on Avenue of the Giants. The park has more than 100 miles of hiking trails, many of them amid spectacular giant redwoods, including the Bull Creek Flats Trail and Founders Grove Nature Trail. Bears are occasionally spotted by mountain bikers on rides out to the park's outskirts. In winter, nearby High Rock on the Eel River is one of the better shoreline fishing spots for steelhead. (For more information on Humboldt Redwoods, see notes for Albee Creek and Burlington campgrounds in this chapter.)

RV sites, facilities: There are 154 sites for RVs up to 33 feet, trailers up to 24 feet, or tents. Picnic tables, fire grills, and food lockers are provided. Drinking water, flush toilets, and showers are available. A grocery store and a coin-operated laundry are within one mile in Myers Flat. Leashed pets are permitted.

Reservations, fees: Reservations are accepted with a $7.50 reservation fee at 800/444-PARK (800/444-7275) or www.reserveamerica.com. The fee is $12–15 per night. A senior discount is available. Open May through September.

Directions: From Eureka, drive south 50 miles on U.S. 101 to the Myers Flat/Avenue of the Giants exit. Continue south and drive less than a mile to the campground entrance on the left.

Contact: Humboldt Redwoods State Park, 707/946-2409, fax 707/946-2326.

46 GIANT REDWOODS RV AND CAMP

Rating: 8

on the Eel River
See map pages 430–431

This privately operated park is in a grove of redwoods and covers 23 acres, much of it fronting the Eel River. Trip options include the scenic drive on Avenue of the Giants.

RV sites, facilities: There are 57 RV sites (34 drive-through), many with partial or full hookups (30 amps), and 26 tent sites. Picnic tables and fire rings are provided. Drinking water, restrooms, showers, modem hookups, a store, ice, a coin-operated laundry, limited cell phone reception, a playground, and a recreation room are available. An ATM is nearby. Pets are welcome with a dog "freedom area" available at the river bar.

Reservations, fees: Reservations are recommended in the summer. The fee is $20–30 per night, plus $2.50 per person per night for more than two people and $2 per pet per night. The seventh night is free. Major credit cards are accepted. A senior discount is available. Open year-round, with limited facilities in winter.

Directions: From Eureka, drive south 50 miles on U.S. 101 to the Myers Flat/Avenue of the Giants exit. Turn right on Avenue of the Giants and make a quick left onto Myers Avenue. Drive .25 mile on Myers Avenue to the campground entrance.

Contact: Giant Redwoods RV and Camp, 707/943-3198, fax 707/943-3359, website: www.giantredwoodsrvcamp.com.

47 SHELTER COVE CAMPGROUND & DELI

Rating: 9

overlooking the Pacific Ocean
See map pages 430–431

This is a prime oceanside spot to set up a base

CALIFORNIA

camp for deep-sea fishing, whale-watching, tide-pool gazing, beachcombing, and hiking. A six-lane boat ramp makes it perfect for campers who have trailered boats and don't mind the long drive. Reservations are strongly advised here. The park's backdrop is the King Range National Conservation Area, offering spectacular views. The deli is well known for its fish and chips. The salmon and halibut fishing is quite good here in the summer season; always call first for current regulations and seasons, which change every year. Crabbing is good in December, clamming is best during winter's low tides, and hiking is good in the King Mountain Range during the summer. There is heavy rain in winter. On occasional Saturday nights from Memorial Day through Labor Day, there are barbecues with live entertainment, weather permitting. Note that two miles north is one of the only black sand beaches in the continental United States.

RV sites, facilities: There are 103 sites, many with full hookups (30, 50 amps), for RVs or tents, including 15 drive-through sites. These include some long-term renters. Picnic tables and fire rings are provided. Restrooms, showers, an RV dump station, a coin-operated laundry, a grocery store, a deli, modem access, limited cell phone reception, propane, ice, and RV supplies are available. A boat ramp and marina is across the street. An ATM is within two miles. Leashed pets are permitted.

Reservations, fees: Reservations are recommended. The fee is $20–30 per night, plus $3 per person per night for more than two people. Major credit cards are accepted. Open year-round.

Directions: From Eureka, drive 60 miles south on U.S. 101 to the Redway/Shelter Cove exit. Take that exit and drive 2.5 miles north on Redwood Road to Briceland–Shelter Cove Road. Turn right (west) and drive 24 miles (following the truck/RV route signs) to Upper Pacific Drive. Turn left (south) on Upper Pacific Drive and proceed (it becomes Machi Road) .5 mile to the park on the right.

Contact: Shelter Cove Campground & Deli, 707/986-7474, fax 707/986-7101.

48 DEAN CREEK RESORT

Rating: 7

on the South Fork of the Eel River

See map pages 430–431

This year-round RV park is set on the South Fork of the Eel River. This is a very family-oriented resort. In the summer, it makes a good base camp for a redwood park adventure, with Humboldt Redwoods State Park (well north of here) providing 100 miles of hiking trails, many routed through awesome stands of giant trees. In the winter, heavy rains feed the South Fork Eel, inspiring steelhead upstream on their annual winter journey. Fishing is good in this area, best by shore at nearby High Rock. Bank access is good at several other spots, particularly upstream near Benbow and in Cooks Valley. An excellent side trip is to drive three miles south to the Avenue of the Giants, a tour through giant redwood trees. The campground also offers volleyball, shuffleboard, badminton, and horseshoes. You get the idea.

RV sites, facilities: There are 64 sites with partial or full hookups (30, 50 amps) for RVs or tents, 12 drive-through sites, and an 11-unit motel. Picnic tables and fire grills are provided. Restrooms, showers, a recreation room, a coin-operated laundry, a store, RV supplies, modem access, limited cell phone reception, wood, ice, a giant spa, a sauna, a pool (heated only in summer), an RV dump station, and a playground are available. Mini-golf is available on-site. An ATM is nearby. Some facilities are wheelchair-accessible. Leashed pets are permitted.

Reservations, fees: Reservations are recommended in the summer and may be made at 877/923-2555. The fee is $26–36 per night, plus $3.50 per person per night for more than two people, $1.50 per pet, and $1.50 per each additional vehicle per night. A senior discount is available. Major credit cards are accepted. Open year-round.

Directions: From Eureka, drive 60 miles south on U.S. 101 to the Redwood Drive exit. Exit onto Redwood Drive and continue about a half block to the campground entrance on the right.

Contact: Dean Creek Resort, 707/923-2555, fax 707/923-2547, website: www.deancreekresort.com.

CALIFORNIA

49 BENBOW LAKE STATE RECREATION AREA

Rating: 7

on the Eel River
See map pages 430–431

This camp is set along the South Fork of the Eel River, with easy access from U.S. 101. It gets heavy use in the summer. In theory, Benbow Lake is created each summer when the river is dammed on a temporary basis, creating a 1,000-acre lake for swimming and light boating. This seasonal dam is projected to be installed in mid-June and kept in place until mid-September. However, there is no guarantee this will occur. There was no lake in 2000 or 2002 because of dam repairs and ensuring downstream passage of steelhead smolts. If you're making a vacation planned around lake recreation, always call first. In the winter, this stretch of river can be quite good for steelhead fishing.

RV sites, facilities: There are 77 sites for RVs up to 30 feet or tents; two sites have full hookups. Picnic tables, food lockers, and fire grills are provided. Drinking water, flush toilets, and coin-operated showers are available. A boat ramp (no motors) and boat rentals are available nearby. There is an RV dump station at the park entrance. Supplies and a coin-operated laundry are available in Garberville. Leashed pets are permitted at campsites only.

Reservations, fees: Reservations are accepted with a $7.50 reservation fee at 800/444-PARK (800/444-7275) or www.reserveamerica.com. The fee is $12–17 per night. A senior discount is available. Open April through October, weather permitting.

Directions: From the junction of U.S. 101 and Highway 1 in Leggett, drive north on U.S. 101 past Richardson Grove State Park to the Benbow exit (two miles south of Garberville). Take that exit and drive 2.7 miles to the park entrance.

Contact: Benbow Lake State Recreation Area, 707/923-3238.

50 BENBOW VALLEY RV RESORT & GOLF COURSE

Rating: 7

on the Eel River
See map pages 430–431

This is an RV park set along U.S. 101 and the South Fork Eel River, with both a pretty nine-hole regulation golf course and little Benbow Lake providing nearby recreation options. It takes on a dramatically different character in the winter, when the highway is largely abandoned, the river comes up, and steelhead migrate upstream to the stretch of water here. Cooks Valley and Benbow provide good shore fishing access. Note that fishing restrictions for steelhead are extremely severe and subject to constant change; always check with the Department of Fish and Game before fishing for steelhead. (See the note in the previous listing for Benbow Lake State Recreation Area on the status of Benbow Lake.)

RV sites, facilities: There are 112 RV sites (60 drive-through) with full hookups (20, 30, 50 amps), including three "VIP" sites, plus cottage and RV cabin rentals. Picnic tables are provided. Drinking water, restrooms, cable TV, cell phone reception, modem access, showers, a coin-operated laundry, a grocery store, an ATM, a snack bar, a playground, a recreation room, a heated swimming pool, a whirlpool, RV supplies, and a nine-hole golf course are available. A boat dock and boat rentals (in summer) are within 100 feet at Benbow Lake. Leashed pets are permitted. A doggy playground and pet wash are available.

Reservations, fees: Reservations are accepted. The fee is $30–40 per night, plus $2.50 per person per night for more than two people and $2 per pet per night. A senior discount is available. Major credit cards are accepted. Open year-round.

Directions: From the junction of U.S. 101 and Highway 1 in Leggett, drive north on U.S. 101 past Richardson Grove State Park to the Benbow exit (two miles south of Garberville). Take that exit and turn north on Benbow Drive and drive a short distance to the campground.

Contact: Benbow Valley RV Resort & Golf Course, 707/923-2777, fax 707/923-2821, website: www.benbowrv.com.

CALIFORNIA

51 MADRONE AND HUCKLEBERRY

🧍🏊🎣🐕♿🚐⛺

Rating: 8

in Richardson Grove State Park
See map pages 430–431

The highway cuts a swath right through Richardson Grove State Park, and everyone slows to gawk at the tallest trees in the world, one of the most impressive groves of redwoods you can drive through in California. To explore further, there are several campgrounds available at the park, as well as a network of outstanding hiking trails. The best of these are the short Redwood Exhibit Trail, Settlers Loop, and Toumey Trail. The park is one of the prettiest and most popular state parks, making reservations a necessity from Memorial Day through Labor Day weekend. When arriving from points south on U.S. 101, this is the first park in the Redwood Empire where you will encounter significant old-growth redwood. There are nine miles of hiking trails, fishing in the winter for steelhead, and several trees of significant note. These include the ninth-tallest coast redwood, results of a tree ring study conducted on fallen trees in 1933, and a walk-through tree.

RV sites, facilities: At Madrone Camp, there are 40 sites for RVs up to 30 feet or tents. At Huckleberry, there are 36 sites for RVs up to 30 feet or tents. Picnic tables, food lockers, and fire grills are provided. Drinking water, flush toilets, limited cell phone reception, and coin-operated showers are available. A mini-mart, an ATM, and an RV dump station are nearby (three miles away). Some facilities are wheelchair-accessible. Leashed pets are permitted at campsites only.

Reservations, fees: Reservations are accepted with a $7.50 reservation fee at 800/444-PARK (800/444-7275) or www.reserveamerica.com. The fee is $12–15 per night. A senior discount is available. Open year-round, but subject to occasional winter closures.

Directions: From the junction of U.S. 101 and Highway 1 in Leggett, drive north on U.S. 101 for 20 miles (past Piercy) to the park entrance along the west side of the road (note: Garberville is nine miles north on U.S. 101).

Contact: Richardson Grove State Park, 707/247-3318.

52 OAK FLAT

🧍🏊🎣🐕♿🚐⛺

Rating: 8

in Richardson Grove State Park
See map pages 430–431

Oak Flat is on the eastern side of the Eel River in the shade of forest and provides easy access to the river. The campground is open only in the summer. (For side-trip information, see the previous listing for Madrone and Huckleberry.)

RV sites, facilities: There are 100 sites for RVs up to 21 feet, trailers up to 18 feet, or tents. Picnic tables, food lockers, and fire grills are provided. Drinking water, flush toilets, limited cell phone reception, and coin-operated showers are available. A grocery store, an ATM, and propane are nearby. Leashed pets are permitted.

Reservations, fees: Reservations are accepted with a $7.50 reservation fee at 800/444-PARK (800/444-7275) or www.reserveamerica.com. The fee is $15 per night. A senior discount is available. Open mid-June to mid-September.

Directions: From the junction of U.S. 101 and Highway 1 in Leggett, drive north on U.S. 101 for 20 miles (past Piercy) to the park entrance on the west side of the road (nine miles south of Garberville).

Contact: Richardson Grove State Park, 707/247-3318.

53 RICHARDSON GROVE CAMPGROUND & RV PARK

🧍🎣🐕🛝🚐⛺

Rating: 7

on the Eel River
See map pages 430–431

This private camp provides a nearby alternative to Richardson Grove State Park, complete with cabin rentals. The state park, with its grove of giant redwoods and excellent hiking, is the primary attraction. The park is family-oriented, with volleyball and basketball courts and horseshoes. The adjacent South Fork Eel River may look like a trickle in the summer, but there are some good swimming holes. It also provides good steelhead fishing in January and February, with especially good shore fishing access here as well as to the south in Cooks Valley (check DFG regulations before fishing). This campground is owned and operated by the Northern California/Nevada District Assemblies of God.

RV sites, facilities: There are 91 sites for RVs or tents (28 drive-through), many with partial or full hookups (30 amps), and two log cabins. Picnic tables and fire rings are provided. Drinking water, restrooms, showers, limited cell phone reception, modem access, an RV dump station, a playground, a coin-operated laundry, a grocery store, propane, and ice are available. An ATM is nearby. Leashed pets are permitted.

Reservations, fees: Reservations are recommended. The fee is $15–22 per night for individual sites. Group rates are available. A senior discount is available. Major credit cards are accepted. Open year-round.

Directions: From the junction of U.S. 101 and Highway 1 in Leggett, drive north on U.S. 101 (one mile before reaching Richardson Grove State Park) to the camp entrance on the west side (left) of the road.

Contact: Richardson Grove Campground & RV Park, 707/247-3380, fax 707/247-9806, website: www.redwoodfamilycamp.com.

54 REDWOODS RIVER RESORT

Rating: 8

on the Eel River
See map pages 430–431

This resort is situated in a 21-acre grove of redwoods on U.S. 101 and features 3,000 feet of river frontage. Many of the campsites are shaded. A hiking trail leads from the resort to the Eel River, a walk of just over a quarter mile. This is one in a series of both public and private campgrounds along the highway between Leggett and Garberville. Steelhead and salmon fishing are popular here in the winter, and the resort provides nearby access to state parks. The elevation is 700 feet.

RV sites, facilities: There are 27 RV sites with full hookups (20, 30, 50 amps), including nine drive-through sites, 14 tent sites, eight cabins, and eight lodge rooms. Cabins and lodge rooms have fully furnished kitchenettes and private bathrooms. Lodge rooms have decks with barbecues and picnic tables. Cabins have wood-burning

stoves. At campsites, picnic tables and fire rings are provided. Restrooms, hot showers, a heated pool (summer only), a playground, a recreation room, a mini-mart, a coin-operated laundry, limited cell phone reception, modem access, a group kitchen, an RV dump station, an ice-cream social, Karaoke, arts and crafts (summer), and an evening campfire (in summer) are available. An ATM is nearby. Some facilities are wheelchair-accessible. Leashed pets are permitted.

Reservations, fees: Reservations are recommended in the summer. The fee is $12–30 per night, plus $3 per person for more than two people and $1 for pets. Major credit cards are accepted. Open year-round.

Directions: From the junction of U.S. 101 and Highway 1 in Leggett, drive north on U.S. 101 for seven miles to the campground entrance on the left.

Contact: Redwoods River Resort, 707/925-6249, fax 707/925-6413, website: www.redwoodriver resort.com.

55 REDWOOD CAMPGROUND

Rating: 8

on the Eel River in Standish-Hickey State Recreation Area
See map pages 430–431

This is one of three camps in Standish-Hickey State Recreation Area, and it is by far the most unusual. To reach Redwood Campground requires driving over a temporary "summer bridge," which provides access to a pretty spot along the South Fork Eel River. In early September, out comes the bridge and up comes the river. The elevation is 800 feet. Standish-Hickey is the gateway to the tall trees country. It covers 1,012 acres set in an inland river canyon. The South Fork Eel provides two miles of river frontage. One of the few virgin stands of redwoods in this area can be seen on the Grove Trail. Note that two other campgrounds are available at this park, and that this camp is open only in summer.

RV sites, facilities: There are 63 sites for RVs up to 18 feet or tents. No trailers, including pop-up tent trailers, are permitted. Picnic tables and fire rings are provided. Drinking water, coin-operated showers, and flush toilets are available. Some facilities are wheelchair-accessible. Leashed pets are permitted.

Reservations, fees: Reservations are accepted with a $7.50 reservation fee at 800/444-PARK (800/444-7275) or www.reserveamerica.com. The fee is $15 per night. Open July through Labor Day weekend.

Directions: From the junction of U.S. 101 and Highway 1 in Leggett, drive north on U.S. 101 for one mile to the park entrance.

Contact: Standish-Hickey State Recreation Area, 707/925-6482, fax 707/925-6402.

56 ROCK CREEK

Rating: 8

on the Eel River in Standish-Hickey State Recreation Area

See map pages 430–431

This is one of two main campgrounds set in a redwood grove at Standish-Hickey State Recreation Area (the other is Hickey). It is the classic state park camp, with numbered sites, flat tent spaces, picnic tables, and food lockers. Hiking is only fair in this park, but most people enjoy the short tromp down to the nearby South Fork Eel River. In the winter, steelhead migrate through the area. (See the previous listing for Redwood Campground for more details on this park.)

RV sites, facilities: There are 35 sites for RVs up to 27 feet, trailers to 24 feet, or tents. There is one hike-in/bike-in site that accommodates up to eight people. Picnic tables and fire rings are provided. Drinking water, coin-operated showers, limited cell phone reception, and flush toilets are available. An ATM is nearby. Some facilities are wheelchair-accessible. Leashed pets are permitted.

Reservations, fees: Reservations are accepted with a $7.50 reservation fee at 800/444-PARK (800/444-7275) or www.reserveamerica.com. The fee is $15 per night. The hike-in, bike-in site is

$2 per person per night. A senior discount is available.

Directions: From the junction of U.S. 101 and Highway 1 in Leggett, drive north on U.S. 101 for one mile to the park entrance on the west side of the road.

Contact: Standish-Hickey State Recreation Area, 707/925-6482, fax 707/925-6402.

57 HICKEY

Rating: 8

on the Eel River in Standish-Hickey State Recreation Area

See map pages 430–431

This is an ideal layover for U.S. 101 cruisers yearning to spend a night in the redwoods. The park is best known for its campsites set amid redwoods and for the nearby South Fork Eel River with its steelhead fishing in the winter. The elevation is 800 feet. (See the listing for Redwood Campground in this chapter for details about Standish-Hickey State Recreation Area.)

RV sites, facilities: There are 65 sites for RVs up to 27 feet, trailers to 24 feet, or tents. Picnic tables and fire rings are provided. Drinking water, coin-operated showers, limited cell phone reception, and flush toilets are available. A grocery store and an ATM are nearby. Some facilities are wheelchair-accessible. Leashed pets are permitted.

Reservations, fees: Reservations are accepted with a $7.50 reservation fee at 800/444-PARK (800/444-7275) or www.reserveamerica.com. The fee is $15 per night. A senior discount is available. Open year-round.

Directions: From the junction of U.S. 101 and Highway 1 in Leggett, drive north on U.S. 101 for one mile to the park entrance on the left.

Contact: Standish-Hickey State Recreation Area, 707/925-6482, fax 707/925-6402.

CALIFORNIA

California

Chapter 14
Shasta and Trinity

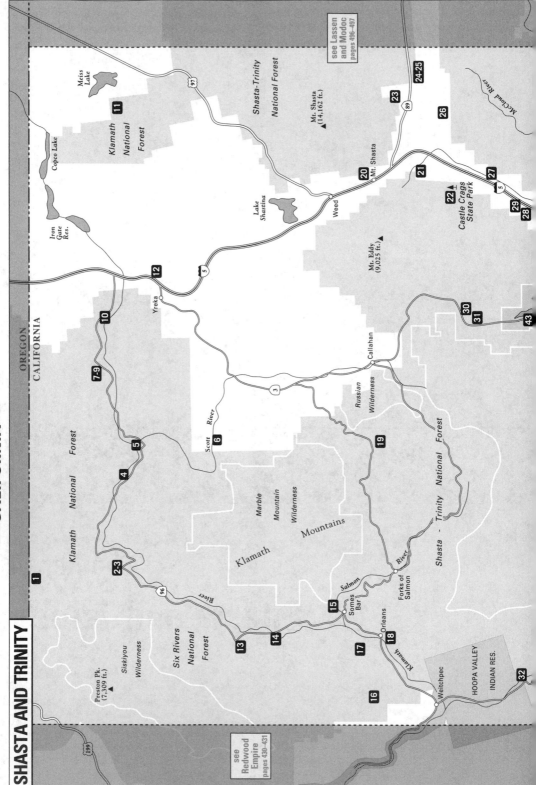

SHASTA AND TRINITY

see Lassen and Modoc pages 496-497

see Redwood Empire pages 430-431

OREGON
CALIFORNIA

Meiss Lake

Copco Lake

Iron Gate Res.

Klamath National Forest

Shasta-Trinity National Forest

Mt. Shasta ▲14,162 ft.

McCloud River

Lake Shastina

Weed

Mt. Shasta

Castle Crags State Park

Mt. Eddy ▲9,025 ft.

Yreka

Callahan

Scott River

Russian Wilderness

Klamath National Forest

Marble Mountain Wilderness

Klamath Mountains

Shasta - Trinity National Forest

Salmon River

Forks of Salmon

Somes Bar

Orleans

Klamath River

Six Rivers National Forest

Siskiyou Wilderness

Preston Pk. (7,309 ft.) ▲

Weitchpec

HOOPA VALLEY INDIAN RES.

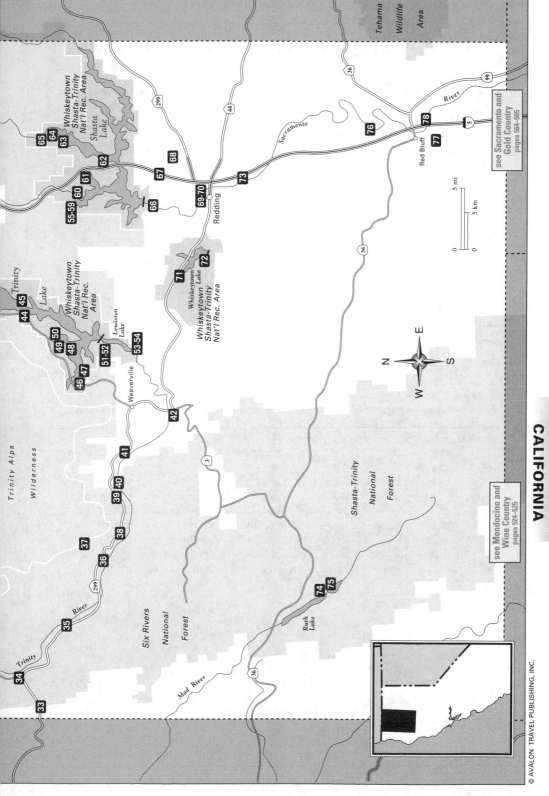

CALIFORNIA

Tehama
Wildlife
Area

Whiskeytown
Shasta-Trinity
Nat'l Rec. Area

Shasta
Lake

65 64 63

62

61

60

55–59

66

68

67

69–70

73

Redding

Sacramento

River

76

78

77

Red Bluff

5

see Sacramento and
Gold Country
pages 564–565

5 mi

5 km

0

0

Trinity

Lake

44 45

49 50

48

46 47

51–52

53–54

Lewiston
Lake

Weaverville

42

Whiskeytown
Shasta-Trinity
Nat'l Rec.
Area

71

72

Whiskeytown Lake
Shasta-Trinity
Nat'l Rec. Area

N E S W

41

40

39

38

37

36

35

34

33

299

River

Trinity

Trinity Alps

Wilderness

Six Rivers

National

Forest

Mad River

Shasta-Trinity

National

Forest

Ruth
Lake

74 75

see Mendocino and
Wine Country
pages 524–525

36

36

36

3

44

299

99

Chapter 14—Shasta and Trinity

At 14,162 feet, Mount Shasta rises like a diamond in a field of coal. Its sphere of influence spans a radius of 125 miles, and its shadow is felt everywhere in the region. This area has much to offer with giant Shasta Lake, the Sacramento River above and below the lake, the McCloud River, and the wonderful Trinity Divide country with dozens of pretty backcountry lakes and several wilderness areas. This is one of the best regions anywhere for an outdoor adventure—especially hiking, fishing, power-boating, rafting, and exploring.

In this area you can find campgrounds that are truly remote, set near quiet wilderness, and that offer the potential for unlimited adventures. It's easy to find a campground in a secluded setting near great recreation opportunities. That is the main reason people visit.

There are hundreds of destinations, but the most popular are Shasta Lake, the Trinity Alps and its surrounding lakes and streams, and the Klamath Mountains, known as "Bigfoot Country" by the locals.

Shasta Lake is one of America's top recreation lakes. It is the one destination that is big enough to handle all who love it. The massive reservoir boasts 370 miles of shoreline, 1,200 campsites, 21 boat launches, 11 marinas, 35 resorts, and numerous houseboat and cabin rentals. A remarkable 22 species of fish live in the lake. Many of the campgrounds feature lake views. In addition, getting here is easy—a straight shot off I-5.

At the charmed center of this beautiful region is the Trinity Alps, where lakes are sprinkled everywhere. It's also home to the headwaters for feeder streams to the Trinity River, Klamath River, New River, Wooley Creek, and others. Trinity Lake provides outstanding boating and fishing, and, just downstream, smaller Lewiston Lake offers a quiet alternative. One advantage to Lewiston Lake is that it is always full of water, even all summer long, making for a very pretty scene. Downstream of Lewiston, the Trinity River provides low-cost rafting and outstanding shoreline access along Highway 299 for fishing for salmon and steelhead.

The neighboring Klamath Mountains are well known as Bigfoot Country. If you drive up the Forest Service road at Bluff Creek, just off Highway 96 upstream of Weitchpec, you can even find the spot where the famous Bigfoot home film footage was shot in the 1960s. Well, I haven't seen Bigfoot, but I have discovered tons of outdoor recreation. This remote region features miles of the Klamath and Salmon Rivers, as well as the Marble Mountain Wilderness. Options include canoeing, rafting, and fishing for steelhead on the Klamath River, or hiking to your choice of more than 100 wilderness lakes.

1 WEST BRANCH

Rating: 6

in Klamath National Forest

See map pages 460–461

This is a virtually unknown, low-charge camp, set in a canyon near Indian Creek. This is deep in Klamath National Forest at 2,200 feet in elevation. The best side trip here is the winding four-mile drive on a bumpy dirt road to Kelly Lake, little known and little used. A remote Forest Service station is on the opposite side of Indian Creek Road from the campground. This camp is a 20-minute drive from the town of Happy Camp.

RV sites, facilities: There are 15 sites for RVs up to 32 feet or tents. Picnic tables and fire grills are provided. Drinking water, vault toilets, garbage service, and cell phone reception are available. There are RV dump stations in Happy Camp at the Elk Creek Campground and the Happy Camp Open Dump. Leashed pets are permitted.

Reservations, fees: Reservations are not accepted. The fee is $8 per night, with two vehicles maximum per site. A senior discount is available. Open May through October.

Directions: From Happy Camp on Highway 96, turn north on Indian Creek Road (a paved road) and drive 12.5 miles to the camp on the right side of the road.

Contact: Klamath National Forest, Happy Camp Ranger District, 530/493-2243, fax 530/493-1796.

2 CURLY JACK

Rating: 7

on the Klamath River in Klamath National Forest

See map pages 460–461

This campground is set at 1,075 feet elevation on the Klamath River, providing opportunities for fishing, light rafting, and kayaking. What's special about Curly Jack, though, is that the water is generally warm enough through the summer for swimming.

RV sites, facilities: There are 14 sites for RVs up to 22 feet or tents, with some specially designed sites for RVs up to 60 feet, and three group sites. Fire grills are provided. Drinking water, vault

toilets, garbage service, and cell phone reception are available. A camp host is on-site in summer. An RV dump station and an ATM are within two miles. Some facilities are wheelchair-accessible. Leashed pets are permitted.

Reservations, fees: Reservations are required for group camps only. The fees are $10 per night or $30 per night for a group campsite. A maximum of two vehicles is allowed per site. A senior discount is available. Open year-round, but services are available only from May through September.

Directions: From the town of Happy Camp on Highway 96, turn south on Elk Creek Road and drive about one mile. Turn right on Curly Jack Road and drive one block to the campground entrance.

Contact: Klamath National Forest, Happy Camp Ranger District, 530/493-2243, fax 530/493-1796.

3 ELK CREEK CAMPGROUND

Rating: 8

on the Klamath River

See map pages 460–461

Elk Creek Campground is a year-round RV park set where Elk Creek pours into the Klamath River. It is a beautiful campground, with sites right on the water in a pretty, wooded setting. The section of the Klamath River nearby is perfect for inflatable kayaking and rafting. Guided trips are available for families or experts, with a wide scope of white water available, rated all the way from the easy Class I stuff all the way to the Class V to-hell-and-back rapids. In addition, the water is quite warm in the summer and flows are maintained throughout the year, making it ideal for water sports. The park also has 25 miniature show horses boarded on the property with surreys and buckboards. In addition, horseshoe tournaments are occasionally held.

RV sites, facilities: There are 45 sites, including some drive-through sites and 10 long-term rentals, for RVs up to 60 feet, many with partial or full hookups (30, 50 amps), and a separate area for tents. Three vacation rentals are also available. Picnic tables and fire grills are provided. Drinking water, restrooms, hot showers, limited cell phone reception, modem access, a recreation room, a beach, a coin-operated laundry, an RV dump station, ice, propane, and wood are available. An ATM is nearby. Private horse boarding is available. Leashed pets are permitted.

Reservations, fees: Reservations are accepted. The fees are $7 per person for tent campers and $20 for RVs, plus $3 per person for more than two people. Major credit cards are accepted. Open year-round.

Directions: From Highway 96 in the town of Happy Camp, turn south on Elk Creek Road and drive one mile to the campground on the right.

Contact: Elk Creek Campground, 530/493-2208, fax 530/493-2029, website: www.elkcreekcamp ground.com.

4 O'NEIL CREEK

Rating: 7

in Klamath National Forest
See map pages 460–461

This camp is set near O'Neil Creek, and though it's not far from the Klamath River, access to the river is not easy. To fish or raft, most people will use this as a base camp, then drive out for recreation during the day. That creates a predicament for RV owners, who lose their campsites every time they drive off. During the fall hunting season, this is a good base camp for hunters branching out into the surrounding national forest. Historic mining sites are also nearby.

RV sites, facilities: There are 18 sites for RVs up to 22 feet or tents. Picnic tables and fire grills are provided. Drinking water and vault toilets are available. Garbage service is also available. Supplies can be obtained in Seiad Valley. Leashed pets are permitted.

Reservations, fees: Reservations are not accepted. The fee is $8 per night. A maximum of two vehicles is allowed per site. A senior discount is available. Open May through October.

Directions: From Yreka drive north on I-5 to the junction with Highway 96. Turn west on Highway 96 and drive past Hamburg, continuing west for three miles to the campground.

Contact: Klamath National Forest, Happy Camp Ranger District, 530/493-2243, fax 530/493-1796.

5 SARAH TOTTEN

Rating: 7

on the Klamath River in Klamath National Forest
See map pages 460–461

This is one of the more popular Forest Service camps on the Klamath River, and it's no mystery why. In the summer, its placement is perfect for rafters, who camp here and use it as a put-in spot. In fall and winter, fishermen arrive for the steelhead run. It's in the "banana belt," or good weather area, of the Klamath, in a pretty grove of oak trees. Fishing is often good here for salmon in early October and for steelhead from November through spring, providing there are fishable water flows.

RV sites, facilities: There are five sites for RVs up to 22 feet or tents, 12 tent sites, and a group site. Picnic tables and fire grills are provided. Drinking water and vault toilets are available. A small grocery store is nearby. Leashed pets are permitted.

Reservations, fees: Reservations are accepted only for the group site at 877/444-6777. The fees are $10 for family sites, with two vehicles maximum per site, and $30 per night for group sites. A senior discount is available. Open May through October.

Directions: From Yreka, drive north on I-5 to the junction with Highway 96. At Highway 96, turn west and drive to Horse Creek, continuing west for five miles to the campground on the right side of the road. If you reach the town of Hamburg, you have gone .5 mile too far.

Contact: Klamath National Forest, Happy Camp Ranger District, 530/493-2243, fax 530/493-1796.

6 INDIAN SCOTTY

Rating: 7

on the Scott River in Klamath National Forest
See map pages 460–461

This popular camp provides direct access to the adjacent Scott River. Because it is easy to reach (no gravel roads) and shaded, it gets a lot of use. The camp is set at 2,400 feet. The levels, forces, and temperatures on the Scott River fluctuate

CALIFORNIA

greatly from spring to fall. In the spring, it can be a raging cauldron, cold from snowmelt. Come summer it quiets, with some deep pools providing swimming holes. By fall, it can be reduced to a trickle. Keep your expectations flexible according to the season.

RV sites, facilities: There are 28 sites and a group site for RVs up to 38 feet or tents. Picnic tables and fire grills are provided. Drinking water, vault toilets, and a pay phone are available. There is a playground in the group-use area. Leashed pets are permitted.

Reservations, fees: Reservations are accepted for group sites. The fee is $10 per night during summer, free during winter; the group site is $30 per night. There is a $5 day-use fee. A senior discount is available. Open year-round.

Directions: From Redding, drive north on I-5 to Yreka. In Yreka, turn southwest on Highway 3 and travel 16.5 miles to Fort Jones. In Fort Jones, turn right on Scott River Road and drive 14 miles to a concrete bridge and the adjacent signed campground entrance.

Contact: Klamath National Forest, Scott River Ranger District, 530/468-5351, fax 530/468-1290.

7 THE OAKS RV PARK

Rating: 7

on the Klamath River

See map pages 460–461

Fishing? Rafting? Canoeing? Hiking? This camp provides a good headquarters for all of these adventures. This stretch of the Klamath is ideal for boating, with summer flows warm and often at perfect levels for rafting and canoeing, with a small beach area available. Fishing is best in the fall, when salmon, and later steelhead, migrate through the area.

RV sites, facilities: There are 10 sites with full hookups (30 amps) for RVs or tents and 12 sites for RVs. Picnic tables are provided. Drinking water, restrooms, hot showers, ice, and a coin-operated laundry are available. A restaurant and lounge are available within walking distance next door. Groceries can be obtained within three miles in the town of Klamath River. A golf course is nearby. Leashed pets are permitted.

Reservations, fees: Reservations are accepted. The fee is $14 per night. Open year-round.

Directions: From Redding, drive north on I-5 to Highway 96. Turn west on Highway 96 and drive approximately 20 miles to the town of Klamath River. Look for the park entrance on the left, across from the town post office.

Contact: The Oaks RV Park, 530/465-2323, fax 530/465-2312.

8 QUIGLEY'S GENERAL STORE AND TRAILER PARK

Rating: 7

on the Klamath River

See map pages 460–461

This year-round, privately operated park is set along the Klamath River, highlighted by 13 riverfront sites. Many of the parking sites have clear views of the river, as well as good mountain views. Quigley's General Store is well stocked for such a remote little shop, and you can usually get reliable fishing information here, too.

RV sites, facilities: There are 19 sites with full hookups (30 amps) for RVs up to 45 feet, including seven sites with long-term rentals. Picnic tables are provided. Restrooms, hot showers, modem access, a store, a deli, horseshoes, a beach area, canoe rentals, boat access, and a coin-operated laundry are available. Some facilities are wheelchair-accessible. Leashed pets are permitted.

Reservations, fees: Reservations are accepted. The fee is $15 per night, plus $1 per person for more than two people. Monthly rates are available. Major credit cards are accepted. Open year-round.

Directions: From Redding, drive north on I-5 to Highway 96. Turn west on Highway 96 and drive approximately 20 miles to the town of Klamath River. Look for the campground entrance on the left.

Contact: Quigley's General Store and Trailer Park, 530/465-2224, fax 530/465-2422.

9 FISHER'S KLAMATH RIVER TRAILER PARK

Rating: 8

on the Klamath River

See map pages 460–461

This privately operated RV park is in one of the

prettiest areas of the Klamath River. There's a good piece of river here for summer rafting or fall steelhead fishing. For rafting, the river is sprinkled with Class II and III rapids, ideal for inflatable kayaks, and several commercial rafting companies operate in this area. Every site has a view of the river and the beautiful Siskiyou Mountains.

RV sites, facilities: There are 17 sites with full hookups for RVs up to 45 feet. Picnic tables, restrooms, hot showers, and a coin-operated laundry are available. Leashed pets are permitted.

Reservations, fees: Reservations are accepted. The fee is $12–15 per night, plus $1 extra per person per night for over two people. Monthly rates are available. Open year-round.

Directions: From Redding, drive north on I-5 to Highway 96. Turn west on Highway 96 and drive approximately 15 miles to the campground entrance on the left (if you reach the town of Klamath River, you have gone a mile too far).

Contact: Fisher's Klamath River Trailer Park, 530/465-2297.

10 TREE OF HEAVEN

Rating: 7

in Klamath National Forest

See map pages 460–461

This outstanding riverside campground provides excellent access to the Klamath River for fishing, rafting, and hiking. The best deal is to put in your raft, canoe, or drift boat upstream at the ramp below Iron Gate Reservoir, then make the all-day run down to the takeout at Tree of Heaven. This section of river is an easy paddle and also provides excellent steelhead fishing in the winter. There is also a trail out of the camp that is routed along the river and probes through vegetation, ending at a fair fishing spot (a better spot is nearby at the mouth of the Shasta River). On the drive in from the highway, you can watch the landscape turn from high chaparral to forest.

RV sites, facilities: There are 20 sites for moderate-sized RVs or tents. Picnic tables and fire grills are provided. Drinking water and vault toilets are available. A river access spot for put-in and takeout for rafts and drift boats is available

(some facilities are wheelchair-accessible here). Leashed pets are permitted.

Reservations, fees: Reservations are accepted. The fee is $10 per night. A senior discount is available. Open year-round.

Directions: From Redding, drive north on I-5 to Highway 96. Turn west on Highway 96 and drive seven miles to the campground entrance on the left side of the road.

Contact: Klamath National Forest, Scott River Ranger District, 530/468-5351, fax 530/468-1290.

11 JUANITA LAKE

Rating: 7

in Klamath National Forest

See map pages 460–461

Small and relatively unknown, this camp is set along the shore of Juanita Lake at 5,100 feet. It is stocked with rainbow trout, brown trout, bass, and catfish, but a problem with golden shiners has cut into the lake's fishing productivity. It's a small lake and forested, set near the Butte Valley Wildlife Area in the plateau country just five miles to the northeast. The latter provides an opportunity to see waterfowl and, in the winter, bald eagles. Campers will discover a network of Forest Service roads in the area, providing an opportunity for mountain biking. There is also a paved trail around the lake that is wheelchair-accessible and spans approximately 1.25 miles.

RV sites, facilities: There are 11 sites for RVs up to 32 feet, 12 tent sites, and a group site that can accommodate 50 people. Picnic tables and fire grills are provided. Drinking water, vault toilets, and limited cell phone reception are available. Boating is allowed, but no motorboats are permitted on the lake. Many facilities are wheelchair-accessible. Leashed pets are permitted.

Reservations, fees: Reservations are accepted only for the group site. The fee is $10 per night; the group site is $30 per night. A senior discount is available. Open May through October.

Directions: From Redding, drive north on I-5 to Weed. In Weed, turn north on U.S. 97 and drive approximately 37 miles. Turn left on Ball Mountain Road and drive 2.5 miles, veer right at the fork, and continue to the campground entrance at the lake.

Contact: Klamath National Forest, Goosenest Ranger District, 530/398-4391, fax 530/398-5749.

12 WAIIAKA TRAILER HAVEN

Rating: 4

near Yreka
See map pages 460–461

If it's late, you're tired, and you're hunting for a spot to hunker down for the night, this is your only bet in the immediate Yreka vicinity. A string of fast-food restaurants is available nearby on the west side of the highway. A small hill blocks the view of Mount Shasta to the south.

RV sites, facilities: There are 60 drive-through sites with full hookups (30, 50 amps) for RVs of any length, including 30 long-term rentals, and a separate grassy area for tents. Drinking water, restrooms, showers, a playground, horseshoes, a recreation room, web TV, modem access, limited cell phone reception, a coin-operated laundry, and propane are available. An ATM is nearby. No campfires are permitted. Leashed pets are permitted.

Reservations, fees: Reservations are accepted. The fee is $10–25.50 per night, plus $1.50 per person for more than two people. A senior discount is available. Major credit cards are accepted. Open year-round.

Directions: From Redding, drive north on I-5 to Yreka, take the Fort Jones exit, and drive one block east to Fairlane Road. At Fairlane Road, turn left (north) and drive to Sharps Road. At Sharps Road, bear left (east) and drive one block to the RV park entrance (just past the fairgrounds parking lot) on the left.

Contact: Waiiaka Trailer Haven, 530/842-4500.

13 DILLON CREEK

Rating: 7

on the Klamath River in Klamath National Forest
See map pages 460–461

This is a prime base camp for rafting or a steelhead fishing trip. A put-in spot for rafting is adjacent to the camp, with an excellent river run available from here on down past Presido Bar to the takeout at Ti-Bar. If you choose to go on, make absolutely certain to pull out at Green Riffle river access and takeout, or risk death at Ishi Pishi Falls. The water is warm here in the summer, and there are also many excellent swimming holes in the area. In addition, this is a good stretch of water for steelhead fishing from September to February, best in early winter from Dillon Beach to Ti-Bar. The elevation is 800 feet.

RV sites, facilities: There are 11 RV sites and 10 tent sites. Picnic tables and fire grills are provided. Drinking water and vault toilets are available. There is an RV dump station in Happy Camp, 25 miles north of the campground, and at Aikens Creek, nine miles west of the town of Orleans. Leashed pets are permitted.

Reservations, fees: Reservations are not accepted. The fee is $10 per night, plus $5 per additional vehicle over one vehicle and a $5 day-use fee. Open year-round.

Directions: From Yreka on I-5, turn west on Highway 96 and drive to the town of Happy Camp. Continue west from Happy Camp for 35 miles and look for the campground on the right side of the road. Coming from the west, from Somes Bar, drive 15 miles north on Highway 96.

Contact: Six Rivers National Forest, Orleans Ranger District, 530/627-3291, fax 530/627-3401.

14 MARBLE MOUNTAIN RANCH

Rating: 6

near the Klamath River
See map pages 460–461

The lodge is just across the road from the Klamath River, an ideal location as headquarters for a rafting trip in the summer or a steelhead fishing trip in the fall. This ranch is considered a vacation destination, with most people staying for a week. Commercial rafting trips are available here, with guided trips offered by the ranch. This piece of river is beautiful and fresh with lots of wildlife and birds, yet not dangerous. However, be absolutely certain to take out at Green Riffle boat access before reaching Ishi Pishi Falls, which cannot be run. If you like privacy and comfort, the cabin rentals available here are a nice bonus. There's also a full pack station at the ranch for guided trail rides lasting from one hour to overnight. Guided mountain bike trips are also available. In addition, there is a sporting clays target range.

RV sites, facilities: There are 10 RV sites with full hookups, 30 tent sites, 11 cabins, and two houses. Picnic tables and fire grills are provided. Restrooms, drinking water, hot showers, a coin-operated laundry, a swimming pool, a hot tub, ice, wood, a recreation room, a petting zoo, a clay pigeon shooting range, horseshoes, paddleboat and kayak rentals, and volleyball and basketball courts are available. Leashed pets are permitted.

Reservations, fees: Reservations are required. The fees are $5 per person for tent sites and $15 for RV sites, plus $2 per person for more than two people. Cabins are $60–200 per night. Major credit cards are accepted. Open year-round.

Directions: From the junction of U.S. 101 and Highway 299 near Arcata, turn east on Highway 299 and drive to Willow Creek. In Willow Creek, turn north (left) on Highway 96 east and drive to Somes Bar. At Somes Bar, continue for 7.5 miles to Mile Marker 7.5 and Marble Mountain Ranch on the right.

Contact: Marble Mountain Ranch, 530/469-3322 or 800/KLAMATH (800/552-6284), fax 530/469-3357, website: www.marblemountainranch.com.

15 OAK BOTTOM ON THE SALMON RIVER

Rating: 7

in Klamath National Forest
See map pages 460–461

This camp is just far enough off Highway 96 that it gets missed by zillions of out-of-towners every year. It is across the road from the lower Salmon River, a pretty, clean, and cold stream that pours out of the surrounding wilderness high country. Swimming is very good in river holes, though the water is cold, especially when nearby Wooley Creek is full of snowmelt pouring out of the Marble Mountains to the north. In the fall, there is good shoreline fishing for steelhead, though the canyon bottom is shaded almost all day and gets very cold.

RV sites, facilities: There are 26 sites for small RVs or tents. Picnic tables and fire grills are provided. Drinking water, vault toilets, and limited cell phone reception are available. There is an RV dump station at the Elk Creek Campground in Happy Camp and at Aikens Creek, 13 miles southwest of the town of Orleans. Supplies are available in Somes Bar. Leashed pets are permitted.

Reservations, fees: Reservations are not accepted. The fee is $10 per night, plus $5 per additional vehicle over one vehicle and a $5 day-use fee. Open April through November, weather permitting.

Directions: From the junction of U.S. 101 and Highway 299 near Arcata, turn east on Highway 299 and drive to Willow Creek and Highway 96. Turn north on Highway 96 and drive to Somes Bar–Etna Road (.25 mile before Somes Bar). Turn right on Somes Bar–Etna Road and drive two miles to the campground on the left side of the road.

Contact: Klamath National Forest, Ukonom Ranger District, 530/627-3291, fax 530/627-3401.

16 FISH LAKE

Rating: 8

in Six Rivers National Forest
See map pages 460–461

This is a pretty little lake that provides good fishing for stocked rainbow trout from the season opener on Memorial Day weekend through July. The camp gets little pressure in other months. It's in the heart of Bigfoot country, with numerous Bigfoot sightings reported near Bluff Creek. No powerboats are permitted on the lake, but it's too small for that anyway, being better suited for a canoe, float tube, raft, or pram. The elevation is 1,800 feet. The presence here of Port Orford cedar root disease, spread by spores in the mud, forces closure from October through April.

RV sites, facilities: There are 14 sites for RVs up to 35 feet or tents and 10 sites for tents. Picnic tables and fire grills are provided. Drinking water and vault toilets are available; a camp host is on-site. Leashed pets are permitted.

Reservations, fees: Reservations are not accepted. The fee is $9 per night. A senior discount is available. Open May through September, weather permitting.

Directions: From I-5 in Redding, turn west on Highway 299 and drive to Willow Creek. At Willow Creek, turn north on Highway 96 and drive to Weitchpec, continuing seven miles north on Highway 96 to Fish Lake Road. Turn left on Fish Lake Road and drive five miles (stay to the right at the Y) to Fish Lake.

Contact: Six Rivers National Forest, Orleans Ranger District, 530/627-3291, fax 530/627-3401.

17 THE PINES TRAILER PARK

Rating: 6

on the Klamath River
See map pages 460–461

This is an option for RV cruisers touring Highway 96 and looking for a stopover in Orleans. The steelhead fishing is good in this area in the fall. The campground is in a wooded setting, across the highway from the Klamath River.

RV sites, facilities: There are 25 sites with full hookups (30 amps), including some long-term rentals, for RVs up to 40 feet, and a separate area for tents. Picnic tables are provided. Restrooms, showers, cable TV hookups, an RV dump station, and a coin-operated laundry are available. Leashed pets are permitted.

Reservations, fees: Reservations are accepted. The fee is $14 per night, plus $1 per person for more than two people. Monthly rates are available. Open year-round.

Directions: From the junction of U.S. 101 and Highway 299 near Arcata, drive east on Highway 299 to Willow Creek. At Willow Creek, turn north (left) on Highway 96, drive past Weitchpec, and continue to Orleans. In Orleans, look for the park entrance on the left side of the road.

Contact: The Pines Trailer Park, 530/627-3425.

18 KLAMATH RIVERSIDE RV PARK AND CAMPGROUND

Rating: 8

on the Klamath River
See map pages 460–461

Klamath Riverside RV Park and Campground is an option for RV cruisers touring Highway 96—designated the Bigfoot Scenic Byway—and

looking for a place in Orleans. The camp has large grassy sites set amid pine trees, right on the river. There are spectacular views of Mount Orleans and the surrounding hills. A 12-foot Bigfoot statue is on the property. Over the years, I've seen many changes at this park. It has been transformed from a dusty fishing spot to a park more resembling a rural resort. One big plus is that the park offers guided fishing and rafting trips during the season.

RV sites, facilities: There are 45 RV sites, some drive-through, with full hookups (30, 50 amps) and a separate area for tents. Two cabins, a duplex, and five rental trailers are also available. Picnic tables and fire rings are provided. Drinking water, restrooms, showers, a hot tub, a group pavilion, a small store, modem access, and a coin-operated laundry are available. A swimming pool is available in summer. River rafting services and guided drift boat fishing in season are available. An ATM is nearby. Horseback riding is available within 12 miles. Leashed pets are permitted.

Reservations, fees: Reservations are accepted. The fee is $15–22 per night, plus $5 per person for more than two people for tent camping and $2 per person for more than two people for RV camping. Group and monthly rates are available. Open year-round.

Directions: From the junction of U.S. 101 and Highway 299 near Arcata, drive east on Highway 299 to Willow Creek, turn north (left) on Highway 96, and drive past Weitchpec to Orleans. This campground is at the west end of the town of Orleans on Highway 96 on the right.

Contact: Klamath Riverside RV Park and Campground, 530/627-3239 or 800/627-9779, fax 530/627-3755, website: www.klamathriversidervpark.com.

19 IDLEWILD

Rating: 8

on the North Fork of the Salmon River in Klamath National Forest
See map pages 460–461

This is one of the prettiest drive-to camps in the region, set near the confluence of the Salmon River and its south fork, a beautiful, cold, clear stream and a major tributary to the Klamath River. Most campers are using the camp for its nearby trailhead (two miles north on a dirt Forest Service road out of camp). The hike here is routed to the north, climbing alongside the Salmon River for miles into the Marble Mountain Wilderness (wilderness permits are required). It's a rugged 10-mile, all-day climb to Lake of the Island with several other lakes (highlighted by Hancock Lake) to the nearby west, accessible on weeklong trips.

RV sites, facilities: There are 18 sites for RVs up to 22 feet or tents. Picnic tables and fire grills are provided. Drinking water and vault toilets are available. An ATM is within 3.5 miles. Leashed pets are permitted.

Reservations, fees: Reservations are not accepted. The fee is $6 per night. A senior discount is available. Open May to October.

Directions: From Redding, drive north on I-5 to Yreka. In Yreka, turn southwest on Highway 3 and drive to Etna. In Etna, turn west on Etna–Somes Bar Road (Main Street in town) and drive about 16 miles to the campground on the right side of the road. Note: a shorter, more scenic, and more complex route is available from Gazelle (North of Weed on Old Highway 99). Take Gazelle-Callahan Road west over the summit and continue north to Etna.

Contact: Klamath National Forest, Salmon River Ranger District, 530/468-5351, fax 530/468-1290.

20 KOA MOUNT SHASTA

Rating: 7

in Mount Shasta city

See map pages 460–461

Despite this KOA camp's relative proximity to the town of Mount Shasta, the extended driveway, wooded grounds, and view of Mount Shasta offer some feeling of seclusion. A bonus here is that those cute little KOA log cabins are available, providing additional privacy. There are many excellent side trips. The best is driving up Everitt Memorial Highway, which rises up the slopes of Mount Shasta to the tree line at Bunny Flat, where you can take outstanding, short day hikes with great views to the south of the Sacramento River Canyon and Castle Crags. In the winter, you can play in the snow, including heading up to Bunny Flat for snow play or to the Mount

Shasta Board & Ski Park for developed downhill and cross-country skiing. One of the biggest events of the year in Mount Shasta is the Fourth of July Run For Fun and associated parade and fireworks display at nearby Lake Siskiyou.

RV sites, facilities: There are 41 sites with full hookups (20, 30, 50 amps) for RVs, including many drive-through sites, 89 additional sites for RVs or tents (partial hookups), and four camping cabins. Picnic tables and fire grills are provided. Restrooms, showers, limited cell phone reception, a playground, propane, a grocery store, a horseshoe pit, shuffleboard, a swimming pool, and a coin-operated laundry are available. An ATM is nearby. Leashed pets are permitted.

Reservations, fees: Reservations are accepted at 800/562-3617. The fee is $15–27 per night, plus $2–3 per person for more than two people. Major credit cards are accepted. Open year-round.

Directions: From Redding, drive north on I-5 to the town of Mount Shasta. Continue past the first Mount Shasta exit and take the Central Mount Shasta exit. Turn right at the stop sign and drive to Mount Shasta Boulevard. Turn left and drive .5 mile to East Hinckley Boulevard. Turn right (signed KOA) on East Hinckley, drive a very short distance, then turn left at the entrance to the extended driveway for KOA Mount Shasta.

Contact: KOA Mount Shasta, 530/926-4029, website: www.koa.com.

21 LAKE SISKIYOU CAMP-RESORT

Rating: 9

near Mount Shasta

See map pages 460–461

This is a true gem of a lake, a jewel set at the foot of Mount Shasta. The lake level is almost always full and offers a variety of quality recreation options, with great swimming, low-speed boating, and fishing. The campground complexes are huge, yet they are tucked into the forest so visitors don't get their style cramped. The water is clean and fresh, and the swimming can be a euphoric sensation on a hot summer afternoon. There is an excellent beach and swimming area, the latter protected by a buoy line. In spring, the fishing is good for trout, and then, as the water warms, for smallmouth bass. A good boat ramp and boat rentals are available, and a 10 mph speed limit is strictly enforced, keeping the lake pristine and quiet.

RV sites, facilities: There are 150 sites for RVs, 125 with full hookups (20, 30, 50 amps) and 25 with partial hookups, including some drive-through sites, and 225 additional sites for tents, six of which are group areas. There are also 26 cabins and park-model cabins, and 11 RV rentals. Picnic tables and fire grills are provided. Drinking water, flush toilets, showers, a playground, propane, a grocery store, an ATM, limited cell phone reception, modem access, a gift shop, a deli, a coin-operated laundry, and an RV dump station are available. There are also a marina, boat rentals (canoes, kayaks, motorized boats), free boat launching, a fishing dock, a fish-cleaning station, a swimming beach, and a banquet room. A free movie plays every night in the summer. Some facilities are wheelchair-accessible. Leashed pets are permitted.

Reservations, fees: Reservations are accepted. The fee is $18–25 per night, plus $1–2.50 per person for more than two people, $4 per night for each additional vehicle, and $1 per pet per night. Mooring is $7 per night. Major credit cards are accepted. Open April through October, weather permitting.

Directions: From the town of Mount Shasta on I-5, take the Central Mount Shasta exit and drive to the stop sign. Turn west and drive a short distance to Old Stage Road. Turn left and drive .25 mile to a Y at W. A. Barr Road. Bear right on W. A. Barr Road and drive past Box Canyon Dam. Two miles farther, turn right at the entrance road for Lake Siskiyou Campground and Marina and drive a short distance to the entrance station.

Contact: Lake Siskiyou Camp-Resort, 530/926-2618 or 888/926-2618, website: www.lakesis.com.

22 CASTLE CRAGS STATE PARK

Rating: 9

on the Sacramento River
See map pages 460–461

This park is named for the awesome granite spires that tower 6,000 feet above the park. Beyond to the north is giant Mount Shasta (14,162 feet), making for a spectacular natural setting. The camp-

sites are set in forest, shaded, very pretty, and sprinkled along a paved access road. But not a year goes by when people don't write in complaining of the highway noise from I-5 echoing in the Sacramento River Canyon, as well as of the occasional passing freight trains in the night. Pristine quiet, this campground is not. At the end of the access road is a parking area for the two-minute walk to the Crags Lookout, a beautiful view. Nearby is the trailhead (at 2,500 feet elevation) for hikes up the Crags, featuring a 6.2-mile round-trip that rises to Castle Dome at 4,966 feet, the leading spire on the crag's ridge. Again, road noise echoing up the canyon provides a background once you clear the tree line. Trout fishing is good in the nearby Sacramento River but requires driving, walking, and exploring to find the best spots. There are also some good swimming holes, but the water is cold. This is a popular state park, with reservations often required in summer, but with your choice of any campsite even in late spring.

RV sites, facilities: There are 64 sites for RVs up to 27 feet or tents, an overflow area with 12 sites and limited facilities, and six primitive walk-in sites (100-yard walk required). Picnic tables, food lockers, and fire grills are provided. Drinking water, wood, hot showers, and flush toilets are available. Leashed pets are permitted at campsites only.

Reservations, fees: Reservations are accepted with a $7.50 reservation fee at 800/444-PARK (800/444-7275) or www.reserveamerica.com. The fee is $12–15 per night, plus a $4 day-use fee; walk-in sites are $2 per person per night. A senior discount is available. Open year-round.

Directions: From Redding, drive north on I-5 for 45 miles to the Castle Crags State Park exit. Turn west and drive to the well-signed park entrance on the right side of the road.

Contact: Castle Crags State Park, 530/235-2684, fax 530/235-1965.

23 McCLOUD DANCE COUNTRY RV PARK

Rating: 6

in McCloud
See map pages 460–461

Dance Country RV Park is very popular with square dancers in the summer. The town of

McCloud is the home of McCloud Dance Hall, a large dance hall dedicated to square and round dancing. The park is sprinkled with old-growth pine trees and bordered by Squaw Valley Creek, a pretty stream. The RV sites are grassy and manicured, with many shaded sites. McCloud River's three waterfalls are accessible from the McCloud River Loop, five miles south of the park on Highway 89. Mount Shasta Board & Ski Park also offers summer activities such as biking, mountain climbing, and chairlift rides to great views of the surrounding forests. The ski park access road is six miles west of McCloud off Highway 89 at Snowman's Hill Summit. The McCloud River Railroad runs an excursion and a dinner train on summer weekends out of McCloud; reservations are available in town. If you're lucky you might see "Old Engine No. 25," one of the few remaining steam engines in service. (For more information, see the following listing for Fowler's Camp.)

RV sites, facilities: There are 122 sites, most with full hookups (30, 50 amps) and the rest with partial hookups, for RVs up to 60 feet, a grassy area for dispersed tent camping, and seven park-model cabins. Picnic tables are provided. Drinking water, restrooms with hot showers, a central barbecue and campfire area, cable TV, cell phone reception, a coin-operated laundry, an RV dump station, propane, horseshoes, a fish-cleaning station, and two pet walks are available. An ATM is nearby. Large groups are welcome. Some facilities are wheelchair-accessible. Leashed pets are permitted, except in cabins.

Reservations, fees: Reservations are recommended. The fee is $15–25 per night for two people, plus $1.50 for each additional child 6–12 years old and $3 for each additional camper 13 years of age or older. Major credit cards are accepted. Open year-round.

Directions: From Redding, drive north on I-5 and continue just past Dunsmuir to the junction with Highway 89. Turn east on Highway 89 and drive nine miles to McCloud and Squaw Valley Road. Turn right on Squaw Valley Road and then turn immediately left into the park entrance.

Contact: McCloud Dance Country RV Park, 530/964-2252, website: www.mccloudrvpark.com.

24 FOWLER'S CAMP

Rating: 10

on the McCloud River in Shasta-Trinity National Forest

See map pages 460–461

This campground is set beside the beautiful McCloud River, providing the chance for an easy hike to two waterfalls, including one of the most dramatic in Northern California. From the camp, the trail is routed upstream through forest, a near-level walk for only 15 minutes, then arrives at awesome Middle Falls, a wide-sweeping and powerful cascade best viewed in April. By summer, the flows subside and warm to the point that some people will swim in the pool at the base of the falls. Another trail is routed from camp downstream to Lower Falls, an outstanding swimming hole in midsummer. Fishing the McCloud River here is fair, with trout stocks made from Lakim Dam on downstream to the camp. If this camp is full, Cattle Camp and Algoma offer overflow areas.

RV sites, facilities: There are 39 sites for RVs of any length or tents. Picnic tables and fire grills are provided. Drinking water, vault toilets, and limited cell phone reception are available. An ATM is within six miles. Some facilities are wheelchair-accessible. Leashed pets are permitted.

Reservations, fees: Reservations are not accepted. The fee is $12 per night. A senior discount is available. Open May through October.

Directions: From Redding, drive north on I-5 and continue just past Dunsmuir to the junction with Highway 89. Turn east on Highway 89 and drive 12 miles to McCloud. From McCloud, drive five miles southeast on Highway 89 to the campground entrance road on the right. Turn right and drive a short distance to a Y, then turn left at the Y to the campground.

Contact: Shasta-Trinity National Forest, McCloud Ranger District, 530/964-2184, fax 530/964-2938.

CALIFORNIA

25 CATTLE CAMP

Rating: 5

on the McCloud River in Shasta-Trinity National Forest

See map pages 460–461

This campground is ideal for RV campers who want a rustic setting, or as an overflow area if the more attractive Fowler's Camp is filled. One of the best swimming holes in the McCloud River is near the camp, although the water is typically cold. There are several good side trips in the area, including fishing on the nearby McCloud River, visiting the three waterfalls near Fowler's Camp, and exploring the north slopes of Mount Shasta (a map of Shasta-Trinity National Forest details the back roads).

RV sites, facilities: There are 27 sites for RVs or tents. Picnic tables and fire grills are provided. Drinking water, vault toilets, and limited cell phone reception are available. Some facilities are wheelchair-accessible, including toilets. Leashed pets are permitted.

Reservations, fees: Reservations are not accepted. The fee is $12 per night. A senior discount is available. Open late April to October, weather permitting.

Directions: From Redding, drive north on I-5 and continue just past Dunsmuir to the junction with Highway 89. Turn east on Highway 89 and drive to McCloud. From McCloud, drive 11 miles east on Highway 89 to the campground entrance road on the right. Turn right and drive .5 mile to the campground on the left side of the road.

Contact: Shasta-Trinity National Forest, McCloud Ranger District, 530/964-2184, fax 530/964-2938.

26 FRIDAY'S RV RETREAT & McCLOUD FLY FISHING RANCH

Rating: 7

near McCloud

See map pages 460–461

Friday's offers great recreation opportunities for every member of the family. The property features a private fishing pond, a casting pond, 1.5 miles of Squaw Valley Creek frontage, and five miles of hiking trails. In addition, the McCloud River's wild trout section is a half-hour drive to the south, the beautiful McCloud Golf Course (nine holes) is within a five-minute drive, and a trailhead for the Pacific Crest Trail is only five minutes away. The park covers 400 wooded and grassy acres. Owner Bob Friday is quite a character, and he figured out that if he planted giant rainbow trout in the ponds for catch-and-release fishing, fly fishers would stop to catch a monster and take a photograph, and then tell people they caught the fish on the McCloud River, where they are smaller and elusive. Also available is the dinner and excursion train that runs out of McCloud on summer weekends. See McCloud Dance Country RV Park for other information and side trip options.

RV sites, facilities: There are 30 sites with full hookups (30, 50 amps), including mostly drive-through sites, for RVs of any length, a large, grassy area for dispersed tent camping, and two cabins. Picnic tables and fire pits are provided. Drinking water, restrooms with hot showers and flush toilets, satellite TV, a laundry room, a pay phone, cell phone reception, modem access, propane, and a recreation room are available. An ATM is nearby. A fly-fishing school is available by arrangement. Some facilities are wheelchair-accessible. Leashed pets are permitted.

Reservations, fees: Reservations are recommended. The fee is $15–22 per night for two people, plus $3 per person for more than two people. Monthly rates are available. Open mid-May to mid-September, weather permitting.

Directions: From Redding, drive north on I-5 and continue just past Dunsmuir to the junction with Highway 89. Bear right on Highway 89 and drive nine miles to McCloud and Squaw Valley Road. Turn right at Squaw Valley Road and drive six miles to the park entrance on the right.

Contact: Friday's RV Retreat & McCloud Fly Fishing Ranch, 530/964-2878, website: www.fridaysflyshop.com.

27 RAILROAD PARK RV & CAMPGROUND

Rating: 7

south of Dunsmuir

See map pages 460–461

This camp was designed in the spirit of the railroad,

when steam trains ruled the rails. The property features old stage cars (available for overnight lodging) and a steam locomotive. Many good side trips are available in the area, including excellent hiking and sightseeing at Castle Crags State Park (where there is a series of awesome granite spires) and outstanding trout fishing on the upper Sacramento River. At night, the sound of occasional passing trains soothes some, wakes others.

RV sites, facilities: There are 24 sites with full hookups (30 amps) for RVs, including some drive-through sites, four sites for RVs with no hookups, and a separate area with 17 sites for tents only. Restrooms, hot showers, satellite TV hookups, limited cell phone reception, ice, a coin-operated laundry, a recreation room, a playground, and horseshoes are available. A restaurant and lounge and an ATM are within walking distance. Some facilities are wheelchair-accessible. Leashed pets are permitted.

Reservations, fees: Reservations are accepted with a deposit. The fee is $18–25 per night, plus $2 per person per night for more than two people and $2 per each additional vehicle. Major credit cards are accepted. Open April through October.

Directions: From Redding, drive north on I-5 for 45 miles to the exit for Cragview Drive/Railroad Park Road. Take that exit and drive .5 mile (the road becomes Railroad Park Road). Turn left under the freeway and continue to the campground on the left.

Contact: Railroad Park RV & Campground, 530/235-0420, website: www.rrpark.com.

28 BEST IN THE WEST RESORT

Rating: 3

near Dunsmuir

See map pages 460–461

This is a good layover spot for RV cruisers looking to take a break. The proximity to Castle Crags State Park, the Sacramento River, and Mount Shasta makes this location a winner. Trains make regular runs every night in the Sacramento River Canyon and the noise is a problem for some visitors.

RV sites, facilities: There are 16 sites, most with full hookups (30 amps), for RVs, a separate grassy area for dispersed tent camping, five cabins, and a lodge. Picnic tables are provided. Restrooms, hot showers, cable TV, a coin-operated laundry, limited cell phone reception, and a playground are available. An ATM is within five miles. Leashed pets are permitted.

Reservations, fees: Reservations are accepted. The fee is $17 per night. Monthly rates available. Open year-round.

Directions: From Redding, drive north on I-5 for about 40 miles to the Sims Road exit. Take the Sims Road exit and drive one block west on Sims Road to the campground on the left.

Contact: Best in the West Resort, 530/235-2603, website: www.eggerbestwest.com.

29 SIMS FLAT

Rating: 7

on the Sacramento River

See map pages 460–461

The upper Sacramento River is again becoming one of the best trout streams in the West that provides easy and direct access off an interstate highway. This camp is a good example. Sitting beside the upper Sacramento River at an elevation of 1,600 feet, it provides access to some of the better spots for trout fishing, particularly from mid-May through July. The trout population has recovered since the devastating spill from a train derailment that occurred in 1991, and there's good trout fishing in this area. There is a wheelchair-accessible interpretive trail. If you want to literally get away from it all, there is a trailhead about three miles east on Sims Flat Road that climbs along South Fork, including a terrible, steep, one-mile section near the top, eventually popping out at Tombstone Mountain. The noise from passing trains can be a shock for newcomers.

RV sites, facilities: There are 19 sites for RVs up to 16 feet or tents. Picnic tables and fire grills are provided. Drinking water, limited cell phone reception, and flush and vault toilets are available. A grocery store is nearby. Some facilities are wheelchair-accessible. Leashed pets are permitted.

Reservations, fees: Reservations are not accepted. The fee is $12 per night. A senior discount is available. Open April through October.

Directions: From Redding, drive north on I-5 for about 40 miles to the Sims Road exit. Take the Sims Road exit (on the east side of the highway) and drive south for a mile to the campground.

Contact: Shasta-Trinity National Forest, Mount Shasta Ranger District, 530/926-4511, fax 530/926-5120.

30 EAGLE CREEK

Rating: 7

in Shasta-Trinity National Forest
See map pages 460–461

This campground is set where little Eagle Creek enters the north Trinity River. Some campers use it as a base camp for a fishing trip, with the rainbow trout often abundant but predictably small in this stretch of water. The campground is open year-round, but there is no drinking water in the winter. The elevation is 2,800 feet.

RV sites, facilities: There are 12 sites for RVs up to 27 feet or tents and five tent sites. Picnic tables and fire grills are provided. Drinking water (spring, summer, and fall only) and vault toilets are available, and there is a camp host. Leashed pets are permitted.

Reservations, fees: Reservations are not accepted. The fee is $9 per night. A senior discount is available. Open year-round.

Directions: From Redding, drive west on Highway 299 to Weaverville and Highway 3. Turn north on Highway 3 and drive to Trinity Center at the north end of Trinity Lake. From Trinity Center, continue north on Highway 3 for 16.5 miles to the campground on the right side of the road.

Contact: Shasta-Trinity National Forest, Weaverville Ranger Station, 530/623-2121, fax 530/623-6010.

31 TRINITY RIVER

Rating: 7

in Shasta-Trinity National Forest
See map pages 460–461

This camp offers easy access off Highway 3, yet it is fairly secluded and provides streamside access to the upper Trinity River. It's a good base camp for a fishing trip when the upper Trinity is loaded with small trout. The elevation is 2,500 feet.

RV sites, facilities: There are seven sites for RVs up to 32 feet or tents. Picnic tables and fire grills are provided. Drinking water (spring, summer, and fall only) and vault toilets are available, and there is a camp host. Leashed pets are permitted.

Reservations, fees: Reservations are not accepted. The fee is $9 per night. A senior discount is available. Open year-round, but there's no drinking water in the winter.

Directions: From Redding, drive west on Highway 299 to Weaverville and Highway 3. Turn north on Highway 3 and drive to Trinity Center at the north end of Trinity Lake. From Trinity Center, continue north on Highway 3 for 9.5 miles to the campground on the left side of the road.

Contact: Shasta-Trinity National Forest, Weaverville Ranger Station, 530/623-2121, fax 530/623-6010.

32 TISH TANG

Rating: 8

in Six Rivers National Forest
See map pages 460–461

This campground is adjacent to one of the best swimming holes in all of Northern California. By late July the adjacent Trinity River is warm and slow, perfect for tubing, falling in "by accident," or paddling a canoe. There is a large gravel beach, and some people will bring along their shorty lawn chairs and just take a seat on the edge of the river in a few inches of water. Though Tish Tang is a good put-in spot for rafting in the late spring and early summer, the flows are too slow and quiet for most rafters to even ruffle a feather during the summer. The elevation is 400 feet.

RV sites, facilities: There are 19 sites for tents or RVs up to 30 feet and trailers up to 22 feet and 21 sites for tents. Picnic tables and fire grills are provided. Drinking water, vault toilets, and limited cell phone reception are available, and there is a camp host. An ATM is within eight miles. Leashed pets are permitted.

Reservations, fees: Reservations are not accepted. The fees are $10 per night and $15 per night for multiple-family sites, plus $5 for each additional vehicle. Open late May to late October.

Directions: From the junction of U.S. 101 and Highway 299 near Arcata, turn east on Highway 299 and drive to Willow Creek. In Willow Creek, turn north on Highway 96 and drive eight miles north to the campground entrance on the right side of the road.

Contact: Hoopa Valley Tribal Council, Forestry Department, 530/625-4284, fax 530/625-4230.

33 EAST FORK WILLOW CREEK

Rating: 9

on Willow Creek
See map pages 460–461

This is a beautiful spot along Willow Creek. Set at a 2,000-foot elevation, it's one of the prettiest campgrounds in the area. In August and September the river is often quite warm, ideal for swimming or tubing. In the winter it is one of the better camps for shoreline steelhead fishing. Way back in the 1950s and early 1960s this was one of the better-known campgrounds in the area, but the flood of 1964 wiped it out. Only recently have rehabilitation efforts restored it to life.

RV sites, facilities: There are 13 sites for RVs up to 35 feet or tents. Picnic tables and fire rings are provided. Vault toilets with wheelchair access are available. No drinking water is available. Leashed pets are permitted.

Reservations, fees: Reservations are not accepted. The fee is $8 per night, plus $5 per night for additional vehicles, with two vehicles maximum per site. A senior discount is available. Open May through October.

Directions: From the junction of U.S. 101 and Highway 299 near Arcata, turn east on Highway 299 and drive 32 miles (six miles west of Willow Creek) and look for the camp's entrance road (well signed) on the right (south) side of the road.

Contact: Six Rivers National Forest, Lower Trinity Ranger District, 530/629-2118, fax 530/629-2102. For a map, send $6 to U.S. Forest Service, Attn: Map Sales, P.O. Box 9035, Prescott, AZ 86313, 928/433-8285, or website:www.r5.fs.fed.us/maps; ask for the Six Rivers National Forest.

34 BOISE CREEK

Rating: 7

in Six Rivers National Forest
See map pages 460–461

This camp features a quarter-mile-long trail down to Boise Creek and nearby access to the Trinity River. If you have ever wanted to see Bigfoot, you can do it while camping here because there's a giant wooden Bigfoot on display in nearby Willow Creek. After your Bigfoot experience, your best bet during summer is to head north on nearby Highway 96 (turn north in Willow Creek) to the campground at Tish Tang, where there is excellent river access, swimming, and rafting in the late summer's warm flows. The Trinity River also provides good salmon and steelhead fishing during fall and winter, respectively, with the best nearby access upriver along Highway 299 at Burnt Ranch. Note that fishing is prohibited in nearby Willow Creek. Also note that although drinking water was available at this campground in the past, the required repairs to the water system were not scheduled as of the publication date in 2003.

RV sites, facilities: There are 17 sites for RVs up to 35 feet or tents and several sites for bicyclists and hikers. Picnic tables and fire grills are provided. No drinking water is available. Vault toilets are available, and a camp host is on-site. A grocery store, a gas station, a restaurant, and propane are available nearby. Leashed pets are permitted.

Reservations, fees: Reservations are not accepted. The fee is $10 per night, plus $4 per each additional vehicle. A senior discount is available. Open year-round, with limited services in winter.

Directions: From the intersection of U.S. 101 and Highway 299 near Arcata, drive 38 miles east on Highway 299 and look for the campground entrance on the left side of the road. If you reach the town of Willow Creek, you have gone 1.5 miles too far.

Contact: Six Rivers National Forest, Lower Trinity Ranger District, 530/629-2118, fax 530/629-2102.

35 BURNT RANCH

Rating: 7

on the Trinity River in Shasta-Trinity National Forest
See map pages 460–461

This campground is set on a bluff above the Trinity River and is one of its most compelling spots. Burnt Ranch Falls isn't much of a waterfall, but it provides a fantastic spot to watch salmon and steelhead leap like hurdlers to make it past the falls and into a calm pool above. The peak migration periods are in mid-September for salmon and in early winter and early spring for steelhead. On their migratory route, the fish will hold below the falls, gaining strength for their upriver surge, making it a natural fishing spot. This section of river is very pretty, with deep, dramatic canyons nearby. The elevation is 1,000 feet.

RV sites, facilities: There are 16 sites for RVs up to 25 feet or tents and a group site for up to eight people. Picnic tables and fire grills are provided. Drinking water and vault toilets are available. Garbage must be packed out. Supplies can be obtained in Hawkins Bar about one hour away. Leashed pets are permitted.

Reservations, fees: Reservations are not accepted. The fee is $8 per night in season. There is a maximum of two vehicles per unit, except at the group site. A senior discount is available. Open year-round, weather permitting.

Directions: From Redding, take Highway 299 west and drive past Weaverville to Burnt Ranch. In Burnt Ranch, continue a half mile and look for the campground entrance on the right side of the road.

Contact: Shasta-Trinity National Forest, Big Bar Ranger Station, 530/623-6106, fax 530/623-6123.

36 DEL LOMA RV PARK AND CAMPGROUND

Rating: 7

on the Trinity River
See map pages 460–461

RV cruisers looking for a layover spot near the Trinity River will find just that at Del Loma. Shady sites and sandy beaches are available here along the Trinity. Rafting and tubing trips are popular in this area during the summer. Salmon fishing is best in the fall, steelhead fishing in the winter. This camp is popular for family reunions and groups. Salmon fishing can be sensational on the Trinity in the fall and some anglers will book a year in advance to make certain they get a spot. The park was largely remodeled in 2001 and 2002.

RV sites, facilities: There are 41 sites, including two drive-through, with partial or full hookups (50 amps) for RVs and tents, five camping cabins, and 29 apartments. Picnic tables and fire grills are provided. Drinking water, a grocery store, RV supplies, flush toilets, hot showers, an RV dump station, a seasonal swimming pool, firewood, a coin-operated laundry, modem access, a recreation room, volleyball, 18-hole mini-golf, and horseshoes are available. An ATM is within five miles. Leashed pets are permitted.

Reservations, fees: Reservations are accepted at 800/839-0194. The fee is $20 per night, plus $2 per person for more than two people. Group and monthly rates are available. Major credit cards are accepted. Open year-round.

Directions: From the junction of U.S. 101 and Highway 299 in Arcata, turn east on Highway 299 and drive to Burnt Ranch. From Burnt Ranch, continue 10 miles east on Highway 299 to the town of Del Loma and look for the campground entrance on the right.

Contact: Del Loma RV Park and Campground, 530/623-2834 or 800/839-0194, website: www.dellomarv.com.

37 HAYDEN FLAT/GROUP

Rating: 7

on the Trinity River in Shasta-Trinity National Forest
See map pages 460–461

This campground is split into two pieces, with most of the sites grouped in a large, shaded area across the road from the river and a few on the river side. A beach is available along the river; it is a good spot for swimming as well as a popular put-in and takeout for rafters. The elevation is 1,200 feet.

RV sites, facilities: There are 35 sites for RVs up

to 25 feet or tents and five sites for RVs up to 35 feet. Picnic tables and fire grills are provided. Drinking water, vault toilets, and limited cell phone reception are available. An ATM is within a half mile. Some facilities are wheelchair-accessible. Leashed pets are permitted.

Reservations, fees: Reservations are accepted for group sites; the fee is 10–23 with an advance payment of $30 for three sites and up to 24 people. Reservations are not accepted for individual sites; the fee is $10 per night, $6 in off-season. A senior discount is available. Open year-round.

Directions: From the junction of U.S. 101 and Highway 299 in Arcata, head east on Highway 299 and drive to Burnt Ranch. From Burnt Ranch, continue 10 miles east on Highway 299 and look for the campground entrance along the left side of the road. If you reach the town of Del Loma, you have gone a half mile too far.

Contact: Shasta-Trinity National Forest, Big Bar Ranger Station, 530/623-6106, fax 530/623-6123.

38 BIG FLAT

Rating: 6

on the Trinity River in Shasta-Trinity National Forest

See map pages 460–461

This level campground is set off Highway 299, just across the road from the Trinity River. The sites are close together, and it can be hot and dusty in midsummer. No problem. That is when you will be on the Trinity River, taking the lowest-priced rafting trip available anywhere in the West—as low as $25 to rent an inflatable kayak from Trinity River Rafting in nearby Big Bar, which includes shuttle service. It's fun, exciting, easy (newcomers are welcome), and cheap.

RV sites, facilities: There are 10 sites for RVs up to 25 feet or tents. Picnic tables and fire grills are provided. Drinking water and vault toilets are available. Leashed pets are permitted.

Reservations, fees: Reservations are not accepted. The fee is $8 per night in season, $6 in winter. A senior discount is available. Open year-round, weather permitting.

Directions: From Redding, turn west on Highway 299, drive past Weaverville, Junction City, and Helena, and continue for about seven miles.

Look for the campground entrance on the right side of the road. If you reach the town of Big Bar, you have gone three miles too far.

Contact: Shasta-Trinity National Forest, Big Bar Ranger Station, 530/623-6106, fax 530/623-6123.

39 PIGEON POINT

Rating: 7

on the Trinity River in Shasta-Trinity National Forest

See map pages 460–461

In the good old days, huge flocks of bandtail pigeons flew the Trinity River Canyon, swooping and diving in dramatic shows. Nowadays you don't see too many pigeons, but this camp still keeps its name. It is better known for its access to the Trinity River, with a large beach for swimming. The elevation is 1,100 feet.

RV sites, facilities: There are 10 sites for RVs up to 25 feet or tents. Picnic tables and fire grills are provided. Vault toilets are available. No drinking water is available. Supplies can be obtained within 10 miles in Big Bar or Junction City. Some facilities are wheelchair-accessible. Leashed pets are permitted.

Reservations, fees: Reservations are not accepted. The fee is $6 per night. A senior discount is available. Open year-round.

Directions: From Redding, head west on Highway 299 and drive to Weaverville. Continue west on Highway 299 to Helena and continue .5 mile to the campground on the left (south) side of the road.

Contact: Shasta-Trinity National Forest, Big Bar Ranger Station, 530/623-6106, fax 530/623-6123.

40 BIGFOOT CAMPGROUND AND RV PARK

Rating: 8

on the Trinity River

See map pages 460–461

This private RV park is set along the Trinity River and has become one of the most popular spots on the Trinity River. The low-cost raft trips are a feature, along with cabin rentals. It is also a popular layover for Highway 299 cruisers but provides the option for longer stays with rafting, gold panning, and, in the fall and winter, fishing for salmon and steelhead, respectively. RV sites are exceptionally large, and a bonus is that a storage area is available. A three-acre site for tent camping is set along the river.

RV sites, facilities: There are 46 sites with partial or full hookups (20, 30, 50 amps) for RVs, a separate area for tent camping, and four cabins. From December 1 to May 1 no tents are allowed, and restrooms are closed. Picnic tables and barbecues are provided. Drinking water, flush toilets, coin-operated showers, a coin-operated laundry, a grocery store, an RV dump station, television, limited cell phone reception, propane, a solar-heated swimming pool (summer only), and horseshoes are available. Modem hookups, fishing licenses, guide services, and a tackle shop are also available. Some facilities are wheelchair-accessible. Leashed pets are permitted.

Reservations, fees: Reservations are recommended from June through October. The fee is $17–23 per night, plus $2 per night per person for more than two people. Major credit cards are accepted. Open year-round.

Directions: From Redding, turn west on Highway 299 and drive to Junction City. Continue west on Highway 299 for three miles to the camp on the left.

Contact: Bigfoot Campground and RV Park, 530/623-6088 or 800/422-5219, fax 530/623-3573, website: www.bigfootRVcabins.com.

41 JUNCTION CITY

Rating: 7

on the Trinity River
See map pages 460–461

Some of the Trinity River's best fall salmon fishing is in this area in September and early October, with steelhead following from mid-October into the winter. That makes it an ideal base camp for a fishing or camping trip.

RV sites, facilities: There are 22 sites for RVs up to 28 feet or tents. Picnic tables, fire grills, and bear-proof food lockers are provided. Drinking water, vault toilets, and limited cell phone reception are available, and camp hosts are on-site. Note that from November through April, drink-

ing water is available only from the pump house. Groceries and propane are within two miles in Junction City. Leashed pets are permitted.

Reservations, fees: Reservations are not accepted. The fee is $8 per night from May through October. A senior discount is available. Open year-round.

Directions: From Redding, turn west on Highway 299 and drive to Junction City. At Junction City, continue west on Highway 299 for 1.5 miles to the camp on the right.

Contact: Bureau of Land Management, Redding Field Office, 530/224-2100, fax 530/224-2172.

42 DOUGLAS CITY AND STEINER FLAT

Rating: 7

on the Trinity River
See map pages 460–461

If you want to camp along this stretch of the main Trinity River, these camps are your best bet (they're along the river about two miles from each other). They are set off the main road, near the river, with good bank fishing access (the prime season is from mid-August through winter for salmon and steelhead). There's paved parking and two beaches at Douglas City Campground. Steiner Flat, a more primitive camp, provides better access for fishing. This can be a good base camp for an off-season fishing trip on the Trinity River or a lounging spot during the summer. The elevation is 1,700 feet.

RV sites, facilities: There are 18 sites for RVs up to 30 feet or tents at Douglas City, with dispersed camping at Steiner Flat. At Douglas City, picnic tables and fire grills are provided. Restrooms, flush toilets, and sinks are available. Drinking water is available in summer only. At Steiner Flat, a pit toilet is available. No drinking water is available. Supplies are available within one mile in Douglas City. Leashed pets are permitted.

Reservations, fees: Reservations are not accepted. The fee is $10 per night. A senior discount is available. Open year-round.

Directions: From Redding, go west on Highway 299 and continue over the bridge at the Trinity River near Douglas City to Steiner Flat Road. Turn left on Steiner Flat Road and drive .5 mile

to Douglas City campground on the left. To reach
Steiner Flat, continue two more miles and look
for the campground on the left.

Contact: Bureau of Land Management, Redding
Field Office, 530/224-2100, fax 530/224-2172.

43 WYNTOON RESORT

Rating: 8

on Trinity Lake
See map pages 460–461

This huge resort is an ideal family vacation destination. Set in a wooded area covering 70 acres
on the north shore of Trinity Lake, it provides
opportunities for fishing, boating, swimming,
and water-skiing, with access within walking distance. The lake sits at the base of the dramatic
Trinity Alps, one of the most beautiful regions
in the state.

RV sites, facilities: There are 136 sites, including
many drive-through, with full hookups (20, 30,
50 amps) for trailers or RVs, 78 tent sites, 19 cottages, and five trailers. Picnic tables and fire rings
are provided. Drinking water, restrooms, showers, a coin-operated laundry, a playground, a heated pool (Memorial Day through Labor Day), an
RV dump station, limited cell phone reception,
modem access, gasoline, a grocery store, ice, a
snack bar, a fish-cleaning area, boat rentals, slips,
and a boat launch are available. An ATM is within a half mile. Some facilities are wheelchair-
accessible. Leashed pets are permitted.

Reservations, fees: Reservations are accepted.
The fee is $25–29 per night, plus $3 per person
for more than two people and $1 per pet per
night. Monthly rates are available. Major credit
cards are accepted. Open year-round.

Directions: From Redding, turn west on Highway 299 and drive to Weaverville at Highway 3.
Turn north on Highway 3 and drive to Trinity
Lake. At Trinity Center, continue .5 mile north
on Highway 3 to the resort on the right.

Contact: Wyntoon Resort, 530/266-3337 or
800/715-3337, fax 530/266-3820, website: www.
wyntoonresort.com.

44 PREACHER MEADOW

Rating: 7

in Shasta-Trinity National Forest
See map pages 460–461

The winter of 2000 was one of the strangest on
record here, when a localized wind storm knocked
down 66 trees and put this campground temporarily out of commission. It reopened in summer of 2000. The possibility of a tree blow-down
makes a constant subject of discussion for campers
here. But it isn't long and your attention will shift
to the view of the Trinity Alps, excellent from
the right vantage point. Otherwise, compared to
all the other camps in the area so close to Trinity Lake, it has trouble matching up in the quality department. If the lakeside camps are full,
this camp provides an overflow option.

RV sites, facilities: There are 45 sites for RVs up
to 40 feet or tents. Picnic tables and fire grills
are provided. Drinking water, vault toilets, and
limited cell phone reception are available, and a
camp host is on-site. Supplies, a coin-operated
laundry, and a small airport are nearby. Leashed
pets are permitted.

Reservations, fees: Reservations are not accepted. The fee is $10 per night. A senior discount
is available. Open mid-May through October.

Directions: From Redding, turn west on Highway 299 and drive to Weaverville at Highway 3.
Head north on Highway 3 and drive to Trinity
Lake. Continue toward Trinity Center and look
for the campground entrance on the left side of
the road (if you reach Trinity Center you have
gone two miles too far).

Contact: Shasta-Trinity National Forest, Weaverville Ranger Station, 530/623-2121, fax 530/
623-6010.

45 JACKASS SPRINGS

Rating: 6

on Trinity Lake in Shasta-Trinity
National Forest
See map pages 460–461

If you're poking around for a more secluded campsite on this end of the lake, halt your search and
pick the best spot you can find at this campground,

since it's the only one in this area of Trinity Lake. The campground is one mile from Trinity Lake, but you can't see the lake from the camp. It is most popular in the fall as a base camp for deer hunters. The elevation is 2,500 feet.

RV sites, facilities: There are 21 sites for RVs up to 32 feet or tents. Picnic tables and fire grills are provided. Vault toilets are available. No drinking water is available. Garbage must be packed out. Leashed pets are permitted.

Reservations, fees: Reservations are not accepted. There is no fee for camping. Open year-round, weather permitting.

Directions: From Redding head west on Highway 299 and drive to Weaverville and the junction with Highway 3. Turn north on Highway 3 and drive 29 miles to Trinity Center. Continue five miles past Trinity Center to County Road 106. Turn right on County Road 106 and drive 12 miles to the Jackass Springs/County Road 119 turnoff. Turn right on County Road 119 and drive five miles to the campground at the end of the road.

Contact: Shasta-Trinity National Forest, Weaverville Ranger Station, 530/623-2121, fax 530/623-6010.

46 PINEWOOD COVE RESORT

Rating: 7

on Trinity Lake
See map pages 460–461

This is a privately operated camp with full boating facilities at Trinity Lake. If you don't have a boat but want to get on Trinity Lake, this can be a good starting point. A reservation is advised during the peak summer season. The elevation is 2,300 feet.

RV sites, facilities: There are 50 sites with partial or full hookups (30, 50 amps) for RVs up to 40 feet, including 10 RV sites rented for the entire season and wait-listed, and 28 tent sites. There are also eight park-model cabins, six trailer rentals, and one A-frame cabin. Picnic tables and fire grills are provided. Restrooms, showers, a coin-operated laundry, limited cell phone reception, modem access, an RV dump station, RV supplies, free movies three nights a week, a recreation room, pinball and video machines, a grocery store, ice, fishing tackle, a library, a boat dock

with 32 slips, a beach, and boat rentals are available. Some facilities are wheelchair-accessible. Leashed pets are permitted.

Reservations, fees: Reservations are recommended in the summer. The fee is $22–29 per night, plus $4 per person for more than two people and $2 per pet per night. Major credit cards are accepted. A senior discount is available. Open mid-April through October.

Directions: From Redding, turn west on Highway 299 and drive to Weaverville. In Weaverville, turn north (right) on Highway 3 and drive 14 miles to the campground entrance on the right.

Contact: Pinewood Cove Resort, 800/988-5253 (reservations only) or 530/286-2201, fax 530/286-2202, website: www.pinewoodcove.com.

47 TANNERY GULCH

Rating: 8

on Trinity Lake in Shasta-Trinity National Forest
See map pages 460–461

This is one of the more popular Forest Service camps on the southwest shore of huge Trinity Lake. There's a nice beach near the campground, provided the infamous Bureau of Reclamation hasn't drawn the lake level down too far. It can be quite low in the fall. The elevation is 2,400 feet.

RV sites, facilities: There are 87 sites for RVs up to 40 feet or tents and four multifamily sites. Picnic tables and fire grills are provided. Drinking water, flush and vault toilets, and a boat ramp area are available, and a camp host is on-site. A grocery store is nearby. Leashed pets are permitted.

Reservations, fees: Reservations are accepted with a $9 reservation fee at 877/444-6777 or www.reserveusa.com. The fee is $15–20 per night, plus $5 for each additional vehicle. A senior discount is available. Open May through September.

Directions: From Redding, head west on Highway 299 and drive to Weaverville. In Weaverville, turn north on Highway 3 and drive 13.5 miles north to County Road 172. Turn right on County Road 172 and drive 1.5 miles to the campground on the left side of the road.

Contact: Shasta-Trinity National Forest, Weaverville Ranger Station, 530/623-2121, fax 530/623-6010.

CALIFORNIA

48 MINERSVILLE

Rating: 7

on Trinity Lake in Shasta-Trinity National Forest
See map pages 460–461

The setting is near lakeside, quite beautiful when Trinity Lake is fullest in the spring and early summer. This is a good camp for boaters, with a boat ramp in the cove a short distance to the north. But note that the boat ramp is not always functional. When the lake level is 65 feet below full, the ramp is not usable. The elevation is 2,500 feet.

RV sites, facilities: There are 21 sites for RVs up to 18 feet or tents. Picnic tables and fire grills are provided. Drinking water (spring, summer, and fall only), flush toilets, and a low-water boat ramp are provided. A camp host is on-site. Leashed pets are permitted.

Reservations, fees: Reservations are not accepted. The fee is $12–20 per night, free in winter. A senior discount is available. Open year-round, but note that there is no drinking water in the winter.

Directions: From Redding, head west on Highway 299 to Weaverville. Turn north on Highway 3 and drive about 18 miles (if you reach the Mule Creek Ranger Station, you have gone .5 mile too far). Turn right at the signed campground access road and drive .5 mile to the camp.

Contact: Shasta-Trinity National Forest, Weaverville Ranger Station, 530/623-2121, fax 530/623-6010.

49 HAYWARD FLAT

Rating: 7

on Trinity Lake in Shasta-Trinity National Forest
See map pages 460–461

When giant Trinity Lake is full of water, Hayward Flat is one of the prettiest places you could ask for. The camp has become one of the most popular Forest Service campgrounds on Trinity Lake, because it sits right along the shore and offers a "private" beach for Hayward Flat campers only. The elevation is 2,400 feet.

RV sites, facilities: There are 98 sites for tents or RVs up to 40 feet and four multifamily sites. Picnic tables and fire grills are provided. Drinking water and flush toilets are available, and there is a camp host. Supplies and a boat ramp are available nearby. Leashed pets are permitted.

Reservations, fees: Reservations are accepted with a $9 reservation fee at 877/444-6777 or www.reserveusa.com. The fee is $15–20 per night, plus $5 for each additional vehicle. A senior discount is available. Open mid-May through mid-September.

Directions: From Redding, head west on Highway 299 and drive to Weaverville. In Weaverville, turn north on Highway 3 and drive about 20 miles, approximately three miles past the Mule Creek Ranger Station. Turn right at the signed access road for Hayward Flat and drive about three miles to the campground at the end of the road.

Contact: Shasta-Trinity National Forest, Weaverville Ranger Station, 530/623-2121, fax 530/623-6010.

50 ALPINE VIEW

Rating: 9

on Trinity Lake in Shasta-Trinity National Forest
See map pages 460–461

This is an attractive area, set on the shore of Trinity Lake at a creek inlet. The boat ramp nearby provides a bonus. It's a very pretty spot, with views to the west across the lake arm and to the Trinity Alps, featuring Granite Peak. The Forest Service also runs tours from the campground to historic Bowerman Barn, which was built in 1894. The elevation is 2,400 feet.

RV sites, facilities: There are 66 sites for RVs up to 32 feet or tents. Picnic tables and fire grills are provided. Drinking water and flush toilets are available, and a camp host is on-site. The Bowerman Boat Ramp is next to the camp. Some facilities are wheelchair-accessible. Leashed pets are permitted.

Reservations, fees: Reservations are not accepted. The fee is $15–20 per night, plus $5 for each additional vehicle. A senior discount is available. Open mid-May through mid-September (rarely it is closed temporarily when lake levels are extremely low).

Directions: From Redding, turn west on Highway 299 and drive to Weaverville. In Weaverville, turn north on Highway 3 and drive to Covington

Mill (six miles south of Trinity Center). Turn right (south) on Guy Covington Road and drive three miles to the camp (one mile past Bowerman Boat Ramp) on the right side of the road.

Contact: Shasta-Trinity National Forest, Weaverville Ranger Station, 530/623-2121, fax 530/623-6010.

51 LAKEVIEW TERRACE RESORT

Rating: 8

on Lewiston Lake

See map pages 460–461

This might be your Golden Pond. It's a terraced RV park—with cabin rentals also available—that overlooks Lewiston Lake, one of the prettiest drive-to lakes in the region. Fishing for trout is excellent from Lakeview Terrace on upstream toward the dam. Lewiston Lake is perfect for fishing, with a 10 mph speed limit in effect (all the hot boats go to nearby Trinity Lake), along with excellent prospects for rainbow and brown trout. The topper is that Lewiston Lake is always full to the brim, just the opposite of the up-and-down nightmare of its neighboring big brother, Trinity.

RV sites, facilities: There are 85 sites, including some drive-through and 75 with full hookups (20, 30 amps), for RVs up to 40 feet, and cabins with one to five bedrooms. Picnic tables and barbecues are provided. Restrooms, hot showers, a coin-operated laundry, a heated pool (summer only), propane, cell phone reception, an RV dump station, ice, horseshoes, a playground, bait, and boat rentals are available. Supplies and an ATM are available within five miles. Leashed pets are permitted.

Reservations, fees: Reservations are recommended. The fee is $18–21 per night, plus $2 per person for more than two people. Major credit cards are accepted. Open year-round.

Directions: From Redding, drive west on Highway 299, drive over Buckhorn Summit, and continue for five miles to Trinity Dam Boulevard. Turn right on Trinity Dam Boulevard and drive 10 miles (five miles past Lewiston) to the resort on the left side of the road.

Contact: Lakeview Terrace Resort, 530/778-3803, fax 530/778-3960, website: www.lakeviewterraceresort.com.

52 ACKERMAN

Rating: 7

on Lewiston Lake in Shasta-Trinity National Forest

See map pages 460–461

Of the camps and parks at Lewiston Lake, Ackerman is closest to the lake's headwaters. This stretch of water below Trinity Dam is the best area for trout fishing on Lewiston Lake. Nearby Pine Cove boat ramp, two miles south of the camp, offers the only boat launch on Lewiston Lake with docks and a fish-cleaning station—a popular spot for anglers. When the Trinity powerhouse is running, trout fishing is excellent in this area. The elevation is 2,000 feet.

RV sites, facilities: There are 66 sites for RVs up to 40 feet or tents. Picnic tables and fire grills are provided. Drinking water (spring, summer, and fall only), flush toilets, limited cell phone reception, and an RV dump station are available. A camp host is on-site. An ATM is within eight miles. Leashed pets are permitted.

Reservations, fees: Reservations are not accepted. The fee is $6–11 per night. A senior discount is available. Open year-round.

Directions: From Redding, head west on Highway 299, drive over Buckhorn Summit, and continue for five miles to Trinity Dam Boulevard. Turn right on Trinity Dam Boulevard and drive four miles to Lewiston. Continue north on Trinity Dam Boulevard for eight miles to the campground.

Contact: Shasta-Trinity National Forest, Weaverville Ranger Station, 530/623-2121, fax 530/623-6010.

53 OLD LEWISTON BRIDGE RV RESORT

Rating: 7

on the Trinity River

See map pages 460–461

This is a popular spot for calm-water kayaking, rafting, and fishing. Though much of the water from Trinity and Lewiston Lakes is diverted via tunnel to Whiskeytown Lake (en route to the valley and points south), enough escapes downstream to provide a viable stream here near the town of Lewiston. This upstream section below

CALIFORNIA

Lewiston Lake is prime in the early summer for trout, particularly the chance for a huge brown trout (special regulations in effect). The campground is in a hilly area but has level sites, with nearby Lewiston Lake also a major attraction. Damage from a major fire in the general area in summer of 1999, set as a "controlled burn," is still evident.

RV sites, facilities: There are 52 sites with full hookups for RVs, including some long-term rentals, a separate area for tents, and five rental trailers. Picnic tables are provided. Restrooms, hot showers, a coin-operated laundry, a grocery store, ice, RV supplies, and propane refills are available. A group picnic area is available by reservation. Supplies can be obtained within walking distance in Lewiston. Leashed pets are permitted.

Reservations, fees: Reservations are accepted. The fees are $24 per night for RVs and $14 per night per vehicle for tent campers, plus $2 per person for more than two people. Monthly rates are available. Major credit cards are accepted. Open year-round.

Directions: From Redding, head west on Highway 299, drive over Buckhorn Summit, and continue for five miles to Trinity Dam Boulevard. Turn right on Trinity Dam Boulevard and drive four miles to Lewiston, and continue north to Rush Creek Road. Turn left (west) on Rush Creek Road and drive .75 mile to the resort on the left.

Contact: Old Lewiston Bridge RV Resort, 800/922-1924 or tel./fax 530/778-3894, website: www.lewistonbridgerv.com.

54 TRINITY RIVER LODGE RV RESORT

Rating: 7

on the Trinity River

See map pages 460–461

For many, this privately operated park has an ideal location. You get level, grassy sites with shade trees along the Trinity River, yet it is just a short drive north to Lewiston Lake or a bit farther to giant Trinity Lake. Lake or river, take your pick. The resort covers nearly 14 acres and is pretty enough that about half the sites are rented for the entire summer.

RV sites, facilities: There are 60 sites with full hookups (30, 50 amps) for RVs up to 40 feet, including about 30 summer rentals, five tent sites, and one cottage. Furnished trailer rentals are also available. Restrooms, hot showers, a coin-operated laundry, cable TV, modem access, a recreation room, a lending library, a clubhouse, a recreation field, propane, a camp store, ice, wood, boat and trailer storage, horseshoes, and a picnic area are available. An ATM is within one mile. Some facilities are wheelchair-accessible. Leashed pets are permitted.

Reservations, fees: Reservations are recommended. The fee is $14–24 per night. Major credit cards are accepted. Open year-round.

Directions: From Redding, go west on Highway 299, drive over Buckhorn Summit, and continue for five miles to Trinity Dam Boulevard. Turn right on Trinity Dam Boulevard and drive four miles to Lewiston. Continue on Trinity Dam Boulevard to Rush Creek Road. Turn left on Rush Creek Road and drive 2.3 miles to the campground on the left.

Contact: Trinity River Lodge RV Resort, 530/778-3791 or 800/761-2769, website: www.trinityrivercampgrounds.com.

55 LAKESHORE VILLA RV PARK

Rating: 7

on Shasta Lake

See map pages 460–461

This is a large campground with level, graveled, shaded sites for RVs, set near the northern Sacramento River arm of giant Shasta Lake. Most of the campers visiting here are boaters coming for the water sports, water-skiing, wakeboarding, or tubing.

RV sites, facilities: There are 92 sites, including some drive-through sites and 75 with full hookups (30, 50 amps), for RVs and tents, and two RV rentals. Restrooms, hot showers, ice, an RV dump station, cable TV, modem access, a coin-operated laundry, a playground, a recreation room, and a boat dock are available. An ATM is nearby. Leashed pets are permitted.

Reservations, fees: Reservations are accepted with a deposit. The fee is $22–25 per night. A few long-term rentals are available. Major credit cards are accepted. Open year-round.

Directions: From Redding, drive north on I-5 for

24 miles to the Lakeshore-Antlers Road exit in Lakehead. Take that exit, turn left at the stop sign, and drive under the freeway to Lakeshore Drive. Turn left on Lakeshore Drive and drive .5 mile to the campground on the right.
Contact: Lakeshore Villa RV Park, 530/238-8688, website: www.american-rvresorts.com.

56 LAKESHORE INN & RV

Rating: 7

on Shasta Lake
See map pages 460–461
Shasta Lake is a boater's paradise and an ideal spot for campers with boats, with a nearby boat ramp and private marina available. This camp is on the Sacramento River arm of Shasta Lake.
RV sites, facilities: There are 40 sites, including some drive-through sites, with partial or full hookups (20, 30, 50 amps) for RVs and tents, and 10 cabins. Picnic tables are provided. Restrooms, hot showers, a swimming pool (summer only), a playground, a video arcade, a coin-operated laundry, limited cell phone reception, modem access, a bar and restaurant (summer only), and a small convenience store (summer) are available. Family barbecues are held on Sunday in season, from 5 P.M. to P.M. Live music is scheduled most Friday and Saturday nights. An ATM, a marina, and boat rentals are available nearby. Some facilities are wheelchair-accessible. Leashed pets are permitted.
Reservations, fees: Reservations are recommended. The fee is $19–28 per night, plus $2 per person for more than two people and $1 per pet per night. Major credit cards are accepted. Open year-round, with limited winter facilities.
Directions: From Redding, drive north on I-5 for 24 miles to the Lakeshore-Antlers Road exit in Lakehead. Take that exit, turn left at the stop sign, and drive under the freeway to Lakeshore Drive. Turn left on Lakeshore Drive and drive one mile to the campground.
Contact: Lakeshore Inn & RV, 530/238-2003, fax 530/238-2832, website: www.shastacamping.com.

57 SHASTA LAKE RV RESORT AND CAMPGROUND

Rating: 7

on Shasta Lake
See map pages 460–461
Shasta Lake RV Resort and Campground is one of a series on the upper end of Shasta Lake with easy access off I-5 by car, then easy access by boat to premium trout or bass fishing as well as water-skiing.
RV sites, facilities: There are 53 sites, including some drive-through, with full hookups (30 amps) for RVs, 21 tent sites, and four trailers. Picnic tables, barbecues, and fire rings are provided. Restrooms, hot showers, a seasonal convenience store, wood, a coin-operated laundry, a playground, and a swimming pool (summer) are available. An ATM is within one mile. There is also a private dock with 36 boat slips. Leashed pets are permitted.
Reservations, fees: Reservations are accepted with a deposit. The fee is $17–25 per night, plus $1 per pet per night. Major credit cards are accepted. Open year-round.
Directions: From Redding, drive north on I-5 for 24 miles to the Lakeshore-Antlers Road exit in Lakehead. Take that exit, turn left at the stop sign, and drive under the freeway to Lakeshore Drive. Turn left on Lakeshore Drive and drive 1.5 miles to the campground on the right.
Contact: Shasta Lake RV Resort and Campground, 530/238-2370 or 800/374-2782, website: www.shastalakerv.com.

58 ANTLERS RV PARK AND CAMPGROUND

Rating: 7

on Shasta Lake
See map pages 460–461
Antlers Park is set along the Sacramento River arm of Shasta Lake at 1,215 feet. Note that no long-term rentals are allowed, which can be a desirable factor for many visitors. This is a full-service spot for campers, boaters, and anglers, with access to the beautiful Sacramento River

arm. The camp often fills in summer, including on weekdays.

RV sites, facilities: There are 66 sites for RVs, including three drive-through and many with full hookups, and 40 sites for tents. Restrooms, hot showers, a seasonal grocery store and snack bar, ice, a coin-operated laundry, a recreation room, a playground, a volleyball court, and a swimming pool (summer) are available. Boat rentals, house-boats, moorage, and a complete marina are available adjacent to the park. Some facilities are wheelchair-accessible. Leashed pets are permitted.

Reservations, fees: Reservations are accepted with a deposit. The fee is $15–30 per night, plus $3 per person for more than two people and $3 per pet per night. Major credit cards are accepted. Open year-round.

Directions: From Redding, drive north on I-5 for 24 miles to the Lakeshore-Antlers Road exit in Lakehead. Take that exit, turn right at the stop sign, and drive a short distance to Antlers Road. At Antlers Road, turn right and drive 2.5 miles south to the campground on the left.

Contact: Antlers RV Park and Campground, 530/238-2322 or 800/642-6849, website: www.antlersrv.com.

59 ANTLERS

Rating: 7

on Shasta Lake in Shasta-Trinity National Forest
See map pages 460–461

This spot is set on the primary Sacramento River inlet of giant Shasta Lake. Antlers is a well-known spot that attracts returning campers and boaters year after year. It is the farthest upstream marina/camp on the lake. Because of that, lake levels can fluctuate greatly from spring through fall, and the operators will move their docks to compensate. Easy access off I-5 is a big plus for boaters.

RV sites, facilities: There are 41 single sites and 18 double sites for RVs up to 30 feet or tents. Picnic tables and fire grills are provided. Drinking water, flush and vault toilets, and limited cell phone reception are available. A camp host is on-site in summer. A boat ramp, a grocery store, an ATM, and a coin-operated laundry are nearby. Leashed pets are permitted.

Reservations, fees: Reservations are accepted with a $9 reservation fee at 877/444-6777 or www.reserveusa.com. The fees are $16 per night for a single site and $26 for a double site, plus $5 for each additional vehicle. A senior discount is available. Open year-round.

Directions: From Redding, drive north on I-5 for 24 miles to the Lakeshore-Antlers Road exit in Lakehead. Take that exit, turn right at the stop sign, and drive a short distance to Antlers Road. At Antlers Road, turn right and drive one mile south to the campground.

Contact: Shasta-Trinity National Forest, Shasta Lake Ranger District, 530/275-1587, fax 530/275-1512; Shasta Lake Visitor Center, 530/275-1589.

60 LAKESHORE EAST

Rating: 7

on Shasta Lake in Shasta-Trinity National Forest
See map pages 460–461

Lakeshore East is near the full-service community of Lakehead and is on the Sacramento arm of Shasta Lake. It's a nice spot, with a good boat ramp and marina nearby at Antlers or Sugarloaf.

RV sites, facilities: There are 20 single sites and six double sites for RVs up to 30 feet or tents. Picnic tables and fire grills are provided. Drinking water and flush toilets are available, and a camp host is on-site. A boat ramp, a grocery store, and a coin-operated laundry are nearby. Some facilities are wheelchair-accessible. Leashed pets are permitted.

Reservations, fees: Reservations are accepted with a $9 reservation fee at 877/444-6777 or www.reserveusa.com. The fees are $16 per night for single sites and $26 for double sites. A senior discount is available. Open May through September.

Directions: From Redding, drive north on I-5 for 24 miles to the Antlers exit at Lakehead. Take the Antlers exit, turn left at the stop sign, and drive under the freeway to Lakeshore Drive. Turn left on Lakeshore Drive and drive three miles. Look for the campground entrance on the left side of the road.

Contact: Shasta-Trinity National Forest, Shasta Lake Ranger District, 530/275-1587, fax 530/275-1512; Shasta Lake Visitor Center, 530/275-1589.

CALIFORNIA

61 TRAIL IN RV CAMPGROUND

Rating: 7

near Shasta Lake
See map pages 460–461

This is a privately operated campground near the Salt Creek arm of giant Shasta Lake. Open, level sites are available. The lake is about a quarter mile away and offers fishing, boating, and swimming. Its proximity to I-5 makes this a popular spot, fast and easy to reach, which is extremely attractive for drivers of RVs and trailers who want to avoid the many twisty roads surrounding Shasta Lake.

RV sites, facilities: There are 39 sites, including 10 pull-through, with full hookups (30, 50 amps) for RVs, and two sites for tents. Picnic tables and fire grills are provided. Restrooms, hot showers, TV hookups, an RV dump station, a swimming pool, a convenience store, ice, wood, and a coin-operated laundry are available. An ATM is within 4.5 miles. Leashed pets are permitted.

Reservations, fees: Reservations are accepted with a deposit. The fee is $25 per night for RV camping ($16 for tent camping) plus $2 per person per night for more than two people and $1 per pet per night. Monthly rates are available. Major credit cards are accepted. Open year-round.

Directions: From Redding, drive 22 miles north on I-5 to the Gilman Road/Salt Creek Road exit. Take that exit and turn left on Salt Creek Road and drive a short distance to Gregory Creek Road. Turn right and drive .25 mile to the campground on the right.

Contact: Trail In RV Campground, 530/238-8533.

62 HOLIDAY HARBOR

Rating: 7

on Shasta Lake
See map pages 460–461

This camp is one of the more popular family-oriented, all-service resorts on Shasta Lake. It is set on the lower McCloud arm of the lake, which is extremely beautiful with a limestone mountain ridge off to the east. It is an ideal jump-off spot for houseboating, boating, all water sports, and fishing. A good boat ramp, boat rentals, and store with all the goodies are bonuses. Another plus is the nearby side trip to Shasta Caverns, a privately guided adventure (fee charged) into limestone caves. This camp often fills in summer, even on weekdays. I've worked with the management here for years, and everyone has always been friendly, helpful, and smart.

RV sites, facilities: There are 27 sites with full hookups (20 amps) for RVs up to 40 feet, with tents allowed in several sites. Picnic tables and barbecues are provided. Restrooms, hot showers, a grocery store, a coin-operated laundry, boat moorage, an ATM, limited cell phone reception, modem access, a playground, propane, and boat rentals are available. Some facilities are wheelchair-accessible. Leashed pets are permitted.

Reservations, fees: Reservations are recommended. The fee is $17.50–26.75 per night, plus $3.50–5.25 per person for more than two people, $4.50 per night for each additional vehicle, and $6.75–9 per night for boat moorage. Major credit cards are accepted. Open April through October.

Directions: From Redding, drive 18 miles north on I-5 to the Shasta Caverns Road exit. Turn right at Shasta Caverns Road and drive about one mile to the campground entrance on the right.

Contact: Holiday Harbor, 530/238-2383 or 800/776-2628, website: www.lakeshasta.com.

63 HIRZ BAY

Rating: 7

on Shasta Lake in Shasta-Trinity National Forest
See map pages 460–461

This is one of two camps in the immediate area (the other is Hirz Bay Group Camp) that provides nearby access to a boat ramp (a half mile down the road) and the McCloud River arm of Shasta Lake. The camp is set on a point at the entrance of Hirz Bay. This is an excellent spot to make a base camp for a fishing trip, with great trolling for trout in this stretch of the lake.

RV sites, facilities: There are 37 single sites and 11 double sites for RVs up to 30 feet or tents. Picnic tables and fire grills are provided. Drinking water, flush and vault toilets, and limited cell phone reception are available. A boat ramp and an ATM are nearby. Some facilities are wheelchair-accessible. Leashed pets are permitted.

CALIFORNIA

Reservations, fees: Reservations are accepted with a $9 reservation fee at 877/444-6777 or www.reserveusa.com. The fees are $16 per night for a single and $26 for a double, plus $5 for each additional vehicle. A senior discount is available. Open year-round.

Directions: From Redding, drive north on I-5 for about 20 miles to the Salt Creek/Gilman exit. Turn right on Gilman Road/County Road 7H009 and drive northeast for 10 miles to the campground/boat launch access road. Turn right and drive .5 mile to the camp on the left side of the road.

Contact: Shasta-Trinity National Forest, Shasta Lake Ranger District, 530/275-1587, fax 530/275-1512; Shasta Lake Visitor Center, 530/275-1589.

64 ELLERY CREEK

Rating: 7

on Shasta Lake in Shasta-Trinity National Forest
See map pages 460–461

This camp is set at a pretty spot where Ellery Creek empties into the upper McCloud arm of Shasta Lake. Several sites are set on the pavement with an unobstructed view of the beautiful McCloud arm. This stretch of water is excellent for trout fishing in the summer, with bank-fishing access available two miles upstream at the McCloud Bridge. In the spring, there are tons of small spotted bass along the shore from the camp on upstream to the inlet of the McCloud River. Boat-launching facilities are available five miles south at Hirz Bay.

RV sites, facilities: There are 19 sites for RVs up to 30 feet or tents. Picnic tables and fire grills are provided. Drinking water, vault toilets, and limited cell phone reception are available. A camp host is on-site. An ATM is nearby. Toilets are wheelchair-accessible. Leashed pets are permitted.

Reservations, fees: Reservations are accepted with a $9 reservation fee at 877/444-6777 or www.reserveusa.com. The fee is $13 per night, plus $5 for each additional vehicle. A senior discount is available. Open April through September.

Directions: From Redding, drive north on I-5 for about 20 miles to the Salt Creek/Gilman exit. Turn right on Gilman Road/County Road 7H009 and drive northeast for 15 miles to the campground on the right side of the road.

Contact: Shasta-Trinity National Forest, Shasta Lake Ranger District, 530/275-1587, fax 530/275-1512; Shasta Lake Visitor Center, 530/275-1589.

65 PINE POINT

Rating: 7

on Shasta Lake in Shasta-Trinity National Forest
See map pages 460–461

Pine Point is a pretty little camp, set on a ridge above the McCloud arm of Shasta Lake amid oak trees and scattered ponderosa pines. The view is best in spring, when lake levels are generally highest. Boat-launching facilities are available at Hirz Bay; boaters park their boats on shore below the camp while the rest of their party arrives at the camp by car. That provides a chance not only for camping, but also for boating, swimming, water-skiing, and fishing. Note: from July through September, this campground can be reserved as a group site only.

RV sites, facilities: There are 14 sites for RVs up to 24 feet or tents. Picnic tables and fire rings are provided. Drinking water and vault toilets are available. Leashed pets are permitted.

Reservations, fees: Reservations are accepted for group sites only with a $9 reservation fee at 877/444-6777 or www.reserveusa.com. The fee is $13 per night, plus $5 for each additional vehicle; group sites are $90 per night. A senior discount is available. Open May through September.

Directions: From Redding, drive north on I-5 for about 20 miles to the Salt Creek/Gilman exit. Turn right on Gilman Road/County Road 7H009 and drive northeast for 17 miles to the campground entrance road on the right.

Contact: Shasta-Trinity National Forest, Shasta Lake Ranger District, 530/275-1587, fax 530/275-1512; Shasta Lake Visitor Center, 530/275-1589.

66 SHASTA

Rating: 6

on the Sacramento River in Shasta-Trinity National Forest
See map pages 460–461

Because campers must drive across Shasta Dam to reach this campground, access was closed in

2002 for national security reasons. Call before planning a visit. I believe it will reopen to the public since the route also provides access to an adjacent OHV area, one of the few in the north state. When open, this place is mainly for quads and dirt bikes, loud and wild, and hey, it's a perfect spot for them. It's barren because of past mining in the area, but the view of the river and Shasta Dam is incredible. Nearby dam tours are unique and memorable.

RV sites, facilities: There are 22 sites for RVs up to 24 feet or tents. Picnic tables and fire rings are provided. Drinking water and vault toilets are available. A boat ramp is nearby. Groceries and bait are available in Shasta Lake City. Leashed pets are permitted.

Reservations, fees: Reservations are not accepted. The fee is $10 per night, plus $5 for each additional vehicle. Open year-round.

Directions: From I-5 in Redding, drive north for three miles to the exit for the town of Shasta Lake City and Shasta Dam Boulevard. Take that exit and bear west on Shasta Dam Boulevard and drive three miles to Lake Boulevard. Turn right on Lake Boulevard and drive two miles. Cross Shasta Dam and continue four miles to the signed campground.

Contact: Shasta-Trinity National Forest, Shasta Lake Ranger District, 530/275-1587, fax 530/275-1512; Shasta Lake Visitor Center, 530/275-1589; Bureau of Reclamation Visitor Center, 530/275-4463.

67 WONDERLAND MOBILE HOME & RV PARK

Rating: 5

near Shasta Lake
See map pages 460–461
This RV park is within a mobile home park south of Shasta Lake. The tour of Shasta Caverns is a recreation option, via a short drive to Holiday Harbor. Other options include the city of Redding's extensive visitors center, the Turtle Bay Museum and Exploration Park, the Carter House Natural History Museum in Caldwell Park, public golf courses, and the Sacramento River trails, which are paved, making them accessible for wheelchairs and bikes.

RV sites, facilities: There are 30 sites for RVs, many with full hookups (30, 50 amps) and some drive-through, and a grassy area for dispersed tent camping. Drinking water, picnic tables, restrooms, showers, a coin-operated laundry, cable TV, limited cell phone reception, a seasonal swimming pool, and horseshoes are available. An ATM is within 1.5 miles. Some facilities are wheelchair-accessible. Leashed pets are permitted.

Reservations, fees: Reservations are accepted. The fee is $12–15 per night, plus $2.50 per person per night for more than two people. A senior discount is available. Major credit cards are accepted. Open year-round.

Directions: From Redding, drive north on I-5 for 11 miles to the Fawndale exit. Take that exit west onto Wonderland Boulevard and drive .25 mile to the park on the left (15203 Wonderland Boulevard).

Contact: Wonderland Mobile Home & RV Park, 530/275-1281.

68 BEAR MOUNTAIN RV RESORT & CAMPGROUND

Rating: 5

near Shasta Lake
See map pages 460–461
This privately operated park on 52 acres is set up primarily for RVs in the remote Jones Valley area along Shasta Lake. A hiking trail leaves from the campground, rises up a hill, and provides a great view of Redding.

RV sites, facilities: There are 97 sites with partial or full hookups (30 amps) for RVs, including some drive-through sites, 24 tent sites, and four park-model cabins. Picnic tables and fire rings are provided. Drinking water, flush toilets, coin-operated showers, a coin-operated laundry, modem access, a convenience store, an RV dump station, limited cell phone reception, a seasonal pool, a recreation hall, an arcade, a playground, table tennis, volleyball, and a horseshoe pit are available. An ATM is nearby. A boat ramp is within three miles. Some facilities are wheelchair-accessible. Leashed pets are permitted.

Reservations, fees: Reservations are accepted. The fee is $14–20 per night, plus $2 per night for more than two people and $2 per night for each additional vehicle. Monthly rates are available.

Major credit cards are accepted. A senior discount is available. Open year-round.

Directions: From Redding, drive north on I-5 for three miles to the Oasis Road exit. Take that exit and turn right on Oasis Road/Old Oregon Trail and drive 3.5 miles to Bear Mountain Road. Turn right on Bear Mountain Road and drive 3.5 miles to the campground on the left.

Contact: Bear Mountain RV Resort & Campground, 530/275-4728 or 800/952-0551, fax 530/275-8459, website: www.campshasta.com.

69 PREMIERE RV RESORT

Rating: 4

in Redding

See map pages 460–461

If you're stuck with no place to go, this large park could be your savior, but expect very hot weather in the summer. Nearby recreation options include a waterslide park and the Turtle Bay Museum and Exploration Park on the Sacramento River, wehre trout fishing is good. In addition, Whiskeytown Lake is nearby to the west and Shasta Lake to the north. Some campers may remember this park as KOA of Redding; they are no longer associated. The park was renovated in 2002.

RV sites, facilities: There are 111 sites for RVs, most with full hookups (30, 50 amps) and some with partial hookups, a small area for tents, and two yurts. Picnic tables and fire grills are provided. Drinking water, flush toilets, showers, a playground, a seasonal swimming pool, a coin-operated laundry, an RV dump station, satellite TV hookups, limited cell phone reception, modem access, a convenience store, propane, and a recreation room are available. An ATM is within a half mile. Leashed pets are permitted.

Reservations, fees: Reservations are accepted. The fee is $30.25–36.30 per night, plus $3 per person per night for more than two people. Major credit cards are accepted. Open year-round.

Directions: In Redding, drive north on I-5 to the Lake Boulevard/Burney-Alturas exit. Turn west (left) on Lake Boulevard and drive a quarter mile to North Boulder Drive. Turn right (north) on North Boulder Drive and drive one block to the campground on the right.

Contact: Premiere RV Resort, 530/246-0101 or 888/710-8450, fax 530/246-0123, website: www .premierervresort.com.

70 MARINA RV PARK

Rating: 6

on the Sacramento River

See map pages 460–461

The riverside setting is a highlight here, with the Sacramento River providing great trout fishing and relief from the dog days of summer. An easy, paved walking and bike trail is available nearby at the Sacramento River Parkway, providing river views and sometimes a needed breeze on hot summer evenings. A miniature golf course is nearby. It is also two miles away from the Turtle Bay Museum and close to a movie theater.

RV sites, facilities: There are 42 sites, most with full hookups, for RVs. Picnic tables, restrooms, hot showers, a coin-operated laundry, a small store, a seasonal swimming pool, a spa, a boat ramp, and an RV dump station are on park grounds. Leashed pets are permitted.

Reservations, fees: Reservations are accepted. The fee is $22 per night, plus $2 per person for more than two people. Monthly rates are available. A senior discount is available. Open year-round.

Directions: In Redding, turn west on Highway 299 and drive 1.5 miles to Park Marina Drive. At Park Marina Drive turn left (south) and drive one mile to the park.

Contact: Marina RV Park, 530/241-4396.

71 OAK BOTTOM

Rating: 7

on Whiskeytown Lake

See map pages 460–461

The prettiest hiking trails at Whiskeytown Lake are at the far western end of the reservoir, and this camp provides excellent access to them. One hiking and biking trail skirts the north shoreline of the lake and is routed to the lake's inlet at the Judge Carr Powerhouse. The other, with the trailhead just a short drive to the west, is routed along Mill Creek, a pristine, clear-running stream with

CALIFORNIA

the trail jumping over the water many times. The campground sites seem a little close, but the camp is next to a beach area. There are junior ranger programs for youngsters 7 to 12 years old, and evening ranger programs at the Oak Bottom Amphitheater are available three nights a week from mid-June through Labor Day. A self-guided nature trail is five miles away at the visitors center.

RV sites, facilities: There are 22 sites for self-contained RVs or trailers in the large parking area near the launch ramp and 102 walk-in tent sites with picnic tables and fire grills. Drinking water, restrooms, flush toilets, coin-operated showers, limited cell phone reception, groceries, ice, wood, an RV dump station, a boat ramp, and boat rentals are available. An ATM is within 10 miles. Some facilities are wheelchair-accessible. Leashed pets are permitted.

Reservations, fees: Reservations are accepted in the summer at 800/365-CAMP (800/365-2267) or http://reservations.nps.gov; reservations are not accepted in the off-season. The fee is $7–18 per night, plus a park use permit of $5 per day, $10 per week, or $20 per year. A senior discount is available. Open year-round.

Directions: From Redding, drive west on Highway 299 for 15 miles (past the visitors center) to the campground entrance road on the left. Turn left and drive a short distance to the campground.

Contact: Whiskeytown National Recreation Area, 530/242-3400 or 530/246-1225, fax 530/246-5154.

72 BRANDY CREEK

Rating: 7

on Whiskeytown Lake
See map pages 460–461
For campers with boats, this is the best place to stay at Whiskeytown Lake, with a boat ramp less than a quarter mile away. Whiskeytown is popular for sailing and windsurfing, as it gets a lot more wind than other lakes in the region. Fishing for kokanee salmon is good in the early morning before the wind comes up.

RV sites, facilities: There are 37 sites for self-contained RVs and trailers up to 35 feet. Drinking water and an RV dump station are available. Leashed pets are permitted.

Reservations, fees: Reservations are not accepted. The fee is $14 per night during the summer and $7 per night during off-season, plus a park use permit of $5 per day, $10 per week, or $20 per year. A senior discount is available. Open year-round.

Directions: From Redding, drive west on Highway 299 for eight miles to the park entrance center. Turn left at the visitors center (Kennedy Memorial Drive) and drive five miles to the campground entrance road on the right. Turn right and drive a short distance to the camp.

Contact: Whiskeytown National Recreation Area, 530/242-3400, fax 530/246-5154.

73 SACRAMENTO RIVER RV PARK

Rating: 7

south of Redding
See map pages 460–461
This makes a good headquarters for a fall fishing trip on the Sacramento River, where the salmon come big from August through October. In the summer, trout fishing is very good from this area as well, but a boat is a must. No problem; there's a boat ramp at the park. In addition, you can hire fishing guides who launch from here daily. The park is open year-round, and if you want to stay close to home, a three-acre pond with bass, bluegill, and perch is also available at the park. You also get great long-distance views of Mount Shasta and Mount Lassen.

RV sites, facilities: There are 140 sites, including some drive-through sites, with full hookups (30, 50 amps) for RVs and 20 sites for tents in a shaded grassy area. Picnic tables, restrooms, hot showers, a grocery store, a coin-operated laundry, an RV dump station, cable TV, modem access, limited cell phone reception, bait, propane, a boat launch, two tennis courts, and a large seasonal swimming pool are available. A clubhouse is available by reservation. An ATM is within 2.5 miles. Some facilities are wheelchair-accessible. Leashed pets are permitted.

Reservations, fees: Reservations are accepted. The fee is $11–21 per night. Major credit cards are accepted. Open year-round.

Directions: From Redding, drive south on I-5 for five miles to the Knighton Road exit. Turn west

(right) and drive a short distance to Riverland Drive. Turn left on Riverland Drive and drive two miles to the park at the end of the road.
Contact: Sacramento River RV Park, 530/365-6402, fax 530/365-2601.

74 FIR COVE

Rating: 7

on Ruth Lake in Six Rivers National Forest
See map pages 460–461

This spot is situated along Ruth Lake adjacent to Bailey Cove. Groups can reserve a section of the campground Monday through Thursday. The elevation is 2,600 feet.
RV sites, facilities: There are 19 single or three group sites for RVs or tents. Several sites can accommodate RVs up to 22 feet. Picnic tables and fire grills are provided. Drinking water and vault toilets are available. Leashed pets are permitted.
Reservations, fees: Reservations are accepted only for group sites through the Mad River Ranger District station. Reservations are not accepted for single sites. The fee is $12 per night, plus $5 per night for additional vehicles; group sites are $40–50 per night. Open on weekends only, May through October, from Friday after 2 P.M. to Monday at 2 P.M.
Directions: From Eureka, drive south on U.S. 101 to Alton and the junction with Highway 36. Turn east on Highway 36 and drive about 50 miles to the town of Mad River. Turn right at the sign for Ruth Lake/Lower Mad River Road and drive 12 miles to the campground on the right side of the road.
Contact: Six Rivers National Forest, Mad River Ranger District, 707/574-6233, fax 707/574-6273.

75 BAILEY CANYON

Rating: 7

on Ruth Lake in Six Rivers National Forest
See map pages 460–461

Ruth Lake is the only major lake within a reasonable driving distance of U.S. 101, although some people might argue with you over how reasonable this twisty drive is. Regardless, you end up at a camp along the east shore of Ruth Lake,

where fishing for trout or bass and water-skiing are popular. What really wins out is that it is hot and sunny all summer, the exact opposite of the fogged-in Humboldt coast. The elevation is 2,600 feet.
RV sites, facilities: There are 25 sites, a few of which are suitable for RVs up to 22 feet. Picnic tables and fire grills are provided. Drinking water and vault toilets are available. A boat ramp and small marina are nearby. Leashed pets are permitted.
Reservations, fees: Reservations are not accepted. The fee is $12 per night, plus $5 per each additional vehicle. A senior discount is available. Open May through October.
Directions: From Eureka, drive south on U.S. 101 to Alton and the junction with Highway 36. Turn east on Highway 36 and drive about 50 miles to the town of Mad River. Turn right at the sign for Ruth Lake/Lower Mad River Road and drive 13 miles to the campground on the right side of the road.
Contact: Six Rivers National Forest, Mad River Ranger District, 707/574-6233, fax 707/574-6273.

76 BEND RV PARK AND FISHING RESORT

Rating: 7

on the Sacramento River
See map pages 460–461

Here's a spot for RV cruisers to rest their rigs for a while. Big Bend RV Park and Fishing Resort is open year-round and is set beside the Sacramento River. The salmon average 15 to 25 pounds in this area, and anglers typically have the best results from mid-August through October. In recent years, the Bureau of Reclamation has been raising the gates of the Red Bluff Diversion Dam in early September. When that occurs, huge numbers of salmon charge upstream from Red Bluff to Anderson, holding in each deep river hole. Expect very hot weather in July and August.
RV sites, facilities: There are 18 sites with partial or full hookups (30 amps) for RVs up to 40 feet and a separate area for tents only. Picnic tables are provided. Drinking water, showers, flush toilets, a grocery store, a bait and tackle shop, a boat ramp, a boat dock, a coin-operat-

ed laundry, modem access, limited cell phone reception, and an RV dump station are available. An ATM is within six miles. Some facilities are wheelchair-accessible. Leashed pets are permitted.

Reservations, fees: Reservations are accepted. The fee is $17–24 per night. Open year-round.

Directions: From I-5 in Red Bluff, drive four miles north on I-5 to the Jelly's Ferry Road exit. Take that exit and turn northeast on Jelly's Ferry Road and drive 2.5 miles to the resort at 21795 Bend Ferry Road.

Contact: Bend RV Park and Fishing Resort, 530/527-6289.

77 O'NITE PARK

Rating: 4

near the Sacramento River
See map pages 460–461

O'Nite Park is set within a mobile home park with many full-time tenants. Pluses are easy access from the highway, nearby supermarkets and restaurants, and many side trips. The park is only one block from the Sacramento River, which gets a big salmon run from mid-August through October. It's about a 45-minute drive east to Lassen Park. The elevation is approximately 300 feet and temperatures are typically in the 100s from mid-June through August.

RV sites, facilities: There are 74 sites, including some drive-through sites, with full hookups for RVs and a separate area for tents. Picnic tables are provided. Restrooms, coin-operated showers, a seasonal swimming pool, modem access, a coin-operated laundry, propane, and ice are available. Some facilities are wheelchair-accessible. Leashed pets are permitted.

Reservations, fees: Reservations are accepted. The fee is $11–19 per night. Open year-round.

Directions: From I-5 and the junction of Highways 99 and 36 (in Red Bluff), drive west on Highway 36/Antelope Boulevard for one block to Gilmore Road. Turn south on Gilmore Road and drive one block to the camp.

Contact: O'Nite Park, 530/527-5868.

78 LAKE RED BLUFF

Rating: 6

on the Sacramento River near Red Bluff
See map pages 460–461

Lake Red Bluff is created by the Red Bluff Diversion Dam on the Sacramento River, and waterskiing, bird-watching, hiking, and fishing are the most popular activities here. It has become a backyard swimming hole for local residents in the summer when the temperatures reach the high 90s and low 100s almost every day. In early September, the Bureau of Reclamation raises the gates at the diversion dam to allow migrating salmon an easier course on the upstream journey, and in the process, Lake Red Bluff reverts to its former self as the Sacramento River.

RV sites, facilities: There are 30 sites for RVs or tents (Sycamore Camp), a group camp (Camp Discovery) with six screened cabins that can accommodate a maximum of 48 campers, and 30 picnic shelters. Drinking water, showers, vault and flush toilets, picnic areas, two boat ramps, and a fish-viewing plaza are available. There are two large barbecues, electrical outlets, lockable storage, five large picnic tables, a comfort station with showers and sinks, and an amphitheater in the group camp area. Some facilities are wheelchair-accessible. Leashed pets are permitted.

Reservations, fees: Reservations are required only for the group camp. The fee is $10 per night for individual sites; the group camp per night is $100 for up to 50 people, $150 for 51–75 people, and $200 for 76–100 people. A senior discount is available. Open April through October.

Directions: From I-5 at Red Bluff, turn east on Highway 36 and drive 100 yards to the first turnoff at Sale Lane. Turn right (south) on Sale Lane. Turn right and drive 1.5 miles to the campground at the end of the road.

Contact: Mendocino National Forest, Corning Work Station, 530/824-5196, fax 530/824-6034.

CALIFORNIA

California

Chapter 15
Lassen and Modoc

LASSEN AND MODOC

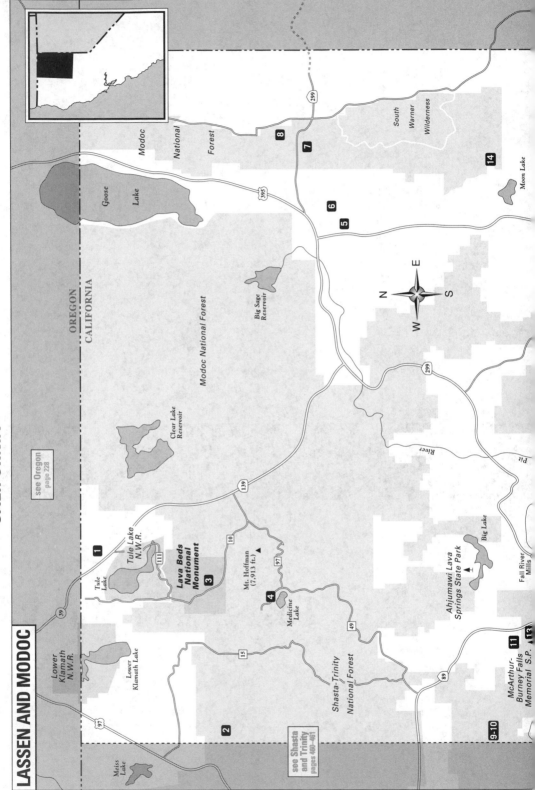

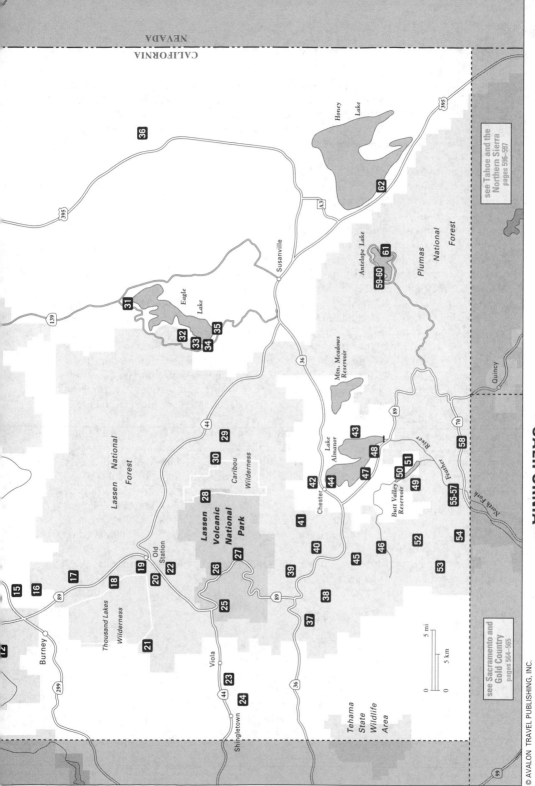

© AVALON TRAVEL PUBLISHING, INC.

CALIFORNIA

see Tahoe and the Northern Sierra pages 596–597

see Sacramento and Gold Country pages 564–565

Chapter 15—Lassen and Modoc

Mount Lassen and its awesome volcanic past seem to cast a shadow everywhere you go in this region. At 10,457 feet, the mountain's domed summit is visible for more than 100 miles in all directions. It blew its top in 1914, with continuing eruptions through 1918. Although now dormant, the volcanic-based geology dominates the landscape everywhere you look.

Of all the areas of California covered in this book, this region has the least number of romantic getaway spots. It caters instead primarily to outdoors enthusiasts. And Lassen Volcanic National Park is one of the best places to lace up the hiking boots or spool new line on a reel. It's often off the radar scope of vacationers, making it one of the few national parks where you can enjoy the wilderness in relative solitude.

The national park is easily explored along the main route, the Lassen Park Highway. Along the way, you can pick a few trails for adventure. The best hikes are the Summit Climb (moderate to challenging), best done first thing in the morning, and Bumpass Hell (easy and great for kids), to see the sulfur vents and boiling mud pots. Another favorite for classic alpine beauty is the Shadow Lake Trail.

Unique features of the region include its pumice boulders, volcanic rock, and spring-fed streams from the underground lava tubes. The highlights include the best still-water canoeing and fly-fishing at Fall River, Big Lake, and Ahjumawi State Park.

Nearby is McArthur–Burney Falls State Park, along with the Pit River and Lake Britton, which together make up one of Northern California's best recreation destinations for families. This is also one of the best areas for fly-fishing, especially at Hat Creek, Pit River, Burney Creek, and Manzanita Lake. For more beautiful settings, you can visit Lake Almanor and Eagle Lake, both of which provide lakeside campgrounds and excellent fishing and boating recreation.

And there's more. In remote Modoc County, you'll find Lava Beds National Monument and the South Warner Wilderness. Lava Beds is a stark, pretty, and often lonely place. It's sprinkled with small lakes full of trout and is home to large-antlered deer that migrate in after the first snow (and after the hunting season has closed), and it features a unique volcanic habitat with huge flows of obsidian (dark, smooth, natural glass formed by the cooling of molten lava) and dacite (gray, craggy volcanic flow). Lava Beds National Monument boasts 445 caves and lava tubes, including the 6,000-foot Catacomb tunnel. Nearby is pretty Medicine Lake, formed in a caldera, which provides good trout fishing, hiking, and exploring.

It seems no matter where you go, there are so many campgrounds that you can always find a match for what you desire.

CALIFORNIA

■ SHADY LANE TRAILER PARK

Rating: 3

in Tulelake
See map pages 496–497
There isn't much shade in some parts of Modoc County, but this private park manages to provide some. Good side trips include the Tule Lake Wildlife Refuge, one of the best places in America (during the winter) to see bald eagles and a good bet year-round for bird-watching. Nearby is Lava Beds National Monument, whose northern edge is an excellent place to see deer in late fall and early winter. There is also a network of lava tubes and ice caves, making for a great getaway adventure. The Tulelake unit of the Klamath National Wildlife Refuge is only four miles away, and the Lower Klamath Lake unit is eight miles away; both provide excellent waterfowl hunting in early fall.

RV sites, facilities: There are 60 RV sites with full hookups, some with long-term renters. Restrooms, showers, patios, and a coin-operated laundry are available. Leashed pets are permitted.

Reservations, fees: Reservations are accepted. The fee is $15 per night. Open year-round.

Directions: From Redding, turn east on Highway 299 and drive to Canby and the junction with Highway 139. Turn left at Highway 139 (north) and drive 52 miles to Tulelake and the south exit of East West Road. Take that exit and drive 1.5 miles to Modoc Avenue. Turn left, and drive a short distance to the trailer park.

Contact: Shady Lane Trailer Park, 795 Modoc Ave., Tulelake, CA 96134, 530/667-2617.

■ SHAFTER

Rating: 4

in Klamath National Forest
See map pages 496–497
This is a little-used camp with trout fishing at nearby Butte Creek for small rainbows, primarily six- to eight-inchers. Little Orr Lake, about a 10-minute drive away on the southwest flank of Orr Mountain, provides fishing for bass and larger rainbow trout, 10- to 12-inchers, as well as a sprinkling of smaller brook trout. A boat ramp

and restroom with vault toilets were opened in 2000. This camp is primitive and not well known, set in a juniper- and sage-filled landscape. A great side trip is to the nearby Orr Mountain Lookout, where there are spectacular views of Mount Shasta. A Forest Service touch that is like gold in the summer is that the road adjacent to the campground is paved, which keeps the dust down.

RV sites, facilities: There are 14 sites for small RVs or tents. Picnic tables and fire grills are provided. Drinking water, a restroom, vault toilets, and a boat ramp are available. Pack out all garbage. Leashed pets are permitted.

Reservations, fees: Reservations are not accepted. The fee is $6 per night. A senior discount is available. Open year-round. Services are available in summer only.

Directions: From Redding, drive north on I-5 to Weed and the exit for Highway 97. Take that exit, turn right at the stop sign, drive through Weed and bear right (north) on Highway 97 and drive 40 miles to Ball Mountain Road. Turn right at Ball Mountain Road and drive 2.5 miles to a T with Old State Highway 97. Turn right and drive 4.25 miles (crossing railroad tracks) to the campground on the right side of the road.

Contact: Klamath National Forest, Goosenest Ranger District, 530/398-4391, fax 530/398-5749.

■ INDIAN WELL

Rating: 9

in Lava Beds National Monument
See map pages 496–497
Lava Beds National Monument is a one-in-a-million spot with more than 500 lava tube caves, Schonchin Butte (a cinder cone with a hiking trail), Mammoth Crater, Native American pictographs, battlefields and campsites from the Modoc War, and wildlife overlooks of Tule Lake. After winter's first snow, this is one of the best places in the West to photograph deer. Nearby is Klamath National Wildlife Refuge, the largest bald eagle wintering area in the lower 48. If you are new to the outdoors, an interpretive center is available to explain it all to you.

RV sites, facilities: There are 43 sites for RVs up to 30 feet or tents. Picnic tables, fire rings, and cooking grills are provided. From Memorial Day

CALIFORNIA

to Labor Day, drinking water, flush toilets, a pay phone, and limited cell phone reception are available. Drinking water and flush toilets are always available in the B Loop and at the visitors center. Note that during the off-season in the A Loop, only pit toilets are available. The town of Tulelake (30 miles north) is the nearest supply station. Some facilities are wheelchair-accessible. Leashed pets are permitted in the campground and roads only.

Reservations, fees: Reservations are not accepted. The fee is $10 per night, plus a $10 per vehicle park entrance fee. A senior discount is available. Open year-round.

Directions: From Redding, drive north on I-5 to Central Weed/Highway 97. Take that exit, turn right and continue for one mile to U.S. 97. Drive north on U.S. 97 for 54 miles to Highway 161. Turn east on Highway 161 and drive 20 miles to Hill Road. Turn right (south) and drive 18 miles to the visitors center and the campground entrance on the left. Turn left and drive .25 mile to the campground.

Contact: Lava Beds National Monument, 530/667-2282, fax 530/667-2737.

4 HARRIS SPRINGS

🚶 🐕 🚐 🏕

Rating: 3

in Shasta-Trinity National Forest

See map pages 496–497

This camp is a hidden spot in remote Shasta-Trinity National Forest, nestled in the long, mountainous ridge that runs east from Mount Shasta to the Lava Beds National Monument. The camp is set at 4,800 feet, with a part-time fire station within a quarter mile on the opposite side of the access road. The area is best explored by four-wheel drive, venturing to a series of small buttes, mountaintops, and lookouts in the immediate area. A map of Shasta-Trinity National Forest is a must.

RV sites, facilities: There are 15 sites for RVs up to 32 feet or tents. Picnic tables and fire grills are provided. Drinking water (spring water, not piped) and vault toilets are available. Garbage must be packed out. Leashed pets are permitted.

Reservations, fees: Reservations are not accepted. There is no fee for camping. Open late May to October, weather permitting.

Directions: From Redding, drive north on I-5 past Dunsmuir to the junction with Highway 89. Turn east on Highway 89 and drive 28 miles to Forest Road 49 (just past Bartle). Turn left on Forest Road 49 and drive five miles to the Y intersection with Harris Springs Road. Turn left at the Y on Harris Springs Road/Forest Road 15 and drive 12 miles to a junction with a forest road signed for the Harris Springs Ranger Station. Turn right and drive a short distance, and look for the campground entrance on the right side of the road.

Contact: Shasta-Trinity National Forest, McCloud Ranger District, 530/964-2184, fax 530/964-2938.

5 BRASS RAIL

🐕 👫 ♿ 🚐 🏕

Rating: 4

near Alturas

See map pages 496–497

This private RV park has easy access from the highway. The elevation is 4,400 feet. Alturas is the biggest "small town" in Modoc County and offers a museum, an old-time saloon, and a nice city park with a playground, and, just south of town, the Modoc National Wildlife Refuge. The Warner Mountains to the distant east provide a backdrop.

RV sites, facilities: There are 70 RV sites, some with full hookups, and a separate tent area. Picnic tables are provided. Hot showers, flush toilets, an RV dump station, a coin-operated laundry, ice, propane, a playground, and a tennis court are available. A restaurant is adjacent to the park. Supplies can be obtained in Alturas, less than a mile away. Some facilities are wheelchair-accessible. Leashed pets are permitted.

Reservations, fees: Reservations are accepted. The fee is $10.50–16 per night, plus $5.50 per person for more than two people and $3–5 per night for each additional vehicle. Major credit cards are accepted. Open March through October.

Directions: In Alturas at the junction of Highway 299 and U.S. 395, turn east on U.S. 395 and drive .5 mile to the signed campground entrance on the right.

Contact: Brass Rail Campground, 530/233-2906.

6 SULLY'S RV PARK

Rating: 4

near Alturas
See map pages 496–497

This privately operated park is next to the playground, the city park, and the Modoc County Museum, which details the history of the area. The surrounding Modoc National Wildlife Refuge is only a short drive away, either a mile southwest of town along the Pit River, or three miles east of town at Dorris Reservoir. Big Sage Reservoir provides another getaway. But alas, what gets most of the traffic is a casino, only one mile from Alturas. The area for tent camping here is grassy and separated from the RV camp.

RV sites, facilities: There are 25 RV sites with full hookups (30, 50 amps) and picnic tables, including 10 drive-through sites, and a separate area for tents. Cable TV, cell phone reception, modem hookups, showers, flush toilets, a coin-operated laundry, and horseshoes are available. Supplies can be obtained in Alturas one block away. An ATM is within seven blocks. Leashed pets are permitted.

Reservations, fees: Reservations are accepted. The fee is $10–17 per night. Monthly rates are available. Open year-round.

Directions: In Alturas, at the junction of Highway 299 and U.S. 395, turn south on U.S. 395 and drive .5 mile (look for the steam engine) to County Road 56. Turn east on County Road 56 and drive one block to the campground on the right.

Contact: Sully's RV Park, 530/233-5347, fax 530/233-2541.

7 CEDAR PASS

Rating: 5

on Cedar Pass in Modoc National Forest
See map pages 496–497

Cedar Pass is at 5,900 feet, set on the ridge between Cedar Mountain (8,152 feet) to the north and Payne Peak (7,618) to the south, high in the north Warner Mountains. Bear Creek enters Thomas Creek adjacent to the camp; both are small streams, but it's a pretty spot.

RV sites, facilities: There are 17 sites for RVs up to 22 feet or tents. Picnic tables and fire grills are provided. Vault toilets are available. No drinking water is available, and garbage must be packed out. Supplies can be obtained in Cedarville or Alturas. Leashed pets are permitted.

Reservations, fees: Reservations are not accepted. There is no fee for camping. Open May through September.

Directions: From Redding drive east on Highway 299 to Alturas. In Alturas continue north on Highway 299/U.S. 395 for five miles to the split for Highway 299. Turn right on Highway 299 and drive about nine miles. Look for the signed entrance road on the right side of the road.

Contact: Modoc National Forest, Warner Mountain Ranger District, 530/279-6116, fax 530/279-8309.

8 STOWE RESERVOIR

Rating: 8

in Modoc National Forest
See map pages 496–497

Stowe Reservoir looks like a large country pond where cattle might drink. You know why? Because it once actually was a cattle pond on a family ranch that has since been converted to Forest Service property. It is in the north Warner Mountains (not to be confused with the South Warner Wilderness), which features many back roads and remote four-wheel-drive routes. The camp is set at an elevation of 6,200 feet. Note that you may find this campground named "Stough Reservoir" on some maps and in previous editions of this book. The name is now officially spelled "Stowe Reservoir," after the family that originally owned the property.

RV sites, facilities: There are 14 sites for RVs up to 22 feet or tents. Picnic tables and fire grills are provided. Drinking water and vault toilets are available. Garbage must be packed out. Supplies can be obtained in Cedarville, six miles away. Leashed pets are permitted.

Reservations, fees: Reservations are not accepted. There is no fee for camping. Open May to October.

Directions: From Redding, drive east on Highway 299 to Alturas. In Alturas, continue north on Highway 299/U.S. 395 for five miles to the

CALIFORNIA

split-off for Highway 299. Turn right on Highway 299 and drive about 12 miles (just past Cedar Pass). Look for the signed entrance road on the left side of the road. Turn left and drive one mile to the campground on the right side of the road.
Contact: Modoc National Forest, Warner Mountain Ranger District, 530/279-6116, fax 530/279-8309.

⑨ DEADLUN

Rating: 8

on Iron Canyon Reservoir in Shasta-Trinity National Forest
See map pages 496–497

Deadlun is a pretty campground set in the forest, shaded and quiet, with a five-minute walk or one-minute drive to the Deadlun Creek arm of Iron Canyon Reservoir. Drive? If you have a canoe to launch or fishing equipment to carry, driving is the choice. Trout fishing is good here, both in April and May, then again in October and early November. One downer is that the shoreline is often very muddy here in March and early April. Because of an engineering error with the dam, the lake never fills completely, causing the lakeshore to be strewn with stumps and quite muddy after spring rains and snowmelt.

RV sites, facilities: There are 30 sites for RVs up to 24 feet or tents. Picnic tables and fire grills are provided. Vault toilets are available. No drinking water is available. A small boat ramp is one mile from the camp. Leashed pets are permitted.

Reservations, fees: Reservations are not accepted. There is no fee for camping. Open year-round.

Directions: From Redding, drive east on Highway 299 for 37 miles to Big Bend Road. At Big Bend Road, turn left and drive 15.2 miles to the town of Big Bend. Continue for five miles to the lake, bearing right at the T intersection, and continue for two miles (past the boat launch turnoff) to the campground turnoff on the left side of the road. Turn left and drive one mile to the campground.

Contact: Shasta-Trinity National Forest, Shasta Lake Ranger District, 530/275-1587, fax 530/275-1512; Shasta Lake Visitor Center, 530/275-1589.

⑩ HAWKINS LANDING

Rating: 7

on Iron Canyon Reservoir
See map pages 496–497

The adjacent boat ramp makes Hawkins Landing the better of the two camps at Iron Canyon Reservoir for campers with trailered boats (though Deadlun is far more secluded). Iron Canyon provides good fishing for trout, has a resident bald eagle or two, and also has nearby hot springs in the town of Big Bend. One problem with this lake is the annual drawdown in late fall, which causes the shoreline to be extremely muddy in the spring. The lake usually rises high enough to make the boat ramp functional by mid-April. This camp is set at an elevation of 2,700 feet.

RV sites, facilities: There are 10 sites for RVs up to 30 feet or tents. Picnic tables and fire grills are provided. Drinking water, vault toilets, and a small boat ramp are available. Supplies can be obtained in Big Bend. Leashed pets are permitted.

Reservations, fees: Reservations are not accepted. The fee is $10 per night, plus $1 dog fee, $3 per night per each additional vehicle, and $7 per night for an extra RV. Open Memorial Day weekend to Labor Day weekend, weather permitting.

Directions: From Redding, drive east on Highway 299 for 37 miles to Big Bend Road. At Big Bend Road turn left and drive 15.2 miles to the town of Big Bend. Continue for 2.1 miles to Forest Road 38N11. Turn left and drive 3.3 miles to the Iron Canyon Reservoir Spillway. Turn right and drive 1.1 miles to a dirt road. Turn left and drive .3 mile to the campground.

Contact: PG&E Land Projects, 916/386-5164.

⑪ BURNEY FALLS TRAILER RESORT

Rating: 5

near Lake Britton
See map pages 496–497

This is a year-round RV park near Lake Britton, Burney Creek, and the Pit River. McArthur–Burney Falls Memorial State Park, with its spectacular waterfall, is within a five-minute drive. The region is loaded with adventure, with Lassen

Volcanic National Park, Hat Creek, and Fall River all within a 30-minute drive.

RV sites, facilities: There are 28 sites with full hookups (30, 50 amps) for RVs or tents, 10 of which are long-term rentals. Picnic tables, restrooms, hot showers, a coin-operated laundry, horseshoes, cell phone reception, modem hookups, and a swimming pool (summer only) are available. An ATM is within nine miles. Leashed pets are permitted.

Reservations, fees: Reservations are accepted. The fee is $18 per night, plus $1 per person per night for more than two people. Monthly rates are available. A senior discount is available. Open year-round.

Directions: From Redding, drive east on Highway 299 to Burney and continue for five miles to the junction with Highway 89. At Highway 89, turn left (north) and drive four miles to Clark Creek Road. Turn left on Clark Creek Road and drive a short distance to the campground entrance on the left.

Contact: Burney Falls Trailer Resort, 530/335-2781.

12 McARTHUR–BURNEY FALLS MEMORIAL STATE PARK

Rating: 9

in McArthur–Burney Falls Memorial State Park
See map pages 496–497

Burney Falls is a 129-foot waterfall, a beautiful cascade split at the top by a little grove of trees, with small trickles oozing and falling out of the adjacent moss-lined wall. Since it is fed primarily by a spring, it runs strong and glorious most of the year, producing 100 million gallons of water every day. The Headwaters Trail provides an outstanding hike, both to see the waterfall and Burney Creek, as well as for an easy adventure and fishing access to the stream. An excellent fly-fishing section of the Pit River is available below the dam. There are other stellar recreation options at this state park. At the end of the campground access road is a boat ramp for Lake Britton, with rentals available for canoes, paddleboats, and small fishing boats. This is a beautiful lake, with pretty canyon walls on its upper end, and good smallmouth bass (at rock piles) and crappie fishing (near the train trestle). There is also a good swimming beach. The Pacific Crest Trail is routed right through the park and provides an additional opportunity for a day hike, best explored downstream from the dam. Reservations for sites are essential during the summer. This park features 910 acres of forest and five miles of stream and lakeshore. The park's landscape was created by volcanic activity, as well as erosion from weather and stream action.

RV sites, facilities: There are 128 sites for RVs up to 35 feet or tents. Picnic tables and fire grills are provided. Drinking water, flush toilets, hot showers, and an RV dump station are available. A grocery/gift store and boat rentals are available in the summer. Some facilities are wheelchair-accessible. Leashed pets are permitted, except on the trails and the beach.

Reservations, fees: Reservations are accepted with a $7.50 reservation fee at 800/444-PARK (800/444-7275) or www.reserveamerica.com. The fee is $15 per night. A senior discount is available. Open year-round.

Directions: From Redding, drive east on Highway 299 to Burney and then continue for five miles to the junction with Highway 89. At Highway 89, turn north (left) and drive six miles to the campground entrance on the left side of the road.

Contact: McArthur–Burney Falls Memorial State Park, 530/335-2777.

13 NORTHSHORE

Rating: 8

on Lake Britton
See map pages 496–497

This peaceful campground is set among the woodlands near the shore of Lake Britton, directly across the lake from McArthur–Burney Falls Memorial State Park. Boating and fishing are popular here, and once the water warms up in midsummer, swimming is also a winner. The best trout fishing in the area is on the Pit River near Powerhouse Number Three, but skilled and aggressive wading is required. A hot spring is available in Big Bend, about a 30-minute drive from camp.

RV sites, facilities: There are 30 sites for RVs up to 30 feet or tents. Picnic tables and fire grills are provided. Drinking water and vault toilets are available. An unimproved boat ramp is available near the camp, and an improved boat ramp is available in McArthur–Burney Falls State Park (about four miles away). Supplies can be obtained in Fall River Mills or Burney. Leashed pets are permitted.

Reservations, fees: Reservations are not accepted. The fee is $13 per night, plus $1 per pet per night. Open mid-May to mid-October, weather permitting.

Directions: From Redding, drive east on Highway 299 to Burney and then continue for five miles to Highway 89. Turn left (north) and drive 9.7 miles (past the state park entrance and over the Lake Britton Bridge) to Clark Creek Road. Turn left (west) and drive about a mile to the camp access road. Turn left and drive one mile to the camp.

Contact: PG&E Land Projects, 916/386-5164, fax 916/923-7044, website: www.pge.com/recreation.

14 BLUE LAKE

Rating: 6

in Modoc National Forest
See map pages 496–497

You won't believe this: the Blue Fire of 1991 burned 35,000 acres in this area, including the east and west slopes adjoining Blue Lake. Yet get this: the campground was untouched. It is a strange scene, a somewhat wooded campground (with some level campsites) near the shore of Blue Lake. The lake covers 160 acres and provides fishing for large brown trout and rainbow trout. A 5 mph speed limit assures quiet water for small boats and canoes. A trail circles the lake and takes less than an hour to hike. The elevation is 6,000 feet. A pair of nesting bald eagles lives here; in the last several years there have been several fledged chicks (up to eight by summer of 2002). Their presence negates year-round use of six campsites otherwise available, but the trade-off is an unprecedented opportunity to view the national bird. This lake received national attention when it was uncovered that it received a special large stock of brown trout in the 30-inch class, a plant attributed to the fact that Blue Lake was the boyhood lake and still "secret" fishing

spot of the director of Department of Fish and Game (and his brother).

RV sites, facilities: There are 48 sites for RVs up to 32 feet or tents. Picnic tables and fire grills are provided. Drinking water and vault toilets are available. Supplies are available in Likely. Some facilities are wheelchair-accessible, including a paved boat launch and fishing pier. Leashed pets are permitted.

Reservations, fees: Reservations are not accepted. The fee is $7 per night. A senior discount is available. Open June through October.

Directions: From Alturas, drive south on U.S. 395 for seven miles to the town of Likely, where you'll come to Jess Valley Road. Turn left on Jess Valley Road/County Road 64 and drive nine miles to the fork. At the fork, bear right on Forest Road 64 and drive seven miles to Forest Road 38N60. Turn right on Forest Road 38N60 and drive two miles to the campground.

Contact: Modoc National Forest, Warner Mountain Ranger District, 530/279-6116, fax 530/279-8309.

15 PIT RIVER

Rating: 6

on the Pit River
See map pages 496–497

Very few out-of-towners know about this hidden and primitive campground set along the Pit River. It can provide a good base camp for a fishing trip adventure. The best stretch of trout water on the Pit is near Powerhouse Number Three. In addition to fishing, there are many other recreation options. A parking area and trail along Hat Creek are available where the Highway 299 bridge crosses Hat Creek. Baum Lake, Crystal Lake, and the Cassel section of Hat Creek are all within five miles of this camp.

RV sites, facilities: There are 10 sites for RVs or tents. Picnic tables and fire rings are provided. Vault toilets are available. No drinking water is available. Garbage service is provided only during summer. There are supplies and a coin-operated laundry in Fall River Mills. Leashed pets are permitted.

Reservations, fees: Reservations are not accepted.

There is no fee for camping. Open year-round, weather permitting.

Directions: From Redding, drive east on Highway 299 to Burney and continue for five miles to the junction with Highway 89. At the junction, continue straight on Highway 299, cross the Pit River Bridge, and drive about three miles to Pit One Powerhouse Road on the right. Just before the powerhouse, turn right (at the bend) and drive along the river for about a mile to the campground.

Contact: Bureau of Land Management, Alturas Field Office, 530/233-4666, fax 530/233-5696.

16 CASSEL

Rating: 8

on Hat Creek

See map pages 496-497

This camp is set at 3,200 feet in the beautiful Hat Creek Valley. It is an outstanding location for a fishing trip base camp, with nearby Crystal Lake, Baum Lake, and Hat Creek (all set in the Hat Creek Valley) providing trout fishing. This section of Hat Creek is well known for its challenging fly-fishing, typically with an excellent evening hatch and surface rise. Long leaders and very small flies are critical. A good source of fishing information is Vaughn's Sporting Goods in Burney. Baum Lake is ideal for car-top boats with electric motors.

RV sites, facilities: There are 27 sites for RVs up to 30 feet or tents. Picnic tables and fire grills are provided. Drinking water and vault toilets are available. Leashed pets are permitted.

Reservations, fees: Reservations are not accepted. The fee is $13 per night, plus $3 per night per each additional vehicle, $7 per night per extra RV, and $1 per pet per night. Open mid-April through October, weather permitting.

Directions: From Redding, drive east on Highway 299 to Burney and continue for five miles to the junction with Highway 89. At the junction, continue straight on Highway 299 for two miles to Cassel Road. At Cassel Road, turn right and drive 3.6 miles to the campground entrance on the left.

Contact: PG&E Land Projects, 916/386-5164, fax 916/923-7044, website: www.pge.com/recreation.

17 HAT CREEK HEREFORD RANCH RV PARK & CAMPGROUND

Rating: 8

near Hat Creek

See map pages 496-497

This privately operated campground is set in a working cattle ranch. Campers are not allowed near the cattle pasture or cattle. Fishing is available in Hat Creek or in the nearby stocked trout pond. Sightseeing is excellent with Burney Falls, Lassen Volcanic National Park, and Subway Caves all within 30 miles.

RV sites, facilities: There are 40 RV sites (30 amps), including some drive-through sites, with partial or full hookups and 40 tent sites. Restrooms, hot showers, an RV dump station, a coin-operated laundry, a playground, modem hookups, and a grocery store are available. Some facilities are wheelchair-accessible. Leashed pets are permitted.

Reservations, fees: Reservations are recommended. The fee is $17.95–22.95 per night, plus $2 per adult and $1.50 per child per night for more than two people and $.50 per night per pet. Major credit cards are accepted. Open April through October.

Directions: From Redding, drive east on Highway 299 to Burney and continue for five miles to the junction with Highway 89. Turn right (south) on Highway 89 and drive 12 miles to the second Doty Road exit and the entrance to the campground.

Contact: Hat Creek Hereford Ranch RV Park & Campground, 530/335-7171 or 877/459-9532, website: www.hatcreekrv.com.

18 BRIDGE CAMP

Rating: 7

on Hat Creek in Lassen National Forest

See map pages 496-497

This camp is one of four along Highway 89 in the area along Hat Creek. It is set at 3,800 feet elevation, with shaded sites and the stream within very short walking distance. Trout are stocked on this stretch of the creek, with fishing access available out of camp, as well as at Rocky and

CALIFORNIA

Cave camps to the south and Honn to the north. In one weekend, fishermen might hit all four.

RV sites, facilities: There are 25 sites for RVs up to 22 feet or tents. Picnic tables and fire grills are provided. Drinking water, vault toilets, and limited cell phone reception are available. An ATM and an RV dump station are within five miles. Leashed pets are permitted.

Reservations, fees: Reservations are not accepted. The fee is $13 per night, plus $5 for each additional vehicle. A senior discount is available. Open late April through October, weather permitting.

Directions: From Redding, drive east on Highway 299 to Burney and continue for five miles to the junction with Highway 89. Turn right (south) on Highway 89 and drive 19 miles to the campground entrance on the right side of the road. If you reach Old Station, you have gone five miles too far.

Contact: Lassen National Forest, Hat Creek Ranger District, 530/336-5521, fax 530/336-5758.

19 CAVE CAMP

Rating: 7

on Hat Creek in Lassen National Forest
See map pages 496–497

Cave Camp is set right along Hat Creek, with both easy access off Highway 89 and an anglers' trail available along the stream. This stretch of Hat Creek is planted with rainbow trout twice a month by the Department of Fish and Game, starting with the opening of trout season on the last Saturday of April. Nearby side trips include Lassen Volcanic National Park, about a 15-minute drive to the south on Highway 89, and Subway Caves (turn left at the junction just across the road from the campground). A rare bonus at this camp is that wheelchair-accessible fishing is available.

RV sites, facilities: There are 46 sites for RVs up to 22 feet or tents. Picnic tables and fire grills are provided. Drinking water, flush toilets, vault toilets, and limited cell phone reception are available. An ATM and an RV dump station are within five miles. Supplies can be obtained in Old Station. Some facilities are wheelchair-accessible. Leashed pets are permitted.

Reservations, fees: Reservations are not accepted. The fee is $15 per night, plus $5 for each

additional vehicle. A senior discount is available. Open May through October.

Directions: From Redding, drive east on Highway 299 to Burney and continue for five miles to the junction with Highway 89. Turn right (south) on Highway 89 and drive 23 miles to the campground entrance on the right side of the road. If you reach Old Station, you have gone one mile too far.

Contact: Lassen National Forest, Hat Creek Ranger District, 530/336-5521, fax 530/336-5758.

20 HAT CREEK

Rating: 7

on Hat Creek in Lassen National Forest
See map pages 496–497

This is one in a series of Forest Service camps set beside beautiful Hat Creek, a good trout stream stocked regularly by the Department of Fish and Game. The elevation is 4,400 feet. The proximity to Lassen Volcanic National Park to the south is a big plus.

RV sites, facilities: There are 75 sites for RVs up to 22 feet or tents and three group camp loops, each of which accommodates 15 to 20 vehicles. Picnic tables and fire grills are provided. Drinking water, an RV dump station, and vault toilets are available. A grocery store, a coin-operated laundry, and propane are available nearby. An ATM and an RV dump station are within five miles. Supplies are available in the little town of Old Station one mile to the north. Leashed pets are permitted.

Reservations, fees: Reservations are only required for campsites 1–9 and for group camps with a $9 reservation fee at 877/444-6777 or www.reserveusa.com. The fee is $15 per night for family sites, plus $5 for each additional vehicle, and $80 per night for group camps. A senior discount is available. Open May through October.

Directions: From Redding, drive east on Highway 44 to the junction with Highway 89 (near the entrance to Lassen Volcanic National Park). Turn left (north) on Highway 89 and drive about 12 miles to the campground entrance on the left side of the road. Turn left and drive a short distance to the campground.

Contact: Lassen National Forest, Hat Creek Ranger District, 530/336-5521, fax 530/336-5758.

21 NORTH BATTLE CREEK RESERVOIR

Rating: 7

on Battle Creek Reservoir
See map pages 496–497

This little-known lake is at 5,600 feet in elevation, largely surrounded by Lassen National Forest. No gas engines are permitted on the lake, making it ideal for canoes, rafts, and car-top aluminum boats equipped with electric motors. When the lake level is up in early summer, it is a pretty setting with good trout fishing.

RV sites, facilities: There are 10 sites for RVs or tents and five walk-in tent sites. Picnic tables and fire grills are provided. Drinking water and vault toilets are available. A car-top boat launch is available nearby. Leashed pets are permitted.

Reservations, fees: Reservations are not accepted. The fee is $11 per night, plus $3 per night per each additional vehicle, $7 per night per extra RV, and $1 per pet per night. Open mid-May to mid-September, weather permitting.

Directions: From Redding, drive east on Highway 44 to Viola. From Viola, continue east for 3.5 miles to Forest Road 32N17. Turn left on Forest Road 32N17 and drive five miles to Forest Road 32N31. Turn left and drive four miles to Forest Road 32N18. Turn right and drive .5 mile to the reservoir and the campground on the right side of the road.

Contact: PG&E Land Projects, 916/386-5164, website: www.pge.com/recreation.

22 BIG PINE CAMP

Rating: 7

on Hat Creek in Lassen National Forest
See map pages 496–497

This campground is set on the headwaters of Hat Creek, a pretty spot amid ponderosa pines. A dirt road out of camp parallels Hat Creek, providing access for trout fishing. A great vista point is on the highway, a mile south of the campground entrance road. It is only a 10-minute drive south

to the Highway 44 entrance station for Lassen Volcanic National Park.

RV sites, facilities: There are 19 sites for RVs up to 22 feet or tents. Picnic tables and fire grills are provided. Drinking water (at two hand pumps), vault toilets, and limited cell phone reception are available. An RV dump station, a grocery store, and propane are available nearby. An ATM is within 10 miles. Leashed pets are permitted.

Reservations, fees: Reservations are not accepted. The fee is $11 per night, plus $5 for each additional vehicle. A senior discount is available. Open May to October, weather permitting.

Directions: From Redding, drive east on Highway 44 to the junction with Highway 89 (near the entrance to Lassen Volcanic National Park). Turn left (north) on Highway 89 and drive about eight miles (one mile past the vista point) to the campground entrance on the right side of the road. Turn right and drive .5 mile to the campground.

Contact: Lassen National Forest, Hat Creek Ranger District, 530/336-5521, fax 530/336-5758.

23 MOUNT LASSEN KOA

Rating: 6

near Lassen Volcanic National Park
See map pages 496–497

This popular KOA camp is 14 miles from the entrance of Lassen Volcanic National Park and has pretty, wooded sites. Location is always the critical factor on vacations, and this park is set up perfectly for launching trips to the nearby east. Hat Creek provides trout fishing along Highway 89, and just inside the Highway 44 entrance station to Lassen Park is Manzanita Lake, providing good fishing and hiking.

RV sites, facilities: There are 45 sites for RVs or tents, including some drive-through sites, with partial or full hookups (30 amps), and five cabins. Picnic tables and fire grills are provided. Flush toilets, hot showers, a playground, a heated pool (summer only), an RV dump station, groceries, ice, wood, a coin-operated laundry, modem access, a video arcade and recreation room, and propane are available. An ATM is within four miles. Leashed pets are permitted.

Reservations, fees: Reservations are accepted with a deposit at 800/562-3403. The fee is $20–33 per night, plus $2 per person for more than two people. Cabins are $40–85 per night. Major credit cards are accepted. Open year-round.

Directions: From Redding, turn east on Highway 44 and drive to Shingletown. In Shingletown, continue east for four miles and look for the park entrance on the right (signed KOA).

Contact: Mount Lassen KOA, 530/474-3133, website: www.koa.com.

24 MILL CREEK PARK

Rating: 7

near Shingletown
See map pages 496–497

Mill Creek Park is a year-round park set up primarily for RVs, yet it has sites for tents as well as cabins. It is set amid conifers on the western slopes of Mount Lassen. A creek and pond for fishing are a plus. Its proximity to Lassen Volcanic National Park is a key attraction. The elevation is 4,000 feet. Note that adjacent to the park is a mobile home park with 10 sites for permanent residents.

RV sites, facilities: There are 16 sites with partial or full hookups for RVs, seven sites for tents, and four cabins. Picnic tables and fire rings are provided. Restrooms, drinking water, flush toilets, and showers are available. A coin-operated laundry and an RV dump station are on-site. Leashed pets are permitted.

Reservations, fees: Reservations are accepted. The fee is $14–18 per night. Monthly rates are available. Major credit cards are accepted. Open year-round.

Directions: From Redding, drive east on Highway 44 to Shingletown. Continue east on Highway 44 for two miles to the park on the right.

Contact: Mill Creek Park, 530/474-5384, fax 530/474-1236, website: www.MillCreekrvPark.org.

25 MANZANITA LAKE

Rating: 9

in Lassen Volcanic National Park
See map pages 496–497

Manzanita Lake, set at 5,890 feet, is one of the prettiest lakes in Lassen Volcanic National Park,

and it has good catch-and-release trout fishing for experienced fly fishers in prams and other nonpowered boats. This is no place for a dad, mom, and a youngster to fish from shore with Power Bait. Because of the great natural beauty of the lake, the campground is often crowded. Evening walks around the lake are beautiful. A museum, visitors center, and small store are available nearby. Ranger programs are offered in the summer.

RV sites, facilities: There are 179 sites for RVs up to 35 feet or tents. Picnic tables, fire grills, and bear-proof food lockers are provided. Drinking water, flush toilets, and limited cell phone reception are available. Propane, groceries, showers, an RV dump station, and a coin-operated laundry are available nearby. A boat launch is also nearby (no motors are permitted at Manzanita Lake). Some facilities are wheelchair-accessible. Leashed pets are permitted at campsites only.

Reservations, fees: Reservations are not accepted. The fee is $16 per night, plus a $10 per vehicle park entrance fee. A senior discount is available. Major credit cards are accepted. Open late May to late September, weather permitting (during the fall season, it's open without drinking water until the camp is closed by snow).

Directions: From Redding, drive east on Highway 44 to the junction with Highway 89. Turn right (south) on Highway 89 and drive one mile to the entrance station to Lassen Volcanic National Park (the state highway becomes Lassen Park Highway/Main Park Road). Continue a short distance on Lassen Park Highway/Main Park Road to the campground entrance road. Turn right and drive .5 mile to the campground.

Contact: Lassen Volcanic National Park, 530/595-4444, fax 530/595-3262.

26 CRAGS

Rating: 8

in Lassen Volcanic National Park
See map pages 496–497

Crags is sometimes overlooked as a prime spot at Lassen Volcanic National Park because there is no lake nearby. No problem, because even though this campground is small compared to the giant complex at Manzanita Lake, the campsites are more spacious, do not fill up as quickly, and many are backed by forest. In addition, the Emigrant Trail runs out of camp, routing east and meeting pretty Lost Creek after a little more than a mile, a great short hike. Directly across from Crags are the towering Chaos Crags, topping out at 8,503 feet. The elevation here is 5,720 feet. Crags reopened in 2003 after being closed for one year for the removal of dead trees.

RV sites, facilities: There are 45 sites for RVs up to 35 feet or tents. Picnic tables, fire rings, and bear-proof food lockers are provided. Drinking water, vault toilets, and limited cell phone reception are available. Leashed pets are permitted in the campground and on paved roads only.

Reservations, fees: Reservations are not accepted. The fee is $10 per night, plus a $10 per vehicle park entrance fee. A senior discount is available. Open late June to early September.

Directions: From Redding, drive east on Highway 44 for 42 miles to the junction with Highway 89. Turn right and drive one mile to the entrance station at Lassen Volcanic National Park (the state highway becomes Lassen Park Highway/Main Park Road). Continue on Lassen Park Highway/Main Park Road for about five miles to the campground on the left side of the road.

Contact: Lassen Volcanic National Park, 530/595-4444, fax 530/595-3262.

27 SUMMIT LAKE, NORTH AND SOUTH

Rating: 9

in Lassen Volcanic National Park
See map pages 496–497

Summit Lake is a beautiful spot where deer often visit each evening on the adjacent meadow just east of the campground. The lake is small, and since trout plants were suspended, it has been just about fished out. Evening walks around the lake are perfect for families. A more ambitious trail is routed out of camp and leads past lavish wildflower displays in early summer to a series of wilderness lakes. The campgrounds are set at an elevation of 6,695 feet.

RV sites, facilities: There are 94 sites for RVs up to 35 feet (only at North Summit) or tents. Picnic tables, fire rings, and bear-proof food lockers are

provided. Drinking water and toilets (flush toilets on the north side, vault toilets on the south side) are available. Ranger programs are available in summer. Some facilities are wheelchair-accessible. Leashed pets are permitted at campsites only.

Reservations, fees: Reservations are not accepted. The fees are $14 (South) and $16 (North) per night, plus a $10 per vehicle park entrance fee. Major credit cards are accepted. A senior discount is available. Open late June to mid-September, weather permitting.

Directions: From Redding, drive east on Highway 44 to the junction with Highway 89. Turn south on Highway 89 and drive one mile to the entrance station to Lassen Volcanic National Park (where the state highway becomes Lassen Park Highway/Main Park Road). Continue on Lassen Park Highway/Main Park Road for 12 miles to the campground entrance on the left side of the road.

Contact: Lassen Volcanic National Park, 530/595-4444, fax 530/595-3262.

28 BUTTE LAKE

Rating: 9

in Lassen Volcanic National Park
See map pages 496–497

Butte Lake campground is situated in an open, volcanic setting with a sprinkling of lodgepole pine. The contrast of the volcanics against the emerald greens of the lake is beautiful and memorable. The Cinder Cone Trail can provide an even better look. The trailhead is near the boat launch area, and it's a strenuous hike involving a climb of 800 feet over the course of two miles to the top of the Cinder Cone. The footing is often loose because of volcanic pebbles. At the rim, you can peer inside the Cinder Cone, as well as be rewarded with lake views and a long-distance vista. Trout fishing is poor at Butte Lake, as at nearly all the lakes at this national park, because trout have not been planted for years. The elevation is 6,100 feet.

RV sites, facilities: There are 98 sites for RVs up to 35 feet or tents. Picnic tables, fire rings, and bear-proof food lockers are provided. Drinking water, flush and vault toilets, and limited cell phone reception are available. A boat ramp is nearby. No motors are permitted on the lake. Leashed pets are permitted at campsites only.

Reservations, fees: Reservations are not accepted. The fee is $14 per night, plus a $10 per vehicle park entrance fee. A senior discount is available. Open late May to late September, weather permitting.

Directions: From Redding, drive east on Highway 44 to the junction with Highway 89. Bear north on Highway 89/44 and drive 13 miles to Old Station. Just past Old Station, turn right (east) on Highway 44 and drive 10 miles to Forest Road 32N21/Butte Lake Road. Turn right and drive six miles to the campground.

Contact: Lassen Volcanic National Park, 530/595-4444, fax 530/595-3262.

29 ROCKY KNOLL

Rating: 7

on Silver Lake in Lassen National Forest
See map pages 496–497

This is one of two camps at pretty Silver Lake, set at 6,400 feet elevation at the edge of the Caribou Wilderness. The other camp is Silver Bowl to the nearby north, which is larger and provides better access for hikers. This camp, however, is closer to the boat ramp, which is at the south end of the lake. Silver Lake provides a good summer fishery for campers.

RV sites, facilities: There are 11 sites for RVs up to 27 feet and seven tent sites. Picnic tables and fire grills are provided. Drinking water and vault toilets are available. Leashed pets are permitted.

Reservations, fees: Reservations are not accepted. The fee is $11 per night. A senior discount is available. Open late May through October, weather permitting.

Directions: From Red Bluff, drive east on Highway 36 to the junction with Highway 89. Continue east on Highway 89/36 past Lake Almanor to Westwood. In Westwood, turn left on County Road A21 and drive 12.5 miles to Silver Lake Road. Turn left (west) on Silver Lake Road/County Road 110 and drive 8.5 miles north to Silver Lake. At Silver Lake, turn left and drive a short distance to the campground.

Contact: Lassen National Forest, Almanor Ranger District, 530/258-2141, fax 530/258-5194.

30 SILVER BOWL

Rating: 7

on Silver Lake in Lassen National Forest
See map pages 496–497

Silver Lake is a pretty lake set at 6,400 feet elevation at the edge of the Caribou Wilderness. There is an unimproved boat ramp at the southern end of the lake. The lake is occasionally planted by the Department of Fish and Game with Eagle Lake trout and brown trout, which provides a summer fishery for campers. A trailhead from adjacent Caribou Lake is routed west into the wilderness, with trails available to Emerald Lake to the northwest, and Betty, Trail, and Shotoverin Lakes nearby to the southeast.

RV sites, facilities: There are 18 sites for RVs or tents. Picnic tables and fire grills are provided. Drinking water and vault toilets are available. Leashed pets are permitted.

Reservations, fees: Reservations are not accepted. The fee is $11 per night. A senior discount is available. Open late May through October, weather permitting.

Directions: From Red Bluff, drive east on Highway 36 to the junction with Highway 89. Continue east on Highway 89/36 past Lake Almanor to Westwood. In Westwood, turn left on County Road A21 and drive 12.5 miles to Silver Lake Road. Turn left on Silver Lake Road/County Road 110 and drive 8.5 miles north to Silver Lake. At Silver Lake, turn right and drive a short distance to the campground.

Contact: Lassen National Forest, Almanor Ranger District, 530/258-2141, fax 530/258-5194.

31 NORTH EAGLE LAKE

Rating: 8

on Eagle Lake
See map pages 496–497

This camp provides direct access in the fall to the best fishing area of huge Eagle Lake. When the weather turns cold, the population of big Eagle Lake trout migrate to their favorite haunts just outside the tules, often in water only five to eight feet deep. From shore, try fishing with inflated night crawlers near the lake bottom, just outside the tules. A boat ramp is about 1.5 miles to the southwest on Stone Road. From there, troll a Needlefish along the tules, or anchor or tie up and use a night crawler for bait under a slip bobber. In the summer this area is quite exposed, and the lake can be hammered by west winds, which can howl from midday to sunset. The elevation is 5,100 feet.

RV sites, facilities: There are 20 sites for RVs or tents. Picnic tables and fire grills are provided. Drinking water and vault toilets are available. A private RV dump station and boat ramp are within 1.5 miles. Leashed pets are permitted.

Reservations, fees: Reservations are not accepted. The fee is $8 per night. A senior discount is available. Open Memorial Day through mid-November.

Directions: From Red Bluff, drive east on Highway 36 to Susanville. In Susanville, turn left (north) on Highway 139 and drive 29 miles to County Road A1. Turn left at County Road A1 and drive .5 mile to the campground.

Contact: Bureau of Land Management, Eagle Lake Field Office, 530/257-0456, fax 530/257-4831.

32 EAGLE LAKE RV PARK

Rating: 7

near Susanville

See map pages 496–497

Eagle Lake RV Park has become something of a headquarters for anglers in pursuit of Eagle Lake trout, which typically range from 18 to 22 inches. A nearby boat ramp provides access to Pelican Point and Eagle Point, where the fishing is often best in the summer. In the fall, the north end of the lake provides better prospects (see the previous listing for North Eagle Lake Campground for more information). This RV park has all the amenities, including a small store. That means no special trips into town, just vacation time, lounging beside Eagle Lake, maybe catching a big trout now and then. One downer: the wind typically howls here most summer afternoons. Resident deer can be like pets here on late summer evenings, including bucks with spectacular racks.

RV sites, facilities: There are 69 RV sites with full

hookups (30 amps), including some drive-through sites, a separate grassy area for tents only, and cabin and RV rentals. Picnic tables and fire grills are provided. Restrooms, showers, a coin-operated laundry, satellite TV hookups, limited cell phone reception, an ATM, an RV dump station, a grocery store, propane, diesel, RV supplies, wood, and a recreation room are available. A boat ramp and dock are nearby. Some facilities are wheelchair-accessible. Leashed pets are permitted.

Reservations, fees: Reservations are recommended. The fee is $20–27 per night, plus $1 per pet per night. Major credit cards are accepted. Open late May to late November, weather permitting.

Directions: From Red Bluff, drive east on Highway 36 toward Susanville. Just before reaching Susanville, turn left on County Road A1 and drive to County Road 518 near Spalding Tract. Turn right on County Road 518 and drive through a small neighborhood to Strand Way (the lake frontage road). Turn right on Strand Way and drive about eight blocks to Palmetto Way and the entrance to the store and the RV park at 687-125 Palmetto Way. Register at the store.

Contact: Eagle Lake RV Park, 530/825-3133, website: www.eaglelakeandrv.com.

33 CHRISTIE

Rating: 9

on Eagle Lake in Lassen National Forest

See map pages 496–497

This camp is set along the southern shore of Eagle Lake at 5,100 feet. Eagle Lake is well known for its big trout (yea) and big winds (boo). The camp offers some protection from the north winds. Its location is also good for seeing osprey with the Osprey Management Area, which covers a six-mile stretch of shoreline, just two miles to the north above Wildcat Point. A nearby resort is a bonus. The nearest boat ramp is at Aspen Grove campground.

RV sites, facilities: There are 69 sites for RVs up to 50 feet or tents. Picnic tables and fire grills are provided. Drinking water and flush toilets are available. A grocery store is nearby. An RV dump station is 2.5 miles away at Merrill campground. Some facilities are wheelchair-accessible. Leashed pets are permitted.

Reservations, fees: Reservations are accepted with a $9 reservation fee at 877/444-6777 or www.reserveusa.com. The fee is $14 per night. Open May through September.

Directions: From Red Bluff, drive east on Highway 36 toward Susanville. Three miles before Susanville turn left on Eagle Lake Road/County Road A1 and drive 15.5 miles to County Road 231. Turn right on County Road 231 and drive four miles to the campground on the right side of the road.

Contact: Lassen National Forest, Eagle Lake Ranger District, 530/257-4188, fax 530/252-5803.

34 MERRILL

Rating: 9

on Eagle Lake in Lassen National Forest
See map pages 496–497

This is one of the largest, most developed Forest Service campgrounds in the entire county. It is set along the southern shore of huge Eagle Lake at 5,100 feet. The nearest boat launch is adjacent to Aspen Grove campground.

RV sites, facilities: There are 180 sites for RVs up to 35 feet or tents. Picnic tables and fire grills are provided. Drinking water, flush toilets, and an RV dump station are available. A grocery store and boat ramp are nearby. Some facilities are wheelchair-accessible. Leashed pets are permitted.

Reservations, fees: Reservations are accepted with a $9 reservation fee at 877/444-6777 or www.reserveusa.com. The fee is $14–15 per night. A senior discount is available. Open May through November.

Directions: From Red Bluff, drive east on Highway 36 toward Susanville. Three miles before Susanville, turn left on Eagle Lake Road/County Road A1 and drive 15.5 miles to County Road 231. Turn right on County Road 231 and drive one mile to the campground on the right side of the road.

Contact: Lassen National Forest, Eagle Lake Ranger District, 530/257-4188, fax 530/252-5803.

35 EAGLE

Rating: 9

on Eagle Lake in Lassen National Forest
See map pages 496–497

Eagle is just up the road from Aspen Grove; the latter is more popular because of the adjacent boat ramp but does not have RV sites.

RV sites, facilities: There are 50 sites for RVs up to 35 feet or tents. Picnic tables and fire grills are provided. Drinking water and flush toilets are available. A boat launch is nearby at Aspen Grove. An RV dump station is within 1.5 miles. Some facilities are wheelchair-accessible. Leashed pets are permitted.

Reservations, fees: Reservations are accepted with a $9 reservation fee at 877/444-6777 or www .reserveusa.com. The fee is $14 per night. A senior discount is available. Open May through September.

Directions: From Red Bluff, drive east on Highway 36 toward Susanville. Three miles before Susanville, turn left on Eagle Lake Road/County Road A1 and drive 15.5 miles to County Road 231. Turn right and drive .5 mile to the campground on the left side of the road.

Contact: Lassen National Forest, Eagle Lake Ranger District, 530/257-4188, fax 530/252-5803.

36 RAMHORN SPRINGS

Rating: 3

south of Ravendale
See map pages 496–497

This camp is not even three miles off the biggest state highway in northeastern California, yet it feels remote and is little known. It is way out in Nowhere Land, near the flank of Shinn Peak (7,562 feet). There are large numbers of antelope in the area, along with a sprinkling of large mule deer. Though being drawn for tags for this area is nearly impossible, the hunters lucky enough to get a deer tag can use this camp for their base in the fall. It is also popular for upland game hunters in search of sage grouse.

RV sites, facilities: There are 12 sites for RVs up to 28 feet or tents. Picnic tables and fire grills are provided. Vault toilets and a horse corral are available. There is no drinking water. Leashed pets are permitted.

Reservations, fees: Reservations are not accepted. There is no fee for camping, but donations are accepted. Open year-round, weather permitting.

Directions: From Red Bluff, drive east on Highway 36 to Susanville. In Susanville, turn north on U.S. 395 and drive 45 miles to Post Camp Road. Turn right on Post Camp Road and drive 2.5 miles east to the campground.

Contact: Bureau of Land Management, Eagle Lake Field Office, 530/257-0456, fax 530/257-4831.

37 BATTLE CREEK

Rating: 7

on Battle Creek in Lassen National Forest
See map pages 496–497

This pretty spot offers easy access and streamside camping along Battle Creek. The trout fishing can be good in May, June, and early July, when the creek is stocked by the Department of Fish and Game, which plants 23,000 rainbow trout and 2,000 smaller brook trout. Many people drive right by without knowing there is a stream here and that the fishing can be good. The elevation is 4,800 feet.

RV sites, facilities: There are 38 sites for RVs or tents and 12 tent sites. Picnic tables and fire grills are provided. Drinking water, flush and vault toilets, and a day-use picnic area are available. Supplies can be obtained in the town of Mineral. Leashed pets are permitted.

Reservations, fees: Reservations are not accepted. The fee is $14 per night. A senior discount is available. Open late April through October, weather permitting.

Directions: From Red Bluff, turn east on Highway 36 and drive 39 miles to the campground (if you reach Mineral, you have gone two miles too far).

Contact: Lassen National Forest, Almanor Ranger District, 530/258-2141, fax 530/258-5194.

38 MILL CREEK RESORT

Rating: 7

on Mill Creek near Lassen National Forest
See map pages 496–497

This is a great spot, surrounded by Lassen National Forest and within close range of the southern Highway 89 entrance to Lassen Volcanic National Park. It is set at 4,800 feet along oft-bypassed Highway 172. A highlight here is Mill Creek (to reach it, turn south on the Forest Service road in town and drive to a parking area at the end of the road along the stream), where there is a great easy walk along the stream and fair trout fishing.

RV sites, facilities: There are 16 sites for RVs up to 22 feet or tents, eight with full hookups (30 amps). About half are taken by long-term rentals. Nine one- and two-bedroom cabins are also available. Picnic tables and fire rings are provided. Drinking water and vault toilets are available. Showers, a coin-operated laundry, a small grocery store, limited cell phone reception, and a café are also available. Some facilities are wheelchair-accessible. Leashed pets are permitted.

Reservations, fees: Reservations are accepted. The fee is $12–20 per night. Campsites are open May through October. Cabins are available year-round.

Directions: From Red Bluff, drive 43 miles east on Highway 36 to the town of Mineral and the junction with Highway 172. Turn right and drive six miles to the town of Mill Creek. In Mill Creek, look for the sign for Mill Creek Resort on the right side of the road.

Contact: Mill Creek Resort, 530/595-4449 or 888/595-4449, website: www.millcreekresort.net.

39 CHILDS MEADOW RESORT

Rating: 8

near Mill Creek
See map pages 496–497

Childs Meadow Resort is an 18-acre resort set at 5,000 feet elevation. It features many recreation options, including catch-and-release fishing one mile away at Mill Creek. There are also a number of trails nearby for horseback riding. The trailhead for the Spencer Meadow Trail is just east of the resort along Highway 36. The trail provides a 12-mile route (one-way) to Spencer Meadow and an effervescent spring that is the source of Mill Creek.

RV sites, facilities: There are 26 sites, 12 drive-through sites with full hookups for RVs (20, 30, 50 amps) and 14 sites for tents, with facilities available for groups. Picnic tables and fire rings are provided. Restrooms, drinking water, flush toilets, modem access, limited cell phone reception, and showers are available. A coin-operated laundry, a store, a restaurant, a group picnic area, a meeting room, and horseshoes are on-site. Leashed pets are permitted.

Reservations, fees: Reservations are accepted. The fee is $15–20 per night. Major credit cards are accepted. Open mid-May through October, weather permitting.

Directions: From Red Bluff, drive east on Highway 36 for 43 miles to the town of Mineral. Continue east on Highway 36 for 10 miles to the resort on the left.

Contact: Childs Meadow Resort, 530/595-3383, website: www.ChildsMeadowResort.com.

40 GURNSEY CREEK

Rating: 7

in Lassen National Forest
See map pages 496–497

This camp is set at 4,700 feet in Lassen National Forest, with extremely easy access off Highway 36. The camp is on the headwaters of little Gurnsey Creek, a highlight of the surrounding Lost Creek Plateau. Gurnsey Creek runs downstream and pours into Deer Creek, a good trout stream with access along narrow, winding Highway 32 to the nearby south.

RV sites, facilities: There are 52 sites for RVs or tents. Picnic tables and fire grills are provided. Drinking water and vault toilets are available. Supplies are available in Mineral. Leashed pets are permitted.

Reservations, fees: Reservations are not accepted. The fee is $12 per night. A senior discount is available. Open May through October, weather permitting.

Directions: From Red Bluff, drive east on Highway 36 for 55 miles (five miles east of Childs

Meadow). Turn left at the campground entrance road and drive a short distance to the campground.

Contact: Lassen National Forest, Almanor Ranger District, 530/258-2141, fax 530/258-5194.

41 WARNER CREEK

Rating: 6

in Lassen National Forest
See map pages 496–497

Some people find this camp by accident. They are driving to the Warner/Drakesbad entrance of Lassen Volcanic National Park and discover this small, primitive camp on the way in, always an option during crowded weekends. It is set at 5,000 feet in elevation along little Warner Creek, a tributary of the North Fork Feather River. Warner Valley is two miles to the north, and the entrance to Lassen Park is another six miles.

RV sites, facilities: There are 13 sites for RVs up to 22 feet or tents. Picnic tables and fire grills are provided. Vault toilets are available. No drinking water is available. Leashed pets are permitted.

Reservations, fees: Reservations are not accepted. The fee is $10 per night. A senior discount is available. Open late May through October, weather permitting.

Directions: From Red Bluff, take Highway 36 east to Chester. In Chester, turn left on Feather River Drive and drive .75 mile to County Road 312. Bear left and drive 5.5 miles to a fork. Bear right (still on County Road 312) and drive one mile to the campground on the right.

Contact: Lassen National Forest, Almanor Ranger District, 530/258-2141, fax 530/258-5194.

42 LAST CHANCE CREEK

Rating: 7

near Lake Almanor
See map pages 496–497

This secluded camp is set at 4,500 feet, adjacent to where Last Chance Creek empties into the north end of Lake Almanor. It is an unpublicized PG&E camp that is known primarily by locals and gets missed almost every time by out-of-towners. The adjacent lake area is a breeding ground in the spring for white pelicans, and the beauty of these birds in large flocks can be extraordinary.

RV sites, facilities: There are 12 sites for RVs up to 30 feet or tents, and 13 group campsites. Picnic tables and fire grills are provided. Drinking water and vault toilets are available. Leashed pets are permitted.

Reservations, fees: Reservations are required for the group camps. The fees are $15 per night for individual sites and $20 for group sites, plus $1 per dog per night. Group sites require a two-night minimum stay and a three-night stay on holidays. Open mid-May through September, weather permitting.

Directions: From Red Bluff, take Highway 36 east to Chester and continue for two miles over the causeway (at the north end of Lake Almanor). About .25 mile after crossing the causeway, turn left on the campground access road and drive 2.1 miles to the campground.

Contact: PG&E Land Projects, 916/386-5164, fax 916/923-7044, website: www.pge.com/recreation.

43 LASSEN VIEW RESORT

Rating: 8

at Lake Almanor east of Red Bluff
See map pages 496–497

This is a classic fishing camp, designed from start to finish with fishing in mind, yet with other facilities and recreation available. It is near one of the best fishing spots on the entire lake, Big Springs, at the mouth of the Hamilton Branch. After launching a boat or renting one at Lassen View, Big Springs is just a five-minute ride, "right around the corner," as they say here. This is where salmon congregate in the spring, and big brown and rainbow trout show up in the fall to feed on the lake's huge supply of pond smelt. The camp is rustic but friendly, and the folks here can help put you onto the fish. Lake Almanor is a big, beautiful lake set at 4,600 feet, ringed by conifers and kept full most of the year. Note that the RV sites are often completely booked for the entire summer with long-term rentals.

RV sites, facilities: There are 59 sites, including 10 drive-through sites, with partial or full hookups (30 amps), including cable TV, for RVs or tents, and 13 cabins. Picnic tables and fire rings are provid-

ed. Drinking water, showers, modem access, limited cell phone reception, and flush toilets are available. A small store, tackle shop, a small marina, boat rentals, a boat dock, and a fish-cleaning facility are also available. A fishing guide can be hired through the store. Volleyball and horseshoes are on-site, and a swimming area is nearby. An ATM is within five miles. Leashed pets are permitted.

Reservations, fees: Reservations are recommended. The fee is $23–26 per night, plus $3 per additional vehicle and $5 per pet per day. Long-term rentals are available. Major credit cards are accepted. Open May through October.

Directions: From Red Bluff, take Highway 36 east for 44 miles to the junction with Highway 89. Continue east on Highway 36/89 to Chester and drive through Chester to the junction with County Road A13. Turn right (south) and drive about four miles to the junction with Highway 147. Turn right on Highway 147 and drive .9 mile to the well-signed camp entrance on the right.

Contact: Lassen View Resort, 530/596-3437, fax 530/596-4437.

44 NORTHSHORE CAMPGROUND

Rating: 7

on Lake Almanor
See map pages 496–497

This is a large, privately developed park on the northern shoreline of beautiful Lake Almanor. The park has 37 acres, with the camp set amid pine tree cover.

RV sites, facilities: There are 94 sites, including a few drive-through sites, with partial hookups (20, 30 amps) for RVs up to 40 feet, and 34 tent sites. About 35 of the RV sites are summer rentals. Picnic tables and fire rings are provided. Drinking water, showers, flush toilets, modem access, limited cell phone reception, a boat ramp, and a dock are available. A playground and lending library are nearby. An ATM is within two miles. Leashed pets are permitted.

Reservations, fees: Reservations are accepted. The fee is $21–34 per night, plus $6 per person for more than two people. Monthly rentals are available. Major credit cards are accepted. Open April through October.

Directions: From Red Bluff, take Highway 36

east for 44 miles to the junction with Highway 89. Drive east on Highway 36/89; the camp is two miles past Chester on the right.

Contact: Northshore Campground, 530/258-3376, fax 530/258-2838, website: www.northshore campground.com.

45 ELAM

Rating: 7

on Deer Creek in Lassen National Forest
See map pages 496–497

Of the campgrounds set on Deer Creek along Highway 32, Elam gets the most use. It is the first stopping point visitors arrive at while heading west on narrow, curvy Highway 32, and it has an excellent day-use picnic area. The stream here is stocked with rainbow trout in late spring and early summer, with good access for fishing. It is a pretty area, set where Elam Creek enters Deer Creek. A Forest Service Information Center is nearby in Chester. If the camp has too many people to suit your style, consider other more distant and primitive camps downstream on Deer Creek. The elevation here is 4,600 feet.

RV sites, facilities: There are 15 sites for RVs or tents. Picnic tables and fire grills are provided. Drinking water and vault toilets are available. Leashed pets are permitted.

Reservations, fees: Reservations are not accepted. The fee is $12 per night. A senior discount is available. Open mid-April through October, weather permitting.

Directions: From Red Bluff, take Highway 36 east for 44 miles to the junction with Highway 89. Continue east on Highway 36/89 to the junction with Highway 32. Turn south on Highway 32 and drive three miles to the campground on the right side of the road. Trailers are not recommended.

Contact: Lassen National Forest, Almanor Ranger District, 530/258-2141, fax 530/258-5194.

46 POTATO PATCH

Rating: 7

on Deer Creek in Lassen National Forest
See map pages 496–497

You get good hiking and fishing at this camp. It is set beside Deer Creek at 3,400 feet elevation, with good access for trout fishing. This is a wild trout stream in this area, and the use of artificials with a single barbless hook and catch-and-release are required along much of the river; check DFG regulations. An excellent fisherman's trail is available along the river.

RV sites, facilities: There are 12 sites for RVs or tents and 20 sites for tents. Picnic tables and fire grills are provided. Drinking water and vault toilets are available. Leashed pets are permitted.

Reservations, fees: Reservations are not accepted. The fee is $12 per night. A senior discount is available. Open April through October, weather permitting.

Directions: From Red Bluff, take Highway 36 east for 44 miles to the junction with Highway 89. Continue east on Highway 36/89 to the junction with Highway 32. Turn south on Highway 32 and drive 11 miles to the campground on the right side of the road. Trailers are not recommended.

Contact: Lassen National Forest, Almanor Ranger District, 530/258-2141, fax 530/258-5194.

47 LAKE ALMANOR CAMPGROUND

Rating: 7

on Lake Almanor
See map pages 496–497

What you get here is a series of four campgrounds along the southwest shore of Lake Almanor provided by PG&E as mitigation for its hydroelectric activities on the Feather River system. The camps are set upstream from the dam, with boat ramps available on each side of the dam. This is a pretty spot, with giant Almanor ringed by lodgepole pines and firs. The lake is usually full, or close to it, well into summer, with Mount Lassen in the distance to the north—bring your camera. Though it can take a day or two to find the fish, once that effort is made, fishing is good for large trout and salmon in the spring and fall and for smallmouth bass in the summer.

RV sites, facilities: There are 131 sites for RVs up to 30 feet or tents. Picnic tables and fire grills are provided. Drinking water, vault toilets, and an RV dump station are available. Leashed pets are permitted.

Reservations, fees: Reservations are not accepted.

The fee is $15 per night, plus $3 per night per additional vehicle, $7 per night per extra RV, and $1 per pet per night. Open May through September.

Directions: From Red Bluff, take Highway 36 east for 44 miles to the junction with Highway 89. Continue east on Highway 36/89 to Lake Almanor and the next junction with Highway 89 (two miles before reaching Chester). Turn right on Highway 89 and drive eight miles to the southwest end of Lake Almanor. Turn left at your choice of four campground entrances.

Contact: PG&E Land Projects, 916/386-5164, fax 916/923-7044, website: www.pge.com/recreation.

48 ALMANOR NORTH AND SOUTH

Rating: 8

on Lake Almanor in Lassen National Forest
See map pages 496–497

This is one of Lake Almanor's best-known and most popular Forest Service campgrounds. It is set along the western shore of beautiful Almanor at 4,519 feet elevation, directly across from the beautiful Almanor Peninsula. There is an excellent view of Mount Lassen to the north, along with gorgeous sunrises. A 10-mile recreation trail runs right through the campground and is excellent for biking or hiking. This section of the lake provides good fishing for smallmouth bass in the summer, best using live crickets for bait. There are two linked campgrounds, named North and South.

RV sites, facilities: There are 101 sites for RVs or tents, including 15 sites for tents only, and a group camp for up to 100 people or 20 RVs. Picnic tables and fire grills are provided. Drinking water and vault and pit toilets are available. A boat ramp and beach area is nearby. Some facilities are wheelchair-accessible. Leashed pets are permitted.

Reservations, fees: Reservations are accepted with a $9 reservation fee for some sites at 877/444-6777 or www.reserveusa.com. Other sites are available on a first-come, first-served basis. The fee is $15 per night. Reservations are required for the group camp, which is $88 per night. A senior discount is available. Open May through October, weather permitting.

Directions: From Red Bluff, take Highway 36 east for 44 miles to the junction with Highway

89. Continue east on Highway 36/89 to Lake Almanor and the next junction with Highway 89 (two miles before reaching Chester). Turn right on Highway 89 and drive six miles to County Road 310. Turn left on County Road 310 and drive one mile to the campground.

Contact: Lassen National Forest, Almanor Ranger District, 530/258-2141, fax 530/258-5194.

49 YELLOW CREEK

Rating: 8

in Humbug Valley
See map pages 496–497

Yellow Creek is one of Cal Trout's pet projects. It's a beautiful stream for fly fishers, demanding the best from skilled anglers—approaching with complete stealth, making delicate casts with long leaders and small dry flies during the evening rise. This camp is set at 4,400 feet in Humbug Valley and provides access to this stretch of water. An option is to fish Butt Creek, much easier fishing for small, planted rainbow trout, with access available along the road on the way in.

RV sites, facilities: There are 10 sites for RVs or tents. Picnic tables and fire grills are provided. Drinking water and vault toilets are available. Leashed pets are permitted.

Reservations, fees: Reservations are not accepted. The fee is $13 per night, plus $3 per night per additional vehicle, $7 per night per extra RV, and $1 per pet per night. Open May through September.

Directions: From Oroville, drive north on Highway 70 to Belden. At Belden, turn left on Forest Road 26N26 and drive north about 11 miles to the campground entrance road on the left side of the road.

Contact: PG&E Land Projects, 916/386-5164, fax 916/923-7044, website: www.pge.com/recreation.

50 PONDEROSA FLAT

Rating: 7

on Butt Lake
See map pages 496–497

This camp is at the north end of Butt Lake, the little brother to nearby Lake Almanor. It is a

CALIFORNIA

fairly popular camp, with the boat ramp a prime attraction, allowing campers/anglers a lakeside spot with easy access. Technically, Butt is the "afterbay" for Almanor, fed by a four-mile-long pipe with water from Almanor. What occurs is that pond smelt from Almanor get ground up in the Butt Lake powerhouse, providing a huge amount of feed for trout at the head of the lake; that's why the trout often get huge at Butt Lake. The one downer here is that lake drawdowns are common, exposing tree stumps.

RV sites, facilities: There are 63 sites for RVs or tents. Picnic tables and fire grills are provided. Drinking water, vault toilets, and a boat ramp are available. Leashed pets are permitted.

Reservations, fees: Reservations are not accepted. The fee is $15 per night, plus $3 per additional vehicle per night, $7 per extra RV per night, and $1 per pet per night. Open May through October, weather permitting.

Directions: From Red Bluff, take Highway 36 east for 44 miles to the junction with Highway 89. Continue east on Highway 36/89 to Lake Almanor and the next junction with Highway 89 (two miles before reaching Chester). Turn right on Highway 89 and drive about seven miles to Butt Valley Road. Turn right on Butt Valley Road and drive 3.2 miles to the campground on the right side of the road.

Contact: PG&E Land Projects, 916/386-5164, fax 916/923-7044, website: www.pge.com/recreation.

51 COOL SPRINGS

Rating: 7

on Butt Lake

See map pages 496–497

One of two camps at Butt Lake, Cool Springs is about midway down the lake on its eastern shore, 2.5 miles south of Ponderosa Flat. Cool Springs Creek enters the lake near the camp. (For more information about Butt Lake, see the previous entry for Ponderosa Flat.)

RV sites, facilities: There are 25 sites for RVs or tents and five walk-in sites. Picnic tables and fire grills are provided. Drinking water, vault toilets, and a boat ramp are available. Leashed pets are permitted.

Reservations, fees: Reservations are not accept-

ed. The fee is $15 per night, plus $3 per additional vehicle per night, $7 per extra RV per night, and $1 per pet per night. Open May through October, weather permitting.

Directions: From Red Bluff, take Highway 36 east for 44 miles to the junction with Highway 89. Continue east on Highway 36/89 to Lake Almanor and the next junction with Highway 89 (two miles before reaching Chester). Turn right on Highway 89 and drive about seven miles to Butt Valley Road. Turn right on Butt Valley Road and drive 5.7 miles to the campground on the right side of the road.

Contact: PG&E Land Projects, 916/386-5164, fax 916/923-7044, website: www.pge.com/recreation.

52 CHERRY HILL

Rating: 7

on Butte Creek in Lassen National Forest

See map pages 496–497

The camp is set at 4,700 feet elevation along little Butte Creek at the foot of Cherry Hill, just downstream from the confluence of Colby Creek and Butte Creek. It is also on the western edge of the alpine zone in Lassen National Forest. A four-mile drive to the north, much of it along Colby Creek, will take visitors to the Colby Mountain Lookout at 6,002 feet for a dramatic view of the Ishi Wilderness to the west. Nearby to the south is Philbrook Reservoir.

RV sites, facilities: There are 20 sites for RVs or tents and six walk-in tent sites. Picnic tables and fire grills are provided. Drinking water and vault toilets are available. Supplies are available in the town of Butte Meadows. An ATM is within three miles. Leashed pets are permitted.

Reservations, fees: Reservations are not accepted. The fee is $11 per night. A senior discount is available. Open May through September, weather permitting.

Directions: From Chico, drive north on Highway 32 to the junction with Humboldt Road (well past the town of Forest Ranch). Turn right and drive five miles to Butte Meadows. Continue on Humboldt Road for three miles to the campground on the right side of the road.

Contact: Lassen National Forest, Almanor Ranger District, 530/258-2141, fax 530/258-5194.

53 BUTTE MEADOWS

Rating: 6

on Butte Creek in Lassen National Forest
See map pages 496–497

On hot summer days, when a cold stream sounds even better than a cold drink, Butte Meadows provides a hideout in the national forest east of Chico. This is a summer camp situated along Butte Creek, which is stocked with 5,000 rainbow trout by the Department of Fish and Game. Nearby Doe Mill Ridge and the surrounding Lassen National Forest can provide a good side-trip adventure. The camp elevation is 4,600 feet.

RV sites, facilities: There are 13 sites for RVs or tents. Fire grills and picnic tables are provided. Drinking water and vault toilets are available. Supplies are available in Butte Meadows. Leashed pets are permitted.

Reservations, fees: Reservations are not accepted. The fee is $10 per night. A senior discount is available. Open late April through October, weather permitting.

Directions: From Chico, drive about 15 miles north on Highway 32 to the town of Forest Ranch. Continue on Highway 32 for another nine miles. Turn right on Humboldt Road and drive five miles to Butte Meadows.

Contact: Lassen National Forest, Almanor Ranger District, 530/258-2141, fax 530/258-5194.

54 PHILBROOK RESERVOIR

Rating: 7

in Lassen National Forest
See map pages 496–497

Philbrook Reservoir is set at 5,600 feet on the western mountain slopes above Chico, on the southwest edge of Lassen National Forest. It is a pretty lake, though subject to late-season drawdowns, with a scenic lookout a short distance from camp. The lake is loaded with small trout— a dink here, a dink there, a dink everywhere.

RV sites, facilities: There are 20 sites for RVs up to 30 feet or tents. Picnic tables and fire grills are provided. Drinking water and vault toilets are available. Trailer and car-top boat launches are available. Leashed pets are permitted.

Reservations, fees: Reservations are not accepted. The fee is $15 per night, plus $3 per night per additional vehicle, $7 per night per extra RV, and $1 per pet per night. Open May through September.

Directions: At Orland on I-5, take the Highway 32/Chico exit and drive to Chico and the junction with Highway 99. Turn south on Highway 99 and drive to Skyway Road/Paradise (in south Chico). Turn east on Skyway Road, drive through Paradise, and continue for 27 miles to Humbug Summit Road. Turn right and drive two miles to Philbrook Road. Turn right and drive 3.1 miles to the campground entrance road. Turn right and drive .5 mile to the campground.

Contact: PG&E Land Projects, 916/386-5164, fax 916/923-7044, website: www.pge.com/recreation.

55 QUEEN LILY

Rating: 7

on the North Fork of the Feather River in Plumas National Forest
See map pages 496–497

The North Fork Feather River is a prime destination for camping and trout fishing, especially for families. This is one of three camps along the river on Caribou Road. This stretch of river is well stocked. Insider's note: The first 150 yards of river below the dam at Caribou typically have large but elusive trout.

RV sites, facilities: There are 12 sites for RVs up to 26 feet or tents. Picnic tables and fire grills are provided. Drinking water, flush toilets, and limited cell phone reception are available. A grocery store, a coin-operated laundry, and an RV dump station are within three miles. Leashed pets are permitted.

Reservations, fees: Reservations are not accepted. The fee is $16 per night. A senior discount is available. Open May through September.

Directions: From Oroville, drive north on Highway 70 to Caribou Road (two miles past Belden). Turn left on Caribou Road and drive about three miles to the campground on the left side of the road.

Contact: Plumas National Forest, Mt. Hough Ranger District, 530/283-0555, fax 530/283-1821; Northwest Park Management, 530/283-5559, fax 530/283-0159.

CALIFORNIA

56 NORTH FORK

Rating: 7

on the North Fork of the Feather River in Plumas National Forest

See map pages 496–497

This camp is between Queen Lily to the nearby north and Gansner Bar camp to the nearby south, all three set on the North Fork Feather River. The elevation is 2,600 feet. Fishing access is good and trout plants are decent, making for a good fishing/camping trip. Note: All three camps are extremely popular on summer weekends.

RV sites, facilities: There are 20 sites for RVs up to 32 feet or tents. Picnic tables and fire grills are provided. Drinking water, flush toilets, and an RV dump station are available. A grocery store and a coin-operated laundry are within three miles. Leashed pets are permitted.

Reservations, fees: Reservations are not accepted. The fee is $16 per night. A senior discount is available. Open May through September.

Directions: From Oroville, drive north on Highway 70 to Caribou Road (two miles past Belden at Gansner Ranch Ranger Station). Turn left on Caribou Road and drive about two miles to the campground on the left side of the road.

Contact: Plumas National Forest, Mt. Hough Ranger District, 530/283-0555, fax 530/283-1821; Northwest Park Management, 530/283-5559, fax 530/283-0159.

57 GANSNER BAR

Rating: 7

on the North Fork of the Feather River in Plumas National Forest

See map pages 496–497

Gansner Bar is the first of three camps along Caribou Road, which runs parallel to the North Fork Feather River. Of the three, this one receives the highest trout stocks of rainbow trout in the 10- to 12-inch class. Caribou Road runs upstream to Caribou Dam, with stream and fishing access along almost all of it. The camps often fill on summer weekends.

RV sites, facilities: There are 14 sites for RVs up to 30 feet or tents. Picnic tables and fire grills are

provided. Drinking water and flush toilets are available. A grocery store and a coin-operated laundry are within one mile. An ATM and RV dump station are nearby. Some facilities are wheelchair-accessible. Leashed pets are permitted.

Reservations, fees: Reservations are not accepted. The fee is $16 per night. A senior discount is available. Open April through October.

Directions: From Oroville, drive north on Highway 70 to Caribou Road (two miles past Belden). Turn left on Caribou Road and drive a short distance to the campground on the left side of the road.

Contact: Plumas National Forest, Mt. Hough Ranger District, 530/283-0555, fax 530/283-1821; Northwest Park Management, 530/283-5559, fax 530/283-0159.

58 HALLSTED

Rating: 7

on the North Fork of the Feather River in Plumas National Forest

See map pages 496–497

Easy highway access and a pretty trout stream right alongside have made this an extremely popular campground. It typically fills on summer weekends. Hallsted is set on the East Branch North Fork Feather River at 2,800 feet elevation. The river is stocked with trout by the Department of Fish and Game.

RV sites, facilities: There are 20 sites for RVs up to 30 feet or tents. Picnic tables and fire grills are provided. Drinking water and flush toilets are available. A grocery store and an ATM are within a quarter mile. Leashed pets are permitted.

Reservations, fees: Reservations are accepted with a $9 reservation fee at 877/444-6777 or www.reserveusa.com. The fee is $16 per night. A senior discount is available. Open May through September.

Directions: From Oroville, drive northeast on Highway 70 to Belden. Continue past Belden for about 12 miles to the campground entrance on the right side of the road. Turn right and drive .25 mile to the campground.

Contact: Plumas National Forest, Mt. Hough Ranger District, 530/283-0555, fax 530/283-1821; Northwest Park Management, 530/283-5559, fax 530/283-0159.

CALIFORNIA

59 BOULDER CREEK

Rating: 7

at Antelope Lake in Plumas National Forest
See map pages 496–497

Antelope Lake is a pretty mountain lake circled by conifers with nice campsites and good trout fishing. It is set at 5,000 feet in remote eastern Plumas National Forest, far enough away so the marginally inclined never make the trip. Campgrounds are at each end of the lake (this one is just north of Lone Rock at the north end), with a boat ramp at Lost Cove on the east side of the lake. The lake isn't huge, but it is big enough, with 15 miles of shoreline and little islands, coves, and peninsulas to give it an intimate feel.

RV sites, facilities: There are 70 sites for RVs or tents. Picnic tables and fire grills are provided. Drinking water, vault toilets, and limited cell phone reception are available. An RV dump station, a boat ramp, an ATM, and a grocery store are nearby. Leashed pets are permitted.

Reservations, fees: Reservations are accepted with a $9 reservation fee at 877/444-6777 or www .reserveusa.com. The fee is $16–22 per night, plus $5 per additional vehicle per night. A senior discount is available. Open May through October.

Directions: From Red Bluff, drive east on Highway 36 to Susanville and U.S. 395. Turn south on U.S. 395 and drive about 10 miles (one mile past Janesville) to County Road 208. Turn right on County Road 208 (signed Antelope Lake) and drive about 15 miles to a Y (one mile before Antelope Lake). Turn left at the Y and drive four miles to the campground entrance on the right side of the road (on the northwest end of the lake).

Contact: Plumas National Forest, Mt. Hough Ranger District, 530/283-0555, fax 530/283-1821; Northwest Park Management, 530/283-5559, fax 530/283-0159.

60 LONE ROCK

Rating: 9

at Antelope Lake in Plumas National Forest
See map pages 496–497

This camp provides an option to nearby Boulder Creek, to the immediate north at the northwest shore of Antelope Lake. (For more information, see the previous entry for Boulder Creek.) The elevation is 5,000 feet. Campfire programs are offered in the summer at the on-site amphitheater.

RV sites, facilities: There are 86 sites for RVs up to 30 feet or tents. Picnic tables and fire grills are provided. Drinking water, vault toilets, and limited cell phone reception are available. An RV dump station, a boat ramp, an ATM, and a grocery store are nearby. Leashed pets are permitted.

Reservations, fees: Reservations are accepted with a $9 reservation fee at 877/444-6777 or www .reserveusa.com. The fee is $16–18 per night, plus $4 per additional vehicle per night. A senior discount is available. Open May through October.

Directions: From Red Bluff, drive east on Highway 36 to Susanville and U.S. 395. Go south on U.S. 395 and drive about 10 miles (one mile past Janesville) to County Road 208. Turn right on County Road 208 (signed Antelope Lake) and drive about 15 miles to a Y (one mile before Antelope Lake). Turn left at the Y and drive three miles to the campground entrance on the right side of the road (on the northwest end of the lake).

Contact: Plumas National Forest, Mt. Hough Ranger District, 530/283-0555, fax 530/283-1821; Northwest Park Management, 530/283-5559, fax 530/283-0159.

61 LONG POINT

Rating: 7

at Antelope Lake in Plumas National Forest
See map pages 496–497

Long Point is a pretty camp set on a peninsula that extends well into Antelope Lake, facing Lost Cove. The lake's boat ramp is at Lost Cove, a three-mile drive around the northeast shore. Trout fishing is often good here, with a wide variety of sizes, from the little stocked Slim Jim rainbow trout on up to some large brown trout. A nature trail is also available.

RV sites, facilities: There are 38 sites for RVs up to 30 feet or tents, and four group units for up to 25 people at each. Picnic tables and fire grills are provided. Drinking water, vault toilets, and limited cell phone reception are available. A grocery store, a boat ramp, an ATM, and an

CALIFORNIA

RV dump stations are nearby. Leashed pets are permitted.

Reservations, fees: Reservations are accepted with a $9 reservation fee at 877/444-6777 or www.reserveusa.com. The fees are $16–18 per night for single sites, $28 per night for double sites, and $45 per night for group sites. A senior discount is available. Open May through October.

Directions: From Red Bluff, drive east on Highway 36 to Susanville and U.S. 395. Go south on U.S. 395 and drive about 10 miles (one mile past Janesville) to County Road 208. Turn right on County Road 208 (signed Antelope Lake) and drive about 15 miles to a Y (one mile before Antelope Lake). Turn right at the Y and drive one mile to the campground entrance on the left side of the road.

Contact: Plumas National Forest, Greenville Work Center, Mt. Hough Ranger District, 530/284-7126, fax 530/284-6211; Northwest Park Management, 530/283-5559, fax 530/283-0159.

62 HONEY LAKE CAMPGROUND

Rating: 4

near Milford

See map pages 496–497

For newcomers, Honey Lake is a strange-looking place—a vast, shallow lake set on the edge of the desert of the Great Basin. The campground is set at 4,385 feet and covers 30 acres, most of it overlooking the lake. There are a lot of junipers and a few aspens and pines nearby, and a waterfowl management area is along the north shore of the lake. Fishing is pretty much zilch. The lake is 26 miles across, and on rare flat calm evenings, the sunsets are spectacular here.

RV sites, facilities: There are 62 sites, all drive-through, for RVs or tents, most with partial or full hookups (30 amps), plus 19 mobile homes and trailers available. Picnic tables are provided. Drinking water, restrooms, showers, cell phone reception, a laundry room, an RV dump station, propane, a grocery store, a restaurant, a tavern, a playground, ice, modem hookups, and a game room are available. An ATM is within nine miles. Some facilities are wheelchair-accessible. Leashed pets are permitted.

Reservations, fees: Reservations are accepted. The fee is $12.50–19.95 per night, plus $3.50 per person per night for more than two people. Long-term rentals are available. A senior discount is available. Open year-round.

Directions: From Susanville on U.S. 395, drive 17 miles south (if you reach Milford, you have gone two miles too far) to the campground on the west side of the highway. It is 65 miles north of Reno.

Contact: Honey Lake Campground, 530/253-2508, website: www.honeylakecampground.com.

California

Chapter 16

Mendocino and Wine Country

see Shasta
and Trinity
pages 460–461

see Redwood
Empire
pages 430–431

see Sacramento and
Gold Country
pages 564–565

Black Butte
Lake

East Park
Reservoir

Stony Gorge
Reservoir

Snow
Mountain
Wilderness

Yolla Bolly Middle
Eel Wilderness

Mendocino

National

Forest

6

38
37
36
35

Lake
Pillsbury

17-18
19
20
34
31-33

16

1

C o a s t   R a n g e s

River

Eel

5 mi

5 km

0

0

Lake
Mendocino

27-28
29

Willits

13
14
15

Laytonville

Leggett

Garberville

Westport

MacKerricher
State Park

2
3
4
5

Jackson State
Forest

12
11

7-10

Fort Bragg

21
22
23

Mendocino

Navarro River
Redwoods State Park

25

24

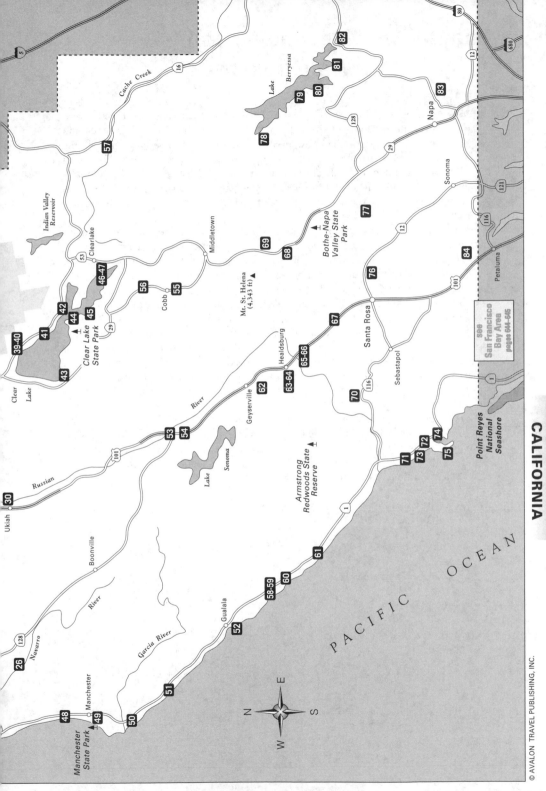

CALIFORNIA

© AVALON TRAVEL PUBLISHING, INC.

Chapter 16—Mendocino and Wine Country

For many people, this region offers the best possible combination of geography, weather, and outdoor activities around. The Mendocino coast is dramatic and remote, with several stellar state parks for hiking, while Sonoma Valley, in the heart of wine country, produces some of the most popular wines in the world. Add in the self-indulgent options of mud baths and hot springs at Calistoga and a dash of mainstream recreation at Clear Lake, Lake Berryessa, or any other lake, and you have a capsule summary of why the Mendocino coast and the wine country have turned into getaway favorites.

For many, this area is where people go for romance, fine cuisine, great wine, mineral springs, and anything else that comes to mind spur-of-the-moment. Such is a vacation in the Napa-Sonoma wine country, or on the beautiful Sonoma and Mendocino coasts.

This region wouldn't be the best of both worlds if there weren't options on the other end of the spectrum. Campgrounds set up primarily for family recreation are available at Clear Lake, Lake Berryessa, and Blue Lakes. If the shoe fits—and for many, it does—you can have a great time fishing, boating, and water-skiing.

The coast features a series of romantic hideaways and excellent adventuring and hiking. The Fort Bragg area alone has three state parks, all with outstanding recreation options, including several easy hikes, many amid redwoods and along pretty streams. Reservations are always required here far in advance for a chance at getting a campsite at a state park on a summer weekend. Fort Bragg also offers excellent fishing out of Noyo Harbor.

The driving tour of Highway 1 along the coast here is the fantasy of many, and it can live up to that fantasy if you don't mind the twists and turns of the road. Along the way, there are dozens of hidden beaches and untouched coastline where you can stop and explore and maybe play tag with the waves. The prize spots are MacKerricher State Park, Salt Point State Park, and Anchor Bay.

1 EEL RIVER

Rating: 8

in Mendocino National Forest
See map pages 524–525

This is a little-known spot, set in oak woodlands at the confluence of the Middle Fork of the Eel River and Black Butte River. The elevation is 1,500 feet, and it's often extremely hot in summer. Eel River is an ancient Native American campsite and a major archaeological site. For this reason, restoration has been limited and at times the camp is overgrown and weedy. Who cares, though? After all, you're camping.

RV sites, facilities: There are 16 sites for RVs up to 21 feet or tents. Picnic tables and fire grills are provided. Drinking water and vault toilets are available. Garbage must be packed out. Leashed pets are permitted.

Reservations, fees: Reservations are not accepted. The fee is $6 per night. A senior discount is available. Open May through October.

Directions: From Willits, drive north on U.S. 101 for 13 miles to Longvale and the junction with Highway 162. Turn northeast on Highway 162 and drive to Covelo. Continue east on Highway 162 for 13 miles to the campground.

Contact: Mendocino National Forest, Covelo Ranger District, 707/983-6118, fax 707/983-8004.

2 WESTPORT UNION LANDING STATE BEACH

Rating: 8

overlooking the Pacific Ocean
See map pages 524–525

The northern Mendocino coast is remote, beautiful, and gets far less people pressure than the Fort Bragg area. That is the key to its appeal. The campsites here are on an ocean bluff. It can get windy, but the reward is the view. This park covers more than three miles of rugged and scenic coastline. There are magnificent views, sunsets, and tree-covered mountains that can provide great opportunities for photos. Several small sandy beaches, and one large beach at the mouth of Howard Creek, provide some good spots for surf fishing. Several species of rockfish and abalone can be taken when tides and ocean conditions are right. But note that the surf here can surge, discouraging all but the hardy. The park was named for two early-day communities, Westport and Union Landing, settlements famous for supply lumber and rail ties.

RV sites, facilities: There are 100 primitive sites for RVs of any length or tents. Picnic tables and fire rings are provided. Drinking water and vault toilets are available. A grocery store is nearby. Leashed pets are permitted.

Reservations, fees: Reservations are not accepted. The fee is $8–11 per night. A senior discount is available. Open year-round.

Directions: From Fort Bragg, drive north on Highway 1 to Westport. In Westport, continue north on Highway 1 for three miles to the campground entrance on the west side of the road.

Contact: Westport Union Landing State Beach, 707/937-5804, fax 707/937-2953.

3 WESTPORT BEACH RV AND CAMPING

Rating: 8

overlooking the Pacific Ocean
See map pages 524–525

Westport Beach RV and Camping is set above the beach near the mouth of Wages Creek, with creekside sites available, some offering glimpses of the ocean. You will notice as you venture north from Fort Bragg that the number of vacationers in the area falls way off, providing a chance for quiet beaches and serene moments. The best nearby hiking is to the north out of the trailhead for the Sinkyone Wilderness. This campground was completely renovated in 2002.

RV sites, facilities: There are 75 sites for RVs with full hookups (30, 50 amps), some drive-through, 22 sites for tents only, and a two-bedroom house for rent. Picnic tables and fire rings are provided. Drinking water, coin-operated showers, flush toilets, an RV dump station, wood, and ice are available. Some facilities are wheelchair-accessible. Leashed pets are permitted.

Reservations, fees: Reservations are accepted. The fees are $28–32 per night for RV sites and $19 per night for tent sites, plus $1 per pet per night. Major credit cards are accepted. Open year-round.

CALIFORNIA

Directions: From Fort Bragg, drive north on Highway 1 to Westport. In Westport, continue north on Highway 1 for a half mile to the campground entrance on the west side of the highway.
Contact: Westport Beach RV and Camping, 707/964-2964, fax 707/964-8185, website: www.westportbeachrv.com.

4 HIDDEN VALLEY CAMPGROUND

Rating: 5

north of Willits

See map pages 524–525

The privately operated park is in a pretty valley, primarily oak/bay woodlands with a sprinkling of conifers. The most popular nearby recreation option is taking the Skunk Train in Willits for the ride out to the coast at Fort Bragg. There are also two golf courses within six miles.

RV sites, facilities: There are 55 sites, 16 with full hookups (30 amps) and 19 with partial hookups, for RVs up to 45 feet and tents. Picnic tables, fire grills, and modem access are provided, and some sites provide satellite TV. Restrooms, ice, firewood, horseshoes, a coin-operated laundry, limited cell phone reception, an RV dump station, and showers are available. An ATM is within 6.5 miles. Leashed pets are permitted.

Reservations, fees: Reservations are accepted. The fee is $18.50–24 per night for two campers, plus $3 per person for more than two people. Open year-round.

Directions: From Willits on U.S. 101, drive north for 6.5 miles on U.S. 101 to the campground on the east side (right) of the road.

Contact: Hidden Valley Campground, 707/459-2521.

5 MACKERRICHER STATE PARK

Rating: 9

overlooking the Pacific Ocean

See map pages 524–525

MacKerricher is a beautiful park on the Mendocino coast, a great destination for adventure and exploration. The camps are set in a coastal forest, with gorgeous walk-in sites. Nearby is a small beach, great tidepools, a rocky point where har-

bor seals hang out in the sun, a small lake (Cleone) with trout fishing, a great bike trail, and outstanding short hikes. The short jaunt around little Cleone Lake has many romantic spots, often tunneling through vegetation, then emerging for lake views. The coastal walk to the point to see seals and tidepools is equally captivating. For wheelchair users, there is a wheelchair-accessible trail to Laguna Point and also a route on a raised boardwalk that runs halfway around Cleone Lake, a former tidal lagoon. This park covers more than 1,530 acres of beach, bluff, headlands, dune, forest, and wetlands. That diverse landscape provides habitat for more than 90 species of birds, most in the vicinity of Cleone Lake. In winter and spring, the headland provides a good lookout for whale-watching.

RV sites, facilities: There are 142 sites for RVs up to 35 feet or tents and 10 walk-in sites. Picnic tables, fire rings, and food lockers are provided. Drinking water, flush toilets, coin-operated showers, and an RV dump station are available. Some facilities are wheelchair-accessible. Leashed pets are permitted.

Reservations, fees: Reservations are accepted with a $7.50 reservation fee at 800/444-PARK (800/444-7275) or www.reserveamerica.com. The fee is $12–15 per night. A senior discount is available. Open year-round.

Directions: From Fort Bragg, drive north on Highway 1 for three miles to the campground entrance on the left side of the road.

Contact: MacKerricher State Park, 707/964-9112; Mendocino District, 707/937-5804, fax 707/937-2953.

6 PLASKETT MEADOWS

Rating: 7

in Mendocino National Forest

See map pages 524–525

This is a little-known camp in the mountains near Plaskett Lakes, a pair of connected dot-sized mountain lakes that form the headwaters of little Plaskett Creek. Trout fishing is best at the westernmost of the two lakes. No motors are permitted on the lakes, and swimming is not recommended. The camp is set at an elevation of 6,000 feet. Note that Plaskett Lakes were drained to kill weeds and were first restocked with trout in summer 2002.

RV sites, facilities: There are 35 sites for RVs up to 20 feet or tents. Fire grills and picnic tables are provided. Drinking water and vault toilets are available. Some facilities are wheelchair-accessible. Leashed pets are permitted.

Reservations, fees: Reservations are not accepted. The fee is $5 per night. Open mid-June through mid-October.

Directions: In Willows on I-5, turn west on Highway 162 and drive toward the town of Elk Creek. Just after crossing the Stony Creek Bridge, turn north on County Road 306 and drive four miles. Turn left on Alder Springs Road/Forest Highway 7 and drive 31 miles to the campground on the left.

Contact: Mendocino National Forest, Grindstone Ranger District, Stonyford Work Center, 530/963-3128, fax 530/963-3173.

◢ WOODSIDE RV PARK AND CAMPGROUND

Rating: 7

in Fort Bragg
See map pages 524–525

This privately operated park is set up primarily for RVs. It covers nine acres, is somewhat wooded, and provides access to nearby Fort Bragg with ocean access close by. Note that about half of the RV sites are long-term rentals.

RV sites, facilities: There are 86 sites, some drive-through, with partial or full hookups (20, 30, 50 amps) for RVs up to 40 feet or tents, 18 sites for tents only, and a group site. Picnic tables and fire rings are provided. Restrooms, coin-operated showers, a recreation room, a sauna, an RV dump station, cable TV, modem access, limited cell phone reception, RV supplies, ice, wood, and a fish-cleaning table are available. Boating and fishing access and an ATM are available within one mile. Leashed pets are permitted.

Reservations, fees: Reservations are accepted at 800/207-8772. The fee is $19–27 per night, plus $5 per person per night for more than two people and $1 per pet per night. Major credit cards are accepted.

Directions: In Fort Bragg at the junction of High-

way 1 and Highway 20, drive south on Highway 1 for one mile to the campground on the west side of the highway.

Contact: Woodside RV Park and Campground, 707/964-3684, website: www.infortbragg.com /woodsiderv.

◪ DOLPHIN ISLE MARINA

Rating: 7

on the Noyo River in Fort Bragg
See map pages 524–525

Noyo Harbor is the headquarters of Fort Bragg—the place where everything begins in this area. For vacationers that includes wharfside restaurants, fishing trips, boat docks, and a chance for a nice stroll out to the Noyo Harbor jetty. This RV park is right at the marina, providing an ideal jump-off point for all of those adventures. Beach access is available one mile away. Note that half of the sites are booked for the entire summer season.

RV sites, facilities: There are 84 sites with partial or full hookups (30 amps) for RVs. Picnic tables are provided. Restrooms, hot showers (coin-operated), an RV dump station, a coin-operated laundry, cable TV, limited cell phone reception, a delicatessen, propane, a marina with gas and diesel, bait and tackle, a boat ramp, and a dock are available. An ATM is within one mile, and modem access is available within two miles. Some facilities are wheelchair-accessible. Leashed pets are permitted.

Reservations, fees: Reservations are accepted. The fee is $25 per night, plus $2 per person for more than two people, $6 for a second vehicle, and $2 per pet per night. Long-term rates are available. Major credit cards are accepted. Open year-round.

Directions: In Fort Bragg at the junction of Highway 1 and Highway 20, drive east on Highway 20 for .25 mile to South Harbor Drive. Turn left on South Harbor Drive and drive .25 mile to Basin Street. Turn right on Basin Street and drive one mile to the campground at the end of the road.

Contact: Dolphin Isle Marina, 707/964-4113, fax 707/964-7136.

CALIFORNIA

9 FORT BRAGG LEISURE TIME RV PARK

Rating: 5

in Fort Bragg
See map pages 524–525

This privately operated park offers horseshoes, badminton, and a covered group picnic area. The drive from Willits to Fort Bragg on Highway 20 is always a favorite, a curving two-laner through redwoods, not too slow, not too fast, best seen from the saddle of a Harley-Davidson. At the end of it is the coast, and just three miles inland is this campground in the sun belt, said to be out of the fog by breakfast. Within short drives are Noyo Harbor in Fort Bragg, Russian Gulch State Park, Mendocino to the south, and MacKerricher State Park to the north. In fact, there's so much in the area, you could explore for days.

RV sites, facilities: There are 82 sites, all drive-through, many with partial or full hookups (30 amps), for RVs up to 40 feet or tents. Picnic tables and fire rings are provided. Restrooms, coin-operated showers, cell phone reception, satellite TV, modem access, an RV dump station, and a coin-operated laundry are available. An ATM is within three miles. Some facilities are wheelchair-accessible. Leashed pets are permitted.

Reservations, fees: Reservations are accepted at 800/700-8542. The fee is $19.50–27.50 per night, plus $1 per additional vehicle per night and $2 per pet per night. A senior discount is available. Major credit cards are accepted. Open year-round.

Directions: In Fort Bragg at the junction of Highway 1 and Highway 20, turn east on Highway 20 and drive 2.5 miles to the campground entrance on the right side of the road.

Contact: Fort Bragg Leisure Time RV Park, 707/964-5994.

10 POMO CAMPGROUND AND RV PARK

Rating: 7

in Fort Bragg
See map pages 524–525

This park, covering 17 acres of lush, native vegetation near the ocean, is one of several camps on the Fort Bragg and Mendocino coast. Nearby Noyo Harbor offers busy restaurants, deep-sea fishing, a boat ramp, harbor, and a nice walk out to the Noyo Harbor jetty. Huckleberry picking is also an option. Many of the RV spaces are quite wide at this park.

RV sites, facilities: There are 94 sites, a few drive-through, with partial or full hookups (20, 30, 50 amps) for RVs, and 30 sites for tents. Picnic tables and fire rings are provided. Restrooms, hot showers (coin-operated), cable TV hookups, a convenience store, firewood, ice, RV supplies, modem access, limited cell phone reception, propane, a coin-operated laundry, an RV dump station, a fish-cleaning table, horseshoes, and a large grass playing field are available. An ATM is within two miles. Leashed pets are permitted.

Reservations, fees: Reservations are recommended in the summer. The fee is $22–30 per night, plus $3–10 per person for more than two people and $1 per pet per night. Open year-round.

Directions: In Fort Bragg at the junction of Highway 1 and Highway 20, drive south on Highway 1 for one mile to Tregoning Lane. Turn left (east) and drive a short distance to the park at the end of the road (17999 Tregoning Lane).

Contact: Pomo Campground and RV Park, 707/964-3373, fax 707/964-0619, website: www.infortbragg.com/pomorvpark.

11 JACKSON DEMONSTRATION STATE FOREST, CAMP 1

Rating: 7

near Fort Bragg
See map pages 524–525

Primitive campsites set in a vast forest of redwoods and Douglas fir are the prime attraction at Jackson Demonstration State Forest. Even though Highway 20 is a major connecting link to the coast in the summer, these camps get bypassed because they are primitive and largely unknown. Why? Because reaching them requires driving on dirt roads sometimes frequented by logging trucks, and there are no campground signs along the highway. This camp features lots of tree cover, with oaks, redwoods, and madrones. Some of the campsites are along the Noyo River, well-known among locals but completely missed by most others. A one-mile trail circles the campground. A DFG hatchery is next to the camp-

CALIFORNIA

ground, but note that no fishing is permitted in the river.

RV sites, facilities: There are 50 primitive sites for RVs up to 27 feet or tents, and one group site for up to 50 people with a minimum of 20. Picnic tables and fire pits are provided. Pit toilets are available. No drinking water is available. Leashed pets are permitted.

Reservations, fees: Reservations are accepted only for the group site. There is no fee for camping. A camping permit is required and a campground map is needed. Both can be obtained from the State Department of Forestry office at 802 N. Main St. (Highway 1) in Fort Bragg, or with a group-site reservation from the campground host in Jackson Demonstration State Forest. Open April to October, weather permitting. Call ahead for status.

Directions: From Willits on U.S. 101, turn west on Highway 20 and drive 27 miles to Forest Road 350 (near the six-mile marker). Turn right and drive 1.3 miles (bear right at the forks on the road) to the campground.

Contact: Jackson Demonstration State Forest, 707/964-5674, fax 707/964-0941.

12 JACKSON DEMONSTRATION STATE FOREST, CAMP 20

Rating: 6

near Fort Bragg

See map pages 524–525

A highlight of Jackson Demonstration Forest is a 50-foot waterfall on Chamberlain Creek. Set in a steep canyon amid giant firs and redwoods, it can be reached with a 10-minute walk. There are also extensive logging roads that are good yet challenging for mountain biking. What to do first? Get a map from the State Forestry Department. For driving, the roads are extremely dusty in summer and muddy in winter. Some locals call this campground "Dunlap Camp."

RV sites, facilities: There are 18 primitive sites for RVs up to 27 feet or tents and six equestrian sites across the road. Picnic tables and fire rings are provided. Pit toilets are available. No drinking water is available. A camp host is onsite from Memorial Day to October. Leashed pets are permitted.

Reservations, fees: Reservations are accepted for equestrian sites only. There is no fee for camping. A camping permit is required and a campground map is needed. Both can be obtained from the State Department of Forestry office at 802 N. Main St. (Highway 1) in Fort Bragg, or from the campground host in Jackson Demonstration State Forest from Memorial Day to October. Open year-round, but subject to closures, especially in winter because of muddy roads. Call ahead for status.

Directions: From Willits on U.S. 101, turn west on Highway 20 and drive 17 miles. At the 16.9-mile marker (just past the Chamberlain Bridge) at Road 200 turn left on Road 200 (the entrance for Jackson State Forest) and Camp 20/Dunlap. Obtain a camping permit and a map from the camp host on the premises at Camp 20.

Contact: Jackson Demonstration State Forest, 707/964-5674, fax 707/964-0941.

13 SLEEPY HOLLOW RV PARK

Rating: 5

north of Willits

See map pages 524–525

This year-round, privately operated park provides easy access off the highway. A nearby recreation option is the Skunk Train in Willits.

RV sites, facilities: There are 24 RV sites (six drive-through) with partial or full hookups and six sites for tents. Picnic tables are provided. Restrooms, showers, a small pond, a recreation room, and an RV dump station are available. Leashed pets are permitted.

Reservations, fees: Reservations are accepted. The fee is $11–15 per night, plus $1 per person for more than two people. Open year-round.

Directions: From Willits on U.S. 101, drive north for 8.5 miles to the 55.5-mile marker (.2 mile beyond the Shimmins Ridge Road sign). At the beginning of the divided four-lane highway, turn right at the signed campground access road and drive to the entrance.

Contact: Sleepy Hollow RV Park, 707/459-0613.

CALIFORNIA

14 QUAIL MEADOWS RV PARK & CAMPGROUND

Rating: 3

in Willits
See map pages 524–525

This is one of several RV parks in the Willits area. Nearby is Lake Emily, set near the Brook Trails development, which is stocked in the spring and early summer with trout by the Department of Fish and Game. It's like a backyard fishing hole for the folks around here. Another recreation option is the Skunk Train from Fort Bragg. Note that of the 49 sites, only 10 are available for overnighters, as the rest are rented for the summer.

RV sites, facilities: There are 49 sites, most drive-through, with partial or full hookups (20, 30 amps) for RVs, and a separate area for tents only. Picnic tables are provided. Patios, restrooms, showers, an RV dump station, a coin-operated laundry, propane, ice, limited cell phone reception, modem access, and TV hookups are available. An ATM is within one mile. Leashed pets are permitted.

Reservations, fees: Reservations are accepted. The fee is $24–28 per night, plus $3 per person for more than two people. A senior discount is available. Open year-round.

Directions: In Willits at the junction of U.S. 101 and Highway 20, drive north on U.S. 101 for one mile to the campground on the east side of the road.

Contact: Quail Meadows RV Park & Campground, 707/459-6006.

15 WILLITS KOA

Rating: 3

near Willits
See map pages 524–525

This is an ideal spot to park your RV if you plan on taking the Skunk Train west to Fort Bragg. A depot for the train is within walking distance of the campground. The campground also offers nightly entertainment in summer. The elevation is 1,377 feet. Tickets are available here for the Skunk Train.

RV sites, facilities: There are 50 RV sites (27 drive-through) with partial or full hookups (30, 50 amps) and 21 sites for tents. Group sites and 12 cabins are available. Picnic tables are provided. Drinking water, flush toilets, modem access, showers, a playground, a swimming pool (heated in summer), hay rides, mini-golf, basketball, volleyball, a fishing pond, a grocery store, limited cell phone reception, RV supplies, a coin-operated laundry, and an RV dump station are available. An ATM is within two miles. Leashed pets are permitted.

Reservations, fees: Reservations are accepted at 800/562-8542. The fee is $35–40 per night, plus $3–4 per person per night for more than two people. Cabins are $51–55 per night. Major credit cards are accepted. Open year-round.

Directions: From Willits at the junction of U.S. 101 and Highway 20, turn west on Highway 20 and drive 1.5 miles to the campground on the left.

Contact: Willits KOA, 707/459-6179, fax 707/459-1489, website: www.koa.com.

16 POGIE POINT

Rating: 7

on Lake Pillsbury in Mendocino National Forest
See map pages 524–525

This camp is set beside Lake Pillsbury in Mendocino National Forest, in the back of a cove at the lake's northwest corner. When the lake is full, this spot is quite pretty. A boat ramp is about a quarter mile to the south, a bonus. The elevation is 1,900 feet.

RV sites, facilities: There are 50 sites for RVs or tents. Picnic tables and fire grills are provided. Drinking water and vault toilets are available. Some facilities are wheelchair-accessible. Leashed pets are permitted.

Reservations, fees: Reservations are not accepted. The fee is $12 per night, plus $3 per additional vehicle, $7 per extra RV, and $1 per pet per night. Open May through October.

Directions: From Ukiah on U.S. 101, drive north to the junction with Highway 20. Turn east (right) on Highway 20 and drive five miles. Turn northwest on East Potter Valley Road toward Lake Pillsbury. Drive 5.9 miles to the town of Potter Valley. Continue on east Potter Valley Road to

Eel River Road. Turn right and drive 15 miles to the Eel River Information Kiosk at Lake Pillsbury. Continue for two miles to the campground access road. Turn right and drive a short distance to the campground.

Contact: Mendocino National Forest, Upper Lake Ranger District, 707/275-2361, fax 707/275-0676; PG&E Land Services, 916/386-5164, fax 916/923-7044, website: www.pge.com/recreation.

17 SUNSET CAMPGROUND

Rating: 7

on Lake Pillsbury in Mendocino National Forest
See map pages 524–525

This camp is on the northeast corner of Lake Pillsbury, with a boat ramp available at the mouth of Squaw Creek Cove less than a quarter mile to the south. The Lakeshore Trail, an adjacent designated nature trail along the shore of the lake here, is accessible to hikers and equestrians only—no bikes. The surrounding national forest offers side-trip possibilities.

RV sites, facilities: There are 54 sites for mid-sized RVs or tents. Picnic tables and fire grills are provided. Drinking water and vault toilets are available. A boat ramp is nearby. Leashed pets are permitted.

Reservations, fees: Reservations are not accepted. The fee is $12 per night, plus $3 per additional vehicle and $1 per pet. A senior discount is available. Open May through October.

Directions: From Ukiah on U.S. 101, drive north to the junction with Highway 20. Turn east (right) on Highway 20 and drive five miles. Turn northwest on East Potter Valley Road toward Lake Pillsbury. Drive 5.9 miles to the town of Potter Valley. Continue on East Potter Valley Road to Eel River Road. Turn right and drive 15 miles to the Eel River Information Kiosk at Lake Pillsbury. Continue east for 4.1 miles to Lake Pillsbury and the junction with Hall Mountain Road. Turn right and drive three miles to the camp entrance.

Contact: Mendocino National Forest, Upper Lake Ranger District, 707/275-2361, fax 707/275-0676; PG&E Land Services, 916/386-5164.

18 NAVY CAMP

Rating: 7

on Lake Pillsbury in Mendocino National Forest
See map pages 524–525

When Lake Pillsbury is full of water, this is one of the most attractive of the many camps here. It is set in the lake's north cove, sheltered from north winds. Surrounded by forest, the camp is in a pretty setting. However, when the lake level is down, as is common in the fall, it can seem as if the camp is on the edge of a dust bowl.

RV sites, facilities: There are 20 sites for RVs or tents. Picnic tables are provided. Drinking water and vault toilets are available. A boat ramp is nearby. Some facilities are wheelchair-accessible. Leashed pets are permitted.

Reservations, fees: Reservations are not accepted. The fee is $12 per night, plus $3 per additional vehicle per night and $1 per pet per night. A senior discount is available. Open Memorial Day weekend through Labor Day weekend.

Directions: From Ukiah on U.S. 101, drive north to the junction with Highway 20. Turn east (right) on Highway 20 and drive five miles to East Potter Valley Road. Turn northwest on East Potter Valley Road toward Lake Pillsbury and drive 5.9 miles to the town of Potter Valley. Continue on East Potter Valley Road to Eel River Road. Turn right and drive 15 miles to the Eel River Information Kiosk at Lake Pillsbury. Continue for four miles around the north end of the lake and look for the campground entrance on the right side of the road. The campground is on the north shore, just west of Oak Flat camp.

Contact: Mendocino National Forest, Upper Lake Ranger District, 707/275-2361, fax 707/275-0676. For a map, send $6 to Upper Lake Ranger Station, 10025 Elk Mountain Rd., Upper Lake, CA 95485, and ask for Mendocino National Forest area.

19 FULLER GROVE AND FULLER GROVE GROUP CAMP

Rating: 7

on Lake Pillsbury in Mendocino National Forest
See map pages 524–525

This is one of several campgrounds bordering

Lake Pillsbury, which at 2,000 acres is by far the largest lake in Mendocino National Forest. It has lakeside camping, good boat ramps, and, in the spring, good fishing for trout, and in the warmer months for bass. This camp is set along the northwest shore of the lake, with a boat ramp only about a quarter mile away to the north. There are numerous backcountry roads in the area, which provide access to a state game refuge to the north and the Snow Mountain Wilderness to the east.

RV sites, facilities: There are 30 sites for RVs up to 22 feet or tents and one group site for up to 100 people. Picnic tables and fire grills are provided. Drinking water, vault toilets, and limited cell phone reception are available. A boat ramp is nearby. Leashed pets are permitted.

Reservations, fees: Reservations are accepted for the group site only at 916/386-5164. The fee is $12 per night for single sites, plus $3 per additional vehicle and $1 per pet; the group site is $100 per night. Open May through October.

Directions: From Ukiah on U.S. 101, drive north to the junction with Highway 20. Turn east (right) on Highway 20 and drive five miles to East Potter Valley Road. Turn northwest on East Potter Valley Road toward Lake Pillsbury and drive 5.9 miles to the town of Potter Valley. Continue on East Potter Valley Road to Eel River Road. Turn right and drive 15 miles to the Eel River Information Kiosk at Lake Pillsbury. Continue for 2.2 miles to the campground access road. Turn right and drive .25 mile to the campground.

Contact: Mendocino National Forest, Upper Lake Ranger District, 707/275-2361, fax 707/275-0676; PG&E Land Services, 916/386-5164.

20 LAKE PILLSBURY RESORT AND MARINA

Rating: 6

on Lake Pillsbury
See map pages 524–525

This is a pretty spot beside the shore of Lake Pillsbury in the heart of Mendocino National Forest. It can be headquarters for a vacation involving boating, fishing, water-skiing, or exploring the surrounding national forest. A boat ramp, small marina, and full facilities make this place

a prime attraction in a relatively remote location. This is the only resort on the lake that accepts reservations, and it has some lakefront sites.

RV sites, facilities: There are 35 sites with partial hookups (30 amps), and two with full hookups, for RVs or tents, and eight cabins. A snack bar, restrooms, flush toilets, coin-operated showers, boat and personal watercraft rentals, fuel, a dock, fishing supplies, and a small marina are available. Leashed pets are permitted.

Reservations, fees: Reservations are recommended. The fee is $18–30 per night, plus $4 per pet per night. Call for cabin prices. A senior discount is available. Major credit cards are accepted. Open year-round.

Directions: From Ukiah on U.S. 101, drive north to the junction with Highway 20. Turn east (right) on Highway 20 and drive five miles to East Potter Valley Road (toward Lake Pillsbury). Turn northwest on East Potter Valley Road and drive 5.9 miles to the town of Potter Valley. Continue on East Potter Valley Road to Eel River Road. Turn right and drive 15 miles to Lake Pillsbury and Forest Road 301F. Turn right at Forest Road 301F and drive two miles to the resort.

Contact: Lake Pillsbury Resort and Marina, 707/743-1581, fax 707/743-2666.

21 CASPAR BEACH RV PARK

Rating: 8

near Mendocino
See map pages 524–525

This privately operated park has ocean frontage and opportunities for beachcombing, fishing, abalone and scuba diving, and good lookouts for whale-watching. The park is somewhat wooded, with a small, year-round creek running behind it. The park is about midway between Fort Bragg and Mendocino, with Fort Bragg five miles to the north. Note that a 30-site mobile home park is adjacent to this park.

RV sites, facilities: There are 59 sites, some drive-through, with partial or full hookups (30 amps) for RVs, and 30 sites for tents only. Picnic tables and fire rings are provided. Cable TV, modem access, flush and pit toilets, showers (coin-operated), and an RV dump station are available. A convenience store, firewood, a playground, a

CALIFORNIA

video arcade, and a coin-operated laundry are available nearby. An ATM is within three miles. Some facilities are wheelchair-accessible. Leashed pets are permitted.

Reservations, fees: Reservations are accepted. The fee is $25–33 per night, plus $3–5 per person for more than two people and $2 per pet per night. Monthly rates are available. Major credit cards are accepted. Open year-round.

Directions: From Mendocino on Highway 1, drive north for 3.5 miles to the Point Cabrillo exit. Turn west on Point Cabrillo Drive and continue .75 mile to the campground on the left.

From Fort Bragg on Highway 1, drive south for 4.5 miles. Turn right on Point Cabrillo Drive and continue .75 mile to the campground.

Contact: Caspar Beach RV Park, 707/964-3306, fax 707/964-0526, website: www.casparbeachrv park.com.

22 RUSSIAN GULCH STATE PARK

Rating: 9

near the Pacific Ocean
See map pages 524–525

Russian Gulch State Park is set near some of California's most beautiful coastline, but the camp speaks to the woods, not the water, with the campsites set in a wooded canyon. They include some of the prettiest and most secluded drive-in sites available on the Mendocino coast. There is a great hike here, an easy hour-long walk to Russian Gulch Falls, a wispy 36-foot waterfall that falls into a rock basin. Although it's always pretty, it's awesome in late winter. Much of the route is accessible by bicycle; there's a rack where you can leave your bike where the trail narrows and turns to dirt. The park covers more than 1,100 acres with about 1.5 miles of ocean frontage, with its rugged headlands thrusting into the Pacific. It rivals Point Lobos for coastal beauty. And yet the park is better known for its heavily forested canyon, Russian Gulch Creek Canyon, and a headland that features the Devil's Punchbowl. The latter is a large collapsed sea cove with churning water that acts as a blowhole. It was created by the pounding of waves against the coastal headlands, gouging a 200-foot tunnel that ends where the earth caved away. That forms a hole

100 feet across and 60 feet deep, called Devil's Punchbowl, where one can look right into it and watch the surge. A beach offers tidepool exploring, swimming, diving, and rock fishing. There are miles of trails, with the best family outing being the three-mile bicycle trail called the North Boundary Trail.

RV sites, facilities: There are 30 sites for RVs up to 24 feet or tents, one hike-in/bike-in site, and one group site. Picnic tables, fire grills, and food lockers are provided. Drinking water, coin-operated showers, limited cell phone reception, and flush toilets are available. A day-use picnic area, beach access, and a recreation hall are nearby. An ATM is within two miles. Some facilities are wheelchair-accessible. Leashed pets are permitted.

Reservations, fees: Reservations are accepted with a $7.50 reservation fee at 800/444-PARK (800/444-7275) or www.reserveamerica.com. The fees are $12–15 per night for campsites, $30 for the group site (up to 40 people), and $2 per night for hike-in, bike-in site. A senior discount is available. Open mid-March to mid-October.

Directions: From Mendocino, drive two miles north on Highway 1 to the campground entrance on the west side of the highway.

Contact: Russian Gulch State Park, 707/937-4296; Mendocino District, 707/937-5804, fax 707/937-2953.

23 VAN DAMME STATE PARK

Rating: 10

near Mendocino
See map pages 524–525

The campsites at Van Damme are extremely popular, usually requiring reservations, but with a bit of planning your reward is a base of operations in a beautiful park with redwoods and a remarkable fern understory. The hike-in sites on the Fern Canyon Trail are perfectly situated for those wishing to take one of the most popular hikes in the Mendocino area, with the trail crossing the Little River several times and weaving among old trees. Just across from the entrance of the park is a small but beautiful coastal bay with a pretty beach, ideal for launching sea kayaks. The park covers 1,831 acres. A sidelight is the Pygmy Forest, where mature cone-bearing cypress

CALIFORNIA

and pine trees are only six inches to eight feet tall. Another favorite is the Cabbage Patch, where skunk cabbage grows in abundance, most striking when seen in May and June. The park has 10 miles of trails along the fern-carpeted canyon along the Little River. A paved road is used by joggers and bicyclists. The beach is popular with abalone divers. Kayak tours are available at the beach parking lot in the summer.

RV sites, facilities: There are 74 sites for RVs up to 35 feet or tents, 10 primitive environmental sites, one hike-in/bike-in site, and one group campsite for up to 50 people. Picnic tables and fire grills are provided. Drinking water, flush toilets, limited cell phone reception, an RV dump station, and coin-operated showers are available. A grocery store, a coin-operated laundry, and propane are available nearby. An ATM is within three miles. Leashed pets are permitted at campsites, but not in environmental sites.

Reservations, fees: Reservations are accepted with a $7.50 reservation fee at 800/444-PARK (800/444-7275) or www.reserveamerica.com. The fees are $12–15 per night, $7 per night for environmental sites, $37 per night for group site, and $2 per night per person for hike-in site. A senior discount is available. Open year-round.

Directions: From Mendocino on Highway 1, drive south for three miles to the town of Little River and the park entrance road on the left (east) side of the road.

Contact: Mendocino District, State Parks, 707/937-5804, fax 707/937-2953.

24 NAVARRO BEACH

Rating: 6

near the mouth of the Navarro River
See map pages 524–525

Navarro Beach is a primitive campground that can bail out drivers stuck for a night without a spot. It is small and open, with no tree cover, set near the ocean and the Navarro River. The camps are just south of the Navarro River Bridge.

RV sites, facilities: There 10 primitive sites for RVs up to 35 feet or tents. Picnic tables and fire grills are provided. No drinking water is available. Pit toilets are available. Leashed pets are permitted.

Reservations, fees: Reservations are not accepted. The fee is $5 per night. A senior discount is available. Open year-round.

Directions: Drive on U.S. 101 to the turnoff for Highway 128 (two miles north of Cloverdale). Turn west on Highway 128 and drive 55 miles to Highway 1. Turn south on Highway 1 and almost immediately, take the exit for Navarro Bluffs Road. Drive a short distance on Navarro Bluffs Road to the campground (on the south side of the Navarro River Bridge).

Contact: Navarro River Redwoods State Park, c/o Hendy Woods, 707/895-3141; Mendocino District, 707/937-5804, fax 707/937-2953.

25 PAUL M. DIMMICK

Rating: 7

on the Navarro River in Navarro River Redwoods State Park
See map pages 524–525

A pretty grove of second-growth redwood trees and the nearby Navarro River are the highlights of this campground at Navarro River Redwoods State Park. It's a nice spot but, alas, lacks any significant hiking trails that could make it an overall spectacular destination; all the trailheads along Highway 128 turn out to be just little spur routes from the road to the river. That is because the park consists of an 11-mile "redwood tunnel" along the Navarro River in its course to the ocean. The river provides swimming in summer but is better suited for easy kayaking and canoeing in later winter and spring.

RV sites, facilities: There are 27 sites for RVs up to 30 feet or tents. Picnic tables and fire grills are provided. Drinking water (summer only) and vault toilets are available. Leashed pets are permitted.

Reservations, fees: Reservations are not accepted. The fee is $11 per night, plus $4 per night per additional vehicle. A senior discount is available. Open March through October.

Directions: From Cloverdale on U.S. 101, drive north for two miles to Highway 128. Turn west on Highway 128 and drive 49 miles. Look for the signed campground entrance on the left side of the road.

Contact: Navarro River Redwoods State Park,

c/o Hendy Woods State Park, 707/895-3141; Mendocino District, 707/987-5804, fax 707/937-2953.

26 HENDY WOODS STATE PARK

Rating: 7

near Boonville
See map pages 524–525

This is a remarkable setting where the flora changes from open valley grasslands and oaks to a cloaked redwood forest with old growth, as if you had waved a magic wand. The campsites are set in the forest, with a great trail routed amid the old redwoods and up to the Hermit Hut (a fallen redwood stump covered with branches), where a hobo lived for 18 years. No, it wasn't me. The park features two virgin redwood groves, Big Hendy (80 acres with a self-guided discovery trail available) and Little Hendy (20 acres). The headwaters of the Navarro River run through the length of the park, but note that fishing is forbidden in the park and that catch-and-release fishing is the law from the bridge at the park entrance on downstream; check regulations. The park is in the middle of the Anderson Valley wine district, which will at first seem an unlikely place to find an 845-acre redwood park, far warmer and less foggy than the redwood parks along the coast.

RV sites, facilities: There are 92 sites for RVs up to 35 feet or tents, two hike-in/bike-in sites, and four cabins. Picnic tables, food lockers, and fire grills are provided. Drinking water, flush toilets, coin-operated showers, firewood, and an RV dump station are available. A seasonal Junior Ranger program with nature walks, campfire programs, and exhibits is also available. A grocery store and propane station are nearby. An ATM is within three miles. Some facilities are wheelchair-accessible. Leashed pets are permitted.

Reservations, fees: Reservations are accepted with a $7.50 reservation fee at 800/444-PARK (800/444-7275) or www.reserveamerica.com. The fees are $14 per night for campsites and $2 per person for hike-in/bike-in sites, plus $4 per night per additional vehicle. A senior discount is available. Open year-round.

Directions: From Cloverdale on U.S. 101, turn northwest on Highway 128 and drive about 35 miles to Philo Greenwood Road. Turn left on Philo Greenwood Road and drive .5 mile to the park entrance.

Contact: Hendy Woods State Park, 707/895-3141; Mendocino District, 707/937-5804, fax 707/937-2953.

27 BU-SHAY

Rating: 7

at Lake Mendocino
See map pages 524–525

Bu-Shay, on the northeast end of Lake Mendocino, is set on a point that provides a pretty southern exposure when the lake is full. The lake is five miles long and one mile wide. It offers fishing for striped bass, largemouth bass, catfish, and bluegill, as well as water-skiing and powerboating. A nearby visitors center features exhibits of local Native American history. The elevation is 750 feet. (For more information about Lake Mendocino, see the entry for Che-Ka-Ka in this chapter.)

RV sites, facilities: There are 164 sites for RVs up to 35 feet or tents and three group sites for up to 120 people each. Picnic tables, fire rings, and lantern holders are provided. Drinking water, restrooms, coin-operated showers, a playground (in the adjacent day-use area), limited cell phone reception, and an RV dump station are available. The boat ramp is two miles from camp near Ky-En campground. An ATM is within 10 miles. Some facilities are wheelchair-accessible. Leashed pets are permitted.

Reservations, fees: Reservations are accepted with a $9 reservation fee at 877/444-6777 or www.reserveusa.com. The fee is $18–20 per night; group sites are $110–200 per night. A senior discount is available. Major credit cards are accepted. Open mid-April through September.

Directions: From Ukiah, drive north on U.S. 101 for 1.5 miles to the Highway 20 turnoff. Drive five miles east on Highway 20. Just after crossing the Russian River bridge, turn left (Inlet Road) and drive approximately one mile to the campground.

Contact: U.S. Army Corps of Engineers, Lake Mendocino, 707/462-7581, fax 707/462-3372.

CALIFORNIA

28 KY-EN

Rating: 7

at Lake Mendocino
See map pages 524–525
This camp is on the north shore of Lake Mendocino. With the access road off Highway 20 instead of U.S. 101 (as with Che-Ka-Ka), it can be overlooked by newcomers. A nearby boat ramp makes it especially attractive. (For more information, see the following entry for Che-Ka-Ka.)
RV sites, facilities: There are 101 sites for RVs up to 35 feet or tents. Picnic tables, fire grills, and lantern holders are provided. Restrooms, coin-operated showers, a playground (in the adjacent day-use area), an RV dump station, a boat ramp, boat rentals, and limited cell phone reception are available. Limited supplies are available at the nearby marina. An ATM is within 10 miles. Some facilities are wheelchair-accessible. Leashed pets are permitted.
Reservations, fees: Reservations are accepted with a $9 reservation fee at 877/444-6777 or www.reserveusa.com. The fee is $18–22 per night. A senior discount is available. Major credit cards are accepted. Open year-round.
Directions: From Ukiah, drive north on U.S. 101 for five miles to the Highway 20 turnoff. Drive east on Highway 20 one mile to Marina Drive. Turn right and drive 200 yards (past the boat ramp) to the campground.
Contact: U.S. Army Corps of Engineers, Lake Mendocino, 707/462-7581, fax 707/462-3372.

29 CHE-KA-KA

Rating: 7

at Lake Mendocino
See map pages 524–525
Lake Mendocino is known for good striped bass fishing, water-skiing, and boating. Nearby, upstream of the lake, is Potter Valley and the East Fork Russian River (also called Cold Creek), which provides trout fishing in the summer. A boat ramp adjacent to the dam is a bonus. The elevation is 750 feet. This campground sits beside the dam at the south end of Lake Mendocino.
RV sites, facilities: There are 22 sites for RVs up

to 35 feet or tents. Picnic tables and fire grills are provided. Drinking water, vault toilets, limited cell phone reception, and lantern holders are available. A boat ramp is nearby. An ATM is within 10 miles. Leashed pets are permitted.
Reservations, fees: Reservations are accepted with a $9 reservation fee at 877/444-6777 or www.reserveusa.com. The fee is $10 per night. A senior discount is available. Major credit cards are accepted. Open mid-April through September.
Directions: From Ukiah, drive north on U.S. 101 to Lake Mendocino Drive. Exit right on Lake Mendocino Drive and continue to the first stoplight. Turn left on North State Street and drive to the next stoplight. Turn right (which will put you back on Lake Mendocino Drive) and drive about one mile to the signed entrance to the campground at Coyote Dam.
Contact: U.S. Army Corps of Engineers, Lake Mendocino, 707/462-7581, fax 707/462-3372.

30 MANOR OAKS RV PARK

Rating: 2

in Ukiah
See map pages 524–525
Manor Oaks RV Park is a drive-in park in an urban setting for U.S. 101 motor-home cruisers. Nearby Lake Mendocino provides a nearby side-trip option, with access to boating, water-skiing, and fishing. Note that about half of the sites are long-term rentals for the summer.
RV sites, facilities: There are 53 sites, 15 drive-through, with full hookups (30 amps) for RVs. Picnic tables and fire grills are provided. Restrooms, showers, a heated swimming pool (in summer), a coin-operated laundry, cell phone reception, and ice are available. An ATM is within one mile. Some facilities are wheelchair-accessible. Leashed pets are permitted.
Reservations, fees: Reservations are accepted at 800/357-8772. The fee is $25 per night, plus $1 per person for more than two people. Open year-round.
Directions: From U.S. 101 in Ukiah, take the Central Ukiah/Gobbi Street exit and drive east for a short distance to 700 E. Gobbi St. on the left.
Contact: Manor Oaks RV Park, 707/462-0529.

CALIFORNIA

31 LE TRIANON RESORT

Rating: 6

on Lower Blue Lake
See map pages 524–525

Le Trianon Resort is the biggest of the camps on the Blue Lakes, the overlooked lakes not far from giant Clear Lake. It is an angler's special with good trout fishing in spring and no water-skiing permitted. The better fishing is in Upper Blue Lake, which is stocked with 28,000 trout per year and where the water is much clearer than at the lower lake. The best fishing is in the spring, in April, May, and June.

RV sites, facilities: There are 100 sites for RVs with partial hookups (30 amps) or tents and 14 cabins. Picnic tables are provided. Flush toilets, showers, an RV dump station, a playground, a boat ramp, limited cell phone reception, boat rentals, fishing supplies, a coin-operated laundry, a snack bar, and a convenience store are available. An ATM is within seven miles. No pets, skateboards, or motorcycles are allowed.

Reservations, fees: Reservations are not accepted. The fee is $25 per night, plus $5 per child and $5 per person for more than two people. A senior discount is available. Major credit cards are accepted. Open April through October.

Directions: From Ukiah, drive north on U.S. 101 for five miles to the junction with Highway 20. Turn east on Highway 20 and drive 12 miles to the resort on the right (5845 W. Hwy. 20).

Contact: Le Trianon Resort, 707/275-2262, fax 707/275-9416.

32 PINE ACRES BLUE LAKES RESORT

Rating: 8

on Upper Blue Lake
See map pages 524–525

Because of their proximity to Clear Lake, the Blue Lakes are often overlooked. But these lovely lakes offer good fishing for trout, especially in spring and early summer on Upper Blue Lake, and a decent chance the rest of the year. With a speed limit (5 mph) in place, quiet boating is the rule. Swimming is good here, and visitors often find a fun surprise in the gentle wild pigs that occa-

sionally roam into the park, looking for handouts. For tent camping, a lawn area is available here.

RV sites, facilities: There are 30 sites, two drive-through, with partial or full hookups (30, 50 amps) for RVs, a lawn area for dispersed tent camping, five cabins, and six lodge rooms. Picnic tables and fire grills are provided. Flush toilets, coin-operated showers, limited cell phone reception, an RV dump station, a clubhouse for groups, boat rentals, boat launching, moorings, a boat ramp, a convenience store, fishing supplies, and lake frontage sites are available. An ATM is within one mile. Leashed pets are permitted.

Reservations, fees: Reservations are accepted for RV sites, cabins, and lodge rooms, but not for tent camping. The fee is $18–25 per night, plus $3.50 per person for more than two people and $5–10 per pet per night. Major credit cards are accepted. Open year-round.

Directions: From Ukiah, drive north on U.S. 101 for five miles to the junction with Highway 20. Turn east on Highway 20 and drive about 13 miles to Irvine Street. Turn right on Irvine Street and drive one block to Blue Lakes Road. Turn right and drive a short distance to the resort on the right.

Contact: Pine Acres Blue Lakes Resort, 707/275-2811, website: www.bluelakepineacres.com.

33 NARROWS RESORT

Rating: 8

on Upper Blue Lake
See map pages 524–525

This is one of four campgrounds in the immediate vicinity at Blue Lakes. This campground is a good fish camp with boat docks and a fish-cleaning station. The Blue Lakes are often overlooked because of their proximity to Clear Lake, but they are a quiet and pretty alternative, with good trout fishing in the spring and early summer, and decent prospects year-round.

RV sites, facilities: There are 48 sites with partial or full hookups (30, 50 amps) for RVs or tents, five park-model cabins, and 14 motel rooms. Picnic tables are provided. Flush toilets, showers, an RV dump station, modem access, a recreation room, boat rentals, a pier, a boat ramp,

CALIFORNIA

limited cell phone reception, fishing supplies, a picnic area, and ice are available. An ATM is within six miles. Leashed pets are allowed, but not in motel rooms or cabins.

Reservations, fees: Reservations are accepted at 800/476-2776. The fee is $22–33 per night, plus $3 per person for more than two people and $3 per pet per night. Major credit cards are accepted. Open year-round.

Directions: From Ukiah, drive north on U.S. 101 for five miles to the junction with Highway 20. Turn east on Highway 20 and drive about 11.5 miles to Blue Lakes Road. Turn right and drive one mile to the resort (5690 Blue Lakes Road).

Contact: Narrows Resort, 707/275-2718, website: www.thenarrowsresort.com.

34 KELLY'S FAMILY KAMPGROUND & RV PARK

Rating: 6

on Scotts Creek near Clear Lake
See map pages 524–525

This privately operated park is set beside Scotts Creek, within short driving range of Blue Lakes to the north on Highway 20 and the north end of Clear Lake to the south.

RV sites, facilities: There are 75 sites for RVs or tents, many with partial hookups (20, 30 amps). Picnic tables, fire pits, and barbecues are provided. Flush toilets, coin-operated showers, an RV dump station, a coin-operated laundry, limited cell phone reception, ice, and a small camp store are available. An ATM is within one mile. Leashed pets are permitted.

Reservations, fees: Reservations are accepted. The fee is $19.25 per night, plus $2 per night per additional vehicle and $1 per pet per night. Open April through October.

Directions: From Ukiah on U.S. 101, drive north to the junction with Highway 20. Turn east and drive 14 miles (five miles from Upper Lake) to Scotts Valley Road. Turn right (south) and drive to the park on the left (at 8220 Scotts Valley Road).

Contact: Kelly's Family Kampground & RV Park, 707/263-5754.

35 MIDDLE CREEK CAMPGROUND

Rating: 6

in Mendocino National Forest
See map pages 524–525

This camp is not widely known, but it's known well enough as an off-highway-vehicle staging area. Some call it "CC Camp." It is set at 2,000 feet at the confluence of the West and East Forks of Middle Creek.

RV sites, facilities: There are 23 sites for small RVs or tents. Picnic tables and fire grills are provided. Drinking water and vault toilets are available. Leashed pets are permitted.

Reservations, fees: Reservations are not accepted. The fees are $4 for single sites and $8 for double sites per night, plus $2 per additional vehicle. Open year-round.

Directions: From Ukiah on U.S. 101, drive north to the junction with Highway 20. Turn east on Highway 20 and drive to the town of Upper Lake and Mendenhall Road. Turn left on Mendenhall Avenue (which becomes Forest Road M1) and drive eight miles to the camp on the right side of the road.

Contact: Mendocino National Forest, Upper Lake Ranger District, 707/275-2361, fax 707/275-0676.

36 DAVIS FLAT

Rating: 1

in Mendocino National Forest
See map pages 524–525

This camp was also a victim of the forest fire that swept through this area in August 2001. It is in a designated off-highway-vehicle area, so expect OHVers, especially in the winter. This isn't the quietest camp around, but there is some good hiking in the area to the immediate west in the Snow Mountain Wilderness. The elevation is 1,700 feet.

RV sites, facilities: There are 70 dispersed sites for RVs of any length or tents. Picnic tables and fire grills are provided. Drinking water and vault toilets are available. Leashed pets are permitted.

Reservations, fees: Reservations are not accepted. There is no fee for camping. Open year-round.

Directions: From I-5 at Maxwell, turn west on

CALIFORNIA

Maxwell-Sites Road and drive to Sites. Turn left on Sites-Lodoga Road and continue to Lodoga. Turn right on Lodoga-Stonyford Road and loop around East Park Reservoir to reach Stonyford. From Stonyford, turn west on Fouts Springs Road/County Road M10 and drive about eight miles. Turn right on Forest Road 18N03 and drive one mile to the campground on your left.

Contact: Mendocino National Forest, Grindstone Ranger District, Stonyford Work Center, 530/963-3128, fax 530/963-3173.

37 LETTS LAKE COMPLEX

Rating: 9

in Mendocino National Forest
See map pages 524–525

Not too many folks know about Letts Lake, a 30-acre, spring-fed lake set in a mixed conifer forest at 4,500 feet just south of the Snow Mountain Wilderness. There are four main loops, each with a separate campground: Main, Stirrup, Saddle, and Spillway. The complex is set on the east side of the lake. No motors are allowed at Letts Lake, making it ideal for canoes, rafts, and float tubes. This lake is stocked with rainbow trout in the early summer and is also known for black bass. It's a designated historical landmark, the site where the homesteaders known as the Letts brothers were murdered. While that may not impress you, the views to the north of the Snow Mountain Wilderness will. In addition, there are several natural springs that can be fun to hunt up. By the way, after such a long drive to get here, don't let your eagerness cause you to stop at Lily Pond (on the left, one mile before reaching Letts Lake), because there are no trout in it.

RV sites, facilities: There are four campgrounds with 44 sites for RVs up to 20 feet or tents. Picnic tables and fire rings are provided. Drinking water and vault toilets are available. A wheelchair-accessible fishing pier is available. There is also an 11-unit picnic area with tables and barbecues on the left side of the lake, open during the day only. Some facilities are wheelchair-accessible. Leashed pets are permitted.

Reservations, fees: Reservations are not accepted. The fee is $8 per night with a 14-day limit. A senior discount is available. Open mid-April through October.

Directions: From I-5 at Maxwell, turn west on Maxwell-Sites Road and drive to Sites and Sites-Lodgoa Road. Turn left on Sites-Lodoga Road and continue to Lodoga and Lodoga-Stonyford Road. Turn right on Lodoga-Stonyford Road and loop around East Park Reservoir to reach Stonyford and Fouts Spring Road. Turn west on Fouts Springs Road/County Road M10 and drive about 17 miles into national forest (where the road becomes Forest Service 17N02) to the campground on the east side of Letts Lake.

Contact: Mendocino National Forest, Grindstone Ranger District, Stonyford Work Center, 530/963-3128, fax 530/963-3173.

38 MILL VALLEY

Rating: 5

near Letts Lake in Mendocino National Forest
See map pages 524–525

This camp is set beside Lily Pond, a little, teeny guy, with larger Letts Lake just a mile away. Since Lily Pond does not have trout and Letts Lake does, this camp gets far less traffic than its counterpart. The area is crisscrossed with numerous creeks, OHV routes, and Forest Service roads, making it a great adventure for owners of four-wheel drives. The elevation is 4,200 feet.

RV sites, facilities: There are 15 sites for RVs up to 18 feet or tents. Picnic tables and fire stoves are provided. Vault toilets are available. Drinking water is available seasonally. Leashed pets are permitted.

Reservations, fees: Reservations are not accepted. Fees range from free to $5 per night, depending upon water availability. A senior discount is available. Open mid-April through October, weather permitting.

Directions: From I-5 at Maxwell, turn west on Maxwell-Sites Road and drive to Sites and Sites-Lodgoa Road. Turn left on Sites-Lodoga Road and continue to Lodoga and Lodoga-Stonyford Road. Turn right on Lodoga-Stonyford Road and loop around East Park Reservoir to reach Stonyford and Fouts Spring Road. Turn west on Fouts Springs Road/County Road M10 and drive about 16 miles into national forest (where the road becomes Forest Service 17N02) to the camp access road on the left. Turn left and drive .5 mile to the camp.

Contact: Mendocino National Forest, Grindstone Ranger District, Stonyford Work Center, 530/963-3128, fax 530/963-3173.

39 SANDPIPER RV PARK

Rating: 7

on Clear Lake
See map pages 524–525
Sandpiper provides boating access to the northern end of Clear Lake. Fishing for catfish is good near here, both in Rodman Slough and just outside the mouth of the slough. This is where the legendary Catfish George Powers caught 4,000 to 5,000 catfish per year, using dead minnows for bait. In addition, the old submerged pilings in this area provide good bass fishing for boaters casting spinner baits. Several beaches are also available at the north end of the lake. Note that most sites are filled with long-term rentals, with six to 10 sites available for overnighters.

RV sites, facilities: There are 30 sites with partial or full hookups (30 amps) for RVs and three cabins. Picnic tables are provided. Drinking water, restrooms, flush toilets, showers, modem access, cell phone reception, and a coin-operated laundry are available. Moorings, a pier, and a boat ramp are nearby. Leashed pets are permitted.

Reservations, fees: Reservations are accepted. The fee is $17–21 per night, plus $3 for each additional vehicle and $2–3 per person for more than two people. A senior discount is available. Open year-round.

Directions: From Ukiah on U.S. 101, drive north to the junction with Highway 20. Turn east on Highway 20 and drive to the town of Nice and Hammond Avenue. Turn right on Hammond Avenue and drive .5 mile to Lakeshore Boulevard. Turn left and drive a short distance to 2630 Lakeshore Boulevard.

Contact: Sandpiper RV Park, 707/274-4448.

40 HOLIDAY HARBOR RV PARK AND MARINA

Rating: 7

on Clear Lake
See map pages 524–525
This is one of the most popular resorts at the north end of Clear Lake. It is ideal for boaters, with marina gas and a major docking complex. Fishing for bass is good in this area, along old docks and submerged pilings. Water-skiing just offshore is also good, with the north end of the lake often more calm than the water at points south. The elevation is about 2,000 feet. Unlike in several privately owned campgrounds in this area, no long-term rentals are permitted, a plus for vacationers.

RV sites, facilities: There are 30 sites, some drive-through, with partial or full hookups (30 amps) for RVs. Picnic tables are provided. Restrooms, showers, a recreation room, modem access, an RV dump station, limited cell phone reception, a coin-operated laundry, and ice are available. An enclosed marina with 150 boat slips, a boat ramp, and an adjacent beach are also available. An ATM is within one mile. Leashed pets are permitted.

Reservations, fees: Reservations are accepted. The fee is $18–19.50 per night, plus $2.50 per person per night for more than two people. Open year-round.

Directions: From north of Ukiah on U.S. 101, drive north to the junction with Highway 20. Turn east on Highway 20 and drive to the town of Nice and Howard Avenue. Turn left on Howard Avenue and drive 200 feet to the park at the end of the road.

Contact: Holiday Harbor RV Park and Marina, 707/274-1136, website: www.niceholidayharbor.com.

41 ARROW RV PARK AND MARINA

Rating: 6

on Clear Lake
See map pages 524–525
Lucerne is known for its harbor and its long stretch of well-kept public beaches along the shore of Clear Lake. The town offers a shopping district, restaurants, and cafés. In summer, crappie fishing is good at night from the boat docks, as long

as there are bright lights to attract gnats, which in turn attract minnows, the prime food for crappie. Some sites here are filled with long-term rentals.

RV sites, facilities: There are 14 sites, two drive-through and many with partial or full hookups, for RVs (30, 50 amps). Picnic tables, barbecues, restrooms, showers, a coin-operated laundry, moorings, fishing supplies, a fish-cleaning station, a boat ramp, a convenience store, and ice are available. Leashed pets are permitted.

Reservations, fees: Reservations are accepted. The fee is $40–45 per night. Weekly and monthly rates are available. A senior discount is available. Open year-round.

Directions: From north of Ukiah on U.S. 101 (or from Williams on I-5), turn on Highway 20 and drive to the town of Lucerne. Continue on Highway 20 to the east side of Lucerne and the campground at 6720 E. Hwy. 20.

Contact: Arrow RV Park and Marina, 707/274-7715.

42 GLENHAVEN BEACH CAMP AND MARINA

Rating: 6

on Clear Lake

See map pages 524–525

This makes a good base camp for all boaters, water-skiers, and anglers. It is set on a peninsula on the eastern shore of Clear Lake, with nearby Indian Beach providing a good recreation and water-play spot. In addition, it is a short boat ride out to Anderson Island, Weekend Island, and Buckingham Point, where bass fishing can be excellent along shaded tules.

RV sites, facilities: There are 21 sites with partial or full hookups (30 amps) for RVs up to 26 feet and tents. Picnic tables and fire rings are provided. Drinking water, restrooms, showers, flush toilets, limited cell phone reception, and a recreation room are available. A boat ramp and boat rentals are available nearby. An ATM is within three miles. Leashed pets are permitted.

Reservations, fees: Reservations are accepted. The fee is $18–20 per night, plus $1 per person for more than two people. Major credit cards are accepted. Open February through November.

Directions: From north of Ukiah on U.S. 101 (or I-5 at Williams), turn on Highway 20 and drive to Clear Lake and the town of Glenhaven (four miles northwest of Clearlake Oaks). In Glenhaven, continue on Highway 20 to the camp (lakeside) at 9625 E. Hwy. 20.

Contact: Glenhaven Beach Camp and Marina, 707/998-3406, website: www.glenhavenbeach.ohgolly.com.

43 U-WANNA CAMP

Rating: 3

near Clear Lake

See map pages 524–525

Whether U-Wanna or not, this could be where you end up if you're hunting for a site on a good-weather summer weekend. The camp is about two miles from Clear Lake, with a boat ramp at nearby Lakeport. A small fishing pond here is a plus. Note that there are 10 permanent rentals.

RV sites, facilities: There are 30 sites, four drive-through and all with partial hookups (30 amps), for RVs or tents. Picnic tables and fire rings are provided. Drinking water, restrooms, flush toilets, limited cell phone reception, showers, an RV dump station, a coin-operated laundry, and two playgrounds are available. A fishing pond, horseshoes, basketball, shuffleboard, and Ping-Pong are available. An ATM is within two miles. Leashed pets are permitted.

Reservations, fees: Reservations are accepted at 888/892-6622. The fee is $18–20 per night, plus $1–2 per person for more than two people, $1 for each additional vehicle, and $1 per pet per night. Open year-round.

Directions: From Highway 29 in Lakeport, go to 11th Street. Turn west and drive .5 mile to Riggs Road. Turn left and go .75 mile to Scotts Creek Road. Turn right and go .75 mile to the camp on the left (2699 Scotts Creek Road).

Contact: U-Wanna Camp, 707/263-6745.

44 CLEAR LAKE STATE PARK

Rating: 9

in Kelseyville at Clear Lake

See map pages 524–525

If you have fallen in love with Clear Lake and its

surrounding oak woodlands, it is difficult to find a better spot than at Clear Lake State Park. It is on the western shore of Clear Lake, and though the oak woodlands flora means you can seem quite close to your camping neighbors, the proximity to quality boating, water sports, and fishing makes the lack of privacy worth it. Reservations are a necessity in summer. That stands to reason, with excellent bass fishing from boats beside a tule-lined shoreline near the park and good catfishing in the sloughs that run through the park. Some campsites have water frontage. The elevation is 2,000 feet. Clear Lake is California's largest natural freshwater lake within state borders. Despite its name, the lake is not clear but green, and in late summer, rather soupy with algae and water grass. The high nutrients in the lake give rise to a flourishing aquatic food chain. With that comes the highest number of large bass of any lake in Northern California. A few short hiking trails are also available at the park. The self-guided Indian Nature Trail passes through the site of what was once a Pomo village. Rangers here are friendly, helpful, and provide reliable fishing information. Junior Ranger programs and guided walks for bird and flower identification are also available.

RV sites, facilities: There are 147 sites for RVs up to 35 feet or tents in four campgrounds, and two hike-in/bike-in sites. Picnic tables and fire rings are provided. Drinking water, restrooms, limited cell phone reception, showers, flush toilets, and an RV dump station are available. A boat ramp, a dock, a fish-cleaning station, and a swimming beach are nearby. A grocery store, a coin-operated laundry, propane, a restaurant, and a gas station are available within three miles. An ATM is within one mile. The boat ramp, picnic area, and some campsites are wheelchair-accessible. Leashed pets are permitted.

Reservations, fees: Reservations are accepted with a $7.50 reservation fee at 800/444-PARK (800/444-7275) or www.reserveamerica.com. The fees are $12–15 per night and $2 per person per night for hike-in/bike-in sites, plus a $4 boat-launch fee. A senior discount is available. Open year-round.

Directions: From Vallejo, drive north on Highway 29 to Lower Lake. Turn left on Highway 29 and drive seven miles to Soda Bay Road. Turn right on Soda Bay Road and drive 11 miles to the park entrance on the right side of the road.

From Kelseyville on Highway 29, take the Kelseyville exit and turn north on Main Street. Drive a short distance to State Street. Turn right and drive .25 mile to Gaddy Lane. Turn right on Gaddy Lane and drive about two miles to Soda Bay Road. Turn right and drive one mile to the park entrance on the left.

Contact: Clear Lake State Park, 707/279-4293.

45 EDGEWATER RESORT AND RV PARK

Rating: 7

on Clear Lake

See map pages 524–525

Soda Bay is one of Clear Lake's prettiest and most intimate spots, and this camp provides excellent access. Both water-skiing and fishing for bass and bluegill are excellent in this part of the lake, sheltered from north winds for quiet water, with a tule-lined shore from Henderson Point all the way around to Dorn Bay—nearly three miles of prime fishing territory. This resort specializes in groups and gatherings. Nearby Konocti Harbor features year-round classic rock concerts.

RV sites, facilities: There are 61 sites with full hookups (20, 30, 50 amps) for RVs and tents, and eight cabins (sleep 4 to 12 people) with air-conditioning and heat, kitchenettes, color TV, and cable. Picnic tables and fire grills are provided. Some sites have cable TV. Restrooms, showers, modem access, limited cell phone reception, an ATM, a general store, a coin-operated laundry, a clubhouse, a seasonal swimming pool, horseshoes, volleyball, and Ping-Pong are available. A seasonal swimming beach, a boat ramp, a fishing pier, boat docking, a fish-cleaning station, firewood, and watercraft rentals are available on premises. Leashed pets are permitted. There is a dog run at the beach.

Reservations, fees: Reservations are accepted at 800/396-6224. The fee is $28–38 per night, plus $5 per person per night for more than two people, $2.50 per pet per night, and $5 per pet per night in cabins. Boat launch, park, and dock is $5 per night. Major credit cards are accepted. Open year-round.

Directions: In Kelseyville on Highway 29, take

the Merritt Road exit and drive on Merritt Road for two miles (it becomes Gaddy Lane) to Soda Bay Road. Turn right on Soda Bay Road and drive three miles to the campground entrance on the left.

Contact: Edgewater Resort and RV Park, 707/279-0208, fax 707/279-0138, website: www.edgewaterresort.net.

46 SHAW'S SHADY ACRES

Rating: 7

on Cache Creek
See map pages 524–525

Shaw's Shady Acres is set beside Cache Creek, just south of Clear Lake. The fishing for catfish is often quite good on summer nights in Cache Creek, a deep green, slow-moving water that looks more like a slough in a Mississippi bayou than a creek. Waterfront campsites with scattered walnut, ash, and oak trees are available. Clear Lake (the lake, not the town) is a short drive to the north.

RV sites, facilities: There are 13 sites, six with full hookups (20, 30 amps) and seven with partial hookups, for RVs up to 38 feet and tents. Picnic tables and fire grills are provided. Restrooms, showers, an RV dump station, limited cell phone reception, a pier, boat rentals, a boat ramp, a coin-operated laundry, a swimming pool (seasonal), a recreation patio, a beer and wine bar, fishing supplies, and a convenience store are available. An ATM is within 1.5 miles. Pets must be leashed and may not be left unattended in camp.

Reservations, fees: Reservations are recommended. The fee is $20 per night, plus $3 per person per night for more than two people and $.50 per pet per night. Open year-round.

Directions: From the town of Lower Lake, drive north on Highway 53 for 1.3 miles to Old Highway 53. Turn left on Old Highway 53 and then almost immediately you will arrive at Cache Creek Way. Turn left and drive .25 mile to the park entrance.

Contact: Shaw's Shady Acres, 707/994-2236.

47 FUNTIME RV PARK & WATERSPORTS

Rating: 7

on Clear Lake
See map pages 524–525

This is one of several privately operated parks near the mouth of Cache Creek at the southern end of Clear Lake. The park offers sites for tents as well as RVs, many near Cache Creek, which actually looks more like a slough—deep, wide, green, and slow-moving. Some may remember this park as "Garner's Resort." It was purchased and renamed in 2002. Note that a mobile home park is on the premises.

RV sites, facilities: There are 40 sites, most drive-through, with full hookups (30, 50 amps) for RVs, 25 tent sites, and six cabins. Picnic tables, barbecues, and cable TV are provided at some sites. Flush toilets, showers, an RV dump station, boat rentals, a pier, a boat ramp, a fish-cleaning station, a swimming pool (seasonal), basketball, horseshoes, fishing supplies, a coin-operated laundry, and a convenience store are available. Some facilities are wheelchair-accessible. Leashed pets are permitted.

Reservations, fees: Reservations are accepted. The fee is $20–26 per night, plus $3 per person per night for more than two people. A senior discount is available. Major credit cards are accepted. Open year-round.

Directions: From the town of Lower Lake, drive north on Highway 53 for 1.3 miles to Old Highway 53. Turn left on Old Highway 53 and drive 1.2 miles to the resort entrance on the left.

Contact: Funtime RV Park & Watersports, 707/994-6267, fax 707/994-6248, website: www.funtimervparks.com.

48 MANCHESTER BEACH KOA

Rating: 7

north of Point Arena at Manchester
State Beach
See map pages 524–525

This is a privately operated KOA park set beside Highway 1 and near the beautiful Manchester State Beach. A great plus here is the cute little log cabins, complete with electric heat. They can provide a great sense of privacy, and after a good sleep, campers are ready to explore the adjacent state park.

RV sites, facilities: There are 43 sites with partial or full RV hookups (20, 30, 50 amps) and 100 tent sites. There are also two cottages and 27 cabins. Picnic tables and fire rings are provided. Drinking water, restrooms, flush toilets, showers, modem access, a heated pool (seasonal), a hot tub and spa, a recreation room, a playground, an RV dump station, a convenience store, ice, firewood, a coin-operated laundry, and propane are available. An ATM is within six miles. Some facilities are wheelchair-accessible. Leashed pets are permitted.

Reservations, fees: Reservations are accepted at 800/562-4188. The fee is $30–45 per night, plus $3–5 per person for more than two people. Major credit cards are accepted. Open year-round.

Directions: On U.S. 101 north of Santa Rosa, turn west on River Road and drive 13 miles to Guerneville and Highway 116. Continue west on Highway 116 and drive about 20 miles to Highway 1 at Jenner. Turn north on Highway 1 and drive 55 miles to Point Arena. From Point Arena, continue north about six miles to the park on the left (west) side of the road.

Contact: Manchester Beach KOA, 707/882-2375, fax 707/882-3104, website: www.manchester beachkoa.com.

49 MANCHESTER STATE PARK

Rating: 8

near Point Arena

See map pages 524–525

Manchester State Park is a beautiful park on the Sonoma coast, set near the Garcia River with the town of Point Arena to the nearby north providing a supply point. If you hit it during one of the rare times when the skies are clear and the wind is down, the entire area will seem aglow in magical sunbeams. The park features 760 acres of beach, sand dunes, and grasslands, with 18,000 feet of ocean frontage and five miles of gentle sandy beach stretching southward toward the Point Arena Lighthouse. The beach curves to form a catch basin for sea debris, which explains

the high volume of driftwood here. The Alder Creek Trail is a great hike here, routed north along beachfront to the mouth of Alder Creek and its beautiful coastal lagoon. This is where the San Andreas Fault heads off from land and into the sea. In winter, the main attraction is steelhead fishing in the Garcia River. In spring and early summer, there is a variety of coastal wildflowers, including sea pinks, poppies, lupines, baby blue eyes, and blue iris. The park provides habitat for tundra swans. The region near the park is grazing land for sheep and cattle.

RV sites, facilities: There are 46 sites for RVs up to 35 feet or tents, 10 environmental sites, and one group site for up to 40 people and RVs up to 21 feet. Picnic tables and fire grills are provided. Drinking water, vault toilets, and an RV dump station are available. Leashed pets are permitted, but no dogs are allowed in environmental sites.

Reservations, fees: Reservations are accepted with a $7.50 reservation fee at 800/444-PARK (800/444-7275) or www.reserveamerica.com. The fees are $12–15 per night, $7 per night for environmental sites, and $30 per night for the group site. A senior discount is available. Open year-round.

Directions: On U.S. 101 north of Santa Rosa, turn west on River Road and drive 16 miles to Guerneville and Highway 116. Continue west on Highway 116 and drive about 20 miles to Highway 1 at Jenner. Turn north on Highway 1 and drive 55 miles to Point Arena. From Point Arena, continue north about five miles to Kinney Lane. Turn left and drive one mile to the campground entrance on the right.

Contact: Manchester State Park, Mendocino District, 707/937-5804, fax 707/937-2953.

50 ROLLERVILLE JUNCTION

Rating: 7

near Point Arena

See map pages 524–525

This privately operated campground has gone through recent renovation, including a new restaurant in 2002. Its location makes it an attractive spot, with the beautiful Manchester State Beach, Alder Creek, and Garcia River all available nearby on one of California's most attractive stretches of coastline. Point Arena Lighthouse and a fishing pier are also nearby. The elevation of the camp is 220 feet.

RV sites, facilities: There are 34 sites, some drive-through, with full hookups (30, 50 amps) for RVs, 10 tent sites, five sleeping cabins, and two park-model cabins. Picnic tables and fire rings are provided. Drinking water, restrooms, flush toilets, hot showers, a hot tub, a heated swimming pool (seasonal), cable TV hookups, modem access, limited cell phone reception, an RV dump station, a coin-operated laundry, a restaurant, a small store, and propane are available. An ATM is within two miles. Some facilities are wheelchair-accessible. Leashed pets are permitted.

Reservations, fees: Reservations are accepted at 800/910-4317. The fee is $27–35 per night, plus $3–5 per person for more than two people. A senior discount is available. Major credit cards are accepted. Open year-round.

Directions: On U.S. 101 north of Santa Rosa, turn west on River Road and drive 16 miles to Guerneville and Highway 116. Continue west on Highway 116 and drive about 20 miles to Highway 1 at Jenner. Turn north on Highway 1 and drive 55 miles to Point Arena. From Point Arena, continue north for 1.5 miles to Point Arena Lighthouse Road and the campground on the left (west side).

Contact: Rollerville Junction, 707/882-2440, fax 707/882-3049, website: www.campingfriend.com/rollervillejunction.

51 ANCHOR BAY CAMPGROUND

Rating: 8

near Gualala
See map pages 524–525

This is a quiet and beautiful stretch of California coast. The campground is on the ocean side of Highway 1 north of Gualala, with sites set at ocean level as well as amid redwood trees—take your pick. Nearby Gualala Regional Park, six miles to the south, provides an excellent easy hike (the headlands-to-beach loop with coastal views), a lookout of the Gualala River, and many giant cypress trees. In winter, the nearby Gualala River attracts large but elusive steelhead.

RV sites, facilities: There are 33 sites, 20 with partial hookups, for RVs or tents. Picnic tables and fire rings are provided. Drinking water, restrooms, flush toilets, coin-operated showers, firewood, and an RV dump station are available. An ATM is within four miles. Leashed pets are permitted.

Reservations, fees: Reservations are accepted. The fee is $27–38 (30 amps), plus $2–5 per person for more than two people, $10–20 for additional vehicles, and $1 per pet per night. A senior discount is available. Major credit cards are accepted. Open year-round.

Directions: On U.S. 101 north of Santa Rosa, turn west on River Road and drive 16 miles to Guerneville and Highway 116. Continue west on Highway 116 and drive about 20 miles to Highway 1 at Jenner. Turn north on Highway 1 and drive 38 miles to Gualala. Continue four miles north on Highway 1 to the campground on the left (west) side of the road.

Contact: Anchor Bay Campground, 707/884-4222, website: www.abcamp.com.

52 GUALALA POINT PARK

Rating: 8

at Sonoma County Regional Park
See map pages 524–525

This is a dramatic spot right on the ocean, adjacent to the mouth of the Gualala River. A trail along the bluff provides an easy hiking adventure; on the west side of the highway other trails to the beach are available.

RV sites, facilities: There are 15 sites for RVs up to 25 feet or tents, five walk-in tent sites, and one hike-in/bike-in site. Picnic tables and fire rings are provided. Drinking water, restrooms, flush toilets, coin-operated showers, an RV dump station, and wood are available. Some facilities are wheelchair-accessible. Leashed pets are permitted.

Reservations, fees: Reservations are accepted with a $7 reservation fee on weekdays at 707/656-2267. The fees are $16 per night and $3 per person per night for hike-in/bike-in site, plus $5 per additional vehicle per night and $1 per pet per night. Open year-round.

Directions: On U.S. 101 north of Santa Rosa, turn west on River Road and drive 16 miles to

Guerneville and Highway 116. Continue west on Highway 116 and drive about 20 miles to Highway 1 at Jenner. Turn north on Highway 1 and drive 38 miles to Gualala. Turn right at the park entrance (a day-use area is on the west side of the highway).

Contact: Gualala Point Park, 707/785-2377, website: www.sonoma-county.org.

53 CLOVERDALE KOA

Rating: 7

near the Russian River
See map pages 524–525

This KOA campground is set just above the Russian River in the Alexander Valley wine country, just south of Cloverdale. The park is both rustic and tidy, with little camping cabins and lodges a great bonus. In addition, a fishing pond is stocked with largemouth bass, bluegill, catfish, and, when water temperatures are cool enough, trout. On moonless nights, this is a great place for stargazing. The nearby Russian River is an excellent beginner's route in an inflatable kayak or canoe. The nearby winery in Asti makes for a popular side trip.

RV sites, facilities: There are 98 sites, six drive-through, with full hookups (30, 50 amps) for RVs, 49 sites for tents, 14 cabins, and three lodges. Picnic tables and fire grills are provided. Flush toilets, showers, modem access, cell phone reception, an ATM, a solar-heated swimming pool, a spa, a playground, an RV dump station, a coin-operated laundry, a recreation room, mini-golf, nature trails, a catch-and-release fish pond, nightly entertainment on weekends in the summer, and a grocery and gift store are available. Leashed pets are permitted.

Reservations, fees: Reservations are accepted at 800/562-4042. The fee is $32–48 per night, plus $7 per person for more than two people and $6 per night for additional vehicle. Major credit cards are accepted. Open year-round.

Directions: From Cloverdale on U.S. 101, take the Central Cloverdale exit, which puts you on Asti Road. Drive straight on Asti Road to 1st Street. Turn right (east) and drive a short distance to River Road. Turn right (south) and drive

four miles to KOA Road. Turn left and drive to the campground entrance.

In summer/fall: south of Cloverdale on U.S. 101, take the Asti exit and drive a short distance to Asti Road. Turn right (south) and drive 1.5 miles to Washington School Road. Turn left (east) and drive 1.5 miles to KOA Road. Turn right and drive to the campground entrance. (Note: This route is open Memorial Day Weekend to late November, when a seasonal bridge is in place.) Both routes are well signed.

Contact: Cloverdale KOA, 707/894-3337 or 800/368-4558 for reservations only, website: www.winecountrykoa.com.

54 DUTCHER CREEK RV PARK AND CAMPGROUND

Rating: 6

near Lake Sonoma
See map pages 524–525

This privately operated campground provides a layover for U.S. 101 cruisers. It has both native and seasonal plant displays, exceptional opportunities for native bird-watching, and the nearby Asti Vineyard provides a side trip. It is set on 25 acres. Lake Sonoma is seven miles to the west, with the best access provided to the south out of Dry Creek Road. The elevation is 385 feet. Note that new owners took over in 2001 and added a swimming pool—a plus—but the majority of sites are long-term rentals, with some mobile homes on the premises—a downer.

RV sites, facilities: There are 38 sites, two drive-through, most with full hookups for RVs up to 36 feet and six tent sites. Picnic tables are provided. Drinking water, restrooms, flush toilets, showers, a heated swimming pool (seasonal), an RV dump station, a pay phone, and a coin-operated laundry are available. Leashed pets are permitted.

Reservations, fees: Reservations are accepted. The fee is $25–35 per night, plus $4 per person for more than two people. Open year-round.

Directions: From Santa Rosa, drive north on U.S. 101 beyond Healdsburg to the Dutcher Creek exit (just south of Cloverdale). Take the Dutcher Creek exit, drive west on Theresa Drive under the freeway, continue .5 mile to the end of Theresa Drive, and follow signs to the park office at 230 Theresa Drive.

Contact: Dutcher Creek RV Park and Campground, 707/894-4829, fax 707/894-4196.

55 BEAVER CREEK RV PARK

Rating: 7

near Cobb Mountain

See map pages 524–525

This camp has a trout creek, a pond with canoes and kayaks in summer, plus plenty of hiking and bird-watching opportunities. In addition, horseback riding and hot-air balloon rides are available nearby. This is one of the few campgrounds in California with tepees. This camp is set near Highway 175 between Middletown and Clear Lake, and while there is a parade of vacation traffic on Highway 29, relatively few people take the longer route on Highway 175. Cobb Mountain looms nearby.

RV sites, facilities: There are 97 sites, most drive-through and all with full hookups, for RVs (30, 50 amps), 10 tent sites, four cabins, and two tepees. Picnic tables and fire rings are provided. Drinking water, restrooms, showers, a group area, a coin-operated laundry, limited cell phone reception, an ATM, modem access, a pool, kayaks and paddleboats, a boating pond, a playground, firewood, propane, horseshoes, a recreation hall, and a store are available. Some facilities are wheelchair-accessible. Leashed pets are permitted.

Reservations, fees: Reservations are accepted at 800/307-2267. The fee is $20–25 per night, plus $2 per person per night for more than two people. Tepees are $25 per night. A senior discount is available. Major credit cards are accepted. Open year-round.

Directions: From Vallejo, drive north on Highway 29 past Calistoga to Middletown and the junction with Highway 175. Turn north on Highway 175 and drive 8.5 miles to Bottle Rock Road. Turn left and drive three miles to the campground entrance on the left side of the road.

Contact: Beaver Creek RV Park, 707/928-4322, fax 707/928-5341, website: www.campbeavercreek .com.

56 BOGGS MOUNTAIN DEMONSTRATION STATE FOREST

Rating: 5

near Middletown

See map pages 524–525

This overlooked spot is set in a state forest that covers 3,500 acres of pine and Douglas fir. There are two adjoining campgrounds here. This is a popular destination for the region's equestrians. There are numerous trails for horses, hikers, and bikers, and there have been some trail conflicts between the groups. Remember: equestrians have the right of way over hikers and bikers, and hikers have the right of way over bikers. Got it? Apparently not, because too many mountain bikers are not yielding out here, and there have been some shouting matches over close calls. Note that in early fall, this area is open to deer hunting, and everybody yields to the guys with rifles. Boggs is one of nine state forests managed with the purpose of demonstrating economical forest management, which means there is logging along with compatible recreation. There is a 14-mile trail system available that started as a series of hand-built fire lines.

RV sites, facilities: There are 20 sites for RVs up to 22 feet or tents. No drinking water is available. Picnic tables and fire pits are provided. Vault toilets are available. Garbage must be packed out. A coin-operated laundry, pizza parlor, and gas station are within two miles. Horses are permitted. Leashed pets are permitted.

Reservations, fees: Reservations are not accepted. There is no fee for camping. Self-registration is required. Open year-round.

Directions: From Vallejo, drive north on Highway 29 past Calistoga to Middletown and the junction with Highway 175. Turn left (north) on Highway 175 and drive seven miles (through the town of Cobb) to Forestry Road. Turn right and drive one mile to the campgrounds on the left.

Contact: Boggs Mountain Demonstration State Forest, 707/928-4378.

CALIFORNIA

57 CACHE CREEK CANYON REGIONAL PARK

Rating: 7

near Rumsey

See map pages 524–525

This is the best campground in Yolo County, yet it's known by few out-of-towners. It is set at 1,300 feet beside Cache Creek, which is the closest river to the Bay Area that provides white-water rafting opportunities. This section of river features primarily Class I and II water, ideal for inflatable kayaks and overnight trips. One rapid, Big Mother, is sometimes considered Class III, though that might be a stretch. Occasionally, huge catfish are caught in this area.

RV sites, facilities: There are 45 sites for RVs or tents and three group sites that can accommodate 20 to 30 people. Picnic tables and fire rings are provided. Drinking water, flush toilets, firewood, and an RV dump station are available. Some facilities are wheelchair-accessible. Leashed pets are permitted.

Reservations, fees: Reservations are not accepted except for group sites. The fee is $15–17 per night, plus $5 per night per additional vehicle and $2 per pet per night. Group sites are $100–150 per night, plus a $25 deposit. A senior discount is available. Open year-round.

Directions: From Vacaville on I-80, turn north on I-505 and drive 21 miles to Madison and the junction with Highway 16 west. Turn northwest on Highway 16 and drive northwest for about 45 miles to the town of Rumsey. From Rumsey, continue west on Highway 16 for five miles to the park entrance on the left.

Contact: Cache Creek Canyon Regional Park, 530/666-8115, fax 530/666-8837.

58 SALT POINT STATE PARK

Rating: 9

near Fort Ross

See map pages 524–525

This is a gorgeous piece of Sonoma coast, highlighted by Fisk Mill Cove, inshore kelp beds, outstanding short hikes, and abalone diving. There is an underwater reserve for divers. In fact, this is one of the finest diving areas for red abalone in the state. Unfortunately there are also diving accidents that are due to the occasional large surf, strong currents, and rocky shoreline. There are two campgrounds here, Gerstle Cove Campground and the much larger Woodside Campground. Great hikes include the Bluff Trail and Stump Beach Trail (great views). During abalone season, this is one of the best and most popular spots on the Northern California coast. The Kruse Rhododendron Reserve is within the park and definitely worth the stroll. This is a 317-acre conservation reserve that features second-growth redwoods, Douglas firs, tan oak, and many rhododendrons, with five miles of hiking trails. After the fall rains, this area is popular for mushroom hunters. Mushroom hunters must park in the area open to picking and be limited to five pounds per day. Of course, this can be a dangerous hobby; only eat mushrooms you can identify as safe. But you knew that, right?

RV sites, facilities: At Gerstle Cove Campground, there are 30 sites for RVs up to 31 feet or tents. At Woodside Campground, there are 79 sites for RVs up to 31 feet or tents, 20 walk-in tent sites (about a 300-yard walk), 10 hike-in/bike-in sites, a group site that can accommodate up to 40 people, and a primitive overflow area for self-contained vehicles. Picnic tables and fire rings are provided. Drinking water, flush toilets, and firewood are available. Summer interpretive programs are also available. An ATM is within two miles. The picnic area and one hiking trail are wheelchair-accessible. Leashed pets are permitted, except on trails.

Reservations, fees: Reservations are accepted with a $7.50 reservation fee at 800/444-PARK (800/444-7275) or www.reserveamerica.com. The fees are is $12 per night, $2 per night for hike-in/bike-in sites, $90 for the group site, and $10 per night for overflow sites. A senior discount is available. Open year-round.

Directions: On U.S. 101 north of Santa Rosa, turn west on River Road and drive 16 miles to Guerneville and Highway 116. Continue west on Highway 116 and drive about 20 miles to Highway 1 at Jenner. Turn north on Highway 1 and drive about 20 miles to the park entrance; Woodside Campground on the right and Gerstle Cove on the left.

Contact: Salt Point State Park, 707/847-3221; Duncan Mills District, 707/865-2391, fax 707/847-3843.

59 OCEAN COVE CAMPGROUND

Rating: 8

on the ocean five miles north of Fort Ross
See map pages 524–525

The highlights here are the campsites on a bluff overlooking the ocean. Alas, it can be foggy during the summer. A good side trip is to Fort Ross, with a stellar easy hike available on the Fort Ross Trail, which features a walk through an old colonial fort as well as great coastal views, excellent for whale-watching. There is also excellent hiking at Stillwater Cove Regional Park, just a mile to the south off Highway 1.

RV sites, facilities: There are 125 drive-through sites for RVs or tents. Picnic tables and fire grills are provided. Drinking water, chemical toilets, limited cell phone reception, an ATM, and coin-operated showers are available. A boat launch, a grocery store, fishing supplies, and diving gear sales are available nearby. Leashed pets are permitted.

Reservations, fees: Reservations are not accepted. The fee is $14 per night per vehicle, plus $1 per pet per night. Major credit cards are accepted. Open April through November.

Directions: On U.S. 101 north of Santa Rosa, turn west on River Road and drive 16 miles to Guerneville and Highway 116. Continue west on Highway 116 and drive about 20 miles to Highway 1 at Jenner. Turn north on Highway 1 and drive 17 miles (five miles north of Fort Ross) to the campground entrance on the left.

Contact: Ocean Cove Campground, 707/847-3422, website: www.ocean-cove.com.

60 STILLWATER COVE REGIONAL PARK

Rating: 8

near Fort Ross
See map pages 524–525

Stillwater Cove has a dramatic rock-strewn cove and sits on a classic chunk of Sonoma coast. The campground is sometimes overlooked, since it is a county-operated park and not on the state park reservation system. One of the region's great hikes is available here: the Stockoff Creek Loop, with the trailhead at the day-use parking lot. In a little over a mile, the trail is routed through forest with both firs and redwoods, and then along a pretty stream. To get beach access, you will need to cross Highway 1 and then drop to the cove.

RV sites, facilities: There are 20 sites for RVs up to 35 feet or tents and a hike-in/bike-in site. Picnic tables and fire rings are provided. Drinking water, flush toilets, coin-operated showers, limited cell phone reception, firewood, and RV dump station are available. Supplies can be obtained in Ocean Cove (one mile north) and Fort Ross. Some facilities are wheelchair-accessible. Leashed pets are permitted.

Reservations, fees: Reservations are accepted with a $7 reservation fee at 707/565-2267 on weekdays. The fee is $16 per night, plus $5 per night for each additional vehicle and and $1 per pet per night. The hike-in/bike-in site is $3 per night. Open year-round.

Directions: On U.S. 101 north of Santa Rosa, turn west on River Road and drive 16 miles to Guerneville and Highway 116. Continue west on Highway 116 and drive about 20 miles to Highway 1 at Jenner. Turn north on Highway 1 and drive 16 miles north on Highway 1 (four miles north of Fort Ross) to the park entrance.

Contact: Stillwater Cove Regional Park, Sonoma County, 707/847-3245, website: www.sonoma-county.org.

61 FORT ROSS REEF

Rating: 8

at Fort Ross State Historic Park
See map pages 524–525

Fort Ross is just as it name announces: an old fort, in this case, an old Russian fort from 1812. The campground is two miles south of the north entrance station, less than a quarter mile from the ocean. Some redwoods and pines provide cover, and some sites are open. The privacy and beauty of the campsites vary as much as any state park camp in California. The sites at the end of the road fill up very quickly. Though the weather is relatively benign, there is often fog.

From camp, a trail leads down to a beach, more rocky than sandy, and a quarter-mile trail leads to the fort. As a destination site, Fort Ross is known as a popular abalone diving spot, with the best areas below the campground and also at nearby Reef Terrace. It also provides good, easy hikes amid its 3,386 acres. The park features a museum in the visitors center, which is always a must-see for campers making the tour up Highway 1.

RV sites, facilities: There are 20 sites for RVs up to 17 feet or tents. Picnic tables and fire rings are provided. Drinking water and flush toilets are available. Supplies can be obtained nearby. A visitors center and guided tours and programs are available. An ATM is within two miles. Some facilities are wheelchair-accessible. Leashed pets are permitted.

Reservations, fees: Reservations are not accepted. The fee is $10 per night, plus $2 per additional vehicle and a $4 day-use fee. A senior discount is available. Open April through November, weather permitting.

Directions: On U.S. 101 north of Santa Rosa, turn west on River Road and drive 16 miles to Guerneville and Highway 116. Continue west on Highway 116 and drive about 20 miles to Highway 1 at Jenner. Turn north on Highway 1 and drive 10 miles north on Highway 1 to the Fort Ross State Park. The campground entrance is two miles north of the main state park entrance.

Contact: Fort Ross State Historic Park, 707/847-3286 or 707/847-3708.

62 FAERIE RING CAMPGROUND

Rating: 7

near the Russian River
See map pages 524–525

If location is everything, then this privately operated campground is set right in the middle of the best of it in the Russian River region. It is a half mile north of the Russian River and a half mile south of Armstrong Redwoods State Park.

RV sites, facilities: There are nine sites with partial or full hookups for RVs up to 35 feet, 33 sites for tents, and several lodging rooms. Picnic tables and fire rings are provided. Drinking water, flush toilets, coin-operated showers, and an RV dump station are available. A clubhouse with exercise area and a meeting room with kitchen facilities are available for groups. Leashed pets are permitted.

Reservations, fees: Reservations are accepted. The fee is $20–25 per night, plus $3–5 per person for more than two people and $2 per pet per night. Group and monthly rates are available. Major credit cards are accepted. Open year-round.

Directions: On U.S. 101 north of Santa Rosa, turn west on River Road and drive 15 miles to Guerneville and Armstrong Woods Road. At Armstrong Woods Road, turn right and drive 1.5 miles to the campground on the right.

Contact: Faerie Ring Campground, 707/869-2746.

63 HILTON PARK FAMILY CAMPGROUND

Rating: 6

on the Russian River
See map pages 524–525

This lush, wooded park is set on the banks of the Russian River, with a choice of open or secluded sites. The highlight of the campground is a large, beautiful beach that offers access for swimming, fishing, and canoeing. The folks here are very friendly, and you get a choice of many recreation options in the area.

RV sites, facilities: There are five sites for RVs up to 33 feet and 20 tent sites. Picnic tables and fire rings are provided. Restrooms, coin-operated showers, a dishwashing area, an ATM, an arcade, a playground, firewood, and ice are available. A beach is nearby. Canoe rentals are available within three miles. Leashed pets are permitted.

Reservations, fees: Reservations are recommended. The fee is $30–40 per night, plus $5 per person per night for more than three people. Pets are $5 per night. A senior discount is available. Open year-round.

Directions: From U.S. 101 north of Santa Rosa, take the River Road/Guerneville exit. Drive west for 11.5 miles (one mile after the metal bridge) to the campground on the left side of the road (just before the Russian River Pub).

Contact: Hilton Park Family Campground, 707/887-9206, website: www.hiltonparkcampground.com.

64 BURKE'S CANOE TRIPS

Rating: 7

on the Russian River
See map pages 524–525

The catch here is that if you want to camp, you have go on a canoe trip. That's just the deal you might be looking for, a fantastic overnighter for many. Burke's is the long-established canoe rental service and campground on the Russian River. The favorite trip is the 10-miler from Burke's in Forestville to Guerneville, which is routed right through the heart of the area's redwoods, about a 3.5-hour paddle trip with plenty of time in the day for sunbathing, swimming, or anything else you can think of. The cost is $42, including a return by shuttle. Many other trips are available.

RV sites, facilities: There are 60 sites for RVs or tents. Picnic tables and fire rings are provided. Flush toilets, showers, wood, limited cell phone reception, and canoe rentals are available. An ATM is within two miles. Pets are not allowed.

Reservations, fees: Reservations are required. The fee is $18 per night, plus $9 per person per night for more than two people. Open May through mid-October.

Directions: From the Bay Area, drive north on U.S. 101 to the junction with Highway 116 West (just north of Petaluma). Take Highway 116 West and drive 15 miles to Forestville and Mirabel Road (at the gas station). Turn right and drive 1.5 miles until it dead-ends at Burke's and the Russian River.

Contact: Burke's Canoe Trips, 707/887-1222, website: www.burkescanoetrips.com.

65 SCHOOLHOUSE CANYON CAMPGROUND

Rating: 8

in the Russian River Valley
See map pages 524–525

This campground comprises 210 acres and features a mile of river access along the Russian River, campsites in a grove of large redwoods, and a parklike setting on land originally homesteaded in the 1850s. A scenic hiking trail, two miles round-trip, is routed up to a ridge for some nice views of the countryside. This overlooks Korbel Winery and vineyards, with long-distance views of four counties. Touring the adjacent Korbel Winery is a popular side trip.

RV sites, facilities: There are 45 sites, some with partial hookups (30 amps), for RVs up to 24 feet or tents. Picnic tables and fire grills are provided. Drinking water, flush toilets, coin-operated showers, limited cell phone reception, and firewood are available. An ATM is within four miles. Some facilities are wheelchair-accessible. Leashed pets are permitted.

Reservations, fees: Reservations are accepted. The fee is $25 per night for two people, plus $5 for each additional person, $5 per night for additional vehicle, and $4 per pet per night. Open May through October.

Directions: From Santa Rosa, drive north on U.S. 101 about 2.5 miles and take the River Road/Guerneville exit. Drive to the stop sign, turn left on River Road, and drive 12.5 miles to the campground entrance (next to Korbel Winery) on the right.

Contact: Schoolhouse Canyon Campground, 707/869-2311.

66 MIRABEL TRAILER PARK AND CAMP

Rating: 7

on the Russian River
See map pages 524–525

The big attraction here during the summer is swimming and paddling around in canoes or kayaks. The campsites are shaded by redwood, pine, and bay trees. This privately operated park is near the Russian River, but in the summer the "river" is actually a series of small lakes, with temporary dams stopping most of the water flow. In winter, out come the dams, up comes the water, and in come the steelhead, migrating upstream past this area. Armstrong Redwoods State Park just north of Guerneville provides a nearby side trip. Note that about half of the sites are booked for the entire summer.

RV sites, facilities: There are 125 sites with partial or full hookups (20, 30, amps) for RVs up to 35 feet and tents. Picnic tables and fire grills are provided. Flush toilets, showers, a coin-operated laundry, an RV dump station, horseshoes,

CALIFORNIA

shuffleboard, limited cell phone reception, a small video arcade, and canoe and kayak rentals are available. An ATM is within two miles. Leashed pets, except pit bulls (which are prohibited), are allowed.

Reservations, fees: Reservations are recommended. The fee is $20–25 per night, plus $3 per person per night for more than two people, $3 per additional vehicle per night, and $3 per pet per night. Open March through October.

Directions: North of Santa Rosa on U.S. 101, take the River Road exit and head west. Drive eight miles to the campground on the right at 8400 River Road.

Contact: Mirabel Trailer Park and Camp, tel./fax 707/887-2383.

67 WINDSORLAND RV PARK

Rating: 3

near Santa Rosa
See map pages 524–525

This developed park is close to the Russian River, the wine country to the east, redwoods to the west, and Lake Sonoma to the northwest. But with a swimming pool, playground, and recreation room, many visitors are content to stay right here, spend the night, then head out on their vacation. Note that some sites are long-term rentals.

RV sites, facilities: There are 55 sites with full hookups (30 amps) for RVs up to 35 feet and a separate area for tents. Patios are provided. Flush toilets, showers, a heated swimming pool (seasonal), an RV dump station, cell phone reception, a coin-operated laundry, a recreation room, a picnic area, and a playground are available. An ATM and modem access are available within a half mile. Leashed pets are permitted.

Reservations, fees: Reservations are accepted. The fee is $25–30 per night. Monthly rates are available. A senior discount is available. Open year-round.

Directions: From Santa Rosa on U.S. 101, drive north for nine miles to Windsor. Take the Windsor exit, turn north on Old Redwood Highway, and drive .5 mile to the park on the right (9290 Old Redwood Highway).

Contact: Windsorland RV Park, 707/838-4882 or 800/864-3407, website: www.windsorland.com.

68 BOTHE–NAPA VALLEY STATE PARK

Rating: 7

near Calistoga
See map pages 524–525

It's always a stunner for newcomers to discover this beautiful park with redwoods and a pretty stream so close to the Napa Valley wine and spa country. Though the campsites are relatively exposed, they are set beneath a pretty oak/bay/madrone forest, with trailheads for hiking nearby. One trail is routed south from the day-use parking lot for 1.1 mile to the restored Bale Grist Mill, a giant partially restored waterwheel on a pretty creek. Weekend tours of the Bale Grist Mill are available in summer. Another, more scenic, route, the Redwood Trail, heads up Ritchey Canyon, amid redwoods and towering Douglas fir, and along Ritchey Creek, all of it beautiful and intimate. The park covers 2,000 acres. Most of it is rugged, with elevations ranging from 300 feet to 2,000 feet. In summer, temperatures can reach the 100s, which is why finding a redwood grove can be stunning. The park has 10 miles of trails. Those who explore will find that the forests are on the north-facing slopes while the south-facing slopes tend to be brushy. The geology here is primarily volcanic, yet the vegetation hides most of it. Bird-watchers will note that this is one of the few places where you can see six species of woodpeckers, including the star of the show, the pileated woodpecker (the size of a crow).

RV sites, facilities: There are 40 sites for RVs up to 31 feet or tents, one hike-in/bike-in site, and one group tent site for up to 30 people. Picnic tables and fire grills are provided. Drinking water, flush toilets, coin-operated showers, limited cell phone reception, and a swimming pool in the summer are available. Supplies can be obtained four miles away in Calistoga. Some facilities are wheelchair-accessible. Leashed pets are permitted.

Reservations, fees: Reservations are accepted with a $7.50 reservation fee at 800/444-PARK (800/444-7275) or www.reserveamerica.com. The fees are $16 per night, $2 for hike-in/bike-in site, and $22 for the group site, plus a $2 pool fee (free for children 16 and under). A senior discount is available. Open year-round.

Directions: From Napa on Highway 29, drive north to St. Helena and continue north for five miles (one mile past the entrance to Bale Grist Mill State Park) to the park entrance road on the left.

Contact: Bothe–Napa Valley State Park, 707/942-4575, website: www.napanet.net/~bothe.

69 NAPA COUNTY FAIRGROUNDS

Rating: 2

in Calistoga

See map pages 524–525

What this really is, folks, is just the county fairgrounds, converted to an RV park. It is open year-round, including when the county fair is in progress. Who knows, maybe you can win a stuffed animal. What is more likely, of course, is that you have come here for the health spas, with great natural hot springs, mud baths, and assorted goodies at the health resorts in Calistoga. Nearby parks for hiking include Bothe–Napa Valley and Robert Louis Stevenson State Parks.

RV sites, facilities: There are 78 sites, some drive-through, with partial or full hookups for RVs and a lawn area for tents. Group sites are available by reservation only with a 10-vehicle minimum. Restrooms, showers, and an RV dump station are available. No fires are permitted. A nine-hole golf course is adjacent to the campground area. Some facilities are wheelchair-accessible. Leashed pets are permitted.

Reservations, fees: Reservations are accepted and required for groups. The fee is $10–25 per night. Major credit cards are accepted. Open year-round.

Directions: From Napa on Highway 29, drive north to Calistoga, turn right on Lincoln Avenue, and drive four blocks to Fairway. Turn left and drive about four blocks to the end of the road to the campground.

Contact: Napa County Fairgrounds, 707/942-5221 (reservations) or 707/942-5111, fax 707/942-5125, website: www.napacountyfairgrounds.com.

70 CASINI RANCH FAMILY CAMPGROUND

Rating: 8

on the Russian River

See map pages 524–525

Woods and water—this campground has both, with sites set near the Russian River in both sun-filled and shaded areas. Its location on the lower river makes a side trip to the coast easy, with the Sonoma Coast State Beach about a 15-minute drive to the nearby west. No long-term rentals are available.

RV sites, facilities: There are 225 sites, some drive-through and many with partial or full hookups (30 amps), for RVs and tents. Picnic tables and fire grills are provided. Flush toilets, showers, a playground, an RV dump station, a coin-operated laundry, cable TV, modem access, limited cell phone reception, an ATM, a video and game arcade, boat and canoe rentals, propane, and a grocery store are available. Some facilities are wheelchair-accessible. Leashed pets are permitted.

Reservations, fees: Reservations are recommended. The fee is $24–32 per night, plus $3 per person for more than two people. Weekly and monthly rates are available. A senior discount is available. Major credit cards are accepted. Open year-round.

Directions: On U.S. 101 north of Santa Rosa, turn west on River Road and drive 16 miles to Guerneville and Highway 116. Continue west on Highway 116 and drive seven miles to Duncan Mills and Moscow Road. Turn left (southeast) on Moscow Road and drive .7 mile to the campground on the left.

Contact: Casini Ranch Family Campground, 707/865-2255 or 800/451-8400 (reservations), fax 707/865-0147.

71 WRIGHTS BEACH

Rating: 8

in Sonoma Coast State Beach

See map pages 524–525

This park provides for more than its share of heaven and hell. This state park campground is at the north end of a beach that stretches south for several miles, yet to the north it is steep and rocky. The campsites are considered a premium because of their location next to the beach. Because the campsites are often full, a key plus is an overflow area available for self-contained vehicles. The beach actually consists of a series of beaches that are separated by rock bluffs and headlands and extends for 17 miles from Bodega Head to Vista Trail (four miles north of Jenner). You can reach the beach from more than a dozen points along the highway. There are many excellent side trips. The best is to the north, where you can explore dramatic Shell Beach (the turnoff is on the west side of Highway 1), or take the Pomo Trail (the trailhead is on the east side of the highway, across from Shell Beach) up the adjacent foothills for sweeping views of the coast. That's the heaven. Now for the hell: more than 125 people have drowned here. Wrights Beach is not for swimming because of rip currents, heavy surf, and surprise rogue waves that can make even surf play dangerous. Many rescues are made each year. The bluffs and coastal rocks can also be unstable and unsafe for climbing. Got it? 1. Stay clear of the water. 2. Don't climb the bluffs. Now it's up to you to get it right.

RV sites, facilities: There are 30 sites for RVs up to 27 feet or tents, with a limit of eight people per site, and an overflow area for self-contained vehicles. Picnic tables and fire rings are provided. Drinking water and flush toilets are available. Showers are available at nearby Bodega Dunes Campground. Leashed pets are permitted.

Reservations, fees: Reservations are accepted with a $7.50 reservation fee at 800/444-PARK (800/444-7275) or www.reserveamerica.com. The fee is $17–20 per night, plus $4 per additional vehicle. A senior discount is available. Open year-round, weather permitting.

Directions: In Petaluma on U.S. 101, take the East Washington exit and turn west (this street becomes Bodega Avenue). Drive west through Petaluma and continue for 17 miles to Highway 1. Turn right (north) on Highway 1 and drive nine miles to Bodega Bay. From Bodega Bay, continue north for six miles to the campground entrance.

Contact: Sonoma Coast State Beach, 707/875-3483.

72 BODEGA DUNES

Rating: 8

in Sonoma Coast State Beach
See map pages 524–525

Sonoma Coast State Beach features several great campgrounds, and if you like the beach, this one rates high. It is set at the end of a beach that stretches for miles, providing stellar beach walks and excellent beachcombing during low tides. For some campers, a foghorn sounding repeatedly through the night can make sleep difficult. The quietest sites here are among the dunes. A day-use area includes a wheelchair-accessible boardwalk that leads out to a sandy beach. In summer, campfire programs and Junior Ranger programs are often available. To the nearby south is Bodega Bay, including a major deep-sea sportfishing operation, crowned by often excellent salmon fishing, best in July. The town of Bodega Bay offers a full marina and restaurants. This beach is far safer than Wrights Beach. (See the previous listing for details about Sonoma Coast State Beach.)

RV sites, facilities: There are 98 sites for RVs up to 31 feet or tents, with a limit of eight people per site, and one hike-in/bike-in site. Picnic tables and fire grills are provided. Drinking water, flush toilets, coin-operated showers, and an RV dump station are available. Laundry facilities, an ATM, supplies, limited cell phone reception, and horse rentals are available within one mile. Some facilities are wheelchair-accessible. Leashed pets are permitted at the campsites only.

Reservations, fees: Reservations are accepted with a $7.50 reservation fee at 800/444-PARK (800/444-7275) or www.reserveamerica.com. The fee is $13–16 per night, plus $4 per additional vehicle and $1 per pet per night. A senior discount is available. Open year-round, weather permitting.

Directions: In Petaluma on U.S. 101, take the East Washington exit and turn west (this street becomes Bodega Avenue). Drive west through Petaluma and continue for 17 miles to Highway 1. Turn right (north) on Highway 1 and drive nine miles to Bodega Bay. In Bodega Bay, drive .5 mile north to the campground entrance on the left (west).

Contact: Sonoma Coast State Beach, 707/875-3483.

73 BODEGA BAY RV PARK

Rating: 8

in Bodega Bay
See map pages 524–525

Bodega Bay RV Park is one of the oldest RV parks in the state, and there are few coastal destinations better than Bodega Bay. Excellent seafood restaurants are available within five minutes, and some of the best deep-sea fishing is available out of Bodega Bay Sportfishing. In addition, there is a great view of the ocean at nearby Bodega Head to the west. It is a 35-minute walk from the park to the beach.

RV sites, facilities: There are 85 sites, some drive-through and most with full hookups, for RVs and one trailer rental. Picnic tables and fire rings are provided. Drinking water, flush toilets, and showers are available. A coin-operated laundry, horseshoes, a video arcade, boccie ball, modem access, and cable TV hookups are available. Some facilities are wheelchair-accessible. Leashed pets are permitted.

Reservations, fees: Reservations are recommended and may be made at 800/201-6864. The fee is $25–31 per night for two people, plus $2 for each additional person. A senior discount is available in the off-season. Major credit cards are accepted. Open year-round.

Directions: In Petaluma on U.S. 101, take the East Washington exit and turn west (this street becomes Bodega Avenue). Drive west through Petaluma and continue for 17 miles to Highway 1. Turn right (north) on Highway 1 and drive nine miles to Bodega Bay. In Bodega Bay, continue north for two miles to the RV park on the left.

Contact: Bodega Bay RV Park, 707/875-3701, website: www.bodegabayrv.com.

74 DORAN REGIONAL PARK

Rating: 7

on Bodega Bay
See map pages 524–525

This campground is set beside Doran Beach on Bodega Bay, which offers complete fishing and marina facilities. In season, it's also a popular clamming and crabbing spot. Salmon fishing is

often excellent during the summer at the Whistle Buoy offshore from Bodega Head, and rock fishing is good year-round at Cordell Bank. Fishing is also available off the rock jetty in the park.

RV sites, facilities: There are 128 sites for RVs or tents and 10 sites for tents. Picnic tables and fire grills are provided. Drinking water, flush toilets, coin-operated showers, RV dump stations, a fish-cleaning station, firewood, limited cell phone reception, and a boat ramp are available. Supplies can be obtained in Bodega Bay. An ATM is within one mile. Some facilities are wheelchair-accessible. Leashed pets are permitted.

Reservations, fees: Reservations are accepted with a $7 reservation fee on weekdays at 707/565-2267. The fee is $16 per night, plus $5 per additional vehicle per night and $1 per pet per night. Open year-round.

Directions: In Petaluma on U.S. 101, take the East Washington exit and turn west (this street becomes Bodega Avenue). Drive west through Petaluma and continue for 17 miles to Highway 1. Turn right (north) on Highway 1 and drive toward Bodega Bay and look for the campground entrance on the right. If you reach the town of Bodega Bay, you have gone a mile too far.

Contact: Sonoma County Parks Department, 707/875-3540, website: www.sonoma-county.org.

75 WESTSIDE REGIONAL PARK

Rating: 7

on Bodega Bay
See map pages 524–525

This campground is on the west shore of Bodega Bay. One of the greatest boat launches on the coast is nearby to the south, providing access to prime fishing waters. Salmon fishing is excellent from mid-June through August. A small, protected beach (for kids to dig in the sand and wade) is available at the end of the road beyond the campground.

RV sites, facilities: There are 43 sites for RVs or tents. Picnic tables and fire grills are provided. Drinking water, flush toilets, coin-operated showers, limited cell phone reception, a fish-cleaning station, firewood, and a boat ramp are available. An ATM is within one mile. Supplies can be obtained in Bodega Bay, less than one mile away.

CALIFORNIA

Some facilities are wheelchair-accessible. Leashed pets are permitted.

Reservations, fees: Reservations are accepted with a $7 reservation fee on weekdays at 707/565-2267. The fee is $16 per night, plus $5 per additional vehicle and $1 per pet per night. Open year-round.

Directions: In Petaluma on U.S. 101, take the East Washington exit and turn west (this street becomes Bodega Avenue). Drive west through Petaluma and continue for 17 miles to Highway 1. Turn right (north) on Highway 1 and drive nine miles to Bodega Bay. In Bodega Bay, continue north to Bay Flat Road. Turn left on Bay Flat Road and drive two miles (looping around the bay) to the campground on the right.

Contact: Westside Regional Park, Sonoma County Parks Department, 707/875-3540, website: www.sonoma-county.org.

76 SPRING LAKE REGIONAL PARK

Rating: 6

at Spring Lake near Santa Rosa
See map pages 524–525

Spring Lake is one of the few lakes in the greater Bay Area that provides lakeside camping. Not only that, Spring Lake is stocked twice each month in late winter and spring with rainbow trout by the Department of Fish and Game. Only nonpowered boats are permitted on this small, pretty lake, which keeps things fun and quiet for everybody. An easy trail along the west shore of the lake to the dam, then into adjoining Howarth Park, provides a pleasant evening stroll. This little lake is where a 24-pound world-record bass was reportedly caught, a story taken as a hoax by nearly all anglers.

RV sites, facilities: There are 30 sites for RVs up to 44 feet or tents. Picnic tables and fire grills are provided. Drinking water, restrooms with flush toilets, showers, an RV dump station, a boat ramp (no gas-powered motorboats), and boat rentals (in summer) are available. A grocery store, a coin-operated laundry, firewood, and propane are available within five minutes. Some facilities are wheelchair-accessible. Leashed pets are permitted with proof of rabies vaccination.

Reservations, fees: Reservations are accepted at

707/565-2267. The fee is $16 per night, plus $5 per night for second vehicle and $1 per pet per night. There is a 10-day camping limit, with a limit of eight people and two vehicles per campsite. Open daily from mid-May through mid-September and on weekends and holidays only during off-season.

Directions: From Santa Rosa on U.S. 101, turn east on Highway 12 (it will become Hoen Avenue) and continue about .5 mile to Newanga Avenue. Turn left and drive .25 mile to the park at the end of the road.

Contact: Spring Lake Regional Park, Sonoma County Parks, 707/539-8092 or 707/565-2041.

77 SUGARLOAF RIDGE STATE PARK

Rating: 5

near Santa Rosa
See map pages 524–525

Sugarloaf Ridge State Park is a perfect example of a place that you can't make a final judgment about from your first glance. Your first glance will lead you to believe that this is just hot foothill country, with old ranch roads set in oak woodlands for horseback riding and sweaty hiking or biking. A little discovery here, however, is that a half-mile walk off the Canyon Trail will lead you to 25-foot waterfall, beautifully set in a canyon, complete with a redwood canopy. A shortcut to this waterfall is available off the south side of the park's entrance road. Otherwise, it can be a long, hot, and challenging hike. In all, there are 25 miles of trail here for hikers and equestrians. Hikers planning for a day of it should leave early, wear a hat, and bring plenty of water. Rangers report that some unprepared hikers have suffered heat stroke in summer, and many others have just plain suffered. In the off-season, when the air is cool and clear, the views from the ridge are eye-popping—visitors can see the Sierra Nevada, Golden Gate, and a thousand other points of scenic beauty from the top of Bald Mountain at 2,769 feet. For the less ambitious, a self-guided nature trail along Sonoma Creek begins at the campground.

RV sites, facilities: There are 47 sites for RVs up to 27 feet or tents and one group site for tents only for up to 50 people. Picnic tables and fire grills are provided. Drinking water and flush toilets are available. Leashed pets are permitted in campsites only.

Reservations, fees: Reservations are accepted with a $7.50 reservation fee at 800/444-PARK (800/444-7275) or www.reserveamerica.com. The fees are $12 per night, $37 per night for group site. A senior discount is available. Open year-round.

Directions: From Santa Rosa on U.S. 101, turn east on Highway 12 and drive seven miles to Adobe Canyon Road. Turn left and drive 3.5 miles to the park entrance at the end of the road.

Contact: Sugarloaf Ridge State Park, 707/833-5712.

78 PUTAH CREEK RESORT

Rating: 7

on Lake Berryessa
See map pages 524–525

This campground is set at 400 feet elevation on the northern end of Lake Berryessa. The Putah Creek arm provides very good bass fishing in the spring and trout trolling in the summer. The north end of the lake has a buoy line that keeps powerboats out, but it can still be explored by paddling a canoe, which allows you to fish in relatively untouched waters and see deer during the evening on the eastern shore. In the fall, usually by mid-October, the trout come to the surface and provide excellent fishing at the mouth of Pope Creek or Putah Creek for anglers drifting live minnows. The resort also has a small, rustic motel.

RV sites, facilities: There are 55 sites with partial or full hookups, some drive-through, for RVs, 175 sites for tents, and a motel. Picnic tables and barbecues are provided. Restrooms, showers, an RV dump station, a coin-operated laundry, two boat ramps, rowboat rentals, a snack bar, a motel, a cocktail lounge, a restaurant, propane, ice, and a convenience store are available. Leashed pets are permitted; no pit bulls or rottweilers.

Reservations, fees: Reservations are accepted. The fee is $21–26 per night, plus $21 for a second vehicle and $2 per pet per night. There is a two-week camping limit in season. Major credit cards are accepted. Open year-round.

Directions: From Vallejo, drive north on I-80 to the Suisun Valley Road exit. Take Suisun Valley Road and drive north to Highway 121. Turn north on Highway 121 and drive five miles to Highway 128. Turn left on Highway 128, drive five miles to Berryessa-Knoxville Road, and continue 13 miles to 7600 Knoxville Road.

Contact: Putah Creek Resort, 707/966-0794 (reservations) or 707/966-2116, fax 707/966-0593.

79 LAKE BERRYESSA MARINA RESORT

Rating: 7

on Lake Berryessa
See map pages 524–525

Lake Berryessa is the Bay Area's backyard water recreation headquarters, the number one lake (in the greater Bay Area) for water-skiing, loafing, and fishing. This resort is set on the west shore of the main lake, one of several resorts at the lake. The addition of park-model cabins is a great plus here.

RV sites, facilities: There are 45 sites with partial hookups (30 amps) for RVs up to 40 feet, 73 sites for tents, and 15 park-model cabins. Flush toilets, showers, an RV dump station, modem access, limited cell phone reception, a coin-operated laundry, a snack bar, complete marina facilities, RV supplies, and a convenience store are available. Leashed pets are permitted at RV sites (but prohibited at tent sites and cabins).

Reservations, fees: Reservations are recommended. The fee is $30–35 per night, plus $9 per night for additional vehicle and $1 per pet per night. Major credit cards are accepted. Open year-round.

Directions: From Vallejo, drive north on I-80 to the Suisun Valley Road exit. Take Suisun Valley Road and drive north to Highway 121. Turn north on Highway 121 and drive five miles to Highway 128. Turn left on Highway 128, drive five miles to Berryessa-Knoxville Road, turn right, and continue nine miles to 5800 Knoxville Road.

Contact: Lake Berryessa Marina Resort, 707/966-2161, fax 707/966-0761, website: www.lakeberryessa.com.

80 SPANISH FLAT RESORT

Rating: 7

on Lake Berryessa
See map pages 524–525

This is one of several lakeside camps at Lake Berryessa. As at Lake Berryessa Marina Resort, the addition of park-model cabins has given this resort a nice touch. This is one of the most popular because many of the sites are on the waterfront, making it a natural gathering place for water-skiers and powerboaters, and on summer weekends, particularly holidays, it can get rowdy here. Berryessa, considered the Bay Area's backyard fishing hole, is the third largest man-made lake in Northern California (Lakes Shasta and Oroville are larger). Trout fishing is good, trolling deep in the summer in Skier's Cove from dawn to mid-morning, or drifting with minnows in fall and winter. The elevation is approximately 500 feet.

RV sites, facilities: There are 120 sites, a few with partial hookups, for RVs up to 37 feet or tents, two yurts, and 12 park-model cabins. Picnic tables and fire grills are provided. Restrooms, drinking water, flush toilets, showers, a boat launch, complete marina facilities, an ATM, boat rentals, and a convenience store are available. A deli and grill are open on summer weekends. A coin-operated laundry, a restaurant, and RV supplies are available within 1.5 miles. Some facilities are wheelchair-accessible. Leashed pets are permitted.

Reservations, fees: Reservations are accepted. The fees are $24–32 per night and $45 per night for yurts, plus $5 for boat launching and $2 per pet per night. There is a camping limit of two weeks. Major credit cards are accepted. Open year-round.

Directions: From Vallejo, drive north on I-80 to the Suisun Valley Road exit. Take Suisun Valley Road and drive north to Highway 121. Turn north on Highway 121 and drive five miles to Highway 128. Turn north on Highway 128 and drive five miles to Berryessa-Knoxville Road. Turn right on Berryessa-Knoxville Road and continue four miles to 4290 Knoxville Road.

Contact: Spanish Flat Resort, 707/966-7700, fax 707/966-7704, website: www.spanishflatresort.com; Spanish Flat Marina, 707/966-7708.

81 PLEASURE COVE RESORT

Rating: 7

on Lake Berryessa
See map pages 524–525
Pleasure Cove is set deep in an extended lake arm on the south end of Lake Berryessa. This park is family-oriented. Of the resorts at Berryessa, this one is sometimes overlooked because of its off-the-beaten-path location. It is an excellent area of the lake for trout and bass fishing. Top nearby fishing spots include the Monticello Dam and the narrows, as well as beyond to the north at Skier's Cove for trout and salmon, and to the south at the back of the coves of the Markley Cove arm for bass.

RV sites, facilities: There are 105 sites, most with partial hookups, for RVs or tents, and five park-model cabins. Picnic tables, fire rings, and barbecues are provided. Restrooms, showers, ice, a restaurant, a bar, a marina, bait and tackle, a boat ramp, propane, an RV dump station, and a store are available. Some facilities are wheelchair-accessible. Pets are not permitted.

Reservations, fees: Reservations are accepted. The fee is $20–24 per night per vehicle. Major credit cards are accepted. Open year-round.

Directions: From Vallejo, drive north on I-80 about 10 miles to the Suisun Valley Road exit. Take Suisun Valley Road and drive north another 10 miles to Highway 121. Turn north (right) on Highway 121 and drive about eight miles to the end of Highway 121 and the junction with Highway 128. Bear right (southeast) on Highway 128 and proceed four miles to Wragg Canyon Road. Turn left and continue three miles to the resort entrance at the end of the road.

Contact: Pleasure Cove Resort, 707/966-2172, fax 707/966-0320.

82 LAKE SOLANO COUNTY PARK

Rating: 6

near Lake Berryessa
See map pages 524–525
Lake Solano provides a low-pressure option to nearby Lake Berryessa. It is a long, narrow lake set below the outlet at Monticello Dam at Lake Berryessa, technically called the afterbay. Compared to Berryessa, life here moves at a much slower pace and some people prefer it. The lake has fair trout fishing in the spring, and it is known among Bay Area anglers as the closest fly-fishing spot for trout in the region. No motors, including electric motors, are permitted at the lake.

CALIFORNIA

The park covers 177 acres along the river. A swimming pond is available in summer.

RV sites, facilities: There are 50 sites for RVs or tents, and 39 sites, some drive-through, with partial hookups (30 amps) for RVs up to 38 feet and tents. Picnic tables and fire grills are provided. Drinking water, flush toilets, two RV dump stations, showers, limited cell phone reception, a boat ramp (summer weekends only), and boat rentals are available. A grocery store is within walking distance, and firewood and ice are sold on the premises. An ATM is within four miles. Some facilities are wheelchair-accessible. Leashed pets with a proof of rabies vaccination are permitted in the camping area only.

Reservations, fees: Reservations are recommended with a two-night minimum stay on weekends. The fee is $8–21 per night, plus $7 for second vehicle with a maximum of two vehicles per site and $1 per pet per night. A senior discount is available. Major credit cards are accepted. Open year-round.

Directions: In Vacaville, turn north on I-505 and drive 11 miles to the junction of Highway 128. Turn west on Highway 128 and drive about five miles (past Winters) to Pleasant Valley Road. Turn left on Pleasant Valley Road and drive to the park at 8685 Pleasant Valley Road. (well signed).

Contact: Lake Solano County Park, 530/795-2990, fax 530/795-1408, website: www.solanocounty.com.

83 NAPA VALLEY EXPOSITION RV PARK

Rating: 2

in Napa

See map pages 524–525

This RV park is directly adjacent to the Napa County Exposition facility. When the fair is in operation mid-July to mid-August, it is closed for one month. The rest of the year it is simply an RV parking area, and it can come in handy.

RV sites, facilities: There are 100 sites, 40 drive-through, with partial hookups (20, 30 amps) for RVs and a grassy area for up to 100 self-contained RVs. Picnic tables, restrooms, showers, a coin-operated laundry, cell phone reception, modem access, an ATM, and an RV dump station are available. A camp host is on-site. A grocery store and restaurant are within walking distance. Leashed pets are permitted.

Reservations, fees: Reservations are not accepted. The fee is $20 per night, plus $5 per night for additional vehicle. Reservations are required for groups. Open year-round.

Directions: From Napa on Highway 29, drive to the Napa/Lake Berryessa exit. Turn east and drive to 3rd Street. Turn right and drive 1.5 blocks to Burnell Street and the campground entrance on the left.

Contact: Napa Valley Exposition RV Park, 707/253-4900, fax 707/253-4943, website: www.napavalleyexpo.com.

84 SAN FRANCISCO NORTH/PETALUMA KOA

Rating: 3

near Petaluma

See map pages 524–525

This campground is less than a mile from U.S. 101, yet it has a rural feel in a 60-acre farm setting. It's a good base camp for folks who require some quiet mental preparation before heading south to the Bay Area or to the nearby wineries, redwoods, and the Russian River. The big plus here is that this KOA has the cute log cabins called "Kamping Kabins," providing privacy for those who want it. There are recreation activities and live music on-site in summer.

RV sites, facilities: There are 312 sites, 161 drive-through, most with partial or full hookups (30, 50 amps), for RVs or tents, and 34 cabins. Picnic tables and fire grills are provided. Flush toilets, showers, cable TV hookups, modem access, an RV dump station, cell phone reception, an ATM, a playground, recreation rooms, a heated swimming pool (seasonal), a whirlpool, a petting farm, shuffleboard, a coin-operated laundry, propane, and a convenience store are available. Some facilities are wheelchair-accessible. Leashed pets are permitted.

Reservations, fees: Reservations are accepted at 800/562-1233. The fee is $29–70 per night, plus $4–6 per person for more than two people. Major credit cards are accepted. Open year-round.

Directions: From Petaluma on U.S. 101, take the

Penngrove exit and drive west for .25 mile on Petaluma Boulevard to Stony Point Road. Turn right (north) on Stony Point Road and drive .25 mile to Rainsville Road. Turn left (west) on Rainsville Road and drive a short distance to the park entrance (signed, 20 Rainsville Road).

Contact: San Francisco North/Petaluma KOA, 707/763-1492, fax 707/763-2668, website: www .koa.com.

California

Chapter 17
Sacramento and Gold Country

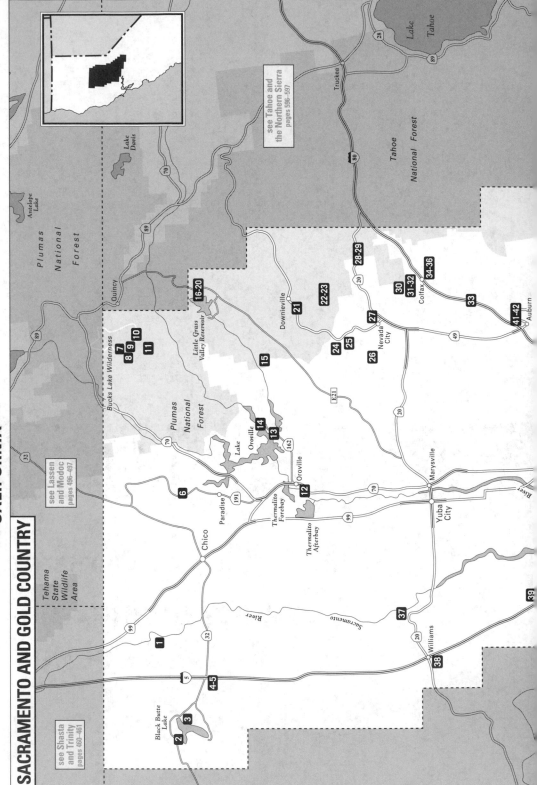

SACRAMENTO AND GOLD COUNTRY

see Shasta
and Trinity
pages 460–461

see Lassen
and Modoc
pages 496–497

see Tahoe and
the Northern Sierra
pages 596–597

Lake
Tahoe

Truckee

Tahoe   National   Forest

Lake
Davis

Antelope
Lake

Plumas   National   Forest

Quincy

Downieville

Little Grass
Valley Reservoir

Bucks Lake Wilderness

Colfax

Nevada
City

Auburn

Plumas
National
Forest

Oroville

Lake
Oroville

Oroville

Marysville

Paradise

Thermalito Forebay

Thermalito
Afterbay

Yuba
City

Chico

Sacramento   River

Williams

Tehama
State
Wildlife
Area

Black Butte
Lake

River

Camp markers: 1, 2, 3, 4-5, 6, 7, 8, 9, 10, 11, 12, 13, 14, 15, 16-20, 21, 22-23, 24, 25, 26, 27, 28-29, 30, 31-32, 33, 34-36, 37, 38, 39, 41-42

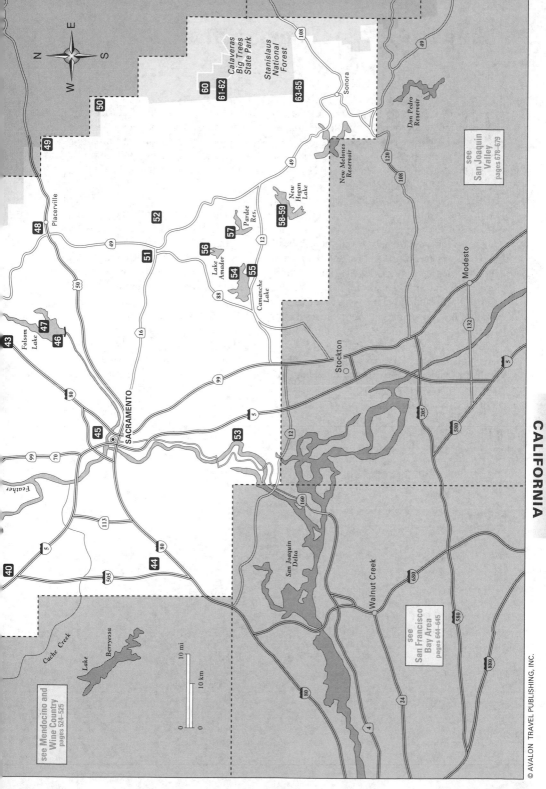

CALIFORNIA

© AVALON TRAVEL PUBLISHING, INC.

Chapter 17—Sacramento and Gold Country

From a distance, this section of the Sacramento Valley looks like flat farmland extending into infinity, with a sprinkling of cities and towns interrupting the view. But a closer look reveals a landscape filled with Northern California's most significant rivers—the Sacramento, Feather, Yuba, American, and Mokelumne. All of these provide water recreation, in both lakes and rivers, as well as serve as the lifeblood for a series of wildlife refuges.

The highlight of the foothill country for lake recreation is the series of great lakes for water sports and fishing. These include Camanche, Rollins, Oroville, and many others. Note that the mapping we use for this region extends up to Bucks Lake, which is set high in Plumas National Forest, the northern start to the Gold Country.

Timing is everything in love and the great outdoors, and so it is in the Central Valley and the nearby foothills. Spring and fall are gorgeous here, along with many summer evenings. But there are always periods of 100-plus temperatures in the summer.

But that's what gives the lakes and rivers such appeal, and in turn, why they are treasured. Take your pick: Lake Oroville in the northern Sierra, Folsom Lake outside Sacramento . . . the list goes on. On a hot day, jumping into a cool lake makes water more valuable than gold, a cold drink on ice worth more than silver. These have become top sites for boating-based recreation and fantastic areas for water sports and fishing.

In the Mother Lode country, three other lakes—Camanche, Amador, and Pardee—are outstanding for fishing. The guidebook *Foghorn Outdoors California Fishing* ranks three of this chapter's lakes among the top 10 lakes for fishing in the state—Lake Oroville and Camanche Lake make the list for bass and Lake Amador makes it for bluegill and catfish—no small feat considering the 300-plus other lakes they were up against.

For touring, the state capital and nearby Old Sacramento are favorites. Others prefer reliving the gold-mining history of California's past or exploring the foothill country, where you'll find Malakoff Diggins State Historic Park.

1 WOODSON BRIDGE STATE RECREATION AREA

Rating: 7

on the Sacramento River

See map pages 564–565

This campground features direct access to the Sacramento River, and a boat ramp makes it an ideal spot for campers with trailered boats. The boat ramp is across the road in the county park, providing easy access for water sports. This is a 328-acre preserve with a dense, native riparian forest, with a sand and gravel beach on the river. The junglelike grove displays some of the last remaining virgin riparian habitat on the 400-mile length of the Sacramento River. In June, the nearby Tehama Riffle is one of the best spots on the entire river for shad. By mid-August, salmon start arriving, en route to their spawning grounds. Summer weather here is hot, with high temperatures commonly 85–100°F and up. In winter, it is home to bald eagles, and in summer, provides a nesting site for the yellow bill cuckoo.

RV sites, facilities: There are 37 sites for tents or RVs up to 31 feet and five boat-in sites. One group site is available. Picnic tables and fire grills are provided. Drinking water, showers, flush toilets, and boat launch (across the street) are available, and there is a camp host. Some facilities are wheelchair-accessible, but the restrooms are not. Leashed pets are permitted.

Reservations, fees: Reservations are accepted with a $7.50 reservation fee at 800/444-PARK (800/444-7275) and www.reserveamerica.com. The fee is $10 per night. A senior discount is available. $30 for the group camp. Open year-round.

Directions: From I-5 in Corning, take the South Avenue exit and drive nine miles east to the campground on the left.

Contact: Woodson Bridge State Recreation Area, 530/839-2112; North Buttes District, 530/538-2200; Bidwell Mansion Visitor Center, 530/895-6144.

2 BUCKHORN

Rating: 7

on Black Butte Lake

See map pages 564–565

Black Butte Lake is in the foothills of the north valley at 500 feet. It is one of the 10 best lakes in Northern California for crappie, best in spring. There can also be good fishing for largemouth, smallmouth, and spotted bass, channel catfish, bluegill, and sunfish. Recreation options include powerboating, sailboating, windsurfing, and hiking nearby. For dirt bikers, an off-highway motorcycle park is available at the Buckhorn Recreation Area.

RV sites, facilities: There are 65 sites for RVs up to 35 feet or tents. Picnic tables and fire grills are provided. Drinking water, flush toilets, an RV dump station, showers, and a playground are available. A boat ramp, propane, and a grocery store are within walking distance. Some facilities are wheelchair-accessible. Leashed pets are permitted.

Reservations, fees: Make reservations at 877/444-6777 or online at www.reserveusa.com. The fee is $14 per night. A senior discount is available. Open year-round.

Directions: From I-5 in Orland, take the Black Butte Lake exit. Drive about 12 miles west on Road 200/Newville Road to Buckhorn Road. Turn left and drive a short distance to the campground on the north shore of the lake.

Contact: Black Butte Lake, U.S. Army Corps of Engineers, 530/865-4781, fax 530/865-5283.

3 ORLAND BUTTES

Rating: 7

on Black Butte Lake

See map pages 564–565

Black Butte Lake isn't far from I-5, but a lot of campers zoom right by it. The prime time to visit is in late spring and early summer, when the bass and crappie fishing can be quite good. Three self-guided nature trails are in the immediate area. (See the prior listing for Buckhorn for more information.) Note: In late winter and early spring, this area is delightful as spring arrives. But from

CALIFORNIA

mid-June through August, expect very hot, dry weather.

RV sites, facilities: There are 35 sites for RVs up to 35 feet or tents. Picnic tables and fire grills are provided. Drinking water, restrooms, showers, a boat ramp, a public telephone, and an RV dump station are available. Leashed pets are permitted.

Reservations, fees: Make reservations at 877/444-6777 or online at www.reserveusa.com. The fee is $14 per night. A senior discount is available. Open April through mid-July.

Directions: From I-5 in Orland, take the Black Butte Lake exit. Drive west on Road 200/Newville Road for eight miles to Road 206. Turn left and drive three miles to the camp entrance on the left.

Contact: Black Butte Lake, U.S. Army Corps of Engineers, 530/865-4781, fax 530/865-5283.

❹ GREEN ACRES RV PARK

Rating: 3

near Orland

See map pages 564–565

This is a layover spot near I-5 in the Central Valley, set in the heart of olive and almond country. It's a restful setting, but hot in summer, at times unbearable without air-conditioning. Salmon fishing is available on the nearby Sacramento River, best from mid-August through October.

RV sites, facilities: There are 68 sites, most drive-through, with partial or full hookups for RVs, and 24 tent sites. A store, a coin-operated laundry, an RV dump station, barbecues, a recreation room, modem access, a seasonal swimming pool, and ice are available. Leashed pets are permitted.

Reservations, fees: Reservations are recommended. The fee is $15–20 per night, plus $3 per person for more than two people. A senior discount is available. Monthly rates available. Open year-round.

Directions: From Orland on I-5, take the Highway 32 exit and drive a half mile west to the campground at 4515 County Road H.

Contact: Green Acres RV Park, 530/865-9188 or 800/468-9452.

❺ OLD ORCHARD RV PARK

Rating: 4

near Orland

See map pages 564–565

Most folks use this as a layover spot while on long trips up or down I-5 in the Central Valley. If you're staying longer than a night, there are two side trips that have appeal for anglers. Nearby Black Butte Lake to the west, with crappie in the early summer, and the Sacramento River to the east, with salmon in the late summer and early fall, can add some spice to your trip. The elevation is 250 feet.

RV sites, facilities: There are 52 sites, all drive-through, with partial or full hookups (30, 50 amps) for RVs up to 60 feet and a large separate site for tents only. Showers, an RV dump station, a coin-operated laundry, cell phone reception, modem access, a clubhouse, and a small store are available. An ATM is within one mile. Some facilities are wheelchair-accessible. Leashed pets are permitted.

Reservations, fees: Reservations are accepted. The fee is $12–24 per night, plus $2 per person for more than two people. Major credit cards are accepted. Open year-round.

Directions: From I-5 at Orland, take the Chico/Highway 32 exit west. Drive west one block to County Road HH. Turn right on County Road HH and drive one block to the park on the right at 4490 County Road HH.

Contact: Old Orchard RV Park, 877/481-9282, fax 530/865-5335.

❻ QUAIL TRAILS VILLAGE

Rating: 4

near Paradise

See map pages 564–565

This is a rural motor home campground, near the west branch of the Feather River, with nearby Lake Oroville as the feature attraction. The Lime Saddle section of the Lake Oroville State Recreation Area is nearby, with a beach, boat-launching facilities, and concessions. Note: Some sites are taken by long-term rentals here.

RV sites, facilities: There are 20 sites, all drive-through, with full hookups for RVs (30 amps) and five tent sites. Picnic tables are provided. Restrooms, hot showers, and a coin-operated laundry are available. An ATM is within four miles. Some facilities are wheelchair-accessible. Leashed pets are permitted.

Reservations, fees: Reservations are accepted. The fee is $12.50–18 per night, plus $2 per person for more than two people. Open year-round.

Directions: From Oroville, drive north on Highway 70 to Highway 191/Clark Road on the left. Turn left on Highway 191 and drive to Paradise and Pearson Road (lighted intersection). Turn right and drive 4.5 miles to the end of the road at Pentz Road. Turn right and drive 1.5 miles south to the park on the left (5110 Pentz Road).

Contact: Quail Trails Village, 530/877-6581, fax 530/876-0516, email: info@quailtrails.com.

▣ MILL CREEK

Rating: 7

at Bucks Lake in Plumas National Forest
See map pages 564–565

When Bucks Lake is full, this is one of the prettiest spots on the lake. The camp is set deep in Mill Creek Cove, adjacent to where Mill Creek enters the northernmost point of Bucks Lake. A boat ramp is a half mile away to the south, providing boat access to one of the better trout fishing spots at the lake. Unfortunately, when the lake level falls, this camp is left high and dry, some distance from the water. The elevation is 5,200 feet.

RV sites, facilities: There are eight sites for RVs up to 27 feet or tents and two walk-in tent sites. Picnic tables and fire grills are provided. Drinking water and vault toilets are available. Groceries are available within five miles. Leashed pets are permitted.

Reservations, fees: Reservations are not accepted. The fee is $16 per night. A senior discount is available. Open mid-May through September, weather permitting.

Directions: From Oroville, drive north on Highway 70 to the junction with Highway 89. Turn south on Highway 89/70 and drive 11 miles to Quincy. In Quincy, turn right at Bucks Lake Road and drive 17 miles to Bucks Lake and the

junction with Bucks Lake Dam Road/Forest Road 33. Turn right, drive around the lake, cross over the dam, and continue for about three miles to the campground.

Contact: Plumas National Forest, Mt. Hough Ranger District, 530/283-0555, fax 530/283-1821; Northwest Park Management, 530/283-5559, website: www.ucampwithus.com.

▣ SUNDEW

Rating: 7

on Bucks Lake in Plumas National Forest
See map pages 564–565

Sundew Camp is on the northern shore of Bucks Lake, just north of Bucks Lake Dam. A boat ramp is about two miles north at Sandy Point Day Use Area at the Mill Creek Cove, providing access to one of the better trout spots on the lake. You want fish? At Bucks Lake you can get fish—it's one of the state's top mountain trout lakes. Sunrises are often spectacular from this camp, with the light glowing on the lake's surface.

RV sites, facilities: There are 20 sites for RVs up to 27 feet or tents. Picnic tables and fire grills are provided. Drinking water, vault toilets, and limited cell phone reception are available. A boat ramp is two miles north of the camp. An ATM is within five miles. Leashed pets are permitted.

Reservations, fees: Reservations are not accepted. The fee is $14 per night, $16 for lakeside sites. A senior discount is available. Open mid-May through September, weather permitting.

Directions: From Oroville, drive north on Highway 70 to the junction with Highway 89. Turn south on Highway 89/70 and drive 11 miles to Quincy. In Quincy, turn right at Bucks Lake Road and drive 17 miles to Bucks Lake and the junction with Bucks Lake Dam Road/Forest Road 33. Turn right, drive around the lake, cross over the dam, continue for .5 mile, and turn right at the campground access road.

Contact: Plumas National Forest, Mt. Hough Ranger District, 530/283-0555, fax 530/283-1821; Northwest Park Management, 530/283-5559, website: www.ucampwithus.com.

CALIFORNIA

Rating: 7

on Bucks Lake
See map pages 564–565

This is the biggest and most popular of the campgrounds at Bucks Lake, a pretty alpine lake with excellent trout fishing and clean campgrounds. A boat ramp is available to the nearby north, along with Bucks Lodge. This camp is set deep in a cove at the extreme south end of the lake, where the water is quiet and sheltered from north winds. Bucks Lake, 5,200 feet elevation, is well documented for excellent fishing for rainbow and Mackinaw trout, with high catch rates of rainbow trout and lake records in the 16-pound class.

RV sites, facilities: There are 65 sites for RVs or tents. Picnic tables and fire grills are provided. Drinking water and vault toilets are available. An RV dump station and a boat ramp are nearby. Leashed pets are permitted.

Reservations, fees: Reservations are not accepted. The fee is $15 per night, plus $3 per additional vehicle per night, $7 per extra RV per night, and $1 per pet per night. Open May through October, weather permitting.

Directions: From Oroville, drive north on Highway 70 to the junction with Highway 89. Turn south on Highway 89/70 and drive 11 miles to Quincy. In Quincy, turn right at Bucks Lake Road and drive 16.5 miles to the campground entrance on the right side of the road.

Contact: PG&E Land Services, 916/386-5164, fax 916/923-7044, website: www.pge.com/recreation.

10 WHITEHORSE

Rating: 7

near Bucks Lake in Plumas National Forest
See map pages 564–565

This campground is set along Bucks Creek, about two miles from the boat ramps and south shore concessions at Bucks Lake. The trout fishing can be quite good at Bucks Lake, particularly on early summer evenings. The elevation is 5,200 feet. (For more information, see the previous listing for Haskins Valley.)

RV sites, facilities: There are 19 sites for RVs up

to 27 feet or tents. Picnic tables and fire grills are provided. Drinking water, vault toilets, and limited cell phone reception are available. A grocery store, an ATM, and a coin-operated laundry are within five miles. Leashed pets are permitted.

Reservations, fees: Reservations are not accepted. The fee is $14 per night. A senior discount is available. Open June through September.

Directions: From Oroville, drive north on Highway 70 to the junction with Highway 89. Turn south on Highway 89/70 and drive 11 miles to Quincy and Bucks Lake Road. Turn right at Bucks Lake Road and drive 14.5 miles to the campground entrance on the right side of the road.

Contact: Plumas National Forest, Mt. Hough Ranger District, 530/283-0555, fax 530/283-1821; Northwest Park Management, 530/283-5559, website: www.ucampwithus.com.

11 GRIZZLY CREEK

Rating: 4

near Bucks Lake in Plumas National Forest
See map pages 564–565

This is an alternative to the more developed, more crowded campgrounds at Bucks Lake. It is a small, primitive camp near Grizzly Creek at 5,400 feet in elevation. Nearby Bucks Lake provides good trout fishing, resorts, and boat rentals.

RV sites, facilities: There are eight sites for RVs up to 35 feet or tents. Picnic tables and fire grills are provided. Drinking water and vault toilets are available. A boat ramp is available at Bucks Lake. A grocery store and coin-operated laundry are within five miles. Leashed pets are permitted.

Reservations, fees: Reservations are not accepted. The fee is $14 per night. A senior discount is available. Open June through October.

Directions: From Oroville, drive north on Highway 70 to the junction with Highway 89. Turn south on Highway 89/70 and drive 11 miles to Quincy and Bucks Lake Road. Turn right at Bucks Lake Road and drive 17 miles to Bucks Lake and the junction with Bucks Lake Dam Road/Forest Road 33. Turn right and drive one mile to the junction with Oroville-Quincy Road/Forest Road

CALIFORNIA

36. Bear left and drive one mile to the campground on the right side of the road.
Contact: Plumas National Forest, Mt. Hough Ranger District, 530/283-0555, fax 530/283-1821; Northwest Park Management, 530/283-5559, website: www.ucampwithus.com.

12 DINGERVILLE USA

Rating: 3

near Oroville
See map pages 564–565
You're right, they thought of this name all by themselves, needed no help. It is an RV park set in the Oroville foothill country—hot, dry, and sticky in the summer, but with a variety of side trips available nearby. It is adjacent to a wildlife area and the Feather River and within short range of Lake Oroville and the Thermalito Afterbay for boating, water sports, and fishing. In the fall, the Duck Club in nearby Richvale is one of the few privately owned properties that offers duck hunting on a single-day basis. The RV park is a clean, quiet campground with easy access from the highway. Half of the sites are taken by long-term renters.
RV sites, facilities: There are 29 sites, all drive-through, with full hookups (30, 50 amps) for RVs. Picnic tables are provided. Restrooms, showers, modem access, cable TV, cell phone reception, a swimming pool, a coin-operated laundry, a horseshoe pit, and a nine-hole executive golf course are available. An ATM is within five miles. Some facilities are wheelchair-accessible. Leashed pets are permitted.
Reservations, fees: Reservations are recommended. The fee is $23 per night. Major credit cards are accepted. Open year-round.
Directions: From Oroville, drive south on Highway 70 to the second Pacific Heights Road turnoff. Turn right at Pacific Heights Road and drive less than one mile to the campground on the left.

From Marysville, drive north on Highway 70 to Palermo-Welsh Road. Turn left on Palermo-Welsh Road and drive to Pacific Heights Road. Turn north on Pacific Heights Road and drive .5 mile to the campground entrance on the right.
Contact: Dingerville USA, 5813 Pacific Heights Rd., Oroville, CA 95965, 530/533-9343.

13 BIDWELL CANYON

Rating: 7

on Lake Oroville
See map pages 564–565
Bidwell Canyon is a major destination at giant Lake Oroville as the campground is near a major marina and boat ramp. It is set along the southern shore of the lake, on a point directly adjacent to the massive Oroville Dam to the west. Many campers use this spot for boating headquarters. Lake Oroville is created from the tallest earth-filled dam in the country, rising 770 feet above the streambed of the Feather River. It creates a huge reservoir, with Oroville covering 28,450 acres when full. It is popular for water-skiing, as the water is warm enough in the summer for all water sports, and there is enough room for both fishermen and water-skiers. Recent habitat work has given the bass fishing a big help, with 30- and 40-fish days possible in the spring, casting plastic worms in the backs of coves where there is floating wood debris. What a lake—there are even floating toilets here (imagine that!). It is very hot in midsummer, with high temperatures ranging from the mid-80s to the low 100s. The area has four distinct seasons—spring is quite beautiful with many wildflowers and greenery. A must-see is the view from the 47-foot tower using the high-powered telescopes, offering a panoramic view of the lake, Sierra Nevada, valley, foothills, and the Sutter Buttes. The Feather River Hatchery is nearby.
RV sites, facilities: There are 75 sites with full hookups (30 amps) for RVs up to 40 feet or tents and trailers up to 31 feet (including boat trailers). Picnic tables and fire grills are provided. Drinking water, flush toilets, and coin-operated showers are available. A grocery store, an ATM, and propane are available within two miles. Leashed pets are permitted, except on trails or beaches; pets must be enclosed at night.
Reservations, fees: Reservations are accepted with a $7.50 reservation fee at 800/444-PARK (800/444-7275) or www.reserveamerica.com. The fee is $16–20 per night. A senior discount is available. Open year-round.
Directions: From Oroville, drive east on Oroville Dam Road/Highway 162 for eight miles to Kelly

CALIFORNIA

Ridge Road. Turn north on Kelly Ridge Road and drive 1.5 miles to Arroyo Drive. Turn right and drive .25 mile to the campground.

Contact: Lake Oroville State Recreation Area, 530/538-2200; Lake Oroville Visitor Center, 530/538-2219.

14 LOAFER CREEK GROUP CAMPS AND EQUESTRIAN CAMPS

Rating: 7

on Lake Oroville

See map pages 564–565

These are three different campground areas that are linked, designed for individual use, groups, and equestrians, respectively. The camps are just across the water at Lake Oroville from Bidwell Canyon, but campers come here for more spacious sites. It's also a primary option for campers with boats, with the Loafer Creek boat ramp one mile away. So hey, this spot is no secret. A bonus here includes an extensive equestrian trail system right out of camp.

RV sites, facilities: There are 137 sites for RVs up to 40 feet or tents and trailers to 31 feet (including boat trailers) and 15 equestrian sites with a two-horse limit per site. Picnic tables and fire grills are provided. Drinking water, flush toilets, coin-operated showers, and an RV dump station are available. A tethering and feeding station is near each site for horses, and a horse-washing station is provided. Propane, groceries, and a boat ramp are available nearby. An ATM is within two miles. Some facilities are wheelchair-accessible. Leashed pets are permitted, but not on trails or beaches.

Reservations, fees: Reservations are accepted with a $7.50 reservation fee at 800/444-PARK (800/444-7275) or www.reserveamerica.com. The fees are $10 per night for single sites, $20 per night for group sites, and $16 per night for equestrian sites. A senior discount is available. Open year-round.

Directions: From Oroville, drive east on Oroville Dam Road/Highway 162 to Kelly Ridge Road. Continue on Highway 162 for two miles to the signed campground entrance on the left.

Contact: Lake Oroville State Recreation Area, 530/538-2200; Lake Oroville Visitor Center, 530/538-2219.

15 SLY CREEK

Rating: 7

on Sly Creek Reservoir in Plumas National Forest

See map pages 564–565

Sly Creek Camp is set on Sly Creek Reservoir's southwestern shore near Lewis Flat, with a boat ramp about a mile to the north. Both camps are well situated for campers/anglers. This camp provides direct access to the lake's main body, with good trout fishing well upstream on the main lake arm. You get quiet water and decent fishing.

RV sites, facilities: There are 26 sites for RVs up to 40 feet, trailers, or tents. Five walk-in tent cabins are also available. Picnic tables and fire grills are provided. Drinking water and vault toilets are available. A car-top boat launch and fish-cleaning stations are available on Sly Creek Reservoir. Leashed pets are permitted.

Reservations, fees: Reservations are not accepted. The fee is $16 per night. A senior discount is available. Open late April to mid-October, weather permitting.

Directions: From Oroville, drive east on Highway 162 for about eight miles to the junction signed Challenge/LaPorte. Bear right (toward LaPorte) and drive east on LaPorte Road past Challenge and continue for 10 miles to Forest Road 16 (a signed turnoff on the left). Turn left and drive 4.5 miles to the campground.

Contact: Plumas National Forest, Feather River Ranger District, 530/534-6500, fax 530/532-1210.

16 BLACK ROCK

Rating: 7

on Little Grass Valley Reservoir in Plumas National Forest

See map pages 564–565

This is the only campground on the west shore of Little Grass Valley Reservoir, with an adjacent boat ramp making it an attractive choice for anglers. The lake is set at 5,060 feet in Plumas National Forest and provides lakeside camping and decent fishing for rainbow trout and kokanee salmon. If you don't like the company, there are seven other camps to choose from at the lake, all on the opposite eastern shore.

RV sites, facilities: There are 20 sites for RVs up to 22 feet or tents and 20 walk-in tent sites. Picnic tables and fire grills are provided. Drinking water, vault toilets, limited cell phone reception, and a fish-cleaning station are available. An RV dump station, a boat ramp, an ATM, and a grocery store are nearby. Leashed pets are permitted.

Reservations, fees: Reservations are not accepted. The fee is $14 per night. A senior discount is available. Open June through October.

Directions: From Oroville, drive east on Highway 162 for about eight miles to the junction signed Challenge/LaPorte. Bear right and drive east past Challenge and Strawberry Valley to LaPorte. Continue two miles past LaPorte to the junction with County Road 514/Little Grass Valley Road. Turn left and drive about five miles to the campground access road on the west side of the lake. Turn right on the access road and drive .25 mile to the campground.

Contact: Plumas National Forest, Feather River Ranger District, 530/534-6500, fax 530/532-1210.

17 RUNNING DEER

Rating: 7

on Little Grass Valley Reservoir in Plumas National Forest

See map pages 564–565

Little Grass Valley Reservoir is a pretty mountain lake set at 5,060 feet in Plumas National Forest, providing lakeside camping, boating, and fishing for rainbow trout and kokanee salmon. Looking straight north from the camp is a spectacular view, gazing across the water and up at Bald Mountain, 6,255 feet in elevation. One of seven campgrounds on the eastern shore, this one is on the far northeastern end of the lake. A trailhead for the Pacific Crest Trail is available nearby at little Fowler Lake about four miles north of Little Grass Valley Reservoir. Note that while no fish-cleaning station is available at Running Deer, there is one nearby at Little Beaver.

RV sites, facilities: There are 40 sites for RVs up to 40 feet or tents. Picnic tables and fire rings are provided. Drinking water, flush toilets, limited cell phone reception, and a nearby fish-cleaning station are available. A boat ramp, grocery store, ATM, and RV dump station are nearby. Leashed pets are permitted.

Reservations, fees: Reservations are accepted with a $9 reservation fee at 877/444-6777 or www.reserveusa.com. The fee is $16–18 per night. A senior discount is available. Open June through September.

Directions: From Oroville, drive east on Highway 162 for about eight miles to the junction signed Challenge/LaPorte. Bear right (to LaPorte) and drive east past Challenge and Strawberry Valley to LaPorte. Continue on County Road 512 (which becomes County Road 514/Little Grass Valley Road) for three miles to Forest Road 22N57. Turn right and drive three miles to the campground on the left.

Contact: Plumas National Forest, Feather River Ranger District, 530/534-6500, fax 530/532-1210.

18 WYANDOTTE

Rating: 8

on Little Grass Valley Reservoir in Plumas National Forest

See map pages 564–565

Of the eight camps on Little Grass Valley Reservoir, this is the favorite. It is set on a small peninsula at 5,100 foot elevation that extends well into the lake, with a boat ramp nearby. (For more information, see the previous listing for Running Deer.)

RV sites, facilities: There are 26 sites and two double sites for RVs up to 22 feet or tents. Picnic tables and fire rings are provided. Drinking water, flush toilets, and limited cell phone reception are available. An RV dump station, boat ramp, fish-cleaning station, ATM, and grocery store are nearby. Leashed pets are permitted.

Reservations, fees: Reservations are not accepted. The fees are $16 per single site and $26 per double site, per night. A senior discount is available. Open May through September.

Directions: From Oroville, drive east on Highway 162 for about eight miles to the junction signed Challenge/LaPorte. Bear right (to LaPorte) and drive east past Challenge and Strawberry

Valley to LaPorte. Continue two miles past LaPorte to the junction with County Road 514/Little Grass Valley Road. Turn left and drive one mile to a junction. Turn left and drive one mile to the campground entrance road on the right.
Contact: Plumas National Forest, Feather River Ranger District, 530/534-6500, fax 530/532-1210.

19 LITTLE BEAVER

Rating: 7

on Little Grass Valley Reservoir in Plumas National Forest
See map pages 564–565

This is one of eight campgrounds on Little Grass Valley Reservoir, set at 5,060 feet. Take your pick. (For more information, see the entry for Running Deer in this chapter.)
RV sites, facilities: There are 120 sites for RVs up to 40 feet or tents. Picnic tables and fire rings are provided. Drinking water, flush toilets, and limited cell phone reception are available. A grocery store, RV dump station, fish-cleaning station, ATM, and boat ramp are nearby. Leashed pets are permitted.
Reservations, fees: Reservations are not accepted. The fee is $16–18 per night. A senior discount is available. Open June through October.
Directions: From Oroville, drive east on Highway 162 for about eight miles to the junction signed Challenge/LaPorte. Bear right (to LaPorte) and drive east past Challenge and Strawberry Valley to LaPorte. Continue two miles past LaPorte to the junction with County Road 514/Little Grass Valley Road. Turn left and drive one mile to a junction. Turn right and drive two miles to the campground entrance road on the left.
Contact: Plumas National Forest, Feather River Ranger District, 530/534-6500, fax 530/532-1210.

20 RED FEATHER CAMP

Rating: 7

on Little Grass Valley Reservoir in Plumas National Forest
See map pages 564–565

This camp is well developed and popular, set on the eastern shore of Little Grass Valley Reser-

voir, just south of Running Deer and just north of Little Beaver. (For more information, see the entry for Running Deer in this chapter.)
RV sites, facilities: There are 60 sites for RVs up to 22 feet or tents. Picnic tables and fire rings are provided. Drinking water, flush toilets, and limited cell phone reception are available. An RV dump station, boat ramp, fish-cleaning station, ATM, and grocery store are nearby. Leashed pets are permitted.
Reservations, fees: Reservations are accepted with a $9 reservation fee at 877/444-6777 or www.reserveusa.com. The fee is $16–18 per night. A senior discount is available. Open June through October.
Directions: From Oroville, drive east on Highway 162 for about eight miles to the junction signed Challenge/LaPorte. Bear right (to LaPorte) and drive east past Challenge and Strawberry Valley to LaPorte. Continue two miles past LaPorte to the junction with County Road 514/Little Grass Valley Road. Turn left and drive one mile to a junction. Turn right and drive three miles to the campground entrance road on the left.
Contact: Plumas National Forest, Feather River Ranger District, 530/534-6500, fax 530/532-1210.

21 INDIAN VALLEY

Rating: 7

on the North Yuba River in Tahoe National Forest
See map pages 564–565

This is an easy-to-reach spot set at 2,200 feet beside the North Yuba River. Highway 49 runs adjacent to the Yuba River for miles eastward, providing easy access to the river in many areas.
RV sites, facilities: There are eight sites for RVs up to 22 feet and nine tent sites. Picnic tables and fire grills are provided. Drinking water and vault toilets are available. Limited supplies are available nearby at the Indian Valley Outpost. Leashed pets are permitted.
Reservations, fees: Reservations are not accepted. The fee is $13 per night. A senior discount is available. Open year-round.
Directions: From Auburn, take Highway 49 north to Nevada City and continue (the road jogs left,

then narrows) to Camptonville. Drive 10 miles to the camp entrance on the right.

Contact: Tahoe National Forest, North Yuba/Downieville Ranger District, 530/288-3231, fax 530/288-0727.

22 MALAKOFF DIGGINS STATE HISTORIC PARK

Rating: 7

near Nevada City
See map pages 564–565

This camp is set near a small lake in the park, but the main attraction of the area is the gold mining history. Tours of the numerous historic sites are available during the summer. The elevation is 3,400 feet. A trip here is like a walk through history. Malakoff Diggins State Historic Park is the site of California's largest "hydraulic" mine. Huge cliffs have been carved by mighty streams of water, a gold-mining technique involving the washing away of entire mountains to find the precious metal. This practice began in the 1850s and continued for many years. Several major gold-mining operations combined hydraulic mining with giant sluice boxes. Hydraulic mining was a scourge to the land, of course, and legal battles between mine owners and downstream farmers eventually ended this method of mining.

The park also contains a 7,847-foot bedrock tunnel that served as a drain. The visitors center has exhibits on life in the old mining town of North Bloomfield.

The cabins here are set near a small lake in the park and are the cheapest deal in California at $10 a night.

RV sites, facilities: There are 30 sites for RVs up to 24 feet or tents, four cabins, and one group tent site for up to 50 people. Picnic tables and fire grills are provided. Drinking water and flush toilets (except mid-November through February) are available. Leashed pets are permitted.

Reservations, fees: Reservations are accepted Memorial Day through Labor Day with a $7.50 reservation fee at 800/444-PARK (800/444-7275) or www.reserveamerica.com. The fees are $10 per night (including cabins) and $37 for the group site. A senior discount is available. Open year-round.

Directions: From Auburn, drive north on High-

way 49 to Nevada City and continue 11 miles to the junction of Tyler Foote Crossing Road. Turn right and drive 16 miles (in the process the road changes names: Cruzon Grade, Back Bone Road, Der Bec Road, North Bloomfield Road) to the entrance on the right. The route is well-signed; the last two miles are quite steep and the last mile is dirt.

Contact: California State Parks, Goldrush District, tel./fax 530/265-2740.

23 SOUTH YUBA

Rating: 7

near the Yuba River
See map pages 564–565

This little-known BLM camp is set next to where little Kenebee Creek enters the Yuba River. The Yuba is about a mile away, with some great swimming holes and evening trout fishing spots to explore. A good side trip is to nearby Malakoff Diggins State Historic Park and the town of North Bloomfield (about a 10-minute drive to the northeast on North Bloomfield Road), which is being completely restored to its 1850s character. Let's hope that does not include the food. The 12-mile-long South Yuba Trail begins at the state park and features outstanding spring wildflower blooms. The elevation is 2,600 feet.

RV sites, facilities: There are 16 sites for RVs up to 27 feet or tents. Picnic tables and fire grills are provided. Drinking water, vault toilets, and limited cell phone reception are available. An ATM is within 10 miles. Some facilities are wheelchair-accessible. Leashed pets are permitted.

Reservations, fees: Reservations are not accepted. The fee is $5 per night. A senior discount is available. Open April through October, weather permitting.

Directions: From Auburn, turn north on Highway 49, drive to Nevada City, and then continue a short distance to North Bloomfield Road. Turn right and drive 10 miles to the one-lane bridge at Edward's Crossing. Cross the bridge and continue 1.5 miles to the campground on the right side of the road (the road becomes quite rough).

Alternate route for RVs or vehicles with trailers: From Auburn turn north on Highway 49 to

CALIFORNIA

Nevada City and continue to Tyler Foote Crossing Road. Turn right and drive to Grizzly Hills Road (just past North Columbia). Turn right and drive three miles to North Bloomfield Road. Turn left and drive to the campground on the right.
Contact: The Bureau of Land Management, Folsom Field Office, 916/985-4474, fax 916/985-3259.

24 SCHOOLHOUSE

Rating: 7

on Bullards Bar Reservoir
See map pages 564–565

Bullards Bar Reservoir is one of the better lakes in the Sierra Nevada for camping, primarily because the lake levels tend to be higher here than at many other lakes. The camp is on the southeast shore, with a trail available out of the camp to a beautiful lookout of the lake. Bullards Bar is known for good fishing for trout and kokanee salmon, water-skiing, and all water sports. A three-lane concrete boat ramp is to the south at Cottage Creek. Boaters should consider the special boat-in camps at the lake. The elevation is 2,200 feet.

RV sites, facilities: There are 56 sites (one triple, 11 double, and 44 single sites) for RVs or tents. Single sites accommodate six people, double sites accommodate 12, and triple sites hold up to 18 people. Picnic tables and fire rings are provided. Drinking water, flush and vault toilets, and limited cell phone reception are available. A boat ramp is nearby. Supplies are available in North San Juan, Camptonville, Dobbins, and at the marina. An ATM is within eight miles. Leashed pets are permitted.

Reservations, fees: Reservations and a shoreline camping permit are required from Emerald Cove Resort. The fee is $14 per night for singles, $28 per night for doubles, and $42 for triples. Open mid-April to mid-October.

Directions: From Marysville, drive east on Highway 20 for 12 miles to Marysville Road (signed Bullards Bar Reservoir). Turn left on Marysville Road and drive 10 miles to Old Marysville Road. Turn right on Old Marysville Road and drive 14 miles to the dam, then continue three miles to the campground entrance road on the left.

Contact: Emerald Cove Resort and Marina,

530/692-3200, website: www.bullardsbar.com; Tahoe National Forest, North Yuba/Downieville Ranger District, 530/288-3231, fax 530/288-0727.

25 MOONSHINE CAMPGROUND

Rating: 7

near the Yuba River and Bullards Bar Reservoir
See map pages 564–565

This campground features shaded sites and a swimming hole on the nearby Middle Fork Yuba River. Both are needed, with the weather hot here in the summer, at 1,430 feet in the Sierra foothills. It's a seven-mile drive to a three-lane boat ramp at Dark Day Picnic Area at Bullards Bar Reservoir, the feature side trip.

RV sites, facilities: There are 25 sites with hookups for water and electricity, for RVs up to 30 feet or tents. Picnic tables and fire rings are provided. Drinking water, vault toilets, ice, and firewood are available. A grocery store and propane are available about three miles away in North San Juan. Some facilities are wheelchair-accessible. Leashed pets are permitted.

Reservations, fees: Reservations are required. The fee is $20–25 per night, plus $2 per person per night for more than four people. Open May through early October.

Directions: From Auburn, drive north on Highway 49 to Nevada City and continue for 17 miles through the town of North San Juan. Continue on Highway 49 and cross a bridge over the Middle Fork Yuba River to Moonshine Road. Turn left on Moonshine Road and drive .75 mile to the campground.

Contact: Moonshine Campground, 530/288-3585, website: www.moonshinecampground.com.

26 COLLINS LAKE RECREATION AREA

Rating: 8

near Marysville on Collins Lake
See map pages 564–565

Collins Lake is in the foothill country east of Marysville at 1,200 feet in elevation, ideal for the camper, boater, and angler. I counted 52 campsites set near the lakefront. This lake is becoming known as an outstanding destination for trophy-sized trout, especially in late spring through early summer, though fishing is often good year-round for know-hows. The lake has 12 miles of shoreline and is quite pretty. In summer, warm water makes the lake exceptional for water-skiing (permitted from May 15 through September 30). A marina is adjacent to the campground, and farther south is a swimming beach and boat ramp. Bonuses for anglers: No personal watercraft are allowed on the lake, and a weekly fishing report is available at the camp's website.

RV sites, facilities: There are 184 sites, including some drive-through, many with partial hookups (20, 30 amps) and a few with full hookups, for RVs or tents, four trailer rentals, and a large overflow camping area. Picnic tables and fire grills are provided. Restrooms, drinking water, flush toilets, an RV dump station, limited cell phone reception, modem access, an ATM, coin-operated showers, a boat ramp, boat rentals, a sandy swimming beach, volleyball, a marina, three group picnic areas, a convenience store, a coin-operated laundry, wood, ice, and propane are available. Some facilities are wheelchair-accessible. Leashed pets are permitted.

Reservations, fees: Reservations are recommended. The fee is $18–35 per night, plus $3 per person for more than two people and $6 per night for a second vehicle. Major credit cards are accepted. Open year-round.

Directions: From Marysville, drive east on Highway 20 for about 12 miles to Marysville Road. Turn north and drive approximately eight miles to the recreation area entrance road on the right. Turn right, drive a mile to the entrance station, and then continue to the campground.

Contact: Collins Lake Recreation Area, 530/692-1600 or 800/286-0576, fax 530/692-1607, website: www.collinslake.com.

27 NEVADA COUNTY FAIRGROUNDS
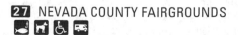

Rating: 6

at the fairgrounds near Grass Valley
See map pages 564–565

The motto here is "California's Most Beautiful Fairgrounds," and that's right. The area is set at 2,300 feet in the Sierra foothills, with a good number of pines sprinkled about. The park is adjacent to the fairgrounds, and even though the fair runs for a week every August, the park is open year-round. A caretaker at the park is available to answer any questions. Kids can fish at a small lake nearby. The Draft Horse Classic is held here every September, and a country Christmas Faire is held Thanksgiving weekend.

RV sites, facilities: There are 15 sites with full hookups (50 amps) and 70 with partial hookups, and an open dirt and grassy area with no hookups available as an overflow area. Two RV dump stations, cell phone reception, showers, and flush toilets are available. A building with kitchen facilities and space for up to 50 people is available for rent. An ATM is within one mile. Some facilities are wheelchair-accessible. Leashed pets are permitted.

Reservations, fees: Reservations are accepted. The fee is $20–25 per night. A 14-day limit is enforced. Major credit cards are accepted. Open year-round.

Directions: From Auburn, drive north on Highway 49 to Grass Valley. Take either the McKnight Way or Empire Street exit and follow the signs to the Nevada County Fairgrounds on the west side of Highway 49.

Contact: Nevada County Fairgrounds, 11228 McCourtney Rd., Grass Valley, CA 95949, 530/273-6217, fax 530/273-1146, website: www.nevadacountyfair.com.

28 WHITE CLOUD

Rating: 5

in Tahoe National Forest
See map pages 564–565

This camp is set along the historic Pioneer Trail, which has turned into one of the top mountain-bike routes in the Sierra Nevada, easy and fast. The trail traces the route of the first wagon road opened by emigrants and gold seekers in 1850. It is best suited for mountain biking, with a lot of bikers taking the one-way downhill ride (with an extra car for a shuttle ride) from Bear Valley to Lone Grave. The Omega Overlook is the highlight, with dramatic views of granite cliffs and the Yuba River. The elevation is 4,600 feet.

RV sites, facilities: There are 46 sites for RVs up

to 26 feet or tents. Picnic tables and fire grills are provided. Drinking water and flush toilets are available. Leashed pets are permitted.

Reservations, fees: Reservations are accepted with a $9 reservation fee at 877/444-6777 or www.reserveusa.com. The fee is $15 per night, plus $6 per additional vehicle. A senior discount is available. Open May through October.

Directions: From Sacramento, drive east on I-80 to Emigrant Gap. Take the off-ramp and then head north on the short connector road to Highway 20. Turn west on Highway 20 and drive about 15 miles to the campground entrance on the left.

Contact: Tahoe National Forest, Nevada City Ranger District, 530/265-4531, fax 530/478-6109; Big Bend Visitor's Center, 530/426-3609, fax 530/426-1744.

29 SCOTTS FLAT LAKE RECREATION AREA

Rating: 8

near Grass Valley
See map pages 564–565

Scotts Flat Reservoir (at 3,100 feet in elevation) is shaped like a large teardrop and is one of the prettier lakes in the Sierra foothills, with 7.5 miles of shoreline circled by forest. Rules prohibiting personal watercraft keep the place sane. The camp is on the lake's north shore, largely protected from spring winds and within short range of the marina and one of the lake's two boat launches. Trout fishing is good here in the spring and early summer. When the lake heats up, water-skiing and powerboating become more popular. Sailing is also good during spring afternoon winds.

RV sites, facilities: There are 185 sites for RVs up to 35 feet or tents. Restrooms, coin-operated showers, a coin-operated laundry, and an RV dump station are provided. A general store, a bait and tackle shop, boat rentals, a boat ramp, and a playground are also available. Some facilities are wheelchair-accessible. Leashed pets are permitted.

Reservations, fees: Reservations are recommended in the summer. The fee is $16–27 per night, plus $5 per night for a second vehicle, $1 per person per night for more than four people, and $3 per pet per night, with a 14-day maximum stay. Major

credit cards are accepted. Open year-round, weather permitting.

Directions: From Auburn, drive north on Highway 49 to Nevada City and the junction with Highway 20. Turn right on Highway 20 and drive five miles (east) to Scotts Flat Road. Turn right and drive four miles to the camp entrance road on the right (on the north shore of the lake).

Contact: Scotts Flat Lake Recreation Area, 530/265-8861.

30 LONG RAVINE

Rating: 7

on Rollins Lake near Colfax
See map pages 564–565

Long Ravine is one of three campgrounds at Rollins Lake, a popular lake for fishing (bass and trout) and water-skiing. The lake, in the Sierra foothills at 2,100 feet, has two extensive lake arms covering 26 miles of shoreline. It also has long stretches of open water near the lower end of the lake, making it excellent for water-skiing, with water surface temperatures ranging from 75 to 80°F in the summer.

RV sites, facilities: There are 84 sites, including some drive-through, for RVs or tents. Flush toilets, picnic tables, and barbecues or fire pits are provided. Hot showers, parking pads, hiking trails, and an RV dump station are available. A full-service marina with a floating gas dock, boat rentals, stores, a restaurant, and a swimming beach and water slide are nearby. Some facilities are wheelchair-accessible. Leashed pets are permitted.

Reservations, fees: Reservations are recommended. The fee is $23–31 per night, plus $6 per night for additional vehicle and $3 per pet per night. Major credit cards are accepted. Open year-round.

Directions: From Auburn, drive northeast on I-80 for about 20 miles to Colfax/Highway 174. Turn north on Highway 174 (a winding, two-lane road) and drive about two miles to Rollins Lake. Turn right on Rollins Lake Road and drive 1.5 miles the campground on the left at 26909 Rollins Lake Road.

Contact: Long Ravine, 530/346-6166, website: www.longravineresort.com.

31 ORCHARD SPRINGS

Rating: 7

on Rollins Lake
See map pages 564–565

Orchard Springs is on the shore of Rollins Lake in the Sierra Nevada foothills among pine, oak, and cedar trees. The summer heat makes the lake excellent for water-skiing, boating, and swimming, and the spring and fall are great for trout and bass fishing.

RV sites, facilities: There are 14 sites, including two drive-through, with full hookups (30 amps) for RVs or tents and 102 tent sites. Picnic tables, fire rings, and barbecues are provided. Drinking water, restrooms, flush toilets, showers, cell phone reception, an ATM, a launch ramp, boat rentals, dock space rentals, bait and tackle, a swimming beach, a group picnic area, and a convenience store are available. A restaurant on-site overlooks Rollins Lake. Some facilities are wheelchair-accessible. Leashed pets are permitted.

Reservations, fees: Reservations are accepted at 530/346-2212. The fee is $23–32 per night, plus $12 for additional vehicles unless towed, $5.75 per boat per night, and $3 per pet per night. Major credit cards are accepted. Open year-round.

Directions: From Auburn, drive northeast on I-80 for about 20 miles to Colfax and Highway 174. Turn north on Highway 174 (a winding, two-lane road) and drive 3.7 miles (bear left at Giovanni's Restaurant) to Orchard Springs Road. Turn right on Orchard Springs Road and drive .5 mile to the road's end. Turn right at the gatehouse and continue to the campground.

Contact: Orchard Springs, 530/346-2837.

32 PENINSULA CAMPGROUND

Rating: 8

on Rollins Lake
See map pages 564–565

Peninsula Campground is on a point that extends into Rollins Lake, flanked on each side by two sprawling lake arms. If you like boating, water-skiing, or swimming, you'll definitely like this place in the summer. This is a family-oriented campground, with lots of youngsters on summer

vacation. If you want trout, prospects are best in April and May. After that the fast boats take over, though there is a good bass bite at dawn and dusk. The boat ramp was remodeled in 2002 and now features two lanes.

RV sites, facilities: There are 78 sites for self-contained RVs up to 40 feet or tents. No RV hookups are available. Groups can be accommodated by reservation. Picnic tables and fire rings are provided. Restrooms with flush toilets and hot showers, drinking water, modem access, an RV dump station, limited cell phone reception, boat rentals (fishing boats, patio boats, canoes, and kayaks), a boat ramp, a fish-cleaning station, a swim beach, volleyball, horseshoes, and a convenience store are available. An ATM is nearby. Leashed pets are permitted.

Reservations, fees: Reservations are recommended. The fee is $21–28 per night, plus $12 per additional vehicle per night, $3 per pet per night, and $5 for the RV dump station. A senior discount is available. Major credit cards are accepted. Open mid-April to September.

Directions: From Auburn, drive northeast on I-80 for about 20 miles to Colfax and Highway 174. Turn north on Highway 174 and drive about eight miles (a winding, two-lane road) to You Bet Road. Turn right and drive 4.3 miles (turning right again to stay on You Bet Road), and continue another 3.1 miles to the campground entrance at the end of the road.

Contact: Peninsula Campground, 530/477-9413 or 866/4MY-CAMP (866/469-2267), website: www.penresort.com.

33 BEAR RIVER CAMPGROUND

Rating: 7

near Colfax on Bear River
See map pages 564–565

This RV park is in the Sierra foothills at 1,800 feet, near Bear River, featuring riverfront campsites. The park covers 200 acres, offers five miles of hiking trails, and is set right on the Placer and Nevada County lines. It fills up on weekends and is popular with both locals and out-of-towners. In the spring, when everything is greened up, it can be a gorgeous landscape. Fishing is okay for trout, noncommercial gold panning is permitted, and some rafting is popular on the river.

RV sites, facilities: There are 25 sites for RVs or tents and one group site for up to 100 people. Picnic tables and fire rings are provided. Drinking water, pit toilets, and limited cell phone reception are available. Supplies and an ATM are available within five miles in Colfax or Bowman. Leashed pets are permitted.

Reservations, fees: Reservations are accepted only for group sites at 530/889-7750 with a $5 reservation fee. The fee is $10 per night, plus $2 for each additional vehicle and $1 per pet. The group site is $40–75. A 14-day maximum stay is enforced. Open year-round.

Directions: From Sacramento, drive east on I-80 east of Auburn to West Weimar Crossroads exit. Take that exit on to Weimar Cross Road and drive north for 1.5 miles to Placer Hills Road. Turn right and drive 2.5 miles to Plum Tree Road. Turn left and drive one mile to the campground on the left. The access road is steep and narrow.

Contact: Bear River Campground, Placer County Facilities Services, 530/886-4900, fax 530/889-6809, website: www.placer.ca.gov.

34 GIANT GAP

Rating: 7

on Sugar Pine Reservoir in Tahoe National Forest
See map pages 564–565

This is a lakeside spot along the western shore of Sugar Pine Reservoir at 3,600 feet in elevation in Tahoe National Forest. For boaters, there is a ramp on the south shore. Note that a 10 mph speed limit is the law, making this lake ideal for anglers in search of quiet water. Other recreation notes: There's a little less than a mile of paved trail, which goes through the day-use area. Big Reservoir, five miles to the east, is the only other lake in the region and also has a campground. The trout fishing at Sugar Pine is fair, not usually great, not usually bad.

RV sites, facilities: There are 30 sites for RVs up to 30 feet or tents. Picnic tables and fire grills are provided. Drinking water and vault toilets are available, and a camp host is on-site. An RV dump station and boat ramp are available on the

south shore. Supplies can be obtained in Foresthill. Some facilities are wheelchair-accessible. Leashed pets are permitted.

Reservations, fees: Reservations are accepted with a $9 reservation fee at 877/444-6777 or www.reserveusa.com. The fees are $12 for a single and $24 for a double, per night, plus $5 per additional vehicle per night. A senior discount is available. Open May through mid-October.

Directions: From Sacramento, drive east on I-80 to the north end of Auburn and the Foresthill Road exit. Take that exit and drive east for 20 miles to Foresthill. Drive through Foresthill (road changes to Foresthill Divide Road) and continue for eight miles to Sugar Pine Road. Turn left and drive five miles to a fork. Turn right and drive one mile to the campground.

Contact: Tahoe National Forest, Foresthill Ranger District, 530/367-2224, fax 530/367-2992.

35 SHIRTTAIL CREEK

Rating: 7

on Sugar Pine Reservoir in Tahoe National Forest
See map pages 564–565

This camp is near the little creek that feeds into the north end of Sugar Pine Reservoir. The boat ramp is all the way around the south side of the lake, near Forbes Creek Group Camp. (For recreation information, see the prior listing for Giant Gap.)

RV sites, facilities: There are 30 sites for RVs up to 30 feet or tents (double and triple sites are available). Picnic tables and fire grills are provided. Drinking water and vault toilets are available, and a camp host is on-site. An RV dump station and boat ramp are available on the south shore. Supplies can be obtained in Foresthill. Some facilities are wheelchair-accessible. Leashed pets are permitted.

Reservations, fees: Reservations are accepted with a $9 reservation fee at 877/444-6777 or www.reserveusa.com. The fees are $12 for single sites, $24 for double sites, and $35 for triple sites, per night. A senior discount is available. Open May through mid-October.

Directions: From Sacramento, drive east on I-80 to the north end of Auburn and the Foresthill

Road exit. Take that exit and drive east for 20 miles to Foresthill. Drive through Foresthill (road changes to Foresthill Divide Road) and continue for eight miles to Sugar Pine Road. Turn left and drive five miles to the campground access road. Turn right (signed) and drive to the campground.

Contact: Tahoe National Forest, Foresthill Ranger District, 530/367-2224, fax 530/367-2992.

36 BIG RESERVOIR

Rating: 7

on Big Reservoir in Tahoe National Forest
See map pages 564–565

Here's a quiet lake where no boat motors are allowed. That makes it ideal for canoeists, row boaters, and tube floaters who don't like the idea of having to dodge water-skiers. The lake is stocked with rainbow trout. Big Reservoir is quite pretty, and a nice beach is available not far from the resort. The elevation is 3,500 feet.

RV sites, facilities: There are 100 sites for RVs up to 25 feet or tents. Picnic tables and fire grills are provided. Drinking water, vault toilets, and limited cell phone reception are available. Firewood is limited. Watercraft rentals are available nearby. A small store is near the campground, and supplies are also available in Foresthill. Leashed pets are permitted.

Reservations, fees: Reservations are accepted at 530/367-2129. The fee is $18 per night. A senior discount is available. Open May through October.

Directions: From Sacramento, drive east on I-80 to the north end of Auburn and the Foresthill Road exit. Take that exit and drive east for 20 miles to Foresthill. Drive through Foresthill (road changes to Foresthill Divide Road) and continue for eight miles to Sugar Pine Road. Turn left and drive about three miles to Forest Road 24 (signed Big Reservoir). Bear right on Forest Road 24 and drive about five miles to the campground entrance road on the right.

Contact: Tahoe National Forest, Foresthill Ranger District, 530/367-2224, fax 530/367-2992.

37 COLUSA–SACRAMENTO RIVER STATE RECREATION AREA

Rating: 5

near Colusa
See map pages 564–565

This region of the Sacramento Valley is well known as a high-quality habitat for birds. This park covers 67 acres and features great bird-watching opportunities. Nearby Delevan and Colusa National Wildlife Refuges are outstanding destinations for wildlife viewing as well, and they provide good duck hunting in December. In summer the nearby Sacramento River is a bonus with fishing for shad in June and July, salmon from August through October, sturgeon in the winter, and striped bass in the spring. The landscape here features cottonwoods and willows along the Sacramento River.

RV sites, facilities: There are 14 sites for RVs up to 30 feet or tents and one group site for a minimum of 10 people and maximum of 40 people. Picnic tables and barbecues are provided. Drinking water, flush toilets, hot showers, and an RV dump station are available. A grocery store, restaurant, gas station, tackle shop, and coin-operated laundry are nearby (within three blocks). A boat ramp for small boats is available. Some facilities are wheelchair-accessible. Leashed pets are permitted.

Reservations, fees: Reservations are accepted with a $7.50 reservation fee at 800/444-PARK (800/444-7275) or www.reserveamerica.com. The fee is $10 per night; $30 per night for the group site. A senior discount is available. Open year-round.

Directions: In Williams, at the junction of I-5 and Highway 20, drive east on Highway 20 for 10 miles to the town of Colusa. Turn north (straight ahead) on 10th Street and drive two blocks, just over the levee, to the park.

Contact: Colusa–Sacramento River State Recreation Area, tel./fax 530/458-4927; North Buttes District, 530/538-2200.

38 ALMOND GROVE MOBILE HOME PARK

Rating: 1

in Williams

See map pages 564–565

The town of Williams is in the middle of the Sacramento Valley, a popular spot to stop and grab a bite at its outstanding delicatessen and restaurant, Granzella's, where there is a gigantic stuffed polar bear in a room filled with about 100 wildlife mounts.

RV sites, facilities: There are seven pull-through RV sites with full hookups. Picnic tables are provided. Restrooms, showers, cable TV (included with hookup), and a coin-operated laundry are available. A store is nearby (within six blocks). Some facilities are wheelchair-accessible. Leashed pets are permitted.

Reservations, fees: Reservations are accepted. The fee is $14 per night. Open year-round.

Directions: In the Sacramento Valley on I-5, drive to Williams and the Central Williams exit. Take that exit and drive west on E Street for eight blocks to 12th Street. Turn left on 12th Street and drive three blocks to the entrance at 880 12th Street.

Contact: Almond Grove Mobile Home Park, 530/473-5620.

39 CAMPERS INN & GOLF COURSE

Rating: 1

near Dunnigan

See map pages 564–565

This private park has a rural valley atmosphere and provides a layover for drivers cruising I-5. The Sacramento River to the east is the closest body of water, but this section of river is hardly a premium side-trip destination. There are no nearby lakes.

RV sites, facilities: There are 72 RV sites (44 drive-through) with partial or full hookups (30, 50 amps) and 13 tent sites. Picnic tables are provided. Restrooms, flush toilets, showers, modem access, a seasonal pool, a clubhouse, horseshoes, a nine-hole golf course, a coin-operated laundry, propane, ice, and groceries are available. Some

facilities are wheelchair-accessible. Leashed pets are permitted.

Reservations, fees: Reservations are accepted. The fee is $16–24 per night, plus $2 per person per night for more than four people. Major credit cards are accepted. Open year-round.

Directions: From I-5, take the Dunnigan exit (just north of the I-505 cutoff). Drive west on County Road E4 for a mile to County Road 88. Turn right and drive for 1.5 miles to the park.

Contact: Campers Inn, 530/724-3350 or 800/79-GOLF3 (800/794-6533), fax 530/724-3110, website: www.campersinnrv.com.

40 HAPPY TIME RV PARK

Rating: 1

near Dunnigan

See map pages 564–565

If you are cruising I-5 and are exhausted or need to take a deep breath before hitting the Bay Area or Sacramento, this private park can provide a respite and, to be honest, not a whole lot more. Restaurants are available in nearby Dunnigan. About one-third of the sites here are long-term rentals.

RV sites, facilities: There are 67 sites with full hookups, including many drive-through, for RVs, and a grassy area for a few tents. Picnic tables are provided. Restrooms, flush toilets, showers, modem access, a playground, a coin-operated laundry, and a seasonal swimming pool are available. Some facilities are wheelchair-accessible. Leashed pets are permitted.

Reservations, fees: Reservations are accepted. The fee is $22 for RVs and $10 for tents. A senior discount is available. Major credit cards are accepted. Open year-round.

Directions: From I-5 near the I-505 intersection, take the County Road 8 exit. Drive east on County Road 8 for a short distance to Road 99W. Turn left on Road 99W and drive to the first driveway (less than one block) and park entrance on the left.

Contact: Happy Time RV Park, 530/724-3336.

CALIFORNIA

41 AUBURN KOA

Rating: 4

near Auburn

See map pages 564–565

This year-round KOA park is set at 1,250 feet and has all the amenities. Hey, a swimming pool is always a bonus in Auburn. An 18-hole golf course is within a half mile.

RV sites, facilities: There are 66 sites with full and partial hookups, including some drive-through, for RVs up to 40 feet, and 10 tent sites, two cabins, and a rental trailer. Picnic tables and fire rings are provided. Restrooms, drinking water, flush toilets, showers, an RV dump station, a playground, a seasonal swimming pool, a whirlpool, a recreation room, a fishing pond, basketball, horseshoes, volleyball, a grocery store, a coin-operated laundry, and propane are available. Some facilities are wheelchair-accessible. Leashed pets are permitted.

Reservations, fees: Reservations are accepted at 800/562-6671. The fee is $25–36 per night. Major credit cards are accepted. Open year-round.

Directions: From Auburn, drive north on Highway 49 for 3.5 miles to Rock Creek Road (one block past Bell Road). Turn right on Rock Creek Road and drive a short distance to the KOA entrance on the left.

Contact: Auburn KOA, 530/885-0990.

42 AUBURN STATE RECREATION AREA

Rating: 8

near Auburn

See map pages 564–565

This state park is a jewel in the valley foothill country, covering more than 35,000 acres along 40 miles of the North and Middle Forks of the American River. This area once teemed with thousands of gold miners, but it is now a natural area offering a wide variety of recreational opportunities and wildlife. The Auburn State Recreation Area is actually made up of land set aside for the Auburn Dam, consisting of 20 miles along two forks of the American River. There are two drive-in campgrounds, Mineral Bar and Rucky-A-Chucky, and two boat-in campgrounds at Lake Clementine. The American River runs through the park, offering visitors opportunities to fish, boat, and raft. In addition, there are more than 100 miles of hiking and horseback riding trails. Lake Clementine offers fishing (not stocked) and water-skiing, with a limit of 25 boats per day; the quota is reached every day on summer weekends. White-water rafting is extremely popular, with more than 30 private outfitters licensed for trips in sections of river through the park.

RV sites, facilities: Mineral Camp provides 16 campsites. Rucky-A-Chucky provides 15 campsites for self-contained RVs up to 20 feet or tents. There are two boat-in campgrounds at Lake Clementine with 20 boat-in sites. Picnic tables and fire grills are provided. Pit toilets are available. No drinking water is available. Garbage must be packed out. Leashed pets are permitted, except at lake Clementine.

Reservations, fees: Reservations are accepted at 800/444-PARK (800/444-7275) or online at www.reserveamerica.com ($7.50 reservation fee). The fee is $7 per night. A senior discount is available. Tent sites are open year-round.

Directions: To Mineral Bar Camp: From I-80 in Auburn, drive east for 15 miles to Colfax. Take the Colfax exit and turn right on the frontage road and drive .5 mile to Iowa Hill Road. Turn left and drive 2.5 miles to the campground on the left.

To Rucky-A-Chucky Camp: From I-80 in Auburn, take the Foresthill Road exit on to Foresthill Road. Continue on Foresthill Road for seven miles to Drivers Flat Road. Turn right and drive 2.8 miles (becomes Rucky-A-Chucky Road) to the campground on the right.

Contact: Auburn State Recreation Area, 530/885-4527, fax 530/885-2798.

43 LOOMIS RV

Rating: 2

in Loomis

See map pages 564–565

This park is in the Sierra foothills, which are known for hot summer weather. The sites are on level gravel and some are shaded. The elevation is 600 feet. Note that about half the sites are long-term rentals.

RV sites, facilities: There are 74 sites, most with full hookups (30 amps), for RVs up to 40 feet, and two one-room cabins. Picnic tables and fire grills are provided. Drinking water, restrooms, flush toilets, showers, an RV dump station, a playground, a seasonal swimming pool, a recreation room, limited cell phone reception, modem access, horseshoes, a convenience store, a coin-operated laundry, and propane are available. An ATM is within a half mile. Some facilities are wheelchair-accessible. Leashed pets are permitted.

Reservations, fees: Reservations are accepted. The fee is $28–40 per night, plus $2–4 per person for more than two people. A senior discount is available. Major credit cards are accepted. Open year-round.

Directions: From Sacramento, drive east on I-80 to Loomis and the junction of Sierra College Boulevard. Take Sierra College Boulevard and drive north for .5 mile to Taylor Road. Turn east and drive a half block to the camp on the right.

Contact: Loomis RV, 916/652-6737.

44 VINEYARD RV PARK

Rating: 2

in Vacaville

See map pages 564–565

This is one of two privately operated parks in the area set up primarily for RVs. It is in a eucalyptus grove, with clean, well-kept sites. If you are heading to the Bay Area, it is late in the day, and you don't have your destination set, this spot offers a chance to hole up for the night and formulate your travel plans. Note that about half the sites are long-term rentals, and the park doesn't take credit cards.

RV sites, facilities: There are 110 sites with full hookups (30, 50 amps) including 26 drive-through, for RVs up to 40 feet. Picnic tables are provided. Restrooms, flush toilets, showers, modem access, a swimming pool, a coin-operated laundry, an RV dump station, cell phone reception, a dog run, a putting green, pay phones, and ice are available. An ATM is within a quarter mile. Some facilities are wheelchair-accessible. Leashed pets are permitted.

Reservations, fees: Reservations are recommended. The fee is $33.25 per night, plus $2 per person

per night for more than two people and $1 per pet per night. Open year-round.

From Vacaville on I-80, turn north on I-505 and drive three miles to Midway Road. Turn right (east) on Midway Road and travel .5 mile to the second campground on the left at 4985 Midway Road.

Contact: Vineyard RV Park, 707/447-8797, website: www.vineyardrvpark.com.

45 SACRAMENTO-METRO KOA

Rating: 1

downtown Sacramento

See map pages 564–565

This is the choice of car and RV campers touring California's capital and looking for a layover spot. It is in downtown Sacramento near the Capitol building, the railroad museum, Sutter's Fort, Old Sacramento, Crocker Museum, and shopping.

RV sites, facilities: There are 95 sites with partial or full hookups (30 amps), most drive-through, for RVs up to 40 feet, 27 tent sites, and 12 cabins. Restrooms, flush toilets, showers, modem access, cable TV, cell phone reception, a playground, a fishing pond, a seasonal swimming pool, a coin-operated laundry, firewood, propane, and a convenience store are available. An ATM is within a quarter mile. Some facilities are wheelchair-accessible. Leashed pets are permitted.

Reservations, fees: Reservations are recommended and may be made at 800/562-2747. The fee is $27–56 per night, plus $5 per person for more than two people. Major credit cards are accepted. Open year-round.

Directions: From Sacramento, drive west on I-80 about four miles to the West Capitol Avenue exit. Exit and turn left onto West Capitol Avenue, going under the freeway to the first stoplight and the intersection with Lake Road. Turn left onto Lake Road and continue a half block to the camp on the right at 3951 Lake Road.

Contact: Sacramento-Metro KOA, 916/371-6771 or 800/545-KAMP (800/545-5267), website: www.koa.com.

CALIFORNIA

46 BEAL'S POINT

Rating: 6

in Folsom Lake State Recreation Area
See map pages 564–565

Folsom Lake State Recreation Area is Sacramento's backyard vacation spot, a huge lake covering about 18,000 acres with 75 miles of shoreline, which means plenty of room for boating, water-skiing, fishing, and sun tanning. This camp is on the lake's southwest side, just north of the dam, with a boat ramp nearby at Granite Bay. The lake has a productive trout fishery in the spring, a fast-growing population of kokanee salmon, and good prospects for bass in late spring and early summer. By summer, water-skiers usually take over the lake each day by about 10 A.M. One problem with this lake is that a minor water drawdown can cause major amounts of shoreline to become exposed on its upper arms. There are opportunities for hiking, biking, running, picnics, and horseback riding. A 32-mile-long trail connects Folsom Lake with many Sacramento County parks before reaching Old Sacramento. This trail is outstanding for family biking and roller blading. Summers are hot and dry. Note that before 2003, there were 15 sites with full hookups for RVs. These hookups were discontinued.

RV sites, facilities: There are 69 sites for RVs up to 31 feet or tents. Picnic tables and fire grills are provided. Drinking water, flush toilets, showers, limited cell phone reception, and an RV dump station are available. A bike path and horseback riding facilities are nearby. An ATM is within four miles. Boat rentals, moorings, a summer snack bar, ice, and bait and tackle are available at the Folsom Lake Marina. Camping, picnicking, and fishing areas are wheelchair-accessible. Leashed pets are permitted.

Reservations, fees: Reservations are accepted April through October with a $7.50 reservation fee at 800/444-PARK (800/444-7275) or www.reserveamerica.com. The fee is $12–15 per night. A senior discount is available. Open year-round.

Directions: From Sacramento, drive east on U.S. 50 to the Folsom Boulevard exit. Turn left at the stop sign and continue on Folsom Boulevard for 3.5 miles, following the road as it curves onto Leidesdorff Street. Head east on Leidesdorff Street for a half mile until it dead-ends into Riley Street. Turn left onto Riley Street and proceed over the bridge to Folsom-Auburn Road. Turn right on Folsom-Auburn Road and drive north for 3.5 miles to the park entrance on the right.

Contact: Folsom Lake State Recreation Area, 916/988-0205, fax 916/988-9062.

47 PENINSULA

Rating: 6

in Folsom Lake State Recreation Area
See map pages 564–565

This is one of the big camps at Folsom Lake, but it is also more remote than the other camps, requiring a circuitous drive. It is on the peninsula on the northeast shore, right where the North Fork American River arm of the lake enters the main lake area. A nearby boat ramp, marina, and boat rentals make this a great weekend spot. Fishing for bass and trout is often quite good in spring and early summer, and water-skiing is popular in the hot summer.

RV sites, facilities: There are 100 sites for RVs or tents. Picnic tables and fire grills are provided. Drinking water, restrooms, flush toilets, and a boat launch are available. A bike path is nearby. Boat rentals, moorings, a snack bar, ice, and bait and tackle are available at the Folsom Lake Marina. Leashed pets are permitted.

Reservations, fees: Reservations are accepted with a $7.50 reservation fee at 800/444-PARK (800/444-7275) or www.reserveamerica.com. The fee is $12–15 per night. A senior discount is available. Open year-round.

Directions: From Placerville, drive east on U.S. 50 to the Spring Street/Highway 49 exit. Turn north on Highway 49 (toward the town of Coloma) and continue 8.3 miles into the town of Pilot Hill and Rattlesnake Bar Road. Turn left on Rattlesnake Bar Road and drive nine miles to the end of the road and the park entrance.

Contact: Folsom Lake State Recreation Area, 916/988-0205, fax 916/988-9062.

CALIFORNIA

48 PLACERVILLE KOA

Rating: 7

near Placerville

See map pages 564–565

This is a classic KOA campground, complete with the cute little log cabins KOA calls "Kamping Kabins." The location of this camp is ideal for many, set near U.S. 50 in the Sierra foothills, the main route up to South Tahoe. Nearby is Apple Hill, where from September to November it is a popular tourist attraction, when the local ranches and orchards sell produce and crafts, often with live music. In addition, the Marshall Gold Discovery Site is 10 miles north, where gold was discovered in 1848, setting off the 1849 gold rush. White-water rafting and gold panning are popular on the nearby American River.

RV sites, facilities: There are 70 sites, 46 with full hookups and 24 with partial hookups, for RVs, 20 sites for tents or RVs, 14 tent sites, including eight with electricity, and eight cabins. Picnic tables and barbecues are provided. Restrooms, drinking water, flush toilets, showers, an RV dump station, a pay phone, cable TV, modem access, a recreation room, a seasonal swimming pool, a spa, a playground, a video arcade, basketball courts, a 19-hole miniature golf course, a convenience store, a snack bar, a dog run, a petting zoo, a fishing pond, bike rentals, pavilion cooking facilities, a volleyball court, and horseshoes are available. Some facilities are wheelchair-accessible. Leashed pets are permitted.

Reservations, fees: Reservations are accepted at 800/562-4197. The fee is $5–38 for RV sites and $22–25 for tent sites, plus $3 per person per night for more than two people. Major credit cards are accepted. Open year-round.

Directions: From U.S. 50 west of Placerville, take the Shingle Springs Drive exit (and not the Shingle Springs/Ponderosa Road exit). Drive one block to Rock Barn Road. Turn left and drive .5 mile to the campground at the end of the road.

Contact: Placerville KOA, 530/676-2267, website: www.koa.com.

49 SLY PARK RECREATION AREA

Rating: 7

on Jenkinson Lake

See map pages 564–565

Jenkinson Lake is set at 3,500 feet in elevation in the lower reaches of Eldorado National Forest, with a climate that is perfect for water-skiing and fishing. The lake covers 640 acres and features eight miles of forested shoreline. Participants of both sports get along, with most water-skiers motoring around the lake's main body, while anglers head upstream into the Hazel Creek arm of the lake for trout (in the spring) and bass (in the summer). Good news for anglers: personal watercraft are not permitted. More good news: this is one of the better lakes in the Sierra for brown trout. The boat ramp is in a cove on the southwest end of the lake, about two miles from the campground. The area also has several hiking trails, and the lake is good for swimming. There are nine miles of trails available for hiking, biking, and equestrians; an equestrian trail also circles the lake. A group camp is available for visitors with horses, complete with riding trails, hitching posts, and corrals. Note: no pets or babies with diapers are allowed on the lake.

RV sites, facilities: There are 155 sites for RVs up to 40 feet or tents. There are five group sites that can accommodate 50 to 100 people and an equestrian camp called Black Oak, which has 12 sites and two youth-group areas. Picnic tables, fire rings, and barbecues are provided. Drinking water, vault toilets, and firewood are available. Two boat ramps are nearby. A grocery store, a snack bar, an RV dump station, bait, and propane are available nearby. Some facilities are wheelchair-accessible. Leashed pets are permitted.

Reservations, fees: Reservations are recommended and may be made at 530/644-2792. The fee is $16–21 per night, plus $2 per person for more than two people, $2 per pet per night, $9 for each additional vehicle, and a $3–6 boat-launch fee; the group site is $160 for up to 50 people. A senior discount is available. Check out by 2 P.M. Open year-round.

Directions: From Sacramento, drive east on U.S. 50 to Pollock Pines and take the exit for Sly Park

CALIFORNIA

Road. Drive south for five miles to Jenkinson Lake and the campground access road. Turn left and drive one mile to the campground.

Contact: Sly Park Recreation Area, El Dorado Irrigation District, 530/644-2545, website: www.eid.org.

50 PIPI

Rating: 7

on the Middle Fork of the Cosumnes River in Eldorado National Forest
See map pages 564–565

This place is far enough out of the way to get missed by most campers. It is beside the Middle Fork of the Cosumnes River at 4,100 feet. There are some good swimming holes in the area, but the water is cold in early summer (after all, it's snowmelt). A trail/boardwalk along the river is wheelchair-accessible. Several sites border a pretty meadow in the back of the camp. This is also a gateway to a vast network of Forest Service roads to the north in Eldorado National Forest.

RV sites, facilities: There are 51 sites for RVs up to 40 feet or tents, including three double-family sites. Picnic tables and fire grills are provided. Drinking water and vault toilets are available. Some camping areas, restrooms, and pathways are wheelchair-accessible. Leashed pets are permitted.

Reservations, fees: Reservations are accepted with a $9 reservation fee for some sites at 877/444-6777 or www.reserveusa.com. The fee is $12 per night for single sites and $24 per night for double sites, plus $5 per night for each additional vehicle. A senior discount is available. Open May through mid-November, weather permitting.

Directions: From Jackson, drive east on Highway 88 to Pioneer and continue for nine miles to Omo Ranch Road. Turn left and drive .8 mile to North-South Road/Forest Road 6. Turn right and drive 5.9 miles to the campground on the left side of the road.

Contact: Eldorado National Forest, Amador Ranger District, 209/295-4251, fax 209/295-5994; Eldorado Information Center, 530/644-6048, fax 530/295-5624.

51 FAR HORIZONS 49ER VILLAGE

Rating: 4

in Plymouth
See map pages 564–565

This is the granddaddy of RV parks, set in the heart of the gold country 40 miles east of Stockton and Sacramento. It is rarely crowded and offers warm pools, a huge spa, and a friendly staff.

RV sites, facilities: There are 329 sites with full hookups (30, 50 amps), including 15 drive-through, for RVs only, 11 park-model cabins, and two RV rentals. Restrooms, flush toilets, showers, an RV dump station, a playground, limited cell phone reception, two heated swimming pools, a hot tub, a recreation room, a TV lounge, a pool room, cable TV, modem access, a coin-operated laundry, a delicatessen, propane, and a general store are available. An ATM is within a quarter mile. Some facilities are wheelchair-accessible. Leashed pets are permitted.

Reservations, fees: Reservations are recommended. The fee is $32–52 per night, plus $2 per night for additional vehicle. Major credit cards are accepted. Open year-round.

Directions: From Sacramento, drive east on U.S. 50 to Watt Avenue. Turn south on Watt Avenue and drive to Highway 16. Turn east on Highway 16 and drive to Highway 49. Turn north on Highway 49 and drive a mile to the campground on the left side of the road at 18265 Hwy. 49. Note: this is a mile south of Main Street in Plymouth.

Contact: Far Horizons 49er Village, 209/245-6981 or 800/339-6981, website: www.49ervillage.com.

52 INDIAN GRINDING ROCK STATE HISTORIC PARK

Rating: 7

near Jackson
See map pages 564–565

Visiting this park is like entering a time machine. It offers a reconstructed Miwok village with petroglyphs, bedrock mortars, a cultural center, a two-mile nature trail, and interpretive talks for groups, by reservation. One unique element is that you will discover *Chaw-se* (grinding rock)

CALIFORNIA

signs about the park. The camp is set at 2,500 feet in the Sierra foothills, about 10 miles from Jackson. It covers 135 acres and is nestled in a small valley with open meadows and large valley oaks. There is a large outcropping of marblized limestone with 1,185 mortar holes, the largest collection of bedrock mortars in North America. Ceremonies are scheduled several times a year by local Native Americans, including the Acorn Harvest Thanksgiving in September. Summers are warm and dry, with temperatures often exceeding 90°F. Spring and fall are ideal, with winters cool, often right on the edge of snow (a few times) and rain (mostly) during most storms.
RV sites, facilities: There are 23 sites for RVs or tents, with some sites available for RVs up to 27 feet, a group primitive tent camping area that can hold up to 44 people, and seven bark houses. Picnic tables, fire grills, and food lockers are provided. Drinking water, flush toilets, limited cell phone reception, and coin-operated hot showers are available. An ATM is within two miles. Some facilities are wheelchair-accessible. Leashed pets are permitted.
Reservations, fees: Reservations are not accepted for single sites. The fee is $12 per night. Reservations are required for bark houses and groups. The group site is $75 per night. A senior discount is available. Open year-round.
Directions: From Jackson, drive east on Highway 88 for 11 miles to Pine Grove–Volcano Road. Turn left on Pine Grove–Volcano Road and drive 1.75 miles to the campground on the left.
Contact: Indian Grinding Rock State Historic Park, 209/296-7488.

53 NEW HOPE LANDING

Rating: 6

on the Mokelumne River north of Stockton
See map pages 564–565
New Hope Landing is a privately operated resort set along the Mokelumne River in the upper San Joaquin Delta. A marina is available, which provides access to 1,000 miles of Delta waterways via the Mokelumne River. The Lower Mokelumne is often an excellent area to troll for striped bass in April and offers great salmon fishing in late summer and early fall. Water-skiing is also pop-

ular in summer, though at this time of year water hyacinth is sometimes a problem farther upstream.
RV sites, facilities: There are 52 sites with full hookups (20, 30, 50 amps) for RVs and 12 sites for tents. Restrooms, showers, ice, bait, propane, cell phone reception, and a marina are available. Some facilities are wheelchair-accessible. Leashed pets are permitted.
Reservations, fees: Reservations are accepted for tent sites only. The fee is $20–27.50 per night, plus $5 for each additional person and $5 for additional vehicle. Open year-round.
Directions: From Stockton, drive north on I-5 for 25 miles to the Thornton exit. Take that exit, turn west on Walnut Grove Road, and drive 3.3 miles to the campground entrance on the left.
Contact: New Hope Landing, tel./fax 209/794-2627.

54 LAKE CAMANCHE NORTH

Rating: 7

on Camanche Lake
See map pages 564–565
The sites at North Shore feature grassy spots with picnic tables set above the lake, and though there are few trees and the sites seem largely exposed, the lake view is quite pretty. The lake will beckon you for water sports and is excellent for boat owners, with a full-service marina available. The warm, clean waters make for good water-skiing (in specified areas) and fishing for trout in spring, bass in early summer, and crappie, bluegill, and catfish in summer. There are five miles of hiking and equestrian trails.
RV sites, facilities: There are 219 sites for RVs or tents, 22 cottages, and some motel rooms. Picnic tables and fire grills are provided. Restrooms, drinking water, showers, an RV dump station, a boat ramp, boat rentals, a laundry room, a grocery store, a café, and a playground are available. Some facilities are wheelchair-accessible. Leashed pets are permitted.
Reservations, fees: Reservations are recommended. The fee is $19 per night, plus $9 per night for each additional vehicle, a $6 boat launch fee, and $2 per pet per night. Major credit cards are accepted. Open year-round.
Directions: From Stockton, drive east on Highway

88 for 24 miles to Clements. Just east of Clements, bear left on Highway 88 and drive six miles to Camanche Parkway. Turn right and drive seven miles to the Camanche North Shore entrance gate.
Contact: Lake Camanche North, 209/763-5121, fax 209/763-5789, website: www.camancherecreation.com.

55 LAKE CAMANCHE SOUTH

Rating: 7

on Camanche Lake
See map pages 564–565
Camanche Lake is a huge, multifaceted facility, covering 7,700 acres with 53 miles of shoreline, set in the foothills east of Lodi at 325 feet in elevation. It is the number one recreation lake for water-skiing and personal watercraft (in specified areas), as well as swimming. In the spring and summer, it provides outstanding fishing for bass, trout, crappie, bluegill, and catfish. There are two campgrounds at the lake, and both have boat ramps nearby and full facilities. This one at South Shore has a large, but exposed, overflow area for camping, a way to keep from getting stuck for a spot on popular weekends.
RV sites, facilities: There are 263 sites for self-contained RVs or tents, 120 sites with full hookups for RVs, and seven cottages. Picnic tables and fire grills are provided. Drinking water, restrooms, showers, an RV dump station, a trout pond, a boat ramp, boat rentals, a coin-operated laundry, a snack bar, and a grocery store are available. Some facilities are wheelchair-accessible. Leashed pets are permitted.
Reservations, fees: Reservations are recommended. The fee is $18–25 per night, plus $9 per night for each additional vehicle, a $6 boat launch fee, and $1 per pet per night. Major credit cards are accepted. Open year-round.
Directions: From Stockton, drive east on Highway 88 for 24 miles to Clements. Just east of Clements continue east on Highway 12 and drive six miles to South Camanche Parkway. Turn left and drive six miles to the entrance gate.
Contact: Lake Camanche South, 209/763-5178, fax 209/763-5724, website: www.camancherecreation.com.

56 LAKE AMADOR RECREATION AREA

Rating: 7

near Stockton
See map pages 564–565
Lake Amador is in the foothill country east of Stockton at an elevation of 485 feet, covering 425 acres with 13 miles of shoreline. Everything here is set up for fishing, with large trout stocks from winter through late spring and the chance for huge bass; plus, water-skiing and personal watercraft are prohibited. The largest two-man bass limit in California was caught here (80 pounds), and the lake record bass weighed 17 pounds, 1.25 ounces. The Carson Creek arm and Jackson Creek arm are the top spots.
RV sites, facilities: There are 150 sites, including 73 with full hookups (20, 30, 50 amps), for RVs up to 40 feet or tents and 12 group sites. Picnic tables and fire grills are provided. Drinking water, restrooms, showers, an RV dump station, a boat ramp, boat rentals, fishing supplies (including bait and tackle), a restaurant, limited cell phone reception, an ATM, a grocery store, propane, a swimming pond, and a playground are available. Some facilities are wheelchair-accessible. Leashed pets are permitted.
Reservations, fees: Reservations are accepted seven days in advance in the summer. The fee is $20–28 per night. Major credit cards are accepted. Open year-round.
Directions: From Stockton, turn east on Highway 88 and drive 24 miles to Clements. Just east of Clements, bear left on Highway 88 and drive 11 miles to Jackson Valley Road. Turn right (well signed) and drive four miles to Lake Amador Drive. Turn right and drive over the dam to the campground office.
Contact: Lake Amador Recreation Area, 209/274-4739, website: www.lakeamador.com.

57 LAKE PARDEE MARINA

Rating: 7

on Pardee Reservoir
See map pages 564–565
Many people think that Pardee is the prettiest lake in the Mother Lode country; it's a big lake

covering 2,257 acres with 37 miles of shoreline. It is a beautiful sight in the spring when the lake is full and the surrounding hills are green and glowing. Water-skiing, personal watercraft, and swimming are prohibited at the lake; it is set up expressly for fishing, with high catch rates for rainbow trout and kokanee salmon. During hot weather, attention turns to bass, both smallmouth and largemouth, as well as catfish.

RV sites, facilities: There are 93 sites with no hookups for RVs up to 40 feet or tents and 12 sites with full hookups for RVs. Picnic tables and fire grills are provided. Drinking water, restrooms, showers (in the RV section), an RV dump station, a boat ramp, boat rentals, a coin-operated laundry, a grocery store, limited cell phone reception, an ATM, propane, RV and boat storage, a wading pool, and a seasonal swimming pool are available. Some facilities are wheelchair-accessible. Leashed pets are permitted.

Reservations, fees: Reservations are accepted for full-hookup RV sites only. The fee is $17–23 per night, plus $8.50 per night for second vehicle and $2 per pet per night. Major credit cards are accepted. Open February through October.

Directions: From Stockton, drive east on Highway 88 for 24 miles to the town of Clements. Just east of Clements, bear left on Highway 88 and drive 11 miles to Jackson Valley Road. Turn right and drive to a four-way stop sign at Buena Vista. Turn right and drive for three miles to Stony Creek Road on the left. Turn left and drive a mile to the campground on the right.

Contact: Pardee Recreation Area, 209/772-1472, fax 209/772-0985, website: www.lakepardee.com.

58 OAK KNOLL

Rating: 7

at New Hogan Reservoir
See map pages 564–565
This is one of three camps at New Hogan Reservoir. The reservoir was created by an Army Corps of Engineers dam project on the Calaveras River. (See the following entry for Acorn West and Acorn East for more information.)

RV sites, facilities: There are 50 sites for RVs or tents. Fire grills and picnic tables are provided. Drinking water and vault toilets are available.

Groceries, propane, an RV dump station, and a four-lane boat ramp are available nearby. Leashed pets are permitted.

Reservations, fees: Reservations are accepted at 877/444-6777 or www.reserveusa.com. The fee is $10 per night. A senior discount is available. Open May to early September.

Directions: From Stockton, drive east on Highway 26 for about 35 miles to Valley Springs and Hogan Dam Road. Turn right and drive 1.5 miles to Hogan Parkway. Turn left and drive one mile to South Petersburg Road. Turn left and drive .5 mile to the campground on the right (adjacent to Acorn campgrounds).

Contact: U.S. Army Corps of Engineers, Sacramento District, 209/772-1343, fax 209/772-9352.

59 ACORN WEST AND ACORN EAST

Rating: 7

at New Hogan Reservoir
See map pages 564–565
New Hogan is a big lake in the foothill country east of Stockton, set at an elevation of 680 feet and covering 4,000 acres with 50 miles of shoreline. Acorn West and Acorn East are two campgrounds on the lake operated by the U.S. Army Corps of Engineers. Boaters might also consider boat-in sites near Deer Flat on the eastern shore. Boating and water-skiing are popular here. Fishing for largemouth bass is off and on, best in the spring up the Bear Creek and Whiskey Creek arms, and again in the fall when the striped bass come to life, chasing bait fish on the surface. Fishing for largemouth bass can be exceptional in spring and summer. An interpretive trail below the dam is worth checking out.

RV sites, facilities: At Acorn West there are 58 sites for RVs or tents. At Acorn East there are 69 sites for RVs or tents. Fire pits and picnic tables are provided. Drinking water, flush toilets, showers, pay telephones, a fish-cleaning station, and an RV dump station are available. A two-lane, paved boat ramp is in Acorn East Campground. Groceries, a restaurant, and propane are available within three miles. Leashed pets are permitted.

Reservations, fees: Reservations are accepted at 877/444-6777 or www.reserveusa.com. The fee

CALIFORNIA

is $12–16 per night. A senior discount is available. Major credit cards are accepted.

Directions: From Stockton, drive east on Highway 26 for about 35 miles to Valley Springs and Hogan Dam Road. Turn right and drive 1.5 miles to Hogan Parkway. Turn left and drive one mile to South Petersburg Road. Turn left and drive .25 mile to the campground on the right.

Contact: U.S. Army Corps of Engineers, Sacramento District, 209/772-1343, fax 209/772-9352.

60 GOLDEN PINES RV RESORT AND CAMP

Rating: 6

near Arnold
See map pages 564–565

This is a privately operated park set at 5,800 feet on the slopes of the Sierra Nevada near Stanislaus National Forest, the North Stanislaus River, and Calaveras Big Trees State Park (two miles away). The latter features 150 giant sequoias, along with the biggest stump you can imagine, and two easy hikes, one routed through the North Grove, another through the South Grove. Note that about half the sites here are long-term rentals.

RV sites, facilities: There are 62 sites with full hookups (30 amps) for RVs, three sites with partial hookups for RVs, 50 tent sites, and two cabins. Picnic tables, fire pits, and barbecues are provided at all RV sites and most tent sites. Drinking water, restrooms, showers, a recreation room, modem access, limited cell phone reception, a seasonal swimming pool, a playground, a convenience store, a coin-operated laundry, and propane are available. An ATM is within a quarter mile. Some facilities are wheelchair-accessible. Leashed pets are permitted.

Reservations, fees: Reservations are recommended. The fee is $18–30 per night, plus $2 per person per night for more than four people and $1 per night for each additional vehicle. A senior discount is available. Major credit cards are accepted. Open year-round.

Directions: From Angels Camp, turn northeast on Highway 4 and drive 22 miles to Arnold. Continue for seven miles to the campground entrance on the left.

Contact: Golden Pines RV Resort and Camp,

209/795-2820, fax 209/795-7432, website: www .goldenpinesrvresort.com.

61 NORTH GROVE

Rating: 7

in Calaveras Big Trees State Park
See map pages 564–565

This is one of two campgrounds at Calaveras Big Trees State Park, the state park known for its two groves of giant sequoias (Sierra redwoods). The park covers 6,500 acres, preserving the extraordinary North Grove of giant sequoias, including the Discovery Tree. Over the years, additional acreage surrounding the grove has been added, providing a mixed conifer forest as a buffer around the giant sequoias. The trailhead for a hike on the North Grove Loop is here; it's an easy 1.5-mile walk that is routed among 150 sequoias, where the sweet fragrance of the huge trees fills the air. These trees are known for their massive diameter, not for their height, as is the case with coastal redwoods. Another hike, a five-miler, is in the South Grove, where the park's two largest sequoias (the Agassiz Tree and the Palace Hotel Tree) can be seen on a spur trail. A visitors center is open during peak periods, offering exhibits on the giant sequoia and natural history. The North Fork Stanislaus River runs near Highway 4, providing trout fishing access. The Stanislaus (near the bridge) and Beaver Creek (about 10 miles away) are stocked with trout in late spring and early summer. In the winter this is a popular spot for cross-country skiing and snowshoeing. The elevation is 4,800 feet.

RV sites, facilities: There are 29 sites for RVs up to 30 feet, 27 sites for tents, five hike-in sites, and two sites designed for wheelchair use. Two group sites are also available for 40 to 60 people each. Fire grills, food lockers, and picnic tables are provided. Drinking water, flush toilets, firewood, coin-operated showers, and an RV dump station are available. No bicycles are allowed on the paths, but they are permitted on fire roads and paved roads. Some facilities are wheelchair-accessible, including a nature trail and exhibits. Leashed pets are permitted, but not on trails.

Reservations, fees: Reservations are accepted with a $7.50 reservation fee at 800/444-PARK

CALIFORNIA

(800/444-7275) or www.reserveamerica.com. The fees are $12 per night, $30–45 for group sites, and $11 for hike-in sites. A senior discount is available. Open year-round, with 12 sites available in winter.

Directions: From Angels Camp, drive east on Highway 4 for 23 miles to Arnold and then continue another four miles to the park entrance on the right.

Contact: Calaveras Big Trees State Park, 209/795-2334; Columbia State Park, 209/532-0150.

62 OAK HOLLOW

Rating: 7

in Calaveras Big Trees State Park
See map pages 564–565
This is one of two campgrounds at Calaveras Big Trees State Park. (See the prior entry for North Grove for recreation information.)

RV sites, facilities: There are 18 sites for RVs up to 30 feet and 23 sites for tents only. Picnic tables, fire rings, and food lockers are provided. Drinking water, flush toilets, and coin-operated showers are available. An RV dump station is four miles away at North Grove. You can buy supplies in Dorrington. Some facilities are wheelchair-accessible, including a nature trail and exhibits. Leashed pets are permitted, except on trails.

Reservations, fees: Reservations are accepted with a $7.50 reservation fee at 800/444-PARK (800/444-7275) or www.reserveamerica.com. The fee is $12 per night. A senior discount is available. Open May through September.

Directions: From Angels Camp, drive east on Highway 4 for 23 miles to Arnold and then continue another four miles to the park entrance on the right. Continue another four miles to the campground on the right.

Contact: Calaveras Big Trees State Park, 209/795-2334; Columbia State Park, 209/532-0150.

63 49ER RV RANCH

Rating: 6

near Columbia
See map pages 564–565
This historic ranch/campground was originally built in 1852 as a dairy farm. Several original barns are still standing. The place has been brought up to date, of course, with a small store on the property providing last-minute supplies. Location is a plus, with the Columbia State Historic Park only a half mile away and the Stanislaus River arm of New Melones Reservoir within a five-minute drive. The elevation is 2,100 feet. Note that there is a separate mobile home park on the premises and that there are long-term rentals in the RV park in the summer.

RV sites, facilities: There are 45 sites with full hookups (30, 50 amps) for RVs up to 40 feet and trailers. Picnic tables and barbecues are provided. Restrooms, drinking water, hot showers, a coin-operated laundry, a convenience store, an RV dump station, cable TV, modem access, limited cell phone reception, propane, and a large barn for group or club activities are available. An ATM is within a half mile. Some facilities are wheelchair-accessible. Leashed pets are permitted.

Reservations, fees: Reservations are accepted. The fee is $25–29.50 per night, plus $2.50 per person for more than two people. Long-term rates and group rates are available. A senior discount is available. Major credit cards are accepted. Open year-round.

Directions: From Sonora, turn north on Highway 49 for 2.5 miles to Parrots Ferry Road. Turn right and drive 1.7 miles to Columbia Street. Turn right and drive .4 mile to Pacific Street. Turn left and drive a block to Italian Bar Road. Turn right and drive .5 mile to the campground on the right.

Contact: 49er RV Ranch, 209/532-4978, website: www.49rv.com.

CALIFORNIA

64 MARBLE QUARRY RV PARK

Rating: 6

near Columbia

See map pages 564–565

This is a family-oriented RV park set at 2,100 feet in the Mother Lode country, within nearby range of several adventures. A quarter-mile trail leads directly to Columbia State Historic Park, and the Stanislaus River arm of New Melones Reservoir is only five miles away.

RV sites, facilities: There are 70 sites with full hookups (30, 50 amps) for RVs or tents, 10 tent sites, a small area for tents, and three sleeping cabins. Drinking water and picnic tables are provided. Restrooms, showers, a seasonal swimming pool, a coin-operated laundry, modem access, limited cell phone reception, a convenience store, an RV dump station, a playground, two clubhouses, a reading/TV room, two full kitchens, satellite TV, and propane are available. An ATM is within a quarter mile. Some facilities are wheelchair-accessible. Leashed pets are permitted.

Reservations, fees: Reservations are accepted. The fee is $21–32 per night, plus $3 per person for more than two people. A senior discount is available. Major credit cards are accepted. Open year-round.

Directions: From Sonora, turn north on Highway 49 and drive 2.5 miles to Parrotts Ferry Road (stop sign). Bear right on Parrotts Ferry Road and drive 1.5 miles to Columbia Street. Turn right and drive a short distance to Jackson Street. Turn right on Jackson Street and drive a quarter mile (becomes Yankee Hill Road) to the campground on the right (at 11551 Yankee Hill Road).

Contact: Marble Quarry RV Park, 209/532-9539, website: www.marblequarry.com.

65 SUGARPINE RV PARK

Rating: 5

in Twain Harte

See map pages 564–565

Twain Harte is a beautiful little town, right at the edge of the snow line in winter, and right where pines take over the alpine landscape. This park is at the threshold of mountain country, with Pinecrest, Dodge Ridge, and Beardsley Reservoir nearby. It sits on 15 acres and features several walking paths. It has a separate 64-site mobile home park for long-term renters.

RV sites, facilities: There are 13 sites with full hookups (30 amps) for RVs, 13 tent sites, and three RV rentals. Picnic tables are provided. Restrooms, showers, a playground, a seasonal pool, a coin-operated laundry, cable TV, limited cell phone reception, and a convenience store are available. An ATM is within two miles. Some facilities are wheelchair-accessible. Leashed pets are permitted.

Reservations, fees: Reservations are accepted. The fee is $20–35 per night, plus $3 per vehicle for more than one vehicle, with exception of towed vehicles. There is a pet fee. A senior discount is available. Major credit cards are accepted. Open year-round.

Directions: From Sonora, drive east on Highway 108 for 17 miles to the park on the right side of the road.

Contact: Sugarpine RV Park, tel./fax 209/586-4631, website: www.rvandcampoutwest.com.

CALIFORNIA

California

Chapter 18

Tahoe and the Northern Sierra

CALIFORNIA

see Lassen and Modoc
pages 496-497

Pyramid Lake

Lahontan Lake

Silver Spring

Truckee River

Carson City

Reno

Plumas National Forest

Frenchman Lake

Lake Davis

Blairsden

Graeagle

Plumas-Eureka State Park

Sierra City

Quincy

Little Grass Valley Res.

Downieville

Yuba River

Truckee

Soda Springs

Emigrant Gap

Tahoe National Forest

Lake Tahoe

Tahoe City

SIERRA

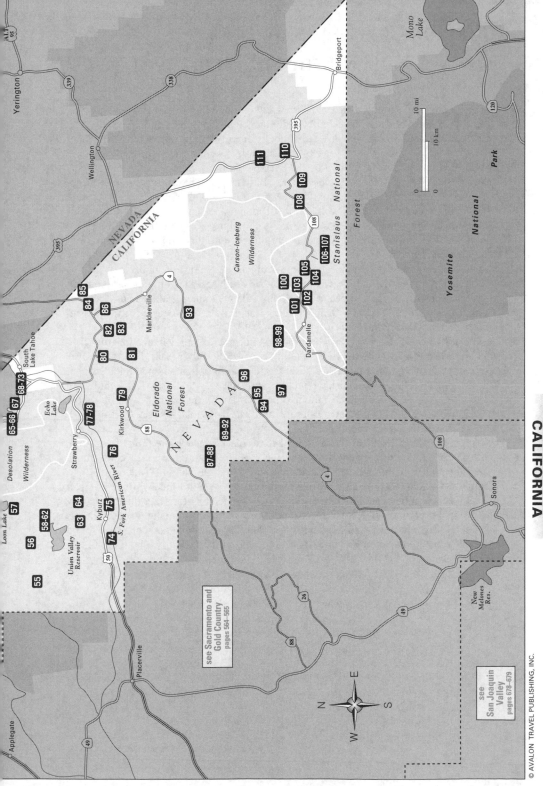

CALIFORNIA

Mono Lake

Bridgeport

Yerington

Wellington

NEVADA
CALIFORNIA

Stanislaus National Forest

Carson-Iceberg Wilderness

Yosemite National Park

111
110
109
108
106-107
105
104
103
100
102
101
98-99

Dardanelle

85
84
86
82
83
80
81
93
96
95
94
97

Markleeville

South Lake Tahoe

68-73
67
65-66

Echo Lake

77-78

Strawberry

79
Kirkwood

88
89-92
87-88

Eldorado National Forest

NEVADA

Desolation Wilderness

Loon Lake
57
56
58-62
63
64
75
74
55

Union Valley Reservoir

Kyburz
S. Fork American River

Placerville

Sonora

New Melones Res.

see Sacramento and Gold Country
pages 564–565

see San Joaquin Valley
pages 678–679

Applegate

10 mi
10 km

Chapter 18—Tahoe and the Northern Sierra

Mount Tallac affords a view across Lake Tahoe like no other: a cobalt blue expanse of water bordered by mountains that span miles of Sierra wildlands. The beauty is stunning. Lake Tahoe is one of the few places on earth where people feel an emotional response just by looking at it. Yosemite Valley, the giant sequoias, the Grand Canyon, a perfect sunset on the Pacific Ocean . . . these are a few other sights that occasionally can evoke the same response. But Tahoe often seems to strike the deepest chord. It can resonate inside you for weeks, even after a short visit.

"What about all the people?" you ask. It's true that people come here in droves. But I found many spots that I shared only with the chipmunks. You can enjoy these spots, too, if you read our books, hunt a bit, and most important, time your trip to span Monday through Thursday.

This area has the widest range and number of campgrounds in California.

Tahoe and the northern Sierra feature hundreds of lakes, including dozens you can drive to. The best for scenic beauty are Echo Lakes, Donner, Fallen Leaf, Sardine, Caples, Loon, Union Valley . . . well, I could go on and on. It is one of the most beautiful regions anywhere on earth.

The north end of the North Sierra starts near Bucks Lake, a great lake for trout fishing, and extends to Bear River Canyon (and Caples Lake, Silver Lake, and Bear River Reservoir). In between are the Lakes Basin Recreation Area (containing Gold, Sardine, Packer, and other lakes) in southern Plumas County, the Crystal Basin (featuring Union Valley Reservoir and Loon Lake, among others) in the Sierra foothills west of Tahoe, Lake Davis (with the highest catch rates for trout) near Portola, and the Carson River Canyon and Hope Valley south of Tahoe.

You could spend weeks exploring any of these places, having the time of your life, and still not get to Tahoe's magic. But it is Tahoe where the adventure starts for many, especially in the surrounding Tahoe National Forest and Desolation Wilderness.

One of California's greatest day trips from Tahoe is to Echo Lakes, where you can take a hiker's shuttle boat across the two lakes to the Pacific Crest Trail, then hike a few miles into Desolation Wilderness and Aloha Lakes. Yet with so many wonderful ways to spend a day in this area, this day trip is hardly a blip on the radar scope.

With so many places and so little time, this region offers what can be the ultimate adventureland.

CALIFORNIA

1 GOLDEN COACH RV RESORT

Rating: 6

near the Feather River
See map pages 596–597

This is a good layover spot for RV cruisers looking to hole up for the night. The park is wooded and set near the Feather River. You'll find mostly older adults here. Some spots at this park are booked for the entire summer.

RV sites, facilities: There are 57 sites, including some drive-through sites, with full hookups for RVs, and two group campgrounds for 10 to 20 people. Picnic tables are provided. Restrooms, showers, modem access, a coin-operated laundry, wood, a convenience store, a café, and propane are available. Leashed pets are permitted.

Reservations, fees: Reservations are recommended. The fee is $15–20 per night, plus $2 per person for more than two people. Long-term rates are available. Major credit cards are accepted. Open May through mid-October.

Directions: In Truckee, at the junction of Highway 80 and Highway 89, take Highway 89 north to the junction with Highway 70. Drive north on Highway 89/Highway 70 for 6.5 miles to Cromberg and look for the signed entrance to the campground on the left at 59704 Highway 70.

Contact: Golden Coach RV Resort, 530/836-2426 or 800/327-0933.

2 LIGHTNING TREE

Rating: 7

on Lake Davis in Plumas National Forest
See map pages 596–597

Lightning Tree campground is near the shore of Lake Davis. Davis is a good-sized lake, with 30 miles of shoreline, set high in the northern Sierra at 5,775 feet. Lake Davis is one of the top mountain lakes for fishing in California, with large rainbow trout in the early summer and fall. This camp is perfectly situated for a fishing trip. It is at Lightning Tree Point on the lake's remote northeast shore, directly across the lake from Freeman Creek, one of the better spots for big trout. This lake is famous for the botched poisoning job in the 1990s by the Department of Fish and Game, and then, in turn, the biggest trout plants in California history at a single lake: more than 1 million trout! It receives lots of snow and often freezes over in the winter. Since pike have reappeared, this future of this lake is one of the biggest environmental time bombs in California; if pike escape downstream, they could invade the Delta and wipe out salmon and other species. There are three boat ramps on the lake.

RV sites, facilities: There are 17 single sites and 21 double sites for RVs up to 50 feet. Vault toilets and garbage service are available from May to October. No drinking water is available. Limited cell phone reception is available. An RV dump station, ATM, and a car-top boat launch are nearby. Leashed pets are permitted.

Reservations, fees: Reserve at 877/444-6777 or online at www.reserveusa.com ($9 reservation fee). The fees are $7 per night or $11 for a double site, plus $3 per night for each additional vehicle. A senior discount is available. Open May to October.

Directions: From Truckee, turn north on Highway 89 and drive to Sattley and County Road A23. Turn right on County Road A23 and drive 13 miles to Highway 70. Turn left on Highway 70 and drive one mile to Grizzly Road. Turn right on Grizzly Road and drive about six miles to Lake Davis. Continue north on Lake Davis Road along the lake's east shore and drive about five miles to the campground entrance on the left side of the road.

Contact: Plumas National Forest, Beckwourth Ranger District, 530/836-2575, fax 530/836-0493.

3 GRASSHOPPER FLAT

Rating: 7

on Lake Davis in Plumas National Forest
See map pages 596–597

Grasshopper Flat provides a nearby alternative to Grizzly at Lake Davis, with the nearby boat ramp at adjacent Honker Cove a primary attraction for campers with trailered boats for fishing. The camp is on the southeast end of the lake, at 5,800 feet elevation. Lake Davis is known for its large rainbow trout that bite best in early summer and fall.

RV sites, facilities: There are 70 sites for RVs up to 32 feet or tents. Picnic tables and fire grills are provided. Drinking water, flush toilets, and limited cell phone reception are available. A boat ramp, grocery store, ATM, and RV dump station are nearby. Leashed pets are permitted.

Reservations, fees: Reservations are accepted at 877/444-6777 or online at www.reserveusa.com ($9 reservation fee). The fee is $14 per night. A senior discount is available. Open May through October.

Directions: From Truckee, turn north on Highway 89 and drive to Sattley and County Road A23. Turn right on County Road A23 and drive 13 miles to Highway 70. Turn left on Highway 70 and drive one mile to Grizzly Road. Turn right on Grizzly Road and drive about six miles to Lake Davis. Continue north on Lake Davis Road for a mile (just past Grizzly) to the campground entrance on the left side of the road.

Contact: Plumas National Forest, Beckwourth Ranger District, 530/836-2575, fax 530/836-0493.

▣ GRIZZLY

Rating: 7

on Lake Davis in Plumas National Forest
See map pages 596–597

This is one of the better developed campgrounds at Lake Davis and is a popular spot for camping anglers. Its proximity to the Grizzly Store, just over the dam to the south, makes getting last-minute supplies a snap. In addition, a boat ramp is to the north in Honker Cove, providing access to the southern reaches of the lake, including the island area, where trout trolling is good in early summer and fall.

RV sites, facilities: There are 55 sites for RVs up to 32 feet or tents. Picnic tables and fire grills are provided. Drinking water and flush toilets are available. A boat ramp, grocery store, and RV dump station are nearby. Leashed pets are permitted.

Reservations, fees: Reservations are accepted at 877/444-6777 or online at www.reserveusa.com ($9 reservation fee). The fee is $14 per night. A senior discount is available. Open May through October.

Directions: From Truckee, turn north on High-way 89 and drive to Sattley and County Road A23. Turn right on County Road A23 and drive 13 miles to Highway 70. Turn left on Highway 70 and drive one mile to Grizzly Road. Turn right on Grizzly Road and drive about six miles to Lake Davis. Continue north on Lake Davis Road for less than a mile to the campground entrance on the left side of the road.

Contact: Plumas National Forest, Beckwourth Ranger District, 530/836-2575, fax 530/836-0493.

▤ COTTONWOOD SPRINGS

Rating: 7

near Frenchman Lake in Plumas National Forest
See map pages 596–597

Cottonwood Springs, elevation 5,700 feet, is largely an overflow camp at Frenchman Lake. It is the only camp at the lake with a group site. The more popular Frenchman, Big Cove, and Spring Creek camps are along the southeast shore of the lake near a boat ramp.

RV sites, facilities: There are 20 sites for RVs up to 50 feet or tents and two group camping areas, which can accommodate up to 25 and 50 people, respectively. Picnic tables and fire rings are provided. Drinking water, flush toilets, limited cell phone reception, and an RV dump station are available. A boat ramp and ATM are nearby. Some facilities are wheelchair-accessible. Leashed pets are permitted.

Reservations, fees: Reserve at 877/444-6777 or online at www.reserveusa.com ($9 reservation fee). The fees are $14 per night or $44–87 per night for groups. A senior discount is available. Open May through October.

Directions: From Reno, drive north on U.S. 395 to the junction with Highway 70. Turn west on Highway 70 and drive to Chilcoot and the junction with Frenchman Lake Road. Turn right on Frenchman Lake Road and drive nine miles to the lake and to a Y. At the Y, turn left and drive 1.5 miles to the campground on the left side of the road.

Contact: Plumas National Forest, Beckwourth Ranger District, 530/836-2575, fax 530/836-0493.

6 BIG COVE

Rating: 7

at Frenchman Lake in Plumas National Forest
See map pages 596–597

Big Cove is one of four camps at the southeastern end of Frenchman Lake, with a boat ramp available about a mile away near the Frenchman and Spring Creek camps. (See the entry for Frenchman for more information.) A trail from the campground leads to the lakeshore. Another trail connects to the Spring Creek Campground, a walk of a half mile.

RV sites, facilities: There are 38 sites for RVs up to 50 feet or tents (19 are multiple-family units; 10 are wheelchair-accessible). Picnic tables and fire rings are provided. Drinking water, flush toilets, and limited cell phone reception are available. A boat ramp, RV dump station, grocery store and ATM (seven miles away), and propane are available nearby. Some facilities are wheelchair-accessible. Leashed pets are permitted.

Reservations, fees: Reserve at 877/444-6777 or online at www.reserveusa.com ($9 reservation fee). The fee is $14–28 per night. A senior discount is available. Open May through September.

Directions: From Reno, drive north on U.S. 395 to the junction with Highway 70. Turn west on Highway 70 and drive to Chilcoot and the junction with Frenchman Lake Road. Turn right on Frenchman Lake Road and drive nine miles to the lake and to a Y. At the Y, turn right and drive two miles to Forest Road 24N01. Turn left and drive a short distance to the campground entrance on the left side of the road (on the east side of the lake).

Contact: Plumas National Forest, Beckwourth Ranger District, 530/836-2575, fax 530/836-0493.

7 SPRING CREEK

Rating: 7

on Frenchman Lake in Plumas National Forest
See map pages 596–597

Frenchman Lake is set at 5,700 feet elevation, on the edge of high desert to the east and forest to the west. This camp is on the southeast end of the lake, where there are three other camp-

grounds, including a group camp and a boat ramp. The lake provides good fishing for stocked rainbow trout, best in the cove near the campgrounds. Trails lead out from the campground, one heading a quarter mile to the Frenchman Campground, the other routed a half mile to Big Cove Campground.

RV sites, facilities: There are 35 sites for RVs up to 55 feet or tents. Picnic tables and fire grills are provided. Drinking water, vault toilets, and limited cell phone reception are available. A boat ramp, ATM, and RV dump station are nearby. Leashed pets are permitted.

Reservations, fees: Reserve at 877/444-6777 or online at www.reserveusa.com ($9 reservation fee). The fee is $14 per night. A senior discount is available. Open May through October.

Directions: From Reno, drive north on U.S. 395 to the junction with Highway 70. Turn west on Highway 70 and drive to Chilcoot and the junction with Frenchman Lake Road. Turn right on Frenchman Lake Road and drive nine miles to the lake and to a Y. At the Y, turn right and drive two miles to the campground on the left side of the road.

Contact: Plumas National Forest, Beckwourth Ranger District, 530/836-2575, fax 530/836-0493.

8 FRENCHMAN

Rating: 7

on Frenchman Lake in Plumas National Forest
See map pages 596–597

Frenchman Lake is set at 5,700 feet in elevation, on the edge of high desert to the east and forest to the west. This camp is on the southeast end of the lake, where there are three other campgrounds, including a group camp and a boat ramp. The lake provides good fishing for stocked rainbow trout. The best fishing is in the cove near the campgrounds and the two inlets, one along the west shore and one at the head of the lake. The proximity to Reno, only 35 miles away, keeps gambling in the back of the minds of many anglers. Because of water demands downstream, the lake often drops significantly by the end of summer. A trail from camp is routed a quarter mile to the Spring Creek Campground.

RV sites, facilities: There are 38 sites for RVs or

tents. Picnic tables and fire grills are provided. Drinking water, vault toilets, and limited cell phone reception are available. An RV dump station, ATM, and boat ramp are nearby. Leashed pets are permitted.

Reservations, fees: Reserve at 877/444-6777 or online at www.reserveusa.com ($9 reservation fee). The fee is $14 per night. A senior discount is available. Open May through October.

Directions: From Reno, drive north on U.S. 395 to the junction with Highway 70. Turn west on Highway 70 and drive to Chilcoot and the junction with Frenchman Lake Road. Turn right on Frenchman Lake Road and drive nine miles to the lake and to a Y. At the Y, turn right and drive 1.5 miles to the campground on the left side of the road.

Contact: Plumas National Forest, Beckwourth Ranger District, 530/836-2575, fax 530/836-0493.

9 CHILCOOT

Rating: 7

on Little Last Chance Creek in Plumas National Forest

See map pages 596–597

This small camp is set along Little Last Chance Creek at 5,400 feet in elevation, about three miles downstream from Frenchman Lake. The stream provides good trout fishing, but access can be difficult at some spots because of brush.

RV sites, facilities: There are 35 sites for RVs up to 45 feet or tents and five walk-in sites for tents. Two sites are wheelchair-accessible. Picnic tables and fire rings are provided. Drinking water and flush toilets are available. A boat ramp, grocery store, ATM, and RV dump station are nearby. Some facilities are wheelchair-accessible. Leashed pets are permitted.

Reservations, fees: Reserve at 877/444-6777 or online at www.reserveusa.com ($9 reservation fee). The fee is $14 per night. A senior discount is available. Open May through October.

Directions: From Reno, drive north on U.S. 395 to the junction with Highway 70. Turn west on Highway 70 and drive to Chilcoot and the junction with Frenchman Lake Road. Turn right on Frenchman Lake Road and drive six miles to the campground on the left side of the road.

Contact: Plumas National Forest, Beckwourth Ranger District, 530/836-2575, fax 530/836-0493.

10 SIERRA SPRINGS TRAILER RESORT

Rating: 5

near Blairsden

See map pages 596–597

This privately operated park is centrally located near fishing, golf, and hiking. A hiking trail is behind the resort. A railroad museum is nearby in Portola. Other possible side trips include the Feather River Park, four miles away in the town of Blairsden. The elevation is 5,000 feet. About half the sites are reserved by long-term tenants for the summer.

RV sites, facilities: There are 40 sites, including some drive-through and 30 with full hookups (20, 30 amps), for RVs up to 40 feet and four tent sites. Picnic tables and fire rings are provided at some sites. Drinking water, flush toilets, showers, an RV dump station, a coin-operated laundry, cable TV, modem access, a playground, limited cell phone reception, a picnic area, horseshoes, a recreation room, and a volleyball net are available. An ATM is within three miles. Leashed pets are permitted.

Reservations, fees: Reservations are accepted. The fee is $19.60–22 per night, plus $2.50 per person per night for more than two people. Open April through October.

Directions: From Truckee, drive northwest on Highway 89 about 50 miles to Blairsden and the junction with Highway 70. Turn right and drive 3.5 miles east to Sierra Springs Drive. Turn left on Sierra Springs Drive and drive a short distance to the resort entrance on the left at 70099 Sierra Springs Road.

Contact: Sierra Springs Trailer Resort, 530/836-2747, fax 530/836-2559, website: www.psln.com/sstr.

11 LITTLE BEAR RV PARK

Rating: 7

on the Feather River

See map pages 596–597

This is a privately operated RV park near the

CALIFORNIA

Feather River. Nearby destinations include Plumas-Eureka State Park and the Lakes Basin Recreation Area. The elevation is 4,300 feet. About half of the sites are taken by full-season rentals.

RV sites, facilities: There are 91 sites, including half taken by full-season rentals, 80 with full hookups for RVs up to 40 feet, and 10 sleeping cabins. Picnic tables and fire rings are provided. Drinking water, showers, flush toilets, a coin-operated laundry, a convenience store, and ice are available. An RV dump station, a clubhouse, Ping-Pong, shuffleboard, and horseshoes are also available. Leashed pets are permitted.

Reservations, fees: Reservations are recommended. The fee is $22–24 per night, plus $4–6 per person for more than two people and $1 per pet per night. Open mid-April to late October.

Directions: In Truckee, drive north on Highway 89 to Blairsden and the junction with Highway 70. Turn north (left) and drive one mile to Little Bear Road. Turn left on Little Bear Road and drive a short distance to the campground on the right.

Contact: Little Bear RV Park, tel./fax 530/836-2774.

12 PLUMAS-EUREKA STATE PARK

Rating: 9

near Graeagle
See map pages 596–597

Plumas-Eureka State Park, covering 5,500 acres, is a beautiful chunk of parkland, featuring great hiking, a pretty lake, and this well-maintained campground. For newcomers to the area, Jamison Camp at the southern end of the park makes for an excellent first stop. So does the nearby hike to Grass Lake, a first-class tromp that takes about two hours and features a streamside walk along Jamison Creek, with the chance to take a five-minute cutoff to see 40-foot Jamison Falls. A historic mine, park museum, blacksmith shop, stable, and stamp mill are also here, with campers provided free admission to the museum. Other must-see destinations in the park include Eureka Lake, and from there, the 1,100-foot climb to Eureka Peak (formerly known as Gold Mountain), 7,447 feet, for a dramatic view of all the famous peaks in this region. Camp elevation is 5,200 feet. Fishing opportunities feature Madora and Eureka Lakes and Jamison Creek, best in May and June. The visitors center was originally constructed as a bunkhouse for miners. More than $8 million of gold was mined here.

RV sites, facilities: There are 67 sites for RVs up to 30 feet, trailers, or tents and one group site for up to 50 people for tent campers only. Picnic tables, food lockers, and fire rings are provided. Drinking water, flush toilets, and showers are available. An RV dump station is nearby. A grocery store, coin-operated laundry, and propane are available within five miles. The group camp is wheelchair-accessible. Leashed pets are permitted.

Reservations, fees: Reservations are not accepted. The fee is $12 per night. Reservations are required for group site; the fee is $100 per night. A senior discount is available. Open mid-May to mid-October, weather permitting.

Directions: In Truckee, drive north on Highway 89 to Graeagle. Just after passing Graeagle (one mile from the junction of Highway 70) turn left on County Road A14/Graeagle-Johnsville Road and drive west for about five miles to the park entrance on the left.

Contact: Plumas-Eureka State Park, 530/836-2380, fax 530/836-0498.

13 MOVIN' WEST RV PARK

Rating: 5

in Graeagle
See map pages 596–597

This RV area set within a mobile home park has become very popular, and about half of the sites are rented for the full summer. A nine-hole golf course is across the road. The elevation is 4,300 feet.

RV sites, facilities: There are 51 sites, including some drive-through, with partial or full hookups (30 amps) for RVs, three tent sites, and two cabins. Picnic tables and fire rings are provided. Drinking water, flush toilets, showers, a pay phone, cable TV, modem access, limited cell phone reception, and a coin-operated laundry are available. A nine-hole golf course, ATM, swimming pond, horse stable, and mini-golf are nearby. Leashed pets are permitted.

Reservations, fees: Reservations are recommended. The fee is $19.73–23.39 per night, plus $3–5 per person for more than two people. Open May through October.

Directions: From Truckee, drive northwest on Highway 89 about 50 miles to Graeagle. Continue just past Graeagle to County Road A14 (Graegle-Johnson Road). Turn left and drive .25 mile northwest to the campground on the left.

Contact: Movin' West RV Park, 530/836-2614.

14 SALMON CREEK

Rating: 9

in Tahoe National Forest
See map pages 596–597

This campground is set at the confluence of Packer and Salmon Creeks, 5,800 feet in elevation, with easy access off the Gold Lakes Highway. It is near the Lakes Basin Recreation Area, with literally dozens of small lakes within five miles, plus great hiking, fishing, and low-speed boating.

RV sites, facilities: There are 31 sites for RVs up to 22 feet or tents. Picnic tables and fire grills are provided. Drinking water and vault toilets are available. Supplies and a coin-operated laundry are available in Sierra City. An ATM is within two miles. Leashed pets are permitted.

Reservations, fees: Reservations are not accepted. The fee is $16 per night. A senior discount is available. Open June through October.

Directions: From Truckee, turn north on Highway 89 and drive 20 miles to Sierraville and Highway 49. Turn left on Highway 49 and drive about 10 miles to the Bassetts Store and Gold Lake Road. Turn right on Gold Lake Road and drive two miles to the campground on the left side of the road.

Contact: Tahoe National Forest, North Yuba/Downieville Ranger District, 530/288-3231, fax 530/288-0727.

15 SARDINE LAKE

Rating: 8

in Tahoe National Forest
See map pages 596–597

Lower Sardine Lake is a jewel set below the Sier- ra Buttes, one of the prettiest settings in California. The campground is actually about a mile east of the lake. Nearby is the beautiful Sand Pond Interpretive Trail. A great hike is routed along the shore of Lower Sardine Lake to a hidden waterfall (in spring) that feeds the lake, and ambitious hikers can explore beyond and discover Upper Sardine Lake. Trout fishing is excellent in Lower Sardine Lake, with a primitive boat ramp available for small boats. The speed limit and small size of the lake keep boaters slow and quiet. A small marina and boat rentals are available.

RV sites, facilities: There are 27 sites for RVs up to 22 feet or tents. Picnic tables and fire grills are provided. Drinking water, vault toilets, and limited cell phone reception are available. An ATM is within three miles. Limited supplies are available at the Sardine Lake Lodge or in Bassetts. Some facilities are wheelchair-accessible. Leashed pets are permitted.

Reservations, fees: Reservations are not accepted. The fee is $16 per night. A senior discount is available. Open June through October.

Directions: From Truckee, drive north on Highway 89 for 20 miles to Sierraville. Turn left on Highway 49 and drive about 10 miles to the Bassetts Store. Turn right on Gold Lake Road and drive 1.5 miles to Packer Lake Road. Turn left, drive a short distance, then bear left at the fork (signed) and drive .5 mile to the campground on the left.

Contact: Tahoe National Forest, North Yuba/Downieville Ranger District, 530/288-3231, fax 530/288-0727.

16 CLIO'S RIVER'S EDGE RV PARK

Rating: 7

on the Feather River
See map pages 596–597

This is a giant RV park adjacent to a pretty and easily accessible stretch of the Feather River. There are many possible side-trip destinations, including Plumas-Eureka State Park, Lakes Basin Recreation Area, and several nearby golf courses. The elevation is about 4,500 feet.

RV sites, facilities: There are 220 sites, including some drive-through, with full hookups (20, 30, 50 amps) for RVs (no tents allowed). Picnic tables are provided. Drinking water, flush toilets, coin-operated showers, a coin-operated laundry, modem access, a clubhouse, and cable TV are available. A grocery store is within three miles. Some facilities are wheelchair-accessible. Leashed pets are permitted.

Reservations, fees: Reservations are accepted. The fee is $24 per night, plus $3–5 per person for more than two people and $1 for additional vehicles not towed. Weekly rates are available. Open mid-April through October.

Directions: From Truckee, drive north on Highway 89 toward Graeagle and Blairsden. Near Clio (4.5 miles south of Highway 70 at Blairsden), look for the campground entrance on the right.

Contact: Clio's River's Edge RV Park, 530/836-2375, fax 530/836-2378, website: www.riversedgerv park.net.

17 LOGANVILLE

Rating: 8

on the North Yuba River in Tahoe National Forest
See map pages 596–597

Nearby Sierra City is only two miles away, meaning you can make a quick getaway for a prepared meal or any food or drink you may need to add to your camp. Loganville is set on the North Yuba River, elevation 4,200 feet. It offers a good stretch of water in this region for trout fishing, with many pools set below miniature waterfalls.

RV sites, facilities: There are 19 sites for RVs up to 22 feet or tents. Picnic tables and fire grills are provided. Drinking water, vault toilets, and limited cell phone reception are available. Supplies and a coin-operated laundry are available in Sierra City. An ATM is within two miles. Leashed pets are permitted.

Reservations, fees: Reservations are not accepted. The fee is $16 per night. A senior discount is available. Open May through October.

Directions: From Auburn, take Highway 49 north to Nevada City and continue (the road jogs left, then narrows) to Downieville. Drive 12 miles east to the campground entrance on the right (two miles west of Sierra City).

Contact: Tahoe National Forest, North Yuba/Downieville Ranger District, 530/288-3231, fax 530/288-0727.

18 WILD PLUM

Rating: 8

on Haypress Creek in Tahoe National Forest
See map pages 596–597

This popular Forest Service campground is set on Haypress Creek at 4,400 feet. There are several hidden waterfalls in the area, which makes this a popular camp for the people who know of them. There's a scenic hike up the Haypress Trail, which goes past a waterfall to Haypress Valley. Two other nearby waterfalls are Loves Falls (on the North Yuba on Highway 49 two miles east of Sierra City) and Hackmans Falls (remote, set in a ravine one mile south of Sierra City; no road access).

RV sites, facilities: There are a total of 44 sites, 19 for RVs up to 22 feet and 25 for tents. Picnic tables and fire grills are provided. Drinking water, vault toilets, and limited cell phone reception are available. Supplies and a coin-operated laundry are available in Sierra City. Leashed pets are permitted.

Reservations, fees: Reservations are not accepted. The fee is $16 per night. A senior discount is available. Open May through October.

Directions: From Auburn, take Highway 49 north to Nevada City and continue (the road jogs left, then narrows) past Downieville to Sierra City at Wild Plum Road. Turn right on Wild Plum Road and drive two miles to the campground entrance road on the right.

Contact: Tahoe National Forest, North Yuba/Downieville Ranger District, 530/288-3231, fax 530/288-0727.

19 CHAPMAN CREEK

Rating: 8

on the North Yuba River in Tahoe National Forest
See map pages 596–597

This campground is set along Chapman Creek at 6,000 feet, just across the highway from where it enters the North Yuba River. A good side trip is to hike the Chapman Creek Trail, which leads out of camp to Beartrap Meadow or to Haskell Peak (8,107 feet).

RV sites, facilities: There are a total of 29 sites, 14 for RVs up to 22 feet and 15 for tents. Picnic tables and fire grills are provided. Drinking water and vault toilets are available. An ATM is within five miles. Supplies are available in Bassetts. Leashed pets are permitted.

Reservations, fees: Reservations are not accepted. The fee is $16 per night. A senior discount is available. Open June through October.

Directions: From Truckee, turn north on Highway 89 and drive 20 miles to Sierraville. At Sierraville, turn left on Highway 49, drive over Yuba Pass, and continue for four miles to the campground on the right.

Contact: Tahoe National Forest, North Yuba/ Downieville Ranger District, 530/288-3231, fax 530/288-0727.

20 YUBA PASS

Rating: 6

in Tahoe National Forest
See map pages 596–597

This camp is set right at Yuba Pass at an elevation of 6,700 feet. In the winter, the surrounding area is a Sno-Park, which gives it an unusual look in summer. Yuba Pass is a popular bird-watching area in the summer.

RV sites, facilities: There are 20 sites for RVs up to 22 feet or tents. Picnic tables and fire grills are provided. Drinking water and vault toilets are available. Supplies are available at Bassetts. Leashed pets are permitted.

Reservations, fees: Reserve at 877/444-6777 or online at www.reserveusa.com ($9 reservation fee). The fee is $16 per night. A senior discount is available. Open late June through October.

Directions: From Truckee, drive north on Highway 89 past Sattley to the junction with Highway 49. Turn west on Highway 49 and drive about six miles to the campground on the left side of the road.

Contact: Tahoe National Forest, Sierraville Ranger District, 530/994-3401, fax 530/994-3143.

21 UNION FLAT

Rating: 8

on the North Yuba River in Tahoe National Forest
See map pages 596–597

Of all the campgrounds on the North Yuba River along Highway 49, this one has the best swimming, if you can stand the cold. The camp has a nice swimming hole next to it. Recreational mining is also an attraction here. The elevation is 3,400 feet.

RV sites, facilities: There are 11 sites for RVs up to 35 feet or tents. Picnic tables and fire grills are provided. Drinking water, vault toilets, and limited cell phone reception are available. An ATM is within six miles. Supplies are available in Downieville. Some facilities are wheelchair-accessible. Leashed pets are permitted.

Reservations, fees: Reservations are not accepted. The fee is $16 per night. A senior discount is available. Open May through October.

Directions: From Auburn, take Highway 49 north to Nevada City and continue (the road jogs left, then narrows) to Downieville. Drive six miles east to the campground entrance on the right.

Contact: Tahoe National Forest, North Yuba/Downieville Ranger District, 530/288-3231, fax 530/288-0727.

22 COLD CREEK

Rating: 8

in Tahoe National Forest
See map pages 596–597

There are four small campgrounds along Highway 89 between Sierraville and Truckee, all within close range of side trips to Webber Lake, Independence Lake, and Campbell Hot Springs in Sierraville. Cold Creek is just downstream of the confluence of Cottonwood Creek and Cold Creek, at 5,800 feet in elevation.

RV sites, facilities: There are 10 sites for RVs up to 22 feet or tents. Picnic tables and fire grills are provided. Drinking water, vault toilets, limited cell phone reception, and firewood are available. Supplies are available in Sierra-

CALIFORNIA

ville. An ATM is within five miles. Leashed pets are permitted.

Reservations, fees: Reserve at 877/444-6777 or online at www.reserveusa.com ($9 reservation fee). The fee is $14 per night, plus $5 for an additional vehicle. Open May through October.

Directions: From Truckee, drive north on Highway 89 for about 20 miles to the campground on the left side of the road. If you reach Sierraville, you have gone five miles too far.

Contact: Tahoe National Forest, Sierraville Ranger District, 530/994-3401, fax 530/994-3143; California Land Management, 530/544-0426.

23 COTTONWOOD CREEK

Rating: 7

in Tahoe National Forest
See map pages 596–597

This camp sits beside Cottonwood Creek at 5,600 feet elevation. An interpretive trail starts at the camp and makes a short loop, and there are several nearby side-trip options, including trout fishing on the Little Truckee River to the nearby south, visiting the Sierra Valley Hot Springs out of Sierraville to the nearby north, or venturing into the surrounding Tahoe National Forest.

RV sites, facilities: There are 24 sites for RVs up to 22 feet or tents. Picnic tables and fire grills are provided. Drinking water, vault toilets, and limited cell phone reception are available. Supplies are available in Sierraville. An ATM is within six miles. Leashed pets are permitted.

Reservations, fees: Reserve at 877/444-6777 or online at www.reserveusa.com ($9 reservation fee). The fee is $14 per night. Open May through October, weather permitting.

Directions: From Truckee, drive north on Highway 89 for about 20 miles to the campground entrance road on the right (.5 mile past Cold Creek Camp). Turn right and drive .25 mile to the campground.

Contact: Tahoe National Forest, Sierraville Ranger District, 530/994-3401, fax 530/994-3143.

24 WOODCAMP

Rating: 7

at Jackson Meadow Reservoir in Tahoe National Forest
See map pages 596–597

Woodcamp and Pass Creek are the best camps for boaters at Jackson Meadow Reservoir because each is directly adjacent to a boat ramp. That is critical because fishing is far better by boat here than from shore, with a good mix of both rainbow and brown trout. The camp is set at 6,100 feet along the lake's southwest shore, in a pretty spot with a swimming beach and short interpretive hiking trail nearby. This is a beautiful lake in the Sierra Nevada, complete with pine forest and a classic granite backdrop.

RV sites, facilities: There are 10 sites for tents or RVs up to 22 feet and 10 sites for tents. Picnic tables and fire grills are provided. Drinking water and flush toilets are available. Supplies are available in Truckee or Sierraville. A boat ramp is adjacent to the camp. Leashed pets are permitted.

Reservations, fees: Reservations are accepted. The fee is $16 per night, plus $5 for each additional vehicle. A senior discount is available. Open June through October.

Directions: From Truckee, drive north on Highway 89 for 17.5 miles to Forest Road 7. Turn left on Forest Road 7 and drive 16 miles to Jackson Meadow Reservoir. At the lake, continue across the dam around the west shoreline and then turn left at the campground access road. The entrance is on the right just before the Woodcamp boat ramp.

Contact: Tahoe National Forest, Sierraville Ranger District, 530/994-3401, fax 530/994-3143.

25 FINDLEY

Rating: 7

at Jackson Meadow Reservoir in Tahoe National Forest
See map pages 596–597

Findley is near Woodcamp Creek, a quarter mile from where it pours into Jackson Meadow Reservoir. Though it is not a lakeside camp, it is quite pretty just the same, and within a half mile of

CALIFORNIA

the boat ramp near Woodcamp. It is set at 6,200 feet. This is one of several camps at the lake.

RV sites, facilities: There are 14 sites for RVs up to 22 feet or tents. Picnic tables and fire grills are provided. Drinking water and flush toilets are available. Supplies are available in Truckee or Sierraville. A boat ramp is nearby. Some facilities are wheelchair-accessible. Leashed pets are permitted.

Reservations, fees: Reserve at 877/444-6777 or online at www.reserveusa.com ($9 reservation fee). The fee is $16 per night. A senior discount is available. Open late June through October.

Directions: From Truckee, drive north on Highway 89 for 17.5 miles to Forest Road 7. Turn left on Forest Road 7 and drive 16 miles to Jackson Meadow Reservoir. Continue across the dam around the lake to the west side. Turn left at the campground access road and drive about .25 mile to the entrance on the left.

Contact: Tahoe National Forest, Sierraville Ranger District, 530/994-3401, fax 530/994-3143.

26 PASS CREEK

Rating: 7

at Jackson Meadow Reservoir in Tahoe National Forest

See map pages 596–597

This is the premium campground at Jackson Meadow Reservoir, a developed site with water, concrete boat ramp, swimming beach nearby at Aspen Creek Picnic Area, and access to the Pacific Crest Trail a half mile to the east (you'll pass it on the way in). This lake has the trademark look of the high Sierra, and the bonus here is that lake levels are often kept higher than at other reservoirs on the western slopes of the Sierra Nevada. Trout stocks are excellent, with 85,000 rainbow and brown trout planted each summer after ice-out. The elevation is 6,100 feet.

RV sites, facilities: There are 15 sites for RVs up to 22 feet and 15 sites for tents. Picnic tables and fire grills are provided. Drinking water, flush toilets, and an RV dump station are available. A boat ramp is available. Supplies are available in Truckee or Sierraville. Leashed pets are permitted.

Reservations, fees: Reserve at 877/444-6777 or online at www.reserveusa.com ($9 reservation

fee). The fee is $10 per night, plus $5 for an additional vehicle. A senior discount is available. Open year-round, with full services June through October.

Directions: From Truckee, drive north on Highway 89 for 17.5 miles to Forest Road 7. Turn left on Forest Road 7 and drive 16 miles to Jackson Meadow Reservoir; the campground is on the left at the north end of the lake.

Contact: Tahoe National Forest, Sierraville Ranger District, 530/994-3401, fax 530/994-3143.

27 EAST MEADOW

Rating: 7

at Jackson Meadow Reservoir in Tahoe National Forest

See map pages 596–597

This camp is in a beautiful setting on the east side of Jackson Meadow Reservoir, on the edge of a sheltered cove. The Pacific Crest Trail passes right by camp, providing access for a day trip, though no stellar destinations are on this stretch of the PCT. The nearest boat ramp is at Pass Creek, two miles away. The elevation is 6,100 feet.

RV sites, facilities: There are 26 sites for RVs or tents and 20 tent sites. (Some sites can accommodate RVs 40 feet in length, most can accommodate 22 feet.) Picnic tables and fire grills are provided. Drinking water and flush toilets are available. An RV dump station and boat ramp are available at Pass Creek. Supplies are available in Truckee or Sierraville. Some facilities are wheelchair-accessible. Leashed pets are permitted.

Reservations, fees: Reserve at 877/444-6777 or online at www.reserveusa.com ($9 reservation fee). The fee is $16 per night, plus $5 for an additional vehicle. A senior discount is available. Open June through October.

Directions: From Truckee, drive north on Highway 89 for 17.5 miles to Forest Road 7. Turn left on Forest Road 7 and drive 15 miles to the campground entrance road on the left (if you reach Pass Creek, you have gone too far). Turn left and drive a mile to the campground on the right.

Contact: Tahoe National Forest, Sierraville Ranger District, 530/994-3401, fax 530/994-3143.

CALIFORNIA

28 UPPER LITTLE TRUCKEE

Rating: 7

on the Little Truckee River in Tahoe National Forest
See map pages 596–597

This camp is set along the Little Truckee River at 6,100 feet. The Little Truckee is a pretty trout stream, with easy access not only from this campground, but also from another three miles northward along Highway 89, then from another seven miles to the west along Forest Road 7, the route to Webber Lake. It is only about a 10-minute drive from this camp to reach Stampede Lake to the east.

RV sites, facilities: There are 26 sites for RVs up to 22 feet or tents. Picnic tables and fire grills are provided. Drinking water and vault toilets are available. Supplies are available in Sierraville. Leashed pets are permitted.

Reservations, fees: Reserve at 877/444-6777 or online at www.reserveusa.com ($9 reservation fee). The fee is $14 per night, plus $5 for an additional vehicle. A senior discount is available. Open year-round, with full services from May through October.

Directions: From Truckee, drive north on Highway 89 for about 11 miles to the campground on the left, a short distance beyond Lower Little Truckee Camp.

Contact: Tahoe National Forest, Sierraville Ranger District, 530/994-3401, fax 530/994-3143; High Sierra Campground Management, 530/544-0426.

29 LOWER LITTLE TRUCKEE

Rating: 7

on the Little Truckee River in Tahoe National Forest
See map pages 596–597

This pretty camp is set along Highway 89 and the Little Truckee River at 6,000 feet. (For more information, see the prior listing for Upper Little Truckee.)

RV sites, facilities: There are 15 sites for RVs up to 22 feet or tents. Picnic tables and fire grills are provided. Drinking water and vault toilets

are available. Supplies are available in Sierraville. Leashed pets are permitted.

Reservations, fees: Reserve at 877/444-6777 or online at www.reserveusa.com ($9 reservation fee). The fee is $14 per night, plus $5 for an additional vehicle. A senior discount is available. Open May through October.

Directions: From Truckee, drive north on Highway 89 for about 12 miles to the campground on the left. If you reach Upper Little Truckee Camp, you have gone .5 mile too far.

Contact: Tahoe National Forest, Sierraville Ranger District, 530/994-3401, fax 530/994-3143; High Sierra Campground Management, 530/544-0426.

30 LAKESIDE

Rating: 7

on Prosser Creek Reservoir in Tahoe National Forest
See map pages 596–597

This primitive camp is in a deep cove in the northwestern end of Prosser Creek Reservoir, near the lake's headwaters. It is a gorgeous lake, set at 5,741 feet, and a 10 mph speed limit keeps the fast boats out. The adjacent shore is decent for hand-launched, car-top boats, providing the lake level is up, and a concrete boat ramp is a mile down the road. Lots of trout are stocked here every year, including 100,000 rainbow trout fingerlings added in an experiment by the Department of Fish and Game to see how fast they will grow. The trout fishing is often quite good after the ice breaks up in late spring; the lake is also popular with ice fishermen in the winter. Sound perfect? Unfortunately for many, the Prosser ORV Park is nearby and can be noisy.

RV sites, facilities: There are 30 sites for RVs up to 33 feet or tents and one group site. Drinking water, vault toilets, and firewood are available. A boat ramp is nearby. Leashed pets are permitted.

Reservations, fees: Reservations are not accepted. The fee is $12 per night, plus $5 for each additional vehicle. A senior discount is available. Open June through October.

Directions: From Truckee, drive north on Highway 89 for three miles to the campground entrance road on the right. Turn right and drive less than a mile to the campground.

Contact: Tahoe National Forest, Truckee Ranger District, 530/587-3558, fax 530/587-6914; California Land Management, 530/544-0426.

31 LOGGER

Rating: 7

at Stampede Lake in Tahoe National Forest
See map pages 596–597

Stampede Lake is a huge lake by Sierra standards, covering 3,400 acres, the largest lake in the region after Lake Tahoe. It is set at 6,000 feet, surrounded by Sierra granite mountains and pines, and is big, and on days when the wind is down, quite beautiful. The campground is also huge, set along the lake's southern shore, a few minutes' drive from the Captain Roberts Boat Ramp. This camp is ideal for campers, boaters, and anglers. The lake is becoming one of the top fishing lakes in California for kokanee salmon (which can be caught only by trolling), and it also has some large Mackinaw trout and a sprinkling of planter-sized rainbow trout. One problem at Stampede is receding water levels from midsummer through fall, a real pain, which puts the campsites some distance from the lake. Even when the lake is full, there are only a few "lakeside" campsites. However, the boat ramp has been extended to assist boaters during drawdowns.

RV sites, facilities: There are 252 sites for RVs up to 32 feet or tents. Picnic tables and fire rings are provided. Drinking water, vault toilets, firewood, and an RV dump station are available. A concrete boat ramp is one mile from camp. A small convenience store and ATM are within seven miles. Some facilities are wheelchair-accessible. Leashed pets are permitted.

Reservations, fees: Reserve at 877/444-6777 or online at www.reserveusa.com ($9 reservation fee). The fee is $15 per night, plus $5 for an additional vehicle. A senior discount is available. Open May through October.

Directions: From Truckee, drive east on I-80 for seven miles to the Boca-Hirschdale/County Road 270 exit. Take that exit and drive north on County Road 270 for about seven miles (past Boca Reservoir) to the junction with County Road

S261 on the left. Turn left and drive 1.5 miles to the campground on the right.

Contact: Tahoe National Forest, Truckee Ranger District, 530/587-3558, fax 530/587-6914; High Sierra Campground Management, 530/544-0426.

32 BOCA REST CAMPGROUND

Rating: 7

on Boca Reservoir in Tahoe National Forest
See map pages 596–597

The Boca Dam faces I-80, so the lake is out of sight of the zillions of highway travelers who would otherwise certainly stop here. Those who do stop find that the lake is very pretty, set at 5,600 feet in elevation and covering 1,000 acres with deep, blue water. This camp is on the lake's northeastern shore, not far from the inlet to the Little Truckee River. The boat ramp is some distance away.

RV sites, facilities: There are 25 sites for RVs up to 22 feet or tents. Picnic tables and fire grills are provided. Drinking water, vault toilets, and firewood are available. A hand-launch boat ramp is also available. A concrete boat ramp is three miles away on the southwest shore of Boca Reservoir. A convenience store is four miles away. An ATM is within 10 miles. Leashed pets are permitted.

Reservations, fees: Reservations are not accepted. The fee is $12 per night, plus $5 for an additional vehicle. A senior discount is available. Open May through October.

Directions: From Truckee, travel east on I-80 for seven miles to the Boca-Hirschdale exit. Take that exit and drive north on County Road 270 for about 2.5 miles to the campground on the right side of the road.

Contact: Tahoe National Forest, Truckee Ranger District, 530/587-3558, fax 530/587-6914; California Land Management, 530/544-0426.

33 BOCA

Rating: 7

on Boca Reservoir in Tahoe National Forest
See map pages 596–597

Boca Reservoir is known as a "big fish factory,"

with some huge but rare brown trout and rainbow trout sprinkled among a growing fishery for kokanee salmon. The lake is set at 5,700 feet amid a few sparse pines. Although the surrounding landscape is not in the drop-dead beautiful class, the lake can still seem a Sierra gem on a windless dawn, out on a boat. It is within a few miles of I-80. The camp is the best choice for anglers/boaters, with a launch ramp just down from the campground.

RV sites, facilities: There are 22 sites for RVs up to 16 feet or tents. Picnic tables and fire grills are provided. Vault toilets are available. No drinking water is available. A concrete boat ramp is north of the campground on Boca Reservoir. Truckee is the nearest place for telephones and supplies. Leashed pets are permitted.

Reservations, fees: Reservations are not accepted. The fee is $12 per night, plus $5 for an additional vehicle. A senior discount is available. Open May through October.

Directions: From Truckee, drive east on I-80 for seven miles to the Boca-Hirschdale exit. Take that exit and drive north for a short distance to County Road 73. Turn left and continue for one mile to the campground on the right side of the road.

Contact: Tahoe National Forest, Truckee Ranger District, 530/587-3558, fax 530/587-6914; California Land Management, 530/544-0426.

34 LAKE SPAULDING

Rating: 8

near Emigrant Gap
See map pages 596–597
Lake Spaulding is set at 5,000 feet in the Sierra Nevada, complete with huge boulders and a sprinkling of conifers. Its clear, pure, very cold water has startling effects on swimmers. The lake is extremely pretty, with the Sierra granite backdrop looking as if it has been cut, chiseled, and smoothed. Just one problem. There's no lake view from the campground. In fact, the lake is about a half mile from the campground. The drive here is nearly a straight shot up I-80, the boat ramp is fine for small aluminum boats, and if there is any problem here, it is that there will be plenty of company at the campground. Fish-

ing for kokanee salmon and rainbow trout is often good, as well as fishing for trout at the nearby South Fork Yuba River. There are many other lakes set in the mountain country to the immediate north that can make for excellent side trips, including Bowman, Weaver, and Faucherie Lakes.

RV sites, facilities: There are 25 sites for RVs up to 20 feet or tents. Picnic tables and fire grills are provided. Drinking water, vault toilets, and five day-use picnic sites are available. A boat ramp is nearby. Supplies are available in Nevada City. Leashed pets are permitted.

Reservations, fees: Reservations are not accepted. The fee is $13 per night, plus $3 per night per additional vehicle, $7 per night per extra RV, and $1 per pet per night. Open mid-May through September, weather permitting.

Directions: From Sacramento, drive east on I-80 past Emigrant Gap to Highway 20. Drive west on Highway 20 for 2.3 miles to Lake Spaulding Road. Turn right on Lake Spaulding Road and drive .5 mile to the campground.

Contact: PG&E Land Projects, 916/386-5164; Big Bend Visitor's Center, 530/426-3609, fax 530/426-1744.

35 LODGEPOLE

Rating: 8

on Lake Valley Reservoir in Tahoe National Forest
See map pages 596–597
Lake Valley Reservoir is set at 5,786 feet and covers 300 acres. It is gorgeous when full, its shoreline sprinkled with conifers and boulders. The lake provides decent results for anglers, who have the best luck while trolling. A speed limit prohibits water-skiing and personal watercraft, and that keeps the place quiet and peaceful. The camp is about a quarter mile from the lake's southwest shore and two miles from the boat ramp on the north shore. A trailhead from camp leads south up Monumental Ridge and to Monumental Creek (three miles one-way) on the northwestern flank of Quartz Mountain (6,931 feet).

RV sites, facilities: There are 35 sites for tents or RVs up to 20 feet long. Picnic tables and fire grills are provided. Drinking water and vault toilets are available. A boat ramp is available nearby.

CALIFORNIA

Supplies can be obtained off I-80. Leashed pets are permitted.

Reservations, fees: Reservations are not accepted. The fee is $15 per night, $3 per night per additional vehicle, $7 per night per extra RV, $1 per pet per night. Open late May through September, weather permitting.

Directions: From I-80, take the Yuba Gap exit and drive south for .4 mile to Lake Valley Road. Turn right on Lake Valley Road and drive for 1.2 miles until the road forks. Bear right and continue for 1.5 miles to the campground entrance road to the right on another fork.

Contact: PG&E Land Projects, 916/386-5164, fax 916/386-5164, website: www.pge.com/recreation.

36 INDIAN SPRINGS

Rating: 7

near the Yuba River in Tahoe National Forest
See map pages 596–597

The camp is easy to reach from I-80 yet is in a beautiful setting at 5,600 feet along the South Fork Yuba River. This is a gorgeous stream, running deep blue-green and pure through a granite setting, complete with giant boulders and beautiful pools. Trout fishing is fair. There is a small beach nearby where you can go swimming, though the water is cold. There are also several lakes in the vicinity.

RV sites, facilities: There are 35 sites for RVs up to 25 feet or tents. Picnic tables and fire grills are provided. Drinking water and vault toilets are available. A grocery store, ATM, and propane are available nearby. Leashed pets are permitted.

Reservations, fees: Reservations are not accepted. The fee is $14 per night, plus $6 for each additional vehicle. A senior discount is available. Open June through October.

Directions: From Sacramento, drive east on I-80 to Yuba Gap and continue for about three miles to the Eagle Lakes exit. Head north on Eagle Lakes Road for a mile to the campground on the left side of the road.

Contact: Tahoe National Forest, Nevada City Ranger District, 530/265-4531, fax 530/478-6109; Sierra Recreation Managers, 209/295-4512; Big Bend Visitor's Center, 530/426-3609, fax 530/426-1744.

37 HAMPSHIRE ROCKS

Rating: 8

on the Yuba River in Tahoe National Forest
See map pages 596–597

This camp sits along the South Fork of the Yuba River at 5,900 feet in elevation, with easy access off I-80 and a nearby Forest Service visitor information center. Fishing for trout is fair. There are some swimming holes, but the water is often very cold. Nearby lakes that can provide side trips include Sterling and Fordyce Lakes (drive-to) to the north, and the Loch Leven Lakes (hike-to) to the south.

RV sites, facilities: There are 31 sites for RVs up to 22 feet or tents. Picnic tables and fire grills are provided. Drinking water and vault toilets are available. A grocery store, restaurant, and propane are available nearby. Leashed pets are permitted.

Reservations, fees: Reserve at 877/444-6777 or online at www.reserveusa.com ($9 reservation fee). The fee is $14 per night, plus $6 per night for each additional vehicle. A senior discount is available. Open June through October.

Directions: From Sacramento, drive east on I-80 to Cisco Grove and continue for a mile to the Big Bend exit. Take that exit (remaining just south of the highway), then turn left on the frontage road and drive east for 1.5 miles to the campground.

Contact: Tahoe National Forest, Nevada City Ranger District, 530/265-4531, fax 530/478-6109; Big Bend Visitor's Center, 530/426-3609, fax 530/426-1744.

38 DONNER MEMORIAL STATE PARK

Rating: 9

on Donner Lake
See map pages 596–597

The remarkable beauty of Donner Lake often evokes a deep, heartfelt response. Nearly everybody has looked down and seen it, passing by from nearby I-80. The lake is big, three miles long and three-quarters of a mile wide, gemlike blue, and set near the Sierra crest at 5,900 feet. The area is well developed, with a number of cab-

CALIFORNIA

ins and access roads, and this state park is the feature destination. Along the southeastern end of the lake, it is extremely pretty, but the campsites are set in forest, not along the lake. Fishing is good here (typically only in the early morning), trolling for kokanee salmon or rainbow trout, with big Mackinaw and brown trout providing wild cards. The park features more than three miles of frontage of Donner Creek and Donner Lake, with 2.5 miles of hiking trails. The lake is open to power- and sailboats, but there is no boat launch at the park; a public ramp is available at the northwest corner of the lake. In the summer a wind often comes up in the early afternoon. In the winter a good cross-country ski trail is available. Campers get free admission to Emigrant Trail Museum.

RV sites, facilities: There are 147 sites for RVs up to 28 feet, trailers up to 24 feet, or tents, and two hike-in/bike-in sites. Picnic tables and fire grills are provided. Drinking water and vault toilets are available. Supplies are available about one mile away in Truckee. Some facilities are wheelchair-accessible. Leashed pets are permitted.

Reservations, fees: Reserve at 800/444-PARK (800/444-7275) or online at www.reserveamerica.com ($7.50 reservation fee). The fees are $12 per night and $1 per person for hike-in or bike-in sites. A senior discount is available. Open mid-May to mid-October, weather permitting.

Directions: From Auburn, drive east on I-80 just past Donner Lake to the Donner State Park exit. Take that exit and turn south (right) on Donner Pass Road and drive .5 mile to the park entrance on the left at the southeast end of the lake.

Contact: Donner Memorial State Park, 530/582-7892 or 530/582-7894, fax 530/550-2347. For boat-launching info, call 530/582-7720.

39 GRANITE FLAT

Rating: 6

on the Truckee River in Tahoe National Forest
See map pages 596–597

This camp is set along the Truckee River at 5,920 feet, in an area known for a ton of traffic on adjacent Highway 89, as well as decent trout fishing and, in the spring and early summer, rafting. It is about a 15-minute drive to Squaw Valley or Lake Tahoe. A bike route is also available along the Truckee River out of Tahoe City.

RV sites, facilities: There are 68 sites for RVs up to 30 feet or tents and seven walk-in tent sites. Picnic tables and fire grills are provided. Drinking water, vault toilets, firewood, and limited cell phone reception are available. An ATM is within two miles. Some facilities are wheelchair-accessible. Leashed pets are permitted.

Reservations, fees: Reserve at 877/444-6777 or online at www.reserveusa.com ($9 reservation fee). The fee is $14 per night, plus $5 for an additional vehicle. A senior discount is available. Open May through October.

Directions: From Truckee, drive south on Highway 89 for 1.5 miles to the campground entrance on the right.

Contact: Tahoe National Forest, Truckee Ranger District, 530/587-3558, fax 530/587-6914; California Land Management, 530/544-0426.

40 COACHLAND RV PARK

Rating: 6

in Truckee
See map pages 596–597

Truckee is the gateway to recreation at North Tahoe. Within minutes are Donner Lake, Prosser Creek Reservoir, Boca Reservoir, Stampede Lake, and the Truckee River. Squaw Valley is a short distance to the south off Highway 89, and Northstar is just off Highway 267. The park is set in a wooded area near the junction of I-80 and Highway 89, providing easy access. The downtown Truckee area (with restaurants) is a half mile away. This is one of the only parks in the area that is open year-round. The elevation is 6,000 feet. One problem: Only 25 of the 131 sites are available for overnighters, with the rest taken by long-term rentals.

RV sites, facilities: There are 131 sites with full hookups (30, 50 amps), including many drive-through, with 25 of the sites available for overnighters, for RVs up to 40 feet or trailers. Picnic tables, restrooms, showers, a coin-operated laundry, cable TV, modem access, cell phone reception, and propane are available. An ATM is within one mile. Some facilities are wheelchair-accessible. Leashed pets are permitted.

Reservations, fees: Reservations are recommended. The fee is $32 per night, plus $1 per night for each additional vehicle. Monthly rates are available. Major credit cards are accepted. Open year-round.

Directions: From Truckee, drive north on Highway 89 for a short distance to the park at 10500 Hwy. 89 on the left side of the road.

Contact: Coachland RV Park, 530/587-3071, fax 530/587-6976, website: www.coachlandrvpark.com.

41 MARTIS CREEK LAKE

Rating: 7

near Truckee
See map pages 596–597

If only this lake weren't so often windy in the afternoon, it would be heaven to fly fishers in float tubes, casting out with sinking lines and leech patterns, using a strip retrieve. To some it's heaven anyway, with Lahontan cutthroat trout growing to 25 inches here. This is a special catch-and-release fishery where anglers are permitted to use only artificial lures with single, barbless hooks. The setting is somewhat sparse and open—a small lake on the eastern edge of the Martis Valley. No motors are permitted at the lake, making it ideal (when the wind is down) for float tubes or prams. The lake level can fluctuate daily, which, along with the wind, can be frustrating for those who show up expecting automatic perfection; that just isn't the way it is out there. At times, the lake level can even be very low. The elevation is 5,800 feet.

RV sites, facilities: There are 25 sites, including some drive-through, for RVs or tents. Picnic tables and fire grills are provided. Drinking water, vault toilets, tent pads, limited cell phone reception, and a pay phone are available. An ATM is within five miles. Supplies are available six minutes away in Truckee. Some facilities are wheelchair-accessible. Leashed pets are permitted.

Reservations, fees: No reservations are accepted except for the wheelchair-accessible sites. The fee is $10 per night. Open May through mid-November, weather permitting.

Directions: From Truckee, drive south on Highway 267 for about three miles (past the airport) to the entrance road to the lake on the left. Turn

left and drive another 2.5 miles to the campground at the end of the road.

Contact: U.S. Army Corps of Engineers, Sacramento District, 530/639-2342, fax 530/639-2175.

42 SILVER CREEK

Rating: 8

on the Truckee River in Tahoe National Forest
See map pages 596–597

This pretty campground is set near where Silver Creek enters the Truckee River. The trout fishing is often good in this area. This is one of three campgrounds along Highway 89 and the Truckee River, between Truckee and Tahoe City. The elevation is 6,068 feet. Those who camped here in the past may remember the trailhead at this camp; that trail is closed, the trailhead shut down.

RV sites, facilities: There are 21 sites for RVs up to 30 feet or tents and seven walk-in sites. Picnic tables and fire grills are provided. Drinking water, vault toilets, limited cell phone reception, and firewood are available. An ATM is within six miles. Supplies are available in Truckee and Tahoe City. Leashed pets are permitted.

Reservations, fees: Reserve at 877/444-6777 or online at www.reserveusa.com ($9 reservation fee). The fee is $12 per night, plus $5 for an additional vehicle. Open June through September.

Directions: From Truckee, drive south on Highway 89 for six miles to the campground entrance on the river side of the highway.

Contact: Tahoe National Forest, Truckee Ranger District, 530/587-3558, fax 530/587-6914; California Land Management, 530/544-0426.

43 GOOSE MEADOWS

Rating: 6

on the Truckee River in Tahoe National Forest
See map pages 596–597

There are three campgrounds set along the Truckee River off Highway 89 between Truckee and Tahoe City. Goose Meadows provides good fishing access with decent prospects, despite the high number of vehicles roaring past on the adjacent highway. This stretch of river is also popular for rafting. The elevation is 6,068 feet.

RV sites, facilities: There are 25 sites for RVs up to 30 feet or tents. Picnic tables and fire grills are provided. Drinking water, vault toilets, limited cell phone reception, and firewood are available. An ATM is within four miles. Supplies are available in Truckee and Tahoe City. Leashed pets are permitted.

Reservations, fees: Reserve at 877/444-6777 or online at www.reserveusa.com ($9 reservation fee). The fee is $12 per night, plus $5 for an additional vehicle. A senior discount is available. Open May through October, weather permitting.

Directions: From Truckee, drive south on Highway 89 for four miles to the campground entrance on the left (river) side of the highway.

Contact: Tahoe National Forest, Truckee Ranger District, 530/587-3558, fax 530/587-6914; California Land Management, 530/544-0426.

44 TAHOE STATE RECREATION AREA

Rating: 9

on Lake Tahoe
See map pages 596–597

This is a popular summer-only campground at the north shore of Lake Tahoe. The Tahoe State Recreation Area covers a large area just west of Highway 28 near Tahoe City. There are opportunities for hiking and horseback riding nearby (though not right at the park). It is also near shopping, restaurants, and, unfortunately, traffic jams in Tahoe City. A boat ramp is two miles to the northwest at nearby Lake Forest, and bike rentals are available in Tahoe City for rides along Highway 89 near the shore of the lake. For a more secluded site nearby at Tahoe, get reservations instead for Sugar Pine Point State Park, 11 miles south on Highway 89 (see listing in this chapter).

RV sites, facilities: There are 38 sites for RVs up to 24 feet or tents. Picnic tables, food lockers, barbecues, and fire pits are provided. Drinking water, vault toilets, and coin-operated showers are available. Firewood, other supplies, and a coin-operated laundry are within walking distance. Leashed pets are permitted.

Reservations, fees: Reserve at 800/444-PARK (800/444-7275) or online at www.reserveamerica.com ($7.50 reservation fee). The fee is $12 per

night. A senior discount is available. Open May through October, weather permitting.

Directions: From Truckee, drive south on Highway 89 through Tahoe City. Turn north on Highway 28 and drive .9 mile to the campground entrance on the right side of the road.

Contact: Tahoe State Recreation Area, 530/583-3074 or 530/525-7232.

45 LAKE FOREST CAMPGROUND

Rating: 8

on Lake Tahoe
See map pages 596–597

The north shore of Lake Tahoe provides beautiful lookouts and excellent boating access. The latter is a highlight of this camp, with a boat ramp nearby. From here it is a short cruise to Dollar Point and around the corner north to Carnelian Bay, one of the better stretches of water for trout fishing. The elevation is 6,200 feet.

RV sites, facilities: There are 15 sites for RVs up to 20 feet or tents. Picnic tables and fire grills are provided. Drinking water, vault toilets, and limited cell phone reception are available. An ATM is within one mile. A grocery store, a coin-operated laundry, and propane are available within four miles. Some facilities are wheelchair-accessible. Leashed pets are permitted.

Reservations, fees: Reservations are not accepted. The fee is $15 per night. There is a 10-day camping limit. Open May through October, weather permitting.

Directions: From Truckee, drive south on Highway 89 through Tahoe City to Highway 28. Bear north on Highway 28 and drive four miles to the campground entrance road (Lake Forest Road) on the right.

Contact: Tahoe City Public Utility District, Parks and Recreation, 530/583-3796, ext. 7, fax 530/583-8452, website: www.tahoecity.pud.com.

46 SANDY BEACH CAMPGROUND

Rating: 8

on Lake Tahoe
See map pages 596–597

Sandy Beach Campground is set at 6,200 feet

CALIFORNIA

near the northwest shore of Lake Tahoe. A nearby boat ramp provides access to one of the better fishing areas of the lake for Mackinaw trout. A public beach is across the road. But the water in Tahoe is always cold, and though a lot of people will get suntans on beaches next to the lake, swimmers need to be members of the Polar Bear Club. A short drive to the east will take you past the town of Kings Beach and into Nevada, where there are some small casinos near the shore of Crystal Bay.

RV sites, facilities: There are 44 sites, including some drive-through and some rented for the full summer, with partial or full hookups for RVs up to 40 feet or tents. Picnic tables and fire rings are provided. Drinking water, showers, flush toilets, and a coin-operated laundry are available. A free public boat ramp is a half a block away. A grocery store and propane are available nearby. Leashed pets are permitted.

Reservations, fees: Reservations are recommended. The fee is $20–25 per night for up to six people with two vehicles. There is a two-dog limit. For weeklong stays, the seventh night is free. Major credit cards are accepted. Open May through October.

Directions: From Truckee, drive south on Highway 267 to Highway 28. Turn right and drive one mile to the park on the right side of the road (entrance well signed).

Contact: Sandy Beach Campground, 530/546-7682.

47 FRENCH MEADOWS

Rating: 7

on French Meadows Reservoir in Tahoe National Forest

See map pages 596–597

The nearby boat launch makes this the choice for boating campers. The camp is on French Meadows Reservoir at 5,300 feet. It is on the lake's southern shore, with the boat ramp about a mile to the south (you'll see the entrance road on the way in). This is a big lake set in remote Tahoe National Forest in the North Fork American River Canyon with good trout fishing. The lake level often drops in late summer, and then a lot of stumps and boulders start poking through

the lake surface. This creates navigational hazards for boaters, but it also makes it easier for the anglers to know where to find the fish. If the fish don't bite here, boaters should make the nearby side trip to pretty Hell Hole Reservoir to the south.

RV sites, facilities: There are 75 sites for RVs up to 35 feet or tents. Picnic tables and fire grills are provided. Drinking water and flush toilets are available. A concrete boat ramp is nearby. Supplies are available in Foresthill. Some facilities are wheelchair-accessible. Leashed pets are permitted.

Reservations, fees: Reserve at 877/444-6777 or online at www.reserveusa.com ($9 reservation fee). The fee is $12 per night. A senior discount is available. Open June through October.

Directions: From Sacramento, drive east on I-80 to the north end of Auburn and the Foresthill Road exit. Take that exit and drive east to Foresthill and Mosquito Ridge Road (Forest Road 96). Turn right (east) and drive 40 miles (curvy) to Anderson Dam and to a junction. Turn left (still Mosquito Ridge Road) and then continue along the southern shoreline of French Meadows Reservoir for four miles to the campground.

Contact: Tahoe National Forest, Foresthill Ranger District, 530/367-2224, fax 530/367-2992; American Land & Leisure, 800/342-2267.

48 LEWIS

Rating: 7

on French Meadows Reservoir in Tahoe National Forest

See map pages 596–597

This camp is not right at lakeside but is just across the road from French Meadows Reservoir. It is still quite pretty, set along a feeder creek near the lake's northwest shore. A boat ramp is available only a half mile to the south, and the adjacent McGuire Picnic Area has a trailhead that is routed along the lake's northern shoreline. This lake is big (2,000 acres) and pretty, created by a dam on the Middle Fork American River, with good fishing for rainbow trout.

RV sites, facilities: There are 40 sites for RVs up to 35 feet or tents. Picnic tables and fire grills are provided. Drinking water and flush toilets are available. A concrete boat ramp is nearby. Supplies are available in Foresthill. Leashed pets are permitted.

Reservations, fees: Reservations are not accepted. The fee is $12 per night. A senior discount is available. Open May through October.

Directions: From Sacramento, drive east on I-80 to the north end of Auburn and the Foresthill Road exit. Take that exit and drive east to Foresthill and Mosquito Ridge Road (Forest Road 96). Turn right (east) and drive 40 miles (curvy) to Anderson Dam and to a junction. Turn left (still Mosquito Ridge Road) and then continue along the southern shoreline of French Meadows Reservoir for five miles to a fork at the head of the lake. Bear left at the fork and drive .5 mile to the camp on the right side of the road.

Contact: Tahoe National Forest, Foresthill Ranger District, 530/367-2224, fax 530/367-2992.

49 BIG MEADOWS

Rating: 7

near Hell Hole Reservoir in Eldorado National Forest

See map pages 596–597

This camp sits on a meadow near the ridge above Hell Hole Reservoir (which is about two miles away). (For more information, see the following listing for Hell Hole.)

RV sites, facilities: There are 54 sites for RVs or tents, including some sites for RVs up to 60 feet. Picnic tables and fire grills are provided. Drinking water and flush and vault toilets are available. One wheelchair-accessible campsite and toilet are available. Leashed pets are permitted.

Reservations, fees: Reservations are not accepted. The fee is $8 per night. A senior discount is available. Open May through October.

Directions: From Sacramento, drive east on I-80 to the north end of Auburn. Take the Elm Avenue exit and turn left at the first stoplight onto Elm Avenue. Drive .1 mile, turn left on High Street, and continue through the signal where High Street merges with Highway 49. Travel on Highway 49 for about 3.5 miles, turn right over the bridge, and drive about 2.5 miles into the town of Cool. Turn left on Georgetown Road/Highway 193 and drive about 14 miles into Georgetown. At the four-way stop, turn left on Main Street (which

becomes Wentworth Springs/Forest Road 1) and drive about 25 miles. Turn left on Forest Road 2 and drive 21 miles to the campground on the left.

Contact: Eldorado National Forest, Georgetown Ranger District, 530/333-4312, fax 530/333-5522; Eldorado Information Center, 530/644-6048, fax 530/295-5624.

50 HELL HOLE

Rating: 8

near Hell Hole Reservoir in Eldorado National Forest

See map pages 596–597

Hell Hole is a mountain temple with sapphire blue water. For the most part, there is limited bank access because of its granite-sculpted shore, and that's why there are no lakeside campsites. This is the closest drive-to camp at Hell Hole Reservoir, about a mile away with a boat launch nearby. Be sure to bring a boat and then enjoy the scenery while you troll for kokanee salmon, brown trout, Mackinaw trout, and a sprinkling of rainbow trout. This is a unique fishery compared to the put-and-take rainbow trout at so many other lakes. The lake elevation is 4,700 feet; the camp elevation is 5,200 feet.

RV sites, facilities: There are 10 sites for RVs or tents. Picnic tables and fire grills are provided. Drinking water and vault toilets are available. Supplies can be obtained in Georgetown. A boat launch is nearby at the reservoir. Leashed pets are permitted.

Reservations, fees: Reservations are not accepted. The fee is $8 per night in the summer season. A senior discount is available. Open May through mid-November, weather permitting.

Directions: From Sacramento, drive east on I-80 to the north end of Auburn. Take the Elm Avenue exit and turn left at the first stoplight onto Elm Avenue. Drive .1 mile, turn left on High Street, and continue through the signal where High Street merges with Highway 49. Travel on Highway 49 for about 3.5 miles, turn right over the bridge, and drive about 2.5 miles into the town of Cool. Turn left on Georgetown Road/Highway 193 and drive about 14 miles into Georgetown. At the four-way stop, turn left on Main Street (which becomes Wentworth Springs/Forest Road 1) and drive about

CALIFORNIA

25 miles. Turn left on Forest Road 2 and drive about 22 miles to the campground on the left.

Contact: Eldorado National Forest, Georgetown Ranger District, 530/333-4312, fax 530/333-5522; Eldorado Information Center, 530/644-6048, fax 530/295-5624.

51 WILLIAM KENT

Rating: 8

near Lake Tahoe in the Lake Tahoe Basin
See map pages 596–597

William Kent camp is a little pocket of peace near the busy traffic of Highway 89 on the western shore corridor. It is on the west side of the highway, meaning visitors have to cross the highway to get lakeside access. The elevation is 6,300 feet, and the camp is wooded with primarily lodgepole pines. The drive here is awesome or ominous, depending on how you look at it, with the view of incredible Lake Tahoe to the east, the deepest blue in the world. But you often have a lot of time to look at it, since traffic rarely moves quickly.

RV sites, facilities: There are 36 sites for RVs up to 40 feet and 55 tent sites. Picnic tables and fire grills are provided. Drinking water, flush toilets, and an RV dump station are available. A grocery store, coin-operated laundry, and propane are available nearby. Leashed pets are permitted.

Reservations, fees: Reserve at 877/444-6777 or online at www.reserveusa.com ($9 reservation fee). The fee is $15 per night, plus $5 per night for each additional vehicle. A senior discount is available. Open June through September.

Directions: From Truckee, drive south on Highway 89 to Tahoe City. Turn south on Highway 89 and drive three miles to the campground entrance on the right side of the road.

Contact: Lake Tahoe Basin Management Unit, Visitor Center, 530/543-2674, fax 530/543-2693; California Land Management, 530/583-3642.

52 SUGAR PINE POINT STATE PARK

Rating: 10

on Lake Tahoe
See map pages 596–597

This is one of three beautiful and popular state parks on the west shore of Lake Tahoe. It is just north of Meeks Bay on General Creek, with almost two miles of lake frontage available, though the campground is on the opposite side of Highway 89. General Creek, a feeder stream to Lake Tahoe here, is one of the clearest streams imaginable. A pretty trail is routed seven miles along the creek up to Lost Lake, just outside the northern boundary of the Desolation Wilderness. This stream also provides trout fishing from mid-July to mid-September. This park contains one of the finest remaining natural areas at Lake Tahoe, featuring dense forests of pine, fir, aspen, and junipers, covering more than 2,000 acres of beautiful landscape. There are many hiking trails, a swimming beach, and, in winter, 20 kilometers of cross-country skiing trails and a heated restroom. There is also evidence of occupation of Washoe Indians, with bedrock mortars, or grinding rocks, near the Ehrman Mansion. The elevation is 6,200 feet.

RV sites, facilities: There are 175 sites for RVs up to 32 feet, trailers up to 26 feet, or tents. There are also 10 group sites. Picnic tables and fire rings are provided. Drinking water, restrooms, flush toilets, coin-operated showers (except in winter), an RV dump station, a day-use area, and a nature center with a bird display are available. A grocery store, coin-operated laundry, and propane are available nearby. Some facilities are wheelchair-accessible. Leashed pets are permitted.

Reservations, fees: Reserve at 800/444-PARK (800/444-7275) or online at www.reserveamerica .com ($7.50 reservation fee). The fee is $15 per night; group sites are $37 per night. A senior discount is available. Open year-round.

Directions: From Truckee, drive south on Highway 89 through Tahoe City. Continue south on Highway 89 and drive 9.3 miles to the campground (signed) on the right (west) side of the road.

Contact: Sugar Pine Point State Park, 530/525-7982 or 530/525-7232.

53 MEEKS BAY

Rating: 9

on Lake Tahoe
See map pages 596–597

Meeks Bay is a beautiful spot along the western shore of Lake Tahoe. A bicycle trail is nearby

CALIFORNIA

and is routed along the lake's shore, but it requires occasionally crossing busy Highway 89.

RV sites, facilities: There are 40 sites for RVs up to 20 feet or tents. Picnic tables and fire grills are provided. Drinking water and vault toilets are available. A coin-operated laundry and groceries are available nearby. Leashed pets are permitted.

Reservations, fees: Reserve at 877/444-6777 or online at www.reserveusa.com ($9 reservation fee). The fee is $18–26 per night, plus $5 per night for each additional vehicle (if not towed). A senior discount is available. Open May through September.

Directions: In South Lake Tahoe at the junction of Highway 89 and U.S. 50, turn north on Highway 89 and drive 17 miles to the campground (signed) on the east side of Highway 89.

Contact: Lake Tahoe Basin Management Unit, Visitor Center, 530/543-2674 or fax 530/543-2693; California Land Management, 530/583-3642.

54 MEEKS BAY RESORT & MARINA

Rating: 7

on Lake Tahoe

See map pages 596–597

Prime access for boating makes this a camp of choice for the boater/camper at Lake Tahoe. This campground is extremely popular and often booked well in advance for July and August. A boat launch is not only nearby, but access to Rubicon Bay and beyond to breathtaking Emerald Bay is possible, a six-mile one-way trip for boats. The resort is adjacent to a 20-mile paved bike trail, with a swimming beach also nearby. Also on-site are the historic Kehlet Mansion and Washoe House.

RV sites, facilities: There are 10 sites, including some drive-through, with full hookups (30, 50 amps) for RVs of any length, 24 sites for tents, plus lodge rooms, cabins, and houses for rent. Picnic tables and fire grills are provided. Drinking water, flush toilets, a coin-operated laundry, snack bar, cell phone reception, showers, a gift shop, and groceries are available. A boat ramp, boat rentals (kayaks, canoes, and paddleboats), and boat slips are also available. An ATM is within three miles. No pets are allowed.

Reservations, fees: Reservations are accepted.

The fee is $20–30 per night, plus a $7 day-use fee, $25 per night for boat slips, and $1 per shower. A 14-day stay limit is enforced. Major credit cards are accepted. Open May through October.

Directions: In South Lake Tahoe at the junction of Highway 89 and U.S. 50, turn north on Highway 89 and drive 17 miles to the campground on the right.

Contact: Meeks Bay Resort & Marina, 530/525-6946 or 877/326-3357 (reservations), website: www.meeksbayresort.com.

55 STUMPY MEADOWS

Rating: 7

on Stumpy Meadows Lake in Eldorado National Forest

See map pages 596–597

This is the camp of choice for visitors to Stumpy Meadows Lake. The first thing visitors notice is the huge ponderosa pine trees, noted for their distinctive mosaic-like bark. The lake is set at 4,400 feet in Eldorado National Forest and covers 320 acres with water that is cold and clear. The lake has both rainbow and brown trout and in the fall provides good fishing for big browns (they move up into the head of the lake, near where Pilot Creek enters).

RV sites, facilities: There are 40 sites for RVs or tents, with some sites available for RVs up to 60 feet. Two of the sites are double units. Picnic tables and fire grills are provided. Drinking water, vault toilets, and an RV dump station are available. A boat ramp is nearby. Leashed pets are permitted.

Reservations, fees: Reserve at 877/444-6777 or online at www.reserveusa.com ($9 reservation fee). The fees are $13 per night and $26 for double-unit sites. A senior discount is available. Open April through October.

Directions: From Sacramento on I-80, drive east to the north end of Auburn. Turn left on Elm Avenue and drive about .1 mile. Turn left on High Street and drive through the signal that marks the continuation of High Street as Highway 49. Drive 3.5 miles on Highway 49, turn right over the bridge, and drive 2.5 miles into the town of Cool. Turn left on Georgetown Road/Highway 193 and drive 14 miles into Georgetown. At the

CALIFORNIA

four-way stop, turn left on Main Street, which becomes Georgetown–Wentworth Springs Road/Forest Road 1. Drive about 18 miles to Stumpy Meadows Lake. Continue about a mile and turn right into Stumpy Meadows campground.
Contact: Eldorado National Forest, Georgetown Ranger District, 530/333-4312, fax 530/333-5522; Eldorado Information Center, 530/644-6048, fax 530/295-5624.

56 GERLE CREEK

Rating: 7

on Gerle Creek Reservoir in Eldorado National Forest
See map pages 596–597

This is a small, pretty, but limited spot along the northern shore of little Gerle Creek Reservoir at 5,231 feet in elevation. The lake is ideal for canoes or other small boats because no motors are permitted and no boat ramp is available. That makes for quiet water. It is set in the Gerle Creek Canyon, which feeds into the South Fork Rubicon River. No trout plants are made at this lake, and fishing is correspondingly poor. A network of Forest Service roads to the north can provide great exploring. A map of Eldorado National Forest is a must.
RV sites, facilities: There are 50 sites for RVs up to 22 feet or tents. Picnic tables and fire grills are provided. Drinking water and vault toilets are available. Wheelchair-accessible trails and fishing pier are nearby. Leashed pets are permitted.
Reservations, fees: Reserve at 877/444-6777 or online at www.reserveusa.com ($9 reservation fee). The fee is $15 per night, plus $5 per each additional vehicle. A senior discount is available. Open late May to early September.
Directions: From Sacramento, drive east on U.S. 50 to Riverton and the junction with Ice House Road/Soda Springs–Riverton Road. Turn north and drive 27 miles (past Union Valley Reservoir) to a fork with Forest Road 30. Turn left, drive two miles, bear left on the campground entrance road, and drive a mile to the campground.
Contact: Eldorado National Forest, Pacific Ranger District, 530/644-2349, fax 530/647-5405; Eldorado Information Center, 530/644-6048, fax 530/295-5624.

57 LOON LAKE

Rating: 9

in Eldorado National Forest
See map pages 596–597

Loon Lake is set near the Sierra crest at 6,400 feet, covering 600 acres with depths up to 130 feet. This is the lake's primary campground, and it is easy to see why, with a picnic area, beach (includes a small unit to change your clothes in), and boat ramp adjacent to the camp. The lake provides good trout fishing, and once the access road is clear of snow, the lake can be stocked every week of summer. Afternoon winds drive anglers off the lake but are cheered by sailboarders. An excellent trail is also available here, with the hike routed along the lake's eastern shore to Pleasant Hike-In/Boat-In where there's a trailhead for the Desolation Wilderness.
RV sites, facilities: There are 43 sites for RVs up to 50 feet or tents. Picnic tables and fire grills are provided. Drinking water and vault toilets are available. A boat ramp ($15 use fee) and swimming beach are nearby. Some facilities are wheelchair-accessible. Leashed pets are permitted.
Reservations, fees: Reserve at 877/444-6777 or online at www.reserveusa.com ($9 reservation fee). The fees are $15 per night (single) and $30 per night (double), plus $5 for each additional vehicle. Open June through early September.
Directions: From Sacramento, drive east on U.S. 50 to Riverton and the junction with Ice House Road/Soda Springs–Riverton Road on the left. Turn left and drive 34 miles to a fork at the foot of Loon Lake. Turn right and drive one mile to the Loon Lake Picnic Area or boat ramp.
Contact: Eldorado National Forest, Pacific Ranger District, 530/644-2349, fax 530/644-5405; Eldorado Information Center, 530/644-6048, fax 530/295-5624.

58 WOLF CREEK

Rating: 9

on Union Valley Reservoir in Eldorado National Forest
See map pages 596–597

Wolf Creek Camp is on the north shore of Union

CALIFORNIA

Valley Reservoir. Listen up. Notice that it's quieter? Yep. That's because there are not as many water-skiers in the vicinity. Why? There's no boat ramp in the immediate area. This camp opened in the summer of 1998 and was an immediate hit—hey, maybe it's time to create a major low-speed zone for this lake. The view of the Crystal Range from the campground is drop-dead gorgeous. The elevation is 4,900 feet.

RV sites, facilities: There are 42 sites for RVs up to 50 feet or tents and four double sites. Picnic tables and fire grills are provided. Drinking water and vault toilets are available. A boat ramp is three miles away at the campground at Yellowjacket. Some facilities are wheelchair-accessible. Leashed pets are permitted.

Reservations, fees: Reserve at 877/444-6777 or online at www.reserveusa.com ($9 reservation fee). The fees are $15 for a single site per night and $30 for a double, plus $5 for each additional vehicle. A senior discount is available. Open early May through October, weather permitting.

Directions: From Sacramento, drive east on U.S. 50 to Riverton and the junction with Ice House Road/Soda Springs–Riverton Road. Turn left and drive 21 miles to Union Valley Road (at the head of Union Valley Reservoir). Turn left and drive 2.5 miles to the campground.

Contact: Eldorado National Forest, Pacific Ranger District, 530/644-2349, fax 530/647-5405; Eldorado Information Center, 530/644-6048, fax 530/295-5624.

59 CAMINO COVE

Rating: 10

on Union Valley Reservoir in Eldorado National Forest
See map pages 596–597

Camino Cove camp opened in the summer of 2000, and right off it proved to be the nicest spot at Union Valley Reservoir, a slam dunk. It is set at the north end of the lake on a peninsula, absolutely beautiful, a tree-covered landscape and yet with sweeping views of the Crystal Basin. The nearest boat ramp is 1.5 miles to the west at West Point.

RV sites, facilities: There are 32 sites for RVs or tents, with some sites for RVs up to 50 feet. Fire

rings are provided. Vault toilets are available. No drinking water is available. A swimming beach is nearby, and a boat ramp is 1.5 miles away at the campground at West Point. Leashed pets are permitted.

Reservations, fees: Reservations are not accepted. There is no fee for camping. Open early May through October, weather permitting.

Directions: From Sacramento, drive east on U.S. 50 to Riverton and the junction with Ice House Road/Soda Springs–Riverton Road. Turn north on Ice House Road and drive seven miles to Peavine Ridge Road. Turn left and drive three miles to Bryant Springs Road. Turn right and drive five miles north past the West Point boat ramp, and continue 1.5 miles east to the campground entrance on the right.

Contact: Eldorado National Forest, Pacific Ranger District, 530/644-2349, fax 530/647-5405; Eldorado Information Center, 530/644-6048, fax 530/295-5624.

60 YELLOWJACKET

Rating: 8

on Union Valley Reservoir in Eldorado National Forest
See map pages 596–597

The camp is set at 4,900 feet on the north shore of gorgeous Union Valley Reservoir. A boat launch adjacent to the camp makes this an ideal destination for trout-angling campers with boats. Union Valley Reservoir, a popular weekend destination for campers from the Central Valley, is stocked with brook trout and rainbow trout by the Department of Fish and Game.

RV sites, facilities: There are 40 sites for RVs or tents, with some sites for RVs up to 45 feet. Picnic tables and fire rings are provided. Drinking water, flush and vault toilets, and an RV dump station are available. A boat ramp is nearby. Leashed pets are permitted.

Reservations, fees: Reserve at 877/444-6777 or online at www.reserveusa.com ($9 reservation fee). The fees are $15 per night plus $5 for each additional vehicle. A senior discount is available. Open Memorial Day weekend through Labor Day weekend.

Directions: From Sacramento, drive east on

U.S. 50 to Riverton and the junction with Ice House Road/Soda Springs–Riverton Road. Turn left and drive 21 miles to Union Valley Road (at the head of Union Valley Reservoir). Turn left and drive a mile to the campground entrance road. Turn left and drive a mile to the campground.

Contact: Eldorado National Forest, Pacific Ranger District, 530/644-2349, fax 530/647-5405; Eldorado Information Center, 530/644-6048, fax 530/295-5624.

61 WENCH CREEK

Rating: 7

on Union Valley Reservoir in Eldorado National Forest

See map pages 596–597

Wench Creek is on the northeast shore of Union Valley Reservoir. (For more information, see the next listing.) The elevation is 4,900 feet.

RV sites, facilities: There are 100 sites for RVs or tents, with some sites for RVs up to 55 feet. There are also two group sites for up to 50 people each. Picnic tables and fire grills are provided. Drinking water and flush and vault toilets are available. A boat ramp and an RV dump station are three miles away at the campground at Yellowjacket. Leashed pets are permitted.

Reservations, fees: No reservations are accepted for family sites. Reserve group sites at 877/444-6777 or online at www.reserveusa.com ($9 reservation fee). The fee is $15 for family sites per night, plus $5 for each additional vehicle; group sites are $80. A senior discount is available. Open mid-May through September.

Directions: From Sacramento, drive east on U.S. 50 to Riverton and the junction with Ice House Road/Soda Springs–Riverton Road. Turn left and drive 19 miles to the campground entrance road (four miles past the turnoff for Sunset Camp). Turn left and drive a mile to the campground at the end of the road.

Contact: Eldorado National Forest, Pacific Ranger District, 530/644-2349, fax 530/647-5405; Eldorado Information Center, 530/644-6048, fax 530/295-5624.

62 PENINSULA RECREATION AREA

Rating: 8

on Union Valley Reservoir in Eldorado National Forest

See map pages 596–597

The two campgrounds here, Sunset and Fashoda, are the prettiest of all the camps at Union Valley Reservoir, set at the eastern tip of the peninsula that juts into the lake at the mouth of Jones Fork. A nearby boat ramp (you'll see it on the left on the way in) is a big plus, along with a picnic area and beach. The lake has decent trout fishing, with brook trout, brown trout, rainbow trout, Mackinaw, kokanee salamon, and smallmouth bass. The place is gorgeous, set at 4,900 feet in the Sierra Nevada.

RV sites, facilities: There are 131 sites for RVs up to 50 feet or tents at Sunset Camp and 30 walk-in tent sites at Fashoda Camp. Picnic tables, fire rings, and fire grills are provided. Drinking water and vault toilets are available. A boat ramp and an RV dump station are available. Some facilities are wheelchair-accessible. Leashed pets are permitted.

Reservations, fees: Reserve at 877/444-6777 or online at www.reserveusa.com ($9 reservation fee). The fees are $15 per night plus $5 for a third vehicle. Open late May to early September.

Directions: From Sacramento, drive east on U.S. 50 to Riverton and the junction with Ice House Road/Soda Springs–Riverton Road. Turn left and drive 15 miles to the campground entrance road (a mile past the turnoff for Jones Fork camp). Turn left and drive 1.5 miles to the campground at the end of the road.

Contact: Eldorado National Forest, Pacific Ranger District, 530/644-2349, fax 530/647-5405; Eldorado Information Center, 530/644-6048, fax 530/295-5624.

63 ICE HOUSE

Rating: 8

on Ice House Reservoir in Eldorado National Forest

See map pages 596–597

Along with Loon Lake and Union Valley Reservoir, Ice House Reservoir is a feature destination in the Crystal Basin Recreation Area. Ice House gets most of the fishermen and Union Valley gets most of the campers. The camp here is on the lake's northwestern shore, 5,500 feet in elevation, just up from the dam and adjacent to the lake's boat ramp. The lake was created by a dam on South Fork Silver Creek and covers 650 acres, with the deepest spot about 130 feet deep. It is stocked with rainbow trout, brook trout, and brown trout.

RV sites, facilities: There are 66 sites for RVs up to 50 feet or tents and 17 sites for tents. Picnic tables and fire grills are provided. Drinking water, vault toilets, a boat ramp, and an RV dump station are available. Three sites are wheelchair-accessible. Leashed pets are permitted.

Reservations, fees: Reserve at 877/444-6777 or online at www.reserveusa.com ($9 reservation fee). The fees are $15 per night plus $5 for each additional vehicle. A senior discount is available. Open June through October.

Directions: From Sacramento, drive east on U.S. 50 to Riverton and the junction with Ice House Road/Soda Springs–Riverton Road. Turn left and drive about 11 miles to the junction with Forest Road 3 and Ice House Road. Turn right on Ice House Road and drive two miles to the campground access road on the right.

Contact: Eldorado National Forest, Pacific Ranger District, 530/644-2349, fax 530/647-5405; Eldorado Information Center, 530/644-6048, fax 530/295-5624.

64 WRIGHTS LAKE

Rating: 9

in Eldorado National Forest
See map pages 596–597

This high mountain lake (7,000 feet) has shoreline camping and good fishing and hiking. There is no boat ramp, plus rules do not permit motors, so it is ideal for canoes, rafts, prams, and people who like quiet. Fishing is fair for both rainbow trout and brown trout. It is a classic alpine lake, though small (65 acres), with a trailhead for the Desolation Wilderness at its north end. From here it is only a three-mile hike to the beautiful Twin Lakes and Island Lake, set on the western flank of Mount Price (9,975 feet).

RV sites, facilities: There are 36 sites for RVs up

to 50 feet or tents and 32 sites for tents. Picnic tables and fire grills are provided. Drinking water, vault toilets, and limited cell phone reception are available. Leashed pets are permitted.

Reservations, fees: Reserve at 877/444-6777 or online at www.reserveusa.com ($9 reservation fee). The fees are $13 per night plus $5 for each additional vehicle. A senior discount is available. Open late June to early October, weather permitting.

Directions: From Sacramento, drive east on U.S. 50 about 20 miles beyond Placerville. Turn left on Ice House Road and drive north 11.5 miles to Ice House Reservoir. Turn east on Road 32 and drive 10 miles. Turn left on Wrights Lake Road and drive two miles to the campground on the right side of the road.

Contact: Eldorado National Forest, Pacific Ranger District, 530/644-2349, fax 530/644-5405; Eldorado Information Center, 530/644-6048, fax 530/295-5624.

65 D. L. BLISS STATE PARK

Rating: 10

on Lake Tahoe
See map pages 596–597

D. L. Bliss State Park is set on one of Lake Tahoe's most beautiful stretches of shoreline, from Emerald Point at the mouth of Emerald Bay on northward to Rubicon Point, spanning about three miles. The camp is at the north end of the park, the sites nestled amid pine trees, with 80 percent of the campsites within a half mile to a mile of the beach. The grandeur of this park and landscape is the result of successive upheavals of the mountain-building process that raised the Sierra Nevada range. The park is named for a pioneering lumberman, railroad owner, and banker of the region, whose family donated this 744-acre parcel to California in 1929. There are two great easy hiking trails. The Rubicon Trail is one of Tahoe's most popular easy hikes, a meandering path just above the southwest shore of Lake Tahoe, wandering through pine, cedars, and firs, with breaks for fantastic panoramas of the lake, as well as spots where you can see nearly 100 feet into the lake. Don't be surprised if you are joined by a chipmunk circus, many begging, sitting upright, hoping for their nut for the day. Although this trail is beautiful and solitary at dawn, by noon it can be crowded by hikers and chipmunks alike. Another trail, a great hike for youngsters, is the Balancing Rock Trail, just a half-mile romp, where after about 40 yards you arrive at this 130-ton, oblong granite boulder that is set on a tiny perch, and the whole thing seems to defy gravity. Some day it has to fall, right? Not yet. The Rubicon Trail runs all the way past Emerald Point to Emerald Bay. One major downer: all water must be pump-filtered or boiled before drinking or other use.

RV sites, facilities: There are 165 sites for RVs up to 18 feet, trailers up to 15 feet, or tents, one hike-in or bike-in site, and a group site for up to 50 people. Picnic tables, fire grills, and food lockers are provided. Restrooms, coin-operated showers, and flush toilets are available. All water must be pump filtered or boiled before use. Leashed pets are permitted at campsites only.

Reservations, fees: Reserve at 800/444-PARK (800/444-7275) or online at www.reserveamerica .com ($7.50 reservation fee). The fees are $12 per night, $37 per night for the group site, and $3 per night for the hike-in site. A senior discount is available. Open May through mid-October, weather permitting.

Directions: In South Lake Tahoe at the junction of Highway 89 and U.S. 50, turn north on Highway 89 and drive 10.5 miles to the state park turnoff on the right side of the road. Turn right (east) and drive to the park entrance. (If arriving from the north, drive from Tahoe City south on Highway 89 for 17 miles to park entrance road.)

Contact: D. L. Bliss State Park, 530/525-7232, fax 530/525-7277.

66 EMERALD BAY STATE PARK AND BOAT-IN

Rating: 10

on Lake Tahoe
See map pages 596–597
This is one of the most beautiful and popular state parks on the planet. The campground is set at Eagle Point, near the mouth of Emerald Bay on Lake Tahoe, a place of rare, divine beauty. Although the high number of people at Lake Tahoe, and at this park in particular, present inevitable problems, there are remarkable solu-

tions: 20 boat-in sites and two hike-in sites. There may be no more beautiful place anywhere to run a boat than in Emerald Bay, with its deep cobalt-blue waters, awesome surrounding ridgelines, glimpses of Lake Tahoe out the mouth of the bay, and even a little island. The park also has several short hiking trails. Emerald Bay is a designated underwater park. It features Fanette Island, Tahoe's only island. The park also features Vikingsholm, one of the finest examples of Scandinavian architecture in North America; tours are available and very popular, and the hike here features a two-mile round-trip with 500-foot drop in elevation to the "castle." The boat-in camps are on the northern side of Emerald Bay at the site of the old Emerald Bay Resort.

RV sites, facilities: There are 100 sites for RVs up to 21 feet, trailers up to 18 feet long, or tents, two hike-in sites, and 22 boat-in sites. Picnic tables and fire grills are provided. Drinking water, restrooms, flush toilets, cell phone reception, and coin-operated showers are available. An ATM is within 5.5 miles. Leashed pets are permitted in the campground and on asphalt.

Reservations, fees: Reserve at 800/444-PARK (800/444-7275) or online at www.reserveamerica .com ($7.50 reservation fee). The fees are $15 per night, $10 per night for boat-in sites, and $3 per night for hike-in sites. A senior discount is available. Open mid-June through early September.

Directions: In South Lake Tahoe at the junction of Highway 89 and U.S. 50, turn north on Highway 89 and drive 6.5 miles to the state park entrance turnoff on the right side of the road.

Contact: Emerald Bay State Park, 530/541-3030 or 530/525-7277.

67 CAMP RICHARDSON RESORT

Rating: 7

on Lake Tahoe
See map pages 596–597
Camp Richardson Resort is within minutes of boating, biking, gambling, and, in the winter, skiing. It's a take-your-pick deal. With cabins, a restaurant, and live music (often nightly in summer) also on the property, this is a place that offers one big package. The campsites are set in the woods, not on the lake itself. From here you can gain access

to an excellent bike route that runs for three miles, then loops around by the lake for another three miles, most of it flat and easy, all of it beautiful. Expect company. The elevation is 6,300 feet.

RV sites, facilities: There are 112 sites with partial or full hookups (30 amps), including some drive-through, for RVs up to 35 feet, 223 sites for tents, cabins, and hotel rooms. Picnic tables and fire pits are provided. Restrooms, drinking water, showers, flush toilets, an RV dump station, an ATM, and limited cell phone reception are available. A boat ramp, boat rentals, groceries, a restaurant, an ice-cream parlor, and propane are available nearby. A swimming beach and bike rentals are also available. Some facilities are wheelchair-accessible. No pets are allowed.

Reservations, fees: Reservations are recommended. The fee is $17–28 per night, plus $5 for each additional vehicle. Major credit cards are accepted. Open June through October.

Directions: In South Lake Tahoe at the junction of Highway 89 and U.S. 50, turn north on Highway 89 and drive 2.5 miles to the resort on the right side of the road.

Contact: Camp Richardson Resort, 530/541-1801 or 800/544-1801 (reservations), fax 530/541-1802, website: www.camprichardson.com.

68 CAMP SHELLEY

Rating: 7

near Lake Tahoe in the Lake Tahoe Basin
See map pages 596–597
This campground is near South Lake Tahoe within close range of an outstanding bicycle trail. The camp is set in the woods, with campfire programs available on Saturday nights in summer. Nearby to the west is the drive to Inspiration Point and the incredible lookout of Emerald Bay, as well as the parking area for the short hike to Eagle Falls. Nearby to the east are Fallen Leaf Lake and the south shore of Lake Tahoe.

RV sites, facilities: There are 26 sites for RVs up to 22 feet or tents. Picnic tables and fire grills are provided. Drinking water and vault toilets are available. A boat ramp, groceries, and propane are available nearby at Camp Richardson. Some facilities are wheelchair-accessible. Leashed pets are permitted.

Reservations, fees: Reservations can be made in person, Monday through Friday, 9 A.M. to 4 P.M. at the Livermore Recreation and Park District Office, 71 Trevarno Rd., Livermore, CA 94550. Reservations can also be made at the campground office, which is intermittently staffed during the season. The fee is $25 per night, ($18 for Livermore residents), plus $5 per additional vehicle. Open mid-June through Labor Day weekend.

Directions: In South Lake Tahoe at the junction of U.S. 50 and Highway 89, turn north on Highway 89, drive 2.5 miles to Camp Richardson, and then continue for 1.3 miles to the sign for Mount Tallac. Turn left on Mount Tallac Trailhead Road and drive to the campground on the right.

Contact: Camp Shelley, 530/541-6985; Livermore Area Recreation and Park District, 925/373-5700.

69 FALLEN LEAF CAMPGROUND

Rating: 7

in the Lake Tahoe Basin
See map pages 596–597
This is a large "tent city" near the north shore of Fallen Leaf Lake, set at 6,337 feet. The lake is almost as deep blue as nearby Lake Tahoe. It's a big lake, three miles long, and also quite deep, 430 feet at its deepest point. The campground is operated by the concessionaire, which provides a variety of recreational opportunities, including a boat ramp and horseback riding rentals. Fishing is best in the fall for kokanee salmon. Because Fallen Leaf Lake is circled by forest and much of it is private property, you will need a boat to fish or explore the lake. A visitors center is north of the Fallen Leaf Lake turnoff on Highway 89.

RV sites, facilities: There are 130 sites for RVs up to 40 feet or tents and 75 sites for tents. Picnic tables and fire grills are provided. Drinking water, vault toilets, and limited cell phone reception are available. An ATM is within three miles. A boat ramp, a coin-operated laundry, and supplies are available nearby. Leashed pets are permitted.

Reservations, fees: Reserve at 877/444-6777 or online at www.reserveusa.com ($9 reservation fee). The fee is $16 per night, plus $5 per night for each additional vehicle (unless towed). A senior discount is available. Open May through October, weather permitting.

Directions: In South Lake Tahoe at the junction of U.S. 50 and Highway 89, turn north on Highway 89 and drive two miles to the Fallen Leaf Lake turnoff. Turn left and drive 1.5 miles to the campground.

Contact: Lake Tahoe Basin Management Unit, Visitor Center, 530/543-2674, fax 530/543-2693; California Land Management, 530/544-0426.

70 TAHOE VALLEY CAMPGROUND

Rating: 5

near Lake Tahoe
See map pages 596–597

This is a massive, privately operated park near South Lake Tahoe. The nearby attractions include five golf courses, horseback riding, casinos, and, of course, "The Lake."

RV sites, facilities: There are 305 sites, including some drive-through, with partial or full hookups (30, 50 amps) for RVs, and 77 sites for tents. Picnic tables and fire grills are provided. Restrooms, showers, modem access, an RV dump station, a coin-operated laundry, a seasonal heated swimming pool, a playground, tennis courts, a grocery store, RV supplies, propane, ice, firewood, cable TV, limited cell phone reception, and a recreation room are available. An ATM is within a quarter mile. Some facilities are wheelchair-accessible. Leashed pets are permitted.

Reservations, fees: Reservations are recommended. The fee is $24–40 per night. Monthly rates are available. Major credit cards are accepted. Open year-round.

Directions: Entering South Lake Tahoe on U.S. 50, drive east on U.S. 50 to Meyers. Continue on U.S. 50 about five miles beyond Meyers to the signed entrance on the right.

Contact: Tahoe Valley Campground, 530/541-2222, fax 530/541-1825.

71 CHRIS HAVEN MOBILE HOME AND RV PARK

Rating: 5

near South Lake Tahoe
See map pages 596–597

This is an RV-only park that is set within the boundaries of a mobile home park, within close range of the casinos to the east. About 75 percent of the campsites are long-term rentals for the summer.

RV sites, facilities: There are 30 sites with full hookups, including some drive-through, for RVs up to 40 feet. Patios, restrooms, showers, modem access and telephone hookups, cable TV, and a coin-operated laundry are available. Some facilities are wheelchair-accessible. Leashed pets are permitted.

Reservations, fees: Reservations are recommended. The fee is $28–30 per night. Monthly rates are available. Major credit cards are accepted. Open year-round.

Directions: Entering South Lake Tahoe on U.S. 50, drive east to E Street (.5 mile south of the junction of U.S. 50 and Highway 89). Turn left on E Street and drive one block to the park on the right.

Contact: Chris Haven Mobile Home and RV Park, 530/541-1895, fax 530/541-4248, website: www.chrishaven.com

72 CAMPGROUND BY THE LAKE

Rating: 5

near Lake Tahoe
See map pages 596–597

This city-operated campground provides an option at South Lake Tahoe. It is set at 6,200 feet, across the road from the lake, with pine trees and lake views.

RV sites, facilities: There are 170 sites, including some drive-through and some with partial hookups (30, 50 amps), for RVs up to 40 feet or tents and one cabin. Picnic tables and fire grills are provided. Drinking water, flush toilets, showers, an RV dump station, a playground, cell phone reception, and a boat ramp are available. An indoor ice-skating rink and a public indoor heated pool are nearby (fee for access). An ATM is within one mile. Supplies and a coin-operated laundry are nearby. Some facilities are wheelchair-accessible. Pets are permitted with proof of vaccinations.

Reservations, fees: Reservations are accepted. The fee is $21–29 per night for up to four people with a two-night minimum on holidays, plus $4 for each additional vehicle and $1 per pet per night. Major credit cards are accepted. Open April through October.

CALIFORNIA

Directions: Entering South Lake Tahoe on U.S. 50, drive east on U.S. 50 to Rufus Allen Boulevard. Turn right and drive .25 mile to the campground on the right side of the road.

Contact: Campground by the Lake, City of South Lake Tahoe, 530/542-6096 or 530/542-6055, website: www.ci.south-lake-tahoe.ca.us.

73 KOA SOUTH LAKE TAHOE

Rating: 5

near Lake Tahoe
See map pages 596–597

Like so many KOA camps, this one is on the outskirts of a major destination area, in this case, South Lake Tahoe. It is within close range of gambling, fishing, hiking, and bike rentals. The camp is set at 6,300 feet.

RV sites, facilities: There are 40 sites with full hookups (30 amps), including some drive-through, for RVs up to 40 feet and 16 sites for self-contained RVs or tents. Picnic tables and fire grills are provided. Restrooms, showers, an RV dump station, a recreation room, a seasonal swimming pool, cable TV, modem access, limited cell phone reception, and a playground are available, weather permitting. A coin-operated laundry, groceries, RV supplies, and propane are also available. An ATM is within one mile. Leashed pets are permitted.

Reservations, fees: Reservations are recommended at 800/562-3477. The fee is $29–37 per night, plus $3.50 per person for more than two people, $3.50 per additional vehicles, and $3.50 per pet per night. Major credit cards are accepted. Open April through mid-October.

Directions: From Sacramento, take U.S. 50 and drive east over the Sierra Nevada past Echo Summit to Meyers. As you enter Meyers, it will be the first campground on the right. Turn right and enter the campground.

Contact: KOA South Lake Tahoe, 530/577-3693, website: www.laketahoekoa.com.

74 SAND FLAT

Rating: 7

on the South Fork of the American River in Eldorado National Forest
See map pages 596–597

This first-come, first-served campground often gets filled up by U.S. 50 travelers. And why not? You get easy access, a well-signed exit, and a nice setting on the South Fork of the American River. The elevation is 3,900 feet. The river is very pretty here, but fishing is often poor. In winter the snow level usually starts just a few miles uphill.

RV sites, facilities: There are 28 single and one double site for RVs up to 40 feet or tents. Picnic tables and fire grills are provided. Drinking water and vault toilets are available. Groceries, a restaurant, and gas are available nearby. Leashed pets are permitted.

Reservations, fees: Reservations are not accepted. The fees are $12 per night for single sites and $24 per night for the double site, plus $5 per night for each additional vehicle. A senior discount is available. Open year-round.

Directions: From Sacramento, drive east on U.S. 50 to Placerville and then continue 28 miles to the campground on the right.

Contact: Eldorado National Forest, Placerville Ranger District, 530/644-2324, fax 530/295-5994; Eldorado Information Center, 530/644-6048, fax 530/295-5624.

75 CHINA FLAT

Rating: 7

on the Silver Fork of the American River in Eldorado National Forest
See map pages 596–597

China Flat sits across the road from the Silver Fork American River, with a nearby access road that is routed along the river for a mile. This provides access for fishing, swimming, gold panning, and exploring. The camp feels far off the beaten path, even though it is only five minutes from that parade of traffic on U.S. 50.

RV sites, facilities: There are 18 sites and one double site for RVs up to 60 feet or tents. Picnic tables and fire grills are provided. Drinking water and vault toilets are available. Some facilities are wheelchair-accessible. Leashed pets are permitted.

Reservations, fees: Reservations are not accepted. The fees are $12 per night and $24 per night for the double site, plus $5 per night for each additional vehicle. A senior discount is available. Open May through October.

Directions: From Sacramento, drive east on U.S. 50 to Kyburz and Silver Fork Road. Turn right and drive three miles to the campground on the right side of the road.

Contact: Eldorado National Forest, Placerville Ranger District, 530/644-2324, fax 530/295-5994; Eldorado Information Center, 530/644-6048, fax 530/295-5624.

76 SILVER FORK

🧍🏊🎣🐕♿🚐⛺

Rating: 7

on the Silver Fork of the American River in Eldorado National Forest
See map pages 596–597

The tons of vacationers driving U.S. 50 along the South Fork American River always get frustrated when they try to fish or camp, because there are precious few opportunities for either, with about zero trout and camps alike. But, just 20 minutes off the beaten path, you can find both at Silver Fork camp. The access road provides many fishing opportunities where rainbow trout is stocked by the state. The camp is set right along the river, at 5,500 feet in elevation, in Eldorado National Forest.

RV sites, facilities: There are 31 sites for RVs up to 65 feet or tents and four double sites. Picnic tables and fire grills are provided. Drinking water and vault toilets are available. Some facilities are wheelchair-accessible. Leashed pets are permitted.

Reservations, fees: Reservations are not accepted. The fees are $12 per night and $24 for double sites. A senior discount is available. Open May through October.

Directions: From Sacramento, drive east on U.S. 50 to Kyburz and Silver Fork Road. Turn right and drive eight miles to the campground on the right side of the road.

Contact: Eldorado National Forest, Placerville

Ranger District, 530/644-6048, fax 530/295-5994; Eldorado Information Center, 530/644-6048.

77 SILVER LAKE WEST

🧍🎣🚤🏕️🐕🚐⛺

Rating: 9

on Silver Lake in Eldorado National Forest
See map pages 596–597

The Highway 88 corridor provides access to three excellent lakes: Lower Bear River Reservoir, Silver Lake, and Caples Lake. Silver Lake is difficult to pass by, with cabin rentals, pretty campsites, decent trout fishing, and excellent hiking. The lake is set at 7,200 feet in a classic granite cirque just below the Sierra ridge. This camp is on the west side of Highway 88, across the road from the lake. A great hike starts at the trailhead on the east side of the lake, a two-mile tromp to little Hidden Lake, one of several nice hikes in the area. In addition, horseback riding rentals are available nearby at Plasse's Resort.

RV sites, facilities: There are 35 sites for RVs up to 30 feet or tents. Picnic tables and fire pits are provided. Vault toilets are available. No drinking water is available. An ATM is nearby. Leashed pets are permitted. There is a maximum of six people and two pets per site.

Reservations, fees: Reservations are not accepted. The fee is $15 per night, plus $3 per night for each additional vehicle and $1 per pet per night. A senior discount is available. Open Memorial Day Weekend through October, weather permitting.

Directions: From Jackson, drive east on Highway 88 for 50 miles (to the north end of Silver Lake) to the campground entrance road on the left.

Contact: Eldorado National Forest, Amador Ranger District, 209/295-4257, fax 209/295-5998.

78 EAST SILVER LAKE

🧍🏊🎣🚤🐕🚐⛺

Rating: 7

in Eldorado National Forest
See map pages 596–597

Silver Lake is an easy-to-reach alpine lake set at 7,200 feet, which provides a beautiful setting, good trout fishing, and hiking. This camp is on the northeast side of the lake, with a boat ramp

CALIFORNIA

nearby. (See the previous entry for Silver Lake West for more information.)

RV sites, facilities: There are 34 sites for RVs or tents and 28 sites for tents. Picnic tables and fire grills are provided. Drinking water and vault toilets are available. A grocery store, boat rentals, a boat ramp, and propane are nearby. Leashed pets are permitted.

Reservations, fees: Reserve at 877/444-6777 or online at www.reserveusa.com ($9 reservation fee). The fee is $14 per night, plus $6 per night for additional vehicles. A senior discount is available. Open June through October.

Directions: From Jackson, drive east on Highway 88 for 50 miles (to the north end of Silver Lake) to the campground entrance road on the right.

Contact: Eldorado National Forest, Amador Ranger District, 209/295-4257, fax 209/295-5998; Eldorado Information Center, 530/644-6048, fax 530/295-5624.

79 CAPLES LAKE

Rating: 8

in Eldorado National Forest
See map pages 596–597

Caples Lake, here in the high country at 7,800 feet, is a pretty lake right along Highway 88. It covers 600 acres, has a 10 mph speed limit, and provides good trout fishing and excellent hiking terrain. The camp is set across the highway (a little two-laner) from the lake, with the Caples Lake Resort and boat rentals nearby. There is a parking area at the west end of the lake, and from here you can begin a great 3.5-mile hike to Emigrant Lake, in the Mokelumne Wilderness on the western flank of Mount Round Top (10,310 feet).

RV sites, facilities: There are 15 sites for RVs up to 22 feet or tents and 20 sites for tents. Picnic tables and fire grills are provided. Drinking water and vault toilets are available. Groceries, an ATM, propane, a boat ramp, and boat rentals are nearby. Leashed pets are permitted.

Reservations, fees: Reservations are not accepted. The fees are $13 per night plus $6 per night per additional vehicle and $6 per night per pet. A senior discount is available. Open June through October.

Directions: From Jackson, drive east on Highway 88 for 63 miles (one mile past the entrance road to Kirkwood Ski Area) to the camp entrance road on the left.

Contact: Eldorado National Forest, Amador Ranger District, 209/295-4257, fax 209/295-5998; Eldorado Information Center, 530/644-6048, fax 530/295-5624.

80 HOPE VALLEY

Rating: 7

near the Carson River in Humboldt-Toiyabe National Forest
See map pages 596–597

The West Fork of the Carson River runs right through Hope Valley, a pretty trout stream with a choice of four streamside campgrounds. Trout stocks are made near the campgrounds during summer. The campground at Hope Valley is just east of Carson Pass, at 7,300 feet in elevation, in a very pretty area. A trailhead for the Pacific Crest Trail is three miles south of the campground. The primary nearby destination is Blue Lakes, about a 10-minute drive away. An insider's note is that little Tamarack Lake, just beyond the turnoff for Lower Blue Lake, is excellent for swimming.

RV sites, facilities: There are 20 sites for RVs up to 22 feet or tents and a group area for up to 16 people. Picnic tables and fire grills are provided. Drinking water and vault toilets are available. Leashed pets are permitted.

Reservations, fees: Reserve at 877/444-6777 or online at www.reserveusa.com ($9 reservation fee). The fees are $10 per night and $18 per night for the group camp. A senior discount is available. Open June through September.

Directions: From Sacramento, drive east on U.S. 50 to the junction with Highway 89. Turn south on Highway 89 and drive over Luther Pass to the junction with Highway 88. Turn right (west) and drive two miles to Blue Lakes Road. Turn left (south) and drive 1.5 miles to the campground on the right side of the road.

From Jackson, drive east on Highway 88 over Carson Pass and continue east for five miles to Blue Lakes Road. Turn right (south) and drive

1.5 miles to the campground on the right side of the road.

Contact: Humboldt-Toiyabe National Forest, Carson Ranger District, 775/882-2766, fax 775/884-8199.

81 LOWER BLUE LAKE

Rating: 7

near Carson Pass

See map pages 596–597

This is the high country, 8,100 feet, where the terrain is stark and steep and edged by volcanic ridgelines, and where the deep blue-green hue of lake water brightens the landscape. Lower Blue Lake provides a popular trout fishery, with rainbow trout, brook trout, and cutthroat trout all stocked regularly. The boat ramp is adjacent to the campground. The access road crosses the Pacific Crest Trail, providing a route to a series of small, pretty, hike-to lakes just outside the edge of the Mokelumne Wilderness.

RV sites, facilities: There are 16 sites for RVs to 30 feet or tents. Picnic tables and fire grills are provided. Drinking water and vault toilets are available. Leashed pets are permitted.

Reservations, fees: Reservations are not accepted. The fee is $15 per night, plus $3 per additional vehicle per night and $1 per pet per night, with a 14-day occupancy limit. Open June through September, weather permitting.

Directions: From Sacramento, drive east on U.S. 50 to the junction with Highway 89. Turn south on Highway 89 and drive over Luther Pass to the junction with Highway 88. Turn right and drive 2.5 miles to Blue Lakes Road. Turn left and drive 11 miles (road becomes dirt) to a junction at the south end of Lower Blue Lake. Turn right and drive a short distance to the campground on the left side of the road.

From Jackson, drive east on Highway 88 over Carson Pass and continue east for five miles to Blue Lakes Road. Turn right (south) and drive 11 miles (the road becomes dirt) to a junction at the south end of Lower Blue Lake. Turn right and drive a short distance to the campground on the left.

Contact: PG&E Land Projects, 916/386-5164, fax 916/923-7044, website: www.pge.com/recreation.

82 CRYSTAL SPRINGS

Rating: 8

on the West Fork of the Carson River in Humboldt-Toiyabe National Forest

See map pages 596–597

For many people, this camp is an ideal choice. It is set at an elevation of 6,000 feet, right alongside the West Fork of the Carson River. This stretch of water is stocked with trout by the Department of Fish and Game. Crystal Springs is easy to reach, just off Highway 88, and supplies can be obtained in nearby Woodfords or Markleeville. Grover Hot Springs State Park makes a good side-trip destination.

RV sites, facilities: There are 20 sites for RVs up to 22 feet or tents. Picnic tables and fire grills are provided. Drinking water and vault toilets are available. Leashed pets are permitted.

Reservations, fees: Reservations are not accepted. The fee is $10 per night. A senior discount is available. Open late April through September.

Directions: From Sacramento, drive east on U.S. 50 to the junction with Highway 89. Turn south on Highway 89 and drive over Luther Pass to the junction with Highway 88. Turn left (east) and drive 4.5 miles to the campground on the right side of the road.

From Jackson, drive east on Highway 88 over Carson Pass to the junction with Highway 89 and continue for 4.5 miles to the campground on the right side of the road.

Contact: Humboldt-Toiyabe National Forest, Carson Ranger District, 775/882-2766, fax 775/884-8199.

83 GROVER HOT SPRINGS STATE PARK

Rating: 8

near Markleeville

See map pages 596–597

This is a famous spot for folks who like the rejuvenating powers of a hot spring. Some say they feel a glow about them for weeks. When touring the South Tahoe/Carson Pass area, many vacationers take part of a day to make the trip to the hot springs. This park is set in an alpine meadow at 5,900 feet on the east side of the Sierra at the edge of the Great Basin, and it is surrounded by peaks that top 10,000 feet. The hot springs are green because of the mineral deposits at the bottom of the pools. The landscape is primarily pine forest and sagebrush. This area is well known for the great fluctuations in weather, from major blizzards to dry scorchers, from warm, clear nights to awesome rim-rattling thunderstorms. High winds are occasional but legendary. During thunderstorms, the hot springs pools close because of the chance of lightning strikes. Yet they remain open in snow, even blizzards, when it can be a euphoric experience to sit in the steaming water. A forest fire near here remains in evidence. Side-trip options include a nature trail in the park and driving to the Carson River (where the water is a mite cooler) and fishing for trout.

RV sites, facilities: There are 50 sites for RVs up to 27 feet, trailers up to 24 feet, or tents and 26 sites for tents. Picnic tables, fire rings, and food lockers are provided. Restrooms, drinking water, flush toilets, coin-operated showers (except in the winter), a hot springs pool with wheelchair access, and a swimming pool are available. An ATM and modem access are available within four miles. A grocery store and coin-operated laundry are nearby. Leashed pets are permitted.

Reservations, fees: Reserve at 800/444-PARK (800/444-7275) or online at www.reserveamerica.com ($7.50 reservation fee). The fee is $15 per night, plus $4 per each additional vehicle and a $4 day-use fee; pool fees are $3 per adult, $1 per child 16 or under. Open year-round.

Directions: From Sacramento, drive east on U.S. 50 to the junction with Highway 89. Turn south on Highway 89 and drive over Luther Pass to the junction with Highway 88. Turn left and drive to Woodfords and the junction with Highway 89. Turn right (south) and drive six miles to Markleeville and the junction with Hot Springs Road. Turn right and drive four miles to the park entrance.

Contact: Grover Hot Springs State Park, 530/694-2248 or 530/525-7232, fax 530/694-2502.

84 INDIAN CREEK RECREATION AREA

Rating: 10

near Indian Creek Reservoir and Markleeville
See map pages 596–597

This beautiful campground is set amid sparse pines near Indian Creek Reservoir, elevation 5,600 feet. This is an excellent lake for trout fishing, and the nearby Carson River is managed as a trophy trout fishery. The lake covers 160 acres, with a maximum speed for boats on the lake set at 10 mph. There are several good hikes in the vicinity as well. The best is a short trek, a one-mile climb to Summit Lake, with scenic views of the Indian Creek area. Summers are dry and warm here, with high temperatures typically in the 80s, and nights cool and comfortable. Bears make an occasional visit. The lake freezes over in winter. It is about 35 miles to Carson City, Nevada, and seven miles to Markleeville.

RV sites, facilities: There are 19 sites for RVs up to 30 feet or tents, a secondary area with 10 walk-in sites for tents only, and a group site for up to 40 people. Picnic tables and fire grills are provided. Restrooms with drinking water, flush toilets, and showers are available. A boat ramp is nearby. Leashed pets are permitted.

Reservations, fees: Reservations are not accepted. The fees are $12 per night per vehicle, $8 per night for walk-in sites, and $35 per night for the group site. A senior discount is available. Open early May through September.

Directions: From Sacramento, drive east on U.S. 50 over Echo Summit to Meyers and Highway 89. Turn south on Highway 89 and drive to Highway 88. Turn left (east) on Highway 88/89 and drive six miles to Woodfords and Highway 89. Turn right (south) on Highway 89 and drive about four miles to Airport Road. Turn left on Airport Road and drive four miles to Indian Creek Reservoir. At the fork, bear left and drive to the campground on the west side of the lake.

From Markleeville, drive north on Highway 89 for about four miles to Airport Road. Turn right on Airport Road and drive about three miles to Indian Creek Reservoir. At the fork, bear left and drive to the campground on the west side of the lake.

CALIFORNIA

Contact: Bureau of Land Management, Carson City Field Office, 5665 Morgan Mill Road, Carson City, NV 89701, 775/885-6000.

85 TOPAZ LAKE RV PARK

Rating: 6

on Topaz Lake, near Markleeville
See map pages 596–597

Topaz Lake, set at 5,000 feet, is one of the hidden surprises for California anglers. The surprise is the size of the rainbow trout, with one of the highest rates of 15- to 18-inch trout of any lake in the mountain country. The setting is hardly pretty, a good-sized lake on the edge of barren high desert which also serves as the border between California and Nevada. Wind is a problem for small boats, especially in the early summer. Some of the sites here are rented for the entire summer.

RV sites, facilities: There are 54 sites, including some drive-through, with full hookups (30 amps) for RVs up to 40 feet. Picnic tables are provided. Drinking water, restrooms, coin-operated showers, cable TV, limited cell phone reception, a coin-operated laundry, propane, a small grocery store, and modem access are available. A 40-boat marina with a courtesy launch and boat trailer storage is available at lakeside. Some facilities are wheelchair-accessible. Leashed pets are permitted.

Reservations, fees: Reservations are recommended. The fee is $20–22 per night, plus $2 per person for more than two people. Monthly rates are available. Major credit cards are accepted. Open March through mid-October, weather permitting; owners request a call before visits in the off-season.

Directions: From Carson City, drive south on U.S. 395 for 45 miles to Topaz Lake and the campground on the left side of the road.

From Bridgeport, drive north on U.S. 395 for 45 miles to the campground on the right side of the road (.3 mile south of the California/Nevada border).

Contact: Topaz Lake RV Park, 530/495-2357, fax 530/495-2118.

86 TURTLE ROCK PARK

Rating: 5

near Woodfords
See map pages 596–597

This pretty, wooded campground, set at 6,000 feet, gets missed by a lot of folks—but not by mountain bikers. It gets missed by vacationers because it is administered at the county level and also because most vacationers want the more pristine beauty of the nearby camps along the Carson River. (If it snows, it closes, so call ahead if you're planning an autumn visit.) Mountain bikers travel here for the "Death Ride," an event held July 1 each year, a wild ride over several mountain passes. This camp always fills for this riding event. Nearby side trips include Grover Hot Springs and the hot springs in Markleeville.

RV sites, facilities: There are 28 sites for RVs up to 35 feet or tents. Picnic tables and fire grills are provided. Drinking water, vault toilets, and limited cell phone reception are available. A recreation building is available for rent. A coin-operated laundry, groceries, and propane are available within two miles. An ATM is within five miles. A camp host is on-site. Leashed pets are permitted.

Reservations, fees: Reservations are not accepted. The fee is $8 per night, plus $3 per night for each additional vehicle. A senior discount is available. Open May to mid-October, weather permitting.

Directions: From Sacramento, drive east on U.S. 50 to the junction with Highway 89. Turn south on Highway 89 and drive over Luther Pass to the junction with Highway 88. Turn left (east) and drive to Woodfords and the junction with Highway 89. Turn south and drive 4.5 miles to the park entrance on the right side of the road.

Contact: Alpine County Parks, 530/694-2140.

87 SOUTH SHORE

Rating: 7

on Bear River Reservoir in Eldorado National Forest
See map pages 596–597

Bear River Reservoir is set at 5,900 feet, which means it becomes ice-free earlier in the spring than its uphill neighbors to the east, Silver Lake and Caples Lake. It is a good-sized lake—725 acres—and cold and deep, too. It gets double-barreled trout stocks, receiving fish from the state and from the operator of the lake's marina and lodge. This campground is on the lake's southern shore, just east of the dam. Explorers can drive south for five miles to Salt Springs Reservoir, which has a trailhead and parking area on the north side of the dam for a great day hike along the lake.

RV sites, facilities: There are nine sites for RVs or tents and 13 sites for tents, plus four two-family sites. Picnic tables and fire grills are provided. Drinking water and vault toilets are available. A boat ramp, grocery store, boat rentals, and propane are available at nearby Bear River Lake Resort. Leashed pets are permitted.

Reservations, fees: Reservations are not accepted. The fees are $13 per night and $26 per night for two-family sites, plus $6 per each additional vehicle. A senior discount is available. Open June through October.

Directions: From Stockton, drive east on Highway 88 for about 80 miles to the lake entrance on the right side of the road (well signed). Turn right and drive four miles (past the dam) to the campground entrance on the right side of the road.

Contact: Eldorado National Forest, Amador Ranger District, 209/295-4251, fax 209/295-5994; Eldorado Information Center, 530/644-6048, fax 530/295-5624.

88 BEAR RIVER LAKE RESORT

Rating: 8

on Bear River Reservoir
See map pages 596–597

Bear River Lake Resort is a full-service vacation lodge, with everything you could ask for. A lot of people have been asking in recent years, making this a popular spot that often requires a reservation. The resort also sponsors fishing derbies in the summer and sweetens the pot considerably by stocking exceptionally large rainbow trout. The resort is set at 6,000 feet. The lake freezes over in the winter. (For more information about Bear River Reservoir, see the prior entry for South Shore.)

RV sites, facilities: There are 150 sites, all with partial hookups (30 amps), for RVs up to 35 feet or tents and eight lodging units. Picnic tables and fire grills are provided. Restrooms, drinking water, coin-operated showers, an RV dump station, a boat ramp, boat rentals, firewood, ice, propane, a coin-operated laundry, a pay phone, a restaurant and cocktail lounge, and a grocery store are available. An ATM is within seven miles. Some facilities are wheelchair-accessible. Leashed pets are permitted at campsites, but no pets are allowed in the lodging units.

Reservations, fees: Reservations are recommended. The fee is $25 per night, plus $5 per additional vehicle per night and a $5 one-time pet fee. Major credit cards are accepted. Open year-round (call for access in winter).

Directions: From Stockton, drive east on Highway 88 for about 80 miles to the lake entrance on the right side of the road (well signed). Turn right and drive 2.5 miles to a junction (if you pass the dam, you have gone .25 mile too far). Turn left and drive .5 mile to the campground entrance on the right side of the road.

Contact: Bear River Lake Reservoir, 209/295-4868, fax 209/295-4585, website: www.bear riverlake.com.

89 PINE MARTEN

Rating: 8

near Lake Alpine in Stanislaus National Forest
See map pages 596–597

Lake Alpine is a beautiful Sierra lake surrounded by granite and pines and set at 7,320 feet, just above where the snowplows stop in winter. This camp is on the northeast side, about a quarter mile from the shore. Fishing for rainbow trout is good in May and early June, before the summer crush. Despite the long drive to get here, the lake is becoming better known for its beauty, camping, and hiking. A trailhead out of nearby Silver Valley Camp provides a two-mile hike to pretty Duck Lake and beyond into the Carson-Iceberg Wilderness.

RV sites, facilities: There are 32 sites for RVs up to 27 feet or tents. Picnic tables and fire grills are provided. Restrooms, drinking water, flush toilets, and a boat ramp are available. A grocery store, an ATM, propane, and a coin-operated laundry are nearby. Leashed pets are permitted.

Reservations, fees: Reservations are not accepted. The fee is $14.50 per night. A free campfire permit is required. A senior discount is available. Open June to mid-October.

Directions: From Angels Camp, drive east on Highway 4 to Arnold and continue for 29 miles to Lake Alpine. Drive to the northeast end of the lake to the campground entrance on the right side of the road.

Contact: Stanislaus National Forest, Calaveras Ranger District, 209/795-1381, fax 209/795-6849.

90 SILVER VALLEY

Rating: 8

on Lake Alpine in Stanislaus National Forest
See map pages 596–597

This is one of four camps at Lake Alpine. Silver Valley is on the northeast end of the lake at 7,400 feet in elevation, with a trailhead nearby that provides access to the Carson-Iceberg Wilderness. (For recreation information, see the prior entry for Pine Marten.)

RV sites, facilities: There are 21 sites for RVs up to 27 feet or tents. Picnic tables and fire grills are provided. Drinking water and flush toilets are available. A boat launch is available. A grocery store, an ATM, propane, and a coin-operated laundry are nearby. Some facilities are wheelchair-accessible. Leashed pets are permitted.

Reservations, fees: Reservations are not accepted. The fee is $14.50 per night. A free campfire permit is required. A senior discount is available. Open June through mid-October.

Directions: From Angels Camp, drive east on Highway 4 to Arnold and continue for 29 miles to Lake Alpine. Drive to the northeast end of the lake to the campground entrance on the right side of the road. Turn right and drive .5 mile to the campground.

Contact: Stanislaus National Forest, Calaveras Ranger District, 209/795-1381, fax 209/795-6849.

91 LAKE ALPINE CAMPGROUND

Rating: 8

on Lake Alpine in Stanislaus National Forest
See map pages 596–597

This is the campground that is in the greatest demand at Lake Alpine, and it is easy to see why. It is very small, a boat ramp is adjacent to the camp, you can get supplies at a small grocery store within walking distance, and during the evening rise you can often see the jumping trout from your campsite. Lake Alpine is one of the prettiest lakes you can drive to, set at 7,320 feet amid pines and Sierra granite. A trailhead out of nearby Silver Valley Camp provides a two-mile hike to pretty Duck Lake and beyond into the Carson-Iceberg Wilderness.

RV sites, facilities: There are 25 sites for RVs up to 27 feet or tents. Picnic tables and fire grills are provided. Restrooms, drinking water, flush and vault toilets, limited cell phone reception, and a boat launch are available. A grocery store, an ATM, propane, and a coin-operated laundry are nearby. Some facilities are wheelchair-accessible. Leashed pets are permitted.

Reservations, fees: Reservations are not accepted. The fee is $14.50 per night. A senior discount is available. Open June through October.

Directions: From Angels Camp, drive east on Highway 4 to Arnold and continue for 29 miles to Lake Alpine. Just before reaching the lake turn right and drive .25 mile to the campground on the left.

Contact: Stanislaus National Forest, Calaveras Ranger District, 209/795-1381, fax 209/795-6849.

92 SILVERTIP

Rating: 6

near Lake Alpine in Stanislaus National Forest
See map pages 596–597

This camp is just over a half mile from the shore of Lake Alpine at an elevation of 7,350 feet. Why then would anyone camp here when there are campgrounds right at the lake? Two reasons: one, those lakeside camps are often full on summer weekends; two, Highway 4 is snowplowed to this campground entrance, but not beyond. So in big snow years when the road is still closed in late spring and early summer, you can park your rig here to camp, then hike in to the lake. In the fall, it also makes for a base camp for hunters. (See the previous entry for Lake Alpine Campground for more information.)

RV sites, facilities: There are 24 sites for RVs up to 27 feet or tents. Picnic tables and fire grills are provided. Restrooms, drinking water, limited cell phone reception, and flush toilets are available. A boat launch is about a mile away. A grocery store, an ATM, propane, a coin-operated laundry, and coin-operated showers are nearby. Leashed pets are permitted.

Reservations, fees: Reservations are not accepted. The fee is $14.50 per night. A senior discount is available. Open July through October, weather permitting.

Directions: From Angels Camp, drive east on Highway 4 to Arnold and continue for 29 miles to Lake Alpine. A mile before reaching the lake (adjacent to the Bear Valley/Mt. Reba turnoff), turn right at the campground entrance on the right side of the road.

Contact: Stanislaus National Forest, Calaveras Ranger District, 209/795-1381, fax 209/795-6849.

93 SILVER CREEK

Rating: 6

in Humboldt-Toiyabe National Forest
See map pages 596–597

This pretty spot, set near Silver Creek, has easy access from Highway 4 and, in years without washouts, good fishing in early summer for small trout. It is in the remote high Sierra, east of Ebbetts Pass. A side trip to Ebbetts Pass features Kinney Lake, Pacific Crest Trail access, and a trailhead at the north end of the lake (on the west side of Highway 4) for a mile hike to Lower Kinney Lake. No bikes are permitted on the trails. The elevation is 6,800 feet.

RV sites, facilities: There are 22 sites for RVs up to 22 feet or tents. Picnic tables and fire grills are provided. Drinking water and vault toilets are available. Leashed pets are permitted.

Reservations, fees: Reserve at 877/444-6777 or online at www.reserveusa.com ($9 reservation

fee). The fee is $10 per night. A senior discount is available. Open late May to early September.

Directions: From Angels Camp, drive east on Highway 4 all the way over Ebbetts Pass and continue for about six miles to the campground.

From Markleeville, drive south on Highway 89 to the junction with Highway 4. Turn west on Highway 4 (steep and winding) and drive about five miles to the campground.

Contact: Humboldt-Toiyabe National Forest, Carson Ranger District, 775/882-2766, fax 775/884-8199.

94 WA KA LUU HEP YOO

Rating: 8

on the Stanislaus River in Stanislaus National Forest
See map pages 596–597

This is a riverside Forest Service campground that provides good trout fishing on the Stanislaus River and a put-in for white-water rafting. The highlight for most is the fishing, one of the best spots on the Stanislaus, stocked monthly by Fish and Game, and good for rainbow, brook, and brown trout. It is four miles downstream of Dorrington and was first opened in 1999 as part of the Sourgrass Recreation Complex. There are cultural sites and preserved artifacts, such as grinding rocks. It is a pretty streamside spot, with ponderosa pine and black oak providing good screening. A wheelchair-accessible trail is available along the stream. The camp is set at an elevation of 3,900 feet, but it feels higher. By the way, if anybody knows what the name of this campground means, please enlighten me; so far, nobody has a clue.

RV sites, facilities: There are 22 sites for RVs up to 50 feet or tents and 27 walk-in tent sites. Picnic tables and fire grills are provided. Restrooms, drinking water, showers, and flush and vault toilets are available. A camp host is on-site in summer. Some facilities are wheelchair-accessible. Leashed pets are permitted.

Reservations, fees: Reservations are not accepted. The fee is $13 per night. Free campfire permits are required. A senior discount is available. Open June through October, weather permitting.

Directions: From Angels Camp, drive east on

Highway 4, past Arnold to Dorrington and Boards Crossing Road. Turn right and drive four miles to the campground on the left (just before the bridge that crosses the Stanislaus River).

Contact: Stanislaus National Forest, Calaveras Ranger District, 209/795-1381, fax 209/795-6849.

95 BIG MEADOWS AND BIG MEADOWS GROUP CAMP

Rating: 5

in Stanislaus National Forest
See map pages 596–597

Big Meadows is set at 6,460 feet on the western slope of the Sierra Nevada. There are a number of recreation attractions nearby, the most prominent being the North Fork Stanislaus River two miles to the south in national forest (see the listing for Sand Flat in this chapter), with access available from a four-wheel-drive road just east of camp, or on Spicer Reservoir Road (see the listing for Stanislaus River in this chapter). Lake Alpine, a pretty, popular lake for trout fishing, is nine miles east on Highway 4.

RV sites, facilities: There are 23 sites for RVs up to 27 feet, 42 sites for tents, and an adjacent group campsite for RVs or tents. Picnic tables and fire grills are provided. Drinking water and vault toilets are available. Groceries, an ATM, a coin-operated laundry, and propane are within five miles. Leashed pets are permitted.

Reservations, fees: Reserve at 877/444-6777 or online at www.reserveusa.com ($9 reservation fee). The fees are $11 per night for single sites and $30 per group of 25 people per night, plus $1 per additional camper. Open June through October.

Directions: From Angels Camp on Highway 49, turn east on Highway 4 and drive about 30 miles (three miles past Ganns Meadows) to the campground on the right.

Contact: Stanislaus National Forest, Calaveras Ranger District, 209/795-1381, fax 209/795-6849.

96 BIG MEADOW

Rating: 5

near the Stanislaus River in Stanislaus National Forest
See map pages 596–597

Big Meadow is set at 6,460 feet and features a number of nearby recreation options. The most prominent is the North Fork Stanislaus River, with access available at Sand Flat and Stanislaus River campgrounds (see listings in this chapter). In addition, Lake Alpine is nine miles to the east, and three mountain reservoirs, Spicer, Utica, and Union, are all within a 15-minute drive. Big Meadow is also a good base camp for hunters.

RV sites, facilities: There are 23 sites for RVs up to 27 feet and 42 sites for tents. Picnic tables and fire grills are provided. Drinking water and vault toilets are available. Groceries, a coin-operated laundry, and propane are within five miles. Leashed pets are permitted.

Reservations, fees: Reserve at 877/444-6777 or online at www.reserveusa.com ($9 reservation fee). The fee is $11 per night. A senior discount is available. Open June through October.

Directions: From Angels Camp on Highway 49, turn east on Highway 4 and drive about 30 miles (three miles past Ganns Meadows) to the campground on the right.

Contact: Stanislaus National Forest, Calaveras Ranger District, 209/795-1381, fax 209/795-6849.

97 STANISLAUS RIVER

Rating: 8

in Stanislaus National Forest
See map pages 596–597

As you might figure from its name, this camp provides excellent access to the adjacent North Fork Stanislaus River. The elevation is 6,200 feet, with timbered sites and the river with sandy beach just south of camp.

RV sites, facilities: There are 25 sites for RVs up to 35 feet or tents. Fire grills and picnic tables are provided. Drinking water and vault toilets are available. Supplies are available in Tamarack. Leashed pets are permitted.

Reservations, fees: Reservations are not accepted. The fee is $8 per night. A senior discount is available. Open June through October, weather permitting.

Directions: From Angels Camp on Highway 49, turn east on Highway 4 and drive about 32 miles (five miles past Ganns Meadows) to Spicer Reservoir Road on the right. Turn right and drive four miles to the campground on the right side of the road.

Contact: Stanislaus National Forest, Calaveras Ranger District, 209/795-1381, fax 209/795-6849.

98 SPICER RESERVOIR

Rating: 8

near Spicer Reservoir in Stanislaus
National Forest
See map pages 596–597

Spicer Reservoir, set at 6,200 feet, isn't big by reservoir standards, covering 227 acres, but it is surrounded by canyon walls and is quite pretty from a boat. The beauty is added to by good trout fishing, even awesome, trolling gold Cripplures. A boat ramp is near the campground. Trails along much of the lake provide a day-hiking option. Note: This area can really get hammered with snow in big winters, so in the spring and early summer, always check for access conditions before planning a trip.

RV sites, facilities: There are 60 family sites, two double-family sites, and a triple-family site, all suitable for RVs up to 50 feet or tents. Picnic tables and fire grills are provided. Drinking water, vault toilets, limited cell phone reception, and a pay phone are available. A boat ramp is nearby. Some facilities are wheelchair-accessible. Leashed pets are permitted.

Reservations, fees: Reservations are not accepted. The fee is $12 per night. A senior discount is available. Open June through October, weather permitting.

Directions: From Angels Camp, drive east on Highway 4 for about 32 miles to Spicer Reservoir Road/Forest Road 7N01. Turn right, drive seven miles, bear right at a fork with a sharp right turn, and drive a mile to the campground at the west end of the lake.

Contact: Stanislaus National Forest, Calaveras Ranger District, 209/795-1381, fax 209/795-6849.

For a map, send $6 to U.S. Forest Service, Attn: Map Sales, P.O. Box 9035, Prescott, AZ 86313, 928/443-8285, or visit the website: www.fs.fed.us/maps. Major credit cards are accepted.

99 CLARK FORK AND CLARK FORK HORSE

Rating: 8

on the Clark Fork of the Stanislaus River in
Stanislaus National Forest
See map pages 596–597

Clark Fork borders the Clark Fork of the Stanislaus River and is used both by drive-in vacationers and backpackers. A trailhead for hikers is a quarter mile away on the north side of Clark Fork Road (a parking area is available here). From here the trail is routed up along Arnot Creek, skirting between Iceberg Peak on the left and Lightning Mountain on the right, for eight miles to Wolf Creek Pass and the junction with the Pacific Crest Trail. (For another nearby trailhead, see the following entry for Sand Flat.)

RV sites, facilities: There are 88 sites for RVs up to 22 feet or tents, and at an adjacent area, 14 equestrian sites with water troughs. Picnic tables and fire grills are provided. Drinking water, vault and flush toilets, and an RV dump station are available. At the equestrian site, no drinking water is available. An ATM is nearby. You can buy supplies in Dardanelle. Some facilities are wheelchair-accessible. Leashed pets are permitted.

Reservations, fees: Reservations are not accepted. The fees are $11–12 per night for family sites and $6 per night for the horse camp, plus $5.50–6 for an additional vehicle. A senior discount is available. Open May through mid-October, weather permitting.

Directions: From Sonora, drive east on Highway 108 past the town of Strawberry to Clark Fork Road. Turn left, drive five miles, turn right again, and drive .5 mile to the campground entrance on the right side of the road.

Contact: Stanislaus National Forest, Summit Ranger District, 209/965-3434, fax 209/965-3372. For a map, send $6 to U.S. Forest Service, Attn: Map Sales, P.O. Box 9035, Prescott, AZ 86313, 928/443-8285, or visit the website:

CALIFORNIA

www.fs.fed.us/maps. Major credit cards are accepted.

100 SAND FLAT

Rating: 7

on the Clark Fork of the Stanislaus River in Stanislaus National Forest
See map pages 596–597

Sand Flat Campground, at 6,200 feet, is only three miles (by vehicle on Clark Fork Road) from an outstanding trailhead for the Carson-Iceberg Wilderness. The camp is used primarily by late-arriving backpackers who camp for the night, get their gear in order, then head off on the trail. The trail is routed out of Iceberg Meadow, with a choice of heading north to Paradise Valley (unbelievably green and loaded with corn lilies along a creek) and onward to the Pacific Crest Trail, or east to Clark Fork and upstream to Clark Fork Meadow below Sonora Peak. Two choices, both winners.

RV sites, facilities: There are 53 sites for RVs up to 40 feet or tents and 15 walk-in sites. Picnic tables and fire grills are provided. Drinking water, vault toilets, and limited cell phone reception are available. An ATM is nearby. You can buy supplies in Dardanelle. Leashed pets are permitted.

Reservations, fees: Reservations are not accepted. The fee is $8 per night per vehicle. A senior discount is available. Open May through October.

Directions: From Sonora, drive east on Highway 108 past the town of Strawberry to Clark Fork Road. Turn left on Clark Fork Road and drive six miles to the campground entrance on the right side of the road.

Contact: Stanislaus National Forest, Summit Ranger District, 209/965-3434, fax 209/965-3372.

101 FENCE CREEK

Rating: 4

near the Middle Fork of the Stanislaus River in Stanislaus National Forest
See map pages 596–597

Fence Creek is a feeder stream to Clark Fork, which runs a mile downstream and joins with the Middle Fork Stanislaus River en route to Donnells Reservoir. The camp sits along little Fence Creek, 5,600 feet in elevation. Fence Creek Road continues east for another nine miles to an outstanding trailhead at Iceberg Meadow on the edge of the Carson-Iceberg Wilderness.

RV sites, facilities: There are 38 sites for RVs up to 22 feet or tents. Picnic tables and fire grills are provided. Vault and pit toilets are available. No drinking water is available. You can buy supplies in Pinecrest about 10 miles away. Leashed pets are permitted.

Reservations, fees: Reservations are not accepted. The fee is $5 per night. A senior discount is available. Open May through mid-October, weather permitting.

Directions: From Sonora, drive east on Highway 108 about 49 miles to Clark Ford Road. Turn left and drive a mile to Forest Road 6N06. Turn left again and drive .5 mile to the campground on the right.

Contact: Stanislaus National Forest, Summit Ranger District, 209/965-3434, fax 209/965-3372.

102 BOULDER FLAT

Rating: 7

near the Middle Fork of the Stanislaus River in Stanislaus National Forest
See map pages 596–597

You want camping on the Stanislaus River? As you drive east on Highway 108, this is the first in a series of campgrounds along the Middle Fork Stanislaus. Boulder Flat is set at 5,600 feet and offers easy access off the highway. Here's another bonus: this stretch of river is stocked with trout.

RV sites, facilities: There are 20 sites for RVs up to 22 feet or tents and one double site. Picnic tables and fire grills are provided. Drinking water, vault toilets, and limited cell phone reception are available. An ATM is nearby. You can buy supplies in Dardanelle. Leashed pets are permitted.

Reservations, fees: Reservations are not accepted. The fees are $15 per night and $17 per night for a double site, plus $5 for an additional vehicle. A senior discount is available. Open May through October.

Directions: From Sonora, drive east on Highway 108 past the town of Strawberry to Clark Fork

CALIFORNIA

Road. At Clark Fork Road, continue east on Highway 108 for a mile to the campground on the left side of the road.

Contact: Stanislaus National Forest, Summit Ranger District, 209/965-3434, fax 209/965-3372.

103 BRIGHTMAN FLAT

Rating: 7

on the Middle Fork of the Stanislaus River in Stanislaus National Forest

See map pages 596–597

This camp is on the Middle Fork of the Stanislaus River at 5,700 feet elevation, a mile east of Boulder Flat and two miles west of Dardanelle.

RV sites, facilities: There are 33 sites for RVs up to 22 feet or tents. Picnic tables and fire grills are provided. Vault toilets are available. No drinking water is available. You can buy supplies in Dardanelle. Leashed pets are permitted.

Reservations, fees: Reservations are not accepted. The fee is $11 per night, plus $5 per night for each additional vehicle. A senior discount is available. Open May through mid-October, weather permitting.

Directions: From Sonora, drive east on Highway 108 past the town of Strawberry to Clark Fork Road. At Clark Fork Road continue east on Highway 108 for two miles to the campground entrance on the left side of the road.

Contact: Stanislaus National Forest, Summit Ranger District, 209/965-3434, fax 209/965-3372.

104 DARDANELLE

Rating: 7

on the Middle Fork of the Stanislaus River in Stanislaus National Forest

See map pages 596–597

This Forest Service camp is within walking distance of supplies in Dardanelle and is also right alongside the Middle Fork Stanislaus River. This section of river is stocked with trout by the Department of Fish and Game. The trail to see Columns of the Giants is just 1.5 miles to the east out of Pigeon Flat.

RV sites, facilities: There are 28 sites for RVs up to 22 feet or tents and three double sites. Picnic tables and fire grills are provided. Drinking water, vault toilets, and limited cell phone reception are available. An ATM is nearby. You can buy supplies in Dardanelle. Leashed pets are permitted.

Reservations, fees: Reservations are not accepted. The fees are $17 per night for single sites and $21 per night for double sites, plus $5 for an additional vehicle. A senior discount is available. Open May through October, weather permitting.

Directions: From Sonora, drive east on Highway 108 past Strawberry to Dardanelle and the campground on the left side of the road.

Contact: Stanislaus National Forest, Summit Ranger District, 209/965-3434, fax 209/965-3372.

105 EUREKA VALLEY

Rating: 8

on the Middle Fork of the Stanislaus River in Stanislaus National Forest

See map pages 596–597

There are about a half dozen campgrounds on this stretch of the Middle Fork Stanislaus River near Dardanelle, at 6,100 feet in elevation. The river runs along two sides of this campground, making it quite pretty. This stretch of river is planted with trout by the Department of Fish and Game, but it is hit pretty hard despite its relatively isolated location. A good short and easy hike is to Columns of the Giants, accessible on a quarter-mile-long trail out of Pigeon Flat, a mile to the west.

RV sites, facilities: There are 28 sites for RVs up to 22 feet or tents. Picnic tables and fire grills are provided. Drinking water, vault toilets, and limited cell phone reception are available. An ATM is nearby. You can buy supplies in Dardanelle. Leashed pets are permitted.

Reservations, fees: Reservations are not accepted. The fee is $15 per night, plus $5 for an additional vehicle. A senior discount is available. Open May through mid-October, weather permitting.

Directions: From Sonora, drive east on Highway 108 past the town of Strawberry to Dardanelle. Continue three miles east to the campground on the right.

Contact: Stanislaus National Forest, Summit Ranger District, 209/965-3434, fax 209/965-3372.

CALIFORNIA

106 BAKER

Rating: 7

on the Middle Fork of the Stanislaus River in Stanislaus National Forest
See map pages 596–597

Baker lies at the turnoff for the well-known and popular Kennedy Meadow trailhead for the Emigrant Wilderness. The camp is set along the Middle Fork Stanislaus River, 6,200 feet elevation, downstream a short way from the confluence with Deadman Creek. The trailhead, with a nearby horse corral, is another two miles farther on the Kennedy Meadow access road. From here it is a 1.5-mile hike to a fork in the trail; right will take you two miles to Relief Reservoir, 7,226 feet, and left will route you up Kennedy Creek for five miles to pretty Kennedy Lake, just north of Kennedy Peak (10,716 feet).

RV sites, facilities: There are 44 sites for RVs up to 22 feet or tents. Picnic tables and fire grills are provided. Drinking water, vault toilets, and limited cell phone reception are available. An ATM is nearby. You can buy supplies in Dardanelle. Leashed pets are permitted.

Reservations, fees: Reservations are not accepted. The fee is $13 per night, plus $5 for an additional vehicle. A senior discount is available. Open May to mid-October, weather permitting.

Directions: From Sonora, drive east on Highway 108 past Strawberry to Dardanelle. From Dardanelle, continue 5.5 miles east to the campground on the right side of the road at the turnoff for Kennedy Meadow.

Contact: Stanislaus National Forest, Summit Ranger District, 209/965-3434, fax 209/965-3372.

107 DEADMAN

Rating: 7

on the Middle Fork of the Stanislaus River in Stanislaus National Forest
See map pages 596–597

This is a popular trailhead camp and an ideal jump-off point for backpackers heading into the adjacent Emigrant Wilderness. The camp is a short distance from Baker (see the prior entry for Baker for hiking destinations).

RV sites, facilities: There are 17 sites for RVs up to 22 feet or tents and two walk-in sites for tents only. Picnic tables, fire grills, and limited cell phone reception are provided. Drinking water and vault toilets are available. An ATM is nearby. You can buy supplies in Dardanelle. Leashed pets are permitted.

Reservations, fees: Reservations are not accepted. The fee is $13 per night, plus $5 for an additional vehicle. A senior discount is available. Open May through mid-October, weather permitting.

Directions: From Sonora, drive east on Highway 108 past the town of Strawberry to Dardanelle. From Dardanelle, continue 5.5 miles east to the Kennedy Meadow turnoff. Drive a mile on Kennedy Meadow Road to the campground, which is opposite the parking area for the Kennedy Meadow Trail.

Contact: Stanislaus National Forest, Summit Ranger District, 209/965-3434, fax 209/965-3372.

108 LEAVITT MEADOWS

Rating: 9

on the Walker River in Humboldt-Toiyabe National Forest
See map pages 596–597

While Leavitt Meadows sits right aside Highway 108, a little winding two-laner, there are several nearby off-pavement destinations that make this camp a winner. The camp is set in the high eastern Sierra, east of Sonora Pass at 7,000 feet in elevation, where Leavitt Creek and Brownie Creek enter the West Walker River. There is a pack station for horseback riding nearby. For four-wheel-drive owners, the most popular side trip is driving four miles west on Highway 108, then turning south and driving four miles to Leavitt Lake, where the trout fishing is sometimes spectacular, trolling a gold Cripplure.

RV sites, facilities: There are 16 sites for RVs up to 40 feet or tents. Picnic tables and fire grills are provided. Drinking water and vault toilets are available. Leashed pets are permitted.

Reservations, fees: Reservations are not accepted. The fee is $11 per night. A senior discount is available. Open mid-April to mid-October, weather permitting.

CALIFORNIA

Directions: From the junction of Highway 108 and U.S. 395 north of Bridgeport, turn west on Highway 108 and drive seven miles to the campground on the left side of the road.

Contact: Humboldt-Toiyabe National Forest, Bridgeport Ranger District, 760/932-7070, fax 760/932-1299.

109 SONORA BRIDGE

Rating: 7

near the Walker River in Humboldt-Toiyabe National Forest

See map pages 596–597

The West Walker River is a pretty stream, flowing over boulders and into pools, and each year this stretch of river is well stocked with rainbow trout by the Department of Fish and Game. One of several campgrounds near the West Walker, Sonora Bridge is set at 6,800 feet, about a half mile from the river. The setting is in the transition zone from high mountains to high desert on the eastern edge of the Sierra Nevada.

RV sites, facilities: There are 23 sites for RVs up to 40 feet or tents. Picnic tables and fire grills are provided. Drinking water and vault toilets are available. Leashed pets are permitted.

Reservations, fees: Reservations are not accepted. The fee is $11 per night. A senior discount is available. Open May through mid-October.

Directions: From north of Bridgeport, at the junction of U.S. 395 and Highway 108, turn west on Highway 108 and drive two miles to the campground.

Contact: Humboldt-Toiyabe National Forest, Bridgeport Ranger District, 760/932-7070, fax 760/932-1299.

110 CHRIS FLAT

Rating: 7

on the Walker River in Humboldt-Toiyabe National Forest

See map pages 596–597

This is one of two campgrounds set along U.S. 395 next to the West Walker River, a pretty trout stream with easy access and good stocks of rainbow trout. The plants are usually made at two campgrounds, resulting in good prospects here at Chris Flat and west on Highway 108 at Sonora Bridge. The elevation is 6,600 feet.

RV sites, facilities: There are 15 sites for RVs up to 40 feet or tents. Picnic tables and fire grills are provided. Drinking water and vault toilets are available. Leashed pets are permitted.

Reservations, fees: Reservations are not accepted. The fee is $11 per night. A senior discount is available. Open late April through October.

Directions: From Carson City, drive south on U.S. 395 to Coleville and then continue south for 15 miles to the campground on the east side of the road (four miles north of the junction of U.S. 395 and Highway 108).

Contact: Humboldt-Toiyabe National Forest, Bridgeport Ranger District, 760/932-7070, fax 760/932-1299.

111 BOOTLEG

Rating: 6

on the Walker River in Humboldt-Toiyabe National Forest

See map pages 596–597

Location is always a key, and easy access off U.S. 395, the adjacent West Walker River, and good trout stocks in summer make this a popular spot. (See the previous two entries for Chris Flat and Sonora Bridge for more information.) Note that this camp is on the west side of the highway, and that anglers will have to cross the road to gain fishing access. The elevation is 6,600 feet.

RV sites, facilities: There are 63 paved sites for RVs up to 45 feet or tents. Picnic tables and fire grills are provided. Drinking water and flush toilets are available. Leashed pets are permitted.

Reservations, fees: Reservations are not accepted. The fee is $11 per night. A senior discount is available. Open early May to mid-September.

Directions: From Carson City, drive south on U.S. 395 to Coleville and then continue south for 13 miles to the campground on the west side of the highway (six miles north of the junction of U.S. 395 and Highway 108).

Contact: Humboldt-Toiyabe National Forest, Bridgeport Ranger District, 760/932-7070, fax 760/932-1299.

CALIFORNIA

California

Chapter 19
San Francisco Bay Area

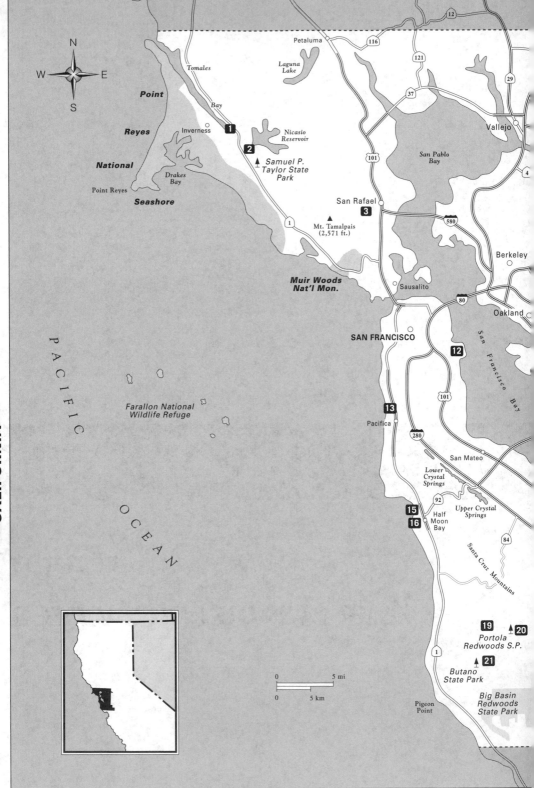

Fairfield

80

680

12

Rio Vista

4-7

160

8-9

Suisun
Bay

Sherman
Island

10

Antioch

Concord

Walnut
Creek

24

13

580

14

San Leandro

Mt. Diablo
State Park

11

Los Vaqueros
Reservoir

680

580

Livermore

580

Pleasanton

92

Del Valle
Res.

17

18

84

Fremont

880

Mission Pk.
(2,517 ft.)

Mountain
View

680

280

SAN JOSE

22

Los Gatos

23

17

24

101

Lake
Anderson

5

see Sacramento and
Gold Country
pages 564–565

12

88

99

Stockton

4

205

5

San

Joaquin

River

132

580

see
San Joaquin
Valley
pages 678–679

Mt. Hamilton
(4,213 ft.)

Henry W. Coe

State Park

25

San Luis
Reservoir

Coyote
Res.

152

© AVALON TRAVEL PUBLISHING, INC.

CALIFORNIA

Chapter 19—San Francisco Bay Area

It's ironic that many people who have chosen to live in the Bay Area are often the ones who complain the most about it. I've even heard some say, "Some day I'm going to get out of here and start having a good time."

I wish I could take anyone who has ever had these thoughts on a little trip in my airplane and circle the Bay Area at 3,000 feet. What you see is that despite strips of roadways and pockets of cities where people are jammed together, most of the region is wild, unsettled, and beautiful. There is no metropolitan area in the world that offers better and more diverse recreation and open space so close to so many.

The Bay Area has 150 significant parks (including 12 with redwoods), 7,500 miles of hiking and biking trails, 45 lakes, 25 waterfalls, 100 miles of coast, mountains with incredible lookouts, bays with islands, and in all, 1.2 million acres of greenbelt with hundreds of acres being added each year with land bought by money earmarked from property taxes. The land has no limit. Enjoy it.

Alongside the unique recreation possibilities remain traditional drive-in sites for RVers at state, county, and regional parks throughout the region.

Note that proximity to a metropolitan area means that the demand is higher. So plan ahead. One shocker is that in spring and fall, there is a huge drop-off in use on weekdays, Sunday through Thursday.

There are many world-class landmarks to see while staying in the Bay Area. In San Francisco alone, there are the Golden Gate Bridge, Fisherman's Wharf, Alcatraz, Ghirardelli Square, Chinatown, SBC Park (formerly Pacific Bell Park), the Crissy Field waterfront, cable cars, Fort Point, the Cliff House and Ocean Beach, and Fort Funston.

■1 OLEMA RANCH CAMPGROUND

Rating: 4

in Olema

See map pages 644–645

If location is everything, then this park should be rated a 10. It is set in Olema, in a valley amid Marin's coastal foothills, an ideal jump-off spot for a Point Reyes adventure, where there's a good chance you'll see tule elk. It borders the Point Reyes National Seashore to the west and the Golden Gate National Recreation Area to the east, with Tomales Bay to the nearby north. There are several excellent trailheads within a 10-minute drive along Highway 1 to the south. But the campsites are small, tightly placed, and I have received complaint letters about the ambience of the place. In the past, when such problems are noted, I have found they are often quickly addressed.

RV sites, facilities: There are 225 sites, some with partial or full hookups (20, 30 amps), for RVs or tents. Picnic tables are provided. Drinking water, restrooms, showers, fire pits, limited cell phone reception, an RV dump station, a coin-operated laundry, an ATM, modem access, an arcade, and a recreation hall (for groups of 25 or more only) are available. Some facilities are wheelchair-accessible. Leashed pets are permitted.

Reservations, fees: Reservations are accepted at 800/655-CAMP (800/655-2267). The fee is $23–32 per night, plus $2 for second vehicle, $3 per person for more than two people, and $1 per pet per night. Major credit cards are accepted. Open year-round.

Directions: From U.S. 101 in Marin, take the San Anselmo/Sir Francis Drake Boulevard exit and drive west for about 20 miles to Highway 1 at Olema. Turn north (right) on Highway 1 and drive .5 mile to the campground on the left.

Contact: Olema Ranch Campground, 415/663-8001, fax 415/663-8832, website: www.olemaranch.com.

■2 SAMUEL P. TAYLOR STATE PARK

Rating: 9

near San Rafael

See map pages 644–645

This is a beautiful park, with campsites set amid redwoods, complete with a babbling brook running nearby. The park covers more than 2,700 acres of wooded countryside in the steep and rolling hills of Marin County, featuring unique contrasts of coast redwoods and open grassland. Hikers will find 20 miles of hiking trails, a hidden waterfall, and some good mountain biking routes on service roads. The paved bike path that runs through the park and parallels Sir Francis Drake Boulevard is a terrific, easy ride. Trees include redwood, Douglas fir, oak, and madrone, and native wildflowers include buttercups, milkmaids, and Indian paintbrush. The section of the park on the north side of Sir Francis Drake (the camp is on the south side) has the best hiking in the park.

RV sites, facilities: There are 35 sites for RVs up to 27 feet or tents, 25 sites for tents, two group sites for 25 and 50 people, one hike-in/bike-in camp, and one equestrian site with corrals at Devil's Gulch Horse Camp. Picnic tables, food lockers, and fire grills are provided. Drinking water, flush toilets, and limited cell phone reception are available. A small store, ATM, and café are four miles away in Lagunitas. Some facilities are wheelchair-accessible. Leashed pets are permitted in campsites only.

Reservations, fees: Reserve at 800/444-PARK (800/444-7275) or online at www.reserveamerica .com ($7.50 reservation fee). The fees are $15 per night, $18–37 per night for group sites, $10 per night for the equestrian camp, and $2 per person per night for hike-in/bike-in site. A senior discount is available. Open year-round.

Directions: From U.S. 101 in Marin, take the Sir Francis Drake Boulevard exit and drive west for about 15 miles to the park entrance on the left side of the road.

Contact: Samuel P. Taylor State Park, 415/488-9897, fax 415/488-4315; California State Parks, Marin District, 415/893-1580, fax 415/893-1583.

■3 MARIN PARK

Rating: 2

in Greenbrae

See map pages 644–645

For out-of-towners with RVs, this can make an ideal base camp for Marin County adventures. To the west are Mt. Tamalpais State Park, Muir

CALIFORNIA

Woods National Monument, Samuel P. Taylor State Park, and Point Reyes National Seashore. To the nearby north is the Loch Lomond Marina on San Pablo Bay, where fishing trips can be arranged for striped bass and sturgeon; phone 415/456-0321. The park offers complete sightseeing information and easy access to buses and ferry service to San Francisco.

RV sites, facilities: There are 89 RV sites with full hookups (30, 50 amps). Showers, a coin-operated laundry, modem access, a swimming pool, cell phone reception, and RV supplies are available. An ATM is within one mile. Some facilities are wheelchair-accessible. Leashed pets are permitted.

Reservations, fees: Reservations are recommended. The fee is $35 per night, plus $2 per person per night for more than two people, with six people maximum per site. Major credit cards are accepted. Open year-round.

Directions: From the south: From the Golden Gate Bridge, drive north on U.S. 101 for 10 miles to Lucky Drive (south of San Rafael). Exit and turn left on Redwood Highway (no sign) and drive three blocks north to the park entrance.

From the north: From San Rafael, drive south on U.S. 101 to the Lucky Drive exit. Take that exit to the first light at Tamal Vista. Turn left and drive to Wornum. Turn left at Wornum and drive under the freeway to Redwood Highway (frontage road). Turn left and drive four blocks north to the park entrance.

Contact: Marin Park, 415/461-5199, fax 415/925-1584, website: www.marinrvpark.com.

4 SANDY BEACH COUNTY PARK

Rating: 6

on the Sacramento River
See map pages 644–645

This is a surprisingly little-known park, especially considering it provides beach access to the Sacramento River. It is a popular spot for sunbathers in hot summer months, but in winter, it is one of the few viable spots where you can fish from the shore for sturgeon. It also provides outstanding boating access to the Sacramento River, including one of the best fishing spots for striped bass in the fall, the Rio Vista Bridge.

RV sites, facilities: There are 42 sites for RVs or tents. Picnic tables and fire grills are provided. Electricity, drinking water, flush toilets, showers, an RV dump station, and a boat ramp are available. Supplies can be obtained nearby (within a mile). Some facilities are wheelchair-accessible. Pets are permitted with proof of rabies vaccination.

Reservations, fees: Reservations are accepted. The fee is $12–18 per night, plus $5 per night for each additional vehicle and $1 per pet per night, with a maximum of 10 people per site. A senior discount is available. Major credit cards are accepted. Open year-round.

Directions: From I-80 in Fairfield, take the Highway 12 exit and drive southeast for 25 miles to Rio Vista and the intersection with Main Street. Turn right on Main Street and drive a short distance to 2nd Street. Turn right and drive .5 mile to Beach Drive. Continue on Beach Drive to the park.

Contact: Solano County Parks, 707/374-2097, fax 707/374-4972, website: www.solanocounty.com.

5 DUCK ISLAND RV PARK

Rating: 6

on the Sacramento River
See map pages 644–645

This pleasant rural park, set up for adults only, has riverside access that provides an opportunity for bank fishing on the Sacramento River. Note that half of the sites are long-term rentals and that this is an adults-only park. A boat ramp is available at the end of Main Street in Rio Vista. Hap's Bait Shop provides reliable fishing information as well as all gear needed for fishing.

RV sites, facilities: There are 51 RV sites with full hookups. Picnic tables are provided. A laundry and recreation room with a kitchen and cell phone reception are available. A small store is available with propane, bait, and RV supplies. Other supplies can be obtained in Rio Vista. Adults only are allowed. Some facilities are wheelchair-accessible. Leashed pets are permitted.

Reservations, fees: Reservations are accepted. The fee is $22 per night. Reservations are required for groups. Major credit cards are accepted. Open year-round.

Directions: In Fairfield on I-80, take the Highway 12 exit and drive 14 miles southeast to Rio Vista and continue to Highway 160 (at the signal

after the bridge). Turn right on Highway 160 and drive just under a mile to the RV park on the right.
Contact: Duck Island RV Park, 916/777-6663 or 800/825-3898.

6 DELTA MARINA RV RESORT

Rating: 6

on the Sacramento River Delta
See map pages 644–645
This is a prime spot for boat campers. Summers are hot and breezy, and water-skiing is popular on the nearby Sacramento River. From November to March, the striped bass fishing is quite good, often as close as just a half mile upriver at the Rio Vista Bridge. The boat launch at the harbor is a bonus.
RV sites, facilities: There are 25 sites with full hookups (30, 50 amps) for RVs. Picnic tables and fire grills are provided. Restrooms, showers, a coin-operated laundry, modem access, cell phone reception, a playground, a boat ramp, ice, and propane are available. Fuel is available 24 hours. An ATM is within a half mile. Some facilities are wheelchair-accessible. Leashed pets (one pet per vehicle) are permitted.
Reservations, fees: Reservations are accepted. The fee is $20–30 per night. Major credit cards are accepted. Open year-round.
Directions: From Fairfield on I-80, take the Highway 12 exit and drive southeast for 14 miles to Rio Vista and the intersection with Main Street. Take the Main Street exit and drive a short distance to 2nd Street. Turn right on 2nd Street and drive to Marina Drive. Turn left on Marina Drive, and continue another short distance to the harbor.
Contact: Delta Marina RV Resort, 707/374-2315, fax 707/374-6471, website: www.deltamarina.com.

7 BRANNAN ISLAND STATE RECREATION AREA

Rating: 7

on the Sacramento River
See map pages 644–645
This state park is perfectly designed for boaters, set in the heart of the Delta's vast waterways. You get year-round adventure: water-skiing and

fishing for catfish are popular in the summer, and in the winter the immediate area is often good for striped bass fishing. The proximity of the campground to the boat launch deserves a medal. What many people do is tow a boat here, launch it, and keep it docked, then return to their site and set up; this allows them to come and go as they please, boating, fishing, and exploring in the Delta. A six-lane boat ramp provides access to a maze of waterways amid many islands, marshes, sloughs, and rivers. Day-use areas include the Windy Cove windsurfing area. Though striped bass in winter and catfish in summer are the most favored fish here, sturgeon, bluegill, perch, bullhead, and bass are also caught. Some sections of the San Joaquin Delta are among the best bass fishing spots in California.
RV sites, facilities: There are 102 sites for RVs up to 36 feet or tents and six group sites for up to 30 people each. Picnic tables and fire grills are provided. Drinking water, restrooms, coin-operated showers (at campground and boat launch), boat berths, an RV dump station, limited cell phone reception, and a boat launch are available. An ATM is within three miles. Supplies can be obtained three miles away in Rio Vista. Some facilities are wheelchair-accessible. Leashed pets are permitted.
Reservations, fees: Reserve at 800/444-PARK (800/444-7275) or online at www.reserveamerica.com ($7.50 reservation fee). The fees are $15 per night and $40 per night for group sites. A senior discount is available. Open year-round.
Directions: In Fairfield on I-80, take the Highway 12 exit, drive southeast 14 miles to Rio Vista, and continue to Highway 160 (at the signal before the bridge). Turn right on Highway 160 and drive three miles to the park entrance on the left.
Contact: Brannan Island State Recreation Area, 916/777-6671; Goldfield District Office, 916/988-0205.

8 SNUG HARBOR MARINA AND RV CAMP/PARK

Rating: 9

near Rio Vista
See map pages 644–645
This year-round resort is an ideal resting place

for families who enjoy water-skiing, boating, biking, swimming, and fishing. After the ferry ride, it is only a few minutes to Snug Harbor, a privately operated resort with a campground, RV hookups, and a separate area with cabins and a cottage. Some say that the waterfront sites with docks give the place the feel of a Louisiana bayou, yet everything is clean and orderly, including a full-service marina, a store, and all facilities—and an excellent location to explore the boating paradise of the Delta. Anglers will find good prospects for striped bass, black bass, blue gill, and catfish. The waterfront sites with docks make Snug Harbor a winner. Snug Harbor was awarded as the "2001 Best Small Park" by the California Travel Parks Association.

RV sites, facilities: There are 38 waterfront sites with docks and full hookups (30, 50 amps) for RVs or tents, 15 inland sites with water hookups only, and 12 park-model cabins. Restrooms, hot showers, an RV dump station, a convenience store, a barbecue, cell phone reception, a swimming beach, a children's play area, a boat launch, paddleboat rentals, propane, and a full-service marina are available. Some facilities are wheelchair-accessible. Leashed pets are permitted.

Reservations, fees: Reservations are recommended. The fee is $27–30 per night, plus $4 per night for each additional vehicle, $7.50 per person per night for more than four people, and $2 per pet per night. Major credit cards are accepted. Open year-round.

Directions: From the Bay Area, take I-80 to Fairfield and Highway 12. Turn east on Highway 12 and drive to Rio Vista and Front Street. Turn left on Front Street and drive under the bridge to River Road. Turn right on River Road and drive two miles to the Real McCoy Ferry (signed Ryer Island). Take the ferry (free) across the Sacramento River to Ryer Island and Levee Road. Turn right and drive 3.5 miles on Levee Road to Snug Harbor on the right.

From Sacramento, drive 26 miles south on I-5 to Highway 12. Drive west on Highway 12 about 20 miles to Rio Vista and then turn north on Route 84 for two miles to the Real McCoy Ferry to Ryer Island. Take the ferry across the Sacramento River (cars are allowed). On Ryer Island, drive 3.5 miles on Levee Road to Snug Harbor.

Contact: Snug Harbor Marina and RV Camp/ Park, 916/775-1455, fax 916/775-1594, website: www.snugharbor.net; Fish Hooker Fishing Charters, 916/777-6498; Waterflies boat rentals (will deliver), 916/777-6431; Herman & Helen's, 209/951-4634.

9 LUNDBORG LANDING

Rating: 5

on the San Joaquin River Delta
See map pages 644–645

This park is on Bethel Island in the heart of the San Joaquin Delta. The boat ramp here provides immediate access to an excellent area for water-skiing, and it turns into a playland on hot summer days. In the fall and winter, the area often provides good striper fishing at nearby Frank's Tract, False River, and San Joaquin River. The fishing for largemouth bass at Frank's Tract is rated among the best in North America. Catfishing in surrounding slough areas is also good year-round. The Delta Sportsman Shop at Bethel Island has reliable fishing information. Live web camera pictures of Frank's Tract are available on the website. Note that some sites are occupied by what appear to be permanent tenants.

RV sites, facilities: There are 76 sites, including some drive-through sites, with full hookups (30, 50 amps) for RVs. Tents are permitted at some sites, and several cabins are available. Restrooms, a laundry room, limited cell phone reception, showers, an RV dump station, propane, a playground, a boat ramp, and a full restaurant and bar are available. An ATM is within two miles. Some facilities are wheelchair-accessible. Leashed pets are permitted.

Reservations, fees: Reservations and deposit are required. The fee is $16–23 per night. Long-term rates are available. Open year-round.

Directions: From Antioch, turn east on Highway 4 and drive to Oakley and East Cypress Road. Turn left on East Cypress Road, drive over the Bethel Island Bridge, and continue .5 mile to Gateway Road. Turn right on Gateway Road and drive two miles to the park entrance on the left (signed well, next to the tugboat).

Contact: Lundborg Landing, P.O. Box 220, Bethel Island, CA 94511, 925/684-9351, website: www .lundborglanding.com.

10 EDDOS HARBOR AND RV PARK

🏊 🛶 🚤 🐕 ♿ 🚐 ⛺

Rating: 6

on the San Joaquin River Delta
See map pages 644–645

This is an ideal spot for campers with boats. Eddos is set on the San Joaquin River, upstream of the Antioch Bridge, in an outstanding region for fishing, powerboating, and water-skiing. In summer, boaters have access to 1,000 miles of Delta waterways, with the best of them in a nearby spiderweb of rivers and sloughs off the San Joaquin to False River, Frank's Tract, and Old River. Hot weather and sheltered sloughs make this ideal for water-skiing. In the winter, a nearby fishing spot called Eddos Bar, as well as the mouth of the False River, attract striped bass.

RV sites, facilities: There are 40 sites with full hookups (30 amps) for RVs and 10 tent sites. Picnic tables are provided. Flush toilets, hot showers, a launch ramp, boat storage, a fuel dock, a coin-operated laundry, modem access, limited cell phone reception, and a small grocery store are available. Some facilities are wheelchair-accessible. Leashed pets are permitted.

Reservations, fees: Reservations are recommended. The fee is $19–22 per night plus $1 per pet per night. Major credit cards are accepted. Open year-round.

Directions: In Fairfield on I-80, take the Highway 12 exit and drive 14 miles southeast to Rio Vista and continue three miles to Highway 160 (at the signal just after the bridge). Turn right on Highway 160 and drive five miles to Sherman Island/East Levee Road. Turn left on East Levee Road and drive five miles to the campground along the San Joaquin River. Note: if arriving by boat, the camp is adjacent to Light 21.

Contact: Eddos Harbor and RV Park, 925/757-5314, fax 925/757-6246, website: www.eddosresort.com.

11 MT. DIABLO STATE PARK

🥾 🚴 🐕 ♿ 🚐 ⛺

Rating: 6

east of Oakland
See map pages 644–645

Mount Diablo, elevation 3,849 feet, provides one of the most all-encompassing lookouts anywhere in America, an awesome 360° on clear mornings. On crystal-clear days you can see the Sierra Nevada and its white, snowbound crest. With binoculars, some claim to have seen Half Dome in Yosemite. The drive to the summit is a must-do trip, and the interpretive center right on top of the mountain is one of the best in the Bay Area. The camps at Mount Diablo are set in foothill/oak grassland country, with some shaded sites. Winter and spring are good times to visit, when the weather is still cool enough for good hiking trips. Most of the trails require long hikes, often including significant elevation gains and losses. No alcohol is permitted in the park. The park offers extensive but challenging hiking, biking, and horseback riding. A museum, visitors center, and gift shop are perched on the Diablo summit. Summers are hot and dry, and in late summer the park can be closed because of fire danger. In winter, snow occasionally falls on the peak—according to my logbook, during the first full moon in February.

RV sites, facilities: There are 64 sites for RVs up to 20 feet or tents (in three campgrounds) and five group sites for 20 to 50 people; one group site is accessible for equestrian use with hitching posts and a water trough. Picnic tables and fire grills are provided. Drinking water and flush and vault toilets are available. Showers are available at Juniper and Live Oak Campgrounds. Leashed pets are permitted in developed areas only.

Reservations, fees: Reserve at 800/444-PARK (800/444-7275) or online at www.reserveamerica.com ($7.50 reservation fee). The fees are $15 per night and $27–67 per night for group sites, plus $4 per additional vehicle. A senior discount is available. Open year-round.

Directions: From Walnut Creek on I-680, take the Diablo Road exit. Turn east on Diablo Road and drive three miles to Mt. Diablo Scenic Boulevard. Turn left and continue 3.5 miles (the road becomes South Gate Road) to the park entrance station. Register at the kiosk, obtain a park map, and drive to the designated campground.

Contact: Mt. Diablo State Park, 925/837-2525 or 925/837-0904; district headquarters, 415/330-6300, website: www.mdia.org.

CALIFORNIA

12 CANDLESTICK RV PARK

Rating: 6

in San Francisco
See map pages 644–645

This RV park is adjacent to Candlestick Park, with the Candlestick State Recreation Area on the other side. It is four miles from downtown San Francisco and an ideal destination for out-of-towners who want to explore the city without having to drive, because the park offers tours and inexpensive shuttles to the downtown area. In addition, there are good hiking opportunities along the shoreline of the bay. On summer afternoons, when the wind howls at 20 to 30 mph here, windsurfers rip by at 50 mph.

RV sites, facilities: There are 165 sites with full hookups (30, 50 amps) for RVs or trailers. Restrooms, showers, a coin-operated laundry, modem access, cell phone reception, a grocery store, a game room, and propane are available. Shuttles and bus tours are also available. An ATM is within one mile. A security officer is posted at the entry station at night. Some facilities are wheelchair-accessible. Small leashed pets are permitted.

Reservations, fees: Reservations are recommended; phone 800/888-CAMP (800/888-2267). The fee is $46–49 per night, plus $3 per person per night for more than two people. Major credit cards are accepted. Open year-round.

Directions: From San Francisco on U.S. 101, take the Candlestick Park exit. Turn east on the stadium entrance road and drive around the parking lot to the far end of the stadium (Gate 4).

Contact: Candlestick RV Park, 415/822-2299, fax 415/822-7638, website: www.sanfranciscorvpark.com.

13 SAN FRANCISCO RV RESORT

Rating: 8

in Pacifica
See map pages 644–645

This has become the best RV park in the Bay Area. It is set on the bluffs just above the Pacific Ocean in Pacifica, complete with beach access, a nearby fishing pier, and sometimes excellent surf fishing. There is also a nearby golf course and the chance for dramatic ocean sunsets. The park is kept clean and in good shape, and though there is too much asphalt, the proximity to the beach overcomes it. It is only 20 minutes from San Francisco. Many RV drivers will remember this park under its former name, Pacific Park RV. It was renamed and renovated in 2002.

RV sites, facilities: There are 182 sites with full hookups, including cable TV, for RVs. Restrooms, showers, a heated swimming a pool, a spa, a group-only recreation room, cable TV, a grocery store, a coin-operated laundry, and propane are available. Some facilities are wheelchair-accessible. Leashed pets are permitted.

Reservations, fees: Reservations are recommended. The fee is $38–69 per night, plus $3.50 per person for more than two people and $3.50 per pet. Major credit cards are accepted. Open year-round.

Directions: From San Francisco, drive south on Highway 280 to Highway 1. Bear west on Highway 1 and drive into Pacifica and to the Manor Drive exit. Take that exit and drive to the stop sign (you will be on the west side of the highway). Continue straight ahead (the road becomes Palmetto Avenue) for about two blocks and look for the entrance to the park on the right side of the road at 700 Palmetto.

From the south, drive north on Highway 1 into Pacifica. Take the Manor Drive exit. At the stop sign, turn left on the frontage road (you will be on the east side of the highway) and drive a block to another stop sign. Turn left, drive a short distance over the highway to a stop sign at Manor/Palmetto, and turn left. Drive about two blocks to the park on the right.

Contact: San Francisco RV Resort, 800/992-0554, fax 650/355-7102, website: www.sanfrancisco rvresort.com.

14 ANTHONY CHABOT REGIONAL PARK

Rating: 7

near Castro Valley
See map pages 644–645

The campground at Chabot Regional Park is set on a hilltop sheltered by eucalyptus, with good views and trails available. The best campsites are the walk-in units, requiring a walk of only a minute or so. Several provide views of Lake Chabot to the south a half mile away. The lake provides

CALIFORNIA

good trout fishing in the winter and spring and a chance for huge but elusive largemouth bass. The Huck Trail is routed down from the campground (near walk-in site 20) to the lake at Honker Bay, a good fishing area. There is also a good 12-mile bike ride around the lake. Boat rentals at a small marina are available.

RV sites, facilities: There are 43 sites for small RVs or tents, 12 sites with full hookups for RVs, and 10 walk-in sites for tents only. Picnic tables and fire grills are provided. Restrooms, drinking water, flush toilets, showers, and an RV dump station are available. Leashed pets are permitted.

Reservations, fees: Reservations are accepted at 510/562-2267 ($6 reservation fee). The fee is $15–20 per night, plus $6 per night for each additional vehicle and $1 per pet per night. Major credit cards are accepted. Open year-round.

Directions: From I-580 in the Oakland hills, drive to the 35th Avenue exit. Take that exit, and at the stop sign, turn east on 35th Avenue and drive up the hill and straight across Skyline Boulevard, where 35th Avenue becomes Redwood Road. Continue on Redwood Road for eight miles to the park and Marciel Road (campground entrance road) on the right.

Contact: Anthony Chabot Regional Park, 510/639-4751; Regional Park Headquarters, 510/635-0135, ext. 2200, fax 510/569-4319.

15 HALF MOON BAY STATE BEACH

Rating: 7

at Half Moon Bay
See map pages 644–645

In summer, this park often fills to capacity with campers touring Highway 1. The campground has level, grassy sites for tents, a clean parking area for RVs, and a state beach available just a short walk away. The feature here is four miles of broad, sandy beaches with three access points with parking. A visitors center opened in 2002. Side trips include Princeton and Pillar Point Marina, seven miles north on Highway 1, where fishing and whale-watching trips are possible. Typical weather is fog in summer, clear days in spring and fall, and wet and windy in the winter—yet occasionally there are drop-dead beautiful days in winter between storms, warm, clear, and wind-less. Temperatures range from lows in the mid-40s in winter to highs in the mid-60s in fall. One frustrating point: the weekend traffic on Highway 1 up and down the coast here is often jammed, with absolute gridlock during festivals.

RV sites, facilities: There are 54 sites for RVs up to 36 feet or tents, four hike-in or bike-in sites, and one group site two miles north of the main campground. Picnic tables, food lockers, and fire grills are provided. Restrooms, drinking water, flush toilets, coin-operated showers, and an RV dump station are available. Leashed pets are permitted.

Reservations, fees: Reservations are not accepted for individual sites. The fees are $12 per night and $1 per person per night for hike-in or bike-in sites. Reserve the group site at 800/444-PARK (800/444-7275) or online at www.reserveamerica.com ($7.50 reservation fee); the fee is $37 per night. A senior discount is available. Open year-round.

Directions: Drive to Half Moon Bay to the junction of Highway 1 and Highway 92. Turn south on Highway 1 and drive one block to Kelly Avenue. Turn right on Kelly Avenue and drive .5 mile to the park entrance at the end of the road.

Contact: Half Moon Bay State Beach, 650/726-8820; Bay Area District, 415/330-6300.

16 PELICAN POINT RV PARK

Rating: 7

in Half Moon Bay
See map pages 644–645

This park is in a rural setting on the southern outskirts of the town of Half Moon Bay, set on an extended bluff near the ocean. The sites consist of concrete slabs with picnic tables. Note that half of RV sites are monthly rentals. All facilities are available nearby, with restaurants available in Half Moon Bay and 10 miles north in Princeton at Pillar Point Harbor. The harbor has an excellent boat launch, a fish-cleaning station, party boat trips for salmon and rockfish and, in the winter, whale-watching trips.

RV sites, facilities: There are 75 sites with full hookups (20, 30 amps) and patios for RVs. Picnic tables are provided. Restrooms, showers, a coin-operated laundry, propane, a small store, a clubhouse, cell phone reception, and an RV dump station are available. An ATM is within three miles. Leashed pets are permitted.

Reservations, fees: Reservations are recommended. The fee is $38–43 per night, plus $2 per night for each additional vehicle, $3 per person per night for more than two people, and $1 per pet. A senior discount is available. Major credit cards are accepted. Open year-round.

Directions: In Half Moon Bay, at the junction of Highway 1 and Highway 92, turn south on Highway 1 and drive 2.5 miles to Miramontes Point Road. Turn right and drive a short distance to the park entrance on the left.

Contact: Pelican Point RV Park, 650/726-9100.

17 DEL VALLE REGIONAL PARK
🏃 🎣 🚣 🛏 🐕 ♿ 🚐 ⛺

Rating: 7

near Livermore
See map pages 644–645
Of the 50 parks in the East Bay Regional Park District, it is Del Valle that provides the greatest variety of recreation at the highest quality. Del Valle Reservoir is the centerpiece, a long narrow lake that fills a canyon, providing a good boat launch for powerboating and fishing for trout, striped bass, and catfish. The sites are somewhat exposed because of the grassland habitat, but they fill anyway on most weekends and three-day holidays. A trailhead south of the lake provides access to the Ohlone Wilderness Trail, and for the well conditioned, there is the 5.5-mile butt-kicker of a climb to Murietta Falls, gaining 1,600 feet in 1.5 miles. Murietta Falls is the Bay Area's highest waterfall, 100 feet tall, though its thin, silvery wisp is difficult to view directly and rarely evokes much emotional response after such an intense climb.

RV sites, facilities: There are 150 sites, including 21 with partial hookups, for RVs or tents. Picnic tables and fire grills are provided. Drinking water, flush toilets, hot showers, an RV dump station, limited cell phone reception, a full marina, and a boat launch are available. An ATM is within 10 miles. Pets are permitted.

Reservations, fees: Reservations are required; phone 510/562-2267 ($7 reservation fee). The fee is $16–20 per night, plus a $3 boat launch fee

and a $1 pet fee. Major credit cards are accepted. Open year-round.

Directions: From I-580 East at Livermore, take the North Livermore Avenue exit and turn right. Drive south for 3.5 miles (the road becomes Tesla Road) to Mines Road. Turn right on Mines Road and drive 3.5 miles to Del Valle Road. Continue on Del Valle Road for three miles to the park entrance.

Contact: Del Valle Regional Park, 925/373-0332; East Bay Regional Park District, 510/635-0135, ext. 2200.

18 JOSEPH GRANT COUNTY PARK
🏃 🚲 🛏 ♿ 🚐 ⛺

Rating: 7

near San Jose
See map pages 644–645
Grant Ranch is a great, wild playland covering 9,000 acres in the foothills of nearby Mount Hamilton to the east. It features 40 miles of hiking trails (horses permitted), 20 miles of old ranch roads that are perfect for mountain biking, a pretty lake (Grant Lake), and miles of foothills, canyons, and grasslands. The campground is set amid oak grasslands, is shaded, and can be used as a base camp for planning the day's recreation. The best hikes are to Halls Valley, especially in the winter and spring when there are many secret little creeks and miniature waterfalls in hidden canyons, the Hotel Trail, and Cañada de Pala Trail, which drops to San Felipe Creek, the prettiest stream in the park. A great side trip is the slow, curvy drive east to Lick Observatory for great views of the Santa Clara Valley. Wood fires are often banned in summer.

RV sites, facilities: There are 40 sites for RVs up to 28 feet or tents. Picnic tables and fire grills are provided. Drinking water, hot showers, an RV dump station, and toilets are available. Pets are permitted.

Reservations, fees: Reservations are not accepted. The fee is $15 per night, plus $6 per night for each additional vehicle and $1 per pet per night, with an eight-person maximum per campsite. Check-in is required before sunset; gates are locked after sunset. Open weekends in March, then daily from April through November.

Directions: In San Jose at the junction of I-680

and U.S. 101, take I-680 north to the Alum Rock Avenue exit. Turn east and drive four miles to Mt. Hamilton Road. Turn right and drive eight miles to the park headquarters entrance on the right side of the road.

Contact: Santa Clara County Parks Department, 408/274-6121, fax 408/270-4808, website: www .parkhere.org.

19 MEMORIAL COUNTY PARK

Rating: 8

near La Honda
See map pages 644–645

This beautiful redwood park is on the western slopes of the Santa Cruz Mountains, tucked in a pocket between the tiny towns of La Honda and Loma Mar. The campground features access to a nearby network of 50 miles of trails, with the best hike along the headwaters of Pescadero Creek. In late winter, it is sometimes possible to see steelhead spawn (no fishing permitted, of course). The trails link with others in nearby Portola State Park and Sam McDonald County Park, providing access to a vast recreation land. The camp is often filled on summer weekends, but the sites are spaced so it won't cramp your style.

RV sites, facilities: There are 156 sites for RVs up to 35 feet or tents, two group sites for up to 75 people, and six youth areas for youth groups of up to 50 people. Picnic tables and fire grills are provided. Drinking water, hot showers, and flush toilets are available. An RV dump station is available from May through October. No pets are allowed.

Reservations, fees: Reservations are not accepted for individual sites. The fee is $15 per night, plus $5 for each additional vehicle. Make reservations for groups at 650/363-4021, Monday through Thursday; group sites are $100. Open year-round.

Directions: Drive to Half Moon Bay at the junction of Highway 1 and Highway 92. Drive south on Highway 1 for 18 miles to the Pescadero Road exit. Turn left on Pescadero Road and drive about 10 miles to the park entrance.

Contact: Memorial County Park, 650/879-0212; San Mateo County Parks and Recreation, 650/363-4021, website: www.sanmateocountyparks.org.

20 PORTOLA REDWOODS STATE PARK

Rating: 9

near Skyline Ridge
See map pages 644–645

Portola Redwoods State Park is very secluded, since visitors are required to travel on an extremely slow and winding series of roads to reach it. The park features redwoods and a mixed evergreen and hardwood forest on the western slopes of the Santa Cruz Mountains, the headwaters of Pescadero Creek, and 18 miles of hiking trails. A literal highlight is a 300-foot-high redwood, one of the tallest trees in the Santa Cruz Mountains. In addition to redwoods, there are Douglas fir and live oak, as well as a riparian zone along the stream. A four-mile hike links up to nearby Pescadero Creek County Park (which, in turn, borders Memorial County Park). At times in the summer, a low fog will move in along the San Mateo coast, and from lookouts near Skyline, visitors can peer to the west at what seems like a pearlescent sea with little islands (hilltops) poking through (this view is available from the access road, not from campsites). Wild pigs are occasionally spotted here, with larger numbers at neighboring Pescadero Creek County Park.

RV sites, facilities: There are 52 sites for RVs up to 24 feet or tents, four walk-in/bike-in sites, one hike-in camp (requires a three-mile hike), and four group sites for 25 to 50 people. Picnic tables and fire grills are provided. Drinking water, flush toilets, coin-operated showers, and firewood are available. Nature hikes and campfire programs are scheduled on weekends from Memorial Day through Labor Day. The nearest gas is 13 miles away. Leashed pets are permitted on paved surfaces only.

Reservations, fees: Reserve at 800/444-PARK (800/444-7275) or online at www.reserveamerica .com ($7.50 reservation fee). The fees are $15 per night, $1 per person per night for walk-in/bike-in sites, $5 per person per night for the hike-in site, and $37–75 per night for group sites. Open March through November.

Directions: From Palo Alto on I-280, turn west on Page Mill Road and drive (slow and twisty) to Skyline Boulevard/Highway 35. Cross Skyline and continue west on Alpine Road (very twisty)

for about three miles to Portola State Park Road. Turn left on Portola State Park Road and drive about three miles to the park entrance at the end of the road.

Contact: Portola Redwoods State Park, 650/948-9098; California State Parks, Santa Cruz District, 831/429-2850, fax 831/429-2876; website: www.santacruzstateparks.org.

21 BUTANO STATE PARK

Rating: 9

near Pescadero
See map pages 644–645

The campground at Butano is set in a canyon filled with a redwood forest, so pretty and with such good hiking that it has become popular enough to make reservations a must. The reason for its popularity is a series of exceptional hikes, including one to the Año Nuevo Lookout (well, the lookout is now blocked by trees, but there are glimpses of the ocean elsewhere along the way), the Mill Ox Loop, and, for the ambitious, the 11-mile Butano Rim Loop. The latter has a backpack camp with seven trail campsites (primitive with pit toilets available) requiring a 5.5-mile hike in the park's most remote area, where no water is available.

RV sites, facilities: There are 21 sites for RVs or tents, 18 walk-in sites, and seven hike-in sites (5.5 miles, with pit toilets available). Picnic tables, food lockers, and fire grills are provided. Restrooms, drinking water, and flush toilets are available. Leashed pets are permitted in campsites.

Reservations, fees: Reserve at 800/444-PARK (800/444-7275) or online at www.reserveamerica.com ($7.50 reservation fee). The fees are $15 per night and $7 per night for hike-in trail sites, plus $4 per additional vehicle. A senior discount is available. Open year-round.

Directions: Drive to Half Moon Bay and the junction of Highway 1 and Highway 92. Drive south on Highway 1 for 18 miles to the Pescadero Road exit and Pescadero Road. Turn left on Pescadero Road and drive past the town of Pescadero to Cloverdale Road. Turn right and drive 5.5 miles to the park entrance on the left.

Contact: Butano State Park, 650/879-2040; California State Parks, Bay Area District, 415/330-6300, fax 415/330-6312.

22 SANBORN-SKYLINE COUNTY PARK

Rating: 8

near Pescadero
See map pages 644–645

This is a pretty camp set in redwood forest, semi-primitive, but like a world in a different orbit compared to the asphalt of San Jose and the rest of the Santa Clara Valley. These campgrounds get heavy use on summer weekends, of course. This is headquarters for a 3,600-acre park that stretches from the foothills of Saratoga up to the Skyline Ridge. Many hiking trails are available, including a trailhead at camp—in all 15 miles of trails. Most explore lush wooded slopes, with redwoods and tan oak. Dogs are prohibited from walk-in sites, and violation of this regulation has created an enforcement situation for rangers. Dogs are permitted, on the other hand, at the RV sites, the main park's grassy area, and day-use sites.

RV sites, facilities: There are 15 sites with full hookups for RVs up to 30 feet, a separate walk-in campground with 33 sites for tents, and a youth group area. Picnic tables and fire pits are provided. Drinking water and flush toilets are available. A youth science center and one-mile nature trail gate close 30 minutes after sunset. Some facilities are wheelchair-accessible. Leashed pets are permitted in the RV campground only.

Reservations, fees: Reservations for RV sites are required, but no reservations are accepted for walk-in sites. The fees are $25 per night, $8 per night for walk-in, and $30 for youth group area for up to 30 people for first night and then $10 for each additional night, plus $1 per pet per night. Major credit cards are accepted. RV sites are open year-round, walk-in sites are open April to mid-October.

Directions: From Highway 17 in San Jose, drive south for six miles to Highway 9/Saratoga Avenue. Turn west and drive to Saratoga, then continue on Highway 9 for two miles to Sanborn Road. Turn left and drive one mile to the park on the right. Walk-in sites require a .1- to .5-mile walk from the parking area.

CALIFORNIA

Contact: Sanborn-Skyline County Park, 408/867-9959, website: www.parkhere.org.

23 BIG BASIN REDWOODS STATE PARK

Rating: 10

near Santa Cruz

See map pages 644–645

Big Basin is one of the best state parks in California, featuring giant redwoods near the park headquarters, secluded campsites set in forest, and rare opportunities to stay in a tent cabin or at a backpacking trail site. The parks covers more than 18,000 acres of redwoods, much of it old-growth, including forest behemoths more than 1,000 years old. It is a great park for hikers, with two waterfalls, one close and one far, making for stellar destinations. The close one is Sempervirens Falls, a long, narrow, silvery stream, an easy 1.5-hour round-trip on the Sequoia Trail. The far one is the famous Berry Creek Falls, a spectacular 70-foot cascade set in a beautiful canyon, framed by redwoods. For hikers in good condition, figure two hours (4.7 miles) to reach Berry Creek Falls, five hours for the round-trip in and out, and six hours for the complete loop (12 miles) that extends into the park's most remote areas. There is also an easy nature loop trail near the park headquarters on the valley floor that is routed past several mammoth redwoods. This is California's oldest state park, established in 1902. It is home to the largest continuous stand of ancient coast redwoods south of San Francisco. There are more than 80 miles of trails with elevations varying from 2,000 feet at the eastern Big Basin Rim on down to sea level. Rainfall averages 48 inches per year, most arriving from December through mid-March.

RV sites, facilities: There are 31 sites for RVs up to 27 feet or tents, 69 sites for tents only, 38 walk-in sites, 36 tent cabins (reservations required), 52 hike-in campsites, and four group sites for 40 to 50 people. Picnic tables, food lockers, and fire grills are provided. Restrooms, drinking water, flush toilets, coin-operated showers, an RV dump station, and groceries are available. Some facilities are wheelchair-accessible. Leashed pets are allowed in campsites and on paved roads only.

Reservations, fees: Reserve at 800/444-PARK (800/444-7275) or online at www.reserveamerica.com ($7.50 reservation fee). The fees are $16 for family sites and walk-in sites, $5 per person for hike-in sites, and $60–75 per night for group sites. Reserve tent cabins at 800/874-8368. A senior discount is available. Open year-round.

Directions: From Santa Cruz, turn north on Highway 9 and drive 12 miles to Boulder Creek and Highway 236 (signed Big Basin). Turn west on Highway 236 and drive nine miles to the park headquarters.

Contact: Big Basin Redwoods State Park, 831/338-8860 or 831/338-8861, fax 831/338-8863; California State Parks, Santa Cruz District, 831/429-2851, website: www.bigbasin.org.

24 PARKWAY LAKES RV PARK

Rating: 3

near Morgan Hill

See map pages 644–645

This RV park provides a spot to park on the southern outskirts of the San Francisco Bay Area. It gets its name from nearby Parkway Lake (408/629-9111), a pay-to-fish lake where for $12 you get a chance to catch rainbow trout up to 10 pounds in the winter and spring, and catfish and sturgeon in the summer. There are several other reservoirs in the nearby foothills, including Coyote, Anderson, Chesbro, Uvas, and Calero. The best nearby source for fishing and recreation information is Coyote Discount Bait and Tackle at 408/463-0711.

RV sites, facilities: There are 113 sites with electricity, including 12 drive-through, for RVs. Restrooms, drinking water, showers, an RV dump station, a heated swimming pool, modem access, a coin-operated laundry, and a recreation room are available. Some facilities are wheelchair-accessible. Leashed pets under 20 pounds are permitted.

Reservations, fees: Reservations are required. The fee is $36 per night, plus $3 per person for more than two people and $1 per pet per night. Major credit cards are accepted. A senior discount is available. Open year-round.

Directions: From San Jose, drive south about 12 miles on U.S. 101 to the Cochrane-Monterey Road exit. Turn right on Cochrane Road and continue about 1.5 miles to the Monterey Highway turnoff. Drive south (right) on Monterey Highway about 3.5 miles to Ogier Road. Turn right on Ogier Road and drive to 100 Ogier Road on the right.

Contact: Parkway Lakes RV Park, 408/779-0244, fax 408/778-7647.

25 HENRY W. COE STATE PARK

Rating: 8

near Gilroy

See map pages 644–645

This is the Bay Area's backyard wilderness, with 100,000 acres of wildlands, including a 23,300-acre wilderness area. There are more than 100 miles of ranch roads and 300 miles of hiking trails, a remarkable network that provides access to 140 ponds and small lakes, hidden streams, and a habitat that is paradise for fish, wildlife, and wild flora. The best camping introduction is at drive-in campsites at park headquarters, set on a hilltop at 2,600 feet that is ideal for stargazing and watching meteor showers. That provides a taste. If you like it, then come back for the full meal. It is the wilderness hike-in and bike-in sites where you will get the full flavor of the park. Before setting out for the outback, always consult with the rangers here—the ambitious plans of many hikers cause them to suffer dehydration and heatstroke. For wilderness trips, the best jump-off point is Coyote Creek and Hunting Hollow trailheads upstream of Coyote Reservoir near Gilroy. The park has excellent pond-style fishing but requires extremely long hikes (typically 10- to 25-mile round-trips) to reach the best lakes, including Mustang Pond, Jackrabbit Lake, Coit Lake, and Mississippi Lake. Expect hot weather in the summer; spring and early summer are the prime times. Even though the park may appear to be 120 square miles of oak foothills, the terrain is often steep, and making ridges often involves climbs of 1,500 feet. There are many great secrets to be discovered here, including Rooster Comb and Coyote Creek. At times on spring days, wild pigs seem to be everywhere. Golden eagles are also abundant. Bring a water purifier for hikes because there is no drinking water in the outback.

RV sites, facilities: There are 10 sites for RVs or tents and 10 sites for tents. There are also eight equestrian campsites, 82 hike-in/bike-in sites, and 10 group sites for 10 to 50 people. At the drive-in site at park headquarters, picnic tables and fire grills are provided. Drinking water and vault toilets are available. Corrals and water troughs are available at the horse camps. Leashed pets are permitted at the drive-in campground only.

Reservations, fees: Reserve at 800/444-PARK (800/444-7275) or online at www.reserveamerica .com ($7.50 reservation fee). The fee is $10 per night. No reservations are accepted for hike-in/bike-in or horse sites; for these sites, a wilderness permit is required from park headquarters. The fees are $12 per night for horse sites and $1 for hike-in/bike-in sites. Reservations are available for the group site at 408/779-2728; the fee is $15 per night. Open year-round.

Directions: From Morgan Hill on U.S. 101, take the East Dunne Avenue exit. Turn east and drive 13 miles (including over the bridge at Anderson Lake, then very twisty and narrow) to the park entrance.

Contact: Henry W. Coe State Park, 408/779-2728 or 408/848-4006; California State Parks, Four Rivers District, 209/826-1196, website: www .coepark.org.

CALIFORNIA

California

Chapter 20

Monterey and Big Sur

Atwater

99

152

Los Baños

see
San Joaquin
Valley
page 678–679

San Joaquin Valley

5

5

San Luis Reservoir

Diablo   Range

25

Salinas

Pinnacles
National
Monument

21

Henry W. Coe
State Park

6

12

156

Hollister

17

15

San Juan Bautista

Fremont Peak
State Park

Soledad

101

14

Salinas

11

Mt. Madonna
County Park

152

5

Pinto
Lake

13

18

68

Carmel River

SAN
JOSE

680

101

Los Gatos

10

9

16

Monterey

Carmel

20

19

1

17

Santa Cruz Mtns.

7 **8**

4

1-2

3

Santa
Cruz

Monterey   Bay

Pt. Lobos
State Reserve

see
San Francisco
Bay Area
pages 664–665

1

N
E
W
S

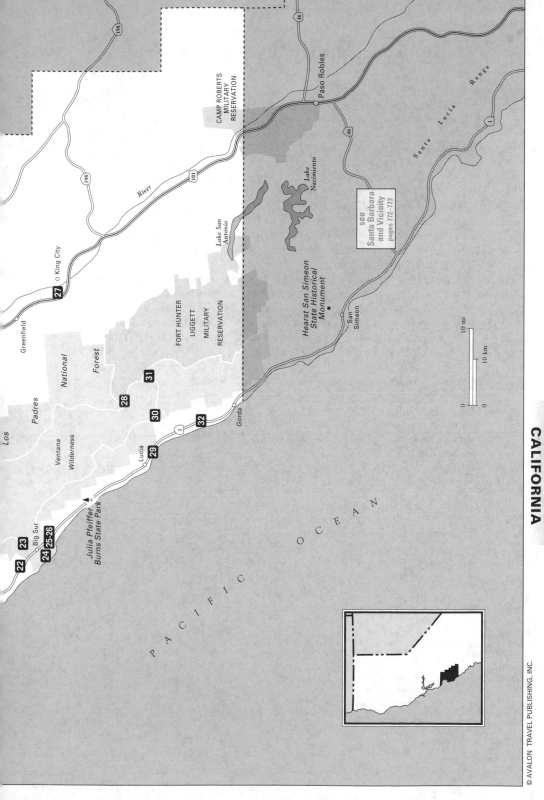

CALIFORNIA

© AVALON TRAVEL PUBLISHING, INC.

see
Santa Barbara
and Vicinity
pages 772–773

Paso Robles

CAMP ROBERTS
MILITARY
RESERVATION

FORT HUNTER
LIGGETT
MILITARY
RESERVATION

Hearst San Simeon
State Historical
Monument

San
Simeon

Lake
Nacimiento

Lake San
Antonio

River

King City

Greenfield

Los

Padres

National

Forest

Ventana
Wilderness

Santa   Lucia   Range

Julia Pfeiffer
Burns State Park

Big Sur

Lucia

Gorda

27

28

29

30

31

32

22

23

24

25-26

198

101

198

46

46

1

1

PACIFIC   OCEAN

10 mi

10 km

Chapter 20—Monterey and Big Sur

The scenic charm seems to extend to infinity from the seaside towns of Santa Cruz, Monterey, and Big Sur. The primary treasure is the coast, which is rock-strewn and sprinkled with inshore kelp beds, where occasionally you can find sea otters playing Pop Goes the Weasel. The sea here is a color like no other, often more of a tourmaline than a straight green or blue.

From Carmel to Lucia alone, touring Big Sur on Highway 1 is one of the most captivating drives anywhere. The inland strip along Highway 1 provides access to state parks, redwoods, coastal streams, Los Padres National Forest, and the Ventana Wilderness. As you explore farther south on the Pacific Coast Highway, you will discover a largely untouched coast.

Most vacations to this region include several must-do trips, often starting in Monterey with a visit to Fisherman's Wharf and its domesticated sea lions, and then to the nearby Monterey Bay Aquarium.

From there, most head south to Big Sur to take in a few brush strokes of nature's canvas, easily realizing why this area is beloved around the world. At first glance, however, it's impossible not to want the whole painting. That is where the campgrounds come in. They provide both the ideal getaway and a launch point for adventure.

At Big Sur, the campgrounds are what many expect: small hideaways in the big redwoods. Most are in a variety of settings, some near Big Sur River, others in the forest.

Other good opportunities are available in Los Padres National Forest and the adjacent Ventana Wilderness, which provides outstanding camping and hiking in the off-season, when the Sierra is buried in snow.

One note of caution: The state park campgrounds on Highway 1 are among the most popular in North America. Reservations far in advance are required all summer, even on weekdays. They are always the first to fill on the state's reservation system. So get the game wired to get your site.

During the summer, only the fog on the coast and the intense heat just 10 miles inland keep this region from attaining perfection.

CALIFORNIA

1 CARBONERO CREEK TRAILER PARK

Rating: 5

near Scotts Valley
See map pages 660–661

This camp is just a short hop from Santa Cruz and the shore of Monterey Bay. There are many side-trip options, making this a prime location for vacationers cruising the California coast. In Santa Cruz there are several quality restaurants, plus fishing trips and boat rentals at Santa Cruz Wharf, as well as the famous Santa Cruz Boardwalk and amusement park.

RV sites, facilities: There are 104 sites with full hookups (30 amps) for RVs and 10 sites for tents. Open fires are prohibited in the campground. Restrooms, showers, cable TV, a coin-operated laundry, modem access (toll-free numbers only), cell phone reception, a recreation room, a hot tub, a whirlpool, and a seasonal swimming pool are available. An ATM is within a quarter mile. Leashed pets are permitted at the RV sites only.

Reservations, fees: Reservations are recommended. The fee is $31–35 per night, plus $3 per person for more than two people and $1 per night for each additional vehicle. Major credit cards are accepted. Open year-round.

Directions: From Santa Cruz, at the junction of Highways 1 and 17 north, turn east on Highway 17 north and drive four miles to the Mt. Hermon/Big Basin exit. Take that exit north onto Mt. Hermon Road and drive to Scotts Valley Drive. Turn right and drive to Disc Drive. Turn right and continue to 917 Disc Drive.

Contact: Carbonero Creek Trailer Park, 831-1288 or 800/546-1288, fax 831/438-2877, website: www.campersworld.com.

2 COTILLION GARDENS RV PARK

Rating: 6

near Santa Cruz
See map pages 660–661

This is a pretty place with several possible side trips. It is set on the edge of the Santa Cruz Mountain redwoods, near Henry Cowell Redwoods State Park and the San Lorenzo River. Monterey Bay is only about a 10-minute drive

from the park. Other side trips include the steam engine ride along the San Lorenzo River out of Roaring Camp Train Rides in Felton and visiting Loch Lomond Reservoir near Ben Lomond for hiking, boat rentals, or fishing. There is a mix of both overnighters and some long-term rentals at this park.

RV sites, facilities: There are 80 sites, including one drive-through, with partial or full hookups (20, 30 amps) for RVs, three sites for tents, and five camping cabins. Picnic tables and fire grills are provided. Restrooms, showers, cable TV, a recreation room, limited cell phone reception, modem access, a seasonally heated swimming pool, and a convenience store are available. An ATM is within one mile. Some facilities are wheelchair-accessible. Leashed pets are permitted.

Reservations, fees: Reservations are recommended. The fee is $33–37 per night, plus $3–5 per person per night for more than two people with a maximum of six. Pets are free if their areas are kept clean. Major credit cards are accepted. Open year-round.

Directions: From Los Gatos, drive west on Highway 17 for 20 miles toward Santa Cruz to the Mt. Hermon Road exit/Scotts Valley (second exit in Scotts Valley). Take the Mt. Hermon Road exit to the stoplight at Mt. Hermon Road. Turn right on Mt. Hermon Road and drive 3.5 miles to Felton and Graham Hill Road. Turn right on Graham Hill Road and drive 50 feet to Highway 9. Turn left on Highway 9 and drive 1.5 miles to the park.

Contact: Cotillion Gardens RV Park, 300 Old Big Trees, Felton, CA 95018, 831/335-7669.

3 SMITHWOODS RV PARK

Rating: 6

near Felton
See map pages 660–661

You get a pretty redwood setting at this privately operated park with its many side-trip possibilities. Henry Cowell Redwoods State Park (good) and Big Basin Redwoods State Park (better) are two nearby parks that provide hiking opportunities. The narrow-gauge train ride through the area is fun, too; it is in Felton at Roaring Camp Train Rides.

CALIFORNIA

RV sites, facilities: There are 142 sites with full hookups (30 amps) for RVs up to 35 feet. No tent camping is allowed. Picnic tables and fire pits are provided. Restrooms, showers, limited cell phone reception, a recreation room, a swimming pool, a coin-operated laundry, modem access, and a convenience store are available. An ATM is within one mile. Some facilities are wheelchair-accessible. Leashed pets are permitted.

Reservations, fees: Reservations are recommended. The fee is $36 per night, plus $2 per person for more than two people, with a maximum of six, and $1 per pet per night. Open year-round.

Directions: From Los Gatos, drive west on Highway 17 for 20 miles toward Santa Cruz to the Mt. Hermon Road exit/Scotts Valley (second exit in Scotts Valley). Take Mt. Hermon Road exit to the stoplight. Turn right on Mt. Hermon Road and drive 3.5 miles to Felton and Graham Hill Road. Turn right on Graham Hill Road and drive 50 feet to Highway 9. Turn left on Highway 9 and drive 1.5 miles to the park entrance on the left.

Contact: Smithwoods RV Park, 831/335-4321.

4 HENRY COWELL REDWOODS STATE PARK

Rating: 8

near Santa Cruz
See map pages 660–661

This is a redwood state park near Santa Cruz with good hiking, good views, and a chance of fishing in the winter for steelhead. The park features a 1,750-acre grove of old-growth redwoods, with 20 miles of trails in the forest, where the old-growth redwoods estimated at 1,400 to 1,800 years old. One great easy hike is a 15-minute walk to a lookout platform over Santa Cruz and the Pacific Ocean; the trailhead is near campsite 49. Another good hike is the Eagle Creek Trail, a three-mile walk that heads along Eagle Creek and the San Lorenzo River, running through a classic redwood canyon. In winter, there is limited steelhead fishing in the San Lorenzo River. A side-trip option is taking the Roaring Camp Big Trees Railroad, which is adjacent to camp, 408/335-4484.

RV sites, facilities: There are 111 sites for RVs up to 40 feet or tents and trailers up to 35 feet,

and one bike-in site. Picnic tables and fire grills are provided. Drinking water, flush toilets, and coin-operated showers are available. A nature center, a book store, and a picnic area are available. Some facilities are wheelchair-accessible. Leashed pets are permitted but must be kept inside tents or vehicles at night.

Reservations, fees: Reservations accepted mid-March through October; reserve at 800/444-PARK or online at www.reserveamerica.com ($7.50 reservation fee). The fees are $16 per night (maximum of eight people) and $2 per person per night for the bike-in site. A senior discount is available. Open mid-February through November.

Directions: In Scotts Valley on Highway 17, take the Mt. Hermon Road exit and drive west toward Felton to Lockwood Lane. Turn left on Lockwood Lane and drive about one mile to Graham Hill Road. Turn left on Graham Hill Road and drive .5 mile to the campground on the right.

Contact: Henry Cowell Redwoods State Park, 831/335-4598 or 831/438-2396.

5 MT. MADONNA COUNTY PARK

Rating: 7

between Watsonville and Gilroy
See map pages 660–661

It's a twisty son-of-a-gun road to reach the top of Mount Madonna, but the views on clear days of Monterey Bay to the west and Santa Clara Valley to the east always make it worth the trip. In addition, a small herd of white deer are kept protected in a pen near the parking area for a rare chance to see unique wildlife. There are many good hiking trails in the park; the best is the Bayview Loop. Elevation in the park reaches 1,896 feet. Insider's notes: campsite 5 at Valley View is the only drive-through site. Although no credit cards are accepted in person, there is a self-pay machine that accepts credit cards, a nice touch.

RV sites, facilities: There are 117 sites for RVs or tents. Picnic tables and fire grills are provided. Drinking water, coin-operated showers, and flush toilets are available. Some facilities are wheelchair-accessible. Leashed pets are permitted.

Reservations, fees: Reservations are not accepted. The fee is $15–25 per night, plus $6 per night for each additional vehicle and $1 per pet per night. There is an eight-person maximum. Major credit cards are accepted at the self-serve machine. Open year-round.

Directions: From U.S. 101 in Gilroy, take the Hecker Pass Highway/Highway 152 exit west. Drive west seven miles to the park entrance on the right.

From Highway 1 in Watsonville, turn east onto Highway 152 and drive about 12 miles east to the park entrance on the left.

Contact: Mt. Madonna County Park, 408/842-2341, fax 408/842-6642, website: www.gooutandplay.org.

6 COYOTE LAKE COUNTY PARK

Rating: 7

near Gilroy
See map pages 660–661

Coyote Lake is a pretty surprise to newcomers, a long, narrow lake set in a canyon just over the ridge east of U.S. 101. It covers 688 acres and is stocked with a total of 24,000 trout on a biweekly basis from late winter through spring; the lake also provides a decent fishery for bass. The campground is nestled in oaks, furnishing some much-needed shade. Note: if you continue east about four miles on the access road that runs past the lake to the Coe State Park Hunting Hollow entrance, you'll come to two outstanding trailheads (one at a parking area, one at the Coyote Creek gate) into that park's wildlands. Wildlife is abundant, including deer and wild turkey.

RV sites, facilities: There are 75 drive-through sites for self-contained RVs or tents. Picnic tables and fire grills are provided. Drinking water, flush toilets, firewood, and a boat ramp are available. A visitors center is on-site. Some facilities are wheelchair-accessible. Leashed pets are permitted.

Reservations, fees: Make reservations at 408/355-2201 or 408/358-3751. The fee is $15 per night, plus $6 for a second vehicle, $4 for boat launching plus $5 for gas motor, and $1 per pet per night. Major credit cards are accepted. Open year-round.

Directions: Drive on U.S. 101 to Gilroy and Leavesley Road. Take that exit and drive east on Leavesley Road to New Avenue. Turn left on New Avenue and drive to Roop Road. Turn right

on Roop Road and drive to Coyote Lake Road. Turn left on Coyote Lake Road and drive to the campground. The park is a total of 5.5 miles from Gilroy.

Contact: Coyote Lake County Park, 408/842-7800, fax 408/842-6439, website: www.gooutandplay.org.

7 SEACLIFF STATE BEACH

Rating: 10

near Santa Cruz
See map pages 660–661

Here is a very pretty spot on a beach along Monterey Bay. Beach walks are great, especially on clear evenings for dramatic sunsets. An interpretive center is available in the summer. This is a popular layover for vacationers touring Highway 1 in the summer, but the best weather is from mid-August to early October. This is a popular beach for swimming and sunbathing, with a long stretch of sand backed by coastal bluffs. A structure called the "old cement ship" by many nearby provides some fascination, but visitors are no longer allowed to walk on it for safety reasons. It is actually an old concrete freighter, the *Palo Alto*. Fishing is often good adjacent to the ship.

RV sites, facilities: There are 26 sites with hookups (30 amps) for RVs up to 40 feet and an overflow area for RVs up to 34 feet. Picnic tables and fire grills are provided. Restrooms, drinking water, flush toilets, and coin-operated showers are available. Propane, groceries, an ATM, a covered picnic area, and a coin-operated laundry are nearby. Some facilities are wheelchair-accessible. Leashed pets are permitted in the camping area and on the beach.

Reservations, fees: Reserve at 800/444-PARK or online at www.reserveamerica.com ($7.50 reservation fee). The fee is $20–26 per night. A senior discount is available. Open year-round.

Directions: From Santa Cruz, drive south on Highway 1 about six miles to State Park Drive/Seacliff Beach exit. Take that exit, turn west, and drive a short distance to the park entrance.

Contact: Seacliff State Beach, 831/685-6500; California State Parks, Santa Cruz District, 831/429-2851, fax 831/429-2876.

CALIFORNIA

8 SANTA CRUZ KOA

Rating: 8

near Watsonville
See map pages 660–661

Bike rentals and nearby access to Manresa State Beach make this KOA campground a winner. The little log cabins are quite cute, and security is first-class. Those who have been here know it is a popular layover spot and weekend vacation destination. The only downer is the amount of asphalt, with everything paved right up to your cabin doorstep.

RV sites, facilities: There are 180 sites, including five drive-through, with partial or full hookups (30, 50 amps), six sites for tents only, 50 camping cabins, and two camping lodges. Picnic tables and fire grills are provided. Restrooms, showers, an RV dump station, modem access, an ATM, limited cell phone reception, a swimming pool, a hot tub, a playground, a recreation room, bicycle rentals, miniature golf, a store, and propane are available. Some facilities are wheelchair-accessible. Leashed pets are permitted.

Reservations, fees: Reservations are advised; call 800/562-7701. The fee is $36–57 per night for two adults, plus $3 per child and $6 per additional adult. Major credit cards are accepted. Open year-round.

Directions: From Santa Cruz, drive 12 miles southeast on Highway 1. Take the San Andreas Road exit and head southwest for 3.5 miles to 1186 San Andreas Road.

Contact: Santa Cruz KOA, 831/722-0551, fax 831/722-0989, website: www.koa.com.

9 SUNSET STATE BEACH

Rating: 9

near Watsonville
See map pages 660–661

On clear evenings, the sunsets here look as if they are imported from Hawaii. The camp is set on a bluff along Monterey Bay. Although there are no ocean views from the campsites, the location makes for easy access down to the beach for beautiful shoreline walks. The beachfront features pine trees, bluffs, and expansive sand dunes. The park is bordered by large agricultural fields. This area was once a good spot for clamming, but they've just about been fished out. The best weather is in late summer and fall. Spring can be windy here, and early summer is often foggy. Reservations are often needed well in advance to secure a spot.

RV sites, facilities: There are 90 sites for RVs up to 31 feet or tents, one hike-in/bike-in site, and one group site for up to 50 people. Picnic tables, food lockers, and fire grills are provided. Restrooms, drinking water, flush toilets, cell phone reception, coin-operated showers, and firewood are available. An ATM is within 2.5 miles. Some facilities are wheelchair-accessible. Leashed pets are permitted, except on the beach.

Reservations, fees: Reserve at 800/444-PARK or online at www.reserveamerica.com ($7.50 reservation fee). The fees are $16 per night, $2 per person per night for the hike-in/bike-in site, and $135 per night for group site. A senior discount is available. Open year-round.

Directions: From Highway 1 near Watsonville, take the Riverside Drive exit toward the ocean to Beach Road. Drive 3.5 miles on Beach Road to the San Andreas Road exit. Turn right on San Andreas Road and drive about three miles to the beach on the left.

Contact: Sunset State Beach, 831/763-7063; California State Parks, Santa Cruz District, 831/429-2851, fax 831/429-2876.

10 PINTO LAKE PARK

Rating: 7

near Watsonville
See map pages 660–661

Pinto Lake can be a real find. Of the seven lakes in the nine Bay Area counties that offer camping, it is the only one where the RV campsites are actually near the lake. For the few who know about it, it's an offer that can't be refused. But note that no tent camping is permitted. From winter to early summer, the Department of Fish and Game stocks the lake twice a month with rainbow trout. A 5 mph speed limit has been established for boaters, and no swimming is permitted. The leash law for dogs is strictly enforced here.

RV sites, facilities: There are 28 sites with full

CALIFORNIA

hookups (30 amps) for RVs. Drinking water, modem access, cell phone reception, and cable TV are available. A boat ramp and boat rentals are available nearby in the summer. An ATM is within one mile. Most facilities are wheelchair-accessible. Leashed pets are permitted.

Reservations, fees: Reservations are recommended. The fee is $25 per night, plus $2 for additional vehicles and $2 per pet per night.

Directions: From Santa Cruz, drive 17 miles south on Highway 1 to the exit for Watsonville/Gilroy-Highway 152. Take that exit and immediately turn left on Green Valley Road and drive 2.7 (.5 mile past Holohan intersection) to the entrance for the lake and campground.

From Monterey, drive north on Highway 1 to the Green Valley Road exit. Take that exit and turn right at the Green Valley Road and drive 2.7 miles (.5 mile past the Holohan intersection) to the entrance for the lake and campground.

Contact: Pinto Lake Park, 831/722-8129, website: www.pintolake.com.

11 McALPINE LAKE AND PARK

Rating: 5

near San Juan Bautista
See map pages 660–661

This is the only privately operated campground in the immediate region that has any spots for tenters. The two camping cabins here look like miniature log cabins, quite cute and comfortable. In addition, the park has a 40-foot-deep lake stocked with trout, bass, bluegill, crappie, and catfish, and since it's privately owned, no fishing license is required. Other highlights of the park are its proximity to Mission San Juan Bautista and the relatively short drive to the Monterey-Carmel area.

RV sites, facilities: There are 27 sites with partial hookups (20, 30, 50 amps) for RVs or tents, 14 sites with full hookups for RVs, 40 sites for tents only, and two cabins. Picnic tables and fire grills are provided. Flush toilets, showers, modem access, limited cell phone reception, an RV dump station, a coin-operated laundry, propane, and groceries are available. An ATM is within three miles. Some facilities are wheelchair-accessible. Leashed pets are permitted.

Reservations, fees: Reservations are accepted. The fee is $25–43 per night, plus $2–4 per person for more than two people and $5 per night for each additional vehicle. Major credit cards are accepted.

Directions: On U.S. 101, drive to the Highway 129 exit. Take Highway 129 west and drive 100 feet to Searle Road (frontage road). Turn left onto Searle Road and drive to the stop sign at Anzar. Turn left again on Anzar and drive under the freeway to the park entrance on the left (900 Anzar Road).

Contact: McAlpine Lake and Park, 831/623-4263, fax 831/623-4559, website: www.mcalpinelake.com.

12 CASA DE FRUTA ORCHARD RESORT

Rating: 1

near Pacheco Pass
See map pages 660–661

This 80-acre RV park has a festival-like atmosphere to it, with country music and dancing every weekend in the summer and barbecues on Sunday. Huge, but sparse, San Luis Reservoir is 20 miles to the east.

RV sites, facilities: There are 300 drive-through sites, most with partial hookups (30 amps) and some with full hookups, for RVs. Picnic tables are provided. Flush toilets, showers, an RV dump station, cable TV, satellite TV, modem access, limited cell phone reception, an ATM, a coin-operated laundry, a playground, a swimming pool, a wading pool, an outdoor dance floor, horseshoes, volleyball courts, baseball diamonds, a wine and cheese tasting room, a candy factory, a bakery, a fruit stand, a petting zoo, a 24-hour restaurant, a gift shop, and a minimart are available. Some facilities are wheelchair-accessible. Leashed pets are permitted.

Reservations, fees: Reservations are accepted. The fee is $30–32 per night, plus $2 per person per night for more than two people and $3 per pet per night. Major credit cards are accepted. Open year-round.

Directions: Drive on U.S. 101 to the junction with Highway 152 (near Gilroy). Take Highway 152 east and drive 13 miles to Highway 156. Turn left (north) on Highway 156 and drive one mile to the park entrance on the right (well signed).

CALIFORNIA

Contact: Casa de Fruta Orchard Resort, 408/842-9316, fax 831/848-3793, website: www.casadefruta.com.

13 CABANA HOLIDAY

Rating: 2

near Salinas
See map pages 660–661
If Big Sur, Monterey, and Carmel are packed, this spot provides some overflow space. It's about a half-hour drive from the Monterey area.

RV sites, facilities: There are 96 sites, including some drive-through, with partial or full hookups (30 amps) for RVs. Picnic tables are provided. Restrooms, showers, a recreation room, modem access, cell phone reception, a swimming pool (heated and open mid-May to mid-October), a playground, and a coin-operated laundry are available. An ATM is within one mile. Some facilities are wheelchair-accessible. Leashed pets are permitted.

Reservations, fees: Reservations are recommended. The fee is $35 per night. A senior discount is available. Major credit cards are accepted.

Directions: From Salinas, drive north on U.S. 101 for seven miles to Highway 156 West. Take the exit for Highway 156 West and drive over the overpass .2 mile to Prunedale North Road to the campground entrance at the intersection.

Contact: Cabana Holiday, 831/663-2886 or 800/541-0085 (reservations), fax 831/663-1660, website: www.reynoldsresorts.com.

14 MONTEREY VACATION RV PARK

Rating: 5

near San Juan Bautista
See map pages 660–661
This RV park has an ideal location for many vacationers. It's a 10-minute drive to San Juan Bautista, 30 minutes to the Monterey Bay Aquarium, and 40 minutes to Monterey's Fisherman's Wharf. It's set in an attractive spot with some trees, but the nearby attractions are what make it a clear winner. The park is well landscaped.

RV sites, facilities: There are 88 drive-through sites for RVs with full hookups (30 amps) and a few tent sites. Flush toilets, showers, a hot tub, a seasonal swimming pool, a coin-operated laun-

dry, modem access (in office), cell phone reception, and propane are available. An ATM is within one mile. Some facilities are wheelchair-accessible. Leashed pets up to 40 pounds are permitted.

Reservations, fees: Reservations are recommended for three-day holiday weekends. The fee is $29–35 per night, plus $1 per pet per night. Major credit cards are accepted.

Directions: On U.S. 101, drive toward San Juan Bautista (between Gilroy and Salinas). The park is on U.S. 101 two miles south of the Highway 156/San Juan Bautista exit at 1400 Hwy. 101.

Contact: Monterey Vacation RV Park, 831/726-9118, fax 831/726-1841.

15 MISSION FARM RV PARK

Rating: 5

near San Juan Bautista
See map pages 660–661
The primary appeal of this RV park is that it is within easy walking distance of San Juan Bautista. The park is set beside a walnut orchard.

RV sites, facilities: There 165 RV sites with full hookups (30 amps) and picnic tables. Flush toilets, showers, a barbecue area, an RV dump station, cell phone reception, a coin-operated laundry, and propane are available. An ATM is within one mile. Leashed pets are permitted; a dog run is available.

Reservations, fees: Reservations are recommended. The fee is $28–31 per night, plus $5 per night for each additional vehicle, $5 per person per night for more than two people, and $1 per pet. Major credit cards are accepted. Open year-round.

Directions: From U.S. 101, drive three miles east on Highway 156. Turn right on The Alameda and drive a block. Turn left on San Juan-Hollister Road and drive .25 mile to the campground at 400 San Juan-Hollister Road.

Contact: Mission Farm RV Park, 831/623-4456.

16 MARINA DUNES RV PARK

Rating: 5

near Monterey Bay
See map pages 660–661
This is a popular park for RV cruisers who are

touring Highway 1 and want a layover spot near Monterey. This place fills the bill, open all year and in Marina, just a short drive from the many side-trip opportunities available in Monterey and Carmel. It is set in the sand dunes, about 300 yards from the ocean.

RV sites, facilities: There are 65 sites, including 61 with full hookups, for RVs and 10 sites for tents. Picnic tables are provided. Restrooms, drinking water, showers, a laundry room, cable TV (some RV sites), modem access, a recreation room, and groceries are available. Some facilities are wheelchair-accessible. Leashed pets are permitted.

Reservations, fees: Reservations are recommended. The fee is $30–58 per night. Major credit cards are accepted.

Directions: From Highway 1 in Marina, drive to the Reservation West Road exit. Take that exit and drive a short distance to Dunes Drive. Turn right on Dunes Drive and drive to the end of the road and the park entrance on the right.

Contact: Marina Dunes RV Park, 831/384-6914, fax 831/384-0285, website: www.marinadunesrv .com.

17 HOLLISTER HILLS STATE VEHICULAR RECREATION AREA

Rating: 4

near Hollister
See map pages 660–661

This unique park was designed for off-highway-vehicle (OHV) enthusiasts. It provides 80 miles of trails for motorcycles and 40 miles of trails for four-wheel-drive vehicles. Some of the trails are accessible directly from the campground. All trails close at sunset. Note that there is no direct access to the Fremont Peak State Park, bordering directly to the west. Elevations at the park range from 800 to 2,600 feet. Visitors are advised to always call in advance because the area is sometimes closed for special events. A sidelight is that a 288-acre area is set aside for hiking and mountain biking. In addition, a self-guided natural history walk is routed into Azalea Canyon and along the San Andreas Fault.

RV sites, facilities: There are four campgrounds with a total of 125 sites for RVs or tents and group sites for up to 300 people. Picnic tables and fire rings are provided. Drinking water, flush toilets, showers, limited cell phone reception, a camp store, and an ATM are available. Leashed pets are permitted.

Reservations, fees: Reservations are not accepted. The fee is $6 per night; the group site is $6 per vehicle. A senior discount is available. Open year-round.

Directions: From Highway 156 northwest of Hollister, drive to Union Road. Turn south on Union Road and drive three miles to Cienega Road. Turn left (south) on Cienega Road and drive five miles to the park on the right.

Contact: Hollister Hills State Vehicular Recreation Area, 831/637-3874 or 831/637-8186; Pit Stop park store, 831/637-3138.

18 LAGUNA SECA RECREATION AREA

Rating: 5

near Monterey
See map pages 660–661

This campground is just minutes away from the sights in Monterey and Carmel. It is situated in oak woodlands overlooking the world-famous Laguna Seca Raceway. It is also near an OHV area.

RV sites, facilities: There are 175 sites, many with partial hookups, for RVs or tents. Picnic tables and fire grills are provided. Restrooms, showers, an RV dump station, a pond, a rifle and pistol range, a clubhouse, and group camping facilities are available. Some facilities are wheelchair-accessible. Leashed pets are permitted.

Reservations, fees: Reservations are accepted at 831/755-4899 or 888/588-2267 ($3.50 reservation fee). The fee is $18–22 per night, plus $10 per additional vehicle and $1 per pet. There is a maximum stay of two nights. Major credit cards are accepted. Open year-round.

Directions: From Monterey, drive east on Highway 68 for nine miles to the park entrance on the left.

Contact: Laguna Seca Recreation Area, 831/758-3604 or tel./fax 831/758-6818, website: www.co .monterey.ca.us/parks.

19 CARMEL BY THE RIVER RV PARK

Rating: 8

on the Carmel River
See map pages 660–661

Location, location, location. That's what vacationers want. Well, this park is set on the Carmel River, minutes away from Carmel, Cannery Row, the Monterey Bay Aquarium, golf courses, and the beach. Each RV site is separated by hedges and flowers.

RV sites, facilities: There are 35 sites with full hookups (20, 30, 50 amps) for RVs. Restrooms, showers, modem access, limited cell phone reception, cable TV, a recreational cabana, a game room with pool tables, a barbecue area, horseshoes, basketball courts, and a river beach are available. A grocery store, coin-operated laundry, and propane are nearby. An ATM is within one mile. Some facilities are wheelchair-accessible. Leashed pets are permitted.

Reservations, fees: Reservations are accepted for two or more nights. The fee is $45–50 per night, plus $1 per pet per night with a limit of three dogs. A senior discount is available. Open year-round.

Directions: In Carmel on Highway 1, drive to Carmel Valley Road. Take Carmel Valley Road southeast and drive 4.5 miles to Schulte Road. Turn right and drive to the end of the road (27680 Schulte Rd. in Carmel).

Contact: Carmel by the River RV Park, 831/624-9329, fax 831/624-8416, website: www.carmelrv.com.

20 SADDLE MOUNTAIN RECREATION PARK

Rating: 6

near the Carmel River
See map pages 660–661

This pretty park is about 100 yards from the Carmel River amid a grove of oak trees. The park offers hiking trails, and if you want to make a buyer's swing into Carmel, it's only a five-mile drive. Note: the Carmel River is reduced to a trickle most of the year.

RV sites, facilities: There are 25 sites with full hookups for RVs up to 40 feet and 25 tent sites.

Picnic tables, food lockers, and fire grills are provided. Restrooms, drinking water, flush toilets, and showers are available. A swimming pool, a playground, horseshoes, a volleyball net, a basketball court, and a game room are nearby. Some facilities are wheelchair-accessible. Leashed pets are permitted in the RV area only.

Reservations, fees: Reservations are accepted for weekends only. The fee is $30–45 per night, plus $5 per person for more than two people. Open year-round.

Directions: In Carmel on Highway 1 drive to Carmel Valley Road. Take Carmel Valley Road southeast and drive 4.5 miles to Schulte Road. Turn right and drive to the park at the end of the road.

Contact: Saddle Mountain Recreation Park, 831/624-1617, fax 831/624-4470.

21 PINNACLES CAMPGROUND

Rating: 7

near Pinnacles National Monument
See map pages 660–661

This is the only camp at the Pinnacles National Monument; a once-great hike-in site was closed by flooding. This private camp has always received a lot more use—it has more facilities, the access road is in better shape, and the campground is closer to Bear Gulch Caves, a prime destination. The jagged pinnacles for which the park was named were formed by the erosion of an ancient volcanic eruption. The Pinnacles National Monument is like a different planet. It's a 16,000-acre park with volcanic clusters and strange caves, all great for exploring. In addition, expansion is imminent. If you are planning to stay a weekend in the spring, arrive early on Friday evening to be sure you get a campsite. In the summer, beware of temperatures in the 90s and 100s. Also note that caves can be closed to access; always check with rangers. Note that a ban on wood fires is in effect. Duraflame logs are permitted as a substitute.

RV sites, facilities: There are 78 sites for RVs or tents, 36 sites with partial hookups for RVs, and 13 group sites. Picnic tables and fire grills are provided. Drinking water, flush toilets, electricity, modem access, an RV dump station, showers, a store, and a swimming pool are available.

Some facilities are wheelchair-accessible. Leashed pets are permitted, except on trails.

Reservations, fees: Reservations ($7 reservation fee) are available by phone, limited hours daily, and online at www.co.monterey.ca.us/parks; reservations are required for group sites. The fee is $7 per person per night for a family site, plus $3 for additional vehicle and a $10 leash deposit; the group site is $6 per person per night with a $60 minimum. Major credit cards are accepted. Open year-round, weather permitting.

Directions: From Hollister, drive south on Highway 25 for 32 miles to Highway 146 (signed Pinnacles). Take Highway 146 and drive 2.5 miles to the campground.

Contact: Pinnacles Campground, 831/389-4462, fax 775/258-7141, website: www.pinncamp.com.

22 BIG SUR CAMPGROUND AND CABINS

Rating: 8

on the Big Sur River

See map pages 660–661

This camp is in the redwoods near the Big Sur River. Campers can stay in the redwoods, hike on great trails through the forest at nearby state parks, or explore nearby Pfeiffer Beach. Los Padres National Forest and Ventana Wilderness in the mountains to the east provide access to remote hiking trails with ridge-top vistas. Cruising Highway 1 south to Lucia and back offers endless views of breathtaking coastal scenery.

RV sites, facilities: There are 40 sites for RVs with partial hookups (30 amps), 40 sites for RVs or tents, 13 cabins, and four tent cabins. Picnic tables and fire grills are provided. Restrooms, drinking water, flush toilets, showers, an RV dump station, an ATM, a playground, a convenience store, and a laundry room are available. Some facilities are wheelchair-accessible. Leashed pets are permitted at campsites but not in cabins.

Reservations, fees: Reservations are recommended. The fee is $26–29 per night, plus $4 per person for more than two people, $8 per night for each additional vehicle, and $4 per pet per night. Major credit cards are accepted. Open year-round.

Directions: From Carmel, drive 27 miles south on Highway 1 to the campground on the right side of the road (two miles north of the state park).

Contact: Big Sur Campground and Cabins, 831/667-2322, fax 831/667-0456, website: www.bigsur.com.

23 PFEIFFER BIG SUR STATE PARK

Rating: 10

in Big Sur

See map pages 660–661

This stretch of coast is one of the most beautiful anywhere. This is one of the most popular state parks in California, and it's easy to see why. You can have it all: fantastic coastal vistas along Highway 1, redwood forests and waterfalls in the Julia Pfeiffer Burns State Park (11.5 miles to the south), expansive beaches with sea otters playing on the edge of kelp beds in the Andrew Molera State Park (4.5 miles north), great restaurants such as Ventana Inn (a few miles south), and private, patrolled sites. Reservations are a necessity. Some campsites in this park are set along the Big Sur River. The park features 800 acres of redwoods, conifers, oaks, sycamores, cottonwoods, maples, alders, and willows, plus open meadows—just about everything, in other words. Wildlife includes wild boar, raccoons, skunk, and many birds, among them water ouzels and belted kingfishers. A number of loop trails provide spectacular views of the Pacific Ocean and the Big Sur Gorge. Big Sur Lodge is within the park.

RV sites, facilities: There are 218 sites for RVs up to 32 feet or tents, two bike-in sites, and two group sites for up to 35 people. Picnic tables and fire grills are provided. Restrooms, drinking water, showers, limited cell phone reception, and flush toilets are available. Groceries, an ATM, a café, a restaurant, and propane are nearby. Some facilities are wheelchair-accessible. Leashed pets are permitted in the campground only.

Reservations, fees: Reserve at 800/444-PARK or online at www.reserveamerica.com ($7.50 reservation fee). The fees are $16–20 per night, $45 per night for group sites, and $2 per person per night for bike-in sites, plus a $5 day-use fee. A senior discount is available. Open year-round, weather permitting.

Directions: From Carmel, drive 26 miles south

on Highway 1 to the park on the left (east side of highway).

Contact: Pfeiffer Big Sur State Park, 831/667-2315, fax 831/667-2886; California State Parks, Monterey District, 831/649-2836.

24 RIVERSIDE CAMPGROUND & CABINS

Rating: 8

on the Big Sur River

See map pages 660–661

This is one in a series of privately operated camps designed for Highway 1 cruisers touring the Big Sur area. This camp is set amid redwoods. Side trips include expansive beaches with sea otters playing on the edge of kelp beds (Andrew Molera State Park), redwood forests and waterfalls (Julia Pfeiffer Burns State Park), and several quality restaurants, including Nepenthe for those on a budget and the Ventana Inn for those who can light cigars with $100 bills.

RV sites, facilities: There are 45 sites, including 16 with partial hookups (20 amps), for RVs or tents. Picnic tables and fire grills are provided. Restrooms, coin-operated showers, limited cell phone reception, and a pay phone are available. An ATM is within one mile. Leashed pets are permitted.

Reservations, fees: Reservations are recommended ($4 reservation fee). The fee is $28–32 per night, plus $3 per person per night for more than two people, $6 per night for each additional vehicle, and $3 per per per night. Major credit cards are accepted. Open April through October.

Directions: From Carmel, drive 25 miles south on Highway 1 to the campground on the right.

Contact: Riverside Campground & Cabins, tel./fax 831/667-2414, website: www.riversidecampground.com.

25 FERNWOOD PARK

Rating: 7

on the Big Sur River

See map pages 660–661

This RV park is on the banks of the Big Sur River in the redwoods of the beautiful Big Sur coast.

Many of the sites are set along the river. A highlight here is live music on Friday and Saturday nights in season. You can crown your trip with a dinner at the Ventana Inn (first-class—bring your bank with you).

RV sites, facilities: There are 28 sites with partial hookups (30 amps) for RVs and 38 sites for tents only. Fire grills and picnic tables are provided. Restrooms with showers, a grocery store, limited cell phone reception, a restaurant, and a bar are available. An ATM is within one mile. Leashed pets are permitted.

Reservations, fees: Reservations are accepted. The fee is $24–27 per night, plus $4 per person for more than two people (maximum of six), $5 per night for each additional vehicle, and $3 per pet per night. Group rates are available. Major credit cards are accepted. Open year-round.

Directions: From Carmel, drive 26 miles south on Highway 1 to the campground on the right.

Contact: Fernwood Park, 831/667-2422, fax 831/667-2663.

26 VENTANA CAMPGROUNDS

Rating: 10

in Big Sur

See map pages 660–661

This rustic camp has wooded sites and is in an ideal location for many. The campsites are private and extremely beautiful, set in the redwoods with a small creek running through camp, with a few small waterfalls nearby. Premium side trips are available, highlighted by the beautiful beach at Andrew Molera State Park (a one-mile hike is necessary), the majestic redwoods, a creek hike, and a bluff-top waterfall in Julia Pfeiffer Burns State Park.

RV sites, facilities: There are 80 sites for self-contained RVs up to 22 feet or tents. Picnic tables and fire grills are provided. A restroom, drinking water, showers, and flush toilets are available. A small store is nearby with firewood and ice. Some facilities are wheelchair-accessible. Leashed pets are permitted.

Reservations, fees: Reservations are accepted. The fee is $25–35 per night, plus $4 per person per night for more than two people and $5 per night for each additional vehicle. There is a three-day minimum stay on holidays. Major credit cards are accepted. Open year-round; call to confirm, may be closed in winter.

Directions: From Carmel, drive 28 miles south on Highway 1 to Big Sur and the campground entrance on the left.

Contact: Ventana Campgrounds, 831/667-2712, website: www.ventanawildernesscampground.com.

27 SAN LORENZO COUNTY PARK

Rating: 3

in King City

See map pages 660–661

A lot of folks cruising up and down the state on U.S. 101 can underestimate their travel time and find themselves caught out near King City, a small city about midpoint between Northern and Southern California. Well, don't sweat it, because San Lorenzo County Park offers a spot to overnight. It's near the Salinas River, which isn't exactly the Mississippi, but it'll do. A museum and visitors center capture the rural agricultural life of the valley. The park covers 200 acres, featuring a playground and ball fields.

RV sites, facilities: There are 99 sites, including 65 drive-through, with partial hookups for RVs or tents. Picnic tables and fire grills are provided. An RV dump station, restrooms, flush toilets, showers, and laundry facilities are available. Leashed pets are permitted.

Reservations, fees: Reservations are accepted at 888/588-2267. The fee is $16–21 per night, plus $2 per pet per night. Group rates are available. Open year-round.

Directions: From King City on U.S. 101, turn left at the Broadway exit and drive to the park at 1160 Broadway.

Contact: San Lorenzo County Park, 831/385-5964.

28 ARROYO SECO

Rating: 8

along Arroyo Seco River in Los Padres National Forest

See map pages 660–661

This pretty spot near the Arroyo Seco River is just outside the northern border of the Ventana

Wilderness. The elevation is 900 feet. Arroyo Seco Group Camp is available to keep the pressure off this campground.

RV sites, facilities: There are 48 sites for RVs up to 26 feet or tents, plus a group site for 25 to 50 people. Picnic tables and fire grills are provided. Restrooms, drinking water, flush toilets, and coin-operated showers are available. Leashed pets are permitted.

Reservations, fees: Reservations are not accepted for individual sites. The fee is $16 per night, plus $4 for each additional vehicle. Reserve the group site at 877/444-6777 ($9 reservation fee) or online at www.reserveusa.com; the group fee is $50 per night. A senior discount is available. Open year-round.

Directions: Drive on U.S. 101 to the town of Greenfield and Greenfield–Arroyo Seco Road. Turn west on Greenfield–Arroyo Seco Road/County Roads G16 and 3050 and drive 19 miles to the camp at the end of the road.

Contact: Los Padres National Forest, Monterey Ranger District, 831/385-5434, fax 831/385-0628.

29 KIRK CREEK

Rating: 8

near the Pacific Ocean in Los Padres National Forest

See map pages 660–661

This pretty camp is set along Kirk Creek as it empties into the Pacific Ocean. There is beach access by a footpath. Another trail from camp branches north through the Ventana Wilderness, which is sprinkled with little-used, hike-in, backcountry campsites. For gorgeous scenery without all the work, a quaint little café in Lucia provides open-air dining on a cliff-top deck, with a dramatic sweeping lookout over the coast.

RV sites, facilities: There are 33 sites for RVs up to 30 feet or tents. Picnic tables and fire grills are provided. Drinking water and flush toilets are available. Leashed pets are permitted.

Reservations, fees: Reservations are not accepted. The fees are $18 per night and $5 per night for bicyclists. A senior discount is available. Open year-round.

Directions: From Monterey, drive south on Highway 1 to Lucia. From Lucia, continue south on

CALIFORNIA

Highway 1 for four miles to the campground on the right.

Contact: Los Padres National Forest, Monterey Ranger District, 831/385-5434, fax 831/385-0628; Parks Management Company, 805/434-1996, fax 805/434-1986.

30 LIMEKILN STATE PARK

Rating: 9

on the Pacific Ocean

See map pages 660–661

Limekiln State Park provides breathtaking views of the Big Sur Coast. This camp provides a great layover spot in the Big Sur area of Highway 1, with drive-in campsites set up both near the beach and the redwoods—take your pick. Several hiking trails are nearby, including one that is routed past some historic lime kilns, which were used in the late 1800s to make cement and bricks. Want more? A short rock hop on a spur trail (just off the main trail) leads to dramatic 100-foot Limekiln Falls, a gorgeous waterfall. This camp was originally called Limekiln Beach Redwoods and was privately operated. It became a state park in 1995. One remaining problem: parking is limited.

RV sites, facilities: There are 18 sites for RVs up to 24 feet or tents and trailers up to 15 feet, and 15 sites for tents. Picnic tables and fire grills are provided. Restrooms, drinking water, showers, flush toilets, and firewood are available. Leashed pets are allowed, except on trails.

Reservations, fees: Make reservations ($7.50 reservation fee) at 800/444-PARK or online at www .reserveamerica.com. The fee is $12 per night. A senior discount is available. Major credit cards are accepted. Open year-round.

Directions: From Big Sur, drive south on Highway 1 for 35 miles (past Lucia) to the park on the left.

Contact: Limekiln State Park, 831/667-2403; California State Parks, Monterey District, 831/649-2836.

31 PONDEROSA

Rating: 4

in Los Padres National Forest

See map pages 660–661

As soon as you turn off Highway 1, you leave behind the crowds and enter a land that is largely unknown to people. This camp is set at 1,500 feet elevation in Los Padres National Forest, not far from the border of the Ventana Wilderness (good hiking and backpacking) and the Hunter Liggett Military Reservation (wild pig hunting is allowed there with a permit). It is one in a series of small camps on Nacimiento-Ferguson Road.

RV sites, facilities: There are 23 sites for RVs up to 32 feet or tents. Picnic tables and fire grills are provided. Vault toilets are available. Drinking water is available March through November. Leashed pets are permitted.

Reservations, fees: Reservations are not accepted. The fee is $15 per night. A senior discount is available. Open year-round.

Directions: From Monterey, drive south on Highway 1 to Lucia. From Lucia, continue south on Highway 1 for four miles to Nacimiento-Ferguson Road. Turn left on Nacimiento-Ferguson Road and drive about 10 miles to the campground on the right.

Contact: Los Padres National Forest, Monterey Ranger District, 831/385-5434, fax 831/385-0628; Parks Management Company, 805/434-1996, fax 805/434-1986, website: www.campone.com.

32 PLASKETT CREEK

Rating: 8

overlooking the Pacific Ocean in Los Padres National Forest

See map pages 660–661

This is a premium coastal camp for Highway 1 cruisers, set at an elevation of just 100 feet along little Plaskett Creek above the Pacific Ocean. The campground provides access to Sand Dollar Beach. It gets overlooked by many for two reasons: it is not listed with a reservation service, and it is farther south of Big Sur than most are willing to drive. A little café in Lucia provides

CALIFORNIA

open-air dining with a dramatic lookout over the coast.

RV sites, facilities: There are 45 sites for RVs up to 26 feet or tents. Picnic tables and fire grills are provided. Drinking water, flush toilets, and firewood are available. Leashed pets are permitted.

Reservations, fees: Reservations are not accepted. The fees are $18 per night and $5 for bicyclists. A senior discount is available. Open year-round.

Directions: From Monterey, drive south on Highway 1 to Lucia. From Lucia, continue south on Highway 1 for 9.5 miles to the campground on the left.

Contact: Los Padres National Forest, Monterey Ranger District, 831/385-5434, fax 831/385-0628; Parks Management Company, 805/434-1996, fax 805/434-1986, website: www.campone.com.

California

Chapter 21
San Joaquin Valley

CALIFORNIA

Mono Lake

CA | NV

see Yosemite and Mammoth Lakes
pages 700–701

see Sequoia and Kings Canyon
pages 732–733

Kings   Canyon   National   Park

Sequoia

Giant Sequoia Nat'l Mon.

Lakeshore

Pine Flat Reservoir

Yosemite   National   Park

168

31 Millerton Lake

Fresno

180

99

30

29 Eastman Lake

Hensley Lake

Madera

32

145

Kings

River

see Sacramento and
Gold Country
pages 564–565

Sonora

4

49

20

25 **19** Lake McClure

18

17 **21**

10 **16**

Don Pedro Reservoir

140

Joaquin

33

San

59

Merced

152

New Melones Res.

8

7 Lake Tulloch

9

5 **6**

120

108

15

14

24

140

152

33

Camanche Reservoir

Modesto

23

Santa Nella

28

13

132

Manteca

5

Stockton

3

4

11 **12**

22

San Luis Reservoir

26 **27**

205

580

5

152

156

Hollister

25

1

2

see Monterey
and Big Sur
pages 660–661

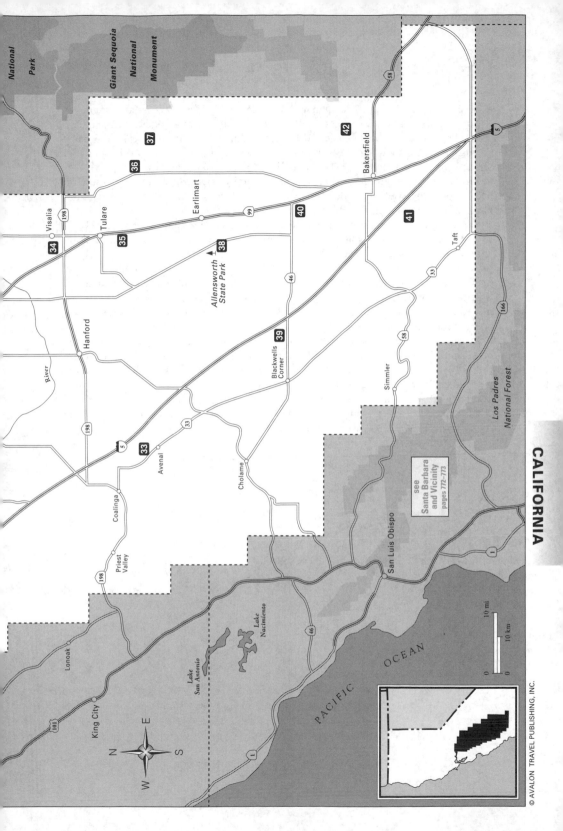

National
Park

Giant Sequoia
National
Monument

CALIFORNIA

58

5

37

42

Bakersfield

36

99

Earlimart

40

41

Visalia

198

Tulare

34

35

38

Taft

Allensworth
State Park

46

33

River

Hanford

198

39

Blackwells
Corner

58

Simmler

166

5

33

Los Padres
National Forest

Avenal

Coalinga

33

Cholame

see
Santa Barbara
and Vicinity
pages 772–773

Priest
Valley

198

San Luis Obispo

1

Lonoak

Lake
San Antonio

Lake
Nacimiento

46

10 mi

10 km

101

King City

PACIFIC OCEAN

1

N
W E
S

0
0

© AVALON TRAVEL PUBLISHING, INC.

Chapter 21—San Joaquin Valley

This section of the San Joaquin Valley is noted for its searing weather all summer long. But that is also when the lakes in the foothills become something like a Garden of Eden for boating and water sports enthusiasts. The region also offers many settings in the Sierra foothills, which can serve as launch points for short drives into the alpine beauty of Yosemite, Sequoia, and Kings Canyon National Parks.

Most of the campgrounds in this region are family oriented. Many of them are on access roads to Yosemite. A bonus is that most have lower prices than their counterparts in the park, and as I said, are more hospitable to children.

The lakes are the primary recreation attraction, with the refreshing, clean water revered as a tonic against the valley heat all summer long. When viewed from the air, the closeness of these lakes to the Sierra Nevada mountain range is surprising to many. Their proximity to the high country results in cool, high-quality water—the product of snowmelt sent down river canyons on the western slope. Some of these lakes are among the best around for water-skiing and powerboat recreation, including Lake Don Pedro east of Modesto, Bass Lake near Oakhurst, Lake McClure near Merced, Pine Flat Reservoir east of Fresno, and Lake Kaweah near Visalia.

In addition, Lake Don Pedro, Pine Flat Reservoir, and Lake Kaweah are among the best fishing lakes in the entire Central Valley; some anglers rate Don Pedro as the number-one all-around fishing lake in the state. The nearby Sierra rivers that feed these lakes (and others) also offer the opportunity to fly-fish for trout. In particular, the Kaweah and Kings Rivers boast many miles of ideal pocket water for fly fishers. Although the trout on these streams are only occasionally large, the catch rates are often high and the rock-strewn beauty of the river canyons is exceptional.

1 WESTGATE LANDING COUNTY PARK

Rating: 6

in the San Joaquin River Delta near Stockton
See map pages 678–679

Summer temperatures typically reach the high 90s and low 100s here, and this county park provides a little shade and boating access to the South Fork Mokelumne River. On hot summer nights, some campers will stay up late and night fish for catfish. Between storms in winter, the area typically gets smothered in dense fog. For RV drivers, the sites are not drive-through but semicircles, which work nearly as well.

RV sites, facilities: There are 14 sites for RVs up to 32 feet or tents. Picnic tables and barbecues are provided. Drinking water and flush toilets are available. Groceries and propane are nearby. There are 24 boat slips available. Leashed pets are permitted.

Reservations, fees: Reservations are accepted with a $10 reservation fee at least three weeks in advance. Less than three weeks in advance, sites are first-come, first-served. The fee is $10 per night, plus $5 per night for each additional vehicle, $10 for a boat slip, and $2 per pet per night. Open year-round.

Directions: On I-5, drive to Lodi and Highway 12. Take Highway 12 west and drive about five miles to Glasscock Road. Turn right and drive about a mile to the park.

Contact: San Joaquin County Parks Department, 209/953-8800.

2 TOWER PARK MARINA AND RESORT

Rating: 6

near Stockton
See map pages 678–679

This huge resort is ideal for boat-in campers who desire a full-facility marina. The camp is set on Little Potato Slough near the Mokelumne River. In the summer, this is a popular water-skiing area. Some hot weekends are like a continuous party. There are no drive-through sites, but access for large RVs is still easy when the adjacent campsite is not taken.

RV sites, facilities: There are 400 sites, most with full hookups (30, 50 amps), for RVs or tents and park-model cabins. Picnic tables and barbecues are provided. Restrooms, showers, an RV dump station, a pavilion, boat rentals, overnight boat slips, a double boat launch, a playground, modem access, limited cell phone reception, an ATM, a restaurant, a bar and nightclub, a seasonal swimming pool, a hot tub, volleyball, horseshoes, baseball, a coin-operated laundry, a gift shop, a store, ice, and propane are available. Some facilities are wheelchair-accessible. Leashed pets are permitted.

Reservations, fees: Reservations are recommended. The fee is $19–27 per night, with a maximum of six people per site, plus $2 per pet per night. Major credit cards are accepted. Open year-round. No tent camping in winter.

Directions: On I-5, drive to Lodi and Highway 12. Take Highway 12 west and drive about five miles to Tower Park Way (before first bridge). Turn left and drive a short distance to the park.

Contact: Tower Park Marina and Resort, 209/369-1041, fax 209/943-5656, website: www.westrec.com.

3 STOCKTON-LODI KOA

Rating: 1

in Lodi
See map pages 678–679

This KOA camp is in the heart of the San Joaquin Valley. The proximity to I-5 and Highway 99 makes it work for long-distance vacationers looking for a spot to park the rig for the night. The San Joaquin Delta is 15 miles to the west, with best access provided off Highway 12 to Isleton and Rio Vista; it's also a pretty drive.

RV sites, facilities: There are 102 sites, most drive-through and many with full hookups (30, 50 amps), for RVs or tents and two cabins. Picnic tables are provided. Restrooms, showers, an RV dump station, a store, propane, a coin-operated laundry, modem access, cell phone reception, a recreation room, a seasonal swimming pool, and a playground are available. An ATM is within one mile. Some facilities are wheelchair-accessible. Leashed pets are permitted.

Reservations, fees: Reservations are accepted at 800/562-1229. The fee is $27–44 per night. Major credit cards are accepted. Open year-round.

Directions: On I-5, drive to Eight Mile Road (five miles north of Stockton). Turn east and drive five miles to the campground at 2851 E. Eight Mile Road.

Contact: Stockton-Lodi KOA, 209/941-2573 (from Stockton), 209/334-0309 (from Lodi), or tel./fax 209/941-2573.

4 DOS REIS COUNTY PARK

Rating: 6

on the San Joaquin River near Stockton
See map pages 678–679

This is a 90-acre county park that has a quarter mile of San Joaquin River frontage, a boat ramp, and nearby access to the eastern Delta near Stockton. The sun gets scalding hot here in the summer, branding everything in sight. That's why boaters make quick work of getting in the water, then cooling off with water sports. In the winter, this area often has zero visibility from tule fog.

RV sites, facilities: There are 26 sites with full hookups for RVs and tents. Picnic tables and fire grills are provided. Restrooms, showers, and a boat ramp are available. A store, a coin-operated laundry, and propane are within three miles. Leashed pets are permitted with a limit of two.

Reservations, fees: Reservations are accepted up to four weeks in advance. The fee is $15 per night, plus $5 per night per additional vehicle and $1 per pet per night. Open year-round.

Directions: Drive on I-5 to Stockton and the Lathrop exit. Turn north on Lathrop and drive 1.5 blocks to Manthy Road. Turn north and drive .5 mile to Dos Rios Road. Turn left and drive to the campground at the end of the road.

Contact: San Joaquin County Parks Department, 209/953-8800, fax 209/331-2012, website: www.co .san-joaquin.ca.us/parks.

5 WOODWARD RESERVOIR COUNTY PARK

Rating: 7

near Oakdale
See map pages 678–679

Woodward Reservoir is a large lake covering 2,900 acres with 23 miles of shoreline, set in the rolling foothills just north of Oakdale. It is a good lake for both water-skiing and bass fishing, with minimal conflict between the two sports. Alas, just when peace was at hand, rentals of personal watercraft are now available here. Two large coves on the south and east ends of the lake, as well as the area behind Whale Island, are for low-speed boats only. That makes for good fishing, while the speedboats have the main lake body to let her rip.

RV sites, facilities: There are 155 sites, 115 with partial hookups (20, 30 amps) and 40 with full hookups, for RVs or tents. Picnic tables and fire grills are provided. Drinking water, flush toilets, showers, an RV dump station, three boat ramps, mooring, dry boat storage, limited cell phone reception, a store, an ATM, bait, fishing licenses, and some equestrian facilities are available. Some facilities are wheelchair-accessible. Leashed pets are permitted.

Reservations, fees: Reservations are not accepted. The fee is $14–20 per night, plus a $7 day-use fee, $6 boat launch fee, and $2 pet fee. A senior discount is available. Major credit cards are accepted. Open year-round.

Directions: Drive on Highway 120 to Oakdale (the road becomes Highway 108/120) and the junction with County Road J14/26 Mile Road. Turn left on 26 Mile Road and drive four miles to the park entrance at Woodward Reservoir (14528 26 Mile Road).

Contact: Woodward Reservoir County Park, 209/847-3304 or 209/525-6750, website: www.co .stanislaus.ca.us.

6 KNIGHTS FERRY RESORT

Rating: 7

on the Stanislaus River
See map pages 678–679

This is a privately run campground in the small historic town of Knights Ferry. The campground has a good number of trees. A nice touch is a restaurant overlooking the Stanislaus River. Side trips include tours of the covered bridge ("the longest west of the Mississippi") and several historic buildings and homes, all within walking distance of the park. River access and hiking trails are available at the east end of town. Raft and canoe rentals are also available nearby.

RV sites, facilities: There are 21 sites for RVs or tents. A community fire pit, restrooms, showers, and a restaurant are available. Some facilities are wheelchair-accessible. No pets are permitted.

Reservations, fees: Reservations are accepted with a deposit. The fee is $20–23 per night, with a two-night minimum stay on weekends and a three-night minimum on holidays. Major credit cards are accepted. Open year-round.

Directions: From Manteca, drive east on Highway 120 to Oakdale (the road becomes Highway 108/120). Continue east on Highway 108 for 12 miles to Knight's Ferry and Kennedy Road. Turn left and drive to a bridge, cross the bridge, and continue a short distance to Sonora Road/Main Street. Turn left and drive to the campground entrance at the Knights Ferry Restaurant.

Contact: Knights Ferry Resort, 209/881-3349.

7 GLORY HOLE

Rating: 7

at New Melones Reservoir
See map pages 678–679

Glory Hole encompasses both Big Oak and Ironhorse Campgrounds. This is one of two major recreation areas on New Melones Reservoir in the Sierra Nevada foothills, a popular spot with a boat ramp nearby for access to outstanding water-skiing and fishing. (See the following entry for Tuttletown Recreation Area for more information.) Some may remember a baseball field that was once here. No more. It was reconstructed into an amphitheater where campfire programs are often available in summer.

RV sites, facilities: Big Oak has 55 sites for RVs or tents, Ironhorse has 89 sites for RVs or tents; 20 sites are for tents only. Picnic tables and fire grills are provided. Drinking water, flush toilets, showers, a marina, boat rentals, an amphitheater, a playground, and horseshoes are available. Some facilities are wheelchair-accessible. Leashed pets are permitted.

Reservations, fees: Reservations are not accepted. The fee is $14 per night. A senior discount is available. Open year-round.

Directions: From Sonora, drive north on High-

way 49 for about 15 miles (Glory Hole Market will be on the left side of the road) to Glory Hole Road. Turn left and drive five miles to the campground, with sites on both sides of the road.

Contact: U.S. Department of Reclamation, 209/536-9094, fax 209/536-9652.

8 TUTTLETOWN RECREATION AREA

Rating: 7

at New Melones Reservoir
See map pages 678–679

Here is a mammoth camping area set on the giant New Melones Reservoir in the Sierra Nevada foothills, a beautiful sight when the lake is full. Tuttletown encompasses three campgrounds (Acorn, Manzanita, and Chamise) and two group camping areas (Oak Knoll and Fiddleneck). New Melones is a huge reservoir that covers 12,250 acres and offers 100 miles of shoreline and good fishing. Water-skiing is permitted in specified areas; a boat ramp is near camp. Although the lake's main body is huge, the better fishing is well up the lake's Stanislaus River arm (for trout) and in its coves (for bass and bluegill), where submerged trees provide perfect aquatic habitat. Trolling for kokanee salmon has also become popular. The lake level often drops dramatically in the fall.

RV sites, facilities: At Acorn there are 69 sites for RVs or tents, at Chamise there are 36 sites for RVs or tents, and at Manzanita there are 55 sites for RVs or tents and 13 walk-in tent sites. Oak Knoll group site holds up to 80 people, and Fiddleneck group site up to 60 people. Picnic tables and fire grills are provided. Drinking water, flush toilets, an RV dump station, showers, a playground, and a boat ramp are available. Some facilities are wheelchair-accessible. Leashed pets are permitted.

Reservations, fees: Reservations are not accepted. The fee is $84–140 per night. A senior discount is available. Open year-round.

Directions: From Sonora, drive north on Highway 49 to Reynolds Ferry Road. Turn left and drive about two miles to the entrance road to the campgrounds.

Contact: U.S. Department of Reclamation, 209/536-9094, fax 209/536-9652.

CALIFORNIA

9 LAKE TULLOCH RV CAMP AND MARINA

Rating: 8

on the south shore of Lake Tulloch
See map pages 678–679

This camp features tons of waterfront on Lake Tulloch, including 20 RV sites with partial hookups, a dispersed tent area, and cabins with direct beach access. Unlike so many reservoirs in the foothill country, this one is nearly always full of water. In addition, it is one of the rare places where fishermen and water-skiers live in harmony. That is due to the many coves and a six-mile-long arm with an enforced 5 mph speed limit. It's a big lake, shaped like a giant X with extended lake arms adding up to 55 miles of shoreline. The campground features mature oak trees that provide shade to most of the developed sites. A secret at Tulloch is that fishing is also good for crawdads. The elevation is 500 feet.

RV sites, facilities: There are 130 sites, including 51 with full hookups (20, 30, 50 amps) and boat sites, 45 sites with partial hookups for RVs or tents, a large area for lakefront tent camping and self-contained RVs, and 10 waterfront cabins. Picnic tables and fire grills are provided. Drinking water, flush toilets, showers, a laundry room, a store, an RV dump station, propane, a playground, a restaurant, volleyball, limited cell phone reception, horseshoes, tetherball, Ping-Pong, a marina, boat and personal watercraft rentals, a boat launch, and a boat ramp are available. An ATM is nearby. Some facilities are wheelchair-accessible, including three cabins. Leashed pets are permitted.

Reservations, fees: Reservations are accepted. The fee is $20–30 per night. Group sites and rates are available. There is no boat berth charge for campers. Major credit cards are accepted. Open year-round.

Directions: From Manteca, drive east on Highway 120 (it becomes Highway 108/120) to Oakdale. Continue east for 13 miles to Tulloch Road on the left. Turn left and drive 4.6 miles to the campground entrance and gatehouse at the south shore of Lake Tulloch.

Contact: Lake Tulloch RV Camp and Marina, 14448 Tulloch Dam Rd., Jamestown, CA 95327, 209/881-0107, website: www.laketullochcampground.com.

10 MOCCASIN POINT

Rating: 7

at Don Pedro Reservoir
See map pages 678–679

This camp is at the north end of Don Pedro Reservoir, adjacent to a boat ramp. Moccasin Point juts well into the lake, directly across from where the major Tuolumne River arm enters the lake. Don Pedro is a giant lake, with nearly 13,000 surface acres and 160 miles of shoreline, but it is subject to drawdowns from midsummer through early fall. At different times, fishing is excellent for salmon, trout, or bass. Houseboating and boat-in camping provide options.

RV sites, facilities: There are 15 sites with full hookups (20, 30 amps) for RVs and 65 sites for tents. Picnic tables, food lockers, and barbecue units are provided at all sites. Ground fires are prohibited. Drinking water, restrooms, showers, a store, an RV dump station, propane, ice, a snack bar, an ATM, limited cell phone reception, a boat ramp, motorboat and houseboat rentals, fuel, moorings, and bait and tackle are available. Some facilities are wheelchair-accessible. No pets are permitted.

Reservations, fees: Reservations are accepted. The fee is $17–25 per night, plus $5 per night for each additional vehicle. Major credit cards are accepted. Open year-round.

Directions: From Manteca, drive east on Highway 120 (it becomes Highway 108/120) for 30 miles to the Highway 120/Yosemite exit. Bear right on Highway 120 and drive 11 miles to Jacksonville Road. Turn left on Jacksonville Road and drive a short distance to the campground on the right.

Contact: Moccasin Point, 209/852-2396, website: www.donpedrolake.com.

11 OAKWOOD LAKE RESORT & MANTECA WATERSLIDES

Rating: 2

near Stockton
See map pages 678–679

This is a huge, privately operated "water theme" park that covers 375 acres and offers a wide array of water-related recreation. It is a great place for families to cool off and have fun on hot summer days, with youngsters lining up for trips down the water slides.

RV sites, facilities: There are 196 sites with full hookups (30, 50 amps) for RVs, 111 sites for tents, and 74 sites with partial hookups for RVs or tents. Picnic tables are provided. Restrooms, showers, an RV dump station, a store, a coin-operated laundry, propane, limited cell phone reception, an ATM, a swimming lagoon, water slides, organized activities, and a stocked 75-acre lake are available. The facilities are wheelchair-accessible. Leashed pets are permitted.

Reservations, fees: Reservations are accepted at 209/239-2500, ext. 308, 301, or 313. The fee is $29–33 per night, plus $16 per person per night for more than four people and $3 per pet per night. A senior discount is available. Open year-round.

Directions: Drive on Highway 120 to Airport Way (two miles east of Manteca). Turn south on Airport Way and drive .5 mile to Woodward Way. Turn right and drive two miles to the park entrance.

Contact: Oakwood Lake Resort, 209/239-9566, fax 209/239-2060, website: www.oakwoodlake.com.

12 ORCHARD RV PARK

Rating: 5

near Stockton
See map pages 678–679

The huge swimming pool and water slides here make this a popular campground for families. Temperatures in the 100-degree range in the summer keep both in constant use. This privately operated park is set up primarily for RV owners. Its location near I-5 makes it a winner for many of them.

RV sites, facilities: There are 88 drive-through RV sites with full hookups (30 amps) and 12 tent sites. Picnic tables and fire grills are provided. Restrooms, showers, a laundry room, an RV dump station, cell phone reception, a seasonal swimming pool, propane, ice, and horseshoes are available. A restaurant is next door. A store, post office, and weekend flea market are nearby. Some

facilities are wheelchair-accessible. Leashed pets are permitted with a two-dog limit.

Reservations, fees: Reservations are accepted. The fee is $22 per night. A senior discount is available. Open year-round.

Directions: Drive on I-5 to Vernalis and Highway 132. Turn east on Highway 132 and drive three miles to the signed campground entrance at 2701 E. Hwy. 132.

Contact: Orchard RV Park, 209/836-2090.

13 CASWELL MEMORIAL STATE PARK

Rating: 7

on the Stanislaus River near Stockton
See map pages 678–679

Caswell Memorial State Park features shoreline frontage along the Stanislaus River, plus an additional 250 acres of parkland. The Stanislaus provides shoreline fishing for catfish on summer nights. Bass and crappie are also occasionally caught. Other recreation options here include a visitors center, an interpretive nature trail, and swimming. Bird-watching is popular; look for red-shouldered and red-tail hawks. During warm months, bring mosquito repellent.

RV sites, facilities: There are 62 sites for RVs up to 24 feet or tents and one group site for up to 50 people. Picnic tables, food lockers, and fire grills are provided. Drinking water, flush toilets, showers, a pay phone, firewood, limited cell phone reception, a swimming beach, and nature trails are available. An ATM is within one mile. Weekend interpretive programs and Junior Ranger programs are available in the summer. Some facilities are wheelchair-accessible. Leashed pets are permitted.

Reservations, fees: Reservations are accepted at 800/444-PARK or online at www.reserveamerica.com. The fee is $14 per night; groups with up to 12 vehicles are $67 per night. A senior discount is available. Open year-round.

Directions: Drive on Highway 99 to Austin Road (1.5 miles south of Manteca). Turn south on Austin Road and drive four miles to the park entrance at the end of the road.

Contact: Caswell Memorial State Park, 209/599-3810; California State Parks, Four Rivers District, 209/826-1197, fax 209/826-0284.

CALIFORNIA

14 MODESTO RESERVOIR REGIONAL PARK

Rating: 7

on Modesto Reservoir
See map pages 678–679

Modesto Reservoir is not well known, but it is a surprisingly big lake, at 2,700 acres with 31 miles of shoreline, set in the hot foothill country. It is one of the first recreation lakes in the Central Valley to advertise "MTBE-free waters." To keep it that way, boaters must buy gas that does not contain MTBE. Some gas stations provide gas that does not contain MBTE. You must show proof that the gas in your boat comes from such a station. Water-skiing is excellent in the main lake body. Anglers head to the southern shore of the lake, which is loaded with submerged trees and coves and is also protected by a 5 mph speed limit. Fishing for bass is good, though the fish are often small.

RV sites, facilities: There are 150 sites with full hookups (20, 30 amps) for RVs and 38 tent sites. Picnic tables and fire grills are provided. Drinking water, flush toilets, an RV dump station, showers, limited cell phone reception, an ATM, two boat ramps, a marina, a store, and propane are available. No gas cans are allowed. Some facilities are wheelchair-accessible. No pets are allowed.

Reservations, fees: Reservations are not accepted. The fee is $12–16 per night, plus $2 per vehicle on holidays. A senior discount is available in winter. Open year-round.

Directions: From Modesto, drive east on Highway 132 for 16 miles past Waterford to Reservoir Road. Turn left and drive to the campground at 18143 Reservoir Road.

Contact: Modesto Reservoir Regional Park, 209/874-9540, fax 209/874-4513, website: www.co.stanislaus.ca.us.

15 TURLOCK LAKE STATE RECREATION AREA

Rating: 6

east of Modesto
See map pages 678–679

This campground is on the shady south shore of the Tuolumne River, about one mile from Turlock Lake. Turlock Lake warms to 65 to 74°F in the summer, cooler than many Central Valley reservoirs, since the water entering this lake is released from the bottom of Don Pedro Reservoir. It often seems just right for boating and all water sports on hot summer days. The lake covers 3,500 surface acres and offers 26 miles of shoreline. A boat ramp is available near the camp, making it ideal for boaters/campers. Bass fishing is fair in the summer. In the late winter and spring, the lake is quite cold, fed by snowmelt from the Tuolumne River. Trout fishing is good year-round as a result. The elevation is 250 feet. The park is bordered by ranches, orchards, and mining tailings along the river.

RV sites, facilities: There are 48 sites for RVs up to 27 feet or tents, 15 sites for tents, and one hike-in/bike-in site. Picnic tables, fire grills, and food lockers are provided. Drinking water, flush toilets, coin-operated showers, a swimming beach, and a boat ramp are available. The boat facilities are wheelchair-accessible. Leashed pets are permitted.

Reservations, fees: Reservations are accepted with a $7.50 reservation fee at 800/444-PARK (800/444-7275) or online at www.reserveamerica.com. The fees are $12 per night and $1 for the hike-in/bike-in site. A senior discount is available. Open year-round.

Directions: From Modesto, drive east on Highway 132 for 14 miles to Waterford, then continue eight miles on Highway 132 to Roberts Ferry Road. Turn right and drive one mile to Lake Road. Turn left and drive two miles to the campground on the left.

Contact: Turlock Lake State Recreation Area, 209/874-2008 or 209/874-2056, fax 209/874-2611.

16 BLUE OAKS

Rating: 7

at Don Pedro Reservoir
See map pages 678–679

Blue Oaks is between the dam at Don Pedro Reservoir and Fleming Meadows. The on-site boat ramp to the east is a big plus here. (See the following entry for Fleming Meadows for more information.)

RV sites, facilities: There are 117 sites, including 29 sites with partial hookups (20, 30 amps) and one drive-through, for RVs or tents. Picnic tables, food lockers, and barbecue units are provided. No ground fires are permitted. Drinking water, flush toilets, showers, limited cell phone reception, an ATM, and an RV dump station are available. A store, coin-operated laundry, and propane are nearby at Fleming Meadows Marina. Some facilities are wheelchair-accessible. No pets are permitted.

Reservations, fees: Reservations are accepted. The fee is $17–25 per night, plus $5 per night for more than one vehicle. Major credit cards are accepted. Open Memorial Day weekend through Labor Day weekend.

Directions: From Manteca, take Highway 120 east to Oakdale (the road becomes Highway 120/108). Continue east on Highway 108 for 20 miles to La Grange Road/J59 (signed Don Pedro Reservoir). Turn right on La Grange Road and drive 10 miles to Bonds Flat Road. Turn left on Bonds Flat Road and drive .5 mile to the campground on the left.

Contact: Blue Oaks, 209/852-2396, website: www.donpedrolake.com.

17 FLEMING MEADOWS

Rating: 7

on Don Pedro Reservoir
See map pages 678–679

Fleming Meadows is on the shore of Don Pedro Reservoir at its extreme south end, just east of the dam. A boat ramp is available in the campground on the southeast side of the dam. This is a big camp at the foot of a giant lake, where hot weather, warm water, water-skiing, and bass fishing make for weekend vacations. Don Pedro has many extended lake arms, providing 160 miles of shoreline and nearly 13,000 surface acres when full.

RV sites, facilities: There are 173 sites, including six drive-through, for RVs or tents and 89 sites with full hookups (20, 30 amps), including eight drive-through, for RVs. Picnic tables, food lockers, and barbecues are provided. Ground fires are prohibited. Restrooms, drinking water, limited cell phone reception, an ATM, flush toilets, showers, and an RV dump station are avail-

able. A coin-operated laundry, a store, ice, a snack bar, a restaurant, bait and tackle, motorboat and houseboat rentals, a boat ramp, berths, engine repairs, and propane are nearby. Some facilities are wheelchair-accessible. No pets are permitted.

Reservations, fees: Reservations are accepted. The fee is $17–25 per night, plus $5 per night for more than one vehicle. Major credit cards are accepted. Open year-round.

Directions: From Manteca, take Highway 120 east to Oakdale (the road becomes Highway 120/108). Continue east on Highway 108 for 20 miles to La Grange Road/J59 (signed Don Pedro Reservoir). Turn right on La Grange Road and drive 10 miles to Bonds Flat Road. Turn left on Bonds Flat Road and drive 2.5 miles to the campground on the left.

Contact: Fleming Meadows, 209/852-2396, website: www.donpedrolake.com.

18 BARRETT COVE RECREATION AREA

Rating: 7

on Lake McClure
See map pages 678–679

Lake McClure is shaped like a giant H, with its lake arms providing 81 miles of shoreline. This camp is on the left side of the H, that is, on the western shore, within a park that provides a good boat ramp. This is the largest in a series of camps on Lake McClure. (See the following listings for McClure Point Recreation Area and Bagby Recreation Area for more information.)

RV sites, facilities: There are 275 sites, 65 with full hookups (30 amps) and two drive-through, for RVs or tents. Picnic tables are provided. Restrooms, showers, boat ramps, an RV dump station, limited cell phone reception, a swimming lagoon, and a playground are available. A store, a coin-operated laundry, boat and houseboat rentals, and propane are also available on-site. An ATM is within four miles. Some facilities are wheelchair-accessible. Leashed pets are permitted.

Reservations, fees: Reservations are accepted. The fee is $16–22 per night, plus $8 per night for each additional vehicle and $2 per pet per night. A senior discount is available. Major credit cards are accepted. Open year-round.

Directions: From Modesto, drive east on Highway 132 for 31 miles to La Grange and then continue for about 11 miles (toward Coulterville) to Merced Falls Road. Turn right and drive three miles to the campground entrance on the left. Turn left and drive a mile to the campground on the left side of the road.

Contact: Barrett Cove Recreation Area, 209/378-2521 or 800/468-8889, fax 209/378-2519, website: www.lakemcclure.com.

19 McCLURE POINT RECREATION AREA

Rating: 7

on Lake McClure
See map pages 678–679

McClure Point Recreation Area is the campground of choice for campers/boaters coming from the Turlock and Merced areas. It is a well-developed facility with an excellent boat ramp that provides access to the main body of Lake McClure. This is the best spot on the lake for water-skiing. For large RVs, the best accessible spots are drive-through sites in what is called the G Loop.

RV sites, facilities: There are 100 sites, all drive-through and many with partial hookups (30 amps), for RVs up to 40 feet or tents. Picnic tables are provided. Restrooms, showers, a boat ramp, limited cell phone reception, a marina, and a laundry room are available. A store is nearby. Leashed pets are permitted.

Reservations, fees: Reservations are accepted. The fee is $16–22 per night, plus $2 per pet. A senior discount is available. Major credit cards are accepted. Open year-round.

Directions: From Turlock, drive east on County Road J16 for 19 miles to the junction with Highway 59. Continue east on Highway 59/County Road J16 for 4.5 miles to Snelling and bear right at Lake McClure Road. Drive seven miles to Lake McSwain Dam and continue for seven miles to the campground at the end of the road.

Contact: McClure Point Recreation Area, 209/378-2521 or 800/468-8889, fax 209/378-2519, website: www.lakemcclure.com.

20 BAGBY RECREATION AREA

Rating: 7

on upper Lake McClure
See map pages 678–679

This is the most distant and secluded camp on Lake McClure. It is set near the Merced River as it enters the lake, way up adjacent to the Highway 49 bridge, nearly an hour's drive from the dam. Trout fishing is good in the area, and it makes sense; when the lake heats up in summer, the trout naturally congregate near the cool incoming flows of the Merced River.

RV sites, facilities: There are 30 sites, 10 with partial hookups (30 amps), for RVs and tents. Drinking water, restrooms with flush toilets and coin-operated showers, a small store, limited cell phone reception, and a boat ramp are available. An ATM is within four miles. Leashed pets are permitted.

Reservations, fees: Reservations are accepted. The fee is $16–22 per night, plus $8 per night for additional vehicle and $2 per pet per night. A senior discount is available. Major credit cards are accepted. Open year-round.

Directions: From Modesto, drive east on Highway 132 for 31 miles to La Grange and then continue for 20 miles to Coulterville and the junction with Highway 49. Turn south on Highway 49, drive about 12 miles, cross the bridge, and look for the campground entrance on the left side of the road. Turn left and drive .25 mile to the campground.

Contact: Bagby Recreation Area, 209/378-2521 or 800/468-8889, fax 209/378-2519, website: www.lakemcclure.com.

21 LAKE McSWAIN RECREATION AREA

Rating: 7

near McSwain Dam on the Merced River
See map pages 678–679

Lake McSwain is actually the afterbay for adjacent Lake McClure, and this camp is near the McSwain Dam on the Merced River. If you have a canoe or car-top boat, this lake is preferable to Lake McClure because water-skiing is not allowed. In terms of size, McSwain is like a puddle com-

CALIFORNIA

pared to the giant McClure, but unlike McClure, the water levels are kept up almost year-round at McSwain. The water is cold here and trout stocks are good in the spring.

RV sites, facilities: There are 112 sites with partial hookups (30 amps) for RVs up to 40 feet or tents. Picnic tables are provided. Drinking water, an RV dump station, restrooms, limited cell phone reception, showers, a boat ramp, boat rentals, a coin-operated laundry, and a playground are available. A store and propane are available nearby. An ATM is within four miles. Leashed pets are permitted.

Reservations, fees: Reservations are accepted. The fee is $16–22 per night, plus $2 per pet. A senior discount is available. Major credit cards are accepted. Open year-round.

Directions: From Turlock, drive east on County Road J16 for 19 miles to the junction with Highway 59. Continue east on Highway 59/County Road J16 for 4.5 miles to Snelling. Continue straight ahead to Lake McClure Road and drive seven miles to the campground turnoff on the right.

Contact: Lake McSwain Recreation Area, 209/378-2521 or 800/468-8889, fax 209/378-2519, website: www.lakemcclure.com.

22 FRANK RAINES REGIONAL PARK

Rating: 4

near Modesto
See map pages 678–679

This park is primarily a riding area for folks with dirt bikes and three- and four-wheel OHVs who take advantage of the rough-terrain riding course available here. A side-trip option is to visit Minniear Park, directly to the east, which is a day-use wilderness park with hiking trails and a creek. This area is very pretty in the spring when the foothills are still green and many wildflowers are blooming.

RV sites, facilities: There are 34 sites, some drive-through and some with full hookups, for RVs or tents. Fire grills and picnic tables are provided. Restrooms, drinking water, showers, and a playground are available. Some facilities are wheelchair-accessible. Pets are permitted.

Reservations, fees: Reservations are not accepted. The fee is $12–16 per night, plus $6–8 per

night for each additional vehicle, $2 for rough-terrain vehicles, and $2 per pet per night. Disabled vets with proof of disability from the Veterans Administration can camp free for 15 days; others with disabilities get a 50 percent discount. Open year-round.

Directions: On I-5, drive to the Patterson exit (south of the junction of I-5 and I-580). Turn west on Patterson and drive to Del Puerto Canyon Road. Turn west and drive 16 miles to the park.

Contact: Frank Raines Regional Park, 408/897-3127, fax 408/897-3127.

23 FISHERMAN'S BEND RIVER CAMP

Rating: 5

on the San Joaquin River
See map pages 678–679

This small, privately operated campground is set along the San Joaquin River on the southern outskirts of the San Joaquin Delta country. The park offers shaded sites and direct river access for boaters. This section of river provides fishing for catfish on hot summer nights.

RV sites, facilities: There are 38 sites, all drive-through, with full hookups (30 amps) for RVs, and 20 sites for tents only. Picnic tables and fire grills are provided. Drinking water, restrooms, showers, an RV dump station, a laundry room, modem access (in office), cell phone reception, a boat ramp, a fish-cleaning station, a seasonal swimming pool, a playground, and horseshoes are available. An ATM is within four miles. Some facilities are wheelchair-accessible. Leashed pets are permitted.

Reservations, fees: Reservations are accepted at 800/862-3731. The fee is $20–28 per night, plus $3 per person per night for more than three people. A senior discount is available. Major credit cards are accepted. Open year-round.

Directions: Drive on I-5 to the exit for Newman/Stuhr Road (south of the junction of I-5 and I-580). Take that exit and turn east on County Road J18/Stuhr Road and drive 6.5 miles to Hills Ferry Road. Turn left and drive a mile to River Road. Turn left on River Road and drive to 26836 River Road.

Contact: Fisherman's Bend River Camp, 209/862-3731, fax 209/862-1684.

CALIFORNIA

24 McCONNELL STATE RECREATION AREA

Rating: 6

on the Merced River
See map pages 678–679

The weather gets scorching hot around these parts in the summer, and a lot of out-of-towners would pay a bunch for a little shade and a river to sit next to. That's what this park provides, with the Merced River flowing past, along with occasional mermaids on the beach. The park covers 70 acres. Fishing is popular for catfish, black bass, and panfish. In high-water years, the Merced River attracts salmon (in the fall).

RV sites, facilities: There are 20 sites for RVs up to 30 feet or tents and two group sites for tents only. Picnic tables, fire grills, and food lockers are provided. Drinking water, flush toilets, coin-operated showers, firewood, and a swimming beach are available. Group sites have an electrical hookup. Supplies can be obtained in Delhi, five miles away. Leashed pets are permitted.

Reservations, fees: Reservations are accepted with a $7.50 reservation fee at 800/444-PARK (800/444-7275) or online at www.reserveamerica.com. The fees are $12 per night for family sites and $18–37 per night for group sites, plus a $4 day-use fee. A senior discount is available. Open year-round.

Directions: From Modesto or Merced, drive on Highway 99 to Delhi and the Shanks Road exit. Take that exit and turn east on Shanks Road and drive a short distance to Vincent Road. Turn right (south) and drive .25 mile to El Capitan Way. Turn left on El Capitan Way and drive three miles to Pepper Street. Turn right and drive one mile to 2nd Avenue. Turn left and drive .5 mile to McConnell Road. Turn right and drive .2 mile to the park entrance at the end of the road.

Contact: McConnell State Recreation Area, 209/394-7755; Four Rivers District, California State Parks, 209/826-1197, fax 209/826-0284.

25 LAKE McCLURE/HORSESHOE BEND RECREATION AREA

Rating: 7

on Lake McClure
See map pages 678–679

Lake McClure is a unique, horseshoe-shaped lake in the foothill country west of Yosemite. It adjoins smaller Lake McSwain, connected by the Merced River. McClure is shaped like a giant H, with its lake arms providing 81 miles of shoreline, warm water for water-skiing, and fishing for bass (on the left half of the H near Cotton Creek) and for trout (on the right half of the H). A boat launch is adjacent to the campground. It's one of four lakes in the immediate area; the others are Don Pedro Reservoir to the north and Modesto Reservoir and Turlock Lake to the west. The elevation is 900 feet.

RV sites, facilities: There are 110 sites, including 35 with partial hookups (30 amps), for RVs or tents. Picnic tables are provided. Restrooms, showers, an RV dump station, a boat ramp, limited cell phone reception, a store, and a coin-operated laundry are available. An ATM is within four miles. Some facilities are wheelchair-accessible. Leashed pets are permitted.

Reservations, fees: Reservations are accepted at 800/468-8889. The fee is $16–22 per night, plus $8 per night for each additional vehicle and $2 per pet per night. A senior discount is available. Major credit cards are accepted. Open year-round.

Directions: From Modesto, drive east on Highway 132 for 31 miles to La Grange and then continue for about 17 miles (toward Coulterville) to the north end of Lake McClure and the campground entrance road on the right side of the road. Turn right and drive .5 mile to the campground.

Contact: Horseshoe Bend Recreation Area, 209/878-3452, fax 209/378-2519, website: www.lakemcclure.com.

26 SAN LUIS CREEK

Rating: 5

on San Luis Reservoir
See map pages 678–679

San Luis Campground is on Los Baños Creek

near San Luis Reservoir. It is one in a series of camps operated by the state in the San Luis Reservoir State Recreation Area, adjacent to the reservoir and O'Neill Forebay, home of the biggest striped bass in California, including the world record for landlocked stripers.

RV sites, facilities: There are 53 sites with partial hookups (30 amps) for RVs or tents and two group sites for 30 to 60 people. Picnic tables and fire pits are provided. Drinking water, pit toilets, limited cell phone reception, and an RV dump station are available. An ATM is within two miles. Leashed pets are permitted.

Reservations, fees: Reservations are accepted with a $7.50 reservation fee at 800/444-PARK (800/444-7275) or online at www.reserveamerica.com. The fees are $14 per night and $44–81 per night for group sites. A senior discount is available. Open year-round.

Directions: Drive on Highway 152 to San Luis Reservoir (12 miles west of Los Baños) and the signed campground entrance road (15 miles west of Los Baños). Turn and drive two miles to the campground on the left.

Contact: San Luis Reservoir State Recreation Area, 209/826-1196; Four Rivers District, 209/826-1197, fax 209/826-0284.

27 BASALT

Rating: 5

on San Luis Reservoir
See map pages 678–679

San Luis Reservoir is a huge, man-made lake, covering 13,800 acres with 65 miles of shoreline, developed among stark foothills to provide a storage facility along the California Aqueduct. It fills by late winter and is used primarily by anglers, water-skiers, and windsurfers. When the Sacramento River Delta water pumps take the water, they also take the fish, filling this lake up with both. Striped bass fishing is best in the fall when the stripers chase schools of bait fish on the lake surface. Spring and early summer can be quite windy, but that makes for good windsurfing. The adjacent O'Neill Forebay is the best recreation bet because of the boat launch and often good fishing. There is a visitors center at the Romero Overlook. The elevation is 575 feet. Summer tem-

peratures can occasionally exceed 100°F, but evenings are usually pleasant. During winter, tule fog is common. Note that in spring and early summer, it can turn windy very quickly. Warning lights mark several spots at the reservoir and forebay.

RV sites, facilities: There are 79 sites for RVs or tents. Picnic tables and fire grills are provided. Drinking water, flush toilets, coin-operated showers, an RV dump station, limited cell phone reception, and a boat ramp are available. A store, ATM, coin-operated laundry, gas station, restaurant, and propane are nearby (about 1.5 miles away). Some facilities are wheelchair-accessible. Leashed pets are permitted.

Reservations, fees: Reservations are accepted with a $7.50 reservation fee at 800/444-PARK (800/444-7275) or online at www.reserveamerica.com. The fee is $12–14 per night. A senior discount is available. Open year-round.

Directions: Drive on Highway 152 to San Luis Reservoir (12 miles west of Los Baños) and the Basalt Campground entrance road. Turn south and drive a short distance to Gonzaga Road. Drive straight on Gonzaga Road and continue 2.5 miles (the road becomes Basalt Road) to the campground on the left.

Contact: San Luis Reservoir State Recreation Area, 209/826-1196; Four Rivers District, 209/826-1197, fax 209/826-0284.

28 LOS BAÑOS CREEK RESERVOIR

Rating: 6

near Los Baños
See map pages 678–679

Los Baños Creek Reservoir is in a long, narrow valley, covering 410 surface acres with 12 miles of shoreline. It provides a smaller, more low-key setting (a 5 mph speed limit is enforced) compared to the nearby giant, San Luis Reservoir. In spring, it can be quite windy and is a popular spot for sailboarding. It is also stocked with trout in late winter and spring. The elevation is 400 feet.

RV sites, facilities: There are 15 sites for RVs up to 30 feet or tents. Picnic tables and fire grills are provided. Chemical toilets are available. No drinking water is available. A boat ramp is nearby. Leashed pets are permitted.

Reservations, fees: Reservations are not accepted. The fee is $7 per night. A senior discount is available. Open year-round.

Directions: Drive on Highway 152 to Volta Road (five miles west of Los Baños). Turn south on Volta Road and drive about a mile to Pioneer Road. Turn left on Pioneer Road and drive a mile to Canyon Road. Turn south (right) onto Canyon Road and drive about five miles to the park.

Contact: San Luis Reservoir State Recreation Area, 209/826-1196; Four Rivers District, 209/826-1197, fax 209/826-0284.

29 CORDORNIZ RECREATION AREA
🚶 🚴 ♨️ 🚣 🛥️ 🐕 🚐 ⛺

Rating: 6

on Eastman Lake
See map pages 678–679

Eastman Lake provides relief on your typical 90- and 100-degree summer day out here. It is tucked in the foothills of the San Joaquin Valley at an elevation of 650 feet and covers 1,800 surface acres. Shade shelters have been added at 12 of the more exposed campsites, a big plus. The warm water in summer makes it good spot for a dip, and it is thus a favorite for water-skiing, swimming, and, in the spring, for fishing. The DFG has established a trophy bass program here, and fishing can be good in the appropriate season for rainbow trout, catfish, bluegill, and sunfish. Check fishing regulations, posted on all bulletin boards. The lake is also a designated "Watchable Wildlife" site with 163 species of birds, and it is home to a nesting pair of bald eagles. A small area near the upper end of the lake is closed to boating to protect a bald eagle nest site. Some may remember the problem that Eastman Lake had with hydrilla, an invasive weed. The problem has been largely solved, with one closed area remaining below Chapman Creek, more than a mile upstream from the main body of the lake. Mild winter temperatures are a tremendous plus at this lake.

RV sites, facilities: There are 62 sites for RVs or tents, 15 with full hookups (50 amps), three group sites for up to 200 people, and three equestrian sites. Picnic tables and fire grills are provided. Drinking water, flush toilets, showers, an RV dump station, limited cell phone reception, and a boat ramp are available. An equestrian staging area is available for overnight use, and there are seven miles of hiking, biking, and equestrian trails. Leashed pets are permitted.

Reservations, fees: Reservations are accepted with a $9 reservation fee at 877/444-6777 or online at www.reserveusa.com. The fees are $14–20 per night, $55–75 per night for group sites, and $8–25 per night for equestrian sites. A senior discount is available. Open year-round.

Directions: Drive on Highway 99 to Chowchilla and the Avenue 26 exit. Take that exit and drive east for 17 miles to County Road 29. Turn left (north) on County Road 29 and drive eight miles to the lake.

Contact: U.S. Army Corps of Engineers, Sacramento District, Eastman Lake, 559/689-3255, fax 559/689-3408.

30 HIDDEN VIEW
🚶 ♨️ 🚣 🛥️ 🐕 🧺 🚐 ⛺

Rating: 5

north of Fresno on Hensley Lake
See map pages 678–679

Hensley Lake is one of two lakes just east of Madera (the other is Millerton Lake). Hensley covers 1,500 surface acres with 24 miles of shoreline and, as long as water levels are maintained, makes for a wonderful water playland. Swimming is good, with the best spot at Buck Ridge on the east side of the lake, where there are picnic tables and trees for shade. The reservoir was created by a dam on the Fresno River. A nature trail is also here. The elevation is 500 feet.

RV sites, facilities: There are 55 sites for RVs or tents, some with electric hookups (30, 50 amps), and two group sites for 25 to 100 people. Picnic tables and fire grills are provided. Restrooms, drinking water, flush toilets, showers, limited cell phone reception, an RV dump station, a playground, and a boat ramp are available. Leashed pets are permitted.

Reservations, fees: Reservations are accepted for groups only with a $9 reservation fee at 877/444-6777 or online at www.reserveusa.com. The fee is $14–20 per night for individual sites, $50 for group sites, plus a $3 boat launch fee. Groups can also reserve the Wakalumi Primitive Area at

CALIFORNIA

559/673-5151. A senior discount is available. Open year-round.

Directions: From Madera, drive northeast on Highway 145 for about six miles to County Road 400. Bear left on County Road 400 and drive to County Road 603 below the dam. Turn left and drive about two miles on County Road 603 to County Road 407. Turn right on County Road 407 and drive .5 mile to the campground.

Contact: U.S. Army Corps of Engineers, Sacramento District, Hensley Lake, 559/673-5151, fax 559/673-2044.

31 MILLERTON LAKE STATE RECREATION AREA

🏃 🏊 🛶 🚤 🎣 🐕 ♿ 🚐 ⛺

Rating: 6

near Madera

See map pages 678–679

As the temperature gauge goes up in the summer, the value of Millerton Lake increases at the same rate. The lake is set at 578 feet in the foothills of the San Joaquin Valley, and the water is like gold here. The campground and recreation area are on a peninsula along the north shore of the lake; there are sandy beach areas on both sides of the lake with boat ramps available near the campgrounds. It's a big lake, with 43 miles of shoreline, from a narrow lake inlet extending to an expansive main lake body. The irony at Millerton is that when the lake is filled to the brim, the beaches are covered, so ideal conditions are actually when the lake level is down a bit, typically from early summer on. Fishing can be good here in spring for bass. Catfish are popular for shoreliners on summer evenings. Water-skiing is very popular in summer, of course. During winter, boat tours are available to view bald eagles. A note of history: The original Millerton County Courthouse, built in 1867, is in the park.

RV sites, facilities: There are 148 sites, 26 with full hookups (20, 30, 50 amps), for RVs up to 36 feet or tents, three boat-in sites, and two group sites for 45 to 75 people. Picnic tables and fire grills are provided. Drinking water, flush toilets, coin-operated showers, an RV dump station, limited cell phone reception, an ATM, and boat ramps are available. You can buy supplies in Fri-

ant. Some facilities are wheelchair-accessible. Leashed pets are permitted.

Reservations, fees: Reservations are accepted with a $7.50 reservation fee at 800/444-7275 or online at www.reserveamerica.com. The fees are $13–22 per night, $7 for boat-in sites, and $54–101 for group sites. A senior discount is available. Open year-round.

Directions: Drive on Highway 99 to Madera at the exit for Highway 145 East. Take that exit east and drive on Highway 145 for 22 miles (six miles past the intersection with Highway 41) to the park entrance on the right.

Contact: Millerton Lake State Recreation Area, 559/822-2332, fax 559/822-2319.

32 COUNTRY LIVING MOBILE HOME AND RV PARK

🏊 🎣 ♿ 🚐

Rating: 1

in Madera

See map pages 678–679

It can be a dry piece of life driving this country on a hot summer afternoon, when you're ready to stop but know of nowhere to go. This RV park gives you an option, one of the scant few on Highway 99 in this region of the San Joaquin Valley. The ambience of the place has been helped by the planting of 34 trees in spring of 2000, along with the removal of 64 dead trees (killed by bug infestation).

RV sites, facilities: There are 49 sites, 25 drive-through and many with full hookups (30, 50 amps), for RVs. Picnic tables are provided at some sites. Restrooms, drinking water, cell phone reception, showers, and a coin-operated laundry are available. A swimming pool and hot tub are open in the summer only. A store and ATM are within 1.5 miles. Leashed pets are permitted.

Reservations, fees: Reservations are accepted. The fee is $15–23 per night, plus $2 per person for more than two people. Open year-round.

Directions: Drive on Highway 99 to Madera and the Avenue 16 exit west. Take that exit and drive west .4 mile to the park entrance on the right (24833 Ave. 16).

Contact: Country Living Mobile Home and RV Park, tel./fax 559/674-5343.

CALIFORNIA

33 TRAVELER'S RV PARK

Rating: 2

near Kettleman City
See map pages 678–679

Being stuck in Kings County looking for a place to park an RV is no picnic. Unless, that is, you are lucky enough to know about Traveler's RV Park. The spaces are wide open with long-distance views of the Sierra. It's literally the "only game in town"; in fact, it's the only camp in the entire county. Another claim to fame: it's eight hours to the Mexican border. Visitors will find access to miles of open paths and roads for hiking or running. Some may remember this park as Kettleman City RV Park. New owners arrived in 2002, new name, too, and an improved attitude with it.

RV sites, facilities: There are 46 sites, all drive-through, with partial or full hookups (30 amps) for RVs and tents. Picnic tables are provided. Restrooms, showers, a seasonal swimming pool, cell phone reception, modem access, an RV dump station, a dog run, and propane are available. A restaurant and snack bar are nearby. An ATM is within a quarter mile. Some facilities are wheelchair-accessible. Leashed pets are permitted.

Reservations, fees: Reservations are accepted at 559/386-0583. The fee is $25 per night, plus $5 per night per additional vehicle. Major credit cards are accepted. Open year-round.

Directions: Drive on I-5 to the junction with Highway 41 (Kettleman Junction). Take Highway 41 north and drive .5 mile to Hubert Way. Turn left on Hubert Way and drive to Cyril Place. Turn right on Cyril Place to the park entrance (30000 Cyril Place).

Contact: Traveler's RV Park, 559/386-0583, fax 559/386-0585.

34 VISALIA/FRESNO SOUTH KOA

Rating: 1

west of Visalia
See map pages 678–679

This is a layover spot for Highway 99 cruisers. If you're looking for a spot to park your rig for the night, you can't get too picky around these parts.

RV sites, facilities: There are 48 sites, all drive-through, with partial or full hookups (20, 30, 50 amps), 38 sites for RVs or tents, and 30 sites for tents only. Restrooms, showers, a swimming pool, cell phone reception, modem access, laundry facilities, a playground, a recreation room, a store, an RV dump station, and propane are available. An ATM is within three miles. Leashed pets are permitted.

Reservations, fees: Reservations are accepted at 800/562-0544. The fee is $22–35 per night, plus $3–5 per person for more than two people. Major credit cards are accepted. Open year-round.

Directions: From Visalia, drive west on Highway 198 to the Plaza exit. Turn right on Plaza and drive five miles to Goshen Road. Turn left on Goshen Road and drive .25 mile to Road 76. Turn right and drive to the camp entrance (well signed).

Contact: Visalia/Fresno South KOA, 559/651-0544, website: www.koa.com.

35 SUN AND FUN RV PARK

Rating: 1

near Tulare
See map pages 678–679

This RV park is just off Highway 99, exactly halfway between San Francisco and Los Angeles. Are you having fun yet? Anybody making the long drive up or down the state on Highway 99 will learn what a dry piece of life the San Joaquin Valley can seem. That's why the swimming pool at this RV park can be a lifesaver.

RV sites, facilities: There are 62 sites with full hookups (30, 50 amps) for RVs. Picnic tables and barbecues are provided. Restrooms, drinking water, showers, modem access, an RV dump station, cell phone reception, a playground, a swimming pool, a spa, laundry facilities, and a recreation room are available. A golf course, restaurant, and store are nearby. An ATM is within a quarter mile. Some facilities are wheelchair-accessible. Leashed pets are permitted.

Reservations, fees: Reservations are accepted. The fee is $25–28 per night. Open year-round.

Directions: From Tulare, drive south on High-

CALIFORNIA

way 99 for three miles to the Avenue 200 exit. Take Avenue 200 west and drive a short distance to the park (1000 Ave. 200).

Contact: Sun and Fun RV Park, 559/686-5779.

36 EAGLE'S NEST ROOST

Rating: 4

near Lake Success

See map pages 678–679

This campground is in a parklike setting with trees and flowers. It is two miles from Lake Success. A small, stocked fishing pond is available, and pet geese and ducks are often wandering around. (For information on Lake Success, see the listing in this chapter for Tule 2.)

RV sites, facilities: There are 250 sites with partial or full hookups (20, 30, 50 amps) for RVs or tents. Picnic tables and barbecues are provided at some sites. Restrooms, hot showers, a recreation room, a playground, a swimming pool, fishing facilities, a laundry room, a store, ice, firewood, limited cell phone reception, an RV dump station, and a dog-walking are available. An ATM is within four miles. Quiet, well-mannered, leashed pets are permitted (no Dobermans, pit bulls, or Rottweilers).

Reservations, fees: Reservations are accepted. The fee is $16–29 per night, plus $3–6 per person for more than two people. A senior discount is available. Major credit cards are accepted. Open year-round.

Directions: Drive on Highway 65 to Porterville and the junction with Highway 190. Turn east on Highway 190 and drive five miles to the park on the left (27798 Hwy. 190).

Contact: Eagle's Nest Roost, 559/784-3948.

37 TULE 2

Rating: 7

on Lake Success

See map pages 678–679

Lake Success is a big lake with many arms, providing 30 miles of shoreline and making the place seem like a dreamland for boaters on hot summer days. The lake is set in the foothill country, at an elevation of 650 feet, where day after day

of 100-degree summer temperatures are common. That is why boating, water-skiing, and personal watercraft are so popular—anything to get wet. In the winter and spring, fishing for trout and bass is good, including the chance for giant bass. No beaches are developed for swimming because of fluctuating water levels, though the day-use area has a decent sloped stretch of shore that is good for swimming. The wildlife area along the west side of the lake is worth exploring, and there is a nature trail below the dam. The campground is the centerpiece of the Tule Recreation Area.

RV sites, facilities: There are 104 sites, some with electrical hookups (30 amps), for RVs up to 35 feet or tents. Picnic tables and fire grills are provided. Restrooms, flush toilets, an RV dump station, limited cell phone reception, and a playground are available. A store, an ATM, a marina, a boat ramp, boat and water-ski rentals, bait and tackle, propane, a restaurant, and a gas station are available nearby. Leashed pets are permitted.

Reservations, fees: Reservations are accepted with a $9 reservation fee at 877/444-6777 or online at www.reserveusa.com. The fee is $16–21 per night. A senior discount is available. Open year-round.

Directions: Drive on Highway 65 to Porterville and the junction with Highway 190. Turn east on Highway 190 and drive eight miles to Lake Success and the campground entrance on the left.

Contact: U.S. Army Corps of Engineers, Sacramento District, 559/784-0215, fax 559/784-5469; Success Marina, 559/781-2078.

38 COLONEL ALLENSWORTH STATE HISTORIC PARK

Rating: 3

near Earlimart

See map pages 678–679

What you have here is the old town of Allensworth, which has been restored as a historical park dedicated to the African-American pioneers who founded it with Colonel Allen Allensworth. He was the highest-ranking army chaplain of his time. Allensworth is the only town in California to founded, funded, and governed by African Americans. One museum is available at the school here and another is at the colonel's house with a 30-minute movie on the history of Allensworth.

Tours are available by appointment. One frustrating element here is that railroad tracks run alongside the park, and the noise can be disruptive. There can be other problems: very hot weather in the summer, and since it is an open area, the wind can blow dust and sand. Are we having fun yet? One nice touch is the addition of shade ramadas at some campsites. A history note: This small farming community was founded in 1908, but a drop in the water table led to its demise.

RV sites, facilities: There are 15 sites for RVs up to 35 feet or tents. Picnic tables and fire grills are provided. Restrooms, drinking water, flush toilets, coin-operated showers, an RV dump station, a visitors center, and a picnic area are available. A store and coin-operated laundry are 12 miles away in Delano. Leashed pets are permitted.

Reservations, fees: Reservations are accepted with a $7.50 reservation fee at 800/444-PARK (800/444-7275) or online at www.reserveamerica.com. The fee is $8 per night. A senior discount is available. Open year-round.

Directions: From Fresno, drive south on Highway 99 about 60 miles to Earlimart and the Alpaugh Road exit. Take that exit and drive to Avenue 56. Turn right (west) on Avenue 56 and drive eight miles to the Highway 43 turnoff. Turn left on Highway 43 and drive two miles to Palmer Avenue. Turn right (and drive over the railroad tracks) to the park entrance.

Contact: Colonel Allensworth State Historic Park, 661/849-3433; San Joaquin South Sector, 661/634-3795.

39 LOST HILLS KOA

Rating: 4

near Kern National Wildlife Refuge
See map pages 678–679

The pickings can get slim around these parts when you're cruising north on I-5, so if it's late, you'll likely be happy to find this KOA camp. The cabin that sleeps four is a nice plus. The nearby Kern National Wildlife Refuge, about a 15-minute drive away, offers a side-trip possibility. It's a waterfowl reserve that attracts ducks, geese, and other waterfowl in the fall and winter.

RV sites, facilities: There are 79 sites, all drive-through, with full hookups (30, 50 amps) for RVs, nine sites for tents only, an overflow area with 20 sites for self-contained RVs and tents, and one cabin. Picnic tables are provided. Restrooms, drinking water, showers, a swimming pool, laundry facilities, a store, an ATM, modem access, cell phone reception, a video room, and propane are available. Restaurants are nearby. Some facilities are wheelchair-accessible. Leashed pets are permitted.

Reservations, fees: Reservations are accepted at 800/562-2793. The fee is $24–30 per night. Major credit cards are accepted. Open year-round.

Directions: Drive on I-5 to the junction with Highway 46 (41 miles south of Avenal near Lost Hills). Turn west on Highway 46 and drive a short distance to the park entrance (near the Carl's Jr.).

Contact: Lost Hills KOA, 661/797-2719, website: www.koa.com.

40 KOA BAKERSFIELD

Rating: 1

north of Bakersfield
See map pages 678–679

If you're stuck in the southern valley and the temperature feels like you're sitting in a cauldron, well, this spot provides a layover for the night near the town of Shafter. It's not exactly a hotbed of excitement.

RV sites, facilities: There are 62 RV sites with partial or full hookups (20, 30, 50 amps) and 12 tent sites. Picnic tables are provided. Restrooms, drinking water, showers, a swimming pool (summer only), a laundry room, a store, an RV dump station, modem access, cell phone reception, an ATM, and propane are available. Some facilities are wheelchair-accessible. Leashed pets are permitted.

Reservations, fees: Reservations are accepted at 800/562-1633. The fee is $26–31 per night, plus $4 per person per night for more than two people. Major credit cards are accepted. Open year-round.

Directions: From Bakersfield, drive north on Highway 99 for 12 miles to the Shafter-Lerdo Highway exit. Take that exit west and drive a mile west on East Lerdo Highway to the park (5101 Lerdo Hwy. in Shafter).

Contact: KOA Bakersfield, 661/399-3107, fax 661/399-8981, website: www.koa.com.

41 BUENA VISTA AQUATIC RECREATION AREA

Rating: 6

near Bakersfield

See map pages 678–679

Buena Vista is actually two connected lakes fed by the West Side Canal, little Lake Evans to the west and larger Lake Webb to the east. Be certain to know the difference between the two: Lake Webb (875 acres) is open to all boating including personal watercraft, and fast boats towing skiers are a common sight in designated ski areas. The speed limit is 45 mph. Lake Evans (85 acres) is small, quiet, and has a strictly enforced 5 mph speed limit, an ideal lake for family water play and fishing. The elevation is 330 feet on the outskirts of Bakersfield.

RV sites, facilities: There are 112 sites with full hookups (30, 50 amps) for RVs or tents. Picnic tables and fire grills are provided. Restrooms, drinking water, flush toilets, showers, cell phone reception, a playground, three boat ramps, a store, an RV dump station, and propane are available. A marina, snack bar, fishing supplies, and groceries are available nearby. An ATM is within two miles. A PGA-rated golf course is two miles west. Leashed pets are permitted.

Reservations, fees: Reservations are accepted at 661/868-7050 Monday through Friday. The fee is $21–32 per night, plus $11 per night per additional vehicle and $3 per night per pet. A senior discount is available. Major credit cards are accepted. Open year-round.

Directions: From I-5 just south of Bakersfield, take Highway 119 west and drive two miles to Highway 43. Turn south (left) on Highway 43 and drive two miles to the campground at the road's end.

Contact: Buena Vista Aquatic Recreation Area, 661/763-1526, website: www.co.kern.ca.us/parks /index.htm.

42 KERN RIVER

Rating: 7

at Lake Ming

See map pages 678–679

The campground is at Lake Ming, a small but exciting place. The lake covers just 205 surface acres, and with the weather so hot, the hot jet boats can make it a wild affair here. It's become a popular spot for southern valley residents, only a 15-minute drive from Bakersfield. It is so popular for water sports that every year the lake is closed to the public one weekend per month for private boat races and water-skiing competitions. Sailing and windsurfing are permitted on the second weekend of every month and on Tuesday and Thursday afternoons. All motorized boating, including water-skiing, is permitted on the remaining days. All boats are required to have a permit; boaters may buy one at the park. Swimming is not allowed. The elevation is 450 feet.

RV sites, facilities: There are 50 sites for RVs up to 28 feet or tents. Picnic tables and fire rings are provided. Restrooms, drinking water, flush toilets, coin-operated showers, an RV dump station, a playground, limited cell phone reception, and a boat ramp are available. A store is nearby. Some facilities are wheelchair-accessible. Leashed pets are permitted.

Reservations, fees: Reservations are not accepted. The fee is $18 per night, plus $9 per night for each additional vehicle (15-person maximum per site) and a $3 pet fee. The maximum stay is 10 days. Open year-round.

Directions: From Bakersfield, drive east on Highway 178 to Alfred Harrell Highway. Turn left (north) on Alfred Harrell Highway and follow the signs to Lake Ming Road. Turn right on Lake Ming Road and follow the signs to the campground on the right.

Contact: Kern County Parks Department, 661/868-7000.

CALIFORNIA

California

Chapter 22

Yosemite and Mammoth Lakes

see Tahoe and
the Northern Sierra
pages 596–597

Bridgeport

Stanislaus

Beardsley
Res.

4

1

Pinecrest

3

2

National

Forest

Dodge Ridge

Yosemite

National

Park

SIERRA

5
6

7-10

Twin Lakes

Hoover
Wilderness

12

Cherry
Lake

13

Lake
Eleanor

16
14 **15**

Hetch Hetchy
Reservoir

Tioga Pass
(9,945 ft.)

River

Grand Canyon of the Tuolumne

Tuolumne
Meadows

Tuolumne

23

25

Mather

TIOGA

21

24

120

20

22

Aspen
Valley

PASS RD.

120

NEVADA

31

Yosemite
Village

33-35

Yosemite
Valley

▲ Glacier Pt.
(7,214 ft.)

140

GLACIER PT. RD.

32

49

see
San Joaquin
Valley
pages 678–679

53

Wawona

54

55

140

41

Sierra

National Forest

San Joaquin River

N
W   E
S

CALIFORNIA

0   5 mi
0   5 km

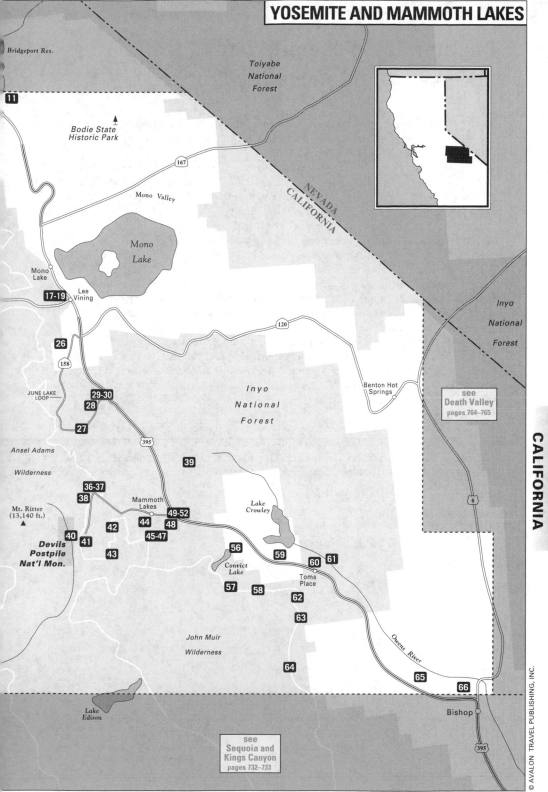

Bridgeport Res.

Toiyabe
National
Forest

11

Bodie State
Historic Park

167

Mono Valley

NEVADA
CALIFORNIA

Mono
Lake

Mono
Lake

Lee
Vining

17-19

120

26

158

Benton Hot
Springs

Inyo

National

Forest

see
Death Valley
pages 764–765

JUNE LAKE
LOOP

29-30
28

27

395

Inyo

National

Forest

Ansel Adams

Wilderness

39

36-37
38

Mt. Ritter
(13,140 ft.)

Mammoth
Lakes

49-52

Lake
Crowley

42

44

48

40
41

45-47

43

**Devils
Postpile
Nat'l Mon.**

56

Convict
Lake

59

60 **61**

Toms
Place

57

58

62

63

John Muir

Wilderness

64

Owens River

65

66

6

CALIFORNIA

Lake
Edison

Bishop

see
**Sequoia and
Kings Canyon**
pages 732–733

395

© AVALON TRAVEL PUBLISHING, INC.

Chapter 22—Yosemite and Mammoth Lakes

Some of nature's most perfect artwork has been created in Yosemite and the adjoining eastern Sierra near Mammoth Lakes, as well as some of the most profound natural phenomena imaginable.

Yosemite Valley is the world's greatest showpiece. It is also among the most highly visited and well-known destinations on earth. Many of the campgrounds listed in this section are within close driving proximity of Yosemite National Park. When it comes to cabin rentals in this region, the variety is extraordinary.

Anything in Yosemite, or in its sphere of influence, is going to be in high demand almost year-round, and the same is true near Mammoth Mountain.

Many family recreation opportunities exist at lake-based settings, including at Lake Alpine, Pinecrest Lake on the western slopes of the Sierra, and at June Lake, Silver Lake, Lake Mary, Twin Lakes, Convict Lake, and Rock Creek Lake on the eastern Sierra. I noticed that the demand for campgrounds is fairly high in the vicinity of Highway 4 and Calaveras Big Trees, and Highway 108 and Pinecrest. That's what happens when you're competing with Yosemite.

Of course, most visits to this region start with a tour of Yosemite Valley. It is framed by El Capitan, the Goliath of Yosemite, on one side and the three-spired Cathedral Rocks on the other. As you enter the valley, Bridalveil Falls comes into view, a perfect free fall over the south canyon rim, then across a meadow. To your left you'll see the two-tiered Yosemite Falls, and finally, Half Dome, the single most awesome piece of rock in the world.

The irony is that this is all most people ever see of the region, even though it represents but a fraction of this fantastic land of wonder, adventure, and unparalleled natural beauty. Though 24,000 people jam into five square miles of Yosemite Valley each summer day, the park is actually 90 percent wilderness. Other landmark areas you can

CALIFORNIA

reach by car include the Wawona Grove of Giant Sequoias, Tenaya Lake, Tuolumne Meadows, and Hetch Hetchy.

But that's still only scratching the surface. For those who hike, another world will open up: Yosemite has 318 lakes, dozens of pristine streams, the Grand Canyon of the Tuolumne River, Matterhorn Peak, Benson Lake (with the largest white sand beach in the Sierra), and dozens of spectacular waterfalls.

If you explore beyond the park boundaries, the adventures just keep getting better. Over Tioga Pass, outside the park and just off Highway 120, are Tioga Lake, Ellery Lake, and Saddlebag Lake (10,087 feet), the latter of which is the highest lake in California accessible by car. To the east is Mono Lake and its weird tufa spires, which create a stark moonscape.

The nearby June Lake Loop and Mammoth Lakes area is a launch point to another orbit. Both have small lakes with on-site cabin rentals, excellent fishing, and great hiking for all levels. In addition, just east of Mammoth Lakes airport is a series of hot springs, including a famous spot on Hot Creek, something of a legend in these parts.

More hiking (and fishing) opportunities abound at Devils Postpile National Monument, where you can hike to Rainbow Falls. At nearby Agnew Meadows, you'll find a trail that hugs the pristine San Joaquin River up to Thousand Island Lake and leads to the beautiful view from Banner and Ritter Peaks in the Ansel Adams Wilderness.

If you didn't already know, this region is home to many of California's best lakes for catching giant rainbow and brown trout. They include Bridgeport Reservoir, Twin Lakes, June Lake, Convict Lake, and Crowley Lake in the eastern Sierra, and Beardsley and Spicer Meadows in the western Sierra.

This region has it all: beauty, variety, and a chance at the hike or fish of a lifetime. There is nothing else like it on earth.

CALIFORNIA

◼ BEARDSLEY

Rating: 6

at Beardsley Lake in Stanislaus National Forest
See map pages 700–701
For years people wondered why there was no campground at Beardsley Reservoir. In fact, some started parking their campers and creating their own. Well, that's why this primitive site is here, used primarily as a base camp for people fishing for trout at Beardsley Reservoir. It is often an outstanding fishery early in the season for brown trout, and then once planted, good for limits of hatchery fish during the evening bite. In winter and spring, as soon as the gate is opened to the boat ramp access road, the fishing is best when the wind blows, believe it or not; let it push your boat while you drift half a nightcrawler behind a set of Half Fast Flashers. The wind always comes up here out of the west, but this is what gets the fish biting. The camp is set at 3,400 feet, but because it is near the bottom of the lake canyon, it actually feels much higher in elevation. Bonus: there is more fishing nearby on the Middle Fork of the Stanislaus.
RV sites, facilities: There are 26 sites for RVs up to 22 feet or tents. Fire rings are provided. Vault toilets are available. No drinking water is available. Leashed pets are permitted.
Reservations, fees: Reservations are not accepted. There is no fee for camping. Open year-round, weather permitting (the road is often gated at the top of the canyon, when the boat ramp road at lake level is iced over).
Directions: From Sonora, drive east on Highway 108 for about 25 miles to Strawberry and the turnoff for Beardsley Reservoir/Forest Road 52. Turn left and drive seven miles to Beardsley Dam. Continue for .25 mile past the dam to the campground.
Contact: Stanislaus National Forest, Summit Ranger District, 209/965-3434, fax 209/965-3372.

◼ FRASER FLAT

Rating: 7

on the South Fork of the Stanislaus River in Stanislaus National Forest
See map pages 700–701
This camp is set at 4,800 feet elevation along the South Fork of the Stanislaus River. If the fish aren't biting, a short side trip via Forest Service roads will route you north into the main canyon of the Middle Fork Stanislaus. A map of Stanislaus National Forest is required for this adventure. Fraser Flat also provides an overflow if the campgrounds at Pinecrest or up at Clark Fork and the upper Highway 108 corridor are filled.
RV sites, facilities: There are 38 sites for RVs up to 22 feet or tents. Picnic tables and fire grills are provided. Drinking water and vault toilets are available. A grocery store and propane are nearby. Some facilities are wheelchair-accessible, including a camping and fishing site. Leashed pets are permitted.
Reservations, fees: Reservations are not accepted. The fee is $13 per night, plus $5 per night for each additional vehicle for more than two vehicles. A senior discount is available. Open May through October, weather permitting.
Directions: From Sonora, drive east on Highway 108 to Long Barn. Continue east for six miles to Spring Gap Road/Forest Road 4N01. Turn left and drive three miles to the campground on the left side of the road.
Contact: Stanislaus National Forest, Mi-Wok Ranger District, 209/586-3234, fax 209/586-0643.

◼ MEADOWVIEW

Rating: 7

near Pinecrest Lake in Stanislaus National Forest
See map pages 700–701
No secret here, folks. This camp is one mile from Pinecrest Lake, a popular weekend vacation area (and there's a trail that connects the camp with the town). Pinecrest Lake is set at 5,621 feet, covers 300 acres, is stocked with rainbow trout, and has a 20 mph speed limit for boaters. This is a family-oriented vacation center, and a popular walk is the easy hike around the lake. If you want something more ambitious, there is a cutoff on the north side of the lake that is routed one mile up to little Catfish Lake. The Dodge Ridge Ski Area is nearby, with many privately owned cabins in the area.
RV sites, facilities: There are 100 sites for RVs up to 22 feet or tents. Picnic tables and fire grills are provided. Drinking water, flush toilets, and

limited cell phone reception are available. A grocery store, an ATM, a coin-operated laundry, a boat ramp, pay showers (in summer only), and propane are nearby. Leashed pets are permitted.

Reservations, fees: Reservations are not accepted. The fee is $13 per night. A senior discount is available. Open May to mid-September.

Directions: From Sonora, drive east on Highway 108 for about 30 miles to the signed road for Pinecrest Lake. Turn right at the sign and drive .5 mile to Pinecrest/Dodge Ridge Road. Turn right and drive about 200 yards to the campground entrance on the right side of the road.

Contact: Stanislaus National Forest, Summit Ranger District, 209/965-3434, fax 209/965-3372.

4 PINECREST

Rating: 7

near Pinecrest Lake in Stanislaus National Forest

See map pages 700–701

This monster-sized Forest Service camp is near Pinecrest Lake. In early summer, there is good fishing for stocked rainbow trout. A launch ramp is available, and a 20 mph speed limit is enforced on the lake. A trail circles the lake and also branches off to nearby Catfish Lake. The elevation is 5,600 feet. Winter camping is allowed near the Pinecrest Day-Use Area.

RV sites, facilities: There are 200 sites for RVs up to 22 feet or tents. Picnic tables and fire grills are provided. Drinking water and toilets are available. There are two winterized restrooms with flush toilets and sinks. A grocery store, an ATM, a coin-operated laundry, pay showers (in summer only), a boat ramp, and propane are nearby. Leashed pets are permitted.

Reservations, fees: Reservations required from mid-May to mid-September at 877/444-6777 or online at www.reserveusa.com ($9 reservation fee). The fee is $19 per night. A senior discount is available. Open April to mid-October, weather permitting.

Directions: From Sonora, drive east on Highway 108 for about 30 miles to the signed turn for Pinecrest Lake on the right. Turn right and drive to the access road (.7 mile past the turnoff signed Pinecrest) for the campground. Turn right and drive a short distance to the campground.

Contact: Stanislaus National Forest, Summit Ranger District, 209/965-3434, fax 209/965-3372.

5 BUCKEYE

Rating: 8

near Buckeye Creek in Humboldt-Toiyabe National Forest

See map pages 700–701

Here's a little secret: a two-mile hike out of camp heads to the undeveloped Buckeye Hot Springs. That is what inspires campers to bypass the fishing at nearby Robinson Creek (three miles away) and Twin Lakes (six miles away). The camp feels remote and primitive, set at 7,000 feet on the eastern slope of the Sierra near Buckeye Creek. Another secret is that brook trout are planted at the little bridge that crosses Buckeye Creek near the campground. A trail that starts near camp is routed through Buckeye Canyon and into the Hoover Wilderness.

RV sites, facilities: There are 65 paved sites for RVs up to 45 feet or tents and one group site. Picnic tables and fire grills are provided. Drinking water and flush toilets are available. Leashed pets are permitted.

Reservations, fees: Reservations are not accepted for individual sites. The fee is $11 per night. Group site reservations can be made at 877/444-6777 or online at www.reserveusa.com ($9 reservation fee); the group site is $50 per night. A senior discount is available. Open early May to mid-October.

Directions: On U.S. 395, drive to Bridgeport and the junction with Twin Lakes Road. Turn west and drive seven miles to Buckeye Road. Turn north on Buckeye Road (dirt, often impassable when wet) and drive 3.5 miles to the campground.

Contact: Humboldt-Toiyabe National Forest, Bridgeport Ranger District, 760/932-7070, fax 760/932-1299.

6 HONEYMOON FLAT

Rating: 8

on Robinson Creek in Humboldt-Toiyabe National Forest

See map pages 700–701

The camp is set beside Robinson Creek at 7,000

CALIFORNIA

feet in elevation, in the transition zone between the Sierra Nevada range to the west and the high desert to the east. It is easy to reach on the access road to Twin Lakes, only three miles farther. The lake is famous for occasional huge brown trout. However, the fishing at Robinson Creek is also often quite good, thanks to the more than 50,000 trout planted each year by the Department of Fish and Game.

RV sites, facilities: There are 19 sites for RVs up to 50 feet or tents. Picnic tables and fire grills are provided. Drinking water, vault toilets, and firewood are available. An ATM is within eight miles. Leashed pets are permitted.

Reservations, fees: Reserve at 877/444-6777 or online at www.reserveusa.com ($9 reservation fee). The fee is $11 per night. A senior discount is available. Open mid-April through October.

Directions: On U.S. 395, drive to Bridgeport and the junction with Twin Lakes Road. Turn west and drive eight miles to the campground.

Contact: Humboldt-Toiyabe National Forest, Bridgeport Ranger District, 760/932-7070, fax 760/932-1299.

7 PAHA

Rating: 8

near Twin Lakes in Humboldt-Toiyabe National Forest

See map pages 700–701

This is one in a series of camps near Robinson Creek and within close range of Twin Lakes. The elevation at the camp is 7,000 feet. (See the entries in this chapter for Lower Twin Lake and Honeymoon Flat for more information.)

RV sites, facilities: There are 20 paved single sites and two double sites for RVs up to 45 feet or tents. Picnic tables and fire grills are provided. Drinking water, flush toilets, and firewood are available. A boat launch, a store, showers, and a coin-operated laundry are available nearby at Twin Lakes Resort. Leashed pets are permitted.

Reservations, fees: Reserve at 877/444-6777 or online at www.reserveusa.com ($9 reservation fee). The fee is $13 per night for single sites and $26 for double sites. A senior discount is available. Open early May to late October, weather permitting.

Directions: On U.S. 395, drive to Bridgeport and the junction with Twin Lakes Road. Turn west and drive 10 miles to the campground.

Contact: Humboldt-Toiyabe National Forest, Bridgeport Ranger District, 760/932-7070, fax 760/932-1299.

8 ROBINSON CREEK

Rating: 9

near Twin Lakes in Humboldt-Toiyabe National Forest

See map pages 700–701

This campground, one of a series in the area, is set at 7,000 feet on Robinson Creek, not far from Twin Lakes. (For recreation options, see the entries in this chapter for Lower Twin Lake and Honeymoon Flat.)

RV sites, facilities: There are 54 paved sites for RVs up to 40 feet or tents. Picnic tables and fire grills are provided. Drinking water and flush and vault toilets are available. An amphitheater is nearby. An ATM is within 10 miles. Some facilities are wheelchair-accessible. Leashed pets are permitted.

Reservations, fees: Reserve at 877/444-6777 or online at www.reserveusa.com ($9 reservation fee). The fee is $13 per night. A senior discount is available. Open mid-April through October.

Directions: On U.S. 395, drive to Bridgeport and the junction with Twin Lakes Road. Turn west and drive 10 miles to the campground.

Contact: Humboldt-Toiyabe National Forest, Bridgeport Ranger District, 760/932-7070, fax 760/932-1299.

9 CRAGS CAMPGROUND

Rating: 8

on Robinson Creek in Humboldt-Toiyabe National Forest

See map pages 700–701

Crags Camp is set at 7,000 feet in the Sierra, one of a series of campgrounds along Robinson Creek near Lower Twin Lake. Although this camp does not offer direct access to Lower Twin, home of giant brown trout, it is very close. (See the entries in this chapter for Lower Twin Lake and Honeymoon Flat for more information.)

RV sites, facilities: There are 23 single sites, two double sites, a triple site, and a group site that can accommodate up to 45 people, for RVs up to 45 feet or tents. Picnic tables and fire grills are provided. A lighted restroom, drinking water, firewood, limited cell phone reception, and flush toilets are available. A boat launch (at Lower Twin Lake), a store, an ATM, a coin-operated laundry, and showers are within a half mile. Some facilities are wheelchair-accessible. Leashed pets are permitted.

Reservations, fees: Reserve at 877/444-6777 or online at www.reserveusa.com ($9 reservation fee). The fees are $13 per night for single sites, $26 for double sites, and 39–73 for triple and group sites. A senior discount is available. Open early May to mid-October, weather permitting.

Directions: On U.S. 395, drive to Bridgeport and the junction with Twin Lakes Road. Turn west and drive 11 miles to a road on the left (just before reaching Lower Twin Lake). Turn left and drive over the bridge at Robinson Creek to another road on the left. Turn left and drive a short distance to the campground.

Contact: Humboldt-Toiyabe National Forest, Bridgeport Ranger District, 760/932-7070, fax 760/932-1299.

10 LOWER TWIN LAKE

Rating: 9

in Humboldt-Toiyabe National Forest
See map pages 700–701

The Twin Lakes are actually two lakes, set high in the eastern Sierra at 7,000 feet. The best of the two is Lower Twin, where a full resort, marina, boat ramp, and some of the biggest brown trout in the West can be found. The state record brown was caught here, 26.5 pounds, and, in 1991, 11-year-old Micah Beirle of Bakersfield caught one that weighed 20.5 pounds, one of the great fish catches by a youngster anywhere in America. Of course, most of the trout are your typical 10- to 12-inch planted rainbow trout, but nobody seems to mind, with the chance of a true monster-sized fish always in the back of the minds of anglers. An option for campers is an excellent

trailhead for hiking near Mono Village at the head of Upper Twin Lake. Here you will find the Barney Lake Trail, which is routed up the headwaters of Robinson Creek, steeply at times, to Barney Lake, an excellent day hike.

RV sites, facilities: There are 12 paved sites for RVs up to 35 feet or tents and three walk-in sites for tents only. Picnic tables and fire grills are provided. Drinking water and flush toilets are available. A boat launch, a store, showers, and a coin-operated laundry are available nearby. Leashed pets are permitted.

Reservations, fees: Reserve at 877/444-6777 or online at www.reserveusa.com ($9 reservation fee). The fee is $13 per night. A senior discount is available. Open early May to mid-October, weather permitting.

Directions: On U.S. 395, drive to Bridgeport and the junction with Twin Lakes Road. Turn west and drive 11 miles to the campground.

Contact: Humboldt-Toiyabe National Forest, Bridgeport Ranger District, 760/932-7070, fax 760/932-1299.

11 WILLOW SPRINGS TRAILER PARK

Rating: 6

near Bridgeport
See map pages 700–701

Willow Springs Trailer Park is set at 6,800 feet along U.S. 395, which runs along the eastern Sierra from Carson City south to Bishop and beyond to Lone Pine. The park is one mile from the turnoff to Bodie ghost town. A nice touch to the place is a central campfire that has been in place for 50 years. The country is stark here on the edge of the high Nevada desert, but there are many side trips that give the area life. The most popular destinations are to the nearby south: Mono Lake, with its tufa towers and incredible populations of breeding gulls and waterfowl, and the Bodie ghost town. For trout fishing, there's Bridgeport Reservoir to the north (good trolling) and downstream to the East Walker River (fly-fishing), both excellent destinations, as well as Twin Lakes to the west (huge brown trout). Ken's Sporting Goods in Bridgeport provides excellent information.

RV sites, facilities: There are 25 sites with full

hookups (30 amps) for RVs and a motel. Picnic tables are provided. Restrooms, showers, limited cell phone reception, a coin-operated laundry, and nightly campfires are available. A restaurant is within walking distance. An ATM is within five miles. Leashed pets are permitted.

Reservations, fees: Reservations are accepted. The fee is $22 per night, plus $3 per person per night for more than two people. Open May through October.

Directions: From Bridgeport on U.S. 395, drive five miles south to the park.

Contact: Willow Springs Trailer Park, 760/932-7725, fax 760/932-1145.

12 TRUMBULL LAKE

Rating: 8

in Humboldt-Toiyabe National Forest
See map pages 700–701

This is a high-mountain camp (9,500 feet) at the gateway to a beautiful Sierra basin. Little Trumbull Lake is the first lake on the north side of Virginia Lakes Road, with Virginia Lakes nearby, along with the Hoover Wilderness and access to many other small lakes by trail. A trail is available that is routed just north of Blue Lake, then leads west to Frog Lake, Summit Lake, and beyond into a remote area of Yosemite National Park. If you don't want to rough it, cabins, boat rentals, and a restaurant are available at Virginia Lakes Resort.

RV sites, facilities: There are 41 single sites, three double sites, and one triple site, for RVs up to 60 feet or tents. Picnic tables and fire grills are provided. Drinking water and vault toilets are available. A store and an ATM are nearby at the resort. Leashed pets are permitted.

Reservations, fees: Reserve at 877/444-6777 or online at www.reserveusa.com ($9 reservation fee). The fees are $11 per night for single sites, $22 for double sites, and $33 for triple sites. A senior discount is available. Open mid-June to mid-October, weather permitting.

Directions: From Bridgeport, drive south on U.S. 395 for 13.5 miles to Virginia Lakes Road. Turn right on Virginia Lakes Road and drive 6.5 miles to the campground entrance road.

Contact: Humboldt-Toiyabe National Forest,

Bridgeport Ranger District, 760/932-7070, fax 760/932-1299.

13 CHERRY VALLEY

Rating: 8

on Cherry Lake in Stanislaus National Forest
See map pages 700–701

Cherry Lake is a mountain lake surrounded by national forest at 4,700 feet in elevation, just outside the western boundary of Yosemite National Park. It is much larger than most people anticipate and provides much better trout fishing than anything in Yosemite. The camp is on the southwest shore of the lake, a very pretty spot, about a mile ride to the boat launch on the west side of the Cherry Valley Dam. The lake is bordered to the east by Kibbie Ridge; just on the other side are Yosemite Park and Lake Eleanor.

RV sites, facilities: There are 46 sites for RVs up to 22 feet or tents. Picnic tables and fire grills are provided. Drinking water and vault toilets are available. A boat ramp is nearby. Leashed pets are permitted.

Reservations, fees: Reservations are not accepted. The fee is $12 per night, $22 for double sites. A senior discount is available. Open April through October.

Directions: From Groveland, drive east on Highway 120 for about 15 miles to Forest Road 1N07/Cherry Lake Road on the left side of the road. Turn left and drive 18 miles to the south end of Cherry Lake and the campground access road on the right. Turn right and drive one mile to the campground.

Contact: Stanislaus National Forest, Groveland Ranger District, 209/962-7825, fax 209/962-7412.

14 SADDLEBAG LAKE

Rating: 10

in Inyo National Forest
See map pages 700–701

This camp is set in spectacular high country above tree line, the highest drive-to camp and lake in California; Saddlebag Lake sits at 10,087 feet. The camp is about a quarter mile from the lake, within walking range of the little store, boat rentals, and a one-minute drive for launching a boat at the ramp. The scenery is stark; everything is granite, ice, or water, with only a few lodgepole pines managing precarious toeholds, sprinkled across the landscape on the access road. An excellent trailhead is available for hiking, with the best hike routed out past little Hummingbird Lake to Lundy Pass. Note that with the elevation and the high mountain pass, it can be windy and cold here, and some people find it difficult to catch their breath on simple hikes. In addition, RV users should note that level sites are extremely hard to come by.

RV sites, facilities: There are 20 sites for RVs up to 30 feet or tents and one group site for up to 25 people. Drinking water, fire grills, and picnic tables are provided. Vault toilets, boat rentals, and a boat launch are available. A grocery store is nearby. Leashed pets are permitted.

Reservations, fees: Reservations are available for the group site only at 877/444-6777 or online at www.reserveusa.com ($9 reservation fee). The fee is $15 per night for single sites, $40–56 per night for the group site. Open July through October, weather permitting.

Directions: On U.S. 395, drive .5 mile south of Lee Vining and the junction with Highway 120. Turn west and drive about 11 miles to Saddlebag Lake Road. Turn right and drive 2.5 miles to the campground on the right.

From Merced, drive east on Highway 140 to the Arch Rock entrance station. Continue east to the Big Oak Flat Road junction (.5 mile before entering Yosemite Valley). Turn left and drive 14 miles to Tioga Road. Turn right and drive about 65 miles (past Tuolumne Meadows) and through the Tioga Pass entrance station. Continue two miles to Saddlebag Lake Road. Turn left and drive 2.5 miles to the campground on the right.

Contact: Inyo National Forest, Mono Lake Visitor Center, 760/647-3044, fax 760/647-3046.

15 TIOGA LAKE

Rating: 9

in Inyo National Forest
See map pages 700–701

Tioga Lake is a dramatic sight, with gemlike blue waters encircled by Sierra granite at 9,700 feet

in elevation. Together with adjacent Ellery Lake, it makes up a pair of gorgeous waters with near-lake camping, trout fishing (stocked with rainbow trout), and access to Yosemite National Park and Saddlebag Lake. The only downers: it can get windy here (no foolin'!) and the camps fill quickly from the overflow crowds at Tuolumne Meadows. (See the following entry for Ellery Lake for more information.)

RV sites, facilities: There are 13 sites for RVs up to 30 feet or tents. Picnic tables and fire grills are provided. Drinking water and vault toilets are available. Leashed pets are permitted.

Reservations, fees: Reservations are not accepted. The fee is $15 per night. A senior discount is available. Open June through October, weather permitting.

Directions: On U.S. 395, drive to just south of Lee Vining and the junction with Highway 120. Turn west on Highway 120 and drive about 11 miles (just past Ellery Lake) to the campground on the left side of the road.

From Merced, drive east on Highway 140 to the Arch Rock entrance station. Continue east to the Big Oak Flat Road junction (.5 mile before entering Yosemite Valley). Turn left and drive 14 miles to Tioga Road. Turn right and drive about 65 miles (past Tuolumne Meadows) and through the Tioga Pass entrance station. Continue one mile to the campground entrance road on the right side of the road.

Contact: Inyo National Forest, Mono Lake Visitor Center, 760/647-3044, fax 760/647-3046.

16 ELLERY LAKE

Rating: 9

in Inyo National Forest
See map pages 700–701

Ellery Lake offers all the spectacular beauty of Yosemite but is two miles outside park borders. That means it is stocked with trout by the Department of Fish and Game (no lakes in Yosemite are planted, hence the lousy fishing). Just like neighboring Tioga Lake, here are deep-blue waters set in rock in the 9,500-foot elevation range, one of the most pristine highway-access lake settings anywhere. Nearby Saddlebag Lake is a common side trip, the highest drive-to lake in California.

Whenever Tuolumne Meadows fills in Yosemite, this camp fills shortly thereafter. Camp elevation is 9,600 feet.

RV sites, facilities: There are 12 sites for RVs up to 30 feet or tents. Picnic tables and fire grills are provided. Drinking water and flush toilets are available. A grocery store and ATM are nearby. Leashed pets are permitted.

Reservations, fees: Reservations are not accepted. The fee is $15 per night. Open late June to mid-October, weather permitting.

Directions: On U.S. 395, drive to just south of Lee Vining and the junction with Highway 120. Turn west on Highway 120 and drive about 10 miles to the campground on the left side of the road.

From Merced, drive east on Highway 140 to the Arch Rock entrance station. Continue east to the Big Oak Flat Road junction (.5 mile before entering Yosemite Valley). Turn left and drive 14 miles to Tioga Road. Turn right and drive about 65 miles (past Tuolumne Meadows) and through the Tioga Pass entrance station. Continue four miles to the campground entrance road on the right.

Contact: Inyo National Forest, Mono Lake Visitor Center, 760/647-3044, fax 760/647-3046.

17 LOWER LEE VINING CAMP

Rating: 7

near Lee Vining

See map pages 700–701

This camp and its neighboring camps—Cattleguard, Moraine, Aspen, Big Bend, and Boulder—can be a godsend for vacationers who show up at Yosemite National Park and make the discovery that there are no sites left, a terrible experience for some late-night arrivals. But these county campgrounds provide a great safety valve, even if they are extremely primitive, on the edge of timber. Lee Vining Creek is the highlight, flowing right past the campgrounds along Highway 120, bound for Mono Lake to the nearby east. It is stocked weekly during the fishing season. A must-do side trip is venturing to the south shore of Mono Lake to walk amid the bizarre yet beautiful tufa towers. There is good rock-climbing and hiking in the area. Although sunshine is the norm,

be prepared for all kinds of weather: it can snow every month of the year here. Short but lively thunderstorms are common in early summer. Other nearby destinations include Mammoth Lakes, June Lake, and Bodie State Park.

RV sites, facilities: There are 59 sites for RVs up to 40 feet or tents. Pit and portable toilets are available. No drinking water is available. You can buy supplies in Lee Vining (about two miles away). Leashed pets are permitted.

Reservations, fees: Reservations are not accepted. The fee is $8 per night. Open May through October, weather permitting.

Directions: On U.S. 395, drive to just south of Lee Vining and the junction with Highway 120. Turn west on Highway 120 and drive about 2.5 miles. Turn left into the campground entrance.

Contact: Mono County Public Works, 760/932-5252, fax 760/932-5248.

18 BIG BEND

Rating: 8

on Lee Vining Creek in Inyo National Forest

See map pages 700–701

This camp is set in sparse but beautiful country along Lee Vining Creek at 7,800 feet elevation. It is an excellent bet for an overflow camp if Tuolumne Meadows in nearby Yosemite is packed. The view from the camp to the north features Mono Dome (10,614 feet) and Lee Vining Peak (11,691 feet).

RV sites, facilities: There are 17 sites for RVs up to 30 feet or tents. Picnic tables and fire grills are provided. Drinking water and vault toilets are available. Leashed pets are permitted.

Reservations, fees: Reservations are not accepted. The fee is $15 per night. A senior discount is available. Open late April to mid-October, weather permitting.

Directions: On U.S. 395, drive to just south of Lee Vining and the junction with Highway 120. Turn west on Highway 120 and drive about 3.5 miles to Poole Power Plant Road and signed campground access road on the right. Turn right and drive a short distance to the camp.

Contact: Inyo National Forest, Mono Lake Visitor Center, 760/647-3044, fax 760/647-3046.

CALIFORNIA

19 ASPEN GROVE

Rating: 8

on Lee Vining Creek
See map pages 700–701
This high-country, primitive camp is set along Lee Vining Creek at 7,500 feet, on the eastern slopes of the Sierra just east of Yosemite National Park. Take the side trip to moonlike Mono Lake, best seen at the south shore's Tufa State Reserve.
RV sites, facilities: There are 58 sites for RVs up to 40 feet or tents. Pit and portable toilets are available. Drinking water is available from a wellhead at the entrance to the camp. You can buy supplies in Lee Vining. Leashed pets are permitted.
Reservations, fees: Reservations are not accepted. The fee is $7 per night, with a limit of two vehicles and six people per site. Open May through October, weather permitting.
Directions: On U.S. 395, drive to just south of Lee Vining and the junction with Highway 120. Turn west on Highway 120 and drive about 3.5 miles. Exit onto Poole Power Plant Road. Turn left and drive about four miles west to the campground on the left.
Contact: Mono County Public Works, 760/932-5451, fax 760/932-5458; Inyo National Forest, Mono Lake Visitor Center, 760/647-3044, fax 760/647-3046.

20 YOSEMITE LAKES

Rating: 7

on Tuolumne River at Groveland
See map pages 700–701
This is a 400-acre park set at 3,400 feet along the South Fork Tuolumne River in the Sierra foothills near Groveland. Its proximity to Yosemite National Park, just five miles from the west entrance station, makes it ideal for many. The park is an affiliate of Thousand Trails, whose facilities usually are open only to members, but in this rare case, it is open to the general public. It is a family-oriented park with a large variety of recreation options and organized activities. Fishing and swimming are popular, and the river is stocked with trout. A plus is 24-hour security.
RV sites, facilities: There are 20 sites with full hookups for RVs and 25 sites for tents available to the public (more sites available to Thousand Trails members only), and cabins, cottages, yurts, rental trailers, and a hostel. Picnic tables and fire rings are provided. Restrooms, drinking water, showers, flush toilets, an RV dump station, a fish-cleaning station, and a coin-operated laundry are available. A store, a weekend restaurant for breakfast and dinner, a TV room, a recreation lodge, a game room, mini-golf, and a playground with basketball, volleyball, and horseshoes are on-site. Kayaks, paddleboats, inner tubes, and bicycles are available for rent. Horseback riding is nearby. Leashed pets are permitted.
Reservations, fees: Reservations are accepted at 800/533-1001. The fee is $30 per night for RVs and $22 per night for tents, plus $10 per additional vehicle unless towed. Major credit cards are accepted. Open year-round, weather permitting.
Directions: Drive east on Highway 120 to Groveland. From Groveland, continue east for 18 miles to the entrance road (signed) for Yosemite Lakes on the right. Turn right and drive a short distance to the park.
Contact: Yosemite Lakes, 209/962-0121, website: www.ThousandTrails.com.

21 DIMOND "O"

Rating: 7

in Stanislaus National Forest
See map pages 700–701
Dimond "O" is set at 4,400 feet in elevation on the eastern side of Stanislaus National Forest—just two miles from the western border of Yosemite National Park.
RV sites, facilities: There are 38 sites suitable for RVs up to 33 feet and trailers. Picnic tables and fire grills are provided. Drinking water and vault toilets are available. Some facilities are wheelchair-accessible. Leashed pets are permitted.
Reservations, fees: Reservations are not accepted. The fee is $13 per night. A senior discount is available. Open April through October.
Directions: From Groveland, drive east on Highway 120 for 25 miles to Evergreen Road/Forest

CALIFORNIA

Road 12. Turn left on Evergreen Road and drive six miles to the campground.

Contact: Stanislaus National Forest, Groveland Ranger District, 209/962-7825, fax 209/962-7412.

22 HODGDON MEADOW

Rating: 7

in Yosemite National Park
See map pages 700–701

Hodgdon Meadow is on the outskirts of Yosemite, just inside the park's borders at the Big Oak Flat (Highway 120) entrance station, at 4,900 feet in elevation. It is near a small feeder creek to the South Fork Tuolumne River. It is about a 20-minute drive on Highway 120 to a major junction, where a left turn takes you on Tioga Road and to Yosemite's high country, including Tuolumne Meadows, and where staying on Big Flat Road routes you toward Yosemite Valley (25 miles from the camp).

RV sites, facilities: There are 105 family sites for RVs up to 35 feet or tents and four group sites for 13 to 30 people. Picnic tables, fire rings, and food lockers are provided. Drinking water and flush toilets are available. Leashed pets are permitted in the campground, but not on trails.

Reservations, fees: Reserve at 800/436-PARK (800/436-7275) or online at http://reservations.nps.gov. Reservations are required May through October. The fees are $18 per night May through October, $12 the remainder of year, and $40 per night for the group campsites, plus a $20 park entrance fee per vehicle. Open year-round.

Directions: From Groveland, drive east on Highway 120 to the Big Oak Flat entrance station for Yosemite National Park. Just after passing the entrance station, turn left and drive a short distance to the campground on the right.

Contact: Yosemite National Park, 209/372-0200, for a touch-tone menu of recorded information.

23 WHITE WOLF

Rating: 8

in Yosemite National Park
See map pages 700–701

This is one of Yosemite National Park's prime mountain camps for people who like to hike, either for great day hikes in the immediate area and beyond, or for overnight backpacking trips. The day hike to Lukens Lake is an easy two-mile trip, the payoff being this pretty little alpine lake set amid a meadow, pines, and granite. Just about everybody who camps at White Wolf makes the trip. Backpackers (wilderness permit required) can make the overnight trip into the Ten Lakes Basin, set below Grand Mountain and Colby Mountain. Bears are common at this camp, so be certain to secure your food in the bear-proof lockers. The elevation is 8,000 feet.

RV sites, facilities: There are 74 sites for RVs up to 27 feet or tents. Picnic tables, fire grills, and food lockers are provided. Drinking water and flush toilets are available. Evening ranger programs are also available. A small store with a walk-up window and limited items is nearby. Leashed pets are permitted in the campground, but not on trails.

Reservations, fees: Reservations are not accepted. The fee is $12 per night, plus a $20 park entrance fee per vehicle. Open July to early September.

Directions: From Merced, drive east on Highway 140 to the Arch Rock entrance station. Continue east to the Big Oak Flat Road junction (a half mile before entering Yosemite Valley). Turn left and drive 14 miles to Tioga Road. Turn right and drive 15 miles to White Wolf Road on the left. Turn left and drive a mile to the campground entrance road on the right.

Contact: Yosemite National Park, 209/372-0200, for a touch-tone menu of recorded information.

24 PORCUPINE FLAT

Rating: 6

near Yosemite Creek in Yosemite National Park
See map pages 700–701

Porcupine Flat, set at 8,100 feet, is southwest of Mount Hoffman, one of the prominent nearby peaks along Tioga Road in Yosemite National Park. The trailhead for a hike to May Lake, set just below Mount Hoffman, is about five miles away on a signed turnoff on the north side of the road. There are several little peaks above the lake where hikers can gain great views, including one of the back side of Half Dome. Tenaya Lake is also nearby.

RV sites, facilities: There are 52 sites for RVs up to 35 feet or tents. There is limited RV space. Picnic tables and fire rings are provided. Pit toilets are available. No drinking water is available. No pets are allowed.

Reservations, fees: Reservations are not accepted. The fee is $8 per night, plus a $20 park entrance fee per vehicle. A senior discount is available. Open July to early September.

Directions: From Merced, drive east on Highway 140 to the Arch Rock entrance station. Continue east to the Big Oak Flat Road junction (a half mile before entering Yosemite Valley). Turn left and drive 14 miles to Tioga Road. Turn right and drive about 25 miles to the campground on the left side of the road (16 miles west from Tuolumne Meadows).

Contact: Yosemite National Park, 209/372-0200, for a touch-tone menu of recorded information.

25 TUOLUMNE MEADOWS

Rating: 8

in Yosemite National Park
See map pages 700–701

This is Yosemite's biggest camp, and for the variety of nearby adventures, it might also be the best. It is set in the high country, at 8,600 feet, and can be used as a base camp for fishing, hiking, and horseback riding, or as a start-up point for a backpacking trip (wilderness permits required). This is one of the top trailheads in North America. There are two outstanding and easy day hikes from here, one heading north on the Pacific Crest Trail for the near-level walk to Tuolumne Falls and Glen Aulin, the other heading south up Lyell Fork (toward Donohue Pass), with good fishing for small brook trout. With a backpack (wilderness permit required), either route can be extended for as long as desired into remote and beautiful country. The campground is huge, and neighbors are guaranteed, but it is well wooded and feels somewhat secluded even with all the RVs and tents. There are lots of food-raiding bears in the area, so use of the food lockers is required.

RV sites, facilities: There are 304 sites for RVs up to 35 feet or tents. Picnic tables, fire grills, and food lockers are provided. An additional 25 hike-in sites are available for backpackers (no parking is available for backpacker campsites, usually reserved for those hiking the Pacific Crest Trail, for which a wilderness permit is required), and seven group sites that can accommodate 30 people each. Drinking water, flush toilets, and an RV dump station are available. No RV hookups are available. Showers and groceries are nearby. Leashed pets are permitted, except in group sites.

Reservations, fees: Reserve at 800/436-PARK (800/436-7275) or online at http://reservations.nps.gov; half of the sites are available through reservations, the other half are first-come, first-served. The fees are $18 per night for family sites, $5 per night per person for walk-in sites, and $40 per night for group sites, plus a $20 per vehicle park entrance fee. Open July through mid-September.

Directions: From Merced, drive east on Highway 140 to the Arch Rock entrance station. Continue east to the Big Oak Flat Road junction (.5 mile before entering Yosemite Valley). Turn left and drive 14 miles to Tioga Road. Turn right and drive 46 miles to the campground on the right side of the road.

From just south of Lee Vining at the junction of U.S. 395 and Highway 120, turn west and drive to the Tioga Pass entrance station for Yosemite National Park. Continue for about 10 miles to the campground entrance on the left.

Contact: Yosemite National Park, 209/372-0200, for a touch-tone menu of recorded information.

26 SILVER LAKE

Rating: 9

in Inyo National Forest
See map pages 700–701

Silver Lake is set at 7,200 feet, an 80-acre lake in the June Lake Loop with Carson Peak looming in the background. Boat rentals, fishing for trout at the lake, a beautiful trout stream (Rush Creek) next to the camp, and a nearby trailhead for wilderness hiking and horseback riding (rentals available) are the highlights. The camp is largely exposed and vulnerable to winds, the only downer. Within

CALIFORNIA

walking distance to the south is Silver Lake, always a pretty sight, especially when afternoon winds cause the lake surface to sparkle in crackling silvers. Just across the road from the camp is a great trailhead for the Ansel Adams Wilderness, with a two-hour hike available that climbs to pretty Agnew Lake overlooking the June Lake basin; a wilderness permit is required for overnight use.

RV sites, facilities: There are 63 sites for RVs up to 40 feet or tents. Picnic tables and fire grills are provided. Drinking water, flush toilets, cell phone reception, and horseback riding facilities are available. A grocery store, an ATM, a coin-operated laundry, motorboat rentals, a boat ramp, bait, a snack bar, boat fuel, and propane are available nearby. Leashed pets are permitted.

Reservations, fees: Reservations are not accepted. The fee is $13 per night. A senior discount is available. Open late April to mid-November.

Directions: From Lee Vining on U.S. 395, drive south for six miles to the first Highway 158 North/June Lake Loop turnoff. Turn west (right) and drive nine miles (past Grant Lake) to Silver Lake. Just as you arrive at Silver Lake (a small store is on the right), turn left at the campground entrance.

Contact: Inyo National Forest, Mono Lake Visitor Center, 760/647-3044, fax 760/647-3046.

27 JUNE LAKE

Rating: 9

in Inyo National Forest
See map pages 700–701

There are three campgrounds at pretty June Lake; this is one of the two operated by the Forest Service (the other is Oh! Ridge). This one is on the northeast shore of the lake at 7,600 feet in elevation, a pretty spot with all supplies available just two miles to the south in the town of June Lake. The nearest boat launch is north of town. This is a good lake for trout fishing, receiving nearly 100,000 stocked trout per year.

RV sites, facilities: There are 28 sites, including 15 available by reservation, for RVs up to 20 feet or tents. Picnic tables and fire grills are provided. Drinking water, flush toilets, limited cell phone reception, and a boat ramp are available. A grocery store, an ATM, a coin-operated laundry, boat

and tackle rentals, moorings, and propane are available nearby. Leashed pets are permitted.

Reservations, fees: Reserve at 877/444-6777 or online at www.reserveusa.com ($9 reservation fee). The fee is $13 per night. A senior discount is available. Open late April to early November, weather permitting.

Directions: From Lee Vining, drive south on U.S. 395 (passing the Highway 158 North) for 20 miles (six miles past Highway 158 North) to June Lake Junction (a sign is posted for "June Lake Village") and Highway 158 South. Turn west (right) on Highway 158 North and drive two miles to June Lake. Turn right (signed) and drive a short distance to the campground.

Contact: Inyo National Forest, Mono Lake Visitor Center, 760/647-3044, fax 760/647-3046.

28 OH! RIDGE

Rating: 8

on June Lake in Inyo National Forest
See map pages 700–701

This is the largest of the campgrounds on June Lake. However, it is not the most popular since it is not right on the lakeshore, but back about a quarter mile or so from the north end of the lake. Regardless, it has the best views of the lake, with the ridge of the high Sierra providing a backdrop. The lake is a good one for trout fishing. The elevation is 7,600 feet.

RV sites, facilities: There are 148 sites, including 74 available for reservation, for RVs up to 40 feet or tents. Picnic tables and fire grills are provided. Drinking water, flush toilets, limited cell phone reception, and a playground are available. A grocery store, an ATM, a coin-operated laundry, a boat ramp, boat and tackle rentals, a swimming beach, moorings, and propane are available nearby. Leashed pets are permitted.

Reservations, fees: Reserve at 877/444-6777 or online at www.reserveusa.com ($9 reservation fee). The fee is $13 per night. A senior discount is available. Open late April to early November.

Directions: From Lee Vining, drive south on U.S. 395 (past the first Highway 158/June Lake Loop turnoff) to June Lake Junction (a gas station/store is on the west side of the road) and Highway 158 South. Turn west on Highway 158 South and

drive two miles to Oh! Ridge Road. Turn right and drive a mile to the campground access road (signed). Turn left and drive to the campground.
Contact: Inyo National Forest, Mono Lake Visitor Center, 760/647-3044, fax 760/647-3046.

29 PINE CLIFF RESORT

Rating: 7

at June Lake
See map pages 700–701
You've found "kid heaven" at Pine Cliff Resort. This camp is in a pretty setting along the north shore of June Lake (7,600 feet in elevation), the feature lake among four in the June Lake Loop. The campsites are nestled in pine trees, designed so each site accommodates different-sized rigs and families, and the campground is about a quarter mile from June Lake. This is the only camp at June Lake Loop that has a swimming beach available. The landscape is a pretty one, with the lake set below snowcapped peaks. The bonus is that June Lake gets large numbers of trout plants each summer, making it extremely popular with anglers. Of the lakes in the June Lake Loop, this is the one that has the most of everything—the most beauty, the most fish, the most developed accommodations, and, alas, the most people. This resort has been operated as a family business for nearly 50 years.
RV sites, facilities: There are 154 sites, including 15 drive-through, with full hookups for RVs, 55 sites for tents and small trailers (18 feet or shorter) only, and 17 sites with partial hookups for RVs or tents. Picnic tables and fire rings are provided. Restrooms, flush toilets, showers, drinking water, a coin-operated laundry, basketball, volleyball, tetherball, horseshoes, a store, and propane are available. A primitive boat ramp, boat and tackle rentals, fish-cleaning facilities, and fuel are available nearby. Some facilities are wheelchair-accessible. Leashed pets are permitted.
Reservations, fees: Reservations are recommended. The fee is $11–20 per night, plus $5 per additional vehicle. Open mid-April through October.
Directions: From Lee Vining, drive south on U.S. 395 (passing the first Highway 158 North/June Lake Loop turnoff) for 20 miles (six miles past Highway 158 North) to June Lake Junction (a

sign is posted for "June Lake Village") and Highway 158 South. Turn right (west) on Highway 158 South and drive a mile to North Shore Drive (a sign is nearby for Pine Cliff Resort). Turn right and drive .5 mile to Pine Cliff Road. Turn left and drive .5 mile to the resort store on the right (route is well signed).
Contact: Pine Cliff Resort, 760/648-7558.

30 HARTLEY SPRINGS

Rating: 8

in Inyo National Forest
See map pages 700–701
Even though this camp is only a five-minute drive from U.S. 395, those five minutes will take you into another orbit. It is in a forest of Jeffrey pine and has the feel of a remote, primitive camp, set in a high-mountain environment at an elevation of 8,400 feet. About two miles to the immediate north at elevation 8,611 feet is Obsidian Dome "Glass Flow," a craggy geologic formation that some people enjoy scrambling around and exploring; pick your access point carefully.
RV sites, facilities: There are 20 sites for RVs up to 40 feet or tents. Picnic tables and fire grills are provided. Vault toilets are available. No drinking water is available. Leashed pets are permitted.
Reservations, fees: Reservations are not accepted. There is no fee for camping. Open late May to late September, weather permitting.
Directions: From Lee Vining, drive south on U.S. 395 (passing the first Highway 158/June Lake Loop turnoff) for 10 miles to June Lake Junction. Continue south on U.S. 395 for six miles to Glass Creek Road (a dirt road on the west side of the highway). Turn west (right) and drive two miles to the campground entrance road on the left.
Contact: Inyo National Forest, Mono Lake Visitor Center, 760/647-3044, fax 760/647-3046.

31 CRANE FLAT

Rating: 6

near Tuolumne Grove of Big Trees in Yosemite National Park
See map pages 700–701
Crane Flat is within a five-minute drive of the

CALIFORNIA

Tuolumne Grove of Big Trees, as well as the Merced Grove to the nearby west. This is the feature attraction in this part of Yosemite National Park, set near the western border in close proximity to the Big Oak Flat entrance station (Highway 120). The elevation is 6,200 feet. Yosemite Valley is about a 25-minute drive away.

RV sites, facilities: There are 166 sites for RVs up to 35 feet or tents. Picnic tables, fire rings, limited cell phone reception, and food lockers are provided. Drinking water and flush toilets are available. Groceries, an ATM, propane, and a gas station are nearby.

Reservations, fees: Reserve at 800/436-PARK (800/436-7275) or online at http://reservations.nps.gov. The fee is $18 per night, plus a $20 park entrance fee per vehicle. A senior discount is available. Open June through September.

Directions: From Groveland, drive east on Highway 120 to the Big Oak Flat entrance station for Yosemite National Park. After passing through the entrance station, drive about 10 miles to the campground entrance road on the right. Turn right and drive .5 mile to the campground.

Contact: Yosemite National Park, 209/372-0200, for a touch-tone menu of recorded information.

32 BRIDALVEIL CREEK
🚶 ⛴ 🐕 🚐 ⛺

Rating: 10

near Glacier Point in Yosemite National Park

See map pages 700–701

There may be no better view in the world than the one from Glacier Point, looking down into Yosemite Valley, where Half Dome stands like nature's perfect sculpture. Then there are the perfect views of Yosemite Falls, Nevada Fall, Vernal Fall, and several hundred square miles of Yosemite's wilderness backcountry. This is the closest camp to Glacier Point's drive-to vantage point, but it is also the closest camp to the best day hikes in the entire park. Along Glacier Point Road are trailheads to Sentinel Dome (incredible view of Yosemite Falls), Taft Point (breathtaking drop, incredible view of El Capitan), and McGurk Meadow (one of the most pristine spots on earth). At 7,200 feet, the camp is more than 3,000 feet higher than Yosemite Valley. A good

day hike out of camp leads you to Ostrander Lake, just below Horse Ridge.

RV sites, facilities: There are 110 sites for RVs up to 35 feet or tents and two group camps that can accommodate up to 30 people. Picnic tables and fire grills are provided. Drinking water and flush toilets are available. Leashed pets are permitted, except in group sites.

Reservations, fees: Reservations are not accepted. The fees are $12 per night and $40 per night for group sites, plus a $20 park entrance fee per vehicle. A 14-day stay limit is enforced. Open July to early September.

Directions: From Merced, drive east on Highway 140 to the Arch Rock entrance station. Continue east (past Big Oak Flat Road junction) to the junction with Wawona Road/Highway 41 (just before Yosemite Valley). Turn right on Highway 41/Wawona Road and drive about 10 miles to Glacier Point Road. Turn left on Glacier Point Road and drive about five miles (a few miles past Badger Pass Ski Area) to Peregoy Meadow and the campground access road on the right. Turn right and drive a short distance to the campground.

Contact: Yosemite National Park, 209/372-0200, for a touch-tone menu of recorded information.

33 LOWER PINES
🚶 🚲 🏊 ⛴ ❄ 🐕 🚐 ⛺

Rating: 9

in Yosemite Valley in Yosemite National Park

See map pages 700–701

Lower Pines sits at 4,000 feet elevation right along the Merced River, quite pretty, in the center of Yosemite Valley. Of course, the tents and RVs are jammed in quite close together. Within walking distance is the trail to Mirror Lake (a zoo on parade), as well as the trailhead at Happy Isles for the hike up to Vernal Fall and Nevada Fall. The park's shuttle bus picks up riders near the camp entrance.

RV sites, facilities: There are 60 sites for RVs up to 40 feet or tents. Fire rings and picnic tables are provided. Drinking water, flush toilets, limited cell phone reception, and food lockers are available. A grocery store, an ATM, a coin-operated laundry, propane, a recycling center, an RV dump station, and horse, bike, and cross-country ski rentals are available nearby. Leashed pets are allowed.

Reservations, fees: Reserve at 800/436-PARK (800/436-7275) or online at http://reservations.nps.gov. The fee is $18 per night, plus a $20 park entrance fee per vehicle. A senior discount is available. Open April through October, weather permitting.

Directions: From Merced, drive east on Highway 140 to the Arch Rock entrance station. Continue east to the Big Oak Flat Road junction (a half mile before entering Yosemite Valley). Continue into Yosemite Valley, drive past Curry Village (on the right) to the campground entrance on the left side of the road (just before Clarks Bridge).

Contact: Yosemite National Park, 209/372-0200, for a touch-tone menu of recorded information.

34 UPPER PINES

Rating: 9

in Yosemite Valley in Yosemite National Park
See map pages 700-701

Of the campgrounds in Yosemite Valley, Upper Pines is the closest trailhead to paradise, providing you can get a campsite at the far south end of the camp. From here it is a short walk to the Happy Isles trailhead and with it the chance to hike to Vernal Fall on the Mist Trail (steep), or beyond to Nevada Fall (very steep) at the foot of Liberty Cap. But crowded this camp is, and you'd better expect it. People come from all over the world to camp here. Sometimes it appears as if they are from other worlds as well. The elevation is 4,000 feet.

RV sites, facilities: There are 238 sites for RVs up to 40 feet or tents. Fire rings and picnic tables are provided. Drinking water, flush toilets, food lockers, limited cell phone reception, and an RV dump station are available. A grocery store, an ATM, a coin-operated laundry, propane, a recycling center, and bike rentals are available nearby. Leashed pets are permitted in the campgrounds, but not on trails.

Reservations, fees: Reserve at 800/436-PARK (800/436-7275) or online at http://reservations.nps.gov. The fee is $18 per night, plus a $20

park entrance fee per vehicle. A senior discount is available. Open year-round.

Directions: From Merced, drive east on Highway 140 to the Arch Rock entrance station. Continue east to the Big Oak Flat Road junction (.5 mile before entering Yosemite Valley). Continue into Yosemite Valley, drive past Curry Village (on the right) to the campground entrance on the right side of the road (just before Clarks Bridge).

Contact: Yosemite National Park, 209/372-0200, for a touch-tone menu of recorded information.

35 NORTH PINES

Rating: 9

in Yosemite Valley in Yosemite National Park
See map pages 700-701

North Pines is set along the Merced River. A trail out of camp heads east and links up the paved road/trail to Mirror Lake, a virtual parade of people. If you continue hiking past Mirror Lake you will get astounding views of Half Dome and then leave the masses behind as you enter Tenaya Canyon. The elevation is 4,000 feet.

RV sites, facilities: There are 81 sites for RVs up to 40 feet or tents. Picnic tables and fire grills are provided. Drinking water, flush toilets, and food lockers are available. A grocery store, a coin-operated laundry, a recycling center, propane, and bike rentals are available nearby. Leashed pets are allowed.

Reservations, fees: Reserve at 800/436-PARK (800/436-7275) or online at http://reservations.nps.gov. The fee is $18 per night, plus a $20 park entrance fee per vehicle. A senior discount is available. Open April through September.

Directions: From Merced, drive east on Highway 140 to the Arch Rock entrance station. Continue east to the Big Oak Flat Road junction (.5 mile before entering Yosemite Valley). Continue into Yosemite Valley, drive past Curry Village (on the right), continue past Upper and Lower Pines Campgrounds, and drive over Clarks Bridge to a junction at the horse stables. Turn left at the horse stables and drive a short distance to the campground on the right.

Contact: Yosemite National Park, 209/372-0200, for a touch-tone menu of recorded information.

CALIFORNIA

36 AGNEW MEADOWS

Rating: 9

in Inyo National Forest
See map pages 700–701

This is a perfect camp to use as a launching pad for a backpacking trip or a day of fly-fishing for trout. It is set along the Upper San Joaquin River at 8,400 feet, with a trailhead for the Pacific Crest Trail available near the camp. From here you can hike seven miles to the gorgeous Thousand Island Lake, a beautiful lake sprinkled with islands set below Banner and Ritter Peaks in the spectacular Minarets. For day hikes, another choice is walking the River Trail, which is routed from Agnew Meadows along the San Joaquin, providing excellent fishing, though the trout are small.

RV sites, facilities: There are 21 sites for RVs or tents, most of which can accommodate RVs up to 46 feet and some up to 55 feet. A group camp is also available (reservations are required for the group camp). Picnic tables and fire grills are provided. Drinking water, chemical and vault toilets, limited cell phone reception, and horseback riding facilities are available (three family sites have hitching racks where horse camping is permitted). An ATM is within 10 miles. Supplies can be obtained at Red's Meadows. Leashed pets are permitted.

Reservations, fees: Reservations are not accepted for single sites. For group camp and horse camping sites, reserve at 877/444-6777 or online at www.reserveusa.com ($9 reservation fee). The fees are $15 per night and $30–50 per night for group and horse camping sites, plus a $5 per person Reds Meadow/Agnew Meadows access fee. A senior discount is available. Open mid-June to late September.

Directions: On U.S. 395, drive to Mammoth Junction/Highway 203. Turn west on Highway 203 and drive four miles, through the town of Mammoth Lakes to Minaret Road (still Highway 203). Turn right and drive five miles to Minaret Station (past the Mammoth Mountain Ski Area). Continue for 2.6 miles to the campground entrance road on the right. Turn right and drive just under a mile to the campground.

Access note: Noncampers are required to use a shuttle bus from the Shuttle Bus Terminal at Mammoth Mountain Main Lodge Gondola Station from 7 A.M. to 7:45 P.M. Space is available for leashed dogs, bikes, and backpacks.

Contact: Inyo National Forest, Mammoth Lakes Visitor Center, 760/924-5500, fax 760/924-5547.

37 PUMICE FLAT

Rating: 8

on the San Joaquin River in Inyo National Forest
See map pages 700–701

Pumice Flat (7,700 feet in elevation) provides roadside camping within short range of several adventures. A trail out of camp links with the Pacific Crest Trail, where you can hike along the Upper San Joaquin River for miles, providing excellent access for fly-fishing, and head north into the Ansel Adams Wilderness. Devils Postpile National Monument is just two miles south, along with the trailhead for Rainbow Falls.

RV sites, facilities: There are 17 sites for RVs or tents, most of which can accommodate RVs up to 47 feet and some up to 55 feet. Picnic tables and fire grills are provided. Drinking water, flush toilets, limited cell phone reception, and horseback riding facilities are available. Limited supplies and an ATM are available at a small store, or full supplies in Mammoth Lakes. Leashed pets are permitted.

Reservations, fees: Reservations are not accepted. The fee is $15 per night, plus a $5 per person Reds Meadow/Agnew Meadows access fee. A senior discount is available. Open mid-June to late September.

Directions: On U.S. 395, drive to Mammoth Junction/Highway 203. Turn west on Highway 203 and drive four miles, through the town of Mammoth Lakes to Minaret Road (still Highway 203). Turn right and drive five miles to Minaret Station (past the Mammoth Mountain Ski Area). Continue for 5.1 miles to the campground on the right side of the road.

Access note: Noncampers are required to use a shuttle bus from the Shuttle Bus Terminal at Mammoth Mountain Main Lodge Gondola Station from 7 A.M. to 7:45 P.M. Space is available for leashed dogs, bikes, and backpacks.

Contact: Inyo National Forest, Mammoth Lakes Visitor Center, 760/924-5500, fax 760/924-5547.

38 UPPER SODA SPRINGS

Rating: 8

on the San Joaquin River in Inyo National Forest
See map pages 700–701

This is a premium location within earshot of the Upper San Joaquin River and within minutes of many first-class recreation options. The river is stocked with trout at this camp, with several good pools within short walking distance. Farther upstream, accessible by an excellent trail, are smaller wild trout that provide good fly-fishing prospects. Devils Postpile National Monument, a massive formation of ancient columnar jointed rock, is only three miles to the south. The Pacific Crest Trail passes right by the camp, providing a trailhead for access to numerous lakes in the Ansel Adams Wilderness. The elevation is 7,700 feet.

RV sites, facilities: There are 29 sites for RVs or tents, most of which can accommodate RVs up to 36 feet and some up to 55 feet. Picnic tables and fire grills are provided. Drinking water, flush toilets, limited cell phone reception, and horseback riding facilities are available. You can buy supplies at Red's Meadows. An ATM is nearby. Leashed pets are permitted.

Reservations, fees: Reservations are not accepted. The fee is $15 per night, plus a $5 per person Reds Meadow/Agnew Meadows access fee. A senior discount is available. Open mid-June to late September.

Directions: On U.S. 395, drive to Mammoth Junction/Highway 203. Turn west on Highway 203 and drive four miles, through the town of Mammoth Lakes to Minaret Road (still Highway 203). Turn right and drive 4.5 miles to the entrance kiosk (adjacent to the Mammoth Mountain Ski Area). Continue for five miles to the campground entrance road on the right. Turn right and drive .25 mile to the campground.

Access note: Noncampers are required to use a shuttle bus from the Shuttle Bus Terminal at Mammoth Mountain Main Lodge Gondola Station from 7 A.M. to 7:45 P.M. Space is available for leashed dogs, bikes, and backpacks.

Contact: Inyo National Forest, Mammoth Lakes Visitor Center, 760/924-5500, fax 760/924-5547.

39 BIG SPRINGS

Rating: 5

on Deadman Creek in Inyo National Forest
See map pages 700–701

Big Springs, at 7,300 feet, is on the edge of the high desert on the east side of U.S. 395. The main attractions are Deadman Creek, which runs right by the camp, and Big Springs, which is just on the opposite side of the river. There are several hot springs in the area, best reached by driving south on U.S. 395 to the Mammoth Lakes Airport and turning left on Hot Creek Road. As with all hot springs, use at your own risk.

RV sites, facilities: There are 26 sites for RVs up to 40 feet or tents. Picnic tables and fire grills are provided. Vault toilets are available. No drinking water is available. Leashed pets are permitted.

Reservations, fees: Reservations are not accepted. There is no fee for camping. Open late April through early November, weather permitting.

Directions: From Lee Vining, drive south on U.S. 395 (past the first Highway 158/June lake Loop turnoff) to June Lake Junction. Continue south for about seven miles to Owens River Road. Turn east (left) and drive two miles to a fork. Bear left at the fork and drive .25 mile to the camp on the left side of the road.

Contact: Inyo National Forest, Mono Lake Visitor Center, 760/647-3044, fax 760/647-3046.

40 MINARET FALLS

Rating: 8

on the San Joaquin River in Inyo National Forest
See map pages 700–701

This camp has one of the prettiest settings of the series of camps along the Upper San Joaquin River and near Devils Postpile National Monument. It is set at 7,700 feet near Minaret Creek, across from where beautiful Minaret Falls pours into the San Joaquin River. Devils Postpile National Monument, one of the best examples in the world of hexagonal, columnar jointed rock, is less than a mile from camp, where there is also a trail to awesome Rainbow Falls. The Pacific Crest Trail runs right through this area as well, and if you hike to the south, there is excellent streamside fishing access.

RV sites, facilities: There are 27 sites for RVs or tents, most of which can accommodate RVs up to 47 feet and some up to 55 feet. Picnic tables and fire grills are provided. Drinking water and vault toilets are available. Chemical toilets and horseback riding facilities are available nearby. You can buy limited supplies at Red's Meadow Store or all supplies in Mammoth Lakes. Leashed pets are permitted.

Reservations, fees: Reservations are not accepted. The fee is $15 per night, plus a $5 per person Reds Meadow/Agnew Meadows access fee. A senior discount is available. Open mid-June to late September.

Directions: On U.S. 395, drive to Mammoth Junction/Highway 203. Turn west on Highway 203 and drive four miles, through the town of Mammoth Lakes to Minaret Road (still Highway 203). Turn right and drive five miles to Minaret Station (past the Mammoth Mountain Ski Area). Continue for six miles to the campground entrance road on the right. Turn right and drive .25 mile to the campground.

Access note: Noncampers are required to use a shuttle bus from the Shuttle Bus Terminal at Mammoth Mountain Main Lodge Gondola Station from 7 A.M. to 7:45 P.M. Space is available for leashed dogs, bikes, and backpacks.

Contact: Inyo National Forest, Mammoth Lakes Visitor Center, 760/924-5500, fax 760/924-5547.

41 DEVILS POSTPILE NATIONAL MONUMENT

🥾 🏕️ ♿ 🚐 ⛺

Rating: 9

near the San Joaquin River
See map pages 700–701

Devils Postpile is a spectacular and rare example of hexagonal, columnar jointed rock that looks like posts, hence the name. The camp is set at 7,600 feet in elevation and provides nearby access for the easy hike to the Postpile. If you keep walking, it is a 2.5-mile walk to Rainbow Falls, a breathtaking 101-foot cascade that pro-

duces rainbows in its floating mist, seen only from the trail alongside the waterfall looking downstream. The camp is also adjacent to the Middle Fork San Joaquin River and the Pacific Crest Trail.

RV sites, facilities: There are 21 sites for RVs or tents. Picnic tables and fire grills are provided. Drinking water and flush toilets are available. Leashed pets are permitted.

Reservations, fees: Reservations are not accepted. The fee is $14 per night, plus a $5 per person Reds Meadow/Agnew Meadows access fee. A senior discount is available. Open mid-June to late October, weather permitting.

Directions: On U.S. 395, drive to Mammoth Junction/Highway 203. Turn west on Highway 203 and drive four miles, through the town of Mammoth Lakes to Minaret Road (still Highway 203). Turn right and drive five miles to Minaret Station (past the Mammoth Mountain Ski Area). Continue for nine miles to the campground entrance road on the right.

Access note: Noncampers are required to use a shuttle bus from the Shuttle Bus Terminal at Mammoth Mountain Main Lodge Gondola Station from 7 A.M. to 7:45 P.M. Space is available for leashed dogs, bikes, and backpacks.

Contact: Devils Postpile National Monument, tel./fax 760/934-2289.

42 RED'S MEADOW

🥾 🏊 🏇 🚐 ⛺

Rating: 6

in Inyo National Forest
See map pages 700–701

Red's Meadow has long been established as one of the best outfitters for horseback riding trips. To get the feel of it, three-mile round-trip rides are available to Rainbow Falls. Multiday trips into the Ansel Adams Wilderness on the Pacific Crest Trail are also available. A small restaurant is a bonus here, always a must-stop for long-distance hikers getting a shot to chomp their first hamburger in weeks, something like a bear finding a candy bar, quite a sight for the drive-in campers. The nearby Devils Postpile National Monument, Rainbow Falls, Minaret Falls, and San Joaquin River provide recreation options. The elevation is 7,600 feet.

RV sites, facilities: There are 56 sites for RVs or tents, most of which can accommodate RVs up to 30 feet and some up to 55 feet. Picnic tables and fire grills are provided. Drinking water, flush toilets, and bear boxes are available. Natural hot springs, a shower house, and horseback riding facilities are also available. You can buy limited supplies at a small store. Leashed pets are permitted.

Reservations, fees: Reservations are not accepted. The fee is $15 per night, plus a $5 per person Reds Meadow/Agnew Meadows access fee. A senior discount is available. Open mid-June to late October.

Directions: On U.S. 395, drive to Mammoth Junction/Highway 203. Turn west on Highway 203 and drive four miles, through the town of Mammoth Lakes to Minaret Road (still Highway 203). Turn right and drive five miles to Minaret Station (past the Mammoth Mountain Ski Area). Continue for 7.4 miles to the campground entrance on the left.

Access note: Noncampers are required to use a shuttle bus from the Shuttle Bus Terminal at Mammoth Mountain Main Lodge Gondola Station from 7 A.M. to 7:45 P.M. Space is available for leashed dogs, bikes, and backpacks.

Contact: Inyo National Forest, Mammoth Lakes Visitor Center, 760/924-5500, fax760/924-5547.

43 LAKE GEORGE

Rating: 8

in Inyo National Forest
See map pages 700–701

The sites here have views of Lake George, a beautiful lake in a rock basin set below the spectacular Crystal Crag. Lake George is at 9,000 feet in elevation, a small lake fed by creeks coming from both Crystal Lake and TJ Lake. Both of the latter make excellent short hiking trips; TJ Lake is only about a 20-minute walk from the campground. Trout fishing at Lake George is decent—not great, not bad, but decent.

RV sites, facilities: There are 16 sites for RVs or tents, most of which can accommodate RVs up to 18 feet and some up to 25 feet. Picnic tables and fire grills are provided. Drinking water, flush toilets, and limited cell phone reception are available. A grocery store, an ATM, a coin-operated laundry, coin-operated showers, and propane are available nearby. Leashed pets are permitted.

Reservations, fees: Reservations are not accepted. The fee is $14 per night with a seven-day limit. A senior discount is available. Open mid-June to mid-September.

Directions: From Lee Vining on U.S. 395, drive south for 25 miles to Mammoth Junction and Highway 203/Minaret Summit Road. Turn west on Highway 203 and drive four miles to Lake Mary Road. Continue straight through the intersection and drive four miles to Lake Mary Loop Drive. Turn left and drive .3 mile to Lake George Road. Turn right and drive .5 mile to the campground.

Contact: Inyo National Forest, Mammoth Lakes Visitor Center, 760/924-5500, fax 760/924-5547.

44 TWIN LAKES

Rating: 8

in Inyo National Forest
See map pages 700–701

From Twin Lakes, you can look west and see pretty Twin Falls, a wide cascade that runs into the head of upper Twin Lake. There are actually two camps here, one on each side of the access road, at 8,600 feet. Lower Twin Lake is a favorite for fly fishers in float tubes.

RV sites, facilities: There are 95 sites for RVs or tents, most of which can accommodate RVs up to 38 feet and some up to 55 feet. Picnic tables and fire grills are provided. Drinking water, flush toilets, a boat launch, and horseback riding facilities are available. A grocery store, an ATM, a coin-operated laundry, coin-operated showers, and propane are available nearby. Some facilities are wheelchair-accessible. Leashed pets are permitted.

Reservations, fees: Reservations are not accepted. The fee is $14 per night with a seven-day limit. A senior discount is available. Open mid-May to late October.

Directions: From Lee Vining on U.S. 395, drive south for 25 miles to Mammoth Junction and Highway 203/Minaret Summit Road. Turn west on Highway 203 and drive four miles to Lake Mary Road. Continue straight through the intersection and drive 2.3 miles to Twin Lakes Loop Road. Turn right and drive .5 mile to the campground.

CALIFORNIA

Contact: Inyo National Forest, Mammoth Lakes Visitor Center, 760/924-5500, fax 760/924-5547.

45 LAKE MARY

Rating: 9

in Inyo National Forest
See map pages 700–701

Lake Mary is the star of the Mammoth Lakes region. Of the 11 lakes in the area, this is the largest. It provides a resort, boat ramp, and boat rentals, and it receives the highest number of trout stocks. It is set at 8,900 feet in a place of incredible natural beauty, one of the few spots that literally has it all. Of course, that often includes quite a few other people. If there are too many for you, an excellent trailhead is available at nearby Coldwater camp.

RV sites, facilities: There are 48 sites for RVs up to 30 feet or tents. Picnic tables and fire grills are provided. Drinking water and flush toilets are available. A grocery store, an ATM, a coin-operated laundry, and propane are nearby. Leashed pets are permitted.

Reservations, fees: Reservations are not accepted. The fee is $14 per night with a 14-day limit. A senior discount is available. Open mid-June to mid-September.

Directions: From Lee Vining on U.S. 395, drive south for 25 miles to Mammoth Junction and Highway 203/Minaret Summit Road. Turn west on Highway 203 and drive four miles to Lake Mary Road. Continue straight through the intersection and drive four miles to Lake Mary Loop Drive. Turn left and drive .25 mile to the campground entrance.

Contact: Inyo National Forest, Mammoth Lakes Visitor Center, 760/924-5500, fax 760/924-5547.

46 PINE CITY

Rating: 7

near Lake Mary in Inyo National Forest
See map pages 700–701

This camp is at the edge of Lake Mary at an elevation of 8,900 feet. It is popular for both families and fly fishers with float tubes.

RV sites, facilities: There are 10 sites for RVs or tents, most of which can accommodate RVs up to 40 feet and some up to 50 feet. Picnic tables and fire grills are provided. Drinking water, flush toilets, and limited cell phone reception are available. A grocery store, an ATM, a coin-operated laundry, and propane are available nearby. Some facilities are wheelchair-accessible. Leashed pets are permitted.

Reservations, fees: Reservations are not accepted. The fee is $14 per night. A senior discount is available. Open late June to mid-September.

Directions: From Lee Vining on U.S. 395, drive south for 25 miles to Mammoth Junction and Highway 203/Minaret Summit Road. Turn west on Highway 203 and drive four miles to Lake Mary Road. Continue straight through the intersection and drive 3.6 miles to Lake Mary Loop Drive. Turn left and drive .25 mile to the campground.

Contact: Inyo National Forest, Mammoth Lakes Visitor Center, 760/924-5500, fax 760/924-5547.

47 COLDWATER

Rating: 7

on Coldwater Creek in Inyo National Forest
See map pages 700–701

While this camp is not the first choice of many simply because there is no lake view, it has a special attraction all its own. First, it is a two-minute drive from the campground to Lake Mary, where there is a boat ramp, rentals, and good trout fishing. Second, at the end of the campground access road is a trailhead for two outstanding hikes. From the Y at the trailhead, if you head right, you will be routed up Coldwater Creek to Emerald Lake, a great little hike. If you head to the left, you will have a more ambitious trip to Arrowhead, Skelton, and Red Lakes, all within three miles. The elevation is 8,900 feet.

RV sites, facilities: There are 77 sites for RVs or tents, most of which can accommodate RVs up to 37 feet and some up to 50 feet. Picnic tables and fire grills are provided. Drinking water, flush toilets, limited cell phone reception, and horse facilities are available. An ATM and supplies are available nearby in Mammoth Lakes. Leashed pets are permitted.

Reservations, fees: Reservations are not accepted. The fee is $14 per night with a 14-day limit.

A senior discount is available. Open mid-June to late September.

Directions: From Lee Vining on U.S. 395, drive south for 25 miles to Mammoth Junction and Highway 203/Minaret Summit Road. Turn west on Highway 203 and drive four miles to Lake Mary Road. Continue straight through the intersection and drive 3.6 miles to Lake Mary Loop Drive. Turn left and drive .6 mile to the camp entrance road.

Contact: Inyo National Forest, Mammoth Lakes Visitor Center, 760/924-5500, fax 760/924-5547.

48 SHERWIN CREEK

Rating: 7

in Inyo National Forest
See map pages 700–701

This camp is set along little Sherwin Creek, at 7,600 feet in elevation, a short distance from the town of Mammoth Lakes. If you drive a mile east on Sherwin Creek Road, then turn right at the short spur road, you will find a trailhead for a hike that is routed up six miles to Valentine Lake in the John Muir Wilderness, set on the northwest flank of Bloody Mountain.

RV sites, facilities: There are 87 sites for RVs or tents, most of which can accommodate RVs up to 34 feet and some up to 50 feet, and 15 walk-in sites for tents only. Picnic tables and fire grills are provided. Drinking water and flush toilets are available. Leashed pets are permitted.

Reservations, fees: Reservations are accepted for 58 sites, including the 15 walk-in sites. The fee is $13 per night with a 21-day limit. A senior discount is available. Open mid-May through mid-September.

Directions: From Lee Vining on U.S. 395, drive south for 25 miles to Mammoth Junction and Highway 203/Minaret Summit Road. Turn west on Highway 203 and drive about three miles to the Mammoth Lakes Visitor Center and continue a short distance to Old Mammoth Road. Turn left and drive about a mile to Sherwin Creek. Turn south and drive two miles on largely unpaved road to the campground on the left side of the road.

Contact: Inyo National Forest, Mammoth Lakes Visitor Center, 760/924-5500, fax 760/924-5547.

49 PINE GLEN

Rating: 6

in Inyo National Forest
See map pages 700–701

This is a well-situated base camp for several side trips. The most popular is the trip to Devils Postpile National Monument, with a shuttle ride from the Mammoth Mountain Ski Area. Other nearby trips include exploring Inyo Craters, Mammoth Lakes, and the hot springs at Hot Creek east of Mammoth Lakes Airport. The elevation is 7,800 feet.

RV sites, facilities: There are 11 family sites (used as overflow from Old Shady Rest and New Shady Rest campgrounds) and six group sites for RVs or tents. Most family sites will accommodate RVs up to 51 feet and some up to 55 feet. Picnic tables and fire grills are provided. Drinking water, flush toilets, limited cell phone reception, and an RV dump station are available. A grocery store, an ATM, a coin-operated laundry, propane, and horseback riding facilities are nearby in Mammoth Lakes. Leashed pets are permitted.

Reservations, fees: Reservations are not accepted for individual sites but are required for group sites; reserve at 877/444-6777 or online at www.reserveusa.com ($9 reservation fee). The fees are $13 per night and $35–50 for group sites. A senior discount is available. Open late May through September.

Directions: From Lee Vining on U.S. 395, drive south for 25 miles to Mammoth Junction and Highway 203/Minaret Summit Road. Turn west on Highway 203 and drive about three miles to the Mammoth Lakes Visitor Center. Just past the visitors center, turn right on Old Sawmill Road and drive a short distance to the campground.

Contact: Inyo National Forest, Mammoth Lakes Visitor Center, 760/924-5500, fax 760/924-5547.

50 NEW SHADY REST

Rating: 6

in Inyo National Forest
See map pages 700–701

This easy-to-reach camp is set at 7,800 feet, not far from the Mammoth Mountain Ski Area. The surrounding Inyo National Forest provides many side-trip opportunities, including Devils Postpile National Monument by shuttle available from near the Mammoth Mountain Ski Area, Upper San Joaquin River, and the Inyo National Forest backcountry trails, streams, and lakes. The camp is open for walk-in, tent-only camping during the winter.

RV sites, facilities: There are 94 sites for RVs or tents, most of which will accommodate RVs up to 38 feet and some up to 55 feet. Picnic tables and fire grills are provided. Drinking water and flush toilets are available. An RV dump station, a playground, a grocery store, a coin-operated laundry, and propane are available nearby. Leashed pets are permitted.

Reservations, fees: Reservations are not accepted. The fee is $13 per night with a 14-day limit. A senior discount is available. Open late May to mid-October, weather permitting.

Directions: From Lee Vining on U.S. 395, drive south for 25 miles to Mammoth Junction and Highway 203/Minaret Summit Road. Turn west on Highway 203 and drive about three miles to the Mammoth Lakes Visitor Center. Just past the visitors center, turn right on Old Sawmill Road and drive a short distance to the campground.

Contact: Inyo National Forest, Mammoth Lakes Visitor Center, 760/924-5500, fax 760/924-5547.

51 OLD SHADY REST

Rating: 6

in Inyo National Forest
See map pages 700–701

Names such as "Old Shady Rest" are usually reserved for mom-and-pop RV parks. The Forest Service respected tradition in officially naming this park what the locals have called it all along. Like New Shady Rest, this camp is near the Mammoth Lakes Visitor Center, with the same side trips available. It is one of three camps in the immediate vicinity. The elevation is 7,800 feet.

RV sites, facilities: There are 51 sites for RVs or tents, most of which can accommodate RVs up to 40 feet and some up to 55 feet. Picnic tables and fire grills are provided. Drinking water, flush toilets, and limited cell phone reception are available. An RV dump station, a playground, a gro-

cery store, an ATM, a coin-operated laundry, and propane are available nearby. Leashed pets are permitted.

Reservations, fees: Reservations are not accepted. The fee is $13 per night with a 14-day limit. A senior discount is available. Open mid-June through early September.

Directions: From Lee Vining on U.S. 395, drive south for 25 miles to Mammoth Junction and Highway 203/Minaret Summit Road. Turn west on Highway 203 and drive about three miles to the Forest Service Visitor Center. Just past the visitors center turn right and drive .3 mile to the campground.

Contact: Inyo National Forest, Mammoth Lakes Visitor Center, 760/924-5500, fax 760/924-5547.

52 MAMMOTH MOUNTAIN RV PARK

Rating: 6

near Mammoth Lakes
See map pages 700–701

This RV park is just across the street from the Forest Service Visitor Center. Got a question? Someone there has got an answer. This camp is open year-round, making it a great place to stay for a ski trip.

RV sites, facilities: There are 185 sites, some with full hookups, including cable TV, for RVs and tents. Fire grills are provided. Restrooms, drinking water, showers, picnic tables, modem access (in office), an RV dump station, a coin-operated laundry, a swimming pool, RV supplies, and a whirlpool are available. Supplies can be obtained in Mammoth Lakes, a quarter mile away. Some facilities are wheelchair-accessible. Leashed pets are permitted.

Reservations, fees: Reservations are accepted. The fee is $25–30 per night, plus $2 per night for each additional vehicle. Major credit cards are accepted. Open year-round.

Directions: From Lee Vining on U.S. 395, drive south for 25 miles to Mammoth Junction and Highway 203. Turn west on Highway 203 and drive three miles to the park on the left.

From Bishop, drive 40 miles north on Highway 395 to Mammoth Lakes exit. Turn west on Highway 203, go under the overpass, and drive three miles to the park on the left.

Contact: Mammoth Mountain RV Park, 760/934-

3822, fax 760/934-1896, website: www.campgrounds.com/mammoth.

53 YOSEMITE-MARIPOSA KOA

Rating: 7

near Mariposa
See map pages 700–701
A little duck pond, cute log cabins, a swimming pool, and proximity to Yosemite National Park make this one a winner. The RV sites are lined up along the entrance road, edged by grass. A 10 P.M. "quiet time" helps ensure a good night's sleep. It's a one-hour drive to Yosemite Valley, and your best bet is to get there early to enjoy the spectacular beauty before the park is packed with people.

RV sites, facilities: There are 49 sites for RVs, including 28 with full hookups and 21 with partial hookups, 26 tent sites, and 12 cabins. Picnic tables and barbecues are provided. Restrooms, showers, an RV dump station, modem access, a coin-operated laundry, a store, propane, a recreation room, a swimming pool, and a playground are available. Leashed pets are permitted in sites for RVs and tents only.

Reservations, fees: Reservations are accepted. The fee is $27–39 per night. Major credit cards are accepted. Open year-round.

Directions: From Merced, drive east on Highway 140 to Mariposa. Continue on Highway 140 for six miles to Midpines and the campground entrance on the left at 6323 Hwy. 140.

Contact: Yosemite-Mariposa KOA, 209/966-2201 or 800/562-9391 (reservations only), website: www.koa.com.

54 WAWONA

Rating: 9

on the South Fork of the Merced River in Yosemite National Park
See map pages 700–701
Wawona camp is an attractive alternative to the packed camps in Yosemite Valley, providing you don't mind the relatively long drives to the best destinations. The camp is pretty, set along the South Fork Merced River, with the sites more spacious than at most other drive-to camps in the

park. The nearest attraction is the Mariposa Grove of Giant Sequoias, but get your visit in early and be out by 9 A.M., because after that it turns into a zoo, complete with shuttle train. The best nearby hike is a strenuous eight-mile round-trip to Chilnualna Falls, the prettiest sight in the southern region of the park; the trailhead is at the east end of Chilnualna Road in North Wawona. It's a 45-minute drive to either Glacier Point or Yosemite Valley. The elevation is 4,000 feet.

RV sites, facilities: There are 93 sites for RVs up to 35 feet or tents and one group campsite. Picnic tables, fire grills, and food lockers are provided. Drinking water and flush toilets are available. A grocery store, propane, a gas station, an RV dump station, a post office, a restaurant, interpretive programs, and horseback riding facilities are available nearby. Leashed pets are permitted in the campground, but not on trails. There are also some stock handling facilities for camping with pack animals; call for further information.

Reservations, fees: Reservations are required from May to September. Reserve at 800/436-PARK (800/436-7275) or online at http://reservations.nps.gov. May to September the fee is $18 per night, plus a $20 park entrance fee per vehicle; the group camp is $40 per night. October to April the fee is $12 per night. A seven-day camping limit is enforced. Open year-round.

Directions: From Oakhurst, drive north on Highway 41 to the Wawona entrance to Yosemite National Park. Continue north on Highway 41 past Wawona (golf course on the left) and drive one mile to the campground entrance on the left.

Contact: Yosemite National Park, 209/372-0200, for a touch-tone menu of recorded information.

55 SUMMERDALE

Rating: 7

on the South Fork of the Merced River in Sierra National Forest
See map pages 700–701
You can't get much closer to Yosemite National Park. This camp is within a mile of the Wawona entrance to Yosemite, about a five-minute drive to the Mariposa Grove. If you don't mind its proximity to the highway, this is a pretty spot in its own right, set along Big Creek, a feeder stream

to the South Fork Merced River. Some good swimming holes are in this area. The elevation is 5,000 feet.

RV sites, facilities: There are nine sites for tents or RVs up to 22 feet and 30 tent sites. Picnic tables and fire grills are provided. Drinking water, vault toilets, firewood, limited cell phone reception, and an amphitheater are available. A grocery store and an ATM are nearby (within one mile). Leashed pets are permitted.

Reservations, fees: Reserve at 877/444-6777 or online at www.reserveusa.com ($9 reservation fee). The fee is $16 per night. A senior discount is available. Open June through October.

Directions: From Oakhurst, drive north on Highway 41 to Fish Camp and continue for one mile to the campground entrance on the left side of the road.

Contact: Sierra National Forest, Bass Lake Ranger District, 559/877-2218, fax 559/877-3108.

56 CONVICT LAKE

Rating: 7

in Inyo National Forest

See map pages 700–701

After driving in the stark desert on U.S. 395 to get here, it is always astonishing to clear the rise and see Convict Lake (7,583 feet) and its gemlike waters set in a mountain bowl beneath a back wall of high, jagged wilderness peaks. The camp is right beside Convict Creek, about a quarter mile from Convict Lake. Both provide very good trout fishing, including some rare monster-sized brown trout below the Convict Lake outlet. Fishing is often outstanding in Convict Lake, with a chance of hooking a 10- or 15-pound trout. A bonus is an outstanding resort with a boat launch, boat rentals, cabin rentals, a small store, a restaurant, and a bar. Horseback rides and hiking are also available, with a trail routed along the north side of the lake, then along upper Convict Creek (a stream crossing is required about three miles in), and into the John Muir Wilderness. This is the most popular camp in the Mammoth area and it is frequently full. Whereas the lake rates a 10 for scenic beauty, the camp itself is in a stark desert setting, out of sight of the lake, and it can get windy and cold here because of the exposed sites.

RV sites, facilities: There are 88 sites for RVs or tents, most of which can accommodate RVs up to 41 feet and some up to 55 feet. Rental cabins are also available through the Convict Lake Resort. Picnic tables and fire grills are provided. Drinking water and flush toilets are available. An RV dump station, a boat ramp, a store, a restaurant, and horseback riding facilities are available nearby. Leashed pets are permitted.

Reservations, fees: Reservations are not accepted. The fee is $13 per night with a seven-day limit. A senior discount is available. For cabins, reservations are advised; phone 800/992-2260 for reservations and fee information. Open late April through October; cabins are open year-round.

Directions: From Lee Vining on U.S. 395, drive south for 31 miles (five miles past Mammoth Junction) to Convict Lake Road (adjacent to Mammoth Lakes Airport). Turn west (right) on Convict Lake Road and drive two miles to Convict Lake. Cross the dam and drive a short distance to the campground entrance road on the left. Turn left and drive .25 mile to the campground.

Contact: Inyo National Forest, Mammoth Lakes Visitor Center, 760/924-5500, fax 760/924-5537; Convict Lake Resort & Cabins, 800/992-2260.

57 McGEE CREEK RV PARK

Rating: 6

near Crowley Lake

See map pages 700–701

This is a popular layover spot for folks visiting giant Crowley Lake. Crowley Lake is still one of the better lakes in the Sierra for trout fishing, with good prospects for large rainbow trout and brown trout, though the 20-pound brown trout that once made this lake famous are now mainly a legend. Beautiful Convict Lake provides a nearby side-trip option. It is also about nine miles to Rock Creek Lake, a beautiful high-mountain destination. The elevation is 7,000 feet.

RV sites, facilities: There are 31 sites with partial or full hookups for RVs or tents. Picnic tables and fire pits are provided. Restrooms, drinking water, showers, and flush toilets are available. Leashed pets are permitted.

Reservations, fees: Reservations are accepted. The fee is $20–30 per night, plus $4 for showers.

Weekly and monthly rates are available. Open late April through mid-October.

Directions: From the junction of U.S. 395 and Highway 203 (the Mammoth Lakes turnoff), drive south on U.S. 395 for 10 miles to the turnoff for McGee Creek Road. Take that exit and look for the park entrance on the left.

Contact: McGee Creek RV Park, 760/935-4233.

58 McGEE CREEK

Rating: 7

in Inyo National Forest
See map pages 700–701

This is a Forest Service camp at an elevation of 7,600 feet, set along little McGee Creek, a good location for fishing and hiking. The stream is stocked with trout, and a trailhead is just up the road. From here you can hike along upper McGee Creek and into the John Muir Wilderness.

RV sites, facilities: There are 28 sites for RVs up to 22 feet or tents. Picnic tables and fire grills are provided. Drinking water, flush toilets, and firewood are available. A small store and an ATM are nearby. Some facilities are wheelchair-accessible. Leashed pets are permitted.

Reservations, fees: Reserve at 877/444-6777 or online at www.reserveusa.com ($9 reservation fee). The fee is $15 per night. A senior discount is available. Open May through September.

Directions: From Mammoth Lakes at the junction of U.S. 395 and Highway 203, drive south on U.S. 395 for 8.5 miles to McGee Creek Road (signed). Turn right (toward the Sierra) and drive 1.5 miles to the campground.

Contact: Inyo National Forest, White Mountain Ranger District, 760/873-2500, fax 760/873-2563.

59 CROWLEY LAKE

Rating: 5

near Crowley Lake
See map pages 700–701

This large BLM camp is across U.S. 395 from the south shore of Crowley Lake. Crowley is the trout-fishing capital of the eastern Sierra, with the annual opener (the last Saturday in April) a great celebration. Though the trout fishing can go through a lull in midsummer, it can become excellent again in the fall when the lake's population of big brown trout heads up to the top of the lake and the mouth of the Owens River. The surroundings are fairly stark; the elevation is 6,800 feet.

RV sites, facilities: There are 47 sites for RVs or tents. Picnic tables and fire grills are provided. Vault toilets are available. No drinking water is available. A grocery store and boat ramp are nearby on Crowley Lake. Leashed pets are permitted.

Reservations, fees: Reservations are not accepted. There is no fee for camping. Open late April through October, weather permitting.

Directions: Drive on U.S. 395 to the Crowley Lake Road exit (21 miles north of Bishop). Take that exit west (toward the Sierra) to Crowley Lake Road and drive northwest for 5.5 miles (past Tom's Place) to the campground entrance on the left (well signed).

Contact: Bureau of Land Management, Bishop Field Office, 760/872-4881, fax 760/872-5050.

60 FRENCH CAMP

Rating: 5

on Rock Creek near Crowley Lake in Inyo National Forest
See map pages 700–701

French Camp is just a short hop from U.S. 395 and Tom's Place, right where the high Sierra turns into high plateau country. Side-trip opportunities include boating and fishing on giant Crowley Lake and, to the west on Rock Creek Road, visiting little Rock Creek Lake 10 miles away. The elevation is 7,500 feet.

RV sites, facilities: There are 84 sites for RVs up to 40 feet or tents and two sites for tents only. Picnic tables and fire grills are provided. Drinking water, flush toilets, and an RV dump station are available. You can buy groceries nearby. Leashed pets are permitted.

Reservations, fees: Reserve at 877/444-6777 or online at www.reserveusa.com ($9 reservation fee). The fee is $11–15 per night. A senior discount is available. Open late April through October.

Directions: From Mammoth Lakes at the junction of U.S. 395 and Highway 203, drive south on U.S. 395 for 15 miles to Tom's Place and Rock Creek Road. Turn right (toward the Sierra) at

Rock Creek Road and drive .25 mile to the campground on the right.

Contact: Inyo National Forest, White Mountain Ranger District, 760/873-2500, fax 760/873-2563.

61 TUFF

Rating: 5

near Crowley Lake in Inyo National Forest
See map pages 700–701

Easy access off U.S. 395 makes this camp a winner, though it is not nearly as pretty as those up Rock Creek Road to the west of Tom's Place. The fact that you can get in and out of here quickly makes it ideal for campers planning fishing trips to nearby Crowley Lake. The elevation is 7,000 feet.

RV sites, facilities: There are 19 sites for RVs up to 22 feet or tents and 15 sites for tents only. Picnic tables and fire grills are provided. Drinking water, flush toilets, and firewood are available. An RV dump station is nearby. Leashed pets are permitted.

Reservations, fees: Reserve at 877/444-6777 or online at www.reserveusa.com ($9 reservation fee). The fee is $11–15 per night. A senior discount is available. Open late April through mid-October.

Directions: From Mammoth Lakes at the junction of U.S. 395 and Highway 203, drive south on U.S. 395 for 15.5 miles (one mile north of Tom's Place) to Rock Creek Road. Turn right (toward the Sierra) on Rock Creek Road and drive .5 mile to the campground.

Contact: Inyo National Forest, White Mountain Ranger District, 760/873-2500, fax 760/873-2563.

62 IRIS MEADOW

Rating: 5

near Crowley Lake in Inyo National Forest
See map pages 700–701

Iris Meadow, at 8,300 feet elevation on the flank of Red Mountain (11,472 feet), is the first in a series of five Forest Service camps set near Rock Creek Canyon on the road leading from Tom's Place up to pretty Rock Creek Lake. Rock Creek is stocked with trout, and nearby Rock Creek Lake also provides fishing and boating for hand-launched boats. This camp also has access to a great trailhead for wilderness exploration.

RV sites, facilities: There are 14 sites for RVs up to 22 feet or tents. Picnic tables and fire grills are provided. Drinking water and flush toilets are available. An ATM and supplies are available in Tom's Place, three miles away. Leashed pets are permitted.

Reservations, fees: Reservations are not accepted. The fee is $16 per night. Open May through October.

Directions: From Mammoth Lakes at the junction of U.S. 395 and Highway 203, drive south on U.S. 395 for 15 miles south to Tom's Place and Rock Creek Road. Turn right (toward the Sierra) at Rock Creek Road and drive three miles to the campground.

Contact: Inyo National Forest, White Mountain Ranger District, 760/873-2500, fax 760/873-2563.

63 EAST FORK

Rating: 8

near Crowley Lake in Inyo National Forest
See map pages 700–701

This is a beautiful, popular campground set along East Fork Rock Creek at 9,000 feet elevation. The camp is only three miles from Rock Creek Lake, where there's an excellent trailhead.

RV sites, facilities: There are 133 sites for RVs up to 40 feet or tents. Picnic tables and fire grills are provided. Drinking water and flush toilets are available. An RV dump station is nearby. An ATM and supplies are available in Tom's Place and at Rock Creek Lake Resort nearby. Leashed pets are permitted.

Reservations, fees: Reservations are accepted for sites 16–57 and 102–127; reserve at 877/444-6777 or online at www.reserveusa.com ($9 reservation fee). The fee is $11–15 per night. A senior discount is available. Open mid-May through November.

Directions: From Mammoth Lakes at the junction of U.S. 395 and Highway 203, drive south on U.S. 395 for 15 miles south to Tom's Place and Rock Creek Road. Turn right (toward the Sierra) at Rock Creek Road and drive five miles to the campground access road on the left.

Contact: Inyo National Forest, White Mountain Ranger District, 760/873-2500, fax 760/873-2563.

CALIFORNIA

64 ROCK CREEK LAKE

Rating: 9

in Inyo National Forest
See map pages 700–701

Rock Creek Lake, set at an elevation of 9,600 feet, is a small but beautiful lake that features cool, clear water, small trout, and a great trailhead for access to the adjacent John Muir Wilderness. The setting is drop-dead beautiful, hence the high rating for scenic beauty, but note that the campsites are set closely together, side by side, in a paved parking area. Note that at times, especially afternoons in late spring, winds out of the west can be cold and pesky at the lake.

RV sites, facilities: There are 28 sites for RVs up to 22 feet or tents and one group site for up to 50 people. Picnic tables and fire grills are provided. Drinking water and flush toilets are available. You can buy supplies in Tom's Place and at the Rock Creek Lake Resort. Leashed pets are permitted.

Reservations, fees: Reservations are not accepted for individual sites but are required for the group site at 877/444-6777 or online at www .reserveusa.com ($9 reservation fee). The fees are $15 per night and $55 per night for group sites. A senior discount is available. Open mid-May through October.

Directions: From the junction of U.S. 395 and Highway 203 (the Mammoth Lakes turnoff), drive 15 miles south on U.S. 395 to Tom's Place. Turn right (toward the Sierra) at Rock Creek Road and drive seven miles to the campground.

Contact: Inyo National Forest, White Mountain Ranger District, 760/873-2500, fax 760/873-2563.

65 HIGHLANDS RV PARK

Rating: 3

near Bishop
See map pages 700–701

This is a privately operated RV park near Bishop that is set up for U.S. 395 cruisers. There is an Indian casino in town. A great side trip is up two-lane Highway 168 to Lake Sabrina. The elevation is 4,300 feet.

RV sites, facilities: There are 103 sites with full hookups, including cable TV, for RVs. Picnic

tables are provided. Restrooms, drinking water, flush toilets, showers, an RV dump station, modem access (in office), propane, ice, a fish-cleaning station, and a coin-operated laundry are available. You can buy groceries nearby (about three blocks away). Leashed pets are permitted.

Reservations, fees: Reservations are recommended. The fee is $25 per night. Weekly and monthly rates are available. Open year-round.

Directions: From Bishop, drive two miles north on U.S. 395/North Sierra Highway to the campground on the right at 2275 N. Sierra Highway.

Contact: Highlands RV Park, 760/873-7616.

66 PLEASANT VALLEY

Rating: 7

near Pleasant Valley Reservoir
See map pages 700–701

Pleasant Valley County Park is adjacent to long, narrow Pleasant Valley Reservoir, created by the Owens River. It is east of the Sierra range in the high desert plateau country; the elevation is 4,200 feet. That makes it available for year-round fishing. The Owens River passes through the park, providing wild trout fishing, with most anglers practicing catch-and-release fly-fishing. This is also near a major jump-off point for hiking, rock-climbing, and wilderness fishing at the Bishop Pass area to the west. Major additional improvements to this campground were planned for 2003 and 2004. One of the first, implemented in late 2002, was replacing the old pit toilets with new vault toilets. People were lined up for miles to try them out.

RV sites, facilities: There are 200 sites for RVs or tents. Picnic tables and fire grills are provided. Drinking water (hand-pumped well water) and vault toilets are available. Leashed pets are permitted.

Reservations, fees: Reservations are not accepted. The fee is $10 per night. Open year-round.

Directions: Drive on U.S. 395 to Pleasant Valley Road (seven miles north of Bishop) on the east side of the road. Turn east and drive one mile to the park entrance.

Contact: Inyo County Parks Department, 760/878-0272, fax 760/873-5599.

California

Chapter 23

Sequoia and Kings Canyon

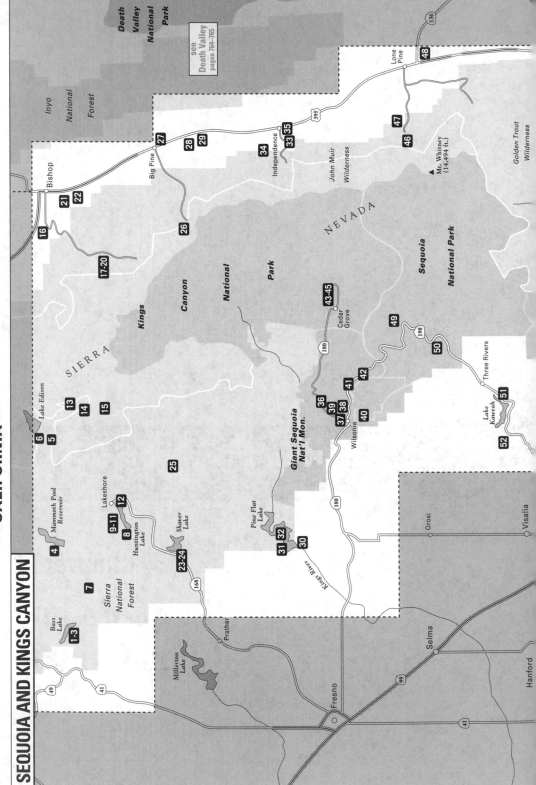

Death Valley National Park

see Death Valley pages 764-765

Inyo National Forest

Bishop

Big Pine

Lone Pine

Independence

NEVADA

John Muir Wilderness

Golden Trout Wilderness

▲ Mt. Whitney (14,494 ft.)

Sequoia National Park

Kings Canyon National Park

SIERRA

Lake Edison

Cedar Grove

Giant Sequoia Nat'l Mon.

Three Rivers

Lake Kaweah

Wilsonia

Mammoth Pool Reservoir

Lakeshore

Huntington Lake

Shaver Lake

Pine Flat Lake

Kings River

Orosi

Visalia

Sierra National Forest

Bass Lake

Millerton Lake

Prather

Selma

Fresno

Hanford

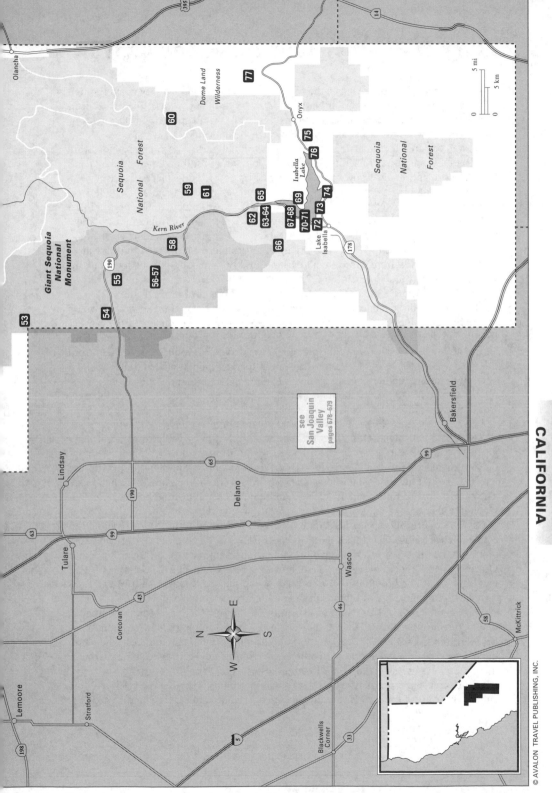

© AVALON TRAVEL PUBLISHING, INC.

Chapter 23—Sequoia and Kings Canyon

There is no place on earth like the high Sierra, from Mount Whitney north through Sequoia and Kings Canyon National Parks. This is a paradise filled with deep canyons, high peaks, and fantastic natural beauty, and sprinkled with groves of the largest living things in the history of the earth—giant sequoias.

Though the area is primarily known for the national parks, the campgrounds available span a great variety of settings. The most popular spots, though, are in the vicinity of Sequoia and Kings Canyon National Parks, or on the parks' access roads.

Sooner or later, everyone will want to see the biggest tree of them all—the General Sherman Tree, estimated to be 2,300 to 2,700 years old with a circumference of 102.6 feet. It is in the Giant Forest at Sequoia National Park. To stand in front of it is to know true awe. That said, I found the Grant Grove and the Muir Grove even more enchanting.

These are among the highlights of a driving tour through both parks. A must for most is taking in the view from Moro Rock, parking, and then making the 300-foot walk up a succession of stairs to reach the 6,725-foot summit. Here you can scan a series of mountain rims and granite peaks, highlighted by the Great Western Divide.

The drive out of Sequoia and into Kings Canyon features rim-of-the-world-type views as you first enter the Kings River canyon. You then descend to the bottom of the canyon, right along the Kings River, gaze up at the high glacial-carved canyon walls, and drive all the way out to Cedar Grove, the end of the road. The canyon rises 8,000 feet from the river to Spanish Peak, the deepest canyon in the continental United States.

Crystal Cave is another point of fascination. Among the formations are adjoined crystal columns that look like the sound pipes in the giant organ at the Mormon Tabernacle. Lights are placed strategically for perfect lighting.

This is only a start. Bears, marmot, and deer are abundant and are commonly seen in Sequoia, especially at Dorst Creek Campground. If you drive up to Mineral King and take a hike, it can seem like the marmot capital of the world.

But this region also harbors many wonderful secrets having nothing to do with the national parks. One of them, for instance, is the Muir Trail Ranch near Florence Lake. The ranch is in the John Muir Wilderness and requires a trip by foot, boat, or horse to reach it. Other unique launch points for trips into the wilderness lie nearby.

On the western slopes of the Sierra, pretty lakes with good trout fishing include Edison, Florence, and Hume Lakes. Hidden spots in Sierra National Forest provide continual fortune hunts, especially up the Dinkey Creek drainage above Courtright Reservoir. On the eastern slopes, a series of small streams offers good vehicle access; here, too, you'll encounter the beautiful Rock Creek Lake, Sabrina and South Lakes (west of Bishop), and great wilderness trailheads at the end of almost every road.

The remote Golden Trout Wilderness on the southwest flank of Mount Whitney is one of the most pristine areas in California. Yet it is lost in the shadow of giant Whitney, elevation 14,494 feet, the highest point in the continental United States, where hiking has become so popular that reservations are required at each trailhead for overnight use, and quotas are enforced to ensure an undisturbed experience for each visitor.

In the Kernville area, there are a series of campgrounds along the Kern River. Most choose this canyon for one reason: the outstanding white-water rafting and kayaking.

1 LUPINE-CEDAR BLUFFS

Rating: 8

on Bass Lake in Sierra National Forest
See map pages 732–733
This is the camping headquarters at Bass Lake and the only camp open year-round, except for the group camp. Bass Lake is a popular vacation spot, a pretty lake, long and narrow, covering 1,200 acres when full and surrounded by national forest. Most of the campgrounds are filled on weekends and three-day holidays. Fishing is best in the spring for rainbow trout and largemouth bass, and by mid-June water-skiers have usually taken over. Boats must be registered at the Bass Lake observation tower after launching.
RV sites, facilities: There are 113 sites for RVs up to 40 feet or tents, and several double- and quadruple-family sites. Picnic tables and fire grills are provided. Drinking water and flush toilets are available. Groceries, an ATM, and a boat ramp are nearby. Some facilities are wheelchair-accessible. Leashed pets are permitted.
Reservations, fees: Reserve at 877/444-6777 or online at www.reserveusa.com ($9 reservation fee). The fees are $18 per night, $36 per night for double-family sites and $72 per night for quadruple-family sites, plus $5 for each additional vehicle. A senior discount is available. Open year-round.
Directions: From Fresno, drive north on Highway 41 to Oakhurst and continue 2.5 miles to Yosemite Forks and Bass Lake Road/County Road 222. Turn right at Bass Lake Road and drive eight miles (staying right at two forks) to the campground (on the south shore of Bass Lake).
Contact: Sierra National Forest, Bass Lake Ranger District, 559/877-2218, fax 559/877-3108.

2 SPRING COVE

Rating: 8

on Bass Lake in Sierra National Forest
See map pages 732–733
This is one of the several camps beside Bass Lake, a long, narrow reservoir in the Sierra foothill country. Expect hot weather in the summer. Boats must be registered at the Bass Lake observation tower after launching. The elevation is 3,400 feet.

RV sites, facilities: There are 11 sites for RVs up to 30 feet and 63 sites for tents only. Picnic tables and fire grills are provided. Drinking water, flush toilets, and firewood are available. Groceries, coin-operated showers, a coin-operated laundry, gasoline, and a marina and boat ramp are available nearby. Leashed pets are permitted.
Reservations, fees: From Memorial Day through Labor Day, reserve at 877/444-6777 or online at www.reserveusa.com ($9 reservation fee). The fee is $18 per night, plus $5 per night for each additional vehicle. A senior discount is available. Open May through September.
Directions: From Fresno, drive north on Highway 41 to Oakhurst and continue 2.5 miles to Yosemite Forks and Bass Lake Road/County Road 222. Turn right at Bass Lake Road and drive 8.5 miles (staying right at two forks) to the campground (on the south shore of Bass Lake).
Contact: Sierra National Forest, Bass Lake Ranger District, 559/877-2218, fax 559/877-3108.

3 WISHON POINT

Rating: 9

on Bass Lake in Sierra National Forest
See map pages 732–733
This camp on Wishon Point is the smallest, and many say the prettiest, of the camps at Bass Lake. The elevation is 3,400 feet.
RV sites, facilities: There are 43 sites for RVs up to 40 feet or tents and several double-family sites. Picnic tables and fire grills are provided. Drinking water, flush toilets, and cell phone reception are available. Groceries, a pay phone, an ATM, and a boat ramp are nearby. Leashed pets are permitted.
Reservations, fees: From Memorial Day through Labor Day, reserve at 877/444-6777 or online at www.reserveusa.com ($9 reservation fee). The fees are $18 per night and $36 per night for double-family sites. A senior discount is available. Open May through September.
Directions: From Fresno, drive north on Highway 41 to Oakhurst and continue 2.5 miles to Yosemite Forks and Bass Lake Road/County Road 222. Turn right at Bass Lake Road and drive nine miles (staying right at two forks) to the campground (on the south shore of Bass Lake).

CALIFORNIA

Contact: Sierra National Forest, Bass Lake Ranger District, 559/877-2218, fax 559/877-3108.

4 MAMMOTH POOL

Rating: 7

near Mammoth Pool Reservoir in Sierra National Forest

See map pages 732–733

Mammoth Pool was created by a dam in the San Joaquin River gorge, a steep canyon, resulting in a long, narrow lake with steep, high walls. The lake seems much higher than its official elevation of 3,330 feet, but that is because of the high ridges. This is the only drive-in camp at the lake, though there is a boat-in camp, China Camp, on the lake's upper reaches. Trout fishing can be good in the spring and early summer, with water-skiing dominant during warm weather. Get this: water sports are restricted from May 1 to June 15 because of deer migrating across the lake—that's right, they're swimming—but the campgrounds here are still open.

RV sites, facilities: There are 29 sites for RVs up to 22 feet or tents, 18 sites for tents only, and five multifamily sites. Picnic tables and fire grills are provided. Drinking water and vault toilets are available. A store and a boat ramp are within a mile. Leashed pets are permitted.

Reservations, fees: Reservations are not accepted. The fees are $13 per night and $24 for the multifamily sites, plus $5 for each additional vehicle. A senior discount is available. Open May through October.

Directions: From Fresno, drive north on Highway 41 for about 25 miles to North Fork Road/County Road 200. Turn right and drive northeast for 17.5 miles to Auberry Road/County Road 222. Turn left (north) and drive one mile to the town of North Fork and Mammoth Pool Road. Turn right and drive 1.5 miles to County Road 225 (still Mammoth Pool Road). Turn right and drive about 37 miles (the road becomes Minarets Road/Forest Road 81) to a junction. Bear right (still Mammoth Pool Road) and drive three miles to Mammoth Pool Reservoir and the campground. The drive from North Fork takes 1.5 to 2 hours.

Contact: Sierra National Forest, Bass Lake Ranger District, 559/877-2218, fax 559/877-3108.

5 MONO HOT SPRINGS

Rating: 8

on the San Joaquin River in Sierra National Forest

See map pages 732–733

The campground is set in the Sierra at 6,500 feet in elevation along the San Joaquin River directly adjacent to the Mono Hot Springs Resort. The hot springs are typically 104°F, with public pools (everybody wears swimming suits) available just above the river on one side, and the private resort (rock cabins available) with its private baths on the other. A small convenience store and excellent restaurant are available at the lodge. The best swimming lake in the Sierra Nevada, Dorris Lake, is a 15-minute walk past the lodge; the lake is clear, clean, and yet not too cold, with walls on one side for fun jumps into deep water. The one downer: the drive in is long, slow, and hellacious, with many blind corners in narrow sections.

RV sites, facilities: There are 26 sites for RVs or tents and four sites for tents only. Picnic tables and fire grills are provided. Drinking water and vault toilets are available. You can buy supplies in Mono Hot Springs. Leashed pets are permitted.

Reservations, fees: Reserve at 877/444-6777 or online at www.reserveusa.com ($9 reservation fee). The fee is $14 per night, plus $5 per night for each additional vehicle. A senior discount is available. Open May through September.

Directions: From the town of Shaver Lake, drive east on Highway 168 for 21 miles to Kaiser Pass Road. Bear northeast on Kaiser Pass Road/Forest Road 80 (slow and curvy) to Mono Hot Springs Campground Road (signed). Turn left and drive a short distance to the campground.

Contact: Sierra National Forest, High Sierra Ranger District, 559/855-5360, fax 559/855-5375.

6 VERMILLION

Rating: 8

on Lake Edison in Sierra National Forest

See map pages 732–733

Lake Edison is a premium vacation destination. It is a large, high-mountain camp set just a few miles from the border of the John Muir Wilderness. The elevation is 7,700 feet. A 15 mph speed limit on the lake guarantees quiet water, and trout fishing is often quite good in early summer, with huge brown trout hooked occasionally. A daytrip option is to hike the trail from the camp out along the north shore of Lake Edison for five miles to Quail Meadows, where it intersects with the Pacific Crest Trail in the John Muir Wilderness. A lodge at the lake provides meals and supplies, with a hiker's boat shuttle available to the head of the lake. Hang out here for long and you are bound to see JMT hikers taking a break. Note that the drive in is long and extremely twisty on a narrow road.

RV sites, facilities: There are 20 sites for RVs up to 16 feet or tents and 11 tent sites. Picnic tables and fire grills are provided. Drinking water and vault toilets are available. A boat ramp and horseback riding facilities are nearby. A small store and restaurant are nearby. Leashed pets are permitted.

Reservations, fees: Reserve at 877/444-6777 or online at www.reserveusa.com ($9 reservation fee). The fee is $14 per night, plus $5 per night for each additional vehicle. Open June through September.

Directions: From the town of Shaver Lake, drive east on Highway 168 for 21 miles to Kaiser Pass Road. Bear northeast on Kaiser Pass Road/Forest Road 80 (slow and curvy) to Mono Hot Springs (the road becomes Edison Lake Road). Continue on Kaiser Pass/Edison Lake Road for five miles to the campground. It is about .25 mile from the west shore of Lake Edison.

Contact: Sierra National Forest, High Sierra Ranger District, 559/855-5360, fax 559/855-5375.

7 ROCK CREEK

Rating: 6

in Sierra National Forest
See map pages 732–733

Drinking water is the big bonus here. It is also why this camp tends to fill up on weekends. A side trip is the primitive road that heads southeast out of camp, switchbacks as its heads east, and drops down the canyon near where pretty Aspen Creek feeds into Rock Creek. The elevation at camp is 4,300 feet. (Note that the best

camp in the immediate region is at Mammoth Pool.)

RV sites, facilities: There are 18 sites for RVs up to 32 feet or tents. Picnic tables and fire grills are provided. Drinking water and vault toilets are available. Leashed pets are permitted.

Reservations, fees: Reserve online at www .reserveusa.com. The fee is $16 per night. A senior discount is available. Open April through October, weather permitting.

Directions: From Fresno, drive north on Highway 41 for about 25 miles to North Fork Road/County Road 200. Turn right and drive northeast for 17.5 miles to Auberry Road/County Road 222. Turn left (north) and drive one mile to the town of North Fork and Mammoth Pool Road. Turn right and drive 1.5 miles to County Road 225 (still Mammoth Pool Road). Turn right and drive about 25 miles (the road becomes Minarets Road/Forest Road 81) to the campground on the right.

Contact: Sierra National Forest, Bass Lake Ranger District, 559/877-2218, fax 559/877-3108.

8 UPPER AND LOWER BILLY CREEK

Rating: 8

on Huntington Lake in Sierra National Forest
See map pages 732–733

Huntington Lake is at an elevation of 7,000 feet in the Sierra Nevada, and this is one of several camps here. These camps are at the west end of the lake along the north shore, where Billy Creek feeds the lake. Of these two adjacent campgrounds, Lower Billy Creek is smaller than Upper Billy and has lakeside sites available. The lake is four miles long and a half mile wide, with 14 miles of shoreline, five resorts, boat rentals, and a trailhead for hiking into the Kaiser Wilderness.

RV sites, facilities: Upper Billy has 20 sites for RVs up to 25 feet or tents and 57 sites for tents only. Lower Billy has 11 sites for RVs or tents. Picnic tables and fire grills are provided. Drinking water and flush and vault toilets are available. A small store is nearby. Leashed pets are permitted.

Reservations, fees: Reserve at 877/444-6777 or online at www.reserveusa.com ($9 reservation fee). The fee is $16 per night, plus $5 for each additional vehicle. A senior discount is available. Open June through September.

Directions: From Fresno, drive east on Highway 168 to Shaver Lake, then continue 21 miles to Huntington Lake and Huntington Lake Road. Turn left on Huntington Lake Road and drive about five miles to the campgrounds on the left.

Contact: Sierra National Forest, High Sierra Ranger District, 559/855-5360, fax 559/855-5375.

9 CATAVEE

Rating: 7

on Huntington Lake in Sierra National Forest
See map pages 732–733

Catavee camp is one of three camps in the immediate vicinity, set on the north shore at the eastern end of Huntington Lake. The camp sits near where Bear Creek enters the lake. Huntington Lake is a scenic, High Sierra Ranger District lake at 7,000 feet, where visitors can enjoy fishing, hiking, and sailing. Sailboat regattas take place here regularly during the summer. A trailhead near camp offers access to the Kaiser Wilderness.

RV sites, facilities: There are 26 sites for RVs up to 25 feet or tents. Picnic tables and fire grills are provided. Drinking water and flush toilets are available. Horseback riding facilities and a small store are nearby. Nearby resorts offer boat rentals and guest docks, and a boat ramp is nearby. Tackle rentals and bait are also available. Some facilities are wheelchair-accessible. Leashed pets are permitted.

Reservations, fees: Reserve at 877/444-6777 or online at www.reserveusa.com ($9 reservation fee). The fee is $20 per night, plus $5 for each additional vehicle. A senior discount is available. Open June through October.

Directions: From Fresno, drive east on Highway 168 to Shaver Lake, then continue 21 miles to Huntington Lake and Huntington Lake Road. Turn left on Huntington Lake Road and drive one mile (just past Kinnikinnick) to the campground on the left.

Contact: Sierra National Forest, High Sierra Ranger District, 559/855-5360, fax 559/855-5375.

10 KINNIKINNICK

Rating: 7

on Huntington Lake in Sierra National Forest
See map pages 732–733

Flip a coin; there are three camps in the immediate vicinity on the north shore of the east end of Huntington Lake and, with a boat ramp nearby, they are all favorites. Kinnikinnick is between Catavee and Deer Creek campgrounds. The elevation is 7,000 feet.

RV sites, facilities: There are 35 sites for RVs up to 22 feet or tents. Picnic tables and fire grills are provided. Drinking water and flush toilets are available. Horseback riding facilities and a store are nearby. Some facilities are wheelchair-accessible. Leashed pets are permitted.

Reservations, fees: Reserve at 877/444-6777 or online at www.reserveusa.com ($9 reservation fee). The fee is $20 per night, plus $5 for each additional vehicle. A senior discount is available. Open June through August.

Directions: From Fresno, drive east on Highway 168 to Shaver Lake, then continue 21 miles to Huntington Lake and Huntington Lake Road. Turn left on Huntington Lake Road and drive one mile to the campground on the left.

Contact: Sierra National Forest, High Sierra Ranger District, 559/855-5360, fax 559/855-5375.

11 DEER CREEK

Rating: 8

on Huntington Lake in Sierra National Forest
See map pages 732–733

This is one of the best camps at Huntington Lake, set near lakeside at Bear Cove with a boat ramp nearby. It is on the north shore of the lake's eastern end. Huntington Lake is four miles long and a half mile wide, with 14 miles of shoreline, five resorts, boat rentals, and a trailhead for hiking into the Kaiser Wilderness. Two other campgrounds are nearby.

RV sites, facilities: There are 34 sites for RVs up to 22 feet or tents. Picnic tables and fire grills are provided. Drinking water and flush toilets are available. A store and propane are available nearby. Some facilities are wheelchair-accessible. Leashed pets are permitted.

Reservations, fees: Reserve at 877/444-6777 or online at www.reserveusa.com ($9 reservation fee). The fee is $20–22 per night, plus $5 for each additional vehicle. A senior discount is available. Open June through September.

Directions: From Fresno, drive east on Highway 168 to Shaver Lake, then continue 21 miles to Huntington Lake and Huntington Lake Road. Turn left on Huntington Lake Road and drive one mile to the campground entrance road on the left.

Contact: Sierra National Forest, High Sierra Ranger District, 559/855-5360, fax 559/855-5375.

12 RANCHERIA

Rating: 8

near Huntington Lake in Sierra National Forest
See map pages 732–733

This is the granddaddy of the camps at Huntington Lake, and also the easiest to reach. It is along the shore of the lake's eastern end. A bonus here is the nearby Rancheria Falls National Recreation Trail, which provides access to beautiful Rancheria Falls. Another side trip is the 15-minute drive to Bear Butte (the access road is across from the campground entrance) at 8,598 feet, providing a sweeping view of the lake below. The elevation at camp is 7,000 feet.

RV sites, facilities: There are 150 sites for RVs up to 22 feet or tents. Picnic tables and fire grills are provided. Drinking water and flush toilets are available. A store and propane are available nearby. Leashed pets are permitted.

Reservations, fees: Reserve at 877/444-6777 or online at www.reserveusa.com ($9 reservation fee). The fee is $18 per night, plus $5 for each additional vehicle. A senior discount is available. Open year-round.

Directions: From Fresno, drive east on Highway 168 to Shaver Lake, then continue 20 miles to Huntington Lake and the campground on the left.

Contact: Sierra National Forest, High Sierra Ranger District, 559/855-5360, fax 559/855-5375.

13 JACKASS MEADOW

Rating: 7

on Florence Lake in Sierra National Forest
See map pages 732–733

Jackass Meadow is a pretty spot adjacent to Florence Lake, near the Upper San Joaquin River. There are good canoeing, rafting, and float-tubing possibilities, all high-Sierra style. The elevation is 7,200 feet. The lake is remote and can be reached only after a long, circuitous drive on a narrow road with many blind turns. A trailhead at the lake offers access to the wilderness and the John Muir Trail.

RV sites, facilities: There are 44 sites for RVs up to 16 feet or tents. Picnic tables and fire grills are provided. Drinking water and vault toilets are available. A wheelchair-accessible fishing pier is nearby. Leashed pets are permitted.

Reservations, fees: Reserve at 877/444-6777 or online at www.reserveusa.com ($9 reservation fee). The fee is $14 per night, plus $5 per night for each additional vehicle. A senior discount is available. Open June through September.

Directions: From the town of Shaver Lake, drive east on Highway 168 for 21 miles to Kaiser Pass Road. Bear northeast on Kaiser Pass Road/Forest Road 80 (slow and curvy) to a junction (left goes to Mono Hot Springs and Lake Edison) with Florence Lake Road. Bear right at the junction and drive five miles to the campground.

Contact: Sierra National Forest, High Sierra Ranger District, 559/855-5360, fax 559/855-5375.

14 TRAPPER SPRINGS

Rating: 8

on Courtright Reservoir in Sierra National Forest
See map pages 732–733

Trapper Springs is on the west shore of Courtright Reservoir, set at 8,200 feet on the west slope of the Sierra. Courtright is a great destination, with excellent camping, boating, fishing, and hiking into the nearby John Muir Wilderness. A 15 mph speed limit makes the lake ideal for fishing, canoeing, and rafting. A trailhead a mile north of camp by car heads around the north end of

CALIFORNIA

the lake to a fork; to the left it is routed into the Dinkey Lakes Wilderness, and to the right it is routed to the head of the lake, then follows Dusy Creek in a long climb into spectacular country in the John Muir Wilderness. There are two driving routes to this lake, one from Shaver Lake and the other from Pine Flat Reservoir; both are very long, slow, and twisty drives.

RV sites, facilities: There are 75 sites for RVs up to 22 feet or tents. Picnic tables and fire grills are provided. Drinking water and vault toilets are available. A boat ramp is nearby. Some facilities are wheelchair-accessible. Leashed pets are permitted.

Reservations, fees: Reservations are not accepted. The fee is $16 per night, plus $7 per extra RV, $3 for additional vehicle, and $1 per pet per night. A senior discount is available. Open June through September.

Directions: From Fresno, drive east on Highway 168 to Dinkey Creek Road (on the right just as you enter the town of Shaver Lake). Turn right and drive 13 miles to McKinley Grove Road (Forest Road 40). Turn right and drive 14 miles to Courtright Road. Turn left (north) and drive 12 miles to the campground entrance road on the right.

Contact: Sierra National Forest, High Sierra Ranger District, 559/855-5360, fax 559/855-5375.

15 WISHON VILLAGE

Rating: 7

near Wishon Reservoir

See map pages 732–733

This privately operated mountain park is set near the shore of Wishon Reservoir, about one mile from the dam. Trout stocks often make for good fishing in early summer, and anglers with boats love the 15 mph speed limit, which keeps personal watercraft off the water. Backpackers and hikers can find a great trailhead at the south end of the lake at Coolidge Meadow, where a trail awaits that is routed to the Woodchuck Creek drainage and numerous lakes in the John Muir Wilderness. The elevation is 6,500 feet.

RV sites, facilities: There are 97 sites with full hookups for RVs and 26 sites for tents. Picnic tables and fire pits are provided. Restrooms, drinking water, coin-operated showers, electrical connections, and sewer hookups are available. A coin-operated laundry, a country store, a bar, ice, a boat ramp, motorboat rentals, bait and tackle, and propane are available nearby. Leashed pets are permitted.

Reservations, fees: Reservations are recommended. The fee is $30 per night for RV sites and $20 per night for tent sites, plus $2 for each additional person up to a six-camper limit per site. Open May through October.

Directions: From Fresno, drive east on Highway 168 to Dinkey Creek Road (on the right just as you enter the town of Shaver Lake). Turn right and drive 13 miles to McKinley Grove Road (Forest Road 40). Turn right and drive 15 miles to the park (66500 McKinley Grove Rd./Forest Road 40).

Contact: Wishon Village, 559/865-5361, fax 559/865-2000, website: www.wishonvillage.com.

16 BROWN'S MILLPOND CAMPGROUND

Rating: 6

near Bishop

See map pages 732–733

This privately operated camp is adjacent to the Millpond Recreation Area, which offers ball fields, playgrounds, and a swimming lake. There is also the opportunity for sailing, archery, tennis, horseshoe games, and fishing.

RV sites, facilities: There are 75 sites, 16 with partial hookups, for RVs or tents. Picnic tables and fire grills are provided. Restrooms, drinking water, flush toilets, coin-operated showers, and a coin-operated laundry are available. A concession stand is nearby. Leashed pets are permitted.

Reservations, fees: Make reservations at 760/872-6911. The fee is $16–19 per night. Open March through October.

Directions: Drive on U.S. 395 to a road signed Millpond/County Park (just north of Bishop). Turn southwest (toward the Sierra) at that road (Ed Powers Road) and drive .25 mile to Sawmill Road. Turn right and drive .25 mile to Millpond Road, then turn left.

Contact: Brown's Millpond Campground, 760/873-5342.

17 SABRINA

Rating: 8

near Lake Sabrina in Inyo National Forest
See map pages 732–733
You get the best of both worlds at this camp. It is set at 9,000 feet on Bishop Creek, just a half mile from Lake Sabrina, a beautiful High Sierra lake. In addition, trails nearby are routed into the high country of the John Muir Wilderness. Take your pick. Whatever your choice, it's a good one.
RV sites, facilities: There are 18 sites for RVs up to 30 feet or tents. Picnic tables and fire grills are provided. Drinking water and vault toilets are available. A boat ramp and boat rentals are available nearby. Supplies are available in Bishop. Leashed pets are permitted.
Reservations, fees: Reservations are not accepted. The fee is $14 per night. A senior discount is available. Open mid-May through October.
Directions: Drive on U.S. 395 to Bishop and Highway 168. Turn northwest (toward the Sierra) on Highway 168 and drive 17 miles (signed Lake Sabrina at a fork) to the campground.
Contact: Inyo National Forest, White Mountain Ranger District, 760/873-2500, fax 760/873-2563.

18 FOUR JEFFREY

Rating: 8

near South Lake in Inyo National Forest
See map pages 732–733
The camp is set on the South Fork of Bishop Creek at 8,100 feet, about four miles from South Lake. If you can arrange a trip in the fall, make sure you visit this camp. The fall colors are spectacular, with the aspen trees exploding in yellows and oranges. It is also the last camp on South Lake Road to be closed in the fall, and though nights are cold, it is well worth the trip. This is by far the largest of the Forest Service camps in the vicinity. There are three lakes in the area: North Lake, Lake Sabrina, and South Lake.
RV sites, facilities: There are 106 sites for RVs up to 50 feet or tents. Picnic tables and fire grills are provided. Drinking water, vault toilets, firewood, and an RV dump station are available. Supplies

are available in Bishop. Some facilities are wheelchair-accessible. Leashed pets are permitted.
Reservations, fees: Reservations are not accepted. The fee is $14 per night. A senior discount is available. Open mid-April through October.
Directions: Drive on U.S. 395 to Bishop and Highway 168. Turn northwest (toward the Sierra) on Highway 168 and drive 14 miles to South Lake Road. Turn left and drive .5 mile to the campground.
Contact: Inyo National Forest, White Mountain Ranger District, 760/873-2500, fax 760/873-2563.

19 BISHOP PARK

Rating: 6

near Lake Sabrina in Inyo National Forest
See map pages 732–733
Bishop Park camp is one in a series of camps along Bishop Creek. This one is just behind the summer community of Aspendell. It is about two miles from Lake Sabrina, an ideal day trip or jump-off spot for a backpacking expedition into the John Muir Wilderness. The elevation is 8,400 feet.
RV sites, facilities: There are 20 sites for RVs up to 22 feet or tents and a group campsite for tents. Picnic tables and fire grills are provided. Drinking water and flush toilets are available. Horseback riding facilities are available at North Lake. Supplies are available in Bishop. Leashed pets are permitted.
Reservations, fees: Reservations are not accepted. The fee is $14 per night, $45 per night for groups. A senior discount is available. Open mid-May through mid-October.
Directions: Drive on U.S. 395 to Bishop and Highway 168. Turn northwest (toward the Sierra) on Highway 168 and drive 15 miles to the campground.
Contact: Inyo National Forest, White Mountain Ranger District, 760/873-2500, fax 760/873-2563.

20 CREEKSIDE RV PARK

Rating: 7

on the South Fork of Bishop Creek
See map pages 732–733
This privately operated park in the high country

CALIFORNIA

is set up primarily for RVs. A lot of folks are surprised to find it here. North, Sabrina, and South Lakes are in the area. The elevation is 8,400 feet.

RV sites, facilities: There are 45 sites with partial or full hookups for RVs, four sites for tents, and rental trailers. Restrooms, drinking water, flush toilets, coin-operated showers, a store, and fish-cleaning facilities are available. A store and propane are available two blocks away. Leashed pets are permitted.

Reservations, fees: Reservations are accepted. The fee is $22–32 per night, plus $2 per pet per night. Open May through October. Major credit cards are accepted.

Directions: Drive on U.S. 395 to Bishop and Highway 168. Turn northwest (toward the Sierra) on Highway 168 and drive 14 miles to South Lake Road. Turn left and drive two miles to the campground entrance on the left (1949 South Lake Road).

Contact: Creekside RV Park, 760/873-4483.

21 BROWN'S TOWN SCHOBER LANE CAMP

Rating: 5

near Bishop
See map pages 732–733

This privately operated campground, one of several in the vicinity of Bishop, is the only one in the area that accepts tents. It's all shade and grass, and it's next to the golf course.

RV sites, facilities: There are 160 sites, 46 with partial hookups, for RVs or tents. Picnic tables are provided. Restrooms, drinking water, flush toilets, coin-operated showers, cable TV at 10 sites, an RV dump station, a museum, a store, and a snack bar are available. Leashed pets are permitted.

Reservations, fees: Reservations are accepted. The fee is $16–21 per night, with a one-vehicle limit per site. Major credit cards are accepted. Open March through Thanksgiving, weather permitting.

Directions: Drive on U.S. 395 to Schober Lane (one mile south of Bishop) and the campground entrance. Turn northwest (toward the Sierra) and into the campground.

Contact: Brown's Town Schober Lane Camp, 760/873-8522.

22 SHADY REST TRAILER PARK

Rating: 3

in Bishop
See map pages 732–733

This is an option for folks who want to find a layover in the Bishop area without going to much trouble to find it. This is a mobile home park with long-term rentals, with some sites available for overnighters. Possible side trips include the Indian Cultural Center in Bishop and the Pleasant Valley Reservoir, about a 15-minute drive from Shady Rest.

RV sites, facilities: There are 25 sites with full hookups for RVs. Restrooms, drinking water, flush toilets, showers, cable TV, and a coin-operated laundry are available. Leashed pets are permitted.

Reservations, fees: Reservations are recommended. The fee is $25 per night. Long-term rates are available. Open year-round.

Directions: Drive on U.S. 395 to Bishop and Yaney Street. Turn southeast (away from the Sierra) and drive .7 mile to the park (399 E. Yaney Street).

Contact: Shady Rest Trailer Park, 760/873-3430.

23 CAMP EDISON

Rating: 8

on Shaver Lake
See map pages 732–733

Camp Edison is the best camp at Shaver Lake, set on a peninsula along the lake's western shore, with a boat ramp and marina. The lake is at an elevation of 5,370 feet in the Sierra, a pretty area that has become popular for its calm, warm days and cool water. Boat rentals and bait and tackle are available at the marina. Newcomers with youngsters will discover that the best area for swimming and playing in the water is on the east side of the lake. Though more distant, this part of the lake offers sandy beaches rather than rocky drop-offs.

RV sites, facilities: There are 252 sites, 43 with

full hookups for RVs up to 60 feet or tents. Picnic tables, fire rings, and barbecues are provided. Restrooms, drinking water, flush toilets, cable TV, electrical connections, coin-operated showers, an RV dump station, a coin-operated laundry, a marina, a boat ramp, and horseback riding facilities are available. In winter, a minimum of 25 sites are kept open. Some facilities are wheelchair-accessible. Leashed pets are permitted.

Reservations, fees: Reservations are accepted. The fee is $22–42 per night, plus $5 for each additional vehicle with a maximum of eight people per site, $5 for a boat, and $4 per pet per night. A senior discount is available. Open year-round with limited winter services.

Directions: From Fresno, drive east on Highway 168 to the town of Shaver Lake. Continue one mile on Highway 168 to the campground entrance road on the right. Turn right and drive to the campground on the west shore of Shaver Lake.

Contact: Camp Edison, 559/841-3134, fax 559/841-3193, website: www.sce.com/campedison.com.

24 DORABELLE

Rating: 7

on Shaver Lake in Sierra National Forest
See map pages 732–733

This is one of the few Forest Service camps in the state that is set up more for RVers than for tenters. The camp is along a long cove at the southwest corner of the lake, well protected from winds out of the northwest. Shaver Lake is a popular lake for vacationers, and it is well stocked with trout during the summer. Boat rentals and bait and tackle are available at the nearby marina. This is also a popular snow-play area in the winter. The elevation is 5,400 feet.

RV sites, facilities: There are 68 sites for RVs up to 30 feet or tents. Picnic tables and fire grills are provided. Drinking water and vault toilets are available. A store is nearby. Leashed pets are permitted.

Reservations, fees: Reserve at 877/444-6777 or online at www.reserveusa.com ($9 reservation fee). The fee is $18 per night, plus $5 for each additional vehicle. A senior discount is available. Open May through September.

Directions: From Fresno, drive east on Highway

168 to Dorabelle Road (on the right just as entering the town of Shaver Lake). Turn right on Dorabelle Road and drive one mile to the campground at the southwest end of Shaver Lake.

Contact: Sierra National Forest, High Sierra Ranger District, 559/855-5360, fax 559/855-5375.

25 DINKEY CREEK

Rating: 7

in Sierra National Forest
See map pages 732–733

This is a huge Forest Service camp set along Dinkey Creek at 5,700 feet, well in the interior of Sierra National Forest. It is a popular camp for anglers who take the trail and hike upstream along the creek for small-trout fishing in a pristine setting. Backpackers occasionally lay over here before driving on to the Dinkey Lakes Parking Area, for hikes to Mystery Lake, Swede Lake, South Lake, and others in the nearby Dinkey Lakes Wilderness.

RV sites, facilities: There are 128 sites for RVs up to 30 feet or tents. Picnic tables and fire grills are provided. Drinking water, flush toilets, showers, and horseback riding facilities are available nearby. You can buy supplies in Dinkey Creek. Leashed pets are permitted.

Reservations, fees: From Memorial Day through Labor Day, reserve at 877/444-6777 or online at www.reserveusa.com ($9 reservation fee). The fee is $18 per night with a 14-day stay limit. A senior discount is available. Open from May through September.

Directions: From Fresno, drive east on Highway 168 to Dinkey Creek Road (on the right just as you enter the town of Shaver Lake). Turn right and drive 14 miles to the campground. A map of Sierra National Forest is advised.

Contact: Sierra National Forest, High Sierra Ranger District, 559/855-5360, fax 559/855-5375.

26 BIG PINE CREEK

Rating: 8

in Inyo National Forest
See map pages 732–733

This is another good spot for backpackers to

launch a multiday trip. The camp is set along Big Pine Creek at 7,600 feet, with trails near the camp that are routed to the numerous lakes in the high country of the John Muir Wilderness.

RV sites, facilities: There are 27 sites for RVs up to 45 feet or tents and three sites for tents only. Picnic tables and fire grills are provided. Drinking water and vault toilets are available. A small convenience store is nearby. Some facilities are wheelchair-accessible. Leashed pets are permitted.

Reservations, fees: Reserve at 877/444-6777 or online at www.reserveusa.com ($9 reservation fee). The fee is $13 per night. A senior discount is available. Open early May through October.

Directions: Drive on U.S. 395 to Big Pine and Crocker Street/Glacier Lodge Road. Turn northwest (toward the Sierra) and drive nine miles (it becomes Glacier Lodge Road) to the campground.

Contact: Inyo National Forest, White Mountain Ranger District, 760/873-2500, fax 760/873-2563.

27 BROWN'S GLACIER
🐕 🚐 ⛰️

Rating: 4

near Big Pine
See map pages 732–733

This is one of two county camps near the town of Big Pine, providing U.S. 395 cruisers with two options. The camp is set along the Big Pine Canal at 3,900 feet. It is owned by the county but operated by a concessionaire. Some may remember this campground as Triangle Campground; it has been renamed and improved for the 2003 season. Brown's runs five small campgrounds in the area named Glacier, Keough Hot Springs, Moll Pond, Brown's Owens River, and Brown's Town.

RV sites, facilities: There are 40 sites, some with partial hookups, for RVs or tents. Picnic tables and fire grills are provided. Restrooms, drinking water, flush toilets, and coin-operated showers are available. Supplies are available in Big Pine. Leashed pets are permitted.

Reservations, fees: Reservations are not accepted. The fee is $14 per night for tent sites, $17 for RV sites with partial hookups. Open April through October.

Directions: Drive on U.S. 395 to the park entrance (.5 mile north of Big Pine) on the southeast side

of the road. Turn east (away from the Sierra) and enter the park.

Contact: Inyo County Parks Department, 760/872-6911, fax 760/873-5599.

28 TINEMAHA CREEK COUNTY PARK
🐕 🚐 ⛰️

Rating: 6

near Big Pine
See map pages 732–733

This primitive, little-known (to out-of-towners) county park campground is on Tinemaha Creek at 4,400 feet. The park's campground will be renovated over the course of several years, with small changes each year. Partial hookups for RVs should be in by summer of 2003.

RV sites, facilities: There are 55 sites, some with partial hookups, for RVs or tents. Picnic tables and fire grills are provided. Pit toilets are available. No drinking water is available. Stream water is available and must be boiled or pump-filtered before use. Leashed pets are permitted.

Reservations, fees: Reservations are not accepted. The fee is $10 per vehicle per night. Open year-round.

Directions: Drive on U.S. 395 to Tinemaha Creek Road (seven miles south of Big Pine and 20 miles north of Independence). Turn west (toward the Sierra) on Tinemaha Creek Road and drive two miles to the park on the left.

Contact: Inyo County Parks Department, 760/878-0272, fax 760/873-5599.

29 TABOOSE CREEK COUNTY CAMPGROUND
🏊 🐕 🚐 ⛰️

Rating: 4

near Big Pine
See map pages 732–733

The eastern Sierra is stark country, but this little spot provides a stream (Taboose Creek) and some trees near the campground. There is an opportunity for trout fishing that's fair, not spectacular. The easy access off U.S. 395 is a bonus. The elevation is 3,900 feet.

RV sites, facilities: There are 55 sites for RVs or tents. Picnic tables and fire grills are provided. Drinking water (hand-pumped from a well) and vault toilets are available. Supplies are available in Big Pine or Independence. Leashed pets are permitted.

Reservations, fees: Reservations are not accepted. The fee is $10 per night. Open year-round.

Directions: Drive on U.S. 395 to Taboose Creek Road (11 miles south of Big Pine). Turn west (toward the Sierra) on Taboose Creek Road and drive 2.5 miles to the campground (straight in).

Contact: Inyo County Parks Department, 760/878-0272, fax 760/873-5599.

30 PINE FLAT RECREATION AREA

Rating: 7

on Pine Flat Reservoir
See map pages 732–733

This is a county park that is open all year, set below the dam of Pine Flat Reservoir, actually not on the lake at all. As a county park campground, it is often overlooked by out-of-towners.

RV sites, facilities: There are 52 sites for RVs or tents. Fire grills and picnic tables are provided. Restrooms, drinking water, flush toilets, an RV dump station, a playground, and a wheelchair-accessible fishing area are available. A store, a coin-operated laundry, and propane are nearby (within a mile). Leashed pets are permitted.

Reservations, fees: Reservations are not accepted. The fee is $11 per night. Open year-round.

Directions: From Fresno, drive east on Highway 180 for 17.5 miles to Trimmer Springs Road. Turn left and drive eight miles to the town of Piedra. Continue on Trimmer Springs Road for one mile to Pine Flat Road. Turn right and drive three miles to the campground on the right.

Contact: Fresno County Parks Department, 559/488-3004, fax 559/488-1988.

31 ISLAND PARK AND DEER CREEK POINT GROUP

Rating: 7

on Pine Flat Reservoir
See map pages 732–733

These are two of four Army Corps of Engineer campgrounds available at Pine Flat Reservoir, a popular lake set in the foothill country east of

Fresno. When Pine Flat is full, or close to full, it is very pretty. The lake is 21 miles long with 67 miles of shoreline and 4,270 surface acres. Right: a big lake with unlimited potential. Because the temperatures get warm in spring here, then smoking hot in summer, the lake is like Valhalla for boating and water sports. The fishing for white bass is often excellent in late winter and early spring and, after that, conditions are ideal for water sports. The elevation is 1,000 feet.

RV sites, facilities: There are 52 sites for self-contained RVs or tents, 60 overflow sites (at Island Park), and two group sites for 50 people each for RVs or tents. Picnic tables and fire grills are provided. Restrooms, drinking water, flush toilets, coin-operated showers, a pay telephone, a boat ramp, a fish-cleaning station, and an RV dump station are available. There is a seasonal store at the campground entrance. Boat rentals are available within five miles. Some facilities are wheelchair-accessible. Leashed pets are permitted.

Reservations, fees: Reservations for Island Park are available at 877/444-6777 or online at www.reserveusa.com ($9 reservation fee); reservations for group sites are required at 559/787-2589. The fees are $10–16 per night and $60 for group sites, plus a $2 boat-launch fee. Open year-round.

Directions: From Fresno, drive east on Highway 180 for 17.5 miles to Trimmer Springs Road. Turn left and drive eight miles to the town of Piedra. Continue on Trimmer Springs Road for one mile to Pine Flat Road. Turn right and drive .25 mile to the park entrance (signed Island Park).

Contact: U.S. Army Corps of Engineers, Sacramento District, Pine Flat Field Office, 559/787-2589, fax 559/787-2773.

32 LAKERIDGE CAMPING AND BOATING RESORT

Rating: 7

on Pine Flat Reservoir
See map pages 732–733

Pine Flat Reservoir is a big lake with seemingly unlimited recreation potential. It is in the foothills east of Fresno at 961 feet elevation, covering 4,270 surface acres with 67 miles of shoreline. The lake's proximity to Fresno has made it a top destination for boating and water sports. Fishing for white bass can also be excellent in the spring and early summer. Note: The one downer is that there are only a few sandy beaches.

RV sites, facilities: There are 108 sites, some with hookups, for RVs up to 32 feet or tents. Picnic tables, restrooms, showers, modem access, a coin-operated laundry, a convenience store, ice, a pay phone, a petting zoo, and houseboat rentals are available.

Reservations, fees: Reservations are recommended at 877/787-2260. The fees are $20 per night for tent sites and $25 per night for RV sites with hookups, plus $2.50 per person per night for more than two people. Major credit cards are accepted.

Directions: From Fresno, drive east on Highway 180 for 17.5 miles to Trimmer Springs Road. Turn left and drive eight miles to the town of Piedra. Continue on Trimmer Springs Road for three miles to Sunnyslope Road. Turn right and drive one mile to the resort on the right.

Contact: Lakeridge Camping and Boating Resort, tel./fax 559/787-2260; marina, 559/787-2506.

33 GRAY'S MEADOW

Rating: 6

on Independence Creek in Inyo National Forest
See map pages 732–733

Gray's Meadow is one of two adjacent camps that are set along Independence Creek. The creek is stocked with small trout by the Department of Fish and Game. The highlight in the immediate area is the trailhead at the end of the road at Onion Valley Camp. For U.S. 395 cruisers looking for a spot, this is a pretty alternative to the camps in Bishop.

RV sites, facilities: There are 52 sites for RVs or tents. Picnic tables and fire grills are provided. Drinking water and flush toilets are available. Supplies and a coin-operated laundry are available in Independence. Leashed pets are permitted.

Reservations, fees: Reserve at 877/444-6777 or online at www.reserveusa.com ($9 reservation fee). The fee is $12 per night. A senior discount is available. Open April through October.

Directions: Drive on U.S. 395 to Independence and Onion Valley Road. Turn west (toward the

Sierra) at Onion Valley Road and drive five miles to the campground on the right.

Contact: Inyo National Forest, Mt. Whitney Ranger District, 760/876-6200, fax 760/876-6202.

34 OAK CREEK

Rating: 6

in Inyo National Forest
See map pages 732–733

Oak Creek is in a series of little-known camps west of Independence that provides a jump-off spot for backpackers. This camp is set at 5,000 feet, with a trail from camp that is routed west (and up) into the California Bighorn Sheep Zoological Area, a rugged, stark region well above the tree line. Caution: plan on a terrible, long, butt-kicker of a climb up to the Sierra crest; stay on the trail. Note that half of the campsites are available by reservation, and half are first-come, first-served.

RV sites, facilities: There are 22 sites for RVs or tents. Picnic tables and fire grills are provided. Drinking water and vault toilets are available. Garbage must be packed out. Supplies and a coin-operated laundry are available in Independence. Some facilities are wheelchair-accessible. Leashed pets are permitted.

Reservations, fees: Reservations are accepted at 877/444-6777. The fee is $12 per night. A senior discount is available. Open year-round, weather permitting.

Directions: Drive on U.S. 395 to North Oak Creek Drive (two miles north of Independence). Turn west (toward the Sierra) at North Oak Creek Drive and drive three miles to the campground on the right.

Contact: Inyo National Forest, Mt. Whitney Ranger District, 760/876-6200, fax 760/876-6202.

35 INDEPENDENCE CREEK COUNTY CAMPGROUND

Rating: 4

in Independence
See map pages 732–733

This unpublicized county park is often overlooked among U.S. 395 cruisers. It is set at 3,900 feet just outside of Independence, which is spiraling downward into something resembling a ghost town. True to form, maintenance is sometimes lacking here. Independence Creek (no fishing) runs through the campground and a museum is within walking distance. At the rate it's going, the whole town could be a museum.

RV sites, facilities: There are 25 sites for RVs or tents. Picnic tables are provided. Drinking water and vault toilets are available. Supplies and a coin-operated laundry are available in Independence. Some facilities are wheelchair-accessible. Leashed pets are permitted.

Reservations, fees: Reservations are not accepted. The fee is $10 per night. Open year-round.

Directions: Drive on U.S. 395 to Independence and Market Street. Turn west (toward the Sierra) at Market Street and drive .5 mile (outside the town limits) to the campground.

Contact: Inyo County Parks Department, 760/878-0272, fax 760/873-5599.

36 PRINCESS

Rating: 7

on Princess Meadow in Giant Sequoia National Monument

See map pages 732–733

This mountain camp is at 5,900 feet. It is popular because of its proximity to both Hume Lake and the star attractions at Kings Canyon National Park. Hume Lake is just four miles from the camp and the Grant Grove entrance to Kings Canyon National Park is only six miles away to the south, while continuing on Highway 180 to the east will take you into the heart of Kings Canyon.

RV sites, facilities: There are 40 sites for RVs up to 22 feet or tents and 50 sites for tents. Picnic tables and fire grills are provided. Drinking water, vault toilets, and an RV dump station are available. A store is four miles away at Hume Lake. Leashed pets are permitted.

Reservations, fees: Reserve at 877/444-6777 or online at www.reserveusa.com ($9 reservation fee). The fee is $14 per night, plus $5 for each additional vehicle and a $10 per vehicle national park entrance fee. A senior discount is available. Open May through September.

Directions: From Fresno, drive east on Highway 180 for 55 miles to the Big Stump Entrance Station at Sequoia–Kings Canyon National Park. Continue 1.5 miles to a junction (signed left for Grant Grove). Turn left and drive 1.5 miles to Grant Grove Village, then continue for 4.5 miles to the campground on the right.

Contact: Sequoia National Forest, Hume Lake Ranger District, 559/338-2251, fax 559/338-2131.

37 AZALEA

Rating: 7

in Kings Canyon National Park

See map pages 732–733

This camp is tucked just inside the western border of Kings Canyon National Park. It is set at 6,600 feet near the General Grant Grove of giant sequoias. (For information on several short, spectacular hikes among the giant sequoias, see the following entry for Sunset.) Nearby Sequoia Lake is privately owned; no fishing, no swimming, no trespassing. To see the spectacular Kings Canyon, one of the deepest gorges in North America, reenter the park on Highway 180.

RV sites, facilities: There are 113 sites for RVs up to 30 feet or tents. Picnic tables and fire grills are provided. Drinking water, flush toilets, and horseback riding facilities are available. Evening ranger programs are often available in the summer. A store is nearby. Showers are available in Grant Grove Village. Some facilities are wheelchair-accessible. Leashed pets are permitted, except on trails.

Reservations, fees: Reservations are not accepted. The fee is $14 per night, plus a $10 per vehicle park entrance fee. A senior discount is available. Open year-round.

Directions: From Fresno, drive east on Highway 180 for 55 miles to the Big Stump entrance station at Sequoia–Kings Canyon National Park. Continue 1.5 miles to a junction (signed left for Grant Grove). Turn left and drive 1.5 miles to Grant Grove Village, then continue for .7 mile to the campground entrance on the left.

Contact: Kings Canyon National Park, 559/565-3341.

38 SUNSET

Rating: 7

in Kings Canyon National Park
See map pages 732–733

This is the biggest of the camps that are just inside the Kings Canyon National Park boundaries at Grant Grove Village, 6,600 feet in elevation. The nearby General Grant Grove of Giant Sequoias is the main attraction, with many short, easy walks among the sequoias, each breathtakingly beautiful. They include the Big Stump Trail, Sunset Trail, North Grove Loop, General Grant Tree, Manzanita and Azalea Loop, and Panoramic Point and Park Ridge Trail. Seeing the General Grant Tree is a rite of passage for newcomers; after a half-hour walk you arrive at a sequoia that is 1,800 years old, 107 feet in circumference, and 267 feet tall.

RV sites, facilities: There are 200 sites for RVs up to 30 feet or tents. Picnic tables and fire grills are provided. Drinking water, flush toilets, and horseback riding facilities are available. A store is nearby. Showers are available in Grant Grove Village. In the summer, evening ranger programs are often available. Some facilities are wheelchair-accessible. Leashed pets are permitted, except on trails.

Reservations, fees: Reservations are not accepted. The fee is $14 per night, plus a $10 per vehicle park entrance fee. A senior discount is available. Open late May to mid-September.

Directions: From Fresno, drive east on Highway 180 for 55 miles to the Big Stump entrance station at Sequoia–Kings Canyon National Park. Continue 1.5 miles to a junction (signed left for Grant Grove). Turn left (still Highway 180) and drive one mile to the campground entrance (.5 mile before reaching Grant Grove Village).

Contact: Kings Canyon National Park, 559/565-3341.

39 CRYSTAL SPRINGS

Rating: 5

in Kings Canyon National Park
See map pages 732–733

Directly to the south of this camp is the General Grant Grove and its giant sequoias. But continuing on Highway 180 provides access to the interior of Kings Canyon National Park, and this camp makes an ideal jump-off point. From here you can drive east, passing Cedar Grove Village, cruising along the Kings River, and finally coming to a dead-end loop, taking in the drop-dead gorgeous landscape of one of the deepest gorges in North America. One of the best hikes, but also the most demanding, is the 13-mile round-trip to Lookout Peak, out of the Cedar Grove Village area. It involves a 4,000-foot climb to 8,531 feet, and with it, a breathtaking view of Sierra ridges, Cedar Grove far below, and Kings Canyon.

RV sites, facilities: There are 62 sites for RVs up to 22 feet or tents. Picnic tables and fire grills are provided. Drinking water, flush toilets, and horseback riding facilities are available. A store is nearby. Showers are available in Grant Grove Village. Evening ranger programs are often available in the summer. Some facilities are wheelchair-accessible. Leashed pets are permitted, except on trails.

Reservations, fees: Reservations are not accepted. The fee is $14 per night, plus a $10 per vehicle park entrance fee. A senior discount is available. Open mid-May to late September.

Directions: From Fresno, drive east on Highway 180 for 55 miles to the Big Stump entrance station at Sequoia–Kings Canyon National Park. Continue 1.5 miles to a junction (signed left for Grant Grove). Turn left and drive 1.5 miles to Grant Grove Village, then continue for .7 mile to the campground entrance on the right.

Contact: Kings Canyon National Park, 559/565-3341.

40 ESHOM CREEK

Rating: 7

on Eshom Creek in Giant Sequoia National Monument
See map pages 732–733

The campground at Eshom Creek is just two miles outside the boundaries of Sequoia National Park. It is well hidden and a considerable distance from the crowds and sights in the park interior. It is set along Eshom Creek at an elevation of 4,800 feet. Many campers at Eshom Creek hike straight into the national park, with a trailhead at Redwood Saddle (just inside the park boundary) providing a route to see the Redwood Mountain Grove, Fallen Goliath, Hart Tree, and Hart Meadow in a sensational loop hike.

RV sites, facilities: There are 17 sites for RVs up to 22 feet or tents and seven group sites for up to 12 people each. Picnic tables and fire grills are provided. Drinking water and vault toilets are available. Leashed pets are permitted.

Reservations, fees: Reservations are not accepted. The fee is $14 per night, $28 per night for group sites. Open May through September.

Directions: Drive on Highway 99 to Visalia and the exit for Highway 198 East. Take that exit and drive east on Highway 198 for 11 miles to Highway 245. Turn left (north) on Highway 245 and drive 18 miles to Badger and County Road 465. Turn right and drive eight miles to the campground.

Contact: Sequoia National Forest, Hume Lake Ranger District, 559/338-2251, fax 559/338-2131.

41 STONY CREEK

Rating: 6

in Giant Sequoia National Monument
See map pages 732–733

Stony Creek camp provides a good option if the national park camps are filled. It is set at creekside at 6,400 feet elevation. Sequoia and Kings Canyon National Parks are nearby.

RV sites, facilities: There are 49 sites for RVs up to 22 feet or tents. Picnic tables and fire grills are provided. Drinking water and flush toilets are available. A store and coin-operated laundry are nearby. Leashed pets are permitted.

Reservations, fees: Reserve at 877/444-6777 or online at www.reserveusa.com ($9 reservation fee). The fee is $16 per night, plus a $10 per vehicle park entrance fee and $5 for each additional vehicle. A senior discount is available. Open June through August.

Directions: From Fresno, drive east on Highway 180 for 55 miles to the Big Stump entrance station at Sequoia–Kings Canyon National Park. Continue 1.5 miles to a junction (signed left for Grant Grove). Turn right at Generals Highway and drive about 13 miles to the campground entrance on the right.

Contact: Sequoia National Forest, Hume Lake Ranger District, 559/338-2251, fax 559/338-2131.

42 DORST CREEK

Rating: 7

on Dorst Creek in Sequoia National Park
See map pages 732–733

Things that go bump in the night swing through Dorst all summer long. That's right, Mr. Bear (a whole bunch of them) makes food raids like a UPS driver on a pick-up route. There are so many bears raiding food here that some years rangers keep a running tally posted on the bulletin board. That's why keeping your food in a bear-proof locker is not only a must, it's the law. The camp is set on Dorst Creek at 6,700 feet, near a trail that is routed into the backcountry and through Muir Grove. It is one in a series of big, popular camps in Sequoia National Park.

RV sites, facilities: There are 204 family sites for RVs up to 30 feet or tents and five group sites. Picnic tables and fire grills are provided. Drinking water, flush toilets, an RV dump station, and evening ranger programs are available. A store and a coin-operated laundry are nearby. Some facilities are wheelchair-accessible. Leashed pets are permitted.

Reservations, fees: Reserve at 800/365-CAMP (800/365-2267) or online at http://reservations.nps.gov. The fees are $16 per night (includes reservation fee) and $38–57 for group sites, plus a $10 per vehicle park entrance fee. Open Memorial Day through Labor Day.

Directions: From Fresno, drive east on Highway 180 for 55 miles to the Big Stump entrance station at Sequoia–Kings Canyon National Park. Continue 1.5 miles to a junction (signed left for Grant Grove). Turn right at Generals Highway and drive about 17 miles to the campground entrance on the right.

Contact: Sequoia National Park, 559/565-3341.

43 SENTINEL

Rating: 8

in Kings Canyon National Park
See map pages 732–733

This camp provides a nearby alternative to Sheep Creek. They both tend to fill up quickly in the summer. It's a short walk to Cedar Grove Village, the center of activity in the park. The elevation is

4,600 feet. Hiking and trout fishing are excellent in the vicinity. The entrance road provides stunning rim-of-the-world views of Kings Canyon, and then drops down right along the Kings River.

RV sites, facilities: There are 82 sites for RVs up to 30 feet or tents. Picnic tables and fire grills are provided. Restrooms, drinking water, flush toilets, and showers are available. A store, a coin-operated laundry, a restaurant, and horseback riding facilities are nearby. Some facilities are wheelchair-accessible. Leashed pets are permitted.

Reservations, fees: Reservations are not accepted. The fee is $14 per night, plus a $10 per vehicle park entrance fee. A senior discount is available. Open late April through mid-November, weather permitting.

Directions: From Fresno, drive east on Highway 180 for 55 miles to the Big Stump entrance station at Sequoia–Kings Canyon National Park. Continue 1.5 miles to a junction (signed left for Grant Grove). Turn left and drive 32 miles to the campground entrance on the left (near Cedar Grove Village).

Contact: Kings Canyon National Park, 559/565-3341.

44 SHEEP CREEK

Rating: 8

in Kings Canyon National Park
See map pages 732–733

This is one of the camps that always fills up quickly on summer weekends. It's a pretty spot and just a short walk from Cedar Grove Village. The camp is set along Sheep Creek at 4,600 feet.

RV sites, facilities: There are 111 sites for RVs up to 30 feet or tents. Picnic tables and fire grills are provided. Restrooms, drinking water, flush toilets, and showers are available. A store, a coin-operated laundry, a restaurant, and horseback riding facilities are available nearby. Leashed pets are permitted.

Reservations, fees: Reservations are not accepted. The fee is $14 per night, plus a $10 per vehicle park entrance fee. A senior discount is available. Open June through September.

Directions: From Fresno, drive east on Highway 180 for 55 miles to the Big Stump entrance station at Sequoia–Kings Canyon National Park. Continue 1.5 miles to a junction (signed left for

Grant Grove). Turn left and drive 31.5 miles to the campground entrance on the left (near Cedar Grove Village).

Contact: Kings Canyon National Park, 559/565-3341.

45 MORAINE

Rating: 8

in Kings Canyon National Park
See map pages 732–733

This is one in a series of camps in the Cedar Grove Village area of Kings Canyon National Park. This camp is used only as an overflow area. Hikers should drive past the Cedar Grove Ranger Station to the end of the road at Copper Creek, a prime jump-off point for a spectacular hike. The elevation is 4,600 feet.

RV sites, facilities: There are 120 sites for RVs or tents. Picnic tables and fire grills are provided. Drinking water and flush toilets are available. Showers, horseback riding facilities, a store, a restaurant, and a coin-operated laundry are nearby. Leashed pets are permitted.

Reservations, fees: Reservations are not accepted. The fee is $14 per night, plus a $10 per vehicle park entrance fee. A senior discount is available. Open June through September, weather permitting.

Directions: From Fresno, drive east on Highway 180 for 55 miles to the Big Stump entrance station at Sequoia–Kings Canyon National Park. Continue 1.5 miles to a junction (signed left for Grant Grove). Turn left and drive 33 miles to the campground entrance (one mile past the ranger station, near Cedar Village).

Contact: Kings Canyon National Park, 559/565-3341.

46 WHITNEY PORTAL AND WHITNEY PORTAL GROUP

Rating: 9

near Mount Whitney in Inyo National Forest
See map pages 732–733

This camp is home to a world-class trailhead. It is regarded as the number one jump-off spot for the hike to the top of Mount Whitney, the highest spot in the continental United States, 14,494 feet, as well as the start of the 211-mile John Muir Trail from Mount Whitney to Yosemite Valley. Hikers planning to scale the summit must have a wilderness permit, available by reservation at the Forest Service office in Lone Pine. The camp is at 8,000 feet, and virtually everyone staying here plans to make the trek to the Whitney summit, a climb of 6,500 feet over the course of 10 miles. The trip includes an ascent over 100 switchbacks (often snow-covered in early summer) to top Wotan's Throne and reach Trail Crest (13,560 feet). Here you turn right and take the Summit Trail, where the ridge is cut by huge notch windows providing a view down more than 10,000 feet to the little town of Lone Pine and the Owens Valley. When you sign the logbook on top, don't be surprised if you see my name in the registry. A plus at the campground is watching the JMT hikers arrive who are just finishing the trail from north to south, that is, from Yosemite to Whitney. There is no comparing the happy look of success when they drop their packs for the last time, head into the little store, and pick a favorite refreshment for celebration.

RV sites, facilities: There are 43 sites for RVs up to 16 feet or tents and three group sites. Picnic tables and fire grills are provided. Drinking water and flush toilets are available. Supplies are available in Lone Pine. Some facilities are wheelchair-accessible. Leashed pets are permitted.

Reservations, fees: Reservations are accepted for 60 percent of the sites. Reserve at 877/444-6777 or online at www.reserveusa.com ($9 reservation fee). The fee is $14 per night, $35 for group sites. Stays are limited to seven days. A senior discount is available. Open late May to mid-October.

Directions: Drive on U.S. 395 to Lone Pine and Whitney Portal Road. Turn west (toward the Sierra) on Whitney Portal Road and drive 13 miles to the campground on the left.

Contact: Inyo National Forest, Mt. Whitney Ranger District, 760/876-6200, fax 760/876-6202.

47 LONE PINE AND LONE PINE GROUP

Rating: 8

near Mount Whitney in Inyo National Forest
See map pages 732–733
This is an alternative for campers preparing to

hike Mount Whitney or start the John Muir Trail. It is set at 6,000 feet, 2,000 feet below Whitney Portal (the hiking jump-off spot), providing a lower-elevation location for hikers to acclimate themselves to the altitude. The camp is set on Lone Pine Creek, with decent fishing and spectacular views of Mount Whitney. Because of its exposure to the east, there are also beautiful sunrises, especially in fall.

RV sites, facilities: There are 43 sites for RVs or tents and one group site. Picnic tables and fire grills are provided. Drinking water and flush toilets are available. Supplies are available in Lone Pine. Leashed pets are permitted.

Reservations, fees: Reservations are accepted for 25 of the sites. Reserve at 877/444-6777 or online at www.reserveusa.com ($9 reservation fee). The fee is $12 per night, $30 for a group site. Stays are limited to 14 days. Open year-round, with no facilities from mid-October through late April.

Directions: Drive on U.S. 395 to Lone Pine and Whitney Portal Road. Turn west (toward the Sierra) on Whitney Portal Road and drive six miles to the campground on the left.

Contact: Inyo National Forest, Mt. Whitney Ranger District, 760/876-6200, fax 760/876-6202.

48 DIAZ LAKE

Rating: 6

near Lone Pine
See map pages 732–733
Diaz Lake, at 3,650 feet in the Owens Valley, is sometimes overlooked by visitors to nearby Mount Whitney. It's a small lake, just 85 acres, and it is popular for trout fishing in the spring, when a speed limit of 15 mph is enforced. In summer when hot weather takes over and the speed limit is bumped to 35 mph, you can say *adios* to the anglers and *hola* to water-skiers. It also becomes a good spot for swimming in the shallows. A 20-foot limit is enforced for boats. Major improvements were planned for this campground starting in 2003.

RV sites, facilities: There are 200 sites, some with partial hookups, for RVs or tents. Picnic tables and fire grills are provided. Restrooms, drinking water, flush toilets, a solar shower, and a boat ramp are available. Supplies and a coin-operated laundry are available in Lone Pine. Leashed pets are permitted.

Reservations, fees: Reservations are accepted for 50 sites at 760/876-5656. The fee is $10 per night. Open year-round.

Directions: Drive on U.S. 395 to the Diaz Lake entrance (two miles south of Lone Pine) on the west side of the road.

Contact: Inyo County Parks Department, 760/878-0272.

49 LODGEPOLE

Rating: 8

on the Marble Fork of the Kaweah River in Sequoia National Park
See map pages 732–733

This giant, pretty camp on the Marble Fork of the Kaweah River is typically crowded. A bonus here is an excellent trailhead nearby that leads into the backcountry of Sequoia National Park. The elevation is 6,700 feet.

RV sites, facilities: There are 214 sites for RVs up to 40 feet or tents. Picnic tables and fire grills are provided. Restrooms, drinking water, flush toilets, pay showers, an RV dump station, horseback riding facilities, a gift shop, and evening ranger programs are available. A store, a deli, and a coin-operated laundry are nearby. Leashed pets are permitted.

Reservations, fees: Reserve at 800/365-CAMP (800/365-2267) or online at http://reservations.nps.gov. The fee is $16 per night (includes reservation fee), plus a $10 per vehicle park entrance fee. A senior discount is available. Open year-round, with limited winter services.

Directions: From Fresno, drive east on Highway 180 for 55 miles to the Big Stump entrance station at Sequoia–Kings Canyon National Park. Continue 1.5 miles to a junction (signed left for Grant Grove). Turn right at Generals Highway and drive about 25 miles to Lodgepole Village and the turnoff for Lodgepole Campground. Turn left and drive .25 mile (past Lodgepole Village) to the campground.

Contact: Sequoia National Park, 559/565-3341.

50 POTWISHA

Rating: 7

on the Marble Fork of the Kaweah River in Sequoia National Park
See map pages 732–733

This pretty spot on the Marble Fork of the Kaweah River is one of Sequoia National Park's smaller drive-to campgrounds. By looking at maps, newcomers may think it is a very short drive farther into the park to see the General Sherman Tree, Giant Forest, and the famous trailhead for the walk-up Moro Rock. Nope. It's a slow, twisty drive, but with many pullouts for great views. A few miles east of the camp, visitors can find Buckeye Flat and a trail that is routed along Paradise Creek.

RV sites, facilities: There are 42 sites for RVs up to 30 feet or tents. Picnic tables and fire grills are provided. Drinking water, flush toilets, an RV dump station, and evening ranger programs are available. Some facilities are wheelchair-accessible. Leashed pets are permitted.

Reservations, fees: Reservations are not accepted. The fee is $14 per night, plus a $10 per vehicle park entrance fee. A senior discount is available. Open year-round.

Directions: From Visalia, drive east on Highway 198 for 36 miles to the Ash Mountain entrance station to Sequoia National Park. Continue into the park (the road becomes Generals Highway) and drive four miles to the campground on the left. Vehicles of 22 feet or longer are not advised on Generals Highway from Potwisha to Giant Forest Village and are advised to use Highway 180 through the Big Stump entrance station.

Contact: Sequoia National Park, 559/565-3341.

51 HORSE CREEK

Rating: 6

on Lake Kaweah
See map pages 732–733

Lake Kaweah is a big lake, covering nearly 2,000 acres with 22 miles of shoreline. This camp is set on the southern shore of the lake. In the spring when the lake is full and the surrounding hills are green, you may even think you have found

CALIFORNIA

Valhalla. With such hot weather in the San Joaquin Valley, it's a boater's heaven, ideal for water-skiers. In spring, when the water is still too cool for water sports, anglers can have the lake to themselves with good bass fishing. By early summer, it's a zoo from the personal watercraft and ski boats. One problem is that the water level drops a great deal during late summer, as thirsty farms suck up every drop they can get, killing prospects of developing beaches for swimming and wading. The elevation is 300 feet.

RV sites, facilities: There are 80 sites for RVs or tents. Picnic tables and fire grills are provided. Restrooms, drinking water, flush toilets, showers, a playground, and an RV dump station are available. Two paved boat ramps are available at Kaweah Recreation Area and Lemon Hill Recreation Area. A store, a coin-operated laundry, boat and water-ski rentals, ice, a snack bar, a restaurant, a gas station, and propane are available nearby. Some facilities are wheelchair-accessible. Leashed pets are permitted.

Reservations, fees: Reservations are accepted with a $9 reservation fee at 877/444-6777 or online at www.reserveusa.com. The fee is $16 per night. A senior discount is available. Major credit cards are accepted. Open year-round.

Directions: From Visalia, drive east on Highway 198 for 25 miles to Lake Kaweah's south shore and the camp on the left.

Contact: U.S. Army Corps of Engineers, 559/597-2301, fax 559/597-2468.

52 LEMON COVE-SEQUOIA

Rating: 5

near Lake Kaweah
See map pages 732–733

This is a privately run, year-round campground in the foothills just west of Lake Kaweah. Some use this park as a base camp for enjoying nearby Lake Kaweah or as a launch point for a trip into the mountains and Sequoia National Park. Compared to many towns in the San Joaquin Valley, Visalia is exceptionally clean and pretty, with greenery from the surrounding farms for many miles. This park is 18 miles from Visalia to the west and three miles from Lake Kaweah to the east (on Highway 198). By the way, the nearby groves of fruit trees along the highway provide a fantastic sideshow.

RV sites, facilities: There are 55 sites, many with partial hookups (50 amps), for RVs or tents, and group camping facilities. Picnic tables and drinking water are provided. Restrooms, showers, a playground, a swimming pool, laundry facilities, a recreation room, cable TV, a store, an RV dump station, and propane are available. Leashed pets are permitted.

Reservations, fees: Reservations are accepted. The fee is $18–22 per night. Open year-round. Major credit cards are accepted.

Directions: From Visalia, drive east on Highway 198 for 18 miles to the campground.

Contact: Lemon Cove-Sequoia, 559/597-2346, website: www.lemoncovesequoiacamp.com.

53 BALCH PARK

Rating: 6

near Mountain Home State Forest
See map pages 732–733

Balch Park is surrounded by Mountain Home State Forest and Sequoia National Forest. A nearby grove of giant sequoias is a featured attraction. The elevation is 6,500 feet. Two fishing ponds are also a feature.

RV sites, facilities: There are 71 sites, a few drive-through, for RVs up to 40 feet or tents. Picnic tables and fire grills are provided. Drinking water and flush and vault toilets are available. Some facilities are wheelchair-accessible. Leashed pets are permitted.

Reservations, fees: Reservations are not accepted. The fee is $14 per night, plus $1 for each additional vehicle and $1 per pet per night. A senior discount is available. Open from May to late October.

Directions: From Porterville, drive east on Highway 190 for 19 miles (a mile past the town of Springville) to Balch Park Road. Turn left (north) at Balch Park Road and drive 40 miles (long and curvy) to the park.

Contact: Balch Park, Tulare County, 559/733-6291.

CALIFORNIA

54 WISHON

Rating: 8

on the Tule River in Giant Sequoia National Monument

See map pages 732–733

Wishon camp is set at 4,000 feet on the Middle Fork of the North Fork Tule River, just west of the Doyle Springs Summer Home Tract. Just down the road to the east, on the left side, is a parking area for a trailhead. The hike here is routed for a mile to the Tule River and then runs along the stream for about five miles, to Mountain Home State Forest.

RV sites, facilities: There are 26 sites for RVs up to 24 feet or tents and nine sites for tents only. Picnic tables and fire grills are provided. Drinking water and vault toilets are available. Leashed pets are permitted.

Reservations, fees: Reserve at 877/444-6777 or online at www.reserveusa.com ($9 reservation fee). The fee is $14 per night, plus $5 for each additional vehicle. A senior discount is available. Open year-round.

Directions: From Porterville, drive east on Highway 190 for 25 miles to County Road 209/Wishon Drive. Turn left at County Road 208/Wishon Drive and drive 3.5 miles (narrow, curvy, RVs not advised).

Contact: Giant Sequoia National Monument, Tule River/Hot Springs Ranger District, 559/539-2607 or 661/548-6503, fax 559/539-2067.

55 QUAKING ASPEN

Rating: 2

in Giant Sequoia National Monument

See map pages 732–733

Quaking Aspen sits at a junction of Forest Service roads at 7,000 feet in elevation, near the headwaters of Freeman Creek. A trailhead for the Summit National Recreation Trail runs right through camp; it's a popular trip on horseback, heading deep into Sequoia National Forest. Another trailhead is a half mile away on Forest Road 21S50. This hike is routed east along Freeman Creek and reaches the Freeman Grove of sequoias in four miles. This camp is in the vicinity of the Sequoia forest fire, named the McNalley Fire, which burned more than 100,000 acres in this area in the summer of 2002. The fire started in the Kern River Canyon near Road's End Resort (which burned down) and then burned up the Kern Canyon north to Forks of the Kern and the surrounding environs. Although 11 groves of giant sequoias here were saved, much of the surrounding forest to the east of the camps was burned.

RV sites, facilities: There are 32 sites for RVs up to 24 feet or tents. Picnic tables and fire grills are provided. Drinking water and vault toilets are available. A store is nearby. Some facilities are wheelchair-accessible. Leashed pets are permitted.

Reservations, fees: Reservations are accepted at 877/444-6777. The fee is $14 per night, plus $5 per additional vehicle. A senior discount is available. Open from May to mid-November, weather permitting.

Directions: From Porterville, drive east on Highway 190 for 34 miles to Camp Nelson. Continue east on Highway 190 for 11 miles to the campground on the right.

Contact: Giant Sequoia National Monument, Tule River/Hot Springs Ranger District, 559/539-2607 or 661/548-6503, fax 559/539-2067.

56 REDWOOD MEADOW

Rating: 7

near Parker Meadow Creek in Giant Sequoia National Monument

See map pages 732–733

The highlight here is the half-mile Trail of the Hundred Giants, which is routed through a grove of giant sequoias and is accessible for wheelchair hikers. This is the site where President Clinton proclaimed the Giant Sequoia National Monument in 2000. The camp is near Parker Meadow Creek at 6,500 feet elevation. Despite its remoteness, this has become a popular place.

RV sites, facilities: There are 15 sites for RVs up to 16 feet or tents. Picnic tables and fire grills are provided. Drinking water and vault toilets are available. Leashed pets are permitted.

Reservations, fees: Reserve at 877/444-6777 or online at www.reserveusa.com ($9 reservation fee). The fee is $14 per night, plus $5 for each additional vehicle. Open from June to September.

CALIFORNIA

Directions: Drive on Highway 99 to Earlimart (about eight miles north of Delano) and the exit for Avenue 56/County Road J22. Take that exit east and drive 39 miles to the town of California Hot Springs and Parker Pass Road/County Road M50. Turn left on Parker Pass Road and drive 12 miles to Western Divide Highway/County Road M107. Turn left on Western Divide Highway and drive three miles to the campground entrance.

Contact: Giant Sequoia National Monument, Tule River/Hot Springs Ranger District, 559/539-2607 or 661/548-6503, fax 559/539-2067.

57 COY FLAT

Rating: 4

in Giant Sequoia National Monument
See map pages 732–733

Coy Flat is set between Coy Creek and Bear Creek, small forks of the Tule River, at 5,000 feet in elevation. The road out of camp is routed five miles (through Rogers' Camp, which is private property) to the Black Mountain Grove of redwoods, with some giant sequoias set just inside the border of the neighboring Tule River Indian Reservation. From camp, a hiking trail (Forest Trail 31S31) is routed east for two miles through the Belknap Camp Grove of sequoias and then turns and heads south for four miles to Slate Mountain, where it intersects with the Summit National Recreation Trail, a steep butt-kicker of a hike that tops out at over 9,000 feet.

RV sites, facilities: There are 20 sites for RVs up to 24 feet or tents. Picnic tables and fire grills are provided. Drinking water and vault toilets are available. Leashed pets are permitted.

Reservations, fees: Reserve at 877/444-6777 or online at www.reserveusa.com ($9 reservation fee). The fee is $14 per night, plus $5 for each additional vehicle. A senior discount is available. Open from mid-April through mid-November.

Directions: From Porterville, drive east on Highway 190 for 34 miles to Camp Nelson and Coy Flat Road. Turn right on Coy Flat Road and drive one mile to the campground.

Contact: Giant Sequoia National Monument, Tule River/Hot Springs Ranger District, 559/539-2607 or 661/548-6503, fax 559/539-2067.

58 FAIRVIEW

Rating: 1

on the Kern River in Sequoia National Forest
See map pages 732–733

Fairview is one of six campgrounds set on the Upper Kern River above Lake Isabella and adjacent to the Kern River, one of the prime rafting rivers in California. This camp sits at 3,500 feet. Many of the rapids are rated Class IV and Class V, for experts with guides only. The favored put-in is at the Johnsondale Bridge, and from here it's a 21-mile run to Kernville. The river eventually pours into Lake Isabella. Two sections are unrunnable, Fairview Dam (Mile 2.5) and Salmon Falls (Mile 8). This campground was one of two burned in the McNalley Fire in the summer of 2002. The fire started near Road's End Lodge (which burned down), 16 miles up the Kern River Highway. Other campgrounds to the south of that were not burned. Even though the canyon has been blackened and left with tree skeletons from the start of the fire on north past Forks of the Kern, the river can still provide an outstanding rafting experience. The sight of the damage from the fire, however, is shocking.

RV sites, facilities: There are 55 sites for RVs up to 45 feet or tents. Picnic tables and fire grills are provided. Drinking water and vault toilets are available. Supplies and a coin-operated laundry are available in Kernville. Some facilities are wheelchair-accessible. Leashed pets are permitted.

Reservations, fees: Reserve at 877/444-6777 or online at www.reserveusa.com ($9 reservation fee). The fee is $14–16 per night, plus $5 for an additional vehicle. A senior discount is available. Open from May to October.

Directions: From Bakersfield, drive east on Highway 178 for about 40 miles to the town of Lake Isabella and Highway 155/Burlando Way. Turn left (north) and drive 10 miles to Kernville and the Kern River Highway/Sierra Way. Turn left on the Kern River Highway and drive 18 miles to the town of Fairview. Continue to the north end of town to the campground entrance.

Contact: Sequoia National Forest, Cannell Meadow Ranger District, 760/376-3781, fax 760/376-3795.

59 HORSE MEADOW

🏃 🎣 🏕 🚐 ⛰

Rating: 8

on Salmon Creek in Sequoia National Forest
See map pages 732–733

This is a little-known spot set along Salmon Creek at 7,600 feet. It is a region known for big meadows, forests, backcountry roads, and plenty of horses. It is just west of the Dome Land Wilderness, and there is a series of three public pastures for horses in the area, as well as trails ideal for horseback riding. From camp, one such trail follows along Salmon Creek to the west to Salmon Falls, a favorite for the few who know of it. A more popular overnight trip is to head to a trailhead about five miles east, which provides a route to Manter Meadows in the Dome Lands.

RV sites, facilities: There are 15 sites for RVs up to 22 feet or tents and 26 sites for tents only. Picnic tables and fire grills are provided. Drinking water and vault toilets are available. Garbage must be packed out. Leashed pets are permitted.

Reservations, fees: Reservations are not accepted. The fee is $5 per night. A senior discount is available. Open from June to November.

Directions: From Bakersfield, drive east on Highway 178 for about 40 miles to the town of Lake Isabella and Highway 155/Burlando Way. Turn left (north) and drive 10 miles to Kernville and the Kern River Highway/Sierra Way. Turn left on the Kern River Highway for about 20 miles to Sherman Pass Road (signed "Highway 395/Black Rock Ranger Station"). Make a sharp right on Sherman Pass Road and drive about 6.5 miles to Cherry Hill Road/Forest Road 22512 (there is a green gate with a sign that says "Horse Meadow/Big Meadow"). Turn right and drive about four miles (the road becomes dirt) and continue for another three miles (follow the signs) to the campground entrance road.

Contact: Sequoia National Forest, Cannell Meadow Ranger District, 760/376-3781, fax 760/376-3795.

60 KENNEDY MEADOW

🏃 🎣 🎣 🏕 ♿ 🚐 ⛰

Rating: 8

on the South Fork of the Kern River in Sequoia National Forest
See map pages 732–733

This is a pretty Forest Service campground set amid piñon pine and sage country, with the Pacific Crest Trail running by the camp. That makes it a great trailhead camp, as well as a refreshing stopover for PCT through-hikers. A highlight is the nearby South Fork Kern River, which provides fishing for rainbow trout. The camp receives moderate use.

RV sites, facilities: There are 15 for RVs up to 30 feet or tents and 23 sites for tents. Picnic tables and fire rings are provided. Drinking water (seasonal) and vault toilets are available. Garbage must be packed out. Leashed pets are permitted.

Reservations, fees: Reservations are not accepted. The fee is $5 per night. A senior discount is available. Open year-round, weather permitting.

Directions: Drive on U.S. 395 to Ninemile Canyon Road (four miles north of the town of Pearsonville, 48 miles south of Lone Pine). Turn west on Ninemile Canyon Road and drive 21 miles to a small store. Bear right at the store (still Ninemile Canyon Road) and continue for three miles to the campground.

Contact: Sequoia National Forest, Cannell Meadow Ranger District, 760/376-3781, fax 760/376-3795.

61 GOLDLEDGE

🎣 🐕 🚐 ⛰

Rating: 7

on the Kern River in Sequoia National Forest
See map pages 732–733

This is another in the series of camps on the Kern River north of Lake Isabella. This one is set at 3,200 feet.

RV sites, facilities: There are 37 sites for RVs up to 30 feet or tents. Picnic tables and fire grills are provided. Drinking water and vault toilets are available. Supplies and a coin-operated laundry are available in Kernville. Leashed pets are permitted.

Reservations, fees: Reserve at 877/444-6777 or

CALIFORNIA

online at www.reserveusa.com ($9 reservation fee). The fee is $14 per night, plus $5 for an additional vehicle. Open from May to September.

Directions: From Bakersfield, drive east on Highway 178 for about 40 miles to the town of Lake Isabella and Highway 155/Burlando Way. Turn left (north) and drive 10 miles to Kernville and the Kern River Highway/Sierra Way. Turn left on the Kern River Highway and drive 10 miles to the campground.

Contact: Sequoia National Forest, Cannell Meadow Ranger District, 760/376-3781, fax 760/376-3795.

62 HOSPITAL FLAT

Rating: 8

on the North Fork of the Kern River in Sequoia National Forest

See map pages 732–733

It's kind of like the old shell game, trying to pick the best of the campgrounds along the North Fork of the Kern River. This one is seven miles north of Lake Isabella. The elevation is 2,800 feet. (For information on rafting on the Kern River, see the entry in this chapter for Fairview.)

RV sites, facilities: There are 40 sites for RVs up to 30 feet or tents. Picnic tables and fire grills are provided. Drinking water and vault toilets are available. Supplies and a coin-operated laundry are available in Kernville. Some facilities are wheelchair-accessible. Leashed pets are permitted.

Reservations, fees: Reserve at 877/444-6777 or online at www.reserveusa.com ($9 reservation fee). The fee is $14 per night, plus $5 for an additional vehicle. A senior discount is available. Open from May to September.

Directions: From Bakersfield, drive east on Highway 178 for about 40 miles to the town of Lake Isabella and Highway 155/Burlando Way. Turn left (north) and drive 10 miles to Kernville and the Kern River Highway/Sierra Way. Turn left on the Kern River Highway and drive seven miles to the campground.

Contact: Sequoia National Forest, Cannell Meadow Ranger District, 760/376-3781, fax 760/376-3795.

63 CAMP 3

Rating: 9

on the North Fork of the Kern River in Sequoia National Forest

See map pages 732–733

This is the second in a series of camps along the Kern River north of Lake Isabella (in this case, five miles north of the lake). If you don't like this spot, Hospital Flat is just two miles upriver and Headquarters is just one mile downriver. The camp elevation is 2,800 feet.

RV sites, facilities: There are 52 sites for RVs up to 30 feet or tents. Picnic tables and fire grills are provided. Drinking water and vault toilets are available. Supplies and a coin-operated laundry are available in Kernville. Leashed pets are permitted.

Reservations, fees: Reserve at 877/444-6777 or online at www.reserveusa.com ($9 reservation fee). The fee is $14 per night, plus $5 for an additional vehicle. A senior discount is available. Open from May to September.

Directions: From Bakersfield, drive east on Highway 178 for about 40 miles to the town of Lake Isabella and Highway 155/Burlando Way. Turn left (north) and drive 10 miles to Kernville and the Kern River Highway/Sierra Way. Turn left on the Kern River Highway and drive five miles to the campground.

Contact: Sequoia National Forest, Cannell Meadow Ranger District, 760/376-3781, fax 760/376-3795.

64 HEADQUARTERS

Rating: 8

on the North Fork of the Kern River in Sequoia National Forest

See map pages 732–733

As you head north from Lake Isabella on Sierra Way, this is the first in a series of Forest Service campgrounds from which to take your pick, all of them set along the North Fork of the Kern River. The North Fork Kern is best known for offering prime white water for rafting. The elevation is 2,700 feet.

RV sites, facilities: There are 44 sites for RVs up

to 27 feet or tents. Picnic tables and fire grills are provided. Drinking water and vault toilets are available. Supplies and a coin-operated laundry are available in Kernville. Some facilities are wheelchair-accessible. Leashed pets are permitted.

Reservations, fees: Reserve at 877/444-6777 or online at www.reserveusa.com ($9 reservation fee). The fee is $14 per night, plus $5 for an additional vehicle. A senior discount is available. Open year-round.

Directions: From Bakersfield, drive east on Highway 178 for about 40 miles to the town of Lake Isabella and Highway 155/Burlando Way. Turn left (north) and drive 10 miles to Kernville and the Kern River Highway/Sierra Way. Turn left on the Kern River Highway and drive three miles to the campground.

Contact: Sequoia National Forest, Cannell Meadow Ranger District, 760/376-3781, fax 760/376-3795.

65 RIVERNOOK CAMPGROUND

Rating: 7

on the North Fork of the Kern River
See map pages 732–733

This is a large, privately operated park set near Lake Isabella a few miles from the head of the lake. Boat rentals are available at one of the nearby marinas. An optional side trip is to visit Keysville, the first town to become established on the Kern River during the gold rush days. The elevation is 2,665 feet.

RV sites, facilities: There are 30 drive-through sites with full hookups for RVs, 41 sites with partial hookups for RVs, and 59 sites for tents. Picnic tables and drinking water are provided. Restrooms, showers, an RV dump station, and cable TV are available. Some facilities are wheelchair-accessible. Leashed pets are permitted.

Reservations, fees: Reservations are recommended. The fee is $25 per night for RVs with full hookups, $19 per night for tents. Major credit cards are accepted. Open year-round.

Directions: From Bakersfield, drive east on Highway 178 for about 40 miles to the town of Lake Isabella and Highway 155/Burlando Way. Turn left (north) and drive 10 miles to Kernville and the Kern River Highway/Sierra Way. Turn left

on Sierra Way and .5 mile to the park entrance (14001 Sierra Way).
Contact: Rivernook Campground, 760/376-2705, fax 760/376-2595.

66 GREENHORN MOUNTAIN PARK

Rating: 7

near Shirley Meadows
See map pages 732–733

This county campground is near the Shirley Meadows Ski Area, a small ski park open on weekends in winter when there is sufficient snow. Greenhorn Mountain Park covers 160 acres, set at 6,000 feet in elevation. The region is filled with a spider-web network of Forest Service roads, detailed on a map of Sequoia National Forest. Lake Isabella is a 15-minute drive to the east.

RV sites, facilities: There are 70 sites for RVs up to 24 feet or tents. Picnic tables and fire grills are provided. Restrooms, drinking water, flush toilets, and two showers are available. Leashed pets are permitted.

Reservations, fees: No reservations are accepted, except for groups. The fee is $20 per night, plus $4 per additional vehicle and $4 per pet per night. A senior discount is available. Open spring through fall, weather permitting.

Directions: From Bakersfield, drive east on Highway 178 for about 40 miles to the town of Lake Isabella and Highway 155/Burlando Way. Turn left (north) and drive six miles to Wofford Heights. Turn left (west) on Highway 155 and drive 10 miles to the park on the left.

Contact: Kern County Parks, 661/868-7000, website: www.co.kern.ca.us/parks/index.htm.

67 LIVE OAK NORTH AND SOUTH

Rating: 8

on Lake Isabella
See map pages 732–733

This is one of two camps set in the immediate area on Lake Isabella's northwest side; the other is Tillie Creek. Live Oak is on the west side of the road, Tillie Creek on the eastern, lake side of the road. (For recreation information, see the following entry for Tillie Creek.)

RV sites, facilities: There are 150 sites for RVs up to 30 feet or tents and one group site. Picnic tables and fire grills are provided. Drinking water, showers, and flush toilets are available. Supplies and a coin-operated laundry are available in nearby Wofford Heights. Leashed pets are permitted.

Reservations, fees: Reservations are required for group sites; reserve at 877/444-6777 or online at www.reserveusa.com ($9 reservation fee). The fee is $16 per night, plus $5 for an additional vehicle; the group site is $200 per night for up to 200 people. Open from May through September.

Directions: From Bakersfield, drive east on Highway 178 for about 40 miles to the town of Lake Isabella and Highway 155/Burlando Way. Turn left (north) and drive 5.5 miles to the campground entrance road on the left (.5 mile before reaching Wofford Heights).

Contact: Sequoia National Forest, Greenhorn Ranger District, 760/379-5646, fax 760/379-8597.

68 TILLIE CREEK

Rating: 9

on Lake Isabella

See map pages 732–733

This is one of two camps (the other is Live Oak) near where Tillie Creek enters Lake Isabella, set on the northwest shore of the lake near the town of Wofford Heights. Lake Isabella is the largest freshwater lake in Southern California, covering 11,400 acres, and with it comes a dynamic array of campgrounds, marinas, and facilities. It is set at 2,605 feet in the foothills east of Bakersfield, fed by the Kern River, and dominated by boating sports of all kinds.

RV sites, facilities: There are 155 family sites and four group sites for RVs up to 45 feet or tents. Picnic tables and fire grills are provided. Restrooms, drinking water, showers, and flush toilets are available. An RV dump station, a playground, an amphitheater, and a fish-cleaning station are nearby. Supplies are available in Wofford Heights. Some facilities are wheelchair-accessible. Leashed pets are permitted.

Reservations, fees: Reservations are required for group sites; reserve at 877/444-6777 or online at www.reserveusa.com ($9 reservation fee). The

fee is $16 per night, plus $5 for an additional vehicle; the group sites are $100–175 per night. A senior discount is available. Open year-round.

Directions: From Bakersfield, drive east on Highway 178 for about 40 miles to the town of Lake Isabella and Highway 155/Burlando Way. Turn left (north) and drive five miles to the campground (one mile before reaching Wofford Heights).

Contact: Sequoia National Forest, Greenhorn Ranger District, 760/379-5646, fax 760/379-8597.

69 CAMP 9

Rating: 8

on Lake Isabella

See map pages 732–733

This campground is primitive and sparsely covered, but it has several bonus features. It is set along the northwest shore of Lake Isabella, known for good boating, water-skiing in the summer, and fishing in the spring. Other options include great rafting waters along the North Fork of the Kern River (north of the lake), a good bird-watching area at the South Fork Wildlife Area (along the northeast corner of the lake), and an off-highway-motorcycle park across the road from this campground. The elevation is 2,650 feet.

RV sites, facilities: There are 109 primitive sites for RVs or tents. Drinking water, flush toilets, an RV dump station, a boat launch, and a fish-cleaning station are available. Supplies and a coin-operated laundry are available nearby in Kernville. Leashed pets are permitted.

Reservations, fees: Reservations are not accepted for individual sites. The fee is $8 per night, plus $5 for each additional vehicle. Phone 760/376-3008 for group reservations. A senior discount is available. Open year-round.

Directions: From Bakersfield, drive east on Highway 178 for about 40 miles to the town of Lake Isabella and Highway 155/Burlando Way. Turn right (south) and drive six miles to the campground entrance on the right (on the northeast shore of Lake Isabella). The campground entrance is just south of the small airport at Lake Isabella.

Contact: Sequoia National Forest, Greenhorn Ranger District, 760/379-5646, fax 760/379-8597.

CALIFORNIA

70 HUNGRY GULCH

Rating: 9

on Lake Isabella, in Sequoia National Forest
See map pages 732–733

Hungry Gulch is on the western side of Lake Isabella, but across the road from the shore. Nearby Boulder Gulch, directly across the road, is an option. There are no boat ramps in the immediate area. (For details about Lake Isabella, see the entry in this chapter for Pioneer Point.)

RV sites, facilities: There are 78 sites for RVs up to 30 feet, trailers, or tents. Picnic tables and fire grills are provided. Restrooms, drinking water, showers, and flush toilets are available. A playground is nearby. Supplies and a coin-operated laundry are available in Lake Isabella. Leashed pets are permitted.

Reservations, fees: Reserve at 877/444-6777 or online at www.reserveusa.com ($9 reservation fee). The fee is $16 per night, plus $5 for each additional vehicle. Open from April through September.

Directions: From Bakersfield, drive east on Highway 178 for about 40 miles to the town of Lake Isabella and Highway 155/Burlando Way. Turn left (north) and drive four miles north on Highway 155 to the campground.

Contact: Sequoia National Forest, Greenhorn Ranger District, 760/379-5646, fax 760/379-8597.

71 BOULDER GULCH

Rating: 8

on Lake Isabella
See map pages 732–733

Boulder Gulch lies fairly near the western shore of Lake Isabella, across the road from Hungry Gulch. Take your pick. Isabella is the biggest lake in Southern California and a prime destination point for Bakersfield area residents. Fishing for trout and bass is best in the spring. By the dog days of summer, when people are bow-wowin' at the heat, water-skiers take over, along with folks just looking to cool off. Like a lot of lakes in the valley, Isabella is subject to drawdowns. The elevation is 2,650 feet. (For more information, see the following entry for Pioneer Point.)

RV sites, facilities: There are 78 sites for RVs up to 45 feet, trailers, or tents. Picnic tables and fire grills are provided. Restrooms, drinking water, flush toilets, showers, a playground, and a fish-cleaning station are available. Supplies and a coin-operated laundry are available in the town of Lake Isabella. Some facilities are wheelchair-accessible. Leashed pets are permitted.

Reservations, fees: Reserve at 877/444-6777 or online at www.reserveusa.com ($9 reservation fee). The fee is $16 per night, plus $5 for each additional vehicle. A senior discount is available. Open from April through September.

Directions: From Bakersfield, drive east on Highway 178 for about 40 miles to the town of Lake Isabella and Highway 155/Burlando Way. Turn left (north) and drive four miles to the campground entrance.

Contact: Sequoia National Forest, Greenhorn Ranger District, 760/379-5646, fax 760/379-8597.

72 PIONEER POINT

Rating: 9

on Lake Isabella, in Sequoia National Forest
See map pages 732–733

Lake Isabella is the largest freshwater lake in Southern California, covering 11,400 acres, and with it comes a dynamic array of campgrounds, marinas, and facilities. It is set at 2,605 feet in the foothills east of Bakersfield, fed by the Kern River, and dominated by boating sports of all kinds. This camp is at the lake's southwest corner, between the spillway and the main dam, with a boat ramp available a mile to the east. Another camp, Main Dam, is nearby. Isabella is a first-class lake for water-skiing, but in the spring and early summer windsurfing is also excellent, best just east of the Auxiliary Dam. Boat rentals of all kinds are available at several marinas.

RV sites, facilities: There are 78 sites for RVs up to 30 feet, trailers, or tents. Picnic tables and fire grills are provided. Restrooms, drinking water, showers, and flush toilets are available. A playground and a fish-cleaning station are nearby. A boat ramp is three miles from camp. Supplies and a coin-operated laundry are available in the town of Lake Isabella. Leashed pets are permitted.

Reservations, fees: Reserve at 877/444-6777 or

online at www.reserveusa.com ($9 reservation fee). The fee is $16 per night, plus $5 for each additional vehicle. A senior discount is available. Open year-round.

Directions: From Bakersfield, drive east on Highway 178 for about 40 miles to the town of Lake Isabella and Highway 155/Burlando Way. Turn left (north) and drive 2.5 miles north on Highway 155 to the campground.

Contact: Sequoia National Forest, Greenhorn Ranger District, 760/379-5646, fax 760/379-8597.

73 MAIN DAM

Rating: 8

on Lake Isabella
See map pages 732–733

This camp is on the south shore of Lake Isabella, just east of Pioneer Point and within a mile of a boat ramp. (For recreation information, see the previous entry for Pioneer Point.)

RV sites, facilities: There are 82 sites for RVs up to 30 feet, trailers, or tents. Picnic tables and fire grills are provided. Drinking water and flush toilets are available. An RV dump station is nearby. Supplies and a coin-operated laundry are available in the town of Lake Isabella. Leashed pets are permitted with proof of shots.

Reservations, fees: Reserve at 877/444-6777 or online at www.reserveusa.com ($9 reservation fee). The fee is $14 per night, plus $5 for each additional vehicle. A senior discount is available. Open May to September.

Directions: From Bakersfield, drive east on Highway 178 for about 40 miles to the town of Lake Isabella and Highway 155/Burlando Way. Turn left (north) and drive 1.5 miles to the campground.

Contact: Sequoia National Forest, Greenhorn Ranger District, 760/379-5646, fax 760/379-8597.

74 PARADISE COVE

Rating: 6

on Lake Isabella
See map pages 732–733

Paradise Cove is on the southeast shore of Lake Isabella. A boat ramp is about two miles away to the east, near the South Fork Picnic Area.

Although the camp is not directly at the lakeshore, it does overlook the broadest expanse of the lake. This part of the lake is relatively undeveloped compared to the areas near Wofford Heights and the dam.

RV sites, facilities: There are 58 sites for RVs or tents, some with picnic tables and fire grills. Flush toilets, showers, and a fish-cleaning station are available. Supplies, an RV dump station, and a coin-operated laundry are available in Mountain Mesa. Some facilities are wheelchair-accessible. Leashed pets are permitted.

Reservations, fees: Reserve at 877/444-6777 or online at www.reserveusa.com ($9 reservation fee). The fee is $16 per night, plus $5 for each additional vehicle. A senior discount is available. Open year-round.

Directions: From Bakersfield, drive east on Highway 178 for about 40 miles to the town of Lake Isabella. Continue east on Highway 178 for six miles to the campground entrance.

Contact: Sequoia National Forest, Greenhorn Ranger District, 760/379-5646, fax 760/379-8597.

75 LAKE ISABELLA RV RESORT

Rating: 5

near Lake Isabella
See map pages 732–733

This quiet, privately operated park set up for RVs is across the street from Lake Isabella. It is one of many camps at the lake, so plan on plenty of company. There is a free public boat ramp 200 yards away within Sequoia National Forest and a full-service marina with watercraft rentals two miles west of the resort. (For details on the immediate area, see the prior entry for Paradise Cove.) The elevation is 2,600 feet.

RV sites, facilities: There are 91 sites with full hookups (30, 50 amps) for RVs, including some permanent residents. Picnic tables and barbecues are provided. Restrooms, showers, a swimming pool, modem access, cell phone reception, a clubhouse, billiards, cable and satellite TV, laundry facilities, and a fish-cleaning station are available. An ATM is within a half mile. Some facilities are wheelchair-accessible. Leashed pets are permitted.

Reservations, fees: Reservations are accepted. The fee is $27 per night, plus $3 per person for

more than two people and $1 per pet per night. Major credit cards are accepted. Open year-round.
Directions: From Bakersfield, drive east on Highway 178 for about 40 miles to the town of Lake Isabella. Continue east on Highway 178 for six miles to the campground entrance on the right (signed).
Contact: Lake Isabella RV Resort, 800/787-9920, website: www.lakeisabellarv.com.

76 KOA LAKE ISABELLA

Rating: 4

on Lake Isabella
See map pages 732–733
This KOA camp provides a good, clean option to the Forest Service camps on the southern end of Lake Isabella, Southern California's largest lake. It is set in South Fork Valley (elevation 2,600 feet), east of the lake off Highway 178. The nearest boat ramp is at South Fork Picnic Area (about a five-minute drive to the west), where there is also a good view of the lake.
RV sites, facilities: There are 104 sites with partial or full hookups for RVs or tents. Picnic tables are provided. Restrooms, drinking water, flush toilets, showers, a playground, a swimming pool, laundry facilities, a store, an RV dump station, and propane are available. Leashed pets are permitted.
Reservations, fees: Reservations are accepted. The fee is $25–35 per night for RVs, $23 per night for tents. Major credit cards are accepted. Open May through September.
Directions: From Bakersfield, drive east on Highway 178 for about 40 miles to the town of Lake Isabella. Continue east on Highway 178 for 10

miles to the campground entrance on the left (well signed).
Contact: KOA Lake Isabella, 760/378-2001.

77 CHIMNEY CREEK

Rating: 5

on the Pacific Crest Trail
See map pages 732–733
This BLM camp is set at 5,900 feet along the headwaters of Chimney Creek, on the southern flank of Chimney Peak (7,990 feet), two miles to the north. This is a trailhead camp for the Pacific Crest Trail, one of its relatively obscure sections. The PCT heads north from camp and in 10 miles it skirts the eastern border of Dome Land Wilderness.
RV sites, facilities: There are 36 sites for RVs up to 25 feet or tents. Picnic tables and fire grills are provided. Vault toilets are available. No drinking water is available. Garbage must be packed out. Leashed pets are permitted.
Reservations, fees: Reservations are not accepted. There is no fee for camping. Open year-round.
Directions: Drive on U.S. 395 to Ninemile Canyon Road (four miles north of the town of Pearsonville, 48 miles south of Lone Pine). Turn west on Ninemile Canyon Road and drive 11 miles to the BLM Work Station and Cane Brake Road. Turn left on Cane Brake Road (the dirt road opposite the BLM station) and drive three miles to the camp on the left.
Contact: Bureau of Land Management, Bakersfield Field Office, 661/391-6000, fax 661/391-6040.

CALIFORNIA

California

Chapter 24
Death Valley

N E S W

15 mi

15 km

0

0

Tonopah

95

6

6

95

95

264

95

168

6

395

Scotty's Junction

Beatty

374

373

95

Death

Valley

Death

VALLEY RD.

DEATH

Scotty's Castle

Eureka
Dunes

Stovepipe
Wells

7

6

Lone Pine

Whitte Mountains

1

2-5

395

Bishop

Lake
Crowley

Inyo

National

Forest

Kings Canyon

National Park

Sequoia

National Park

see
Yosemite and
Mammoth Lakes
pages 700–701

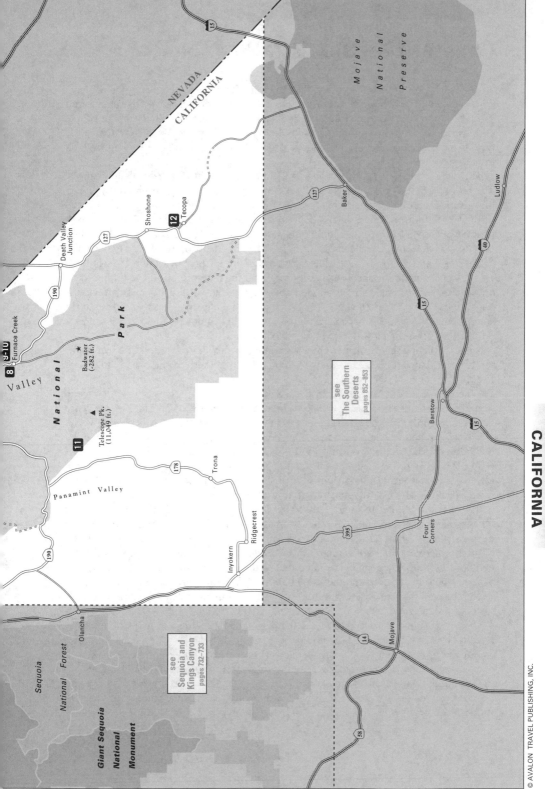

CALIFORNIA

Chapter 24—Death Valley

What good are Death Valley, the Panamint Range, and the nearby desert environs? The answer is that this country is good to look at. On a fall evening, you can take a seat on a ridge, overlooking hundreds of square miles of landscape, and just watch. Every few minutes, you'll find, the view changes. It is like watching the face of someone you care for, one minute joyous, the next pensive, then wondrous, then mysterious.

The desert is like this, always changing the way it looks, just as the sunlight changes. The reason is that as the sun passes through the sky, its azimuth is continuously changing. In turn, that causes a continuous transformation in the way sunlight is refracted through the atmosphere and across the vast landscape. So every few minutes, especially at dawn and dusk in spring and fall, the desert looks different. For those who appreciate this subtlety, the desert calls for them in a way that many others do not understand.

There are other appeals. It is often warm even on the fringe of winter, the wildflowers are small but can be spectacular in spring, and the highways—and everything else—are wide open, at times without another soul for miles in all directions. This region is huge, with Death Valley the largest national park in California, yet there are only 12 campgrounds. Because of the sparse nature of the land, campers should arrive self-contained, that is, equipped with everything they need.

Some of the highlights include the lowest point in the United States, 282 feet below sea level, at Badwater in Death Valley National Park. Yet also in the park is Telescope Peak, towering at 11,048 feet. Crazy? Oh yeah.

When viewed from a distance, in between is a terrain that seems devoid of vegetation. The sub-sea-level salt flats can seem indeed like a bunch of nothing. But they are linked to barren, rising mountains, Eureka Dunes, and surrounding vastness everywhere.

Camping is good at the developed campsites, but this is a great place to leave the RV behind and strike out on your own with a tent to create your own site, do-it-yourself style. One key is to never camp at a water source or in the bottom of ravines. Instead, always camp a good distance from water sources and on shelves or flat spots above ravines. This is why: (1.) If you camp at a water source, you may unintentionally block it from use by wildlife. In their case, it may be life or death, and yet you are in their way—so keep at wide berth from water sources at night. (2.) Never camp at the bottom of ravines in the desert because you can drown. What? Yep. Thunderstorms with tremendous short-term rainfall are common in the desert. If the runoff is blocked, the water can back itself up like a small lake, and then suddenly break through with the force of a small flood. In turn, if you are camped at the bottom of a ravine, you can find yourself in the path of a surprise torrent of water—right in the middle of the desert, the driest place in the state.

Of course, summer is well known for the blazing temperatures, over 100 about every day and occasionally hitting 120 and up.

But that is not when people visit here. They visit in fall, winter, and spring. And if you see somebody sitting on an overlooking ridge at dusk, watching the changing colors of the landscape as if it were created from the palate of an artist, well, don't be surprised. When it comes to beautiful views, the changing colors of the emotion of the land, it doesn't get any better than this.

CALIFORNIA

1 GRANDVIEW

Rating: 6

near Big Pine in Inyo National Forest
See map pages 764–765
This is a primitive and little-known camp, and the folks who find this area earn their solitude. It is in the White Mountains east of Bishop at 8,600 feet along White Mountain Road. The road borders the Ancient Bristlecone Pine Forest to the east and leads north to jump-off spots for hikers heading up Mount Barcroft (13,023 feet) or White Mountain (14,246 feet, the third-highest mountain in California). A trail out of the camp leads up to an old mining site.

RV sites, facilities: There are 26 sites for RVs up to 22 feet or tents. Picnic tables and fire grills are provided. Vault toilets are available. No drinking water is available. Leashed pets are permitted.

Reservations, fees: Reservations are not accepted. There is no fee for camping. Open May through October.

Directions: From Big Pine on U.S. 395, turn east on Highway 168 and drive 13 miles. Turn north on White Mountain/Bristlecone Forest Road (Forest Road 4S01) and drive 5.5 miles to the campground.

Contact: Inyo National Forest, White Mountain Ranger District, 760/873-2500, fax 760/873-2563.

2 PIÑON GROUP CAMP

Rating: 5

near Big Pine in Inyo National Forest
See map pages 764–765
Piñon Group Camp is the first of four group camps set in the immediate area along Highway 168. It is a remote and stark setting, 7,200 feet in elevation, at the foot of the White Mountains on the east side of the Owens Valley. Most campers here will head to the Ancient Bristlecone Pine Forest (turn north on White Mountain Road and drive 10 miles to Schulman Grove Visitor Center), where the oldest tree in the world, nearly 5,000 years old, has been documented. (It is unmarked so some idiot won't cut it down.) The road up here, by the way, provides sweeping views to the west of the Sierra. Hikers can get a similar view by taking the trail out of Cedar Flat to Black Mountain (9,038 feet), about a five-mile tromp one-way, with the trail quite faint, often invisible, over the last mile.

RV sites, facilities: There are five sites for RVs or tents. Picnic tables are provided. Vault toilets are available. No drinking water is available. Leashed pets are permitted.

Reservations, fees: Reservations are accepted with a $9 reservation fee at 877/444-6777 or online at www.reserveusa.com. Open year-round.

Directions: From Big Pine on U.S. 395, head east on Highway 168 for 13 miles to the camp.

Contact: Inyo National Forest, White Mountain Ranger District, 760/873-2500, fax 760/873-2563.

3 FOSSIL GROUP CAMP

Rating: 5

near Big Pine in Inyo National Forest
See map pages 764–765
Fossil Group Camp is a primitive Forest Service group camp set at 7,220 feet in elevation, one of four in the immediate vicinity. (See the prior entry for Piñon Group Camp for side-trip options.)

RV sites, facilities: There are 11 sites for RVs or tents. Picnic tables are provided. Vault toilets are available. No drinking water is available. Leashed pets are permitted.

Reservations, fees: Reservations are accepted with a $9 reservation fee at 877/444-6777 or online at www.reserveusa.com. Open year-round.

Directions: From Big Pine on U.S. 395, head east on Highway 168 and drive 13 miles to the campground.

Contact: Inyo National Forest, White Mountain Ranger District, 760/873-2500, fax 760/873-2563.

4 POLETA GROUP CAMP

Rating: 5

near Big Pine in Inyo National Forest
See map pages 764–765
This is one of four camps in the immediate area, so take your pick. (For side-trip possibilities, see the entry in this chapter for Piñon Group Camp.)

RV sites, facilities: There are eight sites for RVs or tents. Picnic tables are provided. Vault toilets

CALIFORNIA

are available. No drinking water is available. Leashed pets are permitted.

Reservations, fees: Reservations are accepted with a $9 reservation fee at 877/444-6777 or online at www.reserveusa.com. Open year-round.

Directions: From Big Pine on U.S. 395, turn east on Highway 168 and drive 13 miles to the campground.

Contact: Inyo National Forest, White Mountain Ranger District, 760/873-2500, fax 760/873-2563.

5 JUNIPER GROUP CAMP
🚶 🐕 🚐 ⛺

Rating: 5

near Big Pine in Inyo National Forest
See map pages 764–765

Juniper Camp is a nearby option to Poleta Camp for group campers. (See the entry in this chapter for Piñon Group Camp for side-trip details.)

RV sites, facilities: There are five sites for self-contained RVs and tents. Picnic tables are provided. Vault toilets are available. No drinking water is available. Leashed pets are permitted.

Reservations, fees: Reservations are accepted with a $9 reservation fee at 877/444-6777 or online at www.reserveusa.com. Open year-round.

Directions: From Big Pine on U.S. 395, head east on Highway 168 for 13 miles to the camp (signed "Cedar Flat Group Camps").

Contact: Inyo National Forest, White Mountain Ranger District, 760/873-2500, fax 760/873-2563.

6 MESQUITE SPRING
🚶 🏕 ♿ 🚐 ⛺

Rating: 7

in Death Valley National Park
See map pages 764–765

Mesquite Spring is the northernmost and often the prettiest campground in Death Valley, providing you time it right. If you are a lover of desert beauty, then you must make this trip in late winter or early spring, when all kinds of tiny wildflowers can bring the stark valley floor to life. The key is soil moisture, courtesy of rains in November and December. The elevation is 1,800 feet. Mesquite Spring Campground is within short range of two side trips. It is five miles (past the Grapevine entrance station) to Ubehebe Crater,

a scenic point, and four miles to Scotty's Castle, a historic building, where tours are available.

RV sites, facilities: There are 30 sites for RVs or tents. Picnic tables and fire grills are provided. Drinking water, flush toilets, and an RV dump station are available. Some facilities are wheelchair-accessible. Leashed pets are permitted.

Reservations, fees: Reservations are not accepted. The fee is $10 per night, plus a $10 park entrance fee. A senior discount is available. Visitors may pay the entrance fee and obtain a park brochure at the Furnace Creek, Grapevine, Stovepipe Wells, or Beatty Ranger Stations. Open year-round.

Directions: From Furnace Creek Visitor Center, drive north on Highway 190 for 19 miles to Scotty's Castle Road. Turn right and drive 33 miles (three miles before reaching Scotty's Castle) to the campground entrance road on the left. Turn left and drive two miles to the campground.

Contact: Death Valley National Park, 760/786-3200; Furnace Creek Visitor Center, 760/786-3244, fax 760/786-3283.

7 STOVEPIPE WELLS
🚶 🏊 🐕 ♿ 🚐 ⛺

Rating: 4

in Death Valley National Park
See map pages 764–765

Stovepipe Wells is on the major highway through Death Valley. The RV sites consist of an enormous asphalt area with sites simply marked on it. There is no shelter or shade. But note: get fuel here because prices are usually lower than at Furnace Creek. An unusual trail is available off the highway within a short distance; look for the sign for the Mosaic Canyon Trail parking area. From here you can take the easy one-mile walk up a beautiful canyon, where the walls are marble and seem as if they are polished. Rock scramblers can extend the trip for another mile. The elevation is at sea level on the edge of a large expanse of Death Valley below sea level.

RV sites, facilities: There are 200 sites for RVs and 18 sites for tents only. Drinking water, flush toilets, an RV dump station, a swimming pool, a camp store, and gasoline are available. Evening ranger programs are available on winter weekends. Some facilities are wheelchair-accessible. Leashed pets are permitted at campsites only.

Reservations, fees: Reservations are not accepted. The fee is $10 per night, plus a $10 park entrance fee per vehicle. A senior discount is available. Open mid-October to mid-April.

Directions: In Stovepipe Wells Village, drive west on Highway 190 through town to the signed entrance (just before the general store) on the right.

Contact: Death Valley National Park, 760/786-3200; Furnace Creek Visitor Center, 760/786-3244, fax 760/786-3283.

8 FURNACE CREEK

Rating: 5

in Death Valley National Park
See map pages 764–765

This is a well-developed national park site that provides a good base camp for exploring Death Valley, especially for newcomers. The nearby visitors center includes Death Valley Museum and offers maps and suggestions for hikes and drives in this unique wildland. The elevation is 190 feet below sea level. This camp offers shady sites, a rarity in Death Valley. It's open all year, but keep in mind that the daytime summer temperatures commonly exceed 120 degrees, making this area virtually uninhabitable in the summer.

RV sites, facilities: There are 136 sites for RVs or tents. Picnic tables are provided. Drinking water, flush toilets, an RV dump station, and evening ranger programs are available. Some facilities are wheelchair-accessible. Leashed pets are permitted at campsites only.

Reservations, fees: Reservations are recommended mid-October through mid-April at 800/365-CAMP (800/365-2267) or online at http://reservations.nps.gov. The fee is $10–16 per night (includes reservation fee), plus a $10 park entrance fee per vehicle. A senior discount is available. Open year-round.

Directions: From Furnace Creek Ranch, drive one mile north on Highway 190 to the signed campground entrance on the left.

Contact: Death Valley National Park, 760/786-3200; Furnace Creek Visitor Center, 760/786-3244, fax 760/786-3283.

9 TEXAS SPRING

Rating: 2

in Death Valley National Park
See map pages 764–765

This camp is another enormous section of asphalt where the campsites consist of white lines as borders. There's no shade and no shelter. It is open only in winter. The nearby visitors center, which features the Death Valley Museum, offers maps and suggestions for hikes and drives. The lowest point in the United States, Badwater, set 282 feet below sea level, is to the southwest. This camp has one truly unique feature: bathrooms that are listed on the National Historic Register. In summer, you could probably fry an egg on the asphalt here.

RV sites, facilities: There are 92 sites for RVs or tents and two group sites for up to 10 vehicles and 40 people each. Picnic tables are provided. Drinking water, flush toilets, and an RV dump station are available. Some facilities are wheelchair-accessible. Leashed pets are permitted.

Reservations, fees: No reservations are accepted for individual sites but are required for group camp; reserve at 800/365-CAMP (800/365-2267) or online at http://reservations.nps.gov. The fees are $12 per night for individual sites and $50 per night (includes reservation fee) for group sites, plus a $10 park entrance fee per vehicle for all sites. A senior discount is available. Open mid-October to mid-April.

Directions: From Furnace Creek Ranch, drive south on Highway 190 for .25 mile to the signed campground entrance on the left.

Contact: Death Valley National Park, 760/786-3200; Furnace Creek Visitor Center, 760/786-3244, fax 760/786-3283.

10 SUNSET

Rating: 4

in Death Valley National Park
See map pages 764–765

This is one of several options for campers in the Furnace Creek area of Death Valley, with an elevation of 190 feet below sea level. It is advisable to make your first stop at the nearby visitors center for maps and suggested hikes (according to

CALIFORNIA

your level of fitness) and drives. Don't forget your canteen—and if you're backpacking, never set up a wilderness camp closer than 100 yards to water in Death Valley.

RV sites, facilities: There are 1,000 sites for RVs. Drinking water, flush toilets, and an RV dump station are available. Some facilities are wheelchair-accessible. Leashed pets are permitted at campsites.

Reservations, fees: No reservations are accepted for individual sites. The fee is $10 per night, plus a $10 park entrance fee per vehicle. A senior discount is available. Open mid-October through mid-April.

Directions: From Furnace Creek Ranch, turn south on Highway 190 and drive .25 mile to the signed campground entrance and turn left into the campground.

Contact: Death Valley National Park, 760/786-3200; Furnace Creek Visitor Center, 760/786-3244, fax 760/786-3283.

11 WILDROSE

Rating: 4

in Death Valley National Park
See map pages 764–765

Wildrose is on the road that heads out to the primitive country of the awesome Panamint Range, eventually coming within range of Telescope Peak, the highest point in Death Valley National Park (11,049 feet). The elevation at the camp is 4,100 feet.

RV sites, facilities: There are 23 sites for RVs up to 25 feet or tents. Picnic tables are provided. Drinking water (April through November only) and pit toilets are available. Leashed pets are permitted at campsites only.

Reservations, fees: No reservations are accepted and there is no camping fee, however there is a $10 park entrance fee per vehicle. Open year-round.

Directions: From Stovepipe Wells Village, drive 30 miles south on Highway 190 to Wildrose Canyon Road. Turn left and immediately enter the campground entrance road.

Contact: Death Valley National Park, 760/786-3200; Furnace Creek Visitor Center, 760/786-3244, fax 760/786-3283.

12 TECOPA HOT SPRINGS COUNTY CAMPGROUND

Rating: 3

north of Tecopa
See map pages 764–765

This one is out there in no-man's land, and if it weren't for the hot springs and the good rock-hounding, all you'd see around here is a few skeletons. Regardless, it's quite an attraction in the winter, when the warm climate is a plus and the nearby mineral baths are worth taking a dunk in. Rockhounds will enjoy looking for amethysts, opals, and petrified wood in the nearby areas. The elevation is 1,500 feet. Nobody gets here by accident.

RV sites, facilities: There are 340 sites for RVs or tents, some with electrical hookups but no drive-through sites. Picnic tables and fire grills are provided. Drinking water, flush toilets, showers, and an RV dump station are available. A coin-operated laundry, groceries, and propane are available nearby. Some facilities are wheelchair-accessible. Leashed pets are permitted.

Reservations, fees: Reservations are not accepted. The fee is $10–14, plus $5 per person for more than four people. Open year-round.

Directions: From Baker, drive north on I-15 for 52 miles to the Highway 127/Tecopa exit. Turn north on Highway 127 and drive to a county road signed Tecopa Hot Springs (south of the junction of Highway 178 and Highway 127). Turn right (east) and drive three miles to the park and campground entrance.

Contact: Inyo County Parks Department, 760/852-4264, fax 760/852-4243.

CALIFORNIA

California

Chapter 25
Santa Barbara and Vicinity

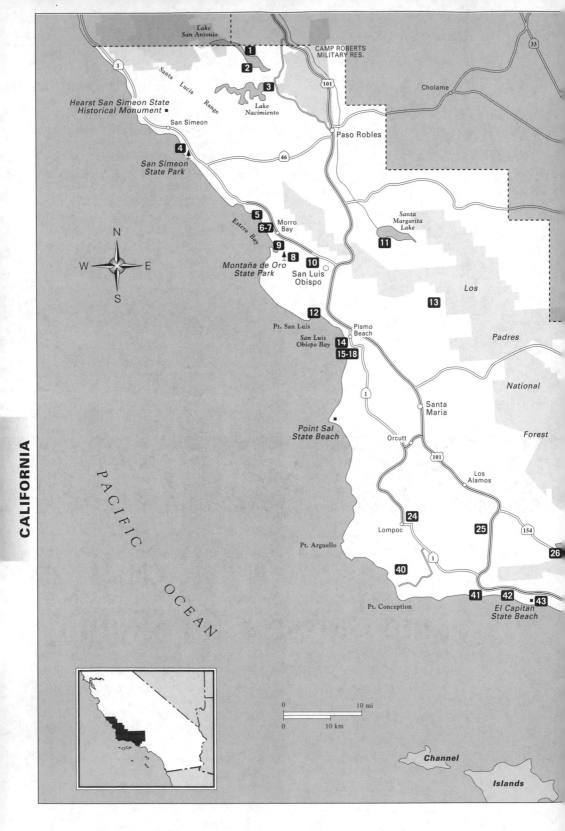

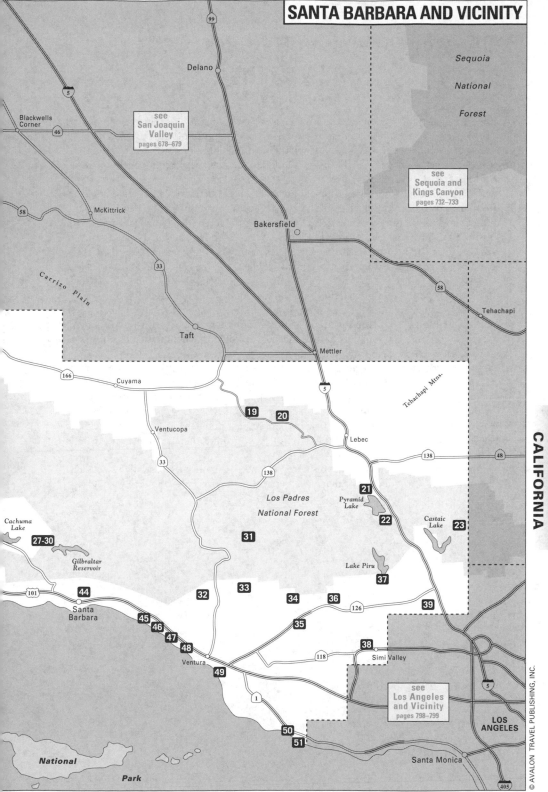

Sequoia

National

Forest

99

Delano

5

Blackwells
Corner

46

see
San Joaquin
Valley
pages 678–679

see
Sequoia and
Kings Canyon
pages 732–733

58

McKittrick

Bakersfield

58

Tehachapi

Carrizo Plain

33

Taft

Mettler

166

Cuyama

5

Tehachapi Mtns.

19 20

Ventucopa

Lebec

138

48

33

138

Los Padres

National Forest

21

Pyramid
Lake

22

Castaic
Lake

23

Cachuma
Lake

27-30

31

Gilbraltar
Reservoir

Lake Piru

37

101

44

32

33

34 36

126

39

Santa
Barbara

45

35

46

47

48

Ventura

38

118

Simi Valley

49

see
Los Angeles
and Vicinity
pages 798–799

5

LOS
ANGELES

1

50

51

Santa Monica

National

Park

405

CALIFORNIA

© AVALON TRAVEL PUBLISHING, INC.

Chapter 25—Santa Barbara
and Vicinity

For many, this region of California coast is like a dream, the best place to live on earth. Visitors, picking one or several of the campgrounds in the region, can get a taste of why it is so special. What you will likely find, however, is that a taste will only whet your appetite. That's how it is here. Many keep coming back for more. Some eventually even move here.

The region is a unique mix of sun-swept sand beaches that stretch 200 miles and surprise inland coastal forests. The coast offers a series of stunning state beaches, where getting a campsite reservation can feel like winning the lottery. If you have a dream trip in mind in which you cruise the coast highway the entire length, you'd better have the reservation system wired from the start. These campsites go fast and are filled every night of the vacation season. There are many highlights on the coast: San Simeon, Hearst Castle, all the state beaches, the stunning towns of Cambria, Goleta, and Cayucos, and the Coast Highway that provides a route through all of it.

Yet as popular as the coast may seem, just inland lie many remote, hidden campsites and destinations. Los Padres National Forest spans a matrix of canyons with small streams, mountaintop lookouts, and wilderness trailheads. The landscape is a mix of pine, deep canyons, chaparral, and foothills.

Two of California's best recreation lakes also provide major destinations, Lake Nacimiento and San Antonio Reservoir. Nacimiento is one of the top family-oriented lakes for water sports, and it also provides sensational fishing for white bass and largemouth bass in the spring. San Antonio is a great lake for bass, at times even rating as one of the best in America, and tours to see bald eagles are also popular in the winter. Cachuma Lake and Lake Casitas near Santa Barbara have produced some of the largest bass caught in history.

The ocean is dramatic here, the backdrop for every trip on the Coast Highway, and it seems to stretch to forever. For many visiting here, forever is how long they wish to stay.

CALIFORNIA

1 NORTH SHORE SAN ANTONIO

Rating: 7

on Lake San Antonio
See map pages 772–773

Lake San Antonio makes a great year-round destination for adventure. It is a big, warm-water lake, long and narrow, set at an elevation of 775 feet in the foothills north of Paso Robles. The camp features four miles of shoreline camping, with the bonus of primitive sites along Pleyto Points. There are four miles of shoreline for camping at North Shore. The lake is 16 miles long, covers 5,500 surface acres, and has 60 miles of shoreline and average summer water temperatures in the 70s, making it an ideal place for fun in the sun. It is one of the top lakes in California for bass fishing, best in spring and early summer. It is also good for striped bass, catfish, crappie, sunfish, and bluegill. It also provides the best wintering habitat in the region for bald eagles, and eagle-watching tours are available from the south shore of the lake. Of course, the size of the lake, along with hot temperatures all summer, make water-skiing and water sports absolutely first-class. Note that boat rentals are not available here, but at South Shore.

RV sites, facilities: There are 200 sites for self-contained RVs or tents, 87 sites with partial hookups (30 amps) for RVs or tents, 20 sites with full hookups for RVs, cabins, and rooms. Picnic tables and fire grills are provided. Restrooms, drinking water, showers, an RV dump station, cell phone reception, a boat ramp, stables, a grocery store, and fishing licenses are available. An ATM is within two miles. Leashed pets are permitted.

Reservations, fees: Reservations are accepted at 888/588-2267. The fee is $22–25 per night, plus $1 per pet per night. A senior discount is available. Major credit cards are accepted. Open year-round.

Directions: On U.S. 101, drive to Jolon Road/G14 exit (just north of King City). Take that exit and turn south on Jolon Road and drive 27 miles to Pleyto Road (curvy road). Turn right and drive three miles to the North Shore entrance of the lake. Note: when arriving from the south or east on U.S. 101 near Paso Robles, it is faster to take the G18/Jolon Road exit.

Contact: North Shore, 805/472-2311, website: www.co.monterey.ca.us/parks.

2 SOUTH SHORE SAN ANTONIO

Rating: 7

on Lake San Antonio
See map pages 772–773

Harris Creek, Redondo Vista, and Lynch are the three campgrounds set near each other along the south shore of Lake San Antonio, a 16-mile reservoir that provides good bass fishing in the spring and water-skiing in the summer. There are also 26 miles of good biking and hiking trails nearby. A museum and visitors center are part of the park's administration building. In the winter, the Monterey County Department of Parks offers a unique eagle-watching program here, which includes boat tours. (See the prior entry for North Shore for more details about the lake.) Note that South Shore has boat rentals, laundry facilities, and a playground.

RV sites, facilities: There are three campgrounds here: Redondo has 86 sites with partial or full hookups for RVs (30 amps) and 173 sites for tents; Lynch has 54 with full hookups for RVs and 52 sites for tents; Harris Creek has 26 sites with full hookups for RVs and 91 sites for tents. Cabin and mobile home rentals are also available. Picnic tables and fire grills are provided. Drinking water and flush toilets are available. Restrooms, hot showers, an RV dump station, cell phone reception, a boat ramp, boat rentals, a playground, a recreation room, laundry facilities, a grocery store, and fishing licenses are available nearby. An ATM is within two miles. Leashed pets are permitted. Note than 20 sites are taken by reservation, and the rest are first-come, first-served.

Reservations, fees: Reservations are accepted at 888/588-2267. The fee is $20–25 per night, plus a $2 pet fee. Group reservations are available at 805/472-2311. A senior discount is available. Open year-round.

Directions: From the north, on U.S. 101 (just north of King City), take the Jolon Road/G14 exit. Turn south on Jolon Road and drive 20 miles to Lockwood and Interlake Road (G14). Turn right and drive 13 miles to San Antonio

CALIFORNIA

Lake Road. Turn left and drive three miles to the South Shore entrance of the lake.

From the south, drive on U.S. 101 to Paso Robles and the 24th Street exit (G14 West). Take that exit and drive 14 miles to Lake Nacimiento Drive. Turn right and drive across Lake Nacimiento Dam to Interlake Road. Turn left and drive seven miles to Lake San Antonio Road. Turn right and drive three miles to the South Shore entrance.

Contact: South Shore, 805/472-2311, website: www.co.monterey.ca.us/parks.

3 LAKE NACIMIENTO RESORT

Rating: 8

at Lake Nacimiento
See map pages 772–773
This is the only game in town at Nacimiento, and the management plays it well. It's an outstanding operation, with headquarters for a great fishing or water sports trip. The fishing for white bass can be incredible, catching dozens, vertical jigging a Horizon jig. And the water play is also great, with such a big lake, 70-degree water temperatures, and some of the best water-skiing in California. The lake has 165 miles of shoreline with an incredible number of arms and lakes, many ideal for bass fishing. Nacimiento hosts 25 fishing tournaments per year. Not only is bass fishing good, but there are also opportunities for trout (in cool months) and bluegill and catfish (in warm months). The resort has a great restaurant with a lake view, and the campsites provide limited tree cover with pines and oaks. Two camps are on the lake's shore, and the rest are set back about three-quarters of a mile from the lake. Lakeview lodging is also available. There are 72 campsites available by reservation and 272 sites that are run on a first-come, first-served basis.

RV sites, facilities: There are 297 campsites at a series of campgrounds operated by the resort at the southeast end of the lake, 19 lodges, eight trailer rentals, two mobile home rentals, and 12 group sites for 15 to 40 people. Oak Knoll Camp has 40 sites with full hookups (30 amps) for RVs. Picnic tables and fire grills are provided. Drinking water and flush toilets are available. Restrooms, showers, an RV dump station, modem access, limited cell phone reception, a boat ramp, boat docks, boat rentals, a playground, a swimming pool, a restaurant, laundry facilities, a general store, and fishing licenses are available. Swimming beaches, basketball and volleyball courts, and horseshoes are also available. Leashed pets are permitted.

Reservations, fees: Reservations are accepted. The fee is $25–35 per vehicle per night, plus $5 per pet per night. A senior discount is available. Major credit cards are accepted. Open year-round.

Directions: On U.S. 101, drive to Paso Robles and the 24th Street/Lake Nacimiento exit. Take that exit, turn west on 24th Street (becomes Lake Nacimiento Road/G14) and drive for nine miles. Bear right on Lake Nacimiento Road G14 for seven miles to the resort entrance on the left. Note: if you cross the Lake Nacimiento dam, you've gone too far.

Contact: Lake Nacimiento Resort, 805/238-3256 (ext. 1 for reservations) or 800/323-3839 (ext. 1 for reservations), website: www.nacimiento resort.com.

4 SAN SIMEON STATE PARK

Rating: 9

in San Simeon State Park
See map pages 772–773
Hearst Castle is only five miles northeast, so San Simeon Creek is a natural for visitors planning to take the tour; for a tour reservation, phone 800/444-4445. San Simeon Creek Campground is across the highway from the ocean, with easy access under the highway to the beach. San Simeon Creek, while not exactly the Mississippi, runs through the campground and adds a nice touch. Washburn Campground provides an option at this park, and while providing better views, the sites are exposed and can be windy. It is one mile inland on a plateau overlooking the Pacific Ocean and Santa Lucia Mountains. The best hike in the area is from Leffingwell Landing to Moonstone Beach, featuring sweeping views of the coast from ocean bluffs and a good chance to see passing whales. There are three preserves in the park, including a wintering site for monarch butterfly populations, and it has an archaeological site dating from more than 5,800 years ago. In the summer, Junior Ranger programs and interpretive programs are available.

CALIFORNIA

RV sites, facilities: At San Simeon Creek Camp, there are 115 sites for RVs up to 35 feet or tents, 14 sites for tents only, and two hike-in/bike-in sites. Picnic tables and fire grills are provided. Drinking water, restrooms, flush toilets, and coin-operated showers are available. At Washburn Camp, there are 70 sites for RVs up to 31 feet or tents. Picnic tables and fire grills are provided. The camp host sells firewood. A pay phone and an RV dump station are available. A grocery store, a coin-operated laundry, a gas station, restaurants, and propane are two miles away in Cambria. Some facilities are wheelchair-accessible. Leashed pets are permitted.

Reservations, fees: Reserve at 800/444-PARK (800/444-7275) or online at www.reserveamerica .com ($7.50 reservation fee). The fees are $12 per night at San Simeon Creek, $7 per night at Washburn, and $1 per person for hike-in/bike-in sites. A senior discount is available. Open year-round.

Directions: From Cambria, drive two miles north on Highway 1 to San Simeon Creek Road. Turn east and drive .2 mile to the park entrance on the right.

Contact: San Simeon State Park, 805/927-2035 or 805/927-2020.

5 MORRO STRAND STATE BEACH

Rating: 7

near Morro Bay

See map pages 772–773

A ton of Highway 1 cruisers plan to stay overnight at this state park. It is set along the ocean near Morro Bay, right on the beach, a pretty spot year-round. The park features a three-mile stretch of beach that connects the southern and northern entrances to the state beach. Fishing, jogging, windsurfing, and kite flying are popular. Side trips include the Morro Bay Wildlife Refuge, the Museum of Natural History, or an ocean fishing trip out of Morro Bay. (See the entry in this chapter for Morro Bay State Park for more information.)

RV sites, facilities: There are 75 sites for RVs up to 24 feet or tents. Picnic tables and fire grills are provided. Drinking water and flush toilets are available. Cold, outdoor showers are also available. Supplies and a coin-operated laundry are available in Morro Bay. Leashed pets are permitted.

Reservations, fees: Reserve at 800/444-PARK (800/444-7275) or online at www.reserveamerica .com ($7.50 reservation fee). The fee is $12 per night. Open year-round.

Directions: On Highway 1, drive to Morro Bay. Take the Yerba Buena Street/Morro Strand State Beach exit. Turn west on Yerba Buena Street and drive one block to the campground.

Contact: Morro Strand State Beach, 805/772-8812 or 805/772-2560, fax 805/772-7434; California State Parks, San Luis Obispo District, 805/549-3312, fax 805/541-4799.

6 RANCHO COLINA RV PARK

Rating: 6

in Morro Bay

See map pages 772–773

This privately operated RV park is one of several camping options in the Morro Bay area. Folks who park here typically stroll the boardwalk, exploring the little shops. (For recreation information, see the entry for Morro Bay State Park in this chapter.) About 20 percent of the sites here are long-term rentals.

RV sites, facilities: There are 57 sites with full hookups (30, 50 amps) for RVs. Picnic tables are provided. Restrooms, showers, laundry facilities, cell phone reception, modem access, and a recreation room are available. An ATM is within one mile. You can buy supplies nearby. Leashed pets are permitted.

Reservations, fees: Reservations are accepted. The fee is $30 per night. Major credit cards are accepted. Open year-round.

Directions: From Morro Bay on Highway 1, drive one mile east on Atascadero Road/Highway 41 to the park at 1045 Atascadero Road.

Contact: Rancho Colina RV Park, 805/772-8420.

7 MORRO DUNES TRAILER PARK AND CAMP

Rating: 6

in Morro Bay

See map pages 772–773

A wide array of side-trip possibilities and great natural beauty make Morro Bay an attractive destination. Most visitors will walk the boardwalk, try at least one of the coastal restaurants, and then head to Morro Bay State Park for hiking or sea kayaking. Other folks will head straight to the port for fishing, or just explore the area before heading north to San Simeon for the Hearst Castle tour. (See the entry in this chapter for Morro Bay State Park for more information.)

RV sites, facilities: There are 139 sites with full hookups including cable TV for RVs and 43 sites for tents. Picnic tables and fire grills are provided. Restrooms, drinking water, showers, electrical connections, modem access, laundry facilities, a store, wood, ice, and an RV dump station are available. Propane can be obtained nearby. Some facilities are wheelchair-accessible. Leashed pets are permitted.

Reservations, fees: Reservations are accepted. The fee is $17–25 per night, plus $1 per pet per night. Major credit cards are accepted. Open year-round.

Directions: Drive on Highway 1 to Morro Bay and the exit for Highway 41. Take that exit and turn west on Atascadero Road/Highway 41 and drive .5 mile to 1700 Embarcadero/Atascadero Road.

Contact: Morro Dunes Trailer Park and Camp, 805/772-2722, fax 805/772-2372, website: www .morrodunes.com.

8 MONTAÑA DE ORO STATE PARK

Rating: 9

near Morro Bay
See map pages 772–773

This sprawling chunk of primitive land includes coastline, 8,500 acres of foothills, and Valencia Peak at 1,347 feet in elevation. The name means "Mountain of Gold," named for the golden wildflowers that bloom here in the spring. The camp is perched near a bluff, and while there are no sweeping views from campsites, they await nearby. The Bluffs Trail is one of the best easy coastal walks anywhere, offering stunning views of the ocean and cliffs and, in the spring, tons of wildflowers over the course of just 1.5 miles. Another hiking option at the park is to climb Valencia Peak, a little butt-kicker of an ascent that tops out at 1,373 feet, providing more panoramic

coastal views. These are the two best hikes among 50 miles of trails for horses, mountain bikers, and hikers, with trails accessible right out of the campground.

RV sites, facilities: There are 50 sites for RVs up to 27 feet or tents, four walk-in environmental sites, four equestrian sites, and two group equestrian sites for up to 50 people and 25 horses. Picnic tables and fire grills are provided. Vault toilets are available. Drinking water is available only at the main campground; stock water is available at the equestrian campground. There is limited corral space and single-site equestrian camps with two stalls each. Garbage from equestrian and environmental sites must be packed out. Supplies and a coin-operated laundry are available five miles away in Los Osos. Leashed pets are permitted.

Reservations, fees: Reserve at 800/444-PARK (800/444-7275) or online at www.reserveamerica .com ($7.50 reservation fee). The fees are $7 per night, $12 for equestrian sites, and $25 for group sites. A senior discount is available. Open year-round.

Directions: From Morro Bay, drive two miles south on Highway 1. Turn on South Bay Boulevard and drive four miles to Los Osos. Turn right on Los Osos Valley Road and drive five miles (it becomes Pecho Valley Road) to the park.

Contact: Montaña de Oro State Park, 805/528-0513; San Luis Obispo District, 805/549-3312.

9 MORRO BAY STATE PARK

Rating: 9

in Morro Bay
See map pages 772–773

Reservations are strongly advised at this popular campground. This is one of the premium stopover spots for folks cruising north on Highway 1. The park offers a wide range of activities and exhibits covering the natural and cultural history of the area. The park features lagoon and natural bay habitat. The most prominent feature is Morro Rock. A "morro" is a small volcanic peak, and there are nine of them along the local coast. The top hike at the park climbs one of them, Black Hill, and rewards hikers with sensational coastal views. The park has a marina

CALIFORNIA

and golf course, with opportunities for sailing, fishing, and bird-watching. Activities include beach walks, kayaking in Morro Bay, fishing the nearby ocean on a party boat, and touring Hearst Castle.

RV sites, facilities: There are 95 sites for RVs up to 31 feet or tents, 30 sites with partial hookups for RVs, two hike-in/bike-in sites, and two group sites for 30 to 50 people. Picnic tables, food lockers, and fire rings are provided. Restrooms, drinking water, flush toilets, coin-operated showers, an RV dump station, museum exhibits, and nature walks and interpretive programs are available. A coin-operated laundry, a grocery store, propane, a boat ramp, mooring, rentals, gas stations, and food service are available in Morro Bay. Some facilities are wheelchair-accessible. Leashed pets are permitted.

Reservations, fees: Reserve at 800/444-PARK (800/444-7275) or online at www.reserveamerica.com ($7.50 reservation fee). The fees are $12–18 per night, $1 per person per night for hike-in/bike-in sites, and $22–37 per night for group sites. A senior discount is available. Open year-round.

Directions: On Highway 1, drive to Morro Bay and take the exit for Los Osos–Baywood Park/Morro Bay State Park. Turn south and drive one mile to State Park Road. Turn right and drive one mile to the park entrance on the right.

Contact: Morro Bay State Park, 805/772-7434, fax 805/772-5760; California State Parks, San Luis Obispo District, 805/549-3312, fax 805/541-4799.

10 EL CHORRO REGIONAL PARK

Rating: 6

near San Luis Obispo
See map pages 772–773

North of Morro Bay on the way to San Simeon and Hearst Castle, this can be a prime spot for RV travelers. Note that the campground isn't in the state park reservation system, which means there are times when coastal state parks can be jammed full and this regional park may still have space. Morro Bay, six miles away, provides many possible side trips. The park has full recreational facilities, including volleyball, horseshoes, softball, hiking trails, and botanical gardens. A golf course is nearby. Note that there's a men's prison

about one mile away. For some people, this can be a real turnoff.

RV sites, facilities: There are 42 sites with full hookups for RVs up to 40 feet or tents and some undesignated overflow sites. Fire grills and picnic tables are provided. Restrooms, drinking water, flush toilets, showers, and recreational facilities are available. Supplies and a coin-operated laundry are nearby in San Luis Obispo. Leashed pets are permitted.

Reservations, fees: Reservations are not accepted. The fee is $18–22 per night, plus a $2 pet fee. Groups may reserve six or more sites three weeks before arrival. Major credit cards are accepted. Open year-round.

Directions: From San Luis Obispo, drive 4.5 miles north on Highway 1 to the park entrance on the right side of the highway.

Contact: El Chorro Regional Park, 805/781-5930, website: www.slocountyparks.com.

11 SANTA MARGARITA KOA

Rating: 6

near Santa Margarita Lake
See map pages 772–773

Santa Margarita Lake should have a sign at its entrance that proclaims, "Fishing Only!" That's because the rules here do not allow water-skiing or any water contact, including swimming, wading, using float tubes, or windsurfing. The excellent prospects for bass fishing, along with the prohibitive rules, make this lake a favorite among anglers. Santa Margarita Lake covers nearly 800 acres, most of it long and narrow and set in a dammed-up valley in the foothill country at an elevation of 1,300 feet, just below the Santa Lucia Mountains. On weekends, this place can turn into another world: paintball war games are often held here, and on Saturday afternoons, a BMX track is popular.

RV sites, facilities: There are 54 sites, some with partial hookups (30 amps) and one drive-through, for RVs or tents, and 11 cabins. Picnic tables and fire grills are provided. Restrooms, drinking water, flush toilets, showers, modem access, a swimming pool, a playground, a coin-operated laundry, a store, an RV dump station, cell phone reception, and propane are available. An ATM is within 8.5 miles. Leashed pets are permitted.

Reservations, fees: Make reservations at 800/562-5619. The fee is $28–34 per night, plus $3–4 per person for more than two people. Major credit cards are accepted. Open year-round.

Directions: From San Luis Obispo, drive north on U.S. 101 for eight miles to the Highway 58/Santa Margarita exit. Take that exit, drive through the town of Santa Margarita to Estrada. Turn right on Estrada and drive seven miles (Estrada becomes Pozo Road) to Santa Margarita Lake Road. Turn left and drive a half mile to the campground on the right.

Contact: Santa Margarita KOA, 805/438-5618, fax 805/438-3576, website: www.koa.com.

12 AVILA VALLEY HOT SPRINGS SPA AND RV PARK

Rating: 6

on San Luis Obispo Bay
See map pages 772–773

The hot mineral pool here is a featured attraction. This is a natural mineral hot springs with an artesian well that produces water directly into the spas at 105°F. A pizza kitchen and snack bar are available as well. Nearby recreation options include Avila State Beach and Pismo State Beach.

RV sites, facilities: There are 50 sites, seven drive-through, with full hookups (30, 50 amps) for RVs, and 25 tent sites in three areas. Picnic tables and fire grills (at some spots) are provided. Restrooms, showers, a swimming pool, a hot mineral pool, a spa, cable TV, an RV dump station, cell phone reception, a recreation room, an arcade, massage service, a golf course, a grocery store, a snack bar, and group barbecue pits are available. An ATM is within five miles. Some facilities are wheelchair-accessible. Leashed pets are permitted.

Reservations, fees: Reservations are recommended at 800/332-2359. The fee is $30–43. Two spa passes come free with campsite. Major credit cards are accepted. Open year-round.

Directions: From San Luis Obispo, drive south on U.S. 101 for nine miles to the Avila Beach Drive exit. Take that exit and drive to the park at 250 Avila Beach Drive.

Contact: Avila Valley Hot Springs Spa and RV Park, 805/595-2359, fax 805/595-2060, website: www.avilahotsprings.com.

13 LOPEZ LAKE RECREATION AREA

Rating: 7

near Arroyo Grande
See map pages 772–773

Lopez Lake has become an example of how to do something right, with special marked areas set aside exclusively for water-skiing, personal watercraft, and windsurfing, and the rest of the lake designated for fishing and low-speed boating. There are also reserved areas for swimming. That makes it perfect for just about everyone and, with good bass fishing, the lake has become very popular, especially on spring weekends when the bite is on. Lopez Lake is set amid oak woodlands southeast of San Luis Obispo. The lake is shaped something like a horseshoe, has 940 surface acres with 22 miles of shoreline when full, and gets excellent weather most of the year. Features of the park in summer are ranger-led hikes and campfire shows.

RV sites, facilities: There are 143 sites with full hookups for RVs, 211 sites with partial hookups for RVs and tents, an overflow site for self-contained RVs of any length, and a group site. Picnic tables and fire rings are provided. Restrooms, showers, a playground, laundry facilities, a store, ice, a snack bar, a marina, a boat ramp, mooring, boat fuel, tackle, boat rentals, and a water slide are available. Some facilities are wheelchair-accessible. Leashed pets are permitted.

Reservations, fees: Reservations are accepted by phone or online. The fee is $14–23 per night, plus $5 per night for each additional vehicle, $2 per pet per night, and a $5 boat launch fee. Group rates are available. Major credit cards are accepted. Open year-round.

Directions: From Arroyo Grande on U.S. 101, take the Grand Avenue exit. Turn east and drive through Arroyo Grande. Turn northeast on Lopez Drive and drive 10 miles to the park.

Contact: Lopez Lake Recreation Area, 805/788-2381, website: www.slocountyparks.com.

14 NORTH BEACH

Rating: 7

in Pismo State Beach
See map pages 772–773
Pismo State Beach is nationally renowned for its beaches, dunes, and, in the good old days, clamming. The adjacent tree-lined dunes make for great walks or, for kids, great rolls. The clamming on minus low tides was legendary. The beach is popular with bird-watchers, and the habitat supports the largest wintering colony of monarch butterflies in the United States. Plan on a reservation and having plenty of company in summer. This is an exceptionally popular state beach, either as an ultimate destination or as a stopover for folks cruising Highway 1. There are four restaurants and ATV rentals within two blocks. A trolley service provides a shuttle to the surrounding community. Poaching has devastated the clamming here, with no legal clams taken for years.

RV sites, facilities: There are 103 sites for RVs up to 31 feet or tents and one hike-in/bike-in site. Fire grills, food lockers, and picnic tables are provided. Restrooms, drinking water, showers, flush toilets, and an RV dump station are available. Horseback riding facilities, a grocery store, ATV rentals, restaurants, a coin-operated laundry, and propane are nearby. Some facilities are wheelchair-accessible, including a fishing pier at Ocean Lagoon. Leashed pets are permitted.

Reservations, fees: Reserve at 800/444-PARK (800/444-7275) or online at www.reserveamerica .com ($7.50 reservation fee). The fee is $12 per night or $1 per person per night for the hike-in/bike-in site. Open year-round.

Directions: On Highway 1 in Pismo Beach, take the North Beach/State Campground exit (well signed) and drive to the park entrance.

Contact: Pismo State Beach, 805/773-2334; California State Parks, San Luis Obispo District, 805/549-3312.

15 PISMO COAST VILLAGE RV RESORT

Rating: 7

in Pismo Beach
See map pages 772–773
This big-time RV park gets a lot of use by Highway 1 cruisers. Its location is a plus, set near the ocean. Pismo Beach is famous for its clamming, sand dunes, and beautiful coastal frontage.

RV sites, facilities: There are 400 sites with full hookups (30, 50 amps) including satellite TV and modem access for RVs. Picnic tables and fire grills are provided. Restrooms, showers, playgrounds, swimming pools, laundry facilities, a store, firewood, ice, a recreation room, cell phone reception, an ATM, propane, recreation programs, a restaurant, and a miniature golf course are available. Some facilities are wheelchair-accessible. Leashed pets are permitted.

Reservations, fees: Reserve at 888/RV-BEACH (888/782-3224). The fee is $29–40 per night. Group discounts are available. Major credit cards are accepted. Open year-round.

Directions: In Pismo Beach, drive on Highway 1 to the park at 165 S. Dolliver St./Hwy. 1.

Contact: Pismo Coast Village RV Resort, 805/773-1811, fax 805/773-1507, website: www.pismocoast village.com.

16 LE SAGE RIVIERA

Rating: 6

near Pismo State Beach
See map pages 772–773
This is a year-round RV park that can serve as headquarters for folks who are interested in visiting several nearby attractions, including neighboring Pismo State Beach and Lopez Lake, 10 miles to the east. The park is on the ocean side of Highway 1, 250 yards from the beach.

RV sites, facilities: There are 60 sites, half drive-through, with full hookups (30 amps) for RVs. No tent camping is permitted. Picnic tables are provided. Restrooms, drinking water, showers, limited cell phone reception, modem access, and laundry facilities are available. Stores, an ATM, restaurants, and golf courses are nearby. Some

CALIFORNIA

facilities are wheelchair-accessible. Leashed pets are permitted with size restrictions.

Reservations, fees: Reservations are accepted. The fee is $30–45 per night. Add $5–10 for holidays. A winter discount is offered. Major credit cards are accepted. Open year-round.

Directions: In Pismo Beach on Highway 1, drive south on Highway 1 for .5 mile to the park on the right (west side) to 319 N. Hwy. 1 (in Grover Beach).

Contact: Le Sage Riviera, 805/489-5506, fax 805/489-2103.

▨ 17 OCEANO MEMORIAL CAMPGROUND

Rating: 7

in Oceano

See map pages 772–773

This county park often gets overlooked because it isn't on the state reservation system. That's other folks' loss and your gain. The location is a bonus, near Pismo State Beach, the site of great sand dunes and wide-open ocean frontage.

RV sites, facilities: There are 22 sites with full hookups for RVs up to 40 feet or tents and a group site. Picnic tables and fire grills are provided. Drinking water and flush toilets are available. A playground, coin-operated laundry, grocery store, and propane are available nearby. Leashed pets are permitted with proof of vaccinations.

Reservations, fees: Reservations are not accepted. The fee is $23 per night, plus $5 per night per additional vehicle and $2 per pet per night. Reservations are required for groups. Open year-round.

Directions: From Pismo Beach, drive south on U.S. 101 to Grand Avenue exit west to Highway 1. Take that exit and turn south on Highway 1 and drive 1.5 miles to Pier Avenue. Turn right on Pier Avenue and drive a short distance. Turn left and drive to the campground on the right at 540 Air Park Drive.

Contact: Oceano Memorial Campground, 805/781-5930, fax 805/781-1102, website: www.slocounty parks.com.

▨ 18 OCEANO

Rating: 6

in Pismo State Beach

See map pages 772–773

This is a prized state beach campground, with Pismo Beach and its sand dunes and coastal frontage a centerpiece for the state park system. Its location on the central coast on Highway 1, as well as its beauty and recreational opportunities, makes it extremely popular. It fills to capacity most nights, and reservations are usually a necessity. (For more information on Pismo State Beach, see the entry for North Beach campground in this chapter.)

RV sites, facilities: There are 82 sites for RVs up to 31 feet, trailers, or tents and 42 with partial hookups for trailers and RVs up to 36 feet. There is also one primitive hike-in/bike-in site. Picnic tables, food lockers, and fire grills are provided. Restrooms, drinking water, flush toilets, and coin-operated showers are available. Horseback riding facilities, a grocery store, a coin-operated laundry, an RV dump station, restaurants, and gas stations are nearby. Leashed pets are permitted.

Reservations, fees: Reserve at 800/444-PARK (800/444-7275) or online at www.reserveamerica .com ($7.50 reservation fee). The fee is $12–18 per night or $1 per night per person for the hike-in/bike-in site, plus $6 per night for a third vehicle. A senior discount is available. Open year-round.

Directions: From Pismo Beach, drive two miles south on Highway 1 to Pier Avenue. Turn right and drive .2 mile to the campground entrance.

Contact: Pismo Beach State Park, 805/489-1869 or 805/473-7220.

▨ 19 MIL POTRERO PARK

Rating: 5

near Mount Piños

See map pages 772–773

This is one of the rare RV parks that provides equal billing for tents. It is set at 5,300 feet, with national forest generally surrounding the area. Nearby side trips worth noting are to the Big

CALIFORNIA

Trees of Pleito Canyon and also the drive on Forest Service roads to the summit of Frazier Mountain at 8,013 feet, where there is a lookout with drop-dead gorgeous 360-degree views.

RV sites, facilities: There are 43 sites for RVs or tents. Picnic tables and fire grills are provided. Restrooms, drinking water, flush toilets, showers, and horse corrals are available. Leashed pets are permitted.

Reservations, fees: Reservations are recommended. The fee is $15 per night, $10 for residents of Taft, with a 10-person maximum per site. Open year-round.

Directions: Drive on I-5 to just south of Lebec to the Frazier Park exit. Take that exit and drive west on Frazier Mountain Road to the town of Lake of the Woods and Cuddy Valley Road. Bear right on Cuddy Valley Road and drive five miles to Mil Potrero Highway. Turn right and drive 5.5 miles to Pine Mountain Village Center. Continue 1.3 miles to the park entrance on the left.

Contact: Mil Potrero Park, 661/763-4246.

20 McGILL

Rating: 6

near Mount Piños in Los Padres National Forest
See map pages 772–773

The camp is set at 7,400 feet, about four miles from the top of nearby Mount Piños. Although the road is closed to the top of Mount Piños, there are numerous hiking and biking trails in the area that provide spectacular views. On clear days, there are vantage points to the high Sierra, the San Joaquin Valley, and Antelope Valley.

RV sites, facilities: There are 73 family sites for RVs up to 16 feet or tents and two group sites for 60 and 80 people. Picnic tables and fire grills are provided. Drinking water and flush toilets are available. A note of caution: The water wells have been known to run dry in the summer, so bring your own water during the summer. Some facilities are wheelchair-accessible. Leashed pets are permitted.

Reservations, fees: Reservations are required for group sites; reserve at 877/444-6777 ($9 group reservation fee). The fees are $8 per night for fam-

ily sites, $75 for a group site. A senior discount is available. Open late May through October.

Directions: Drive on I-5 to just south of Lebec to the Frazier Park exit. Take that exit and drive west on Frazier Mountain Road to the town of Lake of the Woods and Cuddy Valley Road. Turn right on Cuddy Valley Road and drive about six miles to Mt. Piños Highway. Turn left and drive about four miles to the campground on the right.

Contact: Los Padres National Forest, Mt. Piños Ranger District, 661/245-3731, fax 661/245-1526.

21 LOS ALAMOS

Rating: 4

near Pyramid Lake in Angeles National Forest
See map pages 772–773

Los Alamos is set at an elevation of 2,600 feet near the southern border of the Hungry Valley State Vehicular Recreation Area and about 2.5 miles north of Pyramid Lake. Pyramid Lake is a big lake, covering 1,300 acres with 20 miles of shoreline, and is extremely popular for water-skiing and fast boating, as well as for windsurfing (best at the northern launch point), fishing (best in the spring and early summer and in the fall for striped bass), and swimming (best at boat-in picnic sites).

RV sites, facilities: There are 93 family sites and several group sites for RVs or tents. Picnic tables and fire pits are provided. Drinking water and flush toilets are available. A boat ramp is at the Emigrant Landing Picnic Area. Some facilities are wheelchair-accessible. Leashed pets are permitted.

Reservations, fees: Reservations are not accepted for individual sites, but group reservations are required at 800/416-6992. The fees are $12 per night, $50 per night for groups. A senior discount is available. Open April through October.

Directions: Drive on I-5 to eight miles south of Gorman and the Smokey Bear Road exit. Take the Smokey Bear Road exit and drive west about .75 mile and follow the signs to the campground.

Contact: Angeles National Forest, Santa Clara/Mojave Rivers Ranger District, 661/296-9710, fax 661/296-5847.

CALIFORNIA

22 OAK FLAT

Rating: 3

near Pyramid Lake in Angeles National Forest
See map pages 772–773

Oak Flat is just a short drive from Pyramid Lake, at 2,800 feet near the southwestern border of Angeles National Forest. Pyramid is surrounded by national forest, quite beautiful, and is a favorite destination for folks with powerboats, especially those towing water-skiers. The lake covers 1,300 acres and has 20 miles of shoreline. Fishing for striped bass can be good in the spring and fall, but in summer warfare can practically break out between low-speed fishermen and high-speed skiers. (For more information on Pyramid Lake, see the prior entry for Los Alamos.)

RV sites, facilities: There are 27 sites for RVs up to 32 feet or tents. Picnic tables and fire pits are provided. Vault toilets are available. No drinking water is available. Leashed pets are permitted.

Reservations, fees: No reservations are accepted and there is no camping fee. An Adventure Pass ($30 annual fee or $5 daily fee) per parked vehicle is required. A senior discount is available. Open year-round.

Directions: Drive on I-5 to six miles north of Castaic to Templin Highway. Take Templin Highway west and drive three miles to the campground.

Contact: Angeles National Forest, Santa Clara/Mojave Rivers Ranger District, 661/296-9710, fax 661/296-5847.

23 COTTONWOOD

Rating: 5

near the Warm Springs Mountain Lookout in Angeles National Forest
See map pages 772–773

Cottonwood camp is set at 2,680 feet in remote Angeles National Forest along a small stream. The camp is on the north flank of Warm Springs Mountain. A great side trip is to the Warm Springs Mountain Lookout (4,023 feet), about a five-mile drive. Drive south on Forest Road 7N09 for three miles, turn right (west) on Forest Road 6N32, and drive for 1.5 miles to Forest Road 7N13. Turn left (south) and drive a mile to the summit.

RV sites, facilities: There are 22 sites for RVs up to 22 feet or tents. Picnic tables and fire pits are provided. Vault toilets are available. No drinking water is available. Supplies are available less than four miles away in the town of Lake Hughes. Leashed pets are permitted.

Reservations, fees: No reservations are accepted and there is no camping fee. An Adventure Pass ($30 annual fee or $5 daily pass per parked vehicle) is required. Open year-round.

Directions: Drive on I-5 to the Tehachapis near the small town of Castaic and Lake Hughes Road. Turn northeast on Lake Hughes Road and drive 25 miles to the campground on the right.

Contact: Angeles National Forest, Santa Clara/Mojave Rivers Ranger District, 661/296-9710, fax 661/296-5847.

24 RIVER PARK

Rating: 4

in Lompoc
See map pages 772–773

Before checking in here you'd better get a lesson on how to pronounce Lompoc. It's "Lom-Poke." If you arrive and say, "Hey, it's great to be in Lom-Pock," they might just tell ya to get on back to the other cowpokes. The camp is near the lower Santa Ynez River, which looks quite a bit different than it does up in Los Padres National Forest. A small fishing lake within the park is stocked regularly with trout. Side-trip possibilities include the nearby La Purisima Mission State Historic Park.

RV sites, facilities: There are 36 sites with full hookups for RVs and a large open area for tents. Restrooms, drinking water, flush toilets, coin-operated showers, an RV dump station, a fishing pond, and a playground are available. Supplies and a coin-operated laundry are nearby. Leashed pets are permitted.

Reservations, fees: Reservations are not accepted. The fee is $5–15 per night or $5 per night for hike-in/bike-in sites, plus $10 per night for additional vehicles and $1 per pet per night. Reservations are required for groups. Open year-round.

Directions: In Lompoc, drive to the junction of Highway 246 and Sweeney Road at the southwest edge of town and continue to the park at 401 E. Hwy. 246.

Contact: Lompoc Parks and Recreation Department, 805/736-6565, fax 805/736-5195, website: www.ci.lompoc.ca.us.

25 FLYING FLAGS RV PARK

Rating: 3

near Solvang

See map pages 772–773

This is one of the few privately operated parks in the area that welcomes tenters as well as RVers. Nearby side trips include the Santa Ynez Mission, just east of Solvang. The town of Solvang is of interest. It was originally a small Danish settlement that has expanded since the 1920s yet managed to keep its cultural heritage intact over the years. The town is spotless, with no trash of any kind in sight, and an example of how to do something right.

RV sites, facilities: There are 256 sites with partial or full hookups for RVs and 100 sites for tents. Picnic tables are provided. Restrooms, showers, a playground, a swimming pool, two hot therapy pools, a laundry room, a store, an RV dump station, ice, a recreation room, modem access, an arcade, five clubhouses, and propane are available. A nine-hole golf course is nearby. Some facilities are wheelchair-accessible. Leashed pets are permitted.

Reservations, fees: Reservations are recommended. The fee is $18–28.50 per night, plus $3 per person for more than two people, $3 per night for additional vehicle, and $1 per pet per night. Open year-round. Major credit cards are accepted.

Directions: From Santa Barbara, drive 45 miles north on U.S. 101 to Highway 246. Turn west (left) on Highway 246 and drive about .5 mile to Avenue of the Flags (a four-way stop). Turn left on Avenue of the Flags and drive about one block to the campground entrance on the left at 180 Avenue of the Flags.

Contact: Flying Flags RV Park, 805/688-3716, fax 805/688-9245, website: www.flyingflags.com.

26 CACHUMA LAKE RECREATION AREA

Rating: 7

near Santa Barbara

See map pages 772–773

Cachuma has become one of the best lakes in America for fishing big bass, and the ideal climate makes it a winner for camping as well. Cachuma is set at 800 feet in the foothills northwest of Santa Barbara, a big, beautiful lake covering 3,200 acres. The rules are perfect for fishing: no water-skiing, personal watercraft, swimming, canoeing, kayaking, or windsurfing is permitted; for fishing boats there is a 5 mph speed limit in the coves and a 40 mph limit elsewhere. Yeah, let it rip on open water, then quiet down to sneak-fish the coves.

RV sites, facilities: There are 500 sites, some drive-through with full hookups (30 amps), for RVs or tents and three yurts. Picnic tables and fire pits are provided. Restrooms, drinking water, flush toilets, limited cell phone reception, an ATM, and showers are available. A playground, a general store, propane, a swimming pool, a boat ramp, mooring, boat fuel, boat rentals, bicycle rentals, ice, and a snack bar are available nearby. Watercraft under 10 feet are prohibited on the lake. Leashed pets are permitted but must be kept at least 50 feet from the lake.

Reservations, fees: Reservations are not accepted. The fee is $18–25 per night, plus $8 for a second vehicle and $3 per pet per night. Group reservations are available. A senior discount is available. Major credit cards are accepted. Open year-round.

Directions: From Santa Barbara, drive 20 miles north on Highway 154 to the campground entrance on the right.

Contact: Cachuma Lake Recreation Area, 805/686-5053, website: www.cachuma.com.

27 FREMONT

Rating: 7

near the Santa Ynez River in Los Padres National Forest

See map pages 772–773

Traveling west to east, Fremont is the first in a

series of Forest Service campgrounds near the Santa Ynez River. This one is just inside the boundary of Los Padres National Forest at 900 feet in elevation, nine miles east of Cachuma Lake to the west.

RV sites, facilities: There are 15 sites for RVs up to 16 feet or tents. Picnic tables and fire grills are provided. Drinking water and flush toilets are available. Groceries are available within two miles and propane is available at Cachuma Lake nine miles away. Some facilities are wheelchair-accessible. Leashed pets are permitted.

Reservations, fees: Reservations are not accepted. The fee is $12 per night, plus $4 for a second vehicle. A senior discount is available. Open April through September.

Directions: From Santa Barbara, drive northwest on Highway 154 for about 10 miles to Paradise Road/Forest Road 5N18. Turn right on Paradise Road/Forest Road 5N18 and drive 2.5 miles to the campground on the right.

Contact: Los Padres National Forest, Santa Barbara Ranger District, 805/967-3481, fax 805/967-7312.

28 LOS PRIETOS

Rating: 7

near the Santa Ynez River in Los Padres National Forest
See map pages 772–773

Los Prietos is across from the Santa Ynez River at an elevation of 1,000 feet, just upstream from nearby Fremont campground to the west. There are several nice hiking trails nearby; the best starts near the Los Prietos Ranger Station, heading south for two miles to Wellhouse Falls (get specific directions and a map at the ranger station).

RV sites, facilities: There are 37 sites for RVs up to 22 feet or tents. Picnic tables and fire grills are provided. Drinking water and flush toilets are available. Some facilities are wheelchair-accessible. Leashed pets are permitted.

Reservations, fees: Reservations are not accepted. The fee is $12 per night, plus $4 for a second vehicle. A senior discount is available. Open April through September.

Directions: From Santa Barbara, take Highway 154 and drive 10 miles northeast to Paradise

Road/Forest Road 5N18. Turn right on Paradise Road/Forest Road 5N18 and drive 3.8 miles to the campground.

Contact: Los Padres National Forest, Santa Barbara Ranger District, 805/967-3481, fax 805/967-7312.

29 UPPER OSO

Rating: 7

near the Santa Ynez River in Los Padres National Forest
See map pages 772–773

This is one of the Forest Service campgrounds in the Santa Ynez Recreation Area. It is set in Oso Canyon at 1,100 feet, one mile from the Santa Ynez River. This is prime spot for equestrians, with horse corrals and adjacent campsites available. Note that at high water this campground can become inaccessible. A mile north of camp is the Santa Cruz trailhead for a hike that is routed north up Oso Canyon for a mile, then three miles up to Happy Hollow, and beyond that to a trail camp just west of Little Pine Mountain, elevation 4,508 feet. A trailhead into the San Rafael Wilderness is nearby, and once on the trail, you'll find many primitive sites in the backcountry.

RV sites, facilities: There are 28 sites for RVs up to 22 feet or tents. Picnic tables and fire grills are provided. Drinking water and flush toilets are available. Horse corrals are also available. Some facilities are wheelchair-accessible. Leashed pets are permitted.

Reservations, fees: Reservations are not accepted for individual sites. The fee is $12 per night, plus $4 for a second vehicle. Reserve sites with horse corrals at 800/444-6777 or online at www.reserveusa.com ($9 reservation fee); the fee is $14 per night. A senior discount is available. Open year-round, weather permitting.

Directions: From Santa Barbara, take Highway 154 and drive 10 miles northeast to Paradise Road/Forest Road 5N18. Turn right on Paradise Road/Forest Road 5N18 and drive six miles to Upper Oso Road. Turn left on Upper Oso Road and drive one mile to the campground at the end of the road.

Contact: Los Padres National Forest, Santa

CALIFORNIA

Barbara Ranger District, 805/967-3481, fax 805/967-7312.

30 PARADISE

Rating: 7

near the Santa Ynez River in Los Padres National Forest

See map pages 772–773

Here is yet another option among the camps along the Santa Ynez River. As you drive east it is the second camp you will come to, just after Fremont. The best hiking trailheads nearby are at Upper Oso Camp and the Sage Hill Group Campground. Cachuma Lake is six miles to the west.

RV sites, facilities: There are 15 sites for RVs up to 22 feet or tents. Picnic tables and fire grills are provided. Drinking water and flush toilets are available. Groceries are available nearby. Some facilities are wheelchair-accessible. Leashed pets are permitted.

Reservations, fees: Reserve at 877/444-6777 or online at www.reserveusa.com ($9 reservation fee). The fee is $12 per night, plus $4 for a second vehicle. Open year-round.

Directions: From Santa Barbara, take Highway 154 and drive 10 miles northeast to Paradise Road/Forest Road 5N18. Turn right on Paradise Road/Forest Road 5N18 and drive three miles to the campground on the right.

Contact: Los Padres National Forest, Santa Barbara Ranger District, 805/967-3481, fax 805/967-7312.

31 WHEELER GORGE

Rating: 7

on Matilija Creek in Los Padres National Forest

See map pages 772–773

This developed Forest Service camp is set at 2,000 feet and is one of the more popular spots in the area. The North Fork of the Matilija runs beside the camp and provides some fair trout fishing in the spring and good swimming holes in early summer. A camp host is on-site in summer. Interpretive programs are also available, a nice plus, and a nature trail is adjacent to the campground.

RV sites, facilities: There are 73 sites for RVs up to 16 feet or tents. Picnic tables and fire grills are provided. Drinking water and pit toilets are available. Garbage must be packed out. Some facilities are wheelchair-accessible. Leashed pets are permitted.

Reservations, fees: Reserve at 877/444-6777 or online at www.reserveusa.com ($9 reservation fee). The fee is $12–15 per night. A senior discount is available. Open year-round.

Directions: From Ojai, drive northwest on Highway 33 for 8.5 miles to the campground entrance on the right.

Contact: Los Padres National Forest, Ojai Ranger District, 805/646-4348, fax 805/646-0484.

32 LAKE CASITAS RECREATION AREA

Rating: 7

north of Ventura

See map pages 772–773

Lake Casitas is known as one of Southern California's world-class fish factories, with more 10-pound bass produced here than anywhere, including the former state record, a bass that weighed 21 pounds, three ounces. The ideal climate in the foothill country gives the fish a nine-month growing season and provides excellent weather for camping. Casitas is north of Ventura at an elevation of 550 feet in the foothills bordering Los Padres National Forest. The lake has 32 miles of shoreline with a huge number of sheltered coves, covering 2,700 acres. The lake is managed primarily for anglers. Water-skiing, personal watercraft, and swimming are not permitted, and only boats between 11 and 24 feet are allowed on the lake.

RV sites, facilities: There are 400 sites, 150 with partial hookups (30, 50 amps) and 21 with full hookups, for RVs up to 50 feet and tents. Picnic tables and fire grills are provided. Restrooms, drinking water, flush toilets, showers, two RV dump stations, limited cell phone reception, seven playgrounds, a grocery store, propane, ice, a snack bar, a water playground for children 12 and under, and a full-service marina (including boat ramps, boat rentals, slips, fuel, tackle, and bait) are available. An ATM is within two miles.

CALIFORNIA

Some facilities are wheelchair-accessible. Leashed pets are permitted.

Reservations, fees: Reservations are advised 14 days in advance and must be made 72 hours in advance at 805/649-1122. The fees are $24–44 per night for RVs and $16–18 for tents, plus $10 per night for each additional vehicle and $2.50 per pet per night. Major credit cards are accepted. Open year-round.

Directions: From Ventura, drive north on Highway 33 for 11 miles to Highway 150. Turn west on Highway 150 and drive about four miles to the campground entrance at 11311 Santa Ana Road.

Contact: Lake Casitas Recreation Area, 805/649-2233, fax 805/649-4661, website: www.casitas water.org.

33 CAMP COMFORT PARK

Rating: 2

on San Antonio Creek
See map pages 772–773

This park gets missed by many. It's set in a residential area in the foothill country at 1,000 feet along San Antonio Creek in the Ojai Valley. Lake Casitas Recreation Area is 10 miles away.

RV sites, facilities: There are 43 sites for RVs up to 34 feet or tents. Picnic tables and fire grills are provided. Restrooms, drinking water, flush toilets, showers, and a playground are available. Supplies and a coin-operated laundry are nearby. Leashed pets are permitted.

Reservations, fees: Reservations are accepted. The fee is $16–22 per night, plus a $1 pet fee. Open year-round, weather permitting.

Directions: From Ventura, take Highway 33 north to Highway 150. Turn west on Highway 150 and drive three miles to Creek Road. Turn right and drive one mile to the park.

Contact: Camp Comfort Park, 805/654-3951.

34 FAR WEST RESORT

Rating: 7

on Santa Paula Creek
See map pages 772–773

Far West Resort is near little Santa Paula Creek in the foothill country adjacent to Steckel Coun-

ty Park. For those who want a well-developed park with a lot of amenities, the shoe fits. Note that at one time the two campgrounds, Far West Resort and Steckel County Park, were linked. No more, and for good reason. Far West Resort is a tight ship where the gates close at 10 P.M. and quiet time assures campers of a good night's sleep. It is a good place to bring a family. Steckel County Park, on the other hand, has a campground with so many problems that we removed it from the book. Steckel is a beautiful place gone bad, crime-ridden and scary for most visitors, with wild partying, fights, and screaming. Clearly the rangers at Steckel have let down the public. So what do you do? Go next door to Far West where the inmates aren't running the asylum, and the days are fun and nights are peaceful.

RV sites, facilities: There are 72 sites, 15 with full hookups, the rest with partial hookups, for RVs or tents, three group sites for RVs, and a group tent site for up to 400 people. Picnic tables and fire grills are provided. Restrooms, drinking water, flush toilets, a coin-operated laundry, modem access, an RV dump station, a clubhouse, and horseshoes are available. Supplies and a coin-operated laundry are nearby. Leashed pets are permitted.

Reservations, fees: Reservations are recommended. The fee is $15–22 per night, plus $1 per person per night for more than four people and $1 per pet per night. Group sites $3 per person per night. Major credit cards are accepted. Open year-round for RVs and group tent site; individual tent sites are closed in winter.

Directions: From Ventura, drive east on Highway 126 for 14 miles to Highway 150. Turn northwest on Highway 150 and drive four miles to the resort entrance on right.

Contact: Far West Resort, 805/933-3200, website: www.farwestresort.com.

35 MOUNTAIN VIEW RV PARK

Rating: 3

in Santa Paula
See map pages 772–773

The town of Santa Paula is known for its excellent weather and nearby recreation options, including Los Padres National Forest and the beaches at Ventura. Lake Casitas and Cachuma Lake, both known for big Florida bass, are within reasonable driving distance.

RV sites, facilities: There are 31 sites, 20 drive-through, with full hookups (30 amps) for RVs. A swim spa (a giant hot tub, like a small swimming pool), cable TV, cell phone reception, and modem access are available. No showers are available. A coin-operated laundry, restaurant, ATM, and shopping center are nearby. Leashed pets are permitted.

Reservations, fees: Reservations are required. The fee is $25.30–27.50 per night. A senior discount is available. Open year-round.

Directions: From Ventura, drive east on Highway 126 for 11 miles to Peck Road exit. Take that exit and drive a short distance to Harvard Boulevard. Turn right and drive to the park at 714 West Harvard Boulevard.

Contact: Mountain View RV Park, 805/933-1942.

36 KENNEY GROVE

Rating: 4

near Fillmore
See map pages 772–773

A lot of folks miss this spot, a park tucked away among orchards and eucalyptus groves. It's just far enough off the highway to allow for some privacy. Note that groups are given priority over family and individual campers.

RV sites, facilities: There are 33 sites with partial hookups for RVs and 19 sites for tents. Picnic tables and fire grills are provided. Drinking water, flush toilets, and a playground are available. Supplies and a coin-operated laundry are nearby. Leashed pets are permitted.

Reservations, fees: Reservations are required. The fee is $15–20 per night, plus $2 for a second vehicle and a $1 pet fee. Open year-round.

Directions: From Ventura, drive east on Highway 126 for 22 miles to Old Telegraph Road (before the town of Fillmore). Take the Old Telegraph Road exit and turn left and drive to 7th Street. Turn left and drive to Oak. Turn right on Oak and drive to the park on the left.

Contact: Kenney Grove, 805/524-0750.

37 LAKE PIRU RECREATION AREA

Rating: 7

on Lake Piru
See map pages 772–773

Things can get crazy at Lake Piru, but it's usually a happy crazy, not an insane crazy. Lake Piru, at an elevation of 1,055 feet, is shaped like a teardrop and covers 1,200 acres when full. This is a lake set up for water-skiing, with lots of fast boats. All others be forewarned: the rules prohibit boats under 12 feet or over 26 feet, as well as personal watercraft such as Jet Skis, Ski-Doos, and Wave Runners. Bass fishing can be quite good in the spring before the water-skiers take over. From Memorial Day weekend through Labor Day weekend, there is a designated swimming area, safe from the boats. The tent sites here consist of roughly 40-by-40-foot areas amid trees.

RV sites, facilities: There are 235 sites with partial hookups (30, 50 amps) for RVs up to 40 feet or tents, five sites with full hookups for RVs, and two group camps. Fire pits and picnic tables are provided. Restrooms, drinking water, flush toilets, showers, an RV dump station, a snack bar, ice, bait, a boat ramp, temporary mooring, boat fuel, motorboat rentals, and tackle are available. An ATM is within six miles. Some facilities are wheelchair-accessible. Leashed pets are permitted.

Reservations, fees: Reservations are advised at least one week in advance (phone Monday through Thursday). The fee is $18–33, plus $2 per person for more than four people and $2 per pet per night. Special conditions apply on holiday weekends. Reservations are required for group camps; the fee is $214–318 per night. Major credit cards are accepted. Open year-round.

Directions: From Ventura, drive east on Highway 126 for about 30 miles to the Piru Canyon Road exit. Take that exit and drive northeast on Piru Canyon Road for about six miles to the campground at the end of the road.

Contact: Lake Piru Recreation Area, 805/521-1500, website: www.lake-piru.org.

CALIFORNIA

38 OAK PARK

Rating: 3

in Simi Valley near Moorpark
See map pages 772–773

One of the frustrations of trying to find a camp for the night is that so many state and national park campgrounds are full from reservations, especially at the state beaches. The county parks often provide a safety valve, and Oak Park certainly applies. But not always, and that's the catch. This is an oft-overlooked county park in the foothill country of Simi Valley. The park has many trails offering good hiking possibilities. An often-fun distraction is the Simi Flyers, a model-airplane flying club that puts on displays some weekends at the park. The camp is somewhat secluded, more so than many expect. The catch? Sometimes the entire campground is rented to a single group. Note: gates close at dusk and reopen at 7 A.M.

RV sites, facilities: There are 16 sites with partial hookups (30 amps) for RVs up to 40 feet, a group area for up to 22 RVs, and a large group tent area for up to 150 people. Picnic tables and fire grills are provided. Restrooms, drinking water, flush toilets, a pay phone, cell phone reception, and an RV dump station are available. Horsehoe pits, a playground, and basketball and volleyball courts are nearby. Supplies, an ATM, and a coin-operated laundry are within three miles. Leashed pets are permitted.

Reservations, fees: Reservations are accepted. The fees are $10 per night for tents, $12 per night with no hookups for RVs, and $20 per night with partial hookups for RVs, plus $5 per person per night for more than two people and $1 per pet per night. Open year-round, except Christmas Day.

Directions: From Ventura, drive south on U.S. 101 to Highway 23. Turn north on Highway 23 (which becomes Highway 118 E.) and drive about two miles to the Collins Street exit. Continue straight through the intersection for 1.25 miles (it becomes Old Los Angeles Road) and drive 1.2 miles to the park entrance on the right.

Contact: Oak Park, 805/527-6886, website: www.ventura.org/gsa/parks.

39 VALENCIA TRAVEL VILLAGE

Rating: 6

in Valencia
See map pages 772–773

This huge RV park is in the scenic San Fernando foothills, just five minutes from Six Flags Magic Mountain. Lake Piru and Lake Castaic are only 15 minutes away. The camp was built on a 65-acre horse ranch. Some may remember that this park had a large tent camping area. In 2003, that was converted to add 66 new RV sites.

RV sites, facilities: There are 367 sites, most drive-through, with full hookups (30, 50 amps) for RVs. A market and deli, two swimming pools, a spa, a lounge, a video and games arcade, cell phone reception, a playground, shuffleboard, horseshoes, volleyball courts, laundry facilities, modem access, propane, and an RV dump station are available. An ATM is within four miles. Some facilities are wheelchair-accessible.

Reservations, fees: Reservations are recommended at 888/LUV-TORV (888/588-8678). The fee is $37–47 per night, plus $2 per person per night for more than two people. Weekly and monthly rates are available. A senior discount is available. Major credit cards are accepted. Open year-round.

Directions: Drive on I-5 to Santa Clarita and Highway 126/Henry Mayo Road. Take that exit and drive west on Highway 126 for one mile to the camp on the left.

Contact: Valencia Travel Village, 27946 Henry Mayo Rd. (Hwy. 126), Valencia, CA 91384, 661/257-3333, website: www.goodsam.com.

40 JALAMA BEACH COUNTY PARK

Rating: 8

near Lompoc on the Pacific Ocean
See map pages 772–773

This is a pretty spot set where Jalama Creek empties into the ocean, about five miles north of Point Conception and just south of Vandenberg Air Force Base. The area is known for its sunsets and beachcombing, with occasional lost missiles washing up on the beach. The camp is so popular that a waiting list is common in summer.

RV sites, facilities: There are 110 sites, 29 with

water hookups, for RVs up to 35 feet or tents and several group sites. Picnic tables and fire grills are provided. Restrooms, drinking water, flush toilets, showers, an RV dump station, and a grocery store are available. Note that the nearest gas station is 20 miles away. Some facilities are wheelchair-accessible. Leashed pets are permitted.

Reservations, fees: No reservations are accepted except for groups. The fee is $16–22 per night, plus $8 for an additional vehicle (two-vehicle maximum per site) and $2 per pet per night. Group reservations are required at 805/934-2611 ($25 reservation fee). Major credit cards are accepted. Open year-round.

Directions: From Lompoc, drive about five miles south on Highway 1. Turn southwest on Jalama Road and drive 14 miles to the park.

Contact: Jalama Beach County Park, 805/736-6316, fax 805/736-8020 or 805/736-3504, website: www.slocountyparks.com or www.sbpark.org.

41 GAVIOTA STATE PARK

Rating: 10

near Santa Barbara
See map pages 772–773

This is the granddaddy, the biggest of the three state beaches along U.S. 101 northwest of Santa Barbara. Spectacular and beautiful, the park covers 2,700 acres, providing trails for hiking and horseback riding, as well as a mile-long stretch of stunning beach frontage. Gaviota means "seagull" and was first named by the soldiers of the Portola Expedition in 1769, who learned why you always wear a hat (or a helmet) when the birds are passing overhead. The ambitious can hike the beach to get more seclusion. Trails to Gaviota Overlook (1.5 miles) and Gaviota Peak (3.2 miles one-way) provide lookouts with drop-dead gorgeous views of the coast and Channel Islands. Want more? There is also a half-mile trail to the hot springs. This park is known for being windy and for shade being hard to find. Unfortunately, a railroad trestle crosses above the day-use parking lot. You know what that means? Of course you do. It means trains run through here day and night, and with them, noise. This is a popular beach for swimming and surf fishing, as well as fishing from the pier.

RV sites, facilities: There are 42 sites for RVs up to 27 feet or tents and an area with hike-in/bike-in sites. Picnic tables and fire grills are provided. Restrooms, drinking water, flush toilets, coin-operated showers, summer lifeguard service, and a boat hoist are available. A convenience store (open summer only) is nearby. Some facilities are wheelchair-accessible. Leashed pets are permitted at campsites.

Reservations, fees: Reservations are not accepted. The fee is $10 per night or $1 per person per night for hike-in/bike-in sites. A senior discount is available. Open year-round.

Directions: From Santa Barbara, drive north on U.S. 101 for 33 miles to the Gaviota State Beach exit. Take that exit and turn west and drive a short distance to the park entrance.

Contact: Gaviota State Park, Channel Coast District, 805/968-1033 or 805/899-1400.

42 REFUGIO STATE BEACH

Rating: 9

near Santa Barbara
See map pages 772–773

Refugio State Beach is the smallest of the three beautiful state beaches along U.S. 101 north of Santa Barbara. The others are Gaviota and El Capitan, which also have campgrounds. Palm trees planted close to Refugio Creek provide a unique look to this beach and campground. This is a great spot for family campers with bikes, with a paved two-mile bike trail connecting Refugio campground with El Capitan. Fishing is often good in this area of the coast. As with all state beaches and private camps on the Coast Highway, reservations are strongly advised and often a necessity throughout the vacation season.

RV sites, facilities: There are 85 sites for RVs up to 30 feet or tents, five hike-in/bike-in sites, and one group site for up to 80 people and 25 vehicles. Picnic tables and fire grills are provided. Restrooms, drinking water, flush toilets, coin-operated showers, summer lifeguard service, a summer convenience store, and food services are available. An RV dump station is two miles away at El Capitan State Beach. Some facilities are wheelchair-accessible. Leashed pets are permitted at campsites.

CALIFORNIA

Reservations, fees: Reserve at 800/444-PARK (800/444-7275) or online at www.reserveamerica .com ($7.50 reservation fee). The fees are $12 per night, $1 per night per person for hike-in/bike-in sites, $60 per night for the group site. A senior discount is available. Open year-round, weather permitting.

Directions: From Santa Barbara, drive northwest on U.S. 101 for 23 miles to the Refugio State Beach exit. Take that exit and turn west (left) and drive a short distance to the campground entrance.

Contact: Refugio State Beach, 805/899-1400; Channel Coast District, 805/968-1033.

43 EL CAPITAN STATE BEACH

Rating: 10

near Santa Barbara
See map pages 772–773

This is one in a series of beautiful state beaches along the Santa Barbara coast. The water is warm, the swimming good. A stairway descends from the bluffs to the beach, a beautiful setting. El Capitan has a sandy beach, rocky tidepools, and stands of sycamores and oaks along El Capitan Creek. A paved, two-mile bicycle trail is routed to Refugio State Beach, a great family trip. This is a perfect layover for Coast Highway vacationers, and reservations are usually required to assure a spot. Refugio State Beach to the north is another camping option.

RV sites, facilities: There are 142 sites for RVs up to 30 feet or tents, seven hike-in/bike-in sites, and three group sites for tents only for 50 to 125 people. Picnic tables and fire grills are provided. Restrooms, drinking water, flush toilets, coin-operated showers, an RV dump station, summer lifeguard service, and a summer convenience store are available. Some facilities are wheelchair-accessible. Leashed pets are permitted.

Reservations, fees: Reserve at 800/444-PARK (800/444-7275) or online at www.reserveamerica .com ($7.50 reservation fee). The fees are $12 per night, $1 per person per night for hike-in/bike-in sites, $37–93 per night for group sites. A senior discount is available. Open year-round, weather permitting.

Directions: From Santa Barbara, drive north on U.S. 101 for 20 miles to the El Capitan State Beach exit. Turn west (left) and drive a short distance to the campground entrance.

Contact: El Capitan State Beach, 805/968-1033 or 805/899-1400.

44 SANTA BARBARA SUNRISE RV PARK

Rating: 3

in Santa Barbara
See map pages 772–773

Motor-home cruisers get a little of two worlds here. For one thing, the park is close to the beach; for another, the downtown shopping area isn't too far away, either. This is the only RV park in Santa Barbara.

RV sites, facilities: There are 33 sites, three drive-through, with full hookups (30 amps) and patios for RVs, and two tent sites. Restrooms, showers, cable TV, cell phone reception, and laundry facilities are available. A grocery store, golf course, tennis courts, and propane are nearby. An ATM is within one mile. Leashed pets are permitted.

Reservations, fees: Reservations are recommended. The fee is $35 per night and up (depending on size), plus $5 per night for each additional vehicle and $5 per pet per night. Major credit cards are accepted. Open year-round.

Directions: In Santa Barbara on U.S. 101 northbound, drive to the Salinas Street exit. Take that exit and drive to the park (well signed) to 516 S. Salinas Street.

In Santa Barbara on U.S. 101 southbound, drive to the Milpas Street exit. Take that exit and drive to the junction with Salinas Street (signed with blue camper signs).

Contact: Santa Barbara Sunrise RV Park, 805/966-9954 or 800/345-5018, fax 805/966-7950, website: www.santabarbara.com.

45 CARPINTERIA STATE BEACH

Rating: 8

near Santa Barbara
See map pages 772–773

First, plan on reservations, and then, plan on plenty of neighbors. This state beach is one pretty spot, and a lot of folks cruising up the coast

CALIFORNIA

like the idea of taking off their cowboy boots here for awhile. This is an urban park; that is, it is within walking distance of downtown, restaurants, and shopping. You can love it or hate it, but this camp is almost always full. It features one mile of beach. Harbor seals can be seen December through May, along with an occasional passing gray whale. Tidepools here are protected and contain starfish, sea anemones, crabs, snails, octopus, and sea urchins. In the summer, the visitors center features a living tidepool exhibit. Other state beaches to the nearby north are El Capitan State Beach and Refugio State Beach, both with campgrounds.

RV sites, facilities: There are 60 sites with partial or full hookups (30 amps) for RVs up to 21 feet, 119 sites for RVs up to 30 feet or tents, 101 sites for tents, one hike-in/bike-in site, and two group sites for a maximum of 40 and 65 campers. Picnic tables and fire grills are provided. Restrooms, drinking water, flush toilets, limited cell phone reception, and coin-operated showers are available. A convenience store, ATM, coin-operated laundry, restaurants, and propane are nearby in the town of Carpinteria. Some facilities are wheelchair-accessible. Leashed pets are permitted, except on the beach.

Reservations, fees: Reserve at 800/444-PARK (800/444-7275) or online at www.reserveamerica.com ($7.50 reservation fee). The fees are $12–26 per night, $2 per person per night for hike-in/bike-in sites, $90–135 for group sites. A senior discount is available. Open year-round.

Directions: From Santa Barbara, drive south on U.S. 101 for 12 miles to the Casitas Pass exit. Take that exit and turn right on Casitas Pass Road and drive about a block to Carpinteria Avenue. Turn right and drive a short distance to Palm Avenue. Turn left and drive three blocks to the campground at the end of Palm Avenue.

Contact: Carpinteria State Beach, 805/684-2811; Channel Coast District, 805/889-1400.

46 HOBSON COUNTY PARK

Rating: 6

on the Pacific Ocean north of Ventura
See map pages 772–773
This county park is at the end of Rincon Park-

way, kind of like a crowded cul-de-sac, with easy access to the beach and many side-trip possibilities. Emma Wood State Beach, San Buenaventura State Beach, and McGrath State Beach are all within 11 miles of the park.

RV sites, facilities: There are 31 sites for RVs up to 34 feet or tents. Picnic tables and fire grills are provided. Restrooms, drinking water, flush toilets, coin-operated showers, and a snack bar are available. Leashed pets are permitted, but not on the beach.

Reservations, fees: Reservations are accepted. The fee is $22–30 per night, plus $3 per night for additional vehicle and $1 per pet per night. Open year-round.

Directions: From Ventura, drive northwest on U.S. 101 for three miles to the State Beaches exit. Take that exit and turn north on West Pacific Highway and drive five miles to the campground on the left.

Contact: Ventura County Parks Department, 805/654-3951, website: www.ventura.org/gsa/parks.

47 FARIA COUNTY PARK

Rating: 7

on the Pacific Ocean north of Ventura
See map pages 772–773
This county park provides a possible base of operations for beach adventures. It is set along the ocean, with Emma Wood State Beach, San Buenaventura State Beach, and McGrath State Beach all within 10 miles of the park.

RV sites, facilities: There are 42 sites for RVs up to 34 feet or tents. Picnic tables and fire grills are provided. Restrooms, drinking water, flush toilets, coin-operated showers, a playground, and a snack bar are available. Pets are permitted.

Reservations, fees: Reservations are accepted. The fee is $22–35 per night, plus $1 per pet per night. Open year-round.

Directions: From Ventura, drive north on U.S. 101 for three miles to the State Beaches exit. Take that exit and turn north on West Pacific Highway and drive four miles to the campground.

Contact: Ventura County Parks Department, 805/654-3951, website: www.ventura.org/gsa/parks.

CALIFORNIA

48 RINCON PARKWAY

Rating: 5

on the Pacific Ocean north of Ventura
See map pages 772–773

This is basically an RV park near the ocean, where the sites are parking end-to-end along old Highway 1. It is not quiet. Passing trains across the highway vie for noise honors with the surf. Emma Wood State Beach, San Buenaventura State Beach, and McGrath State Beach are all within 10 miles.
RV sites, facilities: There are 127 RV sites for self-contained vehicles up to 34 feet. An RV dump station and supplies are available nearby. Leashed pets are allowed, but not on the beach.
Reservations, fees: Reservations are not accepted. The fee is $18 per night, plus $3 per night for additional vehicle and $1 per pet per night. Open year-round.
Directions: From Ventura, drive northwest on U.S. 101 for three miles to the State Beaches exit. Take that exit and turn north on West Pacific Highway and drive 4.5 miles to the campground on the left.
Contact: Ventura County Parks Department, 805/654-3951, website: www.ventura.org/gsa/parks.

49 McGRATH STATE BEACH

Rating: 9

on the Pacific Ocean south of Ventura
See map pages 772–773

This is a pretty spot just south of Ventura Harbor. Campsites are about 200 yards from the beach. This park features two miles of beach frontage, as well as lush riverbanks and sand dunes along the ocean shore. That gives rise to some of the best bird-watching in California. The north tip of the park borders the Santa Clara River Estuary Natural Preserve, where the McGrath State Beach Nature Trail provides an easy walk (wheelchair-accessible) along the Santa Clara River as it feeds into the estuary and then into the ocean. Rangers caution all considering swimming here to beware of strong currents and rip tides; they can be deadly. Ventura Harbor and the Channel Islands National Park Visitor Center are nearby side trips.

RV sites, facilities: There are 174 sites for RVs up to 34 feet or tents (29 of the sites can be used as group sites) and a hike-in/bike-in site. Picnic tables and fire grills are provided. Restrooms, drinking water, flush toilets, coin-operated showers, an RV dump station, and horseshoes are available. Lifeguard service is provided in summer. Supplies and a coin-operated laundry are nearby. Some facilities are wheelchair-accessible. Leashed pets are permitted in campsites only.
Reservations, fees: Reserve at 800/444-PARK (800/444-7275) or online at www.reserveamerica.com ($7.50 reservation fee). The fee is $12 per night or $1 per person for hike-in/bike-in sites. A senior discount is available. Open year-round.
Directions: Drive on U.S. 101 to south of Ventura and the Seaward exit. Take that exit and turn west on Seaward Avenue and drive one mile to Harbor Boulevard. Bear left on Harbor and drive four miles to the park (signed).
Contact: McGrath State Beach, 805/654-4744 or 805/648-4127; Channel Coast State Park District, 805/899-1400.

50 POINT MUGU STATE PARK/ THORNHILL BROOME

Rating: 7

in Point Mugu State Park
See map pages 772–773

Point Mugu State Park is known for its rocky bluffs, sandy beaches, rugged hills, and uplands. There are two major river canyons and wide grassy valleys sprinkled with sycamores, oaks, and a few native walnut trees. Of the campgrounds at Point Mugu, Thornehill Broome Campground is more attractive than Big Sycamore (see next listing) for many visitors because it is on the ocean side of the highway (Big Sycamore is on the east side of the highway). The beachfront is pretty and you can always just lie there in the sun and pretend you're a beached whale, but the park's expanse on the east side of the highway in the Santa Monica Mountains provides more recreation options. That includes two stellar hikes, the 9.5-mile Big Sycamore Canyon Loop and the seven-mile La Jolla Valley Loop. In all, the park covers 14,980 acres, far more than the obvious strip of beachfront. The park has more than 70 miles of hiking trails and five miles of ocean shoreline. Swimming, body surfing, and surf fishing are available on the beach.

RV sites, facilities: There are 60 primitive sites for RVs up to 31 feet or tents. Picnic tables and fire rings are provided. Drinking water and chemical toilets are available. Supplies can be obtained nearby. Note that nearby Big Sycamore has a restroom with flush toilets and coin-operated showers, an RV dump station, and a nature center. Some facilities are wheelchair-accessible. Leashed pets are permitted.

Reservations, fees: Reserve at 800/444-PARK (800/444-7275) or online at www.reserveamerica .com ($7.50 reservation fee). The fee is $7–12 per night. A senior discount is available. Open year-round.

Directions: From Oxnard, drive 15 miles south on Highway 1 to the camp entrance on the right.

Contact: Thornhill Broome State Beach, 818/880-0350, fax 818/880-6165.

51 POINT MUGU STATE PARK/ BIG SYCAMORE CANYON

Rating: 6

in Point Mugu State Park
See map pages 772–773

While this camp is across the highway from the ocean, it is also part of Point Mugu State Park, which covers 14,980 acres. That gives you plenty of options. One of the best is taking the Big Sycamore Canyon Loop, a long hiking route with great views that starts right at the camp. In all, it's a 9.5-mile loop that climbs to a ridge top and offers beautiful views of nearby canyons and long-distance vistas of the coast. Note: The front gate closes at 10 P.M. and reopens at 8 A.M.

RV sites, facilities: There are 55 sites for RVs up to 31 feet or tents (up to eight campers per site) and one hike-in/bike-in site. Picnic tables and fire grills are provided. Restrooms, drinking water, flush toilets, coin-operated showers, and an RV dump station are available. A nature center is within walking distance. Supplies can be obtained nearby. Some facilities are wheelchair-accessible. Leashed pets are permitted at campsites.

Reservations, fees: Reserve at 800/444-PARK (800/444-7275) or online at www.reserveamerica .com ($7.50 reservation fee). The fee is $12 per night or $1 per person per night for hike-in/bike-in site. A senior discount is available. Open year-round.

Directions: From Oxnard, drive south on Highway 1 for 16 miles to the camp on the left.

Contact: Big Sycamore Canyon, 818/880-0350, fax 818/880-6165.

CALIFORNIA

California

Chapter 26

Los Angeles and Vicinity

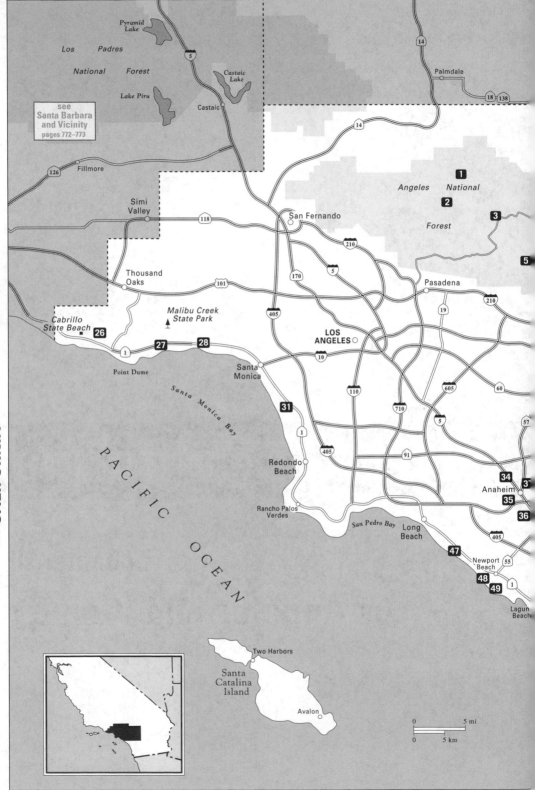

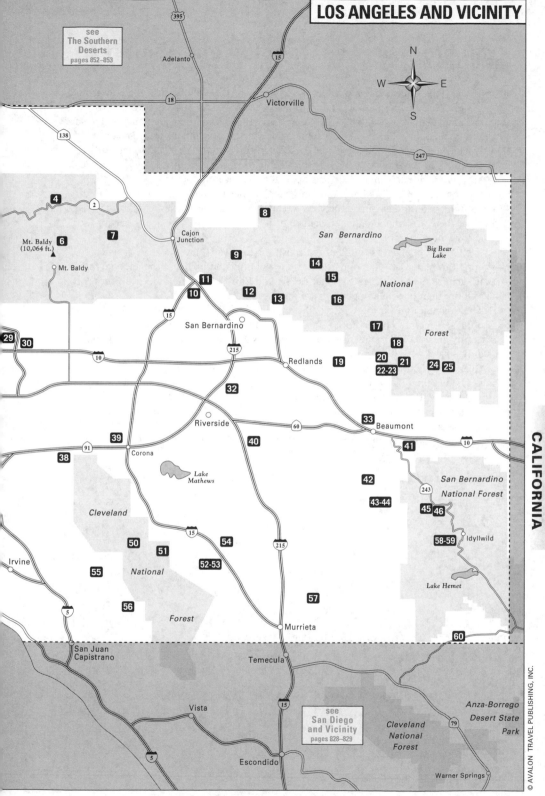

see
The Southern
Deserts
pages 852–853

Adelanto

395

15

N

W E

S

18

Victorville

138

247

4

2

Cajon
Junction

8

San   Bernardino

Big Bear
Lake

Mt. Baldy
(10,064 ft.) **6**

Mt. Baldy

7

9

14

National

15

15

11

10

12

13

16

San Bernardino

17

Forest

18

215

Redlands

19

20

21

24 **25**

22-23

29
30

10

32

Riverside

33 Beaumont

10

39

60

41

91

38

Corona

40

243

San Bernardino

Lake
Mathews

42

National Forest

45 **46**

Cleveland

43-44

15

50

51

54

58-59 Idyllwild

Irvine

55

National

52-53

215

5

56

57

Lake Hemet

Forest

Murrieta

60

San Juan
Capistrano

Temecula

see
San Diego
and Vicinity
pages 828–829

15

Vista

Anza-Borrego
Desert State

79

Park

Cleveland
National
Forest

5

Escondido

Warner Springs

CALIFORNIA

Chapter 26—Los Angeles and Vicinity

The stereotypical image of the region you see on TV—the blonde in a convertible, the surfer with the movie-star jawline—is so flawed as to be ridiculous, pathetic, and laughable. And while there is some classic beach, lifeguards and all, the surrounding area for recreation spans some of the best opportunities in California.

In fact, there are 60 campgrounds for RVs in this region, more than many other of California's 16 geographic regions. It stuns some to learn that Los Angeles and its nearby forests provide this many camping opportunities, even for RVers.

But for those of us who know this landscape, it does not come as a surprise. The area has a tremendous range of national forests, canyons, mountains, lakes, coast, and islands. In fact, there are so many hidden gems that it is like a giant scavenger hunt for those who love the outdoors.

While most people first think of the coast, the highways, and the beaches when envisioning this region, it is the opportunities for camping and hiking in the national forests that surprise most. Angeles National Forest and San Bernardino National Forest provide more than one million acres and a thousand miles of trails.

The mountaintop views are incredible, probably best from Mount Baldy (10,064 feet), Mount San Jacinto (10,804 feet), and Mount San Gorgonio (11,490 feet). There are a series of great campgrounds nestled on the flanks of all three of these destinations. It is only a start.

Even more famous is the region's top recreation lake, Big Bear, for fishing and boating. Though the region is known for its high population, and Big Bear is no exception on weekends, the relatively few people on weekdays, especially Monday to Thursday mornings, can be stunning to discover. Other top lakes include Arrowhead, Castaic, and several smaller reservoirs.

Yet this is not even the best of it. Look over the opportunities and take your pick. People? What people?

■ CHILAO

Rating: 6

near the San Gabriel Wilderness in Angeles National Forest
See map pages 798–799

This popular trailhead camp gets a lot of use. And it's easy to see why, with the Chilao Visitor Center nearby (have any questions—here's where you ask them) and a national recreation trail running right by the camp. Access to the Pacific Crest Trail is two miles north at Three Points, and parking is available there. The elevation is 5,300 feet.

RV sites, facilities: There are 110 sites for RVs up to 36 feet or tents. Picnic tables and fire rings are provided. Drinking water and vault toilets are available. An RV dump station is available at Charlton Flat Picnic Area. There is no drinking water in dry years. Leashed pets are permitted.

Reservations, fees: Reservations are not accepted. The fee is $12 per night. A senior discount is available. Open May through October.

Directions: From Pasadena, drive north on I-210 for four miles to the exit for Highway 2/Angeles Crest Highway. Take that exit and drive northeast on Highway 2 for 26 miles to the campground entrance road (signed) on the left.

Contact: Angeles National Forest, Los Angeles River Ranger District, 818/899-1900, fax 818/896-6727.

■ MONTE CRISTO

Rating: 7

on Mill Creek in Angeles National Forest
See map pages 798–799

This is a Forest Service camp on Mill Creek at 3,600 feet, just west of Iron Mountain. The camp is situated under sycamore trees, which provide great color in the fall. In most years, Mill Creek flows eight months out of the year.

RV sites, facilities: There are 19 sites for RVs up to 30 feet or tents. Picnic tables and fire grills are provided. Drinking water and vault toilets are available, but there is no drinking water in dry years. Some facilities are wheelchair-accessible. Leashed pets are permitted.

Reservations, fees: Reservations are not accepted. The fee is $8 per night, plus $2 for each additional vehicle. Reservations are available for sites with wheelchair facilities. A senior discount is available. Open year-round.

Directions: From Pasadena, drive north on I-210 for four miles to the exit for Highway 2/Angeles Crest Highway. Take that exit and drive northeast on Highway 2 for nine miles to Angeles Forest Highway/County Road N3. Turn left on Angeles Forest Highway and drive about nine miles to the campground.

Contact: Angeles National Forest, Los Angeles River Ranger District, 818/899-1900, fax 818/896-6727.

■ BUCKHORN

Rating: 9

near Snowcrest Ridge in Angeles National Forest
See map pages 798–799

This is a prime jump-off spot for backpackers in Angeles National Forest. The camp is set at 6,300 feet among huge pine and cedar trees, along a small creek near Mount Waterman (8,038 feet). A great day hike begins here, a tromp down to Cooper Canyon and the PCT; hikers will be rewarded by beautiful Cooper Falls on this three-hour round-trip. Want a weekend trip? Got it: the High Desert National Recreational Trail leads north from camp into the backcountry, over Burkhart Saddle, and west around Devil's Punchbowl County Park to South Fork Campground. Then it heads south to the Islip Trailhead, east past Eagle's Roost, and south again for the last mile back to Buckhorn. It's a 20-mile hike, with the South Fork Camp situated 10 miles out, perfect for a weekend trip.

RV sites, facilities: There are 38 sites for RVs up to 18 feet or tents. Picnic tables and fire pits are provided. Drinking water and vault toilets are available, and a camp host is on-site. Leashed pets are permitted.

Reservations, fees: Reservations are not accepted. The fee is $14 per night. A senior discount is available. Open May through November.

Directions: From Pasadena, drive north on I-210 for four miles to the exit for Highway 2/Angeles

CALIFORNIA

Crest Highway. Take that exit and drive northeast on Highway 2 for 34 miles northeast to the signed campground entrance.

Contact: Angeles National Forest, Los Angeles River Ranger District, 818/899-1900, fax 818/896-6727.

❹ TABLE MOUNTAIN

Rating: 6

in Angeles National Forest

See map pages 798–799

This is a family campground that accommodates both tents and RVs. The road leading in is a paved two-lane county road, easily accessible by any vehicle. The nearby Big Pines Visitor Information Center, one mile to the south, can provide maps and information on road conditions. The camp elevation is 7,200 feet. A rough road for four-wheel-drive rigs is available out of camp that leads north along the Table Mountain Ridge.

RV sites, facilities: There are 115 sites for RVs up to 32 feet or tents. Picnic tables and fire pits are provided. Drinking water and vault toilets are available. Leashed pets are permitted.

Reservations, fees: Reserve at 877/444-6777 or online at www.reserveusa.com ($9 reservation fee). The fee is $14 per night. A senior discount is available. Open May through September.

Directions: Drive on I-15 to Cajon Junction (north of San Bernardino) and the exit for Highway 138 West. Take that exit and drive west on Highway 138 to Angeles Crest Highway/Highway 2. Turn west on Angeles Crest Highway and drive five miles to Wrightwood, then continue for three miles to Big Pines and Table Mountain Road. Turn right on Table Mountain Road and drive one mile to the campground.

Contact: Angeles National Forest, Santa Clara/Mojave Rivers Ranger District, 661/296-9710, fax 661/296-5847.

❺ COLDBROOK

Rating: 7

on the North Fork of the San Gabriel River in Angeles National Forest

See map pages 798–799

This roadside camp is set along the North Fork San Gabriel River, with little Crystal Lake to the north. A secret waterfall is hidden off the road, about three miles north on Soldier Creek. To find it, park at the deep bending turn in the road at Soldier Creek, then hike uphill for less than a mile. It's just like a treasure hunt, and it's always a welcome surprise to find the waterfall. The elevation is 3,300 feet.

RV sites, facilities: There are 22 sites for RVs up to 22 feet or tents. Picnic tables and fire rings are provided. Drinking water and vault toilets are available. Leashed pets are permitted.

Reservations, fees: Reservations are not accepted. The fee is $12 per night, plus $5 for each additional vehicle. Discounts are available for those with Adventure Passes and for seniors. Open year-round.

Directions: Drive on I-210 to Azusa and the exit for Azusa Canyon and San Gabriel Canyon Road/Highway 39. Take that exit and drive north on San Gabriel Canyon Road for 18 miles to the campground entrance.

Contact: Angeles National Forest, San Gabriel River Ranger District, 626/335-1251, fax 626/914-3790.

❻ MANKER FLATS

Rating: 7

near Mount Baldy in Angeles National Forest

See map pages 798–799

This camp is best known for its proximity to Mount Baldy and the nearby trailhead to reach San Antonio Falls. The trail to San Antonio Falls starts at an elevation of 6,160 feet, three-tenths of a mile up the road on the left. From here, it's a 1.5-mile saunter on a ski park maintenance road to the waterfall, a pretty 80-footer. The wild and ambitious can continue six more miles and climb to the top of Mount Baldy (10,064 feet) for breathtaking 360-degree views. Making this all-day butt-kicker is like a baptism for Southern California hikers.

RV sites, facilities: There are 21 sites for RVs up to 16 feet or tents. Picnic tables and fire grills are provided. Drinking water and vault toilets are available. There is no drinking water in dry years. Leashed pets are permitted.

Reservations, fees: Reservations are not accepted. The fee is $12 per night, plus $4 for each additional vehicle. Discounts are offered for those with Adventure Passes and for seniors. Open May through September.

Directions: Drive on I-10 to Ontario and the exit for Highway 83. Take that exit and drive north on Highway 83 to Mt. Baldy Road. Continue north on Mt. Baldy Road for nine miles to the campground.

Contact: Angeles National Forest, San Gabriel River Ranger District, 626/335-1251, fax 626/914-3790.

7 APPLE WHITE

Rating: 5

near Lytle Creek in San Bernardino National Forest
See map pages 798–799

Nothing like a little insiders' know-how, especially at this camp, set at 3,300 feet near Lytle Creek. You can reach the Middle Fork of Lytle Creek by driving north from Fontana via Serra Avenue to the Lytle Creek area. To get to the stretch of water that is stocked with trout by the Department of Fish and Game, turn west on Middle Fork Road, which is 1.5 miles before the campground at Apple White. The first mile upstream is stocked in early summer.

RV sites, facilities: There are 42 sites for RVs up to 30 feet or tents. Picnic tables and fire grills are provided. Restrooms, drinking water, and flush toilets are available. A store is nearby. Some facilities are wheelchair-accessible. Leashed pets are permitted.

Reservations, fees: Reservations are not accepted. The fee is $10 per night or $15 for double sites, plus $3 for each additional vehicle. A senior discount is available. Open year-round.

Directions: Drive to Ontario and the junction of I-10 and I-15. Take I-15 north and drive 11 miles

to the Sierra Avenue exit. Turn left, go under the freeway, and continue north for about nine miles (into national forest) to the campground on the right.

Contact: San Bernardino National Forest, Front Country Ranger District, 909/887-2576, fax 909/887-8197.

8 MOJAVE RIVER FORKS REGIONAL PARK

Rating: 5

near Silverwood Lake
See map pages 798–799

The bonuses here are for RV drivers, with the full hookups for RVs and the park's proximity to Silverwood Lake—which is only 15 minutes away but does not have any sites with hookups. The sites here are well spaced, but the nearby "river" is usually dry. The elevation is 3,000 feet.

RV sites, facilities: There are 25 sites, seven drive-through, with full hookups (30 amps) for RVs, 25 sites for RVs or tents, 30 sites for tents only, and four group sites. Picnic tables and fire grills are provided. Restrooms, drinking water, flush toilets, showers, limited cell phone reception, and an RV dump station are available. An ATM is within 10 miles. Leashed pets are permitted.

Reservations, fees: Reservations are accepted. The fees are $10 per night for tent sites and $15 per night for RV sites with hookups, plus $5 per night for each additional vehicle and $1 per pet per night. Open year-round.

Directions: Drive on I-15 to Cajon Junction (north of San Bernardino) and the exit for Highway 138 (Silverwood). Take that exit east and drive nine miles to a fork with Highway 173. Bear left at the fork on Highway 173 and drive six miles to the park on the right.

Contact: Mojave River Forks Regional Park, 760/389-2322.

9 MESA

Rating: 6

on Silverwood Lake
See map pages 798–799

This state park campground is on the west side

of Silverwood Lake at 3,355 feet in elevation, bordered by San Bernardino National Forest to the south and high desert to the north. The hot weather and proximity to San Bernardino make it a winner with boaters, who have 1,000 surface acres of water and 13 miles of shoreline to explore. It's a great lake for water-skiing (35 mph speed limit), water sports (5 mph speed limit in coves), and windsurfing, with afternoon winds usually strong in the spring and early summer. Note that the quota on boats is enforced, with a maximum of 175 boats per day, and that boat launch reservations are required on summer weekends and holidays. There are also designated areas for boating, water-skiing, and fishing, to reduce conflicts. Fishing varies dramatically according to season, with trout planted in the cool months, and largemouth bass, bluegill, and striped bass occasionally caught the rest of the year. The park also has a modest trail system with both nature and bike trails. A bonus is that there are also some hike-in/bike-in campsites.

RV sites, facilities: There are 131 sites for RVs up to 32 feet or tents (with a few for RVs up to 60 feet), four hike-in/bike-in sites, and six group sites for 10 to 100 people. Picnic tables and fire rings are provided. Restrooms, drinking water, flush toilets, coin-operated showers, an RV dump station, a boat ramp, a marina, boat rentals, and a store are available. Some facilities are wheelchair-accessible. Leashed pets are permitted.

Reservations, fees: Reserve at 800/444-PARK (800/444-7275) or online at www.reserveamerica.com ($7.50 reservation fee). The fees are $8 per night, $1 per night per camper for hike-in/bike-in sites, $40–75 for group sites. Open year-round.

Directions: Drive on I-15 to Cajon Junction (north of San Bernardino) and the exit for Highway 138 East. Take that exit and drive east on Highway 138 for 13 miles to the park entrance on the right.

Contact: Silverwood Lake State Recreation Area, 760/389-2303 or 760/389-2281.

10 GLEN HELEN REGIONAL PARK

Rating: 4

near Cajon Pass

See map pages 798–799

The centerpieces of Glen Helen Regional Park are two lakes and this campground. The park covers 1,340 acres in the rolling hills at the mouth of Cajon Pass. The ponds are stocked with trout in winter and with catfish in summer, and bass are also occasionally caught. Both lakes are set up for shore fishing, with no boats allowed on the lakes, except for those little paddleboats, and no swimming or water contact is permitted. Two 350-foot water slides for kids are a great bonus. A major obtrusive problem is the location of the campground, actually set just across the street from the park, near both the freeway and railroad tracks. That's right, drivers in passing cars can actually see you, and at night, passing trains feel and sound like the world is ending. This park is home to the Renaissance Pleasure Faire in May and June. The Blockbuster Pavilion is the largest outdoor amphitheater in the United States and can accommodate up to 65,000 people at major events. An OHV park is also nearby.

RV sites, facilities: There are 48 sites, some drive-through, for RVs or tents and two group sites for 50 to 200 people. Picnic tables and fire rings are provided. Restrooms, drinking water, flush toilets, showers, an RV dump station, and a pay phone are on-site. A swimming lagoon, a picnic area with shelters, bait and tackle, pedal boat rentals, and a playground with volleyball, horseshoes, and water slides are nearby. A snack bar is available on weekends. A store and gas station are a half mile away. Some facilities are wheelchair-accessible. Leashed pets are permitted.

Reservations, fees: Reservations are not accepted for individual sites. The fee is $10 per night, plus $1 per pet per night. Reservations are accepted for group sites ($10 reservation fee); the fee is $3 per person per night. There is a maximum 14-day stay in any 30-day period. A senior discount is available. Open year-round.

Directions: From San Bernardino, drive north on I-215 for nine miles to the exit for Devore Road. Take that exit and turn west on Devore Road and drive one mile to the campground and the park (adjacent to the interchange for I-15 and I-215).

Contact: Glen Helen Regional Park, 909/887-7540 (reservations), fax 909/887-1359; Blockbuster Pavilion, 909/880-6500 or 909/88-MUSIC (909/886-8742); OHV Park, 909/880-3090.

CALIFORNIA

11 SAN BERNARDINO–CABLE CANYON KOA

Rating: 5

near Silverwood Lake

See map pages 798–799
This KOA camp provides space for tents as well as RVs. It is set at 2,200 feet and is virtually surrounded by national forest. Silverwood Lake to the east provides a nearby side trip. (For information on Silverwood Lake, see the entry for Mesa campground earlier in this chapter.)
RV sites, facilities: There are 155 sites, 65 drive-through, with partial or full hookups for RVs or tents, seven RV rentals, and two camping cabins. Picnic tables are provided. Restrooms, drinking water, flush toilets, showers, a coin-operated laundry, modem access, a playground, a swimming pool, a recreation room, a store, and propane are available. Some facilities are wheelchair-accessible. Leashed pets are permitted.
Reservations, fees: Reservations are accepted at 800/KOA-4155 (800/562-4155). The fees are $19 per night for tent sites and $49 per night for RV sites, plus $2–4 per person for more than two people. Weekday discounts are offered. Major credit cards are accepted. Open year-round.
Directions: From San Bernardino, drive north on I-215 for six miles to the exit for Devore and Devore Road (two miles south of the junction of I-15 and I-215). Take that exit to Devore Road. Turn right and drive to Santa Fe Road. Turn right and drive one block to Dement Road. Turn right on Dement Road (which becomes Cable Canyon Road) and continue to the park entrance (1707 Cable Canyon Road).
Contact: San Bernardino–Cable Canyon KOA, 909/887-4098, website: www.sanbernardinokoa .com or www.koa.com.

12 CAMP SWITZERLAND

Rating: 7

near Lake Gregory
See map pages 798–799
Well, it really doesn't look much like Switzerland, but this camp is set in a wooded canyon at 4,500 feet below the dam at little Lake Gregory.

Since it is well below the dam, there are no lake views or even much of a sense that the lake is nearby. Yet it is only a short distance away. Lake Gregory covers just 120 acres, and while no privately owned boats are permitted here, boats can be rented at the marina. No gas motors are permitted at the lake, but electric motors are allowed. It is surrounded by the San Bernardino National Forest. A large swimming beach is available on the south shore (about three-quarters of a mile away) with a water slide and dressing rooms.
RV sites, facilities: There are 30 sites with full hookups for RVs, 10 sites for tents, and two cabins. Picnic tables are provided. Restrooms, drinking water, flush toilets, and coin-operated showers are available. A store and propane are nearby. Leashed pets are permitted, with some restrictions.
Reservations, fees: Reservations are accepted. The fee is $20–25 per night, plus $5 for each additional vehicle and $3 per pet per night. Open year-round, weather permitting.
Directions: Drive on Highway 30 to San Bernardino and Highway 18 (two miles east of the junction of Highway 30 and Highway 259). Turn north on Highway 18/Rim of the World Highway and drive 14 miles to Crestline/Highway 138. Turn north (left) on Highway 138 and drive two miles to Lake Drive. Turn right and drive three miles to the campground entrance (signed, just past the fire station, below the dam at the north end of Lake Gregory).
Contact: Camp Switzerland, P.O. Box 967, Crestline, CA 92325, 909/338-2731.

13 DOGWOOD

Rating: 6

near Lake Arrowhead in San Bernardino National Forest
See map pages 798–799
So close, but yet so far—that's the paradox between Lake Arrowhead and Dogwood. The lake is just a mile away, but no public boating or swimming is permitted and only extremely limited access for shore fishing is permitted, with the lake ringed by gated trophy homes, each worth millions. The elevation is 5,600 feet. Any questions? The rangers at the Arrowhead Ranger Station, about 1.5 miles down the road to the east, can answer them.

CALIFORNIA

RV sites, facilities: There are 90 sites for RVs up to 22 feet or tents. Picnic tables and fire grills are provided. Drinking water, flush toilets, coin-operated showers, and an RV dump station are available. A store and coin-operated laundry are nearby. Some facilities are wheelchair-accessible. Leashed pets are permitted.

Reservations, fees: Reserve at 877/444-6777 or online at www.reserveusa.com ($9 reservation fee). The fee is $20 per night, plus $5 for each additional vehicle. A senior discount is available. Open May through October.

Directions: Drive on Highway 30 to San Bernardino and Highway 18 (two miles east of the junction of Highway 30 and Highway 259). Turn north on Highway 18 and drive 15 miles to Rim of the World Highway. Continue on Highway 18 for .2 mile to Daley Canyon Road. Turn left on Daley Canyon Road and make an immediate right on the Daley Canyon access road. Drive a short distance to the campground entrance on the left.

Contact: San Bernardino National Forest, Mountaintop Ranger Station, 909/337-2444, fax 909/337-1104.

14 NORTH SHORE

Rating: 8

on Lake Arrowhead in San Bernardino National Forest

See map pages 798–799

Of the two camps at Lake Arrowhead, this one is preferable. It is set at 5,300 feet near the northeastern shore of the lake, which provides decent trout fishing in the spring and early summer. To the nearby north, Deep Creek in San Bernardino National Forest is well worth exploring; a hike along the stream to fish for small trout or see a unique set of small waterfalls is highly recommended.

RV sites, facilities: There are 27 sites for RVs up to 22 feet or tents. Picnic tables and fire rings are provided. Drinking water and flush toilets are available. A store and a coin-operated laundry are nearby. Some facilities are wheelchair-accessible. Leashed pets are permitted.

Reservations, fees: Reserve at 877/444-6777 or online at www.reserveusa.com ($9 reservation

fee). The fee is $12 per night, plus $5 per night for each additional vehicle. A senior discount is available. Open May through November.

Directions: Drive on Highway 30 to San Bernardino and Highway 18 (two miles east of the junction of Highway 30 and Highway 259). Turn north on Highway 18/Rim of the World Highway and drive 17 miles to Highway 173. Turn left on Highway 173 and drive north for 1.6 miles to the stop sign. Turn right (still on Highway 173) and drive 2.9 miles to Hospital Road. Turn right and continue .1 mile to the top of the small hill. Turn left just past the hospital entrance and you will see the campground.

Contact: San Bernardino National Forest, Mountaintop Ranger Station, 909/337-2444, fax 909/337-1104.

15 CRAB FLATS

Rating: 4

near Crab Creek in San Bernardino National Forest

See map pages 798–799

Four-wheel-drive cowboys and dirt-bike enthusiasts often make this a base camp, known as a staging area for off-highway vehicles. It is a developed Forest Service camp set at a fork in the road at 6,200 feet. A challenging jeep road and motorcycle trail is available from here, heading west into Deep Creek Canyon. Note that Tent Peg Group Camp is just a half mile to the west on Forest Road 3N34 (hiking trails are available there).

RV sites, facilities: There are 29 sites for RVs up to 15 feet or tents. Drinking water, vault toilets, picnic tables, and fire rings are provided. Leashed pets are permitted.

Reservations, fees: Reserve at 877/444-6777 or online at www.reserveusa.com ($9 reservation fee). The fee is $15 per night. A senior discount is available. Open mid-May through October.

Directions: Drive on Highway 30 to the junction with Highway 330 (east of San Bernardino near Highland). Take Highway 330 North (signed "Mountain Resorts") and drive to Running Springs and the junction with Highway 18. Turn east on Highway 18 and drive to Green Valley Road. Turn left on Green Valley Road and drive

CALIFORNIA

three miles to Forest Road 3N16 (a dirt road). Turn left and drive four miles (you will cross two creeks that vary in depth depending on season; high clearance is recommended but is typically not necessary) to an intersection. Bear left at the intersection and drive a very short distance to the campground entrance on the right.

Contact: San Bernardino National Forest, Mountaintop Ranger Station, 909/337-2444, fax 909/337-1104.

16 GREEN VALLEY

Rating: 7

near Green Valley Lake in San Bernardino National Forest
See map pages 798–799

This camp sits along pretty Green Valley Creek at an elevation of 7,000 feet. Little Green Valley Lake is a mile to the west. The lake is stocked with trout by the Department of Fish and Game and is also a good spot to take a flying leap and belly flop.

RV sites, facilities: There are 37 sites for RVs up to 22 feet or tents. Picnic tables and fire grills are provided. Drinking water and flush toilets are available. A store and coin-operated laundry are nearby. Leashed pets are permitted.

Reservations, fees: Reservations may be made at 877/444-6777 or online at www.reserveusa.com ($9 reservation fee). The fee is $15 per night, plus $5 per night for each additional vehicle. Open May through October.

Directions: Drive on Highway 30 to the junction with Highway 330 (east of San Bernardino near Highland). Take Highway 330 North (signed "Mountain Resorts") and drive to Running Springs and the junction with Highway 18. Turn east on Highway 18 and drive to Green Valley Road. Turn left on Green Valley Road and drive three miles to Forest Road 3N16 (a dirt road). Turn left and drive four miles (you will cross two creeks that vary in depth depending on season; high clearance is recommended but is typically not necessary) to the campground (one mile past the town of Green Valley Lake).

Contact: San Bernardino National Forest, Mountaintop Ranger Station, 909/337-2444, fax 909/337-1104.

17 HANNA FLAT

Rating: 8

near Big Bear Lake in San Bernardino National Forest
See map pages 798–799

This is one of the largest, best maintained, and most popular of the Forest Service camps in the Big Bear Lake District (Serrano Campground is the most popular). All the trees and vegetation provide seclusion for individual sites. There is great forest scenery with many hardwood trees, including oak and mountain mahogany. The camp is set at 7,000 feet on the slopes on the north side of Big Bear Lake, just under three miles from the lake. Big Bear is a beautiful mountain lake covering more than 3,000 acres, with 22 miles of shoreline and often excellent trout fishing and water-skiing. A trailhead for the Pacific Crest Trail is a mile by road north of the camp.

RV sites, facilities: There are 19 sites for RVs up to 32 feet or tents and 69 sites for tents. Picnic tables and fire grills are provided. Drinking water and flush toilets are available. Some facilities are wheelchair-accessible. Leashed pets are permitted.

Reservations, fees: Reserve at 877/444-6777 or online at www.reserveusa.com ($9 reservation fee). The fee is $15 per night, plus $5 for a second vehicle. A senior discount is available. Open May through September.

Directions: Drive on Highway 30 to the junction with Highway 330 (east of San Bernardino near Highland). Take Highway 330 North (signed "Mountain Resorts") and drive 35 miles to the dam on Big Bear Lake and a fork for Highway 38. Take the left fork to Highway 38 and drive about four miles to the town of Fawnskin and Rim of the World Highway. Turn left and drive three miles (after .5 mile, it becomes Forest Road 3N14, a dirt road) to the campground on the left.

Contact: San Bernardino National Forest, Big Bear Ranger District Discovery Center, 909/866-3437, fax 909/866-1781.

CALIFORNIA

18 SERRANO
♟ ≋ ⬛ ⛵ 🐕 ♿ 🚐 ⛺

Rating: 8

on Big Bear Lake in San Bernardino National Forest
See map pages 798–799
This campground opened in the 1990s and became the first National Forest campground to offer state-of-the-art restrooms and hot showers. That is why it costs so much to camp here. Regardless, it has since become the most popular campground in the region. Location is also a big plus, as this is one of the few camps at Big Bear within walking distance of the lakeshore. It covers 60 acres, a big plus. Another bonus is a paved trail that is wheelchair-accessible. Want more? Big Bear is the jewel of Southern California lakes, the Lake Tahoe of the South, with outstanding trout fishing and water-skiing. A trailhead for the Pacific Crest Trail is nearby, and Canada is only 2,200 miles away. The elevation is 6,800 feet.

RV sites, facilities: There are 132 sites, 30 sites with full hookups, for RVs up to 36 feet or tents. Picnic tables and fire rings are provided. Restrooms, drinking water, flush toilets, showers, and an RV dump station are available. A store is nearby. Some facilities are wheelchair-accessible. Leashed pets are permitted.

Reservations, fees: Reserve at 877/444-6777 or online at www.reserveusa.com ($9 reservation fee). The fee is $20 per night or $40 per night for double sites. A senior discount is available. Open mid-April to mid-November.

Directions: Drive on Highway 30 to the junction with Highway 330 (east of San Bernardino near Highland). Take Highway 330 North (signed "Mountain Resorts") and drive 35 miles to the dam on Big Bear Lake and a fork with Highway 38 and Highway 18. Bear left at Highway 38 and drive about 2.5 miles to Fawnskin and North Shore Lane (signed Serrano Campground). Turn on North Shore Lane and drive to the campground entrance.

Contact: San Bernardino National Forest, Big Bear Ranger District Discovery Center, 909/866-3437, fax 909/866-1781.

19 YUCAIPA REGIONAL PARK
♟ ≋ ⬛ 🐕 ♿ 🚐 ⛺

Rating: 7

near Redlands
See map pages 798–799
This is a great family-oriented county park, complete with water slides and paddleboats for the kids and fishing access and hiking trails for adults. Three lakes are stocked weekly with catfish in the summer and trout in the winter, the closest thing around to an insurance policy for anglers. Spectacular scenic views of the Yucaipa Valley, the San Bernardino Mountains, and Mount San Gorgonio are possible from the park. The park covers 885 acres in the foothills of the San Bernardino Mountains. A one-acre swimming lagoon and two 350-foot water slides make this a favorite for youngsters. The Yucaipa Adobe and Mousley Museum of Natural History is nearby.

RV sites, facilities: There are 26 sites, 18 drive-through and 11 with full hookups (20, 50 amps), for RVs, nine sites for tents, and nine group camps. Picnic tables and fire rings are provided. Restrooms, drinking water, flush toilets, and showers are available. A swimming lagoon, fishing ponds, water slides, paddleboat rentals, aquacycle rentals, a pay phone, cell phone reception, a snack bar, a picnic shelter, a playground with volleyball and horseshoes, and an RV dump station are also available. An ATM is within one mile. The water slide is open Memorial Day weekend through Labor Day weekend. Some facilities are wheelchair-accessible. Leashed pets are permitted.

Reservations, fees: Reservations are accepted. The fees are $13 per night for tent sites and $22 per night for RV sites, plus $1 per pet per night. Major credit cards are accepted. There are additional charges for fishing, swimming, and use of the water slide. Open year-round.

Directions: Drive on I-10 to Redlands and the exit for Yucaipa Boulevard. Take that exit and drive east on Yucaipa Boulevard to Oak Glen Road. Turn left and continue two miles to the park on the left.

Contact: Yucaipa Regional Park, 909/790-3127, fax 909/790-3121, website: www.co.san-bernardino.ca.us/parks.

CALIFORNIA

20 HOLLOWAY'S MARINA AND RV PARK

Rating: 6

on Big Bear Lake
See map pages 798–799

This privately operated RV park (no tent sites) is a good choice at Big Bear Lake, the jewel of Southern California's lakes, with more than 3,000 surface acres and 22 miles of shoreline. Its cool waters make for excellent trout fishing, and yet, by summer, it has heated up enough to make for superb water-skiing. A bonus in the summer is that a breeze off the lake keeps the temperature in the mid-80s.

RV sites, facilities: There are 100 sites with full hookups (20, 30, 50 amps) for RVs. Picnic tables and fire grills are provided. Restrooms, drinking water, flush toilets, showers, an RV dump station, cable TV, limited cell phone reception, a convenience store, ice, propane, a coin-operated laundry, a playground, and a full marina with boat rentals, and a ramp are on the premises. An ATM is within 1.5 miles. Leashed pets are permitted.

Reservations, fees: Reservations are accepted. The fee is $40–50 per night, plus $5 for each additional vehicle. Major credit cards are accepted. Open year-round, weather permitting.

Directions: Drive on Highway 30 to the junction with Highway 330 (east of San Bernardino near Highland). Take Highway 330 North (signed "Mountain Resorts") and drive 35 miles to the dam on Big Bear Lake and a fork with Highway 38 and Highway 18 (at Running Springs). Turn right at Highway 18 and drive three miles to Edgemoor Road (at a log cabin restaurant). Turn left at Edgemoor Road and drive .5 mile to the park on the left.

Contact: Holloway's Marina and RV Park, 909/866-5706 or 800/448-5335, fax 909/866-5436.

21 PINEKNOT

Rating: 6

near Big Bear Lake in San Bernardino National Forest
See map pages 798–799

This popular, developed Forest Service camp is just east of Big Bear Lake Village (on the southern shore of the lake) about two miles from the lake. It is a popular spot for mountain biking, with several ideal routes available. Of the camps at Big Bear, this is the closest to supplies. The elevation is 7,000 feet.

RV sites, facilities: There are 52 sites for RVs up to 45 feet or tents. Picnic tables and fire grills are provided. Drinking water and flush toilets are available. A store and coin-operated laundry are nearby. Some facilities are wheelchair-accessible. Leashed pets are permitted.

Reservations, fees: Reserve at 877/444-6777 or online at www.reserveusa.com ($9 reservation fee). The fee is $18 per night. A senior discount is available. Open mid-May through September.

Directions: Drive on Highway 30 to the junction with Highway 330 (east of San Bernardino near Highland). Take Highway 330 North (signed "Mountain Resorts") and drive 35 miles to the dam on Big Bear Lake and a fork with Highway 38 and Highway 18. Turn right at Highway 18 and drive about six miles to Summit Boulevard. Turn right and drive through the parking area to the road on the left (just before the gate to the ski area). Turn left and drive .25 mile to the campground on the right.

Contact: San Bernardino National Forest, Big Bear Ranger District Discovery Center, 909/866-3437, fax 909/866-1781.

22 BARTON FLATS

Rating: 7

near Jenks Lake in San Bernardino National Forest
See map pages 798–799

This is one of the more developed Forest Service camps in San Bernardino National Forest. The camp is set at 6,500 feet near the northwest end of Jenks Lake, a small, pretty lake with good hiking and a picnic area. Barton Creek, a small stream, runs nearby although it may be waterless in late summer. The San Gorgonio Wilderness, one mile to the south, is accessible via Forest Service roads to the wilderness area trailhead. Permits are required for overnight camping within the wilderness boundaries and are available at Forest Service ranger stations. For those driving

CALIFORNIA

in on Highway 38, stop at the Mill Creek Ranger Station in Redlands.

RV sites, facilities: There are 52 sites for RVs up to 55 feet. Picnic tables and fire grills are provided. Drinking water and flush toilets are available. Some facilities are wheelchair-accessible. Leashed pets are permitted.

Reservations, fees: Reserve at 877/444-6777 or online at www.reserveusa.com ($9 reservation fee). The fee is $20 per night or $30 for multi-family sites, plus $5 for each additional vehicle. A senior discount is available. Open mid-May through October.

Directions: Drive on I-10 to Redlands and Highway 38. Take Highway 38 northeast and drive 27.5 miles to the campground on the left.

Contact: San Bernardino National Forest, Mill Creek Ranger Station, 909/794-1123, fax 909/794-1125.

23 SAN GORGONIO

Rating: 7

near the San Gorgonio Wilderness in San Bernardino National Forest
See map pages 798–799

San Gorgonio is one in a series of Forest Service camps along Highway 38 near Jenks Lake. (See the prior entry for Barton Flats for details.) The elevation is 6,500 feet.

RV sites, facilities: There are 54 sites for RVs up to 55 feet. Picnic tables and fire grills are provided. Restrooms, drinking water, flush toilets, and showers are available. Some facilities are wheelchair-accessible. Leashed pets are permitted.

Reservations, fees: Reserve at 877/444-6777 or online at www.reserveusa.com ($9 reservation fee). The fee is $20 per night or $30 for multi-family sites, plus $5 for each additional vehicle. A senior discount is available. Open mid-May through October.

Directions: Drive on I-10 to Redlands and Highway 38. Take Highway 38 northeast and drive 28 miles to the campground.

Contact: San Bernardino National Forest, Mill Creek Ranger Station, 909/794-1123, fax 909/794-1125.

24 SOUTH FORK

Rating: 7

near the Santa Ana River in San Bernardino National Forest
See map pages 798–799

This is an easy-access Forest Service camp just off Highway 38, set at 6,400 feet near the headwaters of the South Fork Santa Ana River. It is part of the series of camps in the immediate area, just north of the San Gorgonio Wilderness. This one is a four-mile drive from little Jenks Lake. (See the entry in this chapter for Barton Flats for more details.)

RV sites, facilities: There are 24 sites for RVs up to 30 feet or tents. Picnic tables and fire rings are provided. Drinking water and vault toilets are available. Leashed pets are permitted.

Reservations, fees: Reservations are not accepted. The fee is $15 per night, plus $5 for each additional vehicle. Open mid-May through mid-October.

Directions: Drive on I-10 to Redlands and Highway 38. Take Highway 38 northeast and drive 29.5 miles to the campground entrance road.

Contact: San Bernardino National Forest, Mill Creek Ranger Station, 909/794-1123, fax 909/794-1125.

25 HEART BAR FAMILY CAMP

Rating: 4

in San Bernardino National Forest
See map pages 798–799

It's a good thing there is drinking water at this camp. Why? Because Heart Bar Creek often isn't much more than a trickle and can't be relied on for water. The camp is set at 6,900 feet near Big Meadows, the location of the Heart Bar Fire Station. A challenging butt-kicker of a hike has a trailhead about a half mile away to the north off a spur road, midway between the camp and the fire station. The trail here is routed along Wildhorse Creek to Sugarloaf Mountain (9,952 feet, about eight or nine miles one-way to the top). Insider's note: just past the midway point on the trail to Sugarloaf Mountain is a trail camp on Wildhorse Creek.

RV sites, facilities: There are 95 sites for RVs up to 50 feet or tents. Picnic tables and fire grills are provided. Drinking water and vault toilets are available. Some facilities are wheelchair-accessible. Leashed pets are permitted.

Reservations, fees: Reserve at 877/444-6777 or online at www.reserveusa.com ($9 reservation fee). The fee is $15 per night for single family sites or $25 for multifamily sites. Open May through November.

Directions: Drive on I-10 to Redlands and Highway 38. Take Highway 38 northeast and drive 33.5 miles to Forest Road 1N02. Turn right and drive a mile to the campground (adjacent to Skyline Group Campground).

Contact: San Bernardino National Forest, Mill Creek Ranger Station, 909/794-1123, fax 909/794-1125.

26 LEO CARRILLO STATE PARK

Rating: 8

north of Malibu

See map pages 798–799

The camping area at this state park is set in a nearby canyon, and reservations are essential for these canyon sites during the summer. Giant sycamores shade the campsites. The Nicholas Flat Trail provides an excellent hike to the Willow Creek Overlook for beautiful views of the beach. In addition, a pedestrian tunnel provides access to a wonderful coastal spot with sea caves, tunnels, tidepools, and patches of beach. This park features 1.5 miles of beach for swimming, surfing, and surf fishing. In the summer, lifeguards are posted at the beach. Many will remember a beach camp that was once popular here. Well, that sucker is gone, wiped out by a storm.

RV sites, facilities: There are 127 sites for RVs up to 31 feet or tents, one hike-in/bike-in site for up to 24 people, and one group tent site for up to 50 people. Picnic tables and fire rings are provided. Restrooms, drinking water, flush toilets, coin-operated showers, an RV dump station, a visitors center, summer programs, and a summer convenience store are available. The front gates close at 10 P.M. and reopen at 8 A.M. Some facilities are wheelchair-accessible. Leashed pets are permitted.

Reservations, fees: Reserve at 800/444-PARK (800/444-7275) or online at www.reserveamerica .com ($7.50 reservation fee). The fees are $12 per night, $1 per person per night for the hike-in/bike-in site, $37 for the group tent site. A senior discount is available. Open year-round.

Directions: From Santa Monica, drive north on Highway 1 for 28 miles north to the park entrance (signed) on the right.

From Oxnard, drive south on Highway 1 for 20 miles to the park entrance (signed) on the left.

Contact: Leo Carrillo State Beach, 818/880-0350, fax 818/880-6165.

27 MALIBU CREEK STATE PARK

Rating: 9

near Malibu

See map pages 798–799

If you plan on staying here, be sure to get your reservation in early. This 6,600-acre state park is just a few miles out of Malibu between Highway 1 and U.S. 101, two major thoroughfares for vacationers. Despite its popularity, the park manages to retain a natural setting, with miles of trails for hiking, biking, and horseback riding, and inspiring scenic views. The park offers 15 miles of streamside trail through oak and sycamore woodlands and also some chaparral covered slopes. It is an ideal spot for a break on a coastal road trip. This park was once used as a setting for the filming of some movies and TV shows, including *Planet of the Apes* and *M*A*S*H*.

RV sites, facilities: There are 63 sites for self-contained RVs up to 24 feet or tents and a group tent site for up to 50 people. Picnic tables are provided. No wood fires are permitted in the summer, but propane or charcoal barbecues are allowed. Restrooms, drinking water, flush toilets, and coin-operated showers are available. Some facilities are wheelchair-accessible. Leashed pets are permitted, but only in the campground area.

Reservations, fees: Reserve at 800/444-PARK (800/444-7275) or online at www.reserveamerica .com ($7.50 reservation fee). The fees are $12 per night and $45 per night for the group site. A senior discount is available. Open year-round.

Directions: From U.S. 101: Drive on U.S. 101 to the exit for Las Virgenes Canyon Road (on the

CALIFORNIA

western border of Calabasas). Take that exit south and drive on Las Virgenes Canyon Road/County Road N1 for four miles to the park entrance on the right.

From Highway 1: Drive on Highway 1 to Malibu and Malibu Canyon Road. Turn north on Malibu Canyon Road and drive north for 5.5 miles (the road becomes Las Virgenes Canyon Road/County Road N1) to the park entrance on the left.

Contact: Malibu Creek State Park, 818/880-0367, fax 818/880-6165.

28 MALIBU BEACH RV PARK

Rating: 7

in Malibu

See map pages 798-799

This is one of the few privately developed RV parks in the region that provides some sites for tent campers as well. It's one of the nicer spots in the area, set on a bluff overlooking the Pacific Ocean, near both Malibu Pier (for fishing) and Paradise Cove. Each site has a view of either the ocean or adjacent mountains. Sites with ocean views are charged a small premium.

RV sites, facilities: There are 140 sites, five drive-through, with partial or full hookups for RVs and 50 sites for tents. Picnic tables and barbecue grills are provided. Restrooms, showers, a hot tub, a recreation room, a playground, a coin-operated laundry, modem access, propane, ice, cable TV, an RV dump station, and a store are available. Some facilities are wheelchair-accessible. Leashed pets are permitted, except in the tent area.

Reservations, fees: Reservations are recommended at 800/622-6052. The fees are $29–47 for RV sites and $20–23 for tent sites, plus $3 per person for more than two people. Reduced rates are offered in winter. Major credit cards are accepted. Open year-round.

Directions: Drive on Pacific Coast Highway/Highway 1 to the Malibu area. The park is two miles north of the intersection of Highway 1 and Malibu Canyon Road on the east side of the road.

Contact: Malibu Beach RV Park, 310/456-6052, fax 310/456-2532, website: www.MalibuRv.com.

29 POMONA-FAIRPLEX KOA
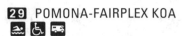

Rating: 4

in Pomona

See map pages 798-799

This is what you might call an urban RV park. Then again, the L.A. County Fairgrounds are right across the street, and there's something going on there every weekend. Fishing at Bonelli Park is only 15 minutes away.

RV sites, facilities: There are 159 drive-through sites with full hookups for RVs and 27 sites with partial hookups for RVs. Restrooms, showers, a heated pool and spa, a convenience store, an RV dump station, and a coin-operated laundry are available. Some facilities are wheelchair-accessible.

Reservations, fees: Reservations are accepted. The fee is $33–40 per night, plus $1 for each additional vehicle and $4 per person for more than two people. Major credit cards are accepted. Open year-round.

Directions: Drive on I-10 to the exit for Fairplex (five miles west of Pomona). Take that exit north (toward the mountain) and drive two miles to McKinley Avenue. Turn right on McKinley Avenue and drive one mile to White Avenue. Turn left and drive about .5 mile (.2 mile south of Arrow Street) to the park on the right (2200 N. White Avenue).

Contact: Pomona-Fairplex KOA, 909/865-4318 or 909/593-8915, website: www.fairplexkoa.com or www.koa.com.

30 EAST SHORE RV PARK

Rating: 7

at Puddingstone Lake

See map pages 798-799

Considering how close Puddingstone Lake is to so many people, the quality of fishing and water-skiing might be a surprise to newcomers. The lake covers 250 acres and is an excellent recreation facility. For the most part, rules permit water-skiing between 10 A.M. and 4 P.M., making it an excellent lake for fishing for bass and trout (in season) during the morning and evening. In addition, even days are set for water-skiing and boating (but no personal watercraft), and odd days for personal watercraft. A ski beach is available on the north shore, and there is a large, sandy swimming beach on the southwest shore about a mile away. The lake is just south of Raging Waters in San Dimas and is bordered to the south by Bonelli Regional County Park; there is also a golf course adjacent to the park. The park is within one mile of the L.A. County Fairgrounds.

RV sites, facilities: There are 519 sites, 14 drive-through, with full hookups (20, 30, 50 amps) for RVs, and 25 walk-in sites for tents. Restrooms, showers, a recreation room, a swimming pool, modem access, cell phone reception, an ATM, cable TV, a store, propane delivery, and a coin-operated laundry are available. A hot tub facility is nearby. Some facilities are wheelchair-accessible. Leashed pets are permitted.

Reservations, fees: Reservations are accepted. The fee is $32–34 per night, plus $2 per person for more than two people and $2 per pet per night. A senior discount is available. Major credit cards are accepted. Open year-round.

Directions: Drive on I-10 to the exit for Fairplex (five miles west of Pomona). Take that exit north to Via Verde (the first traffic light). Turn left on Via Verde and drive to the first stop sign at Campers View. Turn right on Campers View and drive into the park.

Contact: East Shore RV Park, 909/599-8355 or 800/809-3778, fax 909/592-7481, website: www.eastshorervpark.com.

31 DOCKWEILER BEACH RV PARK

Rating: 6

on the Pacific Ocean near Manhattan Beach
See map pages 798–799

This layover spot for coast cruisers is just a hop from the beach and the Pacific Ocean. Access to a 26-mile-long coastal bike path is a plus.

RV sites, facilities: There are 117 sites, 82 with full hookups (30 amps), for RVs up to 35 feet. Picnic tables and barbecue grills are provided. Flush toilets, hot showers, an RV dump station, limited cell phone reception, and a coin-operated laundry are available. An ATM is within one mile. You can buy supplies nearby. Some facilities are wheelchair-accessible. Leashed pets are permitted.

Reservations, fees: Reserve weekdays from 9a.m. to 5p.m. at 800/950-7275 ($7 reservation fee). The fee is $17–27 per night, plus $6 for more than one vehicle and $1 per pet per night. Major credit cards are accepted. Open year-round.

Directions: From Santa Monica and the junction of I-405 and I-10, take I-405 south and drive 12 miles to the exit for Imperial Highway West. Take that exit and drive west on Imperial Highway for four miles to the park (signed) on the left.

Contact: Dockweiler Beach RV Park, Los Angeles County, 310/322-4951 or 800/950-7275, fax 310/322-7036.

32 RANCHO JURUPA COUNTY PARK

Rating: 4

near Riverside
See map pages 798–799

Lord, it gets hot in the summertime, but there is shade and grass here amid cottonwood trees and meadows. This county park stocks a fishing pond, providing trout in the winter and catfish in the summer. Summer is also the best time to explore the park's hiking and equestrian trails. Shaded picnic sites are a plus. Summer visitors will find that the nearest lake for swimming and water sports is Lake Perris, about a 20-minute drive away. The elevation is 780 feet.

RV sites, facilities: There are 72 sites, 12 with full hookups (30 amps), for RVs or tents. Picnic tables and fire grills are provided. Drinking water, flush toilets, showers, cell phone reception, and an RV dump station are available. An ATM is within two miles. Some facilities are wheelchair-accessible. Leashed pets are permitted.

Reservations, fees: Reservations are accepted at 800/234-7275. The fee is $16–18 per night, plus a $5-per-rod fishing fee and a $2 pet fee. Major credit cards are accepted. Open year-round.

Directions: Drive on I-215 to Riverside and Highway 60. Take Highway 60 east and drive seven miles to Rubidoux Boulevard. Turn left on Rubidoux Boulevard and drive .5 mile to Mission Boulevard. Turn left on Mission Boulevard and drive about a mile to Crestmore Road. Turn right and drive 1.5 miles to the park gate on the left (4800 Crestmore Road).

CALIFORNIA

Contact: Rancho Jurupa County Park, 909/684-7032, fax 909/955-4305.

33 BOGART COUNTY PARK

Rating: 4

in Cherry Valley
See map pages 798–799

This county park is overlooked by many vacationers on I-10, and it is as pretty as it gets for this area. There are two miles of horse trails and some hiking trails for a recreation option during the cooler months. It covers 414 acres of Riverside County foothills set at the north end of Cherry Valley. The elevation is 2,800 feet.

RV sites, facilities: There are 38 sites for RVs or tents, a group campground, and an equestrian campground. Fire grills and picnic tables are provided. Drinking water, flush toilets, and a playground are available. Supplies are available in Beaumont. Leashed pets are permitted.

Reservations, fees: Reservations are not accepted for individual sites. The fee is $12 per night, plus $2 per pet per night. Reservations are required for groups at 800/234-7275 ($6.50–12 reservation fee). Open year-round.

Directions: Drive on I-10 to Beaumont and the exit for Beaumont Avenue. Take that exit north and drive four miles to Brookside. Turn right and drive .5 mile to Cherry Avenue. Turn left at Cherry Avenue and drive to the park on the right (9600 Cherry Avenue).

Contact: Bogart County Park, 909/845-3818.

34 ANAHEIM VACATION PARK

Rating: 1

near Knott's Berry Farm
See map pages 798–799

Some of the most popular RV parks in America are in this area, and it's easy to see why. Knott's Berry Farm is within walking distance (five blocks) and Disneyland is nearby. Plus, where else are you going to park your rig? The park has a western theme.

RV sites, facilities: There are 222 sites, 88 drive-through with full hookups (20, 30, 50 amps), for RVs up to 53 feet, and seven sites for tents with barbecues. Restrooms, showers, a spa, satellite TV, cell phone reception, phone and modem access, a swimming pool, a coin-operated laundry, a store, an ATM, a recreation room, and propane are available. A round-trip shuttle service is available to Disneyland for $2. Leashed pets are permitted.

Reservations, fees: Reservations are recommended. The fee is $35–50 for RV sites and $25 for tent sites, plus $2.50 per person for more than two people. Major credit cards are accepted. Open year-round.

Directions: Drive on I-5 to Anaheim and the Beach Boulevard exit. Take that exit south and drive on Beach Boulevard for two miles to the park on the right.

Contact: Anaheim Vacation Park, 714/821-4311, fax 714/761-1743, website: www.anaheimrv.com.

35 TRAVELERS WORLD RV PARK

Rating: 1

near Disneyland
See map pages 798–799

This is one of the most popular RV parks for visitors to Disneyland and other nearby attractions. It is easy to see why, with the park just a half mile from Disneyland. A shuttle service is a great bonus, with buses to Knott's Berry Farm, the Wax Museum, Universal Studios, Marineland, and the *Queen Mary.*

RV sites, facilities: There are 335 sites for RVs or tents with full hookups. Picnic tables and fire grills are provided. Restrooms, showers, a playground, an adult lounge/game room, a swimming pool, a coin-operated laundry, a store, an RV dump station, ice, a recreation room, an RV wash rack, and propane are available. Some facilities are wheelchair-accessible. Leashed pets are permitted.

Reservations, fees: Reservations are required. The fee is $34–38 per night, plus $3 per person for more than two people and $2 per pet. Major credit cards are accepted. Open year-round.

Directions: Drive on I-5 to Anaheim and the exit for Ball Road. Take that exit east and drive to East Vermont Street (from this point, you will be driving in a square in order to make a right turn into the park). Turn right on Vermont and drive to Lemon Street. Turn right on Lemon

Street and drive to Ball Road. Turn right at Ball Road and drive a half block on Ball Road to the park on the right (at 333 W. Ball Road).

Contact: Travelers World RV Park, 714/991-0100, fax 714/991-4939, website: www.travel.to/rv.

36 C. C. CAMPERLAND

Rating: 6

near Disneyland

See map pages 798–799

Camperland is nine blocks south of Disneyland, and that right there is the number-one appeal. Knott's Berry Farm is also close by. This park was renovated in 2002, and in turn, sites have been enlarged and improved, now all with full hookups. The park is clean and quiet, and over 200 trees on the premises offer nice, shaded spaces. The park is one mile from both the Crystal Cathedral and the Anaheim Convention Center.

RV sites, facilities: There are 70 sites with full hookups (30, 50 amps) for RVs or tents. Picnic tables are provided. Restrooms, showers, a solar-heated swimming pool, a coin-operated laundry, an ATM, an RV dump station, and ice are available. Some facilities are wheelchair-accessible. Small, nonaggressive leashed pets are permitted, except in the tent area.

Reservations, fees: Reservations are accepted. The fee is $38–46 per night for RVs and $32 per night for tents, plus $3 per person for more than two people and $3 per pet per night. A senior discount is available. Major credit cards are accepted. Open year-round.

Directions: Drive on I-5 to Garden Grove and the exit for Harbor Boulevard south. Take that exit and drive south on Harbor Boulevard for 1.5 miles to the park on the left (12262 Harbor Boulevard).

Contact: C. C. Camperland, 714/750-6747, website: www.cccamperland.com.

37 ORANGELAND RV PARK

Rating: 1

near Disneyland

See map pages 798–799

This park is about five miles east of Disneyland. If the RV parks on West Street near Disneyland are filled, this is a useful alternative.

RV sites, facilities: There are 212 sites with full hookups (20, 30, 50 amps) for RVs. Picnic tables are provided. Restrooms, showers, a playground, a swimming pool, a therapy pool, an exercise room, a coin-operated laundry, a store, modem access, cell phone reception, an ATM, a car wash, a shuffleboard court, billiards, an RV dump station, ice, and a recreation room are available. Some facilities are wheelchair-accessible. Leashed pets are permitted.

Reservations, fees: Reservations are recommended. The fee is $45–55 per night, plus $2 per person for more than eight people and $1 per pet per night. Major credit cards are accepted. Open year-round.

Directions: Drive on I-5 to Anaheim and the exit for Katella Avenue. Take that exit east for Katella Avenue and drive two miles (Anaheim Stadium and the Santa Ana River) to Struck Avenue. Turn right and drive 200 yards to the park on the right (1600 W. Struck Avenue).

Contact: Orangeland RV Park, 714/633-0414, fax 714/633-9012, website: www.orangeland.com.

38 CANYON RV PARK

Rating: 6

at Featherly Regional Park

See map pages 798–799

This RV park is in Featherly Regional Park, an Orange County park that covers 795 acres. The campground is set in a mature grove of cottonwood and sycamore trees, with natural riparian wildland areas and open spaces nearby. It is near the Santa Ana River (swimming or wading at the lake or creek is prohibited). The Santa Ana River Bicycle Trail runs through this park, which runs from Orange in Riverside County to Huntington Beach and the Pacific Ocean. Side-trip possibilities include Chino Hills State Park to the north, Cleveland National Forest to the south, and Lake Matthews to the southeast. The park is also close to Disneyland and Knott's Berry Farm.

RV sites, facilities: There are 140 sites with partial hookups (20, 30 amps) for RVs up to 40 feet and three cabins. Picnic tables and fire grills are provided. Restrooms, flush toilets, hot showers, modem access, two RV dump stations, a seasonal swimming pool, and a playground are available. A visitors center, summer campfire programs, and guided nature walks are available, and two amphitheaters are on-site. A convenience store, coin-operated laundry, and propane are also available. Restaurants are nearby. Some facilities are wheelchair-accessible. Leashed pets are permitted, with some restrictions.

Reservations, fees: Reservations are accepted. The fee is $35 per night, plus $5 for each additional vehicle, $2 per person for more than two people, and $1 per pet per night. Major credit cards are accepted. Open year-round.

Directions: Drive on I-5 to Highway 91 in Anaheim. Take Highway 91 east and drive 13 miles to the exit for Gypsum Canyon Road. Take that exit to Gypsum Canyon Road. Turn left, drive under the freeway, and drive about one block to the park entrance on the left.

Contact: Canyon RV Park, 714/637-0210, fax 714/637-9317, website: www.canyonrvpark.com or www.ocparks.com.

39 PRADO REGIONAL PARK

Rating: 6

on Prado Park Lake near Corona
See map pages 798–799

Prado Park Lake is the centerpiece of a 2,280-acre recreation-oriented park that features an equestrian center, athletic fields, a shooting range, and a golf course. The lake is small and used primarily for paddling small boats and fishing, which is best in the winter and early spring when trout are planted, and then in early summer for catfish and bass. The shooting facility is outstanding, the site of the 1984 Olympic shooting venue.

RV sites, facilities: There are 35 sites, most drive-through, with full hookups (50 amps) for RVs, 15 tent sites, and 25 group sites. Picnic tables and fire pits are provided. Restrooms, a coin-operated laundry, showers, a pay phone, cell phone reception, a snack bar, a picnic area, playing fields, a boat ramp, a bait shop, and boat rentals are available. A playing field with softball, soccer, and horseshoes is on-site. Some facilities are wheelchair-accessible. Leashed pets are permitted.

Reservations, fees: Reservations are accepted ($2

reservation fee). The fee is $20 per night, plus $1 per pet per night. Long-term rates are available. Proof of insurance for all vehicles is required. Major credit cards are accepted. Open year-round.

Directions: Drive on Highway 91 to Highway 71 (west of Norco and Riverside). Take Highway 71 north and drive four miles to Highway 83/Euclid Avenue. Turn right on Euclid Avenue and drive a mile to the park entrance on the right.

Contact: Prado Regional Park, 909/597-4260, fax 909/393-8428, website: www.san-bernardino.ca.us/parks/prado.

40 LAKE PERRIS STATE RECREATION AREA

Rating: 7

on Lake Perris
See map pages 798–799

Lake Perris is a great recreation lake with first-class fishing for spotted bass and, in the summer, it's an excellent destination for boating and water sports. It is set at 1,500 feet in Moreno Valley, just southwest of the Badlands foothills. The lake has a roundish shape, covering 2,200 acres, with an island that provides a unique boat-in picnic site. There are large ski beaches on the northeast and southeast shores and a designated sailing cove on the northwest side, an ideal spot for windsurfing and sailing. Swimming is also excellent, but it's allowed only at the developed beaches a short distance from the campground. The recreation area covers 8,300 acres and includes 11 miles of paved bike trails, including a great route that circles the lake, 15 miles of equestrian trails, and five miles of hiking trails. Summer campfire and Junior Ranger programs are available. There is also a special area for scuba diving, and a rock-climbing area is just south of the dam.

RV sites, facilities: There are 254 sites with partial hookups for RVs up to 31 feet or tents, 177 sites for tents only, seven primitive horse camps with corrals and water troughs, six group sites for 25 to 85 people each without hookups, and one hike-in/bike-in site. Picnic tables and fire grills are available. Restrooms, drinking water, flush toilets, coin-operated showers, an RV dump station, a playground, a convenience store, two swimming beaches, a boat launch, mooring, and

CALIFORNIA

boat rentals are available. Some facilities are wheelchair-accessible. Leashed pets are permitted, except near the water.

Reservations, fees: Reserve at 800/444-PARK (800/444-7275) or online at www.reserveamerica .com ($7.50 reservation fee) for individual sites and equestrian sites. The fees are $8–14 per night, $12 per night for equestrian sites, and $1 per person per night for hike-in/bike-in site. Reserve group sites at 909/657-0676; the fee is $60 per night. A senior discount is available. Open year-round.

Directions: From Riverside, drive southeast on Highway 215/60 for about five miles to the 215/60 split. Bear south on 215 at the split and drive six miles to Ramona Expressway. Turn left (east) and drive 3.5 miles to Lake Perris Drive. Turn left and drive .75 mile to the park entrance.

Contact: Lake Perris State Recreation Area, 909/657-0676 or 909/940-5603.

41 PINE RANCH RV PARK

Rating: 2

in Banning
See map pages 798–799

Banning may not seem like a hotbed of civilization at first glance, but this clean, comfortable park is a good spot to make camp while exploring some of the area's hidden attractions, including Agua Caliente Indian Canyons and the Lincoln Shrine. It is set at 2,400 feet, 22 miles from Palm Springs. A good side trip is to head south on curving "Highway" 240 up to Vista Point in the San Bernardino National Forest.

RV sites, facilities: There are 106 sites, most drive-through and many with full hookups (30 amps), for RVs. Picnic tables and fire grills are provided. Restrooms, showers, a playground, a swimming pool, a coin-operated laundry, modem access, cell phone reception, cable TV, an RV dump station, ice, horseshoes, and propane are available. An ATM is within two miles. Leashed pets are permitted.

Reservations, fees: Reservations are not accepted. The fee is $23 per night, plus $2 per person for more than two people and $1 per additional vehicle. Major credit cards are accepted. Open year-round.

Directions: Drive on I-10 to Banning and the exit

for Highway 243. Take that exit south and take 8th Avenue south for one block to Lincoln. Turn left on Lincoln and drive two blocks to San Gorgonio. Turn right and drive one mile to the park (1455 S. San Gorgonio Avenue).

Contact: Pine Ranch RV Park, 909/849-7513, fax 909/849-7998, website: www.reynoldsresorts.com.

42 GOLDEN VILLAGE PALMS RV RESORT

Rating: 5

in Hemet
See map pages 798–799

This RV resort is for those ages 55 and over. It is the biggest RV park in Southern California, with major renovation planned for completion in 2003. The grounds are lush, with gravel pads for RVs. It is set near Diamond Valley Lake, about 10 miles south, a new lake that will become the largest reservoir in California. A golf course is nearby, Lake Hemet is 20 miles east, and winery tours are available in Temecula, a 30-minute drive. About 250 of the 1,019 sites are rented on a year-round basis.

RV sites, facilities: There are 1,019 sites, 60 drive-through, all with full hookups for RVs up to 45 feet. No tent sites are available. Restrooms, drinking water, flush toilets, showers, cable TV, modem access, telephones, three swimming pools, a recreation room, a fitness center, a billiard room, three spas, a coin-operated laundry, a large clubhouse, banquet and meeting rooms, shuffleboard, a nine-hole putting green, volleyball courts, and horseshoes are available. A day-use area with propane barbecues is also available. Leashed pets are permitted.

Reservations, fees: Reservations are accepted at 800/323-9610. The fee is $33 per night, plus $10 per person for more than two people. Long-term rates are available. Open year-round.

Directions: Drive to the junction of I-215 and Highway 74 (near Perris). At that junction, take Highway 74 east and drive 15 miles to Hemet (the highway becomes Florida Avenue in Hemet) and continue to the resort on the left.

Contact: Golden Village Palms RV Resort, 909/925-2518, website: www.GoldenVillagePalms .com.

CALIFORNIA

43 CASA DEL SOL RV RESORT

Rating: 3

in Hemet

See map pages 798-799

Hemet is a retirement town, so if you want excitement, the three lakes in the area are the best place to look for it: Lake Perris to the northwest, Lake Skinner to the south, and Lake Hemet to the east. Note that many of the sites are taken by year-round or long-term rentals.

RV sites, facilities: There are 358 sites with full hookups (20, 30, 50 amps) for RVs. Restrooms, drinking water, flush toilets, showers, cable TV, cell phone reception, modem access, telephones, a swimming pool, a recreation room, an exercise room, a billiard room, a hot tub, and a coin-operated laundry are available. An ATM is within one block. Leashed pets are permitted.

Reservations, fees: Reservations are accepted at 888/925-2516. The fee is $27 per night, plus $20 for additional vehicle and $2.50 per person for more than two people. Major credit cards are accepted. Open year-round.

Directions: Drive to the junction of I-215 and Highway 74 (near Perris). At that junction, take Highway 74 east and drive 15 miles to Hemet (the highway becomes Florida Avenue in Hemet) and drive to Kirby Avenue. Turn right (south) on Kirby Avenue and drive a half block to the resort (2750 W. Acacia Avenue).

Contact: Casa del Sol RV Resort, 909/925-2515, website: www.CasadelSolrvpark.com.

44 MOUNTAIN VALLEY RV PARK

Rating: 3

in Hemet

See map pages 798-799

This is one of three RV parks in the Hemet area. Three lakes in the area provide side-trip possibilities: Lake Perris to the northwest, Lake Skinner to the south, and Lake Hemet to the east.

RV sites, facilities: There are 170 sites with full hookups (20, 30, 50 amps) for RVs. Restrooms, drinking water, flush toilets, showers, a fireside room, a swimming pool, an enclosed hot tub, a coin-operated laundry, satellite TV, cell phone reception, modem access, a recreation room, and telephone hookups are available. A store, an ATM, restaurants, and propane are nearby. Some facilities are wheelchair-accessible. Leashed pets are permitted.

Reservations, fees: Reservations are accepted at 800/926-5593. The fee is $29 per night, plus $2.50 per person for more than two people and $2 per pet. Major credit cards are accepted. Open year-round.

Directions: Drive to the junction of I-215 and Highway 74 (near Perris). At that junction, take Highway 74 east and drive 15 miles to Hemet (the highway becomes Florida Avenue in Hemet) and continue to Sanderson Avenue. Turn right on Sanderson Avenue and drive one block to Acacia. Turn left and drive to Lyon Avenue. Turn left on Lyon Avenue and drive to the park at the corner of Lyon and South Acacia (235 S. Lyon).

Contact: Mountain Valley RV Park, 909/925-5812, fax 909/658-6272, website: www.mountainValleyrvp.com.

45 IDYLLWILD COUNTY PARK

Rating: 6

near San Bernardino National Forest

See map pages 798-799

This county park covers 202 acres, set at 5,300 feet and surrounded by Mount San Jacinto State Park, San Jacinto Wilderness, and the San Bernardino National Forest lands. That provides plenty of options for visitors. The park has equestrian trails and an interpretive trail. The top hike in the region is the ambitious climb up the western slopes to the top of Mount San Jacinto (10,804 feet), a terrible challenge of a butt-kicker that provides one of the most astounding views in all the land. (The best route, however, is out of Palm Springs, taking the aerial tramway, which will get you to 8,516 feet in elevation before hiking out the rest.)

RV sites, facilities: There are 60 sites for RVs up to 34 feet or tents and 30 sites for RVs only. Fire grills and picnic tables are provided. Restrooms, drinking water, flush toilets, and showers are available. (There is no drinking water in dry years.) A store, coin-operated laundry, and propane are nearby. Some facilities are wheelchair-accessible. Leashed pets are permitted.

Reservations, fees: Reservations are accepted at 800/234-PARK (800/234-7275) ($6.50 reservation fee). The fee is $15 per night, with a six-person maximum per site. Major credit cards are accepted. Open year-round.

Directions: Drive on I-10 to Banning and Highway 243/Idyllwild Panoramic Highway. Turn south on Idyllwild Panoramic Highway and drive to Idyllwild and Riverside County Playground Road. Turn west on Riverside County Playground Road and drive .5 mile (follow the signs) to the park entrance.

Contact: Idyllwild County Park, 909/659-2656.

46 IDYLLWILD

Rating: 8

in Mount San Jacinto State Park
See map pages 798–799

This is a prime spot for hikers and one of the better jump-off points for trekking in the area, set at 5,400 feet. There are no trails from this campground, but a half mile north is the Deer Spring Trail, which is connected with the Pacific Crest Trail and then climbs on to Mount San Jacinto (10,804 feet) and its astounding lookout.

RV sites, facilities: There are 10 sites for RVs up to 18 feet or tents, 11 sites for RVs only up to 24 feet, 11 sites for tents only, and one hike-in/bike-in site. Fire grills and picnic tables are provided. Piped water, flush toilets, and showers are available. Supplies and a coin-operated laundry are nearby (100 yards). Some facilities are wheelchair-accessible. Leashed pets are permitted.

Reservations, fees: Reserve at 800/444-PARK (800/444-7275) or online at www.reserveamerica.com ($7.50 reservation fee). The fees are $12 per night and $1 per person for the hike-in/bike-in site. A senior discount is available. Open year-round.

Directions: In Idyllwild, drive to the north end of town on Highway 243 to the park entrance on the left (next to the fire station).

Contact: Mount San Jacinto State Park, 909/659-2607, website: www.sanjac.statepark.org; Inland Empire District, 909/657-0676.

47 BOLSA CHICA STATE BEACH

Rating: 7

near Huntington Beach
See map pages 798–799

This state beach extends three miles from Seal Beach to north of the Huntington Beach City Pier. A bikeway connects it with Huntington State Beach, seven miles to the south. Across the road from Bolsa Chica is the 1,000-acre Bolsa Chica Ecological Preserve, managed by the Department of Fish and Game. The campground consists of basically a beachfront parking lot, but a popular one at that. A great little walk is available at the adjacent Bolsa Chica State Reserve, a 1.5-mile loop that provides an escape from the parking lot and entry into the 530-acre nature reserve, complete with egrets, pelicans, and many shorebirds. Lifeguard service is available during the summer. This camp has a seven-day maximum stay during the summer, and a 14-day maximum stay during the winter. Surf fishing is popular here for perch, cabezon, small sharks, and croaker. There are also occasional runs of grunion, a small fish that spawns in hordes on the sandy beaches of Southern California.

RV sites, facilities: There are sites with partial hookups (30 amps) available in a parking lot configuration for RVs up to 48 feet. Fire rings are provided. Restrooms, drinking water, flush toilets, coin-operated showers, an RV dump station, cell phone reception, picnic areas, a bicycle trail, and food service (seasonal) are available. An ATM is within three miles. Some facilities are wheelchair-accessible, including a paved ramp for wheelchair access to the beach. Leashed pets are permitted at campsites.

Reservations, fees: Make reservations at 800/444-PARK (800/444-7275) or online at www.reserveamerica.com ($7.50 reservation fee). The fee is $22–26 per night. A senior discount is available. Open year-round.

Directions: Drive on Highway 1 to the park entrance (1.5 miles north of Huntington Beach).

Contact: Bolsa Chica State Beach, 714/846-3460; Huntington State Beach, 714/536-1454.

48 HUNTINGTON CITY BEACH

Rating: 7

on the Pacific Ocean
See map pages 798–799

This RV park will reopen in fall of 2003, likely with major changes in store. One definite change is that partial hookups will be available for RVs, instead of the previous zilch. In the long term, this park is a helpful layover for Highway 1 cruisers. Bolsa Chica State Beach provides an alternative spot to park an RV. The best nearby adventure is the short loop walk at Bolsa Chica State Reserve (see the prior entry for Bolsa Chica State Beach for more information).

RV sites, facilities: There are 150 sites, 50 with partial hookups, for RVs up to 36 feet and tents. Fire rings are provided. Drinking water, flush toilets, and an RV dump station are available. Supplies are available within a mile. No pets are allowed.

Reservations, fees: Open starting fall of 2003. Call for reservations policy. The fee is $15 per night. Open November through April.

Directions: Drive on I-405 to Huntington Beach and the exit for Beach Boulevard. Take that exit west and drive on Beach Boulevard to Highway 1/Pacific Coast Highway. Turn right (north) and drive to 1st Street. Turn left and drive a short distance to the park entrance.

Contact: Huntington City Beach, City Park Headquarters, 714/536-5286.

49 NEWPORT DUNES WATERFRONT RESORT

Rating: 9

in Newport Beach
See map pages 798–799

This privately operated park is set in a pretty spot on the bay, with a beach, boat ramp, and storage area providing bonuses. It is situated on 100 acres of Newport Bay beach, beautiful and private, without public access. It features one mile of beach and a swimming lagoon, double-wide sites, and 24-hour security. Nearby to the west is Corona del Mar State Beach, and to the south, Crystal Cove State Park. The park is five minutes' walking distance from Balboa Island and is next to the largest estuary in California, the Upper Newport Bay Ecological Reserve.

RV sites, facilities: There are 406 sites with full hookups for RVs up to 50 feet or tents. Picnic tables and fire grills are provided. Restrooms, showers, a swimming pool and spa, a waveless saltwater lagoon, a 450-slip marina, satellite TV, planned activities, beach volleyball, a coin-operated laundry, a store, a waterfront restaurant, a fitness room, and a marina with boat launch ramp are available. Kayaking, windsurfing, and sailing lessons and rentals are also available. Some facilities are wheelchair-accessible. Leashed pets are permitted, with some restrictions.

Reservations, fees: Reserve at 800/765-7661 or 800/288-0770. The fee is $30–145 per night, plus $3 per person for more than two people and $7 for each additional vehicle. Major credit cards are accepted. Open year-round.

Directions: Drive on I-405 to the exit for Highway 55. Take that exit south and drive on Highway 55 to Highway 73. Turn south on Highway 73 and drive three miles to the Jamboree Road exit. Take that exit and drive south on Jamboree Road for five miles to Back Bay Drive. Turn right and drive a short distance to the resort on the left.

Contact: Newport Dunes Waterfront Resort, 949/729-3863, fax 949/729-1133, website: www.newportdunes.com.

50 BLUE JAY

Rating: 4

in the Santa Ana Mountains in Cleveland National Forest
See map pages 798–799

The few hikers who know of this spot like it and keep coming back, provided they time their hikes when temperatures are cool. The trailheads to the San Juan Trail and the Chiquito Trail, both of which lead into the backcountry wilderness and the Santa Ana Mountains, are adjacent to the camp. A Forest Service map is strongly advised. The elevation is 3,400 feet.

RV sites, facilities: There are 43 sites for tents or RVs up to 20 feet and 12 sites for tents only. Picnic tables and fire rings are provided. Drinking

CALIFORNIA

water and vault toilets are available. A store is within five miles. Leashed pets are permitted.

Reservations, fees: Reservations are not accepted. The fee is $15 per night with a two-vehicle maximum. A senior discount is available. Open year-round, weather permitting.

Directions: Drive on I-15 to Lake Elsinore and the Central exit to Highway 74 west. Take that exit and drive west on Highway 74 for 12 miles (the road circles the northwest end of Lake Elsinore, then turns right, away from the lake, to enter national forest) to Forest Road 6S05 (North Main Divide Road). Turn right and drive about seven miles to Falcon Group Camp. Continue .25 mile to the campground entrance on the left.

Contact: Cleveland National Forest, Trabuco Ranger District, 909/736-1811, fax 909/736-3002.

51 EL CARISO NORTH CAMPGROUND
🏕 🚐 ⛰

Rating: 5

near Lake Elsinore in Cleveland National Forest

See map pages 798–799

This pretty, shaded spot at 2,600 feet is just inside the border of Cleveland National Forest with Lake Elsinore to the east. On the drive in there are great views to the east, looking down at Lake Elsinore and across the desert country.

RV sites, facilities: There are 24 sites for RVs up to 22 feet or tents. Picnic tables and fire rings are provided. Drinking water and vault toilets are available. Leashed pets are permitted.

Reservations, fees: Reservations are not accepted. The fee is $15 per night with a two-vehicle maximum. A senior discount is available. Open year-round, weather permitting.

Directions: Drive on I-15 to Lake Elsinore and the Central exit to Highway 74 west. Take that exit and drive west on Highway 74 for 12 miles (the road circles the northwest end of Lake Elsinore, then turns right, away from the lake, to enter national forest) to the campground.

Drive on I-5 to San Juan Capistrano and Highway 74/Ortega Highway. Turn east on the Ortega Highway and drive 24 miles northeast (into national forest) to the campground.

Contact: Cleveland National Forest, Trabuco Ranger District, 909/736-1811, fax 909/736-3002.

52 LAKE ELSINORE WEST MARINA & RV RESORT

Rating: 7

on Lake Elsinore

See map pages 798–799

This privately operated RV park is just a half mile from Lake Elsinore. (For information about Lake Elsinore, see the following entry for Lake Elsinore Recreation Area.)

RV sites, facilities: There are 197 sites with full hookups (30, 50 amps) for RVs or tents. Picnic tables are provided. Restrooms, showers, an RV dump station, a horseshoe pit, a clubhouse, a convenience store, telephone hookups, cell phone reception, modem access, cable TV hookups, and a boat ramp are available. An ATM is within one mile. Some facilities are wheelchair-accessible. Leashed pets are permitted, with some size restrictions.

Reservations, fees: Reservations are accepted. The fee is $35 per night. A senior discount is available. Major credit cards are accepted. Open year-round.

Directions: Drive to the junction of I-15 and Highway 74. At that junction, take Highway 74 west/Central Avenue and drive west for four miles to the entrance to the park on the left (32700 Riverside Drive).

Contact: Lake Elsinore West Marina, 909/678-1300 or 800/328-6844, fax 909/678-6377, website: www.lakeelsinoremarina.com.

53 LAKE ELSINORE RECREATION AREA

Rating: 7

on Lake Elsinore

See map pages 798–799

The weather is hot and dry enough in this region to make the water in Lake Elsinore more valuable than gold. Elsinore is a huge, wide lake, where water-skiers, personal watercraft riders, and windsurfers can find a slice of heaven. This camp is set along the north shore, where there are also several trails for hiking, biking, and horseback riding. There is a designated area near the campground for swimming and water play, with a gently sloping lake bottom a big plus here. If you like thrill sports, hang gliding and parachuting are also available at the lake and, as you scan across the water, you can often look up and see these daredevils soaring overhead. The recreation area covers 3,300 acres. Although the lake is huge when full, an extremely low water level in early 2003 has caused problems with water quality, as well as leaving the campground boat ramps high and dry. This situation is unresolved, with two government entities blaming each other. Boaters planning to visit this lake should call first to get the latest on water levels and quality.

RV sites, facilities: There are 350 sites, many with hookups (30, 50 amps), for RVs up to 40 feet or tents. Picnic tables and fire pits are provided at some sites. Restrooms, drinking water, flush toilets, showers, limited cell phone reception, a bait and snack shop, an ATM, and an RV dump station are available. A coin-operated laundry and a store are nearby. Some facilities are wheelchair-accessible. Leashed pets are permitted.

Reservations, fees: Reservations are accepted at 800/416-6992. The fee is $20–25 per night, plus $10 per vehicle for more than two vehicles. Open year-round.

Directions: Drive to the junction of I-15 and Highway 74. At that junction, take Highway 74 west/Central Avenue. After one block, make a right on Collier Street, then a quick left on Riverside, and drive west for 2.1 miles to the park entrance on the left.

Contact: Lake Elsinore Recreation Area, 909/471-1212; city of Lake Elsinore, 909/674-3124, fax 909/245-9308, website: www.rmrc-recreation.com.

54 PALM VIEW RV PARK

Rating: 5

near Lake Elsinore
See map pages 798–799

This privately operated RV park is in a quiet valley at 700 feet elevation. The sites are fairly rustic, with some shade trees. The park's recreation area offers basketball, volleyball, horseshoes, tetherball, and a playground, which should tell you everything you need to know. For you wonderful goofballs, bungy jumping and parachuting are available in the town of Perris.

RV sites, facilities: There are 50 sites, some drive-through and all with full hookups, for RVs or tents. Restrooms, fire rings, an RV dump station, a recreation area, modem access, a swimming pool, a pond, laundry facilities, a store, ice, and firewood are available. Leashed pets are permitted.

Reservations, fees: Reservations are accepted. The fee is $20–23 per night, plus $3 per person for more than four people. Open year-round.

Directions: Drive to the junction of I-15 and Highway 74. At that junction, take Highway 74/Central Avenue and drive east on Highway 74 for 4.5 miles to River Road. Turn right (south) and drive one mile to the park on the left (22200 River Road).

Contact: Palm View RV Park, 909/657-7791, fax 909/657-7673, website: www.palmviewrvpark.com.

55 O'NEILL REGIONAL PARK

Rating: 6

near Cleveland National Forest
See map pages 798–799

This park is just far enough off the main drag to get missed by most of the RV cruisers on I-5. It is set near Trabuco Canyon, adjacent to Cleveland National Forest to the east. About 70 percent of the campsites are set under a canopy of sycamore and oak, and in general, the park is heavily wooded. The park covers 3,800 acres and features 18 miles of trails, including those accessible by equestrians. Several roads near this park lead to trailheads into Cleveland National Forest. Occasional mountain lion warnings are posted by rangers. The elevation is 1,000 feet.

RV sites, facilities: There are 85 sites, eight drive-through, for RVs up to 35 feet and tents, six equestrian sites for up to three horses per site, and three group camping areas for up to 100 people each. Picnic tables and fire rings are provided. Restrooms, drinking water, flush toilets, showers, a playground, a picnic area, firewood, and an RV dump station are available. Horse corrals, water troughs, and an arena are available at equestrian sites. A nature center is open on weekends. A store is nearby. Some facilities are wheelchair-accessible. Leashed pets are permitted.

Reservations, fees: Reservations are accepted for

group sites only ($25 reservation fee) at 949/923-2260. The fee is $12 per night, plus $4 per additional vehicle, $2 per pet per night, and $3 per horse. Group sites are $12 per vehicle per night. A senior discount is available. Open year-round.
Directions: From I-5 in Laguna Hills, take the County Road S18/El Toro Road exit and drive east (past El Toro) for 7.5 miles. Turn right onto Live Oak Canyon Road/County Road S19 and drive about three miles to the park on the right.
Contact: O'Neill Regional Park, 949/923-2260; Orange County Harbors, Beaches and Parks Department, 714/973-6855, website: www.ocparks.com.

56 CASPERS WILDERNESS PARK

Rating: 6

on the San Juan Creek
See map pages 798–799
This is an 8,000-acre protected wilderness preserve that is best known for coastal stands of live oak and magnificent stands of California sycamore. Highway 74 provides access to this regional park. It is a popular spot for picnics and day hikes, and since the campground is not listed with any of the computer-based reservation services, it is overlooked by most out-of-town travelers. A highlight is 30 miles of trails. Much of the land is pristine and protected in its native state. It is bordered to the south by the San Juan Creek and to the east by the Cleveland National Forest and the San Mateo Canyon Wilderness, adding to its protection.
RV sites, facilities: There are 35 sites for RVs or tents, 22 sites for equestrian campers, six group sites, and 10 sites in an overflow area for RVs. Picnic tables and barbecues are provided. Drinking water, flush toilets, showers, an RV dump station, corrals, stables, a museum with interpretive programs, and a playground are available. Some facilities are wheelchair-accessible. Pets are not allowed.
Reservations, fees: Reservations are not accepted. The fee is $12 per night, plus $4 per additional vehicle and $3 for each horse per night. Reservations are accepted for groups; group fees vary. Open year-round.
Directions: Drive on I-5 to San Juan Capistrano and Highway 74/Ortega Highway. Turn east on

the Ortega Highway and drive 7.5 miles northeast to the signed park entrance on the left.
Contact: Caspers Wilderness Park, Orange County, 949/728-0235, fax 949/728-0346.

57 LAKE SKINNER RECREATION AREA

Rating: 7

on Lake Skinner
See map pages 798–799
Lake Skinner is set within a county park at an elevation of 1,470 feet in sparse foothill country, where the water can sparkle, and it covers 1,200 surface acres. There is a speed limit of 10 mph. Unlike nearby Lake Elsinore, which is dominated by fast boats and water-skiers, no water contact sports are permitted here; hence no water-skiing, swimming, or windsurfing. Afternoon winds make for great sailing, and you can count on consistent midday breezes. The fishing can be good. Many fish are stocked at this lake, including trophy-sized bass and trout, along with catfish, crappie, and bluegill. The fish are stocked biweekly November through May. The fishing records here include a 39.5-pound striped bass and 33-pound catfish. The recreation area also provides hiking and horseback riding trails.
RV sites, facilities: There are 257 sites, many drive-through with full hookups (30, 50 amps), for RVs or tents, an overflow area, and a group camping area. Picnic tables and fire grills are provided. Restrooms, drinking water, flush toilets, coin-operated showers, limited cell phone reception, a playground, a store, ice, bait, an RV dump station, a swimming pool (in the summer), a boat ramp, a marina, mooring, boat rentals, and propane are available. Some facilities are wheelchair-accessible. Leashed pets are permitted.
Reservations, fees: Reservations are accepted at 800/234-7275. The fee is $15–18 per night or $10 per night in the overflow area, plus $4 per night for each additional vehicle and $2 per pet per night. There is a six-person maximum per site. Open year-round. Major credit cards are accepted.
Directions: Drive on I-15 to Temecula and the exit for Rancho California. Take that exit northeast and drive 9.5 miles to the park entrance on the right.

CALIFORNIA

Contact: Lake Skinner Recreation Area, 909/926-1541, website: www.RiversideCountyParks.org.

58 LAKE HEMET

Rating: 7

near Hemet

See map pages 798–799

Lake Hemet covers 420 acres, is set at 4,340 feet, and sits near San Bernardino National Forest just west of Garner Valley. Many campsites have lake views. It provides a good camping/fishing destination, with stocks of 75,000 trout each year, a lot for a lake this size, and yep, catch rates are good. The lake also has bass, bluegill, and catfish. Boating rules prohibit boats under 10 feet, canoes, sailboats, inflatables, and swimming—no swimming or wading at Lake Hemet.

RV sites, facilities: There are 275 sites with full hookups for RVs, an open area for dispersed tent sites, and an open area for groups. Picnic tables and fire rings are provided. Restrooms, drinking water, flush toilets, coin-operated showers, an RV dump station, a playground, a pond, a boat ramp, boat rentals, a store, a coin-operated laundry, and propane are available. Some facilities are wheelchair-accessible. Leashed pets are permitted.

Reservations, fees: No reservations are accepted, except for groups of 20 and up. The fee is $15–18.25 per vehicle per night, plus $2.50 per person for more than two people and $1 per pet per night. Major credit cards are accepted. Open year-round.

Directions: From Palm Desert, drive southwest on Highway 74 for 32 miles (near Lake Hemet) to the campground entrance on the left. For directions if arriving from the west (several options), phone 909/659-2680, ext. 2.

Contact: Lake Hemet, 909/659-2680, website: www.lakehemet.com.

59 HURKEY CREEK COUNTY PARK

Rating: 5

near Lake Hemet

See map pages 798–799

This large county park is just east (across the road) of Lake Hemet, beside Hurkey Creek (which runs in winter and spring). The highlight, of course, is the nearby lake, known for good fishing in the spring. No swimming is permitted. The camp elevation is 4,800 feet. The park covers 59 acres.

RV sites, facilities: There are 107 family sites and 105 group sites for RVs up to 35 feet or tents. Fire grills and picnic tables are provided. Drinking water, flush toilets, and showers are available. An RV dump station is at nearby Lake Hemet. Some facilities are wheelchair-accessible. Leashed pets are permitted.

Reservations, fees: Reserve at 800/234-PARK (800/234-7275) (reservation fee charged). The fee is $15 per night, plus $2 per pet per night. Major credit cards are accepted. Open year-round.

Directions: From Palm Desert, drive southwest on Highway 74 for 32 miles (near Lake Hemet) to the campground entrance on the right.

Contact: Hurkey Creek County Park, 909/659-2050, website: www.riversidecoparks.org.

60 KAMP ANZA RV RESORT

Rating: 4

near Anza

See map pages 798–799

This is a year-round RV park set at 4,100 feet, with many nearby recreation options. Lake Hemet is 11 miles away, with hiking, motorbiking, and jeep trails nearby in San Bernardino National Forest. Pacific Crest Trail hikers are welcome to clean up and to arrange for food and mail pickup here.

RV sites, facilities: There are 116 sites, including some drive-through and many with full hookups, for RVs or tents. Picnic tables and fire grills are provided. Restrooms, showers, a playground, a fishing pond, a hot tub, horseshoes, a coin-operated laundry, a store, an RV dump station, ice, a recreation room, modem access, and propane are available.

Reservations, fees: Reservations are accepted. The fee is $15–18 per night. Open year-round.

Directions: From Palm Desert, drive west on Highway 74 for 24 miles to Highway 371. Turn left on Highway 371 and drive west to the town of Anza and Kirby Road. Turn left on Kirby Road and drive 3.5 miles to the campground on the left at Terwilliger Road (look for the covered wagon out front).

Contact: Kamp Anza RV Resort, 909/763-4819, fax 909/763-0619.

CALIFORNIA

California

Chapter 27
San Diego and Vicinity

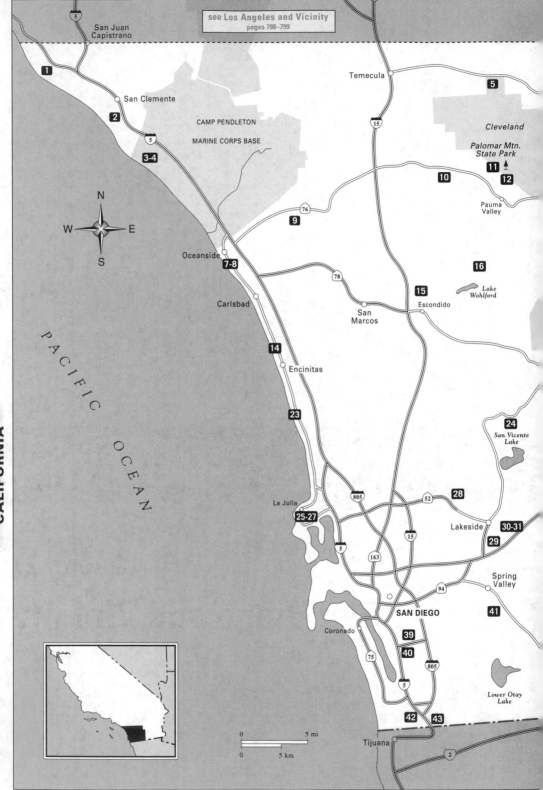

CALIFORNIA

PACIFIC OCEAN

San Juan
Capistrano

San Clemente

CAMP PENDLETON
MARINE CORPS BASE

Temecula

Cleveland

Palomar Mtn.
State Park

Pauma
Valley

Oceanside

Carlsbad

Encinitas

San
Marcos

Escondido

Lake
Wohlford

La Jolla

San Vicente
Lake

Lakeside

Spring
Valley

SAN DIEGO

Coronado

Lower Otay
Lake

Tijuana

0   5 mi

0   5 km

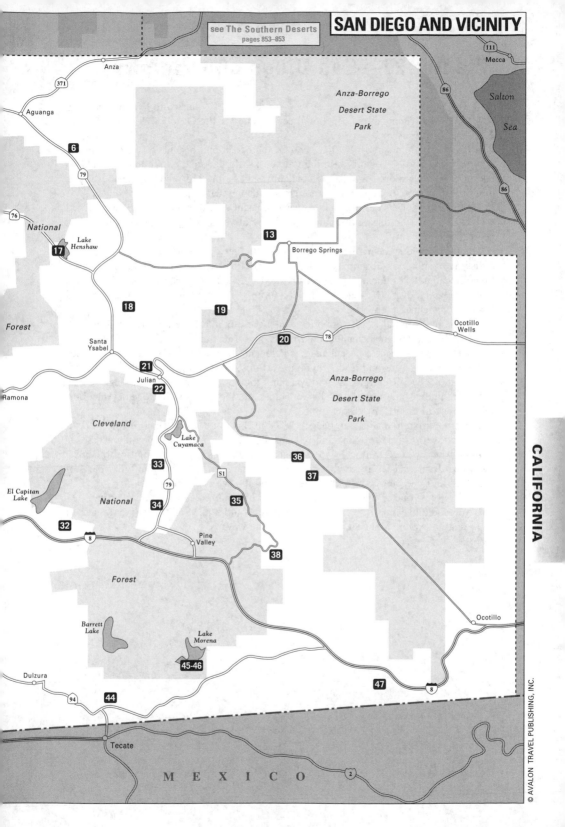

see The Southern Deserts
pages 853–853

111
Mecca

Anza

371

Aguanga

6

79

76

National

Lake
Henshaw

17

18

19

Anza-Borrego

Desert State

Park

86

Salton

Sea

86

13

Borrego Springs

20

78

Ocotillo
Wells

Anza-Borrego

Desert State

Park

Forest

Santa
Ysabel

21

Julian

22

Ramona

Cleveland

Lake
Cuyamaca

33

79

S1

36

37

El Capitan
Lake

National

34

35

32

8

Pine
Valley

38

Forest

Barrett
Lake

Lake
Morena

45-46

Ocotillo

Dulzura

94

44

47

8

Tecate

M E X I C O

2

CALIFORNIA

Chapter 27—San Diego and Vicinity

San Diego was picked as one of the best regions of America to live in according to an unofficial vote at a national conference for the Outdoor Writers Association of America.

It is easy to understand why: the weather, the ocean and beaches, the lakes and the fishing, Cleveland National Forest, the state parks, the Palomar Mountains, the hiking, biking, and water sports. What more could anyone ask for? For many, the answer is you don't ask for more, because it does not get any better than this.

The weather is near perfect. It fits a warm coastal environment with an azure-tinted sea that borders foothills and mountains. In a relatively small geographic spread, you get it all.

The ocean here is warm and beautiful, with 70 miles of beaches and often sensational fishing offshore for albacore, yellowtail, and marlin. The foothills provide canyon settings for many lakes, including Lower Otay, Morena, Barrett, El Capitan, Cuyamaca, San Vicente, Hodges, Henshaw, and several more—with some of the biggest lake-record bass ever caught in the world.

Cleveland National Forest provides a surprise for many—remote mountains with canyons, hidden streams, small campgrounds, and a terrain with a forest of fir, cedar, and hardwoods such as oak. A landmark is Palomar Mountain, with several campgrounds at Palomar State Park and nearby in national forest. This is a great family destination. Long-distance views, stargazing, and watching meteor showers are all among the best anywhere in the state from the 5,000-foot ridges and lookouts on the edge of Anza-Borrego Desert to the nearby east.

For more urban pursuits, San Diego's Mission Bay Park offers a fantastic network of recreation, with trails for biking and rollerblading, plus beaches and boating access.

Everywhere you go, you will find campgrounds and parks, from primitive to deluxe, including developed RV parks that cost as much as fine hotel rooms in other parts of the state, and they're worth it, like silver dollars in a sea of pennies.

The region is one of the few that provides year-round recreation at a stellar level.

If you could live anywhere in America, where would it be? Well, that's what makes it so special to explore and visit, camping along the way.

CALIFORNIA

◼ DOHENY STATE BEACH

🏃 🚴 🏊 🎣 🐕 ♿ 🚐 ⛺

Rating: 8

on Dana Point Harbor

See map pages 828–829

Some campsites are within steps of the beach. Yet this state beach is right in town, set at the entrance to Dana Point Harbor. It is a pretty spot with easy access off the highway. Reservations are needed to guarantee a site at this popular campground. Lifeguard service is available in the summer, and campfire and Junior Ranger programs are also available. A day-use area has a five-acre lawn with a picnic area and volleyball courts. Surfing is popular, but note that it is permitted at the north end of the beach only. San Juan Capistrano provides a nearby side trip, just three miles away.

RV sites, facilities: There are 115 sites for RVs up to 35 feet or tents, and a hike-in/bike-in site is also offered. Picnic tables and fire grills are provided. Restrooms, drinking water, flush toilets, coin-operated showers, cell phone reception, an RV dump station, exhibits, and food service (summer only) are available. Propane and an ATM are nearby. Some facilities are wheelchair-accessible. Leashed pets are permitted in the campground only, not on the beach.

Reservations, fees: Reserve at 800/444-PARK (800/444-7275) or online at www.reserveamerica .com ($7.50 reservation fee). The fees are $12–15 per night and $2 per person for the hike-in/bike-in site (photo ID required). A senior discount is available. Open year-round.

Directions: Drive on I-5 to the exit for Pacific Coast Highway/Camino delas Ramblas (three miles south of San Juan Capistrano). Take that exit and drive to Del Obispo/Dana Point Drive (second light). Turn left and drive one block to Park Lantern/Doheny State Beach Road. Turn left and drive one block to the park entrance. Doheny State Beach is about one mile from I-5.

Contact: Doheny State Beach, 949/496-6172 or 949/492-0802.

◻ SAN CLEMENTE STATE BEACH

🏃 🚴 🏊 🎣 🐕 ♿ 🚐 ⛺

Rating: 8

near San Clemente

See map pages 828–829

The campground at San Clemente State Beach is set on a bluff, not on a beach. A few campsites here have ocean views. Surfing is popular on the north end of a one-mile beach. The beach here is popular for swimming, body surfing, and skin diving. Of the three local state beaches that provide easy access and beachfront camping, this one offers full hookups. The others are Doheny State Beach to the north and San Onofre State Beach to the south. A feature at this park is a two-mile-long interpretive trail, along with hike-in/bike-in campsites. Surfing camp is held here during the summer.

RV sites, facilities: There are 160 sites, 72 with full hookups (20 amps), for RVs up to 30 feet or tents, one hike-in/bike-in site, and one group site with no hookups for up to 50 people and 20 vehicles—RVs or tents. Picnic tables and fire grills are provided. Flush toilets, coin-operated showers, an RV dump station, summer lifeguard service, cell phone reception, and summer programs are available. A store, an ATM, a coin-operated laundry, and propane are nearby. Some facilities are wheelchair-accessible. Leashed pets are permitted.

Reservations, fees: Reserve at 800/444-PARK (800/444-7275) or online at www.reserveamerica .com ($7.50 reservation fee). The fees are $16–20 per night and $2 per person for hike-in/bike-in sites, plus $5 per additional vehicle. A senior discount is available. Open year-round.

Directions: From I-5 in San Clemente, take the Avenida Calafia exit. Drive west for a short distance to the park entrance on the left.

Contact: San Clemente State Beach, 949/492-3156 or 949/492-3281; Orange Coast District, San Clemente Sector, 949/492-0802.

CALIFORNIA

❸ SAN ONOFRE STATE BEACH: BLUFF AREA

Rating: 7

near San Clemente

See map pages 828–829

This camp may appear perfect at first glance, but nope, it is very noisy. Both the highway and train tracks are within very close range; you can practically feel the ground rumble, and that's not all. With Camp Pendleton just on the other side of the freeway, there is considerable noise from helicopters and other operations. Too bad. This is one of three parks set along the beach near San Clemente, just off the busy Coast Highway. The campground is set on top of a 90-foot bluff. This state beach covers more than 3,000 acres, featuring 3.5 miles of sandy beaches and access trails on the neighboring bluffs. This area is one of the most popular in California for surfing, with this state beach also good for swimming. The shadow of the San Onofre Nuclear Power Plant is nearby. Other state beaches in the area are San Clemente State Beach and Doheny State Beach, both situated to the north.

RV sites, facilities: There are 176 sites for RVs up to 36 feet or tents, one group site for up to 50 people, and one hike-in/bike-in site. Picnic tables and fire rings are provided. Drinking water, flush toilets, limited cell phone reception, and cold showers are available. A store, an ATM, a coin-operated laundry, and propane are available within about five miles. Leashed pets are permitted.

Reservations, fees: Reserve at 800/444-PARK (800/444-7275) or online at www.reserveamerica .com ($7.50 reservation fee). The fees are $15 per night, $50 for the group site, and $2 per person per night for the hike-in/bike-in site. Open year-round.

Directions: From San Clemente, drive south on I-5 for three miles to the Basilone Road exit. Take that exit and drive south on Basilone Road for two miles to the park.

Contact: San Onofre State Beach, 949/492-4872; Orange Coast District Office, 949/492-0802 or 909/366-8500.

❹ SAN ONOFRE STATE BEACH: SAN MATEO

Rating: 9

near San Clemente

See map pages 828–829

This state beach is considered one of the best surf breaks in the United States—it's well known as the outstanding Trestles Surfing Area. The camp is set inland and includes a nature trail, featuring a marshy area where San Mateo Creek meets the shoreline. Although this is a state beach, the camp is relatively far from the ocean; it is a 1.1-mile walk to the beach. But it sure is a lot quieter than the nearby option, Bluff Area Campground.

RV sites, facilities: There are 159 sites, 47 with partial hookups (20, 30 amps), for RVs or tents. Picnic tables and fire grills are provided. An RV dump station, showers, limited cell phone reception, and flush toilets are available. A store, an ATM, propane, and a coin-operated laundry are nearby. Some facilities are wheelchair-accessible. Leashed pets are permitted.

Reservations, fees: Reserve at 800/444-PARK (800/444-7275) or online at www.reserveamerica .com ($7.50 reservation fee). The fee is $15–18 per night, plus $5 per additional vehicle and a $5 day-use fee. A senior discount is available. Open year-round.

Directions: Drive on I-5 to the southern end of San Clemente and the Christianitos Road exit. Take that exit and drive east on Christianitos Road for 1.5 miles to the park entrance on the right.

Contact: San Onofre State Beach, 949/492-4872; Orange Coast District Office, 949/492-0802 or 909/366-8500.

❺ DRIPPING SPRINGS

Rating: 7

near the Agua Tibia Wilderness in Cleveland National Forest

See map pages 828–829

This is one of the premium Forest Service camps available, set just inside the national forest border near Vail Lake and adjacent to the Agua Tibia Wilderness. The Dripping Springs Trail is routed south out of camp, starting at 1,600 feet and climbing near the peak of Agua Tibia Mountain, 4,779 feet.

RV sites, facilities: There are 24 sites for RVs up to 32 feet or tents. Picnic tables and fire rings are provided. Drinking water and vault toilets are available. Supplies are available nearby in Temecula. Leashed pets are permitted.

Reservations, fees: Reservations are not accepted. The fee is $12–20 per night, plus $2 per night for additional vehicle. A senior discount is available. Open July through March. Closed April through June for protection of an endangered species, the arroyo southwestern toad.

Directions: From I-15 in Temecula, drive 11 miles east on Highway 79 to the campground.

Contact: Cleveland National Forest, Palomar Ranger District, 760/788-0250, fax 760/788-6130.

6 OAK GROVE

Rating: 4

near Temecula Creek in Cleveland National Forest

See map pages 828–829

Oak Grove camp is on the northeastern fringe of Cleveland National Forest at 2,800 feet. Easy access from Highway 79 makes this a popular camp. The Palomar Observatory is just five miles up the mountain to the west, but there is no direct way to reach it from the campground. Lake Henshaw is about a half-hour drive to the south. A boat ramp and boat rentals are available there.

RV sites, facilities: There are 81 sites for RVs up to 32 feet or tents. Picnic tables and fire grills are provided. Drinking water, flush toilets, and cell phone reception are available. Propane, an ATM, and groceries are nearby. Leashed pets are permitted.

Reservations, fees: Reservations are not accepted. The fee is $15–20 per night. A senior discount is available. Open year-round.

Directions: Drive on I-15 to the Highway 79 exit. Take that exit and drive east on Highway 79 to Aguanga. Continue southeast on Highway 79 for 6.5 miles to the camp entrance.

Contact: Cleveland National Forest, Palomar Ranger District, 760/788-0250, fax 760/788-6130.

7 PARADISE BY THE SEA RV RESORT

Rating: 7

in Oceanside

See map pages 828–829

This is a classic oceanfront RV park, but no tenters need apply. It's an easy walk to the beach. For boaters, Oceanside Marina to the immediate north is the place to go. Oceanside is an excellent headquarters for deep-sea fishing, with charter trips available to Catalina Island and the kelp forests to the north off the shore of Camp Pendleton and San Onofre, as well as points south; contact Helgren's Sportfishing, 760/722-2133, to arrange charters. Camp Pendleton, a huge Marine Corps training complex, is to the north.

RV sites, facilities: There are 102 sites with full hookups (20, 30, 50 amps), four drive-through, for RVs. Restrooms, flush toilets, showers, cable TV hookups, a swimming pool, a spa, modem access, cell phone reception, a whirlpool, a clubhouse, a banquet room, a coin-operated laundry, RV supplies, a pay phone, and a small store are available. Boat rentals are nearby. An ATM is within a quarter mile. Leashed pets are permitted with proof of vaccination.

Reservations, fees: Reservations are recommended. The fee is $45 per night, plus $2.50 per person for more than two people, $5 per night for each additional vehicle, and $1 per pet per night. Major credit cards are accepted. Open year-round.

Directions: Drive on I-5 to Oceanside and the Oceanside Boulevard exit. Take that exit and drive west on Oceanside Boulevard for a half mile to South Coast Highway. Turn left on South Coast Highway and drive to the park on the right (1537 S. Coast Highway).

Contact: Paradise by the Sea RV Resort, 760/439-1376, fax 760/439-1919, website: www.paradisebythesearvresort.com.

8 OCEANSIDE RV PARK

Rating: 7

in Oceanside

See map pages 828–829

There are three options for RV cruisers in the Oceanside area, and this is one of them. It's a short distance to the beach, about a 10-minute walk, where you'll find a snack bar and a lifeguard. A bowling alley is across the street. (For details on the area, see the prior entry for Paradise by the Sea RV Park.) Some may remember this park as "Casitas Poquitos." It has been renamed—same owners, nice folks.

RV sites, facilities: There are 140 sites with full hookups (30 amps) for RVs. Picnic tables and patios are provided. Flush toilets, showers, cable TV hookups, a playground, a coin-operated laundry, an ATM, phone reception, a recreation room, a swimming pool, a spa, a billiard room, propane, a pet run, and a general store are available. Leashed pets are permitted.

Reservations, fees: Reservations are recommended. The fee is $43–46 per night, plus $2 per person per night for more than two people and $1 per pet. A winter discount is available. Major credit cards are accepted. Open year-round.

Directions: Drive on I-5 to Oceanside and the Oceanside Boulevard exit. Take that exit and drive west on Oceanside Boulevard for .5 mile to South Coast Highway. Turn left on South Coast Highway and drive a half block to the park at 1510 S. Coast Highway.

Contact: Oceanside RV Park, 760/722-4404, fax 760/722-4080.

9 GUAJOME COUNTY PARK

Rating: 5

in Oceanside
See map pages 828–829

Guajome means "home of the frog" and, yep, so it is with little Guajome Lake and the adjacent marsh, both of which can be explored with a delightful two-mile hike. The lake provides a bit of fishing for warm-water species, mainly sunfish and catfish. Because of the wetlands, a huge variety of birds will stop here on their migratory journeys, making this a favorite area for bird-watching. Horseback riding trails are also available. A historic adobe house in the park is a must-see. The park covers 557 acres and features several miles of trails for hiking and horseback riding and a nearby museum with antique gas and steam engines.

RV sites, facilities: There are 35 sites, a few drive-through, with partial hookups (20, 30 amps) for

RVs up to 45 feet. Picnic tables and fire grills are provided. Restrooms, drinking water, flush toilets, showers, an RV dump station, cell phone reception, and a playground are available. An enclosed pavilion and gazebo can be reserved for groups. A store, an ATM, and propane are nearby. Leashed pets are permitted.

Reservations, fees: Make reservations at 858/565-3600 or by fax at 619/260-6492 ($3 reservation fee). The fee is $16 per night, with an eight-person maximum per site, plus $1 per pet per night. Major credit cards are accepted. Open year-round.

Directions: From Oceanside, drive east on Highway 76/Mission Avenue for seven miles to Guajome Lakes Road. Turn right (south) on Guajome Lakes Road and drive to the entrance.

Contact: San Diego County Parks Department, 858/694-3049, fax 858/495-5841, website: www .sdparks.org.

10 RANCHO CORRÍDO RV PARK

Rating: 7

near the Pala Mission
See map pages 828–829

This RV layover is 10 miles east of I-15, the main drag. A fishing pond is available for catch-and-release fishing only. This park is very active on summer weekends, with music on Saturday night from May to September, arts and crafts on Saturday, and wagon rides. A full playground makes this a family-oriented camp. It is a short drive to the Pala Indian Reservation and the Pala Mission to the east. The Palomar Observatory is 20 miles to the east, another possible side trip.

RV sites, facilities: There are 210 sites, including 110 with partial hookups (30 amps), for RVs or tents, and 100 sites for tents only. Picnic tables and fire pits are provided. Restrooms, drinking water, flush toilets, showers, an RV dump station, modem access, cable TV hookups, cell phone reception, clubhouses, gazebos, a small store, a fishing pond, and a coin-operated laundry are available. A playground with volleyball, horseshoes, tetherball, and basketball are on-site. An ATM is within a quarter mile. Leashed pets are permitted.

Reservations, fees: Reservations are accepted. The fee is $18–28 per night, plus $7 per person

CALIFORNIA

for more than two people and $3 per pet per night. Weekly rates are available. Major credit cards are accepted. Open year-round.

Directions: Drive on I-15 to the Highway 76 exit (east of Oceanside). Take that exit east and drive on Highway 76 to the town of Pala. Continue east on Highway 76 for four miles to the camp on the right (14715 Hwy. 76).

Contact: Rancho Corrído, 760/742-3755, fax 760/742-3245, website: www.ranchocorrido.com.

11 PALOMAR MOUNTAIN STATE PARK

Rating: 8

near the Palomar Observatory
See map pages 828–829

This is one of the best state parks in Southern California for hiking. It features 14 miles of trails, including several loop trails, often featuring long-distance views. Yet forest covers much of this park, one of the few sites in this Southern California region with a Sierra Nevada–like feel to it This camp offers hiking trails and some fishing in Doane Pond (permit required–great for youngsters learning to fish). There are numerous excellent hikes, including the Boucher Trail (four miles) and Lower Doane Valley Trail (three miles). The view from Boucher Lookout is stunning, at 5,438 feet looking out over the valley below. This developed state park is a short drive from the Palomar Observatory. There are four other campgrounds in the immediate area that are a short distance from the observatory. At the Palomar Observatory (not part of the park) you'll find the 200-inch Hale telescope, America's largest telescope. This is a private, working telescope, run by the California Institute of Technology, so there are no tours or public stargazing through it. The elevation is 4,700 feet.

RV sites, facilities: There are 31 sites for RVs up to 21 feet or tents, three group sites for 15 to 25 people, and one hike-in/bike-in site. Picnic tables, fire grills, and raccoon-resistant food lockers are provided. Drinking water, flush toilets, and coin-operated showers are available. Some facilities are wheelchair-accessible. Leashed pets are permitted.

Reservations, fees: Reserve at 800/444-PARK (800/444-7275) or online at www.reserveamerica

.com ($7.50 reservation fee). The fees are $15 per night, $2 for the hike-in/bike-in site, and $20–32 for group sites. A permit is required for the fishing pond. A senior discount is available. Open year-round.

Directions: Drive on I-15 to the Highway 76 exit (east of Oceanside). Take that exit and drive east on Highway 76 for 25 miles to County Road S6 (which brings you to the top of Palomar Mountain). At the top of the mountain, turn left, drive about 50 feet to State Park Road/County Road S7. Turn left on State Park Road/County Road S7 and drive about 3.5 miles to the park entrance.

Contact: Palomar Mountain State Park, 760/742-3462; Colorado Desert District, 760/767-5311.

12 OAK KNOLL

Rating: 5

near the Palomar Observatory
See map pages 828–829

The camp is set at 3,000 feet in San Diego County foothill country among giant old California oaks. It is at the western base of Palomar Mountain, and to visit the Palomar Observatory and its awesome 200-inch telescope requires a remarkably twisty 10-mile drive up the mountain (the telescope is not open to the public). A good side trip is driving to the Boucher Lookout in Palomar Mountain State Park. Trailheads for excellent hikes on Palomar Mountain include the Observatory Trail (starting at Observatory) and the Doane Valley Loop (starting in Palomar Mountain State Park).

RV sites, facilities: There are 46 sites, many with partial or full hookups (30 amps), for tents or RVs up to 30 feet at all sites and of any size at four sites. There are also several cabins for rent. Restrooms, drinking water, flush toilets, coin-operated showers, a playground, a swimming pool, a clubhouse, a baseball diamond, a video arcade, a coin-operated laundry, propane, and groceries are available. Leashed pets are permitted, but some dogs are prohibited.

Reservations, fees: Call ahead for available space. The fee is $25–35 per night, plus $3 per person for more than two people, $3 per night for additional vehicle, and $2 per pet per night. Cabins are $95 per night. Open year-round.

Directions: Drive on I-15 to the Highway 76 exit (east of Oceanside). Take that exit and drive east on Highway 76 for 25 miles to County Road S6 (which brings you to the top of Palomar Mountain). Turn left and drive a short distance to the campground on the left.

Contact: Oak Knoll, 760/742-3437, website: www .oakknoll.net.

13 BORREGO PALM CANYON

🚶 🐕 ♿ 🚐 ⛺

Rating: 4

in Anza-Borrego Desert State Park
See map pages 828–829

This is one of the best camps in Anza-Borrego Desert State Park with two excellent hikes available. The short hike into Borrego Palm Canyon is like being transported to another world, from the desert to the tropics, complete with a small waterfall, a rare sight in these parts. The Panorama Overlook Trail also starts here. An excellent visitors center is available, offering an array of exhibits and a slide show. The elevation is 760 feet. Anza-Borrego Desert State Park is the largest state park in the continental United States, covering more than 600,000 acres with 500 miles of dirt roads. "Borrego" means bighorn sheep, appropriately named for the desert bighorn sheep that live in the mountains of this park.

RV sites, facilities: There are 65 sites for self-contained RVs up to 31 feet or tents, 52 sites with full hookups (30 amps) for RVs up to 35 feet, and five group sites for up to 24 people with tents. Picnic tables and fire grills are provided. Restrooms, drinking water, flush toilets, showers, and an RV dump station are available. A store, a coin-operated laundry, and propane are nearby. Some facilities are wheelchair-accessible. Leashed pets are permitted.

Reservations, fees: Reserve at 800/444-PARK (800/444-7275) or online at www.reserveamerica .com ($7.50 reservation fee). The fees are $14–20 per night and $32 for the group sites. A senior discount is available. Open year-round.

Directions: From Julian, at the junction of Highway 78 and Highway 79, drive east on Highway 78 for 19.5 miles to Yaqui Pass Road/County Road S3. Turn left (north) and drive six miles to Borrego Springs Road. Turn left and drive five miles to Borrego Springs and Palm Canyon Drive. Turn west and drive 2.5 miles to the campground entrance on the right.

Contact: Anza-Borrego Desert State Park, 760/767-4205; Colorado Desert District, 760/767-5311, fax 760/767-3427.

14 SOUTH CARLSBAD STATE BEACH

🚶 🚴 🏊 🛶 🏕 🐕 ♿ 🚐 ⛺

Rating: 9

near Carlsbad
See map pages 828–829

No reservation? Then likely you can forget about staying here. This is a beautiful state beach and, as big as it is, the sites go fast to the coastal cruisers who reserved a spot. The campground is on a bluff, with half the sites overlooking the ocean. The nearby beach is accessible by a series of stairs. This is a phenomenal place for scuba diving and snorkeling, with a nearby reef available. This is also a popular spot for surfing and body surfing.

RV sites, facilities: There are 222 sites for RVs up to 35 feet or tents and one hike-in/bike-in site. Picnic tables and fire rings are provided. Restrooms, drinking water, flush toilets, cell phone reception, coin-operated showers, and an RV dump station are available. Lifeguard service is provided in summer. Supplies, an ATM, and a coin-operated laundry are available in Carlsbad. Some facilities are wheelchair-accessible. Leashed pets are permitted, but not on the beach.

Reservations, fees: Reserve at 800/444-PARK (800/444-7275) or online at www.reserveamerica .com ($7.50 reservation fee). The fees are $7–14 per night and $2 for the hike-in/bike-in site. A senior discount is available. Open year-round, with the possibility of closing November to January.

Directions: Drive on I-5 to Carlsbad and the exit for Palomar Airport Road. Take that exit and drive .3 mile to Carlsbad Boulevard. Turn south on Carlsbad Boulevard and drive two miles to Poinsettia Avenue. Turn right and drive a short distance to the park entrance.

Contact: South Carlsbad State Beach, 760/438-3143; San Diego Coast District Office, 858/642-4200.

CALIFORNIA

15 DIXON LAKE RECREATION AREA

Rating: 7

near Escondido
See map pages 828–829
Little Dixon Lake is the centerpiece of a regional park in the Escondido foothills. The camp is set at an elevation of 1,405 feet, about 400 feet above the lake's shoreline. No private boats are permitted, and a 5 mph speed limit for rental boats keeps things quiet. The water is clear, with fair bass fishing in the spring and trout fishing in the winter and early spring. Catfish are stocked in the summer, trout in winter and spring. In the summer, the lake is open at night for fishing for catfish. A pretty and easy hike is the Jack Creek Nature Trail, a one-mile walk to a 20-foot waterfall. Note that no wood fires are permitted, but charcoal is allowed.
RV sites, facilities: There are 45 sites, 10 with full hookups (30 amps), for RVs or tents. Group sites are available. Picnic tables and fire grills are provided. Restrooms, drinking water, flush toilets, showers, boat rentals, bait, ice, a snack bar, and a playground are available. No pets are allowed.
Reservations, fees: Reservations are accepted. The fee is $16–24 per night, with a maximum of eight people per site, plus $2 per night for each additional vehicle. Major credit cards are accepted. Open year-round.
Directions: Drive on I-15 to the exit for El Norte Parkway (four miles north of Escondido). Take that exit northeast and drive four miles to La Honda Drive. Turn left and drive to Dixon Lake.
Contact: Dixon Lake Recreation Area, 760/741-3328 or 760/839-4345, website: www.ci.escondido.ca.us.

16 WOODS VALLEY KAMPGROUND

Rating: 5

near Lake Wohlford
See map pages 828–829
This privately operated park is set up primarily for RVs and is a short drive from Lake Wohlford to the south. Lake Wohlford has a 5 mph speed limit, which guarantees quiet water; canoes, inflatables, sailboats, and boats under 10 feet and over

18 feet are prohibited. It provides fair fishing for bass, bluegill, and catfish, best in late winter and spring.
RV sites, facilities: There are 59 sites, many with partial hookups, (20, 30 amps) for RVs of any length, and 30 sites for tents. Picnic tables and fire barrels are provided. Restrooms, drinking water, flush toilets, showers, an RV dump station, cable TV, a kitchen, a coin-operated laundry, a swimming pool, a catch-and-release fishing pond, a small farm with animal pen, a playground, modem access, recreation rooms, volleyball, horseshoes, and supplies are available. Group facilities are also available. Leashed pets are permitted, with some dogs prohibited.
Reservations, fees: Reservations are accepted. The fee is $29–35 per night, plus $3 per person for more than four people, $3 per night for each additional vehicle, $3 per pet per night, and a $5 day-use fee. Monthly rates are available. Open year-round.
Directions: From Escondido, drive south on I-15 past Lake Hodges to the exit for Valley Parkway. Take that exit and drive east on Valley Parkway for about 15 miles to the town of Valley Center and Woods Valley Road. Turn right on Woods Valley Road and drive southeast for two miles the campground entrance on the left (15236 Woods Valley Road).
Contact: Woods Valley Kampground, 760/749-2905, website: www.woodsvalley.com.

17 LAKE HENSHAW RESORT RV

Rating: 7

near Santa Ysabel
See map pages 828–829
Lake Henshaw is the biggest lake in San Diego County, yet it has only one camp. It's a good one, with the cabin rentals a big plus. The camp is on the southern corner of the lake, at 2,727 feet near Cleveland National Forest. Swimming is not permitted and a 10 mph speed limit is in effect. The fishing is best for catfish, especially in the summer, and at times decent for bass, with the lake-record bass weighing 14 pounds, four ounces.
RV sites, facilities: There are 164 sites, many with full hookups (20 amps), for RVs or tents and 17

CALIFORNIA

cabins. Flush toilets, showers, a swimming pool, a whirlpool, a clubhouse, a playground, an RV dump station, limited cell phone reception, a coin-operated laundry, propane, boat and motor rentals, a boat launch, a bait and tackle shop, a restaurant, and a store are available. A golf course is 10 miles away. Some facilities are wheelchair-accessible. Leashed pets are permitted.

Reservations, fees: Reservations are not accepted. The fee is $14–19 per night, plus $1 per pet per night. Reservations are accepted for cabins only. Major credit cards are accepted. Open year-round.

Directions: From El Cajon, drive east on I-8 to Highway 79 (near Descanso Junction). Turn north on Highway 79 and drive to Santa Ysabel. Continue north on Highway 79 for seven miles to Highway 76. Turn left on Highway 76 and drive four miles to the campground on the left.

Contact: Lake Henshaw Resort RV, 760/782-3487 or 760/782-3501, fax 760/782-9224, website: www .lakehenshawca.com.

18 STAGECOACH TRAILS RV, EQUESTRIAN, AND WILDLIFE RESORT

Rating: 6

near Julian
See map pages 828–829

Mention this book and you get a 10 percent discount. You want space? You got space. That includes 600,000 acres of public lands bordering this RV campground, making Stagecoach Trails Resort ideal for those who love horseback riding and hiking. Seventy-five corrals at the campground let you know right away that this camp is very horse-friendly. In addition, Stagecoach Trails Resort provides the perfect jumping-off place for trips into neighboring Anza-Borrego Desert State Park. The resort's name comes from its proximity to the old Wells Fargo Butterfield Stage Route. The scenic rating merits a 6, but if the rating were based purely on cleanliness, professionalism, and friendliness, this resort would rate a 10.

RV sites, facilities: There are 286 sites, most drive-through, with full hookups for RVs (20, 30, 50 amps), and a primitive camping area for tents

with 75 horse corrals and five trailers. Picnic tables and fire rings are provided. Restrooms, drinking water, flush toilets, showers, a heated pool, a recreation room, a banquet room, a store, modem access, a coin-operated laundry, two RV dump stations, and propane are available. The facilities are wheelchair-accessible. Pets are permitted.

Reservations, fees: Reservations are accepted. The fee is $25–30 per night, plus $5 per additional vehicle and $5 per night per horse. Major credit cards are accepted. Open year-round.

Directions: From Escondido, drive east on Highway 78 to Ramona, and continue on Highway 78 for 15 miles to Santa Ysabel and Highway 79. Turn north (left) and drive 14 miles to County Road S2/San Felipe Road. Turn right and drive 17 miles to Highway 78. Turn right (west, toward Julian) and drive .4 mile to County Road S2 (Great Southern Overland Stage Route). Turn left and drive four miles to the resort on the right (at Mile Marker 21 on Road S2).

Contact: Stagecoach Trails Resort, 7878 Overland Stage Route, Julian, CA 92036, 760/765-2197, website: www.stagecoachtrails.com.

19 BUTTERFIELD RANCH

Rating: 3

near Anza-Borrego Desert State Park
See map pages 828–829

Butterfield Ranch is an ideal layover spot for RV cruisers visiting nearby Anza-Borrego Desert State Park who want a developed park in which to spend the night. Note that there is no gas available in Julian after 6 P.M. and that the nearest gas station is 36 miles to the east. This camp was once pretty run-down and we almost removed it from the book, but new owners took over in 2002 and are promising major upgrades, so the future is bright. By early 2003, it was already looking a lot better.

RV sites, facilities: There are 300 sites, most drive-through, with full hookups for RVs, and 200 sites for tents. Restrooms, showers, a playground, a swimming pool, a recreation room, a country store, and a fishing pond for children are available. Leashed pets are permitted.

Reservations, fees: Reservations are accepted. The fee is $16–26 per night, plus $2 per pet per night. Open year-round.

CALIFORNIA

Directions: From Escondido, drive east on Highway 78 to the town of Ramona and continue east on Highway 78 for 14 miles to County Road S2/San Felipe Road. Turn right (south) and drive 12 miles to the campground entrance on the right.

Contact: Butterfield Ranch, 760/765-1463, website: www.butterfieldranch.com.

20 TAMARISK GROVE

Rating: 5

in Anza-Borrego Desert State Park
See map pages 828–829

This is the number-one campground in Anza-Borrego Desert State Park, and it is easy to see why: big tamarisk trees provide shade, and the park provides drinking water. The Cactus Loop Trail, with the trailhead just north of camp, provides a hiking option. This is a 2.5-mile loop that passes seven varieties of cacti, some as tall as people. The elevation is 1,400 feet at this campground.

RV sites, facilities: There are 27 sites for RVs up to 21 feet or tents. Picnic tables and fire grills are provided. Restrooms, drinking water, flush toilets, and coin-operated showers are available. Some facilities are wheelchair-accessible. Leashed pets are permitted.

Reservations, fees: Reserve at 800/444-PARK (800/444-7275) or online at www.reserveamerica .com ($7.50 reservation fee). The fee is $10 per night. Open year-round.

Directions: From Julian, at the junction of Highway 78 and Highway 79, drive east on Highway 78 for 19.5 miles to Yaqui Pass Road/County Road S3. Turn left (north) and drive .25 mile to the campground on the right.

Contact: Anza-Borrego Desert State Park, 760/767-4205; Colorado Desert District, 760/767-5311, fax 760/767-3427.

21 PINEZANITA TRAILER RANCH

Rating: 6

near Julian
See map pages 828–829

Set at an elevation of 4,680 feet in dense pine and oak, this camp has had the same owners, the Stanley family, for more than 30 years. The fishing pond is a great attraction for kids (no license is required); no swimming allowed. The pond is stocked with bluegill and catfish, some of which are 12 inches or longer. Two possible side trips include Lake Cuyamaca, five miles to the south, and William Heise County Park, about 10 miles to the north as the crow flies.

RV sites, facilities: There are 160 sites with full hookups (30 amps), 50 sites with partial hookups, 32 sites for tents, and a few furnished cottages. Picnic tables and fire rings are provided. Restrooms, drinking water, flush toilets, showers, a general store, limited cell phone reception, ice, propane, a fishing pond, and an RV dump station are available. An ATM and supplies are available four miles away in Julian. Leashed pets are permitted.

Reservations, fees: Reservations are accepted. Fees for campsites are $20–26 per night per vehicle (two people) and cottages are $150 per night for two people (no children or pets in the cottages), plus $2 for each additional camper and $2 per pet. Major credit cards are accepted. Open year-round.

Directions: From El Cajon, drive east on I-8 to Highway 79 (near Descanso Junction). Turn north on Highway 79 and drive 20 miles to Julian and the campground on the left.

Contact: Pinezanita Trailer Ranch, P.O. Box 2380, Julian, CA 92036-2380, 760/765-0429, website: www.pinezanita.com.

22 WILLIAM HEISE COUNTY PARK

Rating: 6

near Julian
See map pages 828–829

This is a beautiful county park, set at 4,200 feet, that offers hiking trails and a playground, all amid pretty woodlands with a mix of oak and pine. A great hike starts right at camp (at the tent camping area), signed "Nature Trail." It joins with the Canyon Oak Trail and, after little more than a mile, links with the Desert View Trail. Here you will reach an overlook with a beautiful view of the Anza-Borrego Desert and the Salton Sea. The park features 900 acres of mountain forests of oak, pine, and cedar. A popular

CALIFORNIA

equestrian trail is the Kelly Ditch Trail, which is linked to Cuyamaca Rancho State Park and Lake Cuyamaca. The vast Anza-Borrego Desert State Park lies to the east, and the historic mining town of Julian is five miles away. Julian is known for its Apple Day Festival each fall.

RV sites, facilities: There are 40 sites, one drive-through, for RVs up to 40 feet or tents, 41 sites for tents only, two group sites (tents only) for up to 80 people, and one cabin. Picnic tables and fire grills are provided. Restrooms, drinking water, flush toilets, showers, a coin-operated laundry, an RV dump station, picnic areas, and a playground are available. Supplies are available five miles away in Julian. Leashed pets are permitted.

The Cedar Fire in fall 2003 burned down a cabin and the entry station and damaged some of the surrounding area. As of press time, the status of the remaining cabin was unknown.

Reservations, fees: Reservations are accepted at 858/565-3600. The fee is $14 per night Monday–Thursday and $16 per night Friday–Sunday, plus $1 per pet per night. The tent-only group sites are $50 per night. Cabins are $35 per night. A senior discount is available. Major credit cards are accepted. Open year-round.

Directions: From El Cajon, drive east on I-8 to Highway 79 (near Descanso Junction). Turn north on Highway 79 and drive to Julian and Highway 78. Turn west (left) on Highway 78 and drive to Pine Hills Road. Turn south on Pine Hills Road and drive two miles to Frisius Drive. Turn left on Frisius Drive and drive two miles to the park.

Contact: San Diego County Parks Department, 858/694-3049.

23 SAN ELIJO STATE BEACH

🧍 🚲 🏊 🎣 🛶 🐕 ♿ 🚐 ⛺

Rating: 9

in Cardiff by the Sea
See map pages 828–829

As with South Carlsbad State Beach, about half the sites overlook the ocean, that is, these are bluff-top campgrounds. The swimming and surfing are good here. The narrow bluff-backed stretch of sandy beach has a nearby reef that is popular for snorkeling and diving. What more could you ask for? Well, for one thing, how about not so many trains? Yep, train tracks run nearby and

the trains roll by several times a day. So much for a chance at tranquillity. Regardless, it is a beautiful beach just north of the small town of Cardiff by the Sea. As at all state beaches, reservations are usually required to get a spot between Memorial Day weekend and Labor Day weekend. Nearby San Elijo Lagoon at Solana Beach is an ecological preserve. Though this is near a developed area, there are numerous white egrets, as well as occasional herons and other marine birds.

RV sites, facilities: There are 171 sites, four with full hookups (30 amps), for RVs up to 35 feet (maximum of 24 feet at sites with hookups) or tents and one hike-in/bike-in site. Picnic tables and fire rings are provided. Restrooms, drinking water, flush toilets, coin-operated showers, cell phone reception, a coin-operated laundry, an RV dump station, an ATM, and a small store are available. Lifeguard service is available in the summer. Some facilities are wheelchair-accessible. Leashed pets are permitted, but not on the beach.

Reservations, fees: Reserve at 800/444-PARK (800/444-7275) or online at www.reserveamerica.com ($7.50 reservation fee). The fees are $14–18 per night and $2 per person per night for the hike-in/bike-in site. A senior discount is available. Open year-round.

Directions: Drive on I-5 to Encinitas and the Encinitas Boulevard exit. Take that exit and drive west on Encinitas Boulevard for one mile to U.S. 101 (South Coast Highway). Turn south on U.S. 101 and drive two miles to the park on the right.

Contact: San Elijo State Beach, 760/753-5091; San Diego Coast District Office, 858/642-4200.

24 DOS PICOS COUNTY PARK

🧍 🎣 🐕 🏇 ♿ 🚐 ⛺

Rating: 6

near Ramona
See map pages 828–829

Dos Picos means "two peaks" and is the highlight of a landscape featuring old groves of oaks and steep, boulder-strewn mountain slopes. Some of the oaks are 300 years old. The park covers 78 acres. As a county park, this camp is often missed by folks relying on less complete guides. The park is quite picturesque, with plenty of shade trees and a small pond. Several nearby recreation options are available in the area, including Lake Poway and Lake Sutherland. The elevation is 1,500 feet.

RV sites, facilities: There are 48 sites with partial hookups (30 amps) for RVs up to 40 feet, 12 tent sites, and one group area for up to 55 people. Picnic tables and fire grills are provided. Restrooms, drinking water, flush toilets, showers, an RV dump station, and a playground, horseshoes, and soccer field are available. Supplies, an ATM, and a coin-operated laundry are one mile away in Ramona. Leashed pets are permitted.

Reservations, fees: Make reservations at 858/565-3600. The fee is $12–16 per night, with a maximum of eight people per site, plus $2 per additional vehicle and $1 per pet per night. The group site is $75 per night. A senior discount is available. Major credit cards are accepted. Open year-round.

Directions: Drive on I-8 to El Cajon and the exit for Highway 67. Take that exit and drive north on Highway 67 for 22 miles to Mussey Grade Road. Turn right (a sharp turn) on Mussey Grade Road and drive two miles to the park.

Contact: San Diego County Parks Department, 858/694-3049, fax 858/495-5841, website: www.sdparks.org.

25 DE ANZA HARBOR RESORT

Rating: 5

on Mission Bay

See map pages 828–829

Location means everything in real estate and campgrounds, and this private park passes the test. It is set on a small peninsula that is surrounded on three sides by Mission Bay, Sea World, and the San Diego Zoo. Premium sites overlook Mission Bay, but you pay the highest price for an RV site in California to get it. A beach and golf course are adjacent to the park. Mission Bay has 27 miles of shoreline, expansive beach frontage, great windsurfing, fantastic boating for water-skiing, and ocean access for deep-sea fishing. Note that a 5 mph speed limit is enforced on the northern bay and on the entire bay after sunset.

RV sites, facilities: There are 243 sites with full hookups (30 amps) and patios for RVs. Restrooms, drinking water, flush toilets, showers, a

playground, an RV dump station, a coin-operated laundry, modem access, cell phone reception, a recreation room, pool tables, bike rentals, a boat ramp, propane, and a store are available. An ATM is within one mile. Some facilities are wheelchair-accessible. Leashed pets are permitted.

Reservations, fees: Make reservations at 800/924-7529. The fees are $31–50 per night for sites with no hookups and $51–99 per night with full hookups, plus $3 per person per night for more than four people, a $3 boat fee, and a $3 pet fee. Major credit cards are accepted. Open year-round.

Directions: Drive on I-5 south to San Diego and the Clairemont Drive/Mission Bay exit. Take that exit (stay to your left) to a stop sign at Clairemont Drive. Turn left and drive west to East Mission Bay Drive. Turn right and drive north (the road becomes De Anza Road) .7 mile to the park at the end of the road (2727 De Anza Road).

Contact: De Anza Harbor Resort, 858/273-3211, fax 858/581-5748.

26 CAMPLAND ON THE BAY

Rating: 5

on Mission Bay

See map pages 828–829

No kidding, this is one of the biggest campgrounds on this side of the galaxy. It has space for both tenters and RVers, and you can usually find a spot to shoehorn your way into. The park overlooks Kendall Frost Wildlife Preserve and is set on Mission Bay, a beautiful spot and a boater's paradise; it includes a private beach. Water-skiing, windsurfing, and ocean access for deep-sea fishing are preeminent. Note that a 5 mph speed limit is enforced on the northern bay and on the entire bay after sunset. Sea World, just north of San Diego, offers a premium side trip.

RV sites, facilities: There are 750 sites, most with partial or full hookups and 25 drive-through, for RVs or tents. Picnic tables and fire grills are provided. Restrooms, drinking water, flush toilets, showers, cable TV, a phone, modem access, swimming pools, a hot tub, a recreation hall, an arcade, a playground, an RV dump station, a coin-operated laundry, a store, RV supplies, propane, a boat ramp, boat docks, water toy rentals, boat and bike rentals, and groceries are available. Leashed pets are permitted.

Reservations, fees: Reservations are accepted up to two years in advance at 800/422-9386 ($25 site guarantee fee); up to a 20-minute wait is possible when calling. The fees are $40–75 per night for tent sites and $53–160 per night for RV sites, plus $5 for boats and trailers, $30 for a boat slip up to 20 feet, and $3 per pet per night. There is a maximum of eight people per site. A senior discount is available. Major credit cards are accepted. Open year-round.

Directions: Drive on I-5 south to San Diego and the Balboa-Garnet exit. Take that exit to Mission Bay Drive and drive to Grand Avenue. Turn right and drive one mile to Olney Street. Turn left on Olney Street and drive to Pacific Beach Drive. Turn left and drive a short distance to the campground entrance.

From northbound I-5 in San Diego, take the Grand-Garnet exit. Stay in the left lane to Grand Avenue. Turn left on Grand Avenue and drive to Olney Street. Turn left on Olney Street and continue as above.

Contact: Campland on the Bay, 858/581-4200, fax 858/581-4206, 800/422-9386 (administration office), website: www.campland.com.

27 SANTA FE PARK RV RESORT

Rating: 3

in San Diego
See map pages 828–829

This camp is a short drive from a variety of side trips, including the San Diego Zoo, Sea World, golf courses, beaches, sportfishing, and Tijuana. The owners here are smart and pleasant.

RV sites, facilities: There are 129 RV sites with full hookups (30 amps). No tent camping is allowed. Restrooms, drinking water, flush toilets, showers, a playground, a swimming pool, a hot tub, an RV dump station, cell phone reception, cable TV, a recreation room with a pool table and Ping-Pong, a weight room, and a coin-operated laundry are available. An ATM is within 1.5 miles. Some facilities are wheelchair-accessible. Leashed pets are permitted.

Reservations, fees: Make reservations at 800/959-3787. The fee is $36–52 per night, plus $2.50 per-

son for more than three people and $2 per pet per night. Weekly rates are available. Major credit cards are accepted. Open year-round.

Directions: Drive on I-5 south to San Diego and the Balboa-Garnet exit. Take that exit a short distance to Damon Street (the first left). Turn left and drive .25 mile to Santa Fe Street. Turn left and drive one mile to the camp on the right (5707 Santa Fe Street).

On northbound I-5, drive to the exit for Grand-Garnet. Take that exit and continue as it feeds to East Mission Bay Drive. Continue six blocks to Damon Street. Turn right and drive .25 mile to Santa Fe Street. Turn left and drive one mile to the camp on the right (5707 Santa Fe Street).

Contact: Santa Fe Park RV Resort, 858/272-4051, fax 858/272-2845, website: www.santafeparkrvresort.com.

28 SANTEE LAKES REGIONAL PARK

Rating: 6

near Santee
See map pages 828–829

This is a 190-acre park built around a complex of seven lakes. Most campsites are lakefront, and the park is best known for its fishing. The lakes are stocked with 44,000 pounds of fish, with fantastic lake records including a 39-pound catfish, 16-pound rainbow trout, 12-pound largemouth bass, and 2.5-pound bluegill. Quiet, low-key boating is the name of the game here. Rowboats, pedal boats, and canoes are available for rent. This small regional park is 20 miles east of San Diego. It receives more than 100,000 visitors per year. The camp is set at 400 feet elevation.

RV sites, facilities: There are 172 sites, 23 drive-through, with full hookups (30, 50 amps) for RVs up to 45 feet and 61 sites for tents. Some sites have barbecue grills and picnic tables. Restrooms, drinking water, flush toilets, showers, an RV dump station, boat rentals, a meeting hall, a playground, a swimming pool, a store, a snack bar, a recreation center, modem access, pay phones, propane, and a coin-operated laundry are available. Some facilities are wheelchair-accessible. Leashed pets are permitted at campsites only.

Reservations, fees: Make reservations at 619/596-3141. The fee is $20–35 per night with a six-per-

CALIFORNIA

son maximum, plus $2 per night for each additional vehicle and $1 per pet per night. Monthly rates are available. Major credit cards are accepted. Open year-round.

Directions: Drive on I-8 to El Cajon and Highway 67. Turn north on Highway 67 and drive two miles to Santee and the Prospect Avenue exit. Take that exit and turn left and drive to Magnolia. Turn right on Magnolia and drive to Mission Gorge Road. Turn left on Mission Gorge Road and drive 2.5 miles to Carlton Hills Drive. Turn right and drive to Carlton Oaks Drive. Turn left and drive a mile to the park on the right.

Contact: Santee Lakes Regional Park, 619/596-3141, website: www.santeelakes.com.

29 VACATIONER RV RESORT

Rating: 1

near El Cajon
See map pages 828–829

This camp is 25 minutes from San Diego, 40 minutes from Mexico. Discount tickets to area attractions such as the San Diego Zoo, Sea World, and the Wild Animal Park are available. It's not a real pretty place, and that is compounded with the very real chance of getting highway noise if you have a site at the back of the park. The RV sites are on asphalt and gravel. The elevation is 260 feet.

RV sites, facilities: There are 157 sites with full hookups (30, 50 amps) for RVs up to 40 feet, including 20 pull-through sites. No tent camping is allowed. Restrooms, drinking water, flush toilets, showers, a coin-operated laundry, a recreation room, a volleyball court, horseshoes, modem access, a swimming pool, a hot tub, an RV dump station, satellite TV, a free video library, and a picnic area with barbecues are available. A supermarket and ATM are across the street. Some facilities are wheelchair-accessible. Leashed pets up to 20 pounds are permitted.

Reservations, fees: Reservations are accepted. The fee is $29–36 per night, plus $2 per person for more than two people. Major credit cards are accepted. Open year-round.

Directions: From El Cajon, drive east on I-8 for three miles to the Greenfield Road exit. Take that exit, turn north and drive 100 feet to East Main Street. Turn left (west) and drive .5 mile to the park on the left.

Contact: Vacationer RV Resort, 619/442-0904, fax 619/442-4378, website: www.vacationerrv resort.com.

30 RANCHO LOS COCHES RV PARK

Rating: 2

near Lake Jennings
See map pages 828–829

Nearby Lake Jennings provides an option for boaters and anglers and also has a less developed camp on its northeast shore. Vista Point on the southeastern side of the lake provides a side trip. (For more information, see the following description of Lake Jennings County Park.)

RV sites, facilities: There are 137 sites with full hookups (30, 50 amps) for RVs and four areas for tents. Restrooms, drinking water, flush toilets, showers, an RV dump station, modem access, cable TV, a swimming pool, a hot tub, a recreation hall, a chapel, Ping-Pong, horseshoes, and a coin-operated laundry are available. A store is one mile away. Leashed pets are permitted.

Reservations, fees: Reservations are accepted at 800/630-0448. The fee is $25–38 per night, plus $3 per person for more than two people. Open year-round.

Directions: From El Cajon, drive east on I-8 to the Los Coches Road exit. Take that exit, and drive under the freeway to Highway 8 Business Route. Turn right on Highway 8 Business Route and drive to the park entrance on the left (13468 Hwy. 8 Business).

Contact: Rancho Los Coches RV Park, 619/443-2025, fax 619/443-8440, website: www.rancho loscochesrv.com.

31 LAKE JENNINGS COUNTY PARK

Rating: 6

on Lake Jennings
See map pages 828–829

Lake Jennings is a nice little backyard fishing hole and recreation area set at 850 feet, with easy access from I-8. Most people come here for the fishing. It has quality prospects for giant catfish, as well as largemouth bass, bluegill, and, in cool months, rainbow trout. Note that while shore fishing is available on a daily basis, boats are permitted on the lake only on Saturday, Sunday, and Monday. A fishing permit is required. The highlights here are evening picnics, summer catfishing, and a boat ramp and rentals. Only one campground is right at the lake, and this is it. This lake wasn't named after my late pal, Waylon Jennings, the legendary country singer (he's got a campground named after him in Littlefield, Texas), but he would have approved of it even if it were.

RV sites, facilities: There are 28 sites with full hookups (30 amps), 35 sites with partial hookups for RVs up to 35 feet, and 26 tent sites. Picnic tables and fire grills are provided. Restrooms, drinking water, flush toilets, showers, a playground, and an RV dump station are available. A store is nearby. Leashed pets are permitted.

Reservations, fees: Make reservations at 858/565-3600 or by fax at 619/260-6492. The fee is $14–18 per night, with a maximum of eight people per site, plus $1 per pet per night. Open year-round.

Directions: From El Cajon, drive east on I-8 for 16 miles to Lake Jennings Park Road. Turn north on Lake Jennings Park Road and drive to the park entrance.

Contact: San Diego County Parks Department, 858/694-3049, fax 858/495-5841.

32 ALPINE SPRINGS RV RESORT

Rating: 3

near Lake Jennings
See map pages 828–829

This is one of the few RV parks in the area that welcomes tent campers. It is set in the foothill country in Alpine, eight miles from Lake Jennings to the west. (See the prior entry for Lake Jennings County Park, about 10 minutes away, for more information.) Other nearby lakes include larger El Capitan to the north and Loveland Reservoir to the south. The Viejas Casino and an outlet shopping center are also nearby.

RV sites, facilities: There are 250 sites, 90 with full hookups (50 amps), for RVs or tents. Picnic tables are provided. Restrooms, drinking water, flush toilets, showers, an RV dump station, a coin-operated laundry, and a swimming pool are available. An ATM is within one mile. No pets over 15 pounds are permitted.

Reservations, fees: Reservations are accepted. The fees are $18 per night for tent sites and $25–30 per night for RV sites, plus $3 per person for more than two people. Monthly rates are available. Open year-round.

Directions: From San Diego, drive east on I-8 about 30 miles to Alpine, then continue just east of Alpine to the East Willows exit. Take that exit, cross over the freeway, and drive .3 mile to the park on the left (5635 Willows Drive).

Contact: Alpine Springs RV Resort, 619/445-3162.

33 PASO PICACHO

Rating: 8

in Cuyamaca Rancho State Park
See map pages 828–829

This camp is set at 4,900 feet in Cuyamaca Rancho State Park, best known for Cuyamaca Peak, 6,512 feet. The Stonewall Peak Trail is accessible from across the street. This is a five-mile round-trip, featuring the climb to the summit at 5,730 feet. There are long-distance views from here highlighted by the Salton Sea and the Anza-Borrego State Desert. It's the most popular hike in the park, an easy to moderate grade, and completed by a lot of families. Another more ambitious hike is the trail up to Cuyamaca Peak, starting at the southern end of the campground, a 6.5-mile round-trip tromp (alas, on a paved road; at least it's closed to traffic) with a climb of 1,600 feet in the process. The view from the top is breathtaking, with the Pacific Ocean and Mexico visible to the west and south, respectively. Park headquarters features exhibits about the area's Native Americans, gold mining, and natural history. The Stonewall Mine was once the greatest of gold mines in Southern California. You can also learn here that Cuyamaca means "The Rain Beyond."

RV sites, facilities: There are 85 sites for RVs up to 30 feet or tents, two group camps for up to 60 people each, five cabins, a nature den cabin, and one hike-in/bike-in site. Fire grills and picnic tables are provided. Restrooms, drinking water, flush toilets, coin-operated showers, and an RV dump station are available. Supplies are available nearby in Cuyamaca. Leashed pets are permitted.

Reservations, fees: Reserve at 800/444-PARK (800/444-7275) or online at www.reserveamerica.com ($7.50 reservation fee). The fees are $12–15 per night, $75 for group sites, $27 per night for regular cabins, and $31 for the nature den cabin. A senior discount is available. Open year-round.
Directions: From El Cajon, drive east on I-8 to Highway 79 (near Descanso Junction). Turn north (left) and drive nine miles to the park entrance on the left.
Contact: Cuyamaca Rancho State Park, 760/765-0755, fax 760/765-3021.

34 CUYAMACA RANCHO STATE PARK–GREEN VALLEY

Rating: 8

in Cuyamaca Rancho State Park
See map pages 828–829

Green Valley is the southernmost camp in Cuyamaca Rancho State Park. It is set at 3,900 feet, with Cuyamaca Mountain (6,512 feet) looming overhead to the northwest. A trailhead is available (look for the picnic area) at the camp for an easy five-minute walk to Green Valley Falls, and it can be continued out to the Sweetwater River in a 1.5-mile round-trip. Newcomers should visit the park headquarters, where exhibits detail the natural history of the area. The park covers 25,000 acres with more than 100 miles of trails for hiking, mountain biking, and horseback riding.
RV sites, facilities: There are 81 sites for RVs up to 30 feet or tents and one hike-in/bike-in site. Picnic tables and fire grills are provided. Restrooms, drinking water, flush toilets, coin-operated showers, and an RV dump station are available. A store and propane are nearby. Some facilities are wheelchair-accessible. Leashed pets are permitted.
Reservations, fees: Reserve at 800/444-PARK (800/444-7275) or online at www.reserveamerica.com ($7.50 reservation fee). The fees are $12–15 per night and $2 per person per night for hike-in/bike-in site. plus $4 per additional vehicle. A senior discount is available. Open year-round.
Directions: From El Cajon, drive east on I-8 to Highway 79 (near Descanso Junction). Turn north (left) on Highway 79 and drive seven miles to the campground entrance on the left (near Mile Marker 4).

Contact: Cuyamaca Rancho State Park, 760/765-0755, fax 760/765-3021.

35 LAGUNA

Rating: 4

near Little Laguna Lake in Cleveland National Forest
See map pages 828–829

Laguna is set on Little Laguna Lake, one of the few lakes in America where "Little" is part of its official name. That's because for years everybody always referred to it as "Little Laguna Lake," and it became official. Yep, it's a "little" lake all right, a relative speck, with the camp on its eastern side at an elevation of 5,550 feet. A trailhead for the Pacific Crest Trail is a mile north on the Sunrise Highway/Laguna Mountain Road. Big Laguna Lake, which is actually a pretty small lake, is one mile to the west.
RV sites, facilities: There are 73 sites for RVs up to 50 feet or tents and 30 sites for tents only. Picnic tables and fire grills are provided. Restrooms, drinking water, flush toilets, and coin-operated showers are available. A store and propane are available nearby. Some facilities are wheelchair-accessible. Leashed pets are permitted.
Reservations, fees: Some sites are available by reservation only; reserve at 877/444-6777 or online at www.reserveusa.com ($9 reservation fee). The fee is $14 per night. Open year-round.
Directions: From San Diego, drive east on I-8 about 50 miles to the Laguna Junction exit for the Sunrise Highway. Turn north on the Sunrise Highway and drive 11 miles to the town of Mount Laguna. Continue north on Sunrise Highway/Laguna Mountain Road for 2.5 miles to the campground entrance road on the left.
Contact: Cleveland National Forest, Descanso Ranger District, 619/445-6235, fax 619/445-1753.

36 VALLECITO COUNTY PARK

Rating: 3

near Anza-Borrego Desert State Park
See map pages 828–829

This county park in the desert gets little attention in the face of the other nearby attractions.

This is a 71-acre park built around a sod recon-struction of the historic Vallecito Stage Station. It was part of the Butterfield Overland Stage from 1858 to 1861. The route carried mail and passengers from Missouri to San Francisco in 25 days, covering 2,800 miles. Vallecito means "little valley." It provides a quiet alternative to some of the busier campgrounds in the desert. One bonus is that it is usually 10 degrees cooler here than at Agua Caliente. A covered picnic area is a big plus. Other nearby destinations include Agua Caliente Hot Springs, Anza-Bor-rego Desert State Park to the east, and Lake Cuyamaca and Cuyamaca Rancho State Park about 35 miles away. The elevation is 1,500 feet.

RV sites, facilities: There are 44 primitive sites for RVs up to 40 feet or tents and one large group area. Picnic tables, fire rings, and barbecues are provided. Drinking water, flush toilets, and a play-ground are available. Leashed pets are permitted.

Reservations, fees: Make reservations at 858/565-3600 or by fax at 619/260-6492. The fee is $14–18 per night, with a maximum of eight people per site, plus $1 per pet per night. The group area is $35 per night. Major credit cards are accepted. Open Labor Day weekend through Memorial Day weekend; closed June, July, and August.

Directions: From Julian, at the intersection of Highway 78 and Highway 79, take Highway 78 east and drive 12 miles to San Felipe Road (Coun-ty Road S2). Turn right and drive 18 miles to the park entrance on the right.

Contact: San Diego County Parks Department, 858/694-3049, fax 858/495-5841, website: www .sdparks.org.

nearby. If you would like to see some cold water, Lake Cuyamaca and Cuyamaca Rancho State Park are about 35 miles away. The elevation is 1,350 feet. The park covers 910 acres with sev-eral miles of hiking trails.

RV sites, facilities: There are 20 sites with full hookups (30 amps) and 51 sites with partial hookups for RVs up to 40 feet, 34 tent-only sites, and a caravan area for groups of up to 100 peo-ple. Picnic tables and fire grills are provided. Restrooms, drinking water, flush toilets, show-ers, outdoor and indoor pools, and a playground with horseshoes and shuffleboard are available. Groceries and propane are available nearby. Some facilities are wheelchair-accessible. No pets are allowed.

Reservations, fees: Make reservations at 858/565-3600. The fee is $14–18 per night, with a maxi-mum of eight people per site. The group area is $75 per night. Major credit cards are accepted. Open Labor Day weekend through Memorial Day weekend; closed June, July, and August.

Directions: From El Cajon, drive east on I-8 about 75 miles to the town of Ocotillo (the first town after crossing from San Diego County to Impe-rial County) and County Road S2/Imperial High-way. Turn north on County Road S2/Imperial Highway and drive 25 miles to the park entrance.

From Julian, take Highway 78 east and drive 12 miles to County Road S2/San Felipe Road. Turn right on County Road S2/San Felipe Road and drive 21 miles south to the park entrance.

Contact: San Diego County Parks Department, 858/694-3049, fax 858/495-5841, website: www .sdparks.org.

37 AGUA CALIENTE COUNTY PARK

Rating: 3

near Anza-Borrego Desert State Park
See map pages 828–829

This is a popular park in winter. It has two nat-urally fed pools: a large outdoor pool is kept at its natural 96°F, and an indoor pool is heated and outfitted with jets. Everything is hot here. The weather is hot, the coffee is hot, and the water is hot. And hey, that's what "Agua Caliente" means—hot water, named after the nearby hot springs. Anza-Borrego Desert State Park is also

38 BURNT RANCHERIA

Rating: 6

near the Pacific Crest Trail in Cleveland National Forest
See map pages 828–829

Burnt Rancheria is set high on the slopes of Mount Laguna in Cleveland National Forest, at an elevation of 6,000 feet. The Pacific Crest Trail runs right alongside this camp. It is quiet and private with large, roomy sites. Desert View Pic-nic Area, a mile to the north, provides a good side trip. Wooded Hill Group Campground is less than two miles away.

RV sites, facilities: There are 58 sites for RVs up to 50 feet or tents and 51 sites for tents only. Picnic tables and fire grills are provided. Drinking water and vault toilets are available. Supplies are nearby in Mount Laguna. Leashed pets are permitted.

Reservations, fees: Some sites are available by reservation only; reserve at 877/444-6777 or online at www.reserveusa.com ($9 reservation fee). The fee is $14 per night (two-vehicle maximum). A senior discount is available. Open May through October.

Directions: From San Diego, drive east on I-8 about 50 miles to the Laguna Junction exit for the Sunrise Highway. Turn north on the Sunrise Highway/Laguna Mountain Road and drive about nine miles north to the campground entrance road on the right.

Contact: Cleveland National Forest, Descanso Ranger District, 619/445-6235, fax 619/445-1753.

39 SAN DIEGO METROPOLITAN KOA

Rating: 2

in Chula Vista
See map pages 828–829

This is one in a series of parks set up primarily for RVs cruising I-5. Chula Vista is between Mexico and San Diego, allowing visitors to make side trips east to Lower Otay Lake, north to the San Diego attractions, south to Tijuana, or "around the corner" on Highway 75 to Silver Strand State Beach. Nearby San Diego Bay is beautiful with excellent water-skiing (in designated areas), windsurfing, and a great swimming beach.

RV sites, facilities: There are 206 sites, 100 drive-through, with full hookups (50 amps) for RVs up to 65 feet, 64 sites for tents, and a few cabins. Picnic tables and barbecue grills are provided. Restrooms, drinking water, flush toilets, showers, modem access, a playground, an RV dump station, a coin-operated laundry, a swimming pool, a hot tub, a whirlpool, bike rentals, a kitchen, propane, firewood, and groceries are available. Some facilities are wheelchair-accessible. Leashed pets are permitted.

Reservations, fees: Make reservations at 800/762-

KAMP (800/762-5267). The fees are $28–39 for tent sites and $32–51 per night for RV sites, plus $5 per additional vehicle and $4 per person per night for more than two people. Cabins are $39–75 per night. Major credit cards are accepted. Open year-round.

Directions: Drive on I-5 to Chula Vista and the exit for E Street. Take that exit and drive east on E Street for three miles to 2nd Street. Turn north on 2nd Street and drive to the park on the right (111 N. 2nd Street).

Contact: San Diego Metropolitan KOA, 619/427-3601, fax 619/427-3622, website: www.koa.com.

40 CHULA VISTA MARINA AND RV PARK

Rating: 6

in Chula Vista
See map pages 828–829

This RV park is close to San Diego Bay, a beautiful, calm piece of water where water-skiing is permitted in designated areas. An excellent swimming beach is available, and conditions in the afternoon for windsurfing are also excellent.

RV sites, facilities: There are 237 sites, a few drive-through, with full hookups (30, 50 amps) for RVs up to 60 feet. Restrooms, drinking water, flush toilets, showers, modem access, TV hookups, a playground, a heated swimming pool and spa, a game room, a marina, a fishing pier, a free boat launch, a coin-operated laundry, propane, and groceries are available. Some facilities are wheelchair-accessible. Leashed pets are permitted.

Reservations, fees: Make reservations at 800/770-2878. The fee is $45–61 per night, plus $3 for each additional vehicle, $3 per night for each extra person over two people, and $1 per pet per night. A senior discount is available. Major credit cards are accepted. Open year-round.

Directions: Drive on I-5 to Chula Vista and the exit for J Street/Marina Parkway. Take that exit and drive west a short distance to Sandpiper Way. Turn left and drive a short distance to the park on the left (460 Sandpiper Way).

Contact: Chula Vista Marina and RV Park, 619/422-0111, fax 619/422-8872, website: www .chulavistarv.com.

CALIFORNIA

41 SWEETWATER SUMMIT REGIONAL PARK

Rating: 7

near Sweetwater Reservoir in Bonita
See map pages 828–829

This regional park overlooks the Sweetwater Reservoir in Bonita. The campground is set right on the summit, overlooking the Sweetwater Valley. This camp has equestrian sites with corrals for the horses, and only a $1 fee per horse. There are 15 miles of trails for horseback riding in the park. There are several golf courses nearby, and it is 15 minutes from Tijuana. The Chula Vista Nature Center is nearby on the shore of South San Diego Bay.

RV sites, facilities: There are 58 sites with partial hookups (30 amps) for RVs or tents, including 10 with horse corrals. Picnic tables and fire grills are provided. Restrooms, drinking water, flush toilets, showers, and an RV dump station are available. Leashed pets are permitted.

Reservations, fees: Make reservations at 858/565-3600 or by fax at 619/260-6492. The fee is $16 per night, with a maximum of eight people per site, plus $1 per pet per night. Open year-round.

Directions: From San Diego, drive south on I-805 for 10 miles to Bonita Road. Turn east on Bonita Road and drive to San Miguel Road. Continue on San Miguel Road another two miles to the park entrance on the left.

Contact: San Diego County Parks Department, 858/694-3049, fax 858/495-5841, website: www.sdparks.org.

42 INTERNATIONAL MOTOR INN RV PARK

Rating: 3

near Imperial Beach
See map pages 828–829

Easy access from I-5 is a big plus here, but call ahead for available space. For nearby side trips, head west to Imperial Beach, south to Tijuana, or east to Otay Lake with its megasized bass and catfish.

RV sites, facilities: There are 42 sites, a few drive-through, with full hookups (30 amps) for RVs. Picnic tables and patios are provided. Restrooms, drinking water, flush toilets, showers, a swimming pool, a whirlpool, and a coin-operated laundry are available. An ATM is within one block. Leashed pets are permitted.

Reservations, fees: Reservations are accepted. The fee is $27.60 per night, plus $2 per person per night for more than two people. A senior discount is available. Major credit cards are accepted. Open year-round.

Directions: Drive on I-5 south of the San Diego area to San Ysidro and the Via de San Ysidro exit. Take that exit to Calle Primera. Drive south on Calle Primera to the park (190 E. Calle Primera, next to Motel 6).

Contact: International Motor Inn RV Park, 619/428-4486.

43 LA PACIFICA RV RESORT

Rating: 1

in San Ysidro
See map pages 828–829

This RV park is less than two miles from the Mexican border, with regular Mexicoach bus service from the park to downtown Tijuana and back. Do this trip just once and you will find out how two miles can be the equivalent of a million miles.

RV sites, facilities: There are 177 sites, 72 drive-through, with full hookups (30, 50 amps), individual lawns, and patios for RVs. Flush toilets, showers, a heated swimming pool, cable TV, a whirlpool, a recreation room, a book and video library, an RV dump station, a coin-operated laundry, and propane are available. All facilities are wheelchair-accessible. Leashed pets under 20 pounds are permitted.

Reservations, fees: Reservations are accepted at 888/786-6997. The fee is $32 per night. Major credit cards are accepted. Open year-round.

Directions: From the San Diego area, drive south on I-5 to San Ysidro and the exit for Dairymart Road. Take that exit east to Dairymart Road and drive to San Ysidro Boulevard. Turn left and drive to the park on the left (1010 San Ysidro Boulevard).

Contact: La Pacifica RV Resort, 619/428-4411, fax 619/428-4413, website: www.lapacificarvresort.com.

CALIFORNIA

44 POTRERO COUNTY PARK

Rating: 3

near the Mexican border

See map pages 828–829

If you are looking for a spot to hole up for the night before getting through customs, this is the place. This park covers 115 acres, set at an elevation of 2,300 feet. It is a broad valley peppered with coastal live oaks amid grassy meadows and rocky foothills. The average summer high temperature is in the 90-degree range. Potrero means "pasturing place." Some of the summer grazers are rattlesnakes, occasionally spotted here. Side trips include the railroad museum and century-old historic stone store in Campo and the Mexican community of Tecate. In fact, it is just a heartbeat away from the customs inspection station in Tecate. A good side trip is to the nearby Tecate Mission Chapel, where you can pray that the guards do not rip your car up in the search for contraband.

RV sites, facilities: There are 32 sites with partial hookups (20, 30 amps) for RVs up to 45 feet or tents, seven tent-only sites, and one group camping area. Picnic tables and fire grills are provided. Restrooms, drinking water, flush toilets, showers, a playground, and an RV dump station are available. Picnic areas, ball fields, and a dance pavilion are available. You can buy supplies in Potrero. Leashed pets are permitted.

Reservations, fees: Make reservations at 858/565-3600. The fee is $10–12 per night, with a maximum of eight people per site, plus $1 per pet. Open year-round.

Directions: From El Cajon, drive east on Highway 94 for 42 miles (near the junction of Highway 188) to Potrero Valley Road. Turn north on Potrero Valley Road and drive one mile to Potrero Park Road. Turn east on Potrero Park Road and drive one mile to the park entrance.

Contact: San Diego County Parks Department, 858/694-3049, fax 858/495-5841, website: www.sdparks.org.

45 LAKE MORENA COUNTY PARK

Rating: 7

near Campo

See map pages 828–829

Lake Morena is like a silver dollar in a field of pennies. It's a great lake for fishing and the campground was remodeled in 2002. Yes, Lake Morena is out in the boondocks, but it's well worth the trip. If you like to fish for bass, don't miss it. The county park camp is on the southern shore at an elevation of 3,200 feet. The landscape is chaparral, oak woodlands, and grasslands, and the campsites are set in a grove of oaks. When full, the lake covers 1,500 acres, but water levels can fluctuate a great deal here. Catch rates for bass can be excellent, and some bass are big; the lake record for largemouth bass weighed 19 pounds, two ounces, and the lake record for trout weighed nine pounds, six ounces. Boat rentals are available nearby. The lake is just south of Cleveland National Forest and only seven or eight miles from the California/Mexico border.

RV sites, facilities: There are 58 sites with partial hookups (30 amps) for RVs up to 65 feet, 28 sites with no hookups for RVs or tents, and 10 cabins. Picnic tables and fire grills are provided. Restrooms, drinking water, flush toilets, and showers are available. A store, a boat ramp, and rowboat rentals are nearby. Leashed pets are permitted.

Reservations, fees: Make reservations at 858/565-3600 or by fax at 619/260-6492. The fee is $12–16 per night, with a maximum of eight people per site, plus $1 per pet per night. Cabins are $25 per night. A senior discount is available. Open year-round.

Directions: From El Cajon, drive east on I-8 to Pine Valley, then continue east for four miles to Buckman Springs Road/County Road S1. Take the exit, turn south, and drive 5.5 miles to Oak Drive. Turn right on Oak Drive and drive (well signed) to Lake Morena Drive. Turn left on Lake Morena Drive and drive to the park entrance.

Contact: San Diego County Parks Department, 858/694-3049, fax 858/495-5841, website: www.sdparks.org.

CALIFORNIA

46 LAKE MORENA RV PARK

Rating: 6

near Campo

See map pages 828–829

This camp is near the southern side of Lake Morena, a great lake for fishing and off-season vacations. It is one of three camps near the lake and the best for RVs. Lake Morena, at 3,200 feet, is a large reservoir in the San Diego County foothills and is known for big bass. The lake record weighed 19 pounds, two ounces. The lake has a paved ramp and rowboat rentals.

RV sites, facilities: There are 26 sites with full hookups (30 amps) and 16 with partial hookups for RVs up to 40 feet. Picnic tables are provided. Flush toilets, showers, an RV dump station, modem access, cable TV, limited cell phone reception, propane, and a coin-operated laundry are available. An ATM is within a quarter mile. Some facilities are wheelchair-accessible. Leashed pets are permitted.

Reservations, fees: Reservations are recommended. The fee is $28 per night, plus $2 per person per night for more than four people. A deposit is required on three-day weekends. Open year-round.

Directions: From El Cajon, drive east on I-8 to Pine Valley, then continue east for four miles to Buckman Springs Road/County Road S1. Take the Buckman Springs exit, turn right (south) on Buckman Springs Road, and drive 5.5 miles to Oak Drive. Turn right on Oak Drive and drive 1.5 miles to Lake Morena Drive. Turn left on Lake Morena Drive and drive to the park on the right (2330 Lake Morena Drive).

Contact: Lake Morena RV Park, 619/478-5677, fax 619/478-5031.

47 OUTDOOR WORLD RV PARK AND CAMPGROUND

Rating: 6

in Boulevard

See map pages 828–829

The town of Boulevard is centrally located for a wide variety of recreation possibilities. This park is located on 163 wooded acres and offers large shaded sites. About 10 miles to the north is Mount Laguna, with hiking trails available. About 30 minutes to the south is the nearest point of entry to Mexico at Tecate. Fishing at Lake Morena or Lake Cuyamaca is also a possibility, as is soaking in nearby hot springs. This park is under new ownership as of January 2003, and many extensive improvements are being made throughout. A casino is within five miles, and Lake Morena is a 20-minute drive.

RV sites, facilities: There are 144 sites, 122 with full hookups (30, 50 amps) and 16 with partial hookups, for RVs or tents, four trailer rentals, and a primitive tent camping area. A clubhouse, pool table, restrooms, a store, propane, an espresso stand, showers, a hot tub, modem access, horseshoes, limited cell phone reception, fire rings, and a group camping area are available. An ATM is within four miles. Some facilities are wheelchair-accessible. Leashed pets are permitted, with some dogs prohibited.

Reservations, fees: Reservations are recommended. The fees are $15 per night for tent sites and $25 per night for RV sites, plus $3 per person for more than two people. Weekly and monthly rates are available. A senior discount is available. Major credit cards are accepted. Open year-round.

Directions: From El Cajon, drive east on I-8 for 65 miles (past Alpine) to the Live Oak Springs exit. Take that exit and turn south and drive three miles to Tierra del Sol Road. Turn right and drive .25 mile to Highway 94. Turn right and drive three miles to Shasta Lane. Turn left and drive .75 mile to the campground on the left.

Contact: Outdoor World RV Park and Campground, 37133 Hwy. 94, Boulevard, CA 91905, 619/766-4480, fax 619/766-4480, website: www .outdoorworldretreat.com.

CALIFORNIA

California

Chapter 28

The Southern Deserts

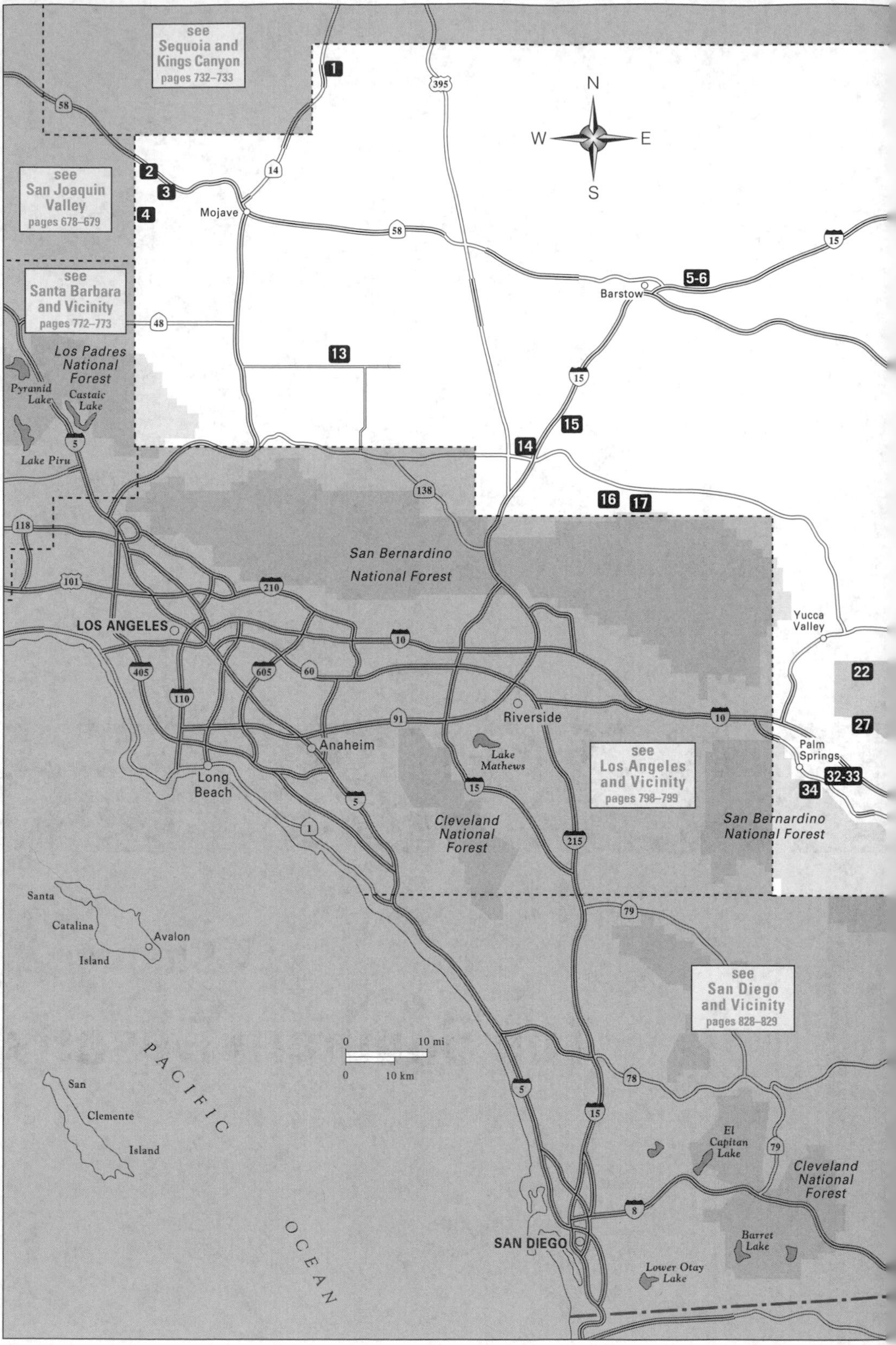
see
Sequoia and
Kings Canyon
pages 732–733
see
San Joaquin
Valley
pages 678–679
see
Santa Barbara
and Vicinity
pages 772–773
see
Los Angeles
and Vicinity
pages 798–799
see
San Diego
and Vicinity
pages 828–829
N
W
E
S
Mojave
Barstow
Los Padres
National
Forest
Pyramid
Lake
Castaic
Lake
Lake Piru
San Bernardino
National Forest
LOS ANGELES
Riverside
Anaheim
Long
Beach
Lake
Mathews
Cleveland
National
Forest
Yucca
Valley
Palm
Springs
San Bernardino
National Forest
Santa
Catalina
Island
Avalon
San
Clemente
Island
PACIFIC
OCEAN
El
Capitan
Lake
Cleveland
National
Forest
SAN DIEGO
Barret
Lake
Lower Otay
Lake
0
10 mi
10 km
1
2
3
4
5-6
13
14
15
16
17
22
27
32-33
34
CALIFORNIA

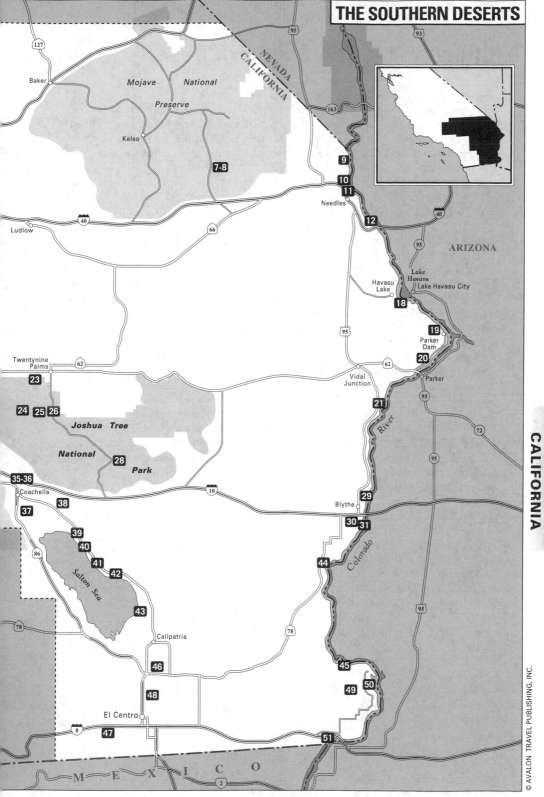

Baker

Mojave National Preserve

Kelso

127

7-8

9

10
11
Needles

12

163

95

NEVADA
CALIFORNIA

93

ARIZONA

95

Lake
Havasu
Lake Havasu City

Havasu
Lake

18

40

66

40

Ludlow

95

19
Parker
Dam

20

Twentynine
Palms

62

62

Vidal
Junction

Parker

95

23

24 25 26

Joshua Tree

21

River

72

National

28

Park

35-36

Coachella

38

10

29

Blythe

30 31

37

86

39

40

41

44

Colorado

95

42

Salton
Sea

43

78

Calipatria

78

45

46

49
50

48

51

El Centro

8

47

CALIFORNIA

M   E   X   I   C   O

2

© AVALON TRAVEL PUBLISHING, INC.

Chapter 28—The Southern Deserts

There is no region so vast in California—yet with fewer people—than the broad expanse of Anza-Borrego State Desert, Joshua Tree National Park, Mojave National Preserve, the Salton Sea, and endless Bureau of Land Management (BLM) land. And yet the area is best-loved not for the desert, but for the boating, water sports, and recreation of the Colorado River. Although these areas are joined at the edges, each has distinct qualities, separate and special.

What often attracts people to this region for the first time is a party at the Colorado River. On big weekends, it can even seem as if there is a party within close vicinity of every boat ramp on the river. The weather is hot, the boats are fast, and the body oil can flow as fast as the liquid refreshments. Campgrounds are available throughout this region for the best access to the water.

The rest of the area is far different.

Anza-Borrego (covered in the San Diego and Vicinity chapter) is so big that it seems to stretch to forever. The park covers 600,000 acres and is the largest state park in California. The landscape features virtually every type of desert terrain, but most obvious are canyons, badlands, and barren ridges. In spring, the blooming cholla can be impressive. This is habitat for the endangered desert bighorn, and seeing one can be the highlight of a lifetime of wildlife viewing.

Joshua Tree National Park, on the other hand, features a sweeping desert landscape edged by mountains and peppered with the peculiar Joshua tree. It is best known by most as the place where the high desert (Mojave Desert, 4,000 feet elevation) meets the low desert (Colorado Desert). This transition and diversity create the setting for a similar diversity in vegetation and habitat. The strange piles of rocks often appear to have been chipped, chiseled, and then left in rows and piles by an ancient prehistoric giant.

The national park is far different than Mojave National Preserve. The highlights here are the Kelso Dunes, a series of volcanic cliffs, and a forest of Joshua trees. It is remote and explored by relatively few visitors. The Mojave is a point of national significance because it is where three major landscapes join: the Sonoran Desert, the Colorado Desert, and the Mojave Desert.

The Salton Sea and endless BLM desert land provide one of the most distinct (and strange) lakes and terrain on earth. The Salton Sea, created in an accident from a broken dike, is one of the largest inland seas in the world. The desert land of the BLM is under BLM control only because no other agency wanted it.

Throughout this barren area, campgrounds are sprinkled in most of the best spots. In all, I found 51 camps for RVs. Somewhere amid all this, a place like no other, you will likely be able to find a match for your desires.

■1 RED ROCK CANYON STATE PARK

Rating: 8

near Mojave

See map pages 852–853

This unique state park is one of the prettiest spots in the region year-round. What makes it worthwhile in any season is the chance to see wondrous geologic formations, most of them tinted red. The park has paleontology sites and the remains of 1890s-era mining operations. A great, easy hike is the two-mile walk to Red Cliffs Natural Preserve, where there are awesome 300-foot cliffs and columns, painted red by the iron in the soil. Part of this area is closed from February through June to protect nesting raptors. For those who don't hike, a must is driving up Jawbone Canyon Road to see Jawbone and Last Chance Canyons. Hikers have it better. The park also has excellent wildflower blooms from March through May. The elevation is 2,600 feet.

RV sites, facilities: There are 50 sites for RVs up to 30 feet or tents. Picnic tables and fire grills are provided. Drinking water, pit toilets, an RV dump station, a picnic area, exhibits, and a nature trail are available. In spring and fall, nature walks led by rangers are available. Some facilities are wheelchair-accessible. Leashed pets are permitted.

Reservations, fees: Reservations are not accepted. The fee is $10 per night. A senior discount is available. Open year-round.

Directions: Drive on Highway 14 to the town of Mojave (50 miles east of the Los Angeles Basin area). Continue northeast on Highway 14 for 25 miles to the park entrance on the left.

Contact: Red Rock Canyon State Park, Mojave Desert Sector, 661/942-0662, fax 661/940-7327.

■2 BRITE VALLEY AQUATIC RECREATION AREA

Rating: 7

at Brite Lake

See map pages 852–853

Brite Valley Lake is a speck of a water hole (90 acres) on the northern flanks of the Tehachapi Mountains in Kern County, at an elevation of 4,000 feet. No gas motors are permitted on the lake, so it's perfect for canoes, kayaks, or inflatables. That makes the campground and lake ideal for a family camping experience. No swimming is permitted. Fishing is fair for trout in the spring, catfish in the summer.

RV sites, facilities: There are 12 sites with partial hookups (20 amps) for RVs and a tent camping area. Picnic tables and fire grills are provided. Restrooms, drinking water, flush toilets, showers, an RV dump station, a playground, three pavilions with electricity and tables, and a fish-cleaning station are available. Supplies and an ATM are available about eight miles away in Tehachapi. Leashed pets are permitted.

Reservations, fees: Reservations are not accepted. The fee is $10–15 per night for each vehicle. Open late April to late October.

Directions: Drive on Highway 58 to Tehachapi and the exit for Tucker Road/Highway 202. Take that exit and drive a short distance to Highway 202. Turn west on Highway 202 and drive 3.5 miles to Banducci Road. Turn left on Banducci Road and follow the signs for about a mile to the park on the right.

Contact: Brite Valley Aquatic Recreation Area, 661/822-3228, fax 661/823-8529, website: www.tvrp.org.

■3 INDIAN HILL RANCH CAMPGROUND

Rating: 7

near Tehachapi

See map pages 852–853

This is a unique park with five ponds, all stocked with trout and catfish. The campground is open year-round and offers spacious, private sites with oak trees and a view of Brite Valley. The elevation is 5,000 feet.

RV sites, facilities: There are 46 sites, 21 drive-through and 37 with full hookups (30, 50 amps), for RVs and a group site for up to 50 people. Picnic tables and fire pits are provided. Flush toilets, showers, an RV dump station, propane, modem access, and five stocked fishing ponds are available. Leashed pets are permitted.

Reservations, fees: Reservations are accepted. The fee is $25–35, plus $6 per additional vehicle and $6 per person for more than four people. The group site is $350 per night, plus $5 per person for more than 50 people. Major credit cards are accepted. Open year-round, with some sites closed from November to mid-May.

Directions: Drive on Highway 58 to Tehachapi and the exit for Tucker Road/Highway 202. Take that exit and drive a short distance to Highway 202. Turn west on Highway 202 and drive 3.5 miles to Banducci Road. Turn left and drive a mile to Indian Hill/Arosa Road. Turn left and drive 1.5 miles to the campground.

Contact: Indian Hill Ranch Campground, 661/822-6613, website: www.IndianHillRanch.com.

4 TEHACHAPI MOUNTAIN PARK

Rating: 5

southwest of Tehachapi

See map pages 852–853

This county park is overlooked by most out-of-towners. It is a pretty spot covering 570 acres, set on the slopes of the Tehachapi Mountains, with elevations in the park ranging from 5,500 to 7,000 feet. The roads to the campgrounds are steep, the sites are flat, and each site has its own toilet, a rarity (yes, it's really true—61 toilets). Trails for equestrians are available. This park is popular not only in spring, but also in winter, with the elevations sometimes high enough to get snow, offering a chance at winter sports (chains often required for access). The park lies eight miles southwest of the town of Tehachapi (pop. 6,550) on the southern side of Highway 58 between Mojave and Bakersfield. Woody's Peak (7,986 feet) overlooks the park from its dominion in the Tehachapi Mountains, the dividing line between the San Joaquin Valley and the Los Angeles Basin.

RV sites, facilities: There are 61 sites for RVs or tents, a group campsite, and 10 cabins with 10 beds each. Picnic tables and fire grills are provided. Restrooms, drinking water (natural spring), and pit and vault toilets are available. Some facilities are wheelchair-accessible. Leashed pets are permitted.

Reservations, fees: Reservations are not accepted. The fee is $10 per night, plus $2 per pet per night. Cabins are $225 per night. Reserve the group site and cabins at 661/868-7002. A senior discount is available. Open year-round.

Directions: In Tehachapi, take Tehachapi Boule-

vard to the Cury Street exit. Take that exit south and drive about three miles to Highline Road. Turn right on Highline Road and drive two miles to Water Canyon Road. Turn left on Water Canyon Road and drive three miles to the park.

Contact: Kern County Parks Department, info line, 661/822-4632, website: www.co.kern.ca.us/parks/index.htm.

5 CALICO GHOST TOWN REGIONAL PARK

Rating: 4

near Barstow

See map pages 852–853

Let me tell you about this ghost town: there are probably more people here now than there have ever been. In the 1880s and 1890s it was a booming silver mine town, and there are still remnants of that. Alas, it now has lots of restaurants and shops. Recreation options include riding on a narrow-gauge railroad, touring what was once the largest silver mine in California, and watching an old-style play with villains and heroes. Whatever you do, don't take any artifacts you may come across, such as an old nail, a jar, or anything; you will be doomed with years of bad luck. No foolin'. This is a 480-acre park with self-guided tours, hiking trails, gold panning, summer entertainment, and a museum, with festivals held through the year.

RV sites, facilities: There are 252 sites, 23 pull-through, 46 with full hookups (30 amps), and 58 with partial hookups, for RVs and tents, three group camping areas, cabins, and a bunkhouse. Fire grills are provided. Restrooms, drinking water, flush toilets, showers, and three RV dump stations are available. A pay phone, restaurants, a saloon, an ATM, and shops are on-site. Groceries, propane, and laundry facilities are 10 miles away. Leashed pets are permitted.

Reservations, fees: Make reservations at 800/TO-CALICO (800/862-2542). The fee is $18–22 per night; cabins are $28 per night. The bunkhouse is $5 per person per night with a minimum charge of $60. Major credit cards are accepted. Open year-round.

Directions: From Barstow, drive northeast on I-15 for seven miles to the exit for Ghost Town Road.

CALIFORNIA

Take that exit and drive north on Ghost Town Road for three miles to the park on the left.
Contact: Calico Ghost Town Regional Park, San Bernardino County, 760/254-2122, fax 760/254-2047, website: www.calicotown.com.

6 BARSTOW CALICO KOA

Rating: 3

near Barstow
See map pages 852-853
Don't blame us if you end up way out here. Actually, for vacationers making the long-distance grind of a drive on I-15, this KOA can seem like the promised land. It's clean, and a nightly quiet time ensures that you have a chance to get rested. It made a Gold Rating in 2002. But hey, as long as you're here, you might as well take a side trip to the Calico Ghost Town, about 10 miles to the northeast at the foot of the Calico Mountains. Rockhounding and hiking are other nearby options. The elevation is 1,900 feet.
RV sites, facilities: There are 78 sites, many drive-through with partial or full hookups (50 amps), for RVs up to 70 feet or tents. Picnic tables and fire grills are provided. Restrooms, drinking water, flush toilets, showers, an RV dump station, modem access, a snack bar, a playground, a swimming pool, a recreation room, a store, propane, firewood, ice, a meeting pavilion, and laundry room facilities are available. Some facilities are wheelchair-accessible. Leashed pets are permitted.
Reservations, fees: Make reservations at 800/KOA-0059 (800/562-0059). The fee is $19-27 per night, plus $2.50 per person for more than two people and $1 per night per additional vehicle for more than two vehicles. Major credit cards are accepted. Open year-round.
Directions: From Barstow, drive northeast on I-15 for seven miles to the exit for Ghost Town Road. Take that exit and drive left under the freeway to a frontage road. Turn left at the frontage road and drive .25 mile to the campground on the right.
Contact: Barstow Calico KOA, 760/254-2311, fax 760/254-2247, website: www.koa.com.

7 MID HILLS

Rating: 5

in the Mojave National Preserve
See map pages 852-853
This is a primitive campground set among the junipers and piñon trees in a mountainous area at 5,600 feet. It is one of two little-known camps in the vast desert that is now managed by the National Park Service. An attraction here is the privacy afforded by the vegetation in the sites. There is an eight-mile one-way trail that starts across from the entrance to Mid Hills and is routed down to the Hole-in-the-Wall Campground. It is a pleasant walk in spring and fall.
RV sites, facilities: There are 35 sites for RVs up to 22 feet or tents. Picnic tables and fire grills are provided. Drinking water and vault toilets are available. Leashed pets are permitted.
Reservations, fees: Reservations are not accepted. The fee is $12 per night. A senior discount is available. Open year-round.
Directions: Drive on I-40 to Essex Road (near Essex, 116 miles east of Barstow). Take that exit and drive north on Essex Road for 10 miles to Black Canyon Road. Turn north and drive nine miles (at Hole-in-the-Wall Campground, the road becomes dirt) and continue seven miles to Wild Horse Canyon Road. Turn right and drive two miles (rough, dirt road) to the campground on the right.
Contact: Mojave National Preserve, 760/928-2572, fax 760/928-2072.

8 HOLE-IN-THE-WALL (AND BLACK CANYON GROUP AND HORSE CAMP)

Rating: 6

in the Mojave National Preserve
See map pages 852-853
This is the largest and best-known of the camps in the vast Mojave National Preserve; the campgrounds are set at 4,400 feet in elevation, with a family camp, group camp, and equestrian camp situated across the road from each other. An interesting side trip is to the Mitchell Caverns in the nearby Providence Mountains State Recreation Area.

RV sites, facilities: There are 35 sites for RVs or tents, one group site for up to 50 people, and an equestrian camp. Picnic tables and fire grills are provided. Drinking water, vault toilets, and an RV dump station are available. Leashed pets are permitted.

Reservations, fees: Reservations are not accepted. The fee is $12 per night. Make reservations for group camp and horse camp at 760/326-6322; the fee is $25 per night, including horse corral if needed. Open year-round.

Directions: Drive on I-40 to Essex Road (near Essex, 116 miles east of Barstow). Take that exit and drive north on Essex Road for 10 miles to Black Canyon Road. Turn north and drive nine miles to the campgrounds.

Contact: Mojave National Preserve, 760/733-4040, fax 760/733-4027.

9 RAINBO BEACH RESORT AND MARINA

Rating: 6

on the Colorado River

See map pages 852–853

The big bonus here is the full marina, making this resort on the Colorado River the headquarters for boaters and water-skiers. And headquarters it is, with tons of happy folks who are extremely well lubed, both inside and out. (For boating details, see the following entry for Needles Marina Park.)

RV sites, facilities: There are 55 sites, 10 drive-through, with full hookups (20, 30, 50 amps) for RVs. Picnic tables are provided except at drive-through sites. Restrooms with showers, a coin-operated laundry, modem access, limited cell phone reception, a swimming pool, a hot tub, a recreation room, a beer bar, and a weekend restaurant are available. A boat dock with gas is nearby. An ATM is within three miles. Leashed pets are permitted.

Reservations, fees: Reservations are accepted. The fee is $24–31 per night. A senior discount is available. Major credit cards are accepted. Open year-round.

Directions: Drive on I-40 to Needles and River Road. Turn north on River Road and drive 1.5 miles to the resort on the right.

Contact: Rainbo Beach Resort and Marina,

760/326-3101, fax 760/326-5085, website: www.coloradoriverinfo.com.

10 NEEDLES MARINA PARK

Rating: 6

on the Colorado River

See map pages 852–853

Bring your suntan lotion and a beach towel. This section of the Colorado River is a big tourist spot where the body oil and beer can flow faster than the river. There are a ton of hot bodies and hot boats, and water-skiing dominates the adjacent calm-water section of the Colorado River. However, note that upstream of the Needles-area put-in is the prime area for water-skiing. Downstream is the chance for canoeing or kayaking. Meanwhile, there's also an 18-hole golf course adjacent to the camp, but most folks head for the river. Compared to the surrounding desert, this park is almost a golden paradise.

RV sites, facilities: There are 190 sites, some drive-through, with full hookups (30, 50) for RVs and six cabins. Picnic tables are provided. Restrooms, drinking water, flush toilets, showers, a heated pool, a whirlpool, a recreation room, modem access, a playground, a boat ramp, boat slips, a store, gas, and laundry facilities are available. Leashed pets are permitted.

Reservations, fees: Reservations are accepted. The fee is $31.50–33.50 per night, plus $7–7.50 per person for more than three people and $2 per pet per night. Major credit cards are accepted. Open year-round.

Directions: Drive on I-40 to Needles and the exit for J Street. Take that exit and drive to Broadway. Turn left on Broadway and drive .75 mile to Needles Highway. Turn right on Needles Highway and drive .5 mile to the park on the left.

Contact: Needles Marina Park, 760/326-2197, fax 760/326-4125, website: www.needlesmarina.com.

11 NEEDLES KOA

Rating: 2

near the Colorado River

See map pages 852–853

At least you've got the Needles KOA out here,

complete with swimming pool, where you can get a new start. Side trips include venturing to the nearby Colorado River or heading north to Lake Mead. Of course, you could always go to Las Vegas. Nah.

RV sites, facilities: There are eight sites with no hookups for RVs or tents, 30 sites with partial hookups, 63 sites with full hookups (50 amps), and several camping cabins. Restrooms, drinking water, flush toilets, showers, a recreation room, a swimming pool, a playground, a store, a snack bar, propane, and laundry facilities are available. Some facilities are wheelchair-accessible. Leashed pets are permitted.

Reservations, fees: Make reservations at 800/562-3407. The fee is $18–26 per night, plus $2 for more than two people. Cabins are $40–60 per night. Major credit cards are accepted. Open year-round.

Directions: Drive on I-40 to Needles and the exit for West Broadway. Take that exit and drive to Needles Highway. Turn left on Needles Highway and drive a short distance to National Old Trails Highway. Turn left and drive to the park on the right (5400 National Old Trails Highway).

Contact: Needles KOA, 760/326-4207, fax 760/326-6329, website: www.koa.com.

12 MOABI REGIONAL PARK

Rating: 7

on the Colorado River
See map pages 852–853

Campsites are situated in the main area of the park along 2.5 miles of shoreline peninsula. One of the features here is 24 group areas. The adjacent Colorado River provides the main attraction, the only thing liquid around these parts that isn't contained in a can or bottle. The natural response when you see it is to jump in the water, and everybody does so, with or without a boat. You'll see lots of wild and crazy types having the times of their lives on the water. The boating season is a long one here, courtesy of that desert climate. Fishing is available for trout, catfish, bass, striped bass, and crappie.

RV sites, facilities: There are more than 600 sites, many with partial or full hookups (20, 30, 50 amps) and 10 drive-through, for RVs or tents, and 24 group camping areas. Picnic tables and fire grills are provided at most sites. Restrooms, flush toilets, showers, laundry facilities, a store, ice, a playground, two RV dump stations, boat rentals (limited), bait, and a boat ramp are available. A softball field, volleyball, basketball, horseshoes, and a putting green are also available. An 18-hole golf course is nearby. Some facilities are wheelchair-accessible. Leashed pets are permitted.

Reservations, fees: Reservations are accepted Monday through Friday, 8 A.M. to 4 P.M.. The fee is $18–35 per night per vehicle, plus $2 per person per night for more than six people and $1 per pet. Long-term rates available, with a five-month limit. Major credit cards are accepted. Open year-round.

Directions: From Needles, drive east on I-40 for 11 miles to Park Moabi Road. Turn left on Park Moabi Road and continue a half mile to the park entrance at the end of the road.

Contact: Moabi Regional Park, 760/326-3831, fax 760/326-3272, website: www.co.san-bernardino.ca.us/parks/moabi.

13 SADDLEBACK BUTTE STATE PARK

Rating: 8

near Lancaster
See map pages 852–853

This 3,000-acre park was originally established to preserve ancient Joshua trees. In fact, it used to be called Joshua Tree State Park, but folks kept getting it confused with Joshua Tree National Park, so it was renamed. The terrain is sparsely vegetated and desertlike, with excellent hiking trails up the nearby buttes. The best hike is the Saddleback Loop, a five-mile trip that features a 1,000-foot climb to Saddleback Summit at 3,651 feet. On rare clear days, there are fantastic views in all directions, including the Antelope Valley California Poppy Preserve, the surrounding mountains, and the Mojave Desert. On the typical hazy day, the poppy reserve might as well be on the moon; you can't even come close to seeing it. The elevation is 2,700 feet.

RV sites, facilities: There are 50 sites for self-contained RVs up to 24 feet, trailers, or tents. A group camp is available for up to 30 people. Picnic tables and fire grills are provided. Drinking water, flush toilets, and an RV dump station are available. A visitors center is nearby. Some facilities are wheelchair-accessible. Leashed pets are permitted.

Reservations, fees: No reservations are accepted for single sites, but the group camp may be reserved at 800/444-PARK (800/444-7275) or online at www.reserveamerica.com ($7.50 reservation fee). The fees are $10 per night for individual sites and $22.50 per night for the group site. A senior discount is available. Open year-round.

Directions: Drive east on Highway 14 to Lancaster and the exit for Avenue J. Take that exit and drive east on Avenue J for 17 miles to the park entrance on the right.

Or drive west on Highway 14 to Lancaster to the exit for 20th Street. Take that exit and drive to Avenue J. Turn east on Avenue J and drive 17 miles to the park entrance on the right.

Contact: Saddleback Butte State Park, Mojave Desert Information Center, 661/942-0662, fax 661/940-7327.

14 DESERT WILLOW RV PARK

Rating: 2

in Hesperia
See map pages 852–853

This is an RV park for I-15 cruisers looking to make a stop. Silverwood Lake, a 1,000-acre recreation lake with fishing, boating, and water sports, is 16 miles to the south. The elevation is 3,200 feet.

RV sites, facilities: There are 176 sites, 24 drive-through, with full hookups (30, 50 amps) for RVs. Restrooms, hot showers, cable TV hookups, a convenience store, groceries, ice, a coin-operated laundry, cell phone reception, modem access, propane, a swimming pool, an indoor spa, a recreation room, and a library are on the premises. An ATM is within one block. Some facilities are wheelchair-accessible. Leashed pets are permitted.

Reservations, fees: Make reservations at 800/900-8114. The fee is $23–26 per night, plus $2 per person for more than two people and $2 per pet per night. Open year-round, with limited winter facilities.

Directions: Drive on I-15 to Hesperia and the exit for Main Street. Take that exit and drive west to the park on the right (12624 Main St. West).

Contact: Desert Willow RV Park, 760/949-0377, fax 760/949-4334.

15 SHADY OASIS VICTORVILLE KOA

Rating: 3

near Victorville
See map pages 852–853

Most long-distance trips on I-15 are grueling endurance tests with drivers making the mistake of trying to get a decent night's sleep at a roadside rest stop. Why endure the torture, especially with a KOA way out here, in Victorville of all places? Where the heck is Victorville? If you are exhausted and lucky enough to find the place, you won't be making any jokes about it. By the way, if you visit, keep your eyes open for the ghost of Roy Rogers, the legendary cowboy singer. He lived just minutes away from this park, where he sat happily in his living room with his horse, Trigger, which he had stuffed. Happy trails to you, until we meet again.

RV sites, facilities: There are 136 sites, many with partial or full hookups (30 amps), some drive-through, for RVs up to 75 feet or tents, and several cabins. Picnic tables and fire grills are provided. Restrooms, drinking water, flush toilets, showers, a recreation room, bicycle rentals, a swimming pool, a playground, modem access, a store, propane, firewood, and a laundry room are available. Some facilities are wheelchair-accessible. Leashed pets are permitted.

Reservations, fees: Make reservations at 800/KOA-3319 (800/562-3319). The fee is $22–26 per night, plus $2 per person for more than two people and $1 per night for additional vehicle. Cabins are $39–43 per night. Major credit cards are accepted. Open year-round.

Directions: Drive on I-15 to Victorville and Stoddard Wells Road (north of Victorville). Turn south on Stoddard Wells Road and drive a short distance to the campground (16530 Stoddard Wells Road).

Contact: Shady Oasis Victorville KOA, 760/245-6867, fax 760/243-2108, website: www.koa.com.

16 HESPERIA LAKE CAMPGROUND

Rating: 5

in Hesperia
See map pages 852–853

This is a slightly more rustic alternative to Desert Willow RV Park in Hesperia. There is a small lake/pond for recreational fishing with a small fishing fee, but no fishing license is required. No boating or swimming are allowed, but youngsters usually get a kick out of feeding the ducks and geese that live at the pond.

RV sites, facilities: There are 53 sites, 30 with partial hookups (50 amps), for RVs or tents, and two group areas for tents. Picnic tables and fire pits are provided. Restrooms, drinking water, flush toilets, showers, a playground, horseshoes, and a fishing pond are available. Some facilities are wheelchair-accessible. Leashed pets are permitted in the camp, but not around the lake.

Reservations, fees: Reservations are not accepted. The fee is $13–20 per night, plus $1 per person for more than six people and $2 per pet. A senior discount is available for fishing on Monday. Major credit cards are accepted. Open year-round.

Directions: Drive on I-15 to Hesperia and the exit for Main Street. Take that exit and drive east on Main Street for 9.5 miles (the road curves and changes names) to the park on the left.

Contact: Hesperia Lake Campground, 760/244-5951 or 800/521-6332.

17 MOJAVE NARROWS REGIONAL PARK

Rating: 7

on the Mojave River
See map pages 852–853

Almost no one except the locals knows about this little county park. It is like an oasis in the Mojave Desert. It is set at 2,000 feet and provides a few recreation options, including a pond stocked in season with trout and catfish, horseback riding facilities, and equestrian trails. Hiking includes a wheelchair-accessible trail. The Mojave River level fluctuates here, almost disappearing in some years in summer and early fall. One of the big events of the year here is on Fathers' Day in June, the Huck Finn Jubilee. Note: the gate closes each evening.

RV sites, facilities: There are 110 sites, seven drive-through, 38 with full hookups (20, 30 amps), for RVs or tents. Picnic tables and barbecue grills are provided. Restrooms, drinking water, flush toilets, showers, an RV dump station, a snack bar, a pay phone, a playground, an archery range, bait, boat rentals, horse rentals, and horseback riding facilities are available. A store, propane, and a coin-operated laundry are available three miles from the campground. Leashed pets are permitted.

Reservations, fees: Reservations accepted for RVs with full hookups. The fee is $10–17 per night, plus $2 per person for more than six people, $1 per pet, and a $3 fishing fee. Weekly rates are available. Major credit cards are accepted. Open year-round.

Directions: Drive on I-15 to Victorville and the exit for Bear Valley Road. Take that exit and drive east on Bear Valley Road for six miles to Ridgecrest. Turn left on Ridgecrest, drive three miles, and make a left into the park.

Contact: Mojave Narrows Regional Park, 760/245-2226, website: www.co.san-bernardino.ca.us/parks/mojave.htm.

18 HAVASU LANDING RESORT & CASINO

Rating: 6

on western shore of Lake Havasu
See map pages 852–853

Located on the western shore of Lake Havasu, this full-service resort is run by the Chemehuevi Indian Tribe. It even includes a casino with slot machines and a card room. The resort is situated in a desert landscape in the Chemehuevi Valley. A boat shuttle operates from the resort to the London Bridge and Havasu City, Arizona. A mobile home park is situated within the resort and an airstrip is nearby. Fifty of the RV sites are rented for the entire winter season. Permits are required for off-road vehicles and can be obtained at the resort. This is one of the most popular boating areas in the southwestern United States. The lake is 45 miles long, covers 19,300

CALIFORNIA

acres, and is located at the low elevation of 482 feet. Havasu was created when the Parker Dam was built across the Colorado River.

RV sites, facilities: There are 130 sites with full hookups (30 amps) for RVs up to 35 feet, three large tent camping areas, and mobile home and RV rentals. Picnic tables, restrooms with flush toilets and showers, an RV dump station, a coin laundry, picnic areas, a restaurant and lounge, a casino, 24-hour security, a marina with gas dock, bait and tackle, a general store and deli, boat launches, boat slips, a fish-cleaning room, dry storage, a boat shuttle, and a boat launch and retrieval service are available. Cellular phone reception is available. An airport is nearby. Leashed pets are permitted.

Reservations, fees: Reservations are accepted; phone 800/307-3610. The fees are $22–$28 per night for RV sites and $10–$15 per night for tent sites, plus $2 per adult per night over two people per site and $6 per night per additional vehicle. Holiday rates are $15 for tent sites and $35–45 per night for RV sites, with a four-night minimum. Weekly and monthly rates are available. A boat launch fee is charged. Major credit cards are accepted. An ATM is on-site. Open year-round.

Directions: From Needles, drive south on Highway 95 for 19 miles to Havasu Lake Road. Turn left and drive 17.5 miles to the resort on the right.

From Blythe, drive north on Highway 95 for 79 miles to Havasu Lake Road. Turn right and drive 17.5 miles to the resort on the right.

Contact: Havasu Landing Resort & Casino, P.O. Box 1707, Havasu Lake, CA 92363, 760/858-4593 or 800/307-3610. For general information about Lake Havasu, contact the Lake Havasu Tourism Bureau, 928/453-3444 or 800/2-HAVASU (242-8278), website: www.golakehavasu.com; Lake Havasu Area Chamber of Commerce, 928/855-4115, website: www.havasuchamber.com.

19 BLACK MEADOW LANDING

Rating: 6

south of Lake Havasu on the Colorado River
See map pages 852–853

This area of the Colorado River attracts a lot of people so reservations are highly recommended.

Hot weather, warm water, and proximity to Las Vegas make this one of the top camping and boating hot spots in the West. Vacationers are here year-round, although fewer people use it in the late winter months. Black Meadow Landing is a large resort with hundreds of RV sites, lodging, and a long list of amenities. Once you arrive, everything you need for a stay should be available within the resort.

RV sites, facilities: There are 450 sites with full hookups (30 amps), tent camping, park model cabins, kitchen cabins, and a motel. Restrooms with flush toilets, drinking water, showers, picnic tables, picnic areas, horseshoe pits, a restaurant, a convenience store, a recreation room (winter only), bait and tackle, propane, a full-service marina, a boat launch, boat slips, boat and RV storage, a swimming lagoon, limited cellular phone reception, and a five-hole golf course are available. Leashed pets are permitted.

Reservations, fees: Reservations are accepted; phone 800/742-8278 (800/7-HAVASU). The fee is $25–$45 per night for two people, plus $6 per person per night and $6 per additional vehicle per night. RVs with air-conditioning are charged $6 per night extra for electricity. Tent camping is $20 per night. Monthly rates are available. Major credit cards are accepted. A senior discount is available during the winter season. Open year-round.

Directions: From Southern California, take I-10 east to Blythe and turn north on U.S. 95. Continue to Vidal Junction at the intersection of U.S. 95 and Highway 62. Turn east on Highway 62 and drive to Earp and Parker Dam Road. Continue straight on Parker Dam Road and drive to a Y intersection and Black Meadow Landing Road (near Parker Dam). Bear left on Black Meadow Landing Road and drive approximately nine miles to the resort at the end of the road.

From Northern California, drive to Barstow and I-40. Turn east on I-40 and drive to Needles. Continue east on I-40 to Arizona 95. Drive south on Arizona 95 to Lake Havasu City. Continue south to the Parker Dam turnoff. Turn west and drive across the dam to a Y intersection and Black Meadow Landing Road. Bear right on Black Meadow Landing Road and drive approximately nine miles to the resort at the end of the road.

Contact: Black Meadow Landing, 156100 Black

Meadow Road, Parker Dam, CA 92267, 760/663-4901 or 800/742-8278(7-HAVASU), website: www.blackmeadowlanding.com. For general information about the Colorado River and Lake Havasu, contact the Lake Havasu Tourism Bureau, 928/453-3444 or 800/2-HAVASU (242-8278), website: www.golakehavasu.com; Lake Havasu Area Chamber of Commerce, 928/855-4115, website: www.havasuchamber.com.

20 RIVER LAND RESORT

Rating: 6

on the Colorado River near Parker Dam
See map pages 852–853

This resort is located in the middle of a very popular boating area, particularly for water-skiing. Summer is the busiest time here because of the sunshine and warm water. In the winter, even though temperatures can get pretty cold, around 40 degrees at night, the campground fills with retirees from the snow or rain country. Even though the resort is located way out there on the Colorado River, there are plenty of services including a convenience store, swimming beach, and full-service marina. Here is a tip for anglers: one of the best spots for catfish is a few miles down the road below Parker Dam.

RV sites, facilities: There are 60 sites with full hookups (30 amps). Picnic tables are provided. Tent camping and park model cabins are available. Restrooms with flush toilets, showers, drinking water, a convenience store, a coin laundry, a full-service marina, a boat launch, boat slips, boat and RV storage, a swimming beach, a fishing pier, bait and tackle, a recreation room, horseshoe pits, and cable television are available. An ATM is within five miles and an 18-hole golf course is seven miles away. Cellular phone service is limited. Leashed pets are permitted.

Reservations, fees: Reservations are accepted; phone 760/663-3733. The fees are $20–30 per night, plus $2 per person per night in summer season and $2 per pet per night. Monthly rates are available. Major credit cards are accepted. Open year-round.

Directions: From Southern California, take I-10 east to Blythe and turn north on U.S. 95. Continue to Vidal Junction at the intersection of U.S.

95 and Highway 62. Turn east on Highway 62 and drive to Earp and Parker Dam Road. Continue straight on Parker Dam Road and drive five miles to the resort on the right.

Contact: River Land Resort, HC20 Box 105, Earp, CA 92242, 760/663-3733.

21 LOST LAKE RESORT

Rating: 6

on the Colorado River in Parker Valley
See map pages 852–853

If you're looking for a remote spot on the Colorado River, this is it. This is one of the only games in town, kind of like an oasis in the middle of the desert. Direct access to the Colorado River is provided, and this is one of the only places around that sells fishing licenses for this stretch of the Colorado River. The Parker Valley portion of the river is part of the Colorado River Indian Reservation, and the tribe requires that all anglers obtain a permit. One of the best spots for big catfish, including large flathead catfish and channel catfish, is below Parker Dam. If you catch a razorback sucker, a rare event, it must be released. It is an endangered species. Note that about half of the sites are filled with long-term or permanent renters. Also note that the resort does not provide refunds for "water conditions."

RV sites, facilities: There are 150 sites with full hookups (30 amps). Tent camping is available. Picnic tables are provided at most sites. Restrooms with flush toilets, showers, a coin laundry, a convenience store, a café, recreation room (winter only), boat and RV storage, a boat launch, bait and tackle, fishing licenses, a full-service marina, and limited cellular phone reception are available. Leashed pets are permitted.

Reservations, fees: Reservations are accepted; phone 760/664-4413. The fee is $20 per night per vehicle for three adults or two adults with two children. Monthly rates are available. Major credit cards are accepted. Open year-round.

Directions: From Southern California, take I-10 east to Blythe and turn north on U.S. 95. Drive for 31 miles to the resort on the right.

Contact: Lost Lake Resort, 42500 Highway 95, Blythe, CA 92225, 760/664-4413.

CALIFORNIA

22 BLACK ROCK CANYON AND HORSE CAMP

🏃 🏕 ♿ 🚐 ⛺

Rating: 4

in Joshua Tree National Park
See map pages 852–853

This is the fanciest darn campground this side of the desert. Why, it actually has drinking water. The camp is set at the mouth of Black Rock Canyon, 4,000 feet elevation, which provides good winter hiking possibilities amid unique (in other words, weird) rock formations. Show up in summer and you'll trade your gold for a sip of water. The camp is near the excellent Black Rock Canyon Visitor Center and a trailhead for a four-mile round-trip hike to a rock wash. If you scramble onward, the route continues all the way to the top of Eureka Peak, 5,518 feet, an 11-mile round-trip. But, hey, why not just drive there?

RV sites, facilities: There are 100 sites for RVs up to 40 feet or tents and 15 equestrian sites for up to six people and four horses per site. Picnic tables and fire grills are provided. Drinking water, flush toilets, and an RV dump station are available. The horse camp has hitching posts and a water faucet, and no tents are allowed. Some facilities are wheelchair-accessible. Leashed pets are permitted, but not on backcountry trails.

Reservations, fees: Reserve at 800/365-CAMP (800/365-2267) or online at http://reservations.nps.gov. The fee is $10 per night, plus a $10 park entrance fee per vehicle. A senior discount is available. Open year-round, weather permitting.

Directions: From the junction of I-10 and Highway 62 near Palm Springs, drive northeast on Highway 62 for 22.5 miles to Yucca Valley and Joshua Lane. Turn right (south) on Joshua Lane and drive about five miles to the campground.

Contact: Joshua Tree National Park, 760/367-5500, fax 760/367-6392; Black Rock Nature Center, 760/365-9585.

23 INDIAN COVE CAMPGROUND

🏃 🏕 🚐 ⛺

Rating: 4

in Joshua Tree National Park
See map pages 852–853

This is one of the campgrounds near the north-ern border of Joshua Tree National Park. The vast desert park, covering 1,238 square miles, is best known for its unique granite formations and scraggly looking trees. If you had to withstand the summer heat here, you'd look scraggly too.

RV sites, facilities: There are 101 sites for RVs up to 40 feet or tents and a group camp with 13 sites for tents only for up to 60 people. Drinking water is available at the Indian Cove Ranger Station. Pit toilets, picnic tables, and fire grills are provided. Gas, groceries, and laundry services are available in Joshua Tree, about 10 miles from camp. Leashed pets are permitted, but not on trails.

Reservations, fees: Reserve at 800/365-CAMP (800/365-2267) or online at http://reservations.nps.gov. The fees are $10 per night and $20–35 for group sites, plus a $10-per-vehicle park entrance fee. A senior discount is available. Open year-round.

Directions: From the junction of I-10 and Highway 62 near Palm Springs, drive northeast on Highway 62 for 22 miles to Yucca Valley, continue to the small town of Joshua Tree, then continue nine miles to Indian Cove Road. Turn right and drive three miles to the campground.

Contact: Joshua Tree National Park, 760/367-5500, fax 760/367-6392.

24 HIDDEN VALLEY

🏃 🏕 🚐 ⛺

Rating: 7

in Joshua Tree National Park
See map pages 852–853

This is one of California's top campgrounds for rock climbers. Set at 4,200 feet in the high desert country, this is one of several camping options in the area. A trailhead is available two miles from camp at Barker Dam, an easy one-mile loop that features the Wonderland of Rocks. The hike takes you next to a small lake with magical reflections of rock formations off its surface. The RV sites here are snatched up quickly, and this campground fills almost daily with rock climbers.

RV sites, facilities: There are 39 sites for RVs up to 40 feet or tents. Picnic tables and fire grills are provided. Pit toilets are available. No drinking water is available. Leashed pets are permitted.

Reservations, fees: No reservations are accepted

CALIFORNIA

and there is no camp fee, but there is a $10 park entrance fee per vehicle. A senior discount is available. Open year-round.

Directions: From the junction of I-10 and Highway 62 near Palm Springs, drive northeast on Highway 62 for 22 miles to Yucca Valley, then continue to the small town of Joshua Tree and Park Boulevard. Turn south on Park Boulevard and drive 14 miles to the campground on the left.

Contact: Joshua Tree National Park, 760/367-5500, fax 760/367-6392.

25 RYAN

Rating: 4

in Joshua Tree National Park
See map pages 852–853

This is one of the high desert camps in the immediate area (another is Jumbo Rocks; see the following listing). Joshua Tree National Park is a forbidding paradise: huge, hot, and waterless (most of the time). The unique rock formations look as if some great artist made them with a chisel. The elevation is 4,300 feet. The best hike in the park starts here—a three-mile round-trip to Ryan Mountain is a 1,000-foot climb to the top at 5,470 feet. The view is simply drop-dead gorgeous, not only of San Jacinto, Tahquitz, and San Gorgonio peaks, but of several beautiful rock-studded valleys as well as the Wonderland of Rocks.

RV sites, facilities: There are 31 sites for RVs up to 40 feet or tents. Picnic tables and fire grills are provided. Pit toilets are available. No drinking water is available. Hitching posts are available (bring water for the horses). Leashed pets are permitted.

Reservations, fees: No reservations are accepted and there is no camp fee, but there is a $10 park entrance fee per vehicle. A senior discount is available. Open year-round.

Directions: From the junction of I-10 and Highway 62 near Palm Springs, drive northeast on Highway 62 to Twentynine Palms and Utah Trail. Turn right (south) on Utah Trail and drive about 20 miles to the campground entrance on the left.

Contact: Joshua Tree National Park, 760/367-5500, fax 760/367-6392.

26 JUMBO ROCKS

Rating: 4

in Joshua Tree National Park
See map pages 852–853

Joshua Tree National Park covers more than 1,238 square miles. It is striking high-desert country with unique granite formations that seem to change color at different times of the day. This camp is one of the higher ones in the park at 4,400 feet, with adjacent boulders and rock formations that look as if they have been strewn about by an angry giant. It is a popular site for rock-climbing.

RV sites, facilities: There are 125 sites for RVs up to 40 feet or tents. Picnic tables and fire grills are provided. Pit toilets are available. No drinking water is available. Leashed pets are permitted.

Reservations, fees: No reservations are accepted and there is no camp fee, but there is $10 park entrance fee per vehicle. A senior discount is available. Open year-round.

Directions: From the junction of I-10 and Highway 62 near Palm Springs, drive northeast on Highway 62 to Twentynine Palms and Utah Trail. Turn right (south) on Utah Trail and drive about nine miles to the campground on the left side of the road.

Contact: Joshua Tree National Park, 760/367-5500, fax 760/367-6392.

27 SKY VALLEY RESORT

Rating: 2

near Palm Springs
See map pages 852–853

This park is a wonderful spot for family fun and relaxation. One of the best adventures in California is just west of Palm Springs, taking the tramway up from Chino Canyon to Desert View, a ride/climb of 2,600 feet for remarkable views to the east across the desert below. An option from there is hiking the flank of Mount San Jacinto, including making the ascent to the summit (10,804 feet), a round-trip butt-kicker of nearly 12 miles.

RV sites, facilities: There are 614 sites with full

hookups for RVs. Restrooms, showers, four swimming pools, nine natural hot mineral whirlpools, two laundry rooms, two large recreation rooms, modem access, cable TV, cell phone reception, a beauty salon, a chapel, a social director, shuffleboard, tennis, horseshoes, a crafts room, and walking paths are available. A store, an ATM, and propane are nearby. Some facilities are wheelchair-accessible. Leashed pets are permitted.

Reservations, fees: Make reservations at 888/893-7727. The fee is $34–36 per night, plus $4 per person for more than two people. Open year-round.

Directions: Drive on I-10 to the Palm Springs area and the Palm Drive exit (to Desert Hot Springs). Take that exit and drive north on Palm Drive to Dillon Road. Turn right on Dillon Road and drive 8.5 miles to the park on the right (74-711 Dillon Road).

Contact: Sky Valley Resort, 760/329-2909, fax 760/329-9473, website: www.skyvalleyresort.com.

28 COTTONWOOD

Rating: 4

in Joshua Tree National Park
See map pages 852–853

If you enter Joshua Tree National Park at its southern access point, this is the first camp you will reach. The park visitors center, where maps are available, is a mandatory stop. This park is vast, high desert country, highlighted by unique rock formations, occasional scraggly trees, and vegetation that manages to survive the bleak, roasting summers. This camp is set at 3,000 feet. A trailhead is available here for an easy one-mile nature trail, where small signs have been posted to identify different types of vegetation. You'll notice, however, that they all look like cacti (the plants, not the signs, heh, heh).

RV sites, facilities: There are 62 sites for RVs up to 40 feet or tents and a group campground with three sites for up to 25 people each. Picnic tables and fire grills are provided. Drinking water and flush toilets are available. Some facilities are wheelchair-accessible. Leashed pets are permitted.

Reservations, fees: No reservations are accepted for individual sites. The fee is $10 per night, plus a $10 park entrance fee per vehicle. Reserve group

sites at 800/365-CAMP (800/365-2267); the fee for group sites is $25 per night, plus a $10 park entrance fee per vehicle. Open year-round.

Directions: From Indio, drive east on I-10 for 35 miles to the exit for El Dorado Mine Road/Twentynine Palms (near Chiriaco Summit). Take that exit and drive north for seven miles (entering the park) to the campground on the right.

Contact: Joshua Tree National Park, 760/367-5500, fax 760/367-6392.

29 MAYFLOWER COUNTY PARK

Rating: 6

on the Colorado River
See map pages 852–853

The Colorado River is the fountain of life around these parts and, for campers, the main attraction of this county park. It is a popular spot for waterskiing, with river access here in the Blythe area. This span of water is flanked by agricultural lands, although there are several developed recreation areas on the California side of the river south of Blythe near Palo Verde.

RV sites, facilities: There are 152 RV sites with partial hookups (30, 50 amps) and 28 tent sites. Picnic tables and fire grills are provided. Restrooms, drinking water, flush toilets, showers, an RV dump station, and a boat ramp and docks are available. Leashed pets are permitted.

Reservations, fees: Reservations are accepted. The fee is $15–18 per night, plus a $2 boat launch fee and a $2 pet fee. Major credit cards are accepted. Open year-round.

Directions: Drive on I-10 to Blythe and Highway 95. Take Highway 95 north (it becomes Intake Boulevard) and drive 3.5 miles to 6th Avenue. Turn right at 6th Avenue and drive three miles to the park entrance directly ahead.

Contact: Mayflower County Park, 760/922-4665; Riverside County, 760/922-9177.

30 DESTINY RIVIERA RESORT

Rating: 6

near the Colorado River
See map pages 852–853

This RV park is set up for camper-boaters who

CALIFORNIA

want to hunker down for awhile along the Colorado River and cool off. Access to the park is easy off I-10, and a marina is available, both big pluses for those showing up with trailered boats. A swimming lagoon is another bonus.

RV sites, facilities: There are 285 sites, some drive-through and many with partial or full hookups, for RVs. Picnic tables are provided. Restrooms, showers, a swimming pool, a spa, cable TV, modem access, a coin-operated laundry, a telephone room, a store, a card room, a boat ramp, boat fuel, and propane are available. A golf course is within five miles. Leashed pets are permitted, with some restrictions.

Reservations, fees: Reservations are accepted at 800/RV-DESTINY (800/783-3784). The fees are $35–39 per night on weekends with a three-day minimum and $18–25 per night on weekdays, plus $4 per person for more than two people and $10 per night for each additional vehicle. A senior discount is available. Major credit cards are accepted. Open year-round.

Directions: Drive on I-10 to Blythe and continue east for two miles to the exit for Riviera Drive. Take that exit east and drive two miles to the park on the right (14100 Riviera Drive).

Contact: Riviera Blythe Marina, 760/922-5350, fax 760/922-6540, website: www.destinyrv.com.

31 DESTINY MCINTYRE PARK

Rating: 3

on the Colorado River

See map pages 852–853

This RV park sits on the outskirts of Blythe on the Colorado River, with this stretch of river providing good conditions for boating, water-skiing, and other water sports. A swimming lagoon is a big plus. Fishing is an option, with a variety of fish providing fair results, including striped bass, largemouth bass, and catfish roaming the area.

RV sites, facilities: There are 160 RV sites, including 11 pull-through sites, with full hookups (20, 30, 50 amps) and 140 tent sites. Picnic tables and fire rings are provided. Restrooms, drinking water, flush toilets, showers, an RV dump station, propane, a snack bar, a store, bait, ice, and a boat ramp and boat fuel are available. Some facilities are wheelchair-accessible. Leashed pets are permitted from November 1 to March 31.

Reservations, fees: Make reservations at 800/RV-DESTINY (800/783-3784). The fees are $35–39 per night on weekends with a three-day minimum and $25 per night on weekdays, plus $4 per person for more than two people and $10 per additional vehicle. A senior discount is available. Major credit cards are accepted. Open year-round.

Directions: Drive on I-10 to Blythe to the exit for Intake Boulevard south. Take that exit and drive south on Intake Boulevard to the junction with 26th Avenue (it takes off to the right) and the park entrance on the left. Turn left and enter the park.

Contact: Destiny McIntyre Resort, 760/922-8205, fax 760/922-5695, website: www.destinyrv.com.

32 OUTDOOR RESORT OF PALM SPRINGS

Rating: 6

near Palm Springs

See map pages 852–853

This is where "every day is considered a holiday." It's considered a Five-Star Resort, beautifully landscaped, huge, and offering many activities: swimming pools galore, three nine-hole golf courses, tons of tennis courts, spas, and on and on. The park is four miles from Palm Springs. One of the best adventures in California is just west of Palm Springs, taking the tramway up from Chino Canyon to Desert View, a ride/climb of 2,600 feet for remarkable views to the east across the desert below. An option from there is hiking the flank of Mount San Jacinto, including making the ascent to the summit (10,804 feet), a round-trip butt-kicker of nearly 12 miles. If you still can't think of anything to do, you can always compare tires. This is the RV park that was voted the "Most Likely to Succeed as a City."

RV sites, facilities: There are 1,213 sites with full hookups for RVs. Restrooms, showers, eight swimming pools, 14 tennis courts, 10 spas, three nine-hole golf courses, two clubhouses, a health club with three saunas, a snack bar, a beauty salon, a coin-operated laundry, modem access, a store, shuffleboard, and planned activities are

available. Some facilities are wheelchair-accessible. Leashed pets are permitted.

Reservations, fees: Make reservations at 800/843-3131 (California only). The fees are $50–60 per night in winter and $35–45 per night in summer, plus $1 per pet per night with a two-pet maximum. Major credit cards are accepted. Open year-round.

Directions: Drive on I-10 to the Palm Springs area and continue to Cathedral City and the exit for Date Palm Drive. Take that exit and drive south on Date Palm Drive for two miles to Ramon Road. Turn left and drive to the resort on the right (69-411) Ramon Road.

Contact: Outdoor Resorts, 760/324-4005 or 800/843-3131, website: www.outdoorresort.com.

33 PALM SPRINGS OASIS RV RESORT

Rating: 2

in Cathedral City
See map pages 852–853

This popular wintering spot is for RV cruisers looking to hole up in the Palm Springs area for awhile. Palm Springs is only six miles away.

RV sites, facilities: There are 140 RV sites with full hookups (20, 30, 50 amps). Restrooms, showers, cable TV and modem access, two swimming pools, a whirlpool, an 18-hole golf course, tennis courts, a coin-operated laundry, and propane are available. Some facilities are wheelchair-accessible. Leashed pets are permitted.

Reservations, fees: Reservations are accepted. The fee is $30–35 per night, plus $2 per person for more than two people. Weekly and monthly rates are available. Major credit cards are accepted. Open year-round.

Directions: Drive on I-10 to the Palm Springs area and continue to Cathedral City and the exit for Date Palm Drive. Take that exit and drive south on Date Palm Drive for four miles to Gerald Ford Drive and the park on the corner (36-100 Date Palm Drive).

Contact: Palm Springs Oasis RV Resort, 760/328-4813 or 800/680-0144, fax 760/328-8455, website: www.mhchomes.com.

34 HAPPY TRAVELER RV PARK

Rating: 1

in Palm Springs
See map pages 852–853

Are we having fun yet? They are at Happy Traveler, which is within walking distance of Palm Springs shopping areas.

RV sites, facilities: There are 130 sites with full hookups (30, 50 amps) for RVs up to 40 feet. Picnic tables are provided. Restrooms, showers, a recreation room, a swimming pool, modem access, cell phone reception, cable TV, a hot tub, and a coin-operated laundry are available. An ATM is within 1.5 miles. Leashed pets are permitted.

Reservations, fees: Reservations are accepted. The fee is $35 per night. Major credit cards are accepted. Open year-round.

Directions: Drive on I-10 to Palm Springs and Highway 111/Palm Canyon Drive. Take Palm Canyon Drive and go one mile south (one block after Ramon) to Mesquite Avenue. Turn right on Mesquite Avenue and drive to the park on the left (211 W. Mesquite).

Contact: Happy Traveler RV Park, 760/325-8518, fax 760/778-6708.

35 INDIAN WELLS RV PARK

Rating: 1

in Indio
See map pages 852–853

Indio is a good-sized town midway between the Salton Sea to the south and Palm Springs to the north. In the summer, it is one of the hottest places in America. In the winter, it is a favorite for "snowbirds," that is, RV and trailer owners from the snow country who migrate south to the desert for the winter. The park provides tons of drive-through sites.

RV sites, facilities: There are 381 RV sites, many drive-through and most with full hookups (50 amps). Picnic tables and fire grills are provided. Restrooms, showers, cable TV hookups, three swimming pools, two therapy pools, a fitness room, horseshoes, shuffleboard courts, a putting green, planned activities, ice, a dog run, a barbecue, and a coin-operated laundry are available.

Some facilities are wheelchair-accessible. Leashed pets are permitted.

Reservations, fees: Reservations are accepted. The fee is $27 per night. Major credit cards are accepted. Open year-round.

Directions: Drive on I-10 to Indio and the exit for Jefferson Street. Take that exit, stay in the right lane, and drive to the light at Jefferson. Turn right at Jefferson and drive south for three miles to the park on the left (47-340 Jefferson Street).

Contact: Indian Wells RV Park, 760/347-0895 or 800/789-0895, fax 760/775-1147.

36 OUTDOOR RESORTS MOTORCOACH RESORT AND SPA

Rating: 7

in Indio

See map pages 852–853

For owners of tour buses, motor coaches, and lavish RVs, it doesn't get any better than this in Southern California. This is the sole motorhome-only park in California, and it is close to golf, shopping, and restaurants. Jeep tours of the surrounding desert canyons and organized recreation events are available.

RV sites, facilities: There are 594 sites with full hookups (20, 30, 50 amps) for RVs only with a minimum length of 25 feet. No trailers or pickup-truck campers are allowed. Restrooms, showers, five swimming pools, six tennis courts, modem access, a sauna, a whirlpool, a coin-operated laundry, two clubhouses, three lakes, 24-hour security, and an 18-hole golf course are available. Some facilities are wheelchair-accessible. Leashed pets are permitted.

Reservations, fees: Reservations are accepted. The fees are $55–65 per night during the winter and $40 per night in the summer. Major credit cards are accepted. Open year-round.

Directions: Drive on I-10 to Indio and the exit for Jefferson Street. Take that exit, stay in the right lane, and drive to the light at Jefferson. Turn right at Jefferson and drive south to Highway 111. Continue on Jefferson for one block to 48th Avenue. Turn left and drive .25 mile to the park on the left side of the road (80-394 48th Avenue).

Contact: Outdoor Resorts Motorcoach, 760/775-7255 or 800/892-2992 (outside California), fax 760/347-0875, website: www.outdoor-resorts.com.

37 LAKE CAHUILLA COUNTY PARK

Rating: 7

near Indio

See map pages 852–853

Lake Cahuilla covers just 135 acres, but those are the most loved 135 acres for miles in all directions. After all, water out here is as scarce as polar bears. This Riverside County park provides large palm trees and a 10-acre beach and waterplay area. In the winter it is stocked with trout, and in the summer, with catfish. No swimming is allowed. Only car-top boats are permitted, and a speed limit of 10 mph is enforced. An equestrian camp is also available, complete with corrals. A warning: the wind can really howl through here, and temperatures well over 100°F are typical in the summer. If it weren't for this lake, they might as well post a sign on I-10 that says, "You are now entering Hell." Actually, there really is a town on I-10 that is named "Hell."

RV sites, facilities: There are 60 sites with partial hookups and 10 sites with no hookups for RVs, a primitive camping area for self-contained RVs and tents, and a group area with horse corrals and equestrian trails. Fire grills and picnic tables are provided. Restrooms, showers, an RV dump station, a playground, a swimming pool, and an unpaved beach boat launch are available. No gas motors are allowed. Leashed pets are permitted.

Reservations, fees: Make reservations at 800/234-PARK (800/234-7275) ($6.50 reservation fee). The fee is $12–16 per night, plus $2 per pet per night. Weekly rates are available. Major credit cards are accepted. Open year-round, but closed Tuesday, Wednesday, and Thursday in summer.

Directions: Drive on I-10 to Indio and the exit for Monroe Street. Take that exit and drive south on Monroe Street to Avenue 58. Turn right and drive three miles to the park at the end of the road.

Contact: Lake Cahuilla County Park, 760/564-4712, fax 760/564-2506, website: www.riverside countyparks.org.

CALIFORNIA

38 HEADQUARTERS

🚶 🚴 🏊 🚣 🎣 🏕 🐕 ♿ 🚐 ⛺

Rating: 5

in the Salton Sea State Recreation Area
See map pages 852–853

This is the northernmost camp on the shore of the giant Salton Sea, one of the campgrounds at the Salton Sea State Recreation Area. The Salton Sea is a vast, shallow, and unique lake, the center of a 360-square-mile basin and one of the world's inland seas. Salton Sea was created in 1905 when a dike broke, and in turn, the basin was flooded with saltwater. It is set at the recreation area headquarters, just south of the town of Desert Beach at an elevation of 227 feet below sea level. Fishing for corvina, tilapia, sargo, and croaker is popular, and it is also one of Southern California's most popular boating areas. Because of the low altitude, atmospheric pressure allows high performance for many ski boats. If winds are hazardous, a red beacon on the northeast shore of the lake will flash. If you see it, get to the nearest shore. The Salton Sea is about a three-hour drive from Los Angeles.

RV sites, facilities: There are 15 sites with full hookups (30 amps) for RVs up to 40 feet, 25 sites for tents, and several hike-in/bike-in sites. Picnic tables and fire grills are provided. Restrooms, drinking water, flush toilets, coin-operated showers, an RV dump station, and a visitors center are available. A store is within two miles. Some facilities are wheelchair-accessible. Leashed pets are permitted.

Reservations, fees: Reserve at 800/444-PARK (800/444-7275) or online at www.reserveamerica.com ($7.50 reservation fee). The fee is $10–16 per night or $1 per person per night for hike-in/bike-in sites. A senior discount is available. Open year-round.

Directions: From Indio, drive south on Highway 111 to Mecca. Continue southeast on Highway 111 for 11 miles to the entrance on the right.

Contact: Salton Sea State Recreation Area, 760/393-3052 or 760/393-3059.

39 MECCA BEACH

🚶 🚴 🏊 🚣 🎣 🏕 🐕 ♿ 🚐 ⛺

Rating: 4

in the Salton Sea State Recreation Area
See map pages 852–853

This is one of the camps set in the Salton Sea State Recreation Area on the northeastern shore of the lake. (For details, see the prior entry for Headquarters.)

RV sites, facilities: There are 110 sites, 10 with full hookups (50 amps), for RVs of any length or tents, and several hike-in/bike-in sites. Picnic tables and fire grills are provided. Restrooms, drinking water, flush toilets, and showers are available. An RV dump station is 1.5 miles north of Headquarters Campground and a store is within 3.5 miles. Leashed pets are permitted.

Reservations, fees: Reservations are not accepted. The fee is $10–16 per night or $1 per night for hike-in/bike-in sites. A senior discount is available. Open year-round.

Directions: From Indio, drive south on Highway 111 to Mecca. Continue southeast on Highway 111 for 12.5 miles to the entrance on the right.

Contact: Salton Sea State Recreation Area, 760/393-3052 or 760/393-3059.

40 CORVINA BEACH

🚶 🚴 🏊 🚣 🎣 🏕 🐕 ♿ 🚐 ⛺

Rating: 5

in the Salton Sea State Recreation Area
See map pages 852–853

This is by far the biggest of the campgrounds on the Salton Sea. The campground is actually more of an open area on hard-packed dirt, best for parking an RV. (For details about the Salton Sea, see the entry for Headquarters earlier in this chapter.)

RV sites, facilities: There are 500 primitive sites in an open area for RVs of any length or tents and several hike-in/bike-in sites. Drinking water and chemical toilets are available. A store and gas station are within five miles. Leashed pets are permitted.

Reservations, fees: Reservations are not accepted. The fee is $7 per night or $1 per night for hike-in/bike-in sites. A senior discount is available. Open year-round.

Directions: From Indio, drive south on Highway

CALIFORNIA

111 to Mecca. Continue southeast on Highway 111 for 14 miles to the entrance on the right.

Contact: Salton Sea State Recreation Area, 760/393-3052 or 760/393-3059.

41 SALT CREEK PRIMITIVE AREA

Rating: 4

in the Salton Sea State Recreation Area
See map pages 852–853

The addition of water at this campground is a big plus, even though the campground consists of just an open area on hard-packed dirt. (For details on the Salton Sea State Recreation Area, see the entry earlier in this chapter for Headquarters.)

RV sites, facilities: There are 150 primitive sites for RVs of any length or tents and several hike-in/bike-in sites. Drinking water and chemical toilets are available. Leashed pets are permitted.

Reservations, fees: Reservations are not accepted. The fee is $7 per night or $1 per night for hike-in/bike-in sites. A senior discount is available. Open year-round.

Directions: From Indio, drive south on Highway 111 to Mecca. Continue southeast on Highway 111 for 17.5 miles to the entrance on the right.

Contact: Salton Sea State Recreation Area, 760/393-3052 or 760/393-3059.

42 BOMBAY BEACH

Rating: 5

in the Salton Sea State Recreation Area
See map pages 852–853

All in all, this is a strange-looking place, with the Salton Sea, a vast body of water, surrounded by stark, barren countryside. This camp is set on a bay along the northeastern shoreline, where a beach and nature trails are available. The campground is a flat, open area. Nearby to the south is the Wister Waterfowl Management Area. The Salton Sea is California's unique saltwater lake set below sea level, where corvina can provide lively sportfishing.

RV sites, facilities: There are 200 sites for RVs of any length or tents and several hike-in/bike-in sites. Drinking water and chemical toilets are available. A store, a restaurant, a marina, and a boat launch are available nearby in Bombay Beach. Leashed pets are permitted.

Reservations, fees: Reservations are not accepted. The fee is $7 per night or $1 per night for hike-in/bike-in sites. A senior discount is available. Open year-round.

Directions: From Indio, drive south on Highway 111 for 19 miles to Mecca. Continue southeast on Highway 11 for 25 miles to the campground entrance on the right.

From Calipatria, drive north on Highway 111 to Niland, then continue north 18 miles to the entrance on the left.

Contact: Salton Sea State Recreation Area, 760/393-3052 or 760/393-3059.

43 RED HILL MARINA COUNTY PARK

Rating: 3

near the Salton Sea
See map pages 852–853

This county park is near the south end of the Salton Sea, one of the weirdest places on earth. Set 228 feet below sea level, it's a vast body of water covering 360 square miles, 35 miles long, but with an average depth of just 10 feet. It's an extremely odd place to swim, where you bob around effortlessly in the highly saline water. Fishing is often good for corvina in spring and early summer. Several wildlife refuges are in the immediate area, including two separate chunks of the Imperial Wildfowl Management Area, to the west and south, and the huge Wister Waterfowl Management Area, northwest of Niland.

RV sites, facilities: There are 40 sites, 10 with partial hookups (30 amps), for RVs or tents. Picnic tables, cabanas, and barbecue pits are provided. Flush toilets, showers, and a boat launch are available. The water at this site is not certified for drinking. Leashed pets are permitted.

Reservations, fees: Reservations are not accepted. The fee is $7–12 per night, plus $2 per night for each additional vehicle, with a 14-day limit. Open year-round.

Directions: From El Centro, drive north on Highway 111 to Brawley and Highway 78/Main Street. Turn west (left) on Highway 78/Main Street and drive a short distance to Highway 111. Turn right (north) and drive to Calipatria. Continue north

CALIFORNIA

on Highway 111 just outside of Calipatria to Sinclair Road. Turn left on Sinclair Road and drive to Garst Road. Turn right and drive 1.5 miles to where it ends at Red Hill Road. Turn left at Red Hill Road and drive to the end of the road and the marina and the campground.

Contact: Red Hill Marina County Park, tel./fax 760/348-2310; Imperial County, 760/482-4384.

44 PALO VERDE COUNTY PARK

Rating: 5

near the Colorado River
See map pages 852–853

This is the only game in town, with no other camp around for many miles. It is set near a bend in the Colorado River, not far from the Cibola National Wildlife Refuge. A boat ramp is available at the park, making it a launch point for adventure. This stretch of river is a good one for powerboating and water-skiing. The best facilities for visitors are available here and on the west side of the river between Palo Verde and Blythe, with nothing available on the east side of the river.

RV sites, facilities: There is an undesignated number of sites for RVs or tents. Picnic tables, fire rings, and shade ramadas are available. Restrooms and flush toilets are available. No drinking water is available. A boat ramp is on-site. A store, a coin-operated laundry, and propane are available in Palo Verde. Leashed pets are permitted.

Reservations, fees: Reservations are not accepted. There is no fee for camping. Open year-round.

Directions: Drive on I-10 to Highway 78 (two miles west of Blythe). Take Highway 78 south and drive about 20 miles (past Palo Verde) to the park entrance road.

Contact: Palo Verde County Park, Imperial County, 760/482-4384.

45 PICACHO STATE RECREATION AREA

Rating: 6

near Taylor Lake on the Colorado River
See map pages 852–853

To get here, you really have to want it. Picacho State Recreation Area is way out there, requiring a long drive north out of Winterhaven on a spindly little road. The camp is on the southern side of Taylor Lake on the Colorado River. The park is the best deal around for many miles, though, with a boat ramp, water-skiing, good bass fishing, and occasionally, crazy folks having the time of their lives. The sun and water make a good combination. This recreation area includes eight miles of the lower Colorado River. Park wildlife includes wild burros and bighorn sheep, with thousands of migratory waterfowl on the Pacific Flyway occasionally taking up residence. More than 100 years ago, Picacho was a gold-mining town with a population of 100 people. Visitors should always carry extra water and essential supplies.

RV sites, facilities: There are 58 sites for RVs up to 40 feet or tents, three group sites for 25 to 100 people, and three boat-in campsites. Picnic tables and fire grills are provided. Drinking water, pit toilets, an RV dump station, solar showers, a camp store, and two boat launches are available. Some facilities are wheelchair-accessible. Leashed pets are permitted.

Reservations, fees: No reservations are accepted except for groups. The fee is $7 per night. Group pricing is based on group size with a $26 minimum. A senior discount is available. Open year-round.

Directions: From El Centro, drive east on I-8 to Winterhaven and the exit for Winterhaven/4th Avenue. Take that exit to 4th Avenue. Turn left and drive .5 mile to County Road S24/Picacho Road. Turn right and drive 18 miles (crossing rail tracks, a railroad bridge, and the American Canal, the road becoming dirt) to the campground. The road is not suitable for large RVs. The drive takes one hour from Winterhaven. In summer, thunderstorms can cause flash flooding, making short sections of the road impassable.

Contact: Picacho State Recreation Area, c/o Salton Sea State Recreation Area, 760/393-3059 or 760/996-2963 (reservations); Colorado Desert District, 760/767-5311.

46 WIEST LAKE COUNTY PARK

Rating: 4

on Wiest Lake
See map pages 852–853

This is a developed county park along the southern shore of Wiest Lake, which adjoins the Imperial Wildfowl Management Area to the north. Wiest Lake is just 50 acres, set 110 feet below sea level, and a prized area with such desolate country in the surrounding region. Water-skiing and windsurfing can be excellent, although few take advantage of the latter. The Salton Sea, about a 20-minute drive to the northwest, is a worthy side trip.

RV sites, facilities: There are 24 RV sites with full hookups (30 amps) and 20 tent sites. Picnic tables and fire grills are provided. Restrooms, flush toilets, showers, and an RV dump station are available. A store, a coin-operated laundry, and propane are nearby. Leashed pets are permitted.

Reservations, fees: Reservations are not accepted. The fee is $7–12 per night, plus $2 per night for each additional vehicle. Open year-round.

Directions: From El Centro, drive north on Highway 111 to Brawley and Highway 78/Main Street. Turn west (left) on Highway 78/Main Street and drive a short distance to Highway 111. Turn right (north) on Highway 111 and drive four miles to Rutherford Road (well signed). Turn right (east) and drive two miles to the park entrance on the right.

Contact: Wiest Lake County Park, 760/344-3712 or 760/339-4384, fax 760/339-4372; Imperial County, 760/482-4384.

47 RIO BEND RV GOLF RESORT

Rating: 5

near El Centro
See map pages 852–853

This RV park is set at 50 feet below sea level near Mount Signal, about a 20-minute drive south of the Salton Sea. For some, this region is a godforsaken wasteland, but, hey, that makes arriving at this park all the more like coming to a mirage in the desert. The park is usually well maintained, and management does what it can to offer visitors recreational options. It's hot out here, sizzling most of the year, but dry and cool in the winter, the best time to visit. New owners took over in 2002, and their first mission was adding 200 sites with full hookups to this large park.

RV sites, facilities: There are 458 sites, 23 drive-through, with full hookups, 42 sites with partial hookups, and a group area with 42 sites with partial hookups for RVs. Picnic tables are provided. A heated pool, a spa, shuffleboard, volleyball, two small stocked lakes, a golf course, a coin-operated laundry, and telephone, cable, and modem access are available. A small store is nearby. Some facilities are wheelchair-accessible. Leashed pets are permitted.

Reservations, fees: Reservations are accepted. The fee is $32 per night, plus $3 per person for more than two people. Major credit cards are accepted. Open year-round.

Directions: From El Centro, drive west on I-8 for seven miles to the Drew Road exit. Take that exit and drive south on Drew Road for .25 mile to the park on the right (1589 Drew Road).

Contact: Rio Bend RV Golf Resort, 760/352-7061, fax 760/352-0055, website: www.riobendrvgolfresort.com.

48 COUNTRY LIFE RV

Rating: 2

near El Centro
See map pages 852–853

You'd better have air-conditioning. This is an RV parking lot on the desert flats about a 10-minute drive north of the Mexican border. Nearby side trips include the Salton Sea to the north, little Sunbeam Lake County Park to the west and, if you need to sober up, the Mexican border customs to the south.

RV sites, facilities: There are 150 sites with full hookups (30, 50 amps) for RVs and six tent sites. Restrooms, drinking water, flush toilets, showers, limited modem access, a swimming pool, a clubhouse, a coin-operated laundry, propane, and groceries are available. Some facilities are wheelchair-accessible. Leashed pets are permitted.

Reservations, fees: Reservations are recommended. The fee is $15–18.50 per night, plus $1 per person per night for more than two people. Major credit cards are accepted. Open year-round.

Directions: Drive on I-8 to El Centro and the Highway 111 exit. Take that exit north and drive .25 mile to Ross road. Turn left on Ross Road and drive a short distance to the campground entrance on the left.

Contact: Country Life RV, 760/353-1040, fax 760/353-1948.

49 SENATOR WASH RECREATION AREA

Rating: 6

near Senator Wash Reservoir
See map pages 852–853

Senator Wash Reservoir Recreation Area features two campgrounds, named (surprise) Senator Wash South Shore and Senator Wash North Shore. This recreation area is approximately 50 acres, with many trees of various types and several secluded camping areas. At Senator Wash North Shore (where there are fewer facilities than South Shore), these campsites are both on the water as well as further inland. Gravel beaches provide access to the reservoir. Boat ramps are nearby. This spot provides boating, fishing, OHV riding, wildlife viewing, and opportunities for solitude and sightseeing.

RV sites, facilities: There is an undesignated number of sites for self-contained RVs or tents. No drinking water is available. At South Shore, two restrooms with flush toilets, outdoor showers, and drinking water are available. At North Shore, there are two vault toilets. A boat ramp is a quarter mile from South Shore. No camping is allowed at the boat ramp. Some facilities are wheelchair-accessible. Leashed pets are permitted.

Reservations, fees: Reservations are not accepted. The fee is $5 per night, plus $1 per person for more than four people, with a maximum 14-day limit. A senior discount is available. Open year-round.

Directions: Drive on I-8 to Yuma, Arizona, and the exit for 4th Avenue. Take that exit and drive to Imperial Highway/County Road S24. Turn north and drive 22 miles to Senator Wash Road. Turn left and drive about three miles to Mesa Campground. Turn left and drive 200 yards to the South Shore Campground access road on the right. Turn right and drive to the reservoir and campground.

Contact: Bureau of Land Management, Yuma Field Office, 520/317-3200, fax 520/317-3250.

50 SQUAW LAKE

Rating: 6

near the Colorado River
See map pages 852–853

Take your pick. There are two camps near the Colorado River in this area (the other is Senator Wash). This one is near Squaw Lake, created by the nearby Imperial Dam on the Colorado River. This sites provides opportunities for swimming, fishing, boating, and hiking, featuring direct boat access to the Colorado River. Wildlife includes numerous waterfowl, as well as quail, coyotes, and reptiles. A speed limit of 5 mph is enforced on the lake; no wakes permitted. The no-wake zone ends at the Colorado River.

RV sites, facilities: There are 125 sites for RVs and dispersed sites for tents. Picnic tables and barbecue grills are provided. Four restrooms with flush toilets and outdoor showers are available. Drinking water is available at a central location. Two boat ramps are nearby. Some facilities are wheelchair-accessible. Leashed pets are permitted.

Reservations, fees: Reservations are not accepted. The fee is $5 per night, plus $1 per person for more than four people, with a maximum 14-day limit. A senior discount is available. Open year-round.

Directions: Drive on I-8 to Yuma, Arizona, and the exit for 4th Avenue. Take that exit and drive to Imperial Highway/County Road S24. Turn north and drive 22 miles to Senator Wash Road. Turn left and drive about four miles (well signed) to the lake and campground on the right.

Contact: Bureau of Land Management, Yuma Field Office, 520/317-3200, fax 520/317-3250.

51 SANS END RV PARK

Rating: 5

in Winterhaven
See map pages 852–853

Sans End is only seven miles from Mexico, and lots of people who stay here like to cross the border for shopping and fun. The high season at this RV park is January to March, and no wonder, because it is blazing hot here in the summer. The Colorado River provides recreational opportunities near Imperial Dam. Boat ramps are available in Yuma and Winterhaven. Some areas of this stretch of water are marshy wetlands that provide an opportunity for duck hunting in the fall and early winter. For anglers, there are some big catfish roaming these waters. The park is surrounded by palm trees, shielding your view of the junkyard across the road.

RV sites, facilities: There are 167 sites for RVs and a few sites for tents. Restrooms, showers, a recreation hall with a pool table, a coin-operated laundry, and shuffleboard are available. Leashed pets are permitted.

Reservations, fees: Reservations are not accepted. The fee is $21 per night. Open year-round.

Directions: Drive on I-8 to the exit for Winterhaven Drive (just west of Yuma, Arizona). Turn left (if arriving from the west) and drive a short distance to the park on the right.

Contact: Sans End RV Park, 2209 W. Winterhaven Dr., Winterhaven, CA 92283, 760/572-0797.

Resources

Resources

National Forests

The Forest Service provides many secluded camps and allows camping anywhere except where it is specifically prohibited. A permit is required when camping in designated wilderness areas; this permit doubles as a campfire permit. If you ever want to clear the cobwebs from your head and get away from it all, this is the way to go.

Many Forest Service campgrounds are quite remote and have no drinking water. You usually don't need to check in or make reservations, and sometimes there is no fee. At many Forest Service campgrounds that provide drinking water, the camping fee is often only a few dollars, with payment made on the honor system. Because most of these camps are in mountain areas, they are subject to winter closure because of snow or mud.

Dogs are usually permitted in national forests with no extra charge and no hassle. Leashes are required for all dogs in some places. Always carry documentation of current vaccinations.

National Forest Adventure Pass—California

Angeles, Cleveland, Los Padres, and San Bernardino National Forests in California require an Adventure Pass for each parked vehicle. Daily passes cost $5; annual passes are available for $30. Adventure Passes can be purchased at national forest offices in Southern California and dozens of retail outlets and on-line vendors. The new charges are use fees, not entrance fees. Holders of Golden Age, Golden Access, and Golden Eagle passports can use these cards in lieu of purchasing an Adventure Pass.

When you purchase an annual Adventure Pass, you can also buy a secondary annual Adventure Pass for $5. Major credit cards are accepted at most retail and on-line outlets, but not at Forest Service offices. Adventure Passes can be purchased by telephone at 909/382-2622, or by mail at San Bernardino National Forest, Fee Project Headquarters, 1824 S. Commercenter Circle, San Bernardino, CA 92408-3430. Checks should be made payable to USDA Forest Service.

You will not need an Adventure Pass while traveling through these forests or when you've paid other types of fees such as camping or ski pass fees. However, if you are camping in these forests and you leave the campground in your vehicle and park outside of the campground for recreation purposes, such as at a trailhead, day-use area, near a fishing stream, etc., you will need an Adventure Pass for your vehicle. You also need an Adventure Pass if camping at a no-fee campground. More information about the Adventure Pass program, including a listing of retail and on-line vendors, can be obtained online at www.fsadventurepass.org.

Northwest Forest Pass—Oregon and Washington

A Northwest Forest Pass is required for certain activities in some Washington and Oregon national forests and at some national parks. The pass is required for parking at participating trailheads, rustic camping areas, boat launches, picnic areas, and interpretive sites. The new charges are use fees, not entrance fees.

Daily passes cost $5 per vehicle; annual passes are $30 per vehicle. You can buy Northwest Forest Passes at national forest offices and dozens of retail outlets. The passes can be purchased by telephone at 800/270-7504 or online at Nature of the Northwest, www.naturenw.org. Holders of Golden Age, Golden Access, and Golden Eagle passports can use these cards in lieu of purchasing a Northwest Forest Pass. Major credit cards are accepted at most retail and online outlets, but not at forest service offices.

More information about the Northwest Forest Pass program, including a listing of retail and online vendors, can be obtained online at www.fs.fed.us/r6/feedemo/ or www.naturenw.org.

National Forest Reservations

Some of the more popular camps, and most of the group camps, are on a reservation system. Reservations can be made up to 240 days in advance, and up to 360 days in advance for groups. To reserve a site, call 877/444-6777 or visit www.ReserveUSA.com. The reservation fee is usually $9 for a campsite in a national forest, and major credit cards are accepted. Holders of Golden Age or Golden Access passports receive a 50 percent discount on fees such as camping (except for group sites), boat launching, and swimming. Golden Eagle Passports can be purchased by telephone at 877/465-2727 or online at www.natlforests.org. Golden Age and Golden Access passports must be obtained in person.

National Forest Maps

National Forest maps are among the best you can get for the price. They detail all backcountry streams, lakes, hiking trails, and logging roads for access. They typically cost $6, sometimes more for wilderness maps, and can be obtained in person at Forest Service offices, or by contacting U.S. Forest Service, Attn: Map Sales, P.O. Box 9035, Prescott, AZ 86313, 928/443-8285, fax 928/443-8207, or online at www.fs.fed.us/maps. Major credit cards are accepted if ordering by telephone.

Forest Service Information

Forest Service personnel are most helpful for obtaining camping, hiking, boating, or fishing information. Unless you are buying a map, Adventure Pass, or Northwest Forest Pass, it is advisable to phone to get the best service. For specific information on a national forest, contact the following offices:

California

Pacific Southwest Region
1323 Club Drive
Vallejo, CA 94592
707/562-USFS (707/562-8737)
website: www.fs.fed.us/r5

Angeles National Forest
701 N. Santa Anita Avenue
Arcadia, CA 91006
626/574-1613
fax 626/574-5233
website: www.fs.fed.us/r5/angeles

Cleveland National Forest
10845 Rancho Bernardo Road, Suite 200
San Diego, CA 92127-2107
858/673-6180
fax 858/673-6192
website: www.fs.fed.us/r5/cleveland

Eldorado National Forest
100 Forni Road
Placerville, CA 95667

530/622-5061 or 530/644-6048
fax 530/621-5297
website: www.fs.fed.us/r5/eldorado

Humboldt-Toiyabe National Forest
1200 Franklin Way
Sparks, NV 89431
775/331-6444
fax 775/355-5399
website: www.fs.fed.us/htnf

Inyo National Forest
351 Pacu Lane, Suite 200
Bishop, CA 93514
760/873-2400
fax 760/873-2458
website: www.fs.fed.us/r5/inyo

Klamath National Forest
1312 Fairlane Road
Yreka, CA 96097-9549
530/842-6131
fax 530/841-4571
website: www.fs.fed.us/r5/klamath

Lake Tahoe Basin Management Unit
35 College Drive
South Lake Tahoe, CA 96150
530/543-2600
fax 530/543-2693
website: www.fs.fed.us/r5/ltbmu

Lassen National Forest
2550 Riverside Drive
Susanville, CA 96130
530/257-2151
fax 530/ 252-6428
website: www.fs.fed.us/r5/lassen

Los Padres National Forest
6755 Hollister Avenue, Suite 150
Goleta, CA 93117
805/968-6640
fax 805/961-5729
website: www.fs.fed.us/r5/lospadres

Mendocino National Forest
825 N. Humboldt Avenue
Willows, CA 95988
530/934-3316
fax 530/934-7384
website: www.fs.fed.us/r5/mendocino

Modoc National Forest
800 W. 12th Street
Alturas, CA 96101
530/233-5811
fax 530/233-8709
website: www.fs.fed.us/r5/modoc

Plumas National Forest
P.O. Box 11500
159 Lawrence Street
Quincy, CA 95971
530/283-2050
fax 530/283-7746
website: www.fs.fed.us/r5/plumas

San Bernardino National Forest
1824 Commercenter Circle
San Bernardino, CA 92408-3430
909/383-5588
fax 909/383-5770
website: www.fs.fed.us/r5/sanbernardino

Sequoia National Forest
Giant Sequoia National Monument
900 W. Grand Avenue
Porterville, CA 93257
559/784-1500
fax 559/781-4744
website: www.fs.fed.us/r5/sequoia

Shasta-Trinity National Forest
2400 Washington Avenue
Redding, CA 96001
530/244-2978
fax 530/242-2233
website: www.fs.fed.us/r5/shastatrinity

Sierra National Forest
1600 Tollhouse Road
Clovis, CA 93611-0532
559/297-0706
fax 559/294-4809
website: www.fs.fed.us/r5/sierra

Six Rivers National Forest
1330 Bayshore Way
Eureka, CA 95501
707/442-1721
fax 707/442-9242
website: www.fs.fed.us/r5/sixrivers

Stanislaus National Forest
19777 Greenley Road
Sonora, CA 95370
209/532-3671
fax 209/533-1890
website: www.fs.fed.us/r5/stanislaus

Tahoe National Forest
631 Coyote Street
Nevada City, CA 95959
530/265-4531
fax 530/478-6109
website: www.fs.fed.us/r5/tahoe
or
Big Bend Visitor Center
49685 Hampshire Rocks Road
Soda Springs, CA 95728
530/426-3609
fax 530/426-1744

Oregon

USDA Forest Service
Pacific Northwest Region
333 SW First Avenue
P.O. Box 3623
Portland, OR 97208-3623
503/808-2971
website: www.fs.fed.us/r6

Deschutes National Forest
1645 Highway 20 East
Bend, OR 97701
541/383-5300
fax 541/383-5531
website: www.fs.fed.us/r6/centraloregon

Fremont National Forest
1301 South G Street
Lakeview, OR 97630
541/947-2151
fax 541/947-6399
website: www.fs.fed.us/r6/fremont

Malheur National Forest
431 Patterson Bridge Road
P.O. Box 909
John Day, OR 97845
541/575-3000
fax 541/575-3001
website: www.fs.fed.us/r6/malheur

Mount Hood National Forest
16400 Champion Way
Sandy, OR 97055
503/622-7674 or 503/668-1700
website: www.fs.fed.us/r6/mthood

Ochoco National Forest
3160 NE Third Street
Prineville, OR 97754
541/416-6500
fax 541/416-6695
website: www.fs.fed.us/r6/centraloregon

Rogue River National Forest
333 W. 8th Street
P.O. Box 520
Medford, OR 97501-0209
541/858-2200
fax 54/858-2220
website: www.fs.fed.us/r6/rogue

Siskiyou National Forest
333 W. 8th Street
Medford, OR 97503
541/858-2200
fax 541/858-2220

Siuslaw National Forest
4077 SW Research Way
P.O. Box 1148
Corvallis, OR 97339
541/750-7000
fax 541/750-7234
website: www.fs.fed.us/r6/siuslaw

Umatilla National Forest
2517 SW Hailey Avenue
Pendleton, OR 97801
541/278-3716
fax 541/278-3730
website: www.fs.fed.us/r6/uma

Umpqua National Forest
2900 NW Stewart Parkway
Roseburg, OR 97470
541/672-6601
fax 541/957-3495
website: www.fs.fed.us/r6/umpqua

Wallowa-Whitman National Forest
1550 Dewey Avenue
P.O. Box 907
Baker City, OR 97814
541/523-6391
fax 541/523-1315
website: www.fs.fed.us/r6/w-w

Willamette National Forest
Federal Building
211 E 7th Avenue
P.O. Box 10607
Eugene, OR 97440
541/225-6300
fax 531/225-6223
website: www.fs.fed.us/r6/willamette

Winema National Forest
2819 Dahlia Street
Klamath Falls, OR 97601
541/883-6714
fax 541/883-6709
website: www.fs.fed.us/r6/winema

Washington

Colville National Forest
765 South Main Street
Colville, WA 99114
509/684-7000
fax 509/684-7280
website: www.fs.fed.us/r6/colville

Gifford Pinchot National Forest
10600 NE 51st Circle
Vancouver, WA 98682
360/891-5000
fax 360/891-5045
website: www.fs.fed.us/r6/gpnf

Mt. Baker–Snoqualmie National Forest
21905 64th Avenue West
Mountlake Terrace, WA 98043-2278
425/775-9702 or 800/627-0062
fax 425/744-3255
website: www.fs.fed.us/r6/mbs

Okanogan and Wenatchee National Forests
215 Melody Lane
Wenatchee, WA 98801-5933
509/662-4335
fax 509/662-4368
website: www.fs.fed.us/r6/okanogan

Olympic National Forest
1835 Black Lake Boulevard SW
Olympia, WA 98512-5623
360/959-2402
fax 360/956-2330
website: www.fs.fed.us/r6/olympic

National Parks and Reservations

The West Coast's national parks are natural wonders, ranging from the spectacular yet crowded Yosemite Valley in California to the breathtaking Crater Lake National Park in Oregon to the often fog-bound Olympic National Park in Washington. Reservations for campsites are available five months in advance for many of the national parks. In addition to campground fees, expect to pay a park entrance fee ranging from $5 to $20 per vehicle (you can buy a National Parks Pass or Golden Eagle annual pass that waives entrance fees). This entrance fee is valid for seven days. Various discounts are available for holders of Golden Age and Golden Access passports, including a 50 percent reduction of camping (group camps not included), parking, boating, and swimming fees and a waiver of park entrance fees. For information about the National Parks Pass, telephone 888/467-2757 (GO-PARKS) or inquire online at www.nationalparks.org.

For Yosemite National Park reservations, call 800/436-PARK (800/436-7275) or visit the website: http://reservations.nps.gov. Major credit cards are accepted.

For all other national parks, call 800/365-CAMP (800/365-2267) or visit the website: http://reservations.nps.gov. Major credit cards are accepted.

For information about each of the national parks in California, Oregon, and Washington, contact the parks directly at the following telephone numbers or addresses:

California

National Park Service
Pacific West Region
One Jackson Center
111 Jackson Street
Suite 700
Oakland, CA 94607
510/817-1300
website: www.nps.gov

Cabrillo National Monument
1800 Cabrillo Memorial Drive
San Diego, CA 92106-3601
619/557-5450 or 619/222-8211
fax 619/557-5469
website: www.nps.gov/cabr

Channel Islands National Park
1901 Spinnaker Drive
Ventura, CA 93001
805/658-5730
fax 805/658-5799
website: www.nps.gov/chis

Death Valley National Park
P.O. Box 579
Death Valley, CA 92328-0579
760/786-3200
fax 760/786-3283
website: www.nps.gov/deva

Devils Postpile National Monument
P.O. Box 3999
Mammoth Lakes, CA 93546
760/934-2289 in summer only
559/565-3341 year-round
website: www.nps.gov/depo

Golden Gate National Recreation Area
Fort Mason, Building 201
San Francisco, CA 94123-0022
415/561-4700
fax 415/561-4750
website: www.nps.gov/goga

Joshua Tree National Park
74485 National Park Drive
Twentynine Palms, CA 92277-3597
760/367-5500
fax 760/367-6392
website: www.nps.gov/jotr

Lassen Volcanic National Park
P.O. Box 100
Mineral, CA 96063-0100
530/595-4444
fax 530/595-3262
website: www.nps.gov/lavo

Lava Beds National Monument
1 Indian Well Headquarters
Tulelake, CA 96134
530/667-2282
fax 530/667-2737
website: www.nps.gov/labe

Mojave National Preserve
222 E. Main Street, Suite 202
Barstow, CA 92311
760/255-8800 or 760/733-4040
fax 760/255-8809
website: www.nps.gov/moja

Pinnacles National Monument
5000 Highway 146
Paicines, CA 95043
831/389-4485
fax 831/389-4489
website: www.nps.gov/pinn

Point Reyes National Seashore
Point Reyes, CA 94956-9799
415/464-5100
fax 415/663-8132
website: www.nps.gov/pore

Redwood National and State Parks
1111 Second Street
Crescent City, CA 95531
707/464-6101
fax 707/464-1812
website: www.nps.gov/redw

Santa Monica Mountains
National Recreation Area
401 W. Hillcrest Drive
Thousand Oaks, CA 91360
805/370-2300 or 805/370-2301
fax 805/370-1850
website: www.nps.gov/samo

Sequoia and Kings Canyon National Parks
47050 Generals Highway
Three Rivers, CA 93271-9651
559/565-3341 or 559/335-2856
fax 559/565-3730
website: www.nps.gov/seki

Smith River National Recreation Area
P.O. Box 228
10600 Highway 199 North
Gasquet, CA 95543
707/457-3131
fax 707/457-3794

Whiskeytown National Recreation Area
P.O. Box 188
14412 Kennedy Memorial Drive
Whiskeytown, CA 96095
530/246-1225 or 530/242-3400
fax 530/246-5154
website: www.nps.gov/whis

Yosemite National Park
P.O. Box 577
Yosemite National Park, CA 95389
209/372-0200 for 24-hour recorded message
fax 209/372-0220
website: www.nps.gov/yose

Oregon
Columbia River Gorge National Scenic Area
902 Wasco Avenue, Suite 200
Hood River, OR 97031
541/386-2333
fax 541/386-1916
website: www.fs.fed.us/r6/columbia

Crater Lake National Park
P.O. Box 7
Crater Lake, OR 97604
541/594-3100
fax 541/594-3010
website: www.nps.gov/crla

Crooked River National Grassland
813 S.W. Highway 97
Madras, OR 97741
541/475-9272
fax 541/416-6694
website: www.fs.fed.us/r6/centraloregon

Hells Canyon National Recreation Area
Wallowa Mountains Visitor Center
88401 Highway 82
Enterprise, OR 97828
541/426-5546 or 541/426-4978
fax 541/426-5522
website: www.fs.fed.us/hellscanyon

Oregon Dunes National Recreation Area
855 Highway Avenue
Reedsport, OR 97467
541/271-3611
fax 541/271-6019
website: www.fs.fed.us/r6/siuslaw/oregondunes

Washington

Hells Canyon National Recreation Area
Snake River Office
2535 Riverside Drive
P.O. Box 699
Clarkston, WA 99403
509/758-0616
fax 509/758-1963
website: www.fs.fed.us/hellscanyon

Lake Roosevelt National Recreation Area
1008 Crest Drive
Coulee Dam, WA 99116-1259
509/633-9441 or 509/738-6266
fax 509/633-9332
website: www.nps.gov/laro

Mount Rainier National Park
Tahoma Woods, Star Route
Ashford, WA 98304-9751
360/569-2211
fax 360/569-2170
website: www.nps.gov/mora

Mount St. Helens National Volcanic Monument
42218 NE Yale Bridge Road
Amboy, WA 98601
360/449-7800
fax 360/449-7801
website: www.fs.fed.us/r6/gpnf/mshnvm

Olympic National Park
600 East Park Avenue
Port Angeles, WA 98362-6798
360/565-3130
fax 360/565-3015
website: www.nps.gov/olym

State Parks

The state parks systems provide many popular camping spots in spectacular settings. These campgrounds include drive-in numbered sites and tent spaces with picnic tables, showers, and restrooms provided nearby. Reservations are often necessary during the summer months. Although many parks are well known, there are still some little-known gems in the state parks systems where campers can enjoy seclusion, even in the summer. Leashed pets are permitted in the campgrounds.

California

Most of the state park campgrounds are on a reservation system, and campsites can be booked up to seven months in advance at these parks. There are also hike-in/bike-in sites at many of the parks, and they are available on a first-come, first-served basis. Reservations can be made by phoning 916/638-5883 or 800/444-PARK (800/444-7275), or visiting the website www.reserveamerica.com. The reservation fee is usually $7.50 for a campsite. Major credit cards are accepted for reservations but are generally not accepted in person at the parks.

Discounts are available for people age 62 and older. Reduced fees are also available to holders of the Disabled Discount Pass. Those with Disabled Veteran/Prisoner of War Passes receive free use of all state park facilities, including camping and day use.

For general information about California State Parks, contact:

California Department of Parks and Recreation
Communications Office
P.O. Box 942896
Sacramento, CA 94296
916/653-6995 or 800/777-0369
fax 916/654-6374
website: www.parks.ca.gov

Oregon

Oregon sponsors a central reservation system. Reservations can be made for many Oregon state parks through Reservations Northwest at 800/452-5687. Online reservations for Oregon state parks can be made at www.oregonstateparks.org. A nonrefundable reservation fee of $6 is charged for a campsite, and the reservation fee for group sites is higher. Major credit cards are accepted for reservations, and credit cards are accepted at some of the parks during the summer. Under this system, reservations can be made throughout the year, up to nine months in advance. Camping fees are discounted during Discovery Season from October through April.

General information regarding Oregon state parks can be obtained by calling 800/551-6949 or visiting the website www.oregonstateparks.org. For more information, contact Oregon State Parks, 1115 Commercial St. NE, Salem, OR 97301-1002.

Washington

More than 50 of the state park campgrounds are on a reservation system, and campsites can be booked up to nine months in advance at these parks. Reservations can be made by telephone at 888/CAMPOUT (888/226-7688) or online at www.parks.wa.gov/reserve.asp. The reservation number is open from 7 A.M. to 8 P.M. (Pacific Standard Time) almost every day of the year. Major credit cards are accepted for reservations, and credit cards are accepted at some of the parks during the summer. A $7 reservation fee is charged for a campsite, and the reservation fee for group sites is higher. Discounts are available for Washington

State pass holders of disabled, limited-income, off-season senior citizen, and disabled veterans status.

General information regarding Washington state parks can be obtained by telephoning 360/902-8844 or visiting the website www.parks.wa.gov. For more information, contact: Washington State Parks and Recreation Commission, 7150 Cleanwater Lane, P.O. Box 42650, Olympia, WA 98504-2669.

Bureau of Land Management

Most of the areas managed by the BLM are primitive and in remote areas. Parking and access are usually free. Often there is also no fee for camping. Holders of Golden Age or Golden Access passports receive a 50 percent discount, except for group camps, at BLM fee campgrounds.

California
Bureau of Land Management
California State Office
2800 Cottage Way, Room W-1834
Sacramento, CA 95825-1886
916/978-4400
website: www.ca.blm.gov

California Desert District Office
22835 Calle San Juan De Los Lagos
Moreno Valley, CA 92553
909/697-5200
fax 909/697-5296
website: www.ca.blm.gov/cdd

Alturas Field Office
708 W. 12th Street
Alturas, CA 96101
530/233-4666
fax 530/233-5696
website: www.ca.blm.gov/alturas

Arcata Field Office
1695 Heindon Road
Arcata, CA 95521-4573
707/825-2300
fax 707/825-2301
website: www.ca.blm.gov/arcata

Bakersfield Field Office
3801 Pegasus Drive
Bakersfield, CA 93308
661/391-6000
fax 661/391-6040
website: www.ca.blm.gov/bakersfield

Barstow Field Office
2601 Barstow Road
Barstow, CA 92311
760/252-6000
fax 760/252-6098
website: www.ca.blm.gov/barstow

Bishop Field Office
351 Pacu Lane, Suite 100
Bishop, CA 93514
760/872-5000
fax 760/872-5050
website: www.ca.blm.gov/bishop

Eagle Lake Field Office
2950 Riverside Drive
Susanville, CA 96130
530/257-0456
fax 530/257-4831
website: www.ca.blm.gov/eaglelake

El Centro Field Office
1661 S. 4th Street
El Centro, CA 92243
760/337-4400
fax 760/337-4490
website: www.ca.blm.gov/elcentro

Folsom Field Office
63 Natoma Street
Folsom, CA 95630
916/985-4474
fax 916/985-3259
website: www.ca.blm.gov/folsom

Hollister Field Office
20 Hamilton Court
Hollister, CA 95023
831/630-5000
fax 831/630-5055
website: www.ca.blm.gov/hollister

Palm Springs/South Coast Field Office
690 W. Garnet Avenue
North Palm Springs, CA 92258-1260
760/251-4800
fax 760/251-4899
website: www.ca.blm.gov/palmsprings

Redding Field Office
355 Hemsted Drive
Redding, CA 96002
530/224-2100

fax 530/224-2172
website: www.ca.blm.gov/redding
Ridgecrest Field Office
300 S. Richmond Road
Ridgecrest, CA 93555
760/384-5400
fax 760/384-5499
website: www.ca.blm.gov/ridgecrest

Ukiah Field Office
2550 N. State Street
Ukiah, CA 95482
707/468-4000
fax 707/468-4027
website: www.ca.blm.gov/ukiah

Oregon
Oregon State Office
3333 W. 1st Ave.
P.O. Box 2965
Portland, OR 97208
503/808-6002
fax 503/808-6308
website: www.or.blm.gov

Burns District
28910 Highway 20 West
Hines, OR 97738
541/573-4400
fax 541/573-4411
website: www.or.blm.gov/burns

Coos Bay District
1300 Airport Lane
North Bend, OR 97459-2000
541/756-0100
fax 541/756-9303
website: www.or.blm.gov/coosbay

Eugene District
2890 Chad Drive
Eugene, OR 97440-2226
541/683-6600
fax 541/683-6981
website: www.edo.or.blm.gov

Lakeview District
1301 South G Street
HC 10 Box 337
Lakeview, OR 97630
541/947-2177
fax 541/947-6399
website: www.or.blm.gov/lakeview

Medford District
3040 Biddle Road
Medford, OR 97504
541/618-2200
fax 541/618-2400
website: www.or.blm.gov/medford

Prineville District
3050 NE Third Street
P.O. Box 550
Prineville, OR 97754
541/416-6700
fax 541/416-6798
website: www.or.blm.gov/prineville

Roseburg District
777 NW Garden Valley Boulevard
Roseburg, OR 97470
541/440-4930
fax 541/440-4948
website: www.or.blm.gov/roseburg

Salem District
1717 Fabry Road SE
Salem, OR 97306
503/375-5646
fax 503/375-5622
website: www.or.blm.gov/salem

Vale District
100 Oregon Street
Vale, OR 97918-9630
531/473-3144
fax 541/473-6213
website: www.or.blm.gov/vale

Spokane District
1103 N. Fancher
Spokane, WA 99212-1275
509/536-1200
fax 509/536-1275
website: www.or.blm.gov/spokane

U.S. Army Corps of Engineers and Reservations

Some of the family camps and most of the group camps operated by the U.S. Army Corps of Engineers are on a reservation system. Reservations can be made up to 240 days in advance, and up to 360 days in advance for groups. To reserve a site, call 877/444-6777 or visit the website www.ReserveUSA.com. Major credit cards are accepted. Holders of Golden Age or Golden Access passports receive a 50 percent discount for campground fees, except for group sites.

California
Los Angeles District
911 Wilshire Boulevard
Los Angeles, CA 90017-3401
213/452-3908
website: www.spl.usace.army.mil

Sacramento District
1325 J Street
Sacramento, CA 95814-2922
916/557-5100
website: www.spk.usace.army.mil

South Pacific Division/San Francisco District
333 Market Street
San Francisco, CA 94105
415/977-8272
website: www.spn.usace.army.mil/

Oregon
Portland District
333 SW First Ave.
P.O. Box 2946
Portland, OR 97208-2946
503/808-5150
fax 503/808-4515
website: www.nwp.usace.army.mil

Washington
Walla Walla District
201 North 3rd Avenue
Walla Walla, WA 99362-1876
509/527-7700

Department of Natural Resources— Washington

The Department of Natural Resources manages more than five million acres of public land in Washington. All of it is managed under the concept of "multiple use," designed to provide the greatest number of recreational opportunities while still protecting natural resources.

The campgrounds in these areas are among the most primitive, remote, and least known of the camps listed in the book. The campsites are usually free, and you are asked to remove all litter and trash from the area, leaving only your footprints behind. Due to budget cutbacks, some of these campgrounds have been closed in recent years; expect more closures in the future.

For more information, contact the Department of Natural Resources at the appropriate state or regional address:

State of Washington
1111 Washington Street SE
P.O. Box 47000
Olympia, WA 98504-7000
360/902-1000 or 800/527-3305
fax 360/902-1775
website: www.dnr.wa.gov

Central Region
1405 Rush Road
Chehalis, WA 98532-8763
360/748-2383
fax 360/748-2387

Northeast Region
225 S. Silke Road
P.O. Box 190
Colville, WA 99114-0190
509/684-7474
fax (509) 684-7484

Northwest Region
919 N. Township Street
Sedro Woolley, WA 98284-9384
360/856-3500
fax 360/856-2150

Olympic Region
411 Tillicum Lane
Forks, WA 98331-9271
360/374-6131
fax 360/374-5446

South Puget Sound Region
950 Farman Avenue North
Enumclaw, WA 98022-9282
360/825-1631
fax 360/825-1672

Southeast Region
713 Bowers Road
Ellensburg, WA 98926-9301
509/925-8510
fax 509/925-8522

Southwest Region
601 Bond Road
P.O. Box 280
Castle Rock, WA 98611-0280
360/577-2025
fax 360/274-4196

State Forests

California
Jackson Demonstration State Forest
802 N. Main Street
Fort Bragg, CA 95437
707/964-5674
fax 707/964-0941

Mountain Home Demonstration State Forest
P.O. Box 517
Springville, CA 93265
559/539-2321 (summer)
or 559/539-2855 (winter)

Oregon
Oregon Department of Forestry
2600 State Street
Salem, OR 97310
503/945-7200
fax 503/945-7212
website: www.odf.state.or.us

Tillamook State Forest
Forest Grove District
801 Gales Creek Road
Forest Grove, OR 97116
503/357-2191
fax 503/357-4548
website: www.odf.state.or.us/areas.northwest
/tillamook/tsf/default.asp

Tillamook State Forest
Tillamook District
5005 E. 3rd Street
Tillamook, OR 97141
503/842-2545
fax 503/842-3143
website: www.odf.state.or.us/areas.northwest
/tillamook/tsf/default.asp

Other Valuable Resources

California Department of Transportation
Highway Information:
916/445-7623 or 800/427-ROAD (800/427-7623)
website: www.dot.ca.gov

Nature of the Northwest Information Center
800 NE Oregon Street, Suite 177
Portland, OR 97232
503/872-2750
fax 503/731-4066
website: www.naturenw.org

Oregon Department of Transportation
355 Capitol Street NE
Salem, OR 97301-3871
503/588-2941 or 800/977-ODOT (800/977-6368)
website: www.odot.state.or.us/home

Tacoma Power
3628 S. 35th Street
P.O. Box 11007
Tacoma, WA 98411
253/502-8000
website: tacomapower.com

Pacific Gas and Electric Company
FERC/Land Projects
2730 Gateway Oaks, Suite 220
Sacramento, CA 95833
916/386-5164
fax 916/923-7044
website: www.pge.com/recreation

U.S. Geological Survey
Branch of Information Services
P.O. Box 25286, Federal Center
Denver, CO 80225
303/202-4700
or 888/ASK-USGS (888/275-8747)
fax 303/202-4693
website: www.usgs.gov

Washington State Department of Transportation
310 Maple Park Avenue SE
P.O. Box 47300
Olympia, WA 98504-7300

Washington State Highway Information:
800/695-ROAD (800/695-7623)

Greater Seattle Area Information:
206/DOT-HIWY (206/368-4499)

Washington State Ferries Information
206/464-6400 or 888/808-7977
website: www.wsdot.wa.gov

Map Resources

U.S. Geological Survey
Branch of Information Services
P.O. Box 25286, Federal Center
Denver, CO 80225
303/202-4700 or 888/ASK-USGS (888/275-8747)
fax 303/202-4693
website: www.usgs.gov

U.S. Forest Service
Attn: Map Sales
P.O. Box 9035
Prescott, AZ 86313
928/443-8285
fax 928/443-8207
website: www.fs.fed.us/maps

Nature of the Northwest Information Center
800 NE Oregon Street, Suite 177
Portland, OR 97232
503/872-2750
fax 503/731-4066
website: www.naturenw.org

Tom Harrison Maps
2 Falmouth Cove
San Rafael, CA 94901-4465
tel./fax 415/456-7940 or 800/265-9090
website: www.tomharrisonmaps.com

Earthwalk Press
5432 La Jolla Hermosa Avenue
La Jolla, CA 92037
800/828-MAPS (800/828-6277)

Map Center
1995 University Avenue, Suite 117
Berkeley, CA 94704
510/841-6277
fax 510/841-0858

Map Link
30 South La Patera Lane, Unit 5
Santa Barbara, CA 93117
800/962-1394 or 805/692-6777
fax 805/692-6787 or 800/627-7768
website: www.maplink.com

Olmstead Maps
P.O. Box 5351
Berkeley, CA 94705
tel./fax 510/658-6534

Index

H

Matilija Creek: 787
Mattole River: **431**, 450
Mauch's Sundown RV Park:
 64–65
Mayfield Lake: **174**, 189–190
Mayfield Lake Park: 190
Mayflower County Park: 866
Mazama: 386
McAlister Creek: 88
McAlpine Lake and Park: 667
McArthur–Burney Falls
 Memorial State Park: **496**,
 503
McCloud: 471, 473
McCloud Dance Country RV
 Park: 471–472
McCloud River: 472–473
McClure Point Recreation
 Area: 688
McConnell State Recreation
 Area: 690
McGee Creek: 727
McGee Creek RV Park:
 726–727
McGill: 783
McGrath State Beach: 794
McKenzie Bridge: 355
McKenzie River: 354–356, 361
McKinleyville: 447
McNeil: 305
McSwain Dam: 688
Meadow Lake: 197
Meadowview: 704–705
Meadow Wood RV Park: 386
Mecca Beach: 870
Medford: **347**
Medford Oaks RV Park: 395
Medicine Lake: **496**
Meeks Bay: 618–619
Meeks Bay Resort & Marina:
 619
Meiss Lake: **460**
Memaloose State Park:
 302–303
Memorial County Park: 655
Mendocino: **524**, 534–535
Mendocino National Forest:
 524, 527–528, 532–533,
 540–541
Merced: **678**
Merced River: 688, 690, 725
Mercer Lake: 253

Mercer Lake Resort: 253–254
Mermaid Inn and Sand-Lo RV
 Park: 61
Merrill: 512
Mesa: 803–804
Mesquite Spring: 768
Methow River: **90**, 99–100,
 103, 106, **134**
Methow River Valley: 101
Metolius River: 351–352
Metzler Park: 282
Mid Hills: 857
Middle Creek Campground: 540
Middle Fork: 339
Middletown: 549
Midway RV Park: 445–446
Midway Village and Grocery:
 115
Milford: 522
Mill Creek (Angeles National
 Forest): 801
Mill Creek (Lassen National
 Forest): 513
Mill Creek (Plumas National
 Forest): 569
Mill Creek Park: 508
Mill Creek Resort: 513
Miller River Group: 119–120
Millersylvania State Park:
 177–178
Millerton Lake: **678**
Millerton Lake State Recre-
 ation Area: 693
Millpond: 375
Mill Valley: 541–542
Milo McIver State Park: 307
Mil Potrero Park: 782–783
Minam State Park: 327
Minaret Falls: 719–720
Mineral Springs: 130
Minersville: 482
Minerva Beach Resort: 44
Mirabel Trailer Park and
 Camp: 553–554
Mission Bay: 841
Mission Farm RV Park: 668
Moabi Regional Park: 859
Moccasin Point: 684
Modesto: **678**, 686, 689
Modesto Reservoir: 686
Modesto Reservoir Regional
 Park: 686

Modoc National Forest: **496**,
 501, 504
Mojave: **852**, 855
Mojave Narrows Regional
 Park: 861
Mojave National Preserve:
 853, 857
Mojave River: 861
Mojave River Forks Regional
 Park: 803
Mokelumne River: 588
Molalla River: 284
Mona: 354
Money Creek Campground: 119
Mono Hot Springs: 736
Mono Lake: **701**
Monroe: **91**
Montaña de Oro State Park:
 772, 778
Monte Cristo: 801
Monterey: **660**, 669
Monterey Bay: **660**, 668
Monterey Vacation RV Park:
 668
Moon Lake: **496**
Moon Reservoir: **408**
Moonshine Campground: 576
Moorpark: 790
Mora: 31–32
Moraine: 750
Moran State Park Ferry-In: 74
Morgan Hill: 657
Morro Bay: **772**, 777–778
Morro Bay State Park:
 778–779
Morro Dunes Trailer Park and
 Camp: 777–778
Morro Strand State Beach:
 777
Moses Lake: **206**
Moses Lake State Park: 211
Moses Mountain: **134**
Moss Creek: 202
Mossyrock Park: 191
Mount Adams: **174**
Mountain Home State Forest:
 753
Mountain Valley RV Park: 818
Mountain View Motel and RV
 Park: 332
Mountain View RV Park:
 788–789

Notes

Notes

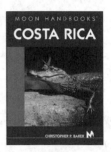

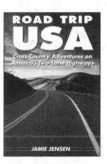